AF730389

PSYCHOLOGY

PSYCHOLOGY

SIXTH EDITION

Lester A. Lefton

University of South Carolina

ALLYN AND BACON

Boston London Toronto Sydney Tokyo Singapore

Executive Editor, Social Sciences: Sean W. Wakely
Developmental Editor: Sue Gleason
Editorial Assistant: Erika Stuart
Marketing Manager: Joyce Nilsen
Sr. Editorial Production Administrator: Susan McIntyre
Editorial Production Service: Jane E. Hoover/Lifland et al., Bookmakers
Text Designer: Deborah Schneck
Photo Researcher: Laurel Anderson/Photosynthesis
Composition and Prepress Buyer: Linda Cox
Manufacturing Buyer: Megan Cochran
Cover Administrator: Linda Knowles
Electronic Production Manager: Tim Ries

Copyright © 1997, 1994, 1991, 1985, 1982, 1979 by Allyn & Bacon
A Viacom Company
160 Gould Street
Needham Heights, MA 02194
Internet: www.abacon.com
America Online: Keyword: College Online

All rights reserved. No part of the material protected by this copyright notice may be reproduced or utilized in any form or by any means, electronic or mechanical, including photocopying, recording, or by any information storage and retrieval system, without written permission from the copyright owner.

Library of Congress Cataloging-in-Publication Data

Lefton, Lester A., 1946–
Psychology / Lefton, Lester A., — 6th ed.
p. cm.
Includes bibliographical references and indexes.
ISBN 0-205-18995-4 (hardcover)
1. Psychology. I. Title.
BF121.L424 1997
150—dc20 96-19231
CIP

Printed in the United States of America

10 9 8 7 6 5 4 01 00 99 98

For Linda, a woman of beauty, courage, strength, and sensitivity; my wife, partner, and friend.

Contents-at-a-Glance

Contents

3 Perception 70

4 States of Consciousness 114

15 Approaches to Treatment 516

16 Social Psychology 554

17 Applied Psychology 600

Appendix Statistical Methods 640

To the Student

Welcome! No matter who you are, this book will have meaning for you.

If you are in a relationship . . .

If you sometimes experience stress (what student doesn't?) . . .

If you expect someday to have children . . .

If you know someone who has contemplated suicide . . .

If anyone in your family has a mental illness . . .

If you have trouble remembering what you have learned . . .

then I can promise that reading this book will give you more than a few insights into such everyday issues of human thought and behavior. Because I believe so fundamentally in helping students glean and retain all the insights they can from a book, I have made a special effort to make psychology both understandable and interesting for you. The first step is for you to be an active learner.

Be an Active Learner

Here are some important study tips that will reduce your stress level and increase your effectiveness as a student:

- Be actively involved in the learning process.
- Make new information meaningful by linking your life experiences and knowledge (what you already know) to new information (what you are learning for the first time).
- Take responsibility for your own learning.

One way to really improve your studying and be an active learner is to use the SQ3R system, which reminds learners to *survey, question, read, recite,* and *review* when reading textbooks (Robinson, 1970). College students have used SQ3R effectively and successfully since 1941—it is a tried-and-true active study method, which is why it is the reading strategy most recommended by psychology teachers. I have modified the original SQ3R method slightly to SQ3R *plus: survey, question, read, recite, review*—plus *write and reflect.* To be an effective learner, use the SQ3R *plus* system when studying psychology—it means putting a little psychology to work.

To use SQ3R *plus*, follow these steps: Before you begin studying, **survey**:

- Quickly read the *outline* at the beginning of the chapter and the chapter's opening paragraphs; this will provide a brief *overview* of the chapter.
- Scan *topic headings* and examine the *Focus* questions that appear throughout the chapter; this will further refine your overview of the chapter's goals.
- Look at the *photos, art, tables,* and *graphs*—these will help you get a more concrete idea of what you will be studying.
- Take time to scan the *tables*, especially the *Building Tables*—these will give you a preview of concepts that you will want to compare and contrast as you read, so that you can learn the similarities and differences among the various theories presented.
- Pay attention to other special features, such as print styles, the use of color in the text, and summaries.
- You also may want to plan a study break at the end of each major section in the chapter.

Next, **question**. Ask yourself questions about the material to be studied. Examine the *Focus* questions that appear every few pages. This step will increase your involvement, interest, and concentration because each question you ask gives you a goal—to find an answer.

Third, **read**. Read the text and answer the questions you asked yourself. Focus on making the material you are reading personally relevant.

Fourth, **recite**. *Recite* means saying things from memory, but being an active learner means putting concepts in your own words.

Fifth, **review**. Double-check the accuracy of your recall and your understanding of the material to be learned. Try to pull together key terms and concepts.

Plus, **write** and **reflect**. When you write a summary of key points, you increase the quality and quantity of your learning. When you reflect on your own learning, you are not only an active learner but also a critical thinker—a person able to make good use of newly learned information.

Use the Pedagogical Features

Several pedagogical features have been integrated in this edition of *Psychology* to stimulate your active involvement with and critical thinking about issues, as well as to help you learn more efficiently and effectively.

Focus. According to learning theory, retention improves if you review and rethink what you have read. Throughout the text, boxed review sections called *Focus* will encourage you to pause, review, question, and think about what you have just learned. Some of the questions review what you have learned, but others do not simply test recall—they encourage you to think critically, to go beyond what you have read to form new connections. The *Focus* boxes are conveniently placed and include page references to show where topics are discussed. Answers to these questions are available from your instructor if you need to check your own answers.

Critical Thinking. Learning about psychology means learning about the thinking process itself. Developing critical thinking skills is thus a major theme—from the introduction to the scientific method and critical thinking in Chapter 1, to the special *Think Critically* questions within Focus boxes, to the *Critical Thinking Connections* page at the end of each chapter. The questions on these pages ask you to think critically about topics across the entire field of psychology and then to actively explore those other topics throughout this book. In addition, special sections called *The Research Process* show you how psychologists use the scientific method.

Key Terms. Key terms are boldfaced in the text and defined in the margins, as well as in the end-of-book *Glossary*; a pronunciation guide is given where appropriate. In addition, the key terms are listed with page references within the chapter's *Summary and Review*, to provide you with an additional review of key concepts after you have finished the chapter.

Building Tables. Presenting major theories and concepts in a way that shows the development of ideas is a major structural and pedagogical element in this text. Pioneered in a previous edition and widely applauded by students and instructors, the *Building Tables* have been visually enhanced and expanded in this edition. As you master one set of concepts, another is added on. These tables allow you to make comparisons and contrasts and provide a means for integrating concepts. They, too, are an excellent study and review aid.

Art. A picture can literally be worth a thousand words if you are one of a growing population of visual learners. With the assistance of a special technical art reviewer, this book's award-winning graphics have been thoroughly redesigned for clarity, accuracy, and consistency. Many figures combine presentation modes and teach through visuals, tables, and detailed explanatory labels. In addition, figures for which animations are presented on the CD-ROM accompanying this book are keyed with a CD icon: 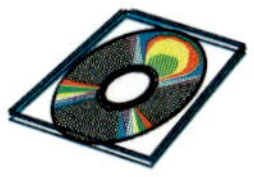

Diversity. A key goal of this edition is to introduce you to the growing diversity in American culture and to show you how multicultural factors must be taken into account when viewing psychological data. This means thinking critically about issues such as gender, ethnicity, age, and socioeconomic status. Diversity topics are featured in a *Diversity* section in most chapters and throughout the text.

Applications. Featuring interesting topics such as improving your memory, eyewitness testimony, questionable "quick-fix" tests of personality, overcoming shyness, and codependence, *Applications* sections focus on how psychology can be applied to everyday life. Applications are also a regular theme throughout the text.

Chapter Summary and Review. Every chapter ends with a carefully structured *Summary and Review*. The summary is organized by section headings with page references to relevant portions of the text. The review is set up in a question-and-answer format, and includes a list of key terms.

Learning Connections. In case you would like additional information on any of the topics in a chapter, each chapter provides *Learning Connections* that refer you to the appropriate sections of the CD-ROM, study guide, audiotape, and World Wide Web site that accompany this book.

Critical Thinking Connections. Because psychology is a broad and multifaceted discipline, introductory students often experience a sense of not seeing the forest for the trees. Too often they have a tendency to focus on one chapter's topics at a time yet miss the connections across chapters. A *Critical Thinking Connections* page at the end of each chapter will prompt you with thought-provoking questions and guide you to other locations in the book where the same or related topics are discussed.

Use the Supplements

You can further reinforce your learning with a variety of supplements available from Allyn and Bacon.

Allyn and Bacon Psychology CD-ROM: "Core Concepts in Psychology" You can take full advantage of the multimedia revolution with this exciting new CD-ROM. It covers 14 core psychology topics.

Through a Central Resource Center, the CD-ROM offers users the following features:

- *Guided Tour,* a brief tutorial.
- *Library* offering key terms, animations and illustrations, video clips, study skills modules, and more. You can browse, sort, and click on any element you wish to view.
- *Topic-by-Topic Exploration,* providing Guided Question reviews with summaries, definitions, and animations to enhance your understanding of psychology's major themes and concepts. A Video Focus for each topic offers related video features with critical thinking questions. Each topic concludes with Test Your Knowledge, multiple-choice questions with feedback on right and wrong answers, and a "score" to show you how you've done.

The CD-ROM runs on either 256-color Macintosh computers (minimum specs equivalent to an LC I) or VGA IBM-compatible computers with *Windows* and a sound board.

Keeping Pace Plus. Written by Andrew Ryan, Jr., who teaches an introductory psychology course with me, *Keeping Pace Plus* is an active reading study guide. Now in its sixth edition, this carefully structured study guide helps you participate actively in learning about psychology. It contains book-specific exercises, learning objectives, review sections, and a practice test section, and a language enrichment section for students who need help with vocabulary. With page-referenced reviews, *Keeping Pace Plus* guarantees learning for anyone who uses it.

SoundGuide. This cassette tape is an audio study guide for the text that will let you review, rehearse, and take practice tests. For use in portable tape players and automobiles, this study aid offers another mode of studying, active learning, and thinking about psychology.

Practice Tests Booklet. If you want extra help preparing for exams, this free booklet provides sample tests, so that you can practice and test what you've learned, and includes answer feedback and page references to the text.

Computerized Study Guide. The computerized study guide includes eight enrichment modules on key topics in psychology. Each module is enhanced with graphics to aid learning and encourage critical thinking. Practice tests that correspond to each chapter in the text are also included. Available for Macintosh and IBM computers.

Studying Psychology. A brief how-to manual, *Studying Psychology: A Manual for Success*, is designed to help you develop the skills to master psychology more effectively. With down-to-earth techniques and ideas, this booklet helps you develop effective strategies for studying, listening, getting the most out of lectures, and preparing for examinations.

Critical Thinking. Developed by James Bell, this booklet focuses on helping you evaluate psychological information. This valuable tool shows you how to evaluate research evidence systematically and improve your critical thinking skills.

Tools of Critical Thinking. A critical thinking text by David A. Levy, this volume provides tools and skills for approaching all forms of problem solving, particularly in psychology.

World of Psychology. A brief series of current articles taken from the *Washington Post*, *World of Psychology* focuses on diversity. High-interest, topical, and provocative, these articles will encourage you to think critically. The readings are cross-referenced to related topics in the text.

Psychology and Culture. Walter Lonner and Roy Malpass have developed a broad-based book of readings that serve as an introduction to the role of culture and ethnicity in human behavior. It features original articles by experts in the field and an extensive introductory overview that sketches conceptual and methodological issues.

Psychologically Speaking: A Self-Assessment. Craig Poulenez Donovan and Peter C. Rosato have prepared a workbook of enjoyable self-assessment exercises paralleling the chapters in the text.

Explore Psychology as a Career

For those who would like to read more about psychology as a profession and potential career, Allyn and Bacon publishes *Preparing for Graduate Study in Psychology: 101 Questions and Answers*, by William Buskist and Thomas R. Sherburne.

The American and Canadian Psychological Associations publish several books and booklets that provide further information. Your school's psychology department or counseling center may have copies of them. Or you may write to the APA or CPA at the addresses given below. The APA publishes the following items:

Is Psychology the Major for You? This 137-page volume is oriented toward students who wish to make a career of psychology. It tells you what careers are available, how to find a job, how to utilize career counseling, and how to survive as a new employee.

Preparing for Graduate Study in Psychology: NOT for Seniors Only! This 96-page source book discusses how to plan the steps that will take you to graduate school, with an emphasis on students who do not yet have the "credentials." It provides help on acquiring recommendations, writing résumés, practicing interviews, and the like.

Graduate Study in Psychology and Associated Fields. This book is a compre hensive guide (over 600 pages) to graduate programs in the United States and Canada. It indicates which schools offer which specialties and discusses admission requirements, housing facilities, financial assistance, tuition, and so on.

Careers in Psychology. This brief (28-page) pamphlet describes the fields of and careers in psychology. Single copies are free to students.

You can also join a national organization as a student affiliate. APA's annual fee for students is $25, for which you get (1) discounts on books published by APA, (2) lower prices on APA journal subscriptions, (3) the *APA Monitor* (the organization's monthly newspaper), and (4) the *American Psychologist* (its official journal) at no extra cost. Write to 750 First Street, NE, Washington, DC 20002.

The Canadian Psychological Association publishes *Graduate Guide: Description of Graduate Psychology Programs in Canadian Universities*. The Canadian Psychological Association's student membership is only $10, for which you receive news in the field and journals. Write to Vincent Road, Old Chelsea, Quebec JOX 2NO.

One Career in Psychology

My own career in psychology has a long history, beginning with a survey of sexual attitudes that I conducted in high school. I passed out questionnaires to the juniors and seniors, who were to respond anonymously. Then I spent days poring over, collating, and summarizing the data—which I, of course, found fascinating.

In college, at Northeastern University in Boston, I majored in psychology and was particularly interested in clinical psychology. I took courses in traditional experimental psychology—learning, physiology, perception—but especially enjoyed abnormal psychology, child development, and personality. In addition to attending classes, I worked in a treatment center for emotionally disturbed children. The work was hard, emotionally grueling, and stressful, and the pay wasn't particularly good—thus the direct delivery of mental health services began to lose some of its appeal for me. Later, as a laboratory assistant, I collected and analyzed data for a psychologist doing research in vision. In contrast to my counseling experience, hunting for answers to scientific questions, speculating about new ideas, designing research questions, and collecting data were activities that held my interest.

My graduate studies at the University of Rochester included research in perception, and I studied visual information processing. In graduate school, my intellectual skills were sharpened, my knowledge base was expanded, and my interests were focused and refined. After earning my PhD, I became a faculty member at the University of South Carolina. My research in cognitive psychology involved studying perceptual phenomena such as eye movements. I now teach, do research in cognitive psychology, and write psychology textbooks. My goal is to share my excitement for psychology in the classroom, in my textbooks, and in professional journals.

Over time, my interests have changed, as I'm sure yours will. At first, I was interested in the delivery of mental health services to children. Later, I focused on applied research issues, such as eye movements among learning disabled readers. But my primary focus remains in basic research issues. My evolving interests have spanned the three major areas in which psychologists work: applied research, human services, and experimental psychology—topics I present throughout this text.

I am married to a wonderful woman and have two college-age daughters. I have applied in my family life much of what I have learned in my profession. My family hasn't been angry about it, although from time to time my "psychologizing" about issues can be annoying, I'm sure. I'm an avid bicyclist and computer hacker and occasional photographer. My life has generally revolved around my work and my family—not necessarily in that order. You'll probably gather that from many of the stories and examples I relate in this text.

I invite you to share my excitement and my enthusiasm for psychology. Stay involved, read closely, focus, and think critically. Try to generate personal meaning from this text. It has generated much for me. And please feel free to write me in care of the Psychology Department, University of South Carolina, Columbia, SC 29208, or send me some E-mail: Lefton@sc.edu.

Good luck!

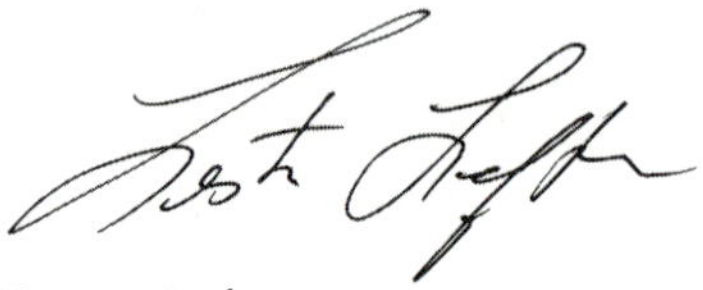

Lester Lefton

To the Instructor

Writing this book was both an adventure and a challenge. Six strategic goals guided my work on *Psychology,* Sixth Edition. First, I wanted to stress *diversity* and sensitivity to culture and gender; I was particularly interested in showing that psychologists must consider the wide range of participants in research. To make reasonable generalizations about human behavior they must consider ethnic, cultural, age, and gender issues. Second, I wanted to show that *research* is a cornerstone of psychology; this revision of *Psychology* reflects an increased emphasis on the role of research in psychology. In emphasizing the importance of research, I especially wanted to focus on *critical thinking* as a key to good scientific thought and research—my third goal. Fourth, I wanted to highlight *ethics* in research. Ethics in research with animals and human participants has been brought to the forefront of psychology and the new edition reflects this concern. Fifth, I wanted to focus on how *applications* grow from research. Last, I wanted to be sure to sustain *student interest* and understanding. To help accomplish this goal, I continued to use a highly personal voice in my writing and to share my own point of view.

A New Edition: Organization, Content, and Diversity

The previous edition of *Psychology* was very well received by both students and instructors. They liked its clarity and appreciated its balance of research and application. They applauded its pedagogical structure, particularly the highly praised graphics, *Building Tables*, and *Connections*. But, for all of its strengths, the text needed to be revised—I wanted to keep it attuned to the needs of students and professors through the year 2000.

To achieve my goals, I enlisted the aid of colleagues, friends, and students who read both the previous edition of the book and new drafts. The publisher sought the help of instructors throughout the country. Psychologists read the manuscript with an eye to accuracy, current trends, sensitivity to gender and diversity issues, pedagogy, and general student interest.

These reviews were extremely helpful. I was buried for months in reams of letters, manuscripts, articles, faxes, and phone calls. The result is a new edition with a spirited and elegant design, an especially clear writing style, and a direct and personal approach to student learning. In addition, the text has been changed in the following specific ways.

Reorganization. The contents have been organized in a new, more logical manner, starting with the basics of psychology (biology, perception, and six chapters on topics from cognitive psychology) and moving to the more applied, clinical, and socially relevant chapters. I responded to professors who preferred that (1) the topic of intelligence be discussed closer to cognition, (2) the topic of development fall later in the book, and (3) the topics of social psychology be more logically collected in a single chapter. Yet every chapter is written so that it can stand alone and be read in any sequence. Every chapter has been rewritten with the aim of providing a more structured approach, with a smoother, more cohesive flow of information. The internal structure of each chapter attempts to match the way teachers present material; editors at Allyn and Bacon and I talked with hundreds of psychology teachers to determine the most logical and sought-after structure.

Content. This new edition covers the core concepts of psychology in addition to emerging, high-interest topics. The traditional areas of learning, memory, cognitive psychology, intelligence, motivation and emotion, development, and social psychology have received thorough scrutiny and revision. Current data and theories from the biological sciences are presented. The applied fields are similarly represented, with complete coverage of topics such as child development, gender differences, performance appraisal, and testing issues. The text covers high-interest topics such as brief therapy, codependence, substance abuse, brain plasticity, and Alzheimer's disease. These topics are presented in an integrated manner by bringing science and application together and showing how they flow directly from traditional psychology. The content of the text reflects the current status of psychological science without being trendy or neglecting the classics. I have also added a chapter on applied psychology, including expanded and strengthened coverage of I/O psychology as well as environmental, legal, community, educational, and sport psychology.

Diversity. This new edition emphasizes diversity and is sensitive to culture, ethnicity, gender, and age. Psychologists now recognize the important role of these factors in psychological phenomena. This makes research more difficult but it also makes the outcomes of that work more relevant. I have attempted to integrate diversity throughout the book and to focus on high-interest topics that combine application and basic research in special sections called *Diversity.*

Annotated Instructor's Edition and Supplements for Instructors

An *Annotated Instructor's Edition* is provided to encourage student involvement and understanding. It includes an instructor's section bound into the front of the book and detailed annotations in the margins that give teaching suggestions, examples, demonstrations, visual aids, and learning objectives. In addition to the *Annotated Instructor's Edition,* a wide array of supplementary materials is available, including an instructor's resource manual filled with activities, handouts, and numerous additional teaching aids; a superb set of transparencies; a lengthy computer-ready test item file; *PsychScience,* an interactive computer simulation of real-life experiments; and custom-edited CNN videos, superb video discs with video segments and graphics, and an extensive videotape library. All of these supplements, and more, are keyed to the *Annotated Instructor's Edition.*

Acknowledgments

The cast of characters who helped me prepare this textbook is extraordinary; some are psychologists, some are students, some are professional textbook developers. I am especially appreciative of the help that instructors and students have given me. They have corrected mistakes, focused my vision, and encouraged me to consider the special needs of diverse populations of students and instructors. A number of these reviewers were my colleagues at the University of South Carolina on whom I prevailed for continual guidance. I especially thank Ernest Furchtgott, who gave me line-by-line comments on the entire book. I also thank Sandra Kelly, Jay Coleman, Jim Appel, Tom Carferty, and Dave Clement, who provided chapter commentaries.

There are two individuals whose contributions to this edition went above and beyond those of traditional reviewers. Dr. David Matsumoto, of San Francisco State University, challenged each chapter's coverage of cross-cultural issues and provided many annotations for the *Annotated Instructor's Edition.* And Dr. Nancy Simpson, of Trident Technical College, acted as a technical art reviewer, subjecting every figure and table to intense scrutiny for pedagogical effectiveness.

I owe a special debt of gratitude to ten reviewers who gave lavishly of their expertise in helping to improve this edition:

Robin M. Akert
Wellesley College

John Benjafield
Brock University

John P. Bruno
Ohio State University

William O. Dwyer
The University of Memphis

Karl Haberlandt
Trinity College

Claire B. Kopp
University of California–Los Angeles

Barbara Hansen Lemme
College of DuPage

Frederick R. Maxwell
Southwest Missouri State University

Robert L. Solso
University of Nevada–Reno

Robert Sternberg
Yale University

Faculty at other institutions, ranging from research universities to teaching-oriented community colleges helped me focus my ideas, pointed me in new research directions, and queried my logic. They met in focus groups, talked with me individually, responded to a survey, and wrote lengthy reviews of each chapter. In immeasurable ways, these reviewers helped make this book better. I thank each of them:

Chapter Reviews

Gerald S. Clack
Loyola University of the South

Verne C. Cox
University of Texas–Arlington

Jan Francis
Santa Rosa Junior College

Phil Goernert
Mankato State University

Laura Green
Florida Atlantic University

Sally Ozonoff
University of Utah

Robert J. Pellegrini
San Jose State University

Allen L. Salo
Fort Hays State University

Sharon A. Wilcox
University of Arkansas

Deborah R. Winters
San Diego, California

Michael York
University of New Haven

Focus Groups, Interviews, Surveys

Tim Babler
Edgewood College

Anne Baden
Western Kentucky University

Frank P. Belcastro
University of Dubuque

David Campbell
Humboldt State University

Kathleen Caproni
Marist College

Cathy Cozzarelli
Kansas State University

John D. Cupp
Tennessee Technological University

Margaret E. Donnelley
Pace University

Richard M. Ehlenz
Lakewood Community College

Martha Ellis
Collin County Community College

Jerome E. Flint
Westminster College

David A. Frieske
Western Kentucky University

Dashiel Geyen
University of Houston–Downtown

Wayne Hall
San Jacinto College

Paul Kasenow
Henderson Community College

Brenda J. Kirby
University of Nebraska–Lincoln

Stephen Kitzis
Fort Hays State University

Charles Ksir
University of Wyoming

R. Langford
California State University–Humboldt

Paulette J. Leonard
University of Central Arkansas

Gary Levy
University of Wyoming

Terry Maul
San Bernardino Valley College

Robert Peters
Highland Park Community College

Marc E. Pratarelli
Fort Hays State University

Dean Richards
California State University–Northridge

Lilia Salazar
Solano Community College

Angela S. Scerbo
Eastern Washington University

Richard A. Scott
University of Central Arkansas

R. R. Vallacher
Florida Atlantic University

George Watson
California State University–Fullerton

I would also like to acknowledge and thank the reviewers of previous editions who helped me build the firm foundation on which this book stands:

Spencer Adams
Salt Lake Community College

Bob Ahlering
Central Missouri State University

Lewis Aiken
Pepperdine University

George Alliger
SUNY–Albany

Georgia Babladelis
California State University

Jean Badry
Indiana University–South Bend

Lew Barker
Baylor University

Brian Bate
Cuyahoga Community College–Western Campus

William Beatty
North Dakota State University

Hal Beck
Appalachian State University

John Best
Eastern Illinois University

Kathleen Bey
Palm Beach Community College

George Bishop
National University of Singapore

Galen Bodenhausen
Michigan State University

Richard Bowen
Loyola University of Chicago

Jay Braun
Arizona State University

Brian Burnie
George Brown College

Edward Caldwell
West Virginia University

Robert B. Cameron
Fairmont State College

John Caruso
Southeastern Massachusetts University

Michael Bernard Casey
Virginia Polytechnic Institute and State University

Lawrence Casler
SUNY–Geneseo

Kathleen Chen
Rochester Institute of Technology

George A. Cicala
University of Delaware

Patrick Conley
University of Illinois–Chicago

Joan Cook
County College of Morris

James Corwin
University of New Orleans

Winifred Curtis
Community College of Rhode Island

Patrick De Boli
Nassau Community College

Donald Devers
Northern Virginia Community College

Terry Devietti
Central Western University

Jadwiga Dolzycki
Tennessee Technological University

Thornton Dozier
Michigan State University

Cheryl Dreut
SUNY–Fredonia

Jane Fillmore
Utah Valley Community College

Leslie Fisher
Cleveland State University

Linda Flickinger
St. Clair Community College

Leonard Flynn
Framingham State College

Mark Garrison
Kentucky State University

Drusilla Glascoe
Salt Lake Community College

James Grosch
SUNY–Geneseo

Ernest Gurman
University of Southern Mississippi

Michael Gurtman
University of Wisconsin–Parkside

Jane Halpert
DePaul University

Joy Hammersla
Seattle Pacific University

Howard Harris
Bronx Community College

Richard J. Harris
Kansas State University

Charles Hinderliter
University of Pittsburgh

Larry Hochhaus
Oklahoma State University

Morton Hoffman
Metropolitan State University

Peter Holland
University of Pittsburgh

Charles A. Homra
Murray State University

Kermit Hoyenga
Western Illinois University

James J. Johnson
Illinois State University

William Kalberer
California State University–Chico

Dennis Karpowitz
University of Kansas

Jane Kelly
Hinds Community College

Arthur D. Kemp
Central Missouri State

Harold Kiess
Framingham State College

Jack Kirshenbaum
Fullerton Community College

James Knight
Humboldt State University

Wayne Lesko
Marymount University

Robert Levy
Indiana State University

Ted Lewandoski
Delaware County Community College

Marjorie Lewis
Illinois State University

Walter J. Lonner
Western Washington University

Sal Macias
University of South Carolina–Sumter

Sheldon Malev
Westchester Community College

Cynthia Margolin
San Jose State College

Duane Martin
University of Texas–Arlington

Richard Maslow
Delta College

James Matiya
Moraine Valley Community College

Robert Meyer
University of Louisville

Jerry Mikosz
Moraine Valley Community College

Linda Musun Miller
University of Arkansas–Little Rock

James Moore, Jr.
Marshall University

Glenda G. Nichols
Tarrant County Junior College

Ronald D. Pearse
Fairmont State College

Harvey Pines
Canisius College

Edward Pollak
West Chester State College

Janet Proctor
Purdue University

Christopher Rhoades
Hilbert College

James Roll
William Rainey Harper College

Peter J. Rowe
College of Charleston

K. Elaine Royal
Middle Tennessee State University

Paul Salmon
University of Louisville

Mike Scoles
University of Central Arkansas

Robert Shaw
Texas Southmost College

Harold I. Siegel
Rutgers University

Gene Smith
Western Illinois University

Janet Sniezak
University of Illinois–Urbana/Champaign

Donald M. Stanley
North Harris College

Dirk Steiner
Louisiana State University

Michael Stevenson
Ball State University

Warren Street
Central Western University

David Townsend
Montclair State University

Frank Vattano
Colorado State University

Benjamin Wallace
Cleveland State University

William Wallace
Marshall University

Charles Weichert
San Antonio College

Andrea Wesley
University of Southern Mississippi

Richard Wesp
Elmira College

David Whitsett
University of Northern Iowa

John Williams
Westchester Community College

Kevin Williams
Rensselaer Polytechnic Institute

Patrick Williams
Wharton County Junior College

Joe Rae Zuckerman
Los Angeles Harbor College

The students who read this book are my greatest friends and my most important audience. For almost two decades, students in my classroom and in classrooms all over the country have read chapters of this text—both previous editions and drafts of new chapters. They provided criticism and help and pointed out areas that needed to be strengthened. I am in their debt.

I also thank Rosa Thorn, my administrative assistant, who makes my life easier by attending to details, keeping up with my correspondence, and facilitating my work flow. Rosa keeps me on an even keel, and her hard work provides me with the time I need to write. My thanks go also to Ian Birnie, who helped with library research and a seemingly endless number of details, and to Jennifer Seidenberg, who worked with me on the tedious task of coordinating permissions. I thank Maggie Haughton and Sheila Pidgeon for their help with finding articles, preparing references, and typing materials for my classes—these ultimately proved useful in the writing of this book. I am also grateful to Mark Garrison, Kentucky State University, who prepared the pedagogically focused *Annotated Instructor's Edition* Instructor's Section, the annotations, and the *Instructor's Resource Manual*; to Celia Reaves, Monroe Community College, for writing a superb test bank; to Andrew Ryan, Jr., University of South Carolina, for his excellent study guide; and to Michael Paolino, University of South Carolina, for preparing thoughtful answers to the focus box questions.

My friends at Allyn and Bacon are an incredibly creative team. Many worked behind the scenes and had limited contact with me directly, but I know of their involvement, and I am appreciative. I thank the sales force and their experienced managers, who gathered information from instructors and students, and Laura Ellingson, Jennifer Normandin, and Erika Stuart, who coordinated reviews and contacted instructors. The marketing team, especially Joyce Nilsen and Lou Kennedy has helped immeasurably in gathering information and setting the agenda for the text. The design of the text is exciting, and I thank Debbie Schneck for her work; I also appreciate the striking cover, which was designed by Linda Knowles.

Production is among the most time-consuming and exacting of the steps in putting a textbook together, and every page of the text shows the superb work of Susan McIntyre, and especially packager Jane Hoover of Lifland et al., Bookmakers. With a fine eye for detail, Susan and Jane managed the specialized elements in this complicated text. They were flexible and responded to dozens of last-minute changes needed to keep the book current despite a breakneck schedule and many technical challenges.

The editorial team at Allyn and Bacon is the best in textbook publishing. I have had the benefit of over a decade of guidance and expertise from top-notch developmental and acquisition editors such as Allen Workman and Bill Barke. They gave crucial input at various points in the production and development of this book. I especially thank Sandi Kirshner, Senior Vice President and Editorial Director, and Bill Barke, President of Allyn and Bacon, respectively, for their continued confidence in me and this project.

On a day-to-day basis, Sue Gleason was the person who made this book happen. She worked with me to ensure the quality, thematic integrity, and overall direction of the text and went over the text line by line to make certain that every thought was precise. She challenged, prodded, and provided advice. Her skill, knowledge, and sound judgment are reflected on every page of text.

Every creative team has to have a leader, and Allyn and Bacon has one of the best: Sean Wakely, Vice President and Editor-in-Chief of the Social Sciences. Sean is dedicated to top-notch bookmaking and has the determination, skills, and creativity not only to look at today's issues but to anticipate future ones.

I dedicate this text to my wife, Linda, a woman of great beauty, courage, strength, and sensitivity. Linda is my wife, my partner, and my friend.

Credits

Figures and Tables

Chapter 3: FIGURE 3.2, p. 78: From Dowling, J. E. and Boycott, B. B. *Proceedings of the Royal Society* (London), B166 (1966), 80–111, Fig. 23. FIGURE 3.3, p. 79: From Pirenne, M. H. (1967). *Vision and the eye,* p. 32. London: Chapman and Hall, Ltd. Reprinted by permission. FIGURE 3.7, p. 83: Adapted from Noton, D., and Stark, L. (1971, June). Eye movements and visual perception. *Scientific American,* pp. 35–44. Copyright 1971 by Scientific American, Inc. All rights reserved. FIGURE 3.10, p. 85: Reprinted from *Vision Research,* vol. 4, MacNichol, E. F., Retinal mechanisms of color vision, pp. 119–133, copyright 1964, with kind permission from Elsevier Science Ltd., The Boulevard, Langford Lane, Kidlington 0X5 1GB, UK. FIGURE 3.15, p. 95: From Beck, J. (1966). Effects of orientation and of shape similarity on perceptual grouping. *Perception and Psychophysics, 1,* pp. 300–302. Reprinted by permission of Psychonomic Society, Inc.

Chapter 4: FIGURE 4.1, p. 122: From *Some must watch while some must sleep,* by William C. Dement. Copyright © 1972 by William C. Dement. Used by permission of the Stanford Alumni Association and William C. Dement. FIGURE 4.2, p. 123: Adapted with changes and data supplied by H. P. Roffwarg from Roffwarg, Muzio, and Dement (1966). Ontogenetic development of human sleep-dream cycle. *Science, 152,* pp. 604–609. Copyright 1966 by the AAAS. FIGURE 4.3, p. 137: From Ray, Oakley, and Ksir (1993). *Drugs, society, and human behavior* (6th ed.), p. 194. St. Louis, MO: Mosby Year Book, Inc. Reprinted by permission.

Chapter 6: FIGURE 6.7, p. 209: Reprinted by permission of Academic Press Inc. from Kosslyn, Stephen M. Information representation in visual images. *Cognitive Psychology ,7,* 341–370.

Chapter 7: FIGURE 7.8, p. 254: Adapted from Moskowitz, B. A. The acquisition of language. *Scientific American,* pp. 92–100. Copyright 1978 by Scientific American, Inc. All rights reserved. FIGURE 7.10, p. 259: Reprinted with permission from Premack, D. (1971). Language in chimpanzees? *Science, 172,* 808–822. Copyright 1971, American Association for the Advancement of Science.

Chapter 8: TABLE 8.1, p. 270: Adapted from Gardner, H., and Hatch, T. (1989). Multiple intelligences go to school: Educational implications of the theory of multiple intelligences. *Educational Researcher, 18* (8), 6. FIGURE 8.5, p. 286: Reprinted with permission from Bouchard, T. J., Jr. and McGue, M. (1981). Familial studies of intelligence: A review. *Science, 212,* 1055–1058. Also from Erlenmeyer-Kimling, L., and Jarvik, L. F. (1963). Genetics and intelligence: A review. *Science,* 142, 1477–1479. Copyright 1963 and 1981, American Association for the Advancement of Science.

Chapter 9: FIGURE 9.3, p. 306: From Lazarus, R. S. and Alfert, E. (1964). Short-circuiting of threat by experimentally altering cognitive appraisal. *Journal of Abnormal and Social Psychology, 69,* 195–205. Copyright © 1964 by the American Psychological Association. Reprinted with permission. FIGURE 9.8, p. 325: Copyright © 1980 by Robert Plutchik. Reprinted by permission of HarperCollins Publishers, Inc. from Plutchik, R. (1980). *Emotion: A psychoevolutionary synthesis.* New York: Harper & Row.

Chapter 10: FIGURE 10.2, p. 347: Reprinted by permission from Berk, Laura. *Infants, Children, and Adolescents.* (1993). Boston, Allyn and Bacon, p. 166. FIGURE 10.4, p. 349: Adapted from Fantz, R. L. (1961, May). The origin of form perception. *Scientific American,* pp. 66–72. Copyright © 1961 by Scientific American, Inc. All rights reserved. FIGURE 10.6, p. 355: © 1995 by Susan Avishai.

Chapter 11: TABLE 11.2, p. 396: Reprinted with the permission of Macmillan Publishing Company from *The journey of adulthood* by Helen L. Bee. Copyright © 1987 by Macmillan Publishing Company.

Chapter 12: TABLE 12.5, p. 440: From the *Minnesota Multiphasic Personality Inventory.* Copyright © the University of Minnesota 1942, 1943 (renewed 1970). MMPI scale names reproduced by permission of the publisher. FIGURE 12.5, p. 443: From Cohen, R. J., Montague, P., Nathanson, L. S., and Swerdlik, M. E. (1988). *Psychological testing.* Mountain View, CA: Mayfield.

Chapter 13: FIGURE 13.4, p. 456: From Selye, H. (1956). *The stress of life.* New York: McGraw-Hill. Used with permission of the McGraw-Hill Companies. TABLE 13.1, p. 457: Reprinted by permission of the publisher from Holmes, T. H., and Rahe, R. H. The Social Readjustment Scale. *Journal of Psychosomatic Research 11,* 213–218. Copyright 1967 by Elsevier Science Inc. TABLE 13.2, p. 458: Reprinted with the permission of Plenum Publishing

Corporation from Kanner, A. D., Coyne, J. C., Schaefer, C., and Lazarus, R. S. (1981). Comparison of two modes of stress measurement: Daily hassles and uplifts versus major life events. *Journal of Behavioral Medicine 4,* 1–39.

Chapter 14: TABLE 14.4, p. 503: From Meyer, R. G., and Salmon, P. (1988). *Abnormal psychology* (2nd ed.). Boston: Allyn and Bacon. Copyright © 1988 by Allyn and Bacon. Reprinted by permission. FIGURE 14.2, p. 505: From Snowden, L. R. and Cheung, F. K. (1990). Use of inpatient mental health services by members of ethnic minority groups. *American Psychologist 45,* 347–355. Copyright © 1990 by the American Psychological Association. Reprinted with permission. FIGURE 14.3, p. 509: From Tsaung, M. T., & Vandermey, R. (1980). *Genes and the mind.* Reprinted by permission of Oxford University Press, Oxford, England.

Chapter 15: TABLE 15.1, p. 521: From Mahrer, A. R., and Nadler, W. P. (1986). Good moments in psychotherapy: A preliminary review, a list, and some promising research avenues. *Journal of Consulting and Clinical Psychology 54,* 10–15. Copyright © 1986 by the American Psychological Association. Reprinted with permission. FIGURE 15.3, p. 534: Reprinted from *Behavior Research and Therapy 2,* Ayllon, T., and Haughton, E., Modification of symptomatic verbal behavior of mental patients, pp. 87–97. Copyright 1964 with permission from Elsevier Science Ltd., Pergamon Imprint, The Boulevard, Langford Lane, Kidlington 0X5 1GB, UK. FIGURE 15.4, p. 535: From Allyon T., & Azrin, N. H. (1965) The measurement and reinforcement of behavior of psychotics. *Journal of the Experimental Analysis of Behavior, 8,* pp. 357–383. Copyright 1965 by the Society for the Experimental Analysis of Behavior, Inc. Reprinted by permission. TABLE 15.4, p. 539: From Ellis, A., and Harper, R. A. (1961). *A guide to rational living.* North Hollywood, CA: Wilshire. Used by permission.

Chapter 16: FIGURE 16.7, p. 578: From Milgram, S. (1963). Behavioral study of obedience. *Journal of Abnormal and Social Psychology 67,* 371–378. Used with permission. TABLE 16.4, p. 590: From Hendrick, C., & Hendrick, S. (1986). A theory and method of love. *Journal of Personality and Social Psychology, 50,* pp. 392–402. Copyright 1986 by the American Psychological Association. Reprinted by permission.

Chapter 17: FIGURE 17.4, p. 615: From Locke, E. A., and Schwieger, D. M. (1979). *Research in organizational behavior.* Used by permission of JAI Press, Inc. FIGURE 17.5, p. 626: From Valins, S., and Baum, A. (1973). Residential group size, social interaction, and crowding. *Environment and Behavior 5,* 421–435. Used by permission of Lawrence Erlbaum Associates, Inc. FIGURE 17.6, p. 628: Reprinted with the permission of Plenum Publishing Corporation from Altman, I., and Vinsel, A. M. (1977). Personal space: An analysis of E. T. Hall's proxemics framework. In I. Altman, A. Rapoport, and J. F. Wohlwill (eds.), *Human behavior and environment: Vol. 2. Advances in theory and research.* New York: Plenum.

Photos

Chapter 1: Opener: Stephen S. Myers/American Museum of Natural History. p. 10 (top): Stephen S. Myers/American Museum of Natural History. p. 10 (middle): Archives of the History of American Psychology, University of Akron (Ohio). p. 12: 1978 Andy Levin/Photo Researchers, Inc. p. 17: AT&T Archives. p. 20: Stephen Marks. p. 21: B. Daemmrich/Stock Boston. p. 23: Steve Winter/Black Star. p. 35 (top): Herchaft/Leo de Wys, Inc. p. 35 (middle): Stan Wayman/Photo Researchers, Inc.

Chapter 2: Opener: The Bridgeman Art Library/British Museum. p. 40 (left): CNRI/Science Photo Library/Photo Researchers, Inc. p. 40 (right): Cindy Karp/Black Star. p. 41: David Teplica, M. D. p. 44 (top): Biophoto/Photo Researchers, Inc. p. 44 (bottom): Omikron/Photo Researchers, Inc. p. 52: A. Glauberman/Photo Researchers, Inc. p. 57 (left): Mulvehill/The Image Works. p. 57 (right): Mallinckrodt Institute of Radiology. p. 64: The Bridgeman Art Library/British Museum. p. 65: M. Gouveneur/Liaison. p. 69 (top): Courtesy of CNN. p. 69 (middle): J. L. Weber/Peter Arnold, Inc. p. 69 (bottom): M. Richards/PhotoEdit.

Chapter 3: Opener: Jerry Jacka/Courtesy Gallery 10. p. 78: J. L. Wver/Peter Arnold, Inc. p. 86: Robert Harbison. p. 87: Superstock. p. 89: Mike Yamashita/Woodfin Camp & Associates. p. 91 (top): Kevin Schafer/Peter Arnold, Inc. p. 91 (bottom): Carol Purcell/Photo Researchers, Inc. p. 93: Baron Wolman/Woodfin Camp & Associates. p. 94 (top): Jerry Jacka/Courtesy Gallery 10. p. 94 (bottom): The Image Works. p. 98: T. Svensson/Stock Market. p. 102: Omikron/Photo Researchers, Inc. p. 109: Rob Schoenbaum/Black Star. p. 113 (top): Ed Kashi. p. 113 (middle): Courtesy of J. Campos, B. Bertenthal, and R. Kermoran. p. 113 (bottom): Robert Harbison.

Chapter 4: Opener: Milan Chuckovich/Tony Stone Images. p. 117: Will Faller. p. 120: Ed Kashi. p. 122: Will & Deni McIntyre/Photo Researchers, Inc. p. 126: Bonnie Kamin. p. 128 (top): Milan Chuckovich/Tony Stone Images. p. 128 (middle): Steve Allen/Peter Arnold, Inc. p. 129: J. Corwin/Stock Boston. p. 130: B. Daemmrich/Stock Boston. p. 133: Ed Kashi. p. 137: M. Richards/PhotoEdit. p. 139: M. Ferri/The Stock Market. p. 147 (top): Gordon Willit/Tony Stone Worldwide. p. 147 (middle): Jonathan Nourok/PhotoEdit. p. 147 (bottom): J. Albertson/Stock Boston.

Chapter 5: Opener: Robert Frerck/Odyssey/Chicago. p. 154: Courtesy of CNN. p. 157: Stan Wayman/Photo Researchers, Inc. p. 164: Courtesy of Pfizer Inc. p. 165: A. Reininger/Woodfin Camp & Associates. p. 168: Radie Nedlin. p. 169 (top left): Brian Smith. p. 169 (top right): Omikron/Photo Researchers, Inc. p. 169 (bottom left): Kevin Horan/Stock Boston. p. 169 (bottom right): Jim Pickerell. p. 177: Will Faller. p. 179: Omikron/Photo Researchers, Inc. p. 180: Robert Frerck/Odyssey/Chicago. p. 181: Will Faller. p. 185: Will Faller. p. 186: Archive. p. 187: Archive. p. 191 (top): Richard Howard/Offshoot Stock. p. 191 (middle): Alexandra Avakian/Woodfin Camp & Associates, Inc.

Chapter 6: Opener: © Mardi Wood. p. 198: Peter Menzel/Stock Boston. p. 200 (top): Peter Menzel/Stock Boston. p. 200 (bottom): Brian Smith. p. 204: Brian Smith. p. 205 (left): Will Faller. p. 205 (right): A. Hvhkihn/Woodfin Camp & Associates. p. 207: B. Daemmrich/The Image Works. p. 208: Bob Daemmrich/The Image Works. p. 211: Stephen Marks. p. 216: Mike Siegel/Seattle Times. p. 219: Harley Soltes/Seattle Times. p. 221: B. Daemmrich/The Image Works. p. 229 (middle): Stephen Marks. p. 229 (bottom): Omikron/Photo Researchers, Inc.

Chapter 7: Opener: Jerry Jacka/Courtesy Dennis Lyon Collection. p. 233: Will Faller. p. 234: Jerry Jacka/Courtesy Dennis Lyon Collection. p. 235: Julie Dennis, Paramount/Shooting Star International. p. 240: Michael Newman/PhotoEdit. p. 245: Robert Harbison. p. 246: Courtesy of Lotus Corporation. p. 249 (top): George Dillon/Stock Boston. p. 249 (bottom): Laima Druskis/Stock Boston. p. 252: K. Kai/Fujifotos/The Image Works. p. 254: Corroon/Monkmeyer Press. p. 260: Courtesy of CNN. p. 263 (top): L. Kolvoord/The Image Works. p. 263 (middle): Ed Kashi. p. 263 (bottom): Archives of the History of American Psychology, University of Akron (Ohio).

Chapter 8: Opener: Robert Frerck/Odyssey/Chicago. p. 271 (top): Jose Azel/Woodfin Camp & Associates. p. 271 (lower left): Robert Harbison. p. 271 (lower right): Jim Pickerell. p. 273: Archives of the History of American Psychology, University of Akron (Ohio). p. 280: Lew Merrim/Monkmeyer Press Photo. p. 284 (top): Robert Frerck/Odyssey/Chicago. p. 284 (middle): Harry Redl/Black Star. p. 286: Robert Azzi/Woodfin Camp & Associates. p. 287: Stephen Marks. p. 292: Bob Daemmrich/The Image Works. p. 293: 1991 Dennis Brack/Black Star. p. 297 (top): Courtesy of James V. Wertsch, Clark University. p. 297 (middle): Renato Rotolo/Gamma Liaison.

Chapter 9: Opener: Hilarie Kavanagh/Tony Stone Worldwide. p. 301: Mary Ellen Lepionka. p. 302: Glyn Kirk/Tony Stone Images. p. 303: Glyn Kirk/Tony Stone Images. p. 304: Stephen Marks. p. 307: Will Faller. p. 308 (upper left): Stephen Marks. p. 308 (lower left): K. Reininger/Black Star. p. 308 (right): Stephen Marks. p. 311: Archive. p. 313: The Bridgeman Art Library/Buehman Collection. p. 315: Superstock. p. 316 (left): Culver Pictures. p. 316 (right): Cesar Vera/Leo de Wys, Inc. p. 323: Robert Harbison. p. 327 (top): Hilarie Kavanagh/Tony Stone Worldwide. p. 327 (middle): Bernstein/Liaison International. p. 328 (left): B. Daemmrich/The Image Works. p. 328 (right): Lisa Rudy Hoke/Black Star. p. 332: Courtesy of David Matsumoto. p. 337 (top): Courtesy of Pfizer Inc. p. 337 (middle): Ed Kashi.

Chapter 10: Opener: "Love Truck" © Jim Wagner 1995/Parks Gallery, Taos, NM. p. 341: Minnesota Twins Study. p. 344 (top and middle): Petit Format-Nestle/Photo Researchers, Inc. p. 344 (bottom): J. Stevenson/Science Library/Photo Researchers, Inc. p. 349 (upper left): Charles Gupton/Stock Boston. p. 349 (upper right): Spencer Grant/Stock Boston. p. 349 (bottom): Courtesy of Dr. David Linton. p. 350: Courtesy of J. Campos, B. Bertenthal, and R. Kermoran. p. 352 (upper left): FourbyFive/Superstock. p. 352 (upper right): Laura Dwight/Peter Arnold, Inc. p. 352 (middle left): James Sugar/Black Star. p. 352 (middle right): Laura Dwight/Peter Arnold, Inc. p. 352 (lower left): Andy Cox/Tony Stone Worldwide, Ltd. p. 352 (lower right): Richard Hutchings/Photo Researchers, Inc. p. 357: B. Daemmrich/Stock Boston. p. 358: Courtesy of James V. Wertsch, Clark University. p. 361 (left): The Bettmann Archive. p. 361 (right): Courtesy of Lawrence Kohlberg. p. 365: Will Faller. p. 371: Liane Enkelis/Stock Boston. p. 373: Stock Boston. p. 377 (top): Corroon/Monkmeyer Press. p. 377 (middle): Michael Newman/PhotoEdit. p. 377 (bottom): Will Faller.

Chapter 11: Opener: Robert Frerck/Odyssey/Chicago. p. 381: Strauss/Curtis/Offshoot Stock. p. 383: Robert Frerck/Odyssey/Chicago. p. 385: Renato Rotolo/Gamma Liaison. p. 387: Will Faller. p. 389 (top): Will Faller. p. 389 (middle): Will Faller. p. 391: Strauss/Curtis/Offshoot Stock. p. 393: Richard Howard/Offshoot Stock. p. 395: Zigy Kalozny/Tony Stone Images, Inc. p. 399: D. Young-Wolff/PhotoEdit. p. 400: D. Young-Wolff/PhotoEdit. p. 401: Ed Kashi. p. 403: Scott Thode/International Stock. p. 407 (top): Will Faller. p. 407 (middle): H. Morgan/Rainbow. p. 407 (bottom): Robert Harbison.

Chapter 12: Opener: Milan Chuckovich/Tony Stone Images. p. 411: Bettmann. p. 417: Ulrike Welsch. p. 419: National Library of Medicine. p. 420: Robert Harbison. p. 421: Mary Evans Picture Library. p. 422: Bettmann. p. 423: Archive. p. 425: Archives of History of American Psychology, University of Akron (Ohio). p. 426: Archive. p. 427: Will Faller. p. 434: B. Aron/PhotoEdit. p. 437: John Coletti. p. 438 (top): Will Faller. p. 438 (bottom): Jose Azel/Woodfin Camp & Associates. p. 447 (top): The Granger Collection. p. 447 (middle): Mary Ellen Lepionka. p. 447 (bottom): Lew Merrim/Monkmeyer Press.

Chapter 13: Opener: Jerry Jacka Photography. p. 451: L. Kolvoord/The Image Works. p. 452: Tom Wagner/Odyssey/Chicago. p. 454: Louisa Preston. p. 456: Courtesy of Hans Selye. p. 458: Jonathan Nourok/PhotoEdit. p. 459 (top): Jerry Jacka Photography. p. 459 (bottom): Michael Newman/PhotoEdit. p. 461: Herchaft/Leo de Wys, Inc. p. 464: H. Morgan/Rainbow. p. 467: Bob Daemmrich/Stock Boston. p. 470: Stephen Marks. p. 475: (top): B. Daemmrich/Stock Boston. p. 475 (middle): David Dempster/Offshoot Stock. p. 475 (bottom): Courtesy of Pfizer Inc.

Chapter 14: Opener: Robert Frerck/Odyssey/Chicago. p. 479: Patrick Ward/Stock Boston. p. 481: AP/Wide World Photos. p. 484: Bettmann. p. 486: David Dempster/Offshoot Stock. p. 487: C. Mellon/Tony Stone Worldwide. p. 488 (top): Robert Frerck/Odyssey/Chicago. p. 488 (middle): Ed Kashi. p. 494: Corbis-Bettmann. p. 495: R. Crandall. p. 501: Gordon Willit/Tony Stone Worldwide/Chicago Ltd. p. 502: Reuters/Corbis-Bettmann. p. 507: Monkmeyer Press Photo. p. 509 (top): Courtesy of the Genain estate. p. 509 (bottom): NIH/Photo Researchers, Inc. p. 515 (middle): Louisa Preston. p. 515 (bottom): Jim Pickerell.

Chapter 15: Opener: Barbara Brown. p. 519 (top): Barbara Brown. p. 519 (middle): Will Faller. p. 524: The Granger Collection. p. 527: Bettmann. p. 528: Michael Rougier/Life Magazine. p. 529: Archive. p. 530: Michael Rougier/Life Magazine. p. 535 (top): Stephen Marks. p. 535 (bottom): Jim Pickerell. p. 536: Richard Howard/Offshoot Stock. p. 538: Stephen Marks. p. 541: The Image Works/Pickerell. p. 542: Ed Kashi. p. 543: The Image Works/Pickerell. p. 545: Mary Kate Denny/PhotoEdit. p. 547: James Wilson/Woodfin Camp & Associates. p. 548: Louisa Preston. p. 553 (middle): Gordon Willitt/Tony Stone Worldwide/Chicago Ltd. p. 553 (bottom): Biophoto/Photo Researchers, Inc.

Chapter 16: Opener: Robert Frerck/Odyssey Productions. p. 557: Courtesy of Gitano. p. 561: J. Albertson/Stock Boston. p. 562: John Coletti. p. 563: Wide World Photos. p. 566 (left): David Austen/Stock Boston. p. 566 (right): Ed Kashi. p. 567: Courtesy of Sue Gleason. p. 569: Robert Harbison. p. 571: D. Greco/The Image Works. p. 572: Alexandra Avakian/Woodfin Camp & Associates. p. 575: William Vandevert/Scientific American. p. 577: Tom Wagner/Odyssey/Chicago. p. 578: Courtesy of the Milgram Estate. p. 582: Michael Newman/PhotoEdit. p. 583: Josh Pulman/Tony Stone Images. p. 587 (left): Joe McDonald/Tom Stack & Associates. p. 587 (right): Barbara Von Hoffmann/Tom Stack & Associates. p. 590: Will Faller. p. 599 (top): Minnesota Twins Study. p. 599 (middle): Richard Howard/Offshoot Stock. p. 599 (bottom): Archive.

Chapter 17: Opener: Jerry Jacka/Arizona State Museum, University of Arizona, Tucson. p. 606: Kerbs/Monkmeyer. p. 608: B. Daemmrich/The Image Works. p. 609: Charles Gupton/Stock Boston. p. 614: Charles Gupton/Tony Stone Worldwide, Ltd. p. 616: Bonnie Kamin. p. 618: Matthew McVay/Tony Stone Images. p. 621: Reprinted with permission from Ergonomics in Design, April 1993. Copyright 1993 by the Human Factors and Ergonomics Society. All rights reserved. p. 628: B. Barnes/PhotoEdit. p. 633: Will Faller. p. 635: L. Kolvoord/The Image Works. p. 639 (top): The Image Works. p. 639 (middle): The Image Works/Pickerell. p. 639 (bottom): Glyn Kirk/Tony Stone Images.

PSYCHOLOGY

1

What Is Psychology?

Middle-class, hard-working, traditional values—these are some of the words that Ralph and Sheila Mattison used to describe themselves. Their son, Alex, could have been described the same way 2 years ago. He was six foot three with a long, lean frame. With his baseball cap slapped on backwards, his T-shirt usually rumpled, and his music turned up a little too loud, Alex was pretty much a typical kid. That was 2 years ago. . . .

The phone roused Ralph and Sheila suddenly out of a deep sleep at 7:00 on Sunday morning. The call was from the police—they insisted on coming over to question Alex. As if straight out of *Columbo,* two rumpled detectives appeared at the Mattisons' door an hour later with a list of terse questions about Alex's whereabouts 3 weeks earlier. It seemed that Alex had been seen with a recently arrested cocaine dealer.

Over the previous 14 months, Alex's normal behavior had deteriorated. At school he fought over trivialities. At home he mouthed off and cursed at his mother. To make matters worse, Alex stopped taking his medication for attention-deficit hyperactivity disorder. His grades tumbled; after-school activities were missed; and, after a major blowup over independence, Alex disappeared for 5 days. At their wits' end, Alex's parents sent him to counseling and later to a special Outward Bound program for youths at risk. Nothing seemed to work. Their son was caught with drugs at school and was seen driving away from the scene of an accident he had caused on the highway; he also withdrew money from his parents' account through an ATM. The Mattisons themselves ended up in counseling.

That Sunday morning, after half an hour of questions by the police, Alex was instructed to meet the detectives at the station the next day for further questioning. Not knowing what was going to happen, already aware that Alex had been getting into trouble at school, the Mattisons hired an attorney, fearing that Alex wasn't being straight with them.

The Mattisons' story is still unfolding. Many of Alex's problems were complicated by his attention-deficit hyperactivity disorder, a neurochemical imbalance that can cause behavior problems. But his problems were clearly more complex than simply his disorder or his medication. Alex could not control his temper, may have self-medicated with illegal drugs, and was too big and too close to adulthood to be forced to do much of anything. Many thousands of families of high school students share similar life experiences.

Psychologists study and try to help people like Alex and his family. They prescribe medications for disorders like Alex's, and they work with whole families to restore them to balance. Perhaps this story about the Mattisons will help you understand why I consider psychology, the science of human behavior and mental processes, so moving, fascinating, and exciting. Psychology helps me understand the nature of human interactions—how parents struggle to help their children grow up and grow independent, how people make their way in the world, form relationships with others, and lead fulfilling lives. I began and continue to study psychology because people fascinate me. You may be taking this course for the same reason.

Before we begin to explore psychology, it is important to carefully define and describe what it is. Many students assume that psychology is the study of Freud, couches, and therapy situations. Although psychology does explore personality, maladjustment, and therapy, it encompasses far more. You will see that psychologists, whether practitioners or researchers, tend to be investigators who carefully and systematically attempt to discover the underpinnings of human behavior and mental processes. Students of psychology often think of themselves as detectives, sifting through facts and theories in an orderly way, attempting to uncover the causes of behavior, so as ultimately to help individuals or organizations become everything they wish to be. Let's begin our exploration with a definition of the science that I find so exciting and that I believe will ultimately help Alex Mattison.

What Is This Science of Psychology?

What exactly is psychology? It is as difficult for me to provide a definition of psychology that includes all its elements as it would be for you to list all the reasons why you might want to study it. We'll begin with a simple definition and gradually expand on it. Broadly defined, **psychology** is the science of behavior and mental processes.

Psychology: The science of behavior and mental processes.

Let's look at the first part of this definition, because it is key to understanding what sets real psychology apart from the pop psychology of talk shows and tabloids. Psychology is a *science*. Because psychology is a science, psychologists use scientific principles, carefully defined methods, and precise procedures to present an organized body of knowledge and to draw inferences, or make predictions, about how people will behave in the future. Predicting behavior is important, for it enables psychologists to help people anticipate their reactions to certain situations and learn how to express themselves in manageable and reasonable ways. For example, because excessive stress can cause anxiety, depression, and even heart attacks, psychologists use theories about stress to devise therapies to help people handle it more effectively.

Interestingly, there remain many people who do not believe that psychology is a science, who see human behavior as either fixed or subject to little change, and who think that people should rely on self-direction rather than on the help of psychologists to reach their potential. This disagreement exists cross-culturally as well; there is not the same degree of consensus about psychology as a meaningful science around the world. Former Soviet bloc nations take a dim view of therapy for emotional disorders, and in some Asian cultures people are expected to be self-reliant and are less likely to seek help from psychologists than are Americans.

Now for the second part of the definition: psychology as the science of *behavior and mental processes*. Psychologists observe not only the mind, but also most other aspects of human functioning—overt actions or behaviors, social relationships, mental processes, emotional responses, and physiological reactions. In cultures other than the United States, psychology also embraces paranormal phenomena such as telepathy and clairvoyance.

Overt actions are directly observable and measurable movements or the results of such movements. Walking, talking, playing, kissing, gestures, and expressions are examples of overt actions. Results or products of overt actions might be the papers you write, the piles of unsorted laundry in your bedroom, or the body you have kept in shape through regular exercise. *Social relationships* are the behaviors we engage in that define our interactions with other people. We make assumptions about the causes of other people's behaviors; we try to change their attitudes; we avoid them or engage them; we date, marry, and have children with them. *Mental processes*, which most of us consider the main grist for the psychological mill, include thoughts and ideas as well as more complex reasoning processes. *Emotional responses* are basically feelings such as anger, regret, lust, happiness, and depression. *Physiological reactions* are closely associated with emotional responses. They include an increased heart rate when you are excited, biochemical changes when light stimulates your eyes, and high blood pressure in response to stress. All of these are fair game for psychological scientists.

Three Principles of Scientific Endeavor

As a science, psychology is committed to objectivity, accuracy, and healthy skepticism about the study of behavior and mental processes. These three basic principles are at the very core of psychology's being a science. These basic principles can help you, too, be a critical thinker in your day-to-day life.

Objectivity. For psychologists, objectivity means evaluating research and theory on their merits, without preconceived ideas. For example, when scientists in 1988 demonstrated through carbon-14 dating techniques that the Shroud of Turin could not have been the burial cloth of Christ, many steadfast believers challenged the accuracy of the carbon-14 dating. Unlike these believers, psychologists attempt to bring scientific objectivity to the research arena.

Accuracy. Psychologists are concerned with gathering data from the laboratory and the real world in precise ways—that is, with accuracy. For instance, to conclude from a small number of eyewitness accounts that whole communities have been abducted by aliens falls considerably short of scientific accuracy. Might there be another plausible explanation for astonishingly similar accounts of small, ghostly figures levitating people to flying-saucer laboratories? Might those reporting such incidents suffer from similar psychological disorders? Rather than relying on limited samples and immediate impressions, psychologists base their thinking on detailed and thorough study that is as precise as possible.

Healthy Skepticism. Most people think twice when they hear stories like that of the woman who reported that she was saved from falling off an alpine precipice by an angelic rescuer who suddenly appeared and then disappeared. Appealing as it may be to believe accounts of alien abductions or angelic rescues, psychologists maintain a healthy skepticism: a cautious view of data, hypotheses, and theory until results are repeated, verified, and proved over time.

The Scientific Method in Psychology

Like other scientists, psychologists use the scientific method in developing theories that describe, explain, predict, and help manage behavior. The **scientific method** in psychology is the technique used to discover knowledge about human behavior and mental processes; in experimentation, it involves *stating the problem*, *forming a theory*, *developing hypotheses*, *observation* (which often includes manipulating some part of the environment to better understand previous conditions that led to a behavior or phenomenon), and *replicating results*.

Let's break down the scientific method into its five basic steps, so that you can have an overview of how psychologists do their work. I will have more to say about the research process later in this chapter.

Stating the Problem. The question a psychologist asks must be stated in such a way that it can be answered; that is, it must be stated in a way that lends itself to investigation. For instance, if you ask the question "What is the mind?" little headway can be made even through rigorous techniques. But if you ask "To what extent is sugar in the diet of 10-year-old boys associated with hyperactive behavior?" the question can be tested with some degree of clarity.

Forming a Theory. After stating the problem, psychologists develop a theory from their current knowledge and past research. A **theory** is a collection of interrelated ideas and facts put forward to explain and predict behavior and mental processes. For example, a theory that a diet high in sugar, caffeine, and red dye causes hyperactivity might put together related facts about personality, gender differences, cultural differences, and the demographics of hyperactivity.

Developing Hypotheses. If a theory is correct, it should allow the psychologist to predict behavior under certain circumstances. In the next step of the scientific method, then, psychologists form educated guesses about how people are likely to react. Such a formulation is called a **hypothesis**—a tentative statement or idea expressing a causal relationship between two events or variables that are to be evaluated in a research study. A hypothesis might be that a specific diet—perhaps one low in refined sugar—is more effective than any other diet in controlling or reducing hyperactive behavior in 10-year-old boys; further, the hypothesis might assert that such a diet will be 10 percent more effective than another diet or no special diet at all.

Observation. After the hypotheses are formed, psychologists carefully observe the variables under different circumstances, usually through research or experimentation. At the outset, the key elements of the study must be defined. The behaviors to be examined have to be carefully specified: How are they to be measured, with what instruments, how frequently, and by whom? In children who suffer from hyperactivity, some behaviors are fairly easily specified—for example, concentration on a task such as addition problems. Other behaviors, such as anxi-

Scientific method: In psychology, the techniques used to discover knowledge about human behavior and mental processes; in experimentation, the scientific method involves stating the problem, forming a theory, developing hypotheses, observation (which often includes manipulating some part of the environment to better understand previous conditions that led to a behavior or phenomenon), and replicating results.

Theory: In psychology, a collection of interrelated ideas and facts put forward to explain and predict behavior and mental processes.

Hypothesis: Tentative statement or idea expressing a causal relationship between two events or variables that are to be evaluated in a research study.

ety and lack of self-esteem, are more difficult to define precisely—in hyperactive children, or in anyone else for that matter.

After researchers have specified the key elements and chosen the participants for an experiment, they conduct the experiment, hoping it will yield interpretable, meaningful results. But extraneous, or irrelevant, variables can make interpretation difficult. *Extraneous variables* are factors that affect the results of an experiment but that are not of interest to the experimenter. An example of an extraneous variable is a lightning storm that occurs during an experiment in which anxiety was being measured through a physical response such as rises in skin conductivity. It would be difficult or impossible for the researchers to ascertain how much of the increased skin conductivity was due to manipulations they created and how much was due to anxiety about lightning. When extraneous variables occur during an experiment (or just before it), they may *confound results*—make data difficult to interpret.

FOCUS

Review

- Why might thought be considered behavior? p. 5
- Identify three key principles to which scientists must be committed. pp. 5–6
- Describe the steps in the scientific method. pp. 6–7
- Why would replicating a research study be so important to scientists? p. 7

Think Critically

- You may have read that scientists have theorized that high levels of aluminum—dietary and environmental—cause Alzheimer's disease, a progressive degenerative disorder affecting memory. What questions would you ask, and what issues would you be concerned with, in attempting to test this hypothesis?

Replicating Results. Most psychologists are aware of their own all-too-human tendency to bias, or subtly predetermine, the outcomes of their research so that they obtain precisely the results they expected. Thus, researchers generally require that an experiment be repeated and that the results be essentially the same. Repeating an experiment, often many times, to verify a result is called *replicating* the experiment. If the results of a replicated experiment are the same, a researcher will generally say that the results are reliable and are likely to occur again given the same set of circumstances.

Discovering Psychology:
Understanding Research

Before we go into the research process in more detail, you may be wondering what kind of people actually do this work of psychology. Let's take a moment to examine who is a psychologist and what a psychologist does on a day-by-day basis.

What Psychologists Do

Sometimes people mistakenly assume that psychologists primarily assist those suffering from debilitating mental disorders, such as schizophrenia and severe depression; but actually there is a world of variety in what psychologists do. Psychologists study nearly every aspect of life, not only to understand how people behave but also to help them lead happier, healthier, more productive lives. Some psychologists practice psychology; others teach or do research. Most are involved in a combination of activities.

And psychologists help not only people with problems but also well-adjusted people. Some psychologists provide services such as career counseling and assistance with community projects. Psychologists seek to provide people with interpersonal skills and knowledge about self-help techniques.

Psychologists, then, are professionals who study behavior and use behavioral principles in scientific research or in applied settings. Most have an advanced degree, usually a PhD (doctor of philosophy). Many psychologists also train for an additional year or two in a specialized area such as mental health, physiology, or child development.

Psychologist: Professional who studies behavior and uses behavioral principles in scientific research or in applied settings.

Founded in 1892, the American Psychological Association (APA) is the oldest and largest professional organization for psychologists. Its purpose is to advance psychology as a science, a profession, and a means of promoting human welfare. Today the APA has more than 68,000 members, with the majority holding doctoral degrees from accredited universities. In addition, there are more than 25,000 student affiliates. The APA disseminates a large number of research publications, which serve as a primary means for many psychologists to present their research to other professionals.

The APA is not the sole voice of psychology. Many specialty groups have emerged over the years. For example, organizations consisting mainly of developmental, behavioral, cognitive, or neuroscience psychologists have been formed. In 1989 the American Psychological Society (APS) was founded; it has a large membership of psychologists with academic interests and focuses on scientific research rather than on practice or applied interests. Two of its goals are to preserve the scientific base of psychology and to promote public understanding of psychology as a science.

Differences among Practitioners

People are often unsure about the differences among clinical psychologists, psychiatrists, and psychoanalysts. All are mental health practitioners who help people with serious emotional and behavior problems, but each looks at behavior differently. **Clinical psychologists** usually have a PhD in psychology and view behavior and emotions from a psychological perspective. In contrast, **psychiatrists** are physicians (medical doctors) who have chosen to specialize in the treatment of emotional disorders. Patients who see psychiatrists often have both physical and emotional problems. Because of their medical training, psychiatrists can prescribe drugs and can admit patients for hospitalization. In 1995 the APA voted to pursue the development of curricula that would prepare psychologists to prescribe drugs.

Clinical psychologists generally have more extensive training than psychiatrists in research, assessment, and psychological treatment of emotional problems. Their nonmedical perspective gives them different roles in hospital settings and encourages them to examine social and interpersonal variables more than psychiatrists do. Psychiatrists use a medical approach, which often involves making assumptions about behavior—for example, that abnormal behavior is diseaselike in nature—that psychologists do not make. Clinical psychologists and psychiatrists often see a similar mix of clients and often work together as part of a mental health team. Most psychologists and psychiatrists support collaborative efforts. However, a friendly rivalry exists between the two orientations because of their sometimes very different points of view.

Psychoanalysts are usually psychiatrists; they have training in the technique of psychoanalysis and use it in treating people with emotional problems. As we'll soon see, psychoanalysis was originated by Sigmund Freud and includes the study of unconscious motivation and dream analysis. It often requires a course of daily therapy sessions; the patient's treatment may last several years. In the past, psychoanalysts had to be physicians. In 1988, however, psychoanalytic institutes began to accept nonphysicians into their training programs. Thus, all practitioners may treat similar clients; but therapists' individual training and assumptions may vary, and this may be reflected in their choice of treatment.

Clinical psychologist: Mental health practitioner who views behavior and mental processes from a psychological perspective and who uses knowledge to treat persons with serious emotional or behavioral problems or to do research into the causes of behavior.

Psychiatrist: Physician (medical doctor) specializing in the treatment of patients with emotional disorders.

Psychoanalyst: Psychiatrist or, occasionally, nonmedical practitioner who has studied the technique of psychoanalysis and uses it in treating people with emotional problems.

Choosing Psychology as a Career

When I was first attracted to psychology as a career, it was because I had a desire to help others. Many psychologists do indeed help others through the delivery of mental health services. But an equal number of psychologists are intrigued by the analysis of data; they focus on research and the discovery of knowledge. These psychologists seek out careers as scientists, practitioners, or consultants because they enjoy the process of searching for and discovering the causes of human behavior.

Psychology attracts many college students who like the idea of understanding human behavior and helping others. These students are intrigued by the causes and implications of behavior; they realize that psychology is part of the fabric of daily life. Psychology is the second most popular undergraduate major—after business administration. And there is good news for those students who go on to graduate school: Almost all of the approximately 3,600 recipients of PhDs in psychology each year find jobs related to their training. There are more than 120,000 psychologists in the United States. If you are considering the field of psychology, you'll be glad to hear that unemployment among psychologists is low. Most experts agree that employment opportunities will continue to improve; psychology is often cited as one of the top 10 growth areas for jobs. Furthermore, compensation for psychologists is good.

Training, of course, is the key to employment. A psychologist who (1) obtains a PhD in clinical psychology from an accredited university, (2) does an internship in a state hospital, and (3) becomes licensed will have a wide variety of job opportunities available in both private and public sectors. Individuals with a master's degree, such as an MSW (master of social work), can function in a variety of settings, and even those with a bachelor's degree can play an important role in delivering psychological services. Salaries, responsibilities, and working conditions tend to be commensurate with level of training in the discipline. In this era of managed care, psychologists with PhDs are increasingly filling supervisory roles in the delivery of mental health services (Humphreys, 1996).

As indicated in Figure 1.1, about 63 percent of the members of the APA who work in the field of psychology deliver human services. About 44 percent are clinical psychologists who work in clinics, community mental health centers, health maintenance organizations, veterans' hospitals, public hospitals, and public and private mental health hospitals. The remainder are private practitioners who maintain offices and work in schools, universities, business, and numerous other public and private settings (American Psychological Association, 1995a).

FIGURE 1.1

What Psychologists Do

Of the members of the American Psychological Association who work in the field of psychology, about 63 percent are involved in the delivery of mental health services—as clinical, counseling, and school psychologists and as other human services providers. The remaining 37 percent focus on research, teaching, and application in university settings, government, and business.

(Data provided by American Psychological Association, 1995.)

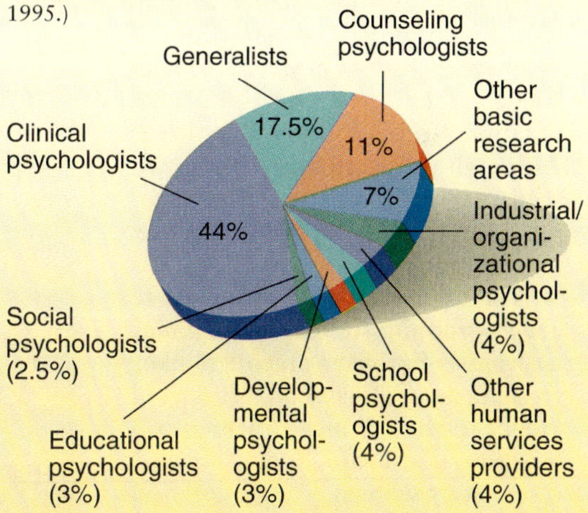

Psychologists with PhDs provide more than 50 million hours of service annually to 4 to 10 million people in the United States (Howard et al., 1986). Most psychologists employed by hospitals spend their time in the direct delivery of human services, including individual and group therapy. About 4 percent of psychologists are employed by business, government, and industry. About 30 percent of the APA's members are employed by universities, nearly half of them in psychology departments. University psychologists spend most of their time researching and teaching.

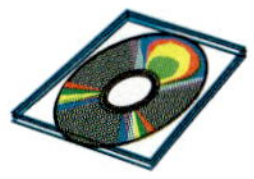

Fig. 1.3

Diversity, on page 10, looks at the current prevalence of women and members of ethnic minorities in the ranks of psychology's practitioners.

Applied Research, Human Services, and Experimental Psychology

Applied research, human services, and experimental psychology have much in common. Actually, human services is a subfield of applied research, but it comprises such a large proportion of psychologists that it is generally viewed as a separate field of

Diversity

Women and Ethnic Minorities Are Hidden No Longer

A helping profession with deep scientific roots, psychology is attracting increasing numbers of women and members of ethnic minorities. For example, 73 percent of bachelor's degrees in psychology are earned by women, and the number of women in graduate training programs has doubled since the mid-1970s (two out of three graduate students in psychology are women). Also, the proportion of full-time faculty who are women is about 27 percent (Kohout, Wicherski, & Cooney, 1992). Data suggest that this trend is likely to continue (Russo & Denmark, 1987). Although proportionately more women than men are entering psychology, women are more likely than men to be employed on a part-time basis.

The first women psychologists received training similar to their male colleagues but were much less likely to achieve professional status equivalent to that of men (Furumoto & Scarborough, 1986). Today, however, research by women is at the forefront of scientific inquiry. Among important women in psychology are Judith Wallerstein and Mavis Hetherington, who have studied the impact of divorce on children; Judith Rodin, who has done important work on eating and eating disorders; Elizabeth Loftus, who has studied the ability of eyewitnesses to remember accurately; and Sandra Scarr, who studies intelligence. Women are presidents of national, regional, and local psychological organizations, and their thoughts and work often dominate psychological journals (Russo & Denmark, 1987).

The number of members of ethnic minorities who become psychologists is small—currently about 8.5 percent—but is slowly growing (Kohout & Pion, 1990). Data indicate that African Americans receive about 3 percent of the PhDs in psychology; Hispanic Americans also earn 3 percent of the PhDs (Smith & Davidson, 1992). In the early part of this century, there was harsh discrimination against members of minority groups. Still, many African Americans overcame the odds; they received PhDs, published scientific research, and made lasting contributions to the discipline.

▲ *Kenneth Clark*

Gilbert Haven Jones was the first African American holder of a PhD to teach psychology in the United States. Albert S. Beckham was a clinician who published studies in the 1930s of socioeconomic status and adolescence among minority groups. Inez Prosser and Howard H. Long are also among the distinguished early psychologists who published in the 1930s. Francis C. Sumner (1895–1954), who chaired the psychology department at Howard University, is considered the father of African American psychology. Kenneth Clark, former president of the American Psychological Association, achieved national prominence for his work on the harmful effects of segregation. The works of Mamie Phipps Clark on self-esteem and racial identification (with her husband, Kenneth Clark) have become classics.

There is less documentation about the role of Hispanic Americans in the history of psychology. Yet we know that prominent Hispanic American psychologists have focused on a variety of psychological issues. Manuel Barrera has done important work in community psychology, especially on social support systems. R. Diaz-Guerrero has examined cultural and personality variables in Hispanic Americans. Jorge Sanchez conducted exemplary research on the role of education in minority achievement and on biased test scores and intelligence testing.

Psychology is strengthened by understanding rather than avoidance of the range of people's abilities. Research and theory become more complete when the multicultural nature of human beings is explored. On a practical level, the effectiveness of the helping professions is enhanced when practitioners understand their clients. The variety of psychologists, of their research interests, and of their socioeconomic and ethnic backgrounds is now contributing to a greater recognition of diversity among people—and this diversity is a strength that psychologists today not only recognize but celebrate.

psychology. All psychologists consider research and theory to be the cornerstones of their approach (Beutler et al., 1995). A human services provider may also do research, and a researcher who works in a university may also provide human services to the university or the community at large. For example, a human services psychologist may help an alcoholic patient by applying learning principles discovered in an experimental laboratory. Similarly, problems discovered by therapists challenge researchers to investigate causes in the laboratory. This cross-fertilization is stimulating. Let's look at each of these areas.

Applied Research. Applied psychologists do research and then use that research to solve practical problems. Many use psychological principles in businesses, government, and institutions, such as hospitals.

Engineering psychologists (sometimes called *human factors psychologists*) use psychological principles to help people design machines for safe and efficient use (for example, an easy-to-use ATM machine). We will discuss this field in Chapter 17.

Educational psychologists focus on such topics as how learning occurs in the classroom, how intelligence affects performance, and the relationship between personality and learning. We will also discuss this field in Chapter 17.

Forensic psychologists deal with legal issues, often working in courts and correctional systems. They evaluate whether inmates are ready for parole, whether a rehabilitation program is achieving its goals, or whether an accused criminal has lied, deserves an "insanity defense," or is likely to give false testimony.

Health psychologists determine how lifestyle changes can improve health. They devise techniques for helping people avoid medical and psychological problems. We will discuss this field further in Chapter 13.

Behavioral medicine psychologists help people who suffer from chronic physical problems such as back pain and migraine headaches learn to cope and develop techniques to manage pain.

Sport psychologists are in an emerging field that focuses on brain–behavior interactions, the role of sports in healthful lifestyles, and the motivation and preparation of athletes. We will also discuss this field in Chapter 17.

Industrial/organizational psychologists help employers evaluate employees; they also focus on personnel selection, employee motivation and training, work behavior, incentives, and work appraisals. They apply psychological research and theory to organizational problems such as productivity, turnover, absenteeism, and management–labor relations. Working in human resources offices and in other departments at universities and businesses, they also evaluate organizational programs. Industrial/organizational psychologists are discussed in greater detail in Chapter 17.

Human Services. Many human services psychologists use behavioral principles to teach people to cope with life more effectively. They try to help people solve problems and to promote well-being. Within the human services area are the subfields of clinical, counseling, community, and school psychology.

Clinical psychologists help clients with behavior problems such as anger, shyness, depression, and marital discord. They work either in private practice or at hospitals, mental institutions, or social service agencies. They administer psychological tests, interview potential clients, and use psychological methods to treat emotional problems. Many universities employ psychologists to help students and staff handle the pressures of academic life.

Surprisingly, the practice of clinical psychology is a relatively recent development. It resulted from the work of Lightner Witmer (1867–1956), a charter member of the APA, who called for the establishment of a field within psychology that would focus on helping people (McReynolds, 1996). Witmer established the first psychological clinic, at the University of Pennsylvania, and coined the term *clinical psychologist*. The field of clinical psychology grew especially rapidly after World War II, when its training began to focus on professional practice and human services needs (Strickland, 1988).

Counseling psychologists, like clinical psychologists, work with people who have behavior problems. They also help people handle career planning, marriage and family problems, and parenting problems. A counselor like this was working with Alex Mattison's family in the chapter opener.

▲ *Community psychologists, such as this counselor working with troubled teenage boys, can be found in a variety of settings. They all share the goal of helping individuals and communities build the networks necessary to help themselves.*

Counseling psychology began in the 1940s, and at first the problems presented by its clients were less serious than those presented by clients of clinical psychologists. However, since the 1980s, the problems of layoffs, spousal abuse, and violence have become more serious, and counseling psychologists have increasingly used psychotherapy and other therapies that were previously used exclusively by clinical psychologists. According to many practitioners and researchers, counseling and clinical psychology are converging (Fitzgerald & Osipow, 1986).

Counseling psychologists may work for public agencies such as mental health centers, hospitals, and universities. Many work in college or university counseling centers, where they help students adjust to the academic atmosphere and provide them with vocational and educational guidance. Like clinical psychologists, many counseling psychologists research the causes and treatment of maladjustment.

Community psychologists strengthen existing social support networks and stimulate the formation of new networks to meet a variety of challenges (L. R. Gonzales et al., 1983). Their goal is to help individuals and their neighborhoods or communities to grow, develop, and plan for the future. Community psychology emerged in response to the widespread desire for an action-oriented approach to individual and social adjustment, and one of its key elements is community involvement to effect social change. For example, community psychologists have been instrumental in organizing social support groups that help AIDS patients and their families handle the stress and loss of self-esteem produced by this catastrophic illness. Community psychologists work in mental health agencies, state governments, and private organizations. We will discuss this field in Chapter 17.

School psychologists help students, teachers, parents, and administrators to communicate effectively with one another and accomplish mutually agreed-upon goals. School psychology began in 1896 at the University of Pennsylvania in a clinic founded to study and treat children considered "morally or mentally defective." Early leaders such as G. Stanley Hall and Lightner Witmer were crucial in promoting psychological interventions and techniques in schools (T. K. Fagan, 1992).

There are more than 30,000 school psychologists, most of whom work in educational systems. They administer and interpret tests, help teachers with classroom-related problems, and influence school policies and procedures (Bardon, 1983). They foster communication among parents, teachers, administrators, and other psychologists at schools. They also provide information to teachers and parents about students' progress and advise them on how to help students achieve more.

Experimental Psychology. Experimental psychologists try to identify and understand the basic elements of behavior and mental processes. Theirs is an approach, not a specific field. That is, experimental psychologists use a set of *techniques*; experimental psychology does not define the topics to be examined. For example, applied psychologists may be involved in experimental research, and experimental psychologists may teach in university settings as well as do research. However, experimental psychologists focus on understanding basic research issues, whereas applied psychologists generally use experimental techniques to improve a specific situation, help a mental health practitioner, or work with an employer.

Experimental psychology covers many areas of interest, some of which overlap with fields outside psychology. Experimental psychologists may be interested, for example, in visual perception, in how people learn language or solve problems, or in how hormones influence behavior. *Physiological psychologists* (sometimes called *neuropsychologists*) try to understand the relationship between the brain and behavior. They may examine drugs, hormones, and even brain transplants. We will examine some of their explorations in Chapter 2. *Cognitive psychologists* focus on thought processes, especially the relationships among learning, memory, and perception. They may, for example, examine how organisms process and interpret information on the basis of some internal representation in memory. We will discuss this field further in Chapter 7. *Developmental psychologists* focus on the emotional, physical, and intellectual changes that take place throughout people's lives. We will return to this field in Chapters 10 and 11. *Social psychologists* study how other people affect an individual's behavior and thoughts and how people interact with one another. For example, they may examine attitude formation, aggressive versus helping behavior, or the formation of intimate relationships. We will discuss this field in Chapter 16.

FOCUS

Review

- Identify the focuses of applied research, human services, and experimental psychology. pp. 11–13
- What makes experimental psychologists different from applied psychologists? p. 12

Think Critically

- Which different kinds of practitioners do you think would be best suited to work with the Mattison family, whose story opened this chapter?
- If you were to seek help for marital conflict, what would be the key reason for choosing a psychologist rather than a psychiatrist?

The Research Process

If you ever have the opportunity to tour a psychologist's laboratory, do so. Even better, if you have the chance to assist a psychologist in research, take advantage of it. Although psychologists use some of the same techniques as other scientists, they refine these techniques to deal with the uncertainties of human behavior. The typical scientific research process in psychology is usually quite systematic and begins with a specific question. This process usually takes the form of an **experiment**—a procedure in which a researcher systematically manipulates and observes elements of a situation in order to answer a question and, usually, to establish causality. For example, if a researcher wants to determine the relationship between an animal's eating behavior and its weight, the researcher could systematically vary (manipulate) how much the animal ate and then weigh (observe) the animal each day to infer that eating behavior and weight are causally related.

Correlation Is Not Causation

Consider this statement: In general, the more education you have, the higher your yearly income. This statement is true, but only up to a point. After a person receives a college degree, adding a professional degree is less likely to add significant additional income to the person's yearly take-home pay. It is not accurate to say that each unit of education causes income to rise; rather, education allows a person to open new doors and creates opportunities to earn more. At a certain point, another master's degree helps little in increasing opportunities. In short, more education does not *cause* more yearly income.

Experiment: Procedure in which a researcher systematically manipulates and observes elements of a situation in order to answer a question and, usually to test hypotheses and make inferences about cause and effect.

Only controlled laboratory experiments permit researchers to make *cause-and-effect statements*—inferences about the causes of behavior. This is a key point:

FIGURE 1.2

Correlations Do Not Show Causation

Although research shows that broken homes and crime are correlated, it does not show causation. Poverty, a third variable, may be the cause of both crime and broken homes.

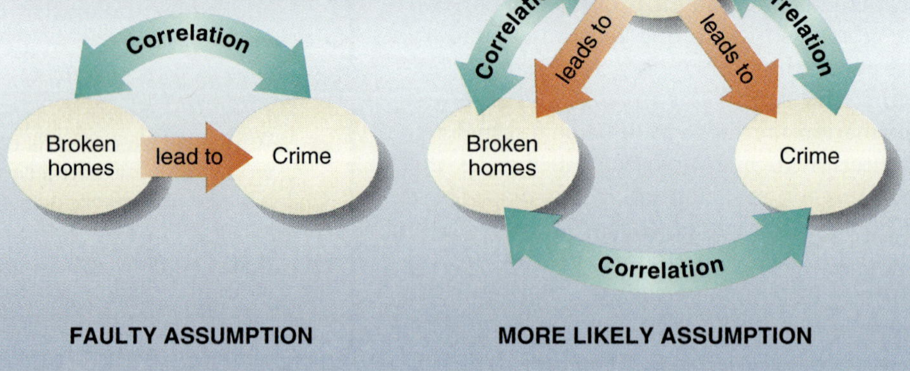

Correlated events are not necessarily causally related. Two events are *correlated* when the increased presence (or absence) of a particular situation is regularly associated with a high (or low) presence of another situation, event, or situational feature. For example, a researcher who finds that children from broken homes have more emotional problems and commit more crimes than other children can state that there is a correlation. However, the researcher cannot conclude that broken homes *cause* emotional problems or crime (see Figure 1.2). By contrast, events are causally related when one event makes another event occur—when one event or situation is contingent on another.

When psychologists suggest that one situation causes another, they have to be sure that several specific conditions are met. They pay close attention to how the data are collected and to whether the results of the study are repeatable in additional experiments. To make meaningful causal inferences, psychologists must create situations in which they can limit the likelihood of obtaining a result that is simply a chance occurrence or due to other irrelevant factors. Only by using carefully formulated experiments can psychologists make sound interpretations of their results and cautiously extend them to other (sometimes therapeutic) situations. Experiments have specific components and requirements, which we'll examine next.

Variable: Condition or characteristic of a situation or person that is subject to change (that varies) within or across situations or individuals.

Independent variable: The variable in a controlled experiment that the experimenter directly and purposely manipulates to see how the variables under study will be affected.

Dependent variable: The variable in a controlled experiment that is expected to change because of the manipulation of the independent variable.

Variables, Hypotheses, and Experimental and Control Groups

Variables. A **variable** is a condition or a characteristic of a situation or person that is subject to change (that varies) either within or across situations or individuals. Researchers manipulate variables in order to measure how the changes in them affect other variables. There are two types of variables in any experiment: independent and dependent variables. The **independent variable** is the variable in a controlled experiment that the experimenter directly and purposely manipulates to see how the variables under study will be affected. The **dependent variable** is the variable that is expected to change because of manipulation of the independent variable. For example, one characteristic of a situation that might change is temperature, and a change in temperature might affect behavior. A researcher might therefore raise the temperature in a room to determine if a person's activity level is increased or decreased by the change.

To see how variables come into play, imagine a simple experiment intended to determine the effects of sleep loss on behavior. The independent (manipulated) variable might be the number of hours college students are allowed to sleep. The dependent variable could be the students' reaction to a stimulus—for example, how quickly they push a button when a light is flashed. The participants in the study might be a large group of college students who normally sleep about 7 hours a night.

Hypotheses. As we saw earlier, a *hypothesis* is a tentative statement or idea expressing a causal relationship between two events or variables that are to be evaluated in a research study. The hypothesis of a sleep experiment might be that students deprived of sleep will react more slowly to a stimulus than will students allowed to sleep their regular 7 hours. Suppose the participants sleep in the laboratory on four successive nights and are tested each morning on a reaction-time task. The participants sleep 7 hours on each of three nights but only 4 hours on the fourth. If the response times after the first three nights are constant and if all other factors are held equal, any observed differences in reaction-time on the fourth test (following the night of 4 hours of sleep) can be attributed to the number of hours of sleep. That is, changes in the independent variable (numbers of hours of sleep) will produce changes in the dependent variable (reaction time). If the results show that students deprived of sleep respond on the reaction-time task a half-second slower than they did after normal sleep, the researcher could feel justified in concluding that sleep deprivation acts to slow down reaction time. The researcher's tentative idea would have been affirmed by the experiment.

Experimental and Control Groups. Researchers must determine whether it is actually the changes in the manipulated variable, and not some unknown extraneous factor, that cause a change in the dependent variable. One way to do this is to set up at the start of the experiment at least two groups of participants who are identical in important ways. **Participants** are individuals who take part in experiments and whose behavior is observed for research data collection (In previous decades, psychologists have called the participants *subjects.*) The attributes participants must have in common will depend on what the experimenter is testing. For example, because reflexes slow down as a person grows older, the researcher in the reaction-time experiment would want to ensure that the two groups were composed of participants of the same or nearly the same age.

Once the participants are known to be identical on important attributes, they are assigned randomly to either the experimental or the control group. *Random assignment* means that the participants are assigned by lottery rather than on the basis of any particular characteristic, preference, or situation that might have even a remote possibility of influencing the outcome. The **experimental group** is the group of participants for whom the independent variable is manipulated. The **control group** is the comparison group—the group of participants tested on the dependent variable in the same way as the experimental group but for whom the independent variable is not manipulated. In the reaction-time experiment, the students who sleep a full 7 hours on all four nights are the control group. Those who are allowed to sleep only 4 hours on the last night are the experimental group. By comparing the reaction times (the dependent variable) for the experimental and control groups, the researcher can determine whether the independent variable is responsible for any differences in the dependent variable between the groups.

If the researcher is confident that all the participants responded with the same reaction time before the experiment—that is, that the two groups are truly comparable—then the person can conclude that sleep deprivation is the cause of the experimen-

Participant: Individual who takes part in an experiment and whose behavior is observed for research data collection. Also known as a *subject*.

Experimental group: In an experiment, the group of participants for whom the independent variable is manipulated.

Control group: In an experiment, the comparison group—the group of participants who are tested on the dependent variable in the same way as the experimental group but for whom the independent variable is not manipulated.

tal group's decreased performance. Without comparable groups, the effect of the independent variable is not clear, and few real conclusions can be drawn from the data.

Operational Definitions, Sample Size, and Significant Differences

Operational Definitions. A key component of successful scientific research is that all terms used in describing the variables and the experimental procedure must be given operational definitions. An **operational definition** is a definition of a variable in terms of a set of methods or procedures used to measure or study that variable. When a researcher manipulates an organism's state of hunger, the concept *hunger* must be defined in terms of the procedures necessary to produce hunger. For example, a researcher might be interested in the effects of hunger (the independent variable) on exploratory behavior (the dependent variable) in mice. The researcher might deprive mice of food for 6, 10, 12, or 24 hours and then record their exploratory behavior. The researcher might operationally define hunger in terms of the number of hours of food deprivation and exploratory behavior in terms of the number of times the mice walked farther than 2 feet down a path.

Sample Size. Another important factor in an experiment is the size and representativeness of the sample. A **sample** is a group of participants who are assumed to be representative of the population about which an inference is being made. For example, a researcher studying schizophrenia has to put together a sample of people with that disorder. A psychologist who wishes to discover whether murderers have low levels of the neurotransmitter serotonin in their brains would have better luck finding a relevant sample at a maximum security penitentiary than at a garden club.

The number of participants in a sample is very important. If an effect is obtained consistently with a large enough number of participants, the researcher can reasonably rule out individual differences and chance as causes. The key assumption is that a large sample better represents the population to which the researcher wishes to generalize the results.

Significant Differences. Researchers want to be sure that the differences they find are significant. For psychologists, a **significant difference** in an experiment is a difference that is statistically unlikely to have occurred because of chance alone and is most likely due to the systematic manipulation of the researcher. For example, when one therapy technique appears to be more effective than another, the researcher wants to be sure that the results with the first technique are significantly different from the results with the second and that the difference is enough to be important. The results are significantly different only if they could not be due to chance, due to the use of only one or two participants, or due to a unique set of participants. Such conclusions can come only from experiments. If experimental results are not statistically significant, they are not considered to have proved or disproved the hypothesis.

Operational definition: Definition of a variable in terms of the set of methods or procedures used to measure or study that variable.

Sample: A group of participants who are assumed to be representative of the population about which an inference is being made.

Significant difference: In an experiment, a difference that is unlikely to have occurred because of chance alone and is most likely due to the systematic manipulations of the researcher.

Successful Experiments Avoid Pitfalls

Good experiments often involve several experimental groups, each tested under different conditions. Another study of the effects of sleep deprivation might involve a control group and five experimental groups. The participants in each of the experimental groups might be deprived of sleep for a different length of time (sleep deprivation operationally defined in terms of number of hours of sleep lost from the normal number of hours slept). In this way, the researcher could examine the effects of several different degrees of sleep deprivation on reaction time.

In a well-designed experiment, the experimenter also looks closely at the nature of the independent variable. Are there actual values for the independent variable above or below which results will differ markedly? For example, the researcher might find that a 1-hour loss of sleep has no effect, that a 2-hour deprivation produces only a modest effect, and that every additional hour of deprivation markedly slows reaction time. These results would show that reaction time is dependent on the amount of sleep deprivation. The use of several experimental groups yields better understanding of how the independent variable (sleep deprivation) affects the dependent variable (reaction time).

▲ *Studies of the effects of various events on worker productivity were conducted at Western Electric's Hawthorne plant between 1924 and 1933. A key finding was that workers performed better simply because they were being given special attention.*

Expectancy Effects. Frequently, things turn out just the way a researcher expects. Researchers are aware, however, that their *expectancies,* or expectations, about results may influence their findings, particularly where human behavior is concerned. A researcher may unwittingly create a situation that leads to specific prophesied results—a **self-fulfilling prophecy**. For example, a teacher may develop expectations about a student's performance early in the year, then unconsciously set low (or high) standards for that student. Sensing those standards, the student will often confirm the teacher's expectations, even when the expectations may not reflect the student's potential ability. In these instances, the student's performance has fulfilled the teacher's prophecy, regardless of other factors.

To avoid the risk of self-fulfilling prophecies, researchers often use a **double-blind technique**—a research technique in which neither the experimenter nor the participants know who is in the control or the experimental group. In this situation, someone who is not connected with the research project keeps track of which participants are assigned to which group. The double-blind technique minimizes the effect that a researcher's subtle cues might have on participants. (In a single-blind experiment, the researcher knows who is in the experimental group and who is in the control group, but the participants do not know who is assigned to which group or whether they are being presented with a manipulated variable.)

Researchers also try to minimize the demand characteristics of studies. **Demand characteristics** are the elements of a study situation that might set things up in a specific way or tip off a participant as to the purpose of the study and perhaps thereby elicit specific behavior from the participant. Participants who even *think* they know the real purpose of a study may try to behave "appropriately" and in so doing may distort the results. Some techniques that minimize the impact of demand characteristics are the use of computers to decrease interaction with people (participants are less likely to want to act appropriately for a computer), of unobtrusive measures such as tape recording rather than note taking, and of deception (concealing the real purpose of the study) until the end of the research session.

Even when a double-blind procedure is used and demand characteristics are minimized, participants often just behave differently when they are in a research study. This finding is known as the **Hawthorne effect**, after some early research studies at the Hawthorne industrial plant that showed that people behave differently (usually better) when they know they are being observed. Researchers therefore attempt to make participants feel comfortable and natural and to create experimental situations that minimize the effects of participation. They often do not collect data until after participants have adapted to the experimental situation and have become less excited about being part of the research study.

Because the topic of this section, the research process, is so central to psychological inquiry and because it can be applied to your own thinking, it will be the focus of special features called *The Research Process* throughout this book—like the one on pages 18 and 19. This first one will remind you to think like a psychological scientist every day.

Self-fulfilling prophecy: The unwitting creation by a researcher of a situation that leads to specific prophesied results.

Double-blind technique: Research technique in which neither the experimenter nor the participants know who is in the control or the experimental group.

Demand characteristics: Elements of a study situation that might set things up in a specific way or tip off a participant as to the purpose of the study and perhaps thereby elicit specific behavior from the participant.

Hawthorne effect: The finding, based on early research studies at the Hawthorne industrial plant, that people behave differently (usually better) when they know they are being observed.

THE RESEARCH PROCESS

Thinking Critically and Evaluating Research

Psychologists, like all scientists, are trained to think, to evaluate research critically, and to put their results into a meaningful framework. Psychologists follow a traditional approach to evaluating research. To benefit from this textbook, you might find it helpful to use the same critical thinking skills and framework in order to follow their logic, to understand their approach, and to evaluate their research.

Critical thinking consists of evaluating the evidence, sifting through the choices, assessing the outcomes, and deciding whether the conclusions make sense. When you think critically, you are being evaluative. You are not accepting glib generalizations; instead you are determining the relevance of facts and looking for biases and imbalances, as well as for objectivity and testable, repeatable results. A critical thinker identifies central issues and is careful not to draw cause-and-effect conclusions from correlations.

When you think critically about research, you become a detective sorting through facts. You look objectively at the facts, question the hypotheses and conclusions, avoid oversimplification, and consider all the arguments, objections, and counter-arguments. You evaluate all assumptions and assertively seek out conflicting points of view. You revise your opinions when the data and conclusions call for it. Whenever you have to evaluate a research study in this text, the popular press, or a psychological publication, you will find it helpful to focus on five research criteria; purpose, methodology, participants, repeatability, and conclusions.

Purpose. What is the purpose of this research? What is the researcher trying to test, demonstrate, or prove? Has the problem been clearly defined? Is the researcher qualified to conduct this research?

Methodology. Is the methodology appropriate and carefully executed? Is the method of investigation used (for example, a case study, survey, or experiment) the most appropriate one for the topic? Has the method been utilized properly? Is there a control group? Have variables been carefully (operationally) defined? Has the researcher followed ethical guidelines?

Participants. Was the sample of participants properly chosen and carefully described? How was the sample selected? Does the sample accurately reflect the characteristics of the population of individuals about which the researcher would like to make generalizations? Will any generalizations be possible from this study?

Repeatability. Are the results repeatable? Has the researcher shown the same finding more than once? Have other investigators made similar findings? Are the results clear and unambiguous—that is, not open to criticism based on poor methodology? What additional evidence will be necessary for a psychologist to support the conclusions?

Conclusions. How logical are the conclusions, implications, and applications suggested by the study? Does the researcher's data support them? Has the researcher gone beyond the data, drawing conclusions

Avoiding Gender, Racial, and Cultural Bias

We just saw that one way to ensure good experiments is have a large enough sample of participants who accurately reflect the population. However, researchers must also be careful to avoid subtle biases that influence results, such as gender, racial, and cultural bias. At any stage of the research endeavor, an experimenter can influence the results and their interpretation by making assumptions about people, their tendencies, and how they might be affected by the variable under study. Such assumptions often include researchers' attitudes about whether to report findings such as gender or racial differences among participants.

Although many behaviors seem universal, truly universal behaviors are those that occur in all human beings regardless of their culture. When research studies are used to draw conclusions and make generalizations about people, it is important to understand that enormous differences exist among both individuals and groups of people. The young and the old may behave differently under similar conditions; research done only on men may yield different results from research done only on women. People are not all alike and do not all behave in the same way, even when in the same situation. Thus, researchers have become especially sensitive to issues of human diversity.

To do effective research, draw meaningful conclusions, and make generalizations that may be wide-ranging, researchers must recognize and test for elements of diversity, even within one society, such as the United States. A society includes indi-

that might fit a predisposed view rather than conclusions that follow logically from the facts of the study? What implications do the data have for psychology as a science and as a profession? What are the potential implications for you as an individual? Has the researcher considered alternative explanations?

Think again about the sleep deprivation experiment described earlier. Use the five criteria to evaluate this research. The participants were college students deprived of sleep and tested on a reaction-time task.

Was the purpose of the study clear? The purpose was to assess the effect of sleep loss on reaction time.

Was the methodology appropriate? The method involved depriving participants of sleep after they had become used to sleeping in a controlled environment; participants were tested each morning. The task was carefully operationally defined.

What about the participants? The participants were college students who were in good health. Reasonable generalizations from their reaction times to the reaction times of other similarly aged people might be possible.

What about repeatability? If the results were obtained with several groups of participants, and if the results were consistent within each of those groups, the repeatability of the results would seem assured.

Last, what about the conclusions? Limited conclusions can be drawn from such a research study. There was only one age group—college students. There were no controls on other factors in the students' environment, such as work loads, school pressure, energy expenditures, and history of sleep loss. A simple conclusion about sleep deprivation could be drawn: In a controlled research study of college students, sleep deprivation tends to slow down reaction time. However, not much more could be said, and no generalizations could be applied to, say, children, older adults, or the chronically mentally ill. The results of the study do not contradict common sense, but they add little to our overall understanding of reaction times.

A key to thinking critically about research is to be evaluative, to question all aspects of the study. Think about the advantages as well as the limitations of the research method used. You can also apply your critical thinking skills to nonacademic material. When a TV commercial tells you that 9 out of 10 doctors recommend Brand X, think critically about that claim. What kind of doctors, for what kind of ailment, for patients of what age, and for what extent of usage?

As you read this text, evaluate research findings. I will present the research to you in ways that allow you to critically evaluate it and to draw your own conclusions. From time to time in each chapter I will also ask you some *Focus* questions, called *Think Critically.* These questions will suggest new ideas and perspectives for you to consider as you evaluate the research studies presented. At the end of each chapter, I will lead you to make *Critical Thinking Connections* between topics spanning the chapters of the text. These are not the only places in the text where you should use your critical thinking skills, but they are places where you can definitely be evaluative.

viduals from many different cultures, races, religions, and so on. Each subgroup has developed its own style of living, which may vary considerably from that of the majority culture and may lead to marked ethnic-related differences in day-to-day behavior and in mental health (Snowden & Cheung, 1990). Psychologists say that a community, organization, or nation is culturally diverse if it has differences in race, ethnicity, language, nationality, age, and religion within it.

Race and Ethnicity. Race refers to a person's ancestry and descent and to a heritable set of traits; race is genetically determined. Ethnicity refers to people's common traits, background, and allegiances, which are often cultural, religious, or language-based; ethnicity is learned from family, friends, and experiences. Families of African American and Asian American descent bring to the American experience a wealth of different worldviews and different ways of bringing up children, based on their particular heritages. The ethnic makeup of the U.S. population is changing rapidly. In the 1980s the non-Hispanic white population grew by less than 8 percent; the African American population increased by 13 percent, to 30 million; and the Hispanic American population grew by 53 percent, to 23 million.

Culture. Culture reflects a person's racial and ethnic background, religious and social values, artistic and musical tastes, and scholarly interests. Culture is the unwritten social and psychological dictionary that each of us has learned and through which we interpret ourselves and others (Landrine, Klonoff, & Brown-

▲ *Researchers must take cultural differences into account when studying all aspects of behavior, including classroom learning.*

Collins, 1992). Various cultural vantage points shape behavior, values, and even mental health. For example, Asian American families have strongly held views about respect for elders and the continuity of the family. Asian American culture, like any culture, helps its group members interpret what they have seen, felt, and experienced; it offers guidelines for interpretation of the world.

Class. Closely tied to culture is a person's class. Although the U.S. class structure is not as rigid as in the last century or in some non-Western countries and class distinctions are somewhat fuzzy, Americans do fall into several socioeconomic classes. Among these classes are the economically poor, the disadvantaged, the educated, and the middle class. In different socioeconomic classes (which include individuals of different races and cultures), people may view the world differently and behave differently primarily because of their socioeconomic status. A research study that is not sensitive to such variables may confuse the causes of its results. For example, not considering socioeconomic class as a key variable in a study of drug use may lead to conclusions that are not true or, at a minimum, not generalizable to all socioeconomic classes.

Gender. Psychologists know that because of both biological and learned reasons, women often react differently than men do in psychological situations. It becomes easy to see that the gender of the population in a research study is crucial (Denmark, 1994). For example, research on morality shows that, in general, women see moral situations differently than men do; research on brain functions shows differences in brain structure between men and women; research on communication styles, aggression, and love shows sharp differences between men and women. Further, more than half of the people seen by mental health practitioners are women—although this may be because men with mental health problems are less likely to seek therapy. These differences must be explored to find their causes.

Age or Disabilities. The exceptional and the elderly are two other groups that shape research results in distinctive ways. The exceptional include individuals diagnosed as having mental retardation, learning disabilities, or physical disabilities. They often require a special sensitivity on the part of professionals. In addition, the elderly are a growing percentage of the general population. More than 30 million Americans are 65 or older, and the aging of the baby boomers means that that number will continue to rise. Psychologists are developing programs that focus on the special needs of the exceptional and the elderly for social support, physical and psychological therapy, and continuing education.

Diversity Within versus Between Groups. The differing perspectives on day-to-day behavior that special groups bring to the fabric of society have not always been appreciated, understood, or even recognized in psychological research or theory. For example, psychologists now take Freud to task for developing a personality theory that is seen as clearly sexist. (We will be evaluating Freud's theory in Chapter 12.) In Freud's day, however, considerations of sexism were unheard of. Further, minorities and special groups such as the exceptional and the elderly were rarely—if ever—included in psychological research studies intended to represent the general population. Today psychologists seek to study all types of people to make valid conclusions based on scientific evidence. They see cultural diversity as an asset for both theorists and practitioners; they also recognize that they must research, learn about, and theorize about this diversity to help individuals optimize their potential (Betancourt & Lopez, 1993). It is crucial to realize, though, that *there are* *usually more differences within a group than between groups.* For example, intelligence test scores differ more among Asian Americans than they do between Asian Americans and any other ethnic group (Zuckerman, 1990).

Individual circumstances exist, and people's individual experiences make glib generalizations impossible. It is true that individuals and special populations often act just as the majority population does, but often with a slightly different twist or variation. Here is the key point to remember as you read this book: While people are very much alike and share many common, even universal, experiences and behaviors, every individual is unique; each person's behavior reflects diverse life experiences.

▲ *Brief questionnaires, like the one being used here to survey passersby during the Olympic games, can help researchers gather a great deal of information quickly.*

Alternative Methods of Psychological Inquiry

Experiments, with their focus on cause-and-effect relationships, are not the only way to collect data about human behavior. Techniques providing information about other than cause-and-effect relationships are also important. These techniques include questionnaires, interviews, naturalistic observation, and case studies.

Questionnaires. A **questionnaire**, or *survey*, is usually a printed form with questions that is given to a large group of people. It is used by researchers to gather a large amount of information from many people in a short time. A questionnaire being used to learn the typical characteristics of psychology students might be sent to students enrolled in an introductory psychology course. It might ask each student to list age, sex, height, weight, previous courses taken, grades in high school, SAT scores, number of brothers and sisters, and parents' financial status. There might also be questions regarding sexual activity, career goals, and personal preferences in TV shows, clothing styles, and music.

One aim of surveys is to discover relationships among variables. For example, a questionnaire designed to assess aggressiveness might ask respondents to list their gender, the number of fights they have had in the past, their feelings of anger, and the sports they enjoy. The researcher who is analyzing the results might check to see whether men and women tend to differ in aggressive behaviors.

The strength of the questionnaire is that it gathers a large amount of information in a short time. Its weaknesses are that it is impersonal, it gathers only the information asked by the questions, it limits the participants' range of responses, it cannot prevent respondents from leaving some questions unanswered or from being untruthful in their responses, and it does not provide a structure from which cause-and-effect relationships can be inferred (although correlations may be found).

Interviews. An **interview** is typically a face-to-face meeting in which a researcher (interviewer) asks an individual a series of standardized questions. The interviewer usually tape-records or writes down the participant's responses. The advantage of an interview over a questionnaire is that it allows for a wider range of responses. An interviewer who notes an exaggerated response, for example, might decide to ask related questions and thus explore more fully an area that seems important to the participant. The interview technique is time-consuming, however, and, as with questionnaires, no cause-and-effect relationships can be inferred.

Naturalistic Observation. A seemingly simple way to find out about behavior is to observe it. As we've seen, however, people who are told they are going to be observed tend to become self-conscious and alter their natural behavior. Therefore,

Questionnaire: Printed form with questions, usually given to a large group of people; used by researchers to gather a substantial amount of data in a short time. Also known as a *survey*.

Interview: Face-to-face meeting in which a series of standardized questions are used to gather detailed information.

Naturalistic observation: Careful and objective observation of events from a distance, without observer intervention.

Case study: Method of interviewing participants to gain information about their background, including data on such factors as childhood, family, education, and social and sexual interactions.

psychologists often use the technique of **naturalistic observation**—careful and objective observation of events from a distance, without observer intervention. The intent is to see how people or animals behave in their natural settings.

A psychologist conducting research on persuasion might act like a browsing shopper at car lots, furniture stores, and appliance centers to discover how salespeople convince customers to buy expensive products. For example, the researcher might observe that one particularly successful car salesperson tends to show budget-minded customers the most expensive automobiles first, so mid-priced models will seem more affordable by comparison. The researcher might also watch a salesperson through a one-way mirror of the kind used to detect thefts in supermarkets.

The strength of naturalistic observation is that the data collected are largely uncontaminated by the researcher's presence or by a laboratory setting. A major weakness is that the behavior the psychologist may wish to examine is not always exhibited. For example, sometimes groups of people do not act persuasively or become aggressive; sometimes animals do not show mating behavior. Naturalistic observation is also very time-consuming.

Naturalistic observers take their data where and how they find them. They cannot manipulate the environment, because that might alter the behavior they are observing. Because variables cannot be manipulated, data from naturalistic observation, like those from questionnaires and interviews, do not permit cause-and-effect conclusions.

Case Studies. The **case study** is a method of interviewing participants to gain information about their background, including data on such factors as childhood, family, education, and social and sexual interactions. The information in a case study describes in detail a specific person's responses to the world; the case study is often used to determine a potential method of treatment.

The strength of the case study is that the information it provides is extensive, for one individual. A weakness is that the information describes only one individual and that person's particular situation. Because the behavior of one person may be like that of others or may be unique, researchers cannot generalize from one individual to an entire population. They must be cautious even when generalizing from a number of case studies.

See Table 1.1 for a summary of the major approaches to data collection.

TABLE 1.1 ***Five Approaches to Collecting Data***

Approach	Strengths	Weaknesses
Experiment	Manipulation of variables to control outside influences; best method for identifying causal relationships.	Laboratory environment is artificial; limited generalizability of findings; manipulation of some variables is unethical or impractical.
Questionnaire	Effective means of measuring actions, attitudes, opinions, preferences, and intentions of large numbers of people.	Lack of explanatory power; validity of findings is limited by sample; reliability is difficult to determine; self-report may be inaccurate or biased.
Interview	Allows a wide range of responses; follow-up questions are possible.	Does not enable researchers to draw conclusions about causal relationships; time-consuming.
Naturalistic observation	Behavior is unaffected by a researcher's manipulations.	Little opportunity to control variables; time-consuming.
Case study	Extensive evidence is gathered on a single person.	Lack of generalizability of findings; time-consuming.

Combined Techniques. Researchers often use several techniques, either at different times or in combination. When I was an undergraduate in a course on research methods, a group of us tried to examine how hitchhikers' attire affects success at getting rides. We posed as hitchhikers and alternated our clothing from grubby to moderately pleasant to dressy. One of us hid behind a billboard and counted the number of cars passing by, the number of drivers who stopped to inquire where we were going, and the number of drivers who offered us a ride (not many). Our experiment had many flaws, but it attempted to use the experimental method; that is, it manipulated an independent variable—type of clothes. It also used naturalistic observation—hiding behind the billboard and counting. The mixing of methods is not only acceptable but often desirable; sometimes it is the only way certain types of research can be conducted.

Ethics: Rules of proper and acceptable conduct that investigators use to guide psychological research; these rules concern the treatment of animals, the rights of human beings, and the responsibilities of investigators.

Ethics in Psychological Research

Some psychologists study behavior by first observing it in animals and then generalizing the principles to human behavior. Research with animals, and with human beings, is extensive, and researchers must pay special attention to ethical considerations in these situations. **Ethics** in research comprises the rules concerning proper and acceptable conduct that investigators use to guide their research; these rules govern the treatment of animals, the rights of human beings, and the responsibilities of investigators.

Research with Animals

Almost everyone has heard about white rats and pigeons being used in psychology labs. Using animals in research studies allows experimenters to isolate simple aspects of behavior and to eliminate the complex distractions and variables that arise in studies involving human beings. The use of animals also enables researchers to conduct studies that could not ethically be conducted with human beings. For example, it would be unethical to deprive human infants of visual stimulation to investigate the effects of visual restriction on their cognitive development. Furthermore, because most animals have shorter life spans than human beings, experimenters can observe and control animals' entire life history, perform autopsies to obtain information, and study several generations in a short time. Research with animals has helped psychologists understand many aspects of human behavior, including eating, learning, perception, and motivation (Baldwin, 1993).

Some people object to the use of animals in research, but at present there are no known realistic alternatives (Gallup & Suarez, 1985). For example, experiments on laboratory rats reveal much about the addictive properties of cocaine and its adverse effects on behavior. Similar experiments with human beings would be unethical. In addition, many people with diseases, such as multiple sclerosis and Alzheimer's disease, are seeing breakthroughs on a daily basis and have legitimate hopes for a cure through animal research and experimentation (Feeney, 1987). Most researchers are sensitive to the needs of animals (Novak & Suomi, 1988); furthermore, the American Psychological Association has strict ethical guidelines for the humane and sensitive care and treatment of animals used in research.

▲ *Research with animals is only a small part of psychological research, but it is invaluable for exploring key issues such as attachment.*

FOCUS

Review

- Distinguish between the independent and the dependent variable as well as the control and the experimental group. pp. 14, 15

- Identify two elements in the design of an experiment that are especially important to making generalizations about the results. p. 16

- Why is it important for psychologists to consider the cultural context in which behavior occurs? pp. 18–19

Think Critically

- Imagine a research study testing the effects of a low dosage of a drug that helps relieve anxiety. The participants are a sample of 50 men who suffer from job-related stress. What are the limitations of such a study? Would you say that such a study is poorly designed, or that it has a flawed methodology?

- Why do you think sample size is so important in psychological research?

Human Participants

Although animal research is an important part of the psychological landscape, psychologists more often work with human participants. In such research, psychologists investigate many of the same processes they study with animals, as well as designing experiments specifically for human participants. A psychologist who wishes to test whether an enhanced environment makes organisms smarter may use both animals and human participants. First, the researcher may first train one rat to run complicated mazes while leaving its littermate in a barren environment. Several months later, the researcher, in examining the two animals, may discover that the brain cells of the maze-running rat are larger and have more internal connections. Along the same lines, the psychologist may test whether a decline in IQ scores among nursing home residents can be halted or reversed by the enrichment of their environment with classes and special activities.

The American Psychological Association (1992) also has strict ethical guidelines for research with human participants: Participants cannot be coerced to do things that are harmful to them, that would have other negative effects, or that would violate standards of decency. The investigator is responsible for ensuring the ethical treatment of the participants in a research study; the participants are free to decline to participate or to withdraw at any time without penalty. In addition, any information gained in an experimental situation is considered strictly confidential. Before a study begins, human participants must also give the researcher their **informed consent**—their agreement through a signature on a document that they understand the nature of their participation in the research and have been fully informed about the general nature of the research, its goals, and its methods. At the end of the project, the participants must go through debriefing. **Debriefing** is a procedure to inform participants about the true nature of an experiment, including hypotheses, methods, and expected or potential results. Debriefing is done *after* the experiment so that the validity of the responses is not affected by participants' knowledge of the experiment's purpose.

Deception in Psychological Research

Is it ever acceptable for researchers to deceive human participants in psychological studies? Imagine a situation in which a researcher tricks a person into believing that she is causing another person pain. Is this acceptable? Or is it acceptable for a researcher to try to change a human participant's views of social or political issues just to see if the researcher can do so? The answer to these questions is generally no. Researchers must not use deception unless the study has important scientific, educational, or applied value. And even then, two key procedures must be followed: obtaining informed consent and providing debriefing.

Many psychologists believe deception is unacceptable under *any* circumstances. They assert that it undermines the public's belief in the integrity of scientists and that its costs outweigh its potential benefits. Today most psychologists do not conduct research in which there is deception; those who do are especially careful to use rigorous informed consent procedures and extensive debriefing to minimize poten-

Informed consent: The agreement of participants expressed through a signed document that indicates that they understand the nature of their participation in upcoming research and have been fully informed about the general nature of the research, its goals, and its methods.

Debriefing: A procedure to inform participants about the true nature of an experiment after its completion.

tially harmful effects. Whenever deception must be used, psychologists go to extraordinary lengths to protect the well-being, rights, and dignity of the participants; anything less is considered a violation of American Psychological Association guidelines (Fisher & Fyrberg, 1994).

Past and Present: Schools of Psychological Thought

Psychology as a discipline and a science would not have been recognized as such 200 years ago. The psychological study of human behavior has evolved over a relatively brief time span, beginning a little more than a century ago. Over that time, psychologists have subscribed to many different perspectives. Once fully developed and presented, these perspectives serve to orient researchers and provide them with a frame of reference in which to do new work. A specific perspective on the study of behavior is called a *school of psychological thought*. This section discusses the development of schools of psychological thought. (A timeline that includes many key events in that development is presented in Figure 1.3 on pages 26 and 27.) You will see that the study of behavior and mental processes, despite its short life, has had a rich and varied history.

The Early Traditions

Structuralism—The Contents of Consciousness. Wilhelm Wundt (1832–1920) developed the first widely accepted school of thought. In Leipzig, Germany, in 1879, the former medical student and physiologist founded the first psychological laboratory; its focus was the study of mental life (Leahey, 1992). Before Wundt, as I have implied, the field of psychology simply did not exist; what are now considered psychological questions lay in the domains of philosophy, medicine, and theology. Wundt was a formal, humorless man, but his lectures were extremely popular, and his dozens of graduate students were admiring followers. One of Wundt's major contributions was teaching his students to use the scientific method when asking psychological questions (Benjamin et al., 1992). Edward B. Titchener (1867–1927), an Englishman, through his writing and talks helped popularize Wundt's ideas, along with his own, in the United States and the rest of the English-speaking world.

What Wundt, Titchener, and others espoused was structuralism. **Structuralism** was the school of psychological thought that considered the organized structure of immediate, conscious experience to be the proper subject matter of psychology. Instead of looking at the broad range of behavior and mental processes that psychologists consider today, the structuralists tried to observe only the inner workings of the mind to find the elements of conscious experience.

To discover these elements of conscious experience, Wundt and Titchener used the technique of **introspection**, or *self-examination*, the description and analysis by a person of what he or she is thinking and feeling. In the process, they also conducted some of the first experiments in psychology. For example, they studied the speed of thought by observing reaction times for simple tasks.

By today's standards, of course, the structuralists focused too narrowly on individuals' conscious experiences. Understanding one person's conscious experiences actually reveals little about another's. Thus, though they represented a beginning, the structuralists' results allowed for few generalizations and the school made little progress in describing the nature of the mind.

Structuralism: The school of psychological thought that considered the organized structure of immediate, conscious experience to be the proper subject matter of psychology.

Introspection: Description and analysis by a person of what he or she is thinking and feeling. Also known as *self-examination*.

Functionalism—How Does the Mind Work? Before long, a new school developed, bringing with it a new, more active way of thinking about behavior. Built

FIGURE 1.3 A Timeline of Key Events in the History of Psychology

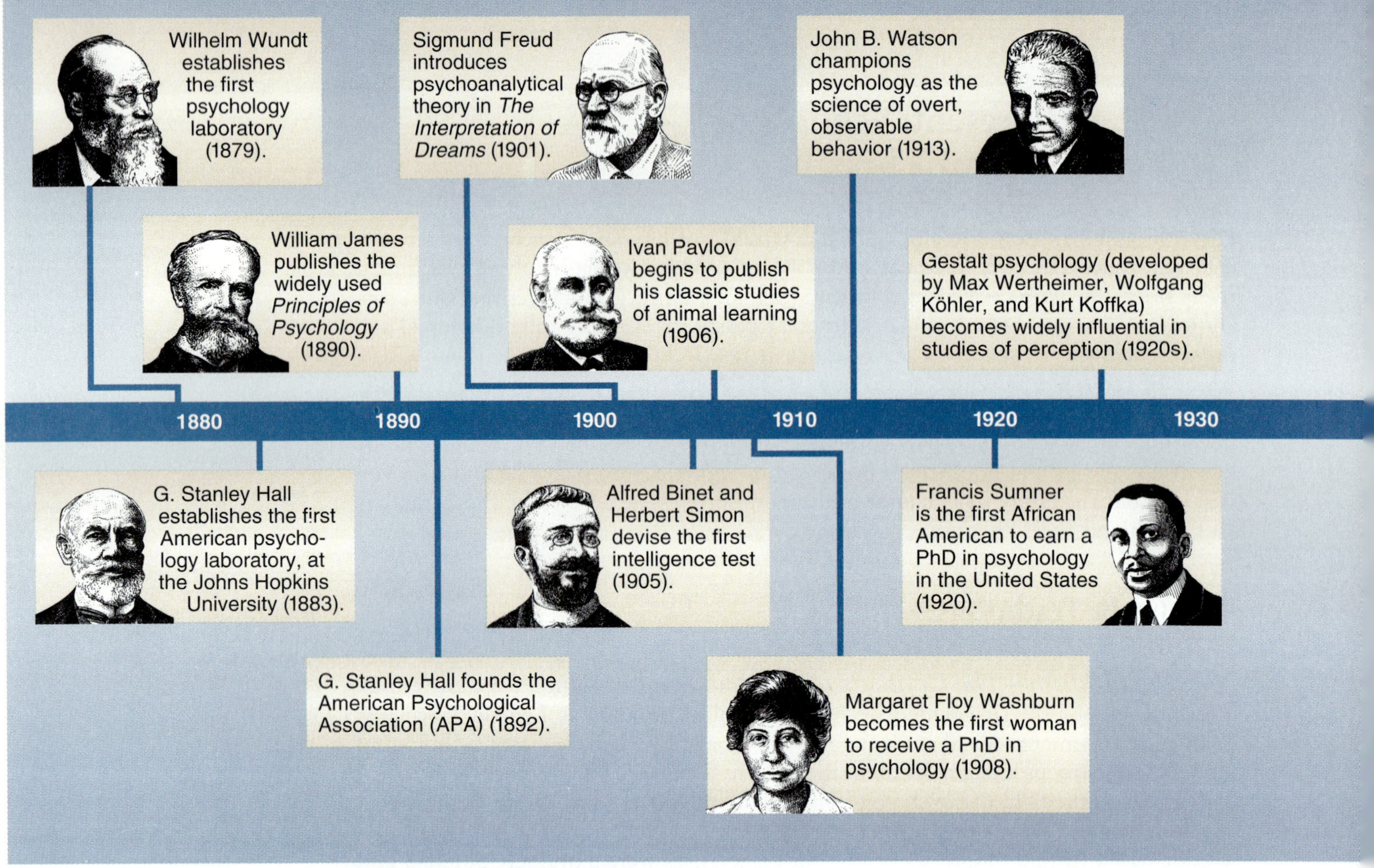

on the basic concepts of structuralism, **functionalism** was the school of psychological thought that tried to discover not just the mind's structures but how and why the mind *functions* and is related to consciousness. It also sought to understand how people adapted to their environment.

This lively new school of thought, with William James (1842–1910) at its head, was the first truly American psychology. James, a physician and professor of anatomy at Harvard University, argued that knowing only the contents of consciousness (structuralism) was too limited. Unlike Wundt, James was charming, informal, outgoing, and vivacious; especially well liked by his students, James argued that a psychologist also had to know how those contents functioned and worked together. Through such knowledge, the psychologist could understand how the mind (consciousness) guided behavior. In 1890 James published *Principles of Psychology*, in which he described the mind as a dynamic set of continuously evolving elements. In this work he coined the phrase *stream of consciousness*, describing the mind as a river, always flowing, never remaining still.

Functionalism: The school of psychological thought (an outgrowth of structuralism) that was concerned with how and why the conscious mind works; its main aim was to know how the contents of consciousness functioned and worked together.

James broadened the scope of structuralism by studying animals, by applying psychology in practical areas such as education, and by experimenting on overt behavior, not just mental processes. James's ideas influenced the life and writing of G. Stanley Hall (1844–1924), another American psychologist who was one of Wundt's early students. Hall, the first person to receive a doctorate in psychology, was the founder of the American Psychological Association (APA) and, like Titchener for structuralism, was an organizer and promoter of functionalist psychology in the United States.

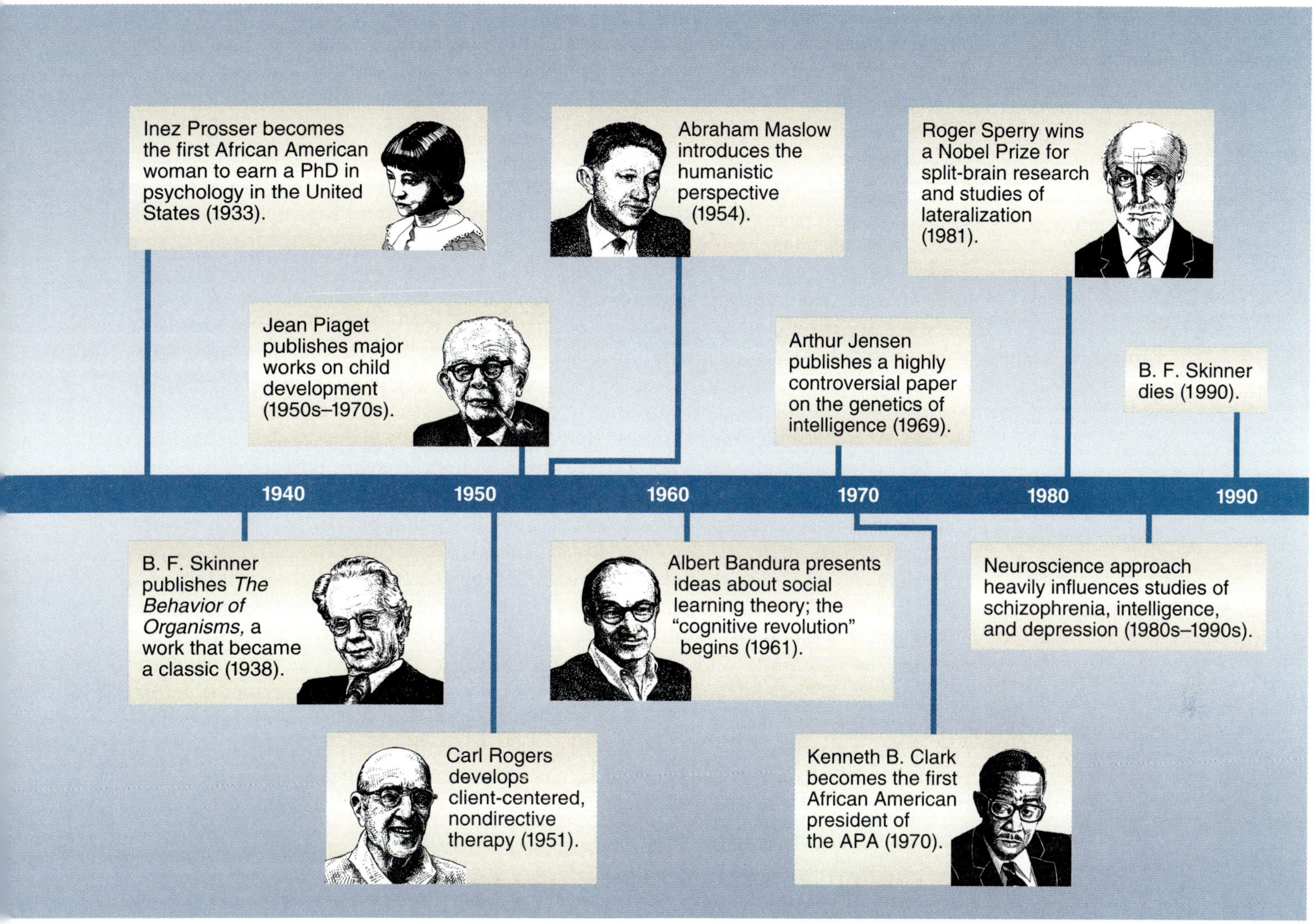

Functionalists continued to use introspection as a technique; for them psychology was still the study of consciousness. For many of the new emerging schools of psychology, however, this scope was too limiting. The early schools of psychological thought were soon replaced by different conceptualizations: Gestalt psychology, psychoanalysis, behaviorism, and humanistic and cognitive approaches to psychology.

Gestalt Psychology—Examining Wholes. In the early 20th century, while some psychologists were feeling their way with structuralism and functionalism, others were developing very different approaches. One such approach was **Gestalt psychology** (*Gestalt* means "configuration")—the school of psychological thought that argued that it is necessary to study a person's total experience, not just parts of the mind or behavior. Gestalt psychologists such as Max Wertheimer (1880–1943) and Kurt Koffka (1886–1941) suggested that conscious experience is more than simply the sum of its individual parts. Arguing that each mind organizes the elements of experience into something unique, by adding structure and meaning to incoming stimuli, Gestalt psychologists analyzed the world in terms of perceptual frameworks. They proposed that people mold simple sensory elements into patterns through which they interpret the world. By analyzing the whole experience—the patterns of a person's perceptions and thoughts—one could understand the mind and its workings.

Eventually Gestalt psychology became a major influence in many areas of psychology—for example, in therapy. A Gestalt-oriented therapist dealing with, say, Alex Mattison, the family member labeled a "problem" in this chapter's opener,

Gestalt psychology [gesh-TALT]: The school of psychological thought that argued that behavior cannot be studied in parts but must be viewed as a whole; the focus was on the unity of perception and thinking.

might call in the rest of the family to see how the "part" (the person seen as the problem) could be better understood in the context of the "whole" (the family configuration). However, as broad as its influence was, Gestalt psychology seemed lacking in scientific rigor and somewhat mystical, and it never achieved as wide a following as did psychoanalysis.

Psychoanalysis—Probing the Unconscious. One of the first researchers to develop a theory about emotional disturbance was Sigmund Freud (1856–1939). Freud grew up during a difficult time in the history of central Europe; he became a dark, brooding, complex, yet charismatic figure. Freud was a physician who was interested in helping people overcome anxiety; he worked in Vienna, Austria, focusing on the causes and treatment of emotional disturbances. Working from the premise that unconscious mental processes direct daily behavior, he developed techniques to explore those unconscious processes; these techniques include free association and dream interpretation. He emphasized that childhood experiences influence future adult behaviors and that sexual energy fuels day-to-day behavior.

Freud created the **psychoanalytic approach**—the school of psychological thought that assumes that psychological maladjustment is a consequence of anxiety resulting from unresolved conflicts and forces of which a person may be unaware. Its therapeutic technique is *psychoanalysis*. The psychoanalytic perspective has undergone many changes since Freud devised it. At times, in fact, it seems only loosely connected to Freud's basic ideas. When this approach was introduced in the United States, most psychologists ignored it. But by the 1920s, when the United States was growing intellectually and fully emerging from the repressed Victorian era, the influence of the psychoanalytic approach spread rapidly. Soon it was so influential and widely studied that it threatened to eclipse research-based laboratory psychology (Hornstein, 1992). Chapter 12 discusses Freud's theory of personality, and Chapter 15 discusses psychoanalysis as the therapeutic technique derived from his theory.

Psychological Schools Grow Broader

The early schools of psychology focused on the mind and how it functioned; for example, psychoanalysis examined how the unconscious operated and shaped later maladjustment. Yet it was not until the mid-1920s that the influences of learning were stressed, and it was not until the 1940s and 1950s that the roles of free will and self-expression were investigated. The 1970s saw the emergence of cognitive psychology, stressing thinking processes; psychology in the 1980s and 1990s has also been heavily influenced by studies of the neurological and biological foundations of behavior. Let's look at these more modern trends in the history of psychology.

Behaviorism—Observable Behavior. Despite their differences in focus, the structuralists, functionalists, Gestaltists, and psychoanalysts were all concerned with the functioning of the mind. They were all interested in private perceptions and conscious or unconscious activity. In the early 20th century, however, American psychology moved from studying the contents of the mind to studying overt behavior. At the forefront of that movement was John B. Watson (1878–1958), the founder of behaviorism. **Behaviorism** is the school of psychological thought that rejects the study of the contents of consciousness and focuses instead on describing and measuring only that which is observable directly or through assessment instruments.

Watson was an upstart—clever, brash, and defiant. Trained as a functionalist, he argued forcefully that there is no reasonable, objective way to study the human mind, particularly through introspection. Watson, flamboyantly and with great self-assurance, contended that behavior, not the private contents of the mind, is the proper subject matter of psychology. According to Watson, psychologists should study only activities that can be objectively observed and measured; prediction and

Psychoanalytic approach [SYE-ko-an-uh-LIT-ick]: The school of psychological thought developed by Freud, which assumes that psychological maladjustment is a consequence of anxiety resulting from unresolved conflicts and forces of which a person may be unaware; includes therapeutic technique known as *psychoanalysis*.

Behaviorism: The school of psychological thought that rejects the study of the contents of consciousness and focuses on describing and measuring only that which is observable directly or through assessment instruments.

control should be the theoretical goals of psychology. This contention was a major break with previous psychological thought. Watson rejected the work of Wundt and most other early psychologists; he argued that psychologists should put the study of consciousness behind them.

After Watson, other American researchers extended and developed behaviorism, so much so that in the United States in the 1920s, behaviorism became the dominant and only acceptable view of psychology. Among those supporting the study of behaviorism was Harvard psychologist B. F. Skinner (1904–1990). In the 1940s Skinner attempted to explain the causes of behavior by cataloging and describing the relations among events in the environment (*stimuli*) and a person's or animal's reactions (*responses*). Skinner's behaviorism led the way for thousands of research studies on conditioning and human behavior, a special focus on stimuli and responses, and the controlling of behavior through learning principles.

Skinner is arguably the most influential psychologist ever trained in the United States. Although he spent his career studying animals, his writings are all about people. His theories about using principles of operant conditioning to design a utopian society brought him lasting fame. But Burrhus Frederic Skinner was more an engineer than a theorist. Determining the best time to get up in the morning, inventing a better hearing aid, designing a comfortable enclosed crib for his daughters—these were the kinds of tasks he found most rewarding. Skinner's thinking classified him as a behaviorist. He believed that we are what we do—that there is no "self," only a collection of possible behaviors. Skinner was also a determinist. In his view, our actions are more a result of past experiences than genetics. But he took the phrase *a result of* very literally. According to Skinner, our environment determines completely what we do. We control our actions about as much as a rock in an avalanche controls its resting place.

Behaviorists focus on how observable responses are learned, modified, and forgotten. They usually emphasize how current behavior is acquired or modified rather than dealing with inherited characteristics or early childhood experiences. One of their fundamental assumptions is that disordered behavior can be replaced with appropriate, worthwhile behavior through traditional learning techniques (described in Chapter 5).

Early behaviorists took a relatively unbending view of the scope of psychology by refusing to study mental phenomena. Nonbehaviorists of their time argued that not all behavior can be explained by stimuli and responses alone. They focused instead on such topics as creativity, the origins of thought, and the expression of love. Today behaviorists are beginning again to study a wider range of human behavior, including mental phenomena such as decision making and maladjustment (Rachlin, 1995).

Humanistic Psychology—Free Will. Another important feature in the landscape of modern psychology is **humanistic psychology**—the school of psychological thought that emphasizes the uniqueness of each human being's experience and the idea that human beings have free will to determine their destiny. Stressing individual free choice, the humanistic approach arose in the post–World War II era. It was in part a response to the psychoanalytic and behavioral views. Humanistic psychologists see people as inherently good and as striving to fulfill themselves; they believe that psychoanalytical theorists misread people as fraught with inner conflict and that behaviorists are too narrowly focused on stimulus–response relations. Humanists focus on individual uniqueness and decision-making ability; they assume that inner psychic forces contribute positively to establishing and maintaining a normal lifestyle.

Humanistic psychologists assert that human beings are conscious, creative, and born with an innate desire to fulfill themselves. They say that psychologists must examine human behavior individually. Proponents of the humanistic view, such as Abraham Maslow and Carl Rogers (both of whom we will study in Chapter 12), believe that human beings have the desire to achieve a state of self-actualization. **Self-actualization** is a final level of psychological development in which a person

Humanistic psychology: The school of psychological thought that emphasizes the uniqueness of each human being and the idea that human beings have free will to determine their destiny.

Self-actualization: The fundamental human need to strive to fulfill one's potential, thus a state of motivation according to Maslow; from a humanist's view, a final level of psychological development in which a person attempts to minimize ill health, be fully functioning, have a superior perception of reality, and feel a strong sense of self-acceptance.

attempts to minimize ill health, be fully functioning, have a superior perception of reality, and feel a strong sense of self-acceptance. Humanistic psychologists think that people create their own perceptions of the world, choose their own experiences, and interpret reality in ways that lead toward becoming self-actualized. Thus, for humanists, self-actualization is not only a final state but also an instinctual and motivational need.

Cognitive Psychology—Thinking Again. In the 1960s and 1970s, many other psychologists realized that behaviorism in its strict forms had limitations, particularly its narrow focus on observable behavior. As an outgrowth of behaviorism (and a reaction to it), these psychologists developed **cognitive psychology**—the school of psychological thought that focuses on the mental processes and activities involved in perception, learning, memory, and thinking. Cognitive psychology goes beyond behaviorism in considering the mental processes involved in behavior—for example, how people solve problems and appraise threatening situations and how they acquire, code, store, and retrieve information. Today cognitive psychology exerts a wide influence on psychological thinking. Cognitive psychology is sometimes seen as antibehaviorist, but it is not. It simply views the strict behavioral approach as missing a key component—mental processes. Cognitive psychology encompasses theory on both symbolic thought processes and the physiological processes that underlie thought; for example, many cognitive theories are put forth to explain how the brain operates.

The cognitive perspective asserts that human beings engage in behaviors, both worthwhile and maladjusted, because of ideas and thoughts. Cognitive psychologists may be clinicians working with maladjusted clients to help them achieve more realistic ideas about the world; the clients then change their thoughts and behavior to adjust to the world more effectively. A cognitively oriented clinician might work to help a client realize that her distorted thoughts about her own importance were interfering with her ability to get along with coworkers, for example. Cognitive psychologists may also be researchers who study intelligence, memory, perception, and the mental processes underlying all thought.

Because cognitive psychology spans many psychological fields and research traditions, it is hard to identify a single person who could be called its leader. However, psychologists Albert Bandura, Albert Ellis, Aaron Beck, George Miller, Ulric Neisser, and Richard Lazarus have all taken prominent roles, and we will encounter their work in later chapters.

Biological Perspective—Predispositions. Increasingly, researchers are turning to biology to explain some human behavior. The **biological perspective**, also referred to as the *neuroscience perspective*, is the school of psychological thought that examines psychological issues based on how heredity and biological structures affect mental processes and behavior and focuses on how physical mechanisms affect emotions, feelings, thoughts, desires, and sensory experiences. Researchers with a biological perspective might study genetic abnormalities, central nervous system problems, brain damage, or hormonal changes, for example. Today exciting research is suggesting that some of the differences between how men and women think about the world may have a biological basis rather than a learned history (e.g., Shaywitz et al., 1995). Other research is investigating whether a person's biological heritage leads to depression, learning disabilities, or homosexuality. Each day, groundbreaking research from a biological perspective is occurring. Researchers Michael Gazzaniga, Seymour Kety, Irving Gottesman, and Robert Plomin are often cited as leaders of the biological perspective.

The biological perspective is especially important in studies of sensation and perception, memory, and some types of maladjustment. It is pivotal in research on abnormal behavior such as schizophrenia, which is linked in part to genetics, or alcoholism, which in many cases has biological underpinnings. We will consider these topics in later chapters.

Cognitive psychology: The school of psychological thought that focuses on the mental processes and activities involved in perception, memory, learning, and thinking.

Biological perspective: The school of psychological thought that examines psychological issues based on how heredity and biological structures affect mental processes and behavior and that focuses on how physical mechanisms affect emotions, feelings, thoughts, desires, and sensory experiences. Also known as the *neuroscience perspective*.

Eclecticism. Psychologists now realize that there are complex relationships among the factors that affect both overt behavior and mental processes. Therefore, most American psychologists involved in applied psychology, especially clinical and counseling psychology, are eclectic in their perspective. **Eclecticism** is a combination of theories, facts, or techniques. In clinical and counseling psychology, eclecticism means using a variety of approaches to evaluate data, theories, and therapies as appropriate for an individual client, rather than relying exclusively on the techniques of one school of psychology.

Eclecticism allows a researcher or practitioner to view a problem from several orientations. For example, consider depression, the disabling mood disorder that affects 10 to 20 percent of men and women in the United States at some time in their lives (Chapter 14 discusses depression at length). From a biological perspective, people become depressed because of changes in brain chemistry. From a behavioral point of view, people learn to be depressed and sad because of faulty reward systems in their environment. From a psychoanalytic perspective, people become depressed because their early childhood experiences caused them to form a negative outlook on life. From a humanistic perspective, depression is often caused by people choosing inaction because they had or have poor role models. From a cognitive perspective, depression is made worse by the interpretations (thoughts) an individual adopts about a situation. An eclectic practitioner recognizes the complex nature of depression and acknowledges each of the possible contributions; the practitioner evaluates the person, the depression, and the context in which it occurs.

FOCUS

Review

- Identify the key assumptions underlying each school of psychological thought. pp. 25–31
- Why was Watson's behaviorism such a departure from other schools of psychological thought? pp. 28–29

Think Critically

- Think about the historical events occurring around the time each school of psychological thought emerged. How might the historical era have helped give birth to each school of thought?
- John B. Watson ultimately went into the advertising business. How might he have applied behaviorist principles in that field?
- Which school of psychology is most likely to be free of cultural biases? Why?

Conclusions and Signposts

A general goal of the discipline of psychology is to combine science, the application of science, and professional practice into one organized endeavor (Stricker, 1992; Strickland, 1988). Psychology is thus a problem-solving science rooted in research and scientific principles. This chapter is meant to give you a broad overview of the methods and procedures used by those detectives who call themselves psychologists. It is meant to orient you to their traditions, their ethical concerns, their past, and potentially their future.

This book will introduce you to the basic theories and principles of psychology. Some of what you learn may help you resolve everyday problems. For example, how does your life history affect your future development? How much do your thoughts about yourself and others determine what you will do tomorrow? How can an understanding of personality and motivation help you interact with other people? How can you apply the principles of memory to improving your skills and grades?

Some of the specific information may help you cope with difficult situations. For example, an understanding of personality and motivation may help some individuals deal with underachieving children. Knowledge about obesity and its causes will help others cope with pressures to become or stay extremely thin. Understanding

Eclecticism [ek-LECK-ti-sizm]: In psychology, a combination of theories, facts, or techniques; the practice of using whatever clinical and counseling techniques are appropriate for an individual client rather than relying exclusively on the techniques of one school of psychology.

the origins, symptoms, and treatment of mental illness may help families deal with feelings about a beloved grandmother who suffers from depression.

Psychologists address all of these issues and many more. In the following chapters we will explore psychological topics such as the effects of drugs on behavior, the various kinds of mental disorders and forms of therapy, the processes of perception and memory, and the physical, mental, and social development of human beings from birth through death.

It is evident that psychology, with its great diversity and its many specialties, is wide-ranging. But with all of its breadth, certain key issues and ideas emerge over and over again and will recur as themes throughout this book's story of psychology:

- The scientific method, based on observation, is a mainstay of psychological critical thinking.
- People's behavior reflects not only their genetic heritage but also their ethnicity, class, culture, race, gender, and age. Human diversity—individual differences and the wide range of human behaviors—is evident to us Americans daily, because those with whom we work, live, and play are more likely than ever to have their origins in diverse cultures.
- Many disorders previously thought to be caused solely by psychological conditions are now known to have a biological component.
- The relative contributions of heredity and environment (nature and nurture), long debated by psychologists, are still under investigation. Even such supposedly inborn aspects of human behavior as intelligence must also be considered within an environmental context.
- Thought (cognition) is becoming an increasingly important topic in the study of behavior, as is the view that human beings are competent and thoughtful and are able to decide their future.
- People continue to grow and mature—physically, socially, and intellectually—throughout their lives.
- Psychological theories are diverse and ever expanding, and they must be considered in the context of the time when they arise.

Summary and Review

What Is This Science of Psychology?

What do psychologists study?

- *Psychology* is the science of behavior and mental processes. Psychologists observe many aspects of human functioning—overt actions, social relationships, mental processes, emotional responses, and physiological reactions. Overt actions are directly observable and measurable movements or the results of such movements. Social relationships are the behaviors people engage in that define their interactions with other people. Mental processes include thoughts, ideas, and reasoning processes. Emotional responses include feelings such as anger, regret, and happiness. Physiological reactions include biochemical changes when light stimulates your eyes and an increased heart rate when you are excited. pp. 4–5

Describe the steps in the scientific method.

- The discipline of psychology is committed to objectivity, accuracy, and healthy skepticism. In their research, psychologists use the *scientific method* to organize their ideas and to develop theories that describe, explain, predict, and help manage behavior. The scientific method's five basic steps are stating a problem clearly, developing a *theory*, forming *hypotheses*, making observations, and replicating experiments. pp. 5–7

KEY TERMS

Psychology, p. 4
Scientific method, p. 6
Theory, p. 6
Hypothesis, p. 6

What Psychologists Do

Distinguish the various types of psychology professionals.

- *Psychologists* are professionals who study behavior and use behavioral principles in scientific research or in applied settings. Most psychologists have an advanced degree, usually a PhD. A *psychiatrist* is a medical doctor who has specialized in the treatment of emotional disorders. *Psychoanalysts* are usually psychiatrists; they have training in the specialized Freudian technique of psychoanalysis for treating people with emotional problems. pp. 7–8

- About 63 percent of psychologists in the American Psychological Association are in human services fields such as clinical, counseling, and school psychology. Most of the rest work in universities, business, and government doing research, teaching, and evaluation of programs. Psychology is attracting an increasing number of women, with the number of women in graduate training programs doubling since the mid-1970s. p. 9

Identify the focuses of applied research, human services, and experimental psychology.

- The three main fields of psychology are applied research, human services, and experimental psychology. All three consider research and theory to be the cornerstone of the psychological approach. Applied researchers use research to solve practical problems. Human services psychologists focus on helping individuals solve problems and on promoting their well-being. Experimental psychologists usually focus on teaching and research. pp. 9–13

KEY TERMS

Psychologist, p. 7
Clinical psychologist, p. 8
Psychiatrist, p. 8
Psychoanalyst, p. 8

The Research Process

Describe an experiment and indicate its key components.

- An *experiment* is a procedure in which a researcher systematically strives to discover and describe the relationship between variables. Only controlled experiments allow for cause-and-effect statements. A *variable* is a characteristic of a situation or person that is subject to change (that varies) either within or across situations or individuals. An *independent variable* is directly and purposely manipulated by the experimenter. The *dependent variable* is expected to change because of manipulations of the independent variable. pp. 13–15

- A *hypothesis* is a tentative statement or idea expressing a causal relationship between two events or variables that are to be evaluated in a research study. p. 15

- An *operational definition* is a definition of a variable in terms of a set of procedures used to measure or study that variable. A *sample* is a group of participants who are assumed to be representative of the population about which an inference is being made. A *significant difference* means that there is a statistically determined likelihood that a behavior has not occurred because of chance alone. p. 16

How do researchers ensure objectivity?

- To ensure objectivity, researchers attempt to minimize *self-fulfilling prophecies* by using carefully controlled situations—for example the *double-blind technique*, in which neither researcher nor participant knows who is assigned to the *experimental* or *control group*. The double-blind technique helps minimize *demand characteristics*—the elements of a study situation that might clue a participant as to the purpose of the study and might thereby elicit specific behavior from the participant. It also helps minimize the *Hawthorne effect*—the tendency of people, as shown in early research studies at the Hawthorne industrial plant, to behave differently (usually better) when they know they are being observed. pp. 16–17

- Critical thinking involves evaluating evidence, sifting through choices, assessing outcomes, and deciding whether conclusions make sense. When evaluating research studies, critical thinkers focus on five research criteria: purpose, methodology, participants, repeatability, and conclusions. pp. 18–19

When is a group considered culturally diverse?

- Psychologists say that a group—for example, a community, organization, or nation—is culturally diverse if it has within it differences in race, ethnicity, language, nationality, age, and religion. p. 19

What are the various other methods of research?

- A *questionnaire*, or survey, is used by researchers to gather a large amount of information from many people in a short time. An *interview* is typically a face-to-face meeting in which a researcher (interviewer) asks an individual a series of standardized questions. In *naturalistic observation*, psychologists observe from a distance how people or animals behave in their natural settings. By contrast, *case study* methods involve interviewing participants to gain information concerning their background, including data on such things as childhood, family, education, and social and sexual interactions. pp. 21–22

KEY TERMS

Experiment, p. 13
Variable, p. 14
Independent variable, p. 14
Dependent variable, p. 14
Participant, p. 15
Experimental group, p. 15
Control group, p. 15
Operational definition, p. 16
Sample, p. 16
Significant difference, p. 16
Self-fulfilling prophecy, p. 17
Double-blind technique, p. 17
Demand characteristics, p. 17
Hawthorne effect, p. 17
Questionnaire, p. 21
Interview, p. 21
Naturalistic observation, p. 22
Case study, p. 22

Ethics in Psychological Research

Describe the ethical considerations in psychological research.

- *Ethics* in research comprises the rules of conduct that investigators use to guide their research; these rules concern the treatment of animals, the rights of human beings, and the responsibilities of investigators. The APA has strict ethical guidelines for animal research. Human participants cannot be coerced to do things that are harmful to themselves, that would have other negative effects, or that would violate standards of decency. In addition, any information gained in an experimental situation is considered strictly confidential. Human participants must give *informed consent* to a researcher and must undergo *debriefing* following an experiment so that they understand the true nature of the research. In general, researchers must not use deception unless the study has highly important scientific, educational, or applied value. pp. 23–25

KEY TERMS

Ethics, p. 23
Informed consent, p. 24
Debriefing, p. 24

Past and Present: Schools of Psychological Thought

Identify the key assumptions underlying each school of psychological thought.

- Psychology became a field of study in the mid-1800s. *Structuralism*, founded by Wundt, focused on the contents of consciousness through *introspection* and was the first true school of psychological thought. *Functionalism*, led by James and others, emphasized how and why the mind works. *Gestalt psychology*, in contrast to structuralism and functionalism, focused on perceptual frameworks and suggested that conscious experience is more than simply the sum of its individual parts. Arguing that each mind organizes the elements of experience into something unique, the early Gestalt psychologists studied perceptual phenomena. The *psychoanalytic approach* developed by Freud is the school of psychological thought that assumes that psychological maladjustment is a consequence of anxiety resulting from unresolved conflicts and forces of which a person may be unaware; its therapeutic technique is psychoanalysis. pp. 25–28

- Watson, the founder of *behaviorism,* argued that the proper subject of psychological study was observable behavior. Skinner took up the behaviorist banner through much of the 20th century. *Humanistic psychology* arose in response to the psychoanalytic and behavioral views and stresses free will and *self-actualization*. *Cognitive psychology* focuses on perception, memory, learning, and thinking and asserts that human beings engage in both worthwhile and maladjusted behaviors because of ideas and thoughts. The *biological perspective* examines how heredity and biological structures affect mental processes and behavior. *Eclecticism* acknowledges the complex relationships among factors affecting behavioral and mental processes and combines theories and techniques as appropriate to the situation. pp. 28–31

KEY TERMS

Structuralism, p. 25
Introspection, p. 25
Functionalism, p. 26
Gestalt psychology, p. 27
Psychoanalytic approach, p. 28
Behaviorism, p. 28
Humanistic psychology, p. 29
Self-actualization, p. 29
Cognitive psychology, p. 30
Biological perspective, p. 30
Eclecticism, p. 31

Learning CONNECTIONS

Some students benefit from extra help with the concept of the scientific method. You can learn more about it in:

- The CD-ROM accompanying this book, Topic 1
- This book's study guide, *Keeping Pace Plus,* or the computerized study guide, Chapter 1
- The audiotape accompanying this book, *SoundGuide for Psychology,* Learning Unit 1
- The study aids found on the World Wide Web site for this book, at http://www.abacon.com/psych/lefton

Critical Thinking CONNECTIONS

Take a moment to think critically about how this chapter's topics are connected with the rest of psychology . . .

If you are interested in . . .	Ask yourself . . .	Then turn to . . .
Careers in clinical, counseling, community, or school psychology 	How can intelligence tests be fairly administered and interpreted?	Chapter 8, pp. 276–278
	Are personality tests an accurate measure of an individual?	Chapter 12, pp. 439–442
	How can psychologists help communities deal with disasters such as hurricanes and floods?	Chapter 13, pp. 461–462; Chapter 17, p. 630
	What sort of coping strategies might clinical psychologists suggest to help people deal with stressful situations?	Chapter 13, pp. 463–465
How psychologists use scientific research methods 	How could the experimental method be used to study phenomena such as learning to avoid poisonous foods?	Chapter 5, p. 157
	How could the experimental method be used to examine the causes of overeating?	Chapter 9, pp. 314–315
	How might the correlational method be used to study the relationship between fathers and their children?	Chapter 10, pp. 370–371
How the schools of psychology influence theory and research 	How might Gestalt psychology influence the study of perception?	Chapter 3, pp. 93–96
	How might cognitive psychology explain the motivation to eat?	Chapter 9, p. 313
	How might Freud's psychoanalytic theory explain the development of your personality?	Chapter 12, pp. 413–417
	What sort of therapy might humanistic theory generate?	Chapter 15, pp. 527–530

2

Biological Bases of Behavior

Oscar winner Patty Duke, who starred in *The Miracle Worker* and *The Patty Duke Show*, lived a double life. As a star, she was glamorous and talented. But in her personal life, she suffered the complex and devastating effects of bipolar disorder. Not accurately diagnosed and treated until she was 35 years old, Duke experienced periods during which she felt euphoric, creative, and energetic. She was also often angry and acted impulsively. Within days of her highs, she would descend into periods of depression and extreme sadness.

The course of Patty Duke's illness is typical of bipolar disorder. People who suffer from this disorder often go through hospitalizations, suicide attempts, panic attacks, crushing depressions, and extraordinary highs. The disorder plays havoc with patients' lives and is often misdiagnosed. This is especially unfortunate because good treatments for bipolar disorder are available. The drug lithium carbonate has been remarkably successful in the treatment of this disorder. Today, Patty Duke no longer suffers from drastic mood swings.

Research on mood disorders will be discussed in detail later in this book. However, Patty Duke's problems highlight an important point: while some problems may be solely psychological, others may be caused by a person's malfunctioning biological systems. A barrage of new research findings shows that chemicals in the brain may hold one of the keys to mood disorders such as depression. Researchers will continue to explore this idea and eventually will confirm, reject, or modify the proposition that mood problems such as depression have strong biological bases and are best treated with medication (Greenberg et al., 1992). This idea challenges the long-held view of many psychologists that mood disorders are unique to each person and must be dealt with through intensive talking therapy.

Psychologists know that biology plays a role—although not necessarily the determining role—in shaping human behavior. However, there is a complex interplay between biology and experience, between inherited traits and encounters in the world—that is, between nature and nurture. **Nature** is a person's inherited characteristics, determined by genetics; **nurture** is a person's experiences in the environment. For example, you can lift weights for years trying to build up your physical strength, but your capabilities are limited by your inherited body structure. Similarly, people try to maximize their intellectual skills through education; yet not everyone can become a nuclear physicist. Also, a person's inherited traits may not become evident in behavior unless the environment supports and encourages those traits. For example, people with special talents must be given opportunities to express and develop them. If Mozart had not had access to musical instruments, his talent might have remained forever untapped.

In this chapter we first examine the issue of nature versus nurture, in order to lay a strong foundation for studying the biological processes that underlie all human behavior and mental processes. Beginning with the smallest of biological building blocks of behavior—genetics and neurons—we follow with the structure and functioning of the brain. We then look at how scientists study brain activity and how chemical substances in our bodies affect our behavior.

Nature versus Nurture

My father always insisted I was a born athlete. He argued that my sister was the scholar in the family; she began reading at a very early age. He reasoned that each of his children had to be born *either* an athlete or a scholar. My father was assuming that what we were was fixed; he allowed little room for environmental influences. My father's beliefs highlight a major question in psychology: What is the relationship between biological mechanisms and environmental mechanisms—between nature and nurture? The debate over what determines abilities and behavior is often talked about as a debate over the relative contributions of these biological and environmental variables. How much of what we are depends on the genes we inherited from our parents? How much is related to the environment in which we are raised—or to our parents' expectations for us? As we shall see, *both* genes and experience are important factors affecting behavior. In fact, it makes little sense to talk about one without talking about the other.

Your genetic heritage is unaffected by day-to-day experiences. Over tens of thousands of years, however, humans have evolved a highly organized brain that does allow learning to affect their behavior. Your brain acts as a library of information. Each new enriching experience affects your later behavior. Some who consider nurture more important than nature suggest that people are not limited by their genetic heritage, because experience, training, and hard work can stretch their potential to amazing lengths. John B. Watson, a pioneer in the field of behaviorism (which we will examine further in Chapter 5), sang the praises of nurture:

Nature: An individual's genetically inherited characteristics.

Nurture: An individual's experiences in the environment.

> Give me a dozen healthy infants, well-formed, and my own specialized world to bring them up in and I'll guarantee to take any one at random and train him to become any type of specialist I might select—doctor, lawyer, artist, merchant-chief, and, yes, even beggar man and thief, regardless of his talents, penchants, tendencies, abilities, vocations, and race of his ancestors. (1924, p. 104)

Psychologists know that biological makeup affects people's intelligence. But can the environment interact with and modify biological makeup, as Watson contended? The truth is that genetic traits provide the framework for behavior; within that framework, experiences ultimately shape what individuals feel, think, and do. Let's take a closer look at the key genetic factors that shape day-to-day behavior.

The Basics of Genetics

Genetics is the study of *heredity*—the biological transmission of traits and characteristics from parents to offspring. Biologists examine such questions as how blue eyes, brown hair, height, and a tendency to develop diabetes or high blood pressure are transmitted from one generation to the next. Behavioral traits such as temperament and intelligence and disorders such as depression also have a genetic basis; this is why psychologists are especially interested in heredity. The field of *behavioral genetics* has thus emerged; its focus is on the relationship of genetics to behavior.

Uniqueness of Human Beings. With the exception of identical twins (discussed on page 41), every human being is genetically unique. Although each of us shares traits with our brothers, sisters, and parents, none of us is identical to them or to anyone else. The reason is that a large number of genes determine, or at least influence, each person's cognitive, personality, and emotional characteristics (Reiss, 1995).

Each human cell normally contains 23 pairs of chromosomes (46 chromosomes in all). **Chromosomes** are microscopic strands of deoxyribonucleic acid (DNA) found in the nucleus (center) of every body cell. Chromosomes carry genetic information in their basic functional units—the genes, thousands of which line up along each chromosome. **Genes** are the units of hereditary transmission, consisting of DNA and protein. Genes control various aspects of a person's physical makeup, including eye color, hair color, and height—and perhaps aspects such as basic intellectual abilities, as well. Every such trait is determined by a pair of genes located in parallel positions on both of the paired chromosomes. Both of these corresponding genes influence the same trait, but they often carry a different form of the genetic code for that trait; and one of the genes may be dominant over the other. For example, if the two genes for eye color carry the genetic codes for blue and brown eyes, respectively, the individual will be brown-eyed, because the brown gene is *dominant*. Different, alternative forms of a gene that occupy the same position on paired chromosomes are called **alleles**. Each allele on a chromosome has a corresponding allele on the other chromosome of the chromosome pair.

Each parent's sperm or ovum (egg) contains 23 chromosomes: half of the final 46. The first 22 pairs of chromosomes carry the same types of genetic information in both males and females. The 23rd pair differs. This pair of chromosomes determines a person's sex. In females, the 23rd pair contains two X chromosomes; in males, it contains one X and one Y chromosome. At the moment of conception, a sperm and an ovum, each containing half of each parent's chromosomes, combine to form a new organism, and the chromosomes recombine to form new pairs. There are 8,388,608 possible recombinations of the 23 pairs of chromosomes, with 70,368,744,000,000 possible combinations of genes. You can see that the chance of any two individuals being exactly alike is exceedingly slim.

Genetic Defects. One goal of genetic research is to prevent *genetic defects*—genetically transmitted diseases, physical defects, or behavioral abnormalities. When

Genetics: The study of heredity, the biological transmission of traits and characteristics from parents to offspring.

Chromosome: Strand of DNA in the nuclei of all cells, which carries genetic information.

Gene: The unit of hereditary transmission carried in chromosomes and consisting of DNA and protein.

Allele [A-leel]: Each member of a pair of genes, which occupies a particular place on a paired chromosome.

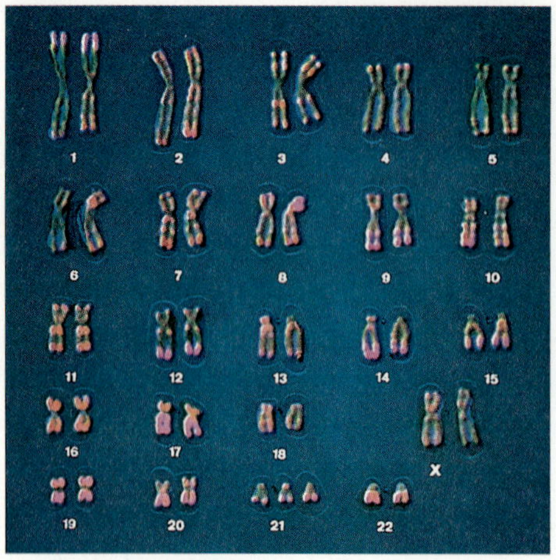

▲ *Down syndrome occurs when every cell in the body has more than two copies of chromosome number 21. This genetic defect causes mental retardation and distinct physical features, including almond-shaped eyes and a stocky physique. Note the three chromosomes at position 21.*

a person is born with the genetic defect of too few or too many genes or chromosomes, the result is usually dramatic.

Down syndrome is a human genetic defect that occurs when every cell in the body has more than exactly two copies of chromosome number 21. There may be an entire extra copy, or a piece of chromosome number 21 may break off and be joined to another chromosome. This genetic accident occurs in 1 out of every 660 live births. Most people with Down syndrome have distinct physical features: a short, stocky build, flattened face, and almond-shaped eyes. Many are born with physical problems such as heart defects, vision problems, and respiratory disorders. People with Down syndrome also have some degree of mental retardation.

Phenylketonuria (PKU) is a human genetic disorder in which the presence of a particular *recessive* gene prevents an individual from metabolizing the amino acid phenylalanine. Unless the disorder is detected soon after birth and the newborn is put on a diet containing very little phenylalanine, levels of that amino acid will increase and can cause irreparable brain damage resulting in mental retardation. Thus, in the United States, all newborns are given a PKU test. In this case, manipulating the physical environment (through diet) can help control the harmful consequences of the genetic disorder.

Mapping the Genome. In an exciting research revolution that has been taking place since the 1980s, biological researchers have been trying to map the specific traits associated with specific chromosomes. That is, they have been trying to map the human *genome*—the total DNA blueprint of heritable traits contained in every cell of the body. They have been modestly successful in this effort. More than 3,400 of the estimated 100,000 human genes have been mapped. Researchers have identified the exact location of genes contributing to the expression of muscular dystrophy, Huntington's disease, some cancers, and some psychological disorders, such as schizophrenia. Today researchers argue that even the nature of family social interactions has a genetic basis, because elements of personality may be genetically determined (Plomin et al., 1994). As McClearn states, "The focus of research has shifted from demonstrating the existence of genetic influence to exploring its details" (McClearn et al., 1991, p. 222). It is important to remember, however, that genetics only lays the framework for our biology and our behavior; so many events, life experiences, and cultural influences affect us that genetic influences must not be considered the determiner of behavior.

By understanding basic biological mechanisms and their relationship to behavior, psychologists can better predict the situations in which maladjustment and behavior disorders may occur. Yet this creates some interesting ethical dilemmas:

Down syndrome: A human genetic defect in which more than two whole chromosomes are present for the 21st pair; usually accompanied by characteristic physical abnormalities and mental retardation.

Phenylketonuria (PKU) [fee-nil-key-ton-NYEW-ree-uh]: A human genetic disorder that prevents an individual from processing the amino acid phenylalanine.

Fraternal twins: Double births resulting from the release of two ova that are fertilized by two sperm; fraternal twins are no more or less genetically similar than non-twin siblings.

Identical twins: Double births resulting from the splitting of a zygote into two identical cells, which then separate and develop independently; identical twins have exactly the same genetic makeup.

What if a particular chromosomal pattern is shown to be associated with aggressiveness? Would it be desirable or ethical to screen newborns to identify those at risk of becoming criminals? Could this information be used to terminate pregnancies? Medical ethicists and psychologists argue that such screening cannot and should not be used for such purposes. Ethical considerations and legislation to guard people's rights must be high on the agenda of genetic researchers.

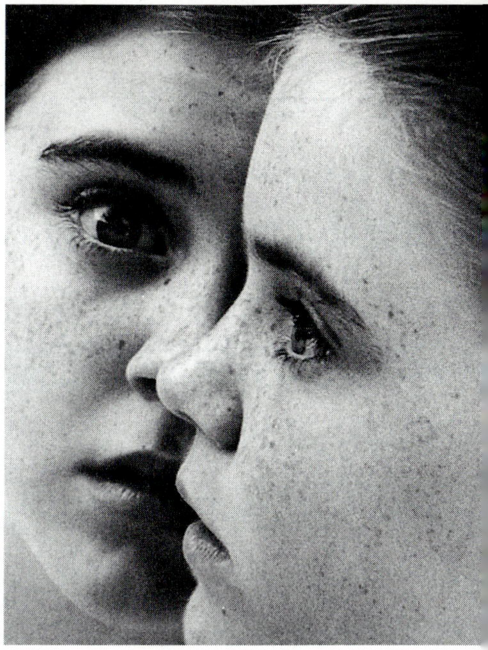

▲ *Identical twins occur when one zygote separates into two identical cells. These twins' genetic make-up is thus identical. Research with twins, particularly identical twins, is useful in exploring the nature-versus-nuture issue.*

Twins and the Nature-versus-Nurture Issue

In addition to studying the impact of biological mechanisms on behavior and mental processes, researchers balance their study by examining the contributions of the environment. One of the best ways psychologists have found to do this is to study twins to assess the contributions of nature and nurture. Twins make ideal subjects for these experiments because they begin life in the same uterine environment and share similar patterns of nutrition and other prenatal influences. **Fraternal twins** are double births that occur when two sperm fertilize two ova (eggs) and the two resulting zygotes (fertilized eggs) implant themselves in the uterus and grow alongside each other. The genes of these types of twins are not identical, so the siblings are only as genetically similar as other brothers and sisters would be. Fraternal twins can be the same or different sexes. Only about 12 sets of fraternal twins occur in every 1,000 births. **Identical twins** are double births that occur when one zygote splits into two identical cells, which then separate and develop independently. The multiplication of these cells proceeds normally, and the cells become two genetically identical organisms, always the same sex. Only 4 sets of identical twins occur in every 1,000 births.

What have twin studies revealed about human behavior? In one study, researchers at the University of Louisville School of Medicine followed 450 sets of twins (half identical and half fraternal) from infancy through adolescence. The study assessed intelligence as well as home and family variables that might influence intellectual development. By adolescence, identical twins had very similar IQs, although not identical levels of intellectual achievement. In contrast, the IQs of fraternal twins were no more similar than those of non-twin siblings. The most important conclusion of the Louisville twins study was that although such environmental variables as family interactions strongly influenced IQ, genetics affected IQ test scores more than environment did (R. S. Wilson, 1983). We will return to heredity and intelligence in Chapter 8.

Twins' genetic factors (nature) are fixed; but if the twins are reared apart, their environments (nurture) are different—that is, they grow up in different families and homes. By comparing psychological characteristics of identical twins reared apart, researchers can assess the extent to which environment affects behavior and perhaps unravel a bit more of the nature–nurture fabric. Researchers have concluded that significant psychological similarities between identical twins are probably due to biological variables, and significant psychological differences are probably due to environmental variables.

There are striking similarities in identical twins, even in those reared apart all of their lives. For example, a long and famous series

FOCUS

Review

- What is the distinction between nature and nurture? p. 38
- What fundamental assumption can researchers make about identical twins that causes them to be ideal participants in nature-versus-nurture studies? p. 41

Think Critically

- What are potential environmental influences that can alter people's inherited characteristics? What can be done to limit such influences, and should it be?
- There are ethical implications to the effort to map the genome and understand the biological characteristics associated with particular gene patterns. What if scientists find genes strongly associated with criminality, for example? What should be done with this knowledge?

of studies, called the Minnesota adoption studies, show that young adopted children are similar intellectually and in personality to other children in their adoptive family. This suggests that family environment exerts a great influence on young children. By adolescence, however, there is greater variation. Teenagers raised in the same family resemble one another intellectually only if they have common genes (Scarr & Weinberg, 1983). Plomin (1989, 1994b) and Bouchard (Bouchard et al., 1990) assert that even though environmental influences on intelligence are strong, heredity exerts a stronger influence (Turkheimer, 1991). But psychologists meet this assertion with healthy skepticism, because the whole story is yet to be told. We will take a closer look at this issue in Chapter 8.

Communication in the Nervous System

The nervous system underlies all of your behavior; it is the communication system that enables you to engage in complex activities. Singing in a choir or even humming along at a concert involves paying attention, listening to the music, producing sound, keeping up with the rhythm, perhaps tapping a foot or clapping your hands. That's a lot of activity, just to sing along! In some ways the nervous system acts like the conductor of a symphony orchestra, sending, receiving, processing, interpreting, and storing vital information—in this case, information about music and/or lyrics. Many psychologists study how electrical and chemical signals in the brain represent and process such information. By studying how the nervous system's components work together and how they are integrated, psychologists learn a great deal about the nature and diversity of human behavior.

The **nervous system** is made up of the structures and organs that allow all behavior and mental processes to take place. The nervous system consists of two divisions—the *central nervous system* (the brain and spinal cord) and the *peripheral nervous system* (all the other parts), which allows the brain to communicate with the rest of the body. We'll examine these two divisions shortly. First, however, you need to understand how communication proceeds within the system as a whole. The nervous system is composed of hundreds of billions of cells, each of which receives information from thousands of other cells. The most elementary unit in the nervous system is the neuron, the building block of the entire system, which is where we will begin our journey.

The Neuron

Nervous system: The structures and organs that act as the communication system for the body, allowing all behavior and mental processes to take place.

Neuron [NEW-ron]: The basic unit (a single cell) of the nervous system, comprising dendrites, which receive neural signals; a cell body, which generates electrical signals; and an axon, which transmits neural signals. Also known as a *nerve cell.*

Afferent neuron: Neurons that send messages to the spinal cord and brain.

Efferent neuron: Neurons that send messages from the brain and spinal cord to other structures in the body.

The basic unit of the nervous system is a single cell: the **neuron**, or *nerve cell.* There are billions of neurons throughout the body (as many as 100 billion in the brain alone), differing in shape, size, and function. Some neurons operate quickly, some relatively slowly. Some neurons are large; others are extremely small. Often neurons are grouped together in bundles; the bundles of neuron fibers are called *nerves* if they exist in the peripheral nervous system and *tracts* if they are in the central nervous system.

Not all of the neurons in your body are especially active at once. Nonetheless, they are always on alert, ready to convey information and signals to some part of the nervous system. Nerve pathways allow signals to flow in two directions: (1) to the brain and spinal cord from the sense organs and muscles, and (2) from the brain and spinal cord to the sense organs and muscles, carrying messages for initiating new behavior. Each type of neuron involved in this two-way neuronal firing has a name: **afferent neurons** (from the Latin *ad*, "to," and *ferre*, "carry") are neurons that send messages to the spinal cord and brain; **efferent neurons** (from Latin *ex*, "out of," and *ferre*, "carry") are neurons that send messages from the brain and spinal cord to other structures in the body (see Figure 2.1).

FIGURE 2.1

The Action of Afferent and Efferent Neurons

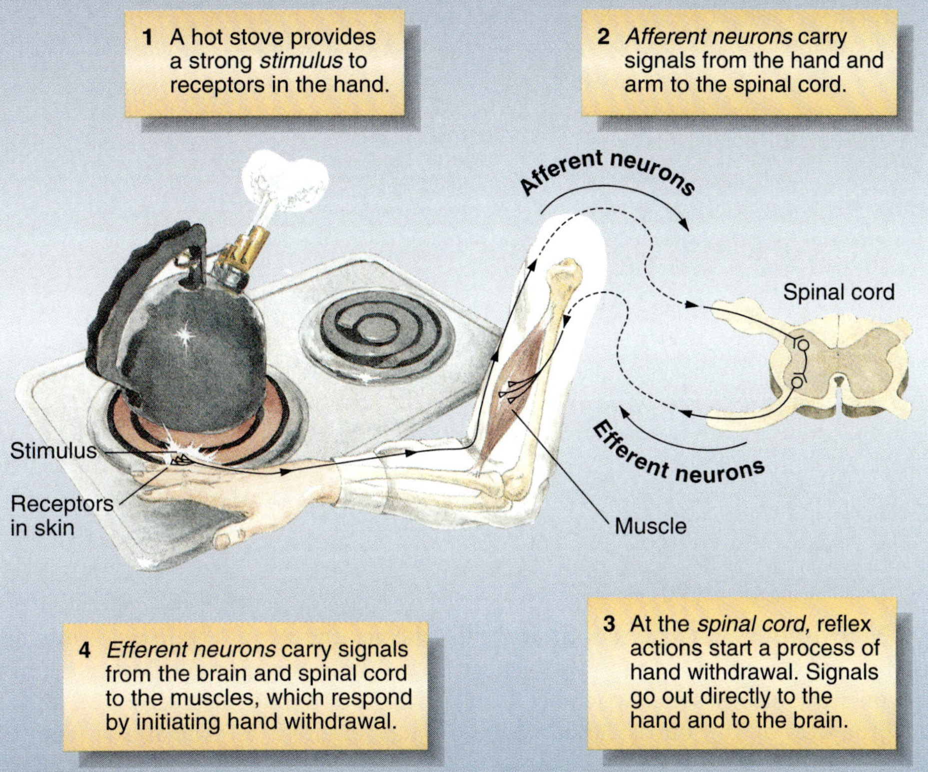

Types of Neurons. There are three types of neurons: sensory neurons, motor neurons, and interneurons. *Sensory neurons* are afferent neurons that convey information from the body's sense organs to the brain and spinal cord. *Motor neurons* are efferent neurons that carry information from the brain and spinal cord to the muscles and glands. *Interneurons* connect neurons together and combine the activities of sensory and motor neurons. There are many more interneurons than sensory or motor neurons; the interneurons form a network that allows the other neurons to interact with one another. The millions of neurons that work together are surrounded by *glial cells*, which nourish the neurons and help hold them in place. Glial cells are small—and 10 times more numerous than sensory, motor, or interneurons. They help insulate the brain from toxins, and they are the basis of the neurons' *myelin sheath*. Many neurons, especially the longer ones, are *myelinated,* or covered with a thin white substance (the myelin sheath) that allows them to conduct signals faster than unmyelinated neurons.

Parts of a Neuron. Typically, neurons are composed of four primary parts: dendrites, a cell body, an axon, and axon terminals (see Figure 2.2 on page 44). **Dendrites** (from the Greek word for "tree," because of their branchlike appearance) are thin, widely branching fibers that become narrower as they spread away from the cell body. Dendrites receive signals from neighboring neurons and carry them back to the cell body. At the *cell body*, the signals are transformed and continue to travel along the long, slim **axon** to the *axon terminals* (the end points of each neuron). Like dendrites, axons have branches at their endings.

Dendrites: Thin, widely branching fibers extending from the neuron cell body, which receive signals from neighboring neurons and carry them back to the cell body.

Axon: A thin, elongated process that leads from the neuron cell body and serves to transmit signals from the cell body and through the axon terminal to adjacent neurons, muscles, or glands.

FIGURE 2.2

The Basic Components of a Neuron

(a) Neurons appear in many forms, but all possess the basic structures shown here: a cell body, an axon (with myelin sheath and axon terminals), and dendrites. (b) Actual human neurons, greatly magnified.

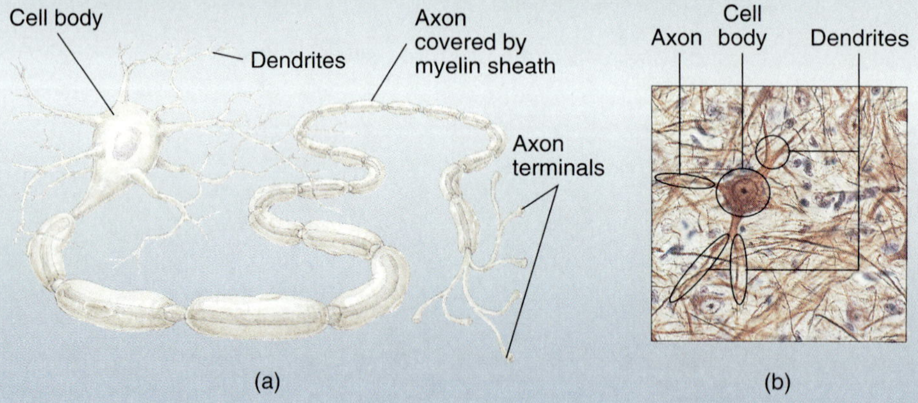

Neuronal Synapses. For almost all neurons, the axon terminals of one neuron lie very close to receptor sites (dendrites, cell body, or axons) of other neurons. The microscopically small space between the axon terminals of one neuron and the receptor sites of another is called a **synapse** (see Figure 2.3). The signal from one neuron may travel across the synapse to another neuron. You can think of many neurons strung together in a long chain as a relay team sending signals, conveying information, or initiating some action in a cell, muscle, or gland. Each neuron receives information from about 1,000 neighboring neurons and may "synapse on" (transmit information to) as many as 1,000 to 10,000 other neurons.

FIGURE 2.3

The Synapse

The synapse is very small. Chemicals released by the axon terminals cross the synapse to stimulate the cell body or the dendrites of another neuron. The photomicrograph shows axon terminals (the orange buttonlike structures) at about 5,000 times their actual size.

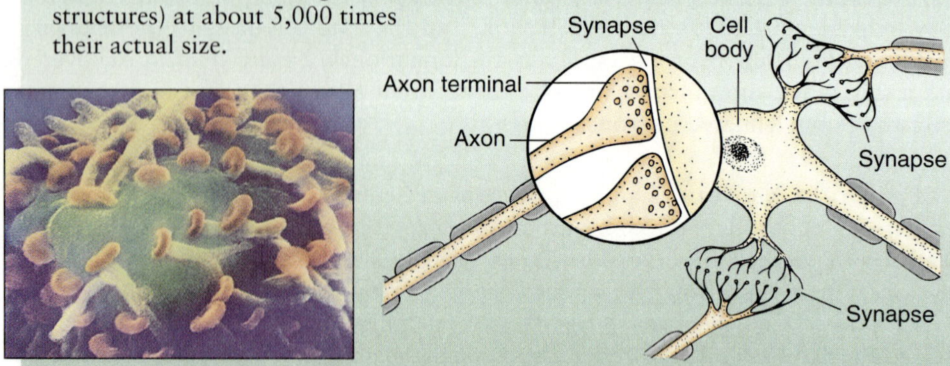

Synapse [SIN-apps]: The microscopically small space between the axon terminals of one neuron and the receptor sites of another neuron.

Electrochemical Processes. How do neurons communicate? What kind of signals do they transmit? Neuroscientists are continually learning more about the nature of the neural impulse and about how information moves from cell to cell across synapses. The process, which involves both electrical and chemical changes, is sometimes termed *electrochemical*. Two types of electrochemical process take place. The first involves activity within a neuron; the second involves transmitter substances (chemicals) that are released from the axons of one neuron and act on neighboring neurons or other targets.

Action potential: An electrical current sent down the axon of a neuron, initiated in an all-or-none fashion by a rapid reversal of the electrical balance of the cell membrane. Also known as a *spike discharge*.

Understanding the electrochemical processes within a cell is essential to understanding the role of neurons in behavior. A widely accepted explanation of these electrochemical processes is the following: An extremely thin (less than 0.00001 millimeter thick) membrane surrounds every neuron; and there are channels, or "gates," in this membrane through which electrically charged ions and small particles can pass. Normally the neuron is in a resting state in which it remains negatively charged inside, relative to the outside. This resting state is maintained by the cell membrane. The difference in electrical charge between inside and outside is a state of *polarization*; that is, the internal state of the neuron (negatively charged) differs from its external state (positively charged).

Action Potentials. When the neuron has been stimulated (its resting state has been disturbed) to the point where it reaches a *threshold* (a level of stimulation intensity below which nothing happens), it is said to be *depolarized*. At this point the sodium "gates" of the cell membrane open. A rapid reversal of electrical polarity occurs, positively charged sodium ions rush through the membrane into the neuron, thereby disturbing the resting state. At this point an action potential has been generated (see Figure 2.4). The **action potential**, or *spike discharge*, is an electrical current that is sent down the axon of a neuron and is initiated by a rapid reversal of the electrical balance of the cell membrane.

A neuron does not necessarily fire or produce an action potential every time it is stimulated. If the level of polarization across the cell membrane has not been disturbed enough to generate an action potential—in other words, if the neuron has not reached its threshold—the cell will not fire. Cells that are highly stimulated are more likely to fire than cells that are less stimulated. For example, a bright flash from a camera will stimulate cells in the visual areas of the brain, but a flicker of a

FIGURE 2.4

Generation of an Action Potential

1 When the neuron is at rest, the inside is negatively charged relative to the outside.

2 When the neuron is stimulated, positively charged particles enter. The action potential is initiated—the neuron is *depolarized.*

3 After a brief period, some positively charged particles are pushed outside the neuron, and the neuron moves back toward its polarized state.

4 The neuron has finally returned to its initial polarized resting state.

Fig. 2.3A

FIGURE 2.5

Major Steps in Neuronal Transmission

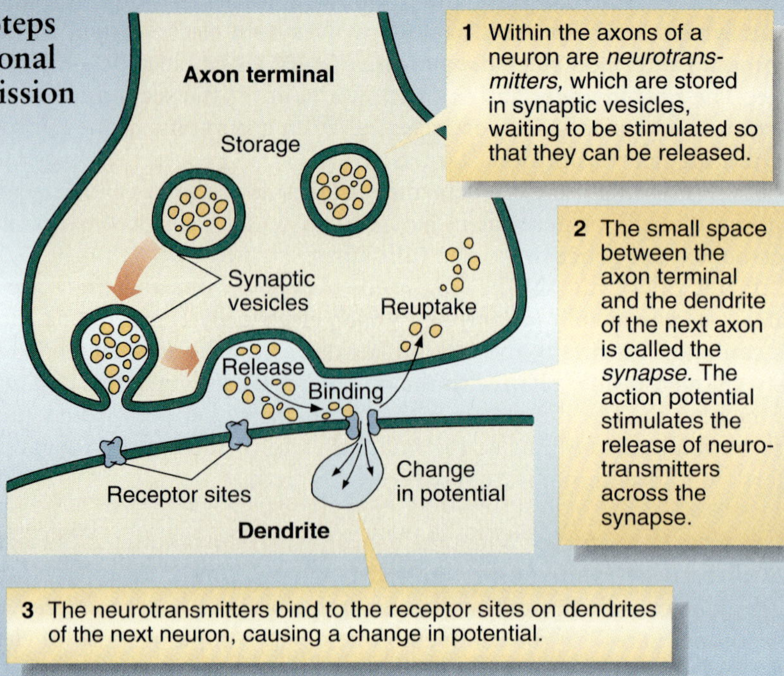

candle may affect far fewer cells. When neurons fire, they generate action potentials in an **all-or-none** fashion—that is, the firing of the neuron, like the firing of a gun, occurs at either full strength or not at all. Action potentials occur in 2 to 4 milliseconds; therefore, neurons cannot normally fire more than 500 times per second. After each firing a neuron needs time to recover, generally just a few thousandths of a second; the time needed for recovery is called the **refractory period.** During this period action potentials are much less likely to occur.

Neurotransmitters. When an action potential moves down to the end of an axon, it initiates the release of **neurotransmitters**—chemicals that normally reside in the axon terminal within synaptic vesicles (small storage structures in the axon terminal) (Dunant & Israel, 1985). The neurotransmitters that are released into the synapse move across the synaptic space and bind to receptor sites on an adjacent cell, thereby conveying information to the neighboring neuron (see Figure 2.5). We will examine the types and various effects of neurotransmitters shortly. When a neurotransmitter has affected the adjacent neuron, it has accomplished its main mission; the neurotransmitter is then either neutralized by an enzyme or taken back up by the neuron that released it, in a process called *reuptake.* Sometimes neurotransmitters cause the receiving neurons to fire more easily, sometimes less easily. A change in the membrane potential of a neuron due to the release of neurotransmitters is called a *postsynaptic potential (PSP).*

Excitatory and Inhibitory Postsynaptic Potentials. There are two kinds of postsynaptic potentials, and they cause opposite effects. *Excitatory PSPs* make it easier for the cell to fire; *inhibitory PSPs* make it harder for the cell to fire. Because thousands of neurons may synapse on a single cell, a single neuron can receive both excitatory and inhibitory PSPs at once. If a neuron receives more excitatory PSPs, then another action potential is likely to be generated. If a neuron receives more inhibitory PSPs, further excitation along the nerve pathway is temporarily inhibited. For example, some neurotransmitters are involved in blocking the perception of

All-or-none: Either at full strength or not at all; a principle by which neurons fire.

Refractory period: The recovery period of a neuron after it fires, during which it cannot fire again; this period allows the neuron to reestablish electrical balance with its surroundings.

Neurotransmitter [NEW-roh-TRANS-mitt-er]: Chemical substance that resides in the axon terminals and within synaptic vesicles and that, when released, moves across the synaptic space and binds to a receptor site on adjacent neurons.

pain; other neurotransmitters enhance such sensory experiences. And some neurotransmitters are excitatory in some situations and inhibitory in others. As another example, when the neurotransmitter acetylcholine attaches to muscle cells, it has an excitatory effect; but in some areas of the brain not related to the excitation of muscles (for example, the visual cortex), acetylcholine can have an inhibitory effect (on, say, vision). Therefore, the effects of a neurotransmitter are determined by the receptor onto which it binds.

Neurotransmitters and Behavior

There are a large number of neurotransmitters; at least 50 have been identified. One of them, gamma-aminobutyric acid (GABA), is involved in virtually every behavior, including anxiety states. Another important neurotransmitter, *serotonin*, is located throughout the brain and is especially important in sleep (McGinty & Szymusiak, 1988). The most well-known neurotransmitter, however, is *acetylcholine,* which is found in neurons throughout the brain and spinal cord. Acetylcholine is crucial to excititation of the skeletal muscles, the muscles that allow you to move. It is also important in such day-to-day functions as memory, learning, and sexual behavior. The memory problems associated with Alzheimer's disease (discussed in Chapter 11) appear to be related to an inability to produce sufficient amounts of acetylcholine. Table 2.1 describes five key neurotransmitters and their effects.

Research on Neurotransmitters. Although scientists have known about the existence of neurotransmitters for a long time, only recently have they realized the significance of these substances in the study of human behavior. For example, researchers have found that serotonin affects motivation and mood (e.g., Young et al., 1985) and that schizophrenia is associated with increased levels of activity in neural circuits that use certain neurotransmitters. In addition, they have found that people with Parkinson's disease, whose symptoms include weakness and uncontrollable shaking, have low levels of the neurotransmitter dopamine. When clinicians give these people drugs that have the same effects as dopamine (such as L-dopa), many of their symptoms are temporarily alleviated. Although it is unlikely that one neurotransmitter alone can cause a disorder such as schizophrenia or Parkinson's disease, a single neurotransmitter may play an important role in the onset or maintenance of such an illness.

Neuropeptides are chains of amino acids that act much like neurotransmitters. The effects of endorphins, one type of naturally produced neuropeptide, are mimicked by the actions of the narcotic morphine. Much as morphine does in hospital-

TABLE 2.1 *Five Key Neurotransmitters*

Neurotransmitter	Location	Effects
Acetylcholine	Brain, spinal cord, autonomic nervous system, selected organs	Excitation in brain and autonomic nervous system; excitation or inhibition in certain organs
Norepinephrine	Brain, spinal cord, selected organs	Inhibition in brain; excitation or inhibition in certain organs
Dopamine	Brain	Inhibition
Serotonin	Brain, spinal cord	Inhibition
GABA	Brain, spinal cord	Inhibition

Neuromodulator: Chemical substance that functions to increase or decrease the sensitivity of widely distributed neurons to the specific effects of neurotransmitters.

Agonist [AG-oh-nist]: Chemical that mimics the actions of a neurotransmitter, usually by occupying receptor sites and facilitating neurochemical transfers.

Antagonist: Chemical that opposes the actions of a neurotransmitter, usually by preventing the neurotransmitter from occupying a receptor site.

ized patients, endorphins inhibit certain synaptic transmissions—particularly those involving pain—and generally make people feel good (e.g., Miller et al., 1993). We will examine pain, endorphins, and pain management in more detail in Chapter 3.

At first, researchers thought that only one type of neurotransmitter existed in each neuron and that each neurotransmitter acted on only one type of receptor. Today researchers know that neurons often hold more than one type of neurotransmitter, and these may act on more than one receptor. Some neurotransmitters (especially neuropeptides) are released into the bloodstream, so their effects may be far-reaching. Researchers now think of such neurotransmitters as neuromodulators. **Neuromodulators** are chemical substances that function to increase or decrease the sensitivity of widely distributed neurons to the specific effects of other neurotransmitters. A neuropeptide released into the bloodstream, for example, affects not only a single cell's immediate ion transfer but whole classes or groups of cells, such as those within the limbic system, a brain structure known to be involved with emotional responses.

The study of neurotransmitters may hold the key to an understanding of drug addiction. It appears that all addictive drugs affect neurotransmitter actions and their likelihood of occurrence; this effect helps explain the addictive nature of the drugs themselves. The study of neurotransmitters and their receptors may also help researchers find drugs that will effectively block the addictive properties of drugs such as cocaine and lead to more successful forms of treatment for addiction (Berridge & Robinson, 1995).

Psychopharmacology. The study of how drugs affect behavior is called *psychopharmacology*. Researchers often study many types of drugs to learn the physiological mechanisms that cause behavioral reactions. Research has shown that many common drugs alter the amount of a neurotransmitter released at synapses; other drugs alter the way neurotransmitters operate. Thus, for example, a drug may change behavior by changing the speed or efficiency with which electrochemical information is transferred from one nerve cell to the next. Chemicals can also be used to mimic or facilitate the actions of neurotransmitters; such chemicals are called **agonists**. When an agonist is administered, it is as if the neurotransmitter itself has been released. Other chemicals, called **antagonists**, oppose the actions of specific neurotransmitters. When an antagonist is administered, a cell's receptor site is blocked and the neurotransmitter cannot have its usual effect. Schizophrenia, a disabling mental disorder, is often treated with antagonists. Cells that normally respond to dopamine are blocked from doing so by being exposed to certain drugs that act as antagonists, and symptoms of schizophrenia are thereby alleviated. (Dopamine in relation to schizophrenia will be discussed in more detail in Chapter 14.) Some drugs block the reabsorption, or reuptake, of neurotransmitters from their receptor sites. This blocking of reuptake has proved highly useful in the treatment of depression, which affects millions of people worldwide.

When neurons fire, information is transferred from the sense organs to the brain and from the brain to the muscular system and the glands. If psychologists knew precisely how

FOCUS

Review

- Describe the full journey of a neural impulse from one neuron to another. pp. 44–47
- What is the difference between excitatory and inhibitory postsynaptic potentials? pp. 46–47
- Distinguish between a neurotransmitter and a neuromodulator. pp. 46–48

Think Critically

- Should scientists try to apply their increasing knowledge of neuronal transmission to build a better human body with faster, more complete analysis and transmission of information, perhaps one in which there exist no feelings of pain?
- What is the downside of the increasing number of drugs that are available for the treatment of mental disorders?

this transfer occurred, they could more successfully predict and manage the behavior of people with neurological damage, mood disorders, or epilepsy. However, the firing of neurons and the release of neurotransmitters and neuromodulators do not in themselves completely explain the biological bases of human behavior. The firing of individual neurons is an incomplete picture because it is the brain as a whole that receives, interprets, and acts on neuronal impulses. It is to the brain and the nervous system that we turn next.

Organization of the Peripheral and Central Nervous Systems

It is a dark, wet evening; you are driving down a deserted road, listening to some 1980s oldies. A truck appears out of nowhere, heading straight toward you. You swerve, brake, turn again, pump the brakes, and then pull over to the side of the road—all within a matter of seconds. On just such a second-by-second basis, the nervous system controls behavior. It is therefore essential for psychologists to understand the organization and functions of the nervous system and its mutually dependent systems and divisions. Recall that the nervous system is made up of the peripheral nervous system and the central nervous system. The central nervous system consists of the brain and spinal cord; the peripheral nervous system connects the central nervous system to the rest of the body. Let's examine them both in detail.

The Peripheral Nervous System

The **peripheral nervous system** is the part of the nervous system that carries information to and from the spinal cord and the brain through spinal nerves attached to the spinal cord and by a system of 12 cranial nerves, which carry signals directly to and from the brain. The peripheral nervous system contains all the nerves that are not in the central nervous system; its nerves focus on the *periphery*, or outer parts, of the body. Its two major divisions are the somatic nervous system and the autonomic nervous system.

The Somatic Nervous System. The **somatic nervous system** is the part of the peripheral nervous system that both responds to the external senses of sight, hearing, touch, smell, and taste and acts on the outside world. Generally considered under the individual's voluntary control, the somatic nervous system is involved in perceptual processing (processing information gathered through one's senses) and in control of movement and muscles. Because it carries information from the sense organs to the brain and from the brain and spinal cord to the consciously controlled muscles, it consists of both sensory (afferent) and motor (efferent) neurons. It is the somatic system that allows you to see an oncoming truck and to get out of its way.

The Autonomic Nervous System. The **autonomic nervous system** is the part of the peripheral nervous system that controls the vital processes of the body, such as heart rate, digestive processes, blood pressure, and functioning of internal organs. In contrast to the somatic nervous system, it operates continuously and involuntarily (although the technique of biofeedback, discussed in Chapter 4, has sometimes proved to be effective in bringing some of these processes under partial voluntary control). The system is called "autonomic" because many of its subsystems are self-regulating, focused on the utilization and conservation of energy resources. The autonomic nervous system is made up of two divisions: the sympathetic nervous system and the parasympathetic nervous system, which work together to control the activities of muscles and glands (see Figure 2.6 on page 50).

Peripheral nervous system [puh-RIF-er-al]: The part of the nervous system that carries information to and from the central nervous system through a network of spinal and cranial nerves.

Somatic nervous system [so-MAT-ick]: The part of the peripheral nervous system that carries information to skeletal muscles and thereby affects bodily movement; it controls voluntary, conscious sensory and motor functions.

Autonomic nervous system [au-toe-NOM-ick]: The part of the peripheral nervous system that controls the vital and automatic processes of the body, such as the heart rate, digestive processes, blood pressure, and functioning of internal organs.

FIGURE 2.6

The Two Divisions of the Autonomic Nervous System

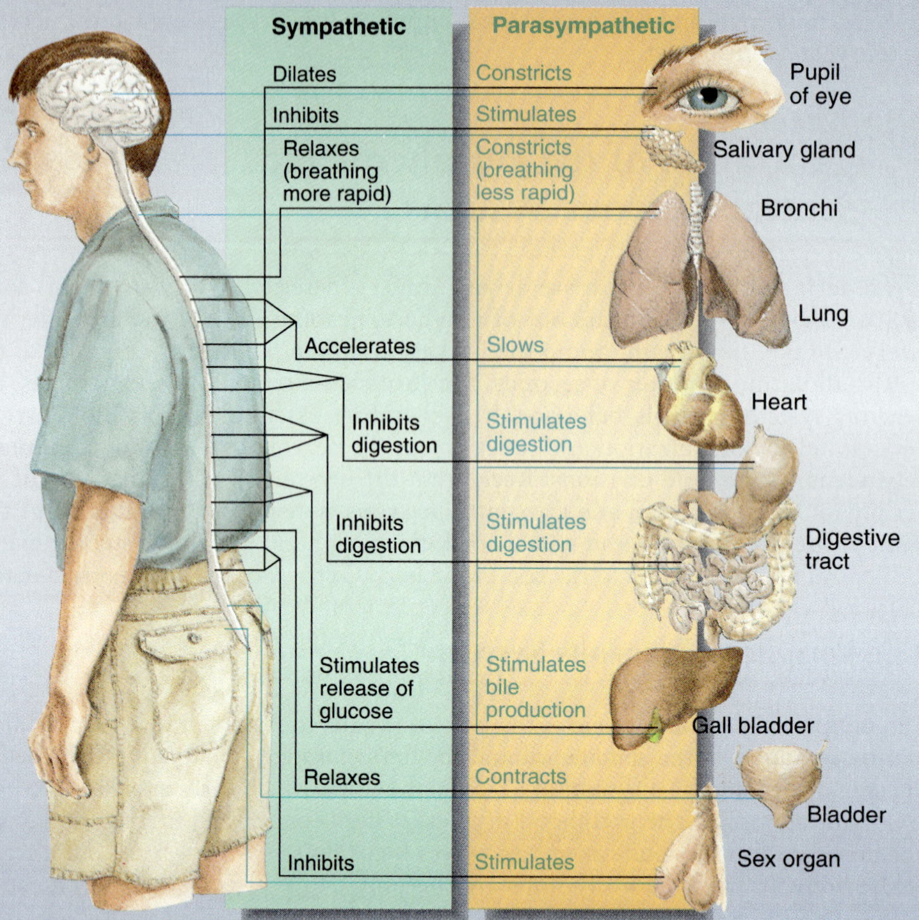

The **sympathetic nervous system** is the part of the autonomic nervous system that responds to emergency situations. Its activities are easy to observe and measure. Activation results in a sharp increase in heart rate and blood pressure, slowing of the digestive processes, dilation of the pupils, and general preparation for an emergency—sometimes called the *fight-or-flight response.* These changes are usually accompanied by an increased flow of epinephrine, or adrenaline, which is a substance released by the adrenal gland (to be discussed later in this chapter), and they are regulated by a set of neurons in the hypothalamus and brain stem (to be discussed shortly) (Jansen et al., 1995). Increased activity of the sympathetic nervous system is what makes your heart pound and your mouth go dry when your car narrowly misses hitting an oncoming truck.

Sympathetic nervous system: The part of the autonomic nervous system that becomes most active in response to emergency situations; it calls up bodily resources as needed for major energy expenditures.

Parasympathetic nervous system [PAIR-uh-sim-puh-THET-ick]: The part of the autonomic nervous system that controls the ongoing maintenance processes of the body, such as the heart rate, digestive processes, and blood pressure.

The **parasympathetic nervous system**, which is active most of the time, is the part of the autonomic nervous system that controls the normal operations of the body, such as digestion, blood pressure, and heart rate. In other words, it keeps the body running smoothly. This system calms everything down and moves the heartbeat back to normal after an emergency. Parasympathetic activity does not show sharp changes on a minute-by-minute basis.

When the sympathetic nervous system is active and the organism is in a fight-or-flight position, the somatic nervous system is also activated. For example, when a

FIGURE 2.7

The Basic Divisions of the Nervous System

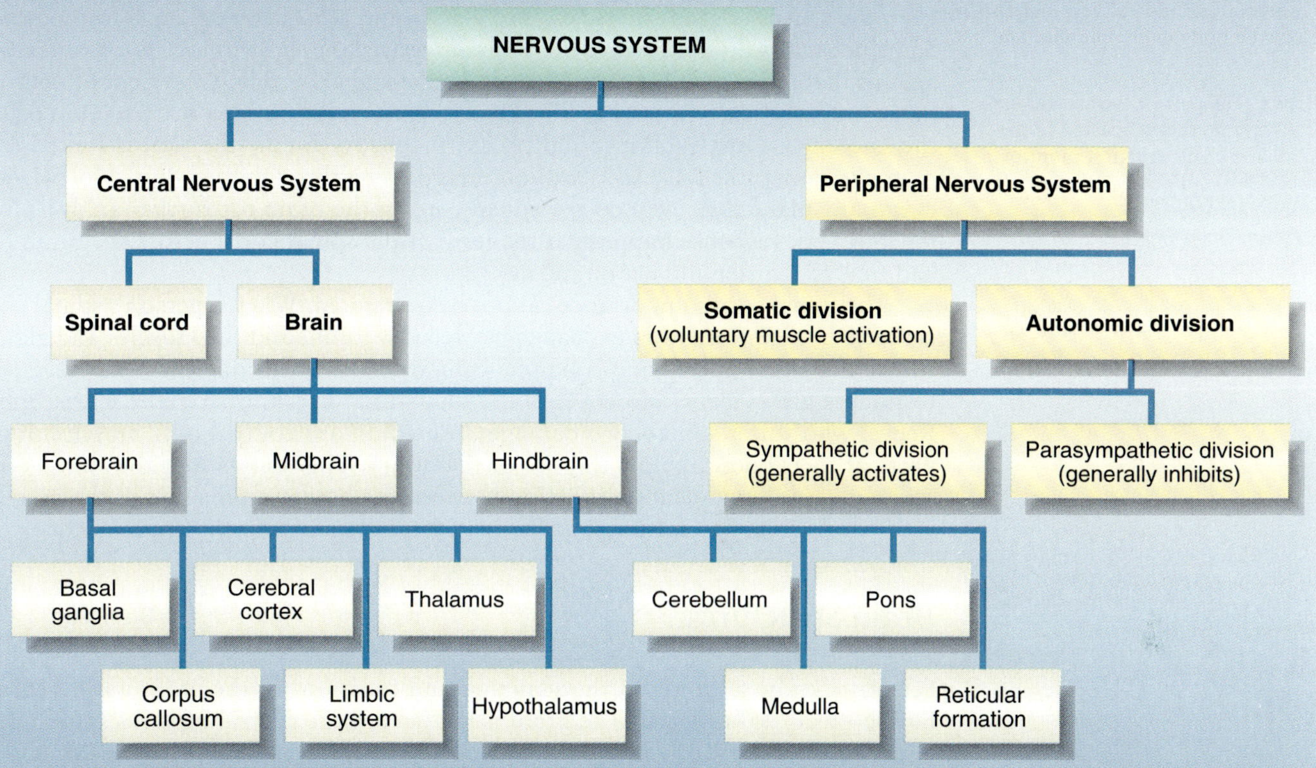

large, snarling dog chases a runner, the runner's adrenal gland is stimulated by the sympathetic nervous system; the burst of energy produced by epinephrine (released by the adrenal gland) affects the somatic nervous system, making the runner's muscles respond strongly and rapidly. Thus, changes in the sympathetic nervous system can produce rapid changes in the organism's somatic nervous system; these changes are usually seen in emotional behavior and in stress reactions (discussed in detail in Chapters 9 and 13). Even simple responses, such as blushing from embarrassment, are regulated by the sympathetic nervous system. Blushing may occur when someone realizes he or she has made a blunder, looks foolish, or is being scrutinized carefully; it occurs automatically.

The Central Nervous System

The **central nervous system** is one of the two major parts of the nervous system. Consisting of the brain and the spinal cord, it serves as the main processing system for most information in the body (see Figure 2.7).

Fig. 2.4

Although exactly how the brain functions remains a mystery that is far from being completely understood, neuroscientists know that the brain operates through many mutually dependent systems and subsystems to affect and control behavior. As you've seen in our discussion of neuronal activity, millions of brain cells are involved in the performance of even simple activities. When you walk, for example, the visual areas of the brain are active and your sight guides you, the brain's motor areas help make your legs move, and the cerebellum helps you keep your balance. It

Central nervous system: One of the two major parts of the nervous system, consisting of the brain and the spinal cord.

Spinal cord: The portion of the central nervous system that is contained within the spinal column and transmits signals from the senses to the brain, controls reflexive responses, and conveys signals from the brain to the muscles and glands.

Brain: The part of the central nervous system that is located in the skull and that regulates, monitors, processes, and guides other nervous system activity.

is the central nervous system communicating with the muscles and glands, under the control of the brain, that allows all these things to happen so effortlessly.

The brain is the control center, but it receives much of its information from the spinal cord, the main communication line to the rest of the body, and from the cranial nerves. The **spinal cord,** contained within the spinal column, receives signals from the sensory organs, muscles, and glands and relays these signals to the brain. Some behaviors do not involve the brain directly. Among them are *spinal reflexes*—actions that are controlled almost solely by the spinal cord and a system of neurons that create a reflexive response. The knee jerk, elicited by a tap on the tendon below the kneecap, is just such a spinal reflex. A sensory input (the tap) is linked to a motor response (the knee jerk) without first passing through the brain. Most signals eventually make their way up the spinal cord to the brain for further analysis, but the knee jerk response happens at the level of the spinal cord, before the brain has had time to register and act on the tap.

The spinal cord's importance cannot be overstated. When a person's spinal cord is severed, the information exchange between the brain and the muscles and glands below the point of damage is halted. Spinal reflexes still operate, and knee jerk responses are evident. However, individuals like well-known actor Christopher Reeve, who suffer spinal cord damage, lose voluntary control over muscles in the parts of their bodies below the site of the injury. This shows that the spinal cord serves a key communication function between the brain and the rest of the body; it is the chief trunk line for neuronal activity. Let's turn next to the brain itself.

Brain Structures

Scientists know a lot about the structure and functions of the brain itself, yet still have a great deal to learn. The **brain** is the part of the central nervous system that regulates, monitors, processes, and guides other nervous system activity. Located in the skull, the human brain is an organ weighing about 3 pounds and composed of two large *cerebral hemispheres*, one on the right side and one on the left. A large, thick dividing structure, the *corpus callosum*, connects the two hemispheres and permits the transfer of information between them. Besides being divided into right and left halves, the brain can be divided into areas with special functions. Some parts are specialized for visual activities; others are involved in hearing, sleeping, breathing, eating, and other important functions. Some brain activities are localized. Most speech and language activity, for example, can be pinpointed to a specific area, usually on the left side of the brain. Other activities may occur in both hemispheres. For example, visual activity occurs in the visual cortex, which occupies both sides of the brain. You will see later in this chapter, however, that psychologists disagree on the extent to which functions are localized within the brain.

In examining the brain, we begin where the spinal cord and the brain meet. Many structures and functions at this juncture deep within the brain are responsible for basic bodily processes, such as breathing, sleeping, and eating. As we move higher up through the brain, we find more complicated structures and functions. So, in embryonic and evolutionary development, the brain grows organizationally and functionally into three fairly discrete sections: the hindbrain, the midbrain, and the fore-

The human brain weighs about 3 pounds and is composed of two large cerebral hemispheres, joined by the corpus callosum. ▶

brain (which includes the cortex). (Follow along in the illustration on pages 64a and 64b, which shows the major sections of the human brain.) Structures in the hindbrain and midbrain are often assumed to be organizationally more primitive than structures in the forebrain and are responsible for more basic, reflexive actions. Structures in the lower portions of the forebrain are organizationally somewhat more complex and involve higher mental functions. Of still higher levels of functioning is the cortex, the deeply fissured gray surface matter that covers the cerebral hemispheres and serves as the basis for thought processing—one of the most advanced abilities of humans.

Hindbrain

The four main structures of the hindbrain receive afferent signals from other parts of the brain and from the spinal cord; they interpret the signals and either relay the information to more complex parts of the brain or immediately cause the body to act. The **hindbrain** (refer to the illustration on pages 64a and 64b) consists of the medulla, the reticular formation, the pons, and the cerebellum.

The **medulla**, through which many afferent and efferent signals pass, is the dense package of nerves lying just above the spinal cord that controls heartbeat and breathing. Within the medulla and extending out into the cortex is a latticelike network of nerve cells, the **reticular formation**, which directly controls a person's state of arousal, waking, and sleeping, as well as responsive bodily functions; damage to it can result in coma and death. The reticular formation extends into and through the pons and the midbrain, with projections toward the cortex (see the illustration on page 64b). The **pons** provides a link between the medulla and the cerebellum and the rest of the brain; and, like the medulla, portions of the pons affect sleep and dreaming.

The **cerebellum** (or "little brain"), a large structure attached to the back surface of the brain stem (the area from the medulla up to the midbrain), influences balance, coordination, and movement. It allows you to do such things as walk in a straight line, type accurately on a keyboard, and coordinate the many movements involved in dancing. The cerebellum may also be involved in a number of cognitive (thinking) operations, including learning, although its functions are not yet clearly established (Daum et al., 1993; Leiner, Leiner, & Dow, 1986).

Midbrain

The **midbrain** (refer to the illustration on page 64b) consists of nuclei (collections of cell bodies) that receive afferent signals from other parts of the brain and from the spinal cord. Like the hindbrain, the midbrain interprets the signals and either relays the information to a more complex part of the brain or causes the body to act at once. One portion of the midbrain is involved in smoothness of movement and another in reflexive movement. Movements of the eyeball in its socket, for example, are controlled by the *superior colliculus*, a structure in the midbrain. The reticular formation continues in the midbrain.

Forebrain

The **forebrain** is the most advanced brain structure organizationally and structurally; it is also the largest and most complicated of the brain structures because of its many interrelated parts: the thalamus and hypothalamus, the limbic system, the basal ganglia and corpus callosum, and the cortex.

Hindbrain: The most primitive organizationally of the three functional divisions of the brain, consisting of the medulla, reticular formation, pons, and cerebellum.

Medulla [meh-DUH-lah]: The most primitive and lowest portion of the hindbrain; controls basic bodily functions such as breathing.

Reticular formation [reh-TICK-you-lar]: Extending out from the medulla, a latticelike network of neurons that directly controls a person's state of arousal, waking, and sleeping, as well as other bodily functions.

Pons: A structure of the hindbrain that connects with the medulla and the cerebellum, provides a link with the rest of the brain, and is involved in sleep.

Cerebellum [seh-rah-BELL-um]: A large structure that is attached to the back surface of the brain stem and that influences balance, coordination, and movement.

Midbrain: The second level of the three organizational structures of the brain, which receives afferent signals from other parts of the brain and from the spinal cord, interprets the signals, and either relays the information to a more complex part of the brain or causes the body to act at once; considered important in the regulation of movement.

Forebrain: The largest, most complicated, and most advanced organizationally and functionally of the three divisions of the brain, with many interrelated parts: the thalamus and hypothalamus, the limbic system, the basal ganglia and corpus callosum, and the cortex.

FIGURE 2.8

Principal Structures of the Limbic System

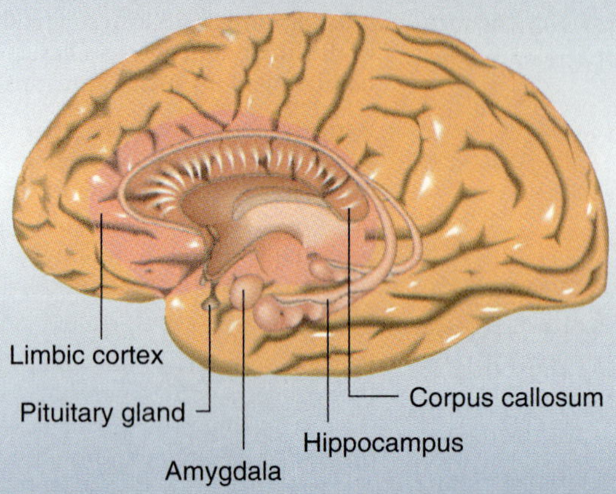

FIGURE 2.9

The Basal Ganglia

The basal ganglia, found deep within the brain, are involved in the regulation and control of gross movement.

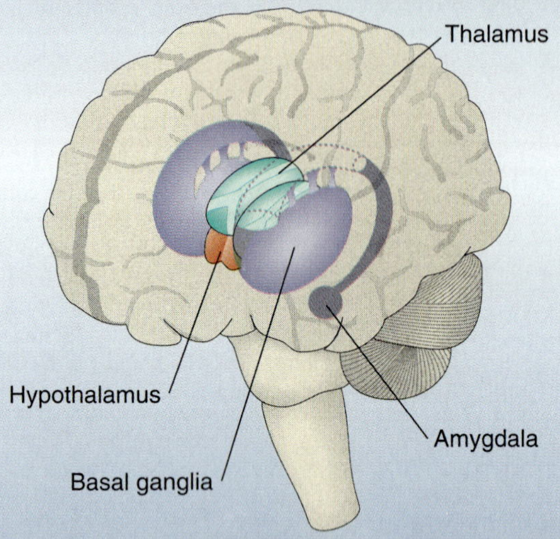

Thalamus and Hypothalamus. The **thalamus** (refer to the illustration on page 64a) acts primarily as a routing station for sending information to other parts of the brain, although it probably also performs some interpretive functions. Nearly all sensory information proceeds through this large structure before going to other areas of the brain. The **hypothalamus,** which is relatively small (pea size) and located just below the thalamus, has numerous connections with the rest of the forebrain and the midbrain and affects many complex behaviors, such as eating, drinking, and sexual activity. It plays a crucial role in the regulation of food intake; disturbances in the hypothalamus often produce sharp changes in eating and drinking behavior. We will examine these topics in more detail in Chapter 9.

Limbic System. One of the most complex and least understood structures of the brain is the **limbic system** (see Figure 2.8). This system, located deep within the temporal lobe, is an interconnected group of structures (including parts of the cortex, thalamus, and hypothalamus) involved in emotions, memory, social behavior, and brain disorders such as epilepsy. Within the limbic system are the hippocampus and the amygdala. In human beings, the *hippocampus* is involved in learning, memory, and some emotional functions. The *amygdala* is a set of cells also involved in the control of some emotional behaviors. Stimulation of the amygdala in animals, for instance, produces attack responses; and surgical removal of the amygdala in human beings was once a radical way of treating people who were extremely violent. The amgydala is now considered important in the recognition of fear, in learning, and in a wide range of other emotions (Bechara et al., 1995; Damasio, 1994). Stimulation of several areas of the limbic system in rats also produces what appear to be highly pleasurable sensations. Olds and Milner (1954) discovered that rats, when given small doses of electrical current in some of the limbic areas as a reward for bar pressing, chose bar pressing over eating, even after having been deprived of food for long periods. The researchers called the areas of the brain being stimulated *pleasure centers.*

The Basal Ganglia and Corpus Callosum. The *basal ganglia* are a series of nuclei located deep in the forebrain to the left and right of the thalamus (see Figure 2.9). They control movements and posture and are also associated with Parkinson's disease. Parts of the basal ganglia influence muscle tone and initiate commands to the cerebellum and to higher brain centers. Damage to this important neurological center can have severe behavioral consequences. The *corpus callosum* is a thick band of cross-hemisphere connections that conveys information between the cerebral hemispheres; damage to it results in essentially two separate brains within one skull. We'll return to the corpus callosum in *The Research Process* on page 58 and 59.

Cortex. The brain has two major portions, referred to as the left and right cere-

Thalamus: A large structure of the forebrain that acts primarily as a routing station to send information to other parts of the brain but probably also performs some interpretive functions; nearly all sensory information proceeds through the thalamus.

Hypothalamus: A relatively small structure of the forebrain, lying just below the thalamus, which acts through its connections with the rest of the forebrain and the midbrain and affects many complex behaviors, such as eating, drinking, and sexual activity.

bral hemispheres (see *The Research Process* for a detailed discussion of brain specialization). The exterior covering of these hemispheres, called the **cortex** (or neocortex), is about 2 millimeters thick and consists of six thin layers of cells. It is *convoluted*, or furrowed. These **convolutions**, folds in the tissue, have the effect of creating more surface area within a small space. The overall surface area of the cortex is at least 1.5 square feet. A highly developed cortex is evident in human beings, but not all mammals show such specialization, and most other mammals' brains are less deeply fissured. The cortex plays a special role in behavior because it is intimately involved in thought.

A traditional way to divide the cortex is to consider it as a series of lobes, or areas, each with characteristic structures and functions. The most prominent structures are two deep fissures (very deep furrows, or folds)—the *lateral fissure* and the *central fissure*—that divide the lobes. These easily recognizable fissures are like deep ravines that run among the convolutions, separating the various lobes; these deep cortical valleys are thought to be especially important in thought (Markowitsch & Tulving, 1994). The *frontal lobe* is in front of the central fissure; the *parietal lobe* is behind it. Below the lateral fissure and the parietal lobe is the *temporal lobe*. And at the back of the head, behind the parietal and temporal lobes, is the *occipital lobe*. Figure 2.10 on page 56 describes each lobe and its primary functions.

Studying the Brain

In the 18th century, people measured the size of heads and examined bumps and prominent features such as a large protruding forehead; their reasoning was that prominent features might be associated with certain kinds of thoughts. Today scientists know that the brain plays a central role in controlling behavior, and they are continually trying to understand it better; but now they use scientific techniques that go far beyond the tape measure. Knowledge of the brain and its relationship to behavior comes about in part through the study of *neuroanatomy*—the structures of the nervous system. Some neuroanatomists study the brains of people who have died of tumors, brain diseases, and trauma (injury) to the brain, hoping to correlate the type of brain damage with the loss of specific abilities, such as seeing, reading, and writing. Some brain damage occurs through accidents, strokes, and brain tumors; observing the behaviors and mental processes of individuals with known damage provides further information (see *The Research Process* on pages 58 and 59). Neuroanatomists who study behavior often use *ablation* as a principal technique. In ablation researchers remove or destroy a portion of an animal's brain and study the animal to determine which behaviors have been disrupted. Today, in addition to ablation, neuroanatomists use electrical recording techniques such as EEGs, MRIs, and CT and PET scans. Still other researchers study brain–behavior relationships by watching animals or children as they interact with their environment and solve problems.

Monitoring Neuronal Activity

Though nonliving brains can be dissected, neuroscientists are becoming more interested in exploring the functions and interconnections of the active central nervous system, a more difficult task. Much of what scientists now know about the electrical activity in the nervous system comes from laboratory studies of abnormalities in brain structure and function. In conducting such studies, scientists use several basic procedures to measure the activity of the nervous system.

One measuring technique is *single unit recording*, in which researchers insert a thin wire, needle, or glass tube containing an electrolyte solution into or next to a

Limbic system: An interconnected group of structures (including parts of the cortex, thalamus, and hypothalamus) located deep within the temporal lobe and involved in emotions, memory, social behavior, and brain disorders such as epilepsy; within the limbic system are the hippocampus and the amygdala.

Cortex: The convoluted, or furrowed, exterior covering of the brain's hemispheres, which is about 2 millimeters thick, consists of six thin layers of cells, and is traditionally divided into a series of lobes, or areas, each with characteristic structures; thought to be involved in both sensory interpretation and complex thought processes. Also known as the *neocortex*.

Convolution: Characteristic fold in the tissues of the cerebral hemispheres and the overlying cortex.

FIGURE 2.10

The Cortex

The cortex is the exterior covering of the cerebral hemispheres. It consists of four major lobes and the association cortex. The cortex plays a special role in behavior because of its intimate involvement in thought.

	Location	Function
Frontal lobe	In front of the central fissure; contains (1) motor cortex and (2) Broca's area	Involved with memory; Concerned with movement; Involved in speech and language production
Parietal lobe	Behind frontal lobe	Associated with activities involved in the sense of touch and body position
Temporal lobe	Below lateral fissure and parietal lobe	Involved with speech, hearing, and some visual information processing
Occipital lobe	Back of head, next to and behind parietal and temporal lobes	Responsible for visual sense
Association cortex	Areas between parietal, temporal, and occipital lobes	Believed to be involved in complex behaviors that involve thinking and sensory processes

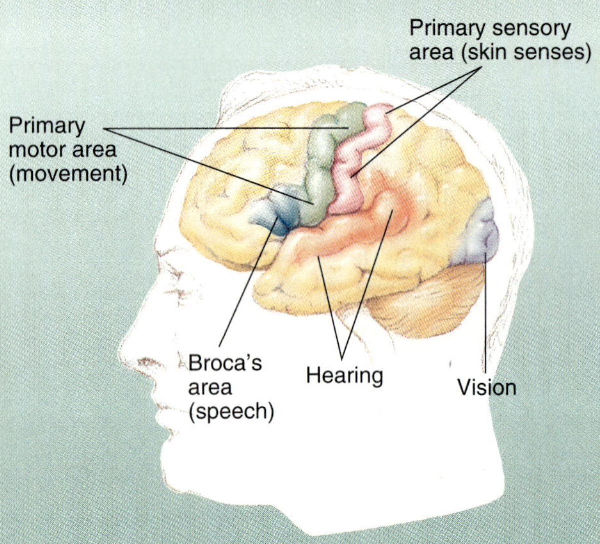

Specific areas of the brain control and influence both sensory and motor functions.

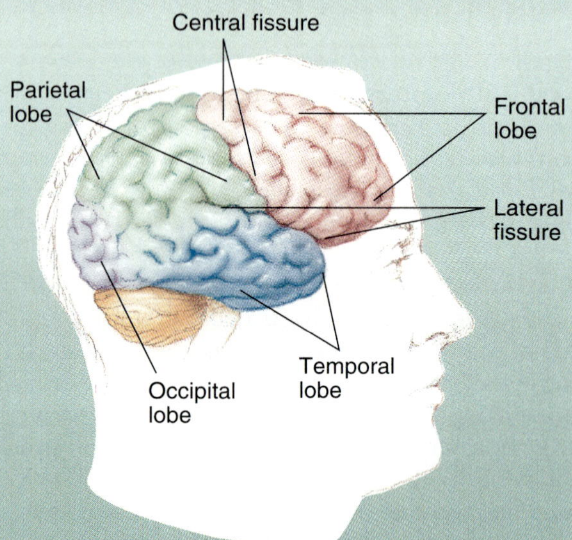

The *lateral fissure* divides the temporal lobe from the parietal lobe; the *central fissure* divides the frontal lobe from the parietal lobe.

single neuron to measure its electrical activity. Because neurons fire extremely rapidly, the data are often fed into a computer, which averages the number of times the cell fires in 1 second or 1 minute. Scientists usually perform this type of recording technique on the neurons of rats, cats, or monkeys.

Electroencephalogram (EEG) [eel-ECK-tro-en-SEFF-uh-low-gram]: Record of electrical brain-wave patterns obtained through electrodes placed on the scalp.

Another technique, *electroencephalography*, measures electrical activity in the nervous systems of both animals and human beings. It produces a record of brain-wave activity called an **electroencephalogram,** or **EEG** (*electro* means "electrical," *encephalon* means "brain," and *gram* means "record"). A small electrode placed on the scalp records the activity of thousands of cells beneath the skull to produce an EEG. EEGs, which are generally computer analyzed, are used for a variety of purposes, including the assessment of brain damage, epilepsy, tumors, and other abnormalities. When brain waves that are normally synchronized become erratic, this is usually evidence of an abnormality requiring further investigation and analysis.

In normal, healthy human beings, EEGs show a variety of characteristic brain-wave patterns, depending on the person's level and kind of mental activity. Researchers usually describe brain waves in terms of their *frequency* (the number of waves in a unit of time) and *amplitude* (the relative height or size of the waves). If people are awake, relaxed, and not engaged in active thinking, their EEGs are predominantly composed of *alpha waves*, which occur at a moderate rate (frequency) of 8 to 12 cycles per second and are of moderate amplitude. When people are excited, their brain waves change dramatically from alpha waves to *beta waves*, which are of high frequency and low amplitude. At different times during sleep, people show varying patterns of high-frequency and low-frequency waves correlated with dreaming activity and restorative functions, both of which are discussed in Chapter 4.

Three significant techniques for measuring the activity of the nervous system have emerged in the last two decades: CT, PET, and MRI scanning. *CT scans* (computerized tomography scans) are computer-assisted X-ray images of the brain (or any area of the body) in three dimensions—essentially a computerized series of X rays that show photographic slices of part of the brain or body. CT scans are especially helpful in locating specific damaged areas and tumors in the brain.

PET scans (positron emission tomography scans) use radioactive markers injected into the bloodstream, enabling researchers to watch the metabolic changes taking place in an organism. PET scans may eventually allow researchers to watch the actual functioning of the brain, to observe how the brain modifies itself as mental activity occurs, and to predict human behavior from brain functioning. PET scans are relatively new to neuroscientists. Their potential has yet to be fully unleashed, but researchers are using them to study a wide range of psychological coding processes as well as psychological disorders such as schizophrenia (Buchsbaum, 1995; Martin et al., 1995).

MRI scans (magnetic resonance imaging scans) use magnetic fields instead of X rays and have far greater clarity and resolution. MRIs can distinguish brain parts as small as 1 or 2 millimeters. Because the magnetic fields can penetrate bone, MRIs are especially useful for diagnosing cartilage and bone marrow problems and tissue damage. Furthermore, because nothing, radioactive or otherwise, needs to be injected to provide results, MRI scans are often preferred to CT scans. Today MRIs

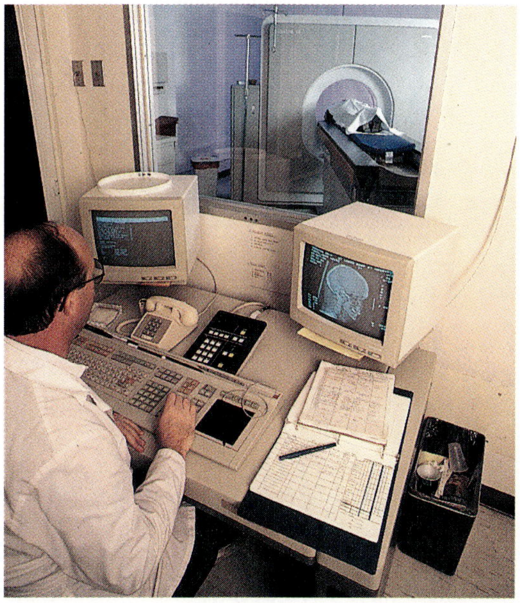

◀ *CT scans (left) are computer-assisted X-ray images that allow researchers to view the brain (or any other part of the body) in three dimensions. MRI scans (below) do not use radiation and have much higher clarity and resolution.* ▼

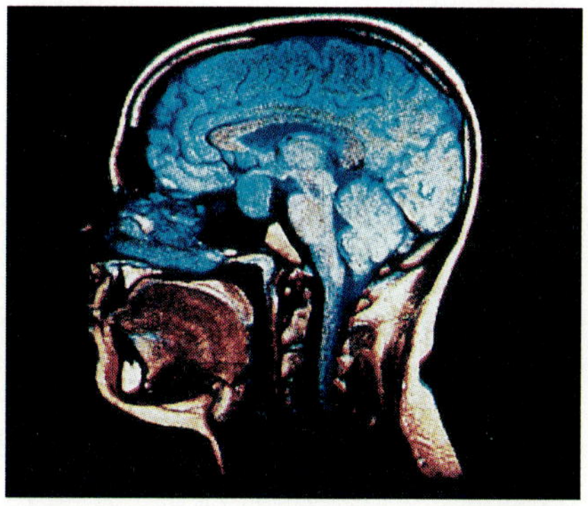

THE RESEARCH PROCESS

Brain Specialization—The Left and Right of Things

The brain's control over other structures of the body is continually evident. This is readily apparent when people take psychoactive drugs (drugs that affect the nervous system, especially the brain). A person takes a drug, which affects the firing of neurons and the flow of neurotransmitters in the brain; these changes make the person feel different. The person responds to the feeling, and further brain changes take place. In other words, the brain affects behavior and behavior in turn affects the brain.

Are there specific places in the brain that control specific behaviors and thoughts? Does one side of the brain have more control over certain behaviors than the other side does? Lavach (1991) says yes, suggesting that brain hemisphere dominance may even affect your choice of occupation, and certainly your worldview. Let's explore the evidence.

Splitting the Brain. Studies of brain structure show that different areas of the brain are responsible for different functions. Since the early 1970s, Roger Sperry (1913–1994) and Michael Gazzaniga have been at the forefront of research in brain organization. Gazzaniga has concluded that the human brain has a modular organization—that it is divided into discrete units that interact to produce mental activity (Gazzaniga, 1989).

Studies by Sperry (1985) and Gazzaniga (1983) show that in most human beings one cerebral hemisphere, usually the left, is specialized for the processing of speech and language; the other, usually the right, appears better able to handle spatial tasks and musical and artistic endeavors. Some of the evidence comes from studies monitoring brain-wave activity in normal participants exposed to different kinds of stimuli. For example, when normal participants are asked to look at or think about letters, or perhaps to rehearse a speech, some characteristic brain-wave activity can be detected on the left side of the brain. When these participants are asked to do creative tasks or are told to reorganize some spatial pattern, brain-wave activity is apparent on the right side of the brain. Although studies of brain waves do not yield complete or thoroughly convincing knowledge of brain function or brain structure, evidence is mounting. For example, research using MRI scans supports a left–right distinction for pitch and music perception and indicates a difference between individuals who have perfect pitch and the rest of us (Schlaug et al., 1995).

What happens to behavior and mental processes when connections between the left and the right sides of the brain are cut? Many important studies have involved **split-brain patients**—often, these are people with uncontrollable, life-threatening epilepsy who have undergone an operation to sever the corpus callosum (the band of fibers that connects the left and right hemispheres of the brain) to prevent seizures from spreading across the hemispheres. Special testing revealed that after the operation there was little or no perceptual or cognitive interaction between the hemispheres; the patients seemed to have two distinct, independent brains, each with its own abilities. Researchers are especially sensitive to fact that nearly all split-brain research has been done with participants whose brains, before surgery, suffered from seizures—this was what brought them to the hospital and the researchers in the first place. But the fact that participants in split-brain research are a specialized patient population does not diminish the importance of this work. Studies of split-brain patients are invaluable to scientists seeking to understand how the brain works—in particular, how the left and right sides function together (e.g., Blanc-Garin, Fauré, & Sabio, 1993).

Each cerebral hemisphere is neurologically connected to the opposite side of the body; thus, the left hemisphere normally controls the right side of the body. Split-brain patients are unable to use the speech and language capabilities located in the left cerebral hemisphere to describe activities carried out by the right one. When stimulus information is presented exclusively to their left hemisphere, they can describe the stimulus, match it, and deal with it in essentially normal ways. But when the same stimulus is presented to their right cerebral hemisphere, they can perform the matching tasks (saying that two items are identical) but are unable to describe the stimulus verbally (a left-hemisphere task). For example, by using simple tests, investigators have found that a split-brain participant holding a pencil that is hidden behind a screen in the left hand (projected onto the *right* visual cortex) cannot describe what is in the hand. However, the participant can easily perform a visual matching task if the pencil is switched to the right hand, which is "viewed" by the left visual cortex.

By studying the two separate hemispheres, researchers are discovering the characteristic functions of each of them and the conditions under which specific functions become associated with one or the other (Kosslyn et al., 1993). (See Figure 2.11.) One relatively new technique used to isolate functions and hemispheres has been to study the time it takes for signals to pass through the corpus callosum to the other hemisphere—some cognitive tasks involve significant and

---

Split-brain patients: People whose corpus callosum, which normally connects the two cerebral hemispheres, has been surgically severed.

are being used to detect signals inaccessible to PET scanners—for example, to pinpoint increases in oxygen in the brain when specific thoughts occur (Raichle, 1994).

CT, PET, and MRI scans are making the examination of brain tissue and its processes easier and more precise, thereby providing more information about the brain and its workings. For example, researchers have been able to show that small

rapid interactions between the hemispheres, whereas others involve little hemispheric communication (Hoptman & Davidson, 1994).

Fig. 2.9

Studies of split-brain patients show two key concepts: (1) localization of specific functions, and (2) the fact that not every behavior is traceable to a single structure in the central nervous system. Most behaviors involve the combined work of several areas. Although there seem to be some specifically left-brain and right-brain activities (e.g., Kingstone et al., 1995) and certain key functions associated with one side of the brain (Metcalfe, Funnell, & Gazzaniga, 1995), which may have developed early in life (McManus & Bryden, 1991) and may be slightly different for men and women (Zaidel et al., 1995), the two halves of the brain still work together (Banich, 1995; Hoptman & Davidson, 1994).

There is no doubt that lateralization and specificity of functions exist. There is also no doubt that the study of brain functions and the work of Sperry and Gazzaniga have been influential in developing current understanding of brain specificity. For example, people with a strong right-brain dominance, who are generally left-handed, may develop differently than right-handers, and this may affect a number of important events in their lives (Coren & Halpern, 1991).

Unfortunately, the popular press and TV newscasters oversimplify the specificity of functions, and in some cases overgeneralize their significance to account for school problems, marital problems, artistic abilities, and even baseball batting averages. The extent of hemispheric specialization is yet to be determined, and most scientists and critical thinkers maintain a healthy skepticism about the existence of "two minds" in one.

FIGURE 2.11

The Effects of Severing the Corpus Callosum

Researchers have developed devices that allow words or pictures to be flashed briefly on a screen. Imagine that a man whose corpus callosum (but not his optic nerve) has been severed is staring directly at such a screen, with his right eye closed or covered with a patch. When a researcher flashes the word *spoon* onto the leftmost side of the screen, it stimulates the man's left eye to send an image exclusively to the right hemisphere of his brain, which is nonverbal. Suppose the man is asked to name what he sees on the screen. Because the right hemisphere is nonverbal, the man will be unable to name the image as the word *spoon*. If he is asked to use his right hand, which is controlled by the left hemisphere, to touch the named object (a spoon) on a tabletop before him, he will not be able to do so because his right hemisphere has been severed from his left and cannot communicate with it. However, if the man is asked to use his left hand to touch the spoon, he will do so. The left hand is controlled by the right hemisphere, which is spatially adept and has been exposed to the word *spoon*. Although the man cannot verbally identify the word as *spoon*, he can locate the spoon with his left hand under the direction of his right hemisphere.

brain lesions (small areas of damaged brain tissue, often due to disease or injury) are common in elderly people and are a natural part of aging. Further, researchers are establishing tentative links among brain lesions, illness, neurochemistry, and depression (Nemeroff et al., 1988). Lawyers are even using brain scans as part of the defense in some criminal trials. For example, an attorney may assert that PET scans show damage to the client's brain that traditional neurological tests could not have found. In one California case, a diagnosis of a mental disorder, confirmed through a PET scan, kept a man from going to the gas chamber.

Plasticity and Change

Do our brains stay the same from birth to death, or can they change through experience or simply through the passage of time? Basic brain organization is established well before birth and does not change in any substantial way after birth; but details of brain structure and functions, particularly in the cerebral cortex, are subject to continued growth and development (Kalil, 1989). Psychologists say that the brain is still *malleable* (teachable) during the formative years. This ability to change is often referred to as *plasticity*. (See *The Research Process.*) Within limits, the nervous system can be modified and fine-tuned by experience—experience that can be acquired over a protracted period, over many years (Shatz, 1992)—and the brain can be trained to relearn and simulate previous learning that may have been lost though an accident or some other brain trauma (Hinton, Plaut, & Shallice, 1993).

Experience with specific stimuli reinforces the development of neural structures. Aoki and Siekevitz (1988) liken the developing brain to a highway system that expands with use. Less traveled roads are abandoned, but popular ones are broadened and new ones are added when needed. When neural structures are used, reused, and constantly updated, they become faster and more easily accessed. During early fetal and infant development, the neural links, connections, and interconnections are embellished. Such elaboration and refinement is greater when organisms are placed in complex, superenriched (e.g., visually stimulating) environments (Chang, Isaacs, & Greenough, 1991). One recent study showed that children with language-based learning impairments can be taught to use repetitive and adaptive training exercises to overcome their problems. The exercises are assumed to change neuronal structures and allow improvement in speech and language processing (Merzenich et al., 1996).

Changes in the brain occur not only in young organisms but in aging ones as well. As human beings grow older, their central nervous systems function differently—sometimes not as well as before. There are decreases in the numbers of neurons and receptors, for example. In addition, some learning tasks become more difficult for aging animals and human beings. Recent research has attempted to identify drugs that facilitate simple learning. For example, nimodipine helped aging rabbits learn simple responses as well as young rabbits do. The drug, used to improve blood flow in stroke patients, may help learning by blocking calcium transmission to areas of the brain involved in memory. Nimodipine is only one of a large number of drugs that are effective in treating age-related learning problems (Deyo, Straube, & Disterhoft, 1989) or that potentially restore brain function after brain damage (LeVere et al., 1989).

Research on the drug enhancement of learning is exciting; finding specific proteins, drugs, and new treatments that alter brain functioning may provide keys to understanding brain development and its effects on behavior. This understanding is especially important in cases of neural diseases such as Alzheimer's or trauma to the nervous system. Early trauma can even have delayed effects (Eslinger et al., 1992). Can damage done to the nervous system be repaired? Injury to the brain early in an organism's life is devastating, but the extent and permanence of the damage depend on the nature of the injury, the age at which it takes place, and the presence of several helping factors, such as the availability of an enriched environment (Kolb, 1989).

Neurotransplants

The idea of replacing body parts is no longer science fiction; physicians routinely conduct kidney and heart transplants. But could the theme of the science fiction movie *Donovan's Brain* be a reality—could you take a brain or a portion of a brain

THE RESEARCH PROCESS

Plasticity—Evidence from Musicians

Our brains are amazingly malleable. For example, at birth, infants' brains are not fully formed; over the ensuing weeks and months, brain organization continues to take place, abilities continue to develop, and significant brain growth occurs. Recent evidence suggests that visual, auditory, and tactile input to the adult brain also changes the central nervous system.

Hypotheses. Thomas Elbert led a group of researchers (Elbert et al., 1995) who asked whether there are special populations of individuals whose experience has resulted in unique brain changes. Reasoning that musicians might be such a group, the researchers decided to examine whether skilled musicians have brains that are specially organized as a result of their musical training.

Elbert and his colleagues specifically asked whether years of practice by violinists and other string players, who do elaborate fingering with the left hand, produce changes in the brain organization of these musicians. String players use the fingers of their left hand continually. By contrast, the right hand moves the bow but does not require such intricate manual dexterity. Do years of practice and experience have an effect on the brain organization of string players? Do these musicians differ from nonmusicians in this regard?

Method. The researchers performed an experiment in which they used MRI scans (which provided records of the functional activity of the brain) to examine the size and strength of changes in the brains of string players. Nine musicians (six violinists, two cellists, and one guitarist), who had played their instruments on the average for over a decade, served as participants in the study. The musicians spent an average of 10 hours per week practicing. Six nonmusicians served as a control group.

The experimenters stimulated the fingers of both the left and the right hands of all participants by applying pressure through a nonpainful stimulator. By examining MRIs, the researchers recorded the strength and location of resulting activity in the brain, especially in the somatosensory areas.

Results and Conclusion. The cortical activity of the musicians was stronger than that of the nonmusicians. Also important was the finding that the location of the tactile stimulation in the brain was shifted for the musicians. Pressure on the left fingers activated more brain cells in the musicians than in the nonmusicians. By contrast, when the right-finger stimulation of the musicians was compared to that of the controls, there were no significant differences in brain organization. There was also a correlation between the age at which the string players began studying their instruments and the magnitude in the change due to stimulation. The earlier the string players began studying, the greater the effect.

Thus, the key finding was that the extent of somatosensory cortical representation of the fingers was greater for musicians than for control subjects, and results of left-finger stimulation were greater than for right-finger stimulation. The researchers concluded that the brain is plastic and continues to be plastic—even in adults the brain continues to modify itself in response to the stimulation brought to it.

Implications. People who are injured in accidents and have to recover from brain trauma are able to do so because of cortical reorganization. The fact that this reorganization occurs at all in adults, whose brains are fully formed, is an important finding. The implications of the work of Elbert and his team of researchers (1995) are that there is continuous plastic reorganization of the somatosensory areas of the brain. Is plasticity in response to tactile stimulation an isolated case? Are other parts of the brain also able to change? Does such cortical reorganization occur only in musicians who have been studying for years? These are questions yet to be answered. But this important new study is an interesting and important beginning.

and move it to another organism? Researchers are focusing on this question in an effort to help patients with brain disorders such as epilepsy and Parkinson's disease. The research is complicated; it also has serious ethical implications.

Can brain tissue that is transplanted from one organism to another survive and develop normally? Research shows the answer depends on the type of tissue and the site where it is transplanted. Some sites prove to be good locations; others are less successful at fostering normal growth. Transplantation is most likely to be successful where cells are clearly organized, as in the visual cortex (Raisman, Morris, & Zhou, 1987). In a series of studies, researchers Fine (1986) and Mikhailova and colleagues (1991) successfully grafted (attached) brain tissue to the central nervous system in rats and other organisms and were able to observe behavior changes associated with the graft. Yet research with animals, however successful, is not the same as research with human beings. People with Parkinson's disease (in which

FOCUS

Review

- Describe the subdivisions of the autonomic nervous system. pp. 49–51
- Identify the differences between single unit recording and the EEG. pp. 55–56
- Why is the corpus callosum so essential to effective communication in the brain? pp. 54, 58–59

Think Critically

- What do you think would happen to behavior if the pons were damaged?
- What is the *potential* function of the convolutions of the cortex?
- If the brain is so malleable and sensitive to change, what can individuals do to optimize their own growth and potential? Or is there anything they can do?

brain tissue no longer secretes sufficient levels of dopamine, causing muscular rigidity and tremors) have been treated with implants of healthy fetal brain tissue with positive results (Bekhtereva et al., 1990). The implants survive, grow naturally, and secrete dopamine, and the patients' condition improves (Lindvall, 1991; Lindvall et al., 1990).

Some day neurotransplants may open up a world of therapeutic possibilities. Victims of head injuries, brain diseases, and birth defects could all benefit. But should the medical and psychological community be allowed to create a more perfect human being? There are surgical risks; many techniques are dangerous and as yet unproven. Physicians and researchers must establish procedures for selecting the best candidates for such experimentation. And what about the source of the transplanted tissue? Implants that have been successful have come from human fetal tissue. Researchers and ethicists alike are unsure under what, if any, conditions fetal tissue should be made available. One possibility that skirts some of the ethical issues is the use of a patient's own dopamine-producing healthy tissue. This procedure is being explored with some success (Madrazo et al., 1987).

Hormones and Glands

In 1978 Dan White fatally shot both San Francisco mayor George Moscone and city supervisor Harvey Milk. In court, White's attorney successfully argued that a diet of junk food had jumbled his client's brain and reduced his capacity for moral behavior. White spent only 3 years in prison for committing the double homicide. Although the "Twinkie defense" is no longer a legal defense in California, White's lawyer capitalized on the fact that a person's body chemistry—even an imbalance in blood sugar levels—can have a dramatic impact on behavior. It is true that body chemistry, hormones, and learned experiences can work together to influence a person. But does this render people unaccountable for their own actions, as Dan White's lawyer claimed?

Combinations of factors are usually the answer to many complex psychological questions, but research shows that some abilities and behaviors have a direct hormonal link—that is, hormones directly affect the behavior. For example, in a paper presented at a scientific meeting in 1988, psychologist Doreen Kimura reported that when some women experience low estrogen levels during and immediately after menstruation, they excel at spatial tasks but perform less well on motor tasks. The differences are small and do not occur with all women. Work in this area is in its early stages, but it is interesting because of the links indicated between hormones and behavior and because of the differences observed between men and women. The links are mediated by the endocrine glands and show the complexity of the relationship of behavior, body structures, and the hormones and other substances that flow through our bodies.

Endocrine Glands

Throughout each day, many of our behaviors are affected by the secretions of *glands*—groups of cells that form structures and secrete substances. Psychologists are particularly interested in the **endocrine glands**—ductless glands that secrete hormones directly into the bloodstream, rather than through a specific duct, or opening, into a target organ. (See Figure 2.12 for the location of several endocrine glands.) **Hormones** are chemicals from the endocrine glands that regulate the activities of specific organs or cells; they travel through the bloodstream to target organs containing cells that respond specifically to particular hormones. Although researchers do not know the extent to which hormones control people's behavior, there is no doubt that the glandular system is interconnected. Each hormone affects behavior and eventually other glands. A disorder in the thyroid, for example, affects not only the metabolic rate but also the pituitary gland, which in turn affects other behaviors. The glands, the hormones, and the target organs interact; the brain initiates the release of hormones, which affect the target organs, which in turn affect behavior, which in turn affects the brain, and so on. *Diversity*, on pages 64 and 65, explores the question of whether gender differences are caused by hormones.

Sexual Behavior. In newborn animals, hormones have an irreversible effect on sexual behavior—they set specific behavior patterns in motion by permanently affecting brain development. In human adults, sexual behavior is to some extent under hormonal control. One study, for example, showed a significant correlation between married couples' hormone levels and frequency of intercourse (Persky,

FIGURE 2.12

The Endocrine Glands

The endocrine glands are situated throughout the body. Though small in size, they exert enormous influence on behavior.

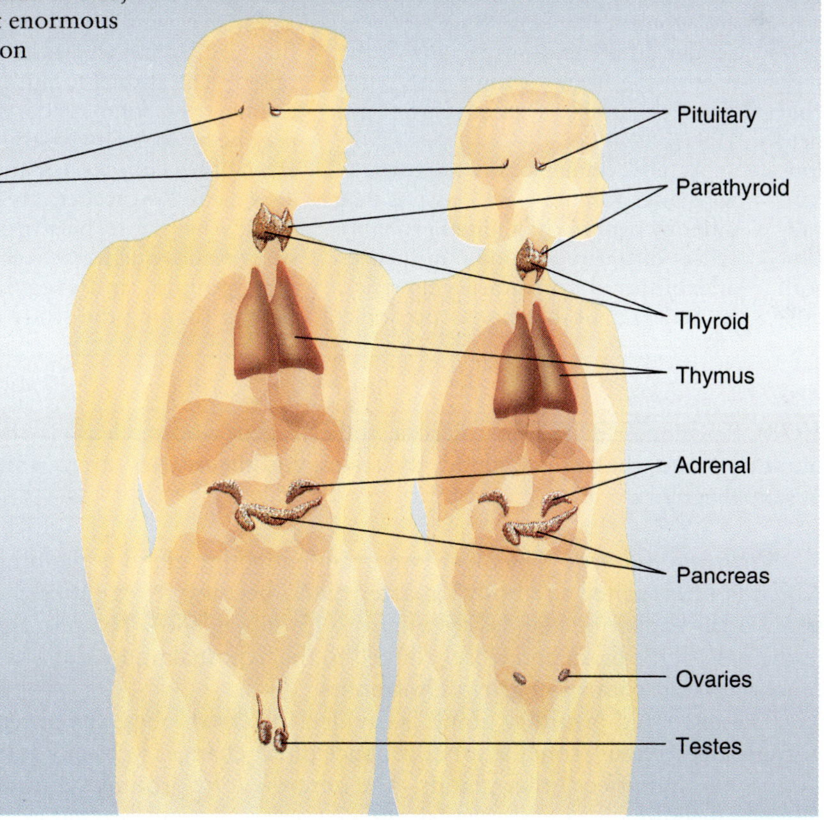

Endocrine glands [END-oh-krin]: Ductless glands that secrete hormones directly into the bloodstream, rather than through a specific duct, or opening, into a target organ.

Hormones: Endocrine gland chemicals that regulate the activities of specific organs or cells.

DIVERSITY

Are Gender Differences Caused by Brain Structures or Hormones?

Some people believe that men and women are essentially the same; however, research does show some important biological and behavioral differences. In recent years, research on gender differences in brain organization has created a volatile debate.

Let's look at some facts. During fetal development, sex hormones are present in the fetus and help create sexual differentiation. Sex hormones are also thought to create permanent changes in brain development that become evident in later behavior. Research shows that, on average, men do better than women on some spatial tasks—for example, the mental rotation of objects (Linn & Petersen, 1985). Across numerous research studies, men do better, on average, in mathematical reasoning and in some motor tasks, such as guiding projectiles through space (Halpern, 1986).

By contrast, women do better than men at some perceptual tasks—for example, the rapid matching of items. Women have greater verbal fluency than men and outperform men in some arithmetic calculations (Hyde, Fennema, & Lamon, 1990). They also do better than men at reading emotions from photographs. For certain other tasks on which both sexes do equally well—for example, rhyming—men and women use different areas of the brain to do the task (Shaywitz et al., 1995).

Women and men perform some tasks differently. Women tend to use both sides of the brain in cognitive tasks such as spelling, for example; men use primarily the left side. While women use both ears equally, men favor the right ear. Not all gender differences appear at all ages and at all phases of learning, however. Gender differences in problem solving, for example, tend to favor females in elementary school and males after puberty (Hyde, Fennema, & Lamon, 1990).

The gender differences in various mental and performance abilities described here are minimal; there is no dramatic difference between men and women on any one task. However, researchers have observed subtle yet potentially important differences. For example, they know that men and women behave differently in many situations, especially emotional ones. While PET scans of adults show similar brain metabolic activity for men and women, there are *some* apparent gender differences—especially in the part of the brain dealing with emotions, the limbic system (Gur et al., 1995).

At birth, human brains are remarkably alike. Kimura (1992) asserts that differing patterns of abilities probably reflect different hormonal influences after birth and structural asymmetries. In males, male hormones predominate; they may affect the size and function of brain structures such as the hypothalamus. For example, when newborn rats are administered large doses of male hormones, their brains develop differently than when they are administered large doses of female hormones, and this difference alters their behavioral abilities permanently.

Of course, making the leap to human beings is difficult, because ethics preclude the manipulation of hormone levels of newborns. However, researchers have been able to measure the abilities of human adults and simultaneously measure their levels of the hormone testosterone. Testosterone is evident in all human beings, although men show significantly higher levels than women. Valerie Shute measured these levels in men and women and found that women with high levels of testosterone performed better on spatial tasks than women with low levels; in men, the reverse was true. Her conclusion was that testosterone levels in men and women affect performance (Shute et al., 1983).

But are gender differences also influenced by the way individuals are raised? The answer to this question is certainly yes. Some gender differences may be biologically based, but Western culture emphasizes and encourages them. Researchers are becoming more sensitive to bias in reports of study results and to the roles that culture, politics, and even economics play in shaping the study of gender

---

1978). Hormones such as testosterone and estrogen, whose release is affected by the pituitary gland, the adrenal gland, the testes, and the ovaries, are certainly involved in sexual activity.

Pituitary Gland. The most important endocrine gland is the **pituitary gland**, which is often called the body's master gland because it regulates the actions of many other endocrine glands (see Figure 2.13 on page 66). The pituitary is located at the base of the brain and closely linked to the hypothalamus, and one of its major functions is the control of growth hormones.

Pituitary gland [pit-YOU-ih-tare-ee]: The body's master gland, located at the base of the brain and closely linked to the hypothalamus; regulates the actions of other endocrine glands; major function is the control of growth hormones.

The pea-sized pituitary gland is divided into two lobes, the anterior and the posterior. Secretions from the lobes produce direct changes in bodily functions, such as growth, and affect other glands. The *anterior lobe* produces a number of hormones—including hormones that stimulate the thyroid and adrenal glands, each of

THE HUMAN BRAIN REVEALED

The human brain is divided into three major sections: the hindbrain, the midbrain, and the forebrain, depicted here from various perspectives.

The *hindbrain* consists of the cerebellum, the medulla, the reticular formation, and the pons. It is shown in progressively more revealed detail in parts (a), (b), and (c).

The *midbrain,* clearly indicated in (c) between the forebrain and the hindbrain, consists of several major structures, as well as a number of smaller, important nuclei (collections of cell bodies). The reticular formation continues from the hindbrain into the midbrain.

The *forebrain* is the largest and most complex of the brain structures, encompassing the thalamus, the hypothalamus, the hippocampus, the amygdala, the basal ganglia (not shown here), the corpus callosum, and the cortex. It, too, is revealed in parts (a)–(c).

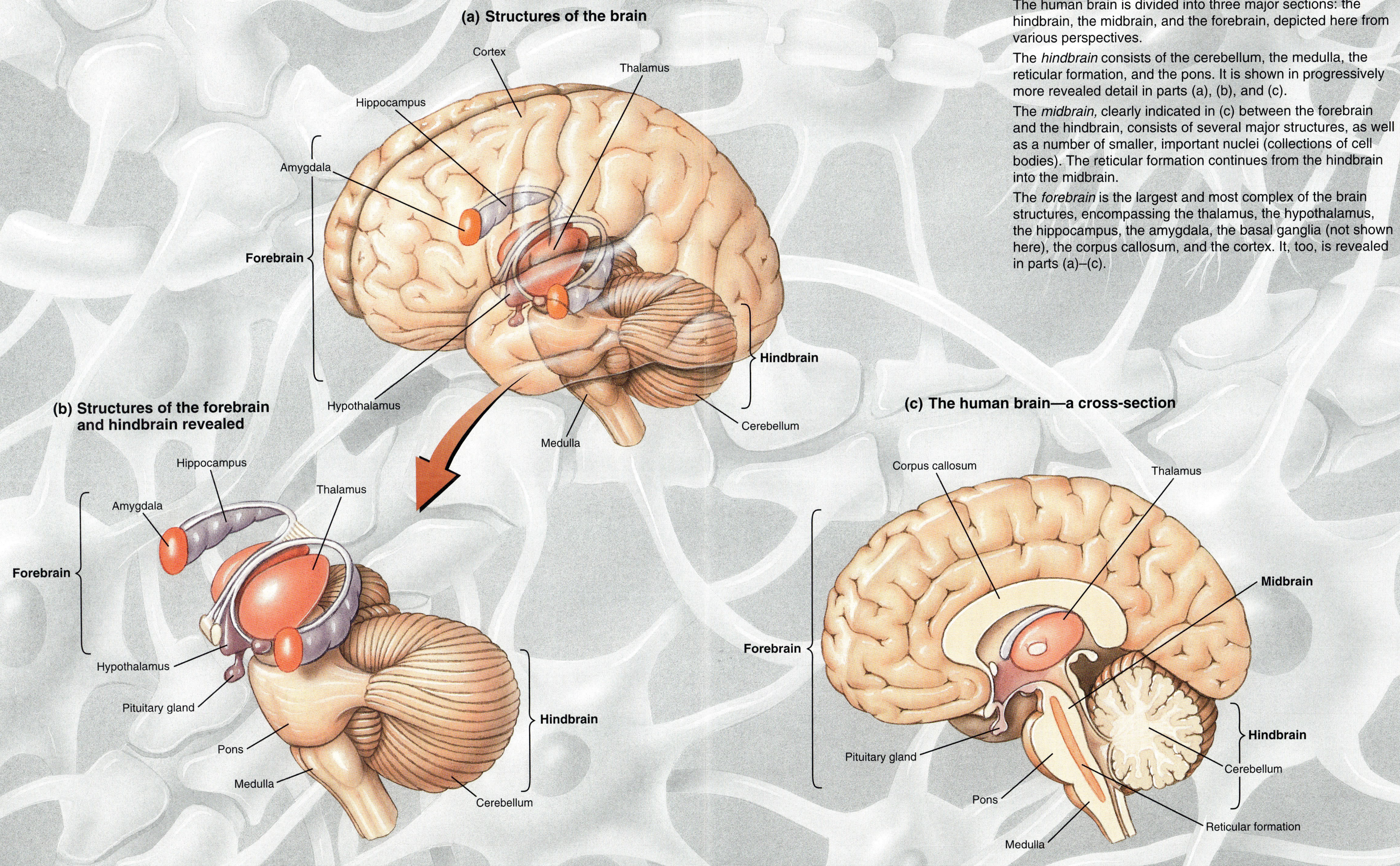

▲ *There are genetic differences between men and women, but society also greatly influences their behavior. And there tend to be more differences among women as a group than between men and women.*

differences (Riger, 1992). Psychologist Sandra Lipsitz Bem (1993) asserts that many traditionally held gender stereotypes are embedded in the culture and in social institutions and perpetuate a society that values males more than females. For example, boys have traditionally been encouraged to participate in physically rough-and-tumble sports; girls have been encouraged to take part in domestic activities. Men have traditionally been expected to be the providers—the wage earners and problem solvers. Today, however, many men and women in Western societies are sharing roles and responsibilities; in raising children, many parents are showing a greater understanding that boys and girls should have equal opportunities.

The effects of changing societal values are becoming more evident in individual behavior. In some Western cultures, differences between men and women that have long been apparent are diminishing; access to and enrollment in courses where problem solving is encouraged—for example, engineering or physics—no longer favor boys. Unfortunately, many girls still shy away from science courses, which helps to perpetuate stereotypes and in some cases causes discrimination. In Chapter 11 we'll see that many of the differences between males and females in mathematical ability are exceedingly small, and the extent of those differences is shrinking each year.

Most important is the fact that *there are usually more differences within a gender than between genders*. For example, there are more differences among individual women's spatial abilities than between women's and men's spatial abilities. This idea is especially important for the relevance of data. It becomes impossible to generalize results to all people if the data are taken only from a small sample of women or men.

Genetics lays the foundation for human development, but hormones affect the process further. Ultimately, how we are raised by our parents, schools, and society shapes our adult abilities. Nature lays the foundation for behavior, and nurture shapes and modifies it. Even psychologists with a strong biological perspective argue that most differences between people are traceable to the environment (Wright, 1994). The gender differences in our abilities lie not only within our genes, but within our society.

which controls specific behaviors; growth hormones (called somatotrophins), which control the body's development; and sex hormones (called gonadotrophins), which are involved in sexual behavior. A person's psychological state influences the secretions from the anterior pituitary; for example, viewing sexually explicit films raises the level of gonadotrophins (LaFerla, Anderson, & Schalch, 1978). The *posterior lobe* of the pituitary gland stores and secretes two major hormones, antidiuretic hormone (ADH) and oxytocin. ADH acts on the kidneys to increase fluid absorption and decrease the amount of urine produced by the body. Oxytocin stimulates uterine contractions in pregnant women and causes labor to begin. It also helps nursing mothers release milk.

Pancreas. Another endocrine gland, the *pancreas*, is involved in regulating the body's sugar levels. Sugar in the blood determines a person's energy level. When blood sugar is high, people are energetic; when it is low, they feel weak and tired.

Insulin: Hormone produced by the pancreas; facilitates the transport of sugar from the blood into body cells, where it is metabolized.

Diabetes mellitus [mel-LIGHT-us]: A condition in which too little insulin is produced, causing sugar to be insufficiently transported out of the blood and into body cells.

Hypoglycemia [hi-po-gly-SEE-me-uh]: A condition in which overproduction of insulin results in very low blood sugar levels.

FIGURE 2.13

The Pituitary Gland

The pituitary gland is often called the body's master gland because it regulates many of the other endocrine glands. Located at the base of the brain, the pea-sized pituitary gland directly affects behavior through control of other glands and through release of hormones—including growth hormones and sex hormones—into the bloodstream.

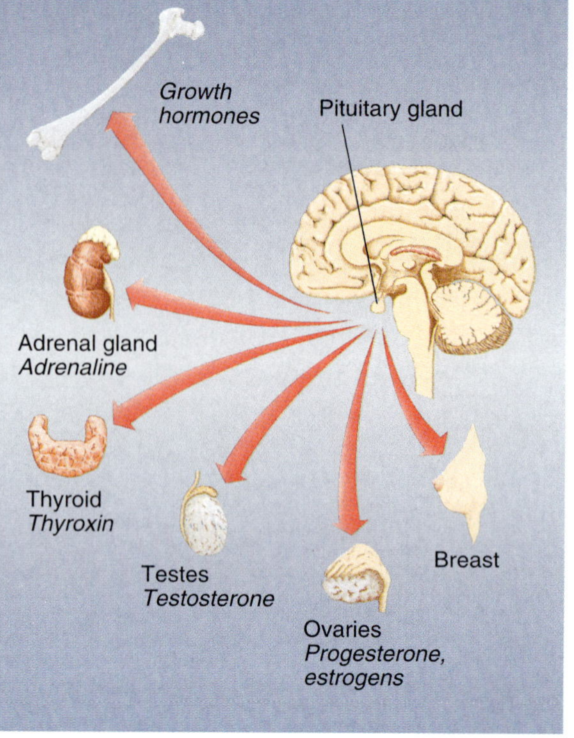

Cells in the pancreas, called the *islets of Langerhans*, control the production of **insulin**—the pancreatic hormone that facilitates the transport of sugar into body cells, where it is metabolized. Two insulin-related problems are diabetes and hypoglycemia. **Diabetes mellitus** is a condition in which an insufficient amount of insulin is produced, causing sugar to be inefficiently transported out of the bloodstream into the cells and thus allowing too much sugar to accumulate in the blood. If the pancreas errs in the opposite direction, the result is hypoglycemia. **Hypoglycemia** is very low blood sugar levels caused by the overproduction of insulin. Hypoglycemic patients have little energy. The condition can usually be controlled through diet, with careful monitoring of types of food eaten and daily calorie intake.

FOCUS

Review

- What evidence has led researchers to conclude that hormonal differences in development affect behavior in adulthood? pp. 63–65
- Why are researchers justified in concluding that the pituitary is the master gland? pp. 64–65

Think Critically

- What are the social implications of the conclusions researchers have reached about gender differences in intellectual and other abilities? Should men or women be expected to do things differently?

Adrenal Glands. The *adrenal glands*, which are also involved in behavior, are located just above the kidneys and are divided into two parts. The *adrenal medulla*, located deep within each adrenal gland, produces epinephrine (adrenaline), a substance that dramatically alters energy levels and affects a person's reactions to stress through stimulation of the sympathetic nervous system. Imagine that you are being chased through a dark alley. The release of epinephrine makes your heart pound and gives you a burst of energy to help you outdistance your pursuer. The *adrenal cortex*, the outer layer that covers each adrenal gland, secretes one hormones is involved in growth and development as well as others that are are involved in cardiovascular functions.

Summary and Review

Nature versus Nurture

What is the distinction between nature and nurture?

- Psychologists generally assert that human behavior is influenced by both *nature* (heredity) and *nurture* (environment). Psychologists study the biological bases of behavior to better understand how these two variables interact. pp. 38–39

What is genetics, and why do psychologists study it?

- *Genetics* is the study of heredity—the biological transmission of traits and characteristics from parents to offspring. The inherited potential of each person is carried by *chromosomes*. Each chromosome contains thousands of *genes*, made up of DNA. Genes are the basic unit of heredity. The 23rd pair of chromosomes determines the gender of a fetus. p. 39
- One goal of genetic research is to help prevent genetic defects such as *Down syndrome* and *phenylketonuria*. pp. 39–40
- *Identical twins* share exactly the same genetic heritage; they come from one ovum and one sperm and are always the same sex. *Fraternal twins* are produced by two ova and two sperm and therefore can be both males, both females, or one male and one female. They share genetic characteristics to the same degree as other siblings do. Studying twins allows researchers to clarify the effects of nature and nurture on developmental processes. pp. 41–42

KEY TERMS

Nature, p. 38
Nurture, p. 38
Genetics, p. 39
Chromosome, p. 39
Gene, p. 39
Allele, p. 39
Down syndrome, p. 40
Phenylketonuria (PKU), p. 40
Fraternal twins, p. 40
Identical twins, p. 40

Communication in the Nervous System

Describe the full journey of a neural impulse from one neuron to another.

- The basic unit of the *nervous system* is the *neuron*, or nerve cell, made up of *dendrites*, a cell body, an *axon*, and axon terminals. The space between the axon terminals and another neuron is the *synapse*. pp. 42–44
- The *action potential* is caused by the stimulation of the neuron. If there is enough stimulation at the cell body, a spike discharge occurs (with a rapid reversal of cell membrane polarity). The neuron fires on an *all-or-none* basis and has a *refractory period*, during which it cannot fire. The action potential propagates down the axon and stimulates the release of *neurotransmitters* that reside in the axon terminal's synaptic vesicles. The neurotransmitters move across the synaptic space and bind to receptor sites on the neighboring cells, thereby conveying information to other neurons. pp. 45–47

What is the focus of psychopharmacology?

- Psychopharmacology is the study of how drugs affect behavior. Research often focuses on *agonists* and *antagonists*. An agonist is a chemical that mimics or facilitates the action of a neurotransmitter, usually by occupying receptor sites. An antagonist is a chemical that opposes the action of a neurotransmitter, usually by blocking it from occupying receptor sites. pp. 48–49

KEY TERMS

Nervous system, p. 42
Neuron, p. 42
Afferent neuron, p. 42
Efferent neuron, p. 42
Dendrites, p. 43
Axon, p. 43
Synapse, p. 44
Action potential, p. 45
All-or-none, p. 46
Refractory period, p. 46
Neurotransmitter, p. 46
Neuromodulator, p. 48
Agonist, p. 48
Antagonist, p. 48

Organization of the Peripheral and Central Nervous Systems

Describe the subdivisions of the nervous system.

- The nervous system is composed of two subsystems: the central and peripheral nervous systems. The *central nervous system* consists of the brain and the spinal cord. The *peripheral nervous system* carries information to and from the spinal cord and brain through spinal and cranial nerves. The peripheral nervous system is further divided into the *somatic* and *autonomic nervous systems*. The autonomic nervous system is made up of two divisions: the *sympathetic* and *parasympathetic nervous systems*, each having different functions. pp. 49–52
- The *brain* is divided into three sections: the hindbrain, the midbrain, and the forebrain (which includes the cortex). The *hindbrain* consists of four main structures: the *medulla*, the *reticular formation*, the *pons*, and the *cerebellum*. The *midbrain* is made up of nuclei that receive afferent signals from other parts of the brain and from the spinal cord, interpret them, and either relay the information to other parts of the brain or cause the body to act at once. The *forebrain* is the largest and most complicated brain structure; it comprises the *thalamus* and the *hypothalamus*, the *limbic system*, the basal ganglia, the corpus callosum, and the *cortex*. The most prominent structures of the cortex are the two deep fissures—the lateral fissure and the central fissure—that divide the cortex's lobes. pp. 52–55

KEY TERMS

Peripheral nervous system, p. 49
Somatic nervous system, p. 49
Autonomic nervous system, p. 49

Sympathetic nervous system, p. 50
Parasympathetic nervous system, p. 50
Central nervous system, p. 51
Spinal cord, p. 52
Brain, p. 52
Hindbrain, p. 53
Medulla, p. 53
Reticular formation, p. 53
Pons, p. 53
Cerebellum, p. 53
Midbrain, p. 53
Forebrain, p. 53
Thalamus, p. 54
Hypothalamus, p. 54
Limbic system, p. 55
Cortex, p. 55
Convolution, p. 55

Studying the Brain

Describe several techniques for studying brain activity and functions.

- One technique for measuring the electrical activity of the nervous system is single unit recording, in which scientists record activity from single cells by placing an electrode within or next to single cells. Another technique is electroencephalography. Researchers can use records of brain-wave patterns, called *electroencephalograms (EEGs)*, to assess neurological disorders and the types of electrical activity that occur during thought, sleep, and other behaviors. Three significant new techniques for measuring the activity of the nervous system have been developed. CT (computerized tomography) scans are created by computer-assisted X-ray procedures. PET (positron emission tomography) scans use radiochemical procedures and allow researchers to observe metabolic changes in progress. MRI (magnetic resonance imaging) scans are similar to CT scans but are not invasive and do not use radiation. pp. 55–58

- Research shows that in most human beings, one cerebral hemisphere—usually the left—is specialized for processing speech and language; the other—usually the right—appears better able to handle spatial tasks and musical and artistic endeavors. p. 58

- Normal cerebral hemispheres are neurologically connected to opposite sides of the body. In laboratory studies, *split-brain patients* are unable to use the speech and language capabilities of the left cerebral hemisphere to describe activities carried out by the right one. pp. 58–59

KEY TERMS

Electroencephalogram (EEG), p. 56
Split-brain patients, p. 58

Hormones and Glands

How does the endocrine system affect behavior?

- The *endocrine glands* are a group of ductless glands that affect behavior by secreting *hormones* into the bloodstream. Each gland may influence different aspects of behavior, but all are related in one way or another to the *pituitary gland*. The pituitary gland is appropriately referred to as the master gland because of its central role in regulating hormones; another important gland is the pancreas, which is involved in regulating the body's sugar levels. pp. 62–66

KEY TERMS

Endocrine glands, p. 63
Hormones, p. 63
Pituitary gland, p. 64
Insulin, p. 66
Diabetes mellitus, p. 66
Hypoglycemia, p. 66

Learning CONNECTIONS

Some students benefit from extra help with the concepts of the action potential and neuronal transmission. You can learn more about them in:

- The CD-ROM accompanying this book, Topic 2

- This book's study guide, *Keeping Pace Plus*, or the computerized study guide, Chapter 2
- The audiotape accompanying this book, *SoundGuide for Psychology*, Learning Unit 2
- The study aids found on the World Wide Web site for this book, at http://www.abacon.com/psych/lefton

Critical Thinking CONNECTIONS

Take a moment to think critically about how this chapter's topics are connected with the rest of psychology . . .

If you are interested in . . .	Ask yourself . . .	Then turn to . . .
The nature-versus-nurture controversy 	What impact might a person's genetic heritage have on the likelihood of his or her becoming an alcoholic?	Chapter 4, pp. 138–139
	Can the "nature" of animals be overcome to the extent that they can be taught to communicate with humans?	Chapter 7, pp. 258–260
	To what extent could a person's home environment predispose him or her to developing a biologically based disease such as schizophrenia?	Chapter 14, pp. 510–512
Communication between brain structures and the nervous system 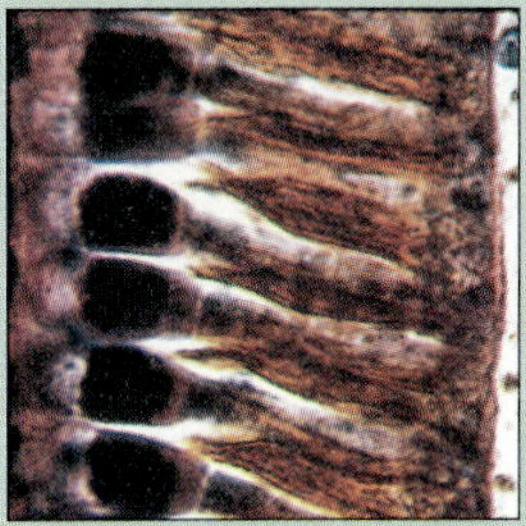	How do the eyes communicate information to the brain, to allow you to perceive the world?	Chapter 3, pp. 80–82
	Can physiological responses be cognitively controlled?	Chapter 9, pp. 305–306
Brain structures and how they affect behavior 	How does alcohol affect higher brain functions and behavior?	Chapter 4, pp. 136–137
	To what extent is it possible to identify the location of memory in the brain?	Chapter 6, pp. 224–225
	What benefit might doctors once have anticipated from removing the frontal lobe in patients suffering from mental illness?	Chapter 15, p. 546

3

Perception

Imagine utter loneliness . . . darkness . . . complete lack of light and sound. Imagine being in an isolation tank where you don't have to adapt to the light—because there is absolutely none. The isolation tank in which you float is relentlessly black and silent. This was the case described in a compelling 1978 novel, a page-turner by Paddy Chayefsky called *Altered States*. I recommend it to all of my students; it is a great novel that raises provocative questions about human perceptual systems and consciousness—and the relationship between the two.

In 1954, neurophysiologist John Lilly enlisted modern technology to find out what would happen if the brain were deprived of all sensory input—he created a situation much like that described by Chayefsky. Lilly actually constructed an isolation tank that excluded all light and sound and was filled with heavily salted water, which allows for easy floating. In this artificial sea, deprived of all external stimuli, Lilly experienced dreams, reveries, hallucinations, and other altered states. Throughout the ages, mystics of all kinds have claimed to achieve such special trance states by purposely limiting their sensory experiences—taking vows of silence, adhering to austere lifestyles, meditating while sitting as still as a stone for hours, and so on.

Clearly, people's view of the world is affected by a wide array of strong, and sometimes subtle, events in the environment. Architects use the laws of perception to affect people's feelings about their work. Spacious atriums create an open look; massive granite walls provide a sense of stability. Theater lighting experts know that a soft pink light makes older people look younger; they also know that sharp contrasts in lighting make for startling and dramatic effects. Similarly, painters use light, shadow, and texture to create various effects. Your perceptions of the world depend on a variety of important variables. Consider what happens when you try to read program notes in a darkened theater. The text and photographs are visible, but you see both with difficulty and with a loss of detail and visual clarity. Coming indoors with dark sunglasses on can affect your perceptual experience in much the same way. Similarly, your hearing may be impaired for a few hours after a rock concert. Tasting the delicacy of a wine may be nearly impossible after eating very spicy food. Your perceptions of the visual, auditory, and taste environment depend not only on light, sound, and food but also on intervening events such as dimming of the lights and eating hot tamales.

This chapter is about such perceptions, and the next chapter is about consciousness; as you study them, you will see their interconnectedness. In fact, this and the following six chapters (on consciousness, learning, memory, cognition, intelligence, and motivation and emotion) all have common roots in the growing field of cognitive psychology: the study of thought and mental processes.

The Perceptual Experience

Whenever you are exposed to a stimulus in the environment, the stimulus initiates an electrochemical change in the receptors in your body. That change in turn initiates the processes of sensation and perception. Psychologists study sensation and perception because what people sense and perceive determines how they will understand and interpret the world. That is, understanding depends on a combination of stimulation, past experiences, and current interpretations. Although the relationship between perception and culture has not been extensively researched, it is clear that culture can affect perception—by telling people what to believe, pay attention to, notice, and expect in the environment. For example, musical composers have long known that a person's experiences with music can make some melodies, especially non-Western ones, sound unfamiliar and dissonant.

Sensation and Perception: Definitions

Traditionally, psychologists have studied sensation and perception together as closely related fields—as we do in this chapter. **Sensation** is the process in which the sense organ receptor cells are stimulated and relay their initial information to higher brain centers for further processing. **Perception** is the process whereby an organism selects and interprets sensory input so that it acquires meaning. Thus, sensation provides the stimulus for further perceptual processing. For example, when light striking the eyeball initiates electrochemical changes, you experience the sensation of light. But your interpretation of the pattern of light and its resulting neural representation as an image is part of perception.

Today, perceptual psychologists generally acknowledge that a strict distinction between sensation and perception is unnecessary. They now think in terms of *perceptual systems*—the sets of structures, functions, and operations by means of which people perceive the world around them. Perception is not merely the firing of a

Sensation: Process by which the sense organ receptor cells are stimulated and relay their initial information to higher brain centers for further processing.

Perception: Process by which an organism selects and interprets sensory input so that it acquires meaning.

single group of neurons; it involves sets of neurons and previous experiences, as well as stimulation that occurs at the eyes or ears. Psychologists are especially aware that perceptual systems interact. Thus, as researchers gather more sophisticated information about sensation and perception, the boundaries between the two begin to fade.

Sensory and perceptual processes rely so closely on each other that many researchers think about the two processes together as perception. For them, perception is the entire process by which an organism acquires sensory input, converts it into electrochemical energy, and interprets it so that it acquires organization, form, and meaning. It is through perception that people explore the world and discover its rules (Gibson, 1988). This complex process involves the nervous system and one or more of the perceptual or sensory systems: vision, hearing, taste, smell, and/or touch.

Psychophysics

Although perceptual systems are different, they share a common process. In each case, an environmental stimulus creates an initial stimulation. Receptor cells translate that form of energy into neuronal impulses, and the impulses are then sent to specific areas of the brain for further processing. Psychologists who study such relationships are using **psychophysics**—the subfield that focuses on the relationship between physical stimuli and people's conscious experience of them.

Psychophysical studies attempt to relate the physical dimension of stimuli to psychological experience. This often begins with studying sensory thresholds. We often speak of a *threshold* as a dividing line, the point at which things become different. In perception, a threshold is the value of a sensory event at the point where things are perceived as different. Early researchers sought to investigate absolute thresholds, the minimum levels of stimulation necessary to excite a perceptual system, such as vision. They asked, for example, what minimum intensity of light is necessary for a person to say, "I see it." It turns out that a true absolute threshold is impossible to determine, because no two individuals see light at exactly the same intensity, because of individuals' many personal variables. The absolute threshold for vision, or any other sense, is thus a statistically determined value that averages how a range of normal people respond. So, for a psychologist, the **absolute threshold** is the statistically determined minimum level of stimulation necessary to excite a perceptual system. Closely related is the *difference threshold*—the amount of change necessary for an observer to report that a level of stimulation (say, a sound) has changed or is different from another value (has gotten louder or softer).

Psychologists have devised a variety of methods for studying perceptual thresholds. In one—the *method of limits*—various values of a signal are presented in ascending or descending order. For example, a psychologist may present lights of very low intensity, then slightly higher intensity, then higher still. A participant's task is to say when he or she finally sees the light—or, in the case of descending limits, no longer sees it. In another method—the *method of constant stimuli*—values of a signal are presented in random (not ascending or descending) order; the participants' task is to respond "yes" or "no," indicating that they have either detected a stimulus or not.

Both the method of limits and the method of constant stimuli have methodological weaknesses—they do not allow for key factors in the human observer. In the last few decades, researchers studying thresholds have used the methods of signal detection theory. **Signal detection theory** holds that an observer's perception is dependent not only on the intensity of a stimulus but on the observer's motivation, on the criteria he or she sets up for saying "Yes, that is enough for me to say that I detect the signal," and on the *noise* (the unstructured, constant background activity) that is present. In addition to manipulating the actual signal intensity, therefore, researchers have manipulated motivation levels (by offering varying rewards), criteria (for example, by telling participants to be *very* sure before they respond, "Yes, I

Psychophysics [SYE-co-FIZ-icks]: The subfield that focuses on the relationship between physical stimuli and people's conscious experience of them.

Absolute threshold: The statistically determined minimum level of stimulation necessary to excite a perceptual system.

Signal detection theory: Theory that holds that an observer's perception is dependent on the intensity of a stimulus, on the observer's motivation, on the criteria he or she sets up, and on the "noise" that is present.

detect the signal"), and levels of noise. It turns out that each variable affects a person's willingness to say "Yes, I detect the signal." This important finding lends support to the idea that there is no finite or absolute threshold—each individual's response will vary.

Subliminal Perception

Subliminal perception is perception below the threshold of awareness. Do subliminal self-help audiotapes do all that they claim? If a visual or auditory stimulus is presented so quickly or at such a low intensity or volume that you cannot consciously perceive it, can it affect your behavior?

Modern studies of this type of perception began in the 1950s with an innovative advertising ploy. A marketing executive superimposed messages on a movie; they said such things as "Buy popcorn." According to some enterprising advertising agents, movie theaters could induce audiences to buy more popcorn by flashing advertisements on the screen at speeds too fast to be consciously observed. Many psychologists dismissed the popcorn marketing story as nonsense, but it did create a stir.

Subliminal perception is possible. In fact, many cognitive scientists take unconscious perception for granted and build theories around it (e.g., Bornstein, 1992; Kihlstrom, Barnhardt, & Tataryn, 1992). However, subliminal perception has had a controversial history. Many of the early (1960s) studies lacked control groups and did not specify the variables being manipulated. Some presented stimuli for durations in which several words might easily be seen by one participant and no words by another. Other studies presented dirty, or taboo, words to see if they affected responses more than neutral or emotionally uncharged words did. Would the dirty words be threatening and emotionally arousing and lead participants to perceptually block out these stimuli? Initial results showed that participants did indeed show increased thresholds and had higher autonomic activity, indicating arousal. Of course, some participants were too embarrassed to repeat the noxious words to the experimenter (often a person of the opposite sex) and denied having seen them.

To avoid some of these methodological problems, later experiments presented participants with both threatening and neutral words for very brief durations. The participants responded by repeating the words or by pressing a button as soon as they saw each word. In these experiments, threatening words had to be presented for a longer time or at a greater intensity level than nonthreatening words in order to be identified.

The presentation of a threatening message—for example, a dirty word—may raise the perceptual threshold above normal levels, making it harder for the participant to perceive subsequent subliminal words. Some researchers suggest that the unconscious or some other personality variable acts as a censor. For example, Silverman (1983) asserts that if an aggressive or sexual message is presented subliminally to participants, it will affect their subsequent behavior—that unconscious processes are at work. Balay and Shevrin (1988) suggest that a stage beyond the sensory or perceptual stages affects the perceptual process. They maintain that subliminal perception can be explained in terms of such nonperceptual variables as motivation, previous experience, repetition, and unconscious or critical censoring processes that influence perceptual thresholds.

In some controlled situations, subliminal stimuli probably can influence perception and behavior (Greenwald, Klinger, & Schuh, 1995; Underwood, 1994). In the real world, however, we are constantly faced with many competing sensory stimuli. Therefore, what grabs our attention depends on many variables, such as importance, prominence, and interest. Should we fear either mind control by advertisers or other unsolicited outside stimuli? The answer is probably no. Can backward speech in rock music be interpreted and understood? Again, the answer is no (Begg, Needham, & Bookbinder, 1993). In the end, subliminal perception, and any learning that results from it, is subtle at most (Smith & Rogers, 1994) and greatly affected by

Subliminal perception: Perception below the threshold of awareness.

such nonperceptual variables as expectation, motivation, previous experience, personality, and other learned, culturally based behaviors (Pratkanis, Eskenazi, & Greenwald, 1994). However, most psychologists argue that more research is needed to determine exactly what is taking place when subliminal perception occurs and to what degree, if any, subliminal stimuli can influence us.

Selective Attention

Have you ever tried to study hard and listen to quiet music at the same time? You may have thought that the music barely reached your threshold of awareness. Yet you may have found your attention wandering. Did melodies or words start to interrupt your studying? Research on attention shows that human beings constantly extract signals from the world around them. Although we receive many different messages at once, we can watch, listen, and attend to only a selected message.

Because people can pay attention to only one or two things at a time, psychologists sometimes call the study of attention the study of *selective attention*. Early researchers in this area discovered the *cocktail party phenomenon*, whereby a person can hear his or her name spoken in a crowded and noisy room. The person cannot discern the content of conversations across the room under such conditions but does hear his or her name.

Perceptual psychologists are interested in the complexities of the processes through which people extract information from the environment. These psychologists hope to answer this question: Which stimuli do people choose to listen to? They focus on the *allocation* of a person's attention. In selective-listening experiments, participants wearing a pair of headphones receive different messages simultaneously in each ear. Their task is often to shadow, or repeat, a message heard in one ear. Typically, they report that they are able to listen to a speaker in *either* the left or the right ear and can provide information about the content and quality of that speaker's voice.

Of the several theories about how people are able to attend selectively, the two described here are the filter theory and the attenuation theory. The *filter theory* states that human beings possess a limited capacity to process information and that perceptual "filters" screen out either information presented to the left ear or information presented to the right ear. The *attenuation theory* states that all the information is analyzed but that intervening factors inhibit (attenuate) attention, so only selected information reaches the highest centers of processing. Hundreds of selective-listening studies have examined the claims of filter versus attenuation theory, and recent research favors attenuation theory (Wood & Cowan, 1995). But regardless of whether people filter or attenuate information, selective-attention studies show that human beings must select among the available stimuli. It is impossible, for example, to pay attention to four lectures at once. A listener can extract information from only one speaker at a time. Admittedly, you can do more than one task at a time—for example, you can drive a car and listen to the radio—but you cannot use the same channel (such as vision) for several tasks simultaneously. You cannot drive a car, read a book, and inspect photographs at the same time.

Clearly, both the auditory and visual systems have limited capacities. People have limited ability to divide their attention between tasks and must allocate their perceptual resources for greatest efficiency. But what happens when the need to divide is not necessary? What occurs when there is a restricted environment?

Restricted Environmental Stimulation

This chapter opened with a situation in which I asked you to consider being completely isolated from sounds and sights. Psychologists call such a situation one of restricted environmental stimulation. And some researchers argue that there are psychological benefits derived from sensory restriction (deprivation)—isolation from sights, sounds, smells, tastes, and feeling. The benefits may have been exaggerated, but such restriction can have profound effects on animals and humans. Heron studied the effects of sensory restriction by isolating individual college students in a comfortable but dull room. To limit their auditory experiences, Heron allowed the students to hear only the continuous hum of an air conditioner; the participants wore translucent plastic visors to limit their vision and tubes lined with cotton around their hands and arms to limit their skin's sensory input. The results were dramatic. Within a few hours, the participants' performance on tests of mental ability was impaired. The students became bored and irritable, and many said they saw "images" (Bexton, Heron, & Scott, 1954).

Several fascinating follow-up studies placed participants in identical conditions *except* that the participants were told that their deprivation would serve as an aid to meditation. How do you think this information affected their response to sensory deprivation? The participants did not hallucinate or become irritable; in fact, their mental ability actually improved (Lilly, 1956; Zuckerman, 1969). These studies suggest that people do not necessarily become bored because of lack of stimulation. Rather, when people *feel* their situation is monotonous, they become bored. Given the opportunity to relax in a quiet place for a long time, many people meditate; they find the "deprivation" relaxing. Such findings indicate the need for caution in interpreting data from sensory deprivation studies involving human beings, particularly because participants approach these situations with powerful expectations (recall the effects of self-fulfilling prophecies mentioned in Chapter 1).

Sensory restriction has proved to have positive effects with some people (Harrison & Barabasz, 1991). The profound relaxation that occurs in an extreme sensory-restricted environment can be highly effective in modifying some existing habits, such as smoking, and in treating such problems as obesity and insomnia (Suedfeld, 1990) and addiction (Borrie, 1991). Men, older individuals, and people with religious backgrounds may be more likely to benefit than others, and some people may be adversely affected. Further, previous experience with sensory restriction may produce a cumulative effect; that is, each time a person undergoes the restriction, it may have a greater effect. In general, the benefits of restricted environmental stimulation are probably underestimated (Suedfeld, 1990).

FOCUS

Review

- Why have modern researchers viewed perception as a unitary rather than a two-step (sensation followed by perception) process? pp. 72–73
- What evidence exists to show that when a person receives more than one incoming message at the same time, the person can attend to only one? p. 75

Think Critically

- How does the culture prime, or precue, individuals to focus their attention in important ways?
- What fundamental assumption does a researcher make when depriving an organism of sensory experience and then measuring behavior?

The Visual System

Imagine that you are in a house at night when the power goes out and you are left in total darkness. You hear creaking sounds but have no idea where they are coming from. You stub your toe on the coffee table, then frantically grope along the walls until you reach the kitchen, where you fumble through the drawers in search of a flashlight. You quickly come to appreciate the sense of sight when you are suddenly without it.

Human beings derive more information through sight than through any other sense. By some estimates, the eyes contain 70 percent of all the body's sense receptors. Although the eyes do respond to pressure, the appropriate stimulus for vision

FIGURE 3.1

The Electromagnetic Spectrum

People can perceive only a small part of the total electromagnetic spectrum.

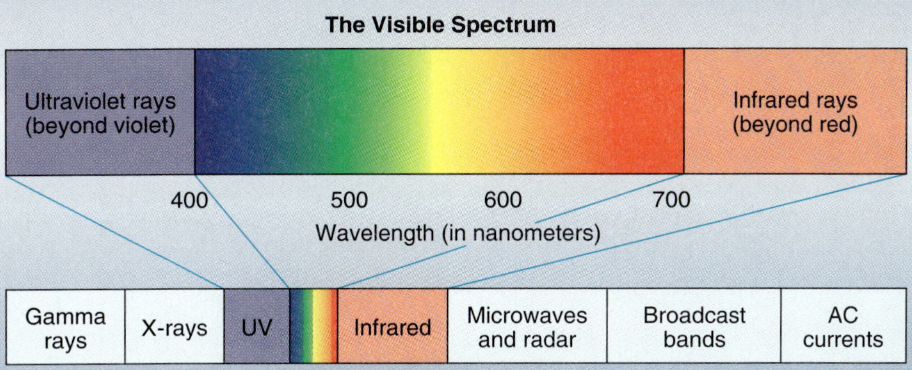

is **electromagnetic radiation**—the entire spectrum of waves initiated by the movement of charged particles. The electromagnetic spectrum includes gamma rays, X rays, ultraviolet rays, visible light, infrared rays, radar, broadcast bands, and AC currents (see Figure 3.1). Note that the visible **light** that can be seen by the human eye is a very small portion of those wavelengths. Light may come directly from a source or may be reflected from an object.

The Structure of the Eye

Figure 3.2, on page 78, shows the major structures of the human eye. Light first passes through the *cornea*—a small, transparent bulge covering both the *pupil* (the dark opening in the center of the eye) and the pigmented *iris*. The iris either constricts to make the pupil smaller or dilates to make it larger. Behind the pupil is the *lens*, which is about 4 millimeters thick. Together, the cornea, the pupil, the iris, and the lens form images in much the same way as a camera shutter and camera lens do. The *retina*, which lines the back of the eye, is like the film in a camera: It captures an image. Constriction of the iris makes the pupil smaller, improving the quality of the image on the retina and increasing the depth of focus—the distance to the part of the visual field that is in sharp focus. This action also helps control the amount of light entering the eye.

When people's eyeballs are not perfectly shaped, their vision is affected. People with elongated eyeballs are **myopic**, or *nearsighted*; they are able to see things that are close to them but have trouble seeing objects at a distance, because the image falls short of the retina. **Hyperopic**, or *farsighted,* people have shortened eyeballs. They have trouble seeing things up close but are able to see objects at a distance, because the image is focused behind the retina.

The *retina* consists of 10 layers of cells. Of these, the most important are the **photoreceptors** (the light-sensitive cells), the bipolar cells, and the ganglion cells. After light passes through several layers of the other kinds of cells (bipolar and ganglion), it strikes the photoreceptor layer, which consists of *rods* (rod-shaped receptors) and *cones* (cone-shaped receptors); these receptors will be described in detail later. In this layer, the light breaks down *photopigments* (light-sensitive chemicals), which causes an electrochemical change in the rods and cones. This electrical energy is transferred back out to the next major layer, the *bipolar cells*. The process by which the perceptual system analyzes stimuli and converts them into electrical impulses is **transduction**, or *coding*.

Electromagnetic radiation [ee-LEK-tro-mag-NET-ick]: The entire spectrum of waves initiated by the movement of charged particles.

Light: The portion of the electromagnetic spectrum visible to the eye.

Myopic [my-OP-ick]: Able to see things that are close but having trouble seeing objects at a distance. Also known as *nearsighted.*

Hyperopic [HY-per-OP-ick]: Having trouble seeing things that are nearby but able to see objects at a distance. Also known as *farsighted.*

Photoreceptors: The light-sensitive cells in the retina: rods and cones.

Transduction: The process by which a perceptual system analyzes stimuli and converts them into electrical impulses. Also known as *coding.*

FIGURE 3.2

The Main Structures of the Eye

The photoreceptors of the retina are connected to higher brain pathways through the optic nerve. Light filters through layers of retinal cells before hitting the receptors (rods and cones), located at the back of the eyeball and pointed away from the incoming light. The rods and cones pass an electrical impulse to the bipolar cells, which in turn relay the impulse back out to the ganglion cells. The axons of the ganglion cells form the fibers of the optic nerve.

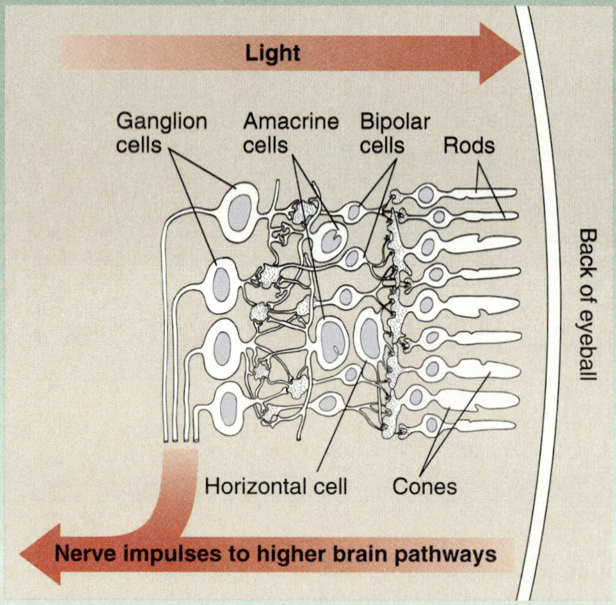

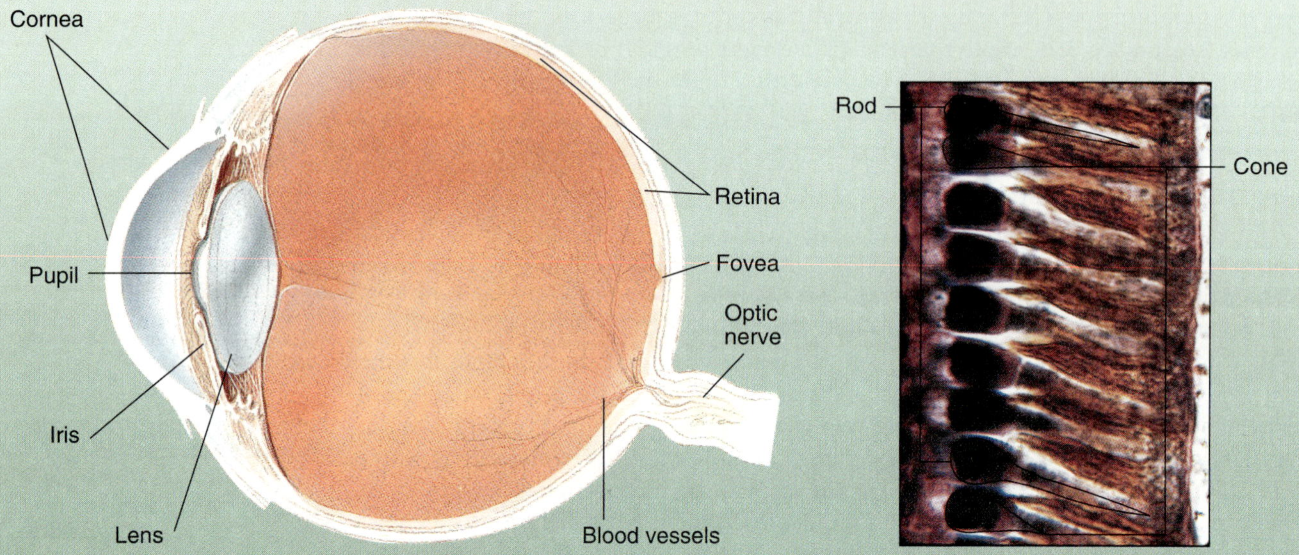

Each eye contains more than 120 million rods and 6 million cones. These millions of photoreceptors do not have individual pathways to the higher visual centers in the brain. Instead, through the process of *convergence*, neural electrochemical signals from rods come together onto a single bipolar cell. At the same time, hundreds of cones synapse and converge onto other bipolar cells. From the bipolar cells, electrochemical energy is transferred to the *ganglion cell layer* of the retina. Dozens of bipolar cells synapse and converge onto each ganglion cell (there are about 1 million ganglion cells). The axons of the ganglion cells make up the *optic nerve*, which carries information that was initially received by the rods and cones to higher pathways in the nervous system. Still further coding takes place at the brain's **visual cortex**, or *striate cortex*. The visual cortex is the most important area of the brain's occipital lobe; it is the location at which signals from the lateral geniculate nucleus (one of the major visual projection areas in the visual system—see page 80) are processed and visual information receives complex analysis.

Visual cortex: The most important area of the brain's occipital lobe, which receives information from the lateral geniculate nucleus. Also known as the *striate cortex*.

FIGURE 3.3

The Number of Rods and Cones and the Blind Spot

The center of the retina (the fovea) contains only cones. At about 18° of visual angle (a measure of the size of images on the retina), there are no receptors at all. This is the place where the optic nerve leaves the eye, called the blind spot. Because the blind spot for each eye is on the nasal side of the eyeball, there is no loss of vision; the two blind spots do not overlap.

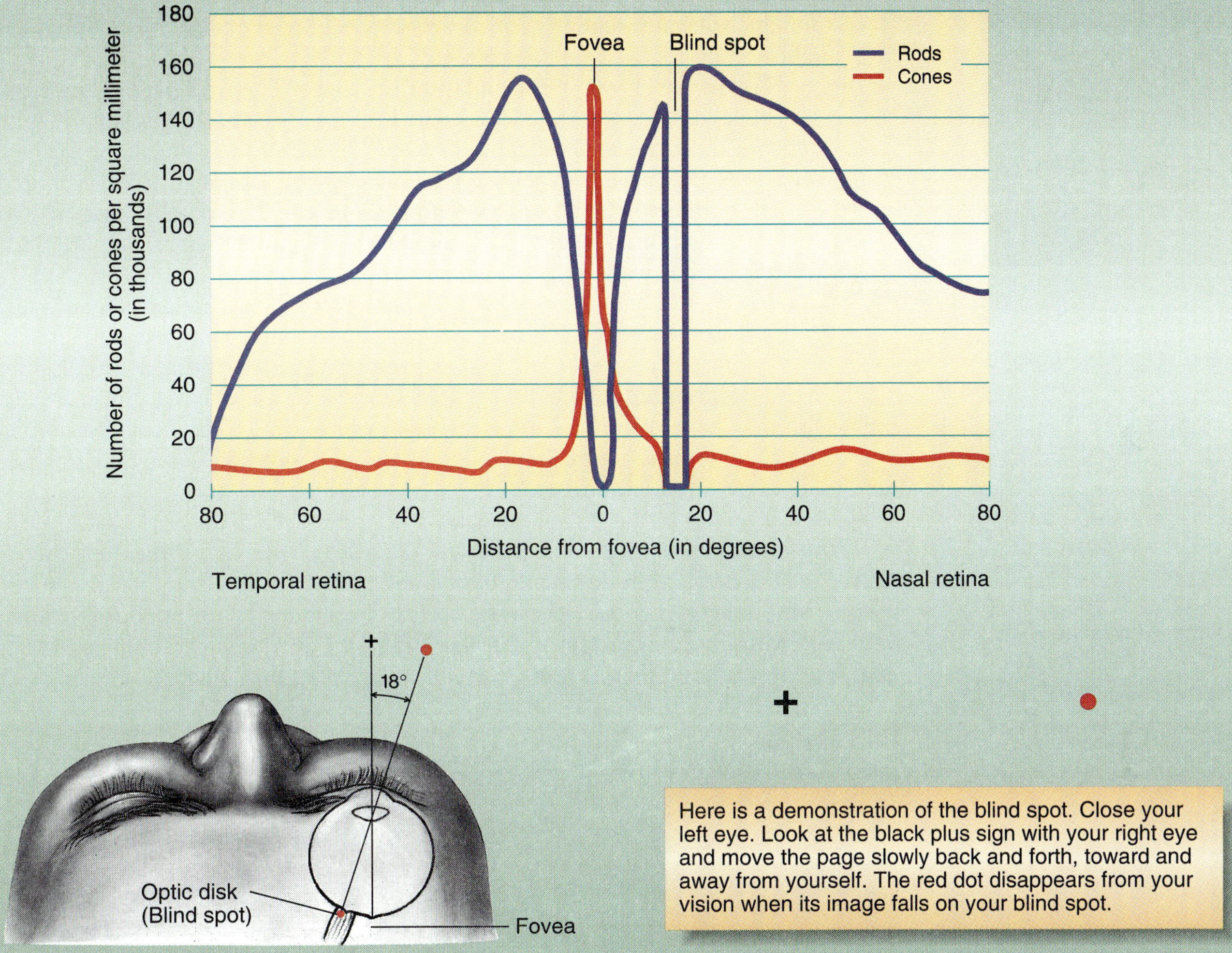

Rods and Cones. The *duplicity theory of vision*, which is now universally accepted, asserts that there are two separate receptor systems in the retina: the rods and the cones. It also states that rods and cones are structurally different and are used to accomplish different tasks. Cones are for the most part tightly packed in the center of the retina, at the *fovea*, and are used for day vision, color vision, and fine visual discrimination. Rods (together with some cones) are found on the rest of the retina (the periphery) and are used predominantly for night vision (see Figure 3.3). The importance of the cones is shown in the visual acuity tests you take when you apply for a driver's license. A *visual acuity test* measures the resolution capacity of the visual system—the ability to see fine details. This ability is principally mediated by cones. You do best on these tests in a well-lit room (cones operate at high light levels) and when the test is presented to your central vision (again, more cones are in the center of the retina than in any other place).

FIGURE 3.4

A Dark Adaptation Curve

The dashed line represents a typical overall dark adaptation curve.

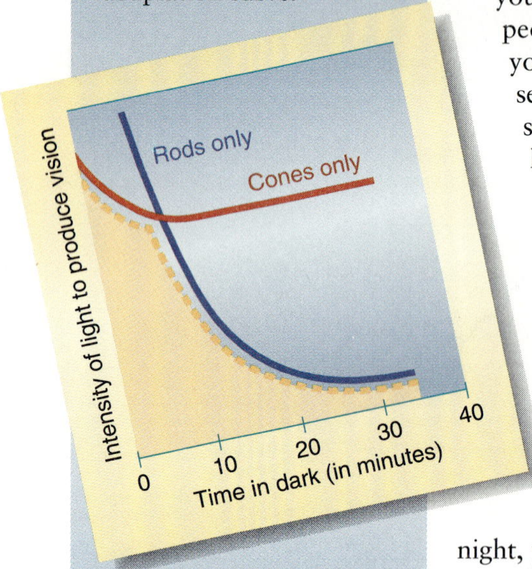

The two solid lines represent separate dark adaptation for rods and cones. Most dark adaptation occurs within 10 minutes. Rods, however, continue to adapt for another 20 minutes, reaching greater levels of sensitivity.

Your eyes are always in some state of light or dark adaptation. Rods and cones are sensitive to light, but in a well-lit room they are less sensitive than they are after having been in the dark. **Dark adaptation** is the increase in sensitivity that occurs when the illumination level changes from high to low. In dark adaptation, chemicals in the photoreceptors (rods and cones) regenerate and return to their inactive state, and light sensitivity increases. If you go from a well-lit lobby into a dark theater, for example, you will experience a brief period of low light sensitivity, during which you will be unable to distinguish empty seats. Your ability to discern objects and people in the theater increases with each passing moment. Within 30 minutes your eyes will have almost fully adapted to the dark and will be far more light-sensitive. Of course, after leaving a dark theater and returning to the afternoon sunlight, you must squint or shade your eyes until they become adapted to the light.

Figure 3.4 shows a dark adaptation curve. The first part of the curve is determined by cones, the second part by rods. The speed at which the photochemicals in the rods and cones regenerate determines the shape of the two parts of the curve. The data for such curves are obtained from experiments with participants who possess only rods or cones. Typically, a participant is first shown bright light for 2 minutes. The light is then turned off, and the participant waits in a totally dark room for 15 seconds. Next, a very dim test spot of light is turned on for half a second, and the participant is asked if he or she sees it. Usually, the participant will report seeing the test spot only after several successive presentations, because dark adaptation occurs gradually. This is why, when you are driving along a road at night, you may have trouble seeing clearly for a brief time after a car drives toward you with its high beams on; the photochemicals in the rods take some time to regenerate to their dark-adapted state.

Higher Pathways. As electrical impulses leave the retina through the optic nerve, they proceed to higher centers of the brain, including the lateral geniculate nucleus and the visual cortex, or striate cortex (see Figure 3.5). Knowledge about the way visual structures are connected to the brain not only aids psychologists but also enables physicians to diagnose many conditions, including whether a stroke victim

Dark adaptation: Increased sensitivity to light in a dark environment; when a person moves from a light environment to a dark one, chemicals in the rods and cones regenerate and return to their inactive state, and light sensitivity increases.

FIGURE 3.5

The Major Components of the Visual System

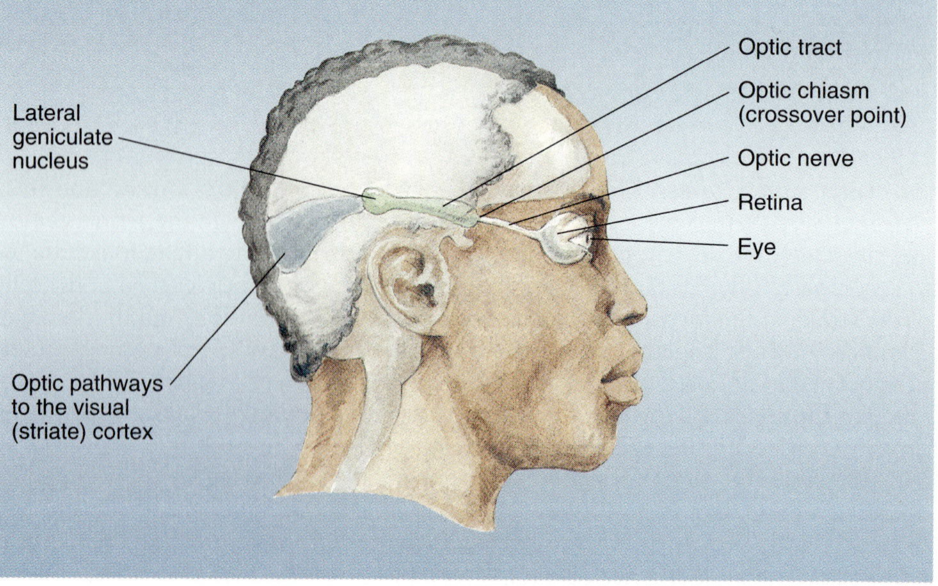

FIGURE 3.6

A Visual Image Is Projected to Both Hemispheres of the Brain

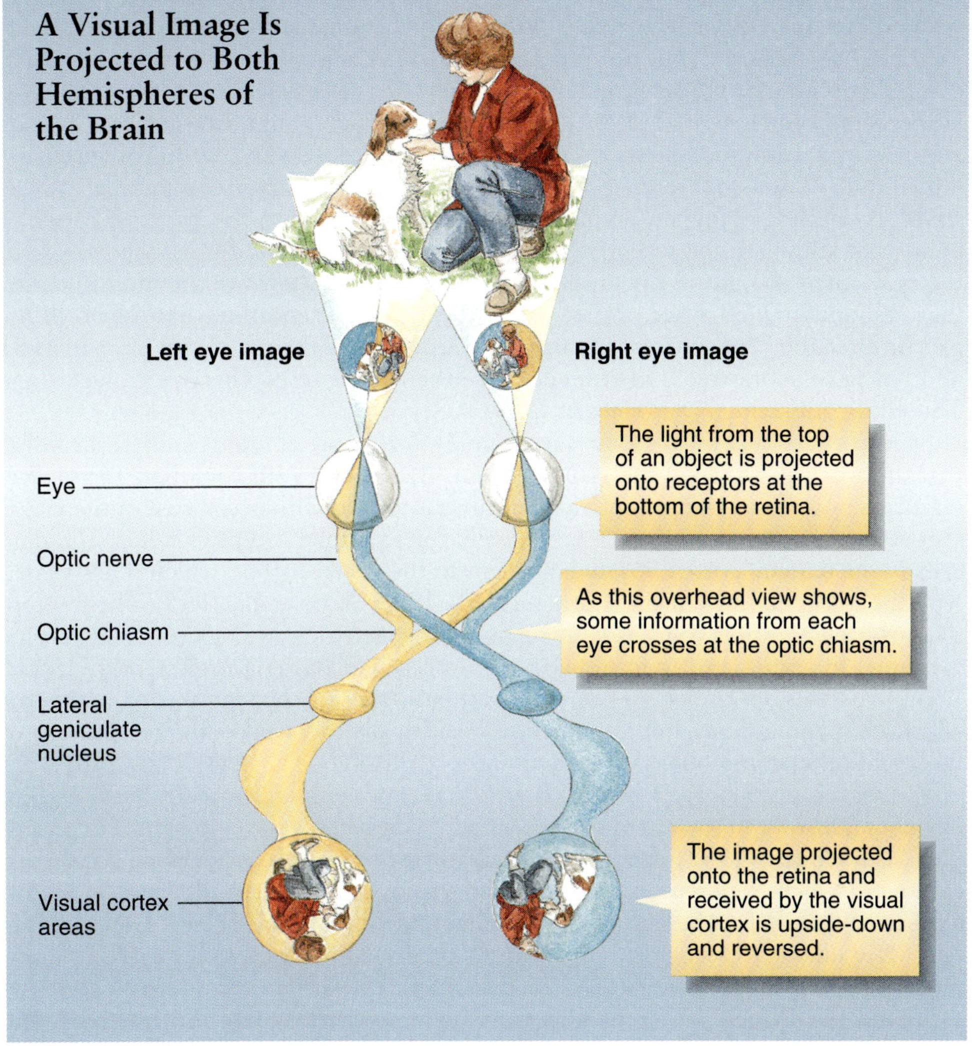

with poor vision has a blood clot that is obstructing circulation in one hemisphere of the brain.

Each eye is connected to both sides of the brain, with half of its optic nerve fibers going to the left side of the brain and the other half crossing over to the right side. The point at which the crossover occurs is called the **optic chiasm** (see Figures 3.5 and 3.6). This crossover of impulses allows the brain to process two sets of signals from an image and helps human beings perceive form in three dimensions. If the optic nerves are severed at the optic chiasm, vision is sharply impaired and tunnel vision results. Normally, however, impulses proceed to higher brain structures.

The Electrical Connection

Vision and other perceptual processes are electrochemical in nature. When receptors in the perceptual systems are stimulated, the information is coded and sent to the brain for interpretation and further analysis. Using this basic information about electrochemical stimulation, researchers are working on a visual prosthesis—a device to help the blind see—which bypasses the eyes and directly stimulates the visual cortex (Bak et al., 1990).

Optic chiasm [KI-azm]: The point at which half of the optic nerve fibers from each eye cross over and project to the other side of the brain.

Most current knowledge about how the brain processes electrochemical signals comes from such studies of receptive fields. **Receptive fields** are the areas of the retina that, when stimulated, produce a change in the firing of cells in the visual system. For example, specific cells will fire, or become active, if a vertical line is presented to the retina but not if a horizontal line is presented. Many perceptual psychologists refer to these stimulated visual system cells as feature detectors. David Hubel and Torsten Wiesel (1962) found receptive fields that are sensitive to such features of a stimulus line as its position, length, movement, color, or intensity. Hubel and Wiesel characterized the responding critical feature-detecting cells as simple, complex, or hypercomplex. *Simple cells* respond to the shape and size of lights that stimulate the receptive field. *Complex cells* respond most vigorously to the movement of light in one direction. *Hypercomplex cells* are the most specific; they respond only to a line of the correct length and orientation that moves in the proper direction. The work of Hubel and Wiesel earned them a Nobel prize in 1981 and has been supported and extended by other noted researchers (e.g., DeValois, Thorell, & Albrecht, 1985; Heeger, 1994).

Electrical coding moves from simple analysis to more complex analysis as information proceeds through the visual system (Maunsell, 1995; Schiller, 1994). Researchers now know that receptive fields are associated with every area of the visual cortex and in some nonvisual areas as well; for example, receptive fields stimulate cells in the parietal cortex, located adjacent to the visual cortex, which is associated with the control of movement (Corbetta et al., 1995; Serno et al., 1995). These receptive fields help to link your visual perception of space to your body movements; for example, in seeing and then moving to catch a ball (Graziano & Gross, 1994). Receptive fields not only help you recognize balls that fly through the air, and vertical and horizontal lines, but also seem to be critically involved in the recognition of faces and other commonly recognized objects (Allison et al., 1994).

Research on the organization of vision, receptive fields, and electrical coding has a long history in a wide range of related fields such as development. For example, Von Senden (1932) reported case histories of people who were born with cataracts (which cloud vision) and had them removed in adulthood. These individuals, seeing clearly for the first time as adults, had several deficiencies. For example, they were unable to recognize simple forms presented in a new color or in an unfamiliar context. Some time later, Hirsch and Spinelli (1971) conducted a series of experiments in which they controlled the visual experiences of newborn kittens. The kittens wore goggles that let them perceive either vertical lines or horizontal lines. When the goggles were later removed, kittens raised with only horizontal experiences bumped into chair legs (vertical) but could leap into a chair seat (horizontal); kittens raised with only vertical experiences had problems with horizontal surfaces (Blakemore & Cooper, 1970). Such studies indicate that, although most of the connections in the visual system are present in newborns, the proper functioning of the system is sensitive to and depends on experience (Wong et al., 1995) and the task given to an organism (Jacobs & Kosslyn, 1994).

Eye Movements

Your eyes are constantly in motion. They search for familiar faces in a crowded classroom, scan a page of headlines and articles in a newspaper, or follow a baseball hit high into right field for a home run. You notice when someone notices something else over your shoulder. You know when someone is fixating on a spot on top of your head (is there a spider there?). Research on eye movements reveals what people are looking at, how long they look at it, and perhaps where they will look next. It also helps psychologists understand some visual problems, such as reading disabilities. Zangwill and Blakemore (1972) studied the eye movements of a man who had difficulty reading. They found that he was moving his eyes from right

Receptive fields: The areas of the retina that, when stimulated, produce a change in the firing of cells in the visual system.

to left across the page, rather than in the usual left-to-right direction. Eye movements also depend on the context in which they are measured. The eye movements of a reader are different from those of a keyboard operator, even when both are examining the same material, because the text viewed by the keyboard operator is processed merely for transcription purposes, not for meaning as it is by a reader (Inhoff, Morris, & Calabrese, 1986).

Saccades are the most common type of eye movement. They are the voluntary eye movements people make when reading, driving, or looking for an object. The eye can make only four or five saccades in a second. Each movement of the eye takes only about 20 to 50 milliseconds, but there is a delay of about 200 to 250 milliseconds before the next movement can be made. During this delay the eye fixates on some part of the visual field. People use eye *fixations* to form representations of the visual world, probably by integrating successive glances into memory. This integration requires that observers move their eyes, pay attention to key elements of a visual scene, and exert eye movement control in a careful, systematic manner (Rayner & Pollatsek, 1992).

Eye movements have been used to determine the *perceptual span*—the size of the region a person sees when fixating, or staring; for example, the perceptual span is the number of letters you see when you fixate at a specific point on this page. Research shows that people use information gathered in both central vision (at the fovea) and peripheral vision (at noncentral regions of the eye) to determine the location of their next eye movements; this ultimately affects the size of the perceptual span (Pollatsek et al., 1993). People also tend to direct their gaze to a point just to the left of center of words when they are reading. This site (left of center) may help them make inferences about the rest of the word (McConkie et al., 1988). A key feature of this whole line of research is that eye movements can tell researchers a great deal about cognitive processes in general, about reading and language in particular (Tanenhaus et al., 1995), and, as we'll see next, about the perception of scenes and pictures.

FIGURE 3.7

Scan Paths Are Highly Individual

Eye movements made by a person viewing a drawing adapted from Paul Klee's *Old Man Figuring*. The numbers show the order of the visual fixations. Lines between the numbers represent saccades, which occupied about 10 percent of the viewing time. The remainder of the time was spent fixating.

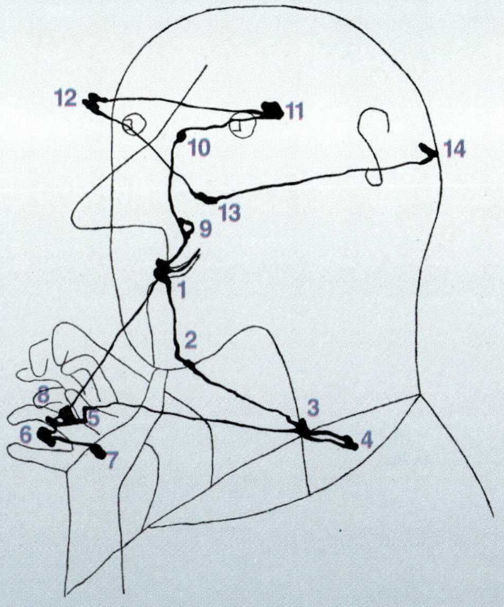

In a classic study of eye movements and perception, Noton and Stark (1971) presented participants with a series of pictures and told them they would have to identify the pictures later in different groupings. The researchers recorded the participants' eye movements during the learning period and in subsequent testing. Each participant fixated on the same area and followed identical scan paths for a specific picture in both phases of the experiment. The researchers suggested that in perceiving and recognizing forms, each person uses a characteristic pattern of eye movement—a pattern that follows a fixed path from one feature to the next (see Figure 3.7). Noton and Stark concluded that eye movements are important to the way the brain stores information and that there are significant individual differences among scan paths. Eye movement research shows more similarities across cultures than between individuals; in cross-cultural research, Western, Middle Eastern, and East Asian cultures show similar eye movement patterns (Abed, 1991).

Color Vision

Think of all the different shades of blue (navy blue, sky blue, baby blue, royal blue, turquoise, aqua). If you are like most people, you have no trouble discriminating among a wide range of colors. Color depends on the wavelength of light particles that stimulate the photoreceptors. It has three psychological dimensions: hue,

Saccades [sack-ADZ]: Rapid voluntary movements of the eyes, to focus on different points.

FIGURE 3.8

Human Beings Are More Sensitive to Yellow Than to Any Other Wavelength

The average observer's sensitivity to visible light during daylight reaches a peak at 555 nanometers. Thus, the normal human eye is more sensitive to yellow wavelengths than to red or blue. The curve in the graph is called a *spectral sensitivity curve.*

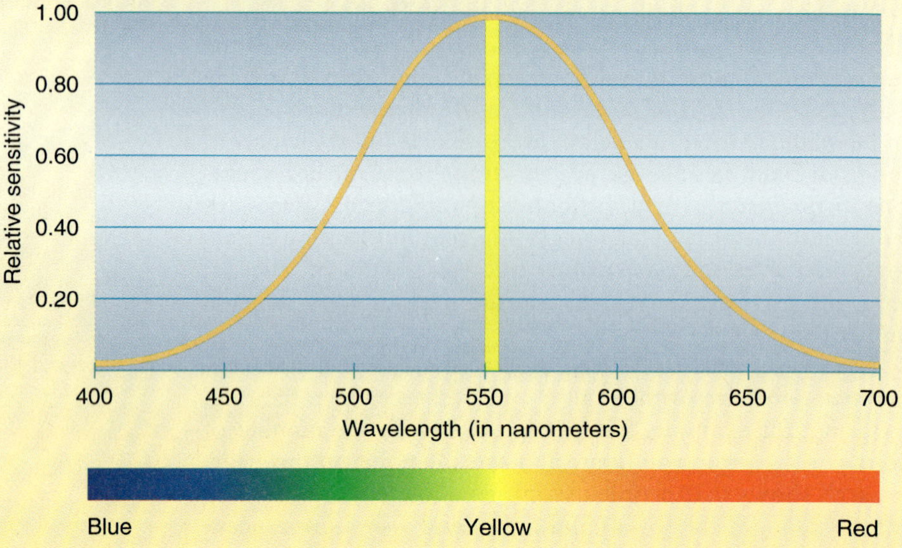

brightness, and saturation. These dimensions correspond to three physical properties of light: wavelength, intensity, and purity.

When people speak of the color of an object, they are referring to its **hue**—whether the light reflected from the object looks red, blue, orange, or some other color. *Hue* is a psychological term, because objects themselves do not possess color. Rather, a person's perception of color is determined by how the eyes and brain interpret reflected wavelengths. In the visible spectrum, a different hue is associated with each wavelength. Light with a wavelength of 400–450 nanometers looks blue; light with a wavelength of 700 nanometers looks red.

The second psychological dimension of color is **brightness**—how light or dark the hue of an object appears. Brightness is affected by three variables: (1) The greater the intensity of reflected light, the brighter the object; (2) the longer the wavelength of reflected light, the less bright the object; (3) the nearer the wavelengths are to being in the 500 to 600 nanometer (yellow) range, the more sensitive the photoreceptors (see Figure 3.8). This is why school buses and fire engines are often painted yellow—they are more visible to motorists.

The third psychological dimension of color is **saturation**, or *purity*—the depth and richness of hue of reflected light, determined by the homogeneity of the wavelengths contained in the light. Few objects reflect light that is totally pure. Usually objects reflect a mixture of wavelengths. Pure, saturated light has a narrow band of wavelengths and, thus, a narrow range of perceived color. A saturated red light with no blue, yellow, or white in it, for example, appears as a very intense red. Unsaturated colors are produced by a wider band of wavelengths. Unsaturated red light can appear to be light pink, dark red, or brownish, because its wider range of wavelengths makes it less pure (see Figure 3.9).

Hue: The psychological property of light referred to as color and determined by the wavelength reflected from an object.

Brightness: The lightness or darkness of reflected light, determined in large part by the light's intensity.

Saturation: The depth of hue of reflected light, as determined by the homogeneity of the wavelengths contained in the light. Also known as *purity*.

Theories of Color Vision. How does the brain code and process color? Two 19th-century scientists, Thomas Young and Hermann von Helmholtz, working independently, proposed that different types of cones provide the basis for color coding in the visual system. *Color coding* is the ability to discriminate among colors on the basis of differences in wavelength. According to the **trichromatic theory**, or the *Young–Helmholtz theory*, all colors can be made by mixing three basic colors: red, green, and blue. (*Trichromatic* means "three colors"; *tri* means "three" and *chroma* means "color.") All cone cells in the retina are assumed to respond to all wavelengths that stimulate them; but there are three types of cones that respond maximally to the red, green, or blue wavelength (see Figure 3.10). The combined neural output of the red-sensitive, green-sensative, and blue-sensative cones provides the information that enables a person to distinguish color. If the neural output of one type of cone is sufficiently greater than that of the others, a person's perception of color will be determined mainly by that type of color receptor. Because each person's neurons are unique, it is likely that each of us sees color somewhat differently.

Unfortunately, the trichromatic theory does not explain some specific visual phenomena well. For example, it does not explain why some colors look more vivid when placed next to other colors (color contrast). It does not explain why people asked to name the basic colors nearly always name more than

FIGURE 3.9

Hue, Brightness, and Saturation

These colors have the same dominant wavelength (hue) but different saturation and brightness.

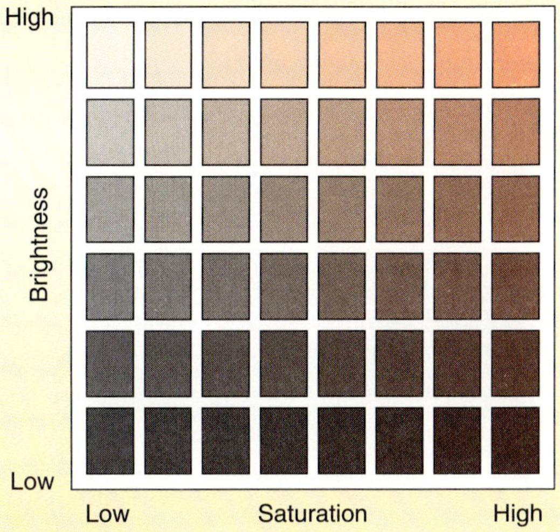

FIGURE 3.10

Three Types of Cones

Each of the three types of cones in the eye has peak sensitivity in a different area of the visible spectrum. Thus, certain cells are more responsive to some wavelengths than to others.

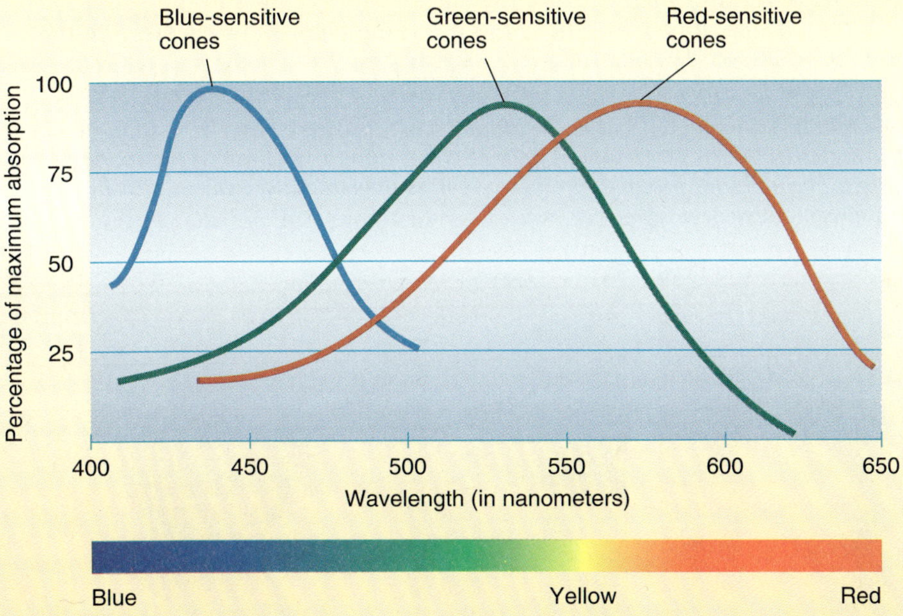

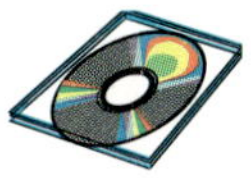

Fig. 3.5

Trichromatic theory [try-kroe-MAT-ick]: The visual theory, stated by Young and Helmholtz, that all colors can be made by mixing three basic colors: red, green, and blue. Also known as the *Young–Helmholtz theory*.

Color blindness: The inability to perceive different hues.

Opponent-process theory: The theory, proposed by Herring, that color is coded by stimulation of three types of paired receptors; each pair of receptors is assumed to operate in an antagonistic way so that stimulation by a given wavelength produces excitation in one receptor of the pair and inhibition of the other receptor.

Trichromats [TRY-kroe-MATZ]: People who can perceive all three primary colors and thus can distinguish any color.

Monochromats [MON-o-kroe-MATZ]: People who cannot perceive any color, usually because their retinas contain only rods.

Dichromats [DIE-kroe-MATZ]: People who can distinguish only two of the three basic hues.

three. Further, the trichromatic theory does not do a good job of explaining aspects of **color blindness**—the inability to perceive different hues (described below). For example, many people with color deficiencies cannot discriminate colors successfully in two areas of the visual spectrum. In 1887, to solve some of the problems left unsolved by the trichromatic theory, Ewald Herring proposed another theory of color vision—the **opponent-process theory**. This theory assumes that there are six basic colors to which people respond and that there are three types of receptors: red–green, blue–yellow, and black–white. Every receptor fires in response to all wavelengths; but in each pair of receptors, one fires maximally to one wavelength. Maximum firing to red, for example, is accompanied by a low rate of firing to green. Opponent-process theory explains color contrast and color blindness better than the trichromatic theory.

Both the trichromatic theory and the opponent-process theory have received support from research (e.g., Hurvich & Jameson, 1974). Studies of the chemistry and absorptive properties of the retina do show three classes of cones. Thus, the trichromatic theory seems to describe accurately the coding at the retina (Marks, Dobell, & MacNichol, 1964). Support for the opponent-process theory comes from microelectrode studies of the lateral geniculate nucleus in monkeys. Cells in this nucleus respond differently to various wavelengths. When the eye is stimulated with light of a wavelength between 400 and 500 nanometers, some cells in the lateral geniculate nucleus decrease their rate of firing. If the eye is stimulated with a longer-wavelength light, the firing rate increases (DeValois & Jacobs, 1968). This change is predicted by the opponent-process theory. Exactly how color information is transferred from the retina to the lateral geniculate nucleus remains to be discovered. Some of the data that helped test the trichromatic and opponent-process theories came from people with abnormal color vision.

Color Blindness. In 1794, John Dalton, formulator of the atomic theory of matter, believed he had figured out why he couldn't distinguish his red stockings from his green ones. He reasoned that something blue in his eyeball absorbed red light and prevented him from seeing red. Dalton was not the first person to suffer from red–green color blindness, but he was the first to try to describe it scientifically.

Most human beings have normal color vision and are considered trichromats. **Trichromats** are people who can perceive all three primary colors and thus can distinguish any color. A very few people (fewer than 1 percent) do not see any color. These people, known as **monochromats**, are totally color-blind and cannot discriminate among wavelengths, often because they lack cone receptors in their retinas (Boynton, 1988). The lack of a specific color-absorbing pigment or chemical in the cones

Color blindness, the inability to see certain colors, is a hereditary condition in which the proteins of one or more types of cones either do not function or are inadequate in number. The balloons are shown on the right as they might appear to a dichromat with a red–green deficiency. ▼

makes accurate color discriminations impossible. Fortunately, most people with color vision deficiencies (about 8 percent of men and 1 percent of women) are only partially color-deficient (Nathans, 1989). **Dichromats** are people who can distinguish only two of the three basic hues; they have deficiencies in either the red–green or the blue–yellow area. About 2 percent of men cannot discriminate between reds and greens (Wyszecki & Stiles, 1967). What does the world look like to a person who is a dichromat? People with a color deficiency see all the colors in a range of the electromagnetic spectrum as the same. For example, to a person with a blue deficiency, all greens, blues, and violets look the same; a person with a red–green deficiency may see red, green, and yellow as yellow. Many color-blind individuals have distorted color responses in several areas of the electromagnetic spectrum; that is, they have trouble with several colors.

The precise role of genetics in color blindness is not clear, but this deficiency is transmitted genetically from mothers to their male offspring. The high number of men who are color-blind, compared to women, is due to the way the genetic information is coded and passed on to each generation. The genetic transmission occurs on the 23rd pair of chromosomes and results from inherited alterations in the genes on the X chromosomes that are responsible for cone pigments (Nathans, 1989).

FOCUS

Review

- Describe how the visual system works when light hits the eye. pp. 76–78
- What is the evidence for the duplicity theory of vision? pp. 79–80
- What do receptive fields tell researchers about the perceptual process? p. 82

Think Critically

- Viewing traditional 3-D comics through special glasses creates the perception of depth. Explain how you think this might work.
- Why do you think that psychologists prefer to use the term *color-deficient* rather than *color-blind* when describing people who have trouble seeing colors?

Visual Perception

Many perceptual experiences involve past events in addition to current stimulation. Integrating previous experiences with new events makes perceptual encounters more meaningful. For example, it is only with experience that children learn that an object stays the same size and shape when it is moved away from their immediate vision. In this section, we will look at a range of visual perceptual phenomena that depend especially on the integration of past and current experiences.

At close range, Georges Seurat's impressionist paintings appear almost unintelligible. However, when seen from a distance, the forms gain definition as complete, familiar objects.

Perception of Form: Constancy

If a friend of yours is wearing dark glasses that conceal much of her face, you will probably still recognize her. Similarly, impressionist artists count on people's ability to infer a complete object from dots of paint on canvas, and cartoonists use exaggerated features to portray well-known people. Understanding how human beings perceive form and space helps architects to design buildings and designers to create furniture and clothes. Perception of form involves the interpretation of stimuli of different sizes, shapes, and depths to create a unit. Two important activities in form perception are recognizing forms at a distance and recognizing forms that appear to have changed size or shape.

Size Constancy. People can generally judge the size of an object, even if the size of its image on the retina changes. For example, you can estimate the height of a 6-foot man who is standing 50 feet away and casts a small image on the retina; you can also estimate his height from only 5 feet away, when he casts a much larger image on the retina. **Size constancy** is the ability of the perceptual system to recognize that an object remains constant in size regardless of its distance from the observer or the size of its image on the retina.

Three variables determine a person's ability to maintain size constancy: (1) previous experience with the true size of objects, (2) the distance between the object and the person, and (3) the presence of surrounding objects. As an object is moved farther away, the size of its image on the retina decreases and its perceived distance increases (see Figure 3.11). These two processes always work together. Moreover, as an object is moved away, its perceived size does not change in relation to that of objects around it. This is why knowing the size of surrounding objects helps people determine the moved object's distance as well as its actual size.

Researchers have studied how experience helps people establish and maintain size constancy. Bower (1966) trained 50- to 60-day-old infants to look toward a specific object by reinforcing their direction of gaze (the reinforcement was an adult saying "peek-a-boo"). He then placed other objects of different sizes at various distances from the infants so that the sizes of their retinal images varied. Finally, he

FIGURE 3.11

Perceptual Constancies

Size constancy is the perceptual system's ability to recognize that an object remains the same size regardless of its distance from an observer or the size of its image on the retina. *Shape constancy* is the perceptual system's ability to recognize a shape despite changes in the angle or position from which it is viewed.

Size constancy: The size of the image on the retina gets larger or smaller as you move closer to or farther away from an object. But thanks to size constancy, you still perceive the object as being the same size.

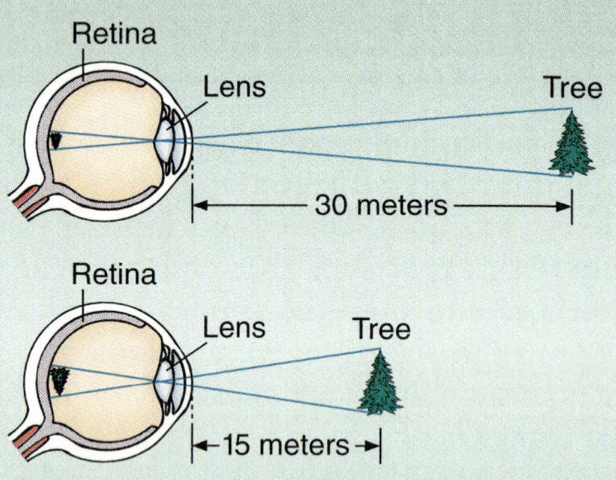

Shape constancy: A door is a door is a door . . . whether it is open, shut, or viewed at an angle.

Size constancy: The ability of the perceptual system to recognize that an object remains constant in size regardless of its distance from the observer or the size of its image on the retina.

arranged the objects so that the small ones were close to the infants and the large ones were farther away, causing the sizes of retinal images to be the same. In all these situations, the infants showed size constancy. They turned their heads only toward the original reinforced object, not toward the other objects that produced images of the same size on the retina. It is clear that infants attain size constancy by the age of 6 months and probably as early as 4 months (Luger, Bower, & Wishart, 1983; McKenzie, Tootell, & Day, 1980).

Hollywood special effects artists have used the brain's tendency to judge an object's size by comparing it with surrounding objects to convince moviegoers that a 6-inch clay model of an ape was the giant King Kong. However, size constancy can also work to a filmmaker's disadvantage. In the early days of Hollywood, a Western was made that attempted to be humorous by starring a cast of dwarfs. The sheriff, the bad guys, and the heroine were all of diminutive stature. However, because the director also downsized all the props and settings (for example, using Shetland ponies for the horses), the characters appeared normal-sized, and the movie lost its potential comic effect.

Shape Constancy. Another important aspect of form perception is **shape constancy**—the ability to recognize a shape despite changes in the angle or position from which it is viewed (see Figure 3.11). For example, even though you usually see trees standing perpendicular to the ground, you can recognize a tree when it has been chopped down and is lying in a horizontal postion. Similarly, an ice cream cone looks triangular when you view it from the side; yet you perceive it as an ice cream cone even when you view it from above, where it appears more circular than triangular.

Depth Perception

For centuries, Zen landscape artists have used the principles of perception to create seemingly expansive, rugged gardens out of tiny plots of land. Although a Zen landscape artist can fool the eye, you judge the distance of objects every day when you drive a car, catch a ball, or take a picture. You estimate your distance from an object and the distance between that object and another one. Closely associated with these two tasks is the ability to see in three dimensions—that is, in terms of height, width,

To create the illusion of depth, Zen gardeners place smaller, less detailed, and darker objects (such as round stones or shrubs) at the rear of the garden and larger, light-colored, and well-textured objects (such as craggy rocks) near the front. They also make a tapering path that winds back to the rear of the garden, seeming to disappear into the distance. ▼

Shape constancy: The ability to recognize a shape despite changes in the orientation or angle from which it is viewed.

FIGURE 3.12

Depth Perception

The ability to see in three dimensions—height, width, and depth—depends on both monocular and binocular cues.

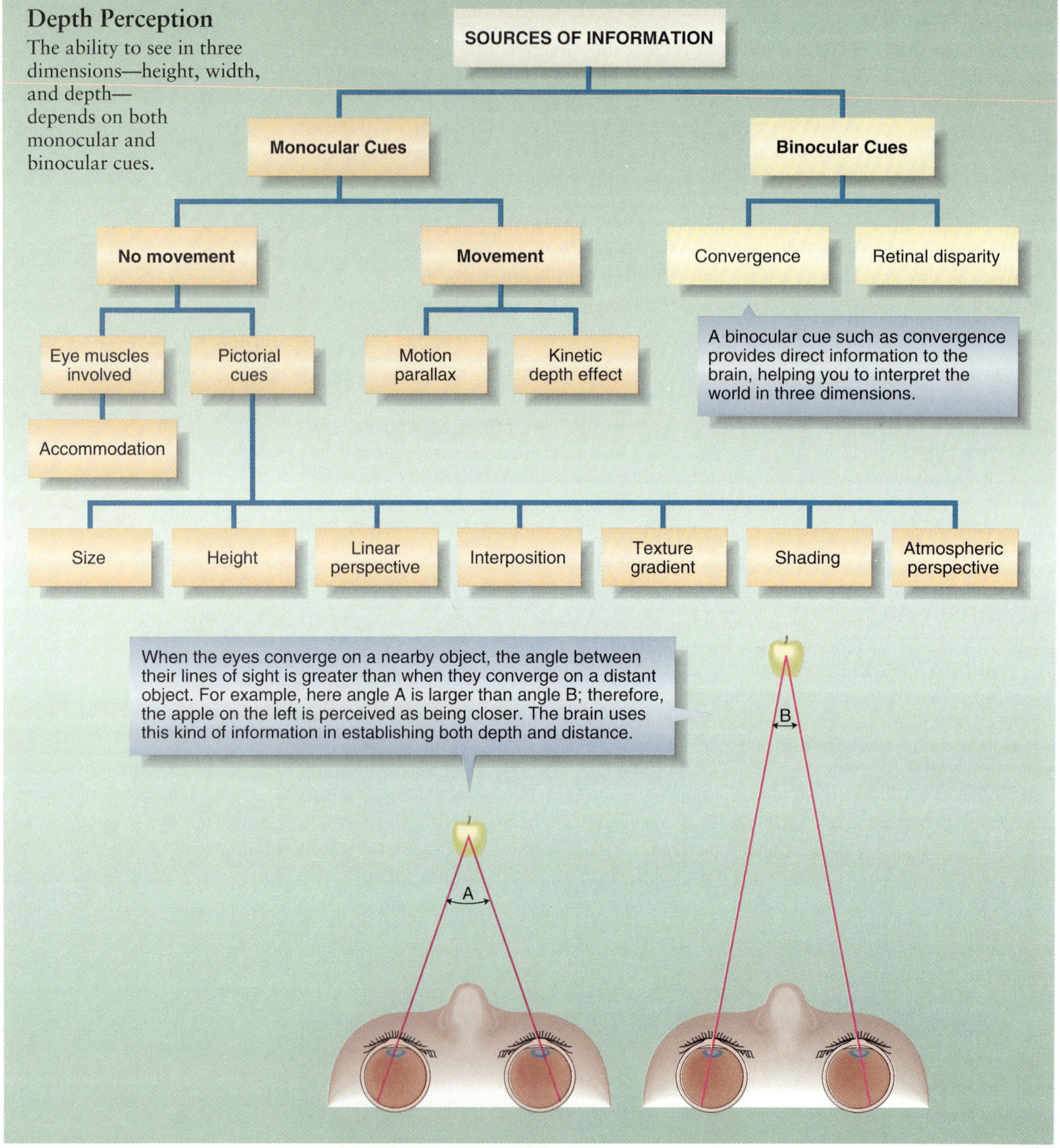

and depth. Both monocular (one-eyed) and binocular (two-eyed) cues are used in depth perception. Binocular cues predominate at close distances, and monocular cues are used for distant scenes and two-dimensional fields of view, such as paintings.

Monocular depth cues [mah-NAHK-you-ler]: Depth cues that do not depend on the use of both eyes.

Monocular Depth Cues. Depth cues that do not depend on the use of both eyes are **monocular depth cues** (see Figure 3.12). Two important monocular depth cues relate to the effects of motion on perception. The first cue, *motion parallax*, occurs when a moving observer stares at a fixed point. The objects behind that point appear to move in the same direction as the observer; the objects in front of the point appear to move in the opposite direction. For example, if you stare at a fence while riding in a moving car, the trees behind the fence rails seem to move in the same direction as the car (forward) and the bushes in front of the rails seem to move in the opposite direction (backward). Motion parallax also affects the speed at which objects appear to move. Objects at a greater distance from the moving observer appear to move more slowly than objects that are closer. The second monocular depth cue derived from movement is the *kinetic depth effect.* Objects that look flat when they are stationary appear to be three-dimensional when set in motion. When two-dimensional projections—such as images of squares or rods shown on a computer screen—are rotated, they appear to have three dimensions.

◀ *A binocular cue such as convergence provides direct information to the brain, helping you interpret the world in three dimensions. You know that a road does not become narrower as it approaches the horizon.*

Monocular cues such as linear perspective and interposition create the illusion of depth in art and in photographs. ▼

Other monocular depth cues come from the stimulus itself; they are often seen in photographs and paintings. For example, larger or taller objects are usually perceived to be closer than smaller ones, particularly in relation to surrounding objects. In addition, *linear perspective* affects perception; this cue is based on the principle that distant objects appear to be closer together than nearer objects. A painter shows distance by making parallel lines converge as they recede. Another monocular cue for depth is *interposition.* When one object blocks out part of another, the first appears to be closer. A fourth monocular cue is *texture;* surfaces that have little texture or detail seem to be in the distance. Artists often use the additional cues of *highlighting* and *shadowing.* Highlighted (light) objects appear close; shadowed (dark) objects appear to be farther away. In addition, the perceptual system picks up other information from shadowing, including the curvature of surfaces (Cavanagh & Leclerc, 1989). Still another monocular depth cue is *atmospheric perspective,* which relates to light wavelengths themselves. Distant mountains often look blue, for example, because long (red) wavelengths are more easily scattered as they pass through the air, allowing more short (blue) wavelengths to reach our eyes. Leonardo da Vinci used this phenomenon in his paintings; he even developed an equation for how much blue pigment should be mixed with the close-up color of an object so the object would appear as far away as he wished. Michelangelo's angels seem to float off the ceiling of the Sistine Chapel because he used color so effectively to portray depth.

All of the preceding monocular depth cues are derived from the stimulus. The monocular depth cue of accommodation, however, is not. If a person looks from one object to another one at a different distance, the lenses of the eye will accommodate—that is, change shape to adapt to the depth of focus. This cue is available from each eye separately. **Accommodation** is the change in the shape of the lens that enables the observer to keep an object in focus on the retina when the object is moved or when the choice of objects for focus changes. This change is controlled by muscles attached to the lens, which provide information about the shape of the lens to the higher processing systems in the brain.

Binocular Depth Cues. Most people, even infants, also use **binocular depth cues**—cues requiring the use of both eyes. One important binocular depth cue is **retinal disparity,** which is the slight difference between the visual images projected on the two retinas. Retinal disparity occurs because the eyes are physically separated (by the bridge of the nose), which causes them to see an object from slightly different angles. To see how retinal disparity works, hold a finger up in front of some distant object. Examine the object first with one eye and then with the other eye. The finger will appear in different positions relative to the object.

Accommodation: The change in the shape of the lens of the eye to keep an object in focus on the retina when the object is moved closer to or farther away from the observer.

Binocular depth cues: Any visual cues for depth perception that require the use of both eyes.

Retinal disparity: The slight difference between the visual images projected on the two retinas.

The closer objects are to the eyes, the farther apart their images on the retinas will be—and the greater the retinal disparity. Objects at a great distance produce little retinal disparity.

Another binocular depth cue is convergence. **Convergence** is the movement of the eyes toward each other in order to keep visual input at corresponding points on the retinas as an object moves closer to the observer. Like accommodation, convergence is controlled by muscles in the eye that convey information to the brain and thus provide a potent physiological depth cue for stimuli close to observers. Beyond 20 or 30 feet, the eyes are aimed pretty much in parallel, and the effect of this cue diminishes.

Illusions

Have you ever seen water ahead on the road, only to find it has disappeared a moment later as you drive by? You most likely also have seen railroad tracks that appear to converge in the distance. When the normal visual process and depth cues seem to break down, you experience an optical illusion. An **illusion** is a perception of a physical stimulus that differs from measurable reality and the commonly expected appearance; many consider it a misperception of stimulation.

FIGURE 3.13

Five Well-Known Illusions

In the Müller-Lyer and Ponzo illusions, lines of equal length appear different in length. The photos with the Müller-Lyer illusion show how the arrows usually represent "near corners" and "far corners." In the Zollner illusion, the short lines make the longer ones seem not parallel, even though they are. In the Wundt illusion, the center horizontal lines are parallel, even though they appear bent. In the Poggendorf illusion, the line disappears behind a solid and reappears in a position that seems wrong.

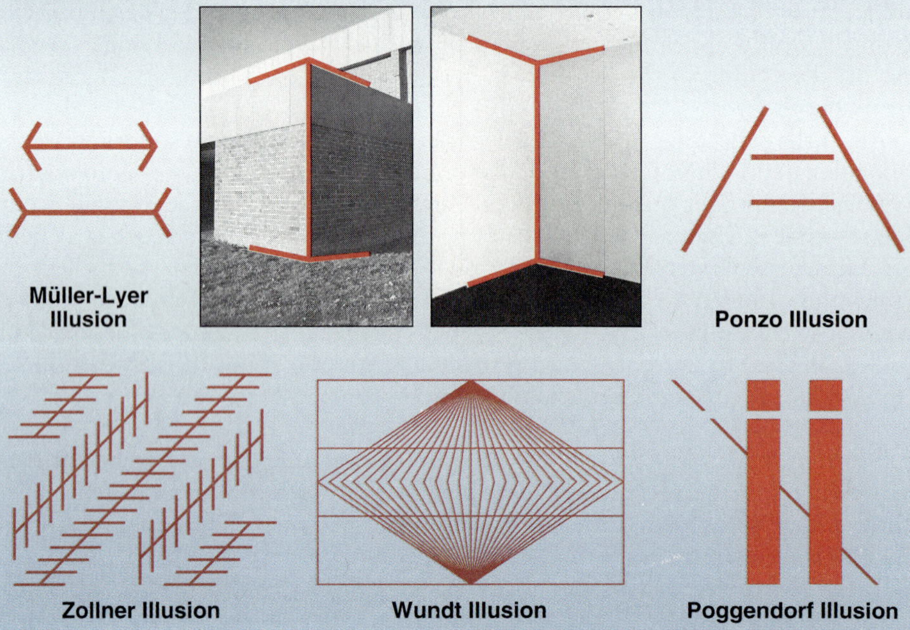

Convergence: The movement of the eyes toward each other to keep information at corresponding points on the retinas as an object moves closer to the observer.

Illusion: A perception of a physical stimulus that differs from measurable reality and normal expectations about its appearance.

A common illusion is the *Müller–Lyer illusion*, in which two equal-length lines with arrows attached to their ends appear to be of different lengths. A similar illusion is the *Ponzo illusion* (sometimes called the railroad illusion), in which two horizontal lines of the same length, bracketed by slanted lines, appear to be of different lengths. (See Figure 3.13 for examples of these two illusions and three others; Figure 3.14 presents another perceptual phenomenon.) One natural illusion is the *moon illusion*. Although the actual size of the moon and the size of its image on the retina do not change, the moon appears about 30 percent larger when it is near the horizon than when it is overhead. The moon illusion is quite striking. In just a few minutes, the size of the moon appears to change from quite large to quite small. The moon illusion is even seen in photographs and paintings (Coren & Aks, 1990).

How do visual illusions work? No completely satisfactory explanations have been found. Recent theories account for them in terms of the backgrounds against which the objects are seen. These explanations are based on the observer's previous experiences and well-developed perceptual constancies. (*Diversity*, on page 94, explores how cultural experiences affect the experience of illusions.) For example, the moon illusion is explained by the fact that, when seen overhead, the moon has a featureless background, whereas at the horizon objects are close to it. Objects in the landscape provide cues about distance that change the observer's perception of the size of the moon (Baird, Wagner, & Fuld, 1990; Restle, 1970). To see how the moon illusion depends on landscape cues, try this: When the moon is at the horizon, bend over and look at it from between your legs. Since that position screens out some of the horizon cues, the magnitude of the illusion will be reduced.

The Ponzo illusion is similarly accounted for by the linear perspective provided by the slanted background lines. The Müller–Lyer illusion occurs because of the angle and shape of the arrows attached to the ends of the lines. Lines angled inward are often interpreted as far corners—those that are most distant from the observer. Lines angled outward are commonly interpreted as near corners—those that are closest to the observer. Therefore, lines with far-corner angles attached to them appear longer because their length is judged in a context of distance.

These are not the only ways of explaining illusions. Some researchers assert that people see the moon as having different sizes on the horizon and overhead because they judge it like they judge other moving objects that pass through space. Because the moon does not get closer to them, they assume it is moving away. Objects that move away get smaller; hence the illusion of a change in the size of the moon (Reed, 1984). This explanation focuses on constancies but also takes account of movement, space, and the atmosphere.

FIGURE 3.14

Impossible Figures

Many types of figures trick the perceiver by being *impossible figures*. The longer you stare at these drawings, the more they seem to have different characteristics.

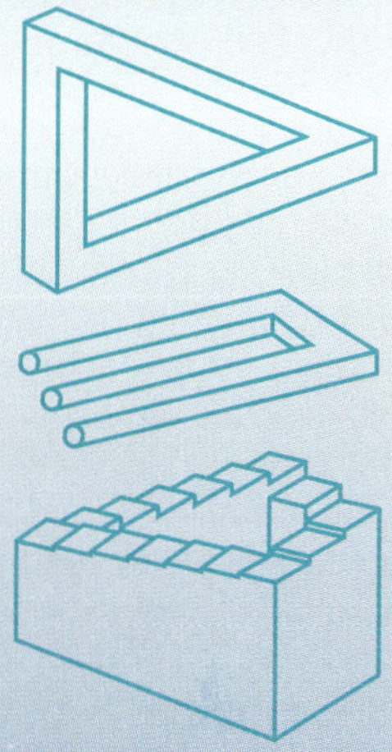

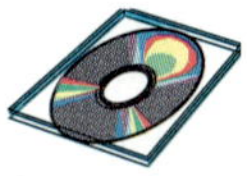

Fig. 3.12

Gestalt Laws of Organization

Gestalt psychologists (see page 27) suggest that conscious experience is more than the sum of its parts. They argue that the mind organizes the elements of experience to form something unique; they thus view the world in terms of perceptual frameworks. Analyzed as a whole experience, the patterns of a person's perceptions make sense. The first Gestalt psychologists—including Max Wertheimer, Kurt Koffka, and Wolfgang Köhler—greatly influenced early theories of form perception. These psychologists assumed (wrongly) that human perceptual processes *solely* reflect brain organization and that they could learn about the workings of the brain by studying perception. Researchers now know, of course, that the relationship between brain structure and function is much more complex—perception is a process that not only represents stimuli but reflects past experiences as well.

The surfaces of this room are arranged at odd angles and depths so that the boy on the right appears to be taller than the woman on the left. In reality, the opposite is true. This is the Ames room illusion.

DIVERSITY

Cross-Cultural Research on Illusions

A wonderful advertisement a number of years ago showed a 12-year-old African American boy eating a thick deli sandwich. The caption was: "You don't have to be Jewish to like Levy's rye bread." You also don't have to be Russian to appreciate Tchaikovsky; nor do you have to be from Ireland to like U2. Yet there is no doubt that artists bring to their work a nationalistic tone. George Gershwin's *Rhapsody in Blue* sounds distinctly American, as does New Orleans jazz.

Each person brings a lifetime of experiences to the perceptual experience. This becomes especially clear from research conducted cross-culturally. Cross-cultural research on illusions, for example, shows that the Müller–Lyer and Ponzo (railroad) illusions are perceived differently by different cultures. Leibowitz (1971) conducted a series of studies on the Ponzo illusion using both American participants and participants from Guam, where there are no railroads and perspective cues are far less prevalent than in the United States. Leibowitz had his participants judge the size of the Ponzo illusion drawn with straight lines; they also judged the illusion in photographs. He found that the size of the illusion increased for the American participants as he added more pictorial depth cues. The participants from Guam showed few differences when more pictorial cues were added. Other differences also existed; for example, the participants from Guam viewed depth differently than did their American counterparts. The different cultures viewed the world in dissimilar ways.

Other illusions have been investigated with different cultural groups. For example, Pedersen and Wheeler (1983) compared the reactions of two groups of Navajos to the Müller–Lyer illusion. One group lived in rectangular houses, where the individuals had extensive experience with corners, angles, and oblique lines. The other group lived in traditional Navajo round houses, where early experiences included far fewer encounters with angles. The researchers found that those who lived in angular houses were more susceptible to the Müller–Lyer illusion, which depends on angles. Some researchers say such illusions depend on the *carpenter effect*, because in Western cultures carpenters use lines, angles, and geometry to build houses.

Although there is little systematic scientific evidence on the topic, musicians have long known that a person's experiences with Western music make 12-tone music and Indian and Asian melodies sound unfamiliar and dissonant. The experience of music, like the experience of illusions, depends on early experiences. Research shows that people's visual and auditory perceptions are also culturally dependent. Deregowski (1980) asserts that there is a dearth of non-Western studies; yet he is able to conclude in his review of studies of language, pictures, smell, and illusions that there exist cross-cultural differences that reflect people's cultures. Individuals from other cultures do not initially see illusions and some features of depth; but when key characteristics of pictures and scenes are pointed out, they often exclaim, "Oh, now I see it!" Yet their initial experiences often show a lack of the recognition that individuals from Western cultures have. Cross-cultural research is exciting and illuminating, though unfortunately limited in its extent. For psychologists to develop truly comprehensive theories of perception, they must incorporate cross-cultural differences into their research.

Law of Prägnanz [PREG-nants]: The Gestalt principle that when items or stimuli *can* be grouped together and seen as a whole, they *will* be.

The early Gestaltists focused their perceptual studies on the ways in which people experience form and organization. These early researchers believed people organize each complex visual field into a coherent whole rather than seeing individual, unrelated elements. That is, they believed people see groups of elements, not fragmented parts. According to this idea, called the **law of Prägnanz,** items or stimuli that *can* be grouped together and seen as a whole, or a form, *will* be seen that way.

FIGURE 3.15

Gestalt Laws

Gestalt principles focus on organizing elements into the coherent wholes by which human beings perceive the world.

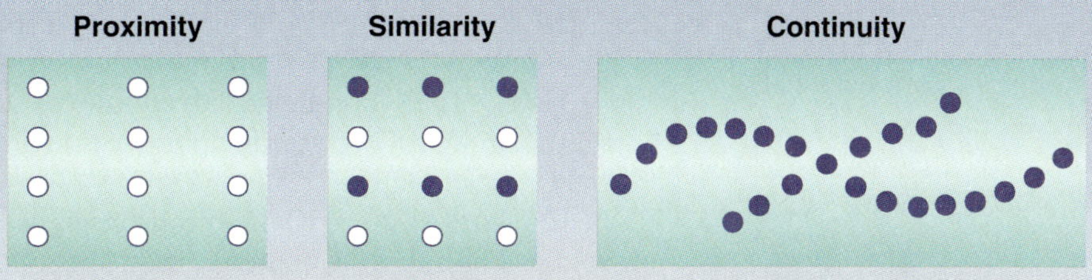

According to the Gestalt law of proximity, the circles in the left panel appear to be arranged in vertical columns because items that are close together tend to be perceived as a unit. According to the law of similarity, the filled and empty circles in the middle panel appear to be arranged in horizontal rows because similar items tend to be perceived in groups. According to the law of continuity, an observer will predict where the next item should occur in the arrangement on the right because the group of items projects into space.

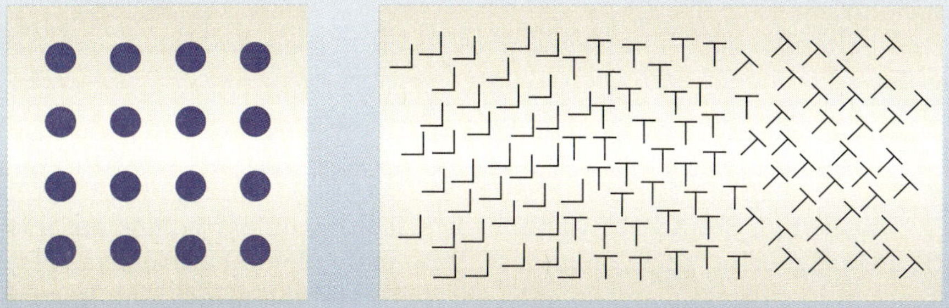

The law of Prägnanz: Items or stimuli that *can* be grouped together as a whole *will* be. These 16 dots are typically perceived as a square.

In a study asking people to divide these lines into two groups, Beck (1966) found that subjects generally placed the boundary between the upright and tilted *T*s rather than between the backward *L*s and upright *T*s. Beck argued that this result supports the law of Prägnanz.

FIGURE 3.16

The Figure–Ground Relationship

Gestalt psychologists studied the figure–ground relationship. In this drawing, figure and ground can be reversed. You can see either two faces against a white background or a goblet against a dark background.

The lower left portion of Figure 3.15 shows a series of 16 dots that people tend to see as a square.

The law of Prägnanz was based on principles of organization for the perception of figures, especially on contours, which help define figure–ground relationships. Gestalt psychologists focused on the nature of *figure–ground relationships*, contending that people perceive *figures* (the main objects of sensory attention—the foregrounds) as distinct from the *grounds* (the backgrounds) on which they are presented (see Figure 3.16). Gestalt psychologists developed the following series of laws, the first three of which are illustrated in the upper part of Figure 3.15, for predicting which areas of an ambiguous pattern would be seen as the figure (foreground) and which as the ground (background):

- *Law of proximity*—elements close to one another in space or time will be perceived as groups.
- *Law of similarity*—similar items will be perceived in groups.

FOCUS

Review

- What are the key variables that allow a person to maintain size constancy? pp. 88–89
- Explain how monocular and binocular depth cues help people see depth. pp. 90–92
- How do perceptual psychologists account for the moon illusion? p. 93

Think Critically

- What do Gestalt researchers mean when they say that the whole is greater than the sum of its parts?
- How do you think culture exerts its influence on your perceptual systems?

- *Law of continuity*—a string of items will indicate where the next item in the string will be found.
- *Common fate principle*—items that move or change together will be perceived as a whole.
- *Law of closure*—parts of a figure that are not presented will be filled in by the perceptual system.

Beck (1966) conducted a well-known study that examined Gestalt principles (see the lower right part of Figure 3.15 on page 95). However, Beck's work showed that Gestalt principles are vague: They apply whether participants choose orientation or shape to break up the figure, but they do not explain why orientation predominated in Beck's study. Gestalt laws are not always obeyed; nor are they consistent with current knowledge of brain organization. Nevertheless, these early investigations continue to influence perceptual psychologists as springboards that have some elements of truth.

Hearing

Listening closely to a Beethoven symphony is delightful and intriguing, but it is difficult because so much is going on at once. With more than 20 instruments playing, the listener must process many sounds, rhythms, and intensities simultaneously. Like seeing, hearing is a complex process that involves converting physical stimuli into a psychological experience. For example, suppose that a tuning fork is struck or a stereo system booms out a bass note. In both cases, sound waves are being created and air is being moved. The movement of the air and the accompanying changes in air pressure (physical stimuli) cause your eardrum to move back and forth rapidly. The movement of the eardrum triggers a series of electromechanical and electrochemical changes that you ultimately experience as sound.

Sound

When a tuning fork, the reed of a clarinet, or a person's vocal cords are set in motion, the resulting vibrations cause sound waves. You can place your hand in front of a stereo speaker and feel the displacement of the sound waves when the volume rises. **Sound** is the psychological experience that occurs when changes in air pressure take place at the receptive organ for hearing; the resulting tones, or sounds, vary in frequency and amplitude. Sound is often thought of in terms of two psychological aspects, pitch and loudness, which are associated with the two physical attributes of frequency and amplitude.

As shown in Figure 3.17, **frequency** is the number of times a complete change in air pressure occurs during a given unit of time. Within 1 second, for example, there may be 50 complete changes (50 cycles per second) or 10,000 complete changes (10,000 cycles per second). Frequency is usually measured in hertz (Hz); 1 Hz equals 1 cycle per second. Frequency determines the pitch, or *tone*, of a sound; **pitch** is the psychological experience that corresponds with the frequency of an auditory stimulus. High-pitched tones usually have high frequencies. When a piano hammer

Sound: The psychological experience that occurs when changes in air pressure take place at the receptive organ for hearing; the resulting tones, or sounds, vary in frequency and amplitude.

Frequency: In sound waves, a measure of the number of times a complete change in air pressure occurs per unit of time; expressed in hertz (Hz), or cycles per second.

Pitch: The psychological experience that corresponds with the frequency of an auditory stimulus. Also known as *tone*.

FIGURE 3.17

The Frequency and Amplitude of Sound Waves

A person's psychological experience of sound depends on the frequency and amplitude of sound waves.

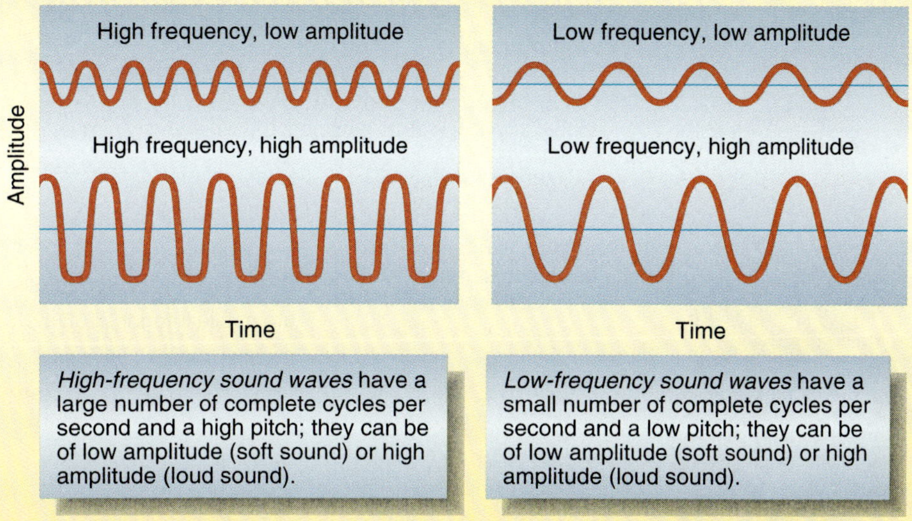

strikes a short string on a piano (at the right), the string vibrates at a high frequency and sounds high in pitch; when a long string (at the far left) is struck, it vibrates less frequently and sounds low in pitch.

Amplitude, or *intensity*, is the total energy of a sound wave, which determines the loudness of a sound. High-amplitude sound waves have more energy than low-amplitude waves; they apply greater force to the ear (see Figure 3.17). Amplitude is measured in *decibels*. Every increase of 20 decibels corresponds to a tenfold increase in intensity. (Decibels are measured on a logarithmic scale, which means that increases are exponential, not linear; thus, increases in sound intensity measured in decibels are quite steep.) As Figure 3.18 on page 98 shows, normal conversation has an amplitude of about 60 decibels, and sounds at about 120 decibels are painfully loud.

Amplitude and frequency are not correlated. A low-frequency sound can be very loud or very soft; that is, it can have either high or low amplitude. Middle C on a piano, for example, can be loud or soft. The frequency (pitch) of the sound stays the same—it is still middle C; only its amplitude (loudness) varies. The psychological perception of loudness depends on other factors, such as background noise and whether the person is paying attention to the sound. Another psychological dimension, *timbre*, is the quality of a sound—the different mixture of amplitudes and frequencies that make up the sound. People's perceptions of all these qualities depend on the physical structure of their ears.

Structure of the Ear

The receptive organ for *audition*, or hearing, is the ear: It translates physical stimuli (sound waves) into electrical impulses that the brain can interpret. The ear has three major parts: the outer ear, the middle ear, and the inner ear. The tissue on the outside of the head is part of the outer ear. The eardrum (*tympanic membrane*) is the boundary between the outer and middle ear. When sound waves enter the ear, they

Amplitude: The total energy of a sound wave, which determines the loudness of a sound. Also known as *intensity*.

FIGURE 3.18

Psychological Responses to Various Sound Intensities

High-amplitude sound waves, such as those generated by a rock band, have greater energy than low-amplitude waves and a greater impact on the sensitive structure of our ears.

Psychological Response	Decibel Scale	Examples
Threshold of severe pain	140	
Painfully loud		Rock band at 15 feet
Very annoying	120	Jet takeoff at 200 feet
		Riveting machine
Prolonged exposure produces damage to hearing	100	Subway train at 15 feet
		Water at foot of Niagara Falls
	80	Automobile interior at 55 mph
		Freeway traffic at 50 feet
Quiet	60	Normal conversation at 3 feet
		Quiet restaurant
Very quiet	40	Quiet office
		Library
Just audible	20	Whisper at 3 feet
		Normal breathing
Threshold of hearing	0	

produce changes in the pressure of the air on the eardrum. The eardrum responds to these changes by vibrating.

The middle ear is quite small. Within it, tiny bones (*ossicles*) known as the *hammer, anvil,* and *stirrup*, help convert the large forces striking the eardrum into a small force. Two small muscles are attached to the ossicles; these muscles contract involuntarily in response to loud vocalizations and especially when they are exposed to an annoyingly loud noise. They help protect the delicate mechanisms of the inner ear from the damaging effects of a loud noise that could overstimulate them (Borg & Counter, 1989). Ultimately, the middle ear bones stimulate the *basilar membrane*, which runs down the middle of the *cochlea*, a spiral tube in the inner ear. Figure 3.19 shows the major structures of the middle and inner ear, and Figure 3.20 shows the basilar membrane.

Fig. 3.7

In the cochlea, which is shaped like a snail's shell and comprises three chambers, sound waves of different frequencies stimulate different areas of the basilar membrane. These areas, in turn, stimulate hair cells, which bring about the initial electrical coding of sound waves. These cells are remarkably sensitive. Hudspeth (1983), for example, found that hair cells respond when they are displaced as little as 100 picometers (trillionths of a meter). These cells are responsible for the transduction of mechanical energy into electrochemical energy.

Electrical impulses make their way through the brain's auditory nervous system in much the same way as visual information proceeds through the visual nervous system. The electrochemical neuronal impulses proceed through the auditory nerve to the midbrain and finally to the auditory cortex. Studies of single cells in the auditory areas of the brain show that some cells are more responsive to certain frequencies than to others. Katsuki (1961) found cells that are maximally sensitive to certain narrow frequency ranges; if a frequency is outside their range, these cells might not fire at all. This finding is analogous to the findings reported by Hubel and Wiesel, who discovered receptive visual fields in which proper stimulation brought

FIGURE 3.19

The Major Structures of the Ear

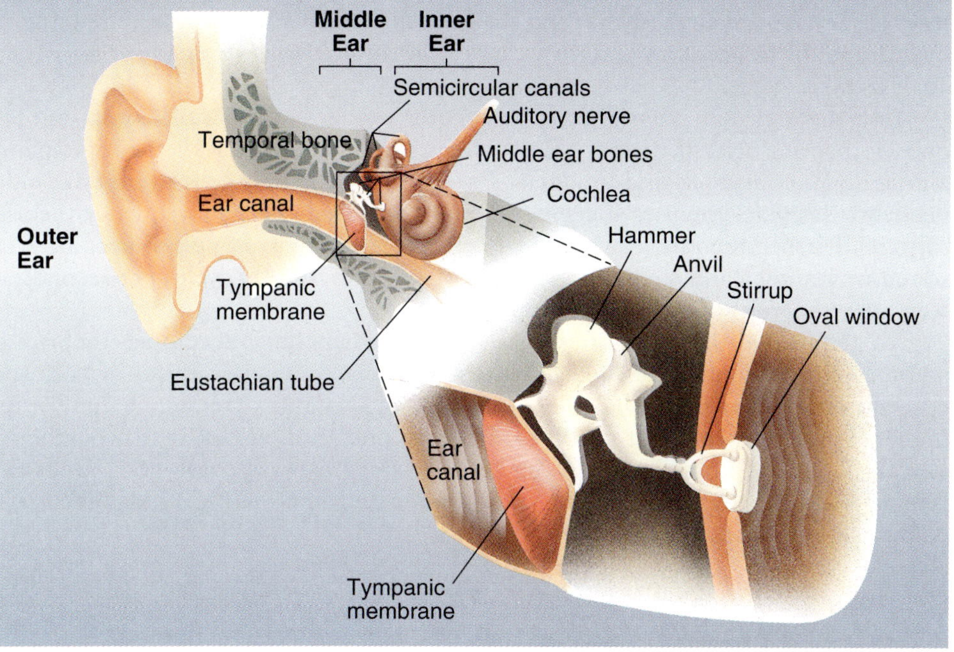

about dramatic changes in the firing of a cell; research supports a highly organized columnar organization in the auditory system, much like that of the visual system (Gray et al., 1989).

Theories of Hearing

Most theories of hearing fall into two major classes: place theories and frequency theories. *Place theories* claim that the analysis of sound occurs in the basilar membrane, with different frequencies and intensities affecting different parts (places) of the membrane. They assert that each sound wave causes a traveling wave on the basilar membrane, which in turn causes changes in the basilar membrane's displacement. The hair

FIGURE 3.20

The Basilar Membrane

In this view, the cochlea has been unwound and cut open to reveal the basilar membrane, which is covered with thousands of hair cells. Pressure variations in the fluid that fills the cochlea cause oscillations to travel in waves along the basilar membrane, stimulating the hair cells.

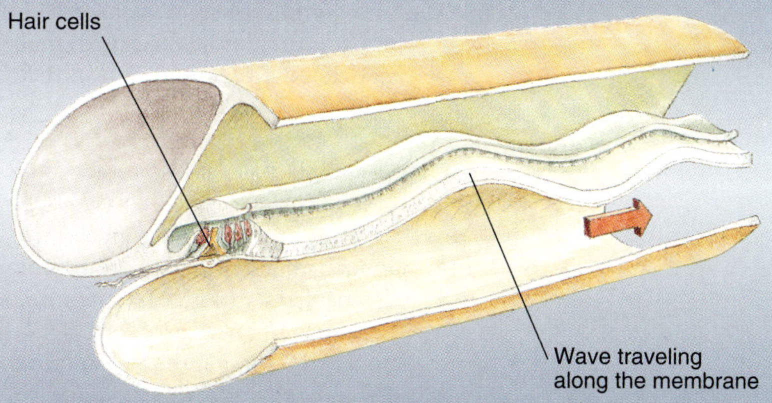

cells on the basilar membrane are displaced by the traveling wave, and the displacement of individual hair cells triggers specific information about pitch.

In contrast, *frequency theories* maintain that the analysis of pitch and intensity occurs at higher centers (levels) of processing, perhaps in the auditory area of the cortex, and that the basilar membrane merely transfers information to those centers. These theories suggest that the entire basilar membrane is stimulated and its overall rate of responding is transferred to the auditory nerve and beyond, where analysis takes place.

Like theories that attempt to explain color vision, both place theories and frequency theories present theoretical problems. And neither class of theory explains all the data about pitch and loudness. For example, the hair cells do not act independently (as place theories suggest) but instead act together (as frequency theories suggest). Further, the rate at which hair cells fire is not fast enough to keep up with sound waves (typically having frequencies of 1,000 to 10,000 cycles per second), as frequency theories suggest.

To get around the difficulties, modern researchers have developed theories of auditory information processing that attempt to explain pitch in terms of both specific action in parts of the basilar membrane and complex frequency analyses at higher levels. Theories that seem at odds with one another can work together to explain pitch and loudness when the best parts of them are combined. (Does this remind you of the debate over the trichromatic and opponent-process theories of color vision we discusses earlier?)

Sound Localization

How do you know where to turn when you hear a baby crying? Although not as direction sensitive as many animals, human beings have amazingly efficient sound localization (direction-determining) abilities. Researchers have learned much about such abilities by presenting sound through headsets, with one sound going to one ear and another sound to the other ear. Such experiments have revealed that there are two key concepts in sound localization: interaural time differences and interaural intensity differences. Because you have two ears, a sound made to the left of your head will arrive at the left ear before the right. Thus, you have an *interaural time difference*. In addition, the sound will reach the two ears at different intensities. A sound made at your left will be slightly more intense to the left ear than to the right; thus, there is an *interaural intensity difference*. These two pieces of information are analyzed in the brain at nuclei that are especially sensitive to time and intensity differences between the ears.

Some potential ambiguities exist in sound localization, however. What happens when the sound source is just in front of you, and thus is equidistant from your two ears? It turns out that head and body movements help resolve the source of a sound. You rotate your head or move your body when you are unsure of the source of a sound. In addition, the external ear has ridges and folds that bounce sounds around just a bit. This creates slight delays that help you localize sounds. Finally, sight and past experiences with sounds aid in the task of localizing sounds in space.

Hearing Impairments

Not everyone has perfect hearing. About 13 million people in the United States have hearing impairments, ranging from minor hearing loss to total deafness. Older individuals sometimes suffer from such impairments, and they are often discriminated against because of their problem. The causes of the impairments are various, and they lead to varying degrees of conduction deafness, sensorineural deafness, or a combination of the two.

Conduction deafness is deafness resulting from interference with the transmission of sound to the neural mechanism of the inner ear. The interference may be caused by something temporary, such as a head cold or a buildup of wax in the outer ear canal. Or it may be caused by something far more serious, such as hardening of the tympanic membrane, destruction of the tiny bones within the ear, or diseases that create pressure in the middle ear. If the person can get help with transmission of the sound past the point of the conduction problem, hearing can be improved.

Sensorineural deafness is deafness resulting from damage to the cochlea, the auditory nerve, or higher auditory processing centers. The most common cause of this type of deafness is ongoing exposure to very high-intensity sound, such as that of rock bands or jet planes. Listening to even moderately loud music for longer than 15 minutes a day can cause permanent deafness.

Hearing loss is measured by an *audiometer*, which presents sounds of different frequencies through a headphone; results are presented as an *audiogram*, which is a graph showing hearing sensitivity at selected frequencies. The audiogram of the person whose hearing is being tested is compared with that of an adult with no known hearing loss. One simpler way to assess and diagnose hearing impairment is to test a person's recognition of spoken words. In a typical test of this sort, a person listens to a tape recording of speech sounds that are standardized in terms of loudness and pitch. Performance is based on the number of words the participant can repeat correctly at various intensity levels. This test is often administered by nonmedical personnel, who then refer individuals who may have hearing problems to a physician.

You can easily see that hearing and vision have many similarities in their perceptual mechanisms. In both perceptual systems, physical energy is transduced into electrochemical energy. Coding takes place at several locations in the brain, and people can have impairments in either visual or auditory abilities.

FOCUS

Review

- What is the difference between pitch and frequency? p. 96
- How does a person locate a sound in space? p. 100
- Distinguish between conduction deafness and sensorineural deafness. p. 101

Think Critically

- Why do scientists consider sound a psychological experience rather than a physical one?
- Why might an inner ear infection cause light headedness?

Taste and Smell

Try the following experiment. Cut a fresh onion in half and inhale its odor while holding a piece of raw potato in your mouth. Now chew the potato. Does the potato taste like an onion? This experiment demonstrates that taste and smell are closely linked. Food contains substances that act as stimuli for both taste and smell.

There is one taste most people have a special fondness for: sweetness. Babies prefer sweet foods; so do great-grandmothers. But researchers know that a sweet tooth involves a craving for more than the taste of sugar. People with a sweet tooth crave candy, cake, ice cream, and sometimes liquor. Their bodies perceive the sweetness and learn that it is associated with many foods that are high in carbohydrates and fat. Carbohydrates act almost as sedatives. So your cravings for some substances—your desire to taste or smell or eat or drink them—are affected by a number of variables, including the composition of the food, its smells, what it ultimately does to you, and your previous experiences with it.

Conduction deafness: Deafness resulting from interference with the transmission of sound to the neural mechanism of the inner ear.

Sensorineural deafness [sen-so-ree-NEW-ruhl]: Deafness resulting from damage to the cochlea, the auditory nerve, or higher auditory processing centers.

FIGURE 3.21

Taste Buds Are Found on the Surface of the Tongue

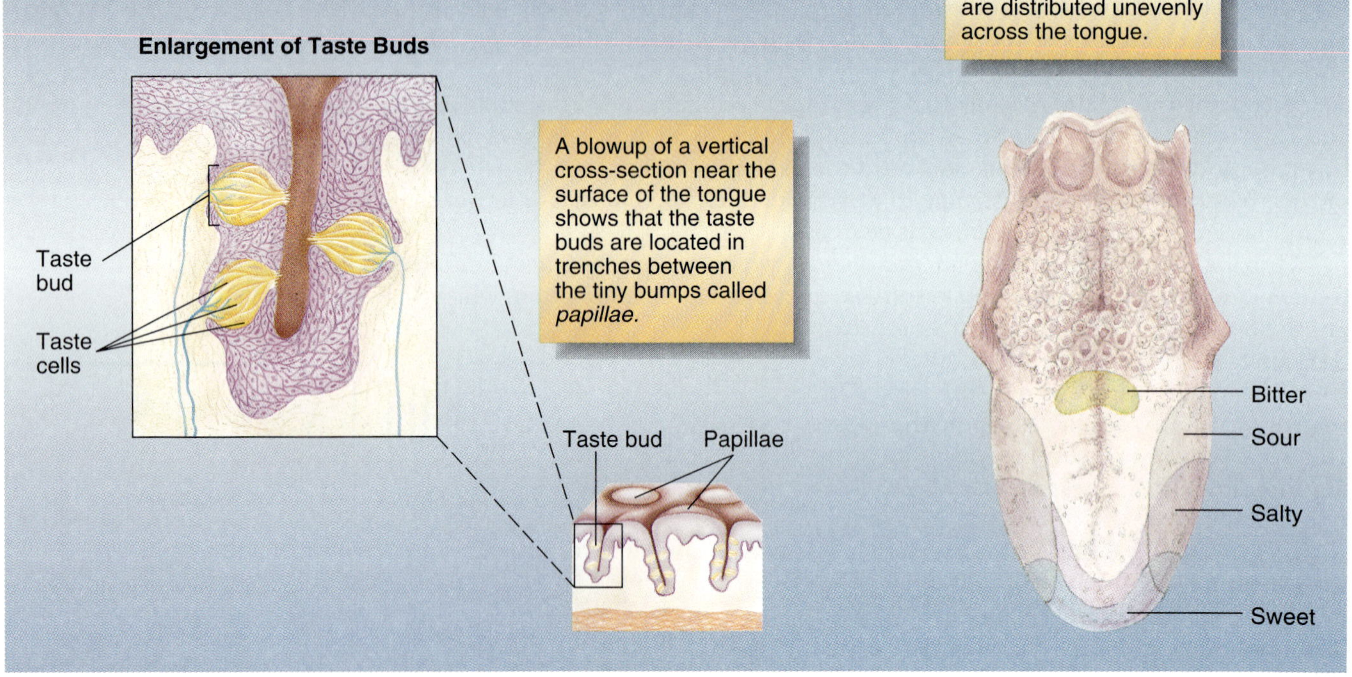

Taste

I remember the first time I was in a cheese store. My father was supposed to buy some cheese and crackers because company was coming for dinner. I was overwhelmed by the quantity of cheeses and their different tastes and smells. The store owner allowed me to sample a variety: Swiss, blue, cheddar, Gruyère, Gorgonzola, and Brie. The cheddar was too sharp, the blue cheese tasted bitter, and the Swiss was bland in comparison. We finally decided on a large slice of Brie; it was soft and creamy, with a slightly sweet, mild flavor.

Taste is a chemical sense; food placed in the mouth is partially dissolved in saliva and stimulates the *taste buds*, the primary receptors for taste stimuli (see Figure 3.21). When substances contact the taste buds, you experience taste. The taste buds are found on small bumps on the tongue—papillae. Each hill-like papilla is separated from the next by a trenchlike moat; on the wall of this moat are located the taste buds, which can be seen only under a microscope. Each taste bud (human beings have about 10,000 of them) consists of 5 to 150 *taste cells*. These cells last only about 10 days and are constantly being renewed.

The papillae, shown here highlighted in purple, are located on the surface of the human tongue. ▼

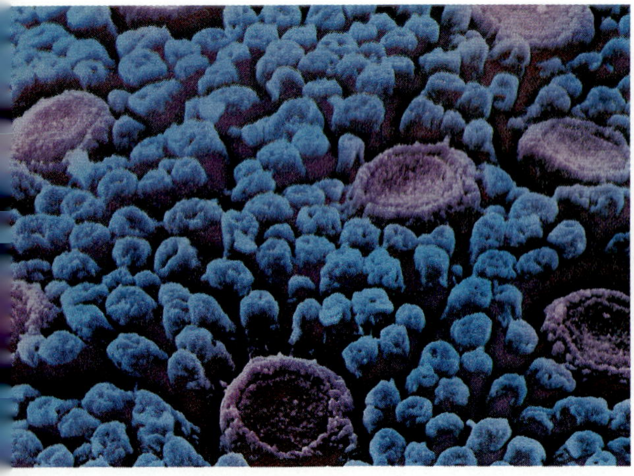

Although psychologists do not know exactly how many tastes there are, most agree that there are four basic ones: sweet, sour, salty, and bitter. Most foods contain more than one primary taste; Hawaiian pineapple pizza, for example, offers a complicated taste stimulus and also stimulates the sense of smell (described in the following section). All taste cells are sensitive to all taste stimuli, but some cells are more sensitive to some stimuli than to others. (In this regard, they are much like the cones in the retina, which are sensitive to all wavelengths but are especially sensitive to a specific range of wavelengths.) By isolating stimuli that initiate only one taste sensation, psychologists have found that some regions of the tongue seem to be more sensitive to particular taste stimuli than others. The tip of the tongue, for example, is more sensitive to sweet tastes than the back of the tongue, and the sides are especially sensitive to sour tastes.

The taste of a particular food depends not only on its chemical makeup but also on your past experiences with this or similar foods, on how much saliva is being mixed into the food as you chew, and on how long you chew the food. A food that is chewed well has a strong taste. A food that rests on the tongue for a long time will lose its ability to stimulate. This is a phenomenon called *sensory adaptation*, or the temporary change in responsiveness of a receptor, often due to repeated high levels of stimulation. A food that loses its texture by being mashed up, blended, or mixed with other foods has less taste and is less appealing to most adults. Thus, a taste experience, much like other perceptual experiences, depends not only on a sensory event but also on past experience and other sensory and perceptual variables.

Smell

Try eating potatoes and onions while holding your nose and you will quickly see that they taste alike, as do carrots and apples. Smell is such an important sense that those who lose it for medical reasons feel disabled. Like the sense of taste, **olfaction**—the sense of smell—is a chemical sense. That is, the stimulus for smell is a chemical in the air. The olfactory system in human beings is remarkably sensitive: humans can distinguish approximately 10,000 different scents and can recognize a smell from as few as 40 or 50 molecules of the chemical. For the sensation of smell to occur, chemicals must move toward the receptor cells located on the walls of the nasal passage. This happens when you breathe them in through your nostrils or take them in through the back of your throat when you chew and swallow. When a chemical substance in the air moves past the receptor cells, it is partially absorbed into the mucus that covers the cells, thereby initiating the process of smell.

For human beings to perceive smell, information must be sent to the brain. At the top of the nasal cavity is the *olfactory epithelium* (see Figure 3.22), a layer of cells that contains the olfactory receptor cells—the nerve fibers that process odors and transmit information about smell to the olfactory bulbs (the enlargements at the end of the olfactory nerve) and on to higher centers of the brain. There can be as

FIGURE 3.22

The Olfactory System

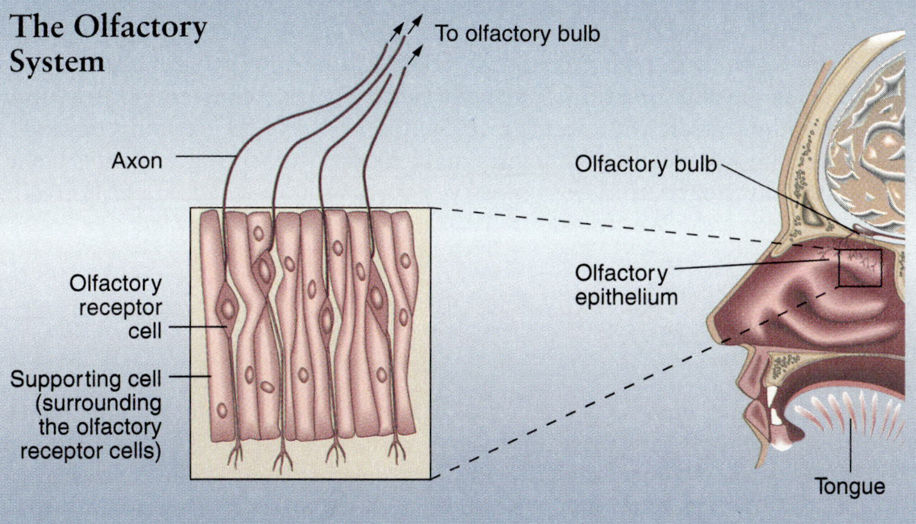

Olfaction [ole-FAK-shun]: The sense of smell.

THE RESEARCH PROCESS

Smell and Communication

Animals secrete *pheromones* (pronounced FER-uh-moans)—scented chemical substances that are detected by other animals. Pheromones act as a means of communication. In fact, scents released by one animal may even influence the physiology of another animal.

Pheromones are widely recognized as initiators of sexual activity among animals. For example, female silkworms release a pheromone that can attract male silkworms from miles away. Similarly, when female hamsters are sexually receptive, they emit a highly odorous substance that attracts males (Montgomery-St. Laurent, Fullenkamp, & Fischer, 1988); mice are similarly equipped (Coppola & O'Connell, 1988).

Many animals emit pheromones to elicit specific behavioral reactions; others, notably dogs, use scents from their feces and urine to maintain territories and identify one another. Beavers attempt to keep strangers out of their territory by depositing foul-smelling substances emitted by sacs near the anus. Reindeer have scent glands between their toes that leave a trail for the rest of the herd. Communication through pheromones is found throughout the animal world. But do human beings share this ability?

Early Ideas. Although people have always believed that a kind of "chemistry" exists between close friends, few really believed that one person's secretions might alter another person's behavior. It was generally thought that human beings do not communicate through smell. However, ground-breaking research in the 1970s began to change psychologists' thinking about smell and communication. McClintock (1971) found that the menstrual periods of women living in a college dormitory who were either roommates or close friends became roughly *synchronous*. That is, after the women lived together for several months, their menstrual cycles began and ended at about the same time. McClintock and others began to question whether the synchronization of the menstrual cycles was due to some type of chemical message.

Research Evidence. In the mid-1980s, two research studies stirred up the pheromone debate. The studies were conducted by two scientists, Cutler and Preti, who focused on a specific issue: Could chemical signals from other people—both men and women—alter women's menstrual cycles? The researchers sought to test McClintock's idea that synchronization of the menstrual cycles was caused by some type of chemical message—pheromones. They used a fascinating technique. They swabbed underarm secretions on the upper lips of women to see whether chemicals in the secretions would affect their menstrual cycles.

many as 30 million olfactory receptor cells in each nostril, making the olfactory system very sensitive. This fact is dramatically illustrated by perfume manufacturing, which is a complex process. Perfume makers may combine hundreds of scents to make one new perfume; dozens of perfumes have the same basic scent and vary only slightly. The manufacturer's task is to generate a perfume that has a distinctive top note—the first impact of a smell. If the substance that creates a smell is not chemically pure, the top note will be followed by a middle and an end note. The middle note follows after the top note fades away, and the end note is long-lasting; it remains long after the top and middle notes have disappeared.

Theories of smell involve both the stimulus for smell and the structure of the receptor system. Some theories posit a few basic smells; others suggest many—including flowery, foul, fruity, resinous, spicy, and burnt. Psychologists have not agreed on a single classification system for smells; nor do they completely understand how odors affect the receptor cells. Research into the coding of smell is intense, and physiological psychologists make headway each year. Another area in which important progress has been made is the question of whether and how odors affect human behavior. We consider this issue in *The Research Process*.

The Skin Senses

Your skin, an organ of your body, contains a wide range of receptors for relaying information about the *skin senses*—pain, touch, and temperature (warmth and cold). In each case a stimulus is converted into neural energy, and then the brain interprets that neural energy as a psychological experience. Skin receptors ultimately send information to the somatosensory cortex of the brain.

In the first study, the scientists gathered underarm secretions from a group of men on swabs (Cutler et al., 1986). They then swabbed the secretions on the upper lips of seven women whose menstrual cycles were either short (under 26 days) or long (over 33 days). The female participants were told that they were receiving a "natural fragrance" that had been injected into alcohol. (Eight additional women in a control group received nothing but alcohol.) The study was double-blind—neither the participants nor the experimenters knew which participants were receiving the underarm secretions and which were receiving the control substance.

Within 3 months, the menstrual cycles of the seven experimental participants became similar; all moved toward the norm of 29.5 days. The researchers did another study, also double-blind, with secretions from other women (Preti et al., 1986). As in the first study, the women were swabbed on the upper lip with either underarm secretions or alcohol. The results were comparable. The times of menstruation became similar and approached the norm. The secretions affected the women's menstrual cycles; pheromones were causing the change.

One Problem, One Strength. A problem with the Cutler and Preti studies is that the researchers used a limited number of participants. The first study used 15 participants and the second 19. Because of this, the researchers were cautious in making generalizations. However, the studies were well designed. The results were highly regarded because the studies were double-blind, used an experimental method with control groups, and produced results that were statistically significant.

Implications. The Cutler and Preti studies suggest that the smell of other human beings affects physiological processes in women. They also indicate that pheromones emitted by a man may alter a woman's menstrual cycle. The data imply that women who live with men may have more regular cycles, and thus may be more fertile, than are those who live alone (see Cutler et al., 1986).

Other people's smells may affect women's physiological processes, but the evidence that smells affect human behavior is still suggestive. The effects of pheromones in animals are profound, but the role of pheromones in human beings remains controversial. Nevertheless, perfume makers have been sent into a frenzy of activity trying to make a perfume with pheromonelike capabilities. Is it reasonable for them to assert that perfumes, like pheromones, can attract members of the opposite sex? Probably not. Pheromones probably are not as powerful in human beings as they are in animals, because so many other environmental stimuli affect human behav ior, attitudes, and interpersonal relations.

Touch

The skin is more than just a binding that holds your body together. It acts as the housing for your *sense of touch*—your tactile system. The skin of an adult human being measures roughly 2 square yards and comprises three layers: the epidermis, the dermis, and the hypodermis. The top layer, the *epidermis* (*epi* means "outer," among other things), consists primarily of dead cells and varies in thickness. On the face it is thin; on the elbows and the heels of the feet it is quite thick. The epidermis is constantly regenerating; in fact, every 28 days or so, all of its cells are replaced. The layer underneath the epidermis—the *dermis (*from *derma,* or "skin")—contains live cells as well as a supply of nerve endings, blood, hair cells, and oil-producing (sebaceous) glands. The dermis and epidermis are resilient, flexible, and quite thick. They protect the body against quick changes in temperature and pressure, and the epidermis in particular guards against pain from small scratches, cuts, and bumps. The deepest layer—the *hypodermis* (*hypo* means "under")—is a thick, insulating cushion.

The specialized receptors for each of the skin senses—pain, touch, and temperature—vary in shape, size, number, and distribution. For example, the body has many more cold receptors than heat receptors; it has more pain receptors behind the knee than on the top of the nose. In the most sensitive areas of the hand, there are as many as 1,300 receptors per square inch.

The skin sense receptors appear to interact with one another; sometimes one sensation seems to combine with or change to another. Thus, increasing pressure can become pain. Similarly, an itch seems to result from a low-level irritation of nerve endings in the skin; however, a tickle can be caused by the same stimulus and produce a reflexlike response. Further, people are far more sensitive to pressure in some parts

FIGURE 3.23

Skin Receptors for Pain Are Not Distributed Evenly

(From Strughold, 1924.)

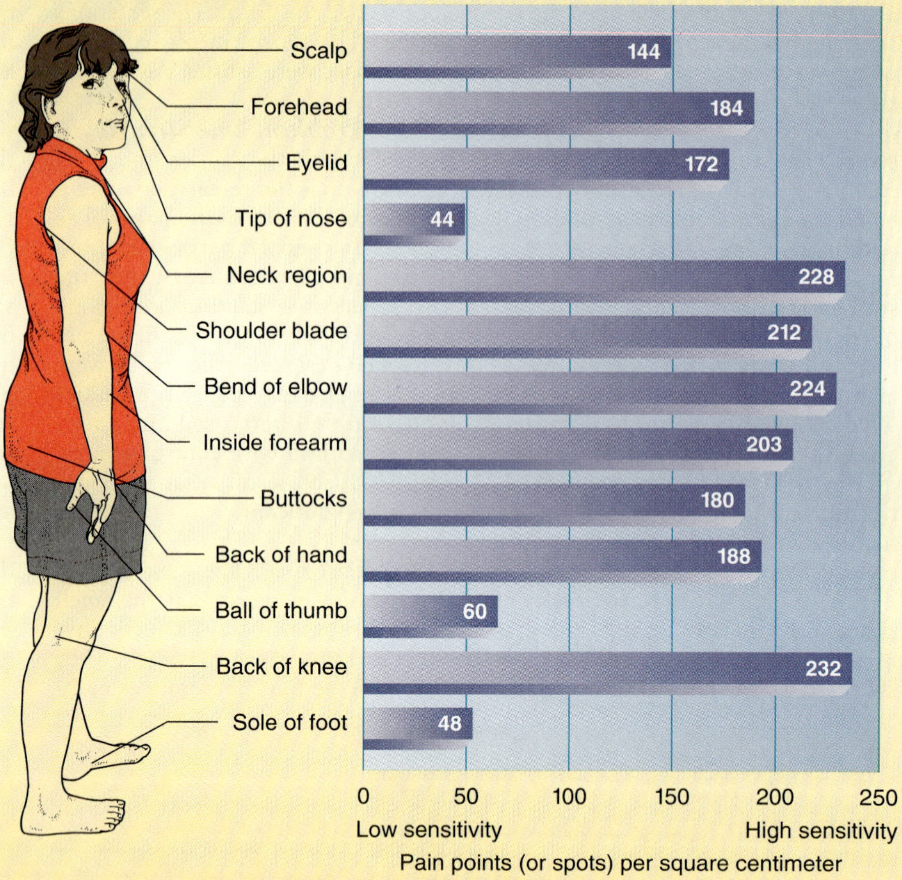

of their bodies than in other parts (compare your fingers to your thigh); the more sensitive areas have more receptors than do the less sensitive areas (see Figure 3.23).

Many of your determinations of how something feels are relative. When you say a stimulus is cold, you mean it is cold compared to normal skin temperature. When you say an object is warm, you mean it feels warmer than normal skin temperature. When you feel a child's head with the back of your hand and say the child has a fever, you are comparing normal skin temperature to a sick child's elevated skin temperature (and you wouldn't make such a determination immediately after coming in from a 20-degree Fahrenheit outdoor temperature).

Pain

Generally, people look forward to sensory experiences: new smells, sights, tastes, and sounds. One exception is pain; pain is a perceptual experience with particular negative qualities (Fernandez & Turk, 1992). Pain is the most common symptom found in medical settings; nevertheless, it is adaptive and necessary. In rare cases, children have been born without the ability to feel pain, which places them in constant danger. Their encounters with caustic substances, violent collisions, and deep cuts elicit no painful cautions to avoid such experiences. Further, they do not recognize serious conditions that would send most of us to the doctor for attention—for example, broken bones, deep burns, or the sharp pains that signal appendicitis.

Studying pain is difficult, because pain can be elicited in so many ways. For example, stomach pains may be caused by hunger or the flu, toothaches by a cavity or an abscess, and headaches by stress or eye strain. Myriad kinds of pain exist, including sunburn pain, pain from terminal cancer, labor pains, pain from frostbite, and even pain in a "phantom limb" lost as a result of trauma or surgery. Psychologists use several kinds of stimuli to study pain. Among them are chemicals, extreme heat and cold, and electric shock (Flor & Turk, 1989).

Most researchers believe the receptors for pain are free nerve endings located throughout the body. Some areas of the body are more sensitive to pain than others, however. For example, the sole of the foot and the ball of the thumb are less sensitive than the back of the knee and the neck. Also, though an individual's pain threshold remains fairly constant, different individuals possess different sensitivities to pain. Some people have a low threshold for pain; they will report a comparatively low-level stimulus as being painful. Others have fairly high pain thresholds.

However, the perception of pain is psychological, and much depends on a person's attitudes, previous experiences, and culture. For example, athletes often report not feeling the pain of an injury until after the competition has ended. Some cultures are more stoical about pain and teach individuals to endure individual suffering; in Western cultures, there is the widespread illusion that pain and suffering are ennobling (Berkowitz, 1993). Also, boys and girls within Western cultures are often taught to respond differently to pain.

What allows pain suppression? How does the body process, interpret, and stop pain? Gate control theory may offer an answer.

Gate Control Theory. One explanation of how the body processes pain is the Melzack–Wall gate control theory (Melzack & Wall, 1970). The theory is complex, taking into account the sizes of nerve fibers, their level of development, and the interplay of excitatory and inhibitory cells that can diminish painful sensations. The theory contends that when a signal that might normally indicate a painful stimulus is sent to the brain, it goes through a series of "gates." These gates can be opened either fully or partially or closed. How far they open determines how much of the original pain signal gets through. A chemical called substance P (standing for pain), which is released by the sensory nerve fibers, transmits pain impulses across the gates. Research support for gate control theory is sparse, although a variety of drugs, as well as electrical stimulation and acupuncture needles, are thought to close the gates, making the original painful stimulus less potent.

Many people who suffer chronic, unrelieved pain have sought help from acupuncture. Initially developed in China thousands of years ago, *acupuncture* is a technique in which long, slender needles are inserted into the body at specific locations in order to relieve particular kinds of pain. Controlled studies of acupuncture have yielded varying results. The National Institutes of Health have reported that acupuncture is ineffective; a few studies, however, have suggested that it helps with mild back pain (Price et al., 1984). Controlled research studies on the results of acupuncture are still inconclusive.

Endorphins. There have been some exciting breakthroughs in research on pain receptors and the nature of pain. Consider, for example, the study of endorphins. **Endorphins** (from *endogenous*, meaning "naturally occurring," and *morphine*, an opiate painkiller usually derived from opium) are painkillers that are produced naturally in the brain and the pituitary gland. There are many kinds of endorphins, and they help regulate several bodily functions, including the control of blood pressure and body temperature (Bloom, 1981). Endorphins also can produce euphoria and a sense of well-being in the way that morphine does, but to an even greater extent. Stress, anticipated pain, and engaging in athletic activities bring about an increased endorphin level. During and after running, runners often report experiencing a "runner's high," a sensation many believe is related to their increased endorphin level.

Endorphins [en-DOR-finz]: Painkillers produced naturally in the brain and pituitary gland.

Endorphins bind themselves to receptor sites in the brain and spinal cord, thereby preventing pain signals from going to higher levels of the nervous system. Naturally produced endorphins include some that increase tolerance to pain and others that actually reduce pain. *Enkephalin*, for example, is an innate brain endorphin that blocks pain signals (Snyder, 1980). Physicians prescribe synthetic endorphins or endorphinlike substances, such as morphine, to block pain.

Pain Management. Usually the pain resulting from a headache, toothache, or small cut is temporary and can be alleviated with a simple pain medication such as aspirin. For millions of people, however, aspirin is not enough. For those who suffer from constant pain caused by back injury, arthritis, or cancer, drug treatment either is not effective or is dangerous because of the high dosages required. Sometimes painkillers are not prescribed because of fear of addiction—in the case of pain relief, a fear that is often exaggerated by caring, well-meaning family and friends (Melzack, 1990). Further, each type of pain may require a different treatment (Flor & Turk, 1989).

New technologies are emerging to help people manage pain. Leaders in pain research reason that something must happen at the site of an injury to trigger endorphin production. What if a drug could stop the whole pain perception process at the actual place where an injury occurs? Researchers are studying the receptor sites in skin tissue and observing how chemicals bind to them. They hope to find compounds that will stop the entire pain perception process, even before endorphin production starts. The compounds they discover may not be total pain relievers; but in combination with other pain medications, such as aspirin, they may be effective.

Practitioners who deal with pain recognize that it can have both physical and psychological sources. Although pain may initially arise from physical complaints, it sometimes continues even after the physical cause abates because it provides other benefits to the sufferer (Fernandez & Turk, 1992). For example, pain may provide the sufferer with attention, which is reinforcing, or it may provide a distraction from other problems. Treatment focuses on helping people cope with pain regardless of its origins.

Hypnosis (which will be examined in more detail in Chapter 4) has been used to treat pain. Patients may be instructed to focus on other aspects of their lives and may be told that after the hypnotic session their pain will be more bearable. Hilgard and Morgan (1975) suggest that two-thirds of patients who are considered highly susceptible to suggestion can experience some relief of pain through hypnosis.

Anxiety and worry can make pain worse. People who suffer from migraine headaches, for example, often make their condition worse by becoming fearful when they feel a headache coming on. Researchers find that biofeedback training, which teaches people how to relax and cope more effectively, can help those who suffer from chronic pain and migraine headaches gain some relief (Nuechterlein & Holroyd, 1980). (Biofeedback will be discussed further in Chapter 4.) Other treatments, closely related to biofeedback, are cognitive coping strategies (discussed in Chapters 13 and 15). A poor or hopeless attitude can make pain worse. Cognitive coping strategies teach patients to have a better attitude about their pain. Patients learn to talk to themselves in positive ways, to divert attention to pleasant images, and to take an active role in managing their pain and transcending the experience.

Kinesthesis and the Vestibular Sense

If you are a dancer or an athlete, you rely mightily on your body to provide you with information about hand, arm, and leg movements. You try to keep your balance, be graceful, and move about with coordinated skill. Two of the sensory systems allow for skilled, accurate, and smooth movement—the often ignored, but vitally important, kinesthetic and vestibular systems.

The kinesthetic and vestibular systems allow these performers to make skilled, smooth movements by providing information about their bodily motion and orientation and their postural adjustment. ▶

Kinesthesis is the awareness aroused by movements of the muscles, tendons, and joints. It is what allows you to touch your finger to your nose with your eyes closed, leap over hurdles during a track-and-field event, and dance without stepping on your partner's feet. The study of kinesthesis provides information about bodily movements. The movements of muscles around your eye, for example, help let you know how far away objects are. Kinesthesia and your other internal sensations (such as an upset stomach) are *proprioceptive cues* (kinesthesia is sometimes called *proprioception*)—sensory cues coming from within your body and providing information about bodily movements and internal sensations.

The **vestibular sense** is the sense of bodily orientation and postural adjustment. It helps you keep your balance and sense of equilibrium. The structures essential to these functions are in the ear. Vestibular sacs and semicircular canals, which are associated with the body wall of the cochlea, provide information about the orientations of the head and body relative to the eye movement and posture systems (Parker, 1980). The vestibular sense allows you to walk on a balance beam without falling off, to know which way is up after diving into the water, and to sense that you are turning a corner when riding in a car, even when your eyes are closed.

Rapid movements of the head bring about changes in the semicircular canals. These changes induce eye movements to help compensate for head changes and changes in bodily orientation. They may also be accompanied by physical sensations ranging from pleasant dizziness to unbearable motion sickness. Studies of the vestibular sense help scientists understand what happens to people during space travel and under conditions of weightlessness.

Extrasensory Perception

Vision, hearing, taste, smell, touch, and even pain are all part of the normal sensory experience of human beings. Some people, however, claim there are other perceptual experiences that not all normal human beings recognize as such. People have been fascinated by *extrasensory perception* (*ESP*) for hundreds of years. The British Society for the Study of Psychic Phenomena has investigated reports of ESP since the 19th century. Early experimenters tested for extrasensory perception by asking participants to guess the symbols on what are now called ESP cards, each marked with a star, a cross, a circle, a square, or a set of wavy lines. One of the most consistently successful guessers once guessed 25 cards in a row, an event whose odds of happening by chance are nearly 300 quadrillion to 1.

ESP includes telepathy, clairvoyance, precognition, and psychokinesis. *Telepathy* is the transfer of thought from one person to another. *Clairvoyance* is the ability to recognize objects or events, such as the contents of a message in a sealed envelope, that are not present to normal sensory receptors. *Precognition* is unexplained knowl-

Kinesthesis [kin-iss-THEE-sis]: The awareness aroused by movements of the muscles, tendons, and joints.

Vestibular sense [ves-TIB-you-ler]: The sense of bodily orientation and postural adjustment.

FOCUS

Review

- Why are taste and smell called chemical senses? pp. 102–103
- What is the evidence that animal behavior is directly affected by pheromones? p. 104
- What are the most and least sensitive parts of the body? p. 105–106
- Why is the study of pain so complicated? p. 107

Think Critically

- Some individuals are born without a sense of smell. What effect would this have on their sense of taste, and why?
- Why do you think the study of endorphins might have relevance to your life?

edge about future events, such as knowing when the phone is about to ring. *Psychokinesis* is the ability to move objects by using only one's mental powers.

Experimental support for the existence of ESP is generally weak, and results have not been repeated very often. Moreover, ESP phenomena such as "reading people's minds" or bending spoons through mental power cannot be verified by experimental manipulations in the way that other perceptual events can be. In addition, the National Research Council has denounced the scientific merit of most of these experiments. None of these criticisms means that ESP does not exist, and active research using scientific methods continues. New techniques include the use of sophisticated electronic detection devices, and attempts to relate ESP phenomena to traditional psychology (as is common in nations of the former Soviet bloc) are underway. However, psychologists see so much trickery and falsification of data and so many design errors in experiments on this subject that they remain skeptical.

Summary and Review

The Perceptual Experience

How does the psychological study of perception help explain individuals' attending to and attaching meaning to stimuli?

- *Perception* is the process through which people attach meaning to sensory stimuli by means of complex processing mechanisms. Each perceptual system operates in a similar way; although all are different, they share common processes. pp. 72–73
- *Psychophysics* is the study of the relationship between physical stimuli and people's conscious experience of them. Psychophysical techniques allow researchers to study and approximate the *absolute threshold* the statistically determined minimum level of stimulation necessary to excite a perceptual system. pp. 73–74
- If a visual or auditory stimulus is presented so quickly or at such a low volume that a person cannot consciously perceive it, psychologists say that it is presented subliminally. Research on *subliminal perception* is controversial, and many researchers maintain that it can be explained in terms of such nonperceptual variables as motivation, previous experience, and unconscious or critical censoring processes. pp. 74–75
- The cocktail party phenomenon, whereby a person can hear his or her name spoken across a crowded and noisy room, is a basic finding of selective attention studies, which show that people have limited-capacity attentional abilities. p. 75
- Studies of sensory deprivation have shown that an organism's early experience is important in the development and proper functioning of its perceptual systems. Profound relaxation can occur in an extreme sensory-restricted environment. pp. 75–76

KEY TERMS

Sensation, p. 72
Perception, p. 72
Psychophysics, p. 73
Absolute threshold, p. 73
Signal detection theory, p. 73
Subliminal perception, p. 74

The Visual System

Describe the structures of the visual system.

- The main structures of the eye are the cornea, pupil, iris, lens, and retina. The retina is made up of 10 layers, of which the most important are the *photoreceptors,* the bipolar cells, and the ganglion cells. The axons of the ganglion cells make up the optic nerve. pp. 77–78

What is the duplicity theory of vision?

- The duplicity theory of vision states that rods and cones are structurally unique and are used to accomplish different tasks. That is, the two types of receptors have special functions and operate differently: Cones are specialized for color, day vision, and fine acuity, and rods are specialized for low light levels but lack color abilities and fine acuity abilities. pp. 79–80

What do receptive fields tell researchers about the perceptual process?

- *Receptive fields* are areas on the retina that, when stimulated, produce changes in the firing of cells in the visual system. Cells at the lateral geniculate nucleus and the *visual cortex* are called feature detectors, and some of them are highly specialized—for example, for motion or color. p. 82

What are the trichromatic and opponent-process theories of color vision?

- The three psychological characteristics of color are *hue, brightness,* and *saturation.* They correspond to the three physical characteristics of light: wavelength, intensity, and purity. Young and Helmholtz's *trichromatic theory* of color vision states that all colors can be made by mixing three basic colors and that the retina has three types of cones. Herring's *opponent-process theory* states that color is coded by a series of receptors that respond either positively or negatively to different wavelengths of light. pp. 83–85

KEY TERMS

Electromagnetic radiation, p. 77
Light, p. 77
Myopic, p. 77
Hyperopic, p. 77
Photoreceptors, p. 77
Transduction, p. 77
Visual cortex, p. 78
Dark adaptation, p. 80
Optic chiasm, p. 81
Receptive fields, p. 82
Saccades, p. 83
Hue, p. 84
Brightness, p. 84
Saturation, p. 84
Trichromatic theory, p. 85
Color blindness, p. 86
Opponent-process theory, p. 86
Trichromats, p. 86
Monochromats, p. 86
Dichromats, p. 86

Visual Perception

What is size constancy?

- *Size constancy* is the ability of the perceptual system to recognize that an object remains constant in size regardless of its distance from the viewer or the size of the retinal image. pp. 88–89

Explain how monocular and binocular depth cues help people see depth.

- The *monocular depth cues* include motion parallax, the kinetic depth effect, linear perspective, interposition, highlighting and shadowing, atmospheric perspective, and *accommodation.* The two primary *binocular depth cues* are *retinal disparity* and *convergence.* pp. 90–92

How do perceptual psychologists account for illusions?

- An *illusion* is a perception of a physical stimulus that differs from measurable reality and the commonly expected appearance; many consider an illusion to be a misperception of stimulation. pp. 92–93

What did the Gestalt psychologists contribute to the understanding of perception?

- According to a Gestalt idea called the *law of Prägnanz,* stimuli that *can* be grouped together and seen as a whole, or a form, *will* be seen that way. Using the law of Prägnanz as an organizing idea, Gestalt psychologists developed principles of organization for the perception of figures, especially figure–ground relationships. pp. 93–96

KEY TERMS

Size constancy, p. 88
Shape constancy, p. 89
Monocular depth cues, p. 90
Accommodation, p. 91
Binocular depth cues, p. 91
Retinal disparity, p. 91
Convergence, p. 92
Illusion, p. 92
Law of Prägnanz, p. 94

Hearing

What are the key characteristics of sound?

- *Sound* refers to changes in pressure passing through a gaseous, liquid, or solid medium—usually air. The *frequency* and *amplitude* of a sound wave determine in large part how a sound will be experienced by a listener. pp. 96–97

Describe the anatomy of the ear and how sound is processed.

- The ear has three main parts: the outer ear, the middle ear, and the inner ear. The eardrum (tympanic membrane) is the boundary between the outer ear and the middle ear. Tiny bones (ossicles) in the middle ear stimulate the basilar membrane in the cochlea, a tube in the inner ear. Place theories of hearing claim that the analysis of sound occurs in the inner ear; frequency theories claim that the analysis of pitch and intensity takes place at higher centers of processing. pp. 97–100
- Because you have two ears, you can locate the source of sound. A sound made to the left of the head will arrive at the left ear before the right. This creates an interaural time difference. In addition, a sound made to the left will be slightly more intense to the left ear than the right; thus, there is an interaural intensity difference. p. 100

Distinguish between conduction deafness and sensorineural deafness.

- *Conduction deafness* results from interference in the delivery of sound to the neural mechanism of the inner ear. *Sensorineural deafness* results from damage to the cochlea, the auditory nerve, or higher auditory processing centers. p. 101

KEY TERMS

Sound, p. 96
Frequency, p. 96
Pitch, p. 96
Amplitude, p. 97
Conduction deafness, p. 101
Sensorineural deafness, p. 101

Taste and Smell

Describe the anatomy of the tongue and how it allows for taste differences.

- The tongue contains thousands of bumps, or papillae, each of which is separated from the next by a "moat." The taste buds are located on the walls of these moats. Each taste bud consists of many taste cells. All taste cells are sensitive to all taste stimuli, but certain cells are more sensitive to some stimuli than to others. pp. 102–103

Why are taste and smell called chemical senses?

- For taste or smell to occur, chemicals must come into contact with the receptor cells. For the sense of smell, the receptors are located on the walls of the nasal passage. When a chemical substance in the air moves past these receptor cells, it is partially absorbed into the mucus that covers the cells, thereby initiating the process of smell. The olfactory epithelium contains the olfactory receptor cells—the nerve fibers that process odors and enable the individual to perceive smell. pp. 103–104

KEY TERM
Olfaction, p. 103

The Skin Senses

Describe the anatomy of the skin.

- The skin is made up of three layers. The top layer is called the epidermis. The layer underneath the epidermis is called the dermis. The deepest layer, called the hypodermis, is a thick insulating cushion. The skin sense receptors appear to interact with one another; sometimes one sensation seems to combine with or change to another. pp. 105–106

What is the most prominent theory of pain?

- A widely accepted explanation of how the body processes pain is the Melzack–Wall gate control theory. It suggests that when a signal that might normally indicate a painful stimulus is sent to the brain, it goes through a series of gates. These gates can be opened or closed, and how far they open determines how much pain signal gets through. This theory helps account for the fact that certain areas of the body are more sensitive to pain than others. p. 107

What are the body's naturally produced painkillers?

- *Endorphins* are painkillers that are naturally produced in the brain and pituitary gland. They help regulate several bodily functions, including blood pressure and body temperature. Stress, anticipated pain, and athletic activities bring about an increased endorphin level. p. 107–108

KEY TERM
Endorphins, p. 107

Kinesthesis and the Vestibular Sense

What sense involves the orientation of the entire body?

- *Kinesthesis* is the awareness that is aroused by movements of the muscles, tendons, and joints. One kinesthetic sense is the *vestibular sense*—the sense of bodily orientation and postural adjustment. This sense helps you keep your balance and sense of equilibrium. p. 109

KEY TERMS
Kinesthesis, p. 109
Vestibular sense, p. 109

Extrasensory Perception

Is there a "sixth sense"—ESP?

- ESP includes telepathy, clairvoyance, precognition, and psychokinesis. Experimental support for the existence of ESP is generally weak. Psychologists remain skeptical about ESP because they see so much trickery and falsification of data, as well as experimental design errors. pp. 109–110

Learning CONNECTIONS

Some students benefit from extra help with the concepts of vision and color perception. You can learn more about them in:

- The CD-ROM accompanying this book, Topic 3 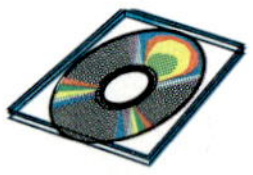
- This book's study guide, *Keeping Pace Plus*, or the computerized study guide, Chapter 3
- The audiotape accompanying this book, *SoundGuide for Psychology*, Learning Unit 3
- The study aids found on the World Wide Web site for this book, at http://www.abacon.com/psych/lefton

Critical Thinking CONNECTIONS

Take a moment to think critically about how this chapter's topics are connected with the rest of psychology . . .

If you are interested in . . .	Ask yourself . . .	Then turn to . . .
Sensory experiences in human beings 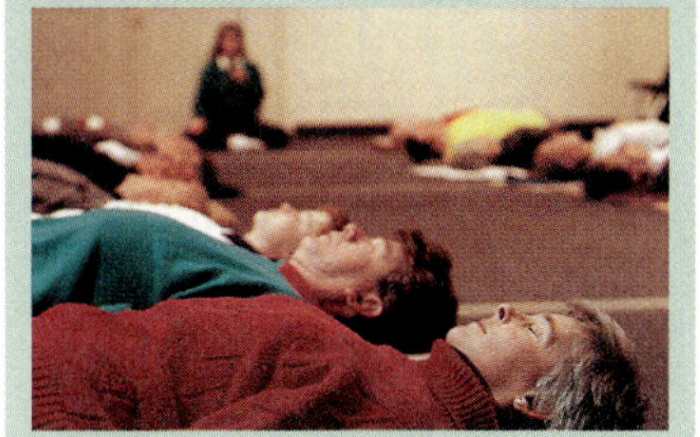	How might altered states of consciousness affect perception in ways that have positive and negative effects?	Chapter 4, pp. 117–118
	What is the impact of too much sensory input, such as noise?	Chapter 17, pp. 624–625
The development of perception 	How might experience alter a child's inborn perceptual abilities?	Chapter 10, pp. 347–350
	When and under what circumstances do sensory and perceptual abilities decline with advancing age?	Chapter 11, pp. 393–394, 400, 401
The operation of the perceptual systems 	How might feedback from perceptual systems help manage certain bodily ailments, such as headaches?	Chapter 4, pp. 130–131
	What are the implications of the finding that *initial* input from the visual and auditory world lasts for only a brief time in the brain?	Chapter 6, pp. 198–199
	What are the implications of the fact that our perceptions of other people often come from nonverbal visual cues in the environment?	Chapter 16, pp. 565–567

4

States of Consciousness

For many Americans, sleep deprivation is a way of life. For many people, mornings start before dawn and bedtime doesn't come until after midnight. In this society, "carrying a schedule" has become a necessity. The day is filled with events: exercise, work, a night class at the community college, aerobics class, shopping, housework, paying the bills. For high schoolers, there are also the requirements of homework, "obligatory" television (*Friends, The Real World, Melrose Place*), and phone contacts with friends. For child-rearing moms and dads, there are getting the kids off to school, driving them to after-school activities, overseeing their homework, and spending "quality time" with them and with each other. And in the downsizing era of the 1990s, this is all accompanied by the stresses of a work world filled with new demands, changing technology, and pressure to do more and more with fewer resources.

When they finally do get to bed, it's no wonder many people have trouble sleeping. Part of the problem is that their lives are filled with stress, irregular meals, and too few hours in which to relax. Along with the rest of the American work force, even college and high school students are working long hours, often at two jobs, and sleeping too little. Tired each morning, people take stimulants such as coffee for a quick jolt of energy. Then they stumble through the day, doing what has to be done. Unfortunately, accidents happen because of sleep deprivation: People fall asleep at the wheel; the oil spill from the *Exxon Valdez* resulted from sleep deprivation among its crew members. And the lack of sleep often causes people to make small mistakes, from missed appointments to typing errors.

Some people are lucky and need only 5 hours of sleep per night—but they are in the minority. Others have the ability to take an occasional "power nap" to revive themselves—but nap opportunities are rare, and in any case such naps work only for a small minority. Most people need 7 to 9 hours of sleep per night. To a great extent, when people are deprived of sleep their normal awareness and responsiveness are altered. Frequently the results of hectic lifestyles, irregular schedules, and use of stimulants create irritability, sleep problems, and strange, disturbing dreams. For these and other reasons, psychologists are interested in sleep, dreams, and alterations in consciousness. By studying sleep and how people move from one conscious state to another, researchers learn more about both individual and human capacities.

Consciousness

The study of consciousness has waxed and waned as a valid pursuit in psychology. Early psychologists, such as Wilhelm Wundt, studied little else but the content of consciousness; later psychologists, such as William James, studied how consciousness operates. But in the 1920s behaviorists, such as John B. Watson, argued that consciousness should be eliminated as a subject of psychological study—because it is not a physical structure that can be examined, probed, or diagrammed. As the behavioral approach came to dominate American psychology, the study of consciousness and thought was all but forgotten. In the free-spirited 1960s and 1970s, however, cognitive psychology emerged as a subdiscipline in its own right, investigating thought, perception, memory, and how they all are interwoven. Consciousness became a viable topic again. The tide had clearly turned; today, consciousness—like other areas of cognitive psychology—is a topic of strong scientific and popular interest.

Defining Consciousness

Almost all psychologists agree that a person who is conscious is aware of the environment; for example, you are conscious when you listen to a lecture (or so your instructor hopes). However, consciousness also refers to inner awareness—knowledge of one's own thoughts, feelings, and memories.

When early psychologists studied the mind and its contents, they were studying consciousness. Wundt and his students in the late 1880s had research participants report the contents of their consciousness while sitting still, while working, and while falling asleep. These were probably fairly boring and unremarkable accounts. At the turn of the century, Sigmund Freud (whom we will study in more depth later) made the study of consciousness quite a bit more interesting. He wrote that deep within a person's consciousness are needs, wishes, and desires that influence feelings and behavior. According to Freud, people have different levels of consciousness—conscious thoughts of which they are aware, as well as unconscious thoughts of which they are unaware.

Today, cognitive psychologists assert that people are aware of certain mental processes and unaware of others. For example, when you drive along a very familiar route, you may suddenly realize that you drove three miles of highway completely unaware of what you passed. You know the route so well that you drove automatically (unconsciously). Cognitive psychologists generally do not speak about the unconscious but instead refer to controlled (deliberate) versus automatic processes. All of these psychologists—the early structuralists, Freud, and today's cognitive researchers—acknowledge that different *levels* of consciousness exist.

As you can see, each view of conscious behavior depends on a person's orientation to psychology. Rather than taking a specific point of view, let's agree to define **consciousness** as the general state of being aware of and responsive to events in the environment, including one's own mental processes.

Consciousness can be seen as a process or a continuum—ranging from the sort of alert attention required to read this textbook to dreaming, hypnosis, or drug-induced states. Following this view of consciousness, a person who does not pay attention or is not alert is not as "conscious" as one who is vigilant and alert. The idea of a continuum of awareness guides many researchers who believe that consciousness is made up of several *levels* of awareness, from alertness to total unresponsiveness. Researchers who favor this view suggest, for example, that a person who is drinking heavily enters, temporarily, a lower (deeper) *level* in the range of conscious levels—that of intoxication. A person who is asleep has pretty much "turned off" consciousness (Hobson, 1994).

▲ *Cognitive psychologists acknowledge that people exhibit different levels of consciousness in their daily lives. For example, when you first learn to ride a bicycle, you are very conscious of every movement. However, once you become an accomplished cyclist, the actions become automatic and unconscious.*

A person who is in a state of consciousness that is dramatically different from ordinary awareness and responsiveness is in an **altered state of consciousness**. Researchers who study altered states often believe that distinctly different conscious *states* explain specific behaviors and attention patterns. Researchers who favor such interpretations believe a heavy drinker has entered a totally different *state* of consciousness. The issue of levels versus states is far from resolved.

Consciousness and the ongoing biological processes in our bodies are closely linked; our biological processes influence how incoming stimuli affect us and our degree of awareness about the world. Thus, as Crick and Koch (1992) argue, perceiving the world and being conscious are constructive processes in which new stimulation, past experience, and an active brain that is attempting to make sense of the world all take part. The study of consciousness has not usually taken into account people's cultural expectations for how the world should look or how the world has generally been experienced. Conscious experiences are often so automatic that the effects of culture often seem routine and habitual; they are experienced with little or no thought.

Theories of Consciousness

As in other areas of psychology, theory guides research in the study of consciousness and its levels or altered states. Several researchers have proposed biologically based theories of consciousness in which understanding the evolution of the human brain is key to understanding consciousness (Jaynes, 1976). Jaynes believes that consciousness (a relatively new phenomenon in the history of humankind) originates in differences in the function and physiology of the two hemispheres of the brain and has emerged based on that architecture (see the discussion in Chapter 2). The human brain, with its two-hemisphere organization, operates on different tasks in different ways with different parts of the brain—some tasks are left-hemisphere tasks, some right-hemisphere. Thus, when the left hemisphere of the brain (often presumed to be language oriented) is operating, one specific kind or level of consciousness will be activated; when the right hemisphere (often presumed to be spatially oriented) is operating, another level will be activated.

Robert Ornstein (1977), in an alternative theory using physiology, suggests that two modes of consciousness exist, each controlled by its own side of the brain.

Consciousness: The general state of being aware of and responsive to events in the environment, including one's own mental processes.

Altered state of consciousness: A state of consciousness that is dramatically different from that of ordinary awareness and responsiveness.

These are the active-verbal-rational mode (called the active mode) and the receptive-spatial-intuitive-holistic mode (called the receptive mode). Ornstein believes evolution has made the active mode automatic; this is the "default," or normal, mode of operation for human beings. Human beings limit their awareness automatically in order to shut out experiences, events, and stimuli that do not directly relate to their ability to survive. When people need to gain perspective and judgment about what they are doing, however, they can expand their normal awareness by using the receptive mode. According to Ornstein, techniques such as meditation, biofeedback, hypnosis, and even the use of certain drugs can help people learn to use the receptive mode, as their primitive ancestors did, to balance the active mode.

Ornstein and his collaborator, David Galin, support many of their ideas with laboratory data showing that the brain is divided and specialized in significant ways. They point out that the left-dominated and the right-dominated modes of consciousness operate in a complementary and alternating fashion, one working while the other is inhibited (Galin, 1974; Ornstein, 1976). In Ornstein's (1977) model, intellectual activities take place in the active, or left-dominated, mode; and intuitive activities take place in the receptive, or right-dominated, mode. The integration of these two modes underlies the highest human accomplishments. Although the existence of two physiological modes of operation in the brain lends support to Ornstein's ideas (Luck et al., 1994), many researchers are skeptical of his theory (Zaidel, 1983). They argue that the structure of the brain does not necessarily explain its function and that insufficient data exist to show how the brain actually operates.

Among the newest explanations of consciousness are those from Daniel Dennett (1991) and Richard Restak (1994). In his best-selling book *Consciousness Explained*, Dennett asserts that human beings possess many sources of information, which together create a conscious experience. He argues that the brain creates multiple drafts (copies) of experiences, which are constantly being reanalyzed. According to Dennett, the brain develops a sense of consciousness as well as a sense of self (which is made up of multiple copies of past experiences) through this constant updating and reanalysis of experience. The theory is as yet untested, is not widely accepted, and has been criticized (Mangan, 1993); however, it takes a new path in bringing together perceptual, physiological, and historical information in one individual to explain consciousness. Such ideas are supported by the arguments of neurologist Restak, who asserts in his book *The Modular Brain* that it is the brain's various modules, sections, or parts that control behavior. Consciousness is not centrally organized but rather is controlled by these modules; lose a module through a car crash or a sports accident and you will lose certain, but not all, key abilities.

Regardless of what theory may explain it, being conscious means being self-aware; and because people are aware, they are able to tell researchers about their experiences. Psychologists can also study consciousness by measuring some specific physiological functions. In the remainder of this chapter, we will focus on a wide array of states of consciousness. Some of these states are desirable and normal; others alter human behavior in less desirable ways. We begin with a very familiar state of consciousness—sleep.

FOCUS

Review

- What are the key characteristics of a definition of consciousness? pp. 116–117
- Explain the theory that two modes of consciousness exist, each controlled by one side of the brain. pp. 117–118

Think Critically

- The differences between levels and states of consciousness may seem slight to you. To help differentiate them, pick one and make a case for it.
- Take a few minutes to jot down the contents of your consciousness right now. What would happen if loud music had been playing while you did this compared to soft background music?

Sleep

In January 1964, at age 17, Randy Gardner made history. He set a world's record by staying awake for more than 260 hours—just short of 11 days. A science fair near his San Diego home was the location of his experiment. He enlisted two friends to help keep him awake, and he took no stimulants, not even coffee. After 6 days, a local physician came to supervise Gardner's progress, much to the relief of his parents. Although he did not suffer any serious physical symptoms, there were marked psychological effects. On day 2, he had trouble focusing his eyes. On day 3, there were mood changes. On day 4, he was irritable and uncooperative; he also began to see images. By day 6, Gardner had speech difficulties and memory lapses. By day 9, his thoughts and speech were incoherent. On day 10, blurred vision became more of a problem and he was regularly forgetting things. Mornings were his most difficult time, but at no time did he behave in a socially deviant manner.

One of the most interesting aspects of Randy Gardner's adventure is what happened to his sleep after his deprivation. Sleep researcher William Dement followed Gardner's sleep, mental health, physical recovery, and electroencephalogram results for days afterward. He wanted to see how Gardner recovered, what happened to his sleep patterns, and whether he made up for lost sleep. Dement found that for the 3 nights following his deprivation, Gardner slept an extra 6.5 hours; and to further aid his recovery on the 4th night, he slept an extra 2.5 hours (Gulevich, Dement, & Johnson, 1966; Johnson, Slye, & Dement, 1965).

These studies of Randy Gardner's sleep loss and his subsequent recovery are part of the history of the study of sleep. Early researchers such as Dement began to realize that sleep and wakefulness follow specific patterns, which can be tracked and predicted. They noted that as you move through the day, your general awareness—responsiveness, thought processes, and physiological responses—changes. On first waking, you may not be fully aware and responsive. You move sluggishly, slow to realize that the coffee is perking and your toast is burning. Later, at a job or in class, you are probably very alert. But as the day wears on, you find your awareness decreasing; and in the evening you may fall asleep in front of the television. Research on sleep is one part of the larger puzzle of human awareness, human consciousness, and altered states of being.

The Sleep–Wakefulness Cycle: Circadian Rhythms

In the casinos of Las Vegas, it is difficult to tell night from day. There are no windows, activity is at fever pitch 24 hours a day, and there are few clocks. People never seem to sleep; it is as if there *is* no day or night. Nevertheless, people do sleep; unlike Randy Gardner, they give in to their bodily urge to rejuvenate themselves. Their bodies tell them they are tired even if there is no clock on the wall to give a reminder. Humans are not at the mercy of light and darkness to control their activities, but seem instead to have an internal biological clock ticking to control the sleep–wakefulness cycle. This clock seems to run in about a 24-hour cycle; thus, the term *circadian* was born—from the Latin *circa diem* ("around a day"). **Circadian rhythms** are internally generated patterns of body functions, including hormonal signals, sleep, blood pressure, and temperature regulation, which have an approximate 24-hour cycle and occur even when normal day and night cues are removed.

Human beings are sensitive to light, which helps keep their biological clocks in sync (Boivin et al., 1996). However, when time cues (clocks, windows, temperature changes as the sun goes down) are removed from the environment for a long time, an interesting event occurs—circadian rhythms run a bit slow. When human beings

Circadian rhythms [sir-KAY-dee-an]: Internally generated patterns of body functions, including hormonal signals, sleep, blood pressure, and temperature regulation, which have an approximate 24-hour cycle and occur even when normal day and night cues are removed.

are placed in artificially lit environments and allowed to sleep, eat, and read whenever they want to, they sleep a constant amount of time; but each "day" they go to sleep a bit later (Foster, 1993). This is because the full sleep–wakefulness cycle runs about 24.5 to 25.5 hours. Body temperature and other bodily functions tend to follow a similar circadian rhythm.

Because you have daylight, clocks, and arbitrary schedules, however, your circadian rhythms alone do not control sleep and wakefulness. You can see the impact of circadian rhythms when your routine is thrown off by having to work through the night, then sleep, then rise, and so forth—your body's clock may not match your work clock. This disruption becomes especially apparent if you are an airline pilot, a surgeon, or a firefighter—one of the approximately 7 million Americans who work at night (Czeisler et al., 1990). When you put in long hours that stretch through the night and into the dawn, and when these hours are not regular, you become less attentive, think less clearly, and may even fall asleep from time to time. Thus, employers, workers, and consumers need to be aware of the potential decreased efficiency of night workers who vary their schedules, especially airline pilots and medical interns.

▲ *Approximately 7 million Americans work at night. Workers such as shift workers, airline pilots, and firefighters, whose schedules are not regular, may become less attentive and efficient as a result of sleep deprivation. In some cases, this can be dangerous, and employers need to be aware of and try to minimize the danger to their employees and the general public.*

Consider the air traveler's common problem—jet lag. If you travel from, say, New York City to London, England, the trip will take about 6 hours. If you leave at 9:00 P.M., you will arrive in London 6 hours later, at 3:00 A.M.—at least as far as your body is concerned. It seems very late at night. But local London time is 8:00 A.M. You are exhausted; people meeting you may want to chat and catch up on gossip or business. You finally go to bed and sleep, but your body still has to adjust. You experience exhaustion and disorientation, a set of feelings referred to as *jet lag*. You may want to sleep during the day and stay up at night. If you are experiencing jet lag or if you work long, irregular shifts, your work performance may not be at its peak. Psychologists have learned this through studying sleep, the sleep–wakefulness cycle, and sleep deprivation.

Sleep: A Restorative Process

Sleep is a natural state of consciousness experienced by everyone. **Sleep** is a nonwaking state of consciousness characterized by general unresponsiveness to the environment and general physical immobility. Some psychologists think sleep allows the body to recover from the day's expenditure of energy; they see it as a restorative process. Others perceive sleep as a holdover from a type of hibernation. They believe an organism conserves energy during sleep, when its expenditure would be inefficient (night is not a good time for animals to catch or produce food). Still others see sleep as a time when the brain recovers from exhaustion and overload. They believe sleep has little effect on basic physiological processes in the rest of the body. Horne (1988) asserts that sleep can be divided into two major types: core and optional. *Core sleep* repairs the effects of waking wear and tear on cerebral functions; it is thus restorative. *Optional sleep* fills the time from the end of core sleep until waking. These views of sleep—as physical restoration, hibernation, brain restoration, and core repairs—guide researchers' investigations into sleep patterns.

Sleep: Nonwaking state of consciousness characterized by general unresponsiveness to the environment and general physical immobility.

Why do some people need more sleep than others? Most people require about 8 hours, but some can function with only 4 or 5 hours, while others need as many as 9 or 10. Young teenagers tend to sleep longer than college students, and elderly people tend to sleep less than young people. Most young adults (65 percent) sleep between 6.5 and 8.5 hours a night, and about 95 percent sleep between 5.5 and 9.5

hours (Horne, 1988). Do you think people who are active and energetic require more sleep than those who are less active? Surprisingly, this is not always the case. Bedridden hospital patients, for example, sleep about the same amount of time as people who are on their feet all day. The amount of sleep a person needs is physiologically determined and depends greatly on sleep cycles.

Sleep Cycles and Stages: REM and NREM Sleep

The sleep–wakefulness cycle is repetitive, determined in part by circadian rhythms, work schedules, and a host of other events. When early sleep researchers such as Nathaniel Kleitman and William Dement studied the sleep–wakefulness cycle, they found stages within sleep that could be characterized through **electroencephalograms (EEGs)**—records of electrical brain patterns—and by eye movements that occur during sleep. Researchers working in sleep laboratories study the EEG patterns that occur in the brain during sleep by attaching electrodes to a participant's scalp and forehead and monitoring the person's brain waves throughout the night. Portable devices now allow the recording of brain waves throughout the day as well (Broughton, 1991).

Recordings of the brain waves of sleeping participants have revealed that during an 8-hour period, people typically progress through five full cycles of sleep (see Figure 4.1 on page 122). A full sleep cycle lasts approximately 90 minutes. We characterize the first four stages within a cycle as **no rapid eye movement (NREM) sleep**. The fifth stage is **rapid eye movement (REM) sleep**—a stage of sleep characterized by high-frequency, low-voltage brain-wave activity, rapid and systematic eye movements, and dreams. When people first fall asleep, they are in stage 1; their sleep is light, and they can be awakened easily. Within the next 30 to 40 minutes, they pass through stages 2, 3, and 4. Stage 4 is very deep sleep; when participants leave that stage, they pass again through stage 3 and then 2 (both are described in the following paragraph) on their way to REM sleep.

The descent into stage 4 sleep may take 40 minutes or longer; then a curious event occurs. People move back through stages 3, 2, and sometimes stage 1 and then nearly awaken when they go into REM sleep for about 10 minutes. Breathing and heart rate increase, eye movements become rapid, imagery becomes vivid, and other physiological excitement occurs. Also, the longer people sleep (and the more sleep cycles they go through), the more REM sleep they experience (Agnew & Webb, 1973; Barbato et al., 1994). Figure 4.1 shows the distinctive brain-wave patterns of wakefulness, the four stages of NREM sleep, and REM sleep in a normal adult. The waking pattern exhibits a fast, regular rhythm. In stage 1, sleep is light; the brain waves are of low amplitude (height) but are relatively fast, with mixed frequencies. Sleepers in stage 1 can be awakened easily. Stage 2 sleep shows low-amplitude, nonrhythmic activity combined with special patterns called sleep spindles and K complexes. A *sleep spindle* is a rhythmic burst of brain waves that wax and wane for 1 or 2 seconds. A *K complex* is a higher-amplitude burst of activity seen in the last third of stage 2. Sleep spindles and K complexes appear only during NREM sleep. Sleepers in stage 2 are in deeper sleep than those in stage 1 but can still be easily awakened. Stage 3 sleep is a transitional stage between stages 2 and 4, with slower but higher-amplitude activity than at stage 2. Stage 4 sleep, the deepest sleep stage, has even higher-amplitude brain-wave traces, called *delta waves*. During this stage, people breathe deeply and have slowed heart rate and lowered blood pressure. Stage 4 sleep has two well-documented behavioral characteristics. First, people are difficult to awaken. People awakened from stage 4 sleep often appear confused and disturbed and take several seconds to rouse themselves fully. Second, people in this stage generally do not dream, although they may report some vague mental activity.

Electroencephalogram (EEG) [eel-ECK-tro-en-SEFF-uh-low-gram]: Record of an organism's electrical brain patterns, obtained through electrodes placed on the organism's scalp.

No rapid eye movement (NREM) sleep: Four distinct stages of sleep during which no rapid eye movements occur.

Rapid eye movement (REM) sleep: Stage of sleep characterized by high-frequency, low-voltage brain-wave activity, rapid and systematic eye movements, and dreams.

FIGURE 4.1

EEG Activity during Sleep

EEGs show distinctive and characteristic patterns for the wakeful state, REM sleep, and each of the four NREM sleep stages. Most people complete about five sleep cycles per night.

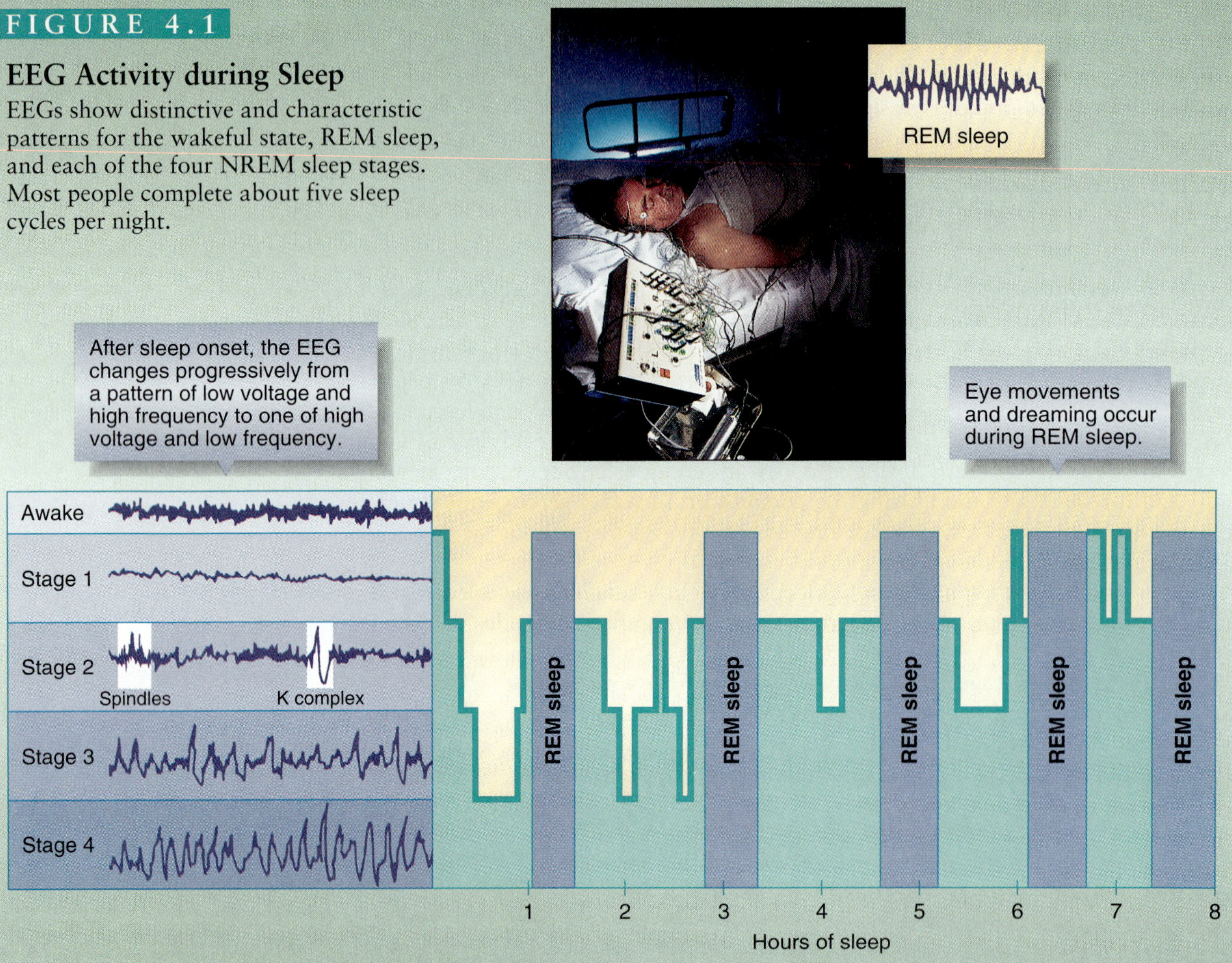

In contrast, research participants who are awakened during REM sleep can report in great detail the imagery and mental activity that are characteristic of a dream state. Because REM sleep is considered necessary for normal physiological functioning and behavior, it might be expected to be a deep sleep; however, it is an active sleep, during which the brain-wave activity resembles that of an aware person (see the pattern at the upper right in Figure 4.1). For this reason, REM sleep is often called *paradoxical sleep*. In REM sleep, participants seem agitated; their eyes move and their heart rate and breathing are variable. Participants are difficult to awaken during REM sleep.

In an EEG recorded during a transition from NREM stage 2 sleep to REM sleep, the first part of the tracing would show a clear K complex, indicating stage 2 sleep; the last part would show waves characteristic of REM sleep. Researchers can identify the stage in which an individual is sleeping by watching an EEG recording. If delta waves are present, the participant is in stage 4 sleep. To confirm this, an experimenter may awaken the participant and ask whether he or she was dreaming.

Sleep cycles develop before birth, and they continue to change into adulthood. Initially, sleeping fetuses show no eye movements. Later, they show eye, facial, and bodily movements. Newborns spend a little less than half their sleep time in REM sleep. From age 1 to age 10, the ratio of REM sleep to stage 4 sleep decreases dra-

FIGURE 4.2

Changes in Sleep Patterns over a Lifetime

Children spend more time in REM sleep than do adults; the proportion of time spent in REM sleep decreases every year. Non-REM sleep accounts for more than half of a newborn's sleep time. In adulthood, 80 to 85 percent of sleep time is non-REM sleep.

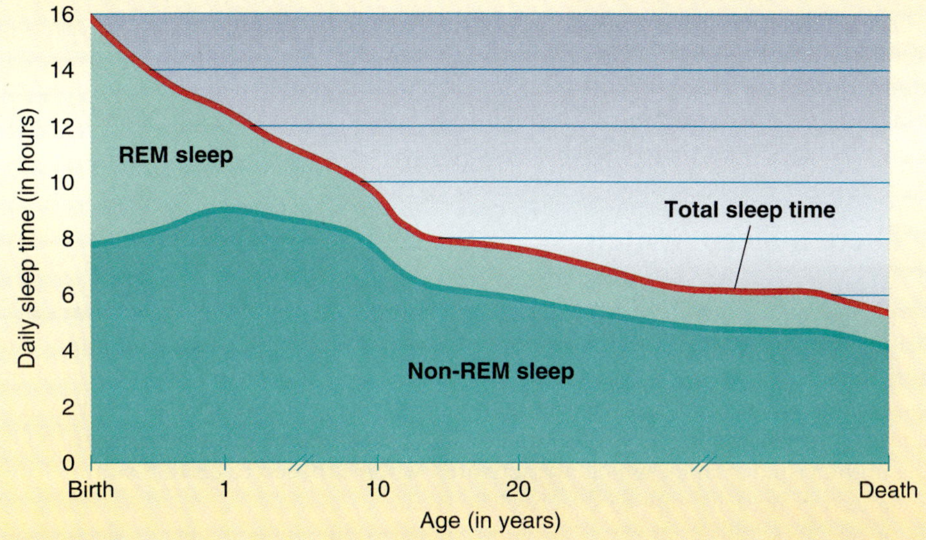

matically; in later adulthood, there is increased fragmentation of sleep patterns (see Figure 4.2).

Sleep Deprivation: Doing without REM

The need for sleep is painfully obvious to anyone who has been deprived of it. Just ask Randy Gardner, who went without sleep for close to 11 days. When people who normally sleep 8 hours miss a few hours on a particular night, they may be tired the following day but can function quite well. However, when people lose a couple hours of sleep for several nights in a row, they often look tired, feel lethargic, and are irritable.

Researchers have investigated what happens to people who are totally or partially deprived of sleep for various amounts of time. The research is generally conducted on laboratory participants who sleep in a sleep laboratory, where their brain-wave activity and eye movements are recorded for several nights. One study deprived participants of all sleep for 205 hours (8.5 days). Researchers found that on the nights immediately after the experiment, participants spent a greater-than-normal amount of time in REM and stage 4 sleep and the least amount of time in stages 1 and 2—the lightest stages of sleep (Kales et al., 1970; Webb & Agnew, 1975). Similar results were obtained in a study in which participants were partially deprived of REM sleep by being awakened when they showed rapid eye movements. They reported feeling sleepy and spent more time in REM sleep on a subsequent night (Dement, Greenberg, & Klein, 1966). According to Horne (1988), only about 30 percent of lost sleep needs to be recovered, mostly stage 4 sleep and REM sleep.

What happens to participants who are regularly deprived of REM sleep? They become anxious and irritable, report difficulty concentrating, and do worse than normal on tests that involve attention and original responses (May & Kline, 1987). As soon as the participants are allowed to have REM sleep again, these psychological ill effects disappear (e.g., Roehrs et al., 1989). Some researchers used to believe that serious disruptions of personality might occur as a result of prolonged REM sleep deprivation. But today it is known that serious maladjustments do not occur with sleep deprivation (Bonnet, 1980). With the exception of brain function effects, especially in the cortex, mild sleep deprivation has surprisingly few effects on the rest of the body (Harrison & Horne, 1996). Even more important, any changes in cerebral functions that do take place with sleep deprivation are quickly reversed after later sleep (Horne, 1988). We saw this in the case of Randy Gardner, who exhibited normal sleep patterns after his deprivation. Some people seem to be able to fall asleep at will—almost as though they had a "sleep switch." Some evidence seems to suggest that there is such a switch.

Is There a Sleep Switch?

If you find yourself in a theater that's a little too hot, watching a film that's a bit boring, after a night in which you haven't had quite enough sleep, you might suddenly doze off. Is there a physiological structure that regulates and initiates sleep? Researchers are now suggesting that there may be certain cells deep within the brain that are "turned on" in such situations, while other brain cells are "shut off." Like cells in the visual system, which are activated when exposed to certain stimuli, these specialized brain cells may be selectively active.

Sherin and colleagues (1996) found that when rats were in various sleep stages, cells in their brains seemed to turn on or off depending on the stage. The specific area of the brain in which these cells are located is the front region of the hypothalamus, called the *ventrolateral preoptic area*, or the VLPO. In rats that were deprived of sleep for 9 to 12 hours, the researchers found that a certain protein was present throughout most of the brain but not in the VLPO; in contrast, in rats that were not sleep-deprived, the protein was found in the VLPO but not in the rest of the brain. According to these researchers, this very small area of the brain may constitute a subpopulation of sleep-controlling cells, whose actions determine the organism's state of consciousness.

In humans, there are about 30,000 cells in the VLPO, which produce neurotransmitters that inhibit the firing of other brain cells. In addition, these VLPO cells have connections with other nearby groups of specialized cells. They are thus strategically placed in the chain of neurological events to initiate or inhibit sleep. The VLPO may modulate all of the neurotransmitters involved in wakefulness, arousal, and consciousness—and thus may indeed be the locus of a "sleep switch."

Of course, rats are not human beings, but the physiological processes of rats and humans have shown many parallels. Whether the VLPO, alone or along with some other center near it, is in fact some kind of master switching mechanism has yet to be determined. Researchers are investigating this hypothesis, looking for alternative explanations, and sorting through the implications for people suffering from sleep disorders as well as those experiencing problems related to jet lag and irregular work schedules.

Sleep Disorders

Do you have trouble falling asleep, snore so loudly that you keep others awake, sleepwalk, or fall asleep at inappropriate times, such as when driving a car? You may have a sleep disorder. People who fall asleep suddenly and unexpectedly have a disorder known as *narcolepsy*. Narcolepsy is probably a symptom of an autonomic nervous system disturbance resulting in lowered arousal, but it may also reflect neurochemical problems (Mamelak, 1991). It is relatively rare, affecting only about 1 in 1,000 people.

Another sleep disorder, *sleep apnea*, causes airflow to stop for at least 15 seconds, so the person ceases breathing. People with this disorder often have as many as 100 apnea episodes in a night; during the day, they are exceedingly sleepy and sometimes have memory losses. People with severe apnea may have work-related accidents and severe headaches, and they may fall asleep during the day. Drug therapy and some minor surgical techniques for creating better airflow have been used to treat those with sleep apnea—and also may relieve the loud snoring that accompanies the disorder. Monitoring equipment for prolonged breathing pauses has also been used to wake the sleeper (Sheridan, 1985). Sleep apnea affects about 40 in 1,000 individuals, but males are more likely than females to suffer from it (Ingbar & Gee, 1985). Sleep apnea has also been proposed as a possible explanation for sudden infant death syndrome (SIDS), in which infants die suddenly during sleep for no obvious reason. Alcohol and other central nervous system depressant drugs often contribute to sleep apnea in adults.

Insomnia, a prolonged inability to sleep, is a very common sleep disorder, often caused by anxiety or depression; 1 in 10 people report suffering from it at some time in their lives. Sleep disturbances and insomnia are especially common among older adults (Prinz et al., 1990). Insomniacs tend to be listless and tired during the day and may use sleeping pills or other drugs to induce sleep at night. Ironically, researchers have found that these drugs do not induce natural sleep; instead, they reduce the proportion of REM sleep (Webb & Agnew, 1975). (Recall that the body's normal response to sleep deprivation is to *increase* REM sleep.) Researchers such as Dement have found that lack of REM sleep may alter normal behavior; accordingly, people with chronic insomnia should not regularly use drugs that force sleep. Various researchers have proposed behavioral methods that do not rely on drugs to help solve the problem; among these methods are relaxation training, thought restructuring, and self-hypnosis (e.g., Morin et al., 1994). Vitiello (1989) asserts that diet affects sleep by affecting sympathetic nervous system activity, which may stimulate people in the middle of the night. Research on diet and insomnia is still in its early stages. But since diet affects mood and sleepiness, this idea does have experimental support, as is discussed in *Applications* on page 126.

Night terrors, another sleep disorder, consist of panic attacks that occur within an hour after a person falls asleep. Sitting up abruptly in a state of sheer panic, a person with a night terror may scream, breathe quickly, and be in a total state of fright. Night terrors are especially common in young children between the ages of 3 and 8. They usually disappear as a child grows older and do not seem to be a symptom of any psychological disorder. The cause of night terrors is not fully established, but they may be due to electrochemical processes overloading during NREM sleep.

In *sleepwalking*, a disorder that tends to run in families, an individual appears both asleep and awake at the same time. Sleepwalking is common among children. A sleepwalking child may reach out to a parent for a hug, navigate a darkened room, avoid a piece of furniture, walk into the street, or seem to be trying to accomplish a task—yet still be asleep. More boys sleepwalk than girls, and children who sleepwalk tend to outgrow it as they mature. Brain activity of sleepwalkers, when recorded with an EEG, shows stage 4 sleep. Research shows that different parts of a sleepwalker's brain display different levels of activity: Motor portions of the brain, lower levels, are active; cognitive portions of the brain, upper levels, are deeply asleep. Contrary to popular belief, there is no danger in waking a sleepwalker. More likely, you may not be able to wake the sleepwalking individual because he or she is so deeply asleep (Hobson, 1994).

Sleep disorders probably have several origins and will require the development of a research methodology, a theory, and a set of treatment plans that reflect the complexity of the problem. To date, no single approach has been found to be universally successful.

Insomnia: Prolonged inability to sleep.

APPLICATIONS

Melatonin—A Drug That Induces Sweet Dreams, Quickly?

If you were a drug researcher seeking a new drug that could make you a billionaire, you might be looking for a drug that has the effect of melatonin. Melatonin induces a sweet and easy sleep without side effects, even among people with insomnia.

Melatonin is a hormone normally released by the pineal gland at the base of the brain. This hormone is involved in helping keep the biological clock in sync, among other things; melatonin levels in a person's bloodstream vary when the amount of light in the person's environment changes (Mishima et al., 1994) and when circadian rhythms are disturbed (Dollins et al., 1993; Härmä et al., 1993). But new research shows that melatonin given in small doses to human beings induces sleep—quickly, easily, even in midday. Richard Wurtman of the Massachusetts Institute of Technology has reported that, given in very small doses, the hormone is a sleep inducer without sleeping pill side effects such as feeling hungover and losing REM sleep (Dollins et al., 1993). Melatonin has proved especially effective in the treatment of sleep disorders (Jan, Espezel, & Appleton, 1994) and for jet lag (Brown, 1994).

Researchers are not sure how melatonin works. It may fool the body into thinking that it is night. It may act on other brain centers. It may affect other natural sleep-inducing hormones. What researchers know is that people who take melatonin in small doses have less trouble sleeping. Currently it is available as a nutritional supplement, not yet as a prescription drug.

Should you take melatonin? Probably not. As a critical thinker, you have to be wary of unproven drugs. Clinical trials with double-blind procedures have yet to be conducted. Dosage levels are untested. Researchers do not know how the hormone affects old people compared with younger ones. Do men and women respond differently? (There is reason to believe that they do.) What about older men versus younger women? Does the drug have any long-term side effects? The potential of melatonin is enormous: It may help people who suffer from sleep disorders; it may aid those who work uncertain shifts, including physicians, nurses, and airline pilots. This drug may revolutionize how and when people sleep—but the operative word is *may*. The outcome must await carefully controlled, scientific double-blind research on human beings.

Dreams

Why do some people rarely remember their dreams while other people can recall theirs in vivid detail? Do dreams contain hidden meanings and mysterious symbols to be deciphered? Sometimes lifelike, sometimes surreal, and sometimes incoherent, dreams may replay a person's life history or venture into the unknown. Dreams have long occupied an important place in psychology, but only since the 1950s have they come under close scientific scrutiny. Dream research is difficult to conduct; in addition, because the data from dream research are always memories of past events, they are sometimes difficult to quantify and verify (Koulack, 1991).

What Is a Dream?

Dream: A state of consciousness that occurs largely during REM sleep and is usually accompanied by vivid visual, tactile, or auditory imagery.

A **dream** is a state of consciousness that occurs largely during REM sleep and is usually accompanied by vivid visual imagery, although the imagery may also be tactile or auditory. During a dream there is an increase in heart rate, the appearance of rapid eye movements, a characteristic brain-wave pattern, and a lack of bodily movements. Although dreams occur most often in REM sleep, they can also occur during NREM sleep; during NREM sleep, they tend to be less visual and more thought-oriented. Dreams during REM sleep are intensely visual, may be action-oriented, and are more likely to be emotional than are NREM dreams.

Most people dream four or five times a night, and their dreams last from a few seconds to several minutes. The first dream of a typical night occurs 90 minutes after a person has fallen asleep and lasts for 10 minutes. With about four dreams per night and 365 days per year, a person dreams more than 100,000 dreams in a lifetime. However, people remember only a few of their dreams. Usually, they recall a dream because they woke in the middle of it or because a specific dream had powerful emotional content or imagery.

Content of Dreams

Sometimes the content of a dream is related to day-to-day events, to a desire a person wishes to fulfill, or to reliving an unpleasant experience. Sometimes a person experiences the same dream or a sequence of related dreams over and over again. Most dreams are commonplace, focusing on events related to people with whom the person comes into contact frequently—family, friends, or coworkers. Common dream themes include sex, aggressive incidents, and misfortunes. Sounds and other sensations from the environment that do not awaken a sleeper are often incorporated into a dream. For example, when a researcher sprayed water on the hands of sleepers, 42 percent (of those who did not awaken) later reported dreaming about swimming pools, baths, or rain (Dement & Wolpert, 1958).

Dreams are mostly visual, and they occur mostly in color. Dement and Kleitman (1957) found in laboratory studies that the patterns of rapid eye movements were related to the visual imagery of participants' dreams. When a participant dreamed about climbing a series of ladders, eye movements were vertical; when a participant dreamed about two people throwing tomatoes at each other, eye movements were horizontal. Not surprisingly, blind individuals, especially those who lost their sight before age 5, tend to have dream imagery that is mostly auditory.

When my younger daughter was 6 years old, she told me about a dream in which she was being chased by a monster, realized that she was dreaming, and turned around (in the dream) and made friends with the monster. Like my daughter, people sometimes report that they are aware of dreaming while the dream is going on; this type of dream is a **lucid dream**. Most people have had a lucid dream at one time or another, particularly as children. When people have experienced a lucid dream, they often report that they were inside and outside the dream at the same time. For some people this is upsetting, and they may wake themselves up from the dream. *Diversity*, on page 128, explores sleeping and dreaming in other cultures.

Dream Theories

Some psychologists assume that dreams express desires and thoughts that may be unacceptable to the conscious mind. Many therapists who interpret and analyze dreams assume that dreams represent some element of a person that is seeking expression. Some psychologists see much symbolism in dreams and assert that the content of a dream hides the dream's true meaning. Other psychologists find dreams meaningless. The suggested meaning of a dream depends on the psychologist's orientation. Two theorists who made much of the meaning of dreams are Freud and Jung; both wrote extensively on the meaning of dreams, yet there is little or no scientific support for their theories of dreams (see Table 4.1 on page 129).

Freudian Theory. Sigmund Freud described dreams as "the royal road to the unconscious." For Freud, a dream expressed desires, wishes, and unfulfilled needs that exist in the unconscious. In his book *The Interpretation of Dreams* (1900/

Lucid dream [LOO-sid]: Dream in which the person is aware of dreaming while it is happening.

DIVERSITY

Sleep and Dreaming in Three Hispanic Cultures

Sleep literature that focuses on the physiology of sleep and dreams is vast, but it includes little cross-cultural information. A study of sleep habits of older adults in three Hispanic cultures, however, offers some interesting data and insights.

George Domino (1986) asked 562 individuals from Mexico, Spain, and Venezuela, as well as additional non-Hispanic U.S. citizens, to fill out a sleep questionnaire. All of the participants in the study were over age 50, natives of their country, city dwellers, in good health, and at similar occupational levels. The questionnaire included such statements as "I am a very light sleeper"; the available responses were "usually," "often," "sometimes," "not usually," and "never." The results were analyzed for each culture and for a number of different groups of questions.

There were several key findings. For example, when the participants rated their feelings about dreams (such as in response to "my dreams are unpleasant"), important cultural differences showed up. While there were no important differences in the number of dreams recalled by the three Hispanic groups, the number recalled by U.S. participants was significantly higher. In addition, both the Mexican and the Venezuelan participants had greater negative emotions associated with their dreams.

It would be difficult to draw sweeping conclusions about Hispanic culture, dreams, and cultural differences from this study; but Domino offers a few conclusions and implications. First, he asserts that all three Hispanic groups are less likely to recall dreams than their non-Hispanic U.S. counterparts because, in general, Hispanic groups are slightly more passive in their coping styles and don't care about the meaning of dreams. This is quite a generalization, but Domino says it explains his data. He also points out that death, sleep, and dreams are often closely related in Hispanic cultures; and dreaming is often seen as an omen. Thus, Hispanic people do not *want* to remember dreams that might carry bad omens. Domino found another important cultural difference as well. Among working people in Mexico, siesta time is looked on as a pleasant interlude; in the United States, taking a nap in midday is considered frivolous. Thus, Hispanic cultures view sleep as necessary and even positive; by contrast, people in the United States often see sleep as a necessary evil, with its enjoyment being a vice not to be condoned.

Of course, some of the differences found by Domino may be due to architectural differences in housing designs, to the sharing of sleeping quarters, and to other domestic and sleeping arrangements. Nevertheless, cultural differences in living styles are important and are reflected in both day-to-day behavior and sleep patterns.

1953), Freud spoke about the manifest and the latent content of dreams. The **manifest content** of a dream consists of its overt story line, characters, and setting—the obvious, clearly discernible events of the dream. The **latent content** of a dream is its deeper meaning, usually involving symbolism, hidden content, and repressed or obscured ideas and wishes—often uncomfortable ones. We will see in Chapters 12 and 15 that Freud used dreams extensively in his theory of personality and in his treatment approach. Freudian psychoanalysts use dream analysis as a therapeutic tool in the treatment of emotional disturbance. Many contemporary therapists use patients' dreams to understand current problems and may see the dreams themselves only as a starting point.

Manifest content: The overt story line, characters, and setting of a dream—the obvious, clearly discernible events of the dream.

Latent content: The deeper meaning of a dream, usually involving symbolism, hidden content, and repressed or obscured ideas and wishes.

Jungian Theory. Carl G. Jung (1875–1961) was trained in Freudian approaches to therapy and personality analysis, and he too considered the dream a crucial way to understand human nature. However, Jung, more than Freud, took for granted

TABLE 4.1
Theories of Dreaming

Psychoanalytic Theory	Jungian Theory	Physiological Model
Psychoanalytic theorists such as Freud view dreams as expressions of desires, wishes, and unfulfilled needs that exist in the unconscious.	Jungian theorists see dreams not only as expressions of needs and desires but as reflections of people's collective unconscious.	Physiological models of dreaming focus on combining neural signals that are randomly generated and on making sense out of random events.

Collective unconscious: In Jung's dream theory, a storehouse of primitive ideas and images in the unconscious that are inherited from one's ancestors; these inherited ideas and images, called *archetypes*, are emotionally charged and rich in meaning and symbolism.

the idea that a dream was nature's way of communicating with the unconscious and focused on the meaning of dreams. Each thing a person dreams has a meaning; dreams are the language through which an individual expresses in an uncensored form the deepest feelings of his or her own mythology. The dream gives visual expression to instinct. Jung asserted that each person shares in the **collective unconscious**, a storehouse of primitive ideas and images that people inherit from their ancestors. These inherited ideas and images, whose representations in the individual are termed *archetypes*, are emotionally charged and rich in meaning and symbolism. The archetypes of the collective unconscious emerge in dreams. One especially important archetype is the *mandala*, a mystical symbol, generally circular in form, that in Jung's view represents the striving for unity within a person's self. Jungian therapy focuses on dream analysis as an approach to understanding the human condition. We will consider how Jung focuses on dreams and the collective unconscious of humankind in more detail in our study of personality in Chapter 12.

Activation–Synthesis Theory. Is it possible that dreams have no underlying meaning at all? Two researchers from Harvard Medical School, Allan Hobson and Robert McCarley (1977), believe dreams have a physiological basis. They argue that during periods of REM sleep, the parts of the brain responsible for long-term memory, vision, audition, and perhaps even emotion are spontaneously *activated* (stimulated) from cells in the hindbrain, especially the pons. The cortex tries to *synthesize*, or make sense out of, the messages. Because this activity is not organized by any external stimuli, the resulting dream is often fragmented and incoherent (Hobson, 1989). Activation–synthesis theory is supported by researchers who assert that the brain (especially the cortex) basically does its daily "housecleaning" during sleep, scanning previous memories, refreshing old storage mechanisms, and maintaining the active memory. Other researchers, however, point out that dreamlike activity occurs even when cells in the pons are not active. In this

FOCUS

Review

- What evidence supports the assertion that people dream in the middle of the night rather than solely at the end? p. 121
- What evidence suggests that sleep disorders have serious implications for day-to-day behavior? pp. 123–125

Think Critically

- What, if anything, would probably happen to you if you cut short your normal sleep time by 2 hours a night for a period of several months?
- Keep a notepad at your bedside, and record several nights' dreams immediately on awakening. (You may otherwise forget them by the time you have breakfast.) Which theory of dreaming seems to explain them best?

view the dream is a random collection of images and means little or nothing of importance. This controversial theory is still being actively researched.

Controlling Consciousness: Biofeedback, Hypnosis, and Meditation

Can you learn to control your own consciousness? Can you manipulate your mental states to achieve certain bodily reactions? Research and anecdotal data suggest that you can. People have long been taught to relax and breathe in special ways so as not to experience pain—for example, during childbirth. Marathons have been won through intense mental concentration that allowed contestants to endure especially difficult physical circumstances. Laboratory research also shows that people can bring some otherwise autonomic bodily states (see Chapter 2), such as blood pressure, under conscious control through a technique called biofeedback.

Biofeedback

Through biofeedback, people attempt to bring normally involuntary functions, such as blood pressure or heart rate, under conscious control.

Imagine a special clinic where people could be taught to treat themselves for headaches, high blood pressure, stress-related illnesses, even nearsightedness. By learning to influence consciously what are normally involuntary reactions, patients might be able to cure themselves. Such a psychological–medical clinic may exist in the future if biofeedback proves to be the healing tool some researchers predict it will be.

Physicians and psychologists once assumed that most biological functions, especially those involving the autonomic nervous system, could not be controlled voluntarily except through drugs or surgery. Since the 1960s, however, studies have explored the extent to which participants can learn to control these functions through biofeedback. **Biofeedback** is a general technique by which individuals can monitor and learn to control the involuntary activity of some of the body's organs and functions. A well-known psychologist, Neal E. Miller, was one of the first researchers to train rats to control certain glandular responses. Miller (1969) suggested that the same techniques could be used to help human beings manage their bodies and behavior. Since then, studies have shown that people can manipulate the electrical activity of their bodies by changing their level of excitation. A relaxed person viewing his or her own alpha waves on a monitor, for example, can change those alpha waves to high-frequency waves by becoming more alert and by paying attention. Similarly, a participant whose heart rate is displayed on a monitor can see the rate decrease as he or she relaxes, thereby learning about the physiological states that allow the body to work easily and efficiently. The person can learn which behaviors relax the heart and lower blood pressure and, in time, can learn to control heart rate and blood pressure by reproducing behaviors associated with reduced heart rate.

Some researchers contend that biofeedback training is not effective (Drennen & Holden, 1984); other researchers point out that the same effects can be obtained without real feedback (Plotkin, 1980). Some are skeptical about the long-term effectiveness of biofeedback. Still others claim to have used biofeedback successfully to treat people with stress-related symptoms, hyperactivity, stuttering, depression, nearsightedness, and learning disabilities. For example, Dietvorst (1978) successfully used biofeedback to help heart attack patients reduce their anxiety and fear of future attacks. He trained participants to decrease their level of arousal, and thus their level of anxiety, by monitoring one measure of their autonomic activity—hand temperature.

Biofeedback: Technique by which individuals can monitor and learn to control the involuntary activity of some of the body's organs and functions.

Many laboratory studies have demonstrated biofeedback's effectiveness in helping people manage a wide range of physiological problems; however, only carefully controlled research will answer persistent questions about its usefulness. For example, under what conditions, with what kinds of problems, and with what types of individuals is biofeedback effective (Middaugh, 1990)? Methodological issues such as those described in Chapter 1 (expectancy effects or attempts to please a researcher, for example) make this a challenging research area.

Hypnosis

"You are falling asleep. Your eyelids are becoming heavy. The weight on your eyes is becoming greater and greater. Your muscles are relaxing. You are feeling sleepier and sleepier. You are feeling very relaxed." These instructions are typical of those used in *hypnotic induction*—the process used to hypnotize people. **Hypnosis** is an altered state of consciousness brought about by procedures that may induce a trance. The generally accepted view of hypnosis is that hypnotized individuals are in a semimystical state of consciousness and give up control over much of their behavior. They are aware of their surroundings and are conscious, but their level of awareness and responses to others are altered. A person's ability to be hypnotized or willingness to follow unconventional instructions given by the hypnotist, such as to make funny noises, is called *hypnotic susceptibility,* or *suggestibility*. Most people can be hypnotized to some extent (Hilgard, 1965). Children between 7 and 14 are the most susceptible; those who daydream are also especially susceptible (Hoyt et al., 1989). Crawford (1994) argues that highly hypnotizable people have stronger attention-focusing abilities than those who are not suggestible—children certainly fit that characterization.

The traditional view of hypnosis is sometimes referred to as a "state" view because it argues that hypnotized individuals are in a state qualitatively different from normal waking consciousness. This view is sometimes distinguished from more social-cognitive views, sometimes referred to as "nonstate" views. But as you will see, such dichotomies are blurred by the data; hypnosis is neither a distinct state nor merely a social phenomenon (Kirsch & Lynn, 1995).

Effects of Hypnosis. People who have been hypnotized report that they know they have been hypnotized and are aware of their surroundings. Some report being in a special, almost mystical state; and most report a sense of time distortion (Bowers, 1979). One reported time distortion effect of hypnosis is *age regression*—the ability to recount details about an experience that took place many years earlier or to feel and act like a child. Because few studies that report age regression during hypnosis have been controlled for accuracy of recall, the authenticity of age regression has been questioned (Nash, 1987). *Heightened memory* is another purported effect of hypnosis. Evidence indicates that hypnosis helps participants recall information (e.g., McConkey & Kinoshita, 1988). However, techniques that do not involve hypnosis may work just as well for this purpose. In fact, in a contradictory study by Putnam (1979), hypnotized and nonhypnotized participants were asked to recall events they had seen earlier on a videotape. Hypnotized participants made more errors when answering leading questions than did nonhypnotized participants. Putnam suggests that hypnotized participants not only make more errors (misrecollection) but also mistakenly believe their memories are accurate (McConkey & Kinoshita, 1988). These results have led researchers to question the use of hypnosis in courtroom settings; in fact, some states do not allow the testimony of hypnotized persons as evidence (Sanders & Simmons, 1983; Smith, 1983).

Hypnosis is also used for pain reduction. In a case reported by E. F. Siegel (1979), hypnosis successfully reduced lower-leg pain in a woman who had undergone an above-the-knee amputation. (The phenomenon of pain in a part of the body that no longer exists is called *phantom pain*; it occurs in some amputees.) Hypnosis has also been used to reduce pain from heat, pressure, and childbirth (Harmon, Hynan, & Tyre, 1990; Miller & Bowers, 1993). Few studies of pain management, however, are conducted with adequate experimental rigor. Critics of hypnosis note that most patients show signs of pain even when hypnotized. Also, in

Hypnosis: Altered state of consciousness brought about by procedures that may induce a trance.

many cases, analgesic drugs (pain relievers) are used along with the hypnotism. Some researchers (especially Barber, considered next) challenge the ability of hypnosis to reduce pain, reasoning that relaxation and a patient's positive attitude and lowered anxiety account for reported reductions in pain.

Challenges to Hypnosis. Theodore Xenophon Barber is one of the major skeptics of the traditional "state" theory of hypnotism; he contends that the concepts of hypnosis and the hypnotic trance are meaningless and misleading. According to Barber, behaviors of hypnotized participants are no different from behaviors of participants willing to think about and imagine themes suggested to them. If participants' attitudes toward a situation lead them to expect certain effects, those effects will be more likely to occur. Barber's approach is called the *cognitive–behavioral viewpoint,* and it stresses the role of social processes in changing people's behavior during hypnosis (Barber, Spanos, & Chaves, 1974).

Barber's studies show that participants given task-motivating instructions (such as to concentrate deeply, fix their attention, or breathe deeply) perform similarly to participants who undergo hypnotic induction. Typically, more than half of the participants in experimental groups showed responsiveness to task suggestions, in contrast to 16 percent in control groups that were given no special instructions. From the results, Barber concluded that task-motivating instructions are almost as effective as hypnotic induction procedures in increasing participants' responsiveness to task suggestions.

Barber's studies have received support from other research. Salzberg and DePiano (1980), for example, found that hypnosis did not facilitate performance any more than task-motivating instructions did. In fact, they argued that for cognitive tasks, task-motivating instructions are more effective than hypnosis. But the evidence showing that effects similar to those from hypnosis can be achieved in various ways (e.g., Bryant & McConkey, 1989) does not mean that psychologists must discard the concept or use of hypnosis. It simply means they should reconsider traditional assumptions and begin to think about hypnosis not in an either/or manner—as existing or not existing—but rather that the data and issues that are debated are not yet resolved. Further, ultimate understanding of hypnosis is unlikely to wind up as a strictly state or social-cognitive view (Kirsh & Lynn, 1995).

Hypnosis continues to be widely used as an aid in psychotherapy. Most clients report that it is, if nothing else, a pleasant experience. Therapists assert that in some cases it can (1) help focus a client's energy on a specific topic, (2) aid memory, or (3) help a child cope with the aftereffects of child abuse. Many therapists use hypnosis to help patients relax, enhance their memory, reduce stress and anxiety, lose weight, or stop smoking (e.g., Somer, 1990). Some psychologists assert that hypnosis can help athletes concentrate (Morgan, 1992). Research into the process and effects of hypnosis continues, with an emphasis on defining critical variables in hypnosis itself and in the participants who are the most and the least easily hypnotized (e.g., Nilsson, 1990) and on ascertaining potential negative effects (e.g., Owens et al., 1989).

Meditation

Meditation has become an important daily routine for a colleague of mine. Previously, searing migraines, stomach pains, and high blood pressure had afflicted her during stressful periods. Despite prescription drugs and frequent visits to the doctor, she had found little relief. Then, at a stress management clinic, she discovered how to ease her tensions through meditation. Now, instead of taking a pill when she feels a migraine coming on, she meditates.

Meditation: State of consciousness induced by a variety of techniques and characterized by concentration, restriction of incoming stimuli, and deep relaxation to produce a sense of detachment.

Meditation is a state of consciousness induced by a variety of techniques and characterized by concentration, restriction of incoming stimuli, and deep relaxation to produce a sense of detachment. For centuries meditation has been used to alter consciousness and help relieve health problems. Practitioners report that it can reduce anxiety, tension headaches, backaches, asthma, and the need for sleep. It can also increase self-awareness and feelings of inner peace (West, 1980, 1982).

Practitioners distinguish between two major types of meditation: *mindful* and *concentrative*. Each form of meditation uses different techniques to induce an altered state of awareness. Both direct the focus of attention away from the outside world through intense concentration. One begins *mindful meditation* by trying to empty the mind and just be still. As random and intrusive thoughts arise, one notices them (becomes mindful of their content) without reacting to them, judging them good or bad, or dwelling on them. They eventually become mere wisps of thought that pass through consciousness while the meditator remains serene. Eventually, one becomes aware that the reaction to the thought is the problem (suffering) and that reaction is not necessary in order to have thoughts. In *concentrative meditation*, on the other hand, one concentrates on a visual image or a mantra (repetition of a phrase) or a name of God, and when the mind wanders to a random thought, one brings the mind back to the image without noticing the content of the thought. In this case, the image (or name of God) is the important thing. This form of meditation is closely tied with religions such as Tibetan Buddhism and Hinduism; but concentrative meditation has also been commercially exploited and because of this has, for some, acquired a bad reputation.

▲ *Participants in Dr. Dean Ornish's Healthy Heart Program practice yoga and meditation to help reduce stress on body and mind. Ornish's program, which involves a low-fat vegetarian diet, exercise, stress management, yoga, and meditation, has been proved to reverse heart disease.*

One concentrative approach, *Zen*, is especially popular among people interested in healing and nutritional approaches to health. People using Zen techniques highlight the experience of enlightenment and the possibility of attaining it in this life. Zen techniques urge people to concentrate on their breathing and count their breaths, with the immediate aim of focusing attention on a specific visual stimulus. The ultimate aim is to achieve a spiritual state of being.

Supporters of meditation claim that it is a unique state, capable of causing profound physiological and psychological changes. They argue that mindful meditation produces a different mode of cognitive processing, by training people to maintain awareness of ongoing events and increasing attention. But a study comparing the physiological responses of meditators with those of hypnotized participants found the responses to be nearly identical (Holmes, 1984). Experimental studies also show that individuals trained simply to relax and concentrate have been able to achieve bodily states similar to those of meditators (Fenwick et al., 1977).

Although most theories that explain the nature and effects of meditation rely on concepts that are not scientifically measurable or observable, some controlled studies have been done. The data from these studies have shown that meditators can alter their physiological responses, including oxygen consumption, brainwave activity, and sleep patterns (Pagano et al., 1976). Such evidence encourages some scientists to continue to investigate meditation for relieving tension, anxiety, and arousal.

FOCUS

Review

- What underlying assumption do biofeedback practitioners make when they treat various disorders? p. 130
- What is the fundamental difference between the "state" view of hypnosis and the cognitive–behavioral view of hypnosis? pp. 131–132

Think Critically

- If daydreamers and those who fantasize easily are ideal participants for hypnosis, does this imply that hypnosis is "made up"?
- Why do you think it is reasonable (or unreasonable) to use hypnosis as an aid in courtroom testimony?
- Can you think of a physiological explanation for the effects of rhythmic breathing in meditation?

Altering Consciousness with Drugs

In each of the past few years, U.S. physicians have written more than 2 billion prescriptions for drugs. Of those, almost 50 million were for the tranquilizer diazepam (Valium). At least one-third of all U.S. citizens between the ages of 18 and 74 regularly use some kind of consciousness-altering drug that changes both brain activity and daily behavior. There is no doubt that the United States is a drug-using culture. Americans use drugs to help them wake up in the morning, to get them through stresses in the day, and to help them sleep. Drugs may be legal or illegal; they may be used responsibly or abused with tragic consequences. A **drug** is any chemical substance that alters normal biological processes. Many widely used drugs are both psychoactive and addictive. A **psychoactive drug** is a drug that alters behavior, thought, or emotions by altering biochemical reactions in the nervous system, thereby affecting consciousness. An **addictive drug** is a drug that causes a compulsive physiological need and that, when withheld, produces withdrawal symptoms (discussed in the next section). Addictive drugs also usually produce tolerance (also discussed in the next section).

In studying drug (or substance) use and abuse, we have to consider the drug itself, its properties, and the context of its use. For example, not all people respond in the same way to the same drug, and one person may respond differently on different occasions. Two important questions we need to ask are the following: Does the drug produce dependence? Are there adverse reactions to the drug for the user or adverse consequences for other people or society (Newcomb & Bentler, 1989)? There is no single explanation for substance use and abuse. Societal factors, individual family situations, medical problems, and genetic heritage are all potentially part of a person's reasons for using or abusing drugs. The use versus abuse issue becomes more sharply delineated with children, who have to sort out the conflicting messages American society delivers. Newcomb and Bentler (1989) argue, "Adolescents are quite adept at spotting hypocrisy and may have difficulty understanding a policy of 'saying no to drugs' when suggested by a society that clearly says 'yes' to the smorgasbord of drugs that are legal as well as the range of illicit drugs that are widely available and used" (p. 242).

What Is Substance Abuse?

Substance abusers are people who overuse and rely on drugs to deal with stress and anxiety. Most substance abusers turn to alcohol, tobacco, and other readily available drugs such as cocaine and marijuana; but substance abuse is not confined to these drugs. Psychologists are seeing a growing number of people abusing legal drugs such as tranquilizers and diet pills, as well as illegal drugs such as amphetamines and heroin. A person is a substance abuser if all three of the following statements apply:

- The person has used the abusive substance for at least a month.
- The use has caused legal difficulties or social or vocational problems.
- There is recurrent use in hazardous situations such as driving a car.

Substance abuse can lead to psychological dependence, pathological use, or both. **Psychological dependence** is a compelling desire to use a drug, along with an inability to inhibit that desire. *Pathological use* involves out-of-control episodes of use, such as alcohol binges. Most drugs produce a physiological reaction when they are no longer administered; in general, this reaction is evidence of physical dependence. Without the drug, a dependent person suffers from withdrawal symptoms. **Withdrawal symptoms** are the physiological reactions that occur when an addictive drug is no longer administered to an addict. The reactions may include headaches,

Drug: Any chemical substance that alters normal biological processes.

Psychoactive drug [SYE-koh-AK-tiv]: A drug that alters behavior, thought, or emotions by altering biochemical reactions in the nervous system, thereby affecting consciousness.

Addictive drug: A drug that causes a compulsive physiological need and that, when withheld, produces withdrawal symptoms.

Substance abusers: People who overuse and rely on drugs to deal with stress and anxiety.

Psychological dependence: A compelling desire to use a drug, along with an inability to inhibit that desire.

Withdrawal symptoms: Physiological reactions that occur when an addictive drug is no longer administered to an addict.

nausea, and an intense craving for the absent drug. In addition, addictive drugs usually produce **tolerance**—progressive insensitivity to repeated use of a specific drug in the same dosage and at the same frequency of use. Tolerance forces an addict to use increasing amounts of the drug or to use the drug at an increased frequency to achieve the same effect. For example, alcoholics must consume larger and larger amounts of alcohol to become drunk. Most addictive drugs produce both dependence and tolerance.

Each time people take a psychoactive drug, they change their ability to function normally. Specifically, psychoactive drugs change behavior by altering a person's physiology and normal state of consciousness. Some drugs increase alertness and performance; others relax people and relieve high levels of arousal and tension. Some produce physical and psychological dependence. All psychoactive drugs alter a person's thoughts and moods; they are all considered consciousness-altering.

Why Do People Abuse Drugs?

Some people are likely to develop a substance abuse problem for physiological and genetic reasons; others may have emotional problems caused by stress, poverty, boredom, loneliness, or anxiety. Sadly, many people believe alcohol and other drugs provide a quick fix for these problems. People may turn to drugs to relax, be sociable, forget their worries, feel confident, or lose weight. Parental drug use, peer drug use, poor self-esteem, stressful life changes, divorce, and social isolation have all been implicated. American society and its materialistic values also contribute to the problem; this culture tends to focus on immediate, pleasurable gratification born of individualism. This factor is culture-specific; not all cultures focus on the individual's wants to such an extent.

In any culture, determining the causes of drug abuse is complicated by the definition of addiction. Addictive drugs are generally defined by saying that they are habit-forming (reinforcing) or that they produce a physiological dependence—for example, dependence on alcohol or barbiturates. These two processes are not independent, however; physiological processes may lead to addictive reinforcement patterns. Many drugs that affect the brain differently all share the property of being addictive—alcohol and cocaine are two examples. In order to help develop drug policies, researchers today are attempting to develop models that account for psychological variables such as cravings, physiological variables such as changes in brain structures and firing patterns, and social variables such as family support and therapy.

Substance abusers rarely have identical abuse patterns. Some people use only one drug—for example, alcohol. Others are *polydrug abusers*, taking several drugs; a heroin addict, for example, might also take amphetamines. When amphetamines are difficult to obtain, the person might switch to barbiturates. Some researchers assert that many people are addiction-prone (Sutker & Allain, 1988). Others note that addicts are often ambivalent about whether they want to give up their drug (Bradley, 1990). Still other researchers note that later addictive behaviors can be predicted from antisocial childhood behavior (Nathan, 1988; Shedler & Block, 1990).

Let's take a closer look at some of the most commonly used drugs and their consciousness-altering properties. We begin with alcohol, the source of one of today's most complicated and widespread drug problems in the United States.

Alcohol

The students at my daughters' high school wore black arm bands to show they mourned the death of their sophomore friend Mark Smoak. At 15 years of age, with a learner's permit to drive, Mark Smoak crashed into a telephone pole on a poorly lit street just two miles from his home. It was later learned that his blood alcohol level was exceedingly high. A high school student crashing a car, getting killed, and

Tolerance: Progressive insensitivity to repeated use of a specific drug in the same dosage and at the same frequency of use.

maybe even killing or seriously injuring a friend in the front seat is a tale told all over this country, every year in every community.

Alcohol consumption in the United States has been at an all-time high for more than a decade. According to the U.S. Department of Health and Human Services, about 80 percent of urban U.S. adults report having used alcohol at some time; it is estimated that 10 million people over age 18 in the United States are problem drinkers or alcoholics (defined and discussed shortly). Each year, surveys show that about one-fourth of 8th-grade students and more than one-third of 10th-grade students reported having had five or more drinks on at least one occasion during the previous 2 weeks.

Alcohol is the most widely used sedative–hypnotic. A **sedative–hypnotic** is any of a class of drugs that relax and calm people and, in higher doses, induce sleep. Because alcohol is readily available, relatively inexpensive, and socially accepted, addiction to this drug is easy to establish and maintain. In fact, most Americans consider some alcohol consumption appropriate; they often consume alcoholic beverages before, during, and after dinner, at weddings and funerals, at religious events, and during sports events.

Effects of Alcohol. Alcohol is a depressant that decreases inhibitions and thus increases some behaviors that are normally under tight control. For example, it may diminish people's social inhibitions and make them less likely to restrain their aggressive impulses (Steele & Josephs, 1990). The physiological effects of alcohol vary, depending on the amount of alcohol in the bloodstream and the gender and weight of the user (see Figure 4.3). After equal amounts of alcohol consumption, women have higher blood alcohol levels than men do, even allowing for differences in body weight; this occurs because men's bodies typically have a higher percentage of fluid than do women's. With less blood and other fluids in which to dilute the alcohol, women may end up with higher blood alcohol concentrations with fewer drinks than men (Frezza et al., 1990; York & Welte, 1994). Figure 4.3 shows the behaviors associated with various blood alcohol levels.

With increasing amounts of alcohol in the bloodstream, people typically exhibit progressively slowed behavior; often they exhibit severe motor disturbances, such as staggering. A blood alcohol level greater than 0.10 percent (0.1 milligram of alcohol per 100 milliliters of blood) usually indicates that the person has consumed too much alcohol to function responsibly. In most states, a 0.10 percent blood alcohol level legally defines intoxication; police officers may arrest drivers who are found to have this level of blood alcohol.

The nervous system becomes less sensitive to, or accommodates, alcohol with increased usage. After months or years of drinking, drug tolerance develops, and a person has to consume ever-increasing amounts of alcohol to achieve the same effect. Thus, when not in an alcoholic state, a heavy drinker develops anxiety, cravings, and other withdrawal symptoms (Levin, 1990).

Problem Drinkers versus Alcoholics. *Alcohol-related problems* are medical, social, or psychological problems associated with alcohol use. A person who shows an alcohol-related problem such as missing work occasionally because of hangovers, spending a paycheck to buy drinks for friends, or losing a driver's license because of drunk driving is abusing alcohol. Alcohol-related problems caused by chronic (repeated) alcohol abuse may include liver deterioration, memory loss, and significant mood swings (Nace, 1987). A person with alcohol-related problems, a problem drinker, who also has a physiological and psychological need to consume alcohol and to experience its effects is an **alcoholic**. All alcoholics are problem drinkers, but not all problem drinkers are alcoholics. Without alcohol, alcoholics develop physiological withdrawal symptoms. In addition, they often develop tolerance; a single drink or even a few will not affect them. *The Research Process* (on pages 138 and 139) examines who is at risk for alcoholism.

Sedative–hypnotic: Drug that relaxes and calms people and, in higher doses, induces sleep.

Alcoholic: A problem drinker who also has both a physiological and a psychological need to consume alcohol and to experience its effects.

FIGURE 4.3

Relationship between Alcohol Consumption and Blood Alcohol Level, by Gender and Weight

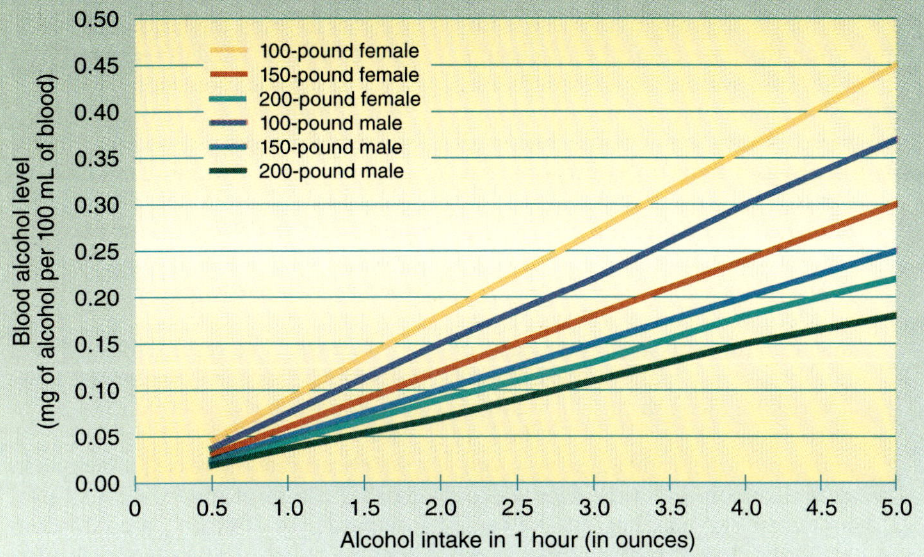

For example, 2.0 ounces of alcohol is equivalent to 4 glasses of wine, 4 cans of beer, or 2 mixed drinks.

Blood Alcohol Level*	Behavioral Effects
0.05	Lowered alertness, impaired judgment, release of inhibitions, good feelings
0.10	Slowed reaction time and impaired motor function, less caution
0.15	Large, consistent increases in reaction time
0.20	Marked depression in sensory and motor capability, decidedly intoxicated behavior
0.25	Severe motor disturbance and impairment of sensory perceptions
0.30	In a stupor but still conscious—no comprehension of events in the environment
0.35	Surgical anesthesia; lethal dose for about 1 percent of adults
0.40	Lethal dose for about 50 percent of adults

*In milligrams of alcohol per 100 milliliters of blood

Social and Medical Problems. From both a medical and a psychological standpoint, alcohol abuse is one of the greatest social problems in the United States. Between 30 and 40 percent of the homeless are people with alcohol problems (McCarty et al., 1991). Drunkenness is the biggest law enforcement problem today, accounting for millions of arrests each year. The Department of Transportation has estimated that alcohol is involved in more than 39,000 automobile deaths each year.

THE RESEARCH PROCESS

Who Is at Risk for Alcoholism?

Are some people more likely than others to become alcoholics? The answer is yes, according to researchers who study the biological side of alcoholism. Researchers assert that genetics, blood and brain chemistry, and specific brain structures predispose some people to alcoholism.

Correlational Studies. Some of the most interesting research on alcoholism comes from studies that focus on *high-risk individuals*—people who seem more at risk for a disorder. (For example, the culturally disadvantaged and the poor are at high risk for substance abuse because they often live in urban environments that expose them to substance abuse, alcoholism, and crime.) Who is at high risk for alcoholism? Children of alcoholics are more likely to be alcoholics, even if they are raised by nonalcoholic adoptive parents. The correlations suggest that the physiology of alcoholics and their children predisposes the children to alcoholism.

Hypotheses. Studies show that alcoholics, more than nonalcoholics, tend to respond with physiological arousal to stress and other disagreeable, aversive stimulation. Finn and Pihl (1987), two McGill University researchers, decided to test the hypothesis that men with extensive family histories of alcoholism are more reactive physiologically to aversive stimulation than are control participants. They also wanted to see whether alcohol reduces physiological responses more for men with a family history of alcoholism than for control participants. Their overall aim was to find out whether certain people are at high risk for alcoholism.

Method. The researchers divided men into three groups on the basis of family history: high, moderate, and low risk for alcoholism. The high-risk participants had alcoholic fathers and grandfathers and at least one other male alcoholic in the family. The moderate-risk participants had one alcoholic parent and no other close alcoholic relative. The low-risk participants had no identifiable alcoholics in the present or the two previous generations of their family.

Finn and Pihl investigated two physiological responses—heart rate and blood volume—of participants who knew they were going to receive mild electrical shocks. Anticipation of a shock induces a physiological response in nearly everybody; the question to be answered was whether the responses were more pronounced in high-risk participants. To add another dimension to the experiment, the researchers gave some participants a moderate amount of alcohol (the amount was adjusted for body weight) to bring the blood alcohol to a level of 0.07 percent—a significant level of intoxication, but not drunk. Would high-risk participants show a greater physiological reaction to the impending shock than low-risk participants? Would alcohol consumption affect the responses of the high-risk participants more than those of the low-risk participants?

Results. The results showed that sober high-risk participants were more cardiovascularly reactive than sober moderate-risk participants—that is, their heart rates increased more quickly than those of moderate-risk participants. In addition, alcohol consumption led to a reduction in physiological response in the high-risk group only. In the moderate- and low-risk groups, alcohol consumption increased physiological responses.

Conclusions and Implications. According to Finn and Pihl, a different pattern of alcohol sensitivity may show up when a strict criterion that requires multigenerational alcoholism, as opposed to a one-generation (alcoholic father only) criterion, is used to select high-risk participants. Men at a high genetic risk for alco-

Although the number of deaths caused by alcohol-related accidents has decreased in the last few years, the number in the next 3 years will still exceed the American death toll of the Vietnam War. In addition, people involved in violent crimes and suicide are often found to have been drinking.

Although alcoholism is seen as a social disease because of its devastating social consequences, it is also a medical problem. Biomedical researchers look for the effects of alcohol on the brain, as well as anything about the brains and basic genetics of alcoholics that may predispose them to alcoholism (Tarter & Vanyukov, 1994). Researchers know that chronic excessive drinking is associated with loss of brain tissue, liver malfunctions, and impaired cognitive and motor abilities (e.g., Ellis & Oscar-Berman, 1989).

Treatment Programs. For some alcoholics, psychological and medical treatment is successful. The most widely known program is Alcoholics Anonymous, which helps individuals abstain from alcohol by providing a therapeutic and emotionally nurturing environment. Treatment programs make abstinence their goal.

holism in stressful situations show a consistent reduction in physiological responses when they consume alcohol. This finding suggests a genetic predisposition to being calmed by alcohol when faced with stressful or aversive stimulation; this conclusion was confirmed and extended by Finn, Kessler & Hussong (1994). The researchers assert that a high-risk label should be assigned to an individual only if two prior generations have been considered. They were able to show a difference between the high-risk (two-generations) group and the moderate-risk (one-generation) group when comparing them to the low-risk control group. Other researchers (Blum et al., 1996; Pickens et al., 1991) lend support to the inheritance factor in alcoholism—especially among young men (McGue, Pickens, & Svikis, 1992). Still further, Schuckit (1994) showed that even when people exhibit a low-level response to alcohol, this may increase their risk of subsequent alcoholism—perhaps because they will later drink more heavily and more often.

Gender and Alcoholism. An important study of the inheritance factor and the vulnerability of women to alcoholism showed similar results. According to Kenneth Kendler and his colleagues (1994), the transmission of vulnerability to alcoholism from parents to their daughters is due largely, and in many cases entirely, to genetic factors. This study showed that genetic vulnerability was equally transmitted from fathers and mothers to their daughters. It may be that a parent's alcohol use affects a woman's ova or a father's sperm (Cicero, 1994).

That inheritance is involved in alcoholism for both men and women is clear; how inheritance interacts with the environment, parental influence (Chassin et al., 1993), and especially thought processes (Goldman et al., 1991) is the question researchers must answer next (Hawkins, Catalano, & Miller, 1992).

A Matter of Ethics. Place a man who is genetically at high risk for alcoholism in a situation of chronic stress, provide that man with alcohol, and the reinforcing effects of stress reduction are likely to make alcohol a highly prized and rewarding substance. Some questions still remain, however. For example, are there high-risk, higher-risk, and extremely high-risk individuals? Are there measures of reactivity that might be more sensitive? The research continues; the Finn and Pihl study is just one of hundreds examining the genetic and other risk factors for alcoholism. Although drug researchers realize the importance of their mission, they also are sensitive to the ethical problems inherent in doing drug research with human beings. Psychologists have ethical guidelines concerning participants in human research, and asking people who are at risk for alcoholism to drink puts them at risk. Today, psychologists insist that research with human participants provide safeguards, treatments, and a thorough risk–benefit analysis for participants

The fundamental assumptions, based on the difficulty alcoholics have controlling their drinking, are that an alcoholic is an alcoholic forever and that alcoholism should be considered diseaselike in nature—and incurable (McCrady, 1994).

Some practitioners, on the other hand, believe that limited, nonproblem drinking should be the goal of treatment programs (Vaillant & Milofsky, 1982). This view assumes that alcohol abuse is a learned behavior and can therefore be unlearned. Those who prefer controlled use with the goal of minimizing the harmful effects of alcohol consumption (Fromme et al., 1994; Marlatt et al., 1993) claim that alcohol abuse is merely a symptom of a larger underlying problem, such as poor self-esteem or family instability (Sobell & Sobell, 1982). Researchers such as Marlatt claim that a controlled drinking model should be preferred to abstinence-only or "zero tolerance" approaches because it supports any behavior change to reduce the harm of problems due to alcohol. However, most researchers hold that controlled drinking is not a reliable answer for most alcoholics, although it may be a reasonable alternative for young heavy drinkers who are not yet alcoholics (Nathan & Skinstad, 1987; Rosenberg, 1993).

TABLE 4.2 *Warning Signs of Alcoholism*

You drink more than you used to and tend to gulp your drinks.
You try to have a few extra drinks before or after drinking with others.
You have begun to drink alone.
You are noticeably drunk on important occasions. You drink the "morning after" to overcome the effects of previous drinking.
You drink to relieve feelings of boredom, depression, anxiety, or inadequacy.
You have begun to drink at certain times, to get through difficult situations, or when you have problems.
You have weekend drinking bouts and Monday hangovers.
You are beginning to lose control of your drinking; you drink more than you planned and get drunk when you did not want to.
You promise to drink less but do not.
You often regret what you have said or done while drinking.
You are beginning to feel guilty about your drinking.
You are sensitive when others mention your drinking.
You have begun to deny your drinking or lie about it.
You have memory blackouts or pass out while drinking.
Your drinking is affecting your relationships with friends or relatives.
You have lost time at work or school because of drinking.
You are beginning to stay away from people who do not drink.

Family therapy is generally considered an important part of treatment for alcoholism, because the alcohol problem of one family member becomes a problem for the entire family. A multimodal treatment approach (one involving many modes of treatment) is often the best plan; the objective is to combine individual or group therapy with participation in Alcoholics Anonymous or some other self-help group (Levin, 1990). Few systematic, carefully controlled studies of alcoholism and procedures for its treatment exist. Some researchers are investigating the use of behavioral therapies and drugs to control alcohol intake—including drugs such as naltrexone, which has been used to treat heroin addiction but shows positive effects for alcoholism (Kranzler & Anton, 1994). Others are studying detoxification centers and halfway houses as treatments for alcoholics. Still others are trying to determine who is at risk (who is likely to become an alcoholic), in the hope that early intervention can prevent alcoholism (e.g., Hawkins, Catalano, & Miller, 1992). Table 4.2 presents some of the warning signs that alcoholism is developing.

Barbiturates and Tranquilizers

Like alcohol, most barbiturates and tranquilizers are considered to be in the sedative–hypnotic class of drugs. They relax or calm people; and when taken in higher doses, they often induce sleep. *Barbiturates* decrease the excitability of neurons throughout the nervous system. They calm the individual by depressing the central nervous system. The use of barbiturates as sedatives, however, has diminished; they have largely been replaced by another class of drugs—tranquilizers.

Tranquilizers are a group of drugs (technically benzodiazepines) that also sedate and calm people. With a somewhat lower potential for abuse, they are sometimes called *minor tranquilizers*. Valium and Librium are two of the most widely used tranquilizers prescribed by physicians for relief of mild stress. Such drugs have been widely abused by all segments of society because of their availability.

Opiates: Heroin

Opiates are a class of drugs with pain-relieving and sedative properties that are addictive and produce tolerance. One opiate is heroin, a derivative of opium that is widely abused. Heroin dulls the senses, relieves pain, tranquilizes, and induces euphoria. Like many other addictive drugs, heroin is considered biologically reinforcing.

Opiates have been used for everything from relieving children's crying to reducing pain from headaches, surgery, childbirth, and menstruation. Today, most opiates are illegal; but heroin and other opiates (such as morphine, which is illegal when not prescribed by a physician) are readily available from drug dealers. The high cost of these illegal drugs leads many addicts to engage in crime to support their habits.

Heroin can be smoked or eaten or, more typically, injected into a vein. (A recent and especially dangerous trend, because of overdose possibilities, is for the user to snort heroin through the nose.) Heroin addicts tend to be young, poor, and undereducated. Most become addicts as a result of peer pressure and a desire for upward mobility among their peers. Estimates of the number of heroin addicts range dramatically from 0.5 million to 13 million. Heroin addicts often use other drugs in combination with heroin; among these are alcohol, barbiturates, amphetamines, and cocaine (the last two drugs will be described in a later section). This polydrug use makes it difficult to classify heroin users as addicts of one drug or another. Moreover, even when classification is possible, treatment is complicated by the medical, psychological, and social problems associated with using many drugs at once.

The major physiological effect of heroin is impaired functioning of the respiratory system. Other effects are some detrimental changes in the heart, arteries, and veins, as well as constipation and loss of appetite. Contrary to popular beliefs, few heroin addicts actually die of overdoses from injections. A lethal dose of the drug would be much larger than that injected even by heavy users. More often than not, heroin addicts die from snorting lethal doses of pure heroin, from taking a mixture of drugs (such as heroin and alcohol), or from disease—especially AIDS, contracted from nonsterile needles and other paraphernalia used in injecting the substance into the bloodstream. Some lawmakers are advocating community programs for distributing sterile needles to drug users to prevent the spread of AIDS. But, as you might expect, such programs are extremely controversial.

The only major successful treatment program for heroin addiction is methadone maintenance. Like heroin, methadone is an addicting drug and must be consumed daily or withdrawal symptoms will occur. Unlike heroin, however, methadone does not produce euphoria or tolerance in the user, and daily dosages do not need to be increased. Because methadone blocks the effects of heroin, a normal injection of heroin has no effect on individuals on methadone maintenance. As a result, many methadone treatment patients (there are about 100,000 in the United States) who might be tempted to use heroin to achieve a high do not do so. Moreover, because methadone is legal, many of the patients are able to hold jobs to support themselves and stay out of jail. Research suggests that methadone treatment combined with psychotherapy and behavior modification techniques to reduce illicit drug use may be far more effective than methadone by itself (Stitzer, 1988). Unfortunately, most methadone treatment programs do not focus on treatment; they simply prescribe methadone and have been criticized as unscrupulous money-making machines that feed an ongoing habit. Thus, methadone treatment programs are seen by many as controversial and potentially unethical.

Marijuana

Consciousness-altering drugs that affect moods, thoughts, memory, judgment, and perception and that are usually self-administered for the purpose of producing those results are called **psychedelics**. Perhaps the most widely used of these drugs is mari-

Opiate: Drugs with pain-relieving and sedative properties that are addictive and produce tolerance.

Psychedelics: Consciousness-altering drugs that affect moods, thoughts, memory, judgment, and perception and that are usually self-administered for the purpose of producing those results.

juana, the dried leaves and flowering tops of the *cannabis sativa* plant, whose active ingredient is *tetrahydrocannabinol* (THC).

Marijuana can be ingested (eaten), but in the United States it is most commonly smoked, a process in which 20 to 80 percent of the THC is lost. People smoke marijuana to alter their consciousness, to alleviate depression, or just as a distraction. Most users report a sense of elation and well-being; others assert that it induces wild flights of fancy. Some users report other, adverse reactions, such as sleeplessness, bad dreams, paranoia, and nausea. Marijuana's effects are felt about 1 minute after smoking, begin to diminish within an hour, and disappear almost completely after 3 to 5 hours—although traces of THC can be detected in the body for weeks. Individuals under the influence of marijuana demonstrate impaired performance on simple intellectual and psychomotor tasks. They become less task-oriented and have slower reaction times. Marijuana also interferes with memory. Little is known about how marijuana affects fetal development and reproductive abilities, and little is known about its long-term effects on those who use it from early adolescence until middle age. Marijuana has been widely used only since the late 1960s; it will take a couple of generations before researchers know all of its long-term effects.

Although researchers agree that marijuana is not physiologically addictive, many argue that it produces psychological dependence. People use and become dependent on marijuana for a variety of reasons. One is that it is more easily available than such substances as barbiturates and cocaine. Another is the relief of tension that marijuana users experience. Further, most people believe the drug has few, if any, long-lasting side effects.

Despite considerable social acceptance of marijuana use in the United States, its sale and possession are still against the law in most states. In several states, the decriminalization of marijuana has meant that possession is treated as a civil violation instead of a crime. There are no arrests, jail sentences, or trials, but its use is still illegal. For the most part, laws against the sale and possession of marijuana have been ineffective, and the drug is widely available across the United States in both urban and rural areas. Legalization is considered a good idea by some experts, although few legislators take the idea seriously.

Amphetamines and Cocaine

Amphetamines and cocaine are considered psychostimulants and are highly addictive. A **psychostimulant** is any drug that increases alertness, reduces fatigue, and elevates mood when taken in low to moderate doses. *Amphetamines* are a group of chemical compounds that act on the central nervous system to increase excitability, depress appetite, and increase alertness and talkativeness. They also increase blood pressure and heart rate. After long-term use of an amphetamine, a person has cravings for the drug and experiences exhaustion, lethargy, and depression without it.

Cocaine is a central nervous system stimulant and an anesthetic. It acts on neurotransmitters such as norepinephrine (noradrenaline) and dopamine. It also stimulates sympathetic activity in the peripheral nervous system, causing dilation of the pupils; increases in heart rate, blood pressure, and blood sugar; and decreased appetite. The drug produces euphoria—a light-headed feeling, a sense of alertness, increased energy, sexual arousal, and sometimes a sense of infallibility—but this euphoria is short-lived.

Cocaine can be sniffed (snorted), smoked, or injected. Sniffing is the most popular method. Once inhaled, the drug is absorbed into the tiny blood vessels that line the nose. Within 5 minutes, the user starts to feel the effects; the peak effect is in 15 minutes and may last for 20 to 30 minutes. The processed, smokable form of cocaine, *crack*, delivers an unusually large dose and induces euphoria in a matter of seconds. Cocaine can also be injected, since it is soluble in water. However, because of concerns about contracting AIDS through infected needles, intravenous injections are less common than they used to be.

Psychostimulant: A drug that in low to moderate doses increases alertness, reduces fatigue, and elevates mood.

TABLE 4.3 *Commonly Abused Drugs*

Types of Drugs	Examples of Drugs	Effects of Drugs	Tolerance?	Physiological Dependence?
Sedative–hypnotics	Alcohol	Reduces tension	yes	yes
	Barbiturates (e.g., Seconal)	Reduce tension; induce sleep	yes	yes
	Tranquilizers (e.g., Valium)	Alleviate tension; induce relaxation	yes	yes
Opiates	Opium Morphine Heroin	Alleviate pain and tension; induce a high	yes	yes
Psychedelics	Marijuana	Changes mood and perception	no	no
Psychostimulants	Amphetamines	Increase excitability, alertness, talkativeness; decrease appetite	yes	yes
	Cocaine	Increases alertness, decreases fatigue, stimulates sexual arousal	yes	yes

Note: Even though a drug may not produce physiological dependence, it may produce a psychological need that compels repeated use.

Cocaine is widely abused. At least 15 percent of high school seniors have used it at least once. Crack is readily available, especially in schools. Admissions to cocaine treatment centers have increased sharply, as have deaths associated with cocaine abuse. (Table 4.3 summarizes the effects of cocaine and other commonly abused drugs.) Why is cocaine use so prevalent in the United States? First, cocaine acts as a powerful reward. In laboratory studies, for example, animals will work incessantly, even to the point of exhaustion, to obtain it. Second, cocaine produces both tolerance and potent urges and cravings. A cocaine high is pleasurable but also brief; users wish to repeat the sensation almost immediately. When the cocaine wears off, its effects give way to unpleasant feelings (known as crashing). These feelings can be alleviated only through more cocaine. Third, in this pleasure-now, pay-later society, instant gratification through drug use seems appropriate to some people (Washton, 1989.)

What are some of the problems of cocaine use? At a minimum, the drug is addictive and produces irritability and eating and sleeping disturbances. It also seems to precipitate other disturbances, such as panic attacks. Further, cocaine can produce serious mental disorders, including paranoia, agitation, and suicidal behavior. Overdosing causes physical problems such as heart attacks, hemorrhages, and heat stroke. Complications associated with cocaine administration include nose sores, lung damage, infection at injection sites, and AIDS. Even those who stop using cocaine often experience medical probems later as a result of damage done to their bodies during the time they were abusing the drug. Also, using cocaine during pregnancy may result in premature birth, malformations of the fetus, and even spontaneous abortions.

FOCUS

Review

- What are the defining characteristics of a substance abuser? p. 134
- How can researchers test the hypothesis that alcoholism may have genetic components? pp. 138–139
- What are the principal risks of cocaine use? p. 143

Think Critically

- To what extent is it true that one can be "born" an alcoholic?
- What do you think is the best way to treat alcoholism, and why? Would you treat cocaine addiction with the same procedures, and why?

Treatment for cocaine addiction first requires getting the addict into therapy (which is difficult, because addicts feel invulnerable), providing a structured program, and making sure the addict refrains from all mood-altering addictive drugs, including alcohol. Blocking the pleasure centers with a drug such as methadone is not feasible: Cocaine (unlike heroin) works through almost all of the major neurotransmitter systems; so even if such a replacement drug could be found, it would probably make the addict listless, since other pleasure centers might similarly be blocked. Because a drug treatment for cocaine addiction is so hard to achieve, a great burden is placed on psychological therapy. Treatment usually includes education, family involvement, group and individual therapy, a focus on abstinence, and long-term follow-up; it is time-intensive and expensive (Hall, Havassy, & Wasserman, 1991).

Summary and Review

Consciousness

What are the key characteristics of a definition of consciousness?

- *Consciousness* is a general state of being aware of and responsive to events in the environment, including one's own mental processes. It can range from alert attention to dreaming, hypnosis, or drug-induced states. An *altered state of consciousness* is a pattern of functioning that is dramatically different from that of ordinary awareness and responsiveness. pp. 116–117

KEY TERMS
Consciousness, p. 117
Altered state of consciousness, p. 117

Sleep

Describe the cycles of sleep and wakefulness.

- A biological clock that ticks within each person controls the sleep–wakefulness cycle; *circadian rhythms* are the internally generated bodily rhythms. When time cues such as daylight and the clock on the wall are removed from the environment, circadian rhythms run a bit slow. pp. 119–120
- Recordings of the brain waves of sleeping participants have revealed distinct cycles of sleep. Each cycle has four stages of *no rapid eye movement* (NREM) *sleep* and one stage of *rapid eye movement* (REM) *sleep*. During REM sleep, rapid and systematic eye movements occur. A full sleep cycle lasts about 90 minutes, so five complete sleep cycles occur in an average night's sleep. People deprived of REM sleep tend to catch up on REM sleep on subsequent nights. pp. 121–123

What happens when someone suffers from a sleep disorder?

- Snoring loudly, sleepwalking, and falling asleep at inappropriate times may be signs of a sleep disorder. People who fall asleep suddenly and unexpectedly have a sleep disorder known as narcolepsy. Narcolepsy is probably a symptom of an autonomic nervous system disturbance and lowered arousal but may also reflect neurochemical problems. Another sleep disorder, *insomnia*, is a prolonged inability to sleep, which is often caused by anxiety or depression. pp. 124–125

KEY TERMS
Circadian rhythms, p. 119
Sleep, p. 120
Electroencephalogram (EEG), p. 121
No rapid eye movement (NREM) sleep, p. 121
Rapid eye movement (REM) sleep, p. 121
Insomnia, p. 125

Dreams

What evidence supports the assertion that people dream in the middle of the night rather than solely at the end?

- A *dream* is a state of consciousness that occurs largely during REM sleep and is usually accompanied by vivid visual imagery, although the imagery may also be tactile or auditory. REM sleep occurs four or five times a night, so most people dream four or five times a night. The first dream of a typical night occurs 90 minutes after a person has fallen asleep and lasts for approximately 10 minutes. pp. 126–127

How have key theorists explained dreaming?

- For Freud, a dream expressed desires, wishes, and unfulfilled needs that exist in the unconscious—dreams were "the royal road to the unconscious." Freud referred to the *manifest content* of a dream (its overt story line, characters, and settings) and the *latent content* of a dream (its deeper meaning, usually involving symbolism, hidden content, and repressed or obscured ideas and wishes). pp. 127–128
- Jung took for granted the idea that a dream was nature's way of communicating with the unconscious and saw dreams as the language through which an individual expresses the deepest feelings of his or her own mythology in an uncensored form. He asserted that each person shares in the *collective unconscious*, a storehouse of primitive ideas and images in people's unconscious that are inherited from their ancestors. pp. 128–129
- Hobson and McCarley believe that dreams have a physiological basis and that, during periods of REM sleep, the parts of the brain responsible for long-term memory, vision, audition, and perhaps even emotion are spontaneously activated

(stimulated) from cells in the hindbrain, especially the pons. The cortex attempts to synthesize, or make sense out of, the messages. pp. 129–130

KEY TERMS

Dream, p. 126
Lucid dream, p. 127
Manifest content, p. 128
Latent content, p. 128
Collective unconscious, p. 129

Controlling Consciousness: Biofeedback, Hypnosis, and Meditation

Differentiate three keys means of controlling consciousness.

- *Biofeedback* is the general technique by which individuals can monitor and learn to control the involuntary activity of some bodily organs and functions. Laboratory studies have demonstrated biofeedback's effectiveness in helping people manage a wide range of physiological problems such as headaches and high blood pressure, but only carefully controlled research will answer persistent questions about its usefulness. pp. 130–131
- *Hypnosis* is an altered state of consciousness brought about by procedures that may induce a trance. Hypnosis can produce special effects such as age regression, heightened memory, and pain reduction. pp. 131–132
- Physical states produced by *meditation* resemble those achieved by individuals trained to relax and concentrate. The two major types of meditation are mindful and concentrative; both induce an altered state of awareness. People using mindful meditation focus on trying to empty the mind and just be still. Concentrative meditation is concentration on a visual image or a mantra; when the mind wanders to random thoughts, the meditator brings it back to the image without noticing the content of the thoughts. pp. 132–133

KEY TERMS

Biofeedback, p. 130
Hypnosis, p. 131
Meditation, p. 132

Altering Consciousness with Drugs

What are the different broad categories of drugs?

- A *drug* is any chemical substance that alters normal biological processes. A *psychoactive drug* is a drug that alters behavior, thought, or emotions by altering biochemical reactions in the nervous system, thereby affecting consciousness. An *addictive drug* is a drug that causes a compulsive physiological need and that, when withheld, produces withdrawal symptoms. p. 134

What are the defining characteristics of a substance abuser?

- *Substance abusers* have used drugs for at least one month, have experienced legal, personal, social, or vocational problems due to drug use, and have used a drug in hazardous situations. Most researchers agree that no single explanation can account for drug use and abuse. pp. 134–135

How does alcohol affect behavior, and who is an alcoholic?

- Alcohol affects behavior in proportion to its level in the bloodstream and the gender and weight of the user. A person with a blood alcohol level of 0.10 percent or more is generally considered intoxicated; if driving, the person can be arrested. p. 136
- An *alcoholic* is a person who has alcohol-related problems and also has a physiological and psychological need to consume alcoholic products and experience their effects. Without alcohol, alcoholics develop physiological *withdrawal symptoms*. In addition, they often develop *tolerance*, whereby a single drink or even a few will not affect them. All alcoholics are problem drinkers, but not all problem drinkers are alcoholics. pp. 136–137

Describe the risks and effects of different classes of drugs.

- Barbiturates and tranquilizers are in the class of drugs called *sedative–hypnotics*. They relax and calm individuals and, when taken in higher doses, can induce sleep. Barbiturates are considered to produce a deeper relaxation than tranquilizers. Tranquilizers are widely overused because of their availability. p. 140
- Heroin is one of the class of drugs called *opiates*. It has become a social problem in part because it is illegal; thus, addicts commit crimes to get money to obtain the drug. Heroin addiction has been treated successfully with methadone, which blocks heroin's effects. Methadone programs are not without critics, however, because of their lack of treatment to help addicts become totally drug-free. p. 141
- *Psychedelics* such as marijuana are consciousness-altering drugs that affect moods, thoughts, memory, judgment, and perception and that are usually self-administered for the purposes of producing those results. p. 142
- In general, a *psychostimulant* is any drug that increases alertness, reduces fatigue, and elevates mood when taken in low to moderate doses. Amphetamines and cocaine are psychostimulants. Cocaine is widely abused in the United States; cocaine addiction is difficult to treat and has numerous medical complications. pp. 142–144

KEY TERMS

Drug, p. 134
Psychoactive drug, p. 134
Addictive drug, p. 134
Substance abusers, p. 134
Psychological dependence, p. 134
Withdrawal symptoms, p. 134
Tolerance, p. 135
Sedative–hypnotic, p. 136
Alcoholic, p. 136
Opiate, p. 141
Psychedelics, p. 141
Psychostimulant, p. 142

Learning CONNECTIONS

Some students benefit from extra help with the concept of sleep cycles. You can learn more about it in:

- The CD-ROM accompanying this book, Topic 4
- This book's study guide, *Keeping Pace Plus*, or the computerized study guide, Chapter 4
- The audiotape accompanying this book, *SoundGuide for Psychology*, Learning Unit 4
- The study aids found on the World Wide Web site for this book, at http://www.abacon.com/psych/lefton

Critical Thinking CONNECTIONS

Take a moment to think critically about how this chapter's topics are connected with the rest of psychology . . .

If you are interested in . . .	Ask yourself . . .	Then turn to . . .
Sleep and dreaming 	How might dreams help explain personality?	Chapter 12, p. 416; Chapter 15, p. 525
	How might stress affect the normal rhythm of sleep and dreams?	Chapter 13, pp. 456–457
	What is the impact of depression on normal sleep?	Chapter 14, pp. 497–498
	In what ways might Freud's interpretation of dreams be used as a therapeutic technique?	Chapter 15, pp. 524–525
Consciousness 	How is everyday awareness adversely affected by stressors in the environment?	Chapter 13, pp. 451–455
	How do treatment procedures take into account the possible role of unconscious day-to-day behavior?	Chapter 15, pp. 524–525
Substance use and abuse 	What are the implications of drug use by pregnant women?	Chapter 10, pp. 344–345
	Why do people turn to substances such as alcohol to help relieve stress?	Chapter 13, pp. 463–464
	How are people's attitudes about lifestyles, including substance use and abuse, influenced by parents and peers?	Chapter 16, pp. 557–558, 574–576

5

Learning

A friend of mine, a Marine, once gave a surprising and public demonstration of the power of learning. He had been a sniper in Vietnam, where he had learned to dive for cover at the sound of gunfire. Shortly after his return to the states, while on leave in Houston, he heard a car backfire as he walked down a sidewalk. He instantly dove for cover, right through a storefront window. Fortunately, he wasn't seriously injured, but he certainly startled those around him. Both common sense and laboratory experimentation tell us that my Marine friend was *conditioned* to behave the way he did.

Like the Marine, we learn a great deal in our lives, including how to protect ourselves from danger. Learning also explains many day-to-day behaviors. Consider, for example, Patrick's behavior. While walking across campus to his psychology class, Patrick wonders how he can get Cathy to notice him. He has made a strategic move to attract her attention by wearing his blue argyle sweater. The sweater became his favorite after several female friends complimented him on it. As Patrick climbs the carpeted stairs to class, he passes Ray, an upperclassman he admires. Noticing that Ray has his jacket collar up, Patrick flips his own collar up. Patrick reaches for the metal knob on the classroom door, touches it, and, expecting a shock, instantly jerks back his hand. Patrick has been shocked often by touching this particular doorknob—but not today. He solves the mystery when he remembers that he is wearing sneakers instead of his leather-soled loafers. It may not be obvious now what all this has to do with learning—but as this chapter progresses, the links between learning and Patrick's behavior will become clear.

By the time we reach adulthood, experience has taught us a large number of simple, predictable associations. We know, for example, that a long day at the beach may result in a painful sunburn and that a gas station should be our next stop when the fuel gauge reads empty. We have also learned sophisticated, complicated processes, such as how to drive a car and how to appreciate music ranging from Bach to Hootie and the Blowfish. Some people learn socially deviant behaviors, such as stealing and drug abuse. In general, learning is the process by which people acquire new knowledge. Psychologists define **learning** as a relatively permanent change in an organism that occurs as a result of experiences in the environment and that is often seen in overt behavior. This definition of *learning* has three important parts: (1) experience in the environment, (2) change in the organism, and (3) permanence.

First, in order for learning to occur, the organism must experience something in the environment. (Patrick observed that Ray was wearing his jacket collar up.) Second, some measurable change in the organism must be evident. (Patrick flipped up his own jacket collar.) Third, the change must be relatively permanent. (Weeks after seeing Ray, Patrick may still be wearing his collar upturned.)

Because the internal processes of learning cannot be seen, psychologists study the results of learning. To do so, they may examine such overt behavior as solving an algebra problem or throwing a ball. They may also measure physiological changes, such as brain-wave activity, heartbeat, and temperature.

Behavior is always being modified; new experiences affect learning, and what is learned may be forgotten. An organism's motivation, abilities, and physiological state influence its ability to learn. For example, if you are tired, learning the material in this chapter will be especially difficult. Also, practice and repeated experiences ensure that you will remember and will easily exhibit newly acquired learning, information, and skills. When learning has occurred, some process within you has changed, and a physiological change has occurred as well.

The factors that affect learning are often studied in animal behavior, because the genetic heritage of animals is easy to control and manipulate and because all details of an animal's history and environmental experiences can be known. Although some psychologists claim that different processes underlie animal and human learning, most believe—and experiments show—that the processes are similar. Differences become apparent and important, however, when complex behaviors are being evaluated and in experiments that require the use of language.

As you read this chapter, keep Patrick in mind. You will see how his actions illustrate the three basic learning processes that are the subject of this chapter: classical conditioning, operant conditioning, and cognitive learning.

Pavlovian, or Classical, Conditioning Theory

Learning: A relatively permanent change in an organism that occurs as a result of experiences in the environment.

When Patrick jerks his hand back from a doorknob in anticipation of a shock, his reaction is elicited by the presence of the doorknob. In the past, Patrick has been shocked when he touched this particular doorknob. Now he reacts in a reflexive manner when he touches it, whether it shocks him or not. He has learned this relationship through a process known as classical conditioning.

In a general sense, psychologists use the term *conditioning* to mean learning. But **conditioning** is actually a systematic procedure through which associations and responses to specific stimuli are learned. It is one of the simplest forms of learning. For example, consider what generally happens when you hear eerie music during a scene on television. You suspect that something supernatural or evil will soon take place, because eerie music usually foreshadows weird events, and you become fearful. You have been *conditioned* to feel that way. In the terminology used by psychologists, the eerie music is the *stimulus*, and fear is the *response*.

When psychologists first studied conditioning, they found relationships between specific stimuli and responses. Each time a certain stimulus occurs, the same reflexive response, or behavior, follows. For example, the presence of food in the mouth leads to salivation; a tap on the knee leads to a knee jerk; a bright light in the eye leads to contraction of the pupil and eye blink. A **reflex** is an involuntary, automatic behavior in response to a stimulus; it occurs without prior learning and usually shows little variability from instance to instance. Conditioned behaviors, in contrast, are learned. Many people have learned the response of fear to the stimulus of sitting in a dentist's chair, since they associate the chair with drilling and pain. A chair by itself (a neutral stimulus) does not elicit fear, but a chair associated with pain becomes a stimulus that can elicit fear. This is an example of *conditioning*.

Conditioned behaviors may occur so automatically that they appear to be reflexive; remember Patrick's jerking his hand away from the doorknob. Like reflexes, conditioned behaviors are involuntary; unlike reflexes, they are learned. In classical conditioning (to be defined shortly), previously neutral stimuli such as chairs, lights, and buzzers become associated with specific events and lead to responses such as fear, eye blinks, and nervousness.

In 1927, Ivan Pavlov (1849–1936), a Russian physiologist, summarized a now famous series of experiments in which he uncovered a basic principle of learning—conditioning. His research began quite by accident in a series of studies on how saliva and gastric secretions work on the digestive processes of dogs. He knew it is normal for dogs to salivate when they eat—salivation is a reflexive behavior that aids digestion—but the dogs were salivating *before* they tasted food. Pavlov reasoned that this might be happening because the dogs had learned to associate the trainers, who brought them food, with the food itself. Anxious to know more about this basic form of learning, Pavlov abandoned his research on gastric processes and redirected his efforts into teaching dogs to salivate to a new stimulus, such as a bell.

What Pavlov discovered was **classical conditioning**, or *Pavlovian conditioning*, in which an originally neutral stimulus, by repeated pairing with a stimulus that naturally elicits a response, comes to elicit a similar or even identical response. The process occurs in this way: When a neutral stimulus (such as a bell, buzzer, or light) is associated with a stimulus that normally brings about a response (such as food), the neutral stimulus over time will come to elicit the same response as the normal stimulus. Pavlov termed the stimulus that normally produces a response (for example, food) an **unconditioned stimulus**; he termed the response to this stimulus (for example, salivating) an **unconditioned response**. The unconditioned response occurs involuntarily, without learning, in response to the unconditioned stimulus.

Pavlov started with a relatively simple experiment—teaching dogs to salivate in response to a bell. First, he surgically altered the location of each dog's salivary gland to make the secretions of saliva accessible. He then attached tubes to the relocated salivary glands to measure precisely the amount of saliva produced by the food—the unconditioned stimulus. Then he introduced a bell—the new stimulus (see Figure 5.1 on page 152). He called the bell a neutral stimulus, because the sound of a bell is not necessarily related to salivation. Pavlov measured the amount of saliva the dogs produced when a bell was rung by itself; the amount was negligible. He then began the conditioning process by ringing the bell and immediately placing food in the dogs' mouths. After he did this several times, the dogs salivated

Conditioning: Systematic procedure through which associations and responses to specific stimuli are learned.

Reflex: Involuntary, automatic behavior that occurs in response to a stimulus without prior learning and usually shows little variability from instance to instance.

Classical conditioning: Conditioning process in which an originally neutral stimulus, by repeated pairing with a stimulus that normally elicits a response, comes to elicit a similar or even identical response. Also known as *Pavlovian conditioning*.

Unconditioned stimulus: A stimulus that normally produces a measurable involuntary response.

Unconditioned response: Unlearned or involuntary response to an unconditioned stimulus.

FIGURE 5.1

Pavlov Measuring Salivation

1 In Pavlov's classical conditioning studies, the dog was restrained in a harness in the cubicle and isolated from all distractions.

2 Pavlov attached a tube to the dog's salivary gland, which had been surgically moved to the outside of the dog's cheek to allow easy collection of saliva. He then measured the number of drops of saliva that occurred naturally when a bell was sounded.

3 Next, Pavlov measured the number of drops of saliva the dog produced when a bell was sounded along with the presentation of food.

4 Pavlov found that after repeated presentation of the bell along with food, salivary production occurred as soon as the bell was sounded, whether or not food was presented. This indicated that the dog had learned to associate the food and the bell—conditioning had occurred.

in response to the sound of the bell alone. Pavlov reasoned that the dogs had learned that the bell meant food was coming. He termed the bell, which elicited salivation as a result of learning, a conditioned stimulus. A **conditioned stimulus** is a neutral stimulus that, through repeated association with an unconditioned stimulus, becomes capable of eliciting a conditioned response. He termed the salivation—the

FIGURE 5.2

The Three Stages of Classical Conditioning

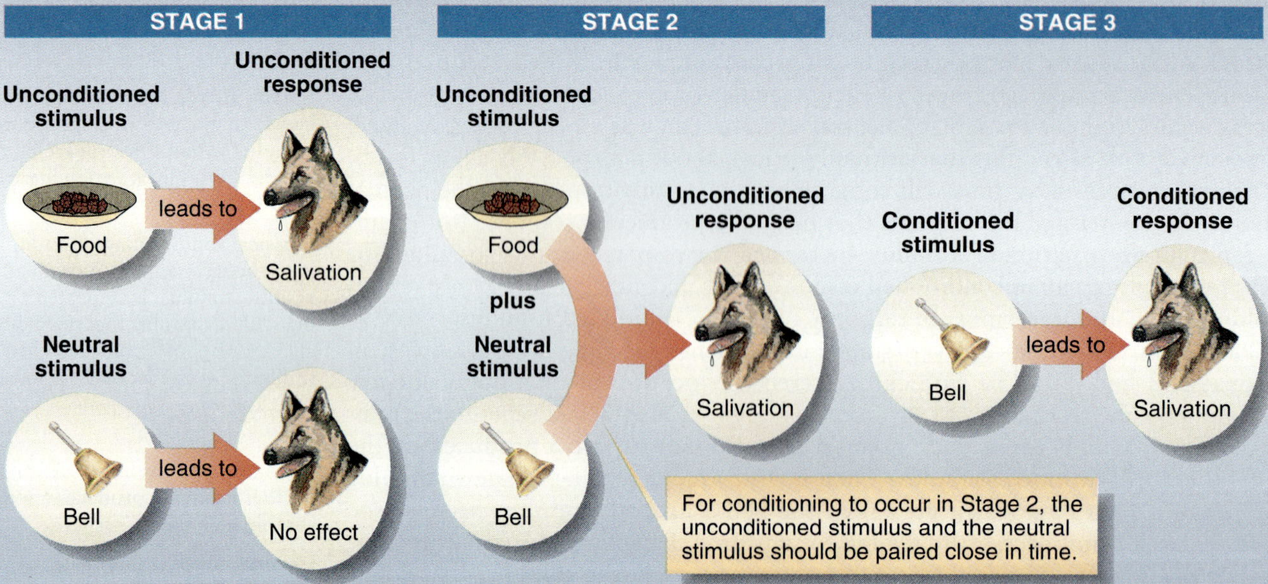

FIGURE 5.3

A Typical Acquisition Curve

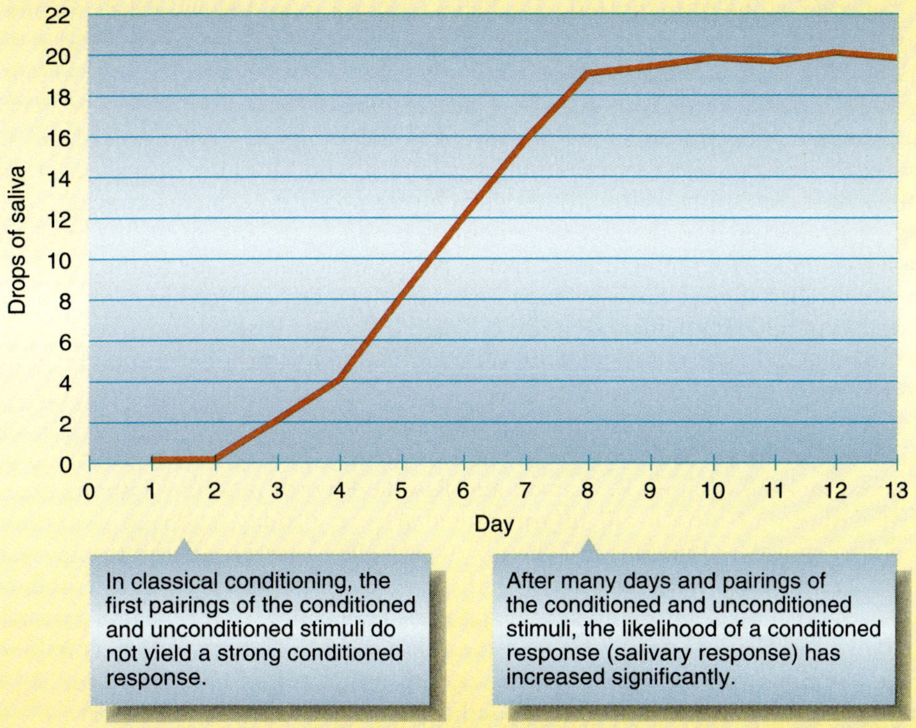

learned response to the sound of the bell—a **conditioned response** (the response elicited by a conditioned stimulus). From his experiments Pavlov discovered that the conditioned stimulus (the bell) brought about a similar but somewhat weaker response than the unconditioned stimulus (the food). The process of Pavlovian conditioning is outlined in Figure 5.2.

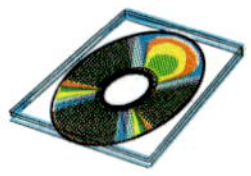

Fig. 5.2

The key characteristic of classical conditioning is the use of an originally neutral stimulus (here, a bell) to elicit a response (here, salivation) through repeated pairing of the neutral stimulus with an unconditioned stimulus that elicits the response naturally (here, food). On the first few trials of such pairings, conditioning is unlikely to occur. With additional trials, there is a greater likelihood that conditioning will occur. After dozens or even hundreds of pairings, the neutral stimulus will yield a conditioned response. Psychologists generally refer to this process as an *acquisition process* and say that an organism has acquired a response. Figure 5.3 shows a typical acquisition curve.

Classical conditioning occurs regularly in the everyday world. Your cat or dog may be conditioned to the sound of an electric can opener, which brings the animal running for food. Similarly, when you enter a dentist's office, your heart rate may increase and you may begin to exhibit nervous behaviors because of learned associations you have developed. When classical conditioning occurs, behavior changes.

Conditioned stimulus: A neutral stimulus that, through repeated association with an unconditioned stimulus, begins to elicit a conditioned response.

Conditioned response: Response elicited by a conditioned stimulus.

Classical Conditioning in Humans

After Pavlov's success with conditioning in dogs, psychologists were able to see that conditioning also occurs in human beings. In 1931, for example, D. P. Marquis showed classical conditioning in infants. Marquis knew that when an object touches

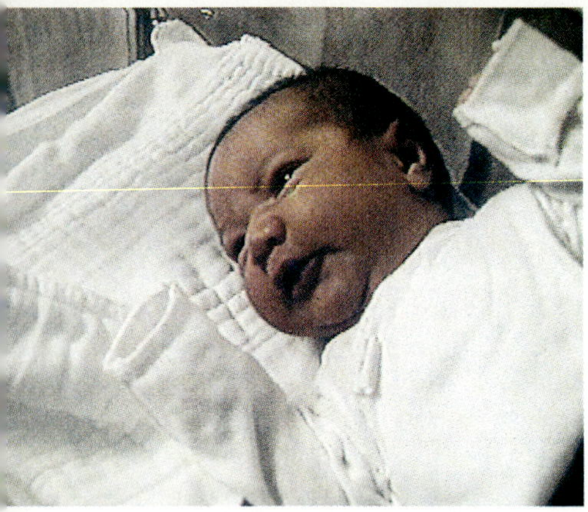

▲ *Classical conditioning appears to play a role in one of the earliest skills learned by newborns—the ability to recognize their mother using their sense of smell. (Photo courtesy of CNN.)*

an infant's lips, the infant immediately starts sucking, because the object is usually the nipple of a breast or bottle, from which the infant gets milk. The nipple, an unconditioned stimulus, elicits sucking, an unconditioned response. After repeated pairings of a sound or light with a nipple, infants were conditioned to suck when only the sound or light was presented.

Sucking is one of many reflexive behaviors in human beings; thus it is one of many responses that can be conditioned. For example, newborns respond reflexively to loud noises. (We'll examine newborns' reflexes in Chapter 10.) A loud noise naturally elicits a startle response—an outstretching of the arms and legs associated with changes in heart rate, blood pressure, and breathing. Any responses of this sort can be elicited through conditioning procedures. And all kinds of neutral stimuli can become conditioned stimuli that elicit either positive or defensive reactions. A puff of air delivered to the eye, for example, produces the unconditioned response of an eye blink. When a light or buzzer is paired with puffs of air to the eye, it will eventually elicit the eye blink by itself. This effect can be produced in many animals, as well as in human adults and infants.

Some psychologists believe both pleasant and unpleasant emotional responses can be classically conditioned. Consider the following: If a child who is playing with a favorite toy is repeatedly frightened by a sudden loud noise, the child may be conditioned to be afraid each time he or she sees the toy. This type of relationship was explored in 1920 by John B. Watson and Rosalie Raynor in a now famous experiment with an 11-month-old infant named Albert. (Today, such an experiment would be considered unethical.) The infant was given a series of toys to play with, including a live white rat. One day, as Albert reached for the rat, the experimenters made a sudden ear-splitting noise that frightened the child. After repeated pairing of the noise and the rat, Albert learned the relationship. The rat served as a conditioned stimulus and the loud noise as the unconditioned stimulus; on each subsequent presentation, the rat evoked a conditioned response of fear in Albert.

Another example: Beer commercials apply conditioning principles by featuring beautiful people enjoying their favorite beer while frolicking on a warm, sunny beach or socializing in a cozy ski chalet. The producers hope that when viewers associate the can of beer (a neutral stimulus) with an unconditioned stimulus that naturally elicits a positive emotional response (the pleasant scene), the beer will similarly elicit a positive response. In other words, they hope to condition people to feel good whenever they think about this beer. The powerful role of classical conditioning in advertising has been supported by experimental studies with adults in the laboratory (Stuart, Shimp, & Engle, 1987).

Higher-Order Conditioning

After a neutral stimulus becomes a conditioned stimulus, it is likely to elicit the conditioned response whenever it is presented. Moreover, another phenomenon that may occur is **higher-order conditioning**—the process by which a neutral stimulus takes on conditioned properties through pairing with another conditioned stimulus. Thus, higher-order conditioning permits increasingly remote associations, which can result in a complex network of conditioned stimuli and responses. At least two factors determine the extent of higher-order conditioning: (1) the similarity between the higher-order stimulus and the original conditioned stimulus, and (2) the frequency and consistency with which the two conditioned stimuli are paired (Rescorla, 1978).

Higher-order conditioning: Process by which a neutral stimulus takes on conditioned properties through pairing with a conditioned stimulus.

Suppose a light is paired with mild electric shocks to a dog. On seeing the light, the dog exhibits fear; the light has thus become a conditioned stimulus that elicits a set of fear responses. If a bell is now paired with or presented just before the light, the new stimulus (the bell) can also take on properties of the conditioned stimulus (the light). After repeated pairings, the dog will learn to associate the two events (the light and the bell), and either event by itself will elicit a fear response. When a third stimulus—say, an experimenter in a white lab coat—is introduced, the dog may learn to associate the experimenter with the bell or light. After enough trials, the dog may have conditioned fear responses to each of the three stimuli: the light, the bell, and the experimenter (Pavlov, 1927; Rescorla, 1977).

Higher-order conditioning is common in daily life and apparent in every culture. For example, a driver who has received several expensive speeding tickets from the highway patrol may reflexively slow down whenever she sees a patrol car, to avoid receiving another ticket. There is a universality to this response—it occurs in Japan as well as in the United States. If the same driver repeatedly observes a highway patrol car parked inconspicuously on a particular stretch of road, she may start slowing down whenever she drives that stretch of road, whether or not she sees a patrol car. The stretch of road becomes another stimulus that induces the driver to ease up on the gas pedal. Even a car that is the same model as those used by the highway patrol may elicit the response. You can see that successful pairing of conditioned and unconditioned stimuli—that is, successful classical conditioning—involves many key variables.

FOCUS

Review

- Identify the fundamental difference between a reflex and a conditioned behavior. p. 151
- Distinguish between a conditioned and an unconditioned response. pp. 151–153

Think Critically

- Provide an example of how classical conditioning and higher-order conditioning occur in your life.
- Can you think of a situation in which you might want to facilitate higher-order conditioning? How you might increase the likelihood of this kind of learning taking place?

Key Variables in Classical Conditioning

Classical conditioning is not a simple process. How loud does the buzzer have to be? How long does the bell have to ring? How sinister must the movie's scary music be? How many times must someone experience pain in a dentist's chair, and how strong does the pain have to be? How would a driver react to the sight of the highway patrol if his only encounter with the police had occurred when his car broke down on a cold, stormy night and he had been aided by an officer? As with other psychological phenomena, situational variables affect when, if, and under what conditions classical conditioning will occur. Cultural variables are also important; while the principles of conditioning are the same in every culture, what constitutes a fear-producing stimulus will vary from culture to culture.

Some of the most important variables in classical conditioning are the strength, timing, and frequency of the unconditioned stimulus. When these variables are optimal, conditioning occurs easily.

Strength, Timing, and Frequency

Strength of the Unconditioned Stimulus. A puff of air delivered to the eye will easily elicit a conditioned response, but only if the puff of air (the unconditioned stimulus) is sufficiently strong. Research shows that when the unconditioned stimulus is strong and elicits a quick and regular reflexive (unconditioned) response, conditioning of the neutral stimulus is likely to occur. On the other hand, when the unconditioned stimulus is weak, it is unlikely to elicit an unconditioned response, and conditioning of the neutral stimulus is unlikely to occur. Thus, pairing a neutral stimulus with a weak unconditioned stimulus will not reliably lead to conditioning.

Timing of the Unconditioned Stimulus. For conditioning to occur, an unconditioned stimulus must usually be paired with a conditioned stimulus close enough in time for the two to become associated; that is, they must be temporally contiguous. (In Pavlov's experiment, conditioning would not have occurred if the bell and the food had been presented an hour apart.) The two stimuli may be presented together or may be separated by a brief interval. The optimal time between the onset of the two stimuli varies from one study to another and depends on many variables, including the type of conditioned response sought (e.g., Schwarz-Stevens & Cunninghan, 1993). Some types of conditioning can occur with fairly long delays, but a general guideline for achieving a strong conditioned response is that the conditioned stimulus should occur about half a second before the unconditioned stimulus and overlap with it, particularly for reflexes such as the eye blink.

Frequency of Pairings. Occasional or rare pairings of a neutral stimulus with an unconditioned stimulus at close intervals usually do not result in conditioning; generally speaking, frequent pairings and pairings that establish a relationship between the unconditioned and the conditioned stimulus are necessary. If, for example, food and the sound of a bell are paired on every trial, a dog is conditioned more quickly than if the stimuli are paired on every other trial. The frequency of the natural occurrence of the unconditioned stimulus is also important. If the unconditioned stimulus does not occur frequently but is always associated with the conditioned stimulus, more rapid conditioning is likely, because one stimulus predicts the other (Rescorla, 1988). Once the conditioned response has reached its maximum strength, additional pairings of the stimuli do not increase the likelihood of a conditioned response. There are exceptions to this general rule, and specific one-time pairings can produce learning.

Predictability

A key factor determining whether conditioning will occur is the predictability of the association of the unconditioned and conditioned stimuli. Closeness in time and regular frequency of pairings promote conditioning, but these are not enough. Predictability facilitates, and turns out to be a central factor in, conditioning (Rescorla, 1988).

Pavlov thought that classical conditioning was based on timing. Research now shows, however, that if the unconditioned stimulus (such as the food) can be predicted by the conditioned stimulus (such as the bell), then conditioning is rapidly achieved. Conditioning is achieved not because of the number of times the two events have occurred but rather because of the reliability with which the conditioned stimulus predicts the unconditioned stimulus. Pavlov's dogs learned that bells were good predictors of food; the conditioned stimulus (bells) reliably predicted the unconditioned one (food), so conditioning was quickly achieved.

In Rescorla's (1988) view, what is learned in conditioning is the predictability of events—bells predicting food, light predicting puffs of air to the eye, dentist chairs predicting pain. Predictability is one of the key elements in classical conditioning, but without other contextual cues it usually is not enough (Papini & Bitterman, 1990). Many learning researchers consider this concept, predictability, a cognitive concept; animals and human beings think about and make predictions about the future based on past events. As we will see in the next two chapters (on memory and cognition), such thought is based on simple learning but becomes even more complex. The predictability of events becomes especially important in some learned behaviors, such as the food aversions considered next.

Taste Aversion

My daughter Sarah has hated mustard ever since her sixth birthday party. After her friends and their mothers left the party, we sat down for ham sandwiches with lettuce and mustard. Two hours later, she was ill—fever, vomiting, chills, and swollen glands. It was the flu. But as far as Sarah was concerned, it was the mustard that had made her sick; 16 years later, she still refuses to eat mustard.

The Garcia Effect. This association of mustard and nausea is an example of a conditioned taste aversion. In a famous experiment, John Garcia gave animals specific foods or liquids to eat or drink and then induced nausea (usually by injecting a drug or by exposing the animals to radiation). He found that after only one pairing of a food or drink (the conditioned stimulus) with the drug or radiation (the unconditioned stimulus), the animals avoided the food or drink that preceded the nausea (see, e.g., Garcia & Koelling, 1971; Linberg et al., 1982).

Two aspects of Garcia's work startled the research community. First, Garcia showed that a conditioned taste aversion could be obtained even if the nausea was induced several hours after the food or drink had been consumed. This contradicted the previously held assumption that the time interval between the unconditioned stimulus and the conditioned stimulus had to be short, especially if conditioning was to occur quickly. Garcia also proved that not all stimuli can serve as conditioned stimuli. He tried to pair bells and lights with nausea to produce an aversion in rats, but he was unable to do so. This led him to conclude that "strong aversions to the smell or taste of food can develop even when illness is delayed for hours after consumption [but] avoidance reactions do not develop for visual, auditory, or tactile stimuli associated with food" (Garcia & Koelling, 1971, p. 461). Garcia had disproved two accepted principles of learning.

Conditioned taste aversion, sometimes called the *Garcia effect*, has adaptive value. In one trial or instance, animals learn to avoid foods that make them sick by associating the smells of poisonous foods with the foods themselves. This clearly has survival value. Conditioned taste aversion is unaffected by intervening events during the delay between the taste and the illness (Holder et al., 1989). Anyone who has suffered from food poisoning will attest to the lasting memory of the food or meal that caused it!

Conditioned taste aversion, or the Garcia effect, has been used successfully to deter coyotes from attacking sheep. ▼

Conditioned taste aversion also has practical uses. Coyotes and wolves often attack sheep and lambs. Garcia laced lamb meat with a substance that causes a short-term illness and put the food on the outskirts of sheep ranchers' fenced-in areas. Coyotes who ate the lamb meat became sick and developed a lamb aversion. After this experience, they approached the sheep as if ready to attack, but they nearly always backed off (see, e.g., Garcia et al., 1976). By using conditioned taste aversion, Garcia deterred coyotes from eating sheep.

Learning, Weight Loss, and Cancer. Cancer patients often undergo chemotherapy; an unfortunate side effect of the therapy is vomiting and nausea. The patients often lose their appetite and lose weight during their treatment. Is it possible that they lose weight because of a conditioned taste aversion? According to researcher Ilene Bernstein (1988), some cancer patients become conditioned to avoid food: They check into a hospital, have a meal, are given chemotherapy, become sick, and then avoid the food that preceded the therapy. Bernstein conducted research with children and adults who were going to receive chemotherapy. Her research showed that patients given foods before therapy developed specific aversions to those foods; control groups who were not given those foods before their therapy did not develop aversions to them. Bovbjerg and colleagues (1992) found similar results.

Patients develop the food aversions even when they know it is the chemotherapy that induces the nausea. Bernstein suggests an intervention based on learning theory: Patients could be given a "scapegoat" food just before chemotherapy, so any conditioned aversion that develops will be to a nutritionally unimportant food rather than to nutritious foods. When Bernstein (1988) tried this procedure, results were successful.

Extinction and Spontaneous Recovery

Some conditioned responses last for a long time; others disappear quickly. Much depends on whether the conditioned response still predicts the unconditioned one. Consider the following: What would have happened to Pavlov's dogs if he had rung the bell each day but never followed the bell with food? What would happen if you went to the dentist every day for 2 months, but the dentist only brushed your teeth with a pleasant-tasting toothpaste and never drilled?

If a researcher continues Pavlov's experiment by presenting the conditioned stimulus (bell) but no unconditioned stimulus (food), the likelihood of a conditioned response decreases with every trial; it undergoes extinction. In classical conditioning, **extinction** is the process through which withholding the unconditioned stimulus gradually reduces the probability (and often the strength) of a conditioned response. Imagine a study in which a puff of air is associated with a buzzer that consistently elicits the conditioned eye-blink response. If the unconditioned stimulus (the puff of air) is no longer delivered in association with the buzzer, the likelihood that the buzzer will continue to elicit the eye-blink response decreases over time (see Figure 5.4). When presentation of the buzzer alone no longer elicits the conditioned response, psychologists say that the response has been *extinguished*.

An extinguished conditioned response can recur, especially after a rest period; this phenomenon is termed **spontaneous recovery**. For example, when a dog has been conditioned to salivate in response to the sound of a bell and then experiences a long series of trials in which food is not paired with the bell, the dog makes few or no responses to the bell. The behavior has been extinguished. If the dog is placed in the experimental situation again after a rest period of 20 minutes, its salivary response to the bell will recur briefly (although less strongly than before). This behavior shows that the effects of extinction are not permanent and that the learned association is not totally forgotten (see Figure 5.5).

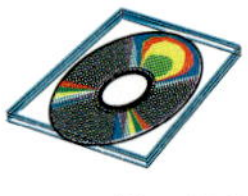

Fig. 5.3

FIGURE 5.4

A Typical Extinction Curve

Numerous experiments have demonstrated that the percentage of times an organism will display a conditioned response decreases over a number of trials in which the unconditioned stimulus is not presented. When presentation of the unconditioned stimulus alone no longer elicits the conditioned response, the response has been extinguished.

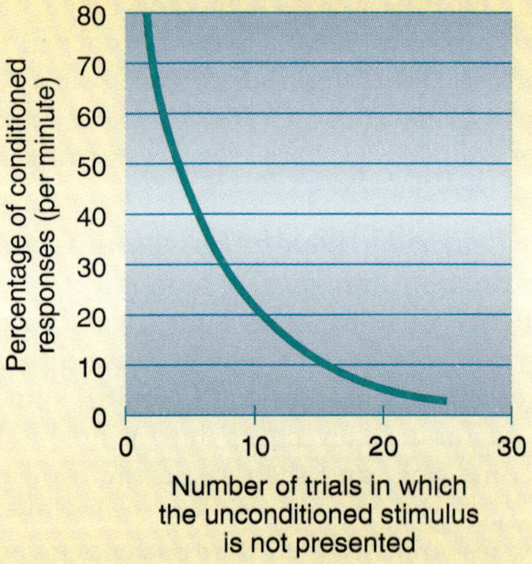

Extinction [egg-STINK-shun]: In classical conditioning, the process through which withholding of the unconditioned stimulus gradually reduces the probability of a conditioned response.

Spontaneous recovery: Recurrence of an extinguished conditioned response following a rest period.

FIGURE 5.5

The Process of Spontaneous Recovery

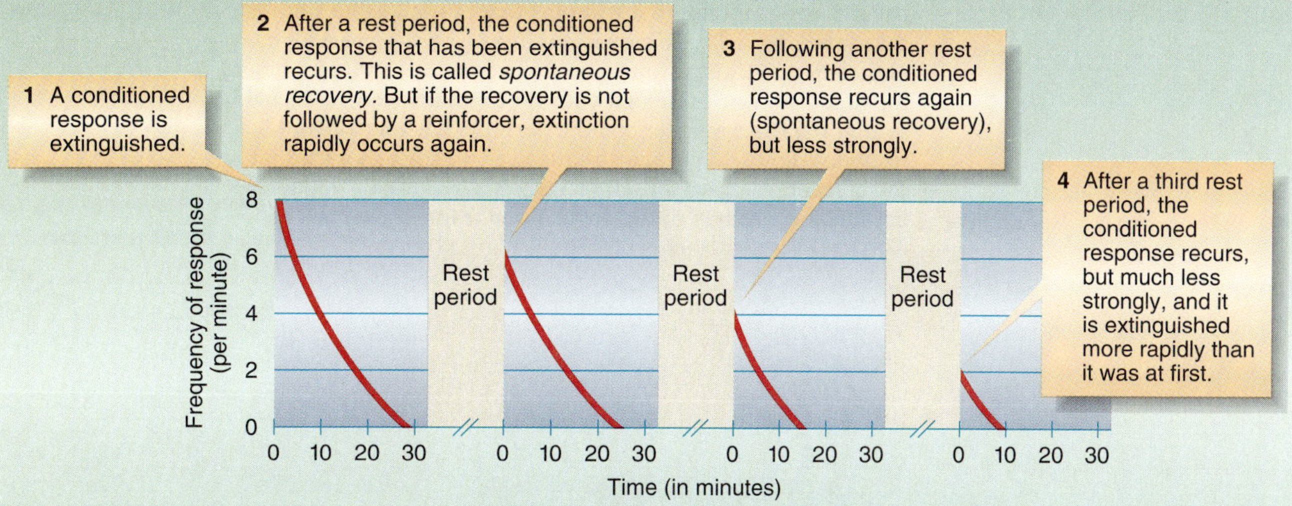

This graph shows some of Pavlov's actual data from an experiment published in 1927. Pavlov brought about extinction in a series of six trials by omitting the presentation of the unconditioned stimulus; but after a 20-minute rest period, spontaneous recovery occurred.

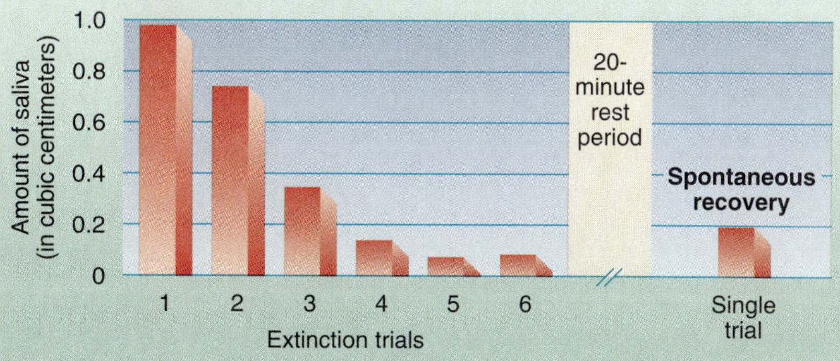

Stimulus Generalization and Stimulus Discrimination

Imagine that a 3-year-old child pulls a cat's tail and gets a painful scratch in return. It will not be surprising if the child develops a fear of that cat; but the child may actually develop a fear of all cats, and even of dogs and other four-legged animals. Adults may respond in the same way to similar stimuli—a phenomenon that psychologists call stimulus generalization.

Stimulus generalization occurs when an organism develops a conditioned response to a stimulus that is similar but not identical to the original conditioned stimulus. The extent to which an organism responds to a stimulus similar to the original one depends on how alike the two stimuli are. If, for example, a loud tone is the conditioned stimulus for an eye-blink response, somewhat lower but similar tones will also produce the response. A totally dissimilar tone will produce little or no response. Likewise, the Marine described at the beginning of the chapter responded to the sound of a car backfiring because it was similar to the sound of gunfire. See Figure 5.6 on page 160 for another example of stimulus generalization.

Stimulus discrimination is the process by which an organism learns to respond only to a specific reinforced stimulus. Pavlov showed that animals that have learned to differentiate between pairs of stimuli display frustration or even aggression when

Stimulus generalization: Occurrence of a conditioned response with a stimulus that is similar but not identical to the original conditioned stimulus.

Stimulus discrimination: Process by which an organism learns to respond only to a specific reinforced stimulus.

FIGURE 5.6

Stimulus Generalization

Stimulus generalization occurs when an organism exhibits a conditioned response to a stimulus that is similar but not identical to the original conditioned stimulus. In this experiment, an organism was trained to respond to a tone of 1,000 Hz. Later, the organism was presented with tones of different frequencies so that the experimenter could determine whether it would respond to those dissimilar frequencies. Results showed that the percentage of responses decreased as the tone's frequency became increasingly different from the training frequency.
(Based on Jenkins & Harrison, 1960.)

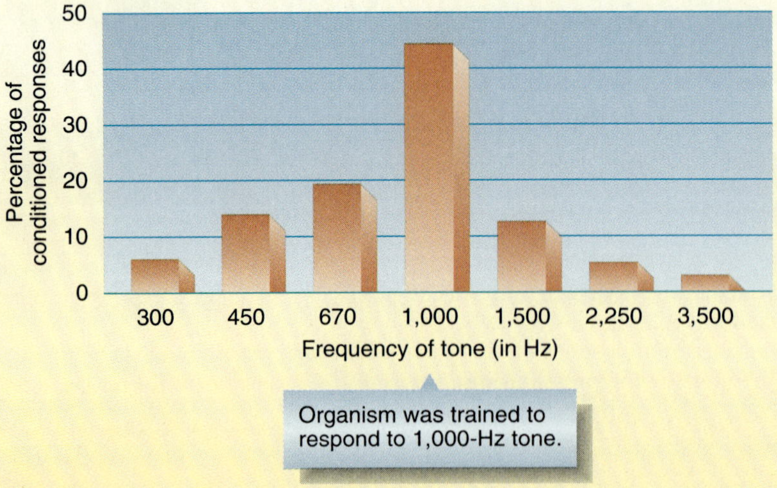

discrimination is made difficult or impossible. He trained a dog to discriminate between a circle and an ellipse and then changed the shape of the ellipse on successive trials to look more and more like the circle. Eventually, the animal was unable to discriminate between the shapes; it randomly chose one or the other and also became aggressive.

Human beings exhibit similar disorganization in behavior when placed in situations in which they feel compelled to make a response but do not know how to respond correctly. In such situations, where discrimination becomes impossible, behavior can become stereotyped and limited in scope; people may choose either not to respond to the stimulus or to respond always in the same way (Lundin, 1961; Maier & Klee, 1941). Often, therapists must teach maladjusted people to learn to be more flexible in their responses to difficult situations.

Table 5.1 summarizes four important concepts in classical conditioning: extinction, spontaneous recovery, stimulus generalization, and stimulus discrimination.

The Conditioning of Physical Symptoms

Think of Patrick's hand on the doorknob, the Marine's reaction to a loud noise, and a person's fear of the dentist chair. You can see that classical conditioning explains a wide range of human behaviors, including some physical responses to the world, such as heart rate acceleration and changes in blood pressure.

Substances such as pollen, dust, animal dander, and mold initiate an allergic reaction in many people. Cat fur, for example, may naturally elicit an allergic

TABLE 5.1 *Four Important Concepts in Classical Conditioning*

Property	Definition	Example
Extinction	The process of reducing the probability of a conditioned response by withholding the unconditioned stimulus (the reinforcer).	An infant conditioned by the stroking of its lips to suck in response to a light is no longer given the unconditioned stimulus of stroking the lips; the infant stops sucking in response to the conditioned stimulus.
Spontaneous recovery	The recurrence of an extinguished conditioned response following a rest period.	A dog's conditioned salivary response has been extinguished. After a rest period, the dog again salivates in response to the conditioned stimulus, though less than before.
Stimulus generalization	The occurrence of a conditioned response to stimuli that are similar but not identical to the original conditioned stimulus.	A dog conditioned to salivate in response to a high-pitched tone also salivates in response to a somewhat lower-pitched tone.
Stimulus discrimination	The process by which an organism learns to respond only to a specific reinforced stimulus.	A goat is conditioned to salivate only in response to lights of high intensity, not to lights of low intensity.

reaction, such as an inability to breathe, in persons with asthma. Asthma attacks, like other behaviors, can be conditioned to occur. If cat fur has *always* been found in Lindsay's house (a regular pairing), classical conditioning theory predicts that even if all the cat hair is removed, an asthmatic individual entering Lindsay's house may have an allergic reaction. (A conditioned stimulus, the house, predicts an unconditioned response, the allergic reaction.) Researchers have shown that people with severe allergies can have an allergic reaction from merely seeing a cat (or entering Lindsay's house, even long after the cat's demise), even if there is no cat fur present.

Even the body's immune system can be conditioned (Ader & Cohen, 1993). Normally, the body releases antibodies to fight disease when toxic substances appear in the blood. This is an involuntary activity that is independent of the nervous system. In a striking series of studies, animals were classically conditioned in a way that altered their immune responses (Ader & Cohen, 1993; Ader, Cohen, & Bovbjerg, 1982). The experimenters paired a sweet-tasting solution with a drug that produced illness and, as a side effect, also suppressed the immune response. The animals quickly learned to avoid the sweet-tasting substance that seemed to predict illness. When later presented with the sweet-tasting substance alone, they showed a reduction in immune system antibodies. The experimenters had classically conditioned an immune system response that was previously thought not to be under nervous system control. This is a striking finding.

New research also shows that drug users condition themselves. When heroin addicts inject heroin, their bodies produce an antiopiate substance to protect them from an overdose; this is a natural response. Siegel (1988) has shown that if the addict always injects the drug in the same room, the place itself may serve to initiate an antiopiate response, without the heroin ever actually being administered.

FOCUS

Review

- How do the variables of strength, timing, and frequency affect learning? pp. 155–156
- What happens to the conditioned response if a researcher in a Pavlovian experiment presents the conditioned stimulus but no unconditioned stimulus? p. 158

Think Critically

- What evidence led Garcia to conclude that taste aversion can occur in one trial or one instance? What other examples of learning could occur in one trial or one instance?

BUILDING TABLE 5.1

Types of Learning: Classical Conditioning

TYPE OF LEARNING	PROCEDURE	RESULT	EXAMPLE
Classical Conditioning	A neutral stimulus (such as a bell) is paired with an unconditioned stimulus (such as food).	The neutral stimulus becomes a conditioned stimulus—it elicits the conditioned response.	A bell elicits a response in a dog. 

Therefore, the location of a user's heroin administration can serve as a conditioned stimulus for the antiopiate response. When this happens, an addict may develop withdrawal symptoms, which in turn may create an even greater "need" for the drug. The stimulus for the increased use may have been merely the location of the drug consumption.

Building Table 5.1 summarizes some of the key elements of classical conditioning. Although classical conditioning explains a wide range of phenomena, not all behaviors are the result of such associations. Many complex behaviors result from another form of learning, operant conditioning, which is discussed next.

Operant Conditioning

Let's return to Patrick, the student described at the beginning of the chapter. Patrick was wearing a blue argyle sweater, which had become his favorite sweater after he had received several compliments on it. Patrick's decision to wear that particular sweater, unlike his jerking away from an electric shock, is a nonreflexive behavior that cannot be attributed to classical conditioning. Rather, Patrick's wearing the blue sweater was reinforced through operant conditioning; that is, Patrick had been rewarded several times for wearing that sweater.

Pioneers: B. F. Skinner and E. L. Thorndike

The process by which Patrick was conditioned to wear his sweater was described in the 1930s by B. F. Skinner (1904–1990), who challenged and began to change the way psychologists think about conditioning and learning. In fact, Skinner questioned whether Pavlovian (classical) conditioning should be studied at all. Like Pavlov, Skinner focused only on an organism's observable behavior. Thought processes, consciousness, brain–behavior relationships, and the mind were not considered the proper subject matter of psychology. Skinner's early work was in the tradition of such strict behaviorists as Watson, although Skinner ultimately modified some of his own most extreme positions. His 1938 book *The Behavior of Organisms* continues to have an impact on studies of conditioning.

According to Skinner, many behaviors are acquired and maintained through operant conditioning, not through Pavlov's classical conditioning. Skinner used the term *operant conditioning* because the organism *operates* on the environment, with every action followed by a specific event, or consequence. **Operant conditioning,** or *instrumental conditioning*, is conditioning in which an increase or decrease in the likelihood that a behavior will recur is affected by the delivery of a rewarding or punishing event as a consequence of the behavior. The conditioned behavior is usu-

Operant conditioning [OP-er-ant]: Conditioning in which the probability that an organism will emit a response is increased or decreased by the subsequent delivery of a reinforcer or punisher. Also known as *instrumental conditioning*.

ally voluntary, not reflex-like as in classical conditioning. Another key difference between classical conditioning and operant conditioning is that the reward or punishment *follows,* rather than coexists with, the behavior.

Consider what happens when a boss rewards and encourages her overworked employees by giving them unexpected cash bonuses. If the bonuses improve morale and induce the employees to work harder, then the employer's conditioning efforts have been successful. In turn, the employees could condition the boss's behavior by rewarding her bonus paying with further increases in productivity, thereby encouraging her to continue giving bonuses. In the laboratory, researchers have studied similar sequences of behaviors followed by rewards. One of the most famous experiments was conducted by the American psychologist E. L. Thorndike (1874–1949), who pioneered the study of operant conditioning during the 1890s and first reported his work in 1898. Thorndike placed hungry cats in boxes and put food outside the boxes. The cats could escape from the boxes and get food by hitting a lever that opened a door in each box. The cats quickly performed the behavior Thorndike was trying to condition (hitting the lever), because doing so (at first by accident and then deliberately) gave them access to food. Because the response (hitting the lever) was important (instrumental) in obtaining the reward, Thorndike used the term *instrumental conditioning* to describe the process and called the behaviors *instrumental behaviors*.

FIGURE 5.7

The Process of Operant Conditioning

Operant conditioning is different from classical conditioning in that the behavior to be conditioned (such as hitting a lever) is reinforced *after* it occurs.

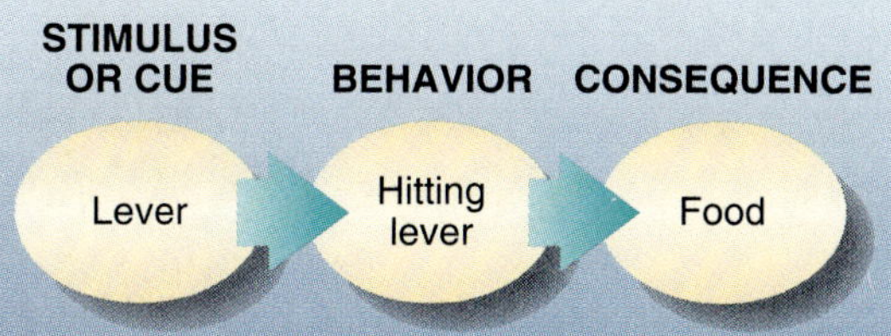

Although Skinner spoke of operant conditioning and Thorndike of instrumental conditioning, the two terms are often used interchangeably. What is important is that both Skinner and Thorndike acknowledged that first the behavior is *emitted* (displayed), and then a consequence (for example, a reward) follows. This is unlike classical (Pavlovian) conditioning, in which first there is a change in the environment (for example, bells and food are paired) and then the conditioned behavior (usually a reflexive response) is *elicited* (see Figure 5.7).

In operant conditioning, such as in Thorndike's experiment with cats, an organism emits a behavior and then a consequence follows. The type of consequence that follows the behavior is a crucial component of the conditioning, because it determines whether the behavior is likely to recur. Principally, the consequence can be a reinforcer or a punisher. As in classical conditioning, a reward acts as a *reinforcer*, increasing the likelihood that the behavior targeted for conditioning will recur; in Thorndike's experiment, food was the reinforcer for hitting the lever. A *punisher*, on the other hand, decreases the likelihood that the targeted behavior will recur. If an electric shock is delivered to a cat's paws each time the cat touches a lever, the cat quickly learns not to touch the lever. Parents use reinforcers and punishers when they link the behavior of their teenagers to the use of the family car. A teenager on a date is more likely to return home at an appropriate hour if doing so will ensure use of the car again. (We will discuss punishment and its consequences in more detail later in this chapter.)

The Skinner Box and Shaping

Much of the research on operant conditioning has used the apparatus that most psychologists call a Skinner box—even though Skinner never approved of the idea of naming it after him. A **Skinner box** is a box that contains a mechanism for delivering a consequence whenever the animal in the box makes a readily identifiable response that the experimenter has decided to reinforce or punish. In experiments that involve rewards, the delivery mechanism is often a small lever or bar in the side of the box; whenever the animal presses it, the pressing behavior is rewarded.

Skinner box: Named (by others) for its developer, B. F. Skinner, a box that contains a responding mechanism (usually a lever) capable of delivering a consequence, often a reinforcer, to an organism.

FIGURE 5.8

A Cumulative Recorder

To record the rate of an organism's responses, a strip of paper is unrolled off a drum at a constant slow rate. Each time the organism makes a response, such as pressing a lever, it initiates an electrical impulse, which makes the recorder's pen move to the side. Subsequent responses move the pen farther to the side, and a steplike slope is drawn. If the organism makes no responses, the pen traces a straight line parallel to the length of the paper. A rapid rate of response produces a steep slope on the resulting tracing; a shallow slope results when the organism has a slow rate of response.

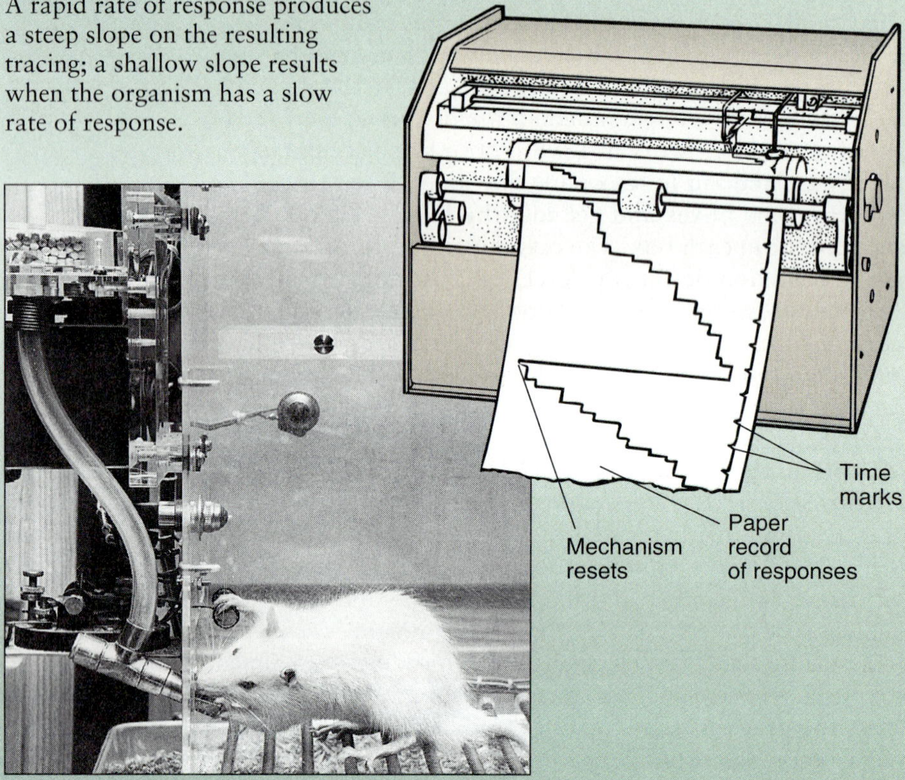

Punishment often takes the form of electric shocks delivered through a grid on the floor of the box.

In a traditional operant conditioning experiment, a rat that has been deprived of food is placed in a Skinner box. The rat moves around the box, often seeking to escape; eventually it stumbles on the lever and presses it. Immediately following that action, the experimenter delivers a pellet of food into a cup. The rat moves about some more and happens to press the lever again; another pellet of food is delivered. After a few trials, the rat learns that pressing the lever brings food. A hungry rat will learn to press the lever many times in rapid succession to obtain food.

To make measuring responses easier, psychologists developed a practical and simple device, a *cumulative recorder.* This device, shown in Figure 5.8, was essential for the early progress made in animal learning laboratories. Today, psychologists use computerized devices to quantify behavior such as bar pressing and to track the progress an organism makes in learning a response.

Shaping: Gradual training of an organism to give the proper responses through selective reinforcement of behaviors as they approach the desired response.

Teaching an organism a complex response takes many trials because most organisms need to be taught in small steps, through *shaping*. **Shaping** is the process of reinforcing behavior that approximates (comes close to) a desired behavior. To teach a hungry rat to press a bar in a Skinner box, for example, a researcher begins by giving the rat a pellet of food each time it enters the side of the box on which the bar is located. Once this behavior is established, the rat receives food only when it touches the wall where the bar is located. It then receives food only when it approaches the bar—and so on, until it receives food only when it actually presses the bar. At each stage the reinforced behavior (entering the half of the box nearest the bar, touching the wall that houses the bar, and so on) more closely approximates the desired behavior (pressing the bar). The sequence of stages used to elicit increasingly closer approximations of a desired behavior is sometimes called the *method of successive approximations,* which means approximately the same thing as *shaping.*

▲ *Trainers use shaping to teach animals tricks. Each time this killer whale makes a closer approximation to the trainer's goal of having it leap through a hoop, she rewards it with a fish.*

Shaping is effective for teaching animals new behaviors; for example, shaping is used to train a dog to sit on command. The trainer generally does this by pairing a dog treat with a push on the dog's rear while verbally commanding "Sit!" With a treat as reinforcer following the sitting, the dog begins to sit with less and less pressure applied to its rear; eventually, it sits on command. Shaping is also helpful in teaching people new behaviors. For example, were you taught how to play baseball? If so, first you were taught how to hold the bat correctly, then how to swing it, then how to make contact with the ball, and finally how to get a base hit.

Teaching new behaviors by means of operant conditioning is time-consuming and often must be done in several stages, especially if the behaviors are complex. For example, a father who wants his son to make his bed neatly will at first reinforce *all* of the child's attempts at bed making, even if the results are sloppy. Over successive weeks, the father will reinforce only the better attempts, until finally he reinforces only neat bed making. Patience is important, because it is essential to reinforce all steps toward the desired behavior, no matter how small (Fischer & Gochros, 1975). Shaping embodies a central tenet of behaviorism—that reinforced behaviors recur. Skinner is the individual most responsible for advancing that notion; psychologists attribute to him the idea that various consequences can redirect the natural flow of behavior. Among the most important of these consequences is reinforcement.

Reinforcement

To really understand operant conditioning, you need to study the basic principles of reinforcement. To psychologists, a **reinforcer** is any event that increases the probability of a recurrence of the response that preceded it. Thus, a behavior followed by a desirable event is likely to recur. Examples of reinforcement abound in daily life: A person works hard in a factory and is rewarded with high pay; a student studies long hours for an examination and is rewarded with a top grade; sales agents call on hundreds of clients and sell lots of their products; young children behave appropriately and receive affection and praise from their parents. The specific behaviors of working hard, studying a great deal, calling on clients, and behaving for parents are established because of reinforcement. Such behaviors can be taught by means of either or both of two kinds of reinforcers: positive and negative.

Reinforcer: Any event that increases the probability of a recurrence of the response that preceded it.

Positive reinforcement: Presentation of a rewarding or pleasant stimulus after a particular response, to increase the likelihood that the response will recur.

Positive Reinforcement. Most people have used positive reinforcement at one time or another. **Positive reinforcement** is the presentation of a rewarding or pleasant stimulus after a particular response, to increase the likelihood that the response will recur. When you are teaching your dog tricks, you reward it with a biscuit or a pat on the head. When a parent is toilet training a 2-year-old, the parent may applaud when the child successfully deposits a bowel movement in the potty;

the applause is a reinforcer. The dog and the child continue the behaviors because they have been rewarded with something that is important or desired; their behaviors have been positively reinforced.

Some reinforcers are more powerful than others, and a reinforcer that rewards one person may not have reinforcing value for another. A smile from an approving parent may be a powerful reinforcer for a 2-year-old; high grades may be the most effective reinforcer for a student; money may be effective for one adult, position or status for another. At many corporations, bonuses for effective performance may include color televisions, stereo systems, or trips to Hawaii.

Negative Reinforcement. Whereas positive reinforcement increases the probability of a response through delivery of a reward, **negative reinforcement** increases the probability of a response through removal of an *aversive* (unpleasant or noxious) stimulus. Negative reinforcement is still reinforcement, because it strengthens or increases the likelihood of a response; its reinforcing properties are associated with its removal. For example, suppose a rat is placed in a maze with an electrified grid that delivers a shock every 50 seconds, and the rat can escape the shock by turning to the left in the maze. The behavior to be conditioned is turning to the left in the maze; the reinforcement is termination of the painful stimulus. In this case, negative reinforcement—termination of the painful stimulus—increases the probability of the response (going left) because that is the way to turn off the unpleasant stimulus.

Noxious or unpleasant stimuli are often used in animal studies of escape and avoidance. In *escape conditioning*, a rat in a Skinner box receives a shock just strong enough to cause it to thrash around until it bumps against a bar, thereby stopping the shock. In just a few trials, the rat learns to press the bar to escape being shocked, to bring an unpleasant situation to an end. In *avoidance conditioning*, the same apparatus is used, but a buzzer or some other cue precedes the shock by a few seconds. In this case, the rat learns that when it is presented with a stimulus or cue such as a buzzer, it should press the bar to prevent the shock from occurring—to avoid it. Avoidance conditioning generally involves escape conditioning as well. First the animal learns how to escape the shock by pressing the bar. Then it learns how to avoid the shock by pressing the bar when it hears the buzzer that signals the oncoming shock.

In avoidance conditioning, the organism learns to respond in such a way that the noxious stimulus is never delivered. For example, to avoid receiving a bad grade on an English quiz, a student may study before an examination. And when an adult develops an irrational fear of airplanes, the person may avoid airplane travel. If the person can get to where he or she needs to go by some other means, the person may never unlearn the fear of planes. Thus, avoidance conditioning can explain adaptive behaviors such as studying before an exam, and it can also explain why some people maintain irrational fears.

Most children master both escape and avoidance conditioning at an early age; appropriate signals from a disapproving parent often elicit an avoidance response so punishment will not follow. Similarly, just knowing the possible effects of an automobile accident will make most cautious adults wear seatbelts. Both positive and negative reinforcements *increase* the likelihood that an organism will repeat a behavior. If the reinforcement is strong enough, is delivered often enough, and is important enough to the organism, it can help maintain behaviors for long periods.

The Nature of Reinforcers. The precise nature of reinforcers is a murky issue. Early researchers recognized that events that satisfy biological needs are powerful reinforcers. Later researchers added events that decrease a person's various needs—for example, conversation that relieves boredom, sounds that relieve sensory deprivation, and money that relieves housing congestion. Then, in the 1960s, researchers acknowledged that an array of events can be reinforcers: *Probable behaviors*—behaviors likely to happen, including biological behaviors such as eat-

Negative reinforcement: Removal of an aversive stimulus after a particular response to increase the likelihood that the response will recur.

ing and social behaviors such as playing tennis, writing letters, or talking—can reinforce less probable or unlikely behaviors such as cleaning closets, studying calculus, or pressing levers. Researchers call this idea the *Premack principle*, after David Premack, whose influential writings and research fostered it (Premack, 1962, 1965). Parents employ the Premack principle when they tell their children that they can go outside to play *after* they clean up their rooms.

The Premack principle and its refinements focus on the problem of determining what is a good reinforcer. Therapists and learning theorists know, for example, that something that acts as a reinforcer for one person may not do so for another, and something that acts as a reinforcer on one day may not do so for the same person on the next day. Therefore, they are very careful about determining what events in a client's life—or a rodent's environment—act as reinforcers. If someone were to offer you a reinforcer for some extraordinary activity on your part, what would be the most effective reinforcer? Do reinforcers change with a person's age and experiences, or do they depend on how often the person has been reinforced? Today, researchers are trying to find out ahead of time what reinforcers will work in practical settings such as the home and the workplace (Timberlake & Farmer-Dougan, 1991).

A reinforcer that is known to be successful may work only in specific situations. The delivery of food pellets to a hungry rat that has just pressed a lever increases the likelihood that the rat will press the lever again. But this reinforcer works only if the rat is hungry; for a rat that has just eaten, food pellets are not reinforcing. Psychologists studying learning and conditioning create the conditions for reinforcement by depriving animals of food or water before an experiment. In doing so, they motivate the animals and allow the delivery of food to take on reinforcing properties. In most experiments, the organism is motivated in some way. Chapter 9 discusses the role of an organism's needs, desires, and physiological state in determining what can be used as a reinforcer.

A **primary reinforcer** is a reinforcer that has survival value for the organism (for example, food, water, or the termination of pain); its value does not have to be learned. Food can be a primary reinforcer for a hungry rat, water for a thirsty one. A **secondary reinforcer** is a neutral stimulus (such as money or grades) that initially has no intrinsic value for the organism but that when linked with a primary reinforcer can become rewarding. Many human pleasures are secondary reinforcers that have acquired value—for example, leather coats that keep people no warmer than cloth ones and sportscars that take people around town no faster than four-door sedans.

Secondary reinforcers are generally used to modify human behavior. Approving nods, unlimited use of the family car, and job promotions are secondary reinforcers that act to establish and maintain a wide spectrum of behavior. Salespeople may work 72-hour weeks to reach their sales objectives. This may happen when their manager, using basic psychology, offers them bonuses for increasing their sales by a specific percentage during a slow month. The manager may reason that increasing the amount of the secondary reinforcer (money) may promote better performance (higher sales). Research shows that increasing or decreasing the amount of a reinforcer can significantly alter an organism's behavior. Of course, what is reinforcing for one person, or one culture for that matter, may not have the same reinforcing properties for another person or another culture. Money may reinforce some behaviors for some individuals; a smile from an approving parent, a salute from a superior officer, or a kiss on the cheek from a loved one may be far more powerful for others.

Superstitious Behaviors. Because reinforcement plays a key role in our learning of new behaviors, parents and educators intentionally try to reinforce children and students on a regular basis. But what happens when a person or animal is *accidentally* rewarded for a behavior—when a reward has nothing to do with the behavior that immediately preceded it? Under this condition, people and animals may develop **superstitious behavior**—behavior learned through coincidental association with reinforcement. For example, a baseball player may try to extend his hitting

Primary reinforcer: A reinforcer (such as food, water, or the termination of pain) that has survival value for an organism and thus its value does not have to be learned.

Secondary reinforcer: A neutral stimulus that has no intrinsic value for an organism initially but that can become rewarding when linked with a primary reinforcer.

Superstitious behavior: Behavior learned through coincidental association with reinforcement.

▲ *Superstitious behaviors are known to run rampant within the great American pastime.*

streak by always using the same "lucky" bat. A student may study at the same table in the library because she earned an A after studying there for the last exam. Many superstitious behaviors—including fear responses to the number 13, black cats, and walking under ladders—are centuries old and have strong cultural associations. Individual superstitious behaviors generally arise from a purely random event that occurred immediately after the behavior. Thus, a person who happens to wear the same pair of shoes in three bicycle races and wins the races may come to believe there is a causal relationship between wearing that pair of shoes and winning bicycle races.

Animals can learn superstitious behaviors even in a Skinner box. For example, on trials in which a pigeon learns the bar-pressing response, the bird may turn its head to the right before pressing the bar and receiving reinforcement. Although the reinforcement is actually contingent only on pressing the bar, to the pigeon it may seem that both the head turning *and* the bar pressing are necessary (Skinner, 1948). Therefore, the pigeon will continue to turn its head before pressing the bar.

Punishment

You already know that the consequences of an action—whether reward or punishment—affect behavior. Clearly, rewards can establish new behaviors and maintain them for long periods. How effective is punishment in manipulating behavior? **Punishment** is the process of presenting an undesirable or noxious stimulus, or removing a desirable stimulus, to decrease the probability that a particular preceding response will recur. Punishment, unlike reinforcement, aims to *decrease* the probability of a particular response. As such, it is a technique people commonly use to try to teach children and pets to control their behavior. For example, when a dog growls at visitors, its owner chastises it or chains it to a post. When children write on the walls with crayons, their parents may scold them harshly or make them scrub the walls clean. In both cases, people indicate displeasure by the delivery of an action in an effort to suppress an undesirable behavior.

Researchers use the same technique to decrease the probability that a behavior will recur. They deliver a noxious or unpleasant stimulus, such as a mild electric shock, when an organism displays an undesirable behavior. If an animal is punished for a specific behavior, the probability that it will continue to perform that behavior decreases.

Another form of punishment involves removal of a pleasant stimulus. For example, if a teenager stays out past her curfew, she may be grounded for a week. If a child misbehaves, he may be forbidden to watch television. One effective punishment is the time-out, in which a person is removed from an environment containing positive events or reinforcers. For example, a child who hits and kicks may be put in a room in which there are no toys, television, or people.

Thus, punishment can involve either adding a noxious event, such as a scolding, or subtracting a positive event, such as TV watching. In both cases, the aim is to decrease the likelihood of a behavior. (See Figure 5.9 for a summary of the effects of adding or subtracting a reinforcer or punisher.)

Punishment: The process of presenting an undesirable or noxious stimulus, or removing a desirable stimulus, to decrease the probability that a particular preceding response will recur.

Primary punisher: Any stimulus or event that is naturally painful or aversive to an organism.

Secondary punisher: A neutral stimulus with no intrinsic negative effect on an organism that acquires punishment value through repeated pairing with a punishing stimulus.

The Nature of Punishers. Just as reinforcers are used for reinforcement, *punishers* are used for punishment. They can be primary or secondary. A **primary punisher** is a stimulus that is naturally painful to an organism; two examples are an electric shock to an animal and visible parental rage to a small child. A **secondary punisher** is a neutral stimulus that takes on punishing qualities; examples are a verbal no, a shake of the head, or indifference. Secondary punishers can be effective means of controlling behavior, especially when used in combination with reinforcers for desired behaviors. But, as with reinforcement, what is punishing for one person or in one culture may not have the same properties for another person or in another culture. Indifference may punish some behaviors for some people; but withholding of approval from a stern authority figure may be far more powerful.

FIGURE 5.9

Effects of Reinforcement and Punishment

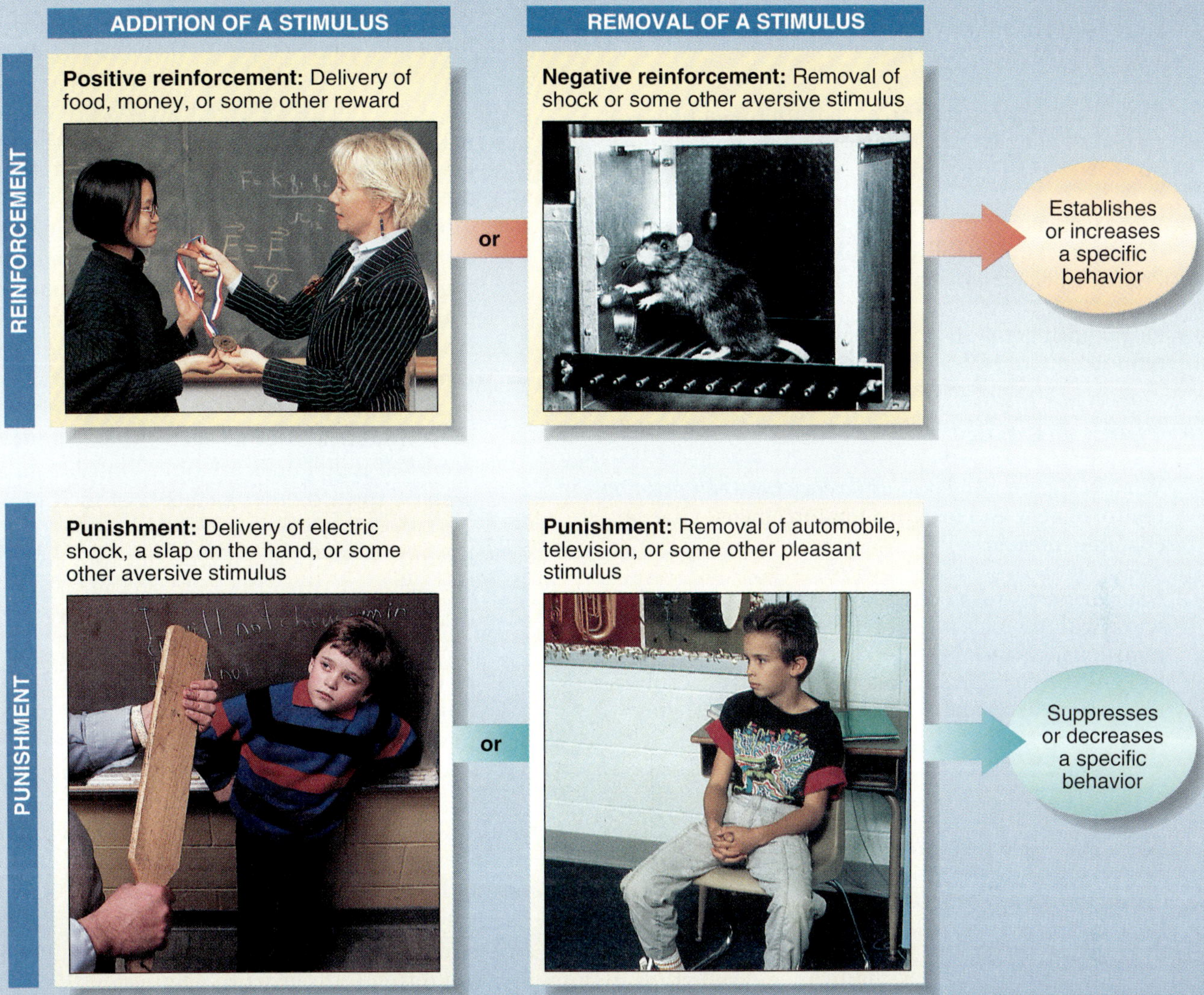

Punishment plus Reinforcement. Some psychologists (e.g., Appel & Peterson, 1965) argue that punishment by itself is not an effective way to control or eliminate behavior. Punishment can suppress simple behavior patterns; but once the punishment ceases, animals and human beings often return to their previous behavior. To be effective, punishment must be continuous, and at the same time the desired alternative behavior should be reinforced. Therefore, those who study children in classrooms urge the combination of punishment for antisocial behavior and reinforcement for prosocial behavior. A combination of private reprimands for disruptive behaviors and public praise for good behaviors is often the most effective method for controlling classroom behavior.

Limitations of Punishment. A serious limitation of punishment as a behavior-shaping device is that it suppresses only existing behaviors. It cannot be used to establish new, desired behaviors. Punishment also has serious social consequences (Azrin & Holtz, 1966). If parents use excessive punishment to control a child's behavior, for

FOCUS

Review

- How could a child's undesirable behavior be shaped to a desired behavior? p. 165
- Why is the type of reinforcer that follows a behavior crucial to whether the behavior will be repeated? pp. 165–166
- What evidence is there that probable behaviors can reinforce less probable or unlikely behaviors (the Premack principle)? pp. 166–167
- Distinguish between primary reinforcers and secondary reinforcers. p. 167

Think Critically

- What is the fundamental difference between positive reinforcement and negative reinforcement? Give an example of each.
- Your neighbor tells you, "Punishment just doesn't work with my kids anymore. I keep escalating the punishments, and they keep acting worse and worse! I'm going to just give up on them!" What do you think is going on here, and what would you advise your neighbor to do?

example, the child may try to escape from the home so that punishment cannot be delivered. Further, children who receive physical punishments often demonstrate increased levels of aggression when they are away from the punisher. Punishment may control a child's behavior while the parents are nearby, but it may also alienate the child from the parents.

Research also shows that children imitate aggression. Thus, parents who punish children physically are likely to have children who are physically aggressive (Mischel & Grusec, 1966). A child (or institutionalized person) may strike out at the person who administers punishment in an attempt to eliminate the source of punishment, sometimes inflicting serious injury. Punishment can also bring about generalized aggression. For example, if two rats in a Skinner box both receive painful shocks, they will strike out at each other. Similarly, punished individuals are often hostile and aggressive toward other members of their group. This is especially true for prison inmates, whose hostility is well recognized, and for class bullies, who are often the children's most strictly disciplined by their parents or teachers. Skinner (1988) believed that punishment in schools is unnecessary and harmful; he advocated nonpunitive techniques, which might involve developing strong bonds between students and teachers and reinforcing school activities at home (Comer, 1988). In general, procedures that lead to a perception of control on the part of an individual are much more likely to lead to nonoccurrence of undesired behavior, even when the disciplining agent (often Mom or Dad) is not around.

Further, if punishment is ineffectively or inconsistently delivered, it may lead to **learned helplessness**, in which a person or animal feels powerless to control the punishment and stops making any response at all. Martin Seligman (1975) and his colleagues showed, for example, that dogs first exposed to a series of inescapable shocks and then given a chance to escape further punishment fail to learn the escape response.

Key Variables in Operant Conditioning

As with classical conditioning, many variables affect operant conditioning. Most important are the strength, timing, and frequency of consequences (either reinforcement or punishment).

Learned helplessness: The behavior of giving up or not responding, exhibited by people or animals exposed to negative consequences or punishment over which they have no control.

Strength, Timing, and Frequency

Strength of Consequences. Studies comparing productivity with varying amounts of reinforcement show that the greater the reward, the harder, longer, and faster a person will work to complete a task (see Figure 5.10). For example, if you

FIGURE 5.10

The Magnitude and Delay of Reinforcement

(a) As the amount of a reinforcer (its magnitude) increases, an organism's time to reach a goal usually decreases. (b) As a delay is placed between a response and reinforcement, the probability that a behavior will occur decreases. Short delays (or no delays) between a response and reinforcement optimize the chances that a behavior will recur.

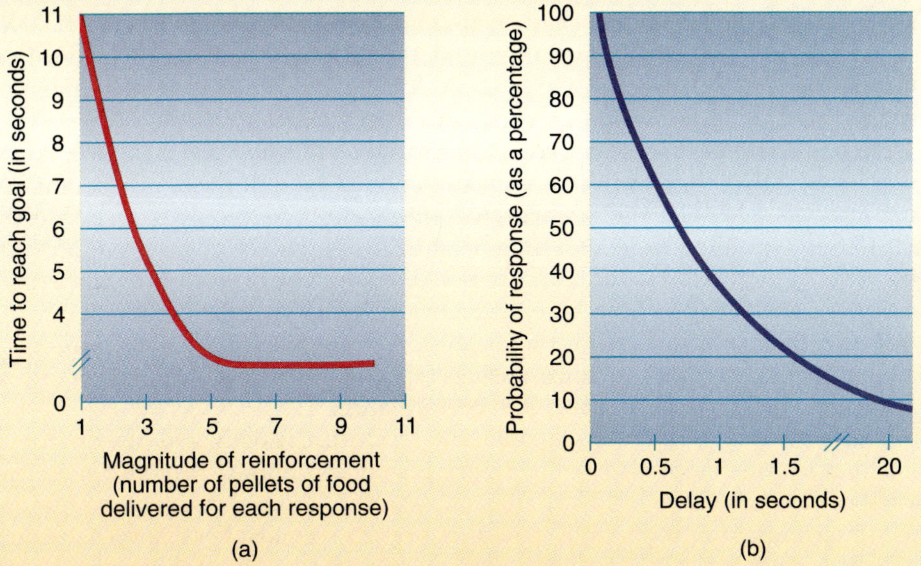

were a gardener, the more money you received for mowing lawns, the more lawns you would want to mow. Similarly, the stronger the punishment, the more quickly and longer the behavior can be suppressed. If you receive a hefty fine for speeding, you probably will start to obey the speed limit.

The strength of a consequence can be measured in terms of either time or degree. For example, the length of time a child stays in a time-out room without positive reinforcements can affect how soon and for how long an unacceptable behavior will be suppressed. Thus, for a given child, a 2-minute stay might not be as effective as a 10-minute stay. Likewise, a half-hearted "Please don't do that, sweetie" is not as effective as a firm "Don't do that again."

Punishment, whatever its form, is best delivered in moderation; too much may be as ineffective as too little. If too much punishment is delivered, it may cause panic, decrease the likelihood of an appropriate response, or even elicit behavior that is contrary to the punisher's goals.

Timing of Consequences. Just as the interval between presenting the conditioned stimulus and the unconditioned stimulus is important in classical conditioning, the interval between a desired behavior and the delivery of the consequence (reward or punishment) is important in operant conditioning. Generally, the shorter the interval, the greater the likelihood that the behavior will be learned (again, see Figure 5.10).

Frequency of Consequences. How often do people need to be reinforced? Is a paycheck once a month sufficient? Will people work better if they receive reinforcement regularly or if they receive it at unpredictable times? Up to this point, our discussion has generally assumed that a consequence follows each response. What if people are reinforced only some of the time, not continually? When a researcher varies the frequency with which an organism is to be reinforced, the researcher is said to manipulate the *schedule of reinforcement*—the pattern of presentation of the reinforcer over time. The simplest and easiest reinforcement pattern is *continuous reinforcement*—reinforcement for every occurrence of the targeted behavior. However, most researchers, or parents for that matter, do not reinforce a behavior every time it occurs; rather, they reinforce occasionally or intermittently. What determines the timetable for reinforcement? Schedules of reinforcement generally are based either on intervals of time or on frequency of response. Some schedules establish a behavior quickly; however, quickly established behaviors are more quickly extinguished than are behaviors that are slower to be established. (We'll discuss extinction further in a few paragraphs.) Researchers have devised four basic schedules of reinforcement; two are *interval schedules* (which deal with time periods), and two are *ratio schedules* (which deal with work output).

Interval schedules can be either fixed or variable. Imagine that a rat in a Skinner box is being trained to press a bar in order to obtain food. If the experiment is on a **fixed-interval schedule**, the reward will follow the first required response that occurs after a specified interval of time. That is, the rat will be given a reinforcer if it presses the bar at least once after a specified time interval, regardless of whether the rat works a great deal or just a little. As Figure 5.11 shows, a fixed-interval schedule produces a scalloped pattern. Just after reinforcement (shown by the tick marks in the figure), both animals and human beings typically respond slowly; just before the reinforcer is due, there is an increase in performance.

Under a **variable-interval schedule**, the reinforcer is delivered after predetermined but varying amounts of time, as long as an appropriate response is made at least once after each interval. The organism may be reinforced if it makes a response after 40 seconds, after 60 seconds, and then after 25 seconds. For example, if grades are posted at unpredictable intervals during a semester, you probably will check the bulletin board at a fairly regular rate. Rats reinforced on a variable-interval schedule work at a slow, regular rate, without showing the scalloped effect of those on a fixed-interval schedule. The work rate is relatively slow, because the delivery of the reinforcer is tied to time intervals rather than to output. Nevertheless, rats on a variable-interval schedule have a better overall rate of response than those on a fixed-interval schedule.

Ratio schedules, which can also be either fixed or variable, deal with output instead of time. In a **fixed-ratio schedule**, the subject is reinforced for a specified number of responses (amount of work). For example, a rat in a Skinner box might be reinforced after every 10th bar press. In this case, the rat will work at a fast, regular rate. It has learned that hard work brings regular delivery of a reinforcer. Figure 5.11 shows that the work rate of a rat on a fixed-ratio schedule is much higher than that of a rat on an interval schedule. In the same way, a teenager who is paid by the job (for the amount of work completed) to mow lawns will probably mow more lawns than one who is paid by the hour.

Variable-ratio schedules can achieve very high rates of response. In contrast to a fixed-ratio schedule, a **variable-ratio schedule** reinforces the subject for a predetermined but variable number of responses (amount of work). Thus, a rat learns that hard work produces a reinforcer, but it cannot predict when the reinforcer will be delivered. Therefore, the rat's best bet is to work at a regular, high rate, thereby generating the highest available rate of response. Sales agents for insurance companies know that the more prospects they approach, the more insurance they will sell. They may not know who will buy, but they do know that a greater number of selling opportunities will ultimately result in more sales. Similarly, gamblers pour quarters into slot machines because they never know when they will be reinforced with a jackpot.

An efficient way to teach a response is to have an organism learn the response on a fixed-ratio schedule, then to introduce a variable-ratio schedule. For example,

Fixed-interval schedule: A reinforcement schedule in which a reinforcer (reward) is delivered after a specified interval of time, provided that the required response occurs at least once after the interval.

Variable-interval schedule: A reinforcement schedule in which a reinforcer (reward) is delivered after predetermined but varying intervals of time, provided that the required response occurs at least once after each interval.

Fixed-ratio schedule: A reinforcement schedule in which a reinforcer (reward) is delivered after a specified number of responses has occurred.

Variable-ratio schedule: A reinforcement schedule in which a reinforcer (reward) is delivered after a predetermined but variable number of responses has occurred.

FIGURE 5.11

The Four Basic Types of Reinforcement Schedules

Each tick mark indicates presentation of a reinforcer. Steep slopes represent high work rates. In general, the rate of response is higher under ratio schedules than under interval schedules.

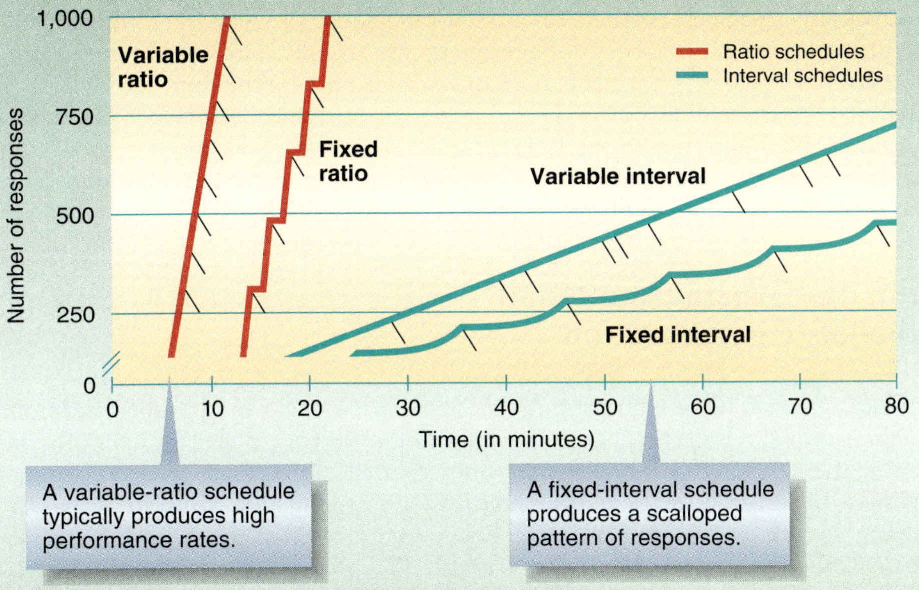

Schedule	Description	Effect
Fixed-interval	Reinforcement is given for the first response after a fixed time.	Response rate drops right after reinforcement but then increases near the end of the interval.
Variable-interval	Reinforcement is given for the first response after a predetermined but variable interval.	Response rate is slow and regular.
Fixed-ratio	Reinforcement is given after a fixed number of responses.	Response rate is fast and regular.
Variable-ratio	Reinforcement is given after a predetermined and variable number of responses.	Response rate is regular and high.

a rat can initially be reinforced on every trial so that it will learn the proper response quickly. It can then be reinforced after every other trial, then after every fifth trial, and then after a variable number of trials. Once the rat has learned the desired response, very high response rates can be obtained even with infrequent reinforcers. When an experimenter implements a *variable*-ratio or a *variable*-interval schedule, the frequency for each ratio or the length of each interval is predetermined, though it will not appear so in the view of the subject. These schedules can easily be combined for maximum effect, depending on the targeted behavior.

Using Schedules of Consequences. The study of reinforcement has many practical implications. Psychologists use the principles of reinforcement to study such frequently asked questions as these: How can I change my little brother's rotten attitude? How can I get more work out of my employees? How do I learn to say no? How do I get my dog to stop biting my ankles? To get your brother to shape up, you can shape his behavior. Each time he acts in a way you like, however slight, reward him with praise or affection. When he acts poorly, withhold attention or rewards and ignore him. Continue this pattern for a few weeks; and as he becomes more pleasant, show him more attention. Remember, reinforced behaviors tend to recur.

Most workers get paid a fixed amount each week. They are on a fixed-interval schedule—regardless of their output, they get their paycheck. One way to increase productivity is to place workers on a fixed-ratio schedule. A worker who is paid by the piece, by the report, by the page, or by the widget is going to produce more pieces, reports, pages, or widgets than one who is paid by the hour and whose productivity therefore does not make a difference. Automobile salespeople, who are known for their persistence, work on a commission basis; their pay is linked to their ability to close a sale. Research in both the laboratory and the business world shows that when pay is linked to output, people generally work harder.

Stimulus Generalization and Stimulus Discrimination

Stimulus generalization and *stimulus discrimination* occur in operant conditioning much as they do in classical conditioning. The difference is that in operant conditioning the reinforcement is delivered only after the animal correctly discriminates between the stimuli. For example, suppose an animal in a laboratory is shown either a vertical or a horizontal line and is given two keys to press—one if the line is vertical, the other if the line is horizontal. The animal gets rewards for correct responses. The animal will usually make errors at first; but after repeated presentations of the vertical and horizontal lines, with reinforcements given only for correct responses, discrimination will occur. Stimulus discrimination can also be established with colors, tones, and more complex stimuli.

The processes of stimulus generalization and discrimination are evident daily. Children often make mistakes by overgeneralizing. For example, a baby who knows that cats have four legs and a tail may call all four-legged animals "cat." With experience and with help, guidance, and reinforcement from his or her parents, the child will learn to discriminate between dogs and cats, using body size, shape, fur, and sounds. Similarly, you may once have been indifferent to distinctions among various Chinese cuisines; but after several experiences, you probably have learned to discriminate among the various dishes. Perhaps you have found that you especially like the Hunan style and don't care for the Szechuan specialties.

Extinction and Spontaneous Recovery

In operant conditioning, if a reinforcer or punisher is no longer delivered—that is, if a consequence does not follow an instrumentally conditioned behavior—the behavior either will not be well established or, if it is already established, will undergo extinction (see Figure 5.12). **Extinction**, in operant conditioning, is the process by which the probability of an organism's emitting a conditioned response is reduced when reinforcement no longer follows the response. Suppose, for example, that a pigeon is trained to peck a key whenever it hears a high-pitched tone. Pecking in response to a high-pitched tone brings reinforcement, but pecking in response to a low-pitched tone does not. If the reinforcement process ceases entirely, the pigeon will eventually stop working. If the pigeon has been on a variable-ratio schedule and thus expects to work for long periods before reinforcement occurs, it will probably work for a very long time before stopping. If it is on a fixed-interval schedule and thus expects reinforcement within a short time, it will stop pecking after just a few unreinforced trials.

Extinction: In operant conditioning, the process by which the probability of an organism's emitting a conditioned response is reduced when reinforcement no longer follows the response.

FIGURE 5.12

The Process of Extinction

When an organism's behavior is no longer reinforced, the likelihood that the organism will continue to respond decreases; psychologists say that the behavior has undergone *extinction.* Extinction is seen with both animals and human beings. In one study, C. D. Williams found that a child was throwing tantrums at bedtime to get attention. Williams instructed the parents to pay no attention to the tantrums. After several days, the number of minutes the child cried decreased to zero. A week later, an aunt put the child to bed; when the child made a fuss (spontaneous recovery), the aunt reinforced the child with attention. The child then had to go through a second extinction process. (Based on data from Williams, 1959, p. 269.)

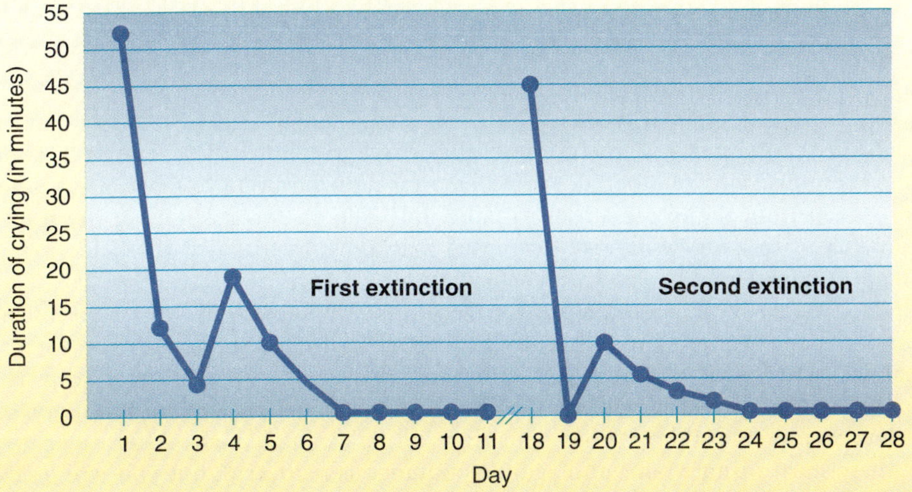

One way to measure the extent of conditioning is to measure how resistant a response is to extinction. *Resistance to extinction* is a measure of how long it takes, or how many trials are necessary, to achieve extinction. Consider a pigeon that is trained to peck when it hears a high-pitched tone and that is rewarded each time it pecks correctly. The pigeon is tested for 30 minutes a day for 60 days. On the 61st day it is not reinforced for its correct behavior. For the first few minutes, the pigeon continues to work normally. But soon its work rate decreases; and by the end of the 30-minute session, it is not pecking at all. When the pigeon is presented with a tone the next day, it again responds with pecking but receives no reinforcer. Within a short time, the pecking behavior is extinguished. People too show extinction; when researchers removed reinforcers from children who were exhibiting self-injurious behavior, the self-injuries decreased (Iwata et al., 1994). Certainly parents know that when they stop reinforcing a child's misbehavior with lots of attention (even if that attention is negative), the misbehaviors often decrease.

Note that the decrease in response is not always immediately apparent, however. When a reinforcer is withheld, organisms sometimes work harder—showing an initial increase in performance. In such cases, the curve depicting the extinction process shows a small initial increase in performance, followed by a decrease (Allen, Turner, & Everett, 1970).

As in classical conditioning, *spontaneous recovery* also occurs in operant conditioning. If an organism's conditioned work behavior has undergone extinction and the organism is given a rest period and then retested, the organism will show spontaneous recovery of the behavior. If the organism is put through this sequence

TABLE 5.2 *Four Important Concepts in Operant Conditioning*

Property	Definition	Example
Extinction	The process of reducing the probability of a conditioned response by withholding the reinforcer after the response.	A rat trained to press a bar stops pressing when it is no longer reinforced.
Spontaneous recovery	The recurrence of an extinguished conditioned response following a rest period.	A rat's continued bar-pressing behavior has undergone extinction; after a rest period, the rat again presses the bar.
Stimulus generalization	The process by which an organism learns to respond to stimuli that are similar but not identical to the original conditioned stimulus.	A cat presses a bar when presented with either an ellipse or a circle.
Stimulus discrimination	The process by which an organism learns to respond only to a specific reinforced stimulus.	A pigeon presses a key only in response to red lights, not to blue or green ones.

several times, its overall work rate in each session will decrease. After one rest period, the organism's work rate will almost equal what it was when the conditioned response was reinforced. However, after a dozen or so rest periods (with no reinforcements), the organism may make only one or two responses; the level of spontaneous recovery will have decreased markedly. Eventually, the behavior will disappear completely.

People also show spontaneous recovery. When you answer a question in class, reinforcement or punishment usually follows: The instructor praises you for your intelligence or berates you for your ignorance. However, if the instructor stops reinforcing correct answers or does not call on you when you raise your hand, you will probably stop responding (your behavior will be extinguished). After a vacation, you may start raising your hand again (spontaneous recovery), but you will quickly stop if your behavior again goes unreinforced. Instructors learn early in their careers that if they want to have lively classes, they need to reinforce not just correct answers but also attempts at correct answers. In doing so, they help shape, or manage, their students' behavior.

Table 5.2 summarizes four important concepts in operant conditioning: extinction, spontaneous recovery, stimulus generalization, and stimulus discrimination.

Intrinsically Motivated Behavior

Psychologists have shown that reinforcement is effective in establishing and maintaining behavior. But some behaviors are intrinsically rewarding—they are pleasurable in themselves. People are likely to repeat intrinsically motivated behaviors for their own sake; for example, they may work on craft projects for the feeling of satisfaction they bring. People are likely to perform extrinsically motivated behavior, such as working for a paycheck, only for the sake of the external reinforcement. Interestingly, if reinforcement is offered for intrinsically motivated behavior, performance may actually decrease. Imagine, for example, that a man does charity work because it makes him feel good. Paying the man could cause him to lose interest in the work, because it would no longer offer the intrinsic reward of selfless behavior. A student pianist may lose her desire to practice when her teacher enters her in a competition; practice sessions become ordeals, and the student may wish to stop playing altogether. For every person and for every culture, rewards are individualistic and determined by a host of learning experiences. *The Research Process* examines the issue of the hidden costs of rewards.

THE RESEARCH PROCESS

Do Rewards Have a Hidden Cost?

A child may love playing checkers, doing puzzles, or coloring in coloring books. But offer her a dime for doing these things and she may no longer want to play. This effect has been called the hidden cost of offering a reward. Why does it occur? And why do some activities seem like fun and others seem like work? Are there things psychologists can do to make activities fun? What are the critical variables?

In general, psychologists find that some activities are intrinsically fun—people like to do them for their own reward. Others, however, are not nearly as much fun; people need to be motivated to perform them, either with reinforcers or with threats of punishment. Psychologists talk about *intrinsic* and *extrinsic* motivation—whether things are done for fun or for rewards. They have found that people are less likely to perform intrinsically motivated activities if offered rewards for them.

On the basis of this fundamental finding, some schools have experimented with a grade-free system. But two researchers from Hebrew University of Jerusalem, Butler and Nisan (1986), have found that in some cases rewards encourage learning and improve performance, although they may decrease creativity.

Hypothesis. Butler and Nisan wanted to know if performance feedback would affect children's willingness to do tasks and how well they did these tasks. They hypothesized that if there is a hidden cost of reward, the feedback should interfere with the students' performance.

Methods. Butler and Nisan asked 6th-grade children to play two word games that involved constructing words from the letters of a longer word. There were two tasks. The first focused on the total number of words constructed. The second involved more creative thinking; the children were asked to use the first and last letter of the longer word as the first and last letters of as many new words as possible. Both tasks were repeated each day over a 3-day period.

The children were divided into three feedback groups. The first of these groups received *written comments* at the end of a session—for example, "The words you wrote were correct, but you did not write many words." The second group were given *numerical grades* on their performance. The third group were given *no feedback* on their performance. Butler and Nisan asked all the students to fill out an attitude questionnaire at the end of the third session in order to help the researchers assess how the students felt about the tasks. The questions included "How interesting were the tasks?" and "How many more would you like to receive?"

Results. The results showed that in the *no feedback* group the number of words for both tasks decreased from the first to the last session; the students became bored with the tasks. The students in the *comments* group improved their overall performance on both tasks from the first to the last session. Providing *numerical grades* improved performance on the first task (quantity of words) but decreased performance on the quality task (creative thinking).

Conclusions and Implications. Contrary to the general finding that a reward sometimes decreases performance, results of the Butler–Nisan study show that rewards improve performance on easier tasks. On more difficult tasks, performance also improves when feedback is in the form of written comments rather than grades.

The implications of this experiment are important. School grades may motivate learners, but on tasks that involve creativity they may decrease motivation. The researchers asked students how they felt about both sets of tasks. Generally speaking, students liked getting feedback and preferred written comments to grades. However, they would rather get grades than no feedback at all. And, like most psychological phenomena, this one is complicated; for some creative tasks, rewards increase children's subsequent originality, especially if the reward is not presented in too obvious a fashion (Eisenberger & Selbst, 1994).

Linney and Seidman (1989) assert: "Now more than ever schools need to examine ways to optimize the learning potential of students and facilitate the creation of learning environments that are best matched to their developmental and sociocultural needs" (p. 339). The hidden cost of reward does not have to exist. School systems that provide interesting tasks are more likely to have motivated students; feedback other than grades can be important in enhancing students' creativity. But most important, learning is facilitated when a task continues to be perceived as interesting and when feedback is given to students who show progress.

Electrical Brain Stimulation

Until the 1950s, researchers assumed that reinforcers were effective because they satisfied some need or drive in an organism, such as hunger. Then James Olds (1955, 1969) found an apparent exception to this assumption. He discovered that rats find electrical stimulation of specific areas of the brain to be rewarding in itself.

Olds implanted electrodes in the hypothalamus of rats and attached the electrodes to a stimulator that provided a small voltage. The stimulator was activated only when the rats pressed a lever in a Skinner box. Olds found that the rats pressed the lever thousands of times in order to continue the self-stimulation. In one study, they pressed it at a rate of 1,920 times per hour (Olds & Milner, 1954). Rats even crossed an electrified grid to obtain this reward. Animals who were rewarded with brain stimulation performed better in a maze, running faster with fewer errors. And hungry rats often chose self-stimulation over food.

Stimulation of specific areas of the brain initiates different drives and activities. In some cases, it reinforces behaviors such as bar pressing; in others, it increases eating, drinking, or sexual behavior. Psychologists are still not sure how electrical stimulation reinforces a behavior such as lever pressing; but they do know that certain neurotransmitters play an important role. For example, when specific neurotransmitters, such as dopamine, are increased after bar pressing, a rat is far more likely to continue bar pressing (P. M. Milner, 1991; White & Milner, 1992). The area of the brain stimulated (initially thought to be the medial forebrain bundle but now recognized to include large parts of the limbic system), the state of the organism, its particular physiological needs, and the levels of various brain neurotransmitters are all important. A hungry rat, for example, will self-stimulate faster than a rat that is not hungry. In addition, a hungry rat will generally choose electrical brain stimulation over food but will not starve to death by always making this choice.

Behavioral Regulation

Behavioral regulation theorists assume that people and animals make choices and that they will choose, if possible, activities that seem optimal to them. Rats, for example, will spend their time eating, drinking, and running on a wheel—activities they find pleasurable. An experiment by Bernstein and Ebbesen (1978) showed that human beings readjust their activities in a systematic manner. The researchers paid participants to live in an isolated room 24 hours a day, 7 days a week, for several weeks. The room had all the usual amenities of a home—bed, tables, shower, books, cooking utensils, and so forth. The experimenters observed the participants through a one-way mirror and recorded their baseline activity—the frequency of participants' specific behaviors when no restrictions were placed on them. The researchers found, for example, that one participant spent nearly twice as much baseline time knitting as studying. The experimenters used the participant's baseline to determine the reinforcing activity—in this case, knitting.

The experimenters then imposed a contingency. In the case of the participant who liked to knit, for example, they insisted that she study for a specific amount of time before she could knit. If she studied only as much as she did before, she would be able to knit for much less time. As a consequence, the subject altered her behavior so that she could knit more. She began to study for longer periods of time—eventually more than doubling the time she spent studying. In other words, she regulated her own behavior through application of the Premack principle (see pages 166–167).

Other techniques of self-regulation are also based on basic psychological learning principles. Here is an illustration. People with Type I diabetes require insulin shots each day. People with Type II diabetes (90 percent of the diabetic population) do not require shots each day but are often obese, must take medication daily, and must follow a strict diet. Both groups show poor adherence to their self-care regime:

BUILDING TABLE 5.2

Types of Learning: Classical Conditioning and Operant Conditioning

TYPE OF LEARNING	PROCEDURE	RESULT	EXAMPLE
Classical Conditioning	A neutral stimulus (such as a bell) is paired with an unconditioned stimulus (such as food).	The neutral stimulus becomes a conditioned stimulus—it elicits the conditioned response.	A bell elicits a response in a dog.
Operant Conditioning	A behavior is followed by a consequence of reinforcement or punishment.	The behavior increases or decreases in frequency. 	A rat will press a bar 120 times per hour to achieve a reward or avoid punishment.

80 percent use unhygienic techniques, 58 percent administer wrong doses of insulin, 75 percent do not eat the prescribed food, and 77 percent test their urine incorrectly (Wing et al., 1986). According to Wing and colleagues (1986), if diabetic individuals are to regulate themselves carefully, they must self-observe, self-evaluate, and then self-reinforce. The researchers assert that when people *self-observe* the target behavior, they are better able to *self-evaluate* their progress. After evaluating their progress, it is crucial that they receive *reinforcement* for adhering to their medical regimen—perhaps by going out for a meal with a friend or by purchasing a long coveted tape or CD. When these procedures are followed, adherence to the medical regimen improves.

Behavioral regulation has other practical applications. For example, members of Weight Watchers may be told to keep track of when and what they eat, when they have the urge to eat, and what feelings or events precede those urges. The organizers seek to help people identify the events that lead to eating so that they can control it. The aim is to help people think clearly, regulate themselves, and thus manage their lives better. This decision process and the focus on thinking are clearly seen in studies of cognitive learning, considered next.

Building Table 5.2 summarizes key points of comparison between classical and operant conditioning.

FOCUS

Review

- Why are variable reinforcement schedules more effective than other reward schedules? pp. 172–173
- What is the evidence that an intrinsically motivated behavior will diminish in frequency when external events reinforce it? pp. 176, 177

Think Critically

- Would you agree or disagree with the view that all intrinsically motivated behavior must at some point have been reinforced?
- When doing human and animal research on learning, researchers often record baseline activity. Why is such evidence important?

Cognitive Learning

"Enough!" shouted Patrick after 4 grueling hours of trying to write a program on his personal computer. Bugs were rampant in his program, all resulting from the same basic problem; but he didn't know what the problem was. After dozens of trial-and-error manipulations, Patrick turned off the computer and went off to

DIVERSITY

Do Men and Women Learn Differently?

Psychologists have been assessing the cognitive learning styles of human beings for decades; in doing so, they have found that males and females *seem* to learn differently. As boys and girls, children are taught different behavior on the playground and in the home, and these behaviors affect the way they learn—at least according to some experts. In general, psychologists argue that boys are more independent and aggressive than girls; girls, by contrast, are more cooperative than boys. In general, boys are taught to win, whereas girls are encouraged to enjoy the game and the process of playing. Thus, cultural styles affect learning in the classroom. As children, both in the classroom and on the playground boys have traditionally been taught to prevail, whereas girls have been taught to get along, communicate, and cooperate (Kohn, 1992). As a consequence, females tend to learn in cooperative learning situations, whereas males tend to learn independently.

Research on the role of learning styles does confirm some differences between men and women—although there are still more differences among women and among men than between men and women. In a study of the test preparation strategies of college students, Speth and Brown (1990) found that men and women differ in how they prepare for multiple-choice versus essay examinations. The women described multiple-choice tests as being more problematic and challenging than did the men. This probably reflects the different approaches to acquiring knowledge, according to Magolda (1990). Magolda found that men viewed learning more as an active, task-oriented process than did women. Magolda also found that men enjoyed the challenge more than the process of learning. Furthermore, according to Crawford and MacLeod (1990), men take a more active participatory role in classrooms than do women, and this role facilitates learning. Yet gender differences in learning styles tend to be small, to be focused on a narrow range of abilities, and to emerge primarily when a particular type of processing is encouraged by test developers, teachers, or employers (Dweck, 1986; Meyers-Levy & Maheswaran, 1991).

Women also view morality differently than do men (morality will be explored in more detail in Chapter 10) and see learning, workplace issues, and relationships differently. These differences show up on the job, where men are more likely than women to focus on winning at all costs. Differences also appear in relationships. Family responsibilities are viewed from sharply different vantage points, as is the raising of children. Parents' well-practiced learning styles encourage children's learning and morality from a sometimes distinctly male or female point of view.

Today, entire curricula are being designed around the idea that gender differences in learning exist. Using

study for his history exam. Then, while staring at a page in the text, he saw a difficult phrase that was set off by commas; he thought about it and suddenly realized his programming mistake. He had mistakenly put commas in his program's if–then statements. It was correct English, but incorrect computer syntax.

Patrick solved his problem by thinking. His learning was not a matter of simple conditioning of a simple response with a simple reinforcer. Learning researchers have actively focused on learning that involves reinforcement. Conditioning processes in studies by Pavlov, Thorndike, and Skinner require a reinforcer for behavior to be maintained. Much of the learning literature has focused on stimuli and responses and their relationship, timing, and frequency. But is a reinforcer always necessary for learning? Can a person learn new behaviors just by thinking or using the imagination? These questions are problematic for traditional learning researchers—but not for cognitive psychologists or learning researchers with a cognitive emphasis.

Thinking about a problem allows you to solve the problem and makes other behaviors possible; thus, thinking and imagination become crucial to learning and problem solving (Skinner, 1989). The importance of thinking—the emphasis of cognitive research—is evident even in early learning studies and will be shown over and over again as we examine such areas of psychology as motivation, maladjustment, and therapy. Some of the most famous psychologists of the early part of this century examined learning when reinforcement was not evident and behavior was not shown. Their early studies focused on insight and latent learning. Some of the studies gave birth to modern studies of cognitive mapping. Recent research has focused on generative learning and observational learning. Still other cognitive research has

research by Belenky and colleagues (1986), faculty at Ohio's Ursuline College are organizing the first-year curriculum of their female students around the idea that women work better in groups, in cooperative efforts, with connections among their ideas, and with a greater emphasis on critical thinking. Critical thinking, which focuses on integrating ideas rather than memorizing information, is the core of the school's approach. It builds on the research finding that women take advantage of cooperative learning and focus on developing their own voice (point of view) in evaluating research findings.

Feminist scholars sometimes assert that an approach that teaches women differently from men reinforces differences between men and women and encourages sexism. Psychologists know that men and women have different approaches in many areas of life—child care and the workplace are two obvious examples. However, there exists no evidence that males and females are born with these differences. Evidence does exist that Americans are raised in a culture that exhibits, lauds, and reinforces gender differences. It is not surprising that men and women learn about the world differently, that they develop distinctly different worldviews, and that these worldviews affect their learning styles and their abilities and desires to determine their own destiny. Of course, as individuals become sensitized to the influences of culture on them, they often seek to gain more freedom from cultural influences so that their destiny will be based on choices made by them.

Nor is a person's learning style inextricably linked to and universally predetermined by his or her gender. In some cultures, male views of the world tend to predominate; in other cultures, female views of the world are most likely to predominate. In American culture, the extent to which any of us takes a masculine or a feminine approach to learning, cooperation, morality, or any other part of development is highly diverse, varying from family to family, region to region. The results of that diversity are seen not only in learning styles but also in morality, in the work force, and in family life.

focused on problem solving, creativity, and concept formation (which will be covered in Chapter 7). All of this work indicates that there are many different aspects to what is learned and how learning takes place, as the discussion in *Diversity* clearly shows.

Insight

When you discover relationships between a series of events, you may say that you have had an *insight*. Insights usually are not taught to people but rather are discovered after a series of events has occurred. Like Patrick's discovery of his extra commas, many types of learning involve both sustained thought and insight.

Discovering the sources of insight was the goal of researchers working with animals during World War I. Wolfgang Köhler, a Gestalt researcher, showed that chimps developed insights into methods of retrieving food that was beyond their reach. The chimps discovered they could pile boxes on top of one another to reach food or attach poles together, making a long stick, to grab bananas. They were never reinforced for the specific behavior, but they learned how to get their food through insight. Once a chimp learns how to pile boxes, or once Patrick realizes his comma error, the insight is not forgotten. The insight occurs through thought, without direct reinforcement. Once it occurs, no further instruction, investigation, or training is necessary. The role of insight is often overlooked in studies of learning; however, it is an essential element in problem solving, a topic discussed in Chapter 7.

Latent Learning

After a person has an insight, learns a task, or solves a problem, the new learning is not necessarily evident. Researchers in the 1920s placed hungry rats in mazes and recorded how many trials it took the rats to reach a "goal"—the spot where food was hidden. It took many days and many trials, but the hungry rats learned the mazes well. Other hungry rats were put into the mazes but were not reinforced with food on reaching the same goal; instead, they were merely removed from the maze. A third group of hungry rats, like the second group, was not reinforced; but after 10 days, these rats were given food on reaching the goal. Surprisingly, in 1 day, the rats in the third group were reaching the goal with few errors. During the first 10 days of maze running, they must have been learning something but not showing it. After being given a reward, they had a reason to reach the goal quickly.

Researchers such as E. C. Tolman (1886–1959) argued that this was **latent learning**—learning that is not demonstrated when it occurs. Tolman showed that when a rat is given a reason (such as food) to show learning, the behavior will become evident. In other words, a rat—or a person—without motivation may not show learning, even if it exists. Tolman's work with rats led him to propose the idea that animals and human beings develop (or generate) a kind of mental map of their world, which allows them to navigate a maze, or even a city street. His early work laid the foundation for more modern studies of latent learning (e.g., Chamizo & Mackintosh, 1989)—and of generative learning, learning to learn, and cognitive maps. We consider each in turn.

Generative Learning

Modern cognitive psychology is changing the way in which educational psychologists think about learning that occurs in school. In addition to realizing that people organize new information in neural structures resembling maps, most cognitive psychologists are suggesting that each individual also places a unique meaning on information being learned. People use existing individual cognitive maps to interpret new information. These psychologists see learning as a *generative process*—that is, the learner generates (constructs) meaning by building relationships between familiar and unfamiliar events (Wittrock, 1987). According to this model, when people are exposed to new information or experiences, they perceive them according to their previous experiences. They then interpret (generate meaning about) the new experiences in ways that are consistent with their prior learning experiences and their memories of those experiences. In other words, they access existing ideas and link new ideas and experiences to them. As a result, they alter their brain structures. These modified structures are then encoded in memory and can be accessed later to interpret more new information. The *generative learning model* asserts that learning with comprehension occurs when a person actively links previously learned ideas to new information. Generative learning is thus seen as a constructive process—a process of constantly remodeling and building on existing knowledge.

According to the generative learning model, classroom learning is not so much a matter of engaging in activities that receive external reinforcement from the teacher or even of receiving thoughts that are transferred from the teacher to the learner. Rather, it is the result of an active process in which the learner plays a critical role in generating meaning and learning. This is because no one other than the learner can build relationships between what the learner already knows and what he or she is currently learning. As a result, what a person actually learns is unique to that person.

Latent learning: Learning that occurs in the absence of any direct reinforcement and that is not necessarily demonstrated in any observable behavior, though it has the potential to be exhibited.

Learning to Learn

Most college seniors believe they are much better students now than they were as first-year students. What makes the difference? How do students learn to learn better? Today, educators and cognitive researchers are focusing on *how* information is learned, as opposed to *what* is learned. To learn new information, students generate hypotheses, make interpretations, make predictions, and revise earlier ideas. They are active learners (Wittrock, 1987).

Human beings learn how to learn; they learn special strategies for special topics, and they devise general rules that depend on their goals (McKeachie, 1988). When you go fishing, you not only catch fish, but you learn something about the sport of fishing. The techniques for learning how to fish are different from those for learning foreign languages and those needed to learn mathematics. But are there general cognitive techniques that span topics, which students can use to learn better? McKeachie, Pintrich, and Lin (1985) have argued that lack of effective learning strategies is a major cause of low achievement by university students. They conducted a study to see whether grades would improve overall when rote learning, repetition, and memorization were replaced by more efficient cognitive strategies. To help students become better learners, McKeachie, Pintrich, and Lin developed a course on learning to learn; it provided a theoretical basis for understanding learning and practical suggestions for studying. Among the suggested techniques were

- *Elaboration*—translating concepts into one's own language and trying actively to relate new ideas to old ones.
- *Attention*—learning to focus one's concentrative abilities and to stay on task.
- *Organization*—developing skills for doing the tasks of learning and concept formation in an orderly manner.
- *Scheduling*—developing routine times in which studying occurs (which turns out to be a key element of both organization and managing anxiety).
- *Managing anxiety*—learning to focus anxiety on getting a task done, rather than becoming paralyzed with fear.
- *Expecting success*—developing an expectation of success rather than failure.
- *Note taking*—acquiring the skills necessary to make note taking a positive and worthwhile tool in learning.
- *Learning in groups*—developing good cooperative learning styles that make the most of interactions with other students (see *Applications,* pages 184–185).

The learning-to-learn course taught by McKeachie and colleagues made students aware of the processes used in learning and remembering. This awareness (thinking about thinking and learning about learning) is called *metacognition*. Learning-skills practice, development of motivation, and development of a positive attitude were also included. Among specific topics were learning from lectures, learning from textbooks, test taking, self-monitoring, reduction of test anxiety, discovering personal learning styles, and learning through such traditional strategies as "SQ3R plus" (Survey, Question, Read, Recite, Review, *plus* Write and Reflect). The course focused on learning in general, not on specific courses such as history or chemistry. The goal was to develop generalized strategies to facilitate learning.

This voluntary learning-to-learn course attracted 180 students. Their test results showed that the learning-to-learn students made gains in several areas, including grades and motivation. And in later semesters the students continued to improve. This straightforward study tells an important story about psychology in general and about learning psychology in particular. First, it shows that psychologists are engaged in activities that help people, not just in esoteric laboratory studies. Second, it shows a shift in emphasis from studies of learning specific kinds of material or studies of specific stimuli and responses to studies of learning strategies. Third, it shows that research into thought processes can lead to more effective thought and, subsequently, to higher levels of motivation. Last, this simple study shows that people can be taught to be more efficient learners.

McKeachie, Pintrich, and Lin argued: "The cognitive approach has generated a richer, deeper analysis of what goes on in learning and memory, increasing our understanding and improving our ability to facilitate retrieval and use of learning. . . .

APPLICATIONS

Cooperative Learning Can Lead to Collaborative Learning

There is no question that the way students learn in school has changed. No longer are they taken to task for helping one another with their work, because there is a movement afoot to help students become part of the learning process in a collaborative way—breaking down barriers between learner and teacher. And one of the first steps in the process of creating a collaborative learning environment is to get students to cooperate with one another. Many American teachers in the past have attempted to motivate students by having them compete against one another. However, research shows that cooperative interactions among students—not just between students and teachers or between students and books—play a significant role in real learning. Teachers who overlook student-to-student teaching may be failing their own courses (Kohn, 1992).

Studies show that forming teams of students in which no one gets credit until everyone understands the material is far more effective than competitive or individualized learning. Whether the students are preschoolers or college age, in English or physics, they have more fun, enjoy the subject matter more, and learn more when they work together. What's the secret? Learning stems more from providing explanations than from receiving them. In a cooperative group, everyone has an incentive to help everyone else. The result is that students of high, medium, and low ability all benefit from a sharing of skills. Groups also facilitate student–teacher dialogues and investigations—a key element of collaborative learning.

American society associates excellence with being Number 1. However, the data show that competition—some students succeeding and others failing—actually impedes collaboration and learning. David Johnson, a social psychologist and education professor at the University of Minnesota, noted that the demonstrated effectiveness of team learning exceeds that of almost everything else that American education has tried (Argyle, 1991; Kohn, 1986). Achievement and attitude of students are both improved through cooperative learning (Hwong et al., 1993).

Cooperative education involves more than just grouping students around a table and telling them to work together. It involves carefully establishing a positive interdependence that makes each student dependent on and accountable to others in the group. The students start to think of themselves as a team, working with their instructors in a collaborative effort at discovery. Knowing that they will sink or swim together—

We need to be aware of several kinds of outcomes—not just *how much knowledge* was learned, but *what kinds of learning* took place" (1985, p. 602). Students can better grasp history, chemistry, or economics if they understand how to go about studying these topics. Law, psychology, and medicine require different learning strategies. After people learn *how* to learn, the differences become obvious; indeed, some researchers think of creativity as a metacognitive process involving thinking about one's own thoughts (Pesut, 1990). Individuals can learn to learn, reason, and make better choices across a variety of domains (Larrick, Morgan, & Nisbett, 1990).

The expectations, both high and low, that individuals have are often set up by teachers and other students. These expectations can be enhanced—and so can learning—through a variety of techniques, as discussed in *Applications*.

Cognitive Maps

Some people are easily disoriented when visiting a new city, while others seem to possess an internal map. These internal maps are sometimes called *cognitive maps*—cognitive representations that enable people to navigate from a starting point to an unseen destination. How are these cognitive routes perceived and learned? Travel routes can be learned through simple associations: This street leads to that street, that street leads to the pizza parlor, and then you go left. But researcher Gary Allen (1987) asserted that learning routes also involves perceptual and cognitive influences, not just rote memorization of turns and signs. He devised a series of studies to demonstrate this. Slides depicting an actual walk through an urban neighborhood were shown in sequential order to a group of research participants; the same slides were shown in random order to a second group. All participants were then asked to make judgments about the distance from the beginning of the walk to a variety of specific locations. Amazingly, the participants who viewed the random presentations

teachers and students—they start swimming.

There are several ways to put cooperative learning theory into practice. One approach, called the *jigsaw method*, was invented by Elliot Aronson, a social psychologist at the University of California, Santa Cruz. He divided a study project into parts and gave one piece to each student in a group. Then he told the students that everyone would be responsible for all the material. Students had to learn from each other, and they did. In addition, Aronson found other results. Self-esteem went up as each student saw that others were depending on him or her. Also, each one realized that being a good student didn't depend on besting others. Moreover, students in the groups grew to like one another more, including those of different races and levels of ability.

Cooperation works in a variety of forums. In industry, for example, cooperative ventures are better than competitive ones when workers and managers are involved (Tjosvold & Chia, 1989). But the structuring of such ventures depends on the makeup of each group, including such variables as gender (McCaslin et al., 1994) and culture (Domino, 1992). So, for example, educators are beginning to use cooperative teaching methods in order to take advantage of women's sense of relationship. For example, at the Emma Willard School, the curriculum has been entirely revised to accentuate cooperative learning and to encourage girls to analyze and express ideas from their own perspective rather than repeat accepted ideology. When U.S. Navy air traffic controller trainees engaged in cooperative learning, achievement was higher, attrition rate was lower, and attitudes were better than among trainees who were not in a cooperative learning situation (Vasquez, Johnson, & Johnson, 1994). Psychologists and educators continue to fine-tune the techniques of cooperative learning in attempts to create truly collaborative learning ventures.

made judgments that were almost as good as those of the participants who saw the sequential walk. How did they do it?

Allen contended that the participants formed a cognitive map by using visual information from some slides that overlapped with information in other slides. From this overlap they pieced together a map of the neighborhood. (Without the overlap among the scenes, the pictures would have appeared to show a random walk through different neighborhoods.) The random-slides participants tried to place the slides in order mentally by paying attention to particular parts of the visual world they had seen in previous slides. In Allen's words, they attempted to impose "order on a collage of perceptual information" (p. 277).

Allen's research showed that in determining routes human beings pay attention to important landmarks, and that not all landmarks are equally useful. People learn the value of various types of landmarks during childhood. In one study, Allen and his colleagues discovered that young children do not value landmarks the same way adults do. As they gain experience, children are more likely to pick landmarks that lead to choices. Human beings also tend to divide portions of a route into segments and learn the map of those segments (Allen, 1981). Allen made a strong case for perceptual and cognitive influences on the learning of routes. His research suggests that people learn routes by integrating segments of routes and landmarks into cognitive maps. Human beings are active processors of information, and that helps them form cognitive maps.

The Theory of Observational Learning

Let's return to Patrick, whose walk to his psychology class was described at the beginning of the chapter. On seeing Ray wearing his jacket collar turned up, Patrick flipped his own collar up to imitate his role model. Patrick learned to change his behavior through observation.

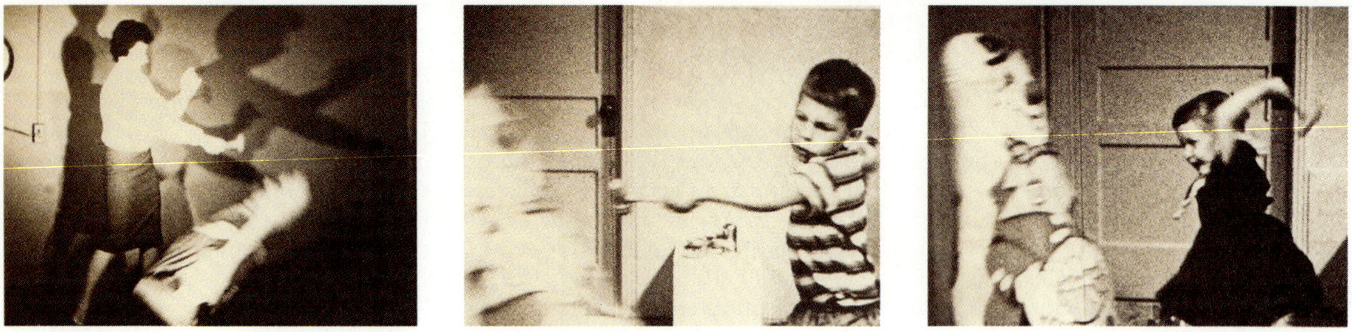

▲ *After watching an adult take aggressive action against a Bobo doll, children imitated the aggressive behavior.*

A truly comprehensive learning theory of behavior must be able to explain how people learn behaviors that are not taught through reinforcement. Although Patrick learned to turn his collar up, he was not taught to do so. Here's another example: Everyone knows that smoking cigarettes is unhealthy. Smokers regularly try to stop smoking, and for most people the first experience with smoking is unpleasant. Nonetheless, 12-year-olds learn to light up anyway. They inhale the smoke, cough for several minutes, and feel nauseated. There is no doubt that it is a punishing experience for them, but they try again. Over time, they master the technique of inhaling and, in their view, look "cool" with a cigarette. That's the key to the whole situation: The 12-year-olds observe other people with cigarettes, think they look cool, want to look cool themselves, and therefore imitate the smoking behavior.

Such situations present a problem for traditional learning theorists, whose theories depend on the concept of reinforcement and give it a central role. There is little reinforcement in establishing smoking behavior; instead, there is punishment (coughing and nausea). Nonetheless, the behavior recurs. To explain this type of learning, Stanford University psychologist Albert Bandura has contended that the principles of classical and operant conditioning are just two of the ways in which people learn. Another way is by observing other people:

> Although it is generally assumed that social behavior is learned and modified through direct reward and punishment of instrumental responses, informal observation and laboratory study of the social learning process reveal that new responses may be rapidly acquired and existing behavioral repertoires may be considerably changed as a function of observing the behavior and attitudes exhibited by models. (Bandura, Ross, & Ross, 1963, p. 527)

During the past 30 years, Bandura's ideas, expressed through observational learning theory, or *social learning theory*, have expanded the range of behaviors that can be explained by learning theory (Woodward, 1982). **Observational learning theory** suggests that organisms learn new responses by observing the behavior of a model and then imitating it. Observational learning theory focuses on the role of thought in establishing and maintaining behavior. Bandura and his colleagues conducted important research to confirm their idea that people can learn by observing and then imitating the behavior of others (Bandura, 1969, 1977b; Bandura, Ross, & Ross, 1963). In their early studies, these researchers showed a group of children some films with aggressive content, in which an adult punched an inflated doll; they showed another group of children some films that had neither aggressive nor passive content. They then compared the play behavior of both groups. The researchers found that the children who had viewed aggressive films tended to be aggressive afterward, whereas the other children showed no change in behavior (Bandura, Ross, & Ross, 1963; Bandura & Walters, 1963). Bandura's research and many subsequent studies have shown that observing aggression creates aggression in children, although children do not imitate aggressiveness when they also see the aggressive model being punished for the aggressive behavior.

Observational learning theory: Theory that suggests that organisms learn new responses by observing the behavior of a model and then imitating it. Also known as *social learning theory*.

Building Table 5.3 compares observational learning with the other two major types of learning discussed in this chapter: classical conditioning and operant conditioning.

BUILDING TABLE 5.3

Types of Learning: Classical Conditioning, Operant Conditioning, and Observational Learning

TYPE OF LEARNING	PROCEDURE	RESULT	EXAMPLE
Classical Conditioning	A neutral stimulus (such as a bell) is paired with an unconditioned stimulus (such as food).	The neutral stimulus becomes a conditioned stimulus—it elicits the conditioned response.	A bell elicits a response in a dog.
Operant Conditioning	A behavior is followed by a consequence of reinforcementm or punishment.	The behavior increases or decreases in frequency.	A rat will press a bar 120 times per hour to achieve a reward or avoid punishment.
Observational Learning	An observer attends to a model to learn a behavior. 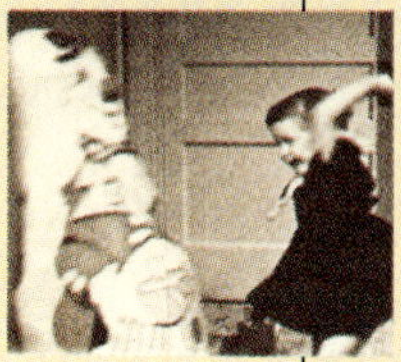	The observer learns a sequence of behaviors and becomes able to perform them at will.	After watching TV violence, children are more likely to show aggressive behaviors.

Everyday experience also shows that people imitate the behavior of others, especially those whom they hold in high esteem. Children emulating Rambo dress in army fatigues, carry toy machine guns, and pretend to launch missiles. You may buy a particular brand of shampoo because your favorite TV star claims to use it. Countless young girls became interested in gymnastics after watching Olympic star Mary Lou Retton and in track events after watching Florence Griffith Joyner. Unfortunately, not all observational learning is positive. Alcohol and other drug use often begins when children and teenagers imitate people they admire.

Laboratory studies of observational learning show that people can learn new behaviors by merely observing them, without being reinforced. For example, in a study by Bernal and Berger (1976), subjects watched a film of other subjects being conditioned to produce an eye-blink response. The filmed subjects had a puff of air delivered to their eyelids; this stimulus was paired with a tone. After a number of trials, the filmed subjects showed an eye-blink response to the tone alone. The subjects who watched the film also developed an eye blink in response to a tone. Other studies show that people who stutter can decrease their stuttering by watching others do so (Martin & Haroldson, 1977). Even children who fear animals can learn to be less fearful by watching other children interact with animals (Bandura & Menlove, 1968). Cats, too, learn by observing. John and colleagues (1968) found that cats can learn to avoid receiving a shock through a grid floor by watching other cats successfully avoid the shocks by performing a task.

FOCUS

Review

- What is the evidence that students who are taught how to learn make gains in many areas, including grades and motivation? pp. 182–184

Think Critically

- What fundamental assumptions do observational learning theorists make about reinforcement in the learning process?
- For a behavior to be learned through observational learning, who would make the best type of model?

A key point to remember is that if a person observes an action that is not reinforced, but rather is punished, the person will not imitate that action—at least not right away. Children who observe aggression that is punished do not immediately behave aggressively; nevertheless, they may learn aggressive responses that may become evident in the future. Learning may take place through observation, but performance of specific learning may depend on a specific setting and a person's expectations about the effect of exhibiting the learned behaviors.

Key Variables in Observational Learning

Observational learning theory has three important elements. One is the *type and power of the model* employed. Nurturing, warm, and caring models, for example, are more likely to be imitated than indifferent, angry ones; authoritative parents are more likely to be imitated than passive ones. In a classroom, children are more likely to imitate peers whom they see as powerful and dominant.

Another element is the *learner's personality and degree of independence*. Dependent children are more likely to imitate models than are independent children. Generally, the less self-confidence a person has, the more likely the person is to imitate a model.

A third factor is the *situation*. People are more likely to imitate others when there is uncertainty about correct behavior. A teenager going on a first date, for example, takes cues about dress from peers and imitates their behavior. A person who has never before been exposed to death but who loses someone close may not know what to say or how to express feelings. Watching other people express their grief provides a model for behavior. But not everyone learns well, and there are sharp differences in how people learn. There is even evidence that men and women learn differently, as discussed in *Diversity* on pages 180 and 181.

Summary and Review

Pavlovian, or Classical, Conditioning Theory

Identify the fundamental difference between learning and reflexes.

- *Learning* is a relatively permanent and stable change in an organism that occurs as a result of experiences in the environment. In contrast, *reflexes* occur involuntarily, quickly, and without prior learning. pp. 150–151

Describe how classical conditioning works.

- *Classical conditioning* involves the pairing of a neutral stimulus (for example, a bell) with an *unconditioned stimulus* (for example, food) so that the *unconditioned response* (for example, salivation) becomes a *conditioned response*. In *higher-order conditioning*, a second neutral stimulus takes on reinforcing properties by being associated with the *conditioned stimulus*. For classical conditioning to occur, the unconditioned stimulus and the conditioned stimulus must usually be presented in rapid sequence, and the conditioned stimulus must predict the occurrence of the unconditioned stimulus. pp. 151–153

KEY TERMS

Learning, p. 150
Conditioning, p. 151
Reflex, p. 151
Classical conditioning, p. 151
Unconditioned stimulus, p. 151
Unconditioned response, p. 151
Conditioned stimulus, p. 152
Conditioned response, p. 153
Higher-order conditioning, p. 154

Key Variables in Classical Conditioning

What are the most important variables in classical conditioning?

- The most important variables in classical conditioning are the strength, timing, and frequency of the unconditioned stimulus. p. 155

What are the key findings in studies of conditioned taste aversion?

- In conditioned taste aversion, or the Garcia effect, it takes only one pairing of a food or drink (the conditioned stimulus) with a nausea-inducing substance (the unconditioned stimulus) to make organisms avoid the food or drink that preceded the subsequent nausea. Taste aversion can be learned even if the nausea is induced several hours after the food or drink has been consumed; this is important because learning theorists had previously assumed that closeness in time between the two events was essential. p. 157

How may conditioned responses vary depending on the situation?

- *Extinction* is the process of reducing the likelihood of a conditioned response by withholding (not pairing) the unconditioned and conditioned stimulus. *Spontaneous recovery* is the recurrence of an extinguished conditioned response following a rest period, showing that previously learned associations are not totally forgotten. p. 158
- *Stimulus generalization* is the occurrence of a conditioned response to stimuli similar to, but not the same as, the training stimulus. In contrast, *stimulus discrimination* is the process by which an organism learns to respond only to a specific reinforced stimulus. p. 159

KEY TERMS

Extinction, p. 158
Spontaneous recovery, p. 158
Stimulus generalization, p. 159
Stimulus discrimination, p. 159

Operant Conditioning

What takes place in operant conditioning?

- *Operant conditioning* is conditioning in which an increase or decrease in the likelihood that a behavior will recur is determined by whether the behavior is followed by a consequence of reward or punishment. The process often occurs through shaping; *shaping* is reinforcing behavior that approximates a desired behavior. A key component of operant conditioning is reinforcement. pp. 162–165

How do reinforcement and punishment work?

- A *reinforcer* is any event that increases the probability that the response that preceded it will recur. *Positive reinforcement* increases the probability that a desired response will occur by introducing a rewarding or pleasant stimulus. *Negative reinforcement* increases the probability that a desired behavior will occur by removing an aversive stimulus. pp. 165–166
- *Primary reinforcers* have survival value for the organism; their value does not have to be learned. *Secondary reinforcers* are neutral stimuli that have no intrinsic value for the organism initially but that become rewards when they are paired with a primary reinforcer. p. 167
- Punishment, unlike reinforcement, decreases the probability of a particular response. *Punishment* is the process of presenting an undesirable or noxious stimulus, or removing a positive desirable stimulus, to decrease the probability that a particular preceding response will recur. p. 168

KEY TERMS

Operant conditioning, p. 162
Skinner box, p. 163
Shaping, p. 164
Reinforcer, p. 165
Positive reinforcement, p. 165
Negative reinforcement, p. 166
Primary reinforcer, p. 167
Secondary reinforcer, p. 167
Superstitious behavior, p. 167
Punishment, p. 168
Primary punisher, p. 168
Secondary punisher, p. 168
Learned helplessness, p. 170

Key Variables in Operant Conditioning

What are the most important variables affecting operant conditioning?

- The most important variables affecting operant conditioning are the strength, timing, and frequency of consequences. Strong consequences delivered quickly yield high work rates. But consequences do not have to be continuous. Studies of schedules of consequences, especially of reinforcement, have shown that consequences can be intermittent. *Fixed-interval* and *variable-interval schedules* provide reinforcement after fixed or variable time periods; *fixed-ratio* and *variable-ratio schedules* provide reinforcement after fixed or variable amounts of work. Variable-ratio schedules produce the highest work rates, while fixed-interval schedules induce the lowest work rates. pp. 170–173

Distinguish between extrinsic and intrinsic motivation.

- Psychologists have shown that reinforcement (extrinsic motivation) is effective in establishing and maintaining behavior. But some behaviors are intrinsically motivated; they are performed because they are pleasurable in themselves. Behavioral regulation theorists assume that organisms make choices and that, if possible, they will engage in the activities that seem optimal to them. If they are prevented from performing a desired activity, they will readjust their activities. pp. 176, 178–179

KEY TERMS

Fixed-interval schedule, p. 172
Variable-interval schedule, p. 172
Fixed-ratio schedule, p. 172
Variable-ratio schedule, p. 172
Extinction, p. 174

Cognitive Learning

What is the focus of cognitive learning psychologists?

- Cognitive learning psychologists focus on thinking processes and on thought that helps process, establish, and maintain learning. Some of the early studies focused on insight and latent learning. When you discover relationships between a series of events, psychologists say that you have had an insight. *Latent learning* is learning that occurs in the absence of any direct reinforcement and that is not necessarily demonstrated in any observable behavior, though it has occurred and has the potential of being exhibited. pp. 180–182

What fundamental assumptions do observational learning theorists make about the learning process?

- *Observational learning theory* (also called social learning theory) suggests that organisms learn new responses by observing the behavior of a model and then imitating it. Observational learning theory has expanded the range of behaviors that can be explained by learning theorists and focuses on the role of thought in establishing and maintaining behavior. p. 186

- Some key elements of observational learning theory are the type and power of the model, the learner's personality and degree of independence, and the situations in which people find themselves. p. 187

KEY TERMS

Latent learning, p. 182

Observational learning theory, p. 186

Learning CONNECTIONS

Some students benefit from extra help with the concept of reinforcement. You can learn more about it in:

- The CD-ROM accompanying this book, Topic 5
- This book's study guide, *Keeping Pace Plus*, or the computerized study guide, Chapter 5
- The audiotape accompanying this book, *SoundGuide for Psychology*, Learning Unit 5
- The study aids found on the World Wide Web site for this book, at http://www.abacon.com/psych/lefton

Critical Thinking CONNECTIONS

Take a moment to think critically about how this chapter's topics are connected with the rest of psychology . . .

If you are interested in . . .	Ask yourself . . .	Then turn to . . .
Classical conditioning 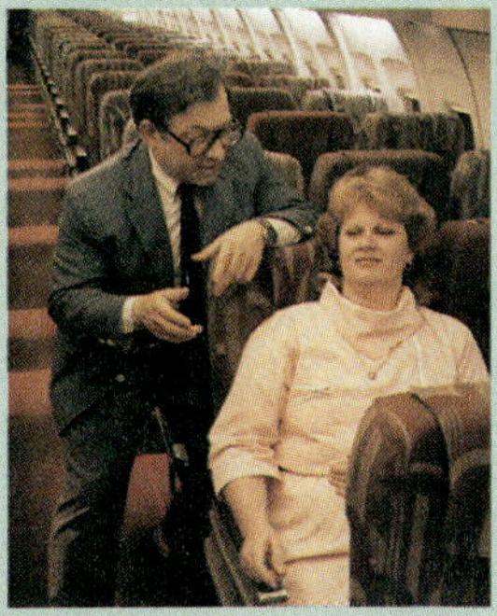	How can a person's physical responses to the stresses in his or her life be conditioned and reversed?	Chapter 13, pp. 463–466
	How might treatment for phobias rely on reconditioning of individuals?	Chapter 15, pp. 535–536
Operant conditioning 	How might conditioning play a role in how people learn language?	Chapter 7, pp. 256–258
	What is the impact of providing reinforcement to people when they already find a behavior rewarding?	Chapter 9, pp. 306–307
	When, and under what conditions, might attitudes such as prejudice be shaped by a parent's use of reinforcement?	Chapter 16, pp. 572–574
Cognitive learning 	Under what conditions might people develop reasoning processes and gain insight into problem-solving tasks?	Chapter 7, pp. 238–241
	Why does behavior that is observed, imitated, and then reinforced become part of an individual's personality?	Chapter 12, p. 431
	What are the implications of watching violence on television for the development of children's behavior?	Chapter 16, p. 582

6

Memory

We were just back from our honeymoon. My wife, Linda, and I were living in a one-room studio apartment. We were waiting to get into married student housing at the University of Rochester, where I was to attend graduate school. I clearly remember listening to a radio announcer, his voice charged with excitement, telling listeners that Neil Armstrong had just landed on the moon in Apollo 11. Linda and I sat on the edge of an oversized single bed in a room crammed with boxes; we were trying to tune in an old black-and-white television, without much success; the room was stuffy and hot.

Those images of events that happened more than 25 years ago are still vivid. But I sometimes have to make a concerted effort to remember how to get to a destination to which I have driven just the day before.

It would be wonderful to have a perfect memory, right? Not necessarily. The Soviet psychologist A. R. Luria studied a man with a memory far surpassing that of normal humans. Shereshevskii, better known as S, could repeat back strings of 70 digits or letters and recite entire conversations verbatim.

Even years after hearing a list, S could repeat it, backward or forward. But his remarkable memory also proved an intellectual hindrance. S had to devise ways to forget lists—for example, by writing down the words and then burning the paper. He found it difficult to carry on a simple conversation, because a single word would trigger a flood of memories, causing him to lose the gist of what was being said. Few people have a memory like S's. Most of us learn things through the processes discussed in Chapter 5. And our learning can be either forgotten or retained.

Psychologists have long recognized that recalling well-learned facts can sometimes be difficult. Even though something has been *learned*, it may not always be *remembered*. You may easily remember the Pledge of Allegiance, for example, but forget the chemical formula for sugar that you memorized for a test last Thursday. Both were learned, but learning and memory are different things. From Chapter 5, recall that learning is a *relatively* permanent change in the organism that occurs as a result of experience; this change is often, but not always, seen in overt behavior. **Memory** is the ability to remember past events, images, ideas, or previously learned information or skills; memory is also the storage system that allows a person to retain and retrieve previously learned information. You may learn something, but it does you little good without the aid of memory

Psychologists have examined memory from a variety of vantage points. Early memory studies at the turn of the century focused on how quickly people learned lists of nonsense words and how long they remembered them or how quickly they forgot them. Later studies, in the post–World War II era, became more practical, focusing on variables such as how the organization of material might affect retention and forgetting. Current research is focusing on how people code information and use memory aids, imagery, and other learning cues to retrieve information from memory. Researchers are also examining the neuroscience of memory and studying what variables determine what is remembered and what is forgotten. Under what conditions is memory enhanced? When are people most likely to forget?

As this chapter unfolds, you will encounter key ideas that may help you improve your memory. I will list some of them now. Even though you won't understand all of them fully until later, keep them in the back of your mind, and look back to see how much you understand after reading the chapter.

- Rehearse often.
- Be an active learner—write down key ideas.
- Generate personal meaning from to-be-learned material.
- Practice to-be-learned material over time.
- Plan on relearning.
- Take advantage of the primacy and recency of events.
- Focus, to prevent interference.
- Make use of chunking by learning key concepts that aid recall.
- Use mnemonics.
- Use mediation as a bridging technique.
- Make use of the von Restorff effect to help you remember.
- Review in different contexts and modalities.
- Prepare the environment to study.

Memory: The ability to remember past events, images, ideas, or previously learned information or skills; the storage system that allows for retention and retrieval of previously learned information.

Approaches to Memory

In the area of memory, as in most areas of psychological investigation, various approaches have been developed to help researchers understand the workings of the topic under study. Four broad views actively dominate psychological thinking on memory: the information-processing approach, the levels-of-processing approach, the parallel distributed processing model, and the neuroscience approach.

The Information-Processing Approach

For many years, researchers thought of the brain as a huge map with certain areas that code vision, others that code auditory events, and still others that code, analyze, and store memory. Their research goal was to discover the spatial layout of the brain and to see how the brain operates. Today, researchers know that the brain is just not that simple.

In the 1960s and 1970s, when the Information Age was still young, researchers began to compare the brain to a computer with complex interconnections and processing abilities. They compared memory in human beings to information processing by computers, with analogies to the basic computer processes of encoding, storage, and retrieval. These three processes are in fact used as a basis for discussions of memory throughout much of this chapter. We will look closely at them in the next section. Human brains, of course, are not computers; nor do they work exactly as computers do. They make mistakes, and they are influenced by biological, environmental, and interpersonal events. Nevertheless, enough similarities exist between human brains and computers for psychologists to discuss learning and memory in terms of information processing.

Information processing in a computer refers to organizing, interpreting, and responding to incoming information. Similiarly, in human beings, information processing has come to mean how environmental stimulation is acted on so that it acquires meaning. The *information-processing approach* analyzes the sequence of steps or stages through which this process occurs (Massaro & Cowan, 1993). The information-processing approach typically describes three stages: sensory memory, short-term memory, and long-term memory. This approach assumes that the stages are separate, though related, and that each can be analyzed by scientific methods. *Sensory memory*, sometimes called the *sensory register*, is the mechanism by which information is entered into the brain, much as you input data when you do word processing on a computer. When you hear a rock band or touch a piece of silk, you start the sensory memory process by entering information. After the information is entered, it is stored for a short time in *short-term memory*, just as a computer keeps your work in temporary random access memory—and if the electricity goes off before you store information, you lose it. In a similar way, if you look at a definition but do not process it adequately, you quickly lose its meaning. The short-term memory storage mechanism is fragile; it requires repetition, further encoding, and transfer of information to a final storage place. In a computer, information is stored for longer periods of time on a floppy or hard disk. In the brain, information is stored in *long-term memory*, from which the person can recall, retrieve, and reconstruct previous experiences.

Three Key Processes: Encoding, Storage, and Retrieval

In virtually every model of memory that has been offered, rejected, or modified, researchers seem to agree that three basic processes must be examined: encoding, storage, and retrieval (see Figure 6.1 on page 196). Like the stages of sensory, short-term, and long-term memory, these processes are the organizing themes around which many psychologists focus their theories. The names of these processes, too, derive from information technologies and will sound familiar to you if you know how computers work.

To a certain extent, the term *encoding* means getting information into the system to be processed. In the psychology of memory, **encoding** is the organizing of

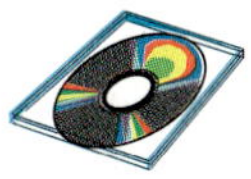

Fig. 6.1

Encoding: The process by which information is put into memory, through conversion of an experience into electrochemical energy.

FIGURE 6.1

The Information-Processing Approach

When information enters the memory's information-processing system, it proceeds from sensory memory to short-term memory and then to long-term memory. Encoding, storage, and retrieval occur in each stage.

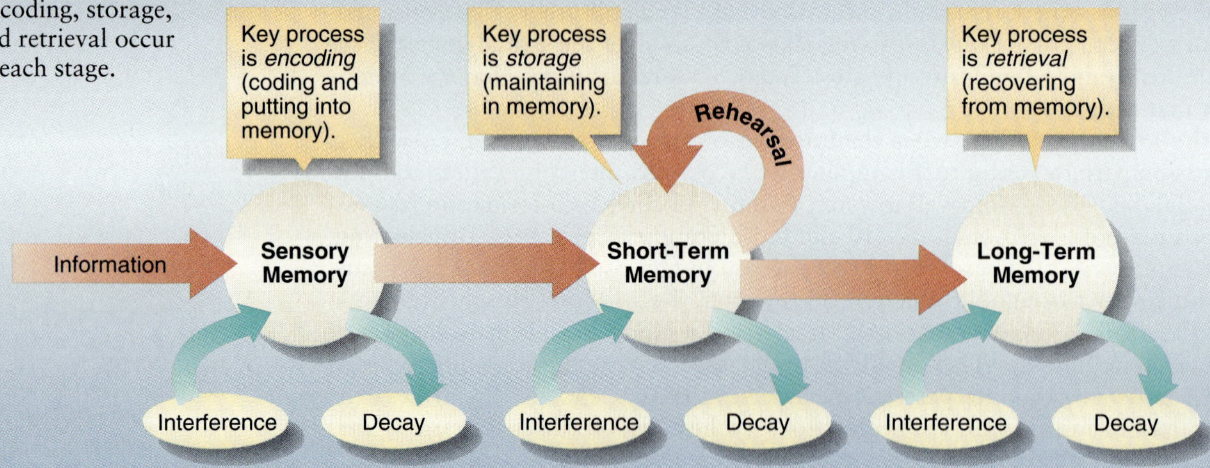

information so that the nervous system can process it, much as a computer programmer devises code to communicate with a computer. The means of organization can be visual or auditory and can include taste, touch, temperature, or other sensory information. The conversion of an experience into electrochemical energy is the first step of encoding and establishing a memory. Sometimes encoding is automatic; at other times it is effortful and requires concentration. Early in their development, people usually have to concentrate to encode information; with practice, such concentrative efforts become more automatic. For example, for young children, reading requires effortful encoding; in older children and adults, reading becomes nearly automatic. **Storage** is the process of maintaining or keeping information in memory. The storage may be for a few seconds (short-term) or for many years (long-term). **Retrieval** is the process by which stored information is recovered from memory. Recalling your Social Security number, remembering the details of a phone call, and listing Disney's names for all of the Seven Dwarfs are retrieval tasks.

Each of the three stages in memory—sensory memory, short-term memory, and long-term memory—focuses to a different extent on encoding, storage, and retrieval. Sensory memory provides some instantaneous, fleetingly temporary storage and retrieval; its main focus, however, is on initial encoding of information. Later, short-term memory provides encoding and temporary storage for about 30 seconds; its main focus is on initial processes, especially storage. Long-term memory may preserve information for a lifetime; its focus is often on retrieval. In later sections we will further examine the three processes—encoding, storage, and retrieval—and how they relate to the stages of memory.

Storage: The process of maintaining information in memory.

Retrieval: The process by which stored information is recovered from memory.

Levels of Processing

Does the human brain process some information at a deeper, more complex level than it does other information? Do thinking processes depend on the depth of storage? From the 1940s on, researchers have tried to distinguish between short-term and long-term memory. But during the 1970s, a new approach to explaining memory encoding and retrieval, the **levels-of-processing approach**, changed the course of research and thinking. This approach was a distinct departure from the traditional information-processing approach, which suggested that information moves from one stage to another in a linear, one-step-at-a-time process.

Researchers Fergus Craik and Robert Lockhart (1972) argued that a person can process a stimulus in different ways, to different extents, and at different levels. For example, a person presented with a computer screen displaying "Cast your vote for Smith, the candidate of distinction" will analyze the display on several levels, in several ways. The lines and angles of the display will be encoded at one level; the words will be encoded for basic meaning and categorized at another level; and the meaning of the display will be encoded, analyzed, and stored at still another, deeper level.

Cognitive psychologists began to equate the level of processing with the degree or depth of analysis involved. When the level of processing becomes more complex, they theorized, the code goes deeper into memory. Thus, the memory for the lines and angles of the computer screen (sensory memory) may be fleeting and short-lived, the memory for the words themselves (short-term memory) may last longer, and the memory for the content of the words (semantic components of long-term memory) may be longest-lasting. According to Craik and Lockhart, encoding in various memory levels involves different operations, and memory features are stored in different ways and for different durations.

The levels-of-processing approach generated an enormous amount of research. It explained why some information, such as your family history, is retained for long periods, and other information, such as the dry cleaner's phone number, is quickly forgotten. It showed that when people are asked to encode information in only one way, they do not encode it in other ways. Thus, when people are not asked to encode words for meaning, just to memorize or quickly repeat them (for example, to remember a list of items to buy at the supermarket), they can later recall very few of them. This helps explain why people tend to solve some problems in only one way.

However, not every researcher accepted the levels-of-processing approach. The reasoning in the levels-of-processing approach was deemed to be circular; the concept was impossible to define. Craik and Lockhart's research finding could be obtained using a number of different methodologies; some researchers did not even obtain the same results. Refinements were suggested; they focused on how memory codes are established, how they are elaborated on or made distinctive, and how recall of codes takes place. The initial levels-of-processing theory dealt primarily with establishing codes in memory. Later research focused on how those codes were used in recall from memory, and we will discuss that later in this chapter.

Despite all the debate, the landmark levels-of-processing research of the early 1970s still shapes the way cognitive researchers think about memory and thought. The traditional distinction between short-term and long-term memory suggested a structural difference in memory stores. The levels-of-processing approach, however, stated that the way information is encoded may determine how it is stored, processed, and recalled. The levels-of-processing approach made researchers aware that encoding processes can be flexible and can vary with the cues provided and the task at hand.

Levels-of-processing approach: A memory theory that is considered a distinct alternative to the information-processing approach and that suggests that information does not move from one stage of memory to another in a linear way but is processed in different ways, to different extents, and at different levels, depending on the degree of analysis.

Parallel distributed processing (PDP): Organization of the brain in neural networks with many operations taking place simultaneously and at many locations within the brain.

Parallel Distributed Processing

It should come as no surprise that many researchers grew to believe that the connections within the brain are so sophisticated and interconnected that any simple three-step model was inadequate to explain human memory. The concept of **parallel distributed processing (PDP)** is an alternative that developed from the notion of the brain being organized in neural networks. This theory suggests that many operations take place simultaneously and at many locations within the brain; a number of PDP theories have been offered, but they share common characteristics.

The PDP concept is appealing because of the analogy to the way so many operations take place in the world. At telephone companies, thousands of calls arrive at switching stations simultaneously. At airline offices, hundreds of requests for information about flights are received simultaneously from all around the world. As you listen to a symphony, you hear dozens of instruments simultaneously. Mainframe computers deal simultaneously with jobs from hundreds of users. PDP models assert that humans, too, can process and store many events simultaneously.

PDP models are models not only of memory but also of perception and learning. PDP models, which focus on the biological bases of memory, are difficult to characterize in traditional terms, are hard to test experimentally, and have not achieved as wide an acceptance as has the traditional information-processing model. Nevertheless, PDP in its various forms has influenced the way psychologists think about memory (Morris, 1989).

As we begin to examine the process and structures of memory, try also thinking of information stored in the brain as books stored in a library. Books can be checked out and new ones added—in parallel, many at a time. Similarly, the books can deteriorate with age, be misplaced, or be difficult to locate. Books that you use frequently are the easiest to find—you know exactly where to look for them. Sometimes the librarians may reorganize the books, storing them differently. We'll return to the library analogy later in this chapter.

The Neuroscience Approach

Memories are stored in electrochemical form in the brain. Most psychologists today believe that most, if not all, memories are retained in some manner. Researchers are exploring the neurobiological bases of memory: How does the brain store memories? Where are memories stored? Are memory traces localized or distributed? Researchers using positron emission tomography techniques (described in Chapter 2) are trying to study the location, extent, and timing of processing in the brain as it occurs. And they are having successes. Toward the end of this chapter, we will explore the neuroscience approach to memory.

Sensory Memory: Focus on Encoding

Sensory memory: The mechanism that performs initial encoding and brief storage of stimuli. Also known as the *sensory register*.

As George Sperling demonstrated in the early 1960s, **sensory memory**, or the *sensory register*, is the mechanism that performs initial encoding and provides brief storage of stimuli from which human beings can retrieve information. The brief image of a stimulus appears the way lightning does on a dark evening; the lightning flashes, and you retain a brief continuing image of it. Sperling (1960) briefly presented to research participants a visual display consisting of three rows of letters. He asked the participants to report one of the three rows and he cued them as to which row to report by using a tone that varied in pitch. Sperling found they were able to recall more than 3 items out of 12 from just a 50-millisecond presentation; as he delayed the cue, recall decreased (see Figure 6.2). From Sperling's studies and others that followed, researchers claimed the existence of a brief (250-millisecond, or 0.25-second), rapidly decaying sensory memory. *Decay* refers to loss of information from memory as a result of disuse and the passage of time. Although some researchers have challenged the exis-

◀ *Sensory memory holds visual images, such as the pattern formed by this moving pen light, for a fraction of a second.*

FIGURE 6.2

Sperling's Discovery of a Visual Sensory Memory

The graph plots participants' accuracy in reporting one row of four letters as a function of the extent of the delay of a tone that signaled to the participants which row to report.
(Based on data from Sperling, 1960, p. 11.)

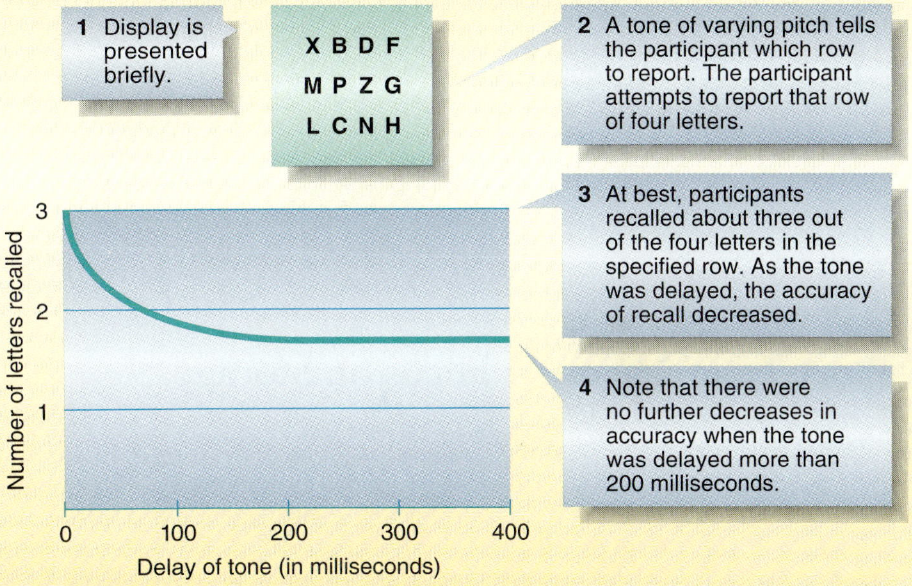

tence and physiological basis of sensory memory (Sakitt & Long, 1979), most researchers still hold that it is the first stage of encoding.

Sensory memory transforms a visual, auditory, or chemical stimulus (such as an odor) into a form the brain can interpret. Consider the visual system. The initial coding usually contains information in a picturelike representation. Sensory memory establishes the visual stimulus in an electrical or neural form and stores it for 0.25 second with little interpretation, in an almost photographic manner. This visual sensory memory is sometimes called an *icon*, and the storage mechanism is called *iconic storage*. For the auditory system the storage mechanism is called *echoic storage*; it stores an auditory representation for about 3 seconds.

Sensory memory is temporary and extremely fragile. Once information is established there, it must be transferred elsewhere for additional encoding and storage, or it will be lost. For example, when you pull a phone number from a rapidly scrolling computer screen display, it is established in visual sensory memory (iconic storage); but unless you quickly transfer it to short-term memory by writing it down or by repeating it over and over to yourself, you will forget it. Building Table 6.1, on page 200, summarizes key processes in sensory memory.

FOCUS

Review

- What are the fundamental assumptions of the information-processing approach? p. 195
- What is the underlying assumption of the levels-of-processing approach to memory? pp. 196–197
- What is the evidence to suggest that sensory memory is temporary and fragile? pp. 198–199

Think Critically

- Why do researchers who focus on parallel distributed processing find the information-processing approach unsatisfactory?

BUILDING TABLE 6.1

Key Processes in Sensory Memory

STAGE	ENCODING	STORAGE	RETRIEVAL	DURATION	FORGETTING
Sensory Memory	Visual or auditory (iconic or echoic storage).	Brief, fragile, and temporary. 	Information is extracted from stimulus presentation and transferred to short-term memory.	Visual: 250 milliseconds; auditory: about 3 seconds.	Rapid decay of information; interference is possible if a new stimulus is presented.

Short-Term Memory: Focus on Storage

After reaching sensory memory, stimuli either decay and are lost or they are transferred to a second stage—short-term memory. **Short-term memory** is the memory storage system that temporarily holds current or recently attended-to information for immediate or short-term use. In short-term memory, information is not simply stored, of course; it is further encoded, then stored or maintained for about 30 seconds. It is here that active processing takes place. A person may decide that a specific piece of information is important; if it is complicated or lengthy enough, it will need to be actively repeated or rehearsed. **Rehearsal** is the process of repeatedly verbalizing, thinking about, or otherwise acting on information in order to keep that information in memory. Researchers generally agree that the more rehearsal, the greater a person's memory for the item to be recalled; also, not all items are recalled equally well. The addition of new information may also *interfere* with the recall of other information in short-term memory.

Lengthy material, such as actors' lines in a play, must be rehearsed repeatedly before it will be passed beyond short-term memory.

Short-term memory: The memory storage system that temporarily holds current or recently attended-to information for immediate or short-term use.

Rehearsal: The process of repeatedly verbalizing, thinking about, or otherwise acting on information in order to keep that information in memory.

To understand how encoding works in short-term memory, just imagine a waiter who is given a lengthy and complex order. Once the order is in short-term memory, it is unlikely that the waiter will remember it after about 2 minutes. Thus, he may repeat the order over and over, rehearsing it until he is able to write it down or give it to the chef. Because of the limitations of short-term memory, rehearsal of information is crucial for encoding and keeping the information active.

FIGURE 6.3

Results of Peterson and Peterson's Classic Experiment

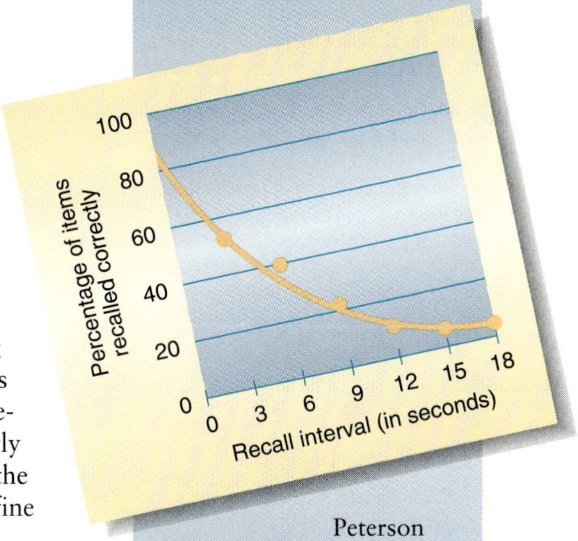

Peterson and Peterson (1959) found that when they delayed the report of three-letter syllables by having subjects count backwards, accuracy of recall decreased over the first 18 seconds.

The Discovery of Short-Term Memory

Researchers had been studying memory and retrieval for decades, but it was not until 1959 that Lloyd and Margaret Peterson, in attempting to define the duration of short-term memory, presented evidence for its existence. In a laboratory study the Petersons asked participants to recall a three-consonant sequence, such as *xbd*, after varying time intervals. During a time that ranged from no delay to 18 seconds, the participants were required to count backward by threes. The aim of asking the participants to count backward was to prevent them from repeating or rehearsing the sequence; the Petersons wanted to examine recall when rehearsal was not possible. Figure 6.3 presents their results. As the interval between presentation and recall increased, accuracy of recall decreased until it fell nearly to levels that could have been due to chance. The Petersons thus showed the duration of short-term memory, although this technique really does not define its complete limits or prove its unique existence (Crowder, 1993).

Thousands of research studies have been done on the components and characteristics of storage in short-term memory. They focus on the importance of duration, capacity, and rehearsal.

Duration. The Petersons' experiment, like many others that followed, showed that information contained in short-term memory is available for less than 20 and no more than 30 seconds. After that, it must be transferred to and stored in long-term memory, or it will be lost. (Of course, it could be maintained indefinitely if a person were to rehearse it over and over again until recall was necessary.)

Capacity. In 1956, George Miller argued that human beings can retain about seven (plus or minus two) items in short-term memory. The limited number of items that can be easily reproduced after presentation in short-term memory is the **memory span**. It usually contains one or two single **chunks**—manageable and meaningful units of information. A chunk can be a letter, a group of numbers and words, or even sentences organized in a familiar way for easy encoding, storage, and retrieval. Many people remember their Social Security number in three chunks and their telephone number in two chunks. Chunks can be made up of groupings based on meaning, past events, associations, perception, rhythm, or some arbitrary strategy devised by a learner to help encode large amounts of data (Schweickert & Boruff, 1986). Research has confirmed the importance of this key idea of chunking and the use of seven plus or minus two units of chunking (Baddeley, 1994). Determining what is a chunk is sometimes difficult, because what is perceptually or cognitively grouped together in one individual may be different in other individuals.

Memory span: The limited number of items that can be easily reproduced after presentation to short-term memory, usually confined to one or two chunks of information.

Chunks: Manageable and meaningful units of information that can be easily encoded, stored, and retrieved.

Rehearsal. As noted earlier, rehearsal is the process of repeatedly verbalizing, thinking about, or otherwise acting on information to be remembered. People will quickly forget a list of meaningless letters or symbols, such as *xbdfmpg*, unless they use rehearsal to maintain the list in short-term memory. Actively rehearsed items can be maintained in short-term memory almost indefinitely. In general, however, the

Maintenance rehearsal: The repetitive review of information (usually in short-term memory) with little or no interpretation.

Elaborative rehearsal: Rehearsal involving repetition (often in short-term memory) in which the stimulus may be associated with other events and be further processed (transferred to long-term memory).

Working memory: A conception of short-term memory that focuses on several subsystems: a component to encode and rehearse auditory information, a visual–spatial scratch pad, and a central processing mechanism, or executive, that balances and controls information flow.

information entered in short-term memory is either transferred to long-term memory or lost.

There are two types of rehearsal: maintenance and elaborative. **Maintenance rehearsal** is the repetitive review of information with little or no interpretation. This shallow form of rehearsal involves the physical stimulus, not its underlying meaning. It goes on principally in short-term memory—for example, when you repeat a phone number you need to recall. **Elaborative rehearsal** involves repetition in which the stimulus may be associated with other events and be further processed. When a shopper attempts to remember items to be purchased to make dinner, she may organize them in a meaningful pattern such as the order of their aisles in the supermarket. This type of rehearsal in short-term memory allows information to be transferred into long-term memory. It is also necessary for understanding a levels-of-processing approach to memory, described earlier (on pages 196–197). Elaborative rehearsal is especially evident in the encoding of information within long-term memory. Maintenance rehearsal alone is usually not sufficient for information to be transferred into long-term memory and permanently stored.

Short-Term Memory as Working Memory

Alan Baddeley and Graham Hitch (1974, 1994) have found existing views of short-term memory too limiting. They reconceptualized short-term memory as a more complex **working memory**, in which several substructures operate simultaneously to maintain information while it is being processed. Earlier, psychologists often concentrated on single memory tasks, trying to understand each of the components in encoding, storage, and retrieval. But the conception of working memory goes beyond individual stages to describe the active integration of both conscious processes (such as repetition) and unconscious processes (those of which a person is unaware). The emphasis of this model of memory is on how the memory system meets the demands of real-life conscious mental activities such as listening to the radio, reading, or mentally calculating the sum of 74 plus 782.

Baddeley and Hitch demonstrated the capabilities of several parallel components of working memory by having participants recall digits while doing some other type of reasoning task. They showed that these components have limited capacities. If one component is given a demanding task, performance by the others will suffer. One subsystem in working memory encodes, rehearses, and holds auditory information such as a phone number. Another is a visual–spatial scratch pad or blackboard that stores visual and spatial information, such as the appearance and location of objects, for a brief time and then is erased to allow new information to be stored. A third subsystem is a central processing mechanism, like an executive, that balances the information flow and allows people to problem solve and make decisions. This notion of an executive suggests that people can control the processing flow of information and adjust it when necessary. Research also shows that the types of information to be learned—for example, textual information versus textual information with pictures—affects the ability to process information accurately (Kruley, Sciama, & Glenberg, 1994).

FOCUS

Review

- How did the Petersons' experiment show that short-term memory exists? p. 201
- In what ways is working memory a broader conception than short-term memory? p. 202

Think Critically

- Provide three examples of information that you have chunked to facilitate recall.

FIGURE 6.4

Short-Term Memory as Working Memory

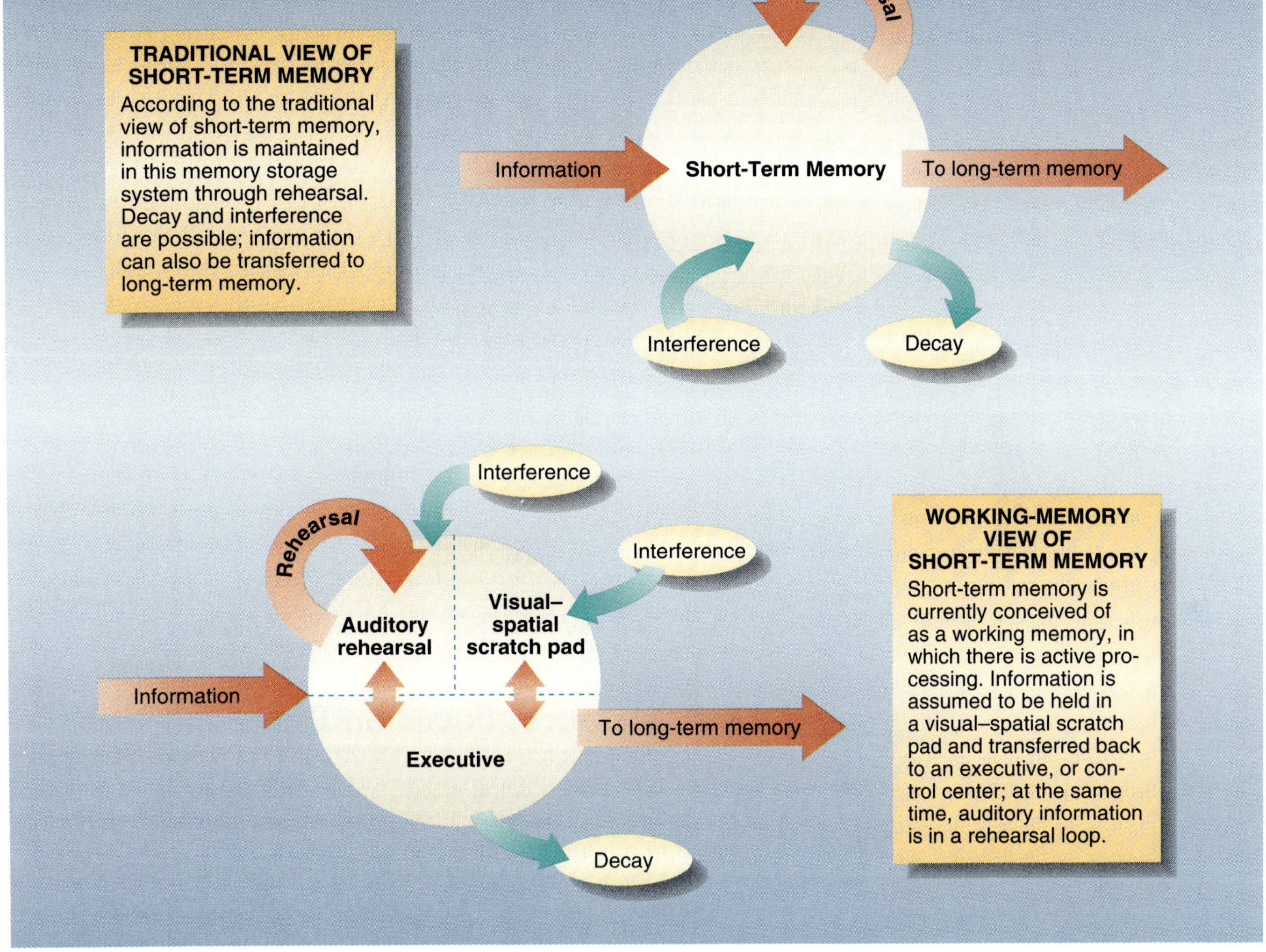

See Figure 6.4 for a comparison of the traditional view of short-term memory with the current view of short-term memory as a working memory.

Some researchers suggest that the traditional view of short-term memory (the information-processing approach) and even the broader view of short-term memory as working memory are still too limiting (Shiffrin, 1993). Both individual differences in working memory and the neural basis of working memory must be considered (D'Esposito et al., 1995). For example, a theory that invokes both neurophysiology and attention asserts that localization of brain functions plays an important role (Schneider & Detweiler, 1987). Other researchers are examining the possibility that animals have a working memory (Green & Stanton, 1989) and the role of working memory in intelligence (Embretson, 1995). Ericsson and Kintsch (1995) assert that conceptions of working memory must include the possibility that working memory can retrieve and use information already in long-term memory—for example, in highly skilled performance where tasks are already learned and well rehearsed but are being refined. These newer theories do not discount existing theories. Rather, they refocus, refine, elaborate, and extend them.

Building Table 6.2, on page 204, summarizes key processes in the first two stages of memory.

BUILDING TABLE 6.2

Key Processes in the First Two Stages of Memory

STAGE	ENCODING	STORAGE	RETRIEVAL	DURATION	FORGETTING
Sensory Memory	Visual or auditory (iconic or echoic storage).	Brief, fragile, and temporary.	Information is extracted from stimulus presentation and transferred to short-term memory.	Visual: 250 milliseconds; auditory: about 3 seconds.	Rapid decay of information; interference is possible if a new stimulus is presented.
Short-Term Memory	Visual and auditory; auditory encoding is especially important. 	Repetitive rehearsal maintains information in storage, perhaps on a visual–auditory scratch pad where further encoding can take place.	Maintenance and elaborative rehearsal can keep information available for retrieval; retrieval is enhanced through elaboration and further encoding.	Less than 20 seconds, no more than 30 seconds; depends on specific task and stimuli.	Interference and decay are operative; new stimulation causes rapid loss of information unless it is especially important.

Long-Term Memory: Focus on Retrieval

Information such as names, faces, dates, places, smells, and events—both important and trivial—can be found in a relatively permanent form in **long-term memory**. The duration of information in long-term memory is indefinite; much of it lasts a lifetime. The capacity for long-term memory is seemingly infinite; the more information a person acquires, the easier it is to acquire information. Using the library analogy again, we can say that long-term memory includes all the books in the library's collection. And as in a library, information can be lost, "misshelved," or for some other reason unavailable—in fact, the information in human the brain is far more fragile than the books in a library.

The information that is typically encoded and stored in long-term memory either is important (a parent's or spouse's birthday, for example) or is used frequently (your telephone number). Maintaining information in long-term memory often involves rehearsal or repetition, but sometimes an important event is immediately etched into long-term memory (Schmidt, 1991).

Types of Long-Term Memory

Long-term memory: The memory storage system that keeps a relatively permanent record of information.

Procedural memory: Memory for the perceptual, motor, and cognitive skills required to complete a task.

Several types of information are stored in long-term memory. For example, a person may remember the words to a Springsteen song, the meaning of the word *sanguine*, and how to operate a CD player. Each of these types of information seems to be stored and called on in a different way. Psychologists therefore split long-term memory into two types: procedural and declarative.

Procedural and Declarative Memory. **Procedural memory** is memory for the perceptual, motor, and cognitive habits or skills required to complete tasks (see Figure 6.5). Learning how to drive an automobile, wash dishes, or swim involves a

FIGURE 6.5

Procedural and Declarative Long-Term Memory

Procedural memory includes cognitive, perceptual, and motor skills (such as dribbling a basketball).

Declarative memory includes what can be brought to mind as a fact (events such as tearing down the Berlin Wall), as well as ideas, rules, and concepts.

series of steps that include perceptual, motor, and cognitive skills—and thus procedural memory. Acquiring such skills is usually time-consuming and difficult at first; but once the skills are learned, they are relatively permanent.

Declarative memory is memory for specific facts (see Figure 6.5) such as Bill Clinton's being elected president in 1992 or Neil Armstrong's being accompanied to the moon by Edwin Aldrin and Michael Collins. The memory is established quickly, and the information is more likely to be forgotten over time than is the information in procedural memory. It is easier to examine declarative memory than procedural memory, though, because people can quickly relate a specific fact but have more trouble explaining how to do something as complex as swimming. We consider declarative memory in more detail next.

Episodic and Semantic Memory. In 1972, Endel Tulving suggested that there are two kinds of declarative long-term memory: episodic memory and semantic memory. **Episodic memory** is chronologically dated memory for specific events, objects, and situations. It might include what you had for breakfast this morning, the movie you saw last night, or what you did on vacation two summers ago. Studies of memory for events in the past show that people remember them well, especially events involving themselves. Episodic memory is often specific; a person can describe not only when something happened but where it happened and the circumstances surrounding it.

When researchers have examined people's ability to remember real-world events (rather than artificially created laboratory events), the results have shown that people have amazingly good memories. These studies are often referred to as

Declarative memory: Memory for specific facts.

Episodic memory [ep-ih-SAH-dick]: Memory for specific events, objects, and situations.

THE RESEARCH PROCESS

Is Flashbulb Memory a Special Kind of Memory?

Where were you when you learned that the Oklahoma City Federal Building had been bombed? How did you hear about the event? What were you doing? What were your first thoughts? Compare the vividness of those memories with your recollection of eating lunch a few days ago.

People vividly remember the circumstances in which they learned of major personal and public events. This phenomenon is often referred to as *flashbulb memory*, and among the first to research it were Brown and Kulik (1977). They argued that there is a special type of memory for events that possess a critical level of surprise and what they called *consequentiality*. Most people believe they have flashbulb memories, and the Brown and Kulik work generated an avalanche of debate and research.

Theories. Two basic theories explain flashbulb memory. The first focuses on emotion, the second on rehearsal. The emotion approach, sometimes called the *now-print theory*, suggests that recall is facilitated when extraordinary cognitive information overactivates the limbic system (the brain's emotion center). In addition, information associated with strong emotions may be talked about more, and the rehearsal of information facilitates its recall. The second theory concerns rehearsal and reconstruction. This *reconstructive-script theory* focuses on people telling and retelling the story and gradually filling in, or reconstructing, their story to match a standard story format.

Research. To determine which of these two theories was correct, J. N. Bohannon (1988) of the Virginia Polytechnic Institute studied 279 people and their memories of the *Challenger* space shuttle disaster. Participants were tested at 2 weeks and then at 8 months following the explosion. They were asked both to evaluate their emotions on hearing the news (to test the now-print theory) and to estimate the number of times that they had retold the story (to test the reconstructive-script theory). Each participant's memory was assessed on three basic aspects: (1) free recall of the story, (2) probed recall of the story (recall when given hints), and (3) probed recall of specific facts concerning the accident itself.

Results. The study's results were dramatic. Participants who rated themselves as more shocked by the shuttle accident remembered more details, were more confident about their answers, and gave more complete stories at both testing times than did participants who rated themselves as less shocked. These results, which focus on emotion, support the now-print approach. However, the study also supported the reconstructive-script theory, which suggests that people organize their memory and fill in the details. The study's results showed that free recall at 8 months was just as good as within 2 weeks of the explosion, but accurate responses to questions asking for specific details declined over testing times. With short delays, either factor (emotion or rehearsal) is sufficient to generate flashbulb memories. But after a delay of 8 months, *both* are required.

autobiographical memory studies, because they often examine people's memories for their own past (Conway, 1991). People can accurately recognize a person, situation, or event years later (Nelson, 1993). Studies of autobiographical memory suggest that long-term memory is especially durable and fairly easy to access if a helpful retrieval cue is available. The more clearly and sharply defined memory cues are and the more often the memories have been recalled or reconstructed, the more vivid the memories are and the less likely it is that a person will experience retrieval failures (Friedman, 1993). (We will look into this issue later in this chapter when we examine forgetting.) *The Research Process* examines flashbulb memory, another type of memory that is related to episodic memory.

Semantic memory is memory of ideas, rules, and general concepts about the world. It is based on a set of generalizations about previous events, experiences, and learned knowledge. It is not time-specific; it refers to knowledge that may have been gathered over days or weeks, and it continues to be modified and expanded over a lifetime. Semantic memory develops earlier in childhood than does episodic memory (Tulving, 1993).

Semantic memory: Memory for ideas, rules, and general concepts about the world.

Semantic memory seems to be stored at different levels of memory, like sections or floors of a library; so a person needing information must go to different levels to access it. At superficial levels of processing, the immediate sensory cues are interpreted. At deeper levels, the cues are encoded and categorized according to the kind of information they give and the meanings for each cue. At still deeper levels, the meanings are analyzed and synthesized. For example, is the following sentence true or false? "U.S. astronauts Armstrong, Collins, and Aldrin were the first to land on

Conclusions. Simple emotional responses without rehearsal, according to Bohannon (1988), produce good short-term recall only. In the same manner, rehearsed information that does not have a strong emotional component results in superior short-lived memory. Bohannon claims that flashbulb memory is maintained over time *only* "if the flashbulb event was important enough to get the person to repeatedly rehearse the information by telling others" (p. 195). Every person experiences emotional events, and some of these the person rehearses. When the experience of learning about an emotional event is especially significant, and when it is repeatedly rehearsed, both the circumstances and the event have a high probability of being remembered in detail. Research on a multinational basis showed that international events are indeed flashbulb memories for people in some countries, but not in others—again, the significance of the event and its emotional impact are key (Conway et al., 1994).

Is flashbulb memory a special kind of memory? McCloskey, Wible, and Cohen (1988) argue, "There is no qualitative distinction . . . between memories for learning about shocking, important events, and memories for learning about expected, trivial events" (p. 181). They assert that flashbulb memory is ordinary memory with no special characteristics. Bohannon's findings on flashbulb memories and the role of emotion and rehearsal in maintaining them are consistent with McCloskey, Wible, and Cohen's argument. Such memories may be vivid, but they must be about emotional events and must be rehearsed. According to Weaver (1993), what makes flashbulb memories special is the undue confidence placed in the accuracy of those memories by those who recall them. The research suggests that there is no special location or encoding mechanism responsible for them.

the moon and did so on July 20, 1969, at 4:18 P.M. Eastern Time." You would need to access several classes of information, including interrelations among times, dates, people, and historic events—which may be complex. The time and effort you will need in order to respond will depend in part on the number of levels of processing required (Tilley & Warren, 1983) and the complexity of the information.

Explicit and Implicit Memory Tasks. Support for a distinction between declarative (both semantic and episodic) and procedural memory also comes from studies that have focused on examining *how* long-term memory responds to different memory tests, especially explicit and implicit memory tasks. **Explicit memory** specifically requires a person to recollect a previous event, such as the presentation of a word in a list; generally speaking, most of the tasks we have been looking at require participants to explicitly recall information. Explicit memory is a conscious, voluntary, active memory store that is relatively easily accessed. In contrast, **implicit memory** is considered a passive, almost unconscious process. Implicit memory tasks *indirectly* test whether a person has knowledge of a previously experienced event that the individual was not required to remember. Thus, you may remember things that you are supposed to (explicit), but you are also likely to recall things you did not deliberately attempt to learn—the color or the publisher of a book you are studying, the height of a cake you may be served, or perhaps the make of a computer in the office of a professor you have visited. Without your specific awareness you learn how people stand and how they gesture, and you also learn how to run better, play golf, or improve your tennis backhand—often without explicit instruc-

Explicit memory: Memory for specific events; a conscious, voluntary, active memory store that is relatively easily accessed.

Implicit memory: Memory for previously experienced events that occurs passively, almost unconsciously, without a person deliberately attempting to learn or remember the event.

tions. Implicit memory occurs without conscious awareness; it demonstrates that people do learn without active effort.

Tulving (Tulving, Schacter, & Stark, 1982) asked research participants to recall long lists of words. In later testing, participants could recall some words and not others; this is no surprise. But Tulving showed that participants could remember superficial characteristics of the previously learned stimuli—even aspects of words that they were unable to recall. This meant that explicit memory (recalling the specific words) was clearly different from implicit memory (having knowledge of the word or event, even without remembering the word or event). Explicit memory is sensitive to the attention paid to a task, the depth of processing, and the retention interval before recall; implicit memory is far more sensitive to the structural and perceptual elements of a stimulus (Parkin, Reid, & Russo, 1990). Lending physiological support to the explicit/implicit distinction is the finding that these memory stores seem to be found in different locations in the brain and each location seems to serve a different memory function (Krupa, Thompson, & Thompson, 1993).

The distinction between explicit and implicit memory adds another dimension to researchers' understanding of long-term memory, refining their understanding of the differences between declarative and procedural memory. This distinction suggests that processes of attention and learning of which people are not aware may affect memory. To a certain extent, implicit memory can be considered to be unconscious memory.

Primacy and Recency Effects

Because of the primacy and recency effects, the first and last speakers will be remembered best and will have the greatest impact on listeners. ▼

Long-term memory studies have brought forth some interesting findings about retrieval and have generated hundreds of research studies focusing on what are called primacy and recency effects. In a typical experiment, a participant may be asked to study 30 or 40 words, with a word presented every 2 seconds. A few seconds or minutes later, the person is asked to recall the words so the researcher can determine whether the information was transferred from short-term to long-term memory. Such experiments typically show an overall recall rate of 20 percent. However, recall is higher for words at the beginning of a list of words than for those at the middle, a phenomenon termed the **primacy effect**. This effect occurs when no information is already stored in short-term memory; at the moment a new task is assigned, the persons's attention to new stimuli is at its peak. Recall is even higher for words at the end of a list, a phenomenon termed the **recency effect**. This effect is due to the active rehearsal of the information in short-term memory and its subsequent encoding into long-term memory. See Figure 6.6 for a graph showing the recall rate for words in various positions in a list. It is called a *serial position curve* and presents the accuracy or speed of recall as a function of item position in a list or series of presented items.

Campaign managers attempt to capitalize on the primacy and recency effects in their candidates' speeches. For example, they urge their candidates to speak both very early in the campaign and very late, just before people vote. If several candidates are to speak back-to-back, campaign managers will try to schedule their candidates either first or last. Primacy effects suggest that attention is at its peak at the beginning; recency effects suggest that speaking last will be effective because other speakers won't interfere with the transfer of information from short-term to long-term memory.

Primacy effect: The more accurate recall of items that were presented first in a series.

Recency effect: The more accurate recall of items presented last in a series.

Imagery: Cognitive process in which a mental picture of a sensory or perceptual experience is created.

Imagery as a Retrieval Device

People use perceptual imagery every day as a long-term memory retrieval aid. In **imagery**, people create, recreate, or conjure up a mental picture of a sensory or perceptual experience to be remembered. People constantly invoke images to recall things they did, said, read, or saw. People's imagery systems can be activated by visual, auditory, or olfactory stimuli or by other images (Tracy & Barker, 1994). Even a lack of sensory stimulation can produce vivid imagery. Imagery helps you answer questions such as these: Which is darker green, a pea or a Christmas tree? Which is bigger, a tennis ball or an orange? Does the person you met last night have brown eyes or blue?

One technique researchers use to measure imagery is to ask participants to imagine objects of various sizes—for example, an animal such as a rabbit next to either an elephant or a fly. In a 1975 study by Stephen Kosslyn of Harvard University, participants reported that when they imagined a fly, plenty of room remained in their mental image for a rabbit. However, when they imagined an elephant, it took up most of the space. One particularly interesting result was that the participants required more time and found it harder to see the rabbit's nose when the rabbit was next to an elephant than when it was next to a fly, because the nose appeared to be extremely small in the first instance (see Figure 6.7). Although they are mental, not physical, phenomena, images have photograph-like "edges"—points beyond which visual information ceases to be represented (Kosslyn, 1987). Thanks to these properties of mental images, imagery has been useful in a wide variety of studies designed to measure the nature and speed of thought (see, for example, Figure 6.8).

Imagery is an important perceptual memory aid. In fact, a growing body of evidence suggests that it is a means of preserving perceptual information that might

FIGURE 6.6

A Serial Position Curve

The probability of recalling an item is plotted as a function of its serial position on a list of items. Generally, the first several items are likely to be recalled (the primacy effect) and the last several are recalled very well (the recency effect).

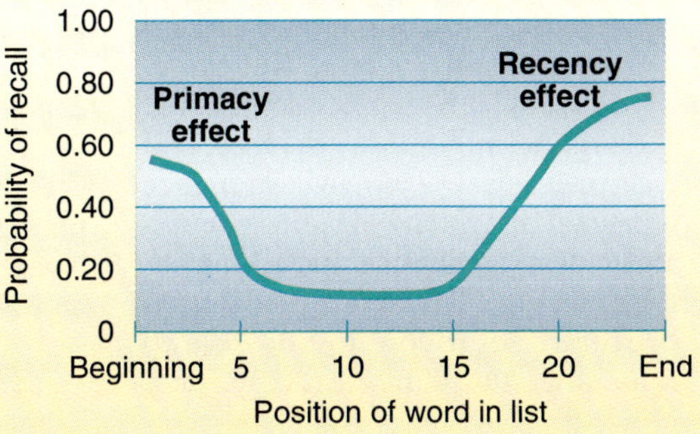

FIGURE 6.7

Kosslyn's Imagery Studies

(Based on Kosslyn, 1975, after Solso, 1979.)

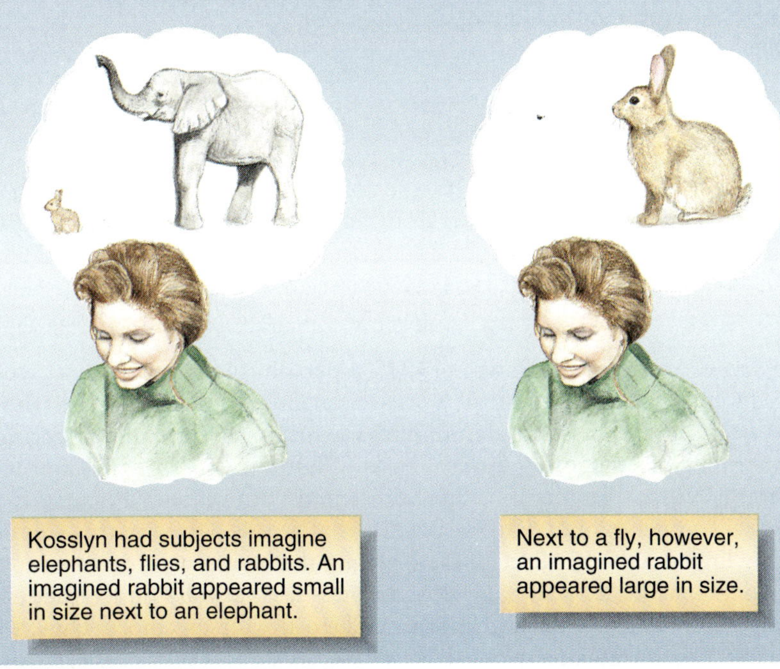

FIGURE 6.8

The Speed of Thought

The speed of thought can be assessed through studies of mental rotation. Shepard and Metzler (1988) asked participants to say as quickly as possible whether visual stimuli were in fact the same stimuli but rotated or were different stimuli.

APPLICATIONS

Improving Your Memory

Several techniques can improve memory. Here are some of the most powerful ones; they move from simple strategies to more complex overall approaches. Try using them to learn this chapter's concepts.

Rehearse, Rehearse, Rehearse. If you want to remember something, there is no substitute for rehearsal (see pages 201–202). Maintenance rehearsal, in which you simply reiterate items without attaching any meaning to them, will facilitate recognition or rote recall if you do not have to remember the items for very long. However, if you really want to remember ideas for a long time, you need to understand them; and this requires the use of elaborative rehearsal. With elaborative rehearsal, you generate meaning as you repeat and think about the information you are learning.

Be an Active Learner. Becoming an active learner means active participation on your part; when you interact with new information, it becomes alive and interesting. By simply using your own thoughts, asking and answering your own questions, and organizing information in ways that make sense to you, you become an active learner. When you are an active learner, the facts become more than facts—they become meaningful and stay with you.

Generate Personal Meaning. To generate personal meaning out of new material (so it becomes relevant to your life and needs), you must find ways to connect yourself, your knowledge, and your life experiences to the material you are studying. People have a natural tendency to do this. But by knowing that learning and memory are enhanced when you create personal meaning, you will become more likely in the future to do so intentionally. When you can relate new information to your own life by connecting it to your past or present, to problems you need to solve, or to events in the world, you make it important. And you are much more likely to understand it, remember it, and use it.

Practice over Time. You will benefit from practice if you review your class notes soon after class or write a summary of an article soon after reading it. When you plan to study, however, distributing practice and rehearsal over time becomes important. Distributing practice means studying a particular subject for a relatively short time every day or every other day, instead of trying to cram all your studying into one long session. If you stick with a schedule for doing schoolwork so that you can avoid cramming, you can make use of the distributed practice principle. In doing so, you will increase the amount of material you learn and remember within the same total amount of study time.

Plan on Relearning. Memory studies show that most forgetting occurs right after something has been learned. They also show that if you go back and relearn (rehearse again) the same material, you learn it more quickly and forget less of it (page 202). Whenever you sit down to work on one of the subjects you are studying, go back and review what you have already studied before you move forward to learn more. In this way, you will be making use of the relearning principle.

Take Advantage of the Primacy and Recency Effects. Research concerning the primacy and recency effects (page 208) shows that you are most likely to remember information received at the beginning and at the end of a study session or lecture. So instead of forcing yourself to have long, drawn-out study sessions, take a short (5- to 10-minute) break after you have studied for 20 to 30 minutes. Taking breaks will enhance your learning and memory because it will increase the number of times that the primacy and recency effects can work for you.

Focus to Prevent Interference. You can facilitate memory storage by doing whatever you can to avoid unnecessary interference (see page 217). For example, when you are studying, focus on one course or one learning task at a time. If you are studying for a big Shakespeare test, stick with Shakespeare until you feel confident you have learned the material.

Make Use of Chunking. Chunking allows us to increase the capacity of our working memory (page 201). For instance, consider the word *psychoneuroendocrinology*. This long word refers to the subfield of psychology ("psycho . . . ology") that in-

otherwise decay. According to Paivio (1971), a person told to remember two words may form an image combining those words. Someone told to remember the words *house* and *hamburger*, for example, might have an easier time remembering those words by forming an image of a house made of hamburgers or of a hamburger on top of a house. When the person is later presented with the word *house*, the word *hamburger* will come to mind. Paivio suggests that words paired in this way become conceptually linked, with the crucial factor being the image.

How images facilitate recall and recognition is not yet fully understood, but one possibility is that an image could add another code to semantic memory. Thus, with two codes, semantic and imaginal, a person has two ways to access previously learned infor-

vestigates the influence on the nervous system ("neuro") of hormones ("endocrin"). What if you had to learn to say this word so that you could spell it on an essay exam? How would you do it with the limited capacity of short-term memory? The answer is that you would use chunking. To remember the long word, you would break it into small chunks: *psycho-neuro-endocrin-ology*.

Another way to use chunking is to group ideas together in organized ways. For example, you might list some factors that increase recall as one chunk of things to remember and some factors that contribute to forgetting as another chunk.

Use Mnemonics. If you transform information that is abstract, difficult, or still unlearned into information that is personally meaningful, it will be easier to remember. Using mnemonics, or memory aids, allows you to combine seemingly unrelated items into an organized format, rhyme, or jingle so you can easily remember all of the items. For example, as a child you may have learned the notes of the treble-clef musical scale, EGBDF, by using the mnemonic jingle "Every Good Boy Does Fine." The more you can relate unfamiliar information that you want to recall to familiar information that you already know, the easier it will be for you to learn and remember it.

Use Mediation. Mediation is a bridging technique that allows you to link two items to be remembered with a third item (or image) that ties them together and serves as a cue for retrieval. Cermak (1975) uses the names *John* and *Tillie* as an example. John reminds someone of a bathroom, which can be associated with the image of tiles, which sounds and is spelled somewhat like Tillie. Therefore, remembering a tiled bathroom helps the person remember the names John and Tillie.

Make Use of the von Restorff Effect. If one item in a group of things to be learned stands out because it differs from the other items, it will be easier to learn and remember; this is known as the *von Restorff effect*. You can make use of this effect by deliberately making an idea you want to remember stand out. Do this by using a colored highlighter on your notes, by exaggerating the meaning of the idea you want to remember, by making the idea seem funny or bizarre in your mind, or by emphasizing the distinctiveness of the idea in your mind as you think about it.

Review in Different Contexts and Modalities. The place where you learned something can be an important retrieval cue. For example, when you see a familiar receptionist in a gymnasium, you may not be able to remember how you knew that person. Try to review and rehearse in different settings. Also, try learning and studying through more than one sensory modality. For example, if you hear (auditory modality) a lecture, write down (tactile–kinesthetic and visual modality) what you heard. If you have been developing mnemonics on paper, try saying them out loud. If you have been outlining a chapter aloud, write down or draw a map of the key ideas.

Prepare the Environment. Because there is so much to learn and remember, you can facilitate the task if you prepare your environment (Brown, 1989). Limit the number of opportunities for people to distract you from your task. Study in a quiet place where there are few people. Avoid visual clutter in your study area; it is a distraction from the task at hand. Limit the number of tasks you are working on so as to focus your attention and thus stay tuned into one task. Finish the tasks that you start so they will not take further attention. Keep a notebook handy to jot down ideas, insights, and potential mnemonics.

mation. Some researchers argue that imagery, verbal encoding mechanisms, and semantic memory operate together to encode and to aid in retrieval (Marschark et al., 1987).

Applications suggests how you can use the information presented in this chapter to help improve your own memory.

Extraordinary Memory

As was noted earlier, nearly perfect recall is rare. But is it possible for an average person to develop a remarkable memory? We saw that the memory span for most

FOCUS

Review

- What evidence supports the existence of episodic memory? Of semantic memory? pp. 205–206
- Differentiate implicit and explicit memory. pp. 207, 208
- What evidence did researchers use to conclude that flashbulb memories are not unique? p. 207

Think Critically

- Is procedural memory more explicit or implicit? What about flashbulb memory? Explain.
- What fundamental assumptions have memory researchers taken from studies of short-term memory and applied to help people improve their memory?

adults is limited to one or two chunks, each chunk containing around seven items, plus or minus two items. Recent research shows, however, that with practice and the use of special chunking strategies, memory span can be increased greatly. In one study, participants' memory spans were increased to 79 digits (Ericsson, Chase, & Faloon, 1980), in another to 106 digits (Staszewski, 1987). The participants in these experiments developed strategies for effective, efficient encoding and efficient retrieval of meaningful chunks of information; the process was effortful, deliberate, and effective. The participants were using exceptionally efficient retrieval structures.

Attempting to increase digit span is a time-consuming process. In the two studies just discussed, the time needed was 20 months in the first case and 5 years in the second—and the results did not carry over to other study materials. But exceptional memory skills can be seen in other research domains. For example, Staszewski (1988) presented research on "lightning mental calculators"—individuals who can solve complex arithmetic problems (such as 54,917 x 63) with remarkable speed and accuracy. The key to such achievement is steady practice, efficient use of memory, and extensive knowledge of numerical relationships. A person can't train to be a lightning mental calculator without extensive daily and weekly practice. Nor can a person learn to calculate calendar date problems (for example, what day of the week was July 27, 1946?) without extensive practice and considerable knowledge of day, date, and calendar rules (Howe & Smith, 1988). Individuals can learn to overcome working memory limitations, but it requires supervised prolonged practice that is maintained at high daily levels (Ericsson, Krampe, & Tesch-Römer, 1993). That an elite, specialized performer requires supervised practice is especially true in music and sports; when high levels of skill training are put into play at a young age, the effects of years of experience become apparent in extraordinary musical skill or sports performance (Ericsson & Charness, 1994).

Forgetting: The Loss of Memory

Quick! Name your first-grade teacher. Your Social Security number. Where you went on your last vacation. In general, your memory serves you amazingly well. Nevertheless, at times you may have trouble recalling the name of someone you know well, where you read an interesting article, or the phone number of a close friend. And have you ever started an exam only to have your mind suddenly go blank?

There are many causes of forgetting, including not rehearsing information well enough and not using it for a long time. Forgetting also occurs because of interference from newly learned or previously learned information, because the information is unpleasant or because of physiological problems. Moreover, forgetting occurs with both short- and long-term memory.

Starting with the pioneering work of Hermann Ebbinghaus and others in the latter part of the 19th century, many psychologists have studied forgetting. Such research has revealed a great deal about memory processes—in particular, those processes that affect learning and the ability to recall what has been learned.

Early Studies

Some of the first experimenters in psychology studied forgetting. Sometimes the tasks they created involved paper and pencil, but more often they merely involved the experimenter, a participant, and some information to be learned. Computers were unheard of, and techniques that psychologists use today would not have made sense.

Relearning. Using the technique of *relearning*, Hermann Ebbinghaus (1850–1909) studied how well people retain stored information. Ebbinghaus earnestly believed that the contents of consciousness could be studied by scientific principles. He tried to quantify how quickly participants could learn, relearn, and forget information. Ebbinghaus was the first person to investigate memory scientifically and systematically, which made his technique as important as his findings.

In his early studies, in which he was both researcher and subject, Ebbinghaus assigned himself the task of learning lists of letters in order of presentation. First he strung together groups of three letters to make nonsense syllables such as *nak*, *dib*, *mip*, and *daf*. He then recorded how many times he had to present lists of these nonsense syllables to himself before he could remember them perfectly. Ebbinghaus found that when the lists were short, learning was nearly perfect in one or two trials. When they contained more than seven items, however, he had to present them over and over for accurate recall.

Later Ebbinghaus did learning experiments with other participants. He had them learn lists of words and then, after varying amounts of time, measured how quickly the participants relearned the original list. If participants relearned the list quickly, Ebbinghaus concluded that they still had some memory of it. He called this learning technique the *saving method,* because what was initially learned was not totally forgotten. (See Figure 6.9 for Ebbinghaus's "forgetting curve.")

FIGURE 6.9

Ebbinghaus's Forgetting Curve

Ebbinghaus found that most forgetting occurs during the first 9 hours after learning.

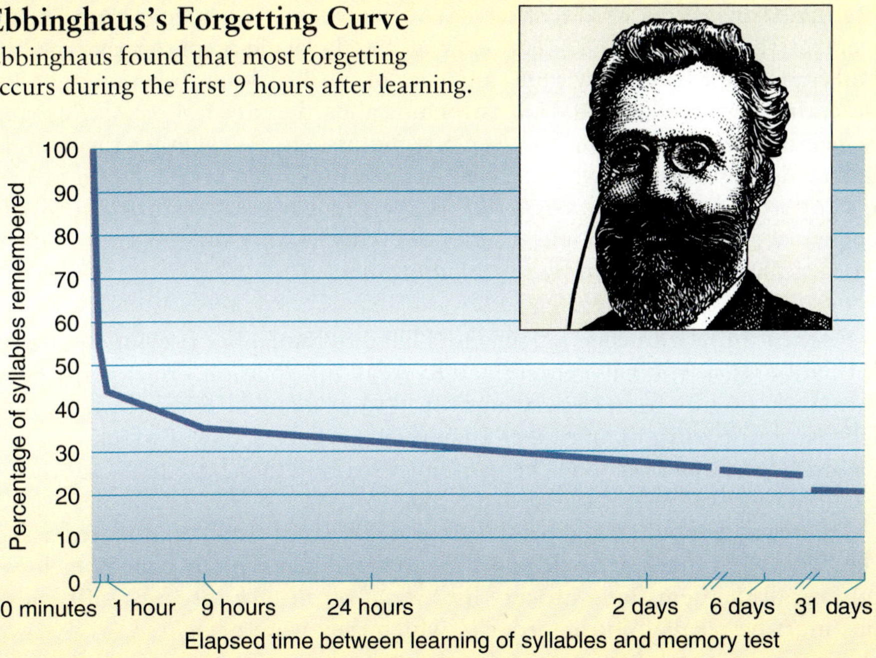

Practice. Following Ebbinghaus's lead, from the 1930s through the 1960s, many researchers investigated the best ways for people to learn new material and relearn forgotten skills. In one study in 1966, Baddeley and Longman wanted to learn which of two types of practice resulted in more optimal learning and retention: intensive practice at one time (massed practice) or the same amount of practice over several intervals (distributed practice). To answer this question, they taught postal workers to touch-type.

The participants were divided into four groups, each member of which practiced the same number of hours: One group practiced typing 1 hour a day (distributed practice), the second practiced 2 hours a day, the third practiced 1 hour twice a day, and the fourth practiced 2 hours twice a day (massed practice). Thus, the participants used either distributed practice or massed practice. The dependent variable was how well they learned to type—that is, the number of accurate keystrokes per minute. A typing test showed that distributed practice (typing 1 hour a day for several days) was more effective. From this experiment and others, researchers have learned that the effectiveness of distributed practice depends on many variables, including the method, order, and speed of presentation. Distributed practice is especially effective for perceptual motor skills, where eye–hand coordination is important.

In the 1970s, researchers began to study the best way to present information to be learned. (This interest paralleled the innovations being carried out at that time in public schools, including open classrooms, the "new math," and cooperative learning.) They found, for example, that if one item in a list differs from the others (say one plant name in a list with nine animal names), the one different item is learned more easily. This is the phenomenon called the *von Restorff effect.*

Measures of Retention

As a teacher, I hope my students will be able to recall key ideas, recognize important concepts, reconstruct elements of my lectures, and be able to visualize key graphs and other images. All of these tasks (recall, recognition, reconstruction, and pictorial memory) are measures of retention—studies of which have allowed researchers to understand how to best improve memory and reduce forgetting. The most widely investigated measures of retention have been recall and recognition. *Recall* is remembering the details of a situation or idea and placing them together in a meaningful framework (usually without any cues or aids). Asking someone to name the spacecraft that exploded with U.S. astronauts aboard is a test of recall. *Recognition* is remembering whether one has seen a stimulus before—whether the stimulus is familiar. Asking someone whether Neil Armstrong landed on the moon in 1969 is a test of recognition. *Reconstruction* is the procedure of restoring a disrupted sequence of events (for example, a series of events in a person's history) to its original order. This is often aided by *pictorial memory.*

Recall. In recall tasks, participants have to remember previously presented information. (Essay exams require you to recall information.) In experiments, the information usually comprises strings (or lists) of digits or letters. A typical study might ask participants to remember 10 nonsense syllables, one of which is presented on a screen every half-second. The participants would then have to repeat the list at the end of the 5-second presentation period.

Three widely used recall tasks are free recall, serial recall, and paired associate tasks. In *free recall tasks*, participants are to recall items in any order, much as you might recall the items on a grocery list. *Serial recall tasks* are more difficult; the items must be recalled in the order in which they were presented, as you would recall a telephone number. In *paired associate tasks*, participants are given a cue to help them recall the second half of a pair of items. In the learning phase of a study, the experimenter might pair the words *tree* and *shoe*. In the testing phase, participants would be presented with the word *tree* and would have to respond with the correct answer, *shoe*.

Recognition. In a multiple-choice test, you are asked to recognize relevant information. Psychologists have found that recognition tasks can help them measure subtle differences in memory ability better than recall tasks can. That's because, although a person may be unable to recall the associated details contained in a previously studied fact, he or she may recognize the fact. Asked to name the capital of Maine, you would probably have a better chance of answering correctly if you were given four names to choose from: Columbus, Annapolis, Helena, or Augusta.

Reconstruction. Here's a test of your memory: What did Neil Armstrong say when he first set foot on the moon? Few people can recall Armstrong's words exactly, but most can probably recognize them or reconstruct them approximately. Researchers have shown that people often "construct" memories of past events; the constructions are close approximations but not exact memories. For example, you might reconstruct the gist of Armstrong's speech by saying that Armstrong said something about man's first steps on the moon being important for all mankind. (Just for the record, his exact words were "That's one small step for man, one giant leap for mankind.")

In 1932, English psychologist Sir Frederick Bartlett reported that when college students tried to recall stories they had just read, they changed them in interesting ways. They shortened and simplified details, a process called *leveling*; they focused on or emphasized certain details, a process called *sharpening*; and they altered facts to make the stories fit their own views of the world, a process called *assimilation*. In other words, the students constructed memories that to some degree distorted the events.

Contemporary explanations of this *reconstructive memory* have centered on the constructive nature of the memory process and on how people develop a **schema**—a conceptual framework that organizes information and makes sense of the world. Because people cannot remember *all* the details of an event or situation, they keep key facts and lose minor details. Schemas group together key pieces of information. In general, people try to fit an entire memory into some framework that will be available for later recall. For example, my schema for life in the United States during 1969, the year the first U.S. astronauts landed on the moon, might include memories of such events as listening to the Beatles' *Abbey Road* album, going on my honeymoon, and reading about the continuing urban unrest in Watts. When people reconstruct memories, however, those reconstructions may not be accurate, as is discussed in *Applications* on page 216.

Pictorial Memory. Related to reconstruction is the study of *pictorial memory*, in which researchers test how well people can remember visual images. The results of these studies show that people are amazingly good at recognizing images they have seen before. In fact, Haber (1979) found that participants can recognize thousands of pictures with almost 100-percent accuracy. In 1970, Standing, Conezio, and Haber showed participants thousands of slides, each for a few seconds. They then presented pairs of slides, only one of which the participants had seen before, and asked the participants to identify which of the pair they had seen. The participants recognized the previously seen slides with greater than 95 percent accuracy. More recent studies have repeated the results of Standing and his colleagues, and researchers have developed other approaches as well. They suggest that pictorial information may be encoded, stored, and retrieved differently from other information; this is why pictorial memory is so good (Intraub, 1980; Intraub & Nicklos, 1985; Standing, 1973).

Schema [SKEEM-uh]: A conceptual framework that organizes information and makes sense of the world by laying out a structure in which events can be encoded.

APPLICATIONS

Eyewitness Testimony

If someone sees an accident or crime, can the witness accurately report the facts of the situation to the police or the courts? The answer is yes and no. The police and the courts have generally accepted *eyewitness testimony* as some of the best evidence that can be presented. Eyewitnesses are people who saw the crime, have no bias or grudge, and are sworn to tell (and recall) the truth. But do they?

Some studies show that eyewitnesses often forget; they recall events incorrectly and identify the wrong people as being involved in the events (Bekerian & Bowers, 1983; E. F. Loftus, 1979). When people make such identifications, they are often confident in their judgments (Wells, Luus, & Windschitl, 1994). Nevertheless, eyewitnesses of the same event often report seeing different things. Langman and Cockburn (1975) recorded the 1968 eyewitness testimony of people who reported seeing Sirhan Sirhan shoot Senator Robert F. Kennedy (brother of President John F. Kennedy). Even though many of the eyewitnesses were standing next to one another, they reported seeing different things. In addition, identification of a criminal, even in a lineup, is prone to significant mistakes (Navon, 1990), although techniques have been developed to improve the accuracy of lineup identifications (Sporer, 1993; Wells, 1993).

To complicate the matter, eyewitnesses often enhance their memories over time (recall Bartlett's theory of assimilation). Harvard law professor Alan Dershowitz (1986) asserts that the memories of witnesses—particularly those with a stake in the eventual outcome—tend to get better with the passage of time. Dershowitz calls this process memory enhancement and argues that it occurs when people fit their hazy memories into a coherent theory and pattern of other results.

A witness's initial recollections of a crime may be vague, for example. However, as a trial approaches, the person is coached and rehearsed and tends to remember better, with more clarity and less ambiguity. According to Dershowitz (1986), what began as a hazy recollection becomes crystal clear. The result in the courtroom may be slightly inaccurate, seriously biased, or largely untrue testimony; that is, it may be constructed testimony. Ironically, the more detailed a witness is (even about irrelevant details), the more credible that witness is assumed to be, even if the witness is recalling things inaccurately (Bell & Loftus, 1989).

Faced with several possible suspects, eyewitnesses often find it difficult to identify the person who committed a crime and may make a mistake. Steve Titus, for example, was wrongly identified (from mugshots) as a rapist; he was convicted of that crime but was later released when the actual rapist was arrested. ▼

Whether the witness's memory is weakened, clouded, or confused or whether retrieval processes are impaired is still not clear; but repeated interrogation of a witness can modify the witness's memory—enhancing the recall of some details and even inducing forgetting of other details —even when no misinformation is contained in the questioning (Shaw, Bjork, & Handal, 1995). When a person feels that another eyewitness has corroborated an identification, his or her confidence increases. However, a witness's confidence is not necessarily related to the accuracy of his or her identification (Sporer et al., 1995); when another witness identifies someone else, that confidence quickly decreases (Luus & Wells, 1994). So witnesses' confidence in their memory is fragile; as Loftus and Hoffman (1989, p. 103) argue, "That people come to accept misinformation and adopt it faithfully as their own is an important phenomenon in its own right."

Despite strong evidence of errors in eyewitness testimony, two researchers from the University of British Columbia believe that eyewitness testimony is accurate and that it is the laboratory studies of eyewitness testimony that may be inaccurate. Yuille and Cutshall (1986) argue that laboratory studies generally use simulated events, films of events, video presentations, and slide shows to study eyewitness testimony—and that this is not the same as actually seeing a crime or accident. They further state that real events are well remembered and that researchers who study eyewitness testimony should do fieldwork before making further claims. This idea is being echoed by other prominent memory researchers who argue that stress and other life events may affect research results (Deffenbacher, 1994; Yuille et al., 1994). Studying real-life everyday memories (Yuille, 1993) may turn out to be crucial to the study of learning and memory and to be a necessary adjunct to traditional laboratory studies (Ceci & Bronfenbrenner, 1991).

Generalizing from field-based situations is difficult because of numerous uncontrolled variables; generalizing from laboratory situations is difficult because of their artificial nature. Today, researchers are insisting on both. Before the issue of eyewitnesses' accuracy is resolved, however, more field-based research and further laboratory simulation studies are needed (Egeth, 1993; Tulving, 1991).

FIGURE 6.10

Decay and Interference in Short-Term and Long-Term Memory

The transfer of information from short-term memory to long-term memory is crucial for accurate recall at a later time. Note that decay and interference affect both short-term and long-term memory.

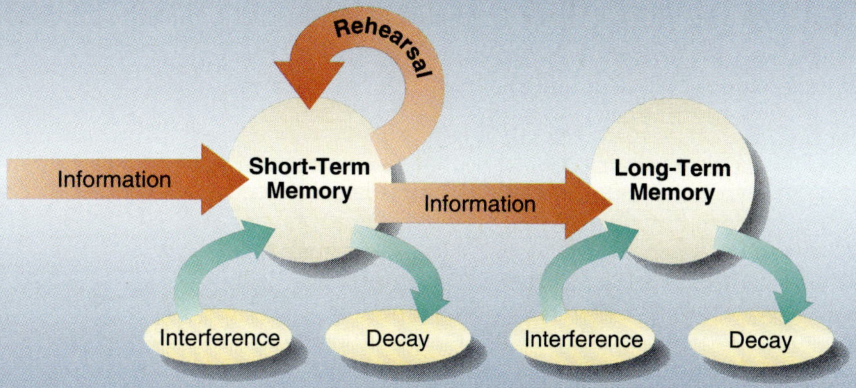

Decay and Interference

Data can be lost from both short-term and long-term memory. Two concepts, decay and interference, help explain the loss (see Figure 6.10).

Decay of Information. **Decay** is the loss of information from memory as a result of disuse and the passage of time. In decay theory, unimportant events fade from memory, and details become lost, confused, or fuzzy. Another way to look at decay theory is this: Memory exists in the brain in a physiological form known as a *memory trace*. With the passage of time and a lack of active use, the trace disintegrates, fades, and is lost.

Decay theory was popular for many years but is not widely accepted today. Many early studies did not consider several important variables that affect memory processes, among them the rate and mode of stimulus presentation. Although decay does form a small part of the final explanation of forgetting, it is probably less important than other factors, such as interference.

Interference in Memory. **Interference** is the suppression or confusion of one bit of information with another that was received either earlier or later. In interference theory, the limited capacity of short-term memory makes it susceptible to interference from, or confusion among, other learned items. That is, when competing information is stored in short-term memory, the crowding that results affects a person's memory for particular items. For example, if someone looks up a telephone number and is then given another number to remember, the second number will probably interfere with the ability to remember the first one. Moreover, interference in memory is more likely to occur when a person is presented with a great deal of new information. (In this text, you are being provided with a great deal of new information. Organizing your studying into coherent chunks will help you avoid confusing the information you are trying to enter into long-term memory.)

Research on interference theory shows that the extent and nature of a person's experiences both before and after learning are important. For example, someone given a list of nonsense syllables may recall 75 percent of the items correctly. However, if that person had earlier been given 20 similar lists to learn, the number of items correctly recalled would be lower; the previous lists would interfere with recall. If the person were subsequently given additional lists to learn, recall would be even lower. Psychologists call these interference effects proactive and retroactive interference (or inhibition). **Proactive interference**, or *proactive inhibition*, is a

Decay: Loss of information from memory as a result of disuse and the passage of time.

Interference: Suppression or confusion of one bit of information with another that was received either earlier or later.

Proactive interference [pro-AK-tiv]: Decrease in accurate recall of information as a result of the effects of previously learned or presented information. Also known as *proactive inhibition.*

FIGURE 6.11

Proactive and Retroactive Interference

In memory, proactive and retroactive interference occur when information interferes with (inhibits recall of) other information.

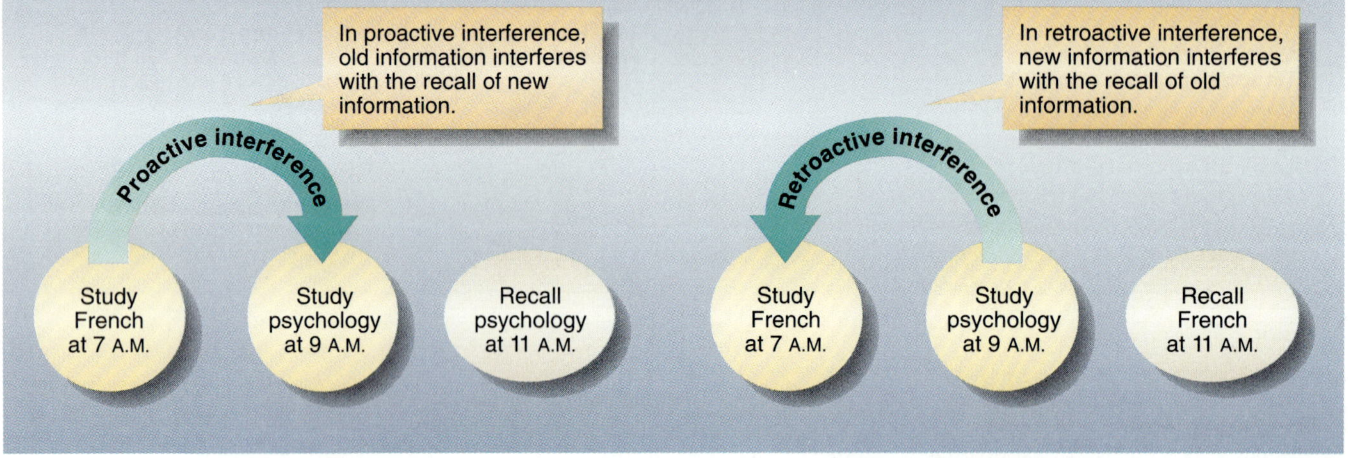

decrease in accurate recall of information as a result of the effects of previously learned or presented information. **Retroactive interference**, or *retroactive inhibition*, is a decrease in accurate recall as a result of the subsequent presentation of different information. (See Figure 6.11 for an illustration of both types of interference.) Proactive and retroactive interference help explain recall failures in long-term memory.

Here is an illustration of proactive and retroactive interference: Suppose that you attend a series of speeches, each 5 minutes long. According to psychological research on proactive and retroactive interference, you will be most likely to remember the first and last speeches. There will be no proactive interference with the first speech and no retroactive interference with the last speech. Your memory of all the middle speeches, however, will suffer from both proactive and retroactive interference.

Interference in Attention. Interference has long been a potent explanatory factor in memory and perception studies. For many years it was used to explain what is called the *Stroop effect* (Stroop, 1935). The Stroop test is a procedure in which people are asked to name colors that are printed in an ink color different from the color being named. For example, the word *red* may be printed in blue ink. Most people find it difficult to attend to the ink color alone when they are asked to name the color in which the word is printed (the Stroop effect). This is because of an assumed automatic tendency to read the word, which produces interference. This explanation has been popular, but attention, rather than interference, is now considered more important in explaining the Stroop effect (MacLeod, 1991).

All of the factors in forgetting are not yet clear, as is shown in the examination of motivated forgetting in *Applications*.

Retroactive interference [RET-ro-AK-tiv]: Decrease in accurate recall of information as a result of the subsequent presentation of different information. Also known as *retroactive inhibition*.

Retrieval Success and Failures: Encoding Specificity

Some contemporary researchers assert that every memory is retained and available but that some memories are less accessible than others. Think of a computer's memory or the library analogy: All the files, or all the books in the library, are there, but

APPLICATIONS

Motivated Forgetting—Memory and Childhood Abuse

Freud (1933) was the first to suggest formally the idea of *motivated forgetting*—the idea that unwanted or unpleasant events might be lost in memory simply because people want to forget them. He stated that such loss occurs through repression—the burying of unpleasant ideas in the unconscious, where they remain inaccessible. Most researchers agree that motivated forgetting probably exists in some form. But they have found it hard to measure and difficult to demonstrate experimentally, even though anecdotal clinical evidence abounds.

For more than a decade Elizabeth Loftus (1991, 1993) has been asking if recall of events, eyewitness ones and other ones—for example, being sexually abused as a child—is due to memory enhancement or outright overinflation of facts. With her data from laboratory situations, she has extrapolated her findings to other such situations—and has caused a furor by viewing with skepticism professionals who treat sexually abused victims and their clients. These professionals assert that their clients' memories, often from many years before, are vivid, accurate, and truthful. Research shows that children and adults can be led to enhance their memories (Lindsay, 1993), and that false memories can remain well preserved over time (Brainerd, Reyna, & Brandse, 1995). However, Ceci and Bruck (1993) hold that adults and even very young children are capable of accurately recalling events that occurred early in their lives.

The debate among professionals has grown intense, dividing the experts and pitting clinical psychologists against researchers. Some memory researchers have asserted that sexually abused victims could not forget their childhood events for long durations (Garry & Loftus, 1994; Loftus, Garry, & Feldman, 1994). Others argue that this is not the case (Williams, 1994). Researchers assert that some misguided therapists are helping some people "recover" events that never occurred (Ofshe & Singer, 1994). Others argue that "a thoughtful review of scientific findings does not support a quick embrace of the simplistic explanation that disclosures of childhood abuse are the result of therapist suggestion" (Olio, 1994, p. 442).

Many have pointed out that there are two key questions: First, can someone forget horrible experiences and remember them years later? And second, is memory fallible? Clinical psychologists speak to the first issue; memory researchers speak to the second. Research shows that memory is indeed fallible; people do forget; and people make mistakes and can be led on. But a long history of clinical experience, case reports, and ethical therapists indicates that many men and women have been abused as children, that such events can be corroborated, and that while there are some misguided therapists (as there are misguided plumbers and physicians), people can repress horrific experiences and have their memories recur when they are adults and can better cope with them.

To be the critical thinkers that they were trained to be, researchers and clinicians alike need to stop talking past one another and listen to the evidence. Is there repressed memory? Sure there is. Are all people who claim that they have been abused making it all up? Surely not. Is memory fallible? Yes. Are some people's memories unreliable and subject to suggestion? Yes, again. The pain of individuals who remember unpleasant events of their childhood, whether accurately or not, is real; where this pain emanates from is not fully resolved.

▲ *Elizabeth Loftus has testified as an expert witness on memory in more than 200 court cases.*

some cannot be found (perhaps because they are mislocated or misshelved), making retrieval difficult or impossible. When retrieval of information is impossible, that information is effectively forgotten.

Research on retrieval focuses on how people encode information and on the cues that act to help in retrieval. If you are given a cue for retrieval and the origi-

FOCUS

Review

- What view of memory reflects the fact that recall and recognition tap different processes? pp. 214–215

Think Critically

- Why do you think distributed practice is more effective than massed practice for learning?
- How do interference explanations of forgetting explain errors in retrieval?

nally stored information contains that cue, retrieval is easier, faster, and more accurate. For example, if I asked you to recall the definition of the word *reinforcement*, it would be easy to recall, because the definition refers to the delivery of a reinforcer. But if I asked you to recall the meaning of *reinforcer,* the definition ("Any event that increases . . .") has no specific cue to help you recall the definition. When a retrieval cue is present, retrieval is easier; this evidence supports the encoding specificity principle.

The **encoding specificity principle** asserts that the value or effectiveness of a specific retrieval cue depends on how well it compares with and contains information from when the original memory was encoded. The more clearly and sharply your memory cues are defined and paired, the better your recall will be and the less likely you will be to experience retrieval failures. To increase your access to information stored in memory, you should match the retrieval situation to the original learning situation as much as possible. The encoding specificity principle is apparent in studies of state-dependent learning.

State-Dependent Learning. Psychologist Gordon Bower (1981) used the following story to describe a phenomenon known as state-dependent learning:

> When I was a kid I saw the movie *City Lights* in which Charlie Chaplin plays the little tramp. In one very funny sequence, Charlie saves a drunk from leaping to his death. The drunk turns out to be a millionaire who befriends Charlie, and the two spend the evening together drinking and carousing. The next day, when sober, the millionaire does not recognize Charlie and even snubs him. Later the millionaire gets drunk again, and when he spots Charlie treats him as his long-lost companion. So the two of them spend another evening together carousing and drinking and then stagger back to the millionaire's mansion to sleep. In the morning, of course, the sober millionaire again does not recognize Charlie, treats him as an intruder, and has the butler kick him out by the seat of his pants. The scene ends with the little tramp telling the camera his opinion of high society and the evils of drunkenness. (p. 129)

The millionaire remembers Charlie only when he is intoxicated, the same state in which he originally met him. Psychologists find that information learned while a person is in a particular physiological state is recalled most accurately when the person is again in that physiological state. This phenomenon, known as **state-dependent learning,** is associated with such states as those involving drugs, time of day (Holloway, 1977), mental illness (Weingartner, 1977), and electroconvulsive shock therapy (discussed in Chapter 15) (Robbins & Meyer, 1970).

In a typical study of state-dependent learning, Weingartner and colleagues (1976) had four groups of participants learn lists of high- and low-imagery words. To induce intoxication, all participants except those in the control group drank vodka and fruit juice. The control group learned and recalled while sober, a second group learned and recalled while intoxicated, a third group learned while sober and recalled while intoxicated, and a fourth group learned while intoxicated and recalled while sober. The results showed that participants recalled the lists best when they were in the same state in which they had learned the lists. (This is not to say that memory is better under intoxicated conditions. All else being equal, retention is better in sober individuals.)

Several theories attempt to explain state-dependent learning. A widely accepted explanation focuses on how altered or drugged states affect the storage process.

Encoding specificity principle: The finding that the value or effectiveness of a specific retrieval cue depends on how well it compares with and contains information from when the original memory was encoded.

State-dependent learning: The tendency to recall information learned in a particular physiological state most accurately when one is again in that physiological state.

BUILDING TABLE 6.3

Key Processes in the Stages of Memory

STAGE	ENCODING	STORAGE	RETRIEVAL	DURATION	FORGETTING
Sensory Memory	Visual or auditory (iconic or echoic storage).	Brief, fragile, and temporary.	Information is extracted from stimulus presentation and transferred to short-term memory.	Visual: 250 milliseconds; auditory: about 3 seconds.	Rapid decay of information; interference is possible if a new stimulus is presented.
Short-Term Memory	Visual and auditory; auditory encoding is especially important.	Repetitive rehearsal maintains information in storage, perhaps on a visual–auditory scratch pad where further encoding can take place.	Maintenance and elaborative rehearsal can keep information available for retrieval; retrieval is enhanced through elaboration and further encoding.	Less than 20 seconds, no more than 30 seconds; depends on specific task and stimuli.	Interference and decay are operative; new stimulation causes rapid loss of information unless it is especially important.
Long-Term Memory	Salient or important information processed by short-term memory is transferred into long-term memory through elaborative rehearsal.	Storage is organized on logical and semantic lines for rapid recall; organization of information by categories, events, and other structures aids retrieval.	Retrieval is aided by cues and careful organization; errors in retrieval can be introduced; long-term memory is fallible.	Indefinite; many events will be recalled in great detail for a lifetime.	Both decay and interference contribute to retrieval failure.

According to this view, part of learning involves the encoding of stimuli in specific ways at the time of learning (encoding specificity principle); to access the stored information, a person must evoke the same context in which the encoding occurred. When you study for an examination with music in the background but are tested in quiet conditions, is your recall not as good? The answer to this question is as yet unresolved, but studies of state-dependent learning may hold the key; and recent studies of mood-dependent memory suggest that the answer may be yes (Eich, 1995).

Building Table 6.3 summarizes key processes in the three stages of memory and forgetting.

The Neuroscience of Memory

We have explored the structure, function, and operation of memory and forgetting. We also need to look at what memories are and where they are found in the brain. Memories are stored in electrochemical form in the brain. Many psychologists who study the biological bases of behavior now believe that most, if not all, memories are retained in some manner. Researchers today are exploring the neurobiological bases of memory. How does the brain store memories? Where are memories stored? Are memory traces localized or distributed?

Studies of Amnesia

Much of the early work on the neuroscience of memory began with the study of patients in hospitals who for one reason or another had developed amnesia, often as the result of an accident. Television soap operas frequently portray people with amnesia, but in fact the condition is relatively rare. **Amnesia** is the inability to remember information, usually because of physiological trauma (such as a blow to the head). Typically, amnesia involves loss of memory for all events within a specific period.

There are two basic kinds of amnesia: retrograde and anterograde. **Retrograde amnesia** is the inability to remember events and experiences that preceded a traumatizing event. The loss of memory can cover the period just before the event, as in the minutes leading up to an accident, or a period of several years before it. Recovery tends to be gradual, with earlier events remembered before more recent ones. **Anterograde amnesia** is the inability to remember events and experiences that occur *after* an injury or brain damage. People suffering from anterograde amnesia are stuck in the lives they lived before being injured; new events are often completely forgotten. For example, if the onset of the amnesia occurred in 1996, the person may be able to remember clearly events of 1995 or earlier but have a difficult time recalling what he or she did only half an hour ago. The person may meet someone for the hundredth time, yet think he or she is being introduced to a perfect stranger. The person is able to learn some new information, but this is highly dependent on how the information is presented (Hamann & Squire, 1995).

In studying patients with brain damage or those who have undergone surgery for major epileptic attacks, researchers have found that the region of the brain called the *hippocampus* may be responsible for the transfer of new information to long-term memory. Milner showed that if certain regions of the brain are damaged or removed, people can remember old information but not new information (Milner, 1966; Milner, Corkin, & Teuber, 1968). The ability to remember remote events seems to depend on brain mechanisms that are separate and distinct from those required for new learning of recent events (Shimamura & Squire, 1986). These studies do not conclusively confirm the existence of separate places or processes in the brain for different types of memory, but they are suggestive. Moreover, research on learning and memory of emotional responses by Kim and Fanselow (1992) supports the idea that memory is not a single process or one encoded in a single place (Shallice et al., 1994). MRI studies are finding that men and women who have undergone traumas show changes in the size of various areas of the brain, especially the hippocampus. All this research supports an important point: Memories may be coded in one or many places, and they may be affected by a range of physical events, past experiences, and current ones—thus, memory is as much a process as it is an event or thing.

Amnesia [am-NEE-zhuh]: Inability to remember information (typically all events within a specific period) usually due to physiological trauma.

Retrograde amnesia [RET-ro-grade]: Loss of memory for events and experiences occurring in a period preceding the amnesia-causing event.

Anterograde amnesia: Loss of memory for events and experiences occurring after the amnesia-causing event.

Consolidation Theory and Coding

Remember, memories are not physical things; rather, they are made up of unique interactions among hundreds and thousands of neurons in the brain. Using this fact, Canadian psychologist Donald Hebb (1904–1985) presented one of the major psychological and physiological theories of memory in 1949. Hebb suggested that when groups of neurons are stimulated, they form patterns of neural activity. If a specific group of neurons fires frequently, a reverberating and regular neural circuit is established. This evolution of a temporary neural circuit into a more permanent circuit is known as **consolidation**. According to Hebb, consolidation serves as the basis of short-term memory and permits the coding (also known as encoding) of information into long-term memory. If Hebb is correct, when people first sense a new stimulus, only temporary changes in neurons take place; but with repetition, consolidation occurs and the temporary circuit becomes a permanent one.

Many psychologists believe that the consolidation process provides the key to understanding both learning and memory—that individual differences in ability to learn or remember may be due to differing abilities to consolidate neural circuits properly. Confirmation of this notion comes from studies using electroconvulsive shock therapy (discussed in Chapter 15) to disrupt consolidation, which results in impaired memory both in human beings and in animals. Further support comes from studies showing that recent memories are more susceptible to amnesia loss than are older memories (Milner, 1989). And there are emerging physiological studies that show that key amino acids have specific roles in memory and in amnesia (Kandel & Abel, 1995).

The consolidation process may even play a role in the physiological development of the brain. Researchers have compared the brains of animals raised in enriched environments with the brains of animals raised in deprived environments. In enriched environments, toys and other objects are available for the animals to play with and to learn from. The brains of animals raised in such environments have more elaborate networks of nerve cells, with more dendrites and more synapses with other neurons (Chang, Isaacs, & Greenough, 1991). This means that when a neuron is stimulated over and over again, it is enriched; and it may branch out and become more easily accessible. Such elaboration is greater when organisms are placed in complex, superenriched visual or auditory environments. These findings may indicate that when key neurons and neurotransmitters are stimulated by reinforcing events, those events may be better remembered and more easily accessed—this may be part of the reason reinforced or practiced events are so easily recalled (Kandel & Abel, 1995).

If a neuron is stimulated, the biochemical processes involved make it more likely to respond again later; further, the number of dendrites of that cell increases because of previous stimulation (Lynch & Baudry, 1984). This suggests that biochemical actions and repeated use may make learning and remembering easier (Kandel & Abel, 1995)—a conception that fits perfectly with Hebb's suggestions. In addition, clear evidence exists that specific protein synthesis occurs just after learning and that long-term memory depends on this synthesis (Matthies, 1989). Psychologists now generally accept the idea that the structure of synapses changes after learning, and especially after repeated learning experiences. As Hebb said (1949, p. 62), "Some memories are both instantaneously established and permanent. To account for the permanence, some structural change seems necessary."

Consolidation theory has been refined, extended, and supported by research. For example, researchers know that a single neuron has many synaptic sites on its dendrites. Alkon (1989) has shown that there is extensive interaction among those sites and with the sites of other neurons. He argues that the spread of electrical and chemical activity from one site to another—without activity or firing of the neurons—seems to be critical for initiating memory storage. He asserts that, on a given neuron, a huge number of different incoming signals can be received and stored. Alkon has been developing mathematical and computer models to simulate neuronal encoding for memory and to study animal memory. This exciting work extends Hebb's ideas.

Also in its infancy but very promising is the finding that there are specific genes necessary for the formation of memories. A research team headed by Alcino Silva has isolated a gene, dubbed the *CREB gene,* which is crucial in the consolidation process. Without the presence of this gene, certain proteins are not activated, and memories are fleeting (Bourtchuladze et al., 1994). The impact of the genetic causes

Consolidation [kon-SOL-ih-DAY-shun]: The evolution of a temporary neural circuit into a more permanent circuit.

of memory and memory loss is yet to be fully understood; the presence of the CREB gene is one link among many in the chain of events from experience to recall, but it seems to be an essential one.

Work on the physiology of memory has expanded on other fronts as well. For example, Schacter (1992) asserts that what researchers need to do is to extend their work by studying memory established in one domain but queried for recall in another domain—for example, to present words visually and test them auditorially or to present words to one hemisphere and test them from the other. This approach is proving fruitful but, like work in genetics, is still in its infancy, and its potential is as yet not fully understood.

Location of Memory in the Brain

Where exactly is memory located? The search for memory—that is, for the memory trace—is long-standing. Early researchers, such as Penfield (1958), looked for a single place in the brain; later researchers discovered that memory resides in many areas. Some areas may involve every type of memory; others may be used for only one type of memory, such as visual or auditory memory. In addition, because of the many steps and the many sensorimotor features involved, procedural (perceptual, motor, and cognitive) information is probably stored in many more locations than is declarative (factual) information. For example, when you load a videocassette into your VCR, you must coordinate your eye and hand to insert the cassette; and you probably listen and feel (kinesthesis) to sense when the cassette has been inserted far enough. Remembering this relatively simple procedure thus requires a great number of neural connections.

In the 1950s, during brain surgery on patients suffering from epilepsy, Wilder Penfield, a surgeon, and his colleagues were able to explore the cortex with electrodes. The electrodes were used to stimulate specific cortical neurons. The patients received only local anesthetic, because the brain contains no pain receptors; and they were therefore conscious during surgery. When Penfield stimulated the temporal lobe cortex (on either the left or the right side), patients reported seeing images—coherent perceptions of experiences. They also reported visual and auditory perceptions that included speech and music. Familiar and unfamiliar experiences were often intermixed with unrealistic and even strange circumstances (Penfield, 1958; Penfield & Jasper, 1954; Penfield & Mathieson, 1974; Penfield & Milner, 1958; Penfield & Perot, 1963).

Penfield interpreted these reports as true perceptions of past events: His patients were reporting memories elicited by the stimulation (Squire, 1987). Penfield concluded that temporal lobe stimulation triggered the memory retrievals. The concept that specific brain locations stored specific memories that could be accessed through stimulation was revolutionary.

The initial excitement soon dissipated, however. Stimulation of different brain sites often brought about the same perceptions. In addition, removal of specific sites (because of the surgery) failed to destroy the memory for the experiences (Squire, 1987). More recent research using similar techniques has shown that when the same site is stimulated repeatedly, different mental images are reported! No consistent mental image has been associated with specific anatomical locations (see Halgren et al., 1978).

Penfield's conclusion that the temporal lobe holds the memory trace has been contested for several reasons. Subsequent work shows that the limbic system and many other brain areas besides the cortex are involved in memory. No single area holds the memory trace. As is often the case with scientific research, although Penfield's work was significant, his conclusions were wrong.

Milner (1966) reported the case of a brain-damaged adult whose short-term memory was intact but who was unable to form new long-term memories. As long as the man was able to rehearse information and keep it in short-term memory, his recall performance was normal. However, as soon as he could no longer rehearse and had to use long-term memory, his recall was poor. Milner's data provide neurological support for a distinction between short- and long-term memory. They also focus researchers' attention on the action of specific brain centers and cells and on how cells may change through time and experience.

Researchers have also sought to determine whether memory traces are localized or distributed throughout the brain. For example, Schacter et al., (1996) and Thompson (1991) assert that the hippocampus plays a key role for certain kinds of memory. But other structures, including the cerebellum, are also important (Thompson & Krupa, 1994). Further, Thompson asserts that procedural memories may be relatively localized but that declarative memories are more widely distributed. Such issues are a long way from being resolved, but research with human beings does show that certain types of memories are stored in certain areas of the brain (Shallice et al., 1994).

Until recently, psychologists concentrated on how cells and synapses changed in response to environmental changes, such as deprivation of sound or light. Now, however, researchers use a variety of techniques to investigate the physiological bases of memory (Zola-Morgan, Squire, & Mishkin, 1982). For example, McGaugh (1990) contends that hormones (chemicals in the bloodstream) may affect the way in which memories are stored. He points out that newly established memories are particularly sensitive to chemical and electrical stimulation of the brain.

Other researchers are attempting to arrange computer models of the neural networks of the brain (often parallel distributed processing models). Their attempts are fascinating, but they are often limited in scope to related groups of brain cells (Sejnowski, Koch, & Churchland, 1988) or to specific types of memories—for example, fearful memories (LeDoux, Romanski, & Xagoraris, 1989) or memory for faces (Damasio, Tranel, & Damasio, 1990). Also, such work doesn't explain many kinds of learning and memory phenomena, such as state-dependent learning, memory for long-forgotten events, or extraordinary memory. A key task for researchers from a neuroscience perspective is to show the relationship between learning and memory and how newly learned information is then stored (Bouton, 1994). The theories that follow from such research help explain a limited range of psychological information about memory (Watkins, 1990), such as learning about smells (Wilson & Sullivan, 1994), but they set the stage for a broader understanding of a more comprehensive, yet to be established, theory of learning and memory.

FOCUS

Review

- Distinguish retrograde from anterograde amnesia. p. 222
- What initial evidence led Penfield to hypothesize that the location of memory could be found? p. 224
- What was Penfield's conclusion about the location of memory? Was he correct? pp. 224–225

Think Critically

- Explain how consolidation plays a role in the development of the brains of animals, and discuss the implications for human beings.
- If you were designing a physiological basis for memory, do you think it would make sense to have memory representations all over the brain, or do you think memory should be located in a specific place? Why?
- At the beginning of this chapter, I asked you to keep in mind a few techniques to help you learn how to study and remember. They are on page 194. Go back now and examine these ideas. Do they make more sense now? I'm sure they do, and you will find that if you use them as study techniques, your recall of explicit to-be-learned information as well as your implicit learning will improve.

Summary and Review

Approaches to Memory

Describe memory.

- *Memory* is the ability to remember past events or previously learned information or skills; it is also the storage system that allows retention and retrieval of information. p. 194

What are the fundamental assumptions and stages of the information-processing approach?

- The information-processing approach assumes that each stage of learning and memory is separate, though related, and is analyzable by scientific methods. p. 195
- *Encoding* is the organizing of information so that the nervous system can process it; it involves the process of getting things into the system. *Storage* is the process of maintaining information in memory for a few seconds (short-term) or for many years (long-term). *Retrieval* is the process by which stored information is recovered from memory. pp. 195–196

What are the underlying assumptions of the levels-of-processing approach? Of parallel distributed processing?

- The *levels-of-processing approach* holds that a person can process a stimulus in different ways, to different extents, and at different levels. When the level of processing becomes more complex, the theory asserts, the code goes deeper into memory. p. 196–197
- The concept of *parallel distributed processing (PDP)* developed from the notion of the brain being organized in neural networks; it suggests that many operations take place simultaneously and at many locations within the brain. p. 197

KEY TERMS

Memory, p. 194
Encoding, p. 195
Storage, p. 196
Retrieval, p. 196
Levels-of-processing approach, p. 197
Parallel distributed processing (PDP), p. 197

Sensory Memory: Focus on Encoding

Describe the role of sensory memory.

- *Sensory memory* is the mechanism that performs initial encoding and brief storage of sensory information. The visual sensory memory is sometimes called the icon, and the storage mechanism is iconic storage. The storage mechanism for the auditory system is echoic storage. Once information is established in sensory memory, it must be transferred elsewhere for additional encoding or it will be lost. pp. 198–199

KEY TERM

Sensory memory, p. 198

Short-Term Memory: Focus on Storage

Describe the differences between short-term and working memory.

- *Short-term memory* is the memory storage system that temporarily holds current or recently acquired information for immediate or short-term use. The duration for which information is maintained in short-term memory is about 30 seconds. In short-term memory, active processing takes place, including rehearsal and the transfer to long-term memory. p. 200
- The brief and limited number of items that can be reproduced easily after presentation is called the *memory span.* The immediate memory span usually contains one or two *chunks*—manageable and meaningful units of information. p. 201
- *Rehearsal* is the process of repeatedly verbalizing, thinking about, or otherwise acting on information to be remembered. *Maintenance rehearsal* is the repetitive review of information with little or no interpretation; this shallow form of rehearsal involves the physical stimulus, not its underlying meaning. *Elaborative rehearsal* involves repetition in which the stimulus may be associated with other events and be further processed; this type of rehearsal is usually necessary to transfer information to long-term memory. pp. 201–202
- *Working memory* is a newer and broader conception of short-term memory that focuses on the real-life capacities of memory. Working memory is seen as being made up of several subsystems: a subsystem to encode and rehearse auditory information; a scratch pad, or holding place for information; and a central processing mechanism, or executive, that balances the information flow. pp. 202–203

KEY TERMS

Short-term memory, p. 200
Rehearsal, p. 200
Memory span, p. 201
Chunks, p. 201
Maintenance rehearsal, p. 202
Elaborative rehearsal, p. 202
Working memory, p. 202

Long-Term Memory: Focus on Retrieval

How does long-term memory operate?

- *Long-term memory* is the memory storage system that keeps a relatively permanent record of information. It is divided into procedural memory and declarative memory. *Procedural memory* is memory for the perceptual, motor, and cognitive skills necessary to complete a task; *declarative memory* is memory for specific facts. Declarative memory is further subdivided into *episodic memory*, or memory for specific events, objects, and situations, and *semantic memory*, or memory for ideas, rules, and general concepts about the world. pp. 204–206

Differentiate between implicit and explicit memory.

- *Explicit memory* requires a person to recollect a previous event, such as the presentation of a word in a list. Explicit memory is a conscious, voluntary, active memory store that is relatively easily accessed. In contrast, *implicit memory* is considered a passive, almost unconscious process. Implicit memory tasks indirectly test whether a person has knowledge of a previously experienced event that the individual was not required to remember. pp. 206, 208

What distinguishes the primacy effect from the recency effect?

- The *primacy effect* results in the more accurate recall of items presented first; the *recency effect* results in the more accurate recall of items presented last. p. 208

What is imagery?

- *Imagery* is a cognitive process in which a mental picture is created of a sensory event. People's imagery systems can be activated by visual, auditory, or olfactory stimuli. Even a lack of sensory stimulation can produce vivid imagery. pp. 208–211

KEY TERMS

Long-term memory, p. 204
Procedural memory, p. 204
Declarative memory, p. 205
Episodic memory, p. 205
Semantic memory, p. 206
Explicit memory, p. 207
Implicit memory, p. 207
Primacy effect, p. 208
Recency effect, p. 208
Imagery, p. 208

Forgetting: The Loss of Memory

How are recall, recognition, and reconstruction different aspects of memory?

- Recall is remembering the details of a situation or idea and placing them together in a meaningful framework (usually without any cues or aids). Recognition is remembering whether one has seen a stimulus before—whether the stimulus is familiar. Research on reconstructive memory focuses on the constructive nature of the memory process and how people develop a *schema*—a conceptual framework that organizes information and makes sense of the world. pp. 214–215

How and why is information lost from memory?

- *Decay* is the loss of information from memory as a result of disuse and the passage of time. According to interference theory, the limited capacity of short-term memory makes it susceptible to *interference* or confusion. *Proactive interference* is a decrease in accurate recall as a result of the effects of previously learned or presented information. *Retroactive interference* is a decrease in accurate recall as a result of the subsequent presentation of different information. pp. 217–218
- The *encoding specificity principle* asserts that the value or effectiveness of a specific retrieval cue depends on how well it compares with and contains information from when the original memory was encoded. The more clearly and sharply memory cues are defined, the better recall will be. p. 220
- *State-dependent learning* is the tendency to recall information learned in a particular physiological state, such as being inebriated, most accurately when one is again in that physiological state. p. 220

KEY TERMS

Schema, p. 215
Decay, p. 217
Interference, p. 217
Proactive interference, p. 217
Retroactive interference, p. 218
Encoding specificity principle, p. 220
State-dependent learning, p. 220

The Neuroscience of Memory

Distinguish retrograde from anterograde amnesia.

- *Amnesia* is the inability to remember information, usually because of some physiological trauma (such as a blow to the head). *Retrograde amnesia* is the inability to remember events that preceded a traumatizing event; *anterograde amnesia* is the inability to remember events that occur after an injury or brain damage. p. 222

How does consolidation affect remembering?

- *Consolidation* is the evolution of a temporary neural circuit into a more permanent circuit. If a neuron is stimulated, the biochemical processes involved make it more likely than nonstimulated neurons to respond later; further, the number of dendrites in the neuron increases because of previous stimulation. pp. 222–224

Can stimulation of specific cortical areas prompt recall from memory?

- When Penfield stimulated the temporal lobe cortex, patients reported seeing images—coherent perceptions of experiences. More recent research shows, however, that no consistent mental images are associated with specific anatomical locations. Further research has proved that no single area holds memory traces. pp. 224–225

KEY TERMS

Amnesia, p. 222
Retrograde amnesia, p. 222
Anterograde amnesia, p. 222
Consolidation, p. 223

Learning CONNECTIONS

Some students benefit from extra help with the concept of memory. You can learn more about it in:

- The CD-ROM accompanying this book, Topic 6
- This book's study guide, *Keeping Pace Plus*, or the computerized study guide, Chapter 6
- The audiotape accompanying this book, *SoundGuide for Psychology*, Learning Unit 6
- The study aids found on the World Wide Web site for this book, at http://www.abacon.com/psych/lefton

Critical Thinking CONNECTIONS

Take a moment to think critically about how this chapter's topics are connected with the rest of psychology . . .

If you are interested in . . .	Ask yourself . . .	Then turn to . . .
The role of memory in everyday life 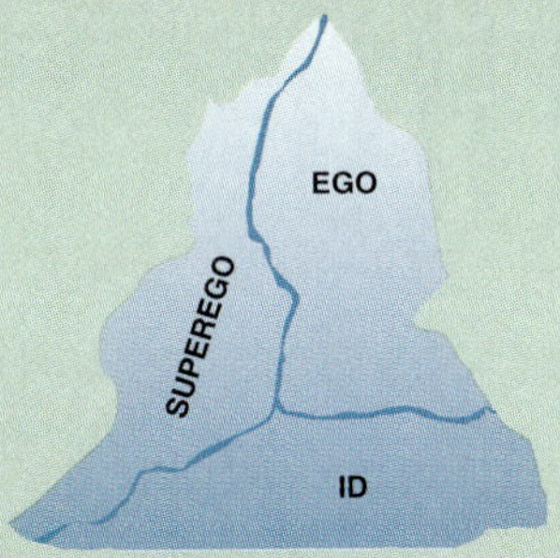	What are the implications of drug use for long-term memory?	Chapter 4, p. 142
	Personality theorists such as Freud suggested that everyday memories are buried deep within the unconscious. What would cognitive or behavioral researchers have to say about such an idea?	Chapter 12, pp. 429–434
Forgetting 	How does Alzheimer's disease affect people's ability to remember past events?	Chapter 11, p. 401
	Why do certain approaches to treatment rely on the ability to recall events that were forgotten, or perhaps relegated to the unconscious?	Chapter 15, pp. 524–525
The biological basis of memory 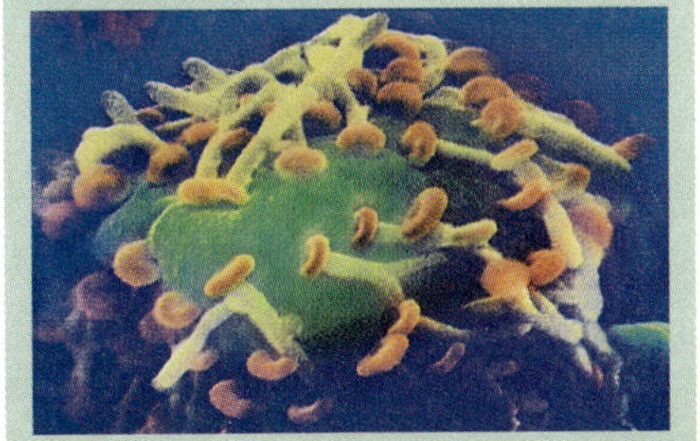	What techniques do psychobiologists use to study the biochemical bases of behavior in order to understand the role of biology in memory?	Chapter 2, pp. 55–59
	How do theories of emotion depend, in part, on a person's memory for past events and the subsequent interpretation of new events?	Chapter 9, pp. 326–330
	What effects does electroconvulsive shock therapy for seriously depressed individuals have on memory?	Chapter 15, p. 546

7

Cognition: Thought and Language

George Koltanowski was a master chess player in the 1950s. He once played 50 opponents simultaneously—blindfolded and with a limit of 10 seconds per move—and won 43 of the games. He was never permitted to view the board, the pieces, or the opponent, but rather was told his opponent's moves by a third person. This amazing ability is a testament to his skill at chess and his extraordinary memory, because chess is a game of skill, knowledge, memory, and imagination.

Chess was one of the first games that human beings played against a computer. It was a logical choice: Chess has a finite number of rules, there is a clear playing field (the chessboard), the game is extremely complex (so the computer doesn't always win), and the rules are rational. Human beings often lose to computers. When I play computer chess, I usually lose, even at low difficulty levels. Nevertheless, by studying the computer's responses, I have learned a great deal. One thing I have learned is that I usually have not looked at all the alternatives before making a move. My computerized chess game allows me to see first-, second-, and third-choice moves. This allows me to trace the logic of the computer program—which is exactly what cognitive psychologists attempt to do when they study thought, reasoning, and language. They try to "see" inside the human brain by devising tasks that will reveal human logic and reasoning. They try to map human strategies and listen to human speech with the aim of getting a glimpse inside the mind.

Thought and language are separate but closely related concepts for cognitive psychologists. Language provides human beings with a unique vehicle for expressing thoughts, planning for the future, and analyzing the past. This chapter therefore covers both cognition (thought)—especially as it relates to perceiving, learning, remembering, and using information, some of the topics of the previous three chapters—and language, the symbolic system people use to communicate their thoughts verbally.

Cognitive Psychology: An Overview

How are a tiger and a domestic cat similar? Who is the U.S. secretary of state? How do you make an omelet? Answering each of these questions requires a different mental procedure. To answer the first question, you probably drew mental images of both felines and then compared the images. In answering the second question, you may simply have known the right name or called forth a list of cabinet members and chosen from the list. The third question may have required you to mentally walk through the procedure of preparing an omelet and describe each step. The thinking you used to answer all the questions required the use of knowledge, language, and images.

Cognitive psychology is the study of the overlapping fields of perception, learning, memory, and thought; it is the study of how people attend to, acquire, transform, store, and retrieve knowledge. So, in a real sense, we have been discussing cognitive psychology for the past three chapters. In this chapter, however, we will zero in on two core topics of cognitive psychology: thought and language. The word *cognition* derives from the Latin *cognoscere*, "to know." Cognitive psychologists are interested primarily in mental processes that influence the acquisition and use of knowledge as well as the ability to *reason*, the process by which people generate logical and coherent ideas, evaluate situations, and reach conclusions. Cognitive researchers assume that mental processes exist, that people are active processors, and that cognitive processes can be studied using techniques that measure time to respond and the accuracy of responses (Ashcraft, 1989).

The history of cognitive psychology began in the late nineteenth century. As we saw in Chapter 1, the main areas of study at the dawn of psychology were mental processes, thought, and the internal workings of the mind, discerned through introspection. In the 1920s, behaviorism—with its focus on directly observable behavior—became the mainstream psychology, and there was little reference to internal cognitive processes. Discussion and research of such "mentalistic" topics as imagery were avoided, because these topics were deemed fleeting and incapable of being observed and measured.

By the late 1940s rudimentary computers, which could store instructions in their memory, were being built—even though they were massive, expensive, and relatively slow. Then, in the late 1950s and early 1960s, roughly parallel with the introduction of high-speed computers, the brain began to be compared to a computer, and research into thought began again in earnest. Jean Piaget (whom we will begin to study in the next chapter) changed the way psychologists thought about children's reasoning abilities; George Miller (1956) published a paper on how humans code information; Noam Chomsky (1957) published an influential work on language; Donald Broadbent (1958) wrote influentially on the nature of attention

Cognitive psychology: The study of the overlapping fields of learning, perception, memory, and thought with a special emphasis on how people attend to, acquire, transform, store, and retrieve knowledge.

and thought; Ulric Neisser (1967) published an important book called *Cognitive Psychology*. Also in 1967, Posner and Mitchell published one of the first true experimental studies of cognitive processes. In 1972 an influential book by Newell and Simon, *Human Problem Solving,* altered the way psychologists thought about the topic. Researchers in cognitive studies came from psychology, biology, linguistics, computer science, and philosophy (especially logic). Research in this emerging area began to examine such questions as these: How does thought develop in children? How many pieces of information can a person code at one time? How much can someone pay attention to? How do the eyes scan text during reading? How do people make decisions such as inferring that, if a bluejay is a bird and all birds have wings, a bluejay has wings? Where and how are memory and thought processes coded?

The areas considered by cognitive psychologists span a range of topics much broader even than the scope of this chapter. Cognitive researchers are interested in, among other things, controlled versus automatic processes. *Controlled processes* require a great deal of effort and attention, whereas *automatic processes* take little effort and happen without conscious awareness—although certain physiological changes accompany both kinds of processes (Strayer & Kramer, 1990). Most complex tasks begin as controlled processes; after hundreds of repetitions, they become automatic and easy, requiring little or no attention. Contemporary cognitive psychologists want to find out how once-difficult tasks such as reading, driving a car, and word processing become automatic. Closely associated with controlled and automatic processes is the role of *attention.* In general, attention refers to the process of directing mental effort to some features of the environment and not to others. People can either focus their attention on one idea, one event, or one person or divide their attention among several tasks or events. Once something is attended to and stored in a person's memory, cognitive researchers want to know how that person makes inferences from the knowledge and *represents knowledge*. Even the monitoring of one's own awareness, a process called *metacognition*, has become a focus for cognitive researchers.

▲ *Complex tasks, such as tying one's shoes, are at first controlled processes requiring a great deal of effort. Over time, with practice, they become automatic.*

It is sometimes hard to pinpoint exactly what cognitive psychology is. But understanding thought, reasoning, and the interplay between human beings and their environment continues to be a central concern for cognitive researchers; this means understanding not only how thought takes place, but how it takes place within a context—the environment—and how people extract information from the environment (E. Gibson, 1992; Neisser, 1992). This chapter concentrates on a series of topics that demonstrate the breadth of cognitive psychology—the diversity of thought processes being examined in the 1990s and how they have grown from their origins in the 1950s. We begin with the study of concept formation, which is crucial for decision making.

Concept Formation

Each day, people make decisions, solve problems, and behave logically; the steps in decision making and problem solving are complicated but orderly. Many researchers conceive of reasoning itself as an orderly process that takes place in discrete steps, one set of ideas leading to another (Rips, 1990). To perform this process, people need to employ rather complex forms of thought—every decision involves the ability to form, manipulate, transform, and interrelate concepts. **Concepts** are the mental categories people use to classify events and objects according to common properties. Many objects with four wheels, a driver's seat, and a steering

Concept: Mental category used to classify an event or object according to some distinguishing property or feature.

DIVERSITY

Sexist Language Affects Thinking

When the pilot episode for the series *Star Trek: The Next Generation* aired in 1987, thousands of viewers of the old *Star Trek* were pleased to hear Captain Jean-Luc Picard announce the mission of the Enterprise: "To boldly go where no one has gone before." Captain James T. Kirk, of the original series, had always said: "To boldly go where no *man* has gone before."

Over the last three decades, psychologists have become particularly aware of the role of language in shaping people's conceptual structures. If you have a concept that all nurses are women, then when a man walks into your hospital room wearing a white lab coat, you assume he is a doctor. Your concept of who fights fires—firemen—is likely to include the idea that only men fight fires. In general, the English language has evolved in such a way that words define many roles as male, except for roles that traditionally have been played by women (nurses, teachers) (Bem, 1993). Walk down any street where work is being done on sidewalks or telephone poles and you are likely to see the warning sign "Men Working." Today, you are just as likely to see women climbing telephone poles, but the sign probably still reads the same.

Concepts of the world first form in childhood, as children hear stories from parents and teachers. They tell of pioneers who traveled to the West with their wives, children, and farm animals. Fairy tales say that it is the king who rules the castle. Children and adults learn that the law was written to be acceptable to a "reasonable man" (lawyers even call it the *reasonable man standard*). Language with a sexist bias expresses stereotypes and expectations about men and women. Thus, many positive descriptive words are thought of as masculine (for example, *successful*, *strong*, *independent*, and *courageous*). Women have traditionally been described as *gentle, loving,* or *patient*. When language indicative of strength or courage is applied to a woman, it is often in the context of incongruity—for example, "She thinks like a man."

That women are thought of as loving and men as successful or that women are thought of as patient and men as strong is important to psychologists who study concept formation, problem solving, and language—the main topics of this chapter—because such concepts set an attitude and an approach on the part of men and women to a whole range of behaviors. Bem (1993) asserts that people view the world through a male point of view and that this is assumed to be the preferred value system. Men in business have been assumed to be task-oriented problem solvers. Women, by contrast, have been assumed to be people-oriented rather than problem-oriented. And, in fact, many men and women do fit such stereotypes; since they were raised in environments where the stereotypes were accepted, it is not surprising that they reflect the stereotypes in their day-to-day behavior.

Research supports the idea that men and women are perceived and treated differently. Frable (1989) concluded that if people believe in

FIGURE 7.1

Classification Tasks Require Choosing among Alternatives That Share Properties

In a typical classification task for children, the objective is to circle the picture that is most like the sample.

wheel are automobiles; automobiles is a concept. More abstract is the concept of justice, which has to do with fairness, ethics, equity. Animals, computers, and lecturers are all examples of concepts that have various exemplars. The study of *concept formation* is the examination of the way people organize and classify events and objects, usually in order to solve problems.

Concepts make events in the world more meaningful by helping people organize their thinking. People develop progressively more complex concepts throughout life. Early on, infants learn the difference between "parent" and "stranger." Within a year, they can discriminate among objects, colors, and people and comprehend such simple concepts as "animal" and "flower." By age 2 they can verbalize these differences.

Much of what young children are taught involves *classification*—the process of organizing things into categories—because this is a key to organizing and understanding this complex world (see Figure 7.1). Think back to your early school years and to TV shows such as *Sesame Street*. You were taught to classify the colors; different farm animals (and their

gender-specific abilities, they are likely to use that belief in making decisions. Frable found that people with strong gender-typed ideas were especially likely to pay attention to the gender of a job applicant and then to devalue the interview performance of women. McDonaugh (1992) found that interviewers not only devalue the resumes of women in general but devalue even more the resumes of women who are African American or who are not beautiful. Thus, gender stereotyping is complicated by racial and physical stereotyping.

While the stereotypes continue to exist in the 1990s—especially with TV reruns reinforcing them—some women and men are becoming more androgynous and are recognizing how stereotypes work (Hale et al., 1990). (*Androgyny* is the state of possessing both male and female characteristics.) Today, people are more accepting of individuals who express androgynous characteristics—for example, men who cook and women who are engineers. Even more importantly, people are becoming more sensitive to how language shapes their concept of the world and their problem-solving abilities. McMinn and colleagues (1990) found that those who used gender-neutral language in writing were also likely to use gender-neutral language in conversation; however, he also found that it is difficult to change the use of sexist language (McMinn et al., 1991). Further, avoiding sexist language is just a beginning; sexism and the behavior that follows from it are deeply embedded in people's thoughts and actions.

▲ *As Captain Janeway's role on* Star Trek Voyager *demonstrates, the* Starship Enterprise *has come a long way since Captain James Kirk first announced its mission in gender-biased terms.*

Western culture has made progress, however. No longer do only men fix telephones and only women work as telephone operators; today people are encouraged to be everything they might be, without regard for gender. Astronauts are both male and female. If Neil Armstrong, referred to in Chapter 6, made his famous "One giant leap for mankind" speech today, he would be more likely to say, "One giant leap for humankind." Despite some lingering sexism, today boys *and* girls in primary school grades are more likely to be encouraged to solve problems creatively, to approach science and math problems with excitement, and to be caring, warm human beings.

sounds); shapes such as triangles, circles, and squares; and the letters in the alphabet. You learned to recognize that the people in your house—mother, father, sister, brother—are a group called a "family." The process of developing concepts through the process of classification is lifelong and always changing. It involves separating dissimilar events and finding commonalities (Medin, 1989). But what is the best way to study the processes by which children and adults classify and organize information? And are there gender-based considerations? *Diversity* examines how words can affect behavior.

Studying Concept Formation

As a type of thinking, concept formation is relatively easy to study in controlled laboratory situations. Psychologists design laboratory studies in which the objective is for participants to form concepts through a wide range of tasks. Suppose you were in a laboratory experiment. You might be asked to make judgments in response to questions such as this: Is a bicycle a toy or a vehicle? The experimenter might time your response and also ask you to express your thought processes out loud.

A key requirement in laboratory situations studying concept formation is that participants understand and be able to form rules—statements of how features are related. For example, if all objects that have four sides and are red are instances, or exemplars, of a concept, then participants can learn that any time they see a red rectangle or square, they should so indicate. Here is a common task used in laboratory investigations of concept formation: An experimenter presents you with objects (stimuli) of different shapes, sizes, and colors and tells you that something about the objects makes them similar. You are asked to identify this characteristic, this rule. Each time the researcher presents a stimulus, you ask whether it has the property (characteristic) being targeted; and the experimenter answers yes or no. Suppose, for example, the first stimulus is a large red triangle. The experimenter tells you that it is a *positive instance* (a stimulus that is an example of the concept under study). You now know that the concept may be largeness, redness, or triangularity. The second stimulus is a small red triangle; the experimenter says that this, too, is a positive instance. You now know that size is not important. The third stimulus is a large blue triangle; it, too, is a positive instance. You surmise that the relevant property is triangularity. When, on the fourth trial, the stimulus is a large blue circle and the experimenter says it is a *negative instance* (a stimulus that is not an example of the concept), you can say with conviction that triangularity is the concept.

There are two broad variations on the procedure for studying concept formation: the reception method and the selection method. In the *reception method*, the researcher presents participants with a series of instances—the task being to classify each as a positive or negative instance. Participants are told after each trial whether their response was correct. For example, a researcher might show a participant 30 objects, 1 at a time. After 10 or 20 correct responses, the researcher can be certain that the participant has learned the concept. In the *selection method*, the researcher presents all the possible instances at once (see Figure 7.2). Usually, the experimenter designates one of the stimuli (instances) as a positive instance at the outset. After guessing what the concept is, the participant chooses a second stimulus and asks whether it is a positive instance. After learning whether the second is positive or negative, the participant picks a third, a fourth, and a fifth instance. This less structured procedure allows the experimenter to examine the hypotheses or strategies that a participant uses in forming a concept, a topic we will consider in the next section.

The laboratory example that we have just considered allows for a careful examination of how concepts work. But the world of concepts is not always so clear-cut. For example, you know that a professor is a teacher and a high school instructor is a teacher, but are ministers teachers? Are den mothers? Is the President of the United States? Each of these individuals acts as a teacher—at least, from time to time. The same problem exists with concepts such as "family." One concept of a family consists of Mom, Dad, and 2.4 kids. But what of single-parent families, blended families, adoptive families, communal families, extended families? Some

FIGURE 7.2

Stimuli in a Concept Formation Task

In a concept formation task, the participant is asked to classify objects of various shapes, sizes, and colors. In a selection task, all the possible instances are shown at once. The participant chooses which instance to examine next.

researchers consider a family any group of people who care about each other in significant ways. You can see that concepts are often fuzzy. Often you must give concepts some massaging to understand and define them.

Eleanor Rosch has asserted that when people are presented with *fuzzy concepts*, they tend to define them in terms of prototypes, or best examples, of a class of items (Rosch, 1973, 1978). A high school English teacher may be a prototype of a teacher; ministers, hiking instructors, and psychologists are also examples, but not "best" examples. Some concepts make for easily defined prototypes; others are hard to define. When you think about the concept of "furniture," you recognize that chairs, sofas, and tables are good examples of furniture—but telephones, stoves, pianos, and mirrors are all furniture as well; this is a concept that is fuzzy. The concept of "computer modem" is much less fuzzy: There may be a few shapes and sizes, but nearly all computer modems do the same thing, in pretty much the same way—they allow for digital computer signals to be reconfigured and sent along analog telephone communication lines. Of course, many variables affect how easily concepts are defined, including properties of the concept as well as an individual's unique experiences with that concept. It is these experiences that help people build strategies and hypotheses about concepts.

Hypothesis-testing theory: A view of concept formation as an active process in which people acquire new information by generating hypotheses about stimuli, testing those hypotheses, discarding old hypotheses if necessary, and making inferences about the stimuli.

Conservative focusing: A hypothesis-testing strategy that involves the successive elimination of alternative possibilities from a narrow range of options.

Hypothesis-Testing Theory

Over the past 50 years, theories of concept formation have changed substantially. The currently held view, **hypothesis-testing theory**, sees concept formation as an active process. According to this theory, people acquire new information by generating hypotheses about stimuli, testing those hypotheses, discarding old hypotheses if necessary, and making an inference about the stimuli.

Levine (1975) identified three hypothesis-testing strategies in adults: hypothesis checking, dimension checking, and global focusing. In *hypothesis checking*, people test one hypothesis at a time. In *dimension checking*, people test a hypotheses about a single dimension or feature. In *global focusing*, the most consistently efficient strategy, people keep all possible hypotheses in mind but focus on one at a time, ruling out alternatives as they are given feedback. To be an efficient global focuser, a person has to be actively involved in seeking solutions and in forming concepts.

Another type of hypothesis-testing strategy, but not necessarily the most efficient, is **conservative focusing**—the successive elimination of possible solutions. It works for a limited range of concepts. If you are given a visual stimulus and asked to find out which of many dimensions is the relevant one, you may try to determine if the relevant dimension has angles in it rather than curves; after this determination, you may try to eliminate another possibility—and on each successive trial you will try to eliminate as many dimensions as possible by narrowing choices. In this way you can determine the relevant dimension or concept most efficiently.

People's hypothesis-testing abilities are determined by the experiences they have had; those with wide experience are more likely to develop interesting, perhaps clever, and good hypotheses. In Chapter 16 you will learn how psychologists study the ability to form concepts about people. This kind of concept formation is *social cognition*—the thought process of

FOCUS

Review

- What is the fundamental difference between a positive and a negative instance in concept formation? p. 236
- In concept formation, what is the most efficient form of hypothesis testing? p. 237

Think Critically

- What are the implications for psychologists of the fact that a dominant new force, cognitive psychology, is so broad and covers so many fields in psychology?
- Where do you think people store information that is fuzzy in its conceptual nature?

making sense of events, other people, self, and the world in general through analyzing and interpreting them. Social cognition focuses on social information in memory and how it affects judgments, choices, evaluations, and, ultimately, behavior (Fiske, 1992). Social cognition is a pragmatic process in which people often use mental shortcuts to help them organize and form concepts about the world.

Using mental shortcuts to help process information decreases the information overload that people might otherwise experience. In forming concepts, people seek to be "cognitive misers," processing information superficially unless they are motivated to do otherwise. In being such a miser, a person develops rules of thumb. One rule of thumb is *representativeness*; individuals or events that appear to be representative of a group are quickly classified as such, often despite a complete lack of evidence. Another rule of thumb is *availability*; the easier it is to bring to mind instances of one category, type, or idea, the more likely it is that that category, type, or idea will be used to describe an event. Of course, this entire process is part of reasoning and decision making, the topic we'll consider next.

Reasoning and Decision Making

You are generally unaware of your cognitive processes; you don't usually think about thinking. And yet you are thinking all the time—sorting through choices, deciding where to go, what to do, and when to do it. When you think, you engage in a wide variety of activities, from daydreaming to planning your next few steps on a mountain path. When cognitive psychologists study *thinking,* however, they generally attempt to study the systematic processes of reasoning, decision making, and problem solving (Galotti, 1989). **Reasoning** is the process by which people generate logical and coherent ideas, evaluate situations, and reach conclusions. The procedure used to reach a valid conclusion is **logic**. You can think about reasoning and logic as proceeding in an ordered way or as comprising a process in which ideas and beliefs are continuously updated in a loose, unstructured way (Rips, 1990)—both approaches are valid, and both types of reasoning occur.

To understand reasoning, researchers have focused on the tasks involved in decision making. **Decision making** means assessing and choosing among alternatives. You make decisions that involve the probability of some event (will my friends want to go on this trip with me?) and others that involve expected value (how important is *this* trip, rather than some other one?). Your decisions vary from the trivial to the complex: what to eat for breakfast, which courses to take, what career to pursue. The trivial decisions are usually made quickly, without much effort, and unconsciously. The complex ones require conscious, deliberate thought and effort. Sometimes your reasoning and decision making are logical. At other times you are not sure how things will work out or whether your reasoning is valid.

Psychologists have devised numerous approaches for looking at the thought processes of individuals. We examine three: (1) formal reasoning, or syllogisms—situations for which there is a single correct answer; (2) logical decision making; and (3) situations in which the answer or decision is less certain and which therefore involve estimating probabilities.

Reasoning: The process by which people generate logical and coherent ideas, evaluate situations, and reach conclusions.

Logic: The procedure used to reach a valid conclusion.

Decision making: Assessing and choosing among alternatives.

Syllogism [SILL-oh-jiz-um]: A sequence of statements, or premises (usually two), followed by a conclusion; the task is to decide (deduce) whether the conclusion is warranted.

Syllogisms: Formal Reasoning

One of the traditional ways to study thinking, reasoning, and decision-making processes is to provide research participants with deduction tasks such as syllogisms. A **syllogism** is a sequence of statements, or *premises* (usually two), followed by a conclusion. The task is to decide (deduce) whether the conclusion is warranted. The assumption in logic is that the premises are true.

By asking participants to describe their thinking and decision-making processes while they contemplate syllogisms, a psychologist can trace their cognitive processes. The psychologist can analyze each decision in the process and thus follow participants' thoughts. People are not especially good at solving abstract syllogisms; more concrete ones are easier to follow. Consider the following syllogism.

Premise 1: All poodles are dogs.

Premise 2: All dogs are animals.

Conclusion: All poodles are animals.

Is the conclusion logical? Do the two premises allow you to conclude that poodles are animals? In the preceding example, it is easy to see that the conclusion is accurate. Because logic assumes that the premises are true, however, you can devise a syllogism in which the conclusion validly follows from the premises but is really false—because one or more of the premises are false. For example, if you changed premise 1 to "All flowers are dogs," you could logically come to the valid (but false) conclusion that "All flowers are animals."

You can learn how to use logic and how to be a better critical thinker and decision maker. One way is to be skeptical about the premises on which conclusions are based. A second way is to systematically evaluate premises for truth. A third way is to think the way a detective does, using logical decision-making skills to eliminate the possibilities one by one.

Logical Decision Making

When making a decision, people are often faced with outcomes that have positive and negative attributes. On the simplest level, they need to add up the positive attributes of the alternatives and then make a decision. For example, when I buy a bicycle, I have to consider its cost, weight, appearance, intended use, and safety, as well as my preference for a specific brand. I must also weigh the relative importance of each of these factors to me. If you were buying the bicycle, you might consider different factors, and you would give each one a different weight in terms of its importance to you.

A decision-making approach in which some factors take on more importance than others is called a *compensatory model*. In the bicycle example, you might do the following (see Figure 7.3 on page 240):

1. Assign a relative importance to each of the factors you have chosen (weight, cost, and appearance, for example), and give each importance level a numerical value, such as 1 to 5.
2. Score each bicycle on the factors themselves. In Figure 7.3, for example, Schwinns are low in cost (good = 5), high in weight (not good = 2), not very good-looking (low = 1), poor as trail bikes (low = 1), and unsafe when used as trail bikes (not good = 2).
3. Multiply the factor scores by the importance values to determine which bicycle has the greatest overall positive score, according to your tastes and criteria.

A problem with compensatory models is that a good value on one attribute sometimes cannot compensate for a poor value on another (Payne, Bettman, & Johnson, 1992). Accordingly, another approach to decision making involves ruling out alternatives that do not meet minimum criteria. For example, if you are interested in purchasing a mountain bike, you need not consider a high-performance racing bike. Further, the low price of a department-store Schwinn cannot compensate for the fact that it's not a rugged mountain bike. If you cannot spend more than $250 for the bicycle, you can rule out all the higher-priced models. This approach, called *elimination by aspects*, is generally a fast and efficient way to make decisions. It is logical, and it helps people reduce the uncertainties about a pending decision.

FIGURE 7.3

The Compensatory Model: Buying a New Trail Bike

Relative importance, or weight, of each factor

Factors	Low 1	2	3	4	High 5
Cost	1	2	3	4	5
Weight	1	2	3	4	5
Appearance	1	2	3	4	5
Intended use	1	2	3	4	5
Safety	1	2	3	4	5

1 First, for each of several factors, a person specifies a weight indicating its relative importance to him or her. This individual assigns the highest importance to intended use as a trail bike, giving that factor a weight of 5. The cost of a bike and how much it weighs are considered to be more important (assigned weights of 4) than appearance and safety (weights of 3).

	Schwinn	Fuji	Trek	Diamond Back
Cost	5 × **4**	2 × 4 = 8	3 × 4	1 × 4
Weight	2 × **4**	5 × 4 = 20	2 × 4	1 × 4
Appearance	1 × **3**	5 × 3 = 15	3 × 3	2 × 3
Intended use	1 × **5**	4 × 5 = 20	5 × 5	3 × 5
Safety	2 × **3**	3 × 3 = 9	5 × 3	1 × 3
Total score	42	**72**	69	32

Choose this bike!

2 Then, the person evaluates how well each type of bike measures up on each factor (cost, weight, appearance, intended use, and safety). If a type of bike measures up well on a particular factor, it gets a value of 5 for that factor. In this example, a Schwinn is inexpensive (earning a value of 5 for the cost factor), and a Diamond Back is relatively costly (a value of 1 for that factor).

3 Next, the person multiplies the value given to each factor times the weight specified for that factor to determine five scores for each bike. The Schwinn, for example, scores 20 points on the cost factor, 8 points on the weight factor, 3 for appearance, and so on.

4 Finally, the five scores for each bike are added up. A high total score reflects good evaluations on relatively important factors. Here, the Fuji has the best overall score—considering all the factors, the person should choose this bike.

Uncertainty: Estimating Probabilities

How do people decide what to wear, where to go, or how to answer a question on the SAT? How do they decide when something is bigger, longer, or more difficult? Many decisions are based on formal logic, some on carefully tested hypotheses, and some on educated guesses. Making an educated guess implies being educated (knowing something) from past experience. When you see rain clouds, for example, you guess—but you cannot be 100 percent sure—that it will rain. The likelihood of rain is expressed as a percentage—that is, as a probability.

Psychological factors, especially previous events, affect how people estimate probabilities of events. Consider a study by Tversky and Kahneman (1973) in which participants were asked to judge if a list of names contained more men than women. Participants were given lists of names of 40 famous people—20 men and 20 women, with a probability of 50 percent of each gender. In one case, the participants read a list in which the men were more famous than the women; in another, the participants read a list in which the women were more famous than the men. After reading their respective lists, the participants were asked if their list contained more names of men or more names of women. The participants who read the list with more famous men said there were more men on the list; those who read the list with more famous women said there were more women on the list. The critical variable affecting the results was the participants' familiarity with the names of the famous people. In other words, the fact that one gender on the list was more famous affected the participants' perceptions and their estimates of probability.

People make probability estimates of all types of behaviors and events. In election years, they guess about the likelihood of a Democratic or a Republican victory. On the basis of past experience, they estimate the probability of staying on a study schedule, an exercise regime, or a diet. They can judge whether a particular event increases or decreases the probability of another event. When several factors are involved, their compounding and mitigating effects alter the probability. For example, the probability that there will be rain when there are thunderclouds, high winds, and low barometric pressure is much higher than the probability of rain when there are only a few thunderclouds.

Subjects asked to make probability judgments about the real world, particularly about fairly rare events, are more likely to fail than are subjects given laboratory problems (Swets, 1992). The farther in the future the event to be predicted is, the more ambiguity exists for the predictor; also, people are likely to be affected by past behavior and therefore make mistakes about the future (Payne, Bettman, & Johnson, 1992). People make mistakes and errors in judgment and may act irrationally. They may ignore key pieces of data and thus make bad (or irrational) decisions that are not based on probability. Sometimes, people's worldviews color their probability decision making. If a moral system, religious belief, or political view is pointed in one direction (for example, Christianity versus Buddhism or capitalism versus communism), a person's strategies and decision estimates will be influenced.

Finally, people are not machines or computers; their creativity, past experiences, and humanness affect results, sometimes in unpredictable ways. However, cognitive psychologists suggest ways for individuals to become the most efficient learners and thinkers they can be, and researchers have found that people can be taught to weigh costs and benefits more accurately and to be less influenced by their past frames of reference (Larrick, Morgan, & Nisbett, 1990; Payne, Bettman, & Johnson, 1992). One way is to use analogies that will help us break out of traditional frames of reference. When researchers examined how students could best learn scientific concepts, they found that analogies and metaphors are especially useful. Details are reported back well through traditional learning of text, but analogies—especially creative ones—provide conceptual bridges that facilitate learning, memory, and concept development (Donnelly & McDaniel, 1993).

FOCUS

Review

- What advantage does using syllogisms in research have for psychologists? pp. 238–239
- What is the fundamental difference between a compensatory model and one based on elimination by aspects? p. 239

Think Critically

- Schooling affects people's ability to solve verbal problems; in a school setting, people answer questions that might be considered silly in most other settings. What does this say about school experiences?
- What evidence exists to support the idea that people are often not good at estimating the probability of events in the world?

Problem Solving

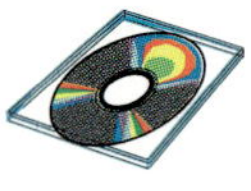

Fig. 7.5A

How do you manage to study for your psychology exam when you have an English paper due tomorrow? How can you arrange your minuscule closet so all of your clothes and other belongings will fit? Your car gets a flat tire on the interstate; what should you do? These are all problems to be solved. In important ways, your approaches to these dilemmas represent some of the highest levels of cognitive functioning. Human beings are wonderful at **problem solving,** at confronting situations that require insight or that call for some unknown elements to be determined. Because you can form concepts and group things together in logical ways, you are able to organize our thoughts and attack a problem to be solved. Psychologists believe that the process of problem solving has four stages, summarized in Figure 7.4.

Huge differences exist in people's problem-solving abilities; but psychologists, with their understanding of the processes of thought and of problem solving, can help people become more effective problem solvers. Recall from Chapters 1 and 3 that Gestalt psychologists analyzed the world in terms of perceptual frameworks and argued that the mind organizes the elements of experience to form something unique. As we saw in Chapter 5, Wolfgang Köhler (1927/1973), a Gestalt researcher, showed that chimps could solve problems by developing *insights* into methods of retrieving food that was beyond their reach. They discovered they could pile up boxes to reach food or attach poles together to make a long stick with which to grab the food. Once the insight occurred, no further instruction, investigation, or training was necessary. Insight is not essential to problem solving; but hints, cues, and prior experience all support the process of developing insight and finding essential elements—an advantage in problem solving (Kaplan & Simon, 1990).

Although people's problem-solving abilities are usually quite good, they may be subject to certain limitations. Among these are functional fixedness and psychological set, which are discussed next. Researchers study these hindrances to gain a better understanding of the processes of problem solving.

Functional Fixedness: Cognition with Constraints

When my daughter Sarah was 4 years old, she saw me taking her raincoat out of the closet before our trip to the zoo. Sarah insisted that it was not raining outside and that raincoats are for rain. I explained that the coat could also be used as a wind breaker or a light spring jacket. Reluctantly, she put on the coat. In this exchange, Sarah was exhibiting a basic characteristic of most people: functional fixedness.

FIGURE 7.4

Stages in Problem Solving

Problem solving can be conceived of as a four-stage process.

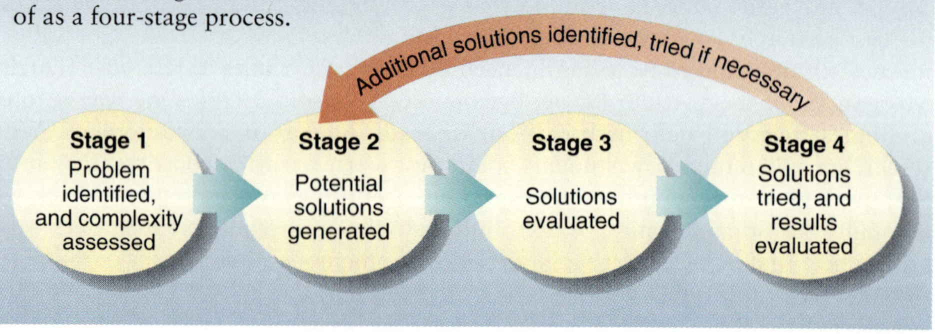

Problem solving: The behavior of individuals when confronted with a situation or task that requires some insight or some unknown elements to be determined.

FIGURE 7.5

The Two-String Problem

In the two-string problem, the person must set one string in motion in order to tie the strings together. This solution illustrates the fact that people need to overcome functional fixedness by using tools in new ways.

Functional fixedness is the inability to see that an object can have a function other than its stated or usual one. When people are functionally fixed, they have limited their choices and conceptual framework. In many ways this constitutes a breakdown in problem solving.

Studies of functional fixedness show that often the name given to a tool limits its function. In a typical study, a subject is presented with a task and provided tools that can be used in various ways. One laboratory problem used to show functional fixedness is the two-string problem (see Figure 7.5). In this task, a person is put in a room in which there are two strings hanging from the ceiling and some objects lying on a table. The task is to tie the two strings together, but it is impossible to reach one string while holding the other. The only solution is to tie a weight (such as a magnet or a pair of pliers) to one string, set it swinging back and forth, take hold of the second string, and wait until the first string swings within reach. This task is difficult because people's previous experiences with objects such as pliers may prevent them from considering them as potential tools in new problem-solving situations.

Psychological Set

Psychologists have found that most individuals are flexible in their approaches to solving problems. In other words, they do not use preconceived, or "set," solutions but often think about objects, people, and situations in new ways. However, sometimes people develop a rigid strategy, or approach, to certain types of problems. Avoiding a rigid approach allows a painter to work in charcoal, pastels, latex, and oils all at once. A flexible scientist will conceive of uses for existing technology, technology that needs to be developed, and even technology beyond the realm of modern science. President John F. Kennedy was able to devise an innovative solution to the complex problem of engendering a better relationship with developing countries: the Peace Corps. All of these solutions require limber thought processes.

Functional fixedness: The inability to see that an object can have a function other than its stated or usual one.

FIGURE 7.6

The Nine-Dot Problem

Because people tend to group things in familiar ways, it is hard for them to overcome their psychological set to connect the nine dots as instructed.

Creative thinking requires that people break out of their *psychological set*—their limited ways of thinking about possibilities. Having a psychological set is the opposite of being creative. According to the principle underlying this problem-solving limitation, prior experience predisposes a person to make a particular response. Most of the time, this predisposition, or readiness, is useful and adaptive; for the most part, what worked in the past will work in the future. Sometimes, however, the biasing effect of a set is not productive. It limits innovation and prevents a person from solving new and complex problems (Holland, 1975). In an increasingly complex and changing world, such limitations are problematic. Here's a problem that is difficult because of a psychological set. In Figure 7.6, draw no more than four lines that will run through all nine dots—without lifting your pen from the paper. The answer is provided in Figure 7.7 on page 247.

Applications offers suggestions for avoiding limitations and barriers to effective critical thinking.

Creative Problem Solving

The owners of a high-rise professional building were deluged with complaints that the building's elevators were too slow. The owners called in a consultant, who researched the problem and discovered that, indeed, tenants often had to wait several minutes for an elevator. Putting in new, faster elevators would cost tens of thousands of dollars, more than the owners could afford. Eventually, the consultant devised a creative solution that ended the complaints but cost only a few hundred dollars: He installed wall mirrors at each elevator stop so people could look at themselves while waiting.

Creativity is the ability to develop original, novel, and appropriate responses to a problem. An *original response* is a response not copied from or imitative of another response; that is, the respondent originated the idea. In this discussion, it means a response that is not usually given. A *novel response* is a response that is new or that has no precedent. Unless an original and novel solution is also appropriate, however, psychologists do not call it creative. An *appropriate response* is a response that is reasonable in terms of the situation. Building your home out of soap bubbles may be an original and novel idea, but it is clearly not appropriate. A key issue in creativity is how people can become more creative in their thinking (Greeno, 1989). You don't have to be an Einstein or a Picasso to be creative, as the building consultant demonstrated. To make sure that a creative solution is appropriate, effective problem solvers form a hypothesis and then test it to evaluate potential solutions. Creativity is simply a different way of thinking.

Creativity as a Three-Stage Process. Morris Stein (1974) defined the creative process as involving three stages: hypothesis formation, hypothesis testing, and communication of results. In hypothesis formation, a person tries to formulate a new response to a problem, which is not an easy task. A person must confront the situation and think of it in nonstereotyped ways, exploring paths not previously explored. This sometimes involves developing guesses based on intuition.

Intuition is an interesting phenomenon; it is often thought of as immediate insight without reasoning processes—you have an intuition, suddenly! But research shows that people who develop intuitions have an orderly memory that is easily activated and has many semantic relationships. It is the automatic activation of clues in a creative or problem-solving context that allows for intuitions and subsequent hypothesis formation (Bowers et al., 1990).

Once an intuition has developed and a hypothesis is formed, the hypothesis must be tested against reality. At this stage, it is crucial to apply the criterion of appropriateness. If the result is original, novel, and appropriate, the person can move toward the third stage—the communication of results. A creative idea or expression is worthless if it is not shared with other people.

Creativity: A quality of thought and problem solving, generally considered to include originality, novelty, and appropriateness.

APPLICATIONS

Be a Critical Thinker

Every day, people have to make judgments, classify ideas, follow logic, and solve complex problems—that is, engage in reasoning. Yet reasoning abilities vary from person to person, and some people are better than others at forming concepts, making decisions, or solving problems. As we saw in Chapter 1, among other things, being a critical thinker means that you have to:

- Avoid biases.
- Be evaluative.
- Avoid oversimplifications.
- Determine the relevance of facts.
- Question facts.
- Consider all arguments.

There are several other key ideas to make you especially good at critical thinking.

Don't fixate on availability. Things that come to mind quickly are not necessarily the best solutions to problems. Don't necessarily choose the first answer.

Don't generalize too quickly. That most elements in a grouping follow a pattern does not mean all elements in the grouping will follow the pattern. For example, the fact that you have seen dozens of red roses does not mean all roses are red.

Don't stick with an easy decision. People often stick with solutions that work, even though other solutions may work even better. Look at all the alternatives.

Don't stick with a decision that fits preexisting ideas. People often accept too quickly ideas that conform to their previously held views. This is a serious mistake for researchers who want to be open to new ideas.

Don't test only some of the available ideas or premises. If you do not evaluate all of the available ideas, premises, alternatives, or conclusions, you are likely to miss the correct, or most logical, answer.

Don't be emotional. Sometimes people become emotionally tied to a specific idea, premise, or conviction. When this happens, the likelihood that they can critically evaluate the evidence drops sharply. Critical thinkers are cool and evaluative, not headstrong and emotional.

Don't be constrained by old ideas. Opening yourself up to new ideas may require conscious effort. For example, committees formed to evaluate problems and recommend solutions often define the problem, write down all possible solutions, order them, and then evaluate the possibilities—an effective problem-solving technique called brainstorming. In **brainstorming,** people consider all possible solutions without making any initial judgments about the worth of those solutions. This procedure can be used to illuminate alternative solutions to problems as diverse as how a city can dispose of its waste and how a topic for a group project can be selected. The rationale behind brainstorming is that people will produce more high-quality ideas if they do not have to evaluate the suggestions immediately. Brainstorming attempts to release the potential of the participants: to free them from potential functional fixedness, increase the diversity of ideas, and promote creativity.

▲ *Sometimes effective problem solving requires two people working together to come up with a solution that neither one of them alone could have discovered.*

When people sort through alternatives to try to solve a problem, they attempt to focus their thinking, discarding inappropriate solutions until a single appropriate option is left. To do so, they *converge* on an answer (or use convergent thinking skills). **Convergent thinking** is narrowing down choices and alternatives to arrive at a suitable answer. **Divergent thinking**, in contrast, is widening the range of possibilities and expanding the options for solutions; this lessens the likelihood of functional fixedness or psychological set. Guilford (1967) defined creative thinking as divergent thinking. According to other psychologists, any solution to a problem that can be worked out only with time and practice is not a creative solution. To foster creativity, people need to rethink their whole approach to a task (Greeno, 1989). Successful entrepreneurs know this to be the case (McClelland, 1987), and those who develop new technologies, products, and services are often well rewarded for their creativity. Business schools are paying closer attention to developing cre-

Brainstorming: A problem-solving technique that involves considering all possible solutions without making prior evaluative judgments.

Convergent thinking: In problem solving, the process of narrowing down choices and alternatives to arrive at a suitable answer.

Divergent thinking: In problem solving, widening the range of possibilities and expanding the options for solutions.

APPLICATIONS

Improve Your Problem-Solving Abilities

Problem solving is a deliberate and time-consuming process and affects your day-to-day life. Therefore, it makes sense to try to become the best problem solver possible. Ashcraft (1989) has suggested the following ways to improve problem-solving abilities.

Increase Your Knowledge. A person with limited knowledge about a topic is far less able to solve problems than is a well-informed person. Learn about bicycles if you are going to buy one. Study computer programming if you are going to program a computer.

Automate Some Tasks. Become an expert at some simple tasks involved in solving your problem. Because you have a limited attention span (see Chapter 3), you should free your mental resources to solve more complex aspects of the problem by automatically solving smaller ones. When playing chess, have a couple of opening moves prepared; in studying, make an outline first. These tasks will then be routine and automatic.

Follow a Plan. Set a plan of action. For example, if your problem is remembering material for an exam, use the SQ3R Plus approach described in "To the Student" at the beginning of this book. Identify the problem, explore alternative approaches, look at the effects, and think critically (see Chapter 1, pages 18–19).

Draw Inferences and Develop Subgoals. Try to draw inferences about the known facts and the possible ways to solve the problem. Then break the large problem down into smaller, more manageable tasks. For example, in planning a Thanksgiving dinner, think first about the appetizers, then about the main course, and finally about the desserts.

▲ *Effective problem solvers often map out their choices before making a decision.*

Work Backwards. Trace a solution in reverse order, working back toward the fact that you know. In writing a computer program, first decide what the output should look like, and then decide on the steps needed to produce that output.

Search for Contradictions and Relations. Are there any possibilities that can be ruled out right away because they violate basic rules, guidelines, or assumptions? Actively consider things you already know that can help you eliminate inconsistencies. This means using your existing framework of knowledge to help you solve new problems.

Reformulate the Problem and Represent It Physically. Go back to the beginning of the problem and try to restate it; rethink it in different terms. For example, if you have been thinking in terms of building with wood, think about other materials to achieve a fresh look. Draw, build, or in some way represent the problem physically—make it tangible and concrete instead of abstract and ethereal. Don't use just your brain to solve a problem. Some of the most creative solutions have been sketched out on napkins by problem solvers attempting to represent a problem in some new way.

Practice. To be good at problem solving, practice doing it. Practice makes perfect—or at least makes you better. For example, the more often you solve algebra word problems that focus on two unknowns, the better you become at solving them.

ativity in marketing courses, and researchers are examining the roles of creativity and insight in solving problems (Kaplan & Simon, 1990).

Applications presents some suggestions for improving your ability to solve problems.

Brain Structure and Creativity. Are some people born creative? It is not clear whether the brain is organized in some special way in highly creative individuals. Researchers have conducted EEG studies to see if there are any observable differences in the brain waves of gifted and talented people. So far, problems in clearly defining the subject population (see Young & Ellis, 1981) and the appropriate testing tasks have called into question the validity of the findings. Moreover, individual differences in the brain-wave patterns of normal people are sufficiently great that a difference in the brain-wave pattern of an especially creative or talented individual would not necessarily be significant. Also, no firm evidence exists that creative individuals are either more or less intelligent than other people. The data relating IQ scores and creativity are inconclusive. However, new research programs for enhancing creativity in adults are showing promising results (Goff, 1992).

Problem Solving and Computers

Because human beings invented computers, it is not surprising that computers handle information in much the same manner as the human brain, though the brain has far more options and strategies for information processing than a computer does. By simulating specific models of the human brain, computers help psychologists understand human thought processes. Specifically, computers help shape theoretical development (as in hypotheses about information processing and about perception), assist researchers in investigating how people solve problems, and enable psychologists to test models of certain aspects of behavior, such as memory. They also assist human beings in performing many real-life chores.

Information Processing. In Chapters 3 and 6, you learned how researchers break down many perception and memory problems into small steps, using the information-processing approach. The information-processing approach to perception, memory, and problem solving is a direct outgrowth of computer simulations. Flowcharts showing how information from sensory memory reaches short- and long-term memory rely implicitly on a computer analogy. Those who study memory extend the computer analogy further by referring to storage areas as "buffers" and information-processing mechanisms as "central processors." The information-processing approach is widely used, although it has come under attack as reducing everything to its smallest element (Bruner, 1990).

Computer Programs. When computer programs implement some types of human activities, they are said to involve *artificial intelligence (AI)*, particularly if the programs are designed to optimize the efficiency of the activities. For example, computers have been programmed to "understand" and produce human language. These programs store information about the rules for generating English sentences and even speech. With programs written for blind people, information can be typed at a keyboard, and the computer vocalizes what has been typed. Researchers who program computers to work like the human brain are designing computer simulations. But the researchers' task is formidable, because, as you saw in Chapter 2, the brain is complex, with billions of interconnections.

The most widely investigated aspect of computer simulation and artificial intelligence is problem solving. As was stated at the beginning of this chapter, chess was one of the first problems attacked by computers. Computers have been taught to play other games, such as checkers and backgammon, and to solve simple number completion tasks. They can also solve complicated problems involving large amounts of memory. The most sophisticated programs include aspects of human memory systems.

Problem-solving programs use two basic approaches: algorithms and heuristics. An **algorithm** is a procedure for solving a problem by using a set of rules to implement particular steps over and over again until the problem is solved. Many mathematics problems (for example, finding a square root) make use of algorithms. Algorithms are precise and are usually implemented exhaustively until the solution is reached. For example, a particular chess algorithm might involve having the computer use a procedure to examine every permutation and combination of possible plays before choosing the one move that has the highest probability of success.

Algorithms are also used in a wide variety of real-life problems, from increasing the yield of a recipe (say by doubling each ingredient) to writing a computer program (even a relatively simple program requires several algorithms). To implement an algorithm, you follow the rules regarding which task to implement at which

FIGURE 7.7

The Nine-Dot Solution

Here is a creative solution to the nine-dot problem presented in Figure 7.6. Note that you have to think beyond your normal psychological set and not see the nine dots as forming a square.

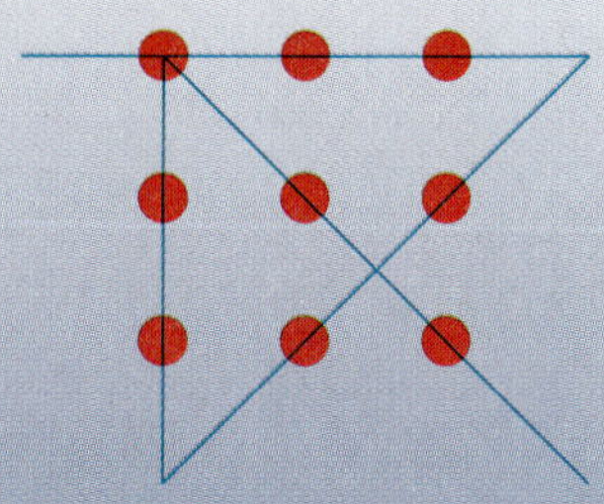

Algorithm [AL-go-rith-um]: A simple, specific, and exhaustive problem-solving procedure that follows a set of rules to implement a step-by-step analysis, as in working out a math problem.

point in the procedure. For example, an algorithm for doubling a recipe might be: "Find the list of ingredients. For each ingredient, find the measured amount of the ingredient, multiply that amount by 2, and use the product as the new amount for the ingredient. Repeat this procedure until there are no more ingredients listed in the recipe." It's monotonous and uninspired, but it works. However, because algorithms are sets of rules and procedures that *must* be followed, the necessary time and effort may make them impractical for some uses. Human problem solvers, such as chess master George Koltanowski, learn things and use rules-of-thumb so that they do not have to follow rigid sets of rules to solve problems. These rules-of-thumb are integral to heuristic strategies.

Heuristics are sets of strategies that act as flexible guidelines—not strict rules and procedures—for discovery-oriented problem solving. Heuristic procedures reflect the processes used by the human brain; they involve making rough estimates, guesses, and subjective evaluations that might be called hunches, or intuitions (Bowers et al., 1990). To contrast heuristics with algorithms, we can return to the chess example. When deciding on a move, a person (or computer) using an algorithm strategy would repeatedly consider every possible move in terms of its probability for success, then choose the one with the highest likelihood of success. A person using a heuristic strategy would consider only the moves he or she believed most likely to be successful. These moves would not be given statistical probabilities of outcomes; instead, the heuristic strategist would ask, "Which move has usually enhanced my strategic position in the game?"

Several different heuristic approaches exist; most of them center on the goal that the problem's solution should achieve. For example, in **subgoal analysis**, a problem is taken apart or broken down into several smaller steps, each of which has a subgoal. In **means–ends analysis**, the person compares the current situation or position with the desired end (the goal) in order to determine the most efficient means for getting from one (the current position) to the other (the goal). The objective is to reduce the number of steps needed to reach the goal. A **backward search** involves working backward from the goal or endpoint to the current position, both to analyze the problem and to reduce the steps needed to get from the current position to the goal. Human beings often use all three of these heuristic approaches; but a person may be limited, by a psychological set, to using only one problem-solving approach. Human beings are also hampered by their limited attention span and their limited ability to work on a number of tasks at one time. In contrast, computers can have hundreds or even thousands of processors operating at once. Today's supercomputers are made up of many powerful computers that operate simultaneously (in parallel) to solve problems.

Although computers can be programmed to process information the way human beings do, they lack human ingenuity and imagination. In addition, computers do not have a referential context in which to interpret situations. When you say to a grocer "Halibut?" and the grocer responds, "Wednesday, after 4, downtown only," you understand the meaning of this answer: Halibut will be available on Wednesday, after 4 o'clock in the afernoon, when the shipment has arrived at the downtown branch of the grocery chain. Human beings understand the context in which fish are shipped only occasionally, to some stores, at certain times during the week. They understand the concepts of branch stores, fresh fish, and selective shipments. Computers do not have such contexts. Further, they cannot evaluate their own ideas or improve their own problem-solving abilities by developing heuristics.

Table 7.1 summarizes the major advantages and disadvantages of algorithms and heuristics.

Heuristics [hyoo-RISS-ticks]: Sets of strategies, not strict rules, that act as guidelines for discovery-oriented problem solving.

Subgoal analysis: Heuristic procedure in which a task is broken down into smaller, more manageable parts.

Means–ends analysis: Heuristic procedure in which the problem solver tries to move closer to a solution by comparing the current situation with the desired goal and determining the most efficient way to get from one to the other.

Backward search: Heuristic procedure in which a problem solver starts at the end of a problem and systematically works in reverse steps to discover the subparts necessary to achieve a solution.

Neural Networks

The comparison of the brain to a computer is a compelling one. Interesting new research has been focusing on the brain's ability to represent information in a num-

TABLE 7.1 ***Algorithms and Heuristics Are Two Different But Equally Viable Approaches to Problem Solving***

Approach	Procedure	Advantages	Disadvantages	Example
Algorithm	Exhaustive, systematic consideration of all possible solutions; a set of rules	Solution is guaranteed.	Can be very inefficient, effortful, time-consuming	Computer chess programs are typically based on a set of predefined rules and moves. 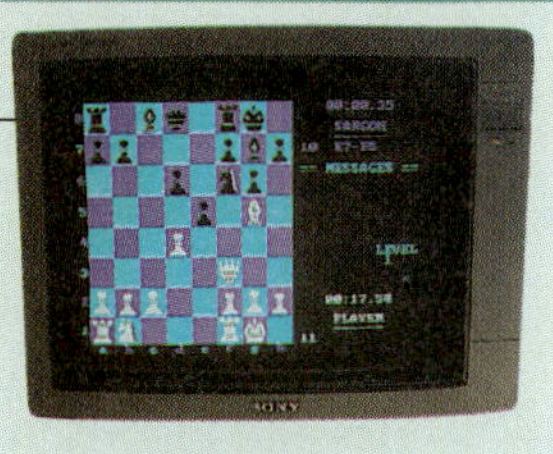
Heuristics	Strategies; rules-of-thumb that have worked in the past	Efficient; saves effort and time	Solution is not guaranteed.	Person attempting to repair a car uses past experience to rule out a whole range of potential problems. 

ber of locations simultaneously. Take a moment and imagine a computer. You may conjure up an image of an IBM or a Macintosh, a laptop or a mainframe terminal. You may also start thinking about programming code, computer screens, even Nintendo. Your images of a specific computer or representations of what the computer can do are stored and coded at different places in the brain. No one suggests that you have a "computer corner" where all information about computers is stored. Since various pieces of information are stored in different portions of the brain, their electrical energy must be combined at some point, in some way, for you to use the word *computer*, understand it, and visualize it.

The brain has specific processing areas. However, these areas themselves are located throughout the brain, and thus a "convergence" zone, or center, is necessary to mediate and organize the information, according to University of Iowa researchers Damasio and Damasio (1992). Thus, signals from physically distant clusters of neuronal activity come together in convergence zones to evoke words, develop sentences, and fully process ideas and images about the subject at hand—such as computers. That convergence zones are located away from specific pieces of information helps explain why some stroke victims and patients with various brain lesions (injuries) can tell you some things about computers but not everything they once knew. For example, a stroke victim may be able to look at a picture and tell you that it has a keyboard and a screen but be unable to say that it is a picture of a computer. According to Damasio and Damasio's view, a key convergence zone has been corrupted. The idea of convergence zones has led to the development of models of where and how the brain operates to represent the world, develop concepts, and solve problems.

In recent years, mathematicians, physiologists, and psychologists have joined forces to develop specific models of how neural structures learn to represent complicated information (e.g., Hinton, 1992). Their work is often based on the concept of *parallel distributed processing* (PDP), which suggests that many operations take place simultaneously and at many locations within the brain (an idea introduced in Chapter 6). The brain in some ways acts as a computer, processing events and information. Unlike most computers used in offices today, the brain can process many operations simultaneously. Most computers can perform only one operation at a time—admittedly very quickly, but still only one at a time. PDP is appealing to theoreticians because in the brain thousands of signals arrive simultaneously. PDP models assert that the brain can process many events, store them simultaneously, and compare

FOCUS

Review

- On the basis of research findings, identify and describe three ways to improve your problem-solving abilities. p. 246
- What are the fundamental differences between heuristics and algorithms? pp. 247–248

Think Critically

- What do you think happens to create functional fixedness? How do you think one might break through it in problem solving?
- If Damasio and Damasio are correct and information is stored all over the brain and brought together in convergence zones, what are the implications for the neuroscience of memory and thought? For locating the memory store?

them to past events (Grossberg, 1995). PDP models are models not only of memory but also of perception and learning; they combine data from studies of eye movements, hearing, the tactile senses, and pattern recognition to present a coherent view of how the brain integrates information to make it meaningful.

To study parallel distributed processing, researchers have devised artificial neural networks. These networks are typically composed of interconnected "units" that serve as model neurons. Each unit, or artificial neuron, receives signals of varying and modifiable weight, to represent signals that would be received by a real neuronal dendrite. Activity generated by the unit is transmitted as a single outgoing signal to other neural units. Both input and output to units can be varied electronically, as can interconnections among units. Layers of units can be connected to other layers, and the output of one layer may be the input to another.

A neural network can be a physical entity, but today researchers prefer to use computers to create complex, fast, electronic neural networks that simulate specific activities. For example, neural networks can be taught to recognize handwritten letters and other simple patterns. A network can be shown a stimulus, say the letter *A*. If the network (the computer program) responds that the stimulus was an *H*, the signal strength of some of the synaptic junctions can be altered to make the network respond appropriately. In addition, a network can learn to recognize a range of forms that look like the letter *A*. We say in this case that the network has learned a *prototype*. The prototypes may constitute the network's basis of form and letter perception.

An interesting aspect of networks is what happens when one portion of a network is partially destroyed: The network does not crash, but it makes some mistakes, much as the brain would. When portions of the brain are ablated (surgically destroyed or removed) or injured in an accident, the person is still able to complete some tasks. (Remember the split-brain patients who could name an object by means of one hemisphere but could only point to the object by means of the other hemisphere—see page 58.)

Language

The doorbell rings. You open the door and see someone wearing sunglasses, a T-shirt, and pink-and-green neon swim trunks. The person says, "Tell your roommate to get her stick. It's 6-foot and glassy." Some people might interpret this to mean that the roommate owns some kind of long Plexiglas pogo stick. A surfer, however, would grab a surfboard (stick) and head out to the beach, where 6-foot-high waves are breaking on a beautiful, windless day (making the ocean's surface "glassy"). Although the words sound the same to surfer and nonsurfer, their interpretation is radically different, because surfers use special expressions when talking about their sport. Linguists even have a name for the study of how the social context of a sentence affects its meaning: *pragmatics.*

Such differences in interpretation highlight the amazing structure of language and people's ability to process it effortlessly despite its complexity. Some researchers have wondered: If two people who speak the same language use different expressions to describe conditions, does this mean they think about the world in different ways? Does language determine thought, or do all people think alike, regardless of their language? Ultimately, what is the influence of culture on language?

Thought, Culture, and Language

In the 1950s researchers discovered that Eskimo language had many more nouns to refer to snow than English does. From this finding, anthropologist and linguist Benjamin Whorf reasoned that the Eskimos' language shaped their thinking about snow—that is, that verbal and language abilities must affect thought directly. In Whorf's view, the structure of the language that people speak directly determines their thoughts and perceptions (Whorf, 1956). To investigate Whorf's claim, cognitive psychologist Eleanor Heider Rosch studied the language structure and color-naming properties of two cultures with different languages (Heider, 1971, 1972; Heider & Olivier, 1972; Rosch, 1973). Every language has ways of classifying colors, although no language includes more than 11 basic colors (Berlin & Kay, 1969). Rosch's research participants were English-speaking Americans and native speakers of Dani, the language of a primitive Stone Age tribe (the Dani) in Indonesian New Guinea. In Dani there are only two basic color names: *mola* for bright colors and *mili* for dark colors. In English there are many ways of classifying colors, usually based on hues; red, blue, yellow, green, turquoise, pink, and brown are examples. If language determines thought, as Whorf claimed, then the English speakers and the Dani would show two different ways of thinking about color.

Rosch showed both groups of participants single-color chips for 5 seconds each. After 30 seconds, she asked the participants to pick the same color from a group of 40 color chips. Whorf's hypothesis predicted that since the Dani have only two basic color-naming words, they would confuse colors within a group. Two different hues from the *mola* category of color would be considered the same basic color, *mola*. Neither the Dani nor the English-speaking participants, however, confused colors within categories. The Dani's two-color language structure did not limit their ability to discriminate, remember, or think about colors.

In the same manner, even though human beings are sensitive to odors, they have an impoverished language structure to describe them. Research shows that although odors are easily detected, descriptions are difficult. They are often based on personal experiences and sometimes are coded in terms of a personal biographical event (for example, Granddad's pipe tobacco, Mother's perfume, Aunt Maria's attic) (Richardson & Zucco, 1989). Linguistic processes play a limited role in the processing of smell; the language of odors is determined by factors other than simply perceptions of odors.

Culture nevertheless has a great influence on both language and thought. In France, for example, fairly rigid linguistic customs reflect hundreds of years of history; so, in the French language, there are formal and informal means of address. The word "you" for friends is *tu*; in more formal settings, one uses *vous*. Japan has even greater culturally determined distinctions in formality of language; who a person is in the workplace—boss, manager, supervisor, worker—affects how he or she is addressed and the extent of deference to that person's position. (In Chapter 17, we will consider workplace psychology in more detail.) Language is thus an expression of racial, geographic, cultural, and religious tendencies (Williamson, 1991).

Americans are in a minority, in that most of us speak only one language; in most other developed countries, people are bilingual, speaking at least two languages. Research shows that when bilingual people are asked to respond to a question, take a personality test, or otherwise interact in the world, they do so in a culturally bound way—depending on the language in which they respond. When responding to a personality inventory written in Chinese, native speakers of Chinese are likely to reflect Chinese values; when they respond to an English version of the

▲ *Language and thought play a role in many forms of unspoken communication. These Japanese coworkers are greeting each other in a traditional manner, which may have been verbally explained to them in childhood, but is now automatic.*

same personality test, their responses are more likely to reflect Western values (Dinges & Hull, 1993).

As Matsumoto (1994) asserts, language and culture are intertwined; so culture affects language, *and* it affects a person's attitudes and worldview. Along with studies of culture, Rosch's studies suggest that language does not determine thought, but rather subtly influences it. Recall from *Diversity* on pages 234–235 that a person's language can shape his or her worldview and expectations—for example, affecting expectations for women or men. Although various languages have developed specific grammars and thought processes, they have probably done so in response to specific environments, events, and cultures. It may be adaptive to discriminate among many kinds of snow or supervisors, but language does not directly determine thoughts. Rather, thoughts about snow and supervisors help shape language and the words in it. Thus, although strong statements about language determining thought are wrong, there is some truth to Whorf's original ideas. As Hunt and Agnoli (1991, p. 377) assert, "The language people speak is a guide to the language in which they think."

Linguistics

Throughout the ages and in every culture, human beings have rendered their thoughts into language and have employed words to order their thoughts. Tens of thousands of years ago, our cave-dwelling ancestors put their thoughts into words to organize hunting parties. Several millennia later, Egyptian scribes used hieroglyphics (writing in pictorial characters) to represent the spoken word. Still later, Socrates was sentenced to drink hemlock for preaching corrupting ideas to the youth of ancient Greece. Today, world leaders employ oratory to rouse their constituencies to moral behavior and social progress, professors verbally instruct students in the various fields of human knowledge, and people from all walks of life use language to exchange ideas with others or to solve problems mentally. Without this ability, human civilization could never exist. In many ways, language and thinking define humanity.

People learn language as children. Children are astonishingly adept at understanding and utilizing the basic rules of language. A 3-year-old, noticing that many nouns can be turned into verbs by the addition of a suffix, may say, "It sunned today," meaning it was a sunny day. The miracle of language acquisition in children has long fascinated linguists and psycholinguists. **Linguistics** is the study of language, including speech sounds, meaning, and grammar. **Psycholinguistics** is the study of how language is acquired, perceived, understood, and produced. Among other things, psycholinguists seek to discover how children learn the complicated rules necessary to speak correctly. Psychological studies since the early 1970s show that children first acquire the simple aspects of language, then learn progressively more complex elements and capabilities. Studies have also revealed *linguistic structures*—the rules and regularities that exist in, and make it possible to learn, a language. This section examines the study of three major areas of psycholinguistic study: *phonology*, the study of the sounds of language; *semantics*, the study of the meanings of words and sentences; and *syntax*, the study of the relationships among words and how they combine to form sentences.

Linguistics [ling-GWIS-ticks]: The study of language, including speech sounds, meaning, and grammar.

Psycholinguistics: The study of how language is acquired, perceived, understood, and produced.

Phonology

The gurgling, spitting, and burping noises infants first make are caused by air passing through the vocal apparatus. At about 6 weeks, infants begin to make speechlike cooing sounds. During their first 12 months, babies' vocalizations become more varied and frequent. Eventually a baby can combine sounds into pronounceable units.

Phonemes. The basic units of sound that compose the words in a language are called **phonemes**. In English, phonemes are the sounds of single letters, such as *b, p, f,* and *v*, and of combinations of letters, such as *t* and *h* in "these." All the sounds in the English language are expressed in 45 phonemes; of those, just 9 make up nearly half of all words.

Morphemes. At about 1 year of age, children make the first sounds that can be classified as real speech. Initially they utter only one word, but soon they are saying as many as four or five words. Words consist of **morphemes**, the basic units of meaning in a language. A morpheme consists of one or more phonemes combined into a meaningful unit. The morpheme *do*, for example, consists of two phonemes, the sounds of the letters *d* and *o*. Other words can be formed by adding prefixes and suffixes to morphemes. Adding *un-* or *-er* to the morpheme *do*, for example, gives *undo* or *doer*. *Morphology* is the study of these meaningful sound units.

No matter what language people speak, one of their first meaningful utterances is the morpheme *ma*. It is coincidental that *ma* is a word in English. Other frequently heard early words of English-speakers are *bye-bye*, *mama*, and *baby*. In any language, the first words often refer to a specific object or person, especially food, toys, and animals. In the second year, a child's vocabulary may increase to more than 200 words, and by the end of the third year, to nearly 900 words. (Figure 7.8, on page 254, shows vocabulary growth through age 7.)

Semantics

At first, babies do not fully understand what their parents' utterances mean. But as more words take on meaning, the growing child develops semantic capability. **Semantics** is the analysis of the meaning of language, but especially of individual words, the relationships among words, and the significance of words within particular contexts.

Consider how a 4-year-old child might misconstrue what her father says to her mother: "I've had a terrible day. First, the morning traffic made me a nervous wreck. Then, I got into an argument with my boss, who became so furious he almost fired me." The child might think her dad got into a car accident and was nearly set on fire. In trying to understand what is being said, a child is faced with understanding not only the meanings of single words but also their relationships to other words. As everyone who has attempted to learn a new language knows, the meaning of a sentence is not always the same as the definitions of the individual words added together. Although children acquire words daily, the words they acquire mean different things, depending on their context. For example, a Chinese exchange student studying English at a California college needed a light for his cigarette and followed these directions printed on a red box: "Pull For Fire."

Syntax

Once children can use words that have distinct meanings, they begin to combine those words into short sentences, such as "Mama look" or "Bye-bye, Mama." That is, they develop a syntactic capability. **Syntax** is the way words and groups of words combine to form phrases, clauses, and sentences. Syntactic capability enables children to convey more meaning. For example, children acquire a powerful new way of making their demands known when they learn to combine the words *I want* or *give me* with appropriate nouns. Suddenly, they can ask for cookies, toys, or Mommy, without any of them being within pointing range. The rewards that such linguistic

Phoneme [FOE-neem]: A basic unit of sound in a language.

Morpheme [MORE-feem]: A basic unit of meaning in a language.

Semantics [se-MAN-ticks]: The analysis of the meaning of language components.

Syntax [SIN-tacks]: The way words and groups of words are related and combine to form phrases and sentences.

FIGURE 7.8

Vocabulary Changes in Childhood

The average size of children's vocabulary increases rapidly from age 1½ until age 6, when children are fully functional—with a vocabulary of more than 2,500 words.
(Adapted from Moskowitz, 1978 on work done by Smith.)

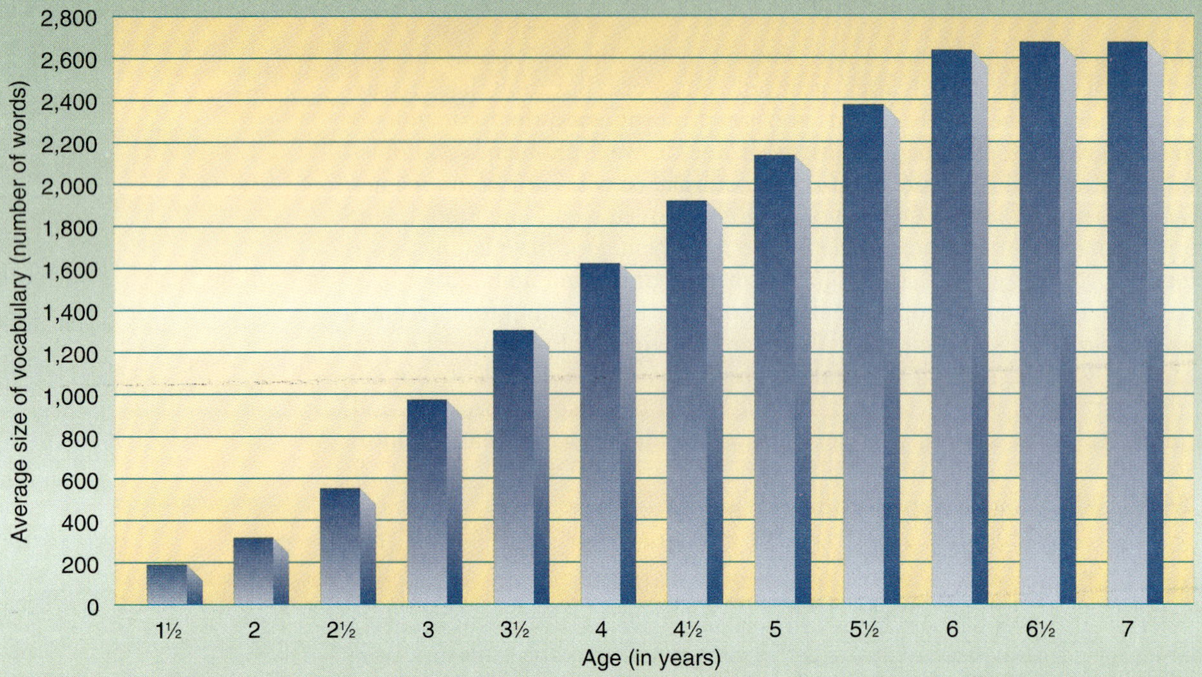

Age	Language Activity
12 weeks	Smiles when talked to; makes cooing sounds spontaneously
16 weeks	Turns head in response to human voices
20 weeks	Makes vowel and consonant sounds while cooing
6 months	Changes from cooing to babbling
12 months	Imitates sounds; understands some words
18 months	Uses from 3–50 words (some babies use very few words at this age—as few as 3—while others use as many as 100); understands basic speech
24 months	Uses between 50 and as much as 250 words; uses two-word phrases
30 months	Uses new words daily; has good comprehension of speech; vocabulary of about 500 words
36 months	Has vocabulary of more than 850 words; makes grammatical mistakes, but their number decreases significantly with each passing week

behavior bring children are powerful incentives for them to learn more language. Children do not really need external rewards to want to learn language, though. (We'll return to the question of incentives for language acquisition later in this chapter when we look at language learning in chimpanzees.) Children begin to use sentences at different ages; but once they begin, they tend to develop at similar rates (R. Brown, 1970). Moreover, the average length of sentences increases at a fairly regular rate as children grow older.

Early studies of children's short sentences suggested that descriptions of the positions and types of words used could characterize early speech, but later analyses showed these descriptions to be inadequate. Later investigations suggested that young children possess an innate grammar and that they use grammatical relationships in much the same ways that adults do (McNeill, 1970). **Grammar** is the linguistic description of how a language functions, especially in terms of the rules and patterns used for generating appropriate and comprehensible sentences.

Figure 7.8 summarizes some of the early linguistic milestones in a child's life.

Transformational Grammar

In 1957 linguist Noam Chomsky, a brilliant theoretician, described a radical approach to grammar that changed many psychologists' views of language development. When it was first introduced, Chomsky's theory was seen as extreme, even reactionary, and, from a behaviorist perspective (then the dominant theory), mentalistic. Chomsky claimed that each person is born with the ability to transform a particular kernel of meaning into an infinite number of meaningful sentences. In Chomsky's grammar, the meaningful message of a sentence is stored differently from the words used to compose it (Chomsky, 1986, 1990). Psychologists are especially interested in transformational grammar because it helps explain unique features of human language.

Surface and Deep Structures. The fundamental idea of Chomsky's **transformational grammar** is that each sentence has both a surface structure and a deep structure. (See Figure 7.9 for an example of how transformational rules work.) The **surface structure** is the organization of a sentence that is closest to its written or spoken form. It is usually the actual sentence, such as *Alex gave Mary a dog*. It shows the words and phrases that can be analyzed through the diagramming procedures often taught in junior high school. The **deep structure** is the underlying mean-

FIGURE 7.9

Chomsky's Concepts of Surface Structure and Deep Structure

Two different surface structures lead to the same meaning through a series of transformational rules.

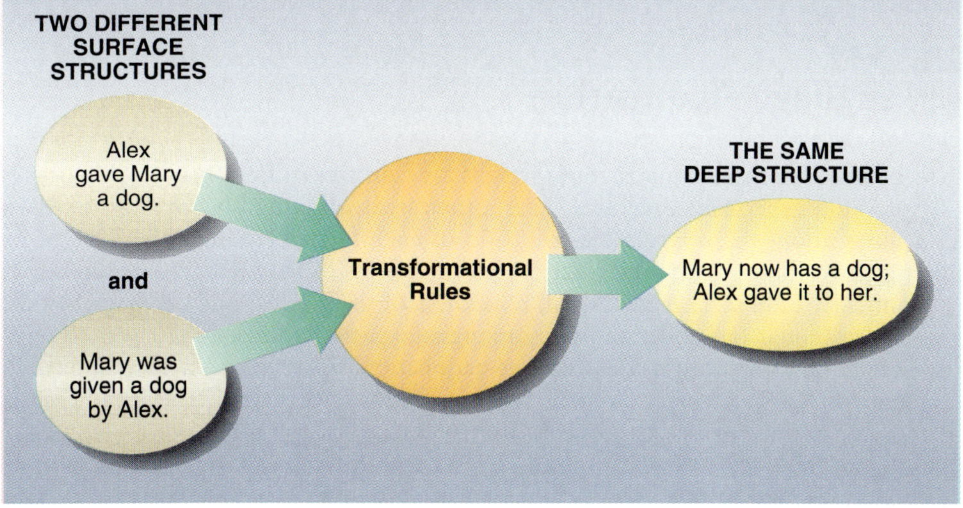

Grammar: The linguistic description of how a language functions, especially the rules and patterns used for generating appropriate and comprehensible sentences.

Transformational grammar: An approach to the study of language that assumes that each surface structure of a sentence has a deep structure associated with it.

Surface structure: The organization of a sentence that is closest to its written or spoken form.

Deep structure: The organization of a sentence that is closest to its underlying meaning.

ing of the sentence. Thus, the sentences *Alex gave Mary a dog* and *Mary was given a dog by Alex* have different surface structures but the same deep structure.

To understand transformational grammar more clearly, consider this sentence: *Visiting relatives can be a pain.* Although the sentence is simple, it has two distinct meanings: that relatives who visit can be annoying guests *or* that going to visit relatives is an annoying chore. Transformational grammar accounts for these two meanings by showing that for the same surface structure, there are two possible deep structures. To a great extent, the meaning of a word or a sentence is far more important than its surface form, or structure.

Abstraction in Language. Imagine that a friend phones you to tell you about a severe-storm warning he just heard over the radio. Most likely, he won't recite the radio announcement verbatim but instead will relay in his own words estimates of the storm's arrival time, wind velocities, and probable amount of precipitation. That is, your friend will tell you what he remembers best from the announcement—its concepts, not its exact wording. This suggests that memory for verbal exchanges is not literal-minded and passive but rather an active compilation of concepts.

Researchers more than 60 years ago made the same argument. In 1932, English psychologist F. C. Bartlett published results from studies that made history and are consistent with recent studies. Bartlett asked people to read a short story packed with plot information. After a few minutes, the participants had to recall the story. They retold the story to another person, who retold it to another, and so forth. Bartlett examined the retelling of the story from person to person to see what happened to the details as time passed. Bartlett found that the stories grew shorter, less detailed, and more informal. Some events in the stories were altered, and others were made up to fit the altered story line. He argued that his participants built a *schema* (an organized structure in memory) of the events of the story, and the schema was what they remembered (see Chapter 6, page 215). Bartlett thus asserted that the participants abstracted the key elements for memory organization and recall; for Bartlett, memory was an active reconstruction.

FOCUS

Review

- What evidence did researchers use to determine whether the structure of spoken language determines people's thoughts and perception? pp. 251–252
- Identify the fundamental difference between surface and deep structure. pp. 255–256
- Summarize Bartlett's evidence for the existence of schemas. p. 256

Think Critically

- If a person is going to learn a second language, where is the best place to do it, and when? Why?

Language Acquisition

Research shows that language and thought are sensitive to both genetic inheritance (nature) and experience (nurture). As in other areas of human behavior, the debate continues about the relative contribution of each factor. If language is based on biology, two things should be true: (1) Many aspects of language ability should be evident early in life. (2) All children, regardless of their culture or language, should develop grammar (an understanding of language patterns) in a similar way. If environmental factors account for language acquisition, the role of learning should be preeminent. Consider what happens when people take their first course in Spanish, French, or Latin. They recognize that they will learn to communicate in a new language that includes a new grammar, new written forms, and new pronunciation. They may buy study aids: books, dictionaries, and tapes. They may read about the country in which the new language is spoken, talk to someone who speaks the language, and rely on foreign language teachers. In general, they prepare to acquire the new language. But when you learned your very first language, how were you prepared to learn it? Were you prepared at all? In trying to resolve the nature–nurture debate over language acquisition, researchers investigate the development of language through observational studies of infants and children, case histories of sensory-deprived infants, studies of reading-disabled or brain-damaged individuals, and experiments with chimpanzees.

Biological Theories

Learning theories emphasize the role of environmental influences, or nurture, in language acquisition. The basic idea is that language is a natural unfolding of traditional learning. But people have the ability to generate an almost infinite number of correctly formed sentences in their native language. Because this ability cannot be acquired solely through imitation or instruction, many researchers, like psychologist George Miller (1965), assert that human beings are biologically equipped with an innate, unique capacity to acquire and develop language.

Although Miller and others do not exclude experience as a factor in shaping children's language, they claim that it is human nature itself that allows children to pay attention to language in their environment and ultimately to use it. Nonetheless, even the strongest proponents of the nature (biological) argument do not contend that a specific language is inborn. Rather, they agree that a predisposition toward language exists and that a blueprint for language is "preprinted." As a child matures, this blueprint provides the framework through which the child learns a language and its rules (e.g., Kuhl et al., 1992). Three major sources of evidence support the biological side of the nature versus nurture debate: (1) studies of brain structure, lateralization, and convergence zones, (2) studies of learning readiness, and (3) studies of language acquisition in children and chimpanzees.

Brain Structure, Lateralization, and Convergence Zones. Even as early as 1800, researchers knew that the brain of a human being was specialized for different functions. At that time, researchers began mapping the brain and discovering that if certain areas were damaged (usually through accidents), the injured person suffered from severe disorders in language abilities. Later work, some of it by Norman Geschwind (1972), led to the idea of *lateralization*—the localization of a particular brain function primarily in one hemisphere. As Chapter 2 showed, considerable evidence suggests that the left and right hemispheres of the brain (normally connected by the corpus callosum) have some distinctly different functions.

Some researchers argue that the brain has unique processing abilities in each hemisphere. For example, important language functions are predominantly, but not exclusively, left hemisphere functions (Corina, Vaid, & Bellugi, 1992). However, the available data do not make an airtight case; each hemisphere seems to play a dominant role in some functions and to interact with the other hemisphere in the performance of others.

Antonio Damasio asserts that the brain has specific language-processing areas, some of which are lateralized (Damasio & Damasio, 1992). So information about any thing or event may be stored in multiple locations through the brain. However, data connect through a convergence zone, or center, that mediates and organizes the information. Thus, signals from physically distant clusters of neuronal activity come together in convergence zones to elicit words, generate sentences, and fully process language.

Learning Readiness. Researcher Eric Lenneberg (1921–1975) claimed that human beings are born with a grammatical capacity and a readiness to produce language (Lenneberg, 1967). He theorized that language simply develops as people interact with their environment. One important aspect of this theory is that a child's capacity to learn language depends on the maturation of specific neurological structures. For example, the structural maturation that has occurred at about 18 to 24 months permits children to acquire grammar so they can interact linguistically with others. On the other hand, lack of maturity in certain structures limits infants' ability to speak in the first months of life. Lenneberg's view derives in part from observations that most children learn the rules of grammar at a very early age.

Lenneberg believed that the brain continues to develop from birth until about age 13, with optimal development at age 2. During this period, children develop grammar and learn the rules of language. After age 13, there is little room for improvement or change in their neurological structure. Lenneberg supported his argument with the observation that brain-damaged children can relearn some speech and language, whereas brain-damaged adolescents or adults who lose language and speech are unable to regain the lost ability completely. Lenneberg's view is persuasive, but some of his original claims have been seriously criticized—particularly his idea of the role of a critical time period in language development (e.g., Kinsbourne, 1975).

Some researchers claim that not only human beings but also other organisms—for example, chimpanzees—are born with a grammatical capacity and a readiness for language.

Language Studies with Chimpanzees

Do animals communicate with one another through language? If they do, is that language the same as, similar to, or totally different from the language of human beings? Most important, what can human beings learn from animals about the inborn aspects of language?

The biological approach to language suggests that human beings are "prewired"—born with a capacity for language. Experience is the key that unlocks this existing capacity and makes it available for expression. The arguments for and against the biological approach to language acquisition use studies showing that chimpanzees naturally develop some language abilities. Chimpanzees are generally considered among the most intelligent animals; in addition, they resemble human beings more closely than any other animal. Playful and curious, chimps share many common physical and mental abilities with human beings. Researchers can also control and shape the environment in which chimps learn language, something they cannot do in studies involving human subjects. For these reasons, chimpanzees have been the species of choice when psychologists have studied language in animals.

However, all attempts to teach animals to talk have failed. Until recently, this failure had led most psycholinguists to conclude that only human beings have the capacity to acquire language. Two decades ago, however, some major research projects showed that even though chimpanzees lack the necessary vocal apparatus to speak, they can learn to use different methods of communication (Rumbaugh & Savage-Rumbaugh, 1978). Scientists have studied chimpanzees both in the field in near-natural environments and in laboratory settings using computer technology. With results from sharply different environments, clear conclusions are emerging.

Washoe. From age 1, the chimpanzee Washoe was raised like a human child in the home of Allen and Beatrice Gardner (1969). During the day, Washoe was in the house or in the large fenced yard. At night, she slept in a trailer. The Gardners and their research assistants did not speak to Washoe. Instead, they used Ameslan (American Sign Language, the sign language used by the deaf) to communicate with her. Rather than being taught to speak words, Washoe was taught to make signs that stood for words as well as for such simple concepts and commands as *more, come, give me, flower, tickle*, and *open*. Within 7 months, Washoe learned 4 signs; after 12 months, she had learned 12 signs. At 22 months, she had a vocabulary of 34 signs; by age 4, she knew 85 signs; and by the end of her 5th year, Washoe had accumulated 160 signs (Fleming, 1974). Washoe learned a large number of signs that refer to specific objects or events. She was able to generalize these signs and to combine them in meaningful order to make sentences. There is no proof, however, that she used a systematic grammar to generate novel kinds of sentences.

Sarah. The chimp Sarah was raised in a cage, with more limited contact with human beings than Washoe had. Psychologist David Premack (1971) used magnetized plastic symbols and instrumental training methods to teach Sarah words and sentences (see Figure 7.10). Initially, Premack placed several plastic symbols on a board in front of Sarah and placed a banana slightly out of reach. Each time Sarah chose the appropriate symbol, he would give her the banana as a reward. Eventually, through shaping, Sarah came to associate a specific symbol with a banana and learned to place the token on the board when she wanted a banana. Gradually Sarah developed a small but impressive vocabulary. She learned to make compound sentences, to answer simple questions, and to substitute words in a sentence construction—for example, "Place banana dish," "Place apple dish," and "Place orange dish." There is no evidence, however, that she could generate a new sentence, such as "Is the apple in the dish?" or "Where are the apples?"

FIGURE 7.10

Symbols Used by Sarah in Premack's Study

Sarah learned to construct sentences using pieces of plastic that varied in color, size, and shape.

Lana. The chimp Lana learned to interact with a computer at the Yerkes Primate Research Center at Emory University. Researchers Rumbaugh, Gill, and Von Glaserfeld (1973) gave Lana 6 months of computer-controlled language training. Lana learned to press a series of keys with imprinted geometric symbols. Each symbol represented a word in an artificial language the researchers called Yerkish. The computer varied the location of each Yerkish word and the color and brightness of the keys. Through instrumental conditioning, Lana was able to demonstrate some of the rudiments of language acquisition. Like Washoe and Sarah, however, Lana did not show that she could manipulate grammatical relations in meaningful and regular ways.

So far, most studies of chimps show that their language usage is similar to that of very young children: It is concrete, specific, and limited. However, chimps do not show the ability to generate an unlimited number of grammatically correct sentences, an ability that human beings acquire with age.

Nim. A Columbia University psychologist, H. S. Terrace (1979, 1980), claims that even the limited results with chimps are greatly overvalued. He suggests that chimps do not have language abilities and that the data reported so far show only that the chimps were mimicking their teachers' signs. Terrace reports significant differences between chimp language and the language of young children. In raising his chimp, Nim Chimpsky (named after the famous linguist Noam Chomsky), Terrace found that Nim's utterances did not increase in length, as young children's do. Nim acquired many words, but she did not use them in longer and longer sentences as time passed. In addition, only 12 percent of Nim's utterances were spontaneous; the remaining 88 percent were responses to her teacher. Terrace points out that a significantly greater percentage of children's utterances are spontaneous. Terrace also found no evidence of grammatical competence either in his own data or in that of other researchers.

Kanzi. Recent work with a little-known species of ape, the pygmy chimpanzee, shows that chimps can acquire symbols without training. According to well-known language researcher Sue Savage-Rumbaugh, these chimps comprehend symbols before they produce them, and they also comprehend human speech. In Savage-Rumbaugh's (1987) view, they have the ability to construct a rudimentary grammar.

Kanzi, a pygmy chimp, uses a keyboard to talk to his human trainers. His keyboard has 256 symbols, and he has mastered more than 200. Recordings of interactions with Kanzi have shown that he comprehends both individual words and

Researchers have gained valuable knowledge about the nature of language by studying chimps and other animals. Researcher Sue Savage-Rumbaugh taught the chimp Kanzi to communicate using a special keyboard. (Photo courtesy of CNN.)

sentences and responds appropriately. He learned his language by being enmeshed in a language environment, not through training procedures. Kanzi's unique contribution is that he understands human speech and syntax and has learned to do so without training. He learned language steadily and rapidly, and Savage-Rumbaugh believes this sets him apart from all other apes who have learned to produce language (Greenfield & Savage-Rumbaugh, 1990) and to comprehend it (Sevcik & Savage-Rumbaugh, 1994).

Chimp Language? Terrace's work challenged the findings of previous investigators and made them think about language in new ways. Other researchers at the Yerkes Primate Center have presented additional challenges to primate language acquisition (Savage-Rumbaugh et al., 1983). They claim not only that chimp language is different from that of human beings but also that the purpose of chimp language is different. Unlike young children, who spontaneously learn to name and to point at objects (often called *referential naming*), chimps do not spontaneously develop such communication skills. Terrace (1985) agrees that the ability to name is a basic part of human consciousness. He argues that, as part of socialization, children learn to refer to various inner states: feelings, thoughts, and emotions. Chimps can be taught some naming skills, but the procedure is long and tedious. Children, on the other hand, develop these skills easily and spontaneously at a young age. Accordingly, researchers such as R. J. Sanders (1985) assert that chimps do not interpret the symbols they use in the same way that children do. These researchers question the comparability of human and chimp language.

Although few psychologists are completely convinced about the role of language in chimp communication, their criticisms do not diminish the chimps' language abilities or their accomplishments in other areas, such as mathematics (Rumbaugh, Savage-Rumbaugh, & Hegel, 1987; Boysen & Berntson, 1989) and comprehension (Sevcik & Savage-Rumbaugh, 1994). They also do not rule out language and speech processing in some chimps. Chimp language remains an emerging part of psychology; researchers such as Savage-Rumbaugh assert that basic ideas about the nature of language must be reevaluated—the linguistic feats of the chimps are just too impressive. The answers are far from complete, but the quest is exciting.

FOCUS

Review

- What is the crucial assumption of biological approaches to language acquisition? p. 257
- Terrace claimed important differences between chimp language and the language of human children. What are those differences? pp. 259–260

Think Critically

- The two learning approaches to language acquisition—conditioning and imitation—operate differently with respect to one key underlying principle. Identify the principle (think back to Chapter 5).

Summary and Review

Cognitive Psychology: An Overview

How do cognitive psychologists approach the field of psychology?

- *Cognitive psychology* is the study of the overlapping fields of perception, learning, memory, and thought. Cognitive psychology focuses on how people attend to, acquire, transform, store, and retrieve knowledge. Cognitive psychologists study thinking; they assume that mental processes exist, are systematic, and can be studied scientifically. Cognitive psychologists believe that individuals are active participants in analyzing their world. pp. 232–233

Concept Formation

What is involved in the process of concept formation?

- *Concepts* are the mental categories used to classify events and objects according to common properties. Concept formation involves classifying and organizing objects by grouping them with or isolating them from others on the basis of a common feature. In studies of concept formation, stimuli vary along dimensions, or features, that set them apart from others. Within each dimension are different values or attributes. pp. 233–235
- Concept-formation studies using the reception method present a subject with a series of instances. The task is to classify the instances as positive or negative. Studies using the selection method present all the possible instances at once. The participant chooses one instance at a time, asking if it is positive or negative. p. 236
- *Hypothesis-testing theory* views concept formation as an active process in which people acquire new information by generating hypotheses, testing those hypotheses, discarding old hypotheses if necessary, and making an inference about the stimuli. p. 237

KEY TERMS

Cognitive psychology, p. 232
Concept, p. 233
Hypothesis-testing theory, p. 237
Conservative focusing, p. 237

Reasoning and Decision Making

Differentiate between reasoning and decision making.

- *Reasoning* is the process by which people generate logical and coherent ideas, evaluate situations, and reach conclusions. The procedure used to reach a valid conclusion is called *logic*. *Decision making* is the assessment of alternatives; people make decisions that sometimes involve the probability of occurrence of an event and the expected value. p. 238

What are some key elements of the decision-making process?

- A *syllogism* is a sequence of statements, or premises (often two, and assumed to be true), followed by a conclusion; the task is to decide (deduce) whether the conclusion is valid. Psychologists analyze the decision-making process by having participants describe the steps of their thinking process. pp. 238–239
- A decision-making approach in which some factors take on more importance than others is called a compensatory model. In elimination by aspects, people rule out alternatives that do not meet minimum criteria; this approach is generally a fast and efficient way to make decisions. p. 239
- Psychological factors, especially previous events, affect how people estimate probabilities of behaviors and events. Sometimes people may ignore key pieces of data, however, and thus make bad (or irrational) decisions not based on probability; at other times, people's worldviews color their probability decision making and strategies. pp. 240–241

KEY TERMS

Reasoning, p. 238
Logic, p. 238
Decision making, p. 238
Syllogism, p. 238

Problem Solving

What are some traditional and nontraditional modes of problem solving?

- *Problem solving* consists of realizing that a problem exists and assessing its complexity, devising solutions, evaluating those solutions, and assessing results. The ability to develop insight into situations gives a person an advantage in problem solving. p. 242
- *Functional fixedness* is the inability to see that an object can have a function other than its stated or usual one. Functional fixedness has been shown to be detrimental to problem solving. To help eliminate functional fixedness, some people use the technique of *brainstorming*. pp. 243, 245
- *Creativity* is the ability to develop responses that are original, novel, and appropriate. According to Guilford, creative thinking is divergent thinking. *Divergent thinking* is the production of new information from known information, or the generation of logical possibilities. In contrast, *convergent thinking* is the process by which possible options are selectively narrowed until they converge onto one answer. pp. 244–245

What are the fundamental differences between algorithms and heuristics ?

- When computer programs implement some types of human activities, they are said to involve artificial intelligence (AI). *Algorithms* are problem-solving procedures that use a set of rules to implement a particular series of steps. *Heuristics* are sets of strategies that act as guidelines, not strict rules, for problem solving. In *subgoal analysis*, a problem is taken apart, or broken down, into several smaller steps, each of which has a subgoal. In *means–ends analysis*, the current situation or position is compared with the desired end in order to determine the most efficient means for getting from one to the other. pp. 247–248

How do PDP models help explain the problem-solving process?

- The study of parallel distributed processing suggests that many operations take place simultaneously and at many locations within the brain. Neural networks have been devised to simulate brain activity. pp. 249–250

KEY TERMS

Problem solving, p. 242
Functional fixedness, p. 243
Creativity, p. 244
Brainstorming, p. 245
Convergent thinking, p. 245
Divergent thinking, p. 245
Algorithm, p. 247
Heuristics, p. 248
Subgoal analysis, p. 248
Means–ends analysis, p. 248
Backward search, p. 248

Language

How are language, thought, and culture interrelated, and what are the key elements of language?

- Whorf assumed that language structure determined thought. However, research shows that language structure alone is unlikely to account for the way people think, because language is also an expression of culture. pp. 251–252
- *Linguistics* is the study of language, including speech sounds, meaning, and grammar. *Psycholinguistics* is the study of how people acquire, perceive, understand, and produce language. *Phonemes* are the basic units of sounds in a language; *morphemes* are the basic units of meaning. *Semantics* is the study of the meaning of language components. *Syntax* is how words and groups of words are related and how words are arranged into phrases and sentences. *Grammar* is the linguistic description of a language, in terms of its rules and patterns for generating comprehensible sentences. pp. 252–254
- *Transformational grammar*, developed by Chomsky, is an approach to studying the structure of a language. It assumes that each sentence has both a *surface structure* and a *deep structure*. In general, researchers conclude that the meaning of a sentence (deep structure) and the level of its analysis are more important than the specific words (surface structure). pp. 255–256

KEY TERMS

Linguistics, p. 252
Psycholinguistics, p. 252
Phoneme, p. 253
Morpheme, p. 253
Semantics, p. 253
Syntax, p. 253
Grammar, p. 255
Transformational grammar, p. 255
Surface structure, p. 255
Deep structure, p. 255

Language Acquisition

How do theorists explain language acquisition?

- Learning plays an important part in language acquisition. However, people have the ability to generate an unlimited number of correctly formed sentences in their language. This ability cannot be acquired solely through imitation or instruction, which suggests the existence of an innate grammar, or language ability. p. 257
- Damasio asserts that the brain has specific language-processing areas, some of which are lateralized. Information about any thing or event may be stored in multiple locations through the brain. However, data are connected through a convergence zone, or center, that mediates and organizes the information. p. 257
- Studies of language ability in chimpanzees have produced some impressive results, although few psychologists are completely convinced about the ways in which chimps use language. The criticisms, however, do not diminish the chimps' language abilities or accomplishments in other areas such as mathematics. p. 260

Learning CONNECTIONS

Some students benefit from extra help with the concepts of decision making and problem solving. You can learn more about them in:

- The CD-ROM accompanying this book, Topic 7

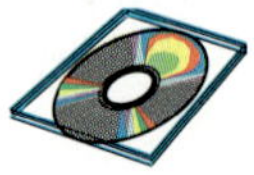

- This book's study guide, *Keeping Pace Plus,* or the computerized study guide, Chapter 7
- The audiotape accompanying this book, *SoundGuide for Psychology,* Learning Unit 7
- The study aids found on the World Wide Web site for this book, at http://www.abacon.com/psych/lefton

Critical Thinking CONNECTIONS

Take a moment to think critically about how this chapter's topics are connected with the rest of psychology . . .

If you are interested in . . .	Ask yourself . . .	Then turn to . . .
Thought as a technique to facilitate improved behavior 	How do motivational researchers consider the role of thought in determining a person's day-to-day decision making?	Chapter 9, pp. 305–306
	Should stress always be considered an interpreted state?	Chapter 13, pp. 450–451
	In what ways do business managers and personnel officers take into account the way people remember, code, and interpret information?	Chapter 17, pp. 603–608
The role of language in everyday life 	How are learning principles used to explain language acquisition?	Chapter 5, pp. 185–187
	What are the implications of an impoverished language environment for a person's intelligence?	Chapter 8, pp. 282–283, 286–287
	What are the various ways of communicating using body language?	Chapter 16, pp. 565–567
Decision making and problem solving 	In what ways can reinforcement for problem solving hinder a person's intrinsic enjoyment of a task?	Chapter 5, p. 177
	How do psychologists use problem solving to help determine intelligence?	Chapter 8, pp. 270–271
	If psychologists consider maladjustment as a series of problems to be solved, what are the implications for cognitive theory?	Chapter 14, pp. 478–479, 481

8

Intelligence

Around an oval table in a classroom washed in the bluish glow of fluorescent lighting, 20 professors were engaged in a heated debate. It was a scheduled discussion among academics. A number of students, and I, looked on.

PROFESSOR JONES: And what about 200 years of oppression?

PROFESSOR SMITH: Forget about the past. The reality is we have hundreds of thousands of people in an underclass who seem unable to get themselves out—no matter what!

PROFESSOR MATTHEWS: Wait a second. You're agreeing with them! You should know better. Intelligence is a reflection of our schooling, our culture, our motivation. It isn't a reflection of innate abilities.

PROFESSOR SMITH: I know the theories, but I also know the realities. You social scientists—especially you psychologists—always believe we can change the way things are. But there are just some truths you won't face up to.

It was starting to become a dreamlike experience. Suddenly I wasn't sure whether this was a meeting of professionals who knew what they were talking about, or a professional wrestling match. The event that had sparked the debate on intelligence and what it means, not only on my campus but also on many radio and TV talk shows, was publication of a book entitled *The Bell Curve* by researchers Richard J. Herrnstein and Charles Murray (1994). In a nutshell, Herrnstein and Murray argue that the United States has a cognitive class structure determined largely by genetic heritability of intelligence—and unlikely to change. It should come as no surprise that their book inspires controversy, even passion—as it did among my colleagues. The book is as political as it is psychological or scientific, presenting an agenda for how American society should respond to known data about intellectual functioning. But perhaps its greatest significance is that it has brought people to the table and gotten them thinking, debating, even yelling about intelligence.

I will have more to say about *The Bell Curve* later (page 288). But for now, it is important to recognize that dealing with intellectual capabilities is a complex task, for there is more to intelligence than test scores. Intelligence tests do not measure other mental characteristics that are important to success, such as motivation, creativity, and leadership skills. People demonstrate effective and intelligent behavior in many ways, but not necessarily in all areas. Some people, for example, can write a complicated computer program but not a short story. Moreover, intelligence must be defined in terms of the situations in which people find themselves. Intelligent behavior for a dancer is very different from intelligent behavior for a scientist, and both types of behavior are different from intelligent behavior for a child with a learning disability.

No single test—such as a test of verbal ability, knowledge of English literature, or math skills—is a clear measure of intelligence. Psychologists therefore use a variety of tests as well as other data—among them interviews, teacher evaluations, and writing and drawing samples—to evaluate an individual's current standing, to make predictions about future performance or behavior, and to offer suggestions for remedial work or therapy. In spite of their drawbacks, tests do have strong predictive value; for example, intelligence tests can generally predict academic achievement, and achievement tests can generally predict whether someone will profit from further training in a specific area.

In this chapter, we will consider individual differences in intelligence by way of theories, tests, and controversies. We also will examine two special populations with respect to intelligence: the gifted and the mentally retarded. But first, let's begin with the very basic, but difficult, question: What is intelligence?

What Is Intelligence?

Why do two students who study the same material for the same amount of time get different scores on an examination? Why do some people succeed in medical school and others have trouble just finishing high school? One factor may be that one person is more intelligent than the other, and higher intelligence increases a person's chances of succeeding academically. Intelligence is one of the most widely used yet hotly debated concepts in science and in everyday life. A group of psychologists attempting to answer the question "What is intelligence?" in 1921 could not reach agreement. Sternberg and Detterman (1986) posed the same question 65 years later to 25 respected researchers who still could not reach agreement.

Defining Intelligence

For some psychologists, intelligence is all mental abilities; for others, it is the basic general factor necessary for all mental activity; for still others, it is a group of specific abilities. J. F. Fagan III (1992) asserts that intelligence is not a trait or a faculty of the mind but instead is processing by the brain. Quinn McNemar (1964) contended, "All intelligent people know what intelligence is—it is the thing that the other guy lacks!" Most psychologists agree, however, that intelligence is a concept, not a thing (Howard, 1993). Most of the various definitions of intelligence share certain qualities: (1) They define intelligence in terms of objectively observable behavior; (2) they include in intelligence both a person's capacity to learn and the person's acquired knowledge; and (3) they view the ability to adapt to the environment as one sign of intelligence.

Perhaps the most widely accepted definition of intelligence is that of the well-known test constructor David Wechsler (1958, p. 7): "**Intelligence** is the aggregate or global capacity of the individual to act purposefully, to think rationally, and to deal effectively with the environment." In Wechsler's definition intelligence is expressed behaviorally. It is shown in the way people act and their ability to learn new things and to use previously learned knowledge. Most important, intelligence has to do with people's ability to adapt to the cultural environment in which they learned about the world. Wechsler's definition has had far-reaching effects on how test developers devise intelligence tests, investigate the nature of intelligence, and interpret intelligence within a cultural context. Intelligence is thus not a thing but a process, a product, and a capacity, which is affected by a person's day-to-day experiences in the environment.

Theories of Intelligence

Psychologists cannot say that all people are intelligent all of the time; nor can they specify the exact conditions under which people will exhibit their intelligence. This realization of individual differences in behavior has been a problem for psychology from its beginnings. E. B. Titchener, an early psychologist, studied the speed of mental processes but paid little or no attention to variations among the people whose mental processes he was studying. John Watson, known as the father of behaviorism, denied the relevance of individual differences in intelligence.

Researchers who examine intelligence today, however, *do* focus on individual differences. In the early 1900s, a large body of data describing the characteristics thought to be involved in intelligence emerged. The data included information on age, race, gender, socioeconomic status, and environmental factors. From these data, researchers developed theories about the nature of intelligence and ways to test it. Today, the most influential approaches to the study of intelligence are Piaget's and Wechsler's theories, factor theories, Jensen's two-level theory, and the relatively new theory proposed by Robert Sternberg.

Piaget's Theory. According to noted Swiss epistemologist and psychologist Jean Piaget (1892–1980), intelligence is a reflection of a person's adaptation to the environment, and intellectual development consists of changes in the way the individual accomplishes that adaptation. Every child goes through invariant (in terms of sequence) stages in intellectual development, with different levels of cognitive processing determining the types of intellectual tasks the child can accomplish. (We will examine this developmental process further in Chapter 10.) Three-year-olds cannot learn calculus, for example, because they are not ready to perform the mental operations needed to grasp the necessary concepts. Piaget's theory of intellectual development focuses on the interaction of biological readiness and learning. In Piaget's view, neither factor predominates in the development of intelligence; they work together.

Wechsler's Theory. David Wechsler viewed intelligence from the perspective of a tester. As one of the developers of a widely used and widely respected intelligence test (which we will examine later), Wechsler knew that tests were made up of many subparts, each measuring a different aspect of a person's functioning and

Intelligence: According to Wechsler, "the aggregate or global capacity of the individual to act purposefully, to think rationally, and to deal effectively with the environment."

resourcefulness. He therefore examined the components of intelligence closely and argued that intelligence tests involving spatial relations and verbal comprehension reveal little about someone's overall capacity to deal with the world. In Wechsler's view, psychologists need to remember that intelligence is more than simply mathematical or problem-solving ability; it is the broader ability to deal with the world.

Factor Theories. Factor theories of intelligence use a correlation technique known as *factor analysis* to discover what makes up intelligence. **Factor analysis** is a statistical procedure designed to discover the mutually independent elements (factors) in any set of data. Results of tests of verbal comprehension, spelling, and reading speed, for example, usually correlate highly, suggesting that some underlying attribute of verbal abilities determines a person's score on those three tests.

Early in this century, Charles E. Spearman (1863–1945) used factor analysis to show that intelligence consists of two parts: a general factor affecting all tasks, which he termed the *g factor*, and several specific factors necessary to perform particular tasks. According to Spearman, some amounts of both the general and the specific factors were necessary for the successful performance of any task. Thus, to do map reading, you need a certain amount of the g factor and a certain amount of specific spatial abilities. This basic approach to intelligence is known as the *two-factor theory of intelligence.*

Louis L. Thurstone (1887–1955) further developed Spearman's work by postulating a general factor analogous to Spearman's, as well as seven other factors, each representing a unique mental ability. Known as the *factor theory approach to intelligence,* this theory included a computational scheme for sorting out the seven factors that Thurstone considered to be the basic abilities of human beings: verbal comprehension, word fluency, number facility, spatial visualization, associative memory, perceptual speed, and reasoning.

Thurstone's factor theory approach led to and culminated in J. P. Guilford's multifactor approach to intelligence testing. Guilford, one of the last students to work with Titchener, focused on individual mental abilities in order to develop a testable scheme of intelligence. Guilford gave large numbers of tests to diverse populations and found a whole range of factors that seemed appropriate in describing intelligence. He looked for a rational scheme of grouping them together and eventually he found it; he called it the *structure of intellect model.* According to Guilford (1967), human intellectual abilities and activities can be described in terms of three major dimensions: the mental operations performed, the contents of those operations, and the resulting products of the operations (see Figure 8.1). Guilford's three-dimensional model produces a minimum of 180 factors, 98 of which have been demonstrated experimentally. These varieties of intelligence are often, but not always, independent of one another.

Guilford (1985) contends that more than a few scores are necessary for a correct assessment of an individual's intellectual abilities. He also asserts that intelligence should be defined as "a systematic collection of abilities or functions for processing information of different kinds in different forms" (p. 231). Research supports Guilford's theory and suggests that optimally weighted composite scores may best predict achievement, school learning, and work performance (Guilford, 1985). The multifactor approach is not universally accepted, however. Some researchers continue to assert that there is a general factor of intelligence and that it cannot be separated into distinct parts accounting for specific processes (Jensen & Weng, 1994); rather, the same overall factor accounts for success in both academic and work pursuits (Kranzler & Jensen, 1991; Ree & Earles, 1992).

Jensen's Two-Level Theory. Arthur Jensen approaches intelligence testing not from the viewpoint of a test constructor but from the viewpoint of a theoretician. Jensen (1969, 1970, 1987) suggests that intellectual functioning consists of associative abilities and cognitive abilities. *Associative abilities* enable people to connect stimuli and events; they require little reasoning or transformation. Questions

Factor analysis: A statistical procedure designed to discover the mutually independent elements (factors) in any set of data.

FIGURE 8.1

Guilford's Model of the Structure of Intellect

Each of Guilford's three dimensions of intellectual abilities and activities—operations, contents, and products—has many attributes. Through various combinations, these dimensions and their attributes produce 180 separate factors. The factor cell illustrated here, a "cognition auditory unit," might be the ability to recognize spoken phonemes.

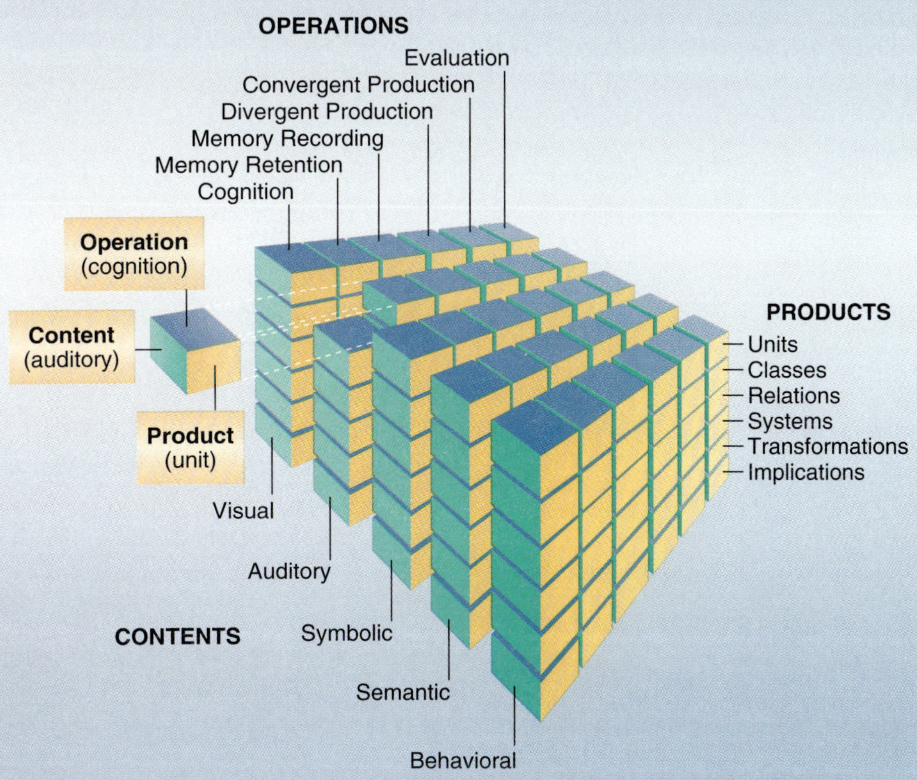

testing associative abilities include, for example, asking someone to repeat from memory a seven-digit number sequence or to name the first president of the United States. *Cognitive abilities*, on the other hand, involve reasoning and problem solving. Solving word problems and defining new words or concepts are examples of cognitive ability tasks. Jensen's idea is not new; even the founders of the testing movement suggested that different kinds of intellectual functioning are involved in intelligence. What is new is Jensen's claim that associative and cognitive abilities are inherited, which adds fuel to the nature-versus-nurture controversy about intelligence (discussed later in this chapter).

Sternberg's View. Robert J. Sternberg takes an information-processing view of intelligence. His view depicts intelligence as having three interacting dimensions. Like Sternberg, other researchers have certainly proposed that there are multiple types of intelligence. Gardner and Hatch (1989) originally presented seven but have recently added an eighth type (see Table 8.1 on page 270). Like Gardner and Hatch, Sternberg believes in multiple types of intelligence, but he focuses on how people's intellectual capacities work together in relation to their internal and external world. Sternberg's ideas, which are relatively new in the domain of intelligence theories, are presented next.

TABLE 8.1 *Gardner and Hatch's Types of Intelligence*

Type of Intelligence	End State	Core Components
Logical–mathematical	Scientist Mathematician	Sensitivity to and capacity to discern logical or numerical patterns; ability to handle long chains of reasoning
Linguistic	Poet Journalist	Sensitivity to the sounds, rhythms, and meanings of words; sensitivity to the different functions of language
Musical	Composer Violinist	Ability to produce and appreciate rhythm, pitch, and timbre; appreciation of the forms of musical expressiveness
Spatial	Navigator Sculptor	Capacity to perceive the visual–spatial world accurately and to perform transformations on initial perceptions
Bodily–kinesthetic	Dancer Athlete	Ability to control bodily movements and to handle objects skillfully
Interpersonal	Therapist Salesperson	Capacity to discern and respond appropriately to the moods, temperaments, motivations, and desires of other people
Intrapersonal	Person with detailed, accurate self-knowledge	Access to one's own feelings and the ability to discriminate among them and draw on them to guide behavior; knowledge of one's own strengths, weaknesses, desires, and intelligence
Naturalist	Botanist Chef	Ability to make fine discriminations among the flora and fauna of the natural world or the patterns and designs of human artifacts

Source: H. Gardner & T. Hatch, Multiple intelligences go to school: Educational implications of the theory of multiple intelligences, *Educational Researcher, 18*(8) (1989), 6; with adaptation based on personal communication from H. Gardner (1996).

A New Theory of Intelligence

A psychologist in search of a field for important research with far-ranging practical implications could confidently choose intelligence and intelligence testing. Robert J. Sternberg of Yale University did—and his life has never been the same. Sternberg has criticized not only today's widely used tests of intellectual ability, which attempt to gauge intelligence on the basis of traditional theories, but also many elements of the theories themselves.

Sternberg (1986a) finds intelligence tests too narrow and contends that they don't adequately account for intelligence in the everyday world. He argues that researchers have focused for too long on how to measure intelligence, rather than on more important questions such as these: What is intelligence? How does it change? What can individuals do to enhance it? Sternberg reasons that some tests measure individual mental abilities, while others measure the way the individual operates in the environment. He asserts that a solid theory of intelligence must account for both individual mental abilities and the ability of people to use their capabilities in the environment. Sternberg focuses not on how much intelligence people have but on how they use it; this makes his theory far more applicable cross-culturally.

FIGURE 8.2

Sternberg's Triarchic Theory of Intelligence

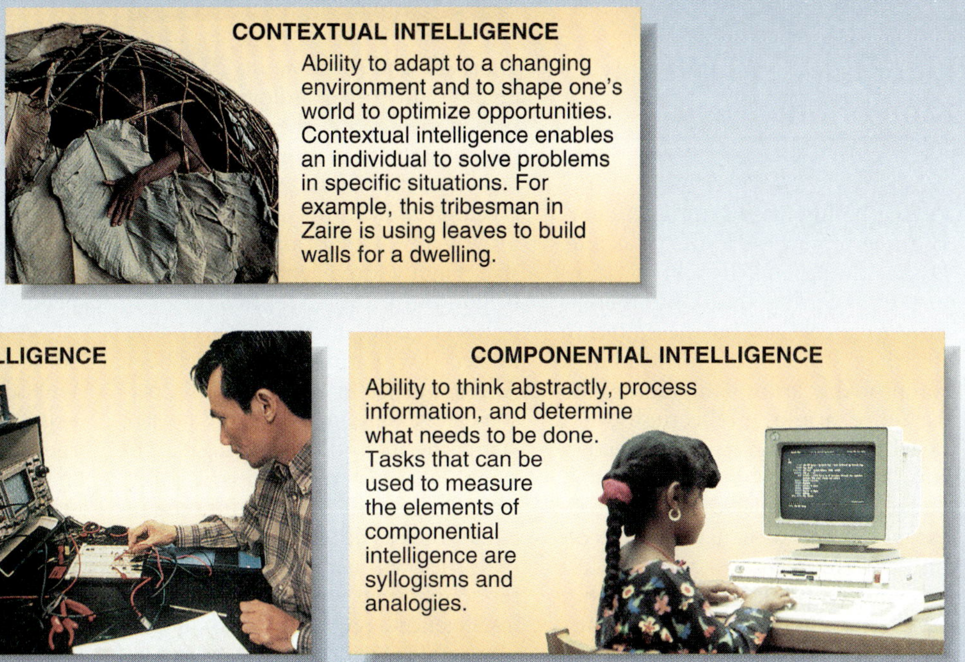

New Ideas. Sternberg (1985, 1986a) has described the new "triarchic" theory of intelligence in his book *Beyond IQ*. The theory presents three dimensions, each covering a different aspect of intelligence: contextual, experiential, and componential (see Figure 8.2).

The *contextual* dimension of the theory deals with an individual's ability to use intelligence for problem solving in specific situations—this is analytic intelligence. This part of the triarchic theory focuses on how people shape their environments so that their competencies can be best utilized. For example, an individual might organize problems in a meaningful way, perhaps by grouping similar items together. The contextual dimension does not refer to any mental operations that are required to carry out problem solving, and thus it is likely to be culture-free. It may apply to an African herdsman staking off territory as well as to a machinist cleaning a well-used lathe.

The *experiential* dimension has to do with a person's application of experience with the external world. According to this part of Sternberg's theory, a test measures intelligence if it assesses both a person's ability to handle novel tasks and the person's mastery of tasks in an automatic manner—this is practical intelligence. An example of such mastery through experience is memorizing verb forms in a foreign language. Initially, remembering them is a new task and tedious, but with practice using the verbs becomes automatic.

The *componential* dimension of Sternberg's theory is the glue that holds the other two subtheories together. It describes the mental mechanisms underlying what are commonly considered intelligent behaviors. A component is a basic method of information processing. Componential intelligence includes a person's ability to determine the tasks that need to be done, to determine the order in which subtasks should be undertaken, to analyze their subparts, to decide which information should be processed, and to monitor performance. This is creative intelligence—the aspect of intelligence necessary to write a love poem, romance novel, or research paper. Tasks that can be used to measure the elements of componential intelligence are analogies, vocabulary, and syllogisms.

To be intelligent, a behavior has to involve all three dimensions of intelligence. For example, Sternberg suggests that eating is a behavior that is adaptive but does

APPLICATIONS

Emotions—A Different Kind of Intelligence

Being highly intelligent is no guarantee of success in life. It is true that doing well in school is important in getting ahead. But there is more to success in business, and in life, than superior cognitive ability. You probably know individuals who are quite bright intellectually, but have little common sense, few leadership skills, or very little motivation. Daniel Goleman (1995), a psychologist who writes a regular science column for the *New York Times*, has published a book titled *Emotional Intelligence*, in which he claims one's emotional life can matter much more than one's intellectual life.

Goleman holds that traditionally defined intelligence stands alongside and separate from emotional intelligence. According to Goleman, emotional intelligence seems to be the key to getting ahead in life. Emotional intelligence includes self-awareness, impulse control, persistence, self-motivation, ability to recognize emotions in others, and social agility. Goleman gives credit to psychologists such as Gardner and Sternberg who stress the multiplicity of intelligence, but he feels that they don't go far enough.

Cognitive ability and emotional intelligence are not mutually exclusive. Highly intelligent people can be bright and productive, but they can be also be cold, unresponsive, and detached (low emotional intelligence). Alternatively, a bright, productive person can be outgoing, cheerful, poised, sympathetic, and caring (high emotional intelligence). Goleman's assertion is that, all other things being equal, those with high emotional intelligence will nearly always do better than those with low emotional intelligence—regardless of their cognitive abilities. Of course, not everyone who is bright has low or high emotional intelligence. Like the other types of intelligence, emotional intelligence is displayed in a wide range of degrees.

Goleman proposes that people who develop a high emotional intelligence can better manage the difficulties of life, such as inappropriate aggression, eating disorders, depression, or alcoholism. He argues that people can be taught to recognize emotions and understand relationships, to develop better frustration tolerance and anger management, to focus better on the task at hand and pay attention (thus becoming less impulsive), and to take another person's perspective.

Students of psychology have to ask some critical questions: To what extent are cognitive ability and emotional intelligence independent? Are they affected by the same environmental variables? Can emotional intelligence be fostered, boosted, or enhanced? (We will see in Chapter 10, page 357, that Head Start programs have successfully enhanced academic skills. Might the same be done for emotional intelligence?) Psychologists know a great deal about both intelligence and emotion, but there is not yet enough research evidence to support this new idea, despite its intuitive appeal. For now, until solid, systematic research is done, it remains an interesting working hypothesis, a good idea that deserves investigation. It will very likely be tested in longitudinal studies over the next decade or two.

not show novelty or the use of nontrivial abilities. Similarly, turning on a light switch is adaptive and automatic but does not demonstrate the other dimensions of intelligence. Few behaviors involve all three dimensions, so Sternberg asserts that various tasks measure intelligence to a different extent.

Ideas like Sternberg's about the multiplicity of intelligence are brought to an even more complex level when emotions enter the equation, as is shown in *Applications*.

FOCUS

Review

- Identify the key qualities of a definition of intelligence. p. 267
- On what fundamental grounds do Wechsler and Sternberg criticize intelligence tests? pp. 268, 270

Think Critically

- What evidence might Sternberg use to argue that existing IQ tests measure some people's behavior only some of the time?

Future Tests. From Sternberg's point of view, new batteries of tests are needed to analyze fully the three basic dimensions of intelligent behavior. Good predictors of a person's academic achievement must look at the person's knowledge of the world—practical intelligence or common sense—in addition to the person's verbal comprehension and mathematical reasoning (Sternberg et al., 1995). Too often, children do poorly in school and society despite having obvious intellectual skills. They often do not know how to allocate their time or how to work effectively with other people.

These skills need to be taught, because some students do not develop them on their own. As Ceci (1991) asserts, schools foster the learning of specific skills, not necessarily general problem-solving abilities. In addition, schools often foster specific ways of thinking about problems, but researchers and tests need to value alternative modes of thought and creativity. Sternberg and Howard Gardner have teamed up on a research project to develop a curriculum to help students develop such practical intelligence by learning to think without boundaries (brainstorm), break down mind-sets (free themselves from functional fixedness), and see novel solutions in the world (exercise creativity).

Principles of Test Development

You probably have taken one or more intelligence tests during your school years. Whether or not you were aware of them, the results of these tests—often rendered in precise numbers—may have determined your educational track from elementary school onward. But psychologists are among the first to admit that intelligence tests have shortcomings, and researchers continue to revise these tests to correct the inadequacies.

Intelligence tests have had a long history. In the late 19th and early 20th centuries, Alfred Binet (1857–1911), a Frenchman, became interested in psychology and began to study behavior. He later employed Theodore Simon (1873–1961), a 26-year-old physician; their friendship and collaboration became famous. Binet and Simon are best known as the founders of the psychological testing movement. Interestingly, however, their first intelligence tests weren't developed for the general population. In 1904, Binet was commissioned to identify procedures for educating children in Paris who suffered from mental retardation. Binet was chosen for the task because he had been lobbying for action to help the schools. (Only recently had schools been made public, and retarded children were doing poorly and dropping out.) In 1905, Binet and Simon set a goal to separate normal children from children with mental retardation. As Stagner (1988) suggests, this may have been the first government-sponsored psychological research. Binet and Simon were concerned only with measuring general intelligence in children, not with why some children were retarded in intellectual development or what their future might be.

Alfred Binet, shown here, collaborated with Theodore Simon on what may have been the first government-sponsored psychological research—working on methods of measuring children's intelligence.

Binet coined the phrase *mental age*, meaning the age level at which a child is functioning cognitively, regardless of chronological age. Binet and Simon developed everyday tasks, such as counting, naming, and using objects, to determine mental age. The scale they developed is often considered the first useful and practical test of intelligence. Ninety years later, psychologists are still following some of their recommendations about how tests should be constructed and administered. In fact, one of the most influential intelligence tests in use today—the Stanford–Binet test—is a direct descendant of Binet's and Simon's early tests.

Developing a Test

Imagine that you are a 7-year-old child taking an intelligence test, and you come to the following question: "Which one of the following tells you the temperature?" Below the question are pictures of the sun, a radio, a thermometer, and a pair of mittens. Is the thermometer the only correct answer? Suppose there are no thermometers in your home, but you often hear the temperature given on radio weather reports. Or imagine that you "test" the temperature each morning by standing outside to feel the sun's strength, or that you know it's cold outside when your parents tell you to wear mittens. According to your experiences, any one of the answers to the question might be an appropriately intelligent response.

What Does a Test Measure? Your predisposition to respond to this hypothetical test question based on your experience—your cultural biases—illustrates the complexity of intelligence test development. In general, a *test* is a standardized device for examining a person's responses to specific stimuli, usually questions or problems. Because there are many potential pitfalls in creating a test, psychologists follow an elaborate set of guidelines and procedures to make certain that their questions are properly constructed. First, a psychologist must decide what the test is to measure. For example, will it measure musical ability or knowledge of geography, mathematics, or psychology? Second, the psychologist needs to construct and evaluate items for the test that will give examiners a reasonable expectation that success on the test will mean something. Third, the test must be standardized.

Standardization. **Standardization** is the process of developing uniform procedures for administering and scoring a test and for establishing norms. **Norms** are the scores and corresponding percentile ranks (see page 275) of a large and representative sample of individuals from the population for which the test was designed. A **representative sample** is a sample of individuals who match the population with whom they are to be compared with regard to key variables such as socioeconomic status and age. Thus, a test designed for all American college freshmen might be given to 2,000 freshmen, including an equal number of males and females, 16 to 20 years old, who were graduated from large and small high schools, from different areas of the United States, and representing different ethnic groups and socioeconomic levels.

Standardization ensures that there is a basis for comparing future test results with those of a standard reference group. After a test is designed and administered to a representative sample, the test developers examine the results to establish norm scores for different segments of the test population. Knowing how people in the representative sample have done allows psychologists and educators to interpret future test results properly. In other words, the scores of those in the representative sample serve as a reference point for comparing individual scores.

Normal Curve. Test developers generally plot the scores of the representative sample on a graph that shows how frequently each score occurs. On most tests some people score very well, some score very poorly, and most score in the middle. When test scores are distributed in that way, psychologists say they are *normally distributed*, or fall on a normal curve. A **normal curve** is a bell-shaped graphic representation of data arranged to show what percentage of the population falls under each part of the curve. As Figure 8.3 shows, most people fall in the middle range, with a few at each extreme. Tests are often devised so that comparisons can be made of individual scores against a normal distribution. (The Appendix discusses the normal distribution in detail.)

Standardization: The process of developing uniform procedures for administering and scoring a test and for establishing norms.

Norms: The scores and corresponding percentile ranks of a large and representative sample of individuals from the population for which a test was designed.

Representative sample: A sample of individuals who match the population with whom they are to be compared with regard to key variables such as socioeconomic status and age.

Normal curve: A bell-shaped graphic representation of data arranged to show what percentage of the population falls under each part of the curve.

FIGURE 8.3

A Normal Distribution

The bell-shaped curve shows a standard normal distribution. As in normal distributions of height, weight, and even intelligence, very few people are represented at the extremes.

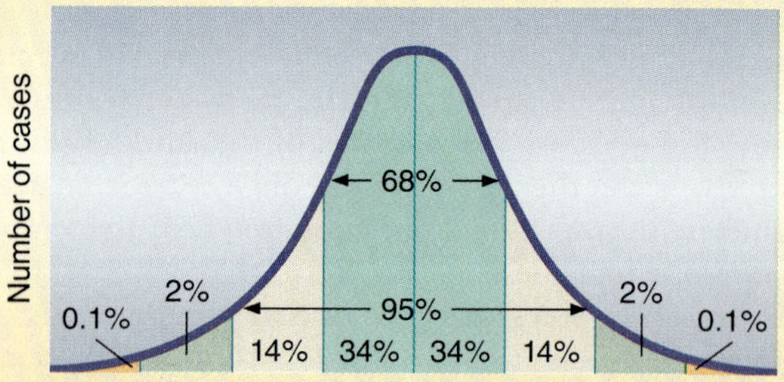

Scores. The simplest score on a test is the **raw score**—the number of correct answers unconverted or transformed in any way. The raw score, however, is seldom a true indicator of a person's ability. For many tests, particularly intelligence tests, raw scores need to be adjusted to take into account a person's age, gender, and grade level. Such scores are commonly expressed in terms of a **standard score**—a score that expresses an individual's position relative to those of others and based on the mean and how scores are distributed around it. If, for example, a 100-item intelligence test is administered to students in the 3rd and 11th grades, test developers expect those in the 11th grade to answer more items correctly than those in the 3rd grade. To adjust for the differences, scoring procedures provide for each student's score to be compared to the score typically achieved by other students at the same grade level. Thus, if 11th-graders typically answer 70 questions correctly, an 11th-grader who answers 90 questions correctly will have done better than most other students at that grade level. Similarly, if 3rd-graders usually answer 25 questions correctly, a 3rd-grader who answers 15 questions correctly will have done worse than most other students in that grade. A standard score is generally a **percentile score**—a score indicating what percentage of the test population obtained a lower score. If, for example, someone's percentile score is 84, then 84 percent of the people taking the test obtained a lower score than that person did.

Intelligence Quotients. Perhaps the oldest and most widely recognized test is the intelligence test. Binet's test clearly qualifies as an intelligence test—even though it was a relatively crude one. In the early part of this century, intelligence was measured by a simple formula. To obtain an intelligence quotient (IQ), a psychologist divided a person's mental abilities, or mental age, by the person's chronological age and multiplied the result by 100. (See Table 8.2 for examples.) Mental ages of children were calculated from the number of correct answers on a series of test items; the higher the number, the higher the mental age.

A problem with the traditional formula—mental age divided by chronological age times 100—is that an intelligence test shows different variability at each age. Young children are far more variable in their answers than are older children or adults; it is as if their intelligence were less stable, less repeatable, and more subject to change. This variability makes predictions and comparisons difficult. To simplify measures of IQ, psychologists and testers began using **deviation IQ**—a standard IQ test score for which the mean and standard deviation remain constant at all ages. (The standard deviation is a measure of variability of scores—see the Appendix.) According to deviation IQs, a child of 9 and an adolescent of 16, each with an IQ of 116, have the same position relative to others who have taken the same IQ test.

TABLE 8.2 ***How to Calculate an Intelligence Quotient***

In the traditional IQ calculation, a person's mental age is divided by his or her chronological age, and the result is multiplied by 100. Three IQs are calculated here.

	Person 1	Person 2	Person 3
Mental Age (MA)	6 years	15 years	15 years
Chronological Age (CA)	6 years	18 years	12 years
MA ÷ CA	6 ÷ 6 = 1	15 ÷ 18 = 0.83	15 ÷ 12 = 1.25
(MA ÷ CA) x 100	1 × 100 = 100	0.83 × 100 = 83	1.25 × 100 = 125
IQ	100	83	125

Raw score: An examinee's test score that has not been transformed or converted in any way.

Standard score: A score that expresses an individual's position relative to the mean, based on the standard deviation.

Percentile score: A score indicating what percentage of the test population would obtain a lower score.

Deviation IQ: A standard IQ test score for which the mean and standard deviation remain constant at all ages.

Both are above the 84th percentile; that is, both scored better than 84 percent of all others their age who took the same IQ test.

Of all the achievements by psychologists in making tests useful, perhaps the most important is ensuring that tests are both reliable and valid. If a student obtains different scores on two versions (or forms) of the same test, which score is correct? Furthermore, does the test measure what it is supposed to measure and only that?

Reliability

Reliability refers to the consistency of test scores. **Reliability** is a test's ability to yield the same score for the same individual through repeated testings. (When a researcher says that test scores have consistency, the researcher is assuming that the person taking the test is in the same emotional and physiological state each time the test is administered.) If a test's results are not consistent over several testing sessions or for two comparable groups of people, useful comparisons are impossible.

Fig. 7.11

There are several ways to determine whether a test is reliable. The simplest, termed *test–retest*, is to administer the same test to the same person on two or more occasions. If, for example, the person achieves a score of 87 one day and 110 another, the test is probably not reliable (see Table 8.3). Of course, the person might have remembered some of the test items from one occasion to the next. To avoid that problem, testers use the *alternative-form method*, which involves giving two different versions of the same test. If the two versions test the same characteristic, differing only in the test items used, both should yield the same result. Another way to test reliability is to use the *split-half method*, which involves dividing a test into two parts; on a reliable test, the scores from the two halves yield similar, if not identical, results.

Even the most reliable test will not yield identical results each time it is taken; however, a good test will have a relatively small standard error of measurement. The *standard error of measurement* is the number of points by which a score varies because of imperfect reliability. Consider an IQ test that has a standard error of measurement of 3, for example. If someone scores 115 on that test, the test developer can state with a high degree of confidence that the individual's real score is between 112 and 118—3 points above or below the obtained score.

Validity

If a psychology exam included questions such as "What is the square root of 647?" and "Who wrote *The Grapes of Wrath*?" it would not be a valid measure of your knowledge of psychology. That is, it would not be measuring what it is supposed to measure. To be useful, a test must have not only reliability, but also **validity**—the

TABLE 8.3 *Test–Retest Reliability*

In *test–retest reliability,* when people are given the same or a similar test on repeated occasions, their scores remain similar.

	High-Reliability Test		Low-Reliabilty Test	
	First Testing	Second Testing	First Testing	Second Testing
Person 1	92	90	92	74
Person 2	87	89	87	96
Person 3	78	77	78	51

Reliability: A test's ability to yield the same score for the same individual through repeated testings.

Validity: The ability of a test to measure what it is supposed to measure and to predict what it is supposed to predict.

ability to measure only what it is supposed to measure and to predict only what it is supposed to predict.

Types of Validity. *Content validity* is a test's ability to measure the knowledge or behavior it is intended to measure. A test designed to measure musical aptitude should not include items that assess mechanical aptitude or personality characteristics. Similarly, an intelligence test should measure only intelligence, not musical training, cultural experiences, or socioeconomic status.

In addition to content validity, a test should have *predictive validity*—the ability to predict a person's future achievements with at least some degree of accuracy. Critics of intelligence tests like to point out, however, that test scores are not always accurate predictors of people's performance. Tests cannot take into account high levels of motivation or creative abilities. Nevertheless, many colleges use the Scholastic Aptitude Test (SAT) scores of high school students to decide which ones should be accepted for admission—thus assuming that the scores accurately predict ability to do college-level work.

Two additional types of validity are *face validity*, the extent to which a person can judge a test's appropriateness by reading or examining the test items, and *construct validity*, the extent to which a test actually measures a particular trait such as intelligence, anxiety, or musical ability.

A Critique of Intelligence Test Validity. There are five basic criticisms of—and defenses for—the validity of intelligence tests and testing. The first is that there is no way to measure intelligence because no clear, agreed-upon definition of intelligence exists. The defense against this argument is that, although different IQ tests seem to measure different abilities, the major tests have face validity. Face validity is the appropriateness of test items "on their face"—that is, their appropriateness to someone examining the items. Intelligence tests generally contain items requiring problem solving and rational thinking, which in white middle-class society are appropriate tests of intelligence.

The second criticism is that because IQ test items usually consist of *learned information*, they reflect the quality of a child's schooling rather than the child's actual intelligence. The response to this challenge is that most vocabulary items on IQ tests are learned in the general environment, not in school; moreover, the ability to learn vocabulary terms and facts seems to depend on the general ability to reason verbally.

The third criticism is that *school settings* may adversely affect IQ and other test scores, not only because tests are often administered inexpertly but also because of the halo effect (e.g., Crowl & MacGinitie, 1974). The **halo effect** is the tendency for one particular or outstanding characteristic about an individual (or a group) to influence the evaluation of other characteristics. A test administrator can develop a positive or negative feeling about a person, a class, or a group of students that may influence the administration of tests or the interpretation of test scores (Nathan & Tippins, 1990). People who defend testing against this charge acknowledge that incorrectly administered tests are likely to result in inaccurate test scores, but they claim that this effect is less powerful than opponents think it is.

The two other criticisms of testing are less directly related to the issue of validity. One claim is that some people are *testwise*. These individuals make better use of their time than others do, guess the tester's intentions, and find clues in the test. Practice in taking tests improves these people's performance. The usual responses are that the items on IQ tests are unfamiliar even to experienced test takers and that the effects of previous practice are seldom or never evident on IQ tests. The final criticism is that individuals' scores often depend on their *motivation to succeed* rather than on actual intelligence. Claude Steele has recently argued that whenever members of minority groups concentrate explicitly on a scholastic task, they worry about the risk of confirming their group's negative stereotype to themselves and others who know the stereotype (Steele & Aronson, 1995). This extra burden may drag down

Halo effect: The tendency for one of an individual's characteristics to influence the evaluation of other characteristics.

FOCUS

Review

- Why is the normal curve an essential part of the process of standardization? p. 274
- What is the fundamental assumption that underlies the use of a representative sample? p. 274

Think Critically

- Which of the basic criticisms of and defenses for the validity of intelligence tests and testing have empirical research support?
- Why might a psychologist not want parents to know their child's IQ score?

their performance, through what Steele calls *stereotype vulnerability*. Stereotype vulnerability probably occurs in part because of subtle instructional differences and in part because of situational pressure in which the test-taking task threatens self-esteem; unless minorities are resilient to such threats, their performance is likely to suffer (Steele, Spencer, & Lynch, 1993). Defenders of IQ tests agree that examinees' motivation and attitudes toward tests are important; however, they deny that the fact of the IQ tests themselves may influence motivation.

Critics of IQ tests are concerned about the interpretation of scores. It is important to remember that intelligence tests are generally made up of different subtests or subscales, each yielding a score. There may also be one general score for the entire test. All these scores require knowledgeable interpretation; that is, test scores must be given a context that is meaningful to the person who receives the information. Without such a context, a score is little more than a number. The interpretation of test scores is the key to understanding IQs; without such interpretation, a single IQ score can be biased, inaccurate, or misleading.

Three Important Intelligence Tests

What is the best intelligence test? What does it measure? Can you study for an intelligence test to get a higher score? As in other areas of science, theory leads to application; many intelligence theorists applied their theoretical knowledge to the development of IQ tests. The three tests we will examine here are all based on the theories of their developers; they are the Stanford–Binet Intelligence Scale, the Wechsler scales, and the Kaufman Assessment Battery for Children.

Stanford–Binet Intelligence Scale

Most people associate the beginning of intelligence testing with Alfred Binet and Theodore Simon. As noted earlier, Binet collaborated with Simon to develop the Binet–Simon Scale in 1905. The original test was actually 30 short tests arranged in order of difficulty and consisting of such tasks as distinguishing food from nonfood and pointing to objects and naming them. The Binet–Simon Scale was heavily biased toward verbal questions and was not well standardized.

From 1912 to 1916, Lewis M. Terman revised the scale and developed an intelligence test now known as the Stanford–Binet Intelligence Scale. (*Stanford* refers to Stanford University, where the test was further developed.) In the Stanford–Binet, a child's mental age (intellectual ability) is divided by chronological age and multiplied by 100 to yield an intelligence quotient (IQ). Decades of psychologists have used the original and revised versions of the Stanford–Binet scale. This test has traditionally been a good predictor of academic performance, and many of its simplest subtests correlate highly with one another.

A new version of the Stanford–Binet Intelligence Scale, published in 1986, contains items that minimize gender and racial characteristics. It is composed of four major subscales and tests individuals aged 2 through 23, yielding one overall IQ

FIGURE 8.4

The Modern Stanford–Binet Intelligence Scale

The most recent version of the Stanford–Binet Intelligence scale measures intelligence with a composite score made up of four scores on broad types of mental activity: verbal reasoning, quantitative reasoning, abstract visual reasoning, and short-term memory. Each of the scores is obtained through a series of subtests that measure specific mental abilities.

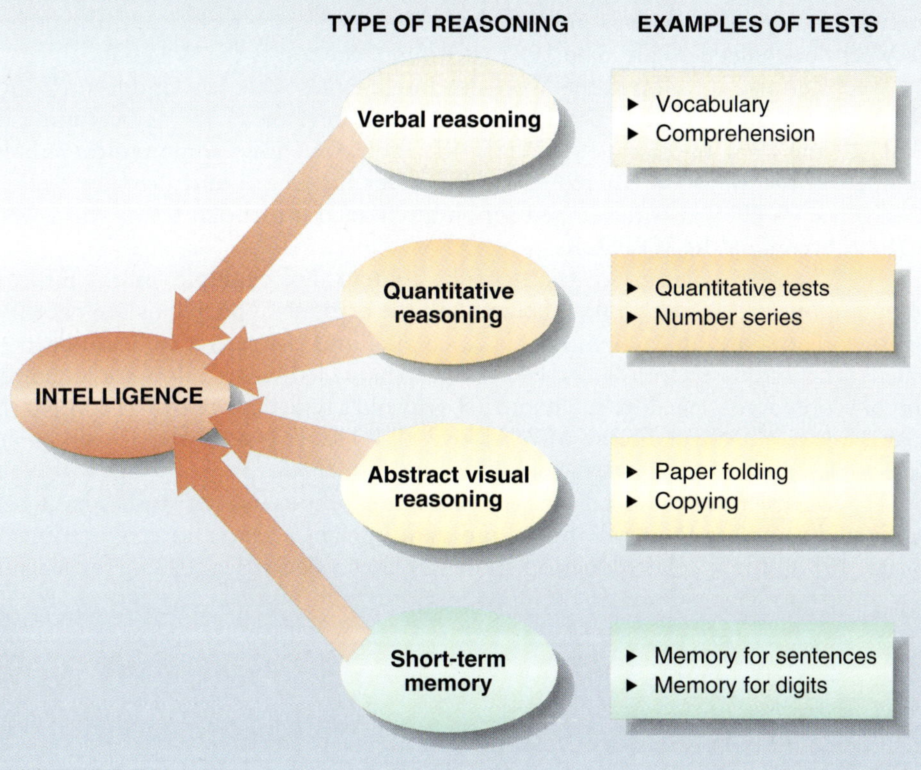

score. The test administration time varies with the examinee's age, because the number of subtests given is determined by age. All examinees are first given a vocabulary test; along with their age, this test determines the level at which all other tests begin. There are 15 possible subtests, which vary greatly in content. Some require verbal reasoning, others quantitative reasoning, and still others abstract visual reasoning. In addition, there are tests of short-term memory. Each of the subtests consists of a series of levels, with two items at each level. The test begins with test items for each subscale at the entry level and continues until a higher level on each subscale is established (until a prescribed number of items are failed). (See Figure 8.4 for a description of the new Stanford–Binet Intelligence Scale.)

Raw scores, determined by the number of items passed, are converted to a standard score for each age group. The new Stanford–Binet scale is a potent test; one of its great strengths is that it can be used over a wide range of ages and abilities. Nonetheless, like all tests, it has limitations. One of these limitations is that examinees are not given the same battery of subtests at different ages; this makes comparisons with other individuals of the same age difficult (Sattler, 1992). However, the new Stanford–Binet scale correlates well with the old one, as well as with the Wechsler scales and the Kaufman Assessment Battery for Children (both of which are examined next).

Wechsler Scales

David Wechsler (1896–1981), a Rumanian immigrant who earned a PhD in psychology from Columbia University, was influenced by Charles Spearman and Karl Pearson, two English statisticians with whom he studied. In 1932, Wechsler was appointed chief psychologist at Bellevue Hospital in New York City; there, he began making history. In the 1930s, Wechsler recognized that the Stanford–Binet Intelligence Scale was inadequate for testing the IQs of adults. He also maintained that some of the Stanford–Binet items lacked validity. In 1939, Wechsler developed the Wechsler–Bellevue Intelligence Scale to test adults. In 1955, the Wechsler Adult Intelligence Scale (WAIS) was published; it eliminated some technical difficulties of the Wechsler–Bellevue scale. The 1981 revision of the test is the WAIS–R.

Wechsler also developed the Wechsler Intelligence Scale for Children (WISC), which covers children aged 6 through 16. It was revised in 1974, becoming the WISC–R; the 1991 revision is the WISC–III. Table 8.4 shows some typical subtests included in the WISC–R. In 1967, the Wechsler Preschool and Primary Scale of Intelligence (WPPSI) was developed for children aged 4 through 6½; it was revised in 1989, becoming the WPPSI–R.

The Wechsler scales group test items by content. For example, all the information questions are presented together, and all the arithmetic problems are presented together. The score on each subtest is calculated and converted to a standard (or scaled) score, adjusted for the test taker's age. The scaled scores allow for a comparison of scores across age levels. Thus, an 8-year-old's scaled score of 7 is comparable to an 11-year-old's scaled score of 7. An overall IQ score is reported as well as subscale scores.

The Wechsler scales have been well researched; thousands of studies have been conducted to assess their reliability and validity. They are valid cross-culturally (Insua, 1983), for special education students (Covin & Sattler, 1985), for learning

TABLE 8.4 *Typical Subtests of the WISC–R*

Verbal Test		PerformanceTest	
Subtest	**Type of Task**	**Subtest**	**Type of Task**
Information	When questioned, recall a general fact that has been acquired in a formal or informal school setting	Picture completion	Point out the part of an incomplete picture that is missing
Similarities	Use another concept in describing how two ideas are alike	Picture arrangement	Put a series of pictures that tell a story in the right sequence
Arithmetic	Solve a word problem without pencil and paper	Block design	Use real blocks to reproduce a picture of a block design ▶
Digit span	Recall an orally presented string of digits	Object assembly	Put the pieces of a jigsaw-type puzzle together to form a complete object
Vocabulary	Define a vocabulary word		
Comprehension	Answer a question requiring practical judgment and common sense	Coding	Given a key that matches numbers to geometric shapes, fill in a blank form with the shapes that go with the numbers

disabled students (Clarizio & Veres, 1984), and for populations of maladjusted individuals (Eppinger et al., 1987).

Kaufman Assessment Battery for Children

Many intelligence tests have been criticized for being biased in that some of their questions are geared toward the white middle-class male experience. Psychologists Alan and Nadeen Kaufman contend that their Kaufman Assessment Battery for Children (K–ABC) uses tasks that tap the experience of all people, regardless of background. A memory task in the K–ABC, for example, might ask a child to look at a picture of a face and a few moments later pick it out from among pictures of other faces.

The K–ABC was designed especially for assessment, intervention, and remediation of school problems. School psychologists, who are the primary users of the K–ABC, act as evaluators and consultants to families and schools, helping them to set and achieve appropriate educational goals. The K–ABC consists of four global scales. Three measure mental processing abilities (sequential processing, simultaneous processing, and a composite of the two); the fourth assesses achievement. The Kaufmans believe that the sequential- and simultaneous-processing scales measure abilities synonymous with intelligence—that is, the ability to process information and the ability to solve problems (Kaufman, 1983). A sequential task requires the manipulation of stimuli in sequential order. For example, a child might be asked to repeat a series of digits in the order in which the examiner presented them. A simultaneous-processing task involves organizing and integrating many stimuli at the same time. Here, a child might be asked to recall the placement of objects on a page that was presented only briefly.

The K–ABC assesses how well and in what way a child solves problems on each task, minimizing the role of language and of acquired facts and skills. A separate part of the test, the achievement scale, involves demonstrating such skills as reading comprehension, letter and word identification, and computation. These tasks resemble those typically found on other IQ tests in that they are heavily influenced by language experience and verbal ability.

Although early research on the K–ABC shows it to be a promising IQ test (German, 1983; Zins & Barnett, 1983), it is not without its critics. A. R. Jensen (1984) and Sternberg (1984) have been especially critical of the assumptions on which the K–ABC is founded, particularly the ideas about how sequential processing proceeds and whether it reflects important elements of thought. Alan Kaufman (1984) wants the K–ABC to be an alternative to the WISC–III and the Stanford–Binet scales; he argues that it is valid and reliable, and he stresses that it is still evolving. Many practitioners consider it child-oriented and easy to administer, but final evaluations of the K–ABC are still probably a decade away.

Controversies about Intelligence

In 1986, a federal court in California upheld a 1979 ruling barring the administration of IQ tests to African American students in the state. According to the judge who made the original ruling, the tests are culturally biased and therefore discriminate against African Americans being evaluated for special education; the result is a disproportionate number of African Americans being assigned to classes for the mentally retarded. The California court case illustrates the kinds of political, cultural, and scientific issues involved in the debate over what intelligence is and what intelligence tests actually measure. Minority groups have joined psychologists and educators in challenging the usefulness of testing in general and of intelligence testing in particular.

Cultural Biases?

A major argument against IQ testing is that the tests are culturally biased and thus effectively discriminate against individuals who do not come from the test makers' environments, which are usually white, male, middle-class, and suburban. A test item or subscale is considered culturally biased when, with all other factors held constant, its content is more difficult for members of one group than for those of other groups. To understand how a test can be culturally biased, imagine that the child of an impoverished migrant worker is given the temperature problem posed earlier. If the child is unfamiliar with thermometers and radios, the child might choose the sun as the best answer. On the basis of experiments that have shown some tests to be culturally biased, some educators and parents have urged a ban on tests in all public schools, especially IQ tests. They argue that some groups of individuals who are not exposed to the same education and experiences as the middle-class group for whom the tests were designed are bound to perform less well.

Clearly, those who interpret IQ tests must be particularly sensitive to any potential biases. Nonetheless, although researchers find differences among the IQ scores of various racial and cultural groups, they find no consistent and conclusive evidence of bias in the tests themselves. Differences between siblings are usually as great as differences between racial groups; there is as great a variability between individuals as between groups. That IQ tests systematically discriminate in terms of race or ethnicity is not true. Biases can exist, but well-respected psychologists (Sattler, 1992; Vernon, 1979) support the view that they do not exist in such tests as the WISC–R. A key to any bias that exists on an IQ test is how the results are used (a point to be examined shortly). When cultural differences occur, they can be eliminated by better test construction, but this still does not explain the meaning of those differences (Helms, 1992).

IQ tests cannot predict or explain all types of intellectual behavior. They are derived from a small sample of a restricted range of cognitive activities. Intelligence can be demonstrated in many ways; an IQ test tells little about someone's ability to be flexible in new situations or to function in mature and responsible ways. Intelligence tests do reflect many aspects of people's environments—how much individuals are encouraged to express themselves verbally, how much time they spend reading, and the extent to which parents have urged them to engage in academic pursuits (e.g., Barrett & Depinet, 1991).

Since the early 1970s, the public, educators, and psychologists have scrutinized the weaknesses of IQ tests and have attempted to eliminate cultural bias in testing by creating better tests and establishing better norms for comparison. The tests have attempted to control the influences of different cultural backgrounds (Helms, 1992). However, even the courts acknowledge the complexity of the issues involved in tests and testing (Elliott, 1987). In isolation, IQ scores mean little. Information about an individual's home environment, personality, socioeconomic status, and special abilities is crucial to understanding intellectual functioning. (*Diversity,* on page 284 and 285, further examines cultural differences in testing.)

Nature or Nurture?

Psychologists have long recognized that both the genetic heritage established before birth (nature) and people's life experiences (nurture) play an important role in intelligence. Researchers have often used child-rearing studies to help unravel the key variables. In a classic environmental study, a researcher administered IQ tests to children reared in different communities in the Blue Ridge Mountains, an isolated area 100 miles west of Washington, D.C. (Sherman & Key, 1932). Most of the adults in each community were illiterate, and communication with the outside world was limited. The investigators concluded that lack of language training and school experience accounted for the children's poor scores on standardized tests, particularly on tests involving calculations and problem solving. Moreover, because the IQ scores of the children were highest in communities with the best social development and lowest in communities with the poorest social development, the researchers concluded that the children's IQs developed only as their environment demanded development. Angoff (1988) has asserted that children from impoverished homes can achieve more on IQ tests, the SAT, and other standardized tests if "cognitive training begins early in life and continues for an extended period . . . and is carried out in a continuously supportive and motivating atmosphere" (p. 719).

However, it is important to remember that tests can be constructed with a bias toward urban or rural children. Myra Shimberg (1929) standardized two tests on urban and rural schoolchildren in New York State. Each test contained 25 questions. The examples in Table 8.5 show clearly that they test for different kinds of information. Shimberg found that rural children scored significantly lower than urban children on Test A but higher than urban children on Test B. The difference between the scores of the two groups was in part a function of the tests themselves, not of any real difference in the children's intellectual capacities. Test A was biased toward urban children, Test B toward rural children.

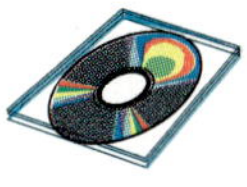

Fig. 7.12

Few would debate the idea that the environment has a potent effect on intellectual tasks. But efforts to unravel the fixed genetic component from the environmental impact have required some sophisticated research and statistical techniques. Such unraveling has often taken place in studies of adopted children, who are raised apart from their biological parents. Researchers examine intelligence test scores and other measures of cognitive ability so as to compare an adopted person's score with those of biological parents, adoptive parents, biological siblings, and adoptive siblings. The goal is to see if scores later in life more greatly resemble those of biological relatives or adoptive relatives. A French adoption study showed a 14-point increase in IQ scores in children from impoverished homes after they were adopted into families in a higher socioeconomic class (Schiff et al., 1982). This study demonstrated that the environment has a strong effect on intellectual abilities. Other data from adoptive homes, however, strongly suggest that the biological mother's IQ score has a more important effect than the adoptive home environment on a child's IQ score (Bouchard et al., 1990; Loehlin, Horn, & Willerman, 1994).

One type of adoptive study compares the intellectual abilities of adopted identical twins who were separated at birth; because the twins share the same genetic heritage, any differences in IQ scores *must* be the result of environmental influences. Figure 8.5, on page 286, summarizes the correlations between IQ scores and child-

TABLE 8.5 ***Tests Can Be Constructed to Have a Bias***

Test A	Test B
1. What are the colors in the American flag?	1. Of what is butter made?
2. Who is the President of the United States?	2. Name a vegetable that grows above ground.
3. What is the largest river in the United States?	3. Why does seasoned wood burn more easily than green wood?
4. How can banks afford to pay interest on the money you deposit?	4. About how often do we have a full moon?
5. What is the freezing point of water?	5. Who was President of the United States during the World War?
6. What is a referendum in government?	6. How can you locate the pole star?

DIVERSITY

Cultural Differences Are Small and Narrowing

Cultural differences, particularly between African Americans and whites, in IQ scores, SAT scores, and other measures of achievement or ability are narrowing. This may be due to a generation of desegregation, more equal opportunities under the law, federal intervention programs for the culturally disadvantaged, socioeconomic factors that affect home environments, or other factors (Jones, 1984). Jones suggests that the more minority-group students enroll in mathematics courses in high school, the better they will do on achievement tests. Consistent with this reasoning is a cross-cultural study comparing Mexican Americans with Caucasian Americans; it showed that with acculturation to U.S. society, the Mexican Americans achieved IQ scores comparable to those of the Caucasian Americans (Gonzales & Roll, 1985). Furthemore, differences within groups are often greater than differences between groups, a fact that minimizes the importance of between-group differences (Zuckerman, 1990).

The relative importance of three factors in creating differences between groups has yet to be established. As a case in point, consider African Americans, who—as a group—do less well on average on intelligence tests than do whites. The first factor being debated is the possibility of a genetic component. The second is that African Americans are disproportionately represented among those who live in culturally impoverished areas. The third is that IQ tests may contain a built-in vocabulary bias against African Americans. Perhaps more important than any of these three factors, however, is the fact that the differences among individuals within a particular racial or ethnic group are greater than the differences among different groups.

People from different backgrounds and cultures differ—there is no doubt about that. A cross-cultural study of 320 Israeli children whose parents had emigrated from Europe, Iraq, North Africa, or Yemen showed that the four groups tended to exhibit four different patterns of cognitive abilities (Burg & Belmont, 1990). Differing patterns of cognitive ability are not surprising; cultures vary considerably in their worldview and in their conception of time, space, people, and what is important. Thus, historical and cultural background has a significant effect on people's patterns of mental ability. When Flynn (1987) showed that IQ scores are changing around the world, he concluded that schooling, educational emphasis, and family values in various cultures were affecting the test scores—not that people in certain cultures were getting smarter. Schooling clearly fosters the cognitive processes that contribute to high IQ scores (Ceci, 1991).

One conclusion is becoming strikingly clear: *Rather than measuring innate intellectual capacity, IQ tests measure the degree to which people adapt to the culture in which they live.* In many cultures, to be intelligent is to be socially adept. In Western society, because social aptitude is linked with schooling, the more schooling you have, the higher your IQ score is likely to be (Ceci, 1991). All individuals have special capabilities (both intellectual and other), and how those capabilities are regarded depends on the social environment. Being a genius in traditional African cultures may include being a good storyteller; in the United States, it may mean being astute and aggressive (Eysenck, 1995). In the United States, however, the concept of giftedness is too often attached to high academic achievement alone. Concern about the implications of this limited conception of intelligence

rearing environments for both related and unrelated children in different studies. If genetics were the sole determinant of IQ scores, the correlation for identical twins should be 1.0 whether they are reared together or apart. Also, the correlation should not decrease when any two siblings (twins or not) are brought up apart from each other. However, identical twins raised together and those raised apart do not have identical IQ scores—although their scores are similar (Bouchard et al., 1990). Bouchard and colleagues conclude that about half of the similarities between identical twins can be accounted for by genetics—not the 70 to 80 percent that some researchers claim. This finding lends strong support to the idea that the environ-

is one reason why educators in some settings are placing less emphasis on IQ scores.

Researchers today assert that the typical intelligence test is too limited because it does not take into consideration the many forms of intelligent behavior that occur outside the testing room, within this diverse culture (Frederiksen, 1986; Sternberg & Wagner, 1993). Frederiksen suggests that real-life problem situations might be used to supplement the usual psychological tests. This view is consistent with Sternberg's (1986a) idea that intelligence must be evaluated on many levels, including the environment in which a person lives and works. If this type of evaluation were to take place, IQ scores could become better at predicting both academic and occupational success (Barrett & Depinet, 1991). Yet, in spite of all the limitations of IQ scores, research continues to show that they are still the best overall predictor of school and job performance (Ree & Earles, 1992, 1993).

Critics of standardized testing have been vocal and persuasive, and their arguments cannot be discounted. Research on test construction, test validation, and the causes of differences among individuals' scores continues. But overall, experts believe that standardized intelligence tests, despite their flaws, adequately measure the most important elements of intelligence (Snyderman & Rothman, 1987). The components of such tests, including their subscales and specific questions, not only help researchers evaluate their validity but also help distinguish the elements most affected by nature from those most affected by nurture. Table 8.6 summarizes some misconceptions about intelligence tests and testing.

TABLE 8.6 *Some Misconceptions about Intelligence Tests and Testing*

Misconception	Reality
Intelligence tests measure innate intelligence.	IQ scores measure some of an individual's interactions with the envronment; they never measure only innate intelligence.
IQs never change.	People's IQs change throughout life, but especially from birth through age 6. Even after this age, significant changes can occur.
Intelligence tests provide perfectly reliable scores.	Test scores are only estimates. Every test score should be reported as a statement of probability, such as: There is a 90 percent chance that the child's IQ falls within a 6-point range of the reported score (from 3 points above to 3 points below).
Intelligence tests measure all aspects of a person's intelligence.	Most intelligence tests do not measure the entire spectrum of abilities related to intellectual behavior. Some stress verbal and nonverbal intelligence but do not adequately measure other areas, such as mechanical skills, creativity, or social intelligence.
A battery of tests can tell us everything we need to know in making judgments about a person's competence.	No battery of tests can give a complete picture of any person. A battery can only illuminate various areas of functioning.

Source: Adapted from Sattler, 1992.

ment must play an equally important role in determining IQ scores (e.g., Johnson, 1991; Plomin et al., 1994). Interestingly, most of the data about IQ scores and the role of genetics come from studies of identical twins and their performance early in life; only recently have data been emerging from studies of older identical twins who have lived full lives and had a wide range of experiences (Pedersen et al., 1992). Some of these data have been explored in *The Bell Curve*, which is discussed in *The Research Process* on pages 288–289.

There are volumes of data from child-rearing studies attempting to demonstrate the genetic and environmental components of intelligence. In general, research shows

FIGURE 8.5

Correlations between IQ Scores of Persons of Varying Relationships

The closer the biological relationship of two individuals, the more similar their IQ scores—strong support for a genetic component to intelligence. (Based on data from Bouchard & McGue, 1981, and Erlenmeyer-Kimling & Jarvik, 1963.)

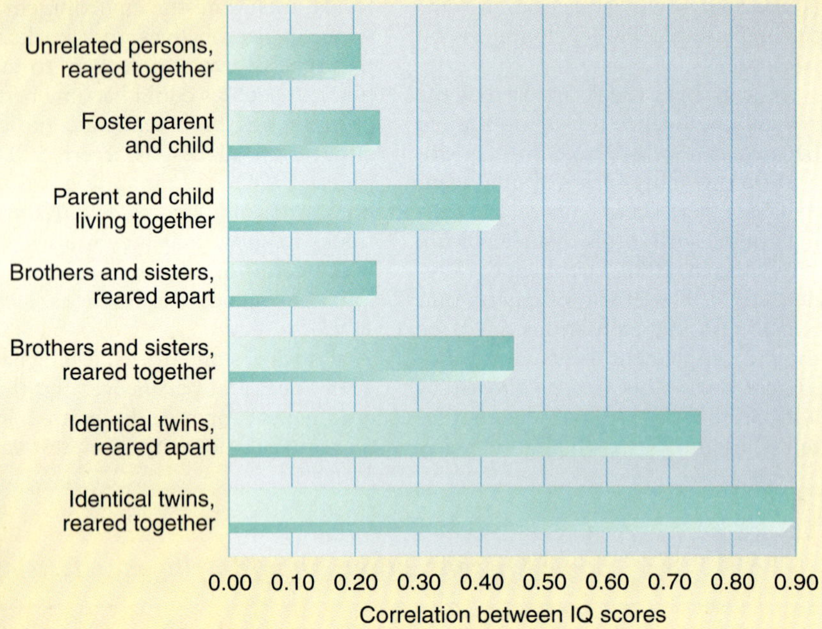

that, to a great extent, genetics and environment contribute equally to IQ scores (Pedersen et al., 1992; Pedersen, Plomin, & McClearn, 1994). However, to frame nature versus nurture as a debate with a winner and a loser is a mistake; the two work together. There is a myth that if a behavior or characteristic is genetic, it cannot be changed. But genes do not fix behavior; instead, they establish a range of possible reactions. Environments determine the extent to which the range of genetic potential will be expressed. Thus, the study of nature, nurture, and social environments together will ultimately answer key questions (Neisser et al., 1996; Plomin, 1994).

Family Structure

An inspiring English teacher, a stimulating TV series, or a friend with a chemistry set may be enough to create differences in the IQ scores of siblings (McCall, 1983). Although siblings are often very similar to one another on a number of dimensions, they are also very different (Dunn & Plomin, 1990). Few doubt that genetic influences are important; the real issue is how important the nonshared environment is (Plomin & Neiderhiser, 1991). Although siblings share a genetic heritage, they experience the same or a similar environment differently (Dunn, 1992). Since a number of variables create differences among brothers and sisters, it is very difficult to estimate the effects of such variables among racial or ethnic groups.

Belmont and Marolla (1973) found that children from large families score lower overall on intelligence tests than do those from smaller families. They suggest that the third and fourth children have a less optimal intellectual environment than does the first or second child. In a later study, Zajonc and Markus (1975) theorized that the intellectual growth of every member within a family depends on the other members. Moreover, they suggested that the overall level of intellectual performance is likely to decrease for each new member of a family. Consider what happens when two adults have a child. The intellectual climate at home becomes that of

TABLE 8.7 *The Zajonc–Markus Model of Intellectual Climate in the Home*

Year of Birth of Child	Number of Children	Value of Intellectual Climate: Formula	Value of Intellectual Climate: Average Number of Units
1976	1	$\frac{\text{Mother (30) + Father (30) + Baby (0)}}{\text{Number in family (3)}}$	= 20.0
1978	2	$\frac{\text{Mother (30) + Father (30) + First Child (2)* + Baby (0)}}{\text{Number in family (4)}}$	= 15.5
1980	3	66 ÷ 5	13.2
1982	4	72 ÷ 6	12.0
1984	5	80 ÷ 7	11.4
1986	6	90 ÷ 8	11.25
1988	7	102 ÷ 9	11.3
1990	8	116 ÷ 10	11.6
1992	9	132 ÷ 11	12.0
1994	10	150 ÷ 12	12.5

*This example assumes that for each 2 years of life, a child is credited with 2 units toward the intellectual climate in the home.

two mature adults and one child. Imagine that each adult is assigned 30 units and the child is assigned 0 units. The average level of intellectual ability in the home drops from 30 to 20. With a second child, the intellectual average decreases again to 15.5. (See Table 8.7 for calculations according to the Zajonc–Markus model.)

Because family size has decreased since the early 1970s and the spacing between children has increased, Zajonc and Markus predicted that the declining trend in SAT scores that began in the late 1960s would be reversed. In fact, SAT scores did decrease from 1973 to 1979 and then rose from 1980 to 1985. Zajonc and his colleagues (1991) claimed that the model predicts the turnaround. His predictions have been confirmed in other cultures as well (Wilson, Mundy-Castle, & Panditji, 1990).

Keep in mind that the family size model is a statistical one; Zajonc (1993) acknowledges that it will not hold true for all individuals and all size families (see also Travis & Kohli, 1995). Even when it does apply, the effects are modest; and many researchers discount its importance because other variables such as emotional climate, touching, health, and schooling are also important (e.g., Sattler, 1992; Wirth & Wolf, 1994). Furthermore, researchers point out that other important factors (Flynn, 1988; Powell & Steelman, 1990), such as increased spacing between the birth of children, can minimize the negative effects. Large families also may contribute to the growth of individual members in areas other than intelligence by nurturing social competence, moral responsibility, and ego strength.

Stability of Intelligence Test Scores

Nearly every American has taken an intelligence test at some time. Was the test you took in second grade a good predictor of your academic ability when you were a sophomore in high school? Or should you have been retested? Does an IQ score remain stable over a long period of time? Early examinations of IQ score stability showed that the IQ scores of infants did not correlate well with their IQ scores when they were school age (Bayley, 1949). Researchers quickly realized that it is not possible to measure the same capabilities in infants that can be measured in older

THE RESEARCH PROCESS

Critical Thinking about *The Bell Curve*

Publication of *The Bell Curve*, by Richard J. Herrnstein and Charles Murray, stirred up a whirlpool of debate in 1994. Among its controversial and debatable positions, the book makes the arguments that IQ is largely genetically determined, that African Americans are trapped in a low-IQ environment from which they are unlikely to emerge, and that any attempts to reverse this situation are doomed to failure. Let's take a look at what these authors claimed and see if critical thinking supports these claims.

Key Arguments. *The Bell Curve* asserts that the United States is ruled by a "cognitive elite" who are selected by IQ tests, SAT scores, and admission to prestigious upper-echelon universities. This supposed cognitive elite is said to occupy the top of the socioeconomic ladder, while the rest of society is assigned to inferior and subordinate status—and, Herrnstein and Murray claim, the situation is likely to stay that way. They write: "Mounting evidence indicates that demographic trends are exerting downward pressure on the distribution of cognitive ability in the United States, and that the pressures are strong enough to have social consequences" (p. 342). They also say that "if women with low scores are reproducing more rapidly than women with high scores, the distribution of scores will, other things equal, decline, no matter whether the woman with the low scores came by them through nature or nurture." Herrnstein and Murray suggest that, unless something is done to correct, alter, or somehow modify the present trends, the United States will be permanently split between a ruling cognitive elite and a large, growing, and powerless underclass made up primarily of low-IQ blacks, whites, Hispanics, and immigrants. Yet Herrnstein and Murray consider it futile to attempt to raise the poor, the disadvantaged, and the cognitively impaired above the limits of their own genetics. They maintain: "The story of attempts to raise intelligence is one of high hopes, flamboyant claims, and disappointing results" (p. 389).

The Bell Curve further asserts that intelligence determines who is rich, middle class, or poor—that is, that the reason the United States has a class structure is mostly determined by genetic causes. Although there is no doubt that there is substantial genetic heritability of ability to score well on intelligence tests—this is well known and acknowledged—as we saw earlier in this chapter, the differences *within* groups of people tend to be greater than the differences *between* groups of people. Any differences between blacks and whites may or may not have a genetic reason; in fact, evidence in favor of a genetic cause is far from conclusive. Thus, the implications of IQ test score differences between blacks and whites are far less meaningful or important than Herrnstein and Murray assert.

Implications. In *The Bell Curve*, Herrnstein and Murray wrote about intelligence with implications for social policy, maintaining that there are problems associated with low cognitive ability—crime and social decay—that are not likely to be solved by outside interventions. To put it bluntly, their argument is that the so-called underclass, as a group, is intellectually inferior. This argument leads them to devalue the potential benefits of affirmative action programs. This is a key point. Ultimately, Herrnstein and

children and adults. Further, correlations of the IQ scores of school-age children and adults show that such scores can change, sometimes substantially. Yet some research indicates that certain predictions from infant to school-age IQ can be made (DiLalla et al., 1990; Rose & Feldman, 1995).

What about the IQ scores of adults? Do IQ scores remain stable throughout adulthood? In general, psychologists have shown that intelligence and achievement test scores at first increase with age, then level off in adulthood, only to decline in late adulthood (Schaie, 1993). The results of a 40-year IQ study showed that, in general, the intellectual functioning of men increased a bit around age 40 and gradually declined to earlier levels when the men were in their 50s (Schwartzman et al., 1987). Despite the passage of 40 years, cognitive performance remained relatively stable. The effect of aging on IQ scores is a complicated issue, because some aspects of the scores decrease more with age than others. For example, numerical-based portions of IQ tests tend to show a more significant decrease with advancing age than do verbal-based portions (Schaie, 1993). In addition, not everyone shows age-related IQ declines; people who continue their education throughout their lives show relatively small decreases.

Ample evidence now exists to confirm that IQ scores remain relatively stable once test subjects reach adulthood. However, the scores of infants and children are so prone to change that they are not reliable predictors of later IQ scores. Of course, a child who achieves a high score on an IQ test at age 9 is likely to do well at

Murray conclude that there is no way out for the underclass; no matter how many remedial educational programs are introduced, individuals will be forever cast within a cognitive disability created by their genetics.

A completely opposite point of view is held by others (e.g., Neisser et al., 1996). For example, Jonathan Crane (1994) argues that the environment is the cause of the black–white gap in test scores; he further asserts that the environment and changes in society are the solution to closing that gap. Crane writes: "There is simply no valid evidence that the race gap in cognitive test scores is caused by genetically determined differences in intellectual capacity. In contrast, there is a good deal of evidence that supports an environmental explanation of the gap" (p. 202).

Critical Analysis. Although any debate about race, IQ, and genetics is inherently controversial, Herrnstein and Murray present data in a way that makes careful critical analysis especially difficult. For example, they omit much historical data, fail to separate the effects of nature and nurture in some early childhood data, present limited new data, and make a series of questionable claims and assumptions. Among their questionable assumptions are the following: that IQ represents a general quality; that IQ largely or solely reflects genetics; that IQ is fixed and immutable; and that a causal relationship exists between IQ and problematic social behaviors.

There have been many—geneticists, biologists, and sociobiologists—who have made the arguments put forth in *The Bell Curve.* Some have been even more extreme (Rushton, 1995). Yet most have not been psychologists, and most have not worked from psychologically relevant data. Rather, they have often taken a political, social, and even moral point of view, with the goal of affecting social policy (e.g., Itzkoff, 1994). Leading psychologists, however, recognize the fallacies, inaccuracies, and weaknesses in such approaches (Sternberg, 1995). They point out the multidimensional nature of intelligence, the modifiability of intelligence, and the fact that IQ is not the only predictor of performance on a job or in life.

Conclusions. A key point to note as students of psychology is that Herrnstein and Murray have not been good critical thinkers or scientists. *The Bell Curve* is based more on a political agenda than on current psychological research. It presents a vision of a future in which people of high and low IQs would have their respective places in society—commensurate with their IQs. But intelligent behavior is not a single thing—it is more a process than a collection of single abilities—and even though everyone cannot be a brain surgeon, there is far more to intelligence than an IQ score reflects. When true equal opportunity is offered, individuals in minority groups improve as much as individuals in other groups. While intelligence may be an important factor in getting a job or moving into a profession, it is less important once you have learned to do the job (Hunt, 1995). Preconceived biases seem to have determined Herrnstein and Murray's conclusions, especially about social policy; in addition, as mentioned before, these authors make misleading assumptions, especially about the heritability and unmodifiability of IQ. The value of *The Bell Curve* is that it raised for debate once again many useful questions about intelligence; the weakness of *The Bell Curve* is that it is not good science, let alone good social policy.

age 18—perhaps even better. The data show enough fluctuation, though, especially at younger ages, to make predictions uncertain.

Gender Differences

Many psychologists believe there are gender differences in verbal ability, with girls surpassing boys in most verbal tasks during the early school years. However, most differences have been due to the cultural expectations of parents and teachers. For example, parents and teachers have long encouraged boys to engage in spatial, mechanical tasks. Two interesting events have occurred in the United States in recent decades, though. First, many parents have been encouraging both girls and boys to acquire math, verbal, and spatial skills; that is, they have endeavored to avoid gender role stereotyping. Second, the observed cognitive differences between boys and girls have been diminishing each year.

It turns out that the old consensus about gender differences is at least exaggerated and at most simply wrong. Hyde and Linn (1988) examined 165 research studies on gender differences in verbal ability; these studies had tested a total of 1,418,899 people. Although Hyde and Linn found a gender difference in favor of females, it was so small that they claimed it is not worth mentioning. They further argued that

FOCUS

Review

- What are the chief differences between the Kaufman Assessment Battery for Children (K–ABC) and the Stanford–Binet and Wechsler scales? pp. 278–281
- If IQ tests do not examine innate ability, what do they measure? p. 285
- What is the evidence to show that cultural variables and gender affect test scores? pp. 284–285, 289–290

Think Critically

- What conclusions about nature versus nurture can be drawn when correlations between IQ scores and child-rearing environments for both related and unrelated children are examined?
- If you had to design a series of selection procedures for a high school, a college, or a program for gifted students, what procedures would you choose?

more refined tests and theories of intelligence are needed to examine any gender differences that may exist. The differences found today exist only in certain special populations; for example, among the very brightest mathematics students, boys continue to outscore girls, although the boys' scores are quite variable (Hedges & Nowell, 1995; Kimball, 1989). Boys are motivated to achieve more and strive harder at math, in part because more of them have career aspirations that involve mathematical skills. As a consequence of these aspirations, boys tend to take additional and more advanced math courses—this puts them still further ahead on standardized tests. But these aspirations have a basis in cultural expectations (Jacklin, 1989). In general, it is fair to say that differences between the test scores of males and those of females are disappearing and that this change has been occurring in many cultures (Lummis & Stevenson, 1990; Skaalvik & Raukin, 1994).

An outcome of Hyde and Linn's findings is the realization that since verbal ability tests provide gender-unbiased measures of cognitive ability, they should be used to select students for academic programs. Selection procedures are especially important for academic programs for special students, such as the gifted.

Giftedness and Mental Retardation

American society is oriented toward looking for, testing, and educating special or exceptional children. As early as the first weeks of the first grade, most children take some kind of reading readiness test; by the end of the fourth grade, students are usually classified and labeled as to their projected future development, again largely on the basis of tests. Educators often use the term *exceptional* to refer to people who are gifted as well as to those who suffer from learning disabilities, physical impairments, and mental retardation.

Giftedness

Gifted individuals represent one end of the continuum of intelligence and talent. Exceptional ability is not limited to cognitive skills, however. Most 6-year-olds enrolled in a ballet class will probably show average ability, but ballet teachers report that an occasional child shows a natural ability for dance. In the same way, many children and adults learn to play the piano, but only a few excel. And over a wide range of behaviors, some people excel in a particular area but are only average in other areas.

The phenomenon of gifted children has been recognized and discussed for centuries. Some gifted children, like Mozart, display their genius musically. Others display it in science; many great scientists made their most important theoretical discoveries very early in their careers. Although there is no universally accepted definition of *giftedness* (just as there is no universally agreed-upon definition of *intelli-*

gence), one was given in section 902 of the federal government's Gifted and Talented Children's Act of 1978:

> The term *gifted and talented* means children and, whenever applicable, youth who are identified at the preschool, elementary, or secondary level as possessing demonstrated or potential abilities that give evidence of high performance responsibility in areas such as intellectual, creative, specific academic or leadership ability, or in the performing or visual arts and who by reason thereof require services or activities not ordinarily provided by the school.

Thus, gifted children may have superior cognitive, leadership, or performing arts abilities. Moreover, they require special schooling that goes beyond the ordinary classroom. Without it, these children may not realize their potential. Even though the federal government acknowledges the need for special education for gifted individuals, states and communities must fund most (about 92 percent) of the cost of their education. Some states—including California, Pennsylvania, and Illinois—spend more per year on educating gifted and talented students than the federal government does. Nearly every state has a special program for the gifted; however, some school systems have none, and others allocate special instruction only in brief periods or to small groups. Some systems provide special schools for children with superior cognitive abilities, performing talents, or science aptitude. Most do not offer gifted programs for all grades (Reis, 1989). However, the special needs of gifted students (and of those with mental retardation—considered next) should not be addressed only 1 day a week or only in grades 1 through 6.

Mental Retardation

The term *mental retardation* covers a wide range of behaviors, from slow learning to severe mental and physical impairment. Many people with mental retardation are able to cope well. Most learn to walk and to feed and dress themselves; many learn to read and are able to work. In 1992, the American Association on Mental Retardation adopted a new formal definition of mental retardation:

> **Mental retardation** refers to substantial limitations in present functioning. It is characterized by significantly subaverage intellectual functioning, existing concurrently with related limitations in two or more of the following applicable adaptive skill areas: communication, self-care, home living, social skills, community use, self-direction, health and safety, functional academics, leisure, and work. Mental retardation manifests before age 18.

This definition requires that practitioners consider (1) cultural and linguistic diversity, (2) how adaptive skills interact with a person's community setting, (3) the fact that specific skills often exist with limitations, and (4) the likelihood that life functioning will generally improve with age.

There are a variety of causes for mental retardation—from deprived environments (especially for those with mild retardation) to genetic abnormalities, infectious diseases, and physical trauma (including that caused by drugs taken by the mother during pregnancy). There are two broad ways to classify retardation. The first focuses on biological versus environmental causes; the second, more prevalent, approach focuses on levels of retardation as reflected in behavior.

Levels of Retardation

A diagnosis of mental retardation involves three criteria: a lower-than-normal (below 70) IQ score as measured on a standardized test such as the WISC–R or the WAIS–R, difficulty adapting to the environment, and the presence of such problems before age 18. There are four basic levels of mental retardation, each corresponding

Mental retardation: Below-average intellectual functioning, as measured on an IQ test, accompanied by substantial limitations in functioning that originate before age 18.

FIGURE 8.6

Mental Retardation as Measured on the Stanford–Binet and Wechsler Scales

Classification	Stanford–Binet IQ Score	Wechsler IQ Score	Percentage of the Mentally Retarded
Mild	52–68	55–69	90
Moderate	36–51	40–54	6
Severe	20–35	25–39	3
Profound	Below 20	Below 25	1

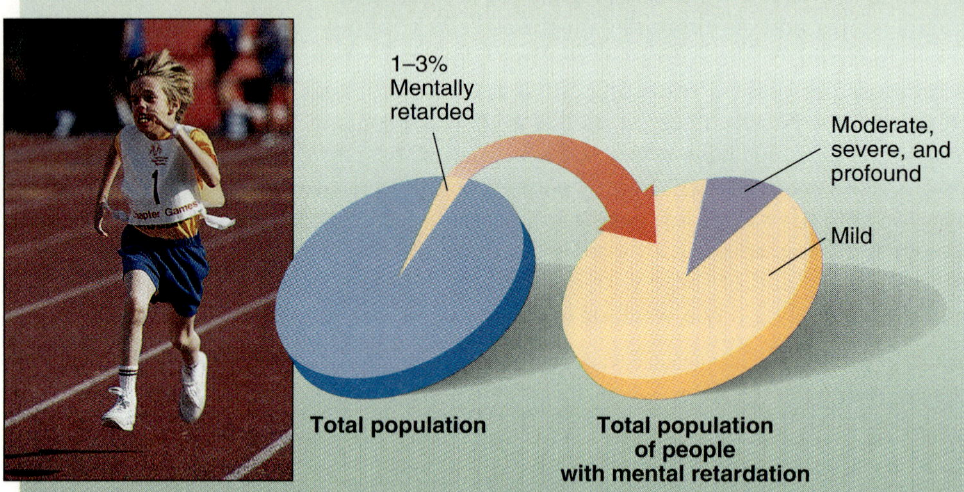

to a different range of scores on a standardized IQ test (see Figure 8.6): mild, moderate, severe, and profound.

Mild Retardation. People with mild mental retardation (Wechsler IQ of 55–69) are approximately 90 percent of those classified as mentally retarded. Through special programs, they are able to acquire academic and occupational skills, but they generally need extra supervision of their work (e.g., Allington, 1981). As adults, people with mild mental retardation function intellectually at about the level of 10-year-olds. Thus, with some help from family and friends, most people with mild mental retardation can cope successfully with their environment. *Applications* examines the employment of people with mental retardation.

Moderate Retardation. People with moderate mental retardation (Wechsler IQ of 40–54) account for approximately 6 percent of those classified as mentally retarded. Most live in institutions or as dependents of their families. Those who are not institutionalized need special classes; some can hold simple jobs, although few are employed. People with moderate mental retardation are able to speak, write, and interact with friends; but their motor coordination, posture, and social skills are clumsy. Their intellectual level is equivalent to that of 5- to 6-year-olds.

Severe Retardation. Only about 3 percent of the people with mental retardation are severely retarded (Wechsler IQ of 25–39). People with severe mental retardation show great motor, speech, and intellectual impairment and are almost totally dependent on others to take care of their basic needs. Severe retardation often results from birth disorders or traumatic injury to the brain.

APPLICATIONS

Employing Workers with Mental Retardation

Companies are realizing that if people with mild mental retardation are placed in the right job, are properly trained, and are effectively motivated, they can be counted on to be good workers. As a result, many companies now hire workers with mental retardation who were once thought unemployable.

There are some drawbacks to hiring such workers. One is that training them often requires extra patience. A more detailed and carefully defined training program is usually necessary; behavioral techniques such as those described in Chapter 5 are used extensively. Even a relatively simple task may have to be broken down into 30 or 40 individual steps. Workers with mental retardation sometimes need help to remain focused on their job; such help might include prompts from supervisors or a checklist to follow. Mentally retarded individuals may work more slowly than others in the same position. They may also require training in social skills—for example, in being friendly toward and smiling at coworkers. Also, workers who have lower IQs may be less adept at personal grooming and may not read, write, tell time, or handle money well.

Nonetheless, there are many great successes. Those workers who have been through training programs do exceptionally well. Workers with mental retardation are likely to stay with jobs others tire of. They may be more dependable, motivated, and industrious than other workers. After they are trained, they have few problems adjusting to the routine of a 9-to-5 job. Owners of fast-food restaurants (such as McDonald's) who hire workers with mental retardation report that these workers rarely come in late or call in sick. The employers consider these workers steady and dependable. Marriott Corporation employs more than 1,000 workers who have been diagnosed as mentally retarded.

All in all, many people diagnosed as mentally retarded are earning wages, and handling their lives impressively. They do far better in their lives outside of their jobs than they ever did before—because of federal law and mainstreaming (discussed on page 294).

The federal government has taken an extensive role in the education and support of individuals with mental retardation. It provides Supplemental Social Security Income payments to unemployed workers with mental retardation. It also provides tax benefits to employers of mentally or physically handicapped workers. Advocates for people with mental retardation are concerned because the costs of such support programs are rising very quickly. Various states are providing funds formerly reserved only for institutions to businesses and colleges for the purpose of training mentally retarded workers. Such programs are money savers for local governments, because workers who earn money pay taxes and do not require support payments. The task for government is substantial; and the challenge, in terms of numbers and cost, is formidable.

Profound Retardation. Only 1 percent of the people with mental retardation are classified as profoundly retarded (Wechsler IQ below 25). These people are unable to master even simple tasks and require total supervision and constant care. Their motor and intellectual development is minimal, and many are physically underdeveloped. Physical deformities and other congenital defects (such as deafness, blindness, and seizures) often accompany profound mental retardation.

The Law and Education

Until recently, thousands of children were given a substandard education after doing poorly on an intelligence test. Labeled as slow learners or perhaps even as mentally retarded, these children received neither special education nor special attention. In 1975, however, the U.S. Congress passed Public Law 94–142 (PL 94–142), the Education for All Handicapped Children Act. Originally intended to improve school programs for physically handicapped children, the law ensures individualized testing and educationally relevant programs for all children.

FOCUS

Review

- What are the implications of the Education for All Handicapped Children Act? p. 294

Think Critically

- A diagnosis of mental retardation involves a lower-than-normal IQ score. What does this imply about IQ tests as a predictor of behavior?

The law requires that all school-age children be provided with an appropriate, free public education. After testing, children with special needs are not to be grouped separately unless they have severe handicaps. Tests for identification and placement must be unbiased. Further, educational programs for special needs children must be arranged to make them as close to normal as possible, with the unique needs of each child considered. An individualized educational program or plan (IEP) must be arranged by the school in consultation with the parents. The law also mandates that schools must follow specific procedures: an explanation of rights, evaluation procedures, regular reevaluation, and explanation for any changes in a student's status. PL 94–142 has significantly increased the amount of testing in public school systems, leading to more classification and labeling. Many see this as a disadvantage. However, the implementation of the law has also guaranteed thousands of children with special needs an appropriate education. This is costly for local school districts; but when students need a special education, they can rely on the courts to make sure that the school system provides it.

Since the passage of PL 94–142, there has been a shift toward **mainstreaming**—the integration of all children with special needs into regular classroom settings, whenever appropriate, with the support of special education services. Technically, the law requires students to be placed in the least restrictive or unusual environment feasible. Its purpose is to make life as normal as possible for these children by requiring that they and their teachers and classmates cope with their current skill level and expand it as much as possible. In mainstreaming, children are assigned to a regular class for at least half of their school day. For the rest of the day, they are often in special education classrooms or in vocational training situations. Although research studies have produced conflicting data on the effectiveness of mainstreaming, psychologists and educators generally support it (Zigler & Hodapp, 1991).

Real progress has been made with mainstreaming, but problems remain in many school settings. Too often children are mainstreamed not into the academic (classroom) side of school, but only into the social side (athletics, lunch). This is being done to avoid stigmatization, but a consequence is a lack of delivery of adequate special academic services to children who require them (Zigler & Hodapp, 1991). Because of problems with mainstreaming, some schools now keep students with special education needs in regular education classrooms and bring support to the special needs child within the class rather than bringing the child to supportive services—an approach called *inclusion*. Not without its critics, the inclusionary approach focuses on the needs of individual children in new ways; research as to its success is still a decade away.

Mainstreaming: The administrative practice of placing children with special needs in regular classroom settings with the support of special education services.

Summary and Review

What Is Intelligence?

Identify the key qualities of a definition of intelligence.

- *Intelligence* is defined in terms of objectively observable behavior, consists of both an individual's capacity to learn and his or her acquired knowledge, and includes an ability to adapt to the environment. A widely accepted definition of intelligence is Wechsler's: "the aggregate or global capacity of the individual to act purposefully, to think rationally, and to deal effectively with the environment." pp. 266–267

Describe several different approaches to intelligence.

- According to Piaget, intelligence is a reflection of a person's adaptation to the environment, and intellectual development consists of changes in the way the individual accomplishes that adaptation. p. 267

- Wechsler examined the components of intelligence closely and argued that intelligence tests made up of subparts involving spatial relations and verbal comprehension reveal little about someone's overall capacity to deal with the world. pp. 267–268

- A *factor analysis approach* to evaluating intelligence uses correlational techniques to determine which tasks are involved in intellectual ability. In factor analysis, many tasks are given to a person, scores are derived for each task, and correlations are computed. The assumption is that tasks with high correlations test similar aspects of intellectual functioning. An example of the factor analysis approach is Guilford's approach. According to Guilford, human intellectual abilities and activities can be described in terms of three major dimensions: the mental operations performed, the contents of those operations, and the resulting products of the operations. p. 268

- Sternberg takes an information-processing view of intelligence. His triarchic theory divides intelligence into three dimensions: componential, experiential, and contextual. Sternberg focuses on adaptation to the world. pp. 269–272

KEY TERMS
Intelligence, p. 267
Factor analysis, p. 268

Principles of Test Development

Why were Binet and Simon significant in the development of intelligence tests?

- Binet coined the phrase *mental age*, meaning the age level at which a child is functioning cognitively. He and Simon developed everyday tasks, such as counting, naming, and using objects, to determine mental age. The scale they developed can be considered the first useful and practical test of intelligence. p. 273

How may intelligence tests be developed fairly and accurately?

- *Standardization* is the process of developing uniform procedures for administering and scoring a test. This includes developing *norms*—the scores and corresponding percentile ranks of a large and representative sample of test takers from the population for which the test was designed. A *representative sample* is a sample of individuals who match the population with whom they are to be compared, with regard to key variables such as socioeconomic status and age. p. 274

- A *normal curve* is a bell-shaped graphic representation of data arranged to show what percentage of the population falls under each part of the curve. The simplest score on a test is the *raw score*—the number of correct answers unconverted or transformed in any way. Scores are commonly expressed in terms of a *standard score*—a score that expresses an individual's position relative to those of others and based on the mean and how scores are distributed around it. A standard score is generally a *percentile score*—a score indicating what percentage of the test population would obtain a lower score. A *deviation IQ* is a standard IQ test score for which the mean and standard deviation remain constant at all ages. pp. 274–276

- A test is considered *reliable* if it yields the same score for the same individual on repeated testings. There are several types of reliability. All tests have some degree of unreliability. The standard error of measurement is the number of points by which a score varies because of the imperfect reliability of a test. A test's *validity* is its ability to measure what it is supposed to measure; without validity, proper inferences from test results cannot be made. pp. 276–277

- There are five basic criticisms of—and defenses for—the validity of intelligence tests and testing. The first focuses on the definition of intelligence. The second focuses on learned information. The third is that school settings may adversely affect IQ scores. The remaining criticisms of testing focus on the fact that some people may be testwise and on people's motivation to succeed. pp. 277–278

KEY TERMS
Standardization, p. 274
Norms, p. 274
Representative sample, p. 274
Normal curve, p. 274
Raw score, p. 275
Standard score, p. 275
Percentile score, p. 275
Deviation IQ, p. 275
Reliability, p. 276
Validity, p. 276
Halo effect, p. 277

Three Important Intelligence Tests

What are the chief differences between the Kaufman Assessment Battery for Children (K-ABC) and the Stanford–Binet and Wechsler scales?

- The Stanford–Binet Intelligence Scale consists of four major subscales and one overall IQ test score. It has been a good predictor of academic performance, and many of its tests correlate highly with one another; its newer items minimize gender and racial characteristics. pp. 278–279

- The Wechsler scales group test items by content. The score on each subtest is converted to a standard (or scaled) score, adjusted for the subject's age. The test yields verbal, performance, and overall IQ scores. p. 280

- The K-ABC consists of four global scales. Three measure mental processing abilities—sequential and simultaneous processing, and a composite of the two; the fourth assesses achievement. p. 281

Controversies about Intelligence

What is the evidence to show that cultural variables and gender affect intelligence test scores?

- Although researchers find differences among the IQ test scores of various racial and cultural groups, they find little or no consistent and conclusive evidence of bias in these tests. The evidence of many studies conducted with a variety of intelligence tests and ethnic minority groups indicates that intelligence tests are not culturally biased. But IQ test scores alone mean little and must be interpreted in the context of a person's life (including schooling). Intelligence can be demonstrated in many ways, including maturity and responsibility. p. 282

- Cultural differences exist and express themselves in IQ test scores; for this reason many psychologists (1) deemphasize overall test scores, (2) focus on interpretation of tests, (3) remember that IQ test scores do not measure innate ability, and (4) focus on intellectual functioning in the context of real-life situations. pp. 284–285

- Proponents of the environmental (nurture) view of intelligence believe that intelligence tests do not adequately measure a person's adaptation to a constantly changing environment. Many researchers claim that current theorizing will never resolve the issue of nature versus nurture, because factors such as family structure, family size, and other environmental variables are important and impossible to measure accurately. Genetics (nature) does not fix a person's intelligence; it sets a framework for environment to shape it. pp. 286–288

- The old consensus about gender differences in verbal and mathematical abilities is at least exaggerated, and at most simply wrong; gender differences in verbal ability are so small that they can be ignored. pp. 289–290

Giftedness and Mental Retardation

Describe the ends of the continuum of intelligence—giftedness and mental retardation—and their implications for educational settings.

- Giftedness is having superior cognitive, leadership, or performing arts abilities. Gifted children represent one end of a continuum of intelligence abilities. Such individuals need special schooling to meet their special needs. pp. 290–291

- *Mental retardation* is below-average intellectual functioning together with substantial limitations in adaptive behavior, originating before age 18. Retardation can affect communication, self-care, home living, social skills, self-direction, health and safety, leisure activities, and work. There are four basic levels of mental retardation; each corresponds to a specific range of scores on a standardized intelligence test. The behaviors associated with mental retardation vary from slow learning to an inability to care for oneself because of impaired physical, motor, and intellectual development. pp. 291–293

- *Mainstreaming* is the integration of all children with special needs into regular classroom settings wherever appropriate and with the support of special services. The purpose of mainstreaming is to help normalize the life experiences of children with special needs; unfortunately this is most often done in social settings rather than academic ones. p. 294

KEY TERMS

Mental retardation, p. 291
Mainstreaming, p. 294

Learning CONNECTIONS

Some students benefit from extra help with the concept of test development. You can learn more about it in:

- The CD-ROM accompanying this book, Topic 7
- This book's study guide, *Keeping Pace Plus*, or the computerized study guide, Chapter 8
- The audiotape accompanying this book, *SoundGuide for Psychology*, Learning Unit 11
- The study aids found on the World Wide Web site for this book, at http://www.abacon.com/psych/lefton

Critical Thinking CONNECTIONS

Take a moment to think critically about how this chapter's topics are connected with the rest of psychology . . .

If you are interested in . . .	Ask yourself . . .	Then turn to . . .
The role intelligence plays in psychological theory 	In what ways does the study of the biological bases of human behavior focus on the extent to which inherited structures determine intelligence?	Chapter 2, pp. 39–41
	What are the implications of child development theories for intellectual functioning?	Chapter 10, pp. 351–359
	How do developmental psychologists study growth and maturation by examining the decline of intellectual functioning that occurs with advanced age and diseases such as Alzheimer's?	Chapter 11, pp. 398–401
The influence of environment on the development of intelligence 	What are the implications of early childhood interactions with parents for intellectual functioning?	Chapter 10, pp. 356–358
	How do gender differences in social development translate into performance differences in the workplace and the classroom?	Chapter 11, pp. 384–385, 392–393
	How many of a person's basic attitudes toward work, school, and intellectual tasks are determined by parents in the early developmental years?	Chapter 16, pp. 557–558
Use of psychological tests 	Do you think that personality can be examined through projective tests?	Chapter 12, pp. 441–442

9

Motivation and Emotion

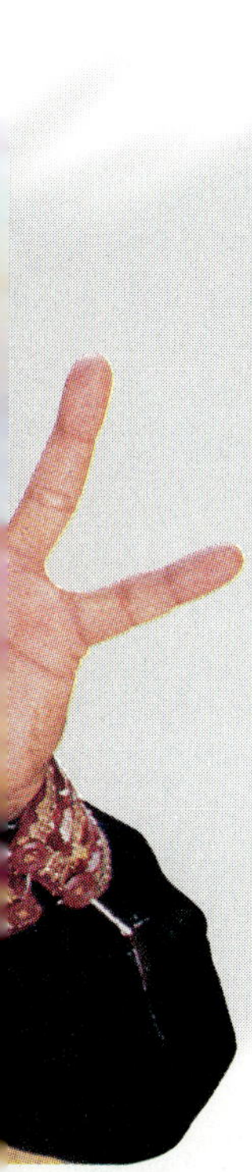

I started taking an evening class in *tae kwon do,* with the superficial goals of pushing my 48-year-old body to do something it had never done before, learning some practical self-defense skills, and breaking through my set point for weight. It took me months to decide to sign up, because not many adults take the class—kids take it and make it look easy (which it isn't). Also I knew that I ran the risk of looking like a total klutz for the first few weeks, if not forever.

Nevertheless, I was motivated to do it, for a number of not-so-superficial reasons. I felt it was a chance to grow by confronting my fears (fears of looking foolish in front of the class, of falling down, of hurting myself, of being the worst student ever to enter the school, of plain failure). I wanted to be part of the group of really good people whom I had seen taking the class together; the atmosphere is very positive and supportive. I wanted to put off the old rocking chair by a few more years (the class makes me feel like a 16-year-old, if I ignore the crackling joints). I also wanted to feel stronger and thereby more self-confident.

You can see that my motivation was personal and very strong. Now, after taking class three times a week and practicing at home, I have made enough progress to test for my yellow belt (the first step in a long journey to black belt, the belt in itself being a form of extrinsic motivation). However, the process is an emotional rollercoaster. When I manage to perform all the techniques properly in a class, I feel on top of the world. On the other hand, there are days when I'm clearly the worst kicker in class and I go home upset. From talking with other students, I've discovered that I'm not alone in reacting this way. Everyone who sticks with it is enormously motivated to succeed, yet even the red belts (just below black) struggle with self-criticism if they don't feel they have performed well enough. And all of this pressure is self-imposed!

Why do some people continue to strive for success while others give up with a single failure or are content to enjoy life at a more relaxed pace? Why will one person spend a free afternoon watching soap operas and munching potato chips while another will use the time for a 5-mile run and a quick study session before dinner? Why do some people crave the excitement of competition while others seem to shy away from it? What drives people to take action, like saving up for *tae kwon do* lessons? And what makes them so emotional about it?

Theories of Motivation

Researchers have always sought to discover what impels people to take various actions—from simple, seemingly instinctual actions such as eating to complex actions such as learning to juggle. Many theories of motivation have been developed to explain human behavior, but no single theory can explain all behavior. An understanding of the interacting forces must begin with a definition of *motivation*. **Motivation** is any condition, although usually an internal one, that appears by inference to initiate, activate, or maintain an organism's goal-directed behavior.

Let's examine the four basic parts of this definition of motivation: (1) internal condition, (2) by inference, (3) initiation, activation, or maintenance, and (4) goal-directed behavior. Motivation reflects an *internal condition*, which cannot be directly observed—that is one reason why its effect has to be inferred. The condition may develop from physiological needs and drives or from complex desires, such as the desire to help others, to obtain approval, or to earn a high income. Motivation is an *inferred concept* that links a person's internal conditions to external behavior. It cannot be observed directly, but an observer can infer its presence by its behavioral effects. Motivation *initiates, activates, or maintains behavior*. Because I am motivated to become a good martial artist, I have initiated a regimen of practice, which I hope to maintain. Motivation generates *goal-directed behavior*. Goals vary widely across individuals and situations. Some goals are concrete and immediate—for example, to get up and eat food, to remove a painful stimulus, or to win a diving match. Other goals are more abstract and long-term; the behavior of someone who studies hard, for example, may be motivated by desires to maximize learning, to obtain good grades, and to get a good job.

Motivation theories fall into five broad categories: drive theory, arousal theory, expectancy theory, cognitive theory, and humanistic theory. We will examine each of these categories of theory in turn and then look at some basic types of motivation, before turning to how emotions and motivation are intertwined.

Motivation: Any internal condition that appears by inference to initiate, activate, or maintain an organism's goal-directed behavior.

Drive theory: An explanation of behavior emphasizing internal factors that energize organisms to attain, reestablish, balance, or maintain some goal that helps with survival.

Drive Theory

Some of the most influential and best-researched motivation theories are forms of drive theory. **Drive theory** is an explanation of behavior that assumes that an organism is motivated to act because of a need to attain, reestablish, balance, or maintain

FIGURE 9.1

An Overview of Drive Theory

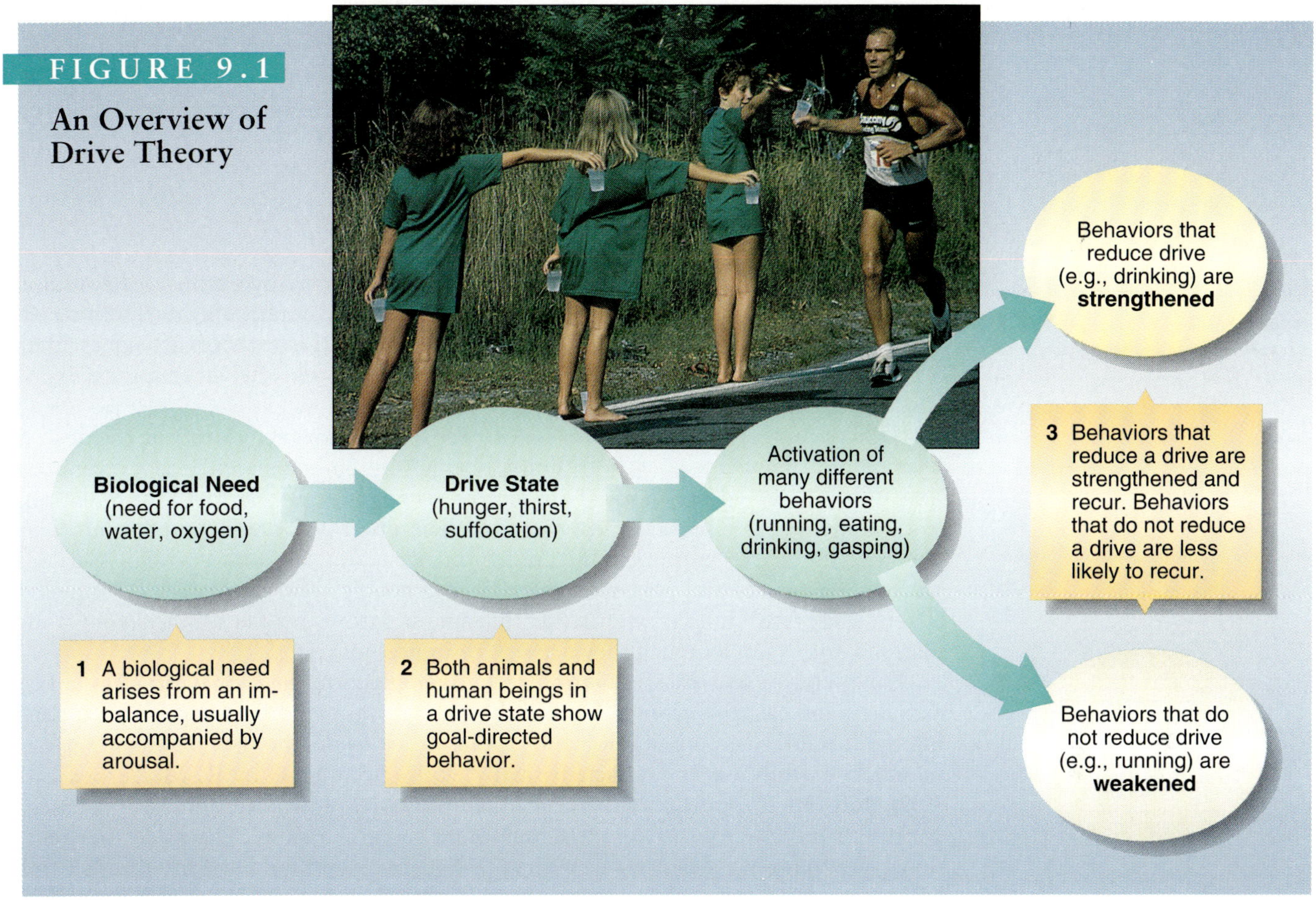

some goal that helps with the survival of the organism or the species. Stimuli such as hunger and pain create, energize, and initiate such behavior. A person who is starving, perhaps a homeless person, may spend most of his or her time looking for food; the individual will be driven to seek food.

A **drive** is an internal aroused condition that directs an organism to satisfy some physiological need. Drive theory focuses on **need**—a state of physiological imbalance usually accompanied by arousal. (We will explore arousal in greater depth in the next section.) Physiological needs are said to be mechanistic, because the organism is pushed, pulled, and energized by them, almost like a machine. The organism motivated by a need is said to be in a *drive state*. Both animals and human beings in that state show goal-directed behavior. Their goal is often to attain *homeostasis*—a state of stability or balance. For example, a thirsty animal—one depleted of its normal level of body fluids—will seek out water to reestablish its body fluid level (psychologists refer to this normally maintained level as a steady state). The processes by which organisms seek to reestablish homeostasis are a key part of drive theory. Behaviors such as eating and drinking, which reduce a biological need (and reestablish homeostasis), are strengthened and are therefore likely to recur. Behaviors such as juggling, which do not reduce a biological need, are less likely to recur. (See Figure 9.1 for an overview and examples of drive theory.)

In examining motivation from a drive reduction point of view, psychologists seek to understand such simple behaviors as eating and drinking. As Abraham Maslow (1962, 1969) suggested, in general, a person's physiological need for food and water must be satisfied before any other needs. However, drive theory clearly does not explain all, or even most, motivated behavior; besides, difficult-to-define concepts such as "need" and "hunger" vary from person to person. The history of motivation theory is marked by distinct shifts from one concept to another. For

Drive: An internal aroused condition that directs an organism to satisfy physiological needs.

Need: A state of physiological imbalance usually accompanied by arousal.

example, though many early researchers focused on the internal conditions—needs—that impel organisms to action, contemporary researchers such as Richard Nisbett recognize and embrace the idea that some human motives are biological, others are learned through conditioning, and still others result from people thinking about and evaluating their needs and their behaviors.

Arousal Theory

A characteristic of all motivational systems is that they involve arousal. **Arousal** is generally thought of as activation of the central nervous system, the autonomic nervous system, and the muscles and glands. Some motivational theorists suggest that organisms seek to maintain optimal levels of arousal by actively varying their exposure to arousing stimuli.

Unlike hunger and thirst, the lack of sensory experience does not result in a physiological imbalance; yet both human beings and animals seek sensory stimulation. When deprived of a normal amount of visual, auditory, or tactile stimulation, some adults become irritable and consider their situation or environment intolerable. Kittens like to explore their environment; young monkeys will investigate mechanical devices and play with puzzles; and people seem motivated or impelled to seek sensory stimulation. (However, in some situations people seek to avoid stimulation—for example, when they are sick or in need of rest.)

But a lack of sensory stimulation and drive reduction theory nevertheless fail to explain many basic behaviors. *Arousal theory* attempts to bridge the gap by explaining the link between a behavior and a state of arousal. The link between performance and arousal was first scientifically explored in 1908 by R. M. Yerkes and J. D. Dodson. They described a relationship involving arousal and performance, called the *Yerkes–Dodson law*. Contemporary researchers have extended that relationship by suggesting that when a person's level of arousal and anxiety is either too high or too low, performance will be poor, especially on complex tasks (e.g., Brehm & Self, 1989). The inverted U-shaped curve in Figure 9.2 shows this relationship between level of arousal and level of performance.

FIGURE 9.2

Performance and Arousal

Performance is at its peak when arousal is at moderate levels; too much or too little arousal results in low performance levels.

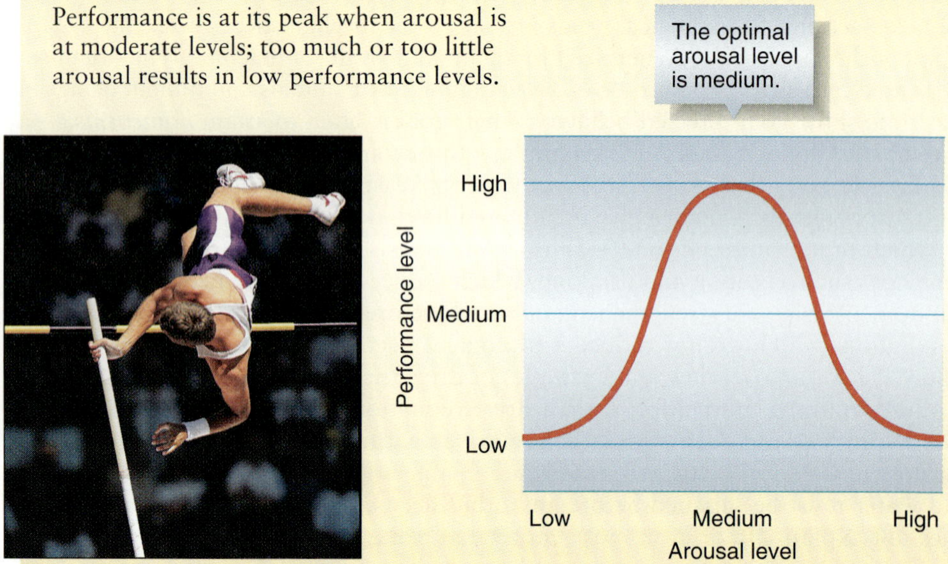

Arousal: Activation of the central nervous system, the autonomic nervous system, and the muscles and glands; according to some motivational theorists, organisms may seek to maintain optimal levels of arousal by actively varying their exposure to arousing stimuli.

BUILDING TABLE 9.1

Drive and Arousal Theories of Motivation

THEORY	THEORIST	PRINCIPALLY EXPLAINS	KEY IDEA	VIEW OF BEHAVIOR
Drive	Nisbett	Obesity	*Homeostasis*—the organism seeks physiological balance.	Partially mechanistic but recognizes the role of learning in hunger and obesity.
Arousal	Hebb	Optimal arousal	Performance depends on level of arousal.	Mostly mechanistic—the efficiency of behavior is determined by the level of physiological arousal.

Thus, people who do not care about what they are doing have little anxiety but also have little arousal and therefore usually perform poorly in both work and play. If arousal increases to the point of high anxiety, performance also suffers. Think of some activity that you practice often and in which you occasionally either compete or perform publicly. For example, you may be a diver, an actor, or a member of a debating team. Chances are you performed most poorly when you were not interested in practicing or when you were exceedingly nervous about your performance, such as during a competition. Conversely, you probably did your best when you were eager to practice or when you were moderately excited by the competition. This phenomenon explains why some baseball players perform exceptionally well at the beginning of the season, when pressure is only moderately high, and then commit numerous errors when pressure increases—for instance, in the final games of the World Series.

Researcher Donald Hebb (1904–1985) suggested that behavior varies from disorganized to effective, depending on a person's level of arousal. He argued that human functioning is most efficient when people are at an optimal level of arousal (Hebb, 1955). People seek, and are most efficient at, specific arousal levels (K. J. Anderson, 1990).

Fundamental to all motivation theories is the notion that it is not the stimulus itself but the organism's internal response to it that determines how the organism behaves. Hebb's idea shifted researchers' focus from stimuli, drives, and needs to the idea that arousal energizes behavior but does not direct it. The development of optimal-arousal theories helped psychologists explain the variation in people's responses to situations in terms of a state of internal arousal rather than solely in terms of responses to stimuli. This shift in emphasis marked a subtle but important transition from a strictly mechanistic drive reduction theory toward learning, expectancy, and more cognitive theories. (See Building Table 9.1 for a comparison of drive and arousal theories.)

Expectancy Theories

Expectancy theories: Explanations of behavior that focus on people's expectations of success in reaching a goal and the need for achievement as energizing factors.

The idea that human beings evaluate and learn from their life situations is most aptly expressed in expectancy theories, which connect thought and motivation. **Expectancy theories** are explanations of behavior that focus on people's expectations

Motive: A specific (usually internal) condition, usually involving some sort of arousal, that directs an organism's behavior toward a goal.

Social need: An aroused condition that directs people toward establishing feelings about themselves and others and toward establishing and maintaining relationships.

of success in reaching a goal and their need for achievement as energizing factors. A key element of these theories, often expressed by achievement researcher David McClelland, is that people's thoughts, their expectations, guide their behaviors. The motives and needs they develop are not initiated because of some physiological imbalance. Rather, people learn through their interactions in the environment to have needs for mastery, affiliation, and competition. These needs are based on their expectations about the future and about how their efforts will lead to various rewarding outcomes.

To understand some important concepts related to expectancy theory, we can consider my desire to be better at *tae kwon do*. That desire means work and hours of practice, which require me to deprive myself of other pleasures. Psychologists think that my motive for striving at *tae kwon do* originates partly in social needs. A **motive** is a specific (usually internal) condition, usually involving some form of arousal, that directs an organism's behavior toward a goal. Unlike a drive, which always has a physiological origin, a motive does not necessarily need to have a physiological explanation. Thus, although I may be motivated to be among the best in my class, there is no urgent physiological need for me to do so. A **social need** is an aroused condition that directs people toward establishing feelings about themselves and others and toward establishing and maintaining relationships. My social needs, for example, probably have included winning approval from family, friends, and other martial artists. The needs for achievement, affiliation, and good feelings about oneself are affected by many factors, including socioeconomic status and race and experiences from birth onward. The need to feel good about oneself often leads to specific behaviors through which a person strive to be evaluated positively (Geen, 1991). This topic will be explored in more detail later in this chapter when we discuss achievement, as well as when we consider social psychology in Chapter 16. (See Building Table 9.2 for a comparison of expectancy theory with drive and arousal theories.)

BUILDING TABLE 9.2

Drive, Arousal, and Expectancy Theories of Motivation

THEORY	THEORIST	PRINCIPALLY EXPLAINS	KEY IDEA	VIEW OF BEHAVIOR
Drive	Nisbett	Obesity	*Homeostasis*—the organism seeks physiological balance.	Partially mechanistic but recognizes the role of learning in hunger and obesity.
Arousal	Hebb	Optimal arousal	Performance depends on level of arousal.	Mostly mechanistic—the efficiency of behavior is determined by the level of physiological arousal.
Expectancy	McClelland	Achievement motivation 	Humans learn the need to achieve.	Partly cognitive, partly mechanistic—achievement is a learned behavior.

Cognitive Theory

In the study of motivation, **cognitive theory** is an explanation of behavior that asserts that people are actively and regularly involved in determining their own goals and the means of achieving them. Like expectancy theory, cognitive theory focuses on thought as an initiator and determinant of behavior. However, more than expectancy theory does, cognitive theory emphasizes the role of conscious decision making in all areas of life. For example, you are actively involved in deciding how much time you will spend studying for a psychology exam, how hard you will work to become an accomplished pianist, or how much commitment you will give to a new diet or exercise routine.

As early as 1949, Donald Hebb anticipated how cognitive theory would influence psychology to move away from mechanistic views of motivation and behavior.

> As far as one can see at present, it is unsatisfactory to equate motivation with biological need. Theory built on this base has a definiteness that is very attractive; but it may have been obtained at too great a cost. (Hebb, 1949, p. 179)

Other factors, such as arousal and attention, are also important determinants of motivation, as we have seen. As a result of Hebb's brilliant theorizing, contemporary researchers emphasize the role of active decision making and the human capacity for abstract thought. These cognitive theorists assume that individuals set goals and decide how to achieve them.

Cognitive Controls. Cognitive theory holds that if you are aware of—and think about—your behavior, motivation, and emotions and you attempt to alter your thoughts, you can control your behavior. Cognitive psychologists maintain that if human beings are aware of their thought patterns, they can control their reasoning and ultimately their overt behavior. We will see in Chapter 15 that this idea is used extensively by therapists to help people with various maladjustments. In explaining motivation, cognitive psychologists show that arousal (which Hebb and other researchers equated with drive) is under voluntary cognitive control.

In a classic study, Lazarus and Alfert (1964) monitored the arousal levels of three groups under conditions capable of inducing great stress. The participants watched a film showing the primitive ritual of subincision, in which an adolescent boy's penis is deeply cut. The film included five such operations. The first group saw a silent film, without any commentary. The second group listened, during the film, to a commentary denying that pain and harm were associated with the operation; this group was termed the *denial commentary group*. The third group listened to the same commentary before the film; this group was termed the *denial orientation group*. The participants' levels of arousal were measured by their electrodermal response (EDR)—a measure of the electrical conductivity of the skin usually correlated with arousal (see Figure 9.3 on page 306).

With the start of the film, the EDR increased in all groups. Levels of arousal varied among the groups, however. The group that heard no commentary had the highest overall level of arousal. The denial commentary group (commentary during the film) had a lower arousal increase than the silent film group. And the denial orientation group (commentary before the film) had the lowest level of increased arousal. Lazarus and Alfert believed the participants in the denial orientation group were able to build up their psychological defenses against the potentially stressful content of the film. In other words, they had some degree of cognitive control to insulate themselves against their physiological and emotional reactions.

Through instruction and self-help techniques, people can alter their behavior by changing their thoughts and thus their expectancies (e.g., Norris, 1989). That thoughts can alter behavior also becomes evident when we consider intrinsic and extrinsic motivation.

Cognitive theory: In motivation, an explanation of behavior that emphasizes the role of thought and individual choices regarding life goals and the means of achieving them.

FIGURE 9.3

Cognitive Controls of Emotional Responses

Lazarus and Alfert (1964) measured the electrodermal response (EDR) of participants viewing a stress-inducing film. The results showed that cognitive processes helped people suppress their stress-related reactions.

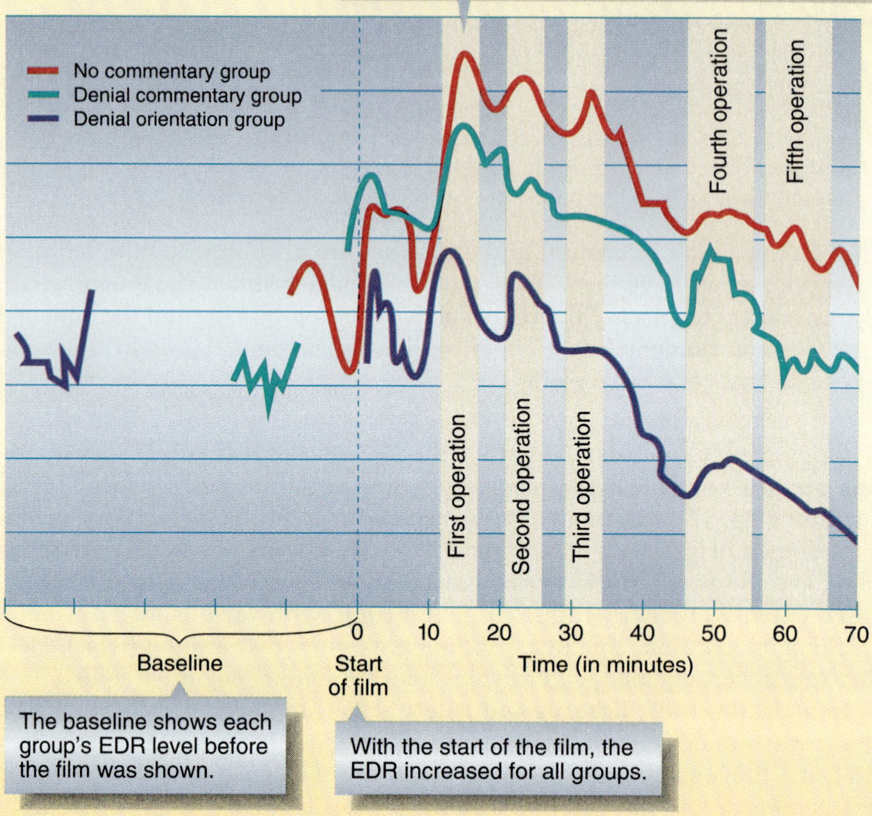

Intrinsic and Extrinsic Motivation. For fun, people engage in a wide variety of behaviors that bring no tangible rewards. Infants play with mobiles, children build Lego cities and then tear them down, and adults do crossword and jigsaw puzzles. Psychologists call behaviors engaged in for no apparent reward except the pleasure and satisfaction of the activity itself **intrinsically motivated behaviors**. Edward Deci (1975) suggests that people engage in such behaviors for two reasons: to obtain cognitive stimulation and to gain a sense of accomplishment, competence, and mastery over the environment. Individuals vary widely with respect to the need for cognitive stimulation; each person's experiences and genetic makeup affect the strength of this need (Cacioppo et al., 1995).

In studies focusing on intrinsic motivation, Deci compared two groups of college-age participants engaged in puzzle solving. One group received no external rewards, and the other group did receive rewards. Deci found that participants who were initially given rewards generally spent less time solving puzzles when rewards were no longer given. Those who were never rewarded, on the other hand, spent the same amount of time solving puzzles on all trials (Deci, 1972). Similar studies of younger children yielded comparable results (Lepper, Greene, & Nisbett, 1973) and also showed that if rewards are expected before the activity is performed, the effect of not

Intrinsically motivated behaviors [in-TRINZ-ick-lee]: Behaviors engaged in for no apparent reward except the pleasure and satisfaction of the activity itself.

◀ *Extrinsic rewards such as recognition on a classroom bulletin board can enhance students' feelings of self-worth.*

giving them is even greater (Ryan, Mims, & Koestner, 1983). Mothers' comments changed the extent of intrinsically motivated behavior in their 6- and 7-year-old children; researchers found a relationship between mothers' being controlling in their words, rather than being supportive or neutral, and the children's low rate of intrinsically motivated play (Deci et al., 1993). Other research (e.g., McGraw & Fiala, 1982) shows that offering rewards for engaging in an already attractive task results in a lower level of involvement and often permanent disengagement. Lepper and Greene (1978) refer to this phenomenon as the *hidden cost of rewards*. When people think about the causes of their actions, such thought will lead to changes in their behavior. (The hidden cost of rewards was also examined in Chapter 5, page 177.)

Extrinsic rewards are rewards that come from the external environment. Praise, a high grade, or money given for a particular behavior are extrinsic rewards. Such rewards can strengthen existing behaviors, provide people with information about their performance, and increase feelings of self-worth and competence. As already noted, however, extrinsic rewards can decrease intrinsic motivation (Pittman & Heller, 1987). Verbal extrinsic rewards (such as praise) are less likely to interfere with intrinsic motivation than are tangible rewards (such as money) (Anderson, Manoogian, & Reznick, 1976).

Psychologists continue to explore the effects of extrinsic rewards for intrinsically motivated behaviors. Baumeister and Tice (1985) showed that when people with high self-esteem are rewarded for intrinsically motivated behaviors, they aspire to excel and seek opportunities to do so. But when people with low self-esteem are rewarded for intrinsically motivated behaviors, they aspire to be only adequate or satisfactory. It is not surprising, then, that intrinsic motivation is, at least in part, related to a person's past experiences and current level of self-esteem. Other variables, such as the type of task undertaken and the type of reward received, can influence the level of intrinsic motivation. The combination of intrinsic motivation, external rewards, self-esteem, and perhaps new and competing needs affect day-to-day behavior. (We will consider in Chapter 13 what happens when goals and needs conflict and how animals and human beings behave in situations that have both positive and negative aspects.)

Humanistic Theory

My physiological readiness, expectations, and learned behavior all work together to determine my success in *tae kwon do*. One of the appealing aspects of humanistic theory is that it recognizes the interplay of behavioral theories and incorporates

Extrinsic rewards [ecks-TRINZ-ick]: Rewards that come from the external environment.

Humanistic theory: An explanation of behavior that emphasizes the entirety of life rather than individual components of behavior; focuses on human dignity, individual choice, and self-worth.

Self-actualization: In humanistic theory, the final stage of psychological development, in which one realizes one's uniquely human potential; the process of achieving everything that one is capable of achieving, including minimizing ill health, attaining a superior perception of reality, and feeling a strong sense of self-acceptance.

some of the best elements of the drive, arousal, expectancy, and cognitive approaches for explaining motivation and behavior.

Humanistic theory is an explanation of behavior that emphasizes the entirety of life rather than individual components of behavior. It focuses on human dignity, individual choice, and self-worth. Humanistic psychologists believe that individuals' behavior must be viewed within the framework of the individuals' environment and values. As we saw in Chapter 1, one of the founders and leaders of the humanistic approach was Abraham Maslow (1908–1970), who assumed that people are essentially good—that they possess an innate inclination to develop their potential and to seek beauty, truth, and harmony.

Like other humanistic theorists, Maslow believed that people are born open and trusting and can experience the world in healthy ways. In his words, people are naturally motivated toward self-actualization. **Self-actualization** is a final level of psychological development in which individuals strive to realize their uniquely human potential—to achieve everything they are capable of achieving. This includes attempts to minimize ill health, to attain a superior perception of reality, and to feel a strong sense of self-acceptance. (Of course, such *self*-preoccupation is a very Western characteristic; many elements of Maslow's theory would not hold up in some Eastern cultures.)

In Maslow's influential theory, people's motives are conceived of as forming a pyramid-shaped structure, with fundamental physiological needs at the base and the needs for love, achievement, understanding, and self-actualization near the top (see Figure 9.4). According to Maslow, as lower-level needs are satisfied, people strive for the next higher level; the pyramid culminates in self-actualization. Maslow even listed the characteristics found in self-actualized people. Although few self-actualized people have all the traits, all such people strive (and are directed) toward acquiring them, he believed. Self-actualized people, according to Maslow:

Are realistically oriented.
Are unconventional.
Have a good sense of humor.
Accept themselves.

FIGURE 9.4

Maslow's Hierarchy of Needs

Physiological needs are at the base of the pyramid. Successive levels above that represent needs that are to an increasing extent learned social needs.

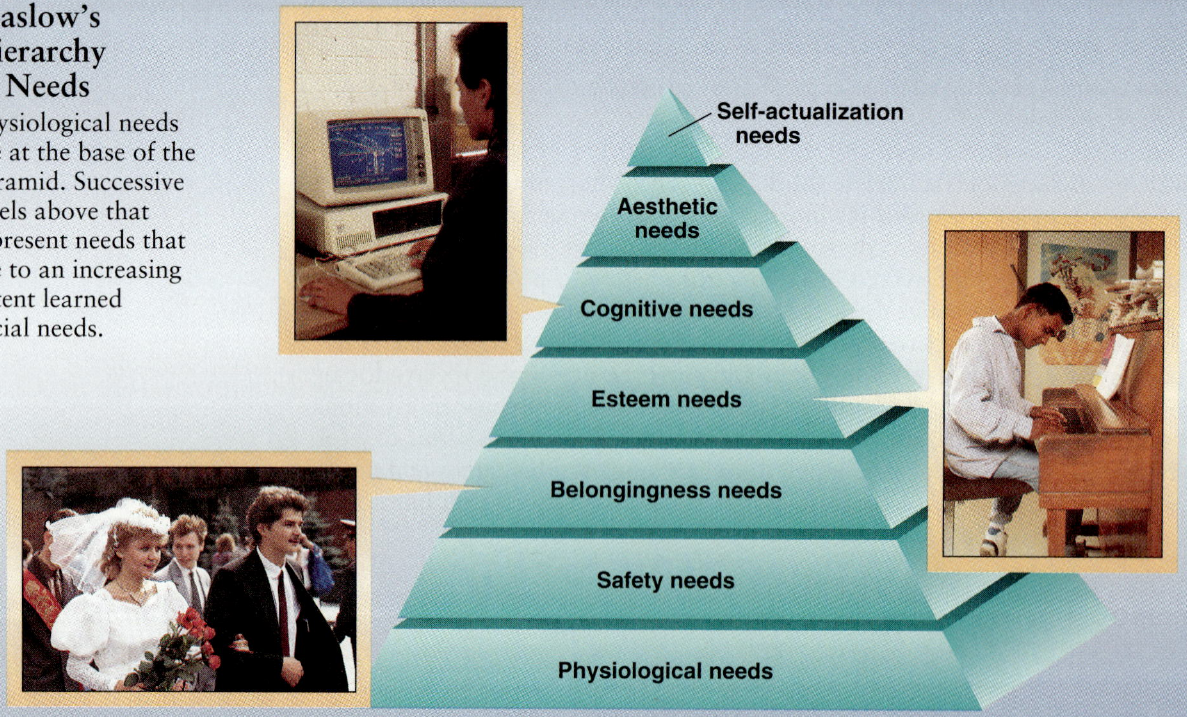

Have a need for privacy.
Are independent.
Identify with people.
Are democratic.
Appreciate the environment.
Are creative and nonconformist.
Are problem-centered.
Have a fresh appreciation of people.
Have spiritual experiences.
Have intimate relationships.
Do not confuse means with ends.
Are spontaneous.

Maslow claimed that once someone's basic physiological needs are met, the person is in a better position to satisfy emotional needs. He did not claim that a person's basic physiological needs have to be satisfied completely before the person can achieve a higher level of fulfillment. Across a lifetime, however, unless basic physiological needs are met, people are unlikely to grow and develop physically or to acquire social and aesthetic motives that might direct behavior. Only if people's needs for food, shelter, and physical safety are met can they attend to developing a sense of self-respect or a sense of beauty.

Building Table 9.3 adds Deci's cognitive theory and Maslow's humanistic theory to the comparative summary of motivation theories.

BUILDING TABLE 9.3

Drive, Arousal, Expectancy, Cognitive, and Humanistic Theories of Motivation

THEORY	THEORIST	PRINCIPALLY EXPLAINS	KEY IDEA	VIEW OF BEHAVIOR
Drive	Nisbett	Obesity	*Homeostasis*—the organism seeks physiological balance.	Partially mechanistic but recognizes the role of learning in hunger and obesity.
Arousal	Hebb	Optimal arousal	Performance depends on level of arousal.	Mostly mechanistic—the efficiency of behavior is determined by the level of physiological arousal.
Expectancy	McClelland	Achievement motivation	Humans learn the need to achieve.	Partly cognitive, partly mechanistic—achievement is a learned behavior.
Cognitive	Deci	Intrinsic motivation	Intrinsic motivation is self-rewarding because it makes people feel competent.	Cognitive—motivation is inborn, but extrinsic rewards often decrease it.
Humanistic	Maslow 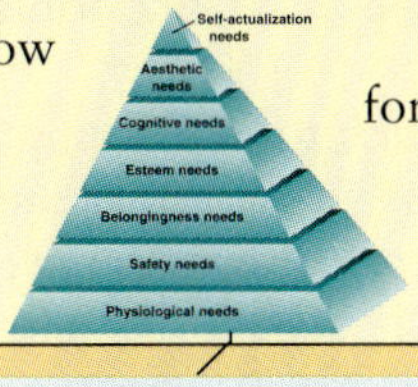	Learned needs for fulfillment and feelings of self-actualization	Self-actualization	Cognitive—humans seek to self-actualize after they have fulfilled basic needs for food and security.

FOCUS

Review

- What is the key aspect of drive theory as an explanation of motivation? p. 301
- What evidence exists to show that intrinsic motivation is lessened when rewards are offered for a behavior? pp. 306–307

Think Critically

- In what way did humanistic theory grow from cognitive theory? Did expectancy theory grow from drive theory?
- Why are humanistic theories difficult to test experimentally?
- Why might self-actualized people not necessarily embody the values that a culture deems "good"?

Although Maslow's theory provides an interesting way to organize aspects of motivation and behavior and their relative importance, its global nature makes experimental verification difficult. Moreover, his levels of motivation seem closely tied to middle-class American cultural experiences; Western cultures are highly individualistic compared to Eastern cultures, which are more collectivistic. So Maslow's theory may not be valid for all cultures or socioeconomic strata. His theory, like many other motivation theories, does not explain how other components of people's lives interact with behavior. For example, how does a person maintain a need for privacy and independence and still have a need to be with other people? Also, humanistic theory does not deal with how people develop the need to seek beauty, truth, and harmony. Again this reveals its culture-bound Western approach—Eastern culture and religion incorporate ways to develop and meet this need, including meditation and exercise.

Hunger: A Physiologically Based Need

Now that you understand the theoretical work that has been done around the subject of motivation, let's look at a few very basic and universal *types* of motivation. All of us have been hungry, felt sexually aroused, and experienced such learned motives as those for achievement. It is to those types of motivation that we turn next, beginning with perhaps the most basic, drive-based motivation—hunger.

Physiological Determinants of Hunger

When you are hungry, you may feel stomach pain or become weak or dizzy—all sensations that impel you to seek food. What causes these sensations? Physiological explanations of hunger focus on the concept of homeostasis and hormones. A delicate balance—a *homeostasis*—of food and fluid intake is necessary for proper physiological functioning; any imbalance results in a drive to restore the balance. For example, when a person experiences fluid deprivation and the resulting cellular dehydration, homeostatic mechanisms come into play. The person is put into a drive state in which the mouth and throat become dry, cueing the person to drink. Thirst is not a result of dryness in the mouth or throat, and simply placing water in the mouth will not reduce thirst. The body seeks to maintain homeostasis, and when the internal regulator drops below a key point—almost like a thermostat—certain actions are put into play.

Similarly, the *glucostatic approach* to explaining hunger argues that the principal physiological cause of hunger is a low blood sugar level, which accompanies food deprivation and creates a chemical imbalance. In the body, sugar is quickly broken down into glucose, which is crucial to cellular activity. When the blood sugar (glucose) level is low, the body sends warning signals to the brain; the brain immediately responds by generating hunger pain in the stomach. Hunger depends directly on levels of blood sugar (and other metabolites), which trigger the central nervous system circuits that control eating. Experiments with animals in which the nerves between stomach and brain were severed show that the animals continued to eat at appropriate times—when their blood sugar levels were low. These experiments provide evidence for the glucostatic approach.

The amount of food people eat does not necessarily affect the feeling of hunger—at least not right away. A hungry adult who eats steadily for 5 minutes may still feel hungry on stopping. But 30 minutes later, after the food has been converted into sugar, the person may no longer feel hungry. The type of food eaten determines how soon the feeling of hunger disappears. A candy bar loaded with easily converted sugar will take away hunger pain faster than will foods high in protein. High-protein foods such as meat, cheese, and milk take more time to digest and to elevate blood glucose.

Much of current knowledge about hunger and eating behavior comes from studies of the brain, particularly of the hypothalamus, a region of the forebrain (see Chapter 2, page 53). Researchers have argued that two areas of the hypothalamus are partly responsible for eating behavior: the ventromedial hypothalamus and the lateral hypothalamus. The *ventromedial hypothalamus* (the "stopeating" center) is activated to stop an organism from eating when the blood sugar level is high, or when this part of the hypothalamus is electrically stimulated. The *lateral hypothalamus* (the "starteating" center) is activated to drive the organism to start eating when the blood sugar level is low, or when this part of the hypothalamus is stimulated. In recent years the lateral hypothalamus has been shown to play a direct role in eating behavior (both hunger and satiety), while the ventromedial hypothalamus has a more indirect role. For example, the ventromedial hypothalamus may influence eating by stimulating the hormonal and metabolic systems (Powley, 1977). As Figure 9.5 shows, researchers have used lesioning (surgical) techniques to destroy

FIGURE 9.5

The Impact of the Hypothalamus on Eating Behavior

The stimulation or destruction (ablation) of a rat's hypothalamus alters the rat's eating behavior; in addition, the location of the hypothalamic stimulation—ventromedial or lateral—affects the results.

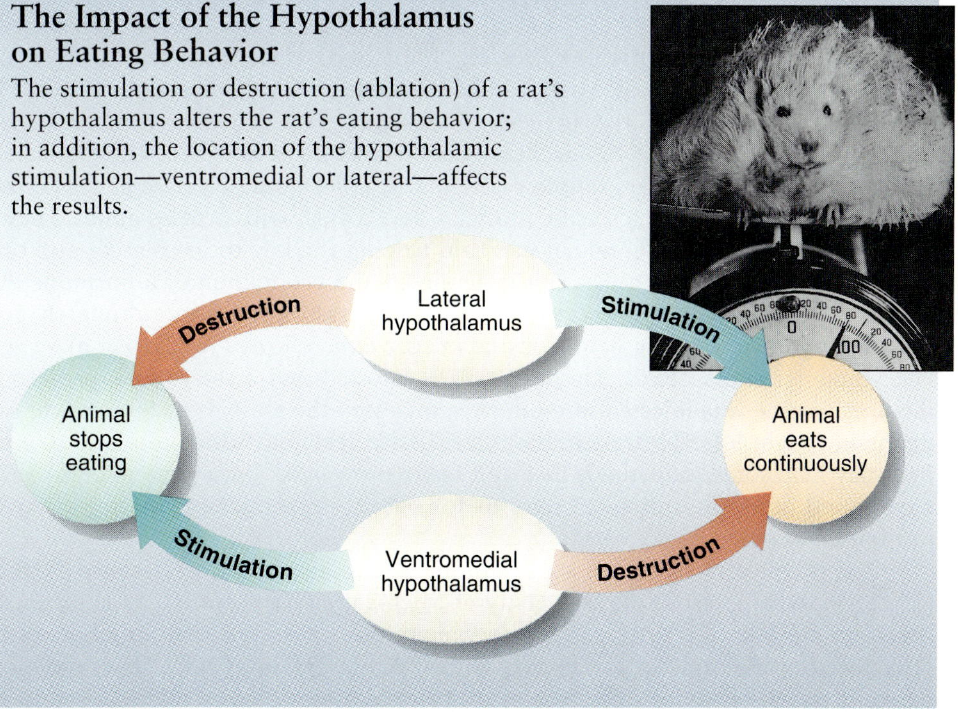

the ventromedial and lateral areas of the hypothalamus in rats. This destruction caused the opposite effects of stimulation.

As we saw in Chapter 2, insulin is a hormone secreted by the pancreas; it is released into the bloodstream when blood sugar (glucose) is present, to allow the blood sugar to be taken into the body's cells. Eating food that quickly increases blood sugar levels, such as candy, also triggers the pancreas to release insulin quickly. The body cells then quickly take in the blood sugar, and the blood sugar level once again falls. Thus, a hungry person who consumes a food high in sugar generally finds that, after an initial feeling of relief from hunger, hunger will rapidly recur; the blood sugar level is now low again, often even lower than before the person ate. Thus, eating a sugar-laden candy bar relieves hunger initially but may cause an even greater level of hunger within a half-hour or so.

What happens when the motivation to eat, the hormonal system, or perhaps genetics leads a person to overeat and eventually to become obese?

Hunger and Obesity

In the 1990s, researchers recognize that there is an ever-growing tendency in the United States to be ever growing; over one-third of Americans are overweight. In an address to the American Psychological Association, Yale University psychologist Judith Rodin (1981, p. 361) summarized the plight of fat people:

> First, heavy people are forced to wear the consequences of their affliction on their body and have probably built up a whole armamentarium of defenses to deal with that circumstance. No other physical characteristic except skin color is so stigmatized in our society. Second is the delightful but problematic fact that food is a positive and reinforcing stimulus for most of us. . . . Third, and probably most unfair of all, obesity is unusual because being fat is one of the factors that may keep one fat. . . . [T]he perverse fact is that it often does take fewer calories to keep people fat than it did to get them fat in the first place. This occurs because obesity itself changes the fat cells and body chemistry and alters levels of energy expenditure.

How do psychologists explain obesity? Two types of explanations are genetic and psychological.

Genetic Explanations of Obesity. Some researchers insist that problems of obesity are genetically based. Grilo and Pogue-Geile (1991) analyzed the results of a series of genetic studies and concluded that inherited traits are the principal determinants of obesity. Other researchers concur, offering a number of explanations including neurotransmitters (Stanley & Gillard, 1994) and defective genes (Zhang et al., 1994). In 1995 the scientific journals were awash with articles about a newly discovered "obesity" gene, which was said to hold the key to overeating and obesity. Researchers suggested that this gene directs the production of a hormone that tells the brain how much fat is stored in the body; this information ultimately governs the organism's eating behavior and energy expenditures (Halaas et al., 1995; Pelleymounter et al., 1995). The researchers reported that if the protein product of the obesity gene was injected into animals, it caused the animals to lose weight and maintain weight loss. The research on the obesity gene may ultimately lead to a pill that may help some individuals lose and maintain weight; but researchers for years have found other physiological reasons for obesity—genetic explanations may be just one cause.

One of the first to offer a physiological explanation was Richard Nisbett (1972), a psychologist at the University of Michigan, who proposed an explanation based on *fat cells*. He asserted that people are born with different numbers of fat cells and that the number of fat cells with which a person is born determines the person's eating behavior and propensity toward obesity. Body fat is stored in fat cells, so people born with many fat cells are more likely to be obese than are those born with few fat cells. Although the number of fat cells a person has is genetically determined, the size of each cell is affected both by genetics and by nutritional experience early in life. Dieting, in this explanation, decreases only the *size*, not the *number*, of fat cells. Moreover, the body "wants" to maintain the size of fat cells at a constant level, so people who have shrunk the normal size of their fat cells by dieting will experience a constant state of food deprivation. In addition, each significant weight gain may add new fat cells. Thus, permanent weight loss becomes extremely difficult. This accounts for the finding that about two-thirds of people who lose weight gain it all back within a year.

Closely associated with the fat cell explanation of eating and obesity is some researchers' view that each person has a *set point*—a level of body weight that is maintained by the body. The central idea of the set point explanation is that the body seeks to maintain and will always reestablish a homeostatic weight. Each individual set point, which differs from person to person, is determined by many factors, including genetics, early nutrition, current environment, and learned habits.

Further, some studies suggest that people can inherit both a tendency to overeat and a slow metabolism. A slow (or low) metabolism uses available energy (calories) from food efficiently; the calories that are left over tend to be stored as fat. For example, the Pima Indians of Arizona are prone to obesity; 80 to 90 percent of the tribe's young adults are dangerously overweight. According to Ravussin (1988), who spent 4 years researching their habits, the Pimas have unusually low metabolisms. During any 24-hour period, the typical Pima (who is as active as the average American) burns about 80 calories less than is considered normal for his or her body size.

▲ *Members of the Pima tribe of Arizona have unusually low metabolisms, resulting in an inherited tendency toward being overweight.*

People don't have the luxury of choosing their genetic heritage, but that does not mean that those who inherit a predisposition toward obesity are condemned to become fat or to lead an otherwise unhealthy lifestyle. Keesey and Powley (1986) agree that the body's natural predisposition is to maintain homeostasis and that therefore attempts to lose weight through intake regulation alone (such as dieting) are prone to failure and tend to lead to what is called *yo-yo dieting*—recurring cycles of dieting and weight gains. However, weight control—even small changes in one's set point—can be achieved through significant increases in one's physical activity.

Psychological Explanations of Obesity. Physiological makeup isn't the only important factor in eating behavior. The social environment is rampant with food-oriented messages that have little to do with nutritional needs. Advertisements proclaim that merriment can be found at a restaurant or a supermarket. Parents coax good behavior from their children by promising them desserts or fat-laden snacks. Thus, eating acquires a significance that far exceeds its role in satisfying physiological needs: It serves as a rationale for social interaction, a means to reward good behavior, and a way to fend off unhappy thoughts and reduce stress (Greeno & Wing, 1994).

Consider my own attempts to maintain my weight after losing 75 pounds through diet and exercise. Suddenly, I noticed food even more than before. Every time I saw food advertised on billboards or television, I wanted to eat. All the social events I attended seemed to feature a delectable spread of appetizers, which I was tempted to sample in order to be "sociable." And whenever I became anxious, my first impulse was to seek the comfort of food. However, by separating eating behaviors linked to hunger from those that were learned responses to emotions, I controlled my eating behavior and avoided gaining weight even 5 years after my major weight loss.

Researchers continue to explore the causes of overeating. Their efforts have led to some interesting findings, especially when dieters are compared to nondieters. This topic is examined in *The Research Process* on pages 314 and 315.

THE RESEARCH PROCESS

What Causes Overeating?

There are laws of nature that cannot be broken. Unfortunately, one law is that calories not expended will be stored as fat; and a continued imbalance between high food intake and low calorie expenditure will result in obesity. Today, one in every five American teenagers is overweight. What causes people to eat more food than they need? Is it junk food, time spent watching television, not enough exercise? Answers to this question have evolved slowly through research spanning three decades.

Initial Studies. Stanley Schachter and colleagues (Schachter, Goldman, & Gordon, 1968) investigated the eating patterns of obese people. The researchers disguised the true purpose of the experiments, because people often alter their behavior when told they are being watched. In one experiment with both obese and normal-weight people, some participants were given roast beef sandwiches to eat and others were not. The participants were then seated in front of bowls of crackers and were presented with rating scales. They were told to eat as many of the crackers as necessary to judge whether each bowl contained crackers that were salty, cheesy, or garlicky. The researchers' actual goal was to observe how many crackers the participants ate in making their judgments.

Initial Results. As you can see in Figure 9.6, the normal-weight participants ate far fewer crackers than they would have if they had not eaten the roast beef sandwiches. In contrast, the obese participants ate even more than they would have if they had not eaten the sandwiches. Schachter and his colleagues concluded that the eating behavior of the obese participants was determined principally by external factors.

Focus on External Cues. In another study, Schachter (1971) asked both obese and normal-weight participants to sit at a desk and fill out a personality test. The participants were invited to munch from a bag of almonds while they completed the task. Schachter set up two situations. In one, the almonds were shelled; in the other, they were unshelled. Schachter's question was whether one group would eat more than the other of each kind of nut.

About half of the normal-weight participants ate nuts, whether or not the nuts were shelled. In contrast, 19 of 20 obese participants ate the shelled nuts, but only 1 of 20 ate the unshelled ones. Schachter concluded that obese people eat more than people of normal weight when food is readily available and less when the food is difficult to get.

Schachter also showed that obese adults will eat more from a bowl of nuts that is brightly illuminated than from a dimly illuminated bowl. Adults of normal weight are unaffected by the degree of illumination. This evidence led Schachter to infer that the sight of food motivates overweight people to eat. He contended that the availability of food, its prominence,

FIGURE 9.6

Eating Behaviors of Normal-Weight and Obese Subjects

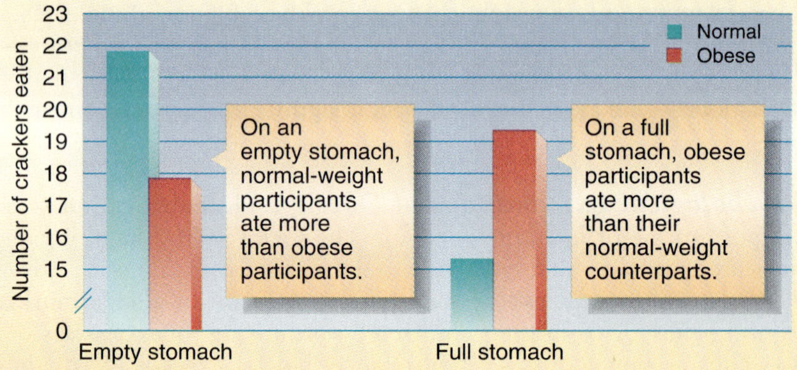

Eating Disorders

In 1994 Christy Henrich, a world-class gymnast, died because of an eating disorder. Henrich, who started training at age 4, was so obsessive a competitor that she was nicknamed E.T.—for Extra Tough. But she dealt with another obsession as well: She always felt that she was too fat. Henrich's anorexia grew so severe that she was eventually too weak to compete. At her death at age 22, she weighed 60 pounds.

Eating disorders: Psychological disorders characterized by gross disturbances in eating behavior and in the way individuals respond to food.

Eating disorders are psychological disorders characterized by gross disturbances in eating behavior and in the way individuals respond to food. Two important eating disorders are anorexia nervosa and bulimia nervosa. These disorders are very much Western diseases; other cultures have their own culture-bound disorders,

and other external cues tell obese individuals when to eat (too much, too fast, and too often). In contrast, normal-weight individuals more often eat in response to internal physiological mechanisms, such as hunger. All in all, under similar conditions, obese participants eat more than normal-weight participants, and the effect is more pronounced when there are external cues to trigger eating.

Contradictions. Schachter's work set off wide-ranging research into the psychological variables that cause overeating. His work focused on external cues, but other researchers argue that obese people are not necessarily more responsive to external cues than are normal-weight people. Stunkard and others suggest that differences between the eating habits of obese and normal-weight individuals are small and inconsistent (Rodin, 1981; Stunkard et al., 1980). They contend instead that the physiological responses of obese individuals may be triggered more quickly than those of normal-weight people.

According to physicians Hirsch and Leibel (1988), people who have lost weight often must take in fewer calories to maintain their weight than do those who have never been obese. This means that formerly obese people have an especially difficult time keeping their weight down. Other researchers agree, asserting that a cycle of dieting and regaining weight makes permanent weight loss difficult because the body burns up fewer calories after a weight loss and that disorders of the autonomic nervous system might play a role in keeping obese people fat (Heatherton, Polivy, & Herman, 1991; Klesges, Isbell, & Klesges, 1992). In addition, researchers Grilo and Pogue-Geile (1991) argue that genetics may play a stronger role than the environment in weight maintenance.

The newest research and assertions are forcing a critical evaluation of all previously collected data. They imply that physiological mechanisms may play a much larger role than psychological ones in eating behavior. Today, there is no simple answer to the nature-versus-nurture question about obesity. Researchers continue to develop multidimensional approaches that examine psychological processes, biological makeup, and sensory aspects of food. In addition, researchers recognize that a person's history with food, level of obesity, response to stress, and current weight all play a role in the likelihood of recurrence or development of obesity (Greeno & Wing, 1994; Lowe, 1993). Some research even suggests a relationship between socioeconomic status and obesity. Sobal and Stunkard (1989) have reported that in developed countries such as the United States, obesity is more common among women of lower socioeconomic status than it is among women of higher socioeconomic status. Research into the possibility of a causal relationship is just beginning (Stunkard & Sørensen, 1993).

Attempts to treat obesity must incorporate a "reasonable weight" that is based on aesthetic and health standards for the wide range of individuals with obesity problems (Brownell & Rodin, 1994; Brownell & Wadden, 1992). Such plans must also incorporate biological and environmental factors as well as cognitive states—the thoughts that the obese have when they are overeating (Grilo & Shiffman, 1994).

but eating disorders such as anorexia nervosa and bulimia nervosa are found in wealthy Western industrialized societies.

Anorexia Nervosa. **Anorexia nervosa**, a starvation disease that affects as many as 40 out of every 10,000 young women in the United States, is an eating disorder characterized by an obstinate and willful refusal to eat. Individuals with the disorder, usually adolescent girls from middle-class families, have a distorted body image. They perceive themselves as fat if they have any flesh on their bones or deviate from their idealized body image. They intensely fear being fat and relentlessly pursue thinness. The anorexic's refusal to eat eventually brings about emaciation and malnutrition (which may bring about a further distortion of body image).

Anorexia nervosa [an-uh-REX-see-uh ner-VOH-suh]: An eating disorder characterized by an intense fear of becoming obese, dramatic weight loss, concern about weight, disturbances in body image, and an obstinate and willful refusal to eat.

▲ *Society contributes to eating disorders by establishing unrealistic standards for the "perfect" female body. In the 1950s, an hourglass figure like that of Jayne Mansfield (left) was the ideal. Today's high-fashion models are much thinner.*

Victims may sustain permanent damage to their heart muscle tissue, sometimes dying as a result.

Many therapists believe that anorexia nervosa has strictly psychological origins. They cite poor mother–daughter relationships, especially overprotective parents, other negative family interactions, and escapes from self-awareness as the main causes (Walters & Kendler, 1995). Others are exploring possible physiological contributions to the disorder, including the many changes taking place at puberty that might influence its emergence (Attie & Brooks-Gunn, 1989), as well as prejudice against the obese (Crandall, 1994). Some psychologists believe that people with eating disorders may lack a hormone that is thought to induce a feeling of fullness after a meal.

People with anorexia nervosa need a structured setting, and therapists often hospitalize them to help them regain weight. To ensure that the setting is reinforcing, hospital staff members are always present at meals. Individual and family therapy is provided. Clients are encouraged to eat and are rewarded for consuming specified quantities of food. Generally, psychotherapy is also necessary to help these people attain a healthy self-image and body weight. Even with treatment, however, as many as 50 percent suffer relapses within a year.

Bulimia Nervosa. **Bulimia nervosa** is an eating disorder characterized by binge eating followed by purging. It tends to occur in normal-weight women with no history of anorexia nervosa (e.g., Garfinkel, Moldofsy, & Garner, 1980). The bingeing (recognized by the person as being abnormal) is accompanied by a fear of not being able to stop eating. Individuals who engage in binge eating become fearful of gaining weight; they become preoccupied with how others see them (Striegel-Moore, Silberstein, & Rodin, 1993). Therefore, they often purge themselves of unwanted calories, mostly through vomiting and the use of laxatives and diuretics. Other methods include compulsive exercising and weight reduction drugs. Bulimics are often depressed (Specker et al., 1994), and the medical complications of bulimia are serious. They include cardiovascular and gastrointestinal problems, menstrual irregularities, blood and hormone dysfunctions, muscular and skeletal problems, and sharp swings in mood and personality (Kaplan & Woodside, 1987).

Men and women are affected by eating disorders in similar ways (Olivardia et al., 1995), but the ratio of female to male bulimics is 10 to 1. Researchers theorize that women believe more readily than men that fat is bad

FOCUS

Review

- What is the evidence that individuals are motivated to eat or drink because of a lack of food or fluid in the body? pp. 310–312
- What evidence is there that the relationship between eating and obesity can be explained by external cues? pp. 314-315

Think Critically

- Individuals do not respond to food in the same way at all times of day. What variables might have affected Schachter's participants to cause them to behave differently in his studies?
- If, as some researchers claim, there is a physiological basis to anorexia, why do you think anorexia is less prevalent in other cultures?

and thin is beautiful. Women of higher socioeconomic classes are at greater risk of becoming bulimic, as are professionals whose weight is directly related to achievement, such as dancers, athletes, and models. Disharmonious family life and maladjusted parents who inflict psychological and physical abuse on a child increase the likelihood of bulimia (Rorty, Yager, & Rossotto, 1994.) Women with bulimia also have lower self-esteem than women who eat normally, and they may have experienced some kind of clinical depression in the past (Klingenspor, 1994).

Bulimia nervosa [boo-LEE-me-uh ner-VOH-suh]: An eating disorder characterized by repeated episodes of binge eating (and a fear of not being able to stop eating) followed by purging.

Some women may eat as a means of lightening their mood, regulating tension, and escaping from self-awareness (Heatherton & Baumeister, 1991). After bingeing, however, they feel guilty. To lessen their guilt and the potential consequence of gaining weight, they purge themselves. Researchers believe the purges reduce postbinge guilt feelings. Bulimics may become so involved in food-related behaviors that they will avoid contact with other people.

Sexual Behavior: Physiology plus Thought

When the Prince of Wales, Prince Charles, was reported to have had a longstanding affair with friend and confidant Camilla Parker-Bowles, the London tabloids had a field day. The affairs of Presidents Franklin Delano Roosevelt and John F. Kennedy had similar effects in the United States. People's preoccupation with the sex lives of national figures indicates that they are fascinated with and often define themselves in terms of their sexuality—a type of motivation that, unlike physiologically based hunger, is not necessary to sustain life. So immediately we see an important difference between sexual behavior and activities like food seeking. The sexual behavior of lower organisms is controlled largely by their physiological and hormonal systems. In human beings, in contrast, the sex drive is to a great extent under psychological control.

This means that not only physiology, especially sex hormones, but ideas, past behaviors, emotions, expectations, and goals all enter into the sexual behavior of human beings. The relative contributions of these factors vary depending on an array of variables. For some people, sights, sounds, and smells are sexual initiators, triggers for sexually motivated behavior. For others, thoughts, feelings, and fantasy either initiate or in many cases satisfy sexual motivation. Men and women respond differently; the old respond differently than the young do; the religious background of individuals affects their sexual behavior; and the culture in which a person is raised has profound influences. Western ideas about sexuality differ significantly from Eastern approaches; and even within Western cultures there exists great diversity. For example, Europeans are more open and expressive sexually than are Americans. But the British find sexual indiscretions among politicians more outrageous and titillating than do Americans, who find financial scandals more difficult to condone. Recognizing this diversity of response, let us first look at some of the initiators of sexual behavior, at the physiology of the behavior itself, and then at the range of sexual behaviors in which human beings engage.

What Initiates the Sex Drive?

Hardly a day goes by that you are not bombarded with sexually suggestive advertisements. Perfume ads abound in magazines; cars are sold by attractive, and often half-clad, models. Sports equipment is sold by youthful, sexually desirable men and women; even toothpaste is sold by alluring women and men. Advertisers use learning principles to pair attractive people and situations with their products in the hope that their products will take on an arousing glamour—and to hint that if you use their product, you may become as alluring as their models. The advertisers are seeking to initiate activity—buying activity—by activating the sexual drive. They know, of course, that people's thoughts, more than their hormones, direct buying behavior. But hormones do play a vital role in sexual behavior.

Sex Hormones. Sexual behavior in human beings is in part under hormonal control, and the hormones are different for men and women. In males, the testes are the principal producer of androgens, the male sex hormones. In females, the ovaries are the principal producer of estrogens, the female hormones. (In reality there are many different male and female sex hormones, but we can refer to them generically as androgens and estrogens.) It is the release of androgens (especially testosterone) and estrogens (especially estradiol) that first signals and accelerates the onset of the secondary sex characteristics in developing teenagers. Once males and females are postpubescent, sufficient levels of androgens and estrogens are present to create a desire and willingness in teenagers to engage in sexual behaviors—if they choose to. In men, androgens (especially testosterone) stay at pretty much the same level on a day-to-day basis; in women, estrogen levels vary throughout the menstrual cycle, and when the menstrual cycle ceases, estrogen levels fall. Both men and women can be receptive and active sexually regardless of their hormone level.

People share with animals a hormonally based sexual urge that is determined, in part, by brain structures such as the hypothalamus (Swaab & Hofman, 1995). But in animals, hormones exert profound effects on behavior, activating an animal toward an organized set of sexual responses. Most of these responses in animals are under direct hormonal control and are not seen without hormonal activation. So, for example, if the hormone-generating testes of male rats are removed, the animals show a marked decrease in sexual activity. Similarly, most female animals are sexually responsive *only* when hormones are released into the bloodstream (when they are "in heat"). Human beings, on the other hand, can choose whether or not to respond sexually to encounters at any given time. In fact, in human beings, the removal of hormone-generating organs may not affect sexual behavior at all (depending on the person's age at removal), because sexual motivation is as much socially and psychologically as physiologically based—or even more so.

Sights, Sounds, Smells, and Fantasy. In animals, a receptive female may show her receptivity by releasing pheromones; this acts as a trigger for sexual activity (see Chapter 3, page 104). Other times, a suggestive movement or circling around a nest may signal receptivity and will trigger sexual behavior from another animal. But human beings, because they are not so directly under hormonal control, can be aroused, become interested, and seek out or be responsive to sexual stimulation because of a sight of something sexual, an erotic sound, or the smell of a familiar and arousing perfume. Thought plays an enormous role in human beings; people's own thoughts, fantasies, emotions, and images initiate and activate sexual desire and activity.

Sexual Response Cycle

Excitement phase: The first phase of the sexual response cycle, during which there are initial increases in heart rate, blood pressure, and respiration.

Vasocongestion: In the sexual response cycle, engorgement of the blood vessels, particularly in the genital area, due to increased blood flow.

When human beings become sexually aroused, they go through a series of four phases (stages). The phases, which together are known as the *sexual response cycle*, are the excitement phase, the plateau phase, the orgasm phase, and the resolution phase.

The **excitement phase** is the first phase of the cycle, during which there are initial increases in heart rate, blood pressure, and respiration. A key characteristic of this phase is **vasocongestion**—engorgement of the blood vessels, particularly in the genital area, due to increased blood flow. In women, the breasts and clitoris swell, the vaginal lips expand, and vaginal lubrication increases; in men, the penis becomes erect. The excitement phase is anticipatory and may last from a few minutes to a few hours. It may be initiated by physical contact, fantasy, or activity in any of the senses.

The **plateau phase** is the second phase of the sexual response cycle, during which the sexual partners are preparing for orgasm. Autonomic nervous system activity, such as the heart rate, increases. In women, the clitoris withdraws, the vagina becomes engorged and fully extended; in men, the penis becomes fully erect, turns a darker color, and may secrete a bit of fluid, which may contain sperm.

The **orgasm phase** is the third phase of the sexual response cycle, during which autonomic nervous system activity reaches its peak and muscle contractions occur throughout the body, especially in the genital area, in spasms. An *orgasm* is the peak of sexual activity. In men, muscles throughout the reproductive system contract to help expel semen; in women, muscles surrounding the outer vagina contract. Although men experience only one orgasm during each sexual response cycle, women are capable of multiple orgasms. An orgasm lasts only a few seconds and is an all-or-none activity; once a threshold for orgasm is reached, the orgasm occurs.

The **resolution phase** is the fourth phase of the sexual response cycle, during which the body naturally returns after orgasm to its resting, or normal, state. This return takes from one to several minutes, varying considerably from person to person. During this phase, men are usually unable to achieve an erection for some period of time, called the *refractory period.*

Like many other physiological events, the sexual response cycle is subject to considerable variation. Some people go through a lengthy plateau phase; others may have a longer resolution phase.

Human Sexual Behavior

While American culture is saturated with sexually suggestive advertisements and sexually explicit movies, television, and other media, this same culture shows considerable reluctance to scientifically examine and talk about sexual behavior. Efforts to examine sexuality in a systematic way are often viewed with skepticism, to the extent that Congress in 1994 sought to ensure that a federally funded sex survey was not conducted.

Sex Surveys: What's Normal? Despite this reluctance to look at the data, over the years various sexual surveys, attitude questionnaires, and in-depth interviews have been conducted. The most famous was conducted by Kinsey and his colleagues (1948, 1953). The Kinsey study used to be the main source of information about human sexual attitudes and behavior. This was unfortunate, because the study, while quite comprehensive, was nonrepresentative of the population; the data were collected in face-to-face interviews with a sample of largely white, middle-class people from the East Coast and the Midwest. In addition, the interviewers often coaxed answers from participants in a belligerent way; this was hardly dispassionate, careful science. But Kinsey's work has now been extended by contemporary researchers such as Morton Hunt (1974), Masters, Johnson, and Kolodny (1994), and especially by Laumann and colleagues (1994).

When the Kinsey studies were first published, the public was shocked. The data regarding homosexuality seemed incredible. Kinsey and his colleagues received considerable criticism from scientists—initially for the data they produced, today for their methods. Now that more than four decades have passed, it is clear that Kinsey's statistics were often accurate but in some cases may have overrepresented or underrepresented contemporary sexual behavior. The Kinsey study overrepresented the number of men who were homosexual (10 percent), for example. The

Plateau phase: The second phase of the sexual response cycle, during which the sexual partners are preparing for orgasm, autonomic nervous system activity increases, and there is further vasoconstriction.

Orgasm phase: The third phase of the sexual response cycle, during which autonomic nervous system activity reaches its peak and muscle contractions occur throughout the body, but especially in the genital area, in spasms.

Resolution phase: The fourth phase of the sexual response cycle, during which the body naturally returns after orgasm to its resting, or normal, state.

most striking example of underrepresentation may be the figures representing the premarital sexual behavior of women. While Kinsey reported some premarital sexual behavior in women, it was, in fact, far more frequent. Since the Kinsey days, major changes in sexual behavior have also taken place and continue to occur. The fear of AIDS during the last decade has caused young men and women to alter their behaviors; among some groups, for example, the number of partners with whom people in their 20s are willing to have sex has decreased. This varies with age, gender, and ethnicity; for example, poor, young, black and Hispanic women are at higher risk for sexually transmitted diseases and for AIDS in particular (Wyatt, 1994). Meanwhile, on many measures, men and women are becoming more alike in attitudes and behaviors (Oliver & Hyde, 1993). Let's examine some of the patterns.

In general, when taken together, reports about sexual practices show that individuals engage in sexual behaviors more when they are younger than when they are older. For example, the frequency of intercourse decreases from a person's early 20s to when he or she is in the 50s or 60s. Similarly, the duration spent in any specific sexual activity decreases with increasing age. Within couples in Western culture, patterns of sexual practices are predictable; elements of sexual activity, particularly foreplay, rarely occur in isolation. One behavior, such as petting, often or at least usually precedes another, such as intercourse. While the sex lives of Americans are predictable, and not as active as is assumed by many, most people are happy with their sex lives (Laumann et al., 1994).

The Laumann study of sexual practices in the United States is the most recent and most comprehensive of the last four decades. In it, 3,432 men and women aged 18 to 59 in randomly selected households throughout the country were administered questionnaires and face-to-face interviews. The results showed that men and women are more likely today than in the 1940s to have intercourse before marriage and that there has been a slow and steady decrease in the age of first intercourse. Men think about sex more than women; about 54 percent of men think about sex daily compared to only 19 percent of women. Interestingly, married men and women have more sex than do nonmarried young people—shattering a myth that the young and footloose are the most active sexually. The truth is that only one-third of people aged 18 to 59 have sex with a partner as often as twice a week. Many behavioral scientists found the results of the Laumann study predictable—but there were some surprises. Most women (90 percent) and most men (75 percent) reported that they had not had extramarital sexual affairs (Laumann et al., 1994, p. 214). This may reflect in part a fear of sexually transmitted diseases; in any case, this society is not as sexually promiscuous as daytime soap operas would have you believe. Another finding that surprised some researchers was that only 5.3 percent of men and 3.5 percent of women had had homosexual intercourse with someone since puberty. More important, only 2.8 percent of men and 1.4 percent of women identified themselves as exclusively homosexual. The Laumann percentages are substantially less than the 10 percent that was reported by Kinsey in the 1950s, and they have been substantiated with similar estimates from other researchers (Sell, Wells, & Wypij, 1995).

A key approach that the Laumann study used was to define sexuality and sexual behavior within the context of how people live. The researchers found that individuals have sex with people they know and live with (most often spouses) and that when people are sexually active, they think about and desire sex more than do individuals who are not sexually active. Further, when people do engage in an extramarital affair, it is usually not a one-night stand with a stranger met on a train but a relationship with someone they know. The Laumann study shows that contemporary sexual behavior has indeed changed. Today, people express their sexuality more often and more openly—and seek to understand their own feelings and behavior. They are also having to pay attention to sexually transmitted diseases, especially to the spread of AIDS, a topic discussed in Chapter 13. Further, people today are confronting more forthrightly, at least more than in previous decades, the issue of sexual orientation.

Sexual Orientation. Sexual orientation is the direction of one's sexual interests. A person with a *heterosexual orientation* has an erotic attraction and preference for members of the opposite sex; an individual with a *homosexual orientation* has an erotic attraction to and preference for members of his or her same sex. A *bisexual orientation* is an erotic attraction to members of both sexes. Before the Kinsey studies, people were considered either heterosexual or homosexual; but Kinsey introduced the idea of a continuum of sexual behaviors: from exclusively homosexual behaviors through some homosexual behaviors, to mostly heterosexual behaviors, to exclusively heterosexual behaviors. Kinsey recognized, and allowed other researchers to realize, that a homosexual encounter does not make a person homosexual. Also, a person may have a homosexual or bisexual orientation without ever having had a homosexual sexual experience. It is thus an overgeneralization and a mistake to label a person as to sexual orientation based solely on a single, or even multiple, sex behaviors.

The Kinsey report startled psychologists when it announced a high frequency of homosexual behavior among men (37 percent) and suggested that 1 in 10 men was primarily homosexual in orientation. The Laumann study has changed the numbers, and researchers and the public are more willing to accept as reasonable estimates the 2.8 percent of men and 1.4 percent of women the study says identify themselves as exclusively homosexual. But Americans, perhaps more than people in other cultures, still have great difficulty with homosexuality. When President Clinton announced soon after he was elected that he was going to change the policy on having gays in the military, it created political furor, intense debate, and research into the effect of having gays in the military (Jones & Koshes, 1995). Further, the high incidence of AIDS among gay men has placed the issues of prevention and homosexuality on the public agenda. Often, however, people have interpreted correlations among AIDS incidence and sexual orientation to draw unwarranted cause-and-effect conclusions.

The causes of homosexuality have been debated for decades, and the argument has developed into a classic nature-versus-nurture debate. The nurture side asserts that homosexual behavior is to a great extent under voluntary control, that it is learned, and that it can be changed by means of effective, consistent, and long-term therapy. Those who support this view see a basic flaw in conclusions from genetic studies, family studies, and research on brain chemistry—they assert that researchers have mixed up the causes of sexual orientation with the effects (Byne, 1994).

On the nature side are those who assert that homosexuality is indeed inborn, fixed, and genetically determined. They cite data showing that homosexual men and women knew when they were young children that they were "different"; they point out that attempts to change gay men and women through therapy, prayer, and drugs are mostly ineffective. Further, recent studies isolating brain structures, genes, and familial patterns of homosexuality (even among twins separated at birth) increasingly lend support to a nature argument (LeVay & Hamer, 1994). The weight of the evidence leans toward the physiological—or nature—side of the debate. Twin studies show a high concordance rate for homosexuality among fraternal and identical twins. In extended families, gay men tend to come from

FOCUS

Review

- What evidence exists to suggest that thought plays an especially important role in human sexual behavior? pp. 317–318
- Describe the evidence that supports the nature and the nurture sides of the debate about the development of sexual orientation. pp. 321–322

Think Critically

- Why do you think the federal government should or should not be engaging in studies of sexual behavior?
- Whenever scientific discoveries dealing with genetics are made, they raise ethical questions. For example, should parents be allowed to prescreen pregnancies for a genetic marker for homosexuality?

families where there are many other gay men; further, Hamer found genetic evidence associated with gay men (Hamer et al., 1993). High levels of specific hormones have been found at birth among babies who later became male homosexuals. Last, both Simon LeVay (1991) and Swaab & Hoffman (1995) found that portions of the hypothalamus of men who were gay differ from those of men who were heterosexual. The impact of this evidence has been profound. Gay men and lesbians are leaving mental health counseling, seeking civil rights protection, and feeling better about themselves and their sexuality.

Achievement: A Social Need

Personality psychologists such as Henry Murray assert that key events and situations in people's environment determine behavior. Murray used the word *press* for the way these environmental situations may motivate a person (Murray, 1938). The environment may *press* an individual to excel at sports, be a loving caretaker to a grandparent, or achieve great wealth. The *press* of poverty may produce a social need for financial security; it may therefore cause a person to work hard, train, and become educated to achieve wealth.

The most notable theories for measuring the results of press are expectancy theories that focus specifically on the **need for achievement**—a social need that directs people to strive constantly for excellence and success. According to such achievement theories, people engage in behaviors that satisfy their desires for success, mastery, and fulfillment. Tasks not oriented toward these goals are not motivating and either are not undertaken or are performed without energy or commitment. There may be even more negative effects when people feel that making an effort is useless. *Applications* discusses what happens when goals, even modest ones, are never achieved.

One of the leaders in early studies of achievement motivation was David C. McClelland, whose early research focused on the idea that people have strong social motives for achievement (McClelland, 1958). McClelland showed that achievement motivation is learned in an individual's home environment during childhood. Adults with a high need for achievement had parents who stressed excellence and who provided physical affection and emotional rewards for high achievement. These adults also generally walked early, talked early, and had a high need for achievement even in elementary school (e.g., Teevan & McGhee, 1972). A high need for achievement is most pronounced in first-born children, perhaps because parents typically have more time to give them direction and praise.

Achievement motives are often measured in terms of scores derived from an analysis of the thought content of imaginative stories. Early studies of people's need for achievement used the *Thematic Apperception Test (TAT)*. In this test, people are shown scenes with no captions and vague themes, which are thus open to interpretation. The test takers are instructed not to think in terms of right or wrong answers but to answer four basic questions for each scene:

1. What is happening?
2. What has led up to this situation?
3. What is being thought?
4. What will happen next?

Using a complex scoring system, researchers analyze participants' descriptions of each scene. They have found that persons with a high need for achievement tell stories that stress success, getting ahead, and competition (Spangler, 1992).

Need for achievement: A social need that directs people to strive constantly for excellence and success.

With tests such as the TAT, a researcher can quickly discern which individuals have a high need for achievement and which have a low need. Lowell (1952), for example, found that when he asked participants to rearrange scrambled letters

APPLICATIONS

Learned Helplessness

People want to have control over their lives so they can determine their own destinies. They want to be able to attribute the causes of their behavior to rational events in the world. Most people believe they can control their environment to a reasonable extent. But what happens to people in a situation in which they feel they have little control? How do they react when negative things happen to them?

Assume that you are a participant in an experiment in which you have to solve puzzles. The puzzles appear to be relatively simple; yet no matter what you do, you cannot solve them. You probably become frustrated. Research shows that, when put in situations in which they have no control over the negative things happening to them, both people and animals often stop responding. Martin Seligman (1975) and his colleagues showed, for example, that dogs first exposed to a series of inescapable shocks and then given a chance to escape further punishment fail to learn the escape response. Seligman termed this behavior *learned helplessness.* **Learned helplessness** is the behavior of giving up or not responding, which is exhibited by organisms exposed to negative consequences or punishment over which they have no control.

According to Seligman, the major cause of learned helplessness is an organism's belief that its response will not affect what happens to it in the future. The result of this belief is anxiety, depression, and, eventually, nonresponsiveness. We will see in Chapter 14 (pages 500–501) that learned helplessness is a key factor underlying depression.

The opposite of learned helplessness is *learned optimism*—a sense that the world has positive outcomes, which leads people to see happy things in their lives (Seligman, 1991). Seligman asserts that *learning* is the key to a sense of doom or optimism.

(such as *wtse*) to construct a meaningful word (*west*), subjects with a low need for achievement improved only slightly at the task over successive testing periods. In contrast, participants who scored high in the need for achievement showed greater ongoing improvement over several periods of testing (see Figure 9.7). The researchers concluded that, when presented with a complex task, persons with a high need for achievement find new and better ways of performing the task as they practice it, whereas those with a low need for achievement try no new methods. People with a high need for achievement constantly strive toward excellence and better performance; they have developed a belief in their self-efficacy and in the importance of effort in determining performance (Carr, Borkowski, & Maxwell, 1991; McClelland, 1961).

FIGURE 9.7

Performance on a Scrambled-Letter Task

The graph shows performance on a scrambled-letter task for successive 2-minute periods. Task achievement is affected by a person's overall approach to achievement-related tasks. Participants with a low need for achievement improved overall; however, those with a high need for achievement improved even more.
(Based on data from Lowell, 1952.)

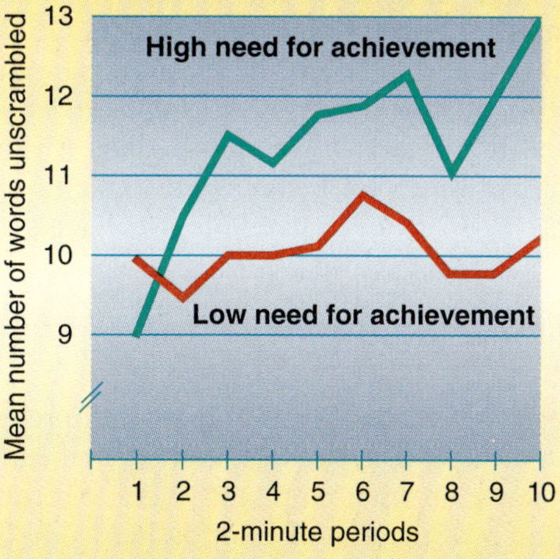

Learned helplessness: Behavior of giving up or not responding, exhibited by organisms exposed to negative consequences or punishment over which they have no control; the major cause is an organism's belief that its response will not affect what happens to it in the future.

The need for achievement seems closely related to the amount of risk people are willing to take. Some researchers claim that children exposed to praise are likely to be more achievement-oriented and thus willing to take on higher levels of risk. To test this idea, Canavan-Gumpert (1977) presented first- and sixth-grade girls in a New York suburban school with math problems, then praised them for correct answers and criticized them for incorrect answers. After a practice task in which they were praised or criticized, the girls chose problems at one of eight levels of difficulty. The praised students had more optimistic expectations, higher standards, and greater confidence about their future performance. They chose problems at the highest level of difficulty, accepting the risk of failure. The criticized students were dissatisfied with their performance and chose problems at the lowest difficulty level. The most important finding of the Canavan-Gumpert study is that praise and criticism directly affected girls' risk-taking behavior and, ultimately, their need for achievement.

The goals people set and the amount of risk they are willing to take are also affected by the kind of needs that motivate them, their experiences, and even their moods (Hom & Arbuckle, 1988). The expression *self-fulfilling prophecy* suggests that those who expect to succeed will do so and those who don't expect to succeed won't. Expectations for success and failure can influence the outcome of an effort if those expectations help shape the person's behavior (Elliott & Dweck, 1988). A teacher who expects a student to fail, for example, may treat the student in ways that increase the likelihood of the student's failure; things tend to turn out just the way the teacher expected (or prophesied) they would. Expectancy thus becomes a key component in explaining behavior, especially in people with a high need for achievement. For example, a person pushed toward success by parents, drama instructors, or sports coaches may develop a high need for achievement; after positive experiences, such an individual will typically set challenging but attainable performance goals (Dweck & Leggett, 1988).

Emotion

In an emotional and tearful scene, Susan Smith, a South Carolina mother of two, convinced not only local townspeople but a nation of TV viewers that her sons had been abducted. People everywhere sympathized and began a nationwide manhunt—only later to find that she had murdered the two little boys. No one understood her motivation. Her emotional display had been largely a lie; her desperation and outrage at her boys' supposed abduction were all an act. How was she able to manipulate a nation's emotional response, let alone her own? The Smith incident demonstrated that outward emotional displays can be manufactured and that the true motivations of behavior and emotional reactions are often difficult to discern.

That motivation and emotion are interconnected, in this chapter as in life, should come as no surprise. Anger can cause you to hurl an object across a room or to lash out at a friend. Happiness can make you smile all day or stop to help a motorist with a flat tire. Fear can electrify you, making your legs pump faster as you sprint down a dark, shadowy alley. Although emotions, including love, joy, and fear, can motivate behavior, these emotional states and categories remain fuzzy (Rosch, 1978). Even psychologists have difficulty agreeing on their definitions.

What Is Emotion?

Emotion: A subjective response, usually accompanied by a physiological change, which is interpreted by an individual and then readies the individual for some action that is associated with a change in behavior.

The word *emotion* is an umbrella term referring to a wide range of subjective states, such as love, fear, sadness, and excitement. We all have emotions, talk about them, and agree on what represents them; but this agreement is not scientific. The psychological investigation of emotion has led to a more precise definition. An **emotion** is a subjective response (feeling), usually accompanied by a physiological change, which is interpreted by the individual and then readies the individual for some action that is associated with a change in behavior. People cry when they are sad, find increased energy when they are excited, and breathe faster, sweat, feel nauseated, and salivate less (causing a dry mouth) when they are afraid (see Kleinginna & Kleinginna, 1981). Some physiological changes precede an emotional response. For example, just before an automobile crashes, the people involved show physiological arousal, muscle tension, and avoidance responses—that is, they brace themselves in anticipation. Other changes are evident only after an emotion-causing event. It is only after the auto accident that people shake with fear, disbelief, or rage.

People often respond to physiological changes by altering their behavior. When they are afraid, they may scream. When they are angry, they may seek revenge or retribution. When they are in love, they may act tenderly toward others. In some situations, people think about acting out their feelings but may not express them in directly observable ways. Emotional expressions sometimes seem contradictory; think about Juliet's claim that "parting is such sweet sorrow." Although emotions may seem to be written all over people's faces, appearances can be deceiving and difficult to interpret.

Psychologists focus on different aspects of emotional behavior. The earliest researchers catalogued and described basic emotions (Bridges, 1932; Wundt, 1896). Others tried to discover the physiological bases of emotion (Bard, 1934). Still others focused on how people perceive bodily movements and on how they convey emotions to others through nonverbal mechanisms such as gestures or eye contact (Ekman, 1992). More recent studies have investigated people's ability to control their emotional responses, as Susan Smith did (Meichenbaum, 1977).

Many psychologists acknowledge that emotion consists of three elements: feelings, physiological responses, and behaviors. People experience the same *kinds* of emotions, but the intensity and quality vary. One person's sense of joy is different from another's. Thus, emotions have a private, personal, and unique component. This subjective element is called *feelings*. Subjective feelings are difficult to measure, so most researchers focus on the other two aspects of emotion—physiological responses and behaviors. This focus shifts research from the internal process to action or readiness for action. Researchers are studying the following observable and measurable aspects of emotions: whether one hemisphere of the brain dominates emotion (R. J. Davidson, 1992; Fox, 1991); the biochemical components of emotions, including blood glucose levels and hormone changes (Baum, Grunberg, & Singer, 1992); physiological responses such as heart rate and blood pressure; and behavioral responses such as smiling and crying.

Robert Plutchik (1980) suggests that emotions can be mixed (just as colors are) to yield new varieties of emotional experience. He has devised a conceptual circle to characterize emotional responses (see Figure 9.8). Neighboring primary emotions (shown inside the circle) are mixed to yield more complex emotions (shown outside the circle). So, for instance, a person experiencing joy and anticipation may feel a sense of optimism; similarly, surprise and sadness when mixed may be experienced as disappointment. Such models are interesting ways to think about the range of human emotional responses; however, there is as yet little data to support them.

Richard Lazarus (1991c) has concluded that there are *four* types of emotions: (1) emotions resulting from harm, loss, or threats; (2) emotions resulting from benefits; (3) borderline emotions, such as hope and compassion; and (4) more complex emotions, such as grief, disappointment, bewilderment, and curiosity. Turner and Ortony (1992) assert that

FIGURE 9.8

An Alternative Conception of Emotional Range: Plutchik's Circle

Plutchik (1980) suggests that human emotions can be mixed (just as colors are) to yield new varieties of emotional experience.

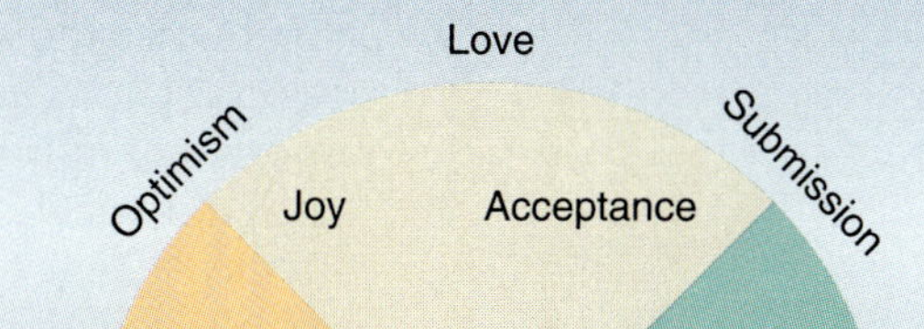

psychologists should think in terms of basic components of emotions rather than basic emotions. Lewis and Saarni (1985) suggest that the following five basic *elements* of emotions must be considered:

1. *Emotional elicitors*—the events that trigger emotions. (These include painful as well as pleasant experiences.)
2. *Emotional receptors (brain mechanisms)*—central nervous system mechanisms responsible for processing emotional reactions. (These mechanisms are discussed later in this chapter.)
3. *Emotional states*—changes in neural, biochemical, and general physiological activity that occur when an organism is activated emotionally.
4. *Emotional expressions*—observable and measurable changes in an organism that convey information to others about emotional states.
5. *Emotional experience*—a subjective state determined by cognitive and social factors. (This is the individual's interpretation and evaluation of an emotional reaction.)

Not all researchers consider all elements of a definition of emotion in their studies. One study may focus on emotional expression; another may focus on emotional experiences. Physiological psychologists sometimes trace neural pathways and confine their research to brain structures such as the hypothalamus. Researchers such as Izard (1993) depict a multistage process of emotion with neural systems at the beginning and cognitive systems at the end. Before going on to the biologically based theories of emotion, read *Diversity*, which examines cultural differences in the use of emotional terms.

Physiological Theories of Emotion

The wide range of emotions that human beings experience and express is in large part controlled by a series of neurons located in an area deep within the brain, the limbic system. The *limbic system* is composed of cells in the hypothalamus, the amygdala, and other cortical and subcortical areas. Studies of these crucial areas began in the 1920s, when Bard (1934) found that the removal of portions of the cortex of cats produced sharp emotional reactions to simple stimuli such as a touch or a puff of air. The cats would hiss, claw, bite, arch their backs, and growl—and their reactions did not seem directed at any specific person or target. Bard referred to this behavior as *sham rage*. Later researchers stimulated portions of the brain with electrical current and found that the visual system was also important in emotions. They deduced that the cortex was integrating visual information and hypothalamic information to produce emotional behavior. In general, two major physiological (biological) approaches to the study of emotion developed: the James–Lange theory and the Cannon–Bard theory. Both are concerned with the physiology of emotions and with whether physiological change or emotional feelings occur first.

The James–Lange Theory. According to a theory proposed by both William James (1842–1910) and Carl Lange (1834–1900) (who are given joint credit since the two approaches were so similar), people experience physiological changes and then interpret them as emotional states (see Figure 9.9 on page 328). People do not cry because they feel sad; they feel sad because they cry. People do not perspire because they are afraid; they feel afraid after they perspire. In other words, the James–Lange theory says that people do not experience an emotion until after their bodies become aroused and begin to respond with physiological changes; that is, feedback from the body produces feelings or emotions (James, 1884; Lange, 1922). For this approach,

Diversity

Cultural Differences in Emotional Terms

If you live in the United States and speak English, your emotional life is categorized differently than if you come from Japan or Indonesia. Some words that describe emotions in the English language have no real equivalent in other languages. Are there emotions that exist in English-speaking people that do not exist in speakers of German, Chinese, or Japanese? If such differences exist, what do they reveal about emotions?

According to James A. Russell (1991, 1994, 1995), who has conducted extensive research into cross-cultural comparisons of emotional terms, enormous differences exist among languages. For example, languages differ in the number of words they provide to categorize emotions. There are 2,000 words to describe emotions in English, but only 1,500 in Dutch, 750 in Taiwanese Chinese, and 230 in Malay.

More important than the number of terms, however, are the categories of emotion. Some English words have no real equivalent in other languages. Russell points out that English distinguishes among *terror, horror, dread, apprehension*, and *timidity* as types of fear. However, in Gidjingali, an Australian aboriginal language, one word, *gurakadj*, suffices. What English treats as different emotions—for example, anger and sadness—other languages treat as one emotion. The English distinction between *shame* and *embarrassment* is not made by the people of Japan. In China, there exists no word for *anxiety*; in Sri Lanka, there is no term for *guilt*. In addition, some languages have words without an equivalent in English.

The categorization of words that describe emotions is important because it shows researchers that the emotional experience across all cultures may not be the same. Cultural differences in emotion are probably due to differences in the way each culture approaches, appraises, and responds to various life events (Mesquita & Frijda, 1992). For example, among the Awlad 'Ali, a tribe of Egyptian Bedouins, the definition of *shameful events* is highly specific: Shameful events are those that injure one's honor; therefore, how a person codes an event is a central element in the person's emotional response to that event (Mesquita & Frijda, 1992). In addition, just because a language does not have a particular word does not mean that the concept does not exist; it may, for example, be expressed in a phrase rather than in a single word.

From psychologists' point of view, the use of language to describe emotions is important because any theoretical discussion that names emotions uses specific words in a specific language. A theory of emotion that aims to be truly universal to all people, in all cultures, in all languages, must be cross-culturally valid—not bound by specific lexical (word) entries in a dictionary. This is an enormous challenge. Most psychologists believe that all human beings experience the same emotions (Mauro, Sato, & Tucker, 1992), but psychologists have to use terminology and methodology that is consistent across cultures. Without such consistency, cross-cultural differences will be hard to separate from cross-cultural similarities (Russell, 1995).

in its most simplified form (Ellsworth, 1994), *feeling* is the essence of emotion. Thus, James (1890, p. 1006) wrote, "Every one of the bodily changes whatsoever it be is felt, acutely or obscurely, the moment it occurs."

A modern physiological approach suggests that facial movements, by their action, can create emotions. In some ways this approach is similar to the James–Lange theory. For example, when specific facial movements create a change in blood flow to and temperature of the brain, pleasant feelings occur. According to Zajonc, Murphy, and Inglehart (1989), a facial movement such as a smile or an eye movement may release the appropriate emotion-linked neurotransmitters. Some neurotransmitters may bring about pleasant emotions and others unpleasant ones. Crying, for example, is associated with a mixture of sympathetic, parasympathetic, and somatic activation (Gross, Fredrickson, & Levenson, 1994). Zajonc and his colleagues argue that facial movements alone are capable of inducing emotions; anecdotally, children (and adults) often do feel a bit happier when their parents and

FIGURE 9.9

Theories of Emotion

In the *James–Lange theory,* arousal precedes interpretation. In the *Cannon–Bard theory,* arousal and emotion occur simultaneously. According to the *Schachter–Singer theory,* the interpretation of arousal depends on the context.

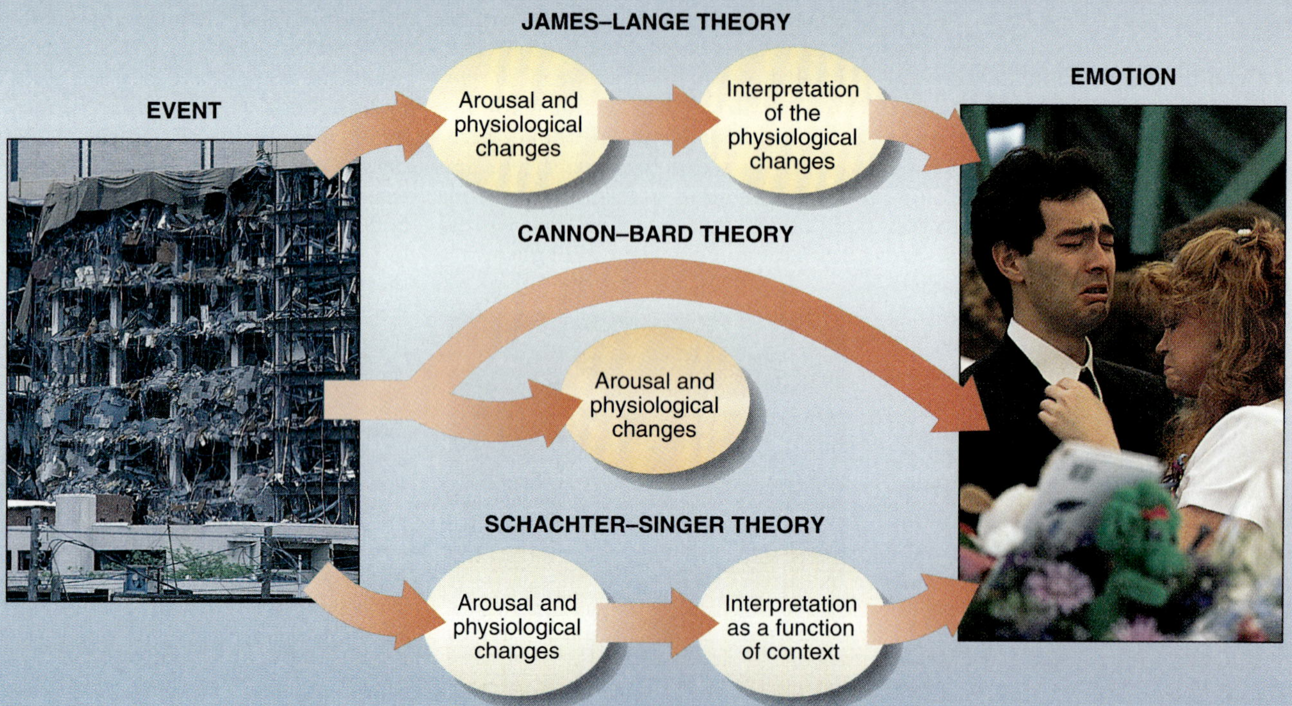

friends coax them to smile. This theory is still relatively new and has not yet been tested extensively by other researchers.

The Cannon–Bard Theory. Physiologists, notably Walter Cannon (1871–1945), were critical of the James–Lange theory. Cannon and P. Bard, a colleague, argued that the physiological changes in many emotional states were identical. They reasoned as follows: If increases in blood pressure and heart rate accompany feelings of both anger and joy, how can people determine their emotional state simply from their physiological state?

Cannon argued that when a person is emotional, two areas of the brain—the thalamus and the cerebral cortex—are stimulated simultaneously (he did not realize the full nature of the limbic system). Stimulation of the cortex produces the emotional component of the experience; stimulation of the thalamus produces physiological changes in the sympathetic nervous system. According to Cannon (1927), emotional feelings *accompany* physiological changes (look again at Figure 9.9); they do not produce such changes.

A problem with the Cannon–Bard approach is that physiological changes in the brain do not happen exactly simultaneously. Further, people report that they often have an experience and then have physiological and emotional reactions to it. Neither the James–Lange nor the Cannon–Bard approach considered the idea that people's interpretations of or thoughts about a situation might alter their physiological reactions and emotional responses. But the James–Lange and Cannon–Bard approaches were appropriate for their time and provided a conceptual bridge to

APPLICATIONS

Lie Detectors

Many physiological changes are due to an increase in activity in the sympathetic branch of the autonomic nervous system. When the sympathetic nervous system is activated, a whole range of responses take place almost simultaneously. Fear, for example, may slow or halt digestion, increase blood pressure and heart rate, deepen breathing, dilate the pupils, decrease salivation (causing a dry mouth), and tense the muscles. Researchers recognized that the autonomic nervous system provides direct, observable, measurable responses that can be quantified in a systematic manner. This realization led to the development of what is commonly called the lie detector, or polygraph device.

The polygraph test (recordings of many physiological responses) is perhaps the most widely recognized recorder of emotion. When people refer to a lie detector test, they are referring to a polygraph test. A polygraph device records changes in the activity of the sympathetic branch of a person's autonomic nervous system. Most autonomic nervous system activity is involuntary, and lying is usually associated with an increase in autonomic activity.

A trained polygraph operator compares a person's autonomic responses to a series of relatively neutral questions to the person's responses to questions about the issue being explored. During noncontroversial questions (such as a request for the person's name or address), autonomic activity remains at what is considered the baseline level. During critical questions (such as whether the person used a knife as a holdup weapon), however, a person with something to hide usually shows a dramatic increase in autonomic nervous system activity.

Not all people, however, show distinct or marked autonomic nervous system changes when they are emotionally aroused (Bashore & Rapp, 1993). Habitual liars show little or no change in autonomic activity when they lie; they seem to be able to lie without becoming emotionally aroused (Honts, 1994). Equally important is the finding that some people who tell the truth may register changes in autonomic nervous system activity because of anxiety. This means that a truthful individual who takes a lie detector test may appear to be lying when the individual is in fact telling the truth. In a study of lie detectors, researchers examined innocent and guilty individuals accused of theft (Kleinmuntz & Szucko, 1984). Although guilty people were often declared guilty by the lie detector and innocent people often were declared innocent, 37 percent of innocent people were declared guilty! In summary, lie detectors are subject to significant errors in both directions—there is no evidence of a unique response to deceit (Kleinmuntz & Szucko, 1984; Patrick & Iacono, 1989; Saxe, 1994).

Today, most states do not accept the results of lie detector tests as valid evidence in court, especially in criminal cases. A federal law now restricts businesses from using the polygraph to test prospective employees. The American Psychological Association has also expressed strong reservations about polygraph tests, asserting that their use may afflict psychological damage on innocent persons. The association's concerns stem in part from the knowledge that some people can control their emotions and do not respond automatically to external stimuli, whereas other people are less able to control their emotions and may overreact to external stimuli.

newer, more modern approaches, often physiological (Lang, 1994). For example, Joseph LeDoux (1993, 1995) has been investigating the physiological bases of emotion—especially fear—and memory and discovering the central role of the amygdala and the structures with which it is connected. LeDoux (1994) asserts that there may be two routes for emotional learning and response, one cortical and one subcortical. He further argues that researchers are well on the way to understanding the cellular level of emotion. Along with studies of brain activity, researchers are now mapping the location of people's emotional lives on a cellular level (George et al., 1995).

An outgrowth of the early researchers' work on the physiology of emotions is an interesting and now controversial use of physiological changes—lie detector tests, which are examined in *Applications*.

Cognitive Theories of Emotion

Fear, sadness, rage, and excitement all have readily recognizable emotional and physiological manifestations. But what about more complex emotions? Consider, for example, pride, shyness, embarrassment, and self-esteem. Consciousness of self requires a far more subtle and complex analysis—one that focuses on thought (Lewis, 1995). Cognitive theories of emotion, focusing on mental interpretation as well as physiology to explain emotions, developed in response to the older physiological approaches. These theories follow logically in the history of psychology, because thought processes have become extremely influential in the past three decades. Cognitive theorists argue that appraisal is a sufficient cause for emotion (R. S. Lazarus, 1991a). So, from a cognitive view, for emotions to function properly, theories must incorporate interpretation, anticipation, and even problem solving (Parrott & Schulkin, 1993).

The Schachter–Singer Approach. The Schachter–Singer view of emotion is a cognitive approach that, focusing on emotional activation, incorporates elements of both the James–Lange and the Cannon–Bard theories. Stanley Schachter and Jerome Singer observed that people do indeed interpret their emotions, but not solely from bodily changes. They argued that people interpret physical sensations within a specific context (refer back to Figure 9.9). Observers cannot interpret what a person's crying means unless they know the situation in which that behavior occurs. If a man cries at a funeral, observers suspect he is sad; if he cries at his daughter's wedding, they suspect he is joyful.

To demonstrate their contention, Schachter and Singer (1962) injected volunteers with epinephrine (adrenaline), a powerful stimulant that increases physiological signs of arousal such as heart rate, excitement, energy, and even sensations of butterflies in the stomach. The participants were not aware of the usual effects of the injection, however. To see if they could affect how participants interpreted their aroused state, Schachter and Singer manipulated the settings in which the volunteers experienced their arousal. The researchers hired undergraduates and paid them to act either happy and relaxed or sad, depressed, and angry. The hired students—called "stooges"—pretended that they too were volunteers in the drug study. However, they were given injections of salt water, not epinephrine. Their emotional behavior was strictly an act. The "happy" stooges shot wads of paper into a wastebasket and flew paper airplanes around the room. The "angry" ones complained about the questionnaire they had to fill out and voiced their dissatisfaction with the experiment.

All the experimental particpants showed increased physiological arousal. Those associated with the happy stooges reported that the drug made them feel good; those with the angry ones reported feeling anger. Schachter and Singer reasoned that when people have no immediate explanation for their physiological arousal (especially when arousal levels are low), they will label their feelings in terms of the thoughts available to them.

The cognitive view receives support from anecdotal data as well as experiments. When people first smoke marijuana or take other psychoactive drugs, for example, they tend to approach the experience with definite expectations. If told the drug will produce feelings of hunger, new users will report feeling hunger; if told the drug is a downer, new users often interpret their bodily sensations as depressive. In Schachter and Singer's view, people experience internal arousal, become aware of the arousal, seek an explanation for it, identify an external cue, and then label the arousal. This labeling determines the emotion that is felt.

Other Cognitive Theories of Emotion. Valins (1966) and Reisenzein (1983) challenged Schachter and Singer's view. Valins showed that thoughts alone are sufficient to produce emotional behavior. He showed groups of men slides of nude women and had them listen to amplifications of what they thought were their own heartbeats. As the men watched the slides, he played a soundtrack of previously recorded heartbeats. The participants were told to ignore their heartbeats. The heartbeats were speeded up or slowed down as the slides were shown. This meant that the subjects were being cued by the heartbeats as to their supposed arousal level, even though their arousal level may not actually have changed. A control group saw the same slides and heard the same sounds, but was told that the sounds were meaningless and to ignore them. When the two groups were asked to judge the attractiveness of the nude women, the experimental group rated them more positively than did the control group. Valins concluded that actual physiological arousal is not a prerequisite for labeling of emotion; cognitive processes alone will suffice (see Harris & Katkin, 1975). Reisenzein (1983) argues that Schachter and Singer's theory overestimates the role of arousal and that arousal at best merely intensifies an emotional experience.

Shaver's Multicultural Prototypes. Phillip Shaver and his colleagues have sought to identify the basic emotions that all people experience and the ways in which they are experienced. Shaver showed that there are six emotions that almost all people will describe when asked to identify emotions: love, joy, anger, sadness, fear, and surprise (Shaver et al., 1987). Of course, these six basic categories can overlap, and many other emotional states can be grouped under them. Schwartz and Shaver (1987) contend that people's emotional knowledge is organized around these six emotional categories and that people exhibit characteristic behaviors with each emotion. Along with others (Ekman, 1994; Izard, 1994), Schwartz and Shaver also assert that these emotions appear cross-culturally and that researchers have to understand this overall structure before they can define an overall theory of emotion. Each culture may put its own value on an emotion and have different traits that trigger it. For example, love is an extremely powerful emotion in the United States; but in Sumatra, one of the chief islands of Indonesia, nostalgia is the most powerful emotion (Heider, 1991).

Shaver asserts that people understand and interpret emotional events by comparing the events to basic emotional concepts. For example, when a mother sees her child fall and start to cry, she rushes toward the child. An observer sees this event and assumes the mother is frightened and concerned. This assumption is based on general knowledge about fear and love. Schwartz and Shaver (1987) claim that people make use of implicit learned knowledge to understand and manage social interactions. Only by understanding this structure of emotion can researchers begin to place cognitive interpretations within a reasonable framework.

Shaver does not deny the role of cognition. On the contrary, he argues that cognitive interpretations are critical. But before psychologists can understand the role of cognition, he believes, they have to understand the overall structure and concept of emotion. To some extent, he argues, they have jumped too far into the analysis of emotion and need to step back and review the basics. Paul Ekman (1993) concurs and asserts that some aspects of emotion may be culture-specific, some may be universal; researchers have just begun to use the proper techniques to ask the proper questions (Russell, 1994).

Frijda: Appraisal and Readiness. Yet another theory of emotion sees appraisal as important but also considers the idea that people ready themselves for action. Nico Frijda (Frijda, Kuipers, & ter Schure, 1989) asserts that each emotional experience is not only a cognitive appraisal of a situation but also a set of action tendencies or behaviors that are being prepared as the cognitive appraisal takes place. Thus, Frijda has introduced responses along with appraisals. This approach looks again at how emotions are expressed—an area of research that has often followed different avenues.

Behavioral Expression of Emotions

Since 1898, psychologists have recognized that facial expressions provide reliable clues to people's feelings. This behavioral expression of emotions is easily observed and interpreted by others. Most important, facial expressions are generally an accurate index of a person's emotional states and are sometimes seen as an index of

FIGURE 9.10

Recognizing and Naming Emotions

Look carefully at the six photographs. Which of the following six emotions is portrayed in each photo?

1. Happiness
2. Sadness
3. Fear
4. Anger
5. Surprise
6. Disgust

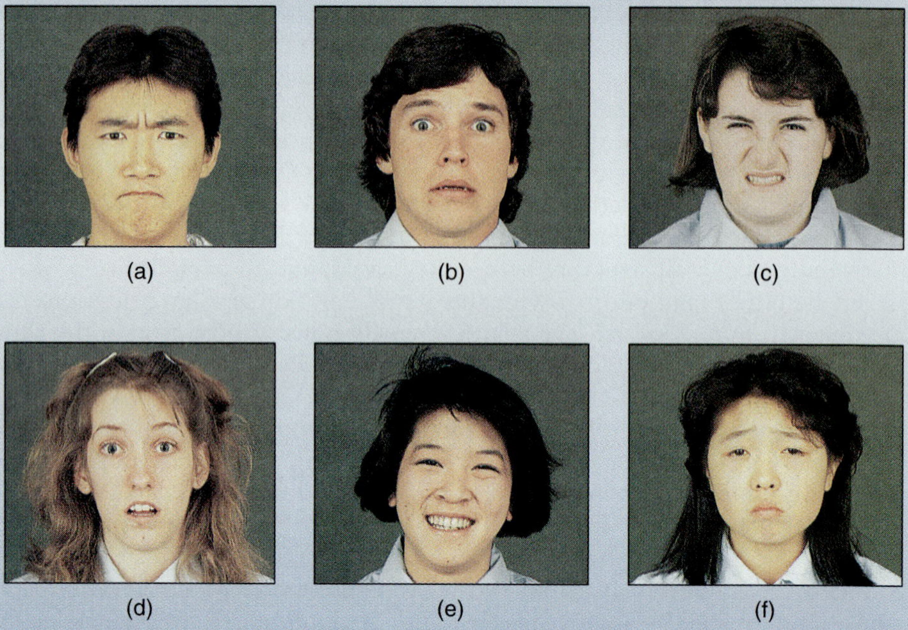

Answers: (a) 4; (b) 3; (c) 6; (d) 5; (e) 1; (f) 2

character (Berry & Wero, 1993). Recent research suggests that there are asymmetries in facial expressions in both infants and adults, and that adults can easily discern those differences. Best and Queen (1989) found that the left side of the face (controlled by the right side of the brain in most people) may be more expressive than the right side of the face, especially in adults (Rothbart, Taylor, & Tucker, 1989). They argue that the right side of the face may be more readily under the control of the left side of the brain, and so people are able to inhibit right-face expression more easily than left-face expression. Nevertheless, though facial expressions (either side) are good indicators of emotion, they are only indicators; a happy face or a turned-down mouth can mask real emotions. For a demonstration that emotions are both easy and difficult to read, see Figure 9.10.

People also display emotion through gestures, body language, and voice tone and volume (Izard & Saxton, 1988). Examples include a lowered head, shaking fists, and laughter, as well as clenched teeth, limpness, and loss of energy. The autonomic nervous system responds differently to differences among emotions (Levenson, 1992). Researchers have studied the smiling responses of infants, children, and adults by examining when and under what conditions smiling is evoked and then lost (Carlson, Gantz, & Masters, 1983). Researchers have also studied smiling cross-culturally (Levenson et al., 1992; Sogon & Masutani, 1989) and have found commonalities in what brings about emotional responses such as smiling, although not all researchers find responses that are the same (Ekman, 1992) or that occur to the same extent (Pittam et al., 1995). Most emotional responses are expressed cross-culturally, but they vary in degree; so while the anthropologist Ruth Benedict characterized Japanese culture as a shame culture and the United States as a guilt culture, it is crucial to note that she overstated the case. The Japanese know guilt, and Americans know shame; the guilt/shame distinction is not an either/or distinction, but rather a gradation of emotional response (Heider, 1994).

Researchers observe animals and human beings in situations that can induce stress and emotional responses. For example, psychologists have studied the emotional expressions of store clerks and their responses to customers. In one study (Rafaeli, 1989), a range of variables was considered: the clerk's gender, the wearing of a smock with a name tag, the presence of other clerks, and the customer's gender. Although the results were complicated, the emotional expressions of clerks were affected by nearly all the variables. Female clerks displayed positive emotions more often than male clerks, male customers received positive emotional responses more often than female customers, and clerks made especially aware of their role (because they were wearing smocks) were more expressive than other clerks. The expression of emotion was thus affected by context and by subtle variables that are still being investigated.

Controlling Emotions

Another aspect of cognitive theory is the self-regulation view of emotional expression, which emphasizes that people are not passive—that they do not respond automatically to environmental or internal stimuli. This view asserts that people manage or determine their emotional states in purposeful ways by constantly evaluating their environment and feelings. Through this appraisal, they alter their level of arousal.

Arousal. Arousal is an essential component in emotion, as we've seen, and researchers show that people can use cognitive means to control their arousal level and therefore their emotions. Even young infants show some forms of emotional restraint and control, and an infant's control of emotion continues to develop, especially at the end of the first year (Kopp, 1989). For psychologists studying the behavior of disturbed individuals, the interaction of arousal, emotion, and thought has become increasingly important. Even in normal individuals, too high a level of arousal can produce extreme emotional responses and lead to disorganized, less effective behavior. Many maladjusted individuals, such as those suffering from the manic stages of bipolar disorders, have so high a level of arousal that they cannot organize their thinking or behavior (see Chapter 14, pages 496–497).

Responses to Emotions. Some studies show that people can control their body's biochemistry. In the study by Lazarus and Alfert (1964) discussed earlier, for example, subjects were able to manipulate their electrodermal response when told in advance about a subincision ritual shown in a film. Thus, emotion and its expression reflect both a person's motivations and basic biochemistry (Carver & Scheier, 1990). People also control their emotions because of strong cultural expectations. In the United States, for example, children and women have greater permission to cry and express emotion than men do. But in Latin America, men are expected to be emotional.

FOCUS

Review

- Identify the fundamental ideas that distinguish the James–Lange, Cannon–Bard, and Schachter–Singer theories of emotion. pp. 327–330
- What is the evidence to suggest that lie detectors are unscientific? p. 329

Think Critically

- Why do you think lie detectors should or should not be used in the public or private sector?
- What are the implications of the idea that there are universal emotions?

Expectations and cognitive appraisals of situations seem to be key elements in physiological and subsequent behavioral expressions of emotion (C. A. Smith, 1989). Expectations that are biased in one direction or another can lead to some unusual consequences; for example, if a person suffers from hypochondriasis (see Chapter 14, page 490), any ache, pain, or quickness of breath may lead the person to experience dire feelings about his or her health.

Summary and Review

Theories of Motivation

Distinguish between a motivation and a need.

- *Motivation* is an internal condition that appears by inference to initiate, activate, or maintain an organism's goal-directed behavior. Motivation is inferred from behavior and is caused by needs, drives, or desires. A *need* is a state of physiological imbalance that is usually accompanied by arousal. pp. 300–301

Differentiate the various theories of motivation.

- *Drive theory* is an explanation of behavior that assumes that an organism is motivated to act because of a need to attain, reestablish, balance, or maintain some goal that helps with the survival of the organism or the species. A mechanistic drive explanation of behavior views the organism as being pushed, pulled, and energized, almost like a machine. pp. 300–301
- According to optimal arousal theories, individuals seek an optimal level of stimulation. The Yerkes–Dodson law basically asserts that behavior varies from disorganized to effective to optimal, depending on the person's level of *arousal*. Contemporary researchers have extended the idea by suggesting that when a person's level of arousal and anxiety is too high or too low, performance will be poor, especially on complex tasks. An inverted U-shaped curve describes the relationship between arousal and effectiveness of behavior. p. 302
- *Expectancy theories* are explanations of behavior that focus on people's expectations of success in reaching a goal and their need for achievement. pp. 303–304
- *Cognitive theory* emphasizes the role of active decision making in all areas of life. It is an explanation of behavior that emphasizes the role of thoughts and individual choices regarding life goals and the means of achieving them. Cognitive theory moves away from mechanistic descriptions of behavior and emphasizes the role of human choice and expression. Cognitive theory focuses on (1) thought as an initiator and determinant of behavior, and (2) the role of active decision making in all areas of life. p. 305
- *Intrinsically motivated behaviors* are behaviors that a person performs in order to feel competent and self-determining. *Extrinsic rewards* are rewards that come from the external environment; they tend to decrease the recurrence of intrinsically motivated behavior. pp. 306–307
- *Humanistic theory* explains behavior by emphasizing the entirety of life rather than the individual components of behavior. Humanistic psychologists believe that individuals' behavior must be viewed within the framework of the individuals' environment and values; humanistic theory focuses on human dignity, individual choice, and self-worth. pp. 307–308

KEY TERMS

Motivation, p. 300
Drive theory, p. 300
Drive, p. 301
Need, p. 301
Arousal, p. 302
Expectancy theories, p. 303
Motive, p. 304
Social need, p. 304
Cognitive theory, p. 305
Intrinsically motivated behaviors, p. 306
Extrinsic rewards, p. 307
Humanistic theory, p. 308
Self-actualization, p. 308

Hunger: A Physiologically Based Need

What causes hunger?

- The glucostatic approach argues that the principal physiological cause of hunger is a low blood sugar level, which accompanies food deprivation. A delicate balance of food and fluid intake—a homeostasis—is necessary for proper functioning. Genetics and disorders of the autonomic nervous system may also play a role in eating behavior. Physiological makeup isn't the only important factor in eating behavior; people's experiences also teach them how to interact with food. pp. 310–311
- There is no clear, convincing, simple answer to the question of nature versus nurture regarding obesity. Genetics plays a role; but a person's history with food, level of obesity, and current weight all play a role in the likelihood of recurrence or development of obesity. pp. 312–313
- *Anorexia nervosa*, a starvation disease, is an eating disorder characterized by the obstinate and willful refusal to eat. *Bulimia nervosa* involves binge eating accompanied by fear of not being able to stop eating. Bulimics often purge themselves of unwanted calories by vomiting and by using laxatives and diuretics. pp. 315–316

KEY TERMS

Eating disorders, p. 314
Anorexia nervosa, p. 315
Bulimia nervosa, p. 317

Sexual Behavior: Physiology plus Thought

What are the rules of thought and of hormonal influences in human sexual behavior?

- Sexual behavior in human beings is in part under hormonal control, and the hormones are different for men and women. In men, the testes are the principal producer of androgens, or male sex hormones; in women, the ovaries are the principal producer of estrogens, or female hormones. p. 318
- Thought plays an enormous role in the sexual behavior of human beings; our own thoughts, fantasies, and images initiate and activate sexual desire and activity. p. 318

How many phases are in the sexual response cycle?

- When human beings become sexually aroused, they go through a series of four phases (stages). The phases, which together are known as the sexual response cycle, are the *excitement phase,* the *plateau phase,* the *orgasm phase,* and the *resolution phase.* p. 319

How have Americans' sex lives changed over the last 40 years?

- The Laumann study, the most recent and comprehensive study of the last four decades, has shown that the sex lives of Americans are predictable and not as active as many assume, although most Americans are happy with their sex lives. The Laumann study showed that men and women are more likely today than they were 40 years ago to have had intercourse before marriage and that there has been a slow and steady decrease in the age of first intercourse. Men think about sex more than women, and married men and women have more sex than do nonmarried young people. p. 320
- A person with a heterosexual orientation has an erotic attraction and preference for members of the opposite sex; an individual with a homosexual orientation has an erotic attraction and preference for members of the same sex. According to the Laumann study, only 2.8 percent of men and 1.4 percent of women identify themselves as exclusively homosexual in orientation. This is substantially less than the 10 percent reported by Kinsey in the 1950s. p. 321

KEY TERMS

Excitement phase, p. 318
Vasocongestion, p. 318
Plateau phase, p. 319
Orgasm phase, p. 319
Resolution phase, p. 319

Achievement: A Social Need

How does expectancy theory explain the need for achievement?

- *Need for achievement* is a social need that directs a person to strive constantly for excellence and success. According to expectancy theory, people engage in behaviors that satisfy their desires for success, mastery, and fulfillment. Tasks not oriented toward these goals are not motivating and either are not undertaken or are done without energy and commitment. Need for achievement can be measured by tests such as the TAT. pp. 322–323

KEY TERMS

Need for achievement, p. 322
Learned helplessness, p. 323

Emotion

Identify the fundamental ideas that distinguish various theories of emotion?

- An *emotion* is a subjective response (feeling), usually accompanied by a physiological change, which is interpreted by the individual and then readies the individual for some action that is associated with a change in behavior. Emotions are aroused internal states; they may occur in response to either internal or external stimuli. pp. 324–325
- The James–Lange theory of emotion states that people experience physiological changes and then interpret those changes as emotions. The Cannon–Bard theory states that when people experience emotions, two areas of the brain are stimulated simultaneously, one creating an emotional response and the other creating physiological change. pp. 327–328
- According to the Schachter–Singer approach, people interpret physiological changes within specific contexts and infer emotions from these cues. p. 330
- Shaver showed that there are six emotions that most people display regardless of their culture: love, joy, anger, sadness, fear, and surprise. These six categories can overlap, and many other emotional states can be grouped under them. p. 331

KEY TERM

Emotion, p. 324

Learning CONNECTIONS

Some students benefit from extra help with motivation theories. You can learn more about them in:

- The CD-ROM accompanying this book, Topic 9
- This book's study guide, *Keeping Pace Plus*, or the computerized study guide, Chapter 9
- The audiotape accompanying this book, *SoundGuide for Psychology*, Learning Unit 10
- The study aids found on the World Wide Web site for this book, at http://www.abacon.com/psych/lefton

Critical Thinking CONNECTIONS

Take a moment to think critically about how this chapter's topics are connected with the rest of psychology . . .

If you are interested in . . .	Ask yourself . . .	Then turn to . . .
The role of motivation in learning, memory, and intelligence 	Is it always true that organisms in a need state (for example, hunger) learn more quickly and better?	Chapter 5, p. 167
	What are some easy ways to improve your memory?	Chapter 6, pp. 210–211
	What characterizes the relationship between innate intelligence and motivation to succeed on a test?	Chapter 8, pp. 277
How thoughts influence motives and behavior 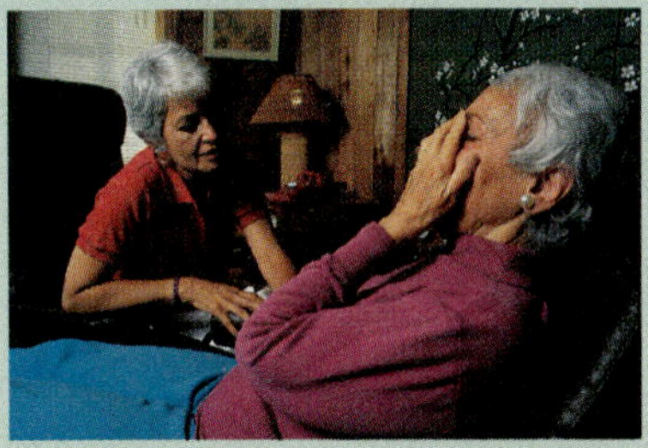	How does cognitive learning take place without specific observable motives or reinforcement?	Chapter 5, pp. 179–182
	How do various treatment approaches consider the role of motivation and a person's appraisal of situations in determining behavior?	Chapter 15, pp. 521–524
The emotional responses people make to various situations 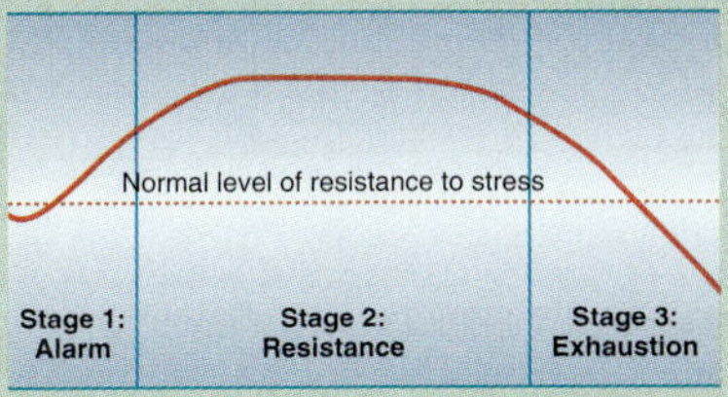	What are the implications if a person can learn to manipulate his or her body's responses and subsequent emotions through techniques such as hypnosis and biofeedback?	Chapter 4, pp. 130–132
	How can people's health be affected by their overall emotional responses when they are faced with stressful situations?	Chapter 13, pp. 466–469
	Is there in fact, any interaction between physiological disorders and emotional responses?	Chapter 13, pp. 456–458

10

Child Development

The Savages, my next-door neighbors, have four children, two boys and two girls. The young Savages were all born within a 4½-year period, the boys first and then the girls. By today's standards, they are a large family. Having lived next door for nearly 20 years, I have watched the family grow in size and change its focus from infant care, to Little League, to the science fair, and now to college tuition. As both neighbor and psychologist, I have been fascinated by how four children could be so different from one another and yet have grown up in the same household. The oldest boy looks like the youngest girl, and they both look like their mother. The second son and the third child, the first girl, also look alike and resemble their dad. It's easy to see that the Savages are a family—but the resemblances end there. Each of the children is unique. Steve and Gene are opposites. Steve, the eldest, lives for rugged team sports; Gene, the second child, enjoys sports but excels at music. Heather and Jenny are different as well. Heather, the third child, has an affinity for sports, especially individual sports like track; while Jenny, the youngest, has strong artistic, visual talent. Cognitively, Heather and Gene are excellent students; Steve has troubles with math; Jenny is considered smart but occasionally unmotivated.

My neighbors were raised in the same household by the same parents and were all born within a short time span. As a psychologist I know that both nature and nurture play key roles in development; in the Savage family, I can see that the environment shaped the lives of the children in specific ways, but there must also have been key biological traits that predisposed them to their various interests and cognitive abilities. The Savage parents have tended to push their children toward excellence, each in his or her own way. This is not unusual in the United States, where individual achievement is so highly valued.

Sometimes, however, parents push their children too fast. According to David Elkind (1987), a well-known psychologist and professor of child development, pushing children can have adverse consequences. Elkind asserts that parents sometimes take a "superkid" approach to child rearing. They hurry their children, expecting them to think, feel, and act much older than they are. Elkind's ideas about such "hurried children" are based on his recognition of individual differences among children and their abilities. Some children develop slowly; others develop rapidly. Some are cognitively advanced; others are average or slow. How much, how well, or how quickly children achieve is affected by family size; for example, language generally emerges earlier in first-borns than in second and subsequent children (Pine, 1995). In general, among women, first-borns tend to be writers more than scientists; second-borns are more likely to be scientists; and last-borns are more likely to be in the performing arts than to be scientists (Bohmer & Sitton, 1993).

Part of the goal of this chapter will be to focus on normal developmental processes in children—in diverse interacting areas such as cognitive, moral, emotional, and social development. We will also see how people's inborn characteristics interact with their environments to produce individuals who are unique in both experience and heredity. Our examination will help explain why the Savage children are so different. The next chapter will look at adolescence, adulthood, and aging—showing that development is a process that lasts a lifetime.

Approaches to Child Development

Psychologists study development to find out how people change throughout their lives and to learn what causes those changes. In their study of development, psychologists adopt various viewpoints and research methods to unravel the causes of behavior.

Views of Development

One way to look at individual development is to consider to what extent the developing person's abilities, interests, and personality are determined by *nature* (at or before birth) or by *nurture* (from experiences after birth). The nature-versus-nurture issue has been raised before, in Chapters 2 and 8. Separating biological from environmental causes of behavior is complicated, and the answer to any specific question about human behavior usually involves the interaction of both nature and nurture.

To assess the roles played by genetics and environment, researchers have studied identical twins (the same genetic makeup) who have been reared apart (different environments), and they have found extraordinary similarities between such siblings (Lykken, McGue, Tellegen, & Bouchard, 1992). In one such study Lykken and his colleagues found an identical twin who was an accomplished storyteller with a collection of amusing anecdotes. Later, his twin brother was asked if he knew any funny stories. "Why, sure," he responded, and leaning back with a practiced air, he continued, "I'll tell you a story." Other twins shared interests in dogs, smoked the same cigarettes, or were both politically conservative. One pair of twins shared a phobia for water at the beach; both would enter the water backward, and then only up to their knees. In the Lykken study there were two firefighters, two gunsmiths, and two people who obsessively counted things; all pairs were identical twins. Lykken and his colleagues (1992) argued that genetics plays an especially important role in human development. But many psychologists—and parents—believe that whereas genetics may play a crucial role, a child's environment has an equal, if not more important, impact. Many parents think they can enhance their children's genetic endowment and optimize the likelihood of their living well-educated, well-reasoned, satisfying lives.

Beyond considering the impact of nature and nurture, most developmental psychologists also have a point of view—a theoretical orientation. Some theorists adopt the mechanistic *reductionistic view*; they believe that if psychologists can reduce an organism's behavior to its essential elements, they can explain the behavior. According to this view, organisms are primarily acted upon by the environment. The mechanistic view holds that all human beings are born alike; differences come about only because of different experiences. The *organismic view*, in contrast, asserts that the organism actively affects its world rather than simply waiting for the world to affect it. Individual people go through developmental stages that are qualitatively different and cannot be reduced to simple elements. Development occurs in a series of stages in which key individual characteristics are likely to emerge. A third way of looking at development is the *contextual view*. This view blends the mechanistic and organismic views with a third element: social and cultural context. Here, all the events in an organism's life are interrelated. The contextualist looks at behavior from the standpoint of the stage of the organism's life and the context in which the behavior occurs. The social and cultural context exerts profound influences on day-to-day development. Children growing up in a culture that respects its elders and views manners, protocol, and hierarchy as important—for example, Japanese culture—develop values and ideas different from those of individuals who mature in an environment stressing individual achievement, such as the United States or Australia (Mann et al., 1994).

▲ *Twins Linda Lackner (left) and April Yamashiro (right) were among those studied by Lykken and his colleagues at the University of Minnesota. Although raised in different environments, many of the twins in the study showed remarkable similarities, which would normally be attributed to environmental influences.*

Two Key Research Methods

Good researchers know that the method that they use to study a problem often influences the results. At the minimum, a researcher must take into account the method used in order to interpret what the results might mean. In developmental research, two widely used methods are the cross-sectional and the longitudinal methods. In the *cross-sectional research method*, a psychologist will compare many individuals of different ages to determine how they differ on some important dimension. In the *longitudinal research method*, the psychologist studies a group of people at different ages to examine changes that have occurred over a long period of time.

Each method has both advantages and disadvantages. For example, the cross-sectional method suffers from the fact that the participants' backgrounds (parents, family income, nutrition) differ and the participants may have learned various things in different ways. Further, a participant's behavior, performance in a specific task, or ability may reflect a predisposition, a liking of the task, or some other variable unrelated to changes that come from development or aging. With this method, individual differences are impossible to assess. But the longitudinal method also has problems. For one thing, it requires repeated access to the same people; but some participants may move, withdraw from the study, or even die. Also, after repeated testing on the same task (even though the tests are months or years apart), participants may do better because of practice. Moreover, longitudinal research sometimes

FIGURE 10.1

Cross-Sectional versus Longitudinal Research

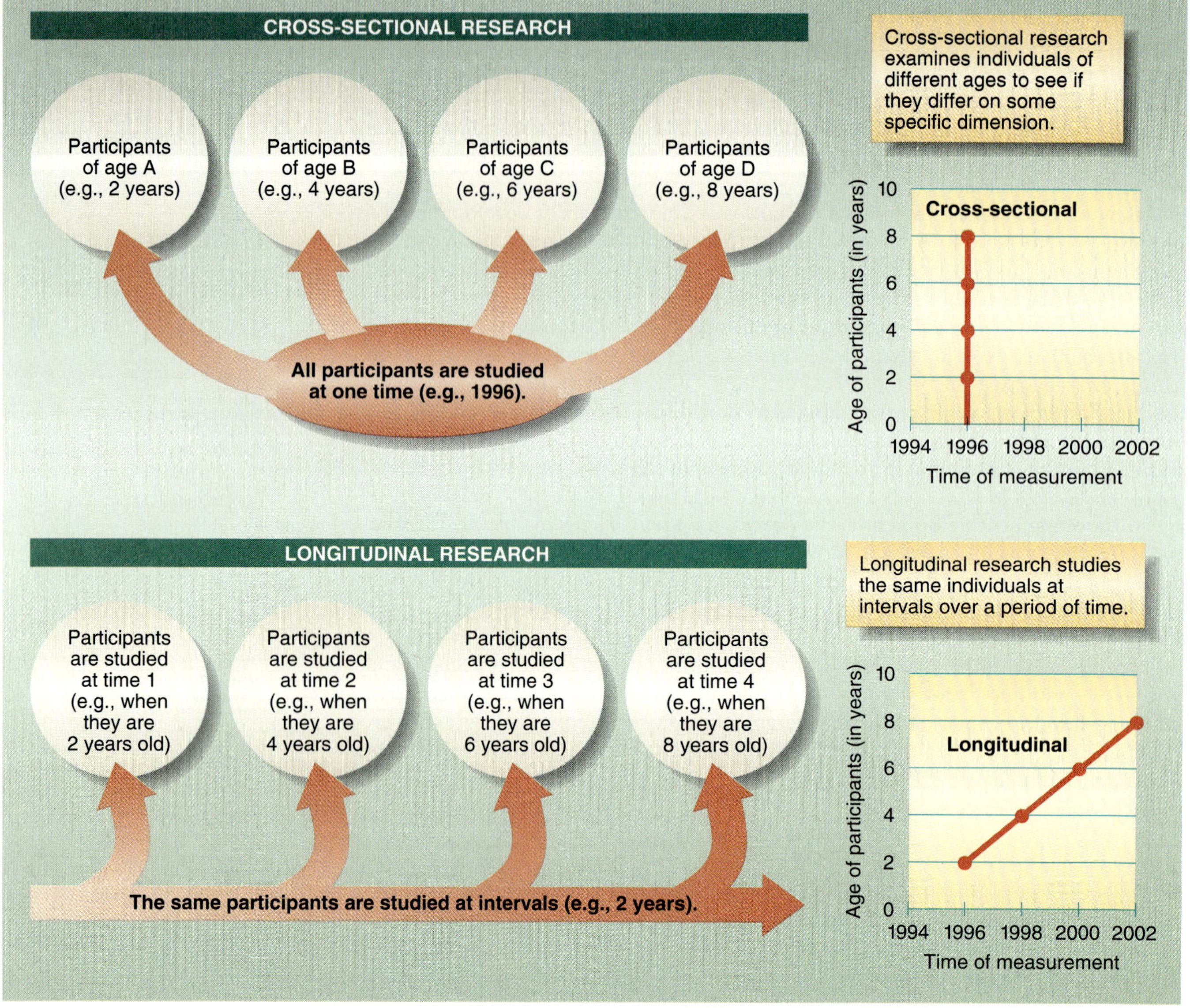

takes years to complete; during that time, important changes may occur in the environment and in the social world of the participants. Finally, such research is time-consuming and expensive. See Figure 10.1 for a comparison of the cross-sectional and longitudinal research methods.

The First Ten Months

The lifelong journey of human development begins with conception. Conception occurs when an ovum and a sperm join in the woman's fallopian tube to form a **zygote**—a fertilized egg. During the next 5 to 7 days, the zygote floats down the fallopian tube to implant itself in the blood-lined wall of the uterus. From that time until the 49th day after conception, the organism is called an **embryo**. Then, from the 8th week until birth, the organism is called a **fetus**. On the average, maturation and development take 266 days, or about 9 months. For descriptive purposes this period is divided into three *trimesters* (3-month periods). Table 10.1 summarizes the prenatal (before birth) and postnatal (after birth) periods of development.

TABLE 10.1 ***Life Stages and Approximate Ages in Human Development***

Life Stage	Approximate Age
Prenatal period	
Zygote	Conception to day 5 to 7
Embryo	To day 49
Fetus	Week 8 to birth
Postnatal period	
Infancy	Birth to 18 months
Toddlerhood	18 months to 3 years
Early childhood	3 to 6 years
Middle childhood	6 to 13 years
Adolescence	13 to 20 years
Young adulthood	20 to 40 years
Middle adulthood	40 to 65 years
Late adulthood	65 plus

Prenatal Development

The First Trimester. Although the prenatal environment can have an influence—especially through the mother's diet (Sigman, 1995)—the basic characteristics of an individual are established as the zygote is formed; these include the color of the hair, skin, and eyes; the sex (gender); the likelihood that the person will be tall or short, fat or lean; and perhaps basic intellectual abilities and personality traits. Within 10 hours, the zygote divides into four cells. During the first week, a cluster of about a dozen cells drifts from the fallopian tube to the uterus. There, the cells begin the process of *differentiation:* Organs and other parts of the body begin to form. Some cells form the *umbilical cord*—a group of blood vessels and tissues that connect the zygote to the placenta. The **placenta** is a mass of tissue in the uterus that acts as the life-support system for the fetus by supplying oxygen, food, and antibodies and by eliminating wastes—all by way of the mother's bloodstream.

By the end of the 1st week, the developing organism is an embryo made up of as many as 150 cells attached to the wall of the uterus. During the 1st month, the embryo begins to take shape. Although it is only a half-inch long, its arms and legs begin to form and it acquires rudimentary eyes, ears, mouth, and brain. By the 25th day, a primitive version of the heart is beating. During the 2nd month, the embryo begins to resemble a human being. Each day it grows about a millimeter, and new parts begin to take shape. The nose begins to form about the 33rd day, and the first true bone cells appear on about the 47th day. In the 3rd month, growth continues, features become more defined, and sex characteristics begin to appear. The digestive, breathing, and musculature systems become stronger. At the end of the 3rd month, the fetus is about 3 inches long and weighs 1 ounce. It can kick its legs, turn its feet, and swallow, although the mother cannot yet feel its movement.

The Second Trimester. During the second 3-month period, the fetus consumes a good deal of food, oxygen, and water through the placenta; and its weight and strength increase. In the 4th or 5th month, it can be up to 10 inches long, its muscles are significantly stronger, and its heartbeat can be heard with a stethoscope. Late in the 4th month or sometimes in the 5th month, the mother begins to feel the movement of the fetus. In the 5th and 6th months, the fetus grows about 2 inches per month. At the end of the second trimester (about 24 weeks), the fetus is about 12 inches long. Its respiratory system is mature enough to enable it to live outside the uterus, increasing the chances of survival if it is born prematurely.

The Third Trimester. In the last trimester, the fetus gains weight rapidly—usually a pound in the 7th month, 2 pounds in the 8th, and a pound a week in the 9th. Its respiratory system and internal organs continue to develop, and its muscles mature significantly. The mother can feel strong kicking and movement.

Table 10.2, on page 344, summarizes the major physical developments during the prenatal period.

Zygote [ZEYE-goat]: A fertilized egg.

Embryo [EM-bree-o]: The human organism from the 5th through the 49th day after conception.

Fetus [FEET-us]: The human organism from the 49th day after conception until birth.

Placenta [pluh-SENT-uh]: A mass of tissue in the uterus connected to the fetus by the umbilical cord and serving as the mechanism for the exchange of nutrients and waste products.

TABLE 10.2 *Major Developments during the Prenatal Period*

	Age	Size	Characteristics
First trimester 1–12 weeks	1 week	150 cells	Zygote attaches to uterine lining
	2 weeks	Several thousand cells	Placental circulation established.
	3 weeks	1/10 inch	Heart and blood vessels begin to develop. Basics of brain and central nervous system form.
	4 weeks	¼ inch	Kidneys and digestive tract begin to form. Rudiments of ears, nose, and eyes are present.
	6 weeks	½ inch	Arms and legs develop. Jaws form around mouth.
	8 weeks	1 inch, 1/30 ounce	Bones begin to develop in limbs. Sex organs begin to form.
	12 weeks	3 inches, 1 ounce	Gender can be distinguished. Kidneys are functioning, and liver is manufacturing red blood cells. Fetal movements can be detected by a physician.
Second trimester 13–24 weeks	16 weeks	6½ inches, 4 ounces	Heartbeat can be detected by a physician. Bones begin to calcify.
	20 weeks	10 inches, 8 ounces	Mother feels fetal movements.
	24 weeks	12 inches, 1½ pounds	Vernix (white waxy substance) protects the body. Eyes open; eyebrows and eyelashes form; skin is wrinkled. Respiratory system is barely mature enough to support life.
Third trimester 25–38 weeks	28 weeks	15 inches, 2½ pounds	Fetus is fully developed but needs to gain in size, strength, and maturity of systems.
	32 weeks	17 inches, 4 pounds	A layer of fat forms beneath the skin to regulate body temperature.
	36 weeks	19 inches, 6 pounds	Fetus settles into position for birth.
	38 weeks	21 inches, 8 pounds	Fetus arrives at full term—266 days from conception.

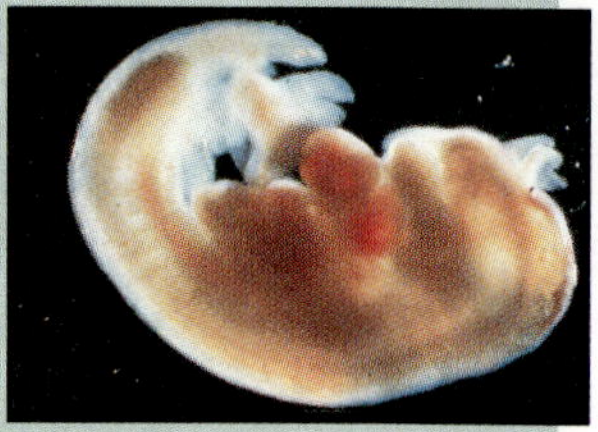

▲ *4 weeks*

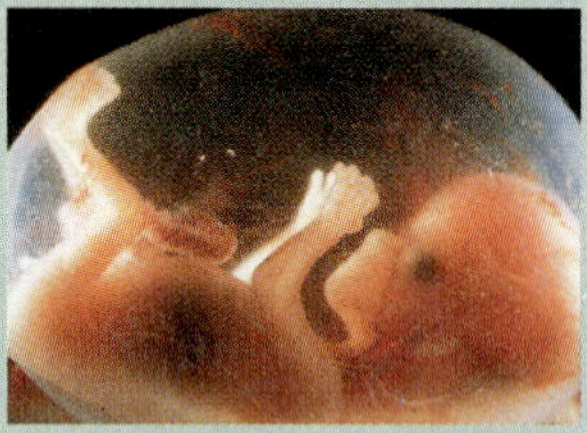

▲ *11 weeks*

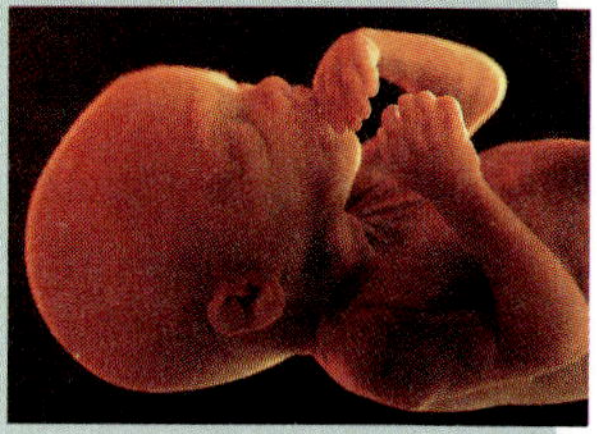

▲ *20 weeks*

Harmful Environmental Influences on the Fetus

People have long assumed that the behavior of a pregnant woman affects her unborn child's development. Medieval European doctors advised pregnant women that uplifting thoughts would help the baby develop into a good, happy person, while fright, despondency, and negative emotions might disrupt the pregnancy and possibly influence the infant to become sad or mean-spirited. Research with animals shows that stress during pregnancy has effects on emotional development of offspring, as indicated when the offspring are later tested as adults (Pfister & Muir, 1992). Generalizing from such data, some pregnant women wear fetal belts that play soothing music to the unborn child, who can listen and thereby gain a benevolent perspective on the outside world.

While a fetus may not be affected by the mother's condition to the extent suggested by medieval doctors, the environment and life-support systems provided by the mother do influence the fetus from conception until birth. Environmental factors such as diet, infection, radiation, and drugs affect both the mother and the fetus. The fetus is especially affected during *critical periods,* during which there is rapid development and special sensitivity to the environment. During the first 2 years of life, the brain is especially sensitive; neuronal connections are undergoing many changes. Although the basic architecture of the brain is in place at birth, how individual connections of neurons are made is subject to considerable influence or damage.

Substances that can produce developmental malformations (birth defects) in a fetus are known as **teratogens**. These defects are the leading cause of death of infants in their first year of life. If the mother drinks alcoholic beverages in early and middle pregnancy, the baby is more likely to be born prematurely, to have a lower birth weight, and to suffer from mental retardation or hyperactivity (Streissguth, Barr, & Martin, 1983). One study showed that the mother's drinking more than 3 ounces of 100-proof liquor per day during pregnancy was significantly related to a small decrease in 4-year-olds' intelligence test scores (Streissguth et al., 1989).

Studies also show that any drug can affect fetal development. High doses of aspirin, for example, may cause fetal bleeding, although the evidence is controversial (Werler, Mitchell, & Shapiro, 1989). Cigarette smoking constricts the oxygen supply to the fetus. Babies born to mothers who smoke cigarettes tend to be smaller and may be at increased risk for cleft palate, mental retardation, and hyperactivity. Certain drugs, including cocaine, marijuana, and tranquilizers, have the possibility of being teratogenic, producing potentially irreversible malformations of the head, face, and limbs as well as neurological disorders (Kopp & Kaler, 1989; Lester & Dreher, 1989). Unfortunately, in recent years, hundreds of thousands of infants have been born each year addicted to cocaine or related drugs. The influence of certain drugs is especially important during the embryonic stage of development, when the mother may not realize she is pregnant—this is usually considered a critical period.

Even a mother's mood during pregnancy or shortly thereafter may have some effect; for example, one study (Dawson et al., 1991) indicated that children of depressed mothers showed unusual brain-wave activity. This study was just a first step in the examination of such relationships.

The Birth Process

Throughout most of human history, women have delivered babies without the aid of doctors, nurses, or medication. Only during the past 70 years have women in developed countries given birth in hospitals, where professionals can respond quickly to complications. In these settings relatively few babies or mothers die in childbirth. Since the 1960s, individuals who consider themselves proponents of prepared, or "natural," childbirth have worked to keep medical interventions, especially medication, to a minimum during the birth process. Part of natural childbirth is the use of a number of techniques to help reduce the pain and discomfort of childbirth without drugs. The best-known technique today is the *Lamaze method.* In the 1990s, there has been an increase in the number of nonmedicated births, home births, and hospital settings that more closely approximate a home setting.

Approximately 9 months after conception, the mother goes into **labor**—the process in which the uterus contracts and the cervix opens so that the fetus can descend through the birth canal to the outside world. The process is divided into three stages: dilation of the cervix, leading up to transition; pushing and birth; and delivery of the placenta. Although each woman's labor is different, most women experience characteristic sensations during the three stages.

In stage 1, the cervix has to open (dilate) to about 10 centimeters (4 inches) to allow the fetus to descend through the birth canal. In *early labor*, the cervix dilates to about 3 centimeters. Labor pains from contractions of the uterine muscles occur at regular intervals, from 5 to 30 minutes apart, and last approximately 30 seconds each. In *active labor*, the cervix dilates to 7 centimeters. Contractions are about 3 to

Teratogen [ter-AT-oh-jen]: Substance that can produce developmental malformations (birth defects) in a fetus.

Labor: The process in which the uterus contracts and the cervix opens so that the fetus can descend through the birth canal to the outside world.

5 minutes apart and more intense. During this stage, the woman usually goes to a hospital or birthing center if she is not giving birth at home. During *transition*, the mother is likely to experience major discomfort or pain. The cervix dilates to the full 10 centimeters, and contractions are much stronger, last longer, and come closer together.

In stage 2, the baby is now ready to be born. When people speak about the birth of a baby, they are usually referring to the slow descent through the birth canal. For anywhere from 5 minutes to about 1 hour, the mother will bear down with her abdominal muscles, pushing the baby from the uterus through the birth canal.

Until delivery, the fetus is attached to its mother by the umbilical cord. In stage 3, within a few minutes after delivery, the placenta at the end of the cord detaches from the wall of the uterus and is also delivered.

The Newborn's Growth, Reflexes, and Perception

Newborns grow rapidly—seemingly almost overnight—and they are not nearly as helpless as many people believe. At birth infants can hear, see, smell, and respond to the environment in adaptive ways; in other words, they have good sensory systems. They also are directly affected by experience. To help infants develop in optimal ways, psychologists try to find out how experience affects their perception. In doing so, psychologists need to discover how infants think, what they perceive, and how they react to the world. Researchers have therefore devised ingenious ways of "asking" newborns questions about their perceptual world, such as these: What are a child's inborn abilities and reflexes? When do inborn abilities become evident? How are inborn abilities affected by the environment?

Growth. An infant who weighs 7.5 pounds at birth may weigh as much as 20 or 25 pounds by 12 months. At 18 months, the infant is usually walking and beginning to talk. For psychologists, infancy continues until the time when the child begins to represent the world abstractly through language. Thus, *infancy* is the period from birth to 18 months; *childhood* is the period from 18 months to about age 13—when *adolescence* begins.

The rapid growth that occurs in the early weeks and months after birth is quite extraordinary and mirrors embryonic development in important ways. A newborn's head is about one-fourth of its body length; a 2-year-old's is only one-fifth. This pattern of growth is called the *cephalocaudal trend* (from the Latin, meaning "head to tail"). Another growth pattern—the *proximodistal trend*—has growth moving from the center (proximal part) of the body outward (to the more "distant" extremities). That is, the head and torso grow before the arms, legs, hands, and feet do. Thus, a newborn's head is about the same circumference as the torso, and an infant's arms and legs are quite short, relatively speaking—but this changes very quickly (see Figure 10.2).

During the period of infancy and childhood, the child grows physically from a being who requires constant care, attention, and assistance to a nearly full-size independent person. This process begins within the 1st year. At the end of the 1st and the beginning of the 2nd year of life, children can walk, climb, and manipulate their environment—skills that often lead to the appearance of safety gates that block stairways, fasteners that lock cabinets, medicine bottles with childproof caps, and a variety of other safety features in the home. There is significant variability in the age at which a child begins to walk or climb. Some babies mature early; others are slow to develop these abilities. The age at which these specific behaviors occur seems unrelated to any other major developmental abilities.

Figure 10.3, on page 348, shows the major achievements in motor development in the first 2 years.

FIGURE 10.2

The Cephalocaudal Trend of Growth

Body proportions change dramatically from fetal stages of development until adulthood.
(From Berk, 1994.)

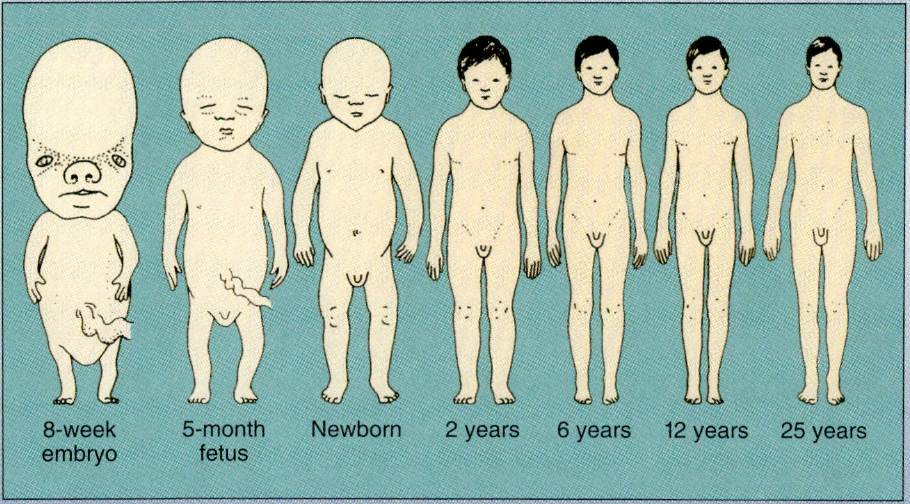

Newborns' Reflexes. Touch the palm of a newborn baby and you'll probably find one of your fingers held in the surprisingly firm grip of a tiny fist. The baby is exhibiting a reflexive reaction. Babies are born with innate *primary reflexes*—unlearned responses to stimuli. Some, such as the grasping reflex, no doubt helped ensure survival in humanity's primate ancestors; most of these reflexes disappear over the course of the first year of life. Physicians use the presence or absence of primary reflexes to assess neurological damage at birth and to evaluate an infant's rate of development. Table 10.3, on page 349, summarizes the primary reflexes and their duration. One primary reflex exhibited by infants is the **Babinski reflex**—a projection of the toes outward and up in response to a touch to the sole of the foot. Another is the **Moro reflex**—an outstretching of the arms and legs and crying in response to a loud noise or a change in the environment. Newborns also exhibit the **rooting reflex**—the turning of the head toward a mild stimulus (such as a breast or hand) that touches their lips or cheek. They show the **sucking reflex** in response to a finger placed in their mouth and the **grasping reflex** in response to an object touching the palms of their hands—infants vigorously grasp objects touching their palm or fingers.

At first, an infant's abilities and reflexes are biologically determined through genetic transmission. Gradually, learned responses, such as reaching for desired objects or grasping a cup, replace reflex reactions. The baby's new experiences in the environment become more important in determining behavior. These complex interactions between nature and nurture follow a developmental time course that continues throughout life.

Infant Perception: Fantz's Viewing Box. An avalanche of research on infant perception shows that newborns have surprisingly well-developed perceptual systems. Some of the early work on infant perception was done by Robert Fantz (1961). Fantz designed a viewing box in which he placed an infant; he then had a hidden observer or camera record the infant's responses to stimuli (see Figure 10.4 on page 349).

Babinski reflex: A reflex in which a newborn projects its toes outward and up when the soles of its feet are touched.

Moro reflex: A reflex in which a newborn stretches out its arms and legs and cries when there is a loud noise or abrupt change in the environment.

Rooting reflex: A reflex in which a newborn turns its head toward a mild stimulus applied to its lips or cheek.

Sucking reflex: A reflex in which a newborn makes sucking motions when presented with a stimulus to the lips, such as a nipple.

Grasping reflex: A reflex in which a newborn grasps vigorously any object touching its palm or fingers or placed in its hand.

FIGURE 10.3

Development of Motor Skills in the First 2 Years

Infants typically develop motor skills in the sequence shown here. Normal, healthy infants may reach any of these milestones earlier or later than these average ages.

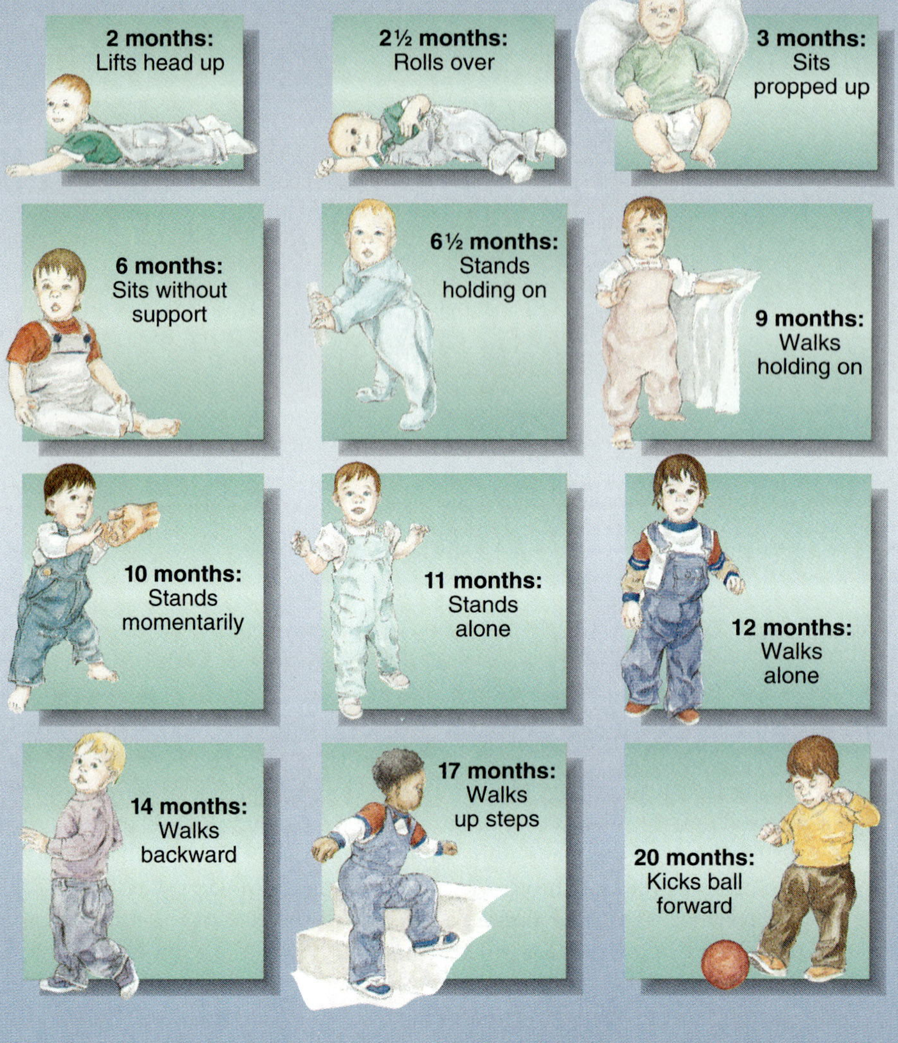

The exciting part of Fantz's work was not so much that he asked interesting questions but that he was able to get "answers" from the infants. By showing infants various pictures of faces and patterns and recording their eye movements, he discovered the infants' visual preferences. He recorded how long and how often the infants looked at each picture and calculated the total time they spent viewing each type of picture. Because they spent more time looking at pictures of faces than at pictures of random squiggles, Fantz concluded not only that they could see different patterns but that they preferred faces.

Other researchers confirm that human and nonhuman infants prefer complex visual fields over simple ones, curved patterns over straight or angular ones, and human faces over random patterns or faces with mixed-up features (Walton & Bower, 1993; Wilson & Goldman-Rakie, 1994). Even in the first few months of life, babies can discriminate among facial features and prefer attractive faces to less attractive

TABLE 10.3 *Newborns' Reflexes*

Reflex	Initiated By	Response	Duration
Eye blink	Flashing a light in the infant's eyes	Closing both eyes	Continues throughout life
Babinski	Gently stroking the sole of the infant's foot	Flexing the big toe; fanning out the other toes	Usually disappears near the end of the first year
Withdrawal	Pricking the sole of the infant's foot	Flexing of the leg	Present during the first 10 days; present but less intense later
Plantar	Pressing a finger against the ball of the infant's foot	Curling all the toes under	Disappears between 8 and 12 months
Moro	Making a sudden loud sound	Extending the arms and legs; then bringing arms toward each other in convulsive manner	Begins to decline in 3rd month; gone by 5th month
Rooting	Stroking the infant's cheek lightly with a finger or a nipple 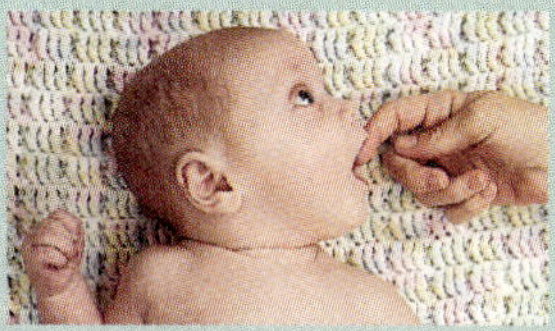	Turning the head toward the finger, opening the mouth, and trying to suck	Disappears at approximately 3 to 4 months
Sucking	Placing a finger in the infant's mouth	Sucking rhythmically 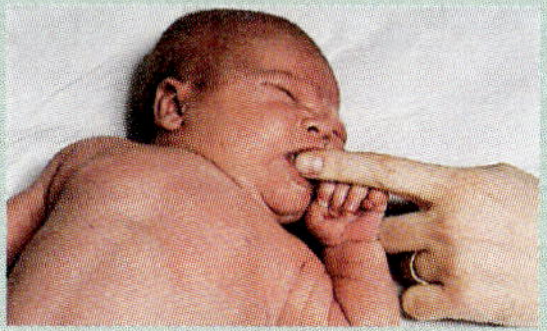	Often less intense and less regular during the first 3 to 4 days of life but continues for several months

FIGURE 10.4

Results of Fantz's Study

Using a viewing box to observe newborns' eye movements, Fantz (1961) recorded the total time infants spent looking at various patterns. He found that they looked at faces or patterned material much more often than they looked at plain fields.

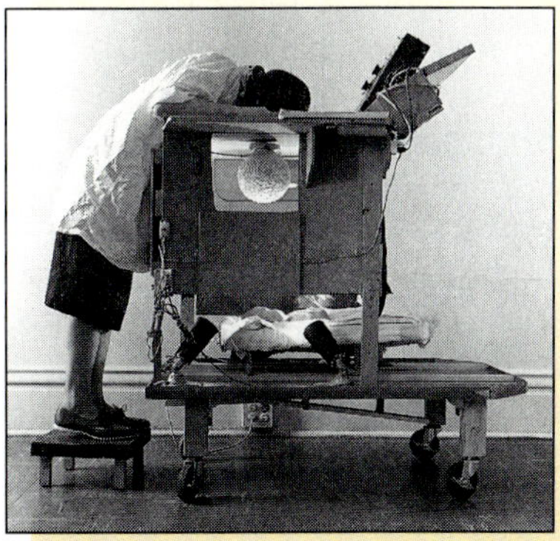

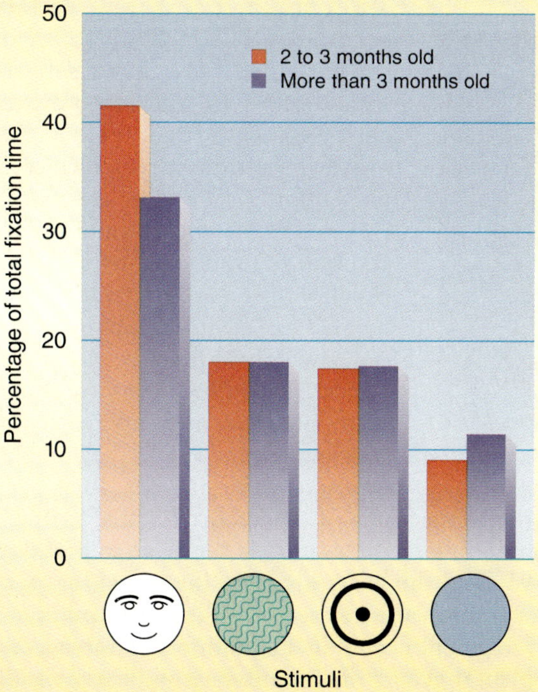

FOCUS

Review

- What are the fundamental differences between the organismic view and the contextual view of development? p. 341
- What is the evidence that the embryonic stage is crucial for fetal development? pp. 343, 345

Think Critically

- Does the Lamaze method actually reduce pain during childbirth, or does it merely help the mother to stand the pain? Explain.
- What ancient survival value did each of the primary reflexes have?
- What survival function might infants' preferences for human faces have?

ones (Langlois et al., 1990, 1991). Newborns look at pictures of their parents more than at pictures of strangers and at eyes more than at other features (Mauer & Salapatek, 1976). Also, babies sometimes respond to caregivers by imitating their facial expressions (pursed lips, stuck-out tongues)—although research in this area is controversial and the findings are not always consistent (Kaitz, Meschulach-Sarfaty, & Auerbach, 1988; Nelson & Ludemann, 1989).

By 7 months, infants know happy faces and happy sounds and can discriminate among them. Using a procedure similar to Fantz's, Walker-Andrews (1986) observed 5- and 7-month-old infants who saw films of people with angry or happy facial expressions making angry or happy sounds. (The lower third of each face was covered so that the infants could not match the sounds to the lips.) Walker-Andrews showed that 7-month-old infants could tell when the sound and facial expression did not match, but 5-month-olds could not. This research supports the idea that infants can make such judgments and suggests a timetable by which infants develop the ability to discriminate among facial expressions.

The Visual Cliff. One of the best-known developmental research studies was done by Walk and Gibson in 1961. They devised the *visual cliff method* to determine the extent of infants' depth perception. In this method the researcher places an infant who can crawl on a glass surface, half of which is covered with a checkerboard pattern. The same pattern is placed several feet below the transparent half of the glass surface. Infants can crawl easily from the patterned area onto the transparent area. Infants who lack depth perception should be willing to crawl onto the transparent side as often as onto the patterned side. Conversely, infants who have depth perception should refuse to crawl onto the transparent side, even when encouraged to do so by their mothers. Walk and Gibson found that infants avoided the transparent surface, thus proving that they have depth perception.

▲ *When placed on the visual cliff, most babies over 6 months of age will not crawl to the "deep" side; this reticence indicates that they have developed depth perception.*

In sum, newborns enter the world with the ability to experience, respond to, and learn from the environment. In general, therefore, psychologists say that the sensory systems of newborns are well formed but still developing; their development is subject to experience, which ultimately alters brain connections permanently (M. Leon, 1992). Newborns are thus genetically equipped and ready to learn, perceive, and experience the world; their brains develop, neurons interconnect, and the complexity of neuronal development continues for several years. Recall from Chapter 3 that, although most of the connections of a newborn's visual system is present at the birth, the proper functioning of the system is sensitive to and depends on experience (Wong et al., 1995) and the tasks given to the individual (Jacobs & Kosslyn, 1995). Without proper and varied experiences, less than optimal brain development occurs. Babies' development occurs in a certain order and according to a rough timetable of developmental events during infancy and early childhood. These events are the topics considered next.

Cognitive Development

Why do some automobiles have childproof locks and windows? Why do parents use gates to guard stairs and gadgets to keep kitchen cabinets closed? Why are young children's toys made so that small parts cannot come off? The answer: Children are inquisitive and much more intelligent than many people give them credit for being.

The physical development of infants is visible and dramatic; parents of infants will tell you that their babies seem to grow and change every day. The changes that occur in young children are less visible but no less dramatic. Children are continually developing, both physically and cognitively; they focus their attention on coping with an ever-expanding world and, as they mature, can determine causes of events. Much of this developing ability is cognitively based (Miller & Aloise, 1989). Figure 10.5, on page 352, shows some of the many cognitive activities of the first 12 months.

The noted Swiss psychologist Jean Piaget came to believe that the fundamental development of all cognitive abilities takes place during the first 2 years of life; many psychologists and educators agree. Piaget devised procedures for examining the cognitive development of young children. He described one such procedure as follows (Piaget, 1963, p. 283):

> Initially we relied exclusively on interviews and asked the children only verbal questions. . . . We now try to start with some action that the child must perform. We introduce him into an experimental setting, presenting him with objects and—after the problem has been stated—the child must do something, he must experiment. Having observed his actions and the manipulation of objects we can then pose the verbal questions that constitute the interview.

Piaget's theory focuses on *how* people think instead of on *what* they think, making it applicable to people in all societies and cultures. Perhaps Piaget's greatest strength, however, was his description of how a person's inherited capacities interact with the environment to produce a cognitively functioning child and adult. Although psychologists were initially skeptical of Piaget's ideas, and some criticisms persist, many researchers have shown that his assumptions are generally correct and can be applied cross-culturally. There are also dissenters (notably Russian psychologist Lev Vygotsky, whose theories we will consider a bit later), who stress society's role in establishing thought processes (Rogoff & Morelli, 1989). Piaget had a strong biological emphasis, asserting that cognitive development proceeds because of biological changes that take place within a child. He did not deny the roles of the environment and of parents and others in providing support for cognitive growth—he just did not focus on these variables.

According to Piaget, both children and adults use two processes to deal with new ideas: assimilation and accommodation. **Assimilation** is the process by which a person absorbs new ideas and experiences, incorporates them into existing cognitive structures (thought processes) and behaviors, and uses them later in similar situations. **Accommodation** is the process of modifying previously developed cognitive structures and behaviors to adapt them to a new concept. A child who learns to grasp a spoon demonstrates assimilation by later grasping similar objects, such as forks, crayons, and sticks. This assimilated behavior then serves as a foundation for accommodation. The child can learn the new and more complex behavior of grasping a sphere (such as a ball) by modifying the earlier response and widening the grasp. People accommodate new information every day by learning new words and then assimilating them by using the words themselves—only to be confronted with more new information. The two processes alternate in a never-ending cycle of cognitive growth, throughout the four stages of development that Piaget described.

Assimilation: According to Piaget, the process by which new concepts and experiences are incorporated into existing mental frameworks so as to be used in a meaningful way.

Accommodation: According to Piaget, the process by which new concepts and experiences modify existing cognitive structures and behaviors.

FIGURE 10.5

Infants' Perceptual and Cognitive Milestones

(After Clarke-Stewart, Friedman, & Koch, 1985, p. 191.)

1 WEEK

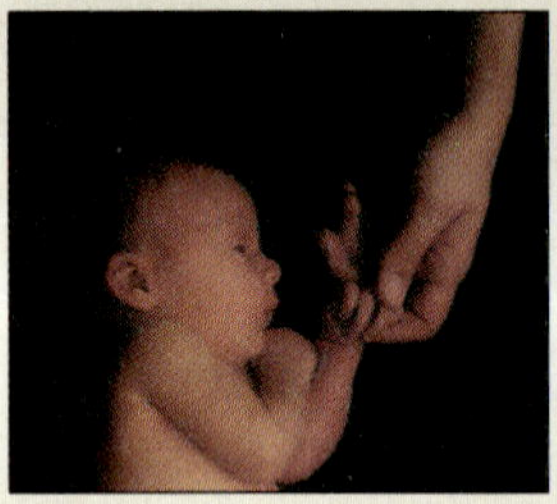

- See patterns, light, and dark
- Are sensitive to the location of a sound
- Distinguish volume and pitch
- Prefer high voices
- Will grasp an object if they touch it accidentally
- Stop sucking to look at a person momentarily

1 MONTH

- Become excited at the sight of a person or a toy
- Look at objects only if in their line of vision
- Prefer patterns to plain fields
- Coordinate eyes sideways, up, and down
- Follow a toy from the side to the center of the body

2 MONTHS

- Prefer people to objects
- Stare at human faces; become quiet at the sound of a human voice
- Are startled at sounds and make a facial response
- Perceive depth
- Coordinate eye movements
- Reach out voluntarily instead of grasping reflexively
- Discriminate among voices, people, tastes, and objects

3 MONTHS

- Follow moving objects
- Glance from one object to another
- Distinguish near objects from distant objects
- Search with eyes for the source of a sound
- Become aware of self through exploration
- Show basic signs of memory

4 TO 7 MONTHS

- See the world in color and with near-adult vision
- Pull dangling objects toward them
- Follow dangling or moving objects
- Turn to follow sound and vanishing objects
- Visually search out fast-moving or fallen objects
- Begin to anticipate a whole object when shown only part of it
- Deliberately imitate sounds and movements
- Recall a short series of actions
- Look briefly for a toy that disappears

8 TO 12 MONTHS

- Put small objects into containers and pull them out of containers
- Search behind a screen for an object after they see it hidden there
- Hold and manipulate one object while looking at another object
- Recognize dimensions of objects

Piaget's Four Stages

Four *stages* of cognitive development are central to Piaget's theory. Piaget believed that just as standing must precede walking, some stages of cognitive development must precede others. For example, if a parent presents an idea that is too advanced, the child will not understand the new concept and no real learning will take place. A 4-year-old who asks how babies are made will probably not understand a biologically accurate explanation and will not learn or remember it. If the same child asks the question a few years later, the explanation will be more meaningful and more likely to be remembered. Piaget's stages are associated with approximate ages. The exact age for each stage will vary with the individual, but children in all cultures go through the same stages. Although Piaget acknowledged the role of environmental influences, he clearly had a strong biological bias, especially in referring to stages of development. The four developmental stages he proposed are the sensorimotor stage, the preoperational stage, the concrete operational stage, and the formal operational stage.

The Sensorimotor Stage. Piaget considered the **sensorimotor stage**, which extends from birth to about age 2, to be the most significant and elaborate, because the foundation for all cognitive development is established during this period. Consider the enormous changes that take place during the first 2 years of life. At birth an infant is a totally dependent, reflexive organism. Within a few weeks, infants learn some simple habits. They smile at their mother or caregiver; they seek the stimulation offered by a colorful musical mobile hanging overhead; they reach out and anticipate events in the environment, such as the mother's breast or a bottle. At 2 to 3 months, infants develop some motor coordination skills (Clifton et al., 1993; Thelen, 1994) and a rudimentary memory for past events, and they are able to predict future visual events (Haith & McCarty, 1990). According to Piaget, the acquisition of memory is a crucial foundation for further cognitive development.

By the age of 6 to 8 months, infants seek new and more interesting kinds of stimulation. They can sit up and crawl. No longer willing just to watch what goes on around them, they begin to manipulate their environment, attempting what Piaget called "making interesting sights last"—they try to manipulate their environment and make interesting events recur. Karen Wynn (1992) suggests that even at this age infants have some key numerical reasoning abilities that lay the foundation for further arithmetic reasoning development. At about 8 months, infants begin to develop a sense of their own intentions, and they attempt to overcome obstacles in order to reach goals. They can now crawl to the other side of a room to where the cat is lying or follow a parent into the next room.

From about 9 months on, babies develop *object permanence*—the ability to realize that objects continue to exist even when they are out of sight. Prior to the development of object permanence, when a mother leaves the room and the baby can no longer see her, she no longer exists. After object permanence develops, the baby realizes that she is just out of view. Although the exact age at which object permanence becomes evident has not yet been established, Renée Baillargeon (1991, 1994) has shown the existence of object permanence for some tasks in 4-month-olds—earlier than Piaget believed possible. Various aspects of object permanence evolve gradually throughout the sensorimotor stage.

In the second half of the sensorimotor stage (from about 12 to 24 months), children begin to walk, talk, and use simple forms of logic. Object permanence is more fully developed; the child can now follow a ball that rolls away and can search for the mother after she has left the room. Children also begin to use language to represent the world, an ability that takes them beyond the concrete world of visual imagery. By age 2, a child can talk about Grandma, Daddy, doggy, cookies, Big Bird, going bye-bye, and other objects and events. No longer an uncoordinated, reflex-oriented organism, the child has become a thinking, walking, talking human

Sensorimotor stage: The first of Piaget's four stages of cognitive development (covering roughly the first 2 years of life), during which the child begins to interact with the environment and the rudiments of memory are established.

being. Simultaneously, children may also become manipulative, difficult to deal with, and belligerent. Parents often describe this stage as the terrible twos; it is characterized by the appearance of the ever-popular "No!" The child's behavior may vacillate between charming and awful. This vacillation and annoying new habits, such as being difficult to dress and bathe, are signs of normal development and mark the beginning of the stage of preoperational thought.

The Preoperational Stage. In the **preoperational stage**, which lasts from about age 2 to age 6 or 7, children begin to represent the world symbolically. As preschoolers, they play with objects in new ways and try, through let's-pretend games, to represent reality. Nonetheless, they continue to think about specifics rather than in the abstract and cannot deal with thoughts that are not easily visually represented. They make few attempts to make their speech more intelligible or to justify their reasoning, and they may develop behavior problems such as inattentiveness, belligerence, and temper tantrums. During this stage, adults often begin trying to teach children how to interact with others, but major social changes will not become fully apparent until the next stage of development.

A key element of the preoperational stage—which affects all of a child's behavior, cognitive and emotional—is egocentrism, or self-centeredness. **Egocentrism** is the inability to perceive a situation or event except in relation to oneself. Children are unable to understand that the world does not exist solely to satisfy their interests and needs. They respond to questions such as "Why does it snow?" with answers such as "So I can play in it." In the preoperational stage, the child is unable to see situations from the point of view of another person. Cognitive immaturity makes a young child continue to pester Mom even after she says she has a headache and wants to be left alone (Elkind, 1981a). Children still cannot usually put themselves in the mother's (or anyone else's) position.

At the end of Piaget's preoperational stage, children are just beginning to understand the difference between their ideas, feelings, and interests and those of others. This process of **decentration** continues for several years. Piaget further held that children's understanding of space and their construction of alternative perspectives is limited during this stage. Recent evidence, however, suggests that Piaget may have underestimated the perspective-taking abilities of children. Researchers now find that even 5-year-olds can solve certain visual and space perspective problems previously thought to be solely in the domain of 9- to 10-year-olds (Newcombe & Huttenlocher, 1992). Also, 4-year-olds have abilities to represent and to remember the past; this is an ability that Piaget suggested was impossible until a later age (Gopnik, 1993).

Preoperational stage: Piaget's second stage of cognitive development (lasting from about age 2 to age 6 or 7), during which initial symbolic thought is developed.

Egocentrism [ee-go-SENT-rism]: The inability to perceive a situation or event except in relation to oneself. Also known as *self-centeredness*.

Decentration: The process of changing from a totally self-oriented point of view to one that recognizes other people's feelings, ideas, and viewpoints.

Concrete operational stage: Piaget's third stage of cognitive development (lasting from approximately age 6 or 7 to age 11 or 12), during which the child develops the ability to understand constant factors in the environment, rules, and higher-order symbolism.

Conservation: The ability to recognize that something that has changed in some way (such as the "shape" of a liquid put in a different container) still has the same weight, substance, or volume.

The Concrete Operational Stage. The **concrete operational stage** is Piaget's third stage of cognitive development, lasting from approximately age 6 or 7 to age 11 or 12; during this stage a child develops the ability to understand constant factors in the environment, rules, and higher-order symbolism such as arithmetic and geography. Children in this stage attend school, have friends, can take care of themselves, and may take on household responsibilities. They can look at a situation from more than one viewpoint and evaluate different aspects of it. The child has gained sufficient mental maturity to be able to distinguish between appearances and reality and to think ahead one or two moves in checkers or other games. During this stage, children discover constancy in the world; they learn rules and understand the reasons for them. For example, a child learns to wear a raincoat on a cloudy morning, anticipating rain later in the day.

The hallmark of this stage is an understanding of **conservation**—the ability to recognize that objects may be transformed, visually or physically, yet still be the same in weight, substance, or volume. This concept has been the subject of considerable research. In a typical conservation task, a child is shown three beakers. Two beakers are short, squat, and half full of water; a third is tall, thin, and empty (see

FIGURE 10.6

Development of Conservation

Conservation is the ability to recognize that an object that has been transformed is still the same object, regardless of any changes it has undergone.

1 A child examines two glasses of juice and sees that they are the same.

2 A researcher pours the contents of one glass into a taller and narrower glass.

3 The child is asked to choose the glass that has "more" in it. Children who have not yet developed the ability to conserve choose the taller glass and often declare, "It has more in it; it's bigger."

Figure 10.6). The experimenter pours the water from one short, squat beaker into the tall, narrow one and asks the child, "Which beaker has more water?" A child who does not understand the principle of conservation will claim that the taller beaker contains more water. A child who is able to conserve volume will recognize that the same amount of water is in both the tall and the short beaker. A child who has mastered one type of conservation (for example, conservation of volume) often cannot immediately transfer that knowledge to other conservation tasks (for example, those involving weight).

A child who masters the concept of conservation realizes that specific facts are true because they follow logically, not simply because they are observed. Abundant research supports this claim. An example is the work of John H. Flavell (1986). Flavell and his colleagues have been studying a phenomenon closely associated with conservation: the ability of children to distinguish between appearance and reality. They assert that by the age of 6 children possess some knowledge of the difference between appearance and reality and can sense what a task is all about.

Cognitive and perceptual cognitive abilities continue to develop as children mature and, slowly and in different ways, begin to grasp new and ever more difficult concepts (Flavell, Green, & Flavell, 1989). For example, at around age 7, children come to realize the connectedness of their thoughts, and they become especially conscious of their inner mental life (Flavell, Green, & Flavell, 1993).

The Formal Operational Stage. The **formal operational stage** is Piaget's fourth and final stage of cognitive development (beginning at about age 12), during which the individual can think hypothetically, can consider all future possibilities, and is capable of deductive logic. Unlike children in the concrete operational stage, whose thought is still tied to immediate situations, adolescents can engage in abstract thought. They do this by forming hypotheses that allow them to think of different

Formal operational stage: Piaget's fourth and final stage of cognitive development (beginning at about age 12), during which the individual can think hypothetically, can consider all future possibilities, and is capable of deductive logic.

FIGURE 10.7

Piaget's Stages of Cognitive Development

ways to represent situations, organizing them into all possible relationships and outcomes. The cognitive world of adolescents is full of informal theories of logic and ideas about themselves and life.

By age 12, the egocentrism of the sensorimotor and preoperational stages has for the most part disappeared, but a new egocentrism has developed. According to Inhelder and Piaget (1958, pp. 345–346): "The adolescent goes through a phase in which he attributes an unlimited power to his own thoughts so that the dream of a glorious future or of transforming the world through ideas (even if this idealism takes a materialistic form) seems to be not only fantasy, but also an effective action which in itself modifies the empirical world." The egocentrism and naive hopes of adolescents eventually decrease as they face and deal with the challenges of life.

Fig. 8.3

Piaget's stages of cognitive development are summarized in Figure 10.7.

Implications and Criticisms of Piaget's Theory. Parents, educators, and psychologists can enhance children's cognitive development by understanding how cognitive abilities develop. For example, Piaget recognized that parental love and parent–child interaction are always important to a child's development, but he asserted that they are *essential* in the first 2 years of life. For a child to develop object permanence, to learn how to make interesting sights last, and to develop the rudiments of numerical reasoning, it is necessary for caregivers to provide abundant physical and cognitive stimuli, especially stimuli that move and change color, shape, and form. Research confirms that children and animals given sensory stimulation from birth through the early months develop more quickly both cognitively and socially than those who are not given such stimulation. Parents and educators who agree with Piaget have devoted their efforts to ensuring that the first years of life are ones in which stimulation is great, curiosity is encouraged, and exploration is maximized. From Piaget's point of view, these efforts optimize children's potential. As *Applications* shows, the psychologists who advised the federal government to begin Project Head Start in the 1960s agreed that an enriched preschool environment could help children from disadvantaged backgrounds.

While acknowledging that it is possible to encourage children's development, Piaget stressed that children should not be pushed too fast. Parents serve a child best by providing cognitive stimulation that is appropriate to the child's current develop-

APPLICATIONS

Project Head Start

Project Head Start was initiated in the 1960s in an effort to break the poverty cycle by raising the social and educational competency of disadvantaged preschool children. Today, Project Head Start enrolls about 750,000 children a year, most of them from the neediest families—mostly African American (65 percent) and from the lower socioeconomic classes (Schnur, Brooks-Gunn, & Shipman, 1992). Head Start has received federal support for more than three decades, has served 13 million children, and is often referred to as a milestone in psychology. The multimillion-dollar project showed what can be done to provide remedial education, social support, and effective use of child development techniques.

Project Head Start gives preschool children an enriched preschool environment. Disadvantaged children are placed in a school with a low teacher–student ratio and are provided nutritional and medical services. Children are given focused, individual attention; efforts are made to help build self-confidence and self-esteem. Basic skills that may lead to more complex learning strategies are taught. Helping preschoolers experience the joy of learning is emphasized. Parent involvement is central; parents work on school boards and in the classroom and also receive related social services such as family counseling. When parents are engaged, they respond more fully to their children's needs, and the children do better (Cronan, Walen, & Cruz, 1994).

While they make significant gains in cognitive abilities, Head Start children still do not do as well as those from homes at higher socioeconomic levels. Why? One reason is that Head Start children tend to be especially disadvantaged, even when compared with other disadvantaged groups. Researchers suggest that a year of Head Start may not be enough to close the gap. Another reason is that about 47 percent of Head Start instructors earn only about $10,000 a year; this pay scale is a serious obstacle to attracting good teachers. Other problems involve lack of training, substandard facilities, and short hours; most programs operate half-days or less. Ed Zigler, the architect of the original program, acknowledges that at best only 40 percent of Head Start centers are of truly high quality (Zigler, 1994). He argues that the data for lack of success should be seen as a mandate for enhancing the program, suggesting that a second year would be likely to magnify and solidify the Head Start advantage. Zigler (1987, p. 258) wrote: "We simply cannot inoculate children in one year against the ravages of a life of deprivation." Clearly, it is essential that disadvantaged children be given an equal educational start in life—not just for a year but throughout their childhood. So if Head Start is less than a complete success, its failures have more to do with its implementation than with its design (Zigler, 1994).

mental level. Noted psychologist David Elkind (1981b), in his book *The Hurried Child*, supports this view; he argues that overacceleration ultimately has deleterious effects. Yale psychologist Edward Zigler (1987, p. 257) concurs: "We are driving our children too hard and thereby depriving them of their most precious commodity—their childhood. . . . Children are growing up too fast today, and prematurely placing four-year-olds and five-year-olds into full-day preschool education programs will only compound the problem." In Zigler's view, developmentally appropriate childcare programs for preschoolers should focus on social interaction and recreation. He asserts that the real business of a preschooler is socialization, not education.

Although Piaget's ideas have had an enormous influence on the ways psychologists think about children's development, some researchers have problems with his approach. For example, Fischer and Silvern (1985) remind psychologists that there is a great deal of variation in maturation and that a strict view of Piaget's stage approach reduces the role of the environment. Other researchers claim that Piaget's specific questions and tasks focus people's thinking about children on the wrong abilities and issues. Many studies of young children measure development by giving the children Piaget-based tasks. Children who cannot do a prescribed task at a given age are thought to be cognitively deficient.

FOCUS

Review

- What is the difference between assimilation and accommodation? p. 351
- From Piaget's view, why are the first 2 years the most important time for cognitive development? pp. 353–354
- How is Vygotsky's approach different from Piaget's? pp. 351, 358

Think Critically

- What does it mean to say that Piaget may have overestimated the extent of egocentrism in young children?
- What are the implications of Vygotsky's view that the most significant moment in intellectual development occurs when speech and practical activity converge?

Psychologist Rochel Gelman argues that researchers tend to underestimate younger children's abilities. Studies by Gelman and others show that to understand cognitive development fully, psychologists should ask children of different ages different questions. For example, Shatz and Gelman (1973) found that 2-year-olds change the length of their sentences on the basis of whom they are talking to, using shorter sentences when speaking to younger children. The researchers point to the cognitive maturity of a child who has decentered enough to make such a shift in point of view. Like Gelman, many other researchers claim that Piaget may have overestimated the degree of egocentrism in young children. Baillargeon asserts that Piaget also underestimated the perceptual abilities of infants to represent space. She holds that abilities such as understanding what actually happens to objects when they are hidden, which Piaget saw as developing at 18 months, can be found at 6 months of age (Miller & Baillargeon, 1990). This is a rather startling finding, and one that needs further research.

Alternatives to Piaget: Vygotsky's Sociocultural Theory

Piaget had a strong biological emphasis; he saw the child as an organism that is self-motivated to abstract reality from the world. The child, he held, is a busy constructor of reality, making interesting sights last, inventing games, and learning abstract rules. But Lev Vygotsky (1896–1934) saw the child not as alone in this task but as part of a social world that includes communication, with the self and with others. Children engage in private speech to plan and guide their own actions and behavior; when they use such speech, they do better in various tasks (Bivens & Berk, 1990). It is important to note that Piaget considered that private speech was egocentric and therefore could not involve perspective taking. Vygotsky suggests just the opposite; private speech helps a child understand his or her world and that of other people. For Vygotsky (1934/1962) even the earliest speech is essentially social and useful; in fact, he asserts that social speech comes first, followed by egocentric, then inner speech. Vygotsky wrote in 1930 that "the most significant moment in the course of intellectual development . . . occurs . . . when speech and practical activity, two previously completely independent lines of development, converge" (Vygotsky, 1930/1978, p. 24).

Lev Vygotsky, shown here with his daughter, thought that children did not face the task of cognitive development alone, but rather as part of a social world that helps them to grow. ▼

Vygotsky held that when children are presented tasks that are outside of their current abilities, they need the help of society—usually parents—to accomplish them. When more skilled individuals help a child, the child then incorporates those new skills and ideas into his or her repertoire of behavior. Children solve practical tasks with the help of their own inner speech, as well as with the help of caregivers. At this point there is a shared understanding of ideas and skills: Adults adjust their helping levels so that the child eventually needs less and less help and instruction to accommodate to the world. In Chapter 5, we considered the role of cooperative learning in education and saw that when students cooperate in teams they do better. Vygotsky's theory would predict such a result.

Moral Reasoning

Few children make it to adolescence without squabbling over who's sitting on which side of the back seat. The adult in charge usually then tells them to stop fighting with their sister or brother and announces that such behavior is "rude" or "unacceptable." As children grow, they develop the capacity to assess for themselves what is right and wrong. From childhood on, individuals develop **morality**—a system of learned attitudes about social practices, institutions, and individual behavior that allows a person to evaluate situations and behavior as being right or wrong, good or bad.

Attitudes about specific behavior—who is sitting on which side—as well as decisions about important moral issues develop and change throughout life. At an early age, children learn from their parents the behaviors, attitudes, and values considered appropriate and correct in their culture. Morality is aided by teachers and bolstered by religious and community leaders as well as by family and friends. As children mature, they acquire attitudes that accommodate an increasingly complex view of the world and of reality. Your views of morality when you were a 10-year-old probably differ from your views today. The U.S. Supreme Court has restricted adolescents' rights to make important life decisions—in part because the court believes adolescents lack moral maturity (Gardner, Scherer, & Tester, 1989). But do they? Or is the reasoning and judgment of a child, a preteen, or an adolescent as sound as that of an adult?

Piaget and Morality

Piaget examined children's ability to analyze questions of morality and found the results to be consistent with his ideas about cognitive development. Young children's ideas about morality are rigid and rule-bound; children expect justice to follow from a particular act. When playing a game, a young child will not allow the rules to be modified. Older children, on the other hand, recognize that rules are established by social convention and may need to be altered, depending on the situation. They have developed a sense of *moral relativity*, which allows them to recognize that situational factors affect the way things are perceived and that people may or may not receive their just reward or punishment (Piaget, 1932).

According to Piaget, as children mature, they move away from inflexibility and toward relativity in their moral judgments; they develop new cognitive structures and assimilate and accommodate new ideas. When young children are questioned about lying, for example, they respond that it is always and under any circumstances bad—a person should never lie. At some time between the ages of 5 and 12, however, children recognize that lying may be permissible in some special circumstances.

Kohlberg: Heinz's Dilemma

Piaget's theory of moral development was based on descriptions of how children respond to specific kinds of questions and the ages at which they switch and use other forms of answers. The research of Harvard psychologist Lawrence Kohlberg (1927– 1987) grew out of Piaget's work. Kohlberg believed that moral development in general proceeds through three levels, each of which is divided into two stages. The central concept in Kohlberg's theory is that of justice. In his studies of moral reasoning, Kohlberg presented different types of stories to people of various ages and asked them to describe what the stories meant to them and how they felt about them (Kohlberg, 1969).

Morality: A system of learned attitudes about social practices, institutions, and individual behavior used to evaluate situations and behavior as being right or wrong, good or bad.

FIGURE 10.8

Development of Morality over Time

In Kohlberg's theory of morality, a distinct progression of moral development emerges over a child's life. The highest, or postconventional, levels of moral reasoning are not often achieved by children.

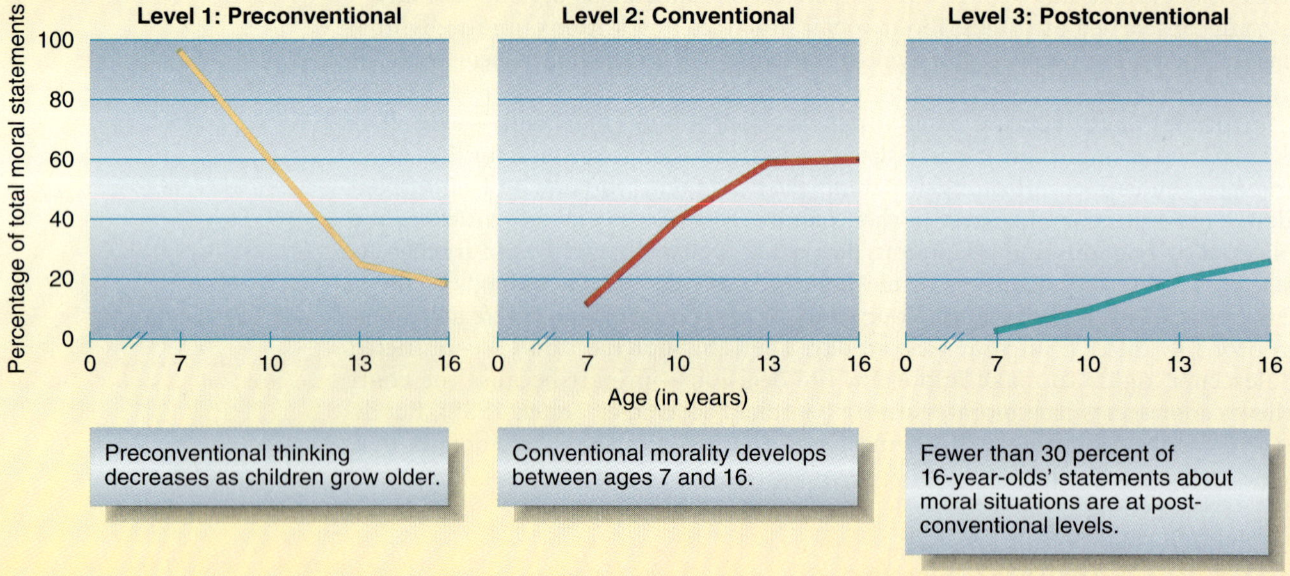

Three Levels of Morality. In one of Kohlberg's stories, Heinz, a poor man, stole a drug for his wife, who would have died without it. Presented with the story of Heinz, children at level 1, *preconventional morality,* either condemn Heinz's behavior (explaining that he should be punished because he stole) or justify it (explaining that Heinz was good because he tried to save his wife's life). People at level 2, *conventional morality,* say that Heinz broke the law by stealing and should go to jail. Only people who have reached level 3, *postconventional morality,* can see that although Heinz's action was illegal, the ethical dilemma is complex (see Figure 10.8).

Young children at level 1, *preconventional morality*, base their decisions about right and wrong on the likelihood of avoiding punishment and obtaining rewards. A child in this stage would say it is "bad" to pull the cat's tail "because Mom will send me to my room." School-age children, who are at level 2, adopt *conventional morality*; they conform in order to avoid the disapproval of other people. At this stage, a 10-year-old might choose not to try cigarettes because his parents and friends disapprove of smoking. Level 2 judgments are also governed by a process that considers the implications of a person's behavior: Why did the person do it? What will be the consequences for that person and for others?

Level 3, or *postconventional morality*, is concerned with contracts, moral conscience, and laws. In level 3 morality, people make judgments on the basis of their perception of the needs of society, with the goal of maintaining community welfare and the legal order. In advanced stages of level 3, people make judgments on the basis of their personal moral beliefs and values rather than those of society. Conscientious objection to legally sanctioned behaviors is associated with this stage. For example, a person may be opposed to capital punishment, even though it is legal in some states. Most adults reach at least the first stage of level 3.

TABLE 10.4 *A Comparison of Piaget and Kohlberg on Moral Development*

Piaget	Kohlberg
Sensorimotor and preoperational (birth–6 or 7 years)	*Level 1—Preconventional morality* Stage 1: Obedience and punishment orientation Stage 2: Naively egoistic orientation
Concrete operational (7–11 or 12 years)	*Level 2—Conventional morality* Stage 3: Good-child orientation Stage 4: Authority-and-social order-maintaining orientation
Formal operations (12 years and beyond	*Level 3—Postconventional morality* Stage 5: Contractual–legalistic orientation Stage 6: Conscience or principle orientation

Extending Initial Ideas. Piaget set the stage for two decades of research by Kohlberg, whose work was monumental in scope. Like other great thinkers, Kohlberg laid down a theory that he knew would be tested, evaluated, and revised—a firm foundation for the next generation of research.

Piaget and Kohlberg studied moral reasoning, not moral behavior. Both theorists focused on how people make decisions, not on the behavior that might result from those decisions. However, their theories differ. Piaget thought of the stages of moral development as discrete, whereas Kohlberg viewed them as overlapping. Table 10.4 compares Piaget's and Kohlberg's theories on moral development.

Kohlberg also went further than Piaget in systematizing the development of morality. He elaborated on ideas about how children's interactions with parents and friends may influence their conceptions of morality. For example, when children realize that working within or around the rules affects other family members, their view of the rules changes. Thus, an older girl will spare her mother embarrassment and respond favorably when asked her opinion about her mother's carefully chosen new dress; a younger child will refuse to break the rules about lying and will tell her mother if she thinks the dress looks ugly (Blasi, 1980).

In Kohlberg's view, children may use earlier levels of moral reasoning from time to time, even though they are capable of higher levels; this finding has been substantiated by the work of DeVries and Walker (1986). They asked university students to fill out an attitude questionnaire and write an essay on capital punishment. The results showed that the students had achieved high levels of moral reasoning but often did not reason at those levels in supporting their positions on capital punishment. In fact, 24 percent of the participants used a level of moral reasoning that was a full stage lower than that which they were capable of using. Researchers are expanding on the original Kohlberg research, using different contexts—for example, perceptions of fairness among schoolchildren of different ages (Thorkildsen, 1989) and religious dogma (Nucci & Turiel, 1993).

Kohlberg's theory has not gone unchallenged. Some have suggested that his views are culturally bound and that he did not examine issues with which normal adults have to deal—for example, what to teach a child about nuclear war and the consequences of dropping the bomb on Hiroshima to end World War II. This criticism of Kohlberg's limitations does not make the work any less important; however, it does raise some significant questions.

Gender Differences: Gilligan's Work

A major addition to the study of morality has been the work done by Carol Gilligan (1982), who found that people look at more than justice when they analyze moral conflicts. She discovered that people are also concerned with caring, with relationships, and with connections with other people.

Though Kohlberg and his colleagues had not generally reported any gender differences, Gilligan did. *Gender differences* are, of course, differences between males and females in behavior or mental processes. Gilligan examined differences between girls and boys in their inclinations toward caring and justice. She found that girls are more concerned with care, relationships, and connections with other people. As younger children, girls gravitate toward a morality of caring, whereas boys gravitate toward a morality of justice. Gilligan asserts that the difference between boys and girls is established by gender and by the child's relationship with the mother. Because of the gender difference between boys and their mothers, boys see that they are essentially different from other people, whereas girls develop a belief in their similarity (connectedness) with others. For older children, Gilligan asserts that the transition to adolescence is a crucial time, during which girls may develop their own voice—a voice too often muted and suppressed (Brown & Gilligan, 1992). Gilligan shows that boys respond to Kohlberg's Heinz dilemma by indicating that sometimes people must act on their own to do the right thing. Girls, in contrast, are more likely to look for ways to talk out differences or to seek some compromise. Like Kohlberg, Gilligan argues that the development of caring follows a time course, with caring initially felt only toward oneself and later toward others as well, and ultimately (in some people) the development of a more mature stage of caring for truth. Gilligan's work has been influential with respect to psychologists' evaluations of morality. Yet her approach fosters a continuation of gender stereotyping—women as nurturing, men as logical. Moreover, her work has been limited to white, middle-class children; it needs a broader, more multicultural perspective.

Does women's inclination toward caring show itself in other cultures? Three researchers from Brigham Young University examined questionnaire responses of women in Korea, China, Thailand, and the United States (Stimpson, Jensen, & Neff, 1992). Their results show that Gilligan's work holds up in the three non-Western cultures, and they suggest that differences in caring between men and women may initially have a biological origin.

The study of morality, justice, and caring has gone beyond Kohlberg's original view. For example, Kitwood (1990) argues that only after people have developed a sense of themselves can they fully care about others; he thus combines personality theory (discussed in Chapter 12) with studies of morality. Moral reasoning and behavior, and especially promoting morality, have to be studied within the context of the total person.

FOCUS

Review

- Distinguish the key differences among preconventional, conventional, and postconventional morality. p. 360
- What was Gilligan's main criticism of Kohlberg's work? p. 362

Think Critically

- What is a potential problem with using Kohlberg's stories in research to study moral development?

Emotional Development

Anne Frank, the young Jewish girl who was hidden from the Nazis during World War II, was eloquently thankful to the people who helped hide her and her family. She wrote extensively of her dedication and gratitude toward people who were making sacrifices and putting their own lives at risk to help her family; she affirmed their morality. For a teenage girl, Anne showed extraordinary emotional maturity. Making moral decisions is not independent of a person's emotional life, an aspect of human behavior that begins its development shortly after birth with the attachments that infants form with caregivers.

Attachment

Attachment is the formal term psychologists use to describe the strong emotional tie that a person feels toward a special other person in his or her life. Attachment theory weighs heavily in the thinking of psychologists about emotional development in children. The understanding of attachment and emotional expression and the bonds that form among people has a long history. Heavily influenced by some classic early work with monkeys done by Harry Harlow, this research was extended in the 1970s by work on bonding.

People's ability to express emotion and form attachments develops from birth through adulthood. Attachment behaviors encouraged in the early weeks and months of life are also nurtured during adolescence and adulthood, when people form close loving bonds with others. Most researchers consider these behaviors innate, even though they unfold slowly over the first year of life and are reinforced by caregivers. The reason is that emotional expressions—including attachment behaviors—not only appear in all cultures (see Chapter 9) but are found in deaf and blind people and in people without limbs, who have limited touch experiences (Izard & Saxton, 1988).

Classic Work: Attachment in Rhesus Monkeys. To find out how people develop attachment behaviors, Harry Harlow (1905–1981), a psychologist at the University of Wisconsin, focused on the development of attachment in rhesus monkeys. Harlow's initial studies were on the nature of early interactions among monkeys. But he found that monkeys raised from birth in isolated bare-wire cages away from their mothers did not survive, even though they were well fed. Other monkeys, raised in the same conditions but with scraps of terry cloth in their cages, survived. Terry cloth is hardly a critical variable in the growth and development of monkeys, yet its introduction into a wire cage made the difference between life and death for these rhesus monkeys. Harlow inferred that the terry cloth provided some measure of security. That conclusion led him to attempt to discover whether infant monkeys had an inborn desire for love or warmth.

In a classic experiment, Harlow placed infant monkeys in cages along with two wire-covered shapes resembling adult monkeys. One figure was covered with terry cloth; the other was left bare. Both could be fitted with bottles to provide milk. In some cases, the wire mother surrogate had the bottle of milk; in other cases, the terry cloth mother surrogate had the bottle. Harlow found that the infant monkeys clung to the terry-cloth mother surrogates whether or not they provided milk. He concluded that the wire mother surrogate, even with a bottle of milk, could not provide the comfort that the terry-cloth mother surrogate could provide (Harlow & Zimmerman, 1958).

Another of Harlow's findings was that neither group of monkeys grew up to be totally normal. Harlow's monkeys were more aggressive and fearful than normally raised monkeys. They were also unable to engage in normal sexual relations. And

Attachment: The strong emotional tie that a person feels toward a special other person in his or her life.

some of the infants raised with wire mother surrogates exhibited self-destructive behaviors (Harlow, 1962).

Bonding. In the 1970s and 1980s, it was widely held that bonding occurs. **Bonding** is a special process of emotional attachment that may occur between parents and babies in the minutes and hours immediately after birth. It is neither a reflex nor a learned behavior, though some psychologists claim that it is inborn. Pediatricians Marshall Klaus and John Kennell (1983) believe that a mother is in a state of heightened sensitivity to her child immediately after delivery and that she begins to form unique, specific attachments to her child. Klaus argues that babies should have as much physical and emotional contact as possible with their mothers and fathers; keeping parents and infants together in the hospital shortly after birth, in rooming-in arrangements, should be the rule, not the exception (Kennell, Voos, & Klaus, 1979). But research has not especially supported claims for bonding. Eyer (1992) asserts that there is no evidence to support bonding's existence and that it is a fictional concept. While the issue of the existence of bonding is not yet resolved, many parents have welcomed the increased contact with their newborns that is reputed to facilitate bonding.

There is no doubt, however, that in the first months of life, the parent–infant attachment deepens as some of the infant's reflexes disappear and new behaviors appear. At about 4 to 8 weeks, an infant may sleep for 4 to 6 hours during the night, uninterrupted by the need to eat, a change that may help weary parents feel a bit more loving toward the infant. When awake, infants smile at the mother and listen attentively to human voices. Between 6 and 9 months, infants begin to crawl, giving them more freedom to seek out favorite people. The ability to crawl is accompanied by important changes in behavior; in fact, some researchers assert that crawling allows for key behavior changes to occur (Bertenthal, Campos, & Kermoian, 1994).

Attachment in Infants. John Bowlby (1907–1990) was one of the first modern psychologists to study the close attachment between mothers and their newborns. Bowlby (1977) argued that the infant's emotional tie with its caregiver evolved as a response that promotes survival. Bowlby asserted that an infant's very early interactions with its parents are crucial to normal development. Research now shows that mothers recognize their infants by smell, touch, and sound (Kaitz et al., 1992), and that infants similarly recognize their mothers (Leon, 1992). Some psychologists consider the establishment of a close and warm parent–child relationship one of the major accomplishments of the first year of life. This attachment is considered a key developmental event that helps an infant develop basic feelings about security.

Attachment to the mother may become so strong that her departure from the room causes a fear response, especially to strangers; this response is known as *separation anxiety* and reflects insecurity on the part of the infant. When infants fear that the principal caregiver, usually the mother, may not be consistently available, they become clingy and vigilant of her disappearing (Bowlby, 1988; Cassidy & Berlin, 1994). In attempting to analyze attachment to parents, researchers have used a procedure called the *strange situation technique,* in which babies from 12 to 24 months old are observed with parents, removed briefly from them, and then reunited. Research with the strange situation technique shows that most babies (65 percent) are *secure;* they are distressed by a parent leaving but are easily comforted. Other babies (about 20 percent) are neither distressed nor comforted by parents going and coming—these babies are categorized as *avoidant* and are considered to have an insecure attachment. Some babies (about 15 percent) are *resistant*; these babies seek closeness to the parent but when separated are angry. Last, some babies (about 5 percent) are characterized as *disoriented*; they show confused, contradictory attachment behaviors and may act angry, sad, or ambivalent at any time.

Researchers consider a secure baby to be one whose mother is affectionate and especially responsive (Isabella, Belsky, & von Eye, 1989). According to some

Bonding: A special process of emotional attachment that may occur between parents and babies in the minutes and hours immediately after birth.

researchers, this mother–child relationship makes later cognitive and emotional development easier (Cassidy & Berlin, 1994). Not all researchers agree, and cross-cultural work shows significant variations (e.g., Tronick, Morelli, & Ivey, 1992), but experimental studies indicate that the quality and nature of the mutual closeness formed between the newborn and the mother can make a difference in later life. Children who have not formed warm, close attachments early in life lack a sense of security and become anxious and overly dependent. As 6-year-olds, they are perceived as more aggressive and less competent than their more secure counterparts (D. A. Cohn, 1990). Those who have close attachments require less discipline and are less easily distracted (Lewis & Feiring, 1989).

▲ *The quality and nature of the bond formed between infant and parents (especially the mother) can make a difference later in childhood. Children who have formed healthy attachments in infancy are less likely to suffer the ill effects of separation during the early school years.*

Once established, early attachment is fairly permanent. Brief separations from parents, as in child-care centers, do not adversely affect it. Influential psychologist Mary Ainsworth (1979) asserts that these parental attachments affect the child's later friendships, relations with relatives, and enduring adult relationships. People's relationships as adults may even be related to the attachment styles they had as children, although this is an untested idea. Can adoptive parents form the same type of secure, close attachment to the child as biological parents? Even without the initial postdelivery bonding that Klaus and Kennell describe, adoptive parents form supportive, healthy family relationships. A caretaking atmosphere that is warm, consistent, and governed by the infant's needs is the key. Both adoptive and biological parents can provide such an atmosphere, and both adoptive and biological children can form strong attachments to their parents (Singer et al., 1985).

Verbal and Emotional Exchanges

Verbal exchanges and other emotional interactions between infants and their caregivers increase significantly as infants mature. Dialogues in the form of gestures, smiles, and vocalizations become more common. Mothers and fathers initiate these interactions as often as the infants do. This early play is good for babies, as long as the babies are not overstimulated and annoyed by too much excitement (Singer & Singer, 1990).

Verbal exchanges help establish ties, teach language, inform infants about the world, and socialize them. These exchanges seem to occur universally, between all infants and parents. In a cross-cultural study, parents in four countries—Argentina, France, Japan, and the United States—all used similar speech categories (Bornstein et al., 1992). There were some differences, too, of course. For example, Japanese mothers were more willing to speak ungrammatically to their infants, using nonsense words, songs, and rhymes more than mothers from the other countries did. But the similarities among cultures outweigh the differences. The researchers concluded: "[The] universal aspects of infancy . . . appear . . . to exert control over the content of maternal speech" (p. 601).

Interactions between parents and babies are especially important in development. In an experiment in which mothers remained still and expressionless, their infants appeared sad and turned away from them (Cohn & Tronick, 1983). The implication is that the mere presence of a parent is not enough; the parent must interact both physically and vocally with the infant (Sorce & Emde, 1981) and must pay attention to the infant (Jones & Raag, 1989). Although infant facial expressions are universal, there are some cultural differences in responsiveness to infants (Camras et al., 1992). In a study of mother–infant interactions with participants from Kenya, Mexico, and the United States, researchers found that a mother's culture and schooling affect her responsiveness. In comparing women from Mexico and the United States, the researchers found that women who had more schooling—

and therefore more institutionalized communication—were more verbally responsive than were women with less schooling (Richman, Miller, & LeVine, 1992). Emotional responsiveness also varied with culture. Women from Kenya were more likely to be soothing and protective to young infants; women from the United States were more verbally active and played a great deal. The cultural differences that appeared were evident at 4 months and were even more pronounced at 9 months. How such verbal and emotional responsiveness on the part of mothers affects later development is a matter of speculation and a promising area for future research.

Several other important variables influence the type and amount of interaction between parents and infants. One is the baby's physical attractiveness, or cuteness (Hildebrandt, 1983). People judge especially beautiful babies as more competent, more likable, and healthier than average or unattractive babies (Stephan & Langlois, 1984). Adults are more likely to play with, speak to, tweak, jiggle, or smile at attractive children (Langlois et al., 1995). This is not surprising; psychologists know that people are biased by the attractiveness of others, whether children or adults (Ritter & Langlois, 1988). The baby's own behavior is also important. Clarke-Stewart (1973) found that the more often the child looked, smiled, or vocalized to the mother, the more affectionate and attached to the child she became and, further, the more responsive she was to her child's distress. Tronick and Cohn (1989) concur. They have found that infants and mothers both change their behavior in reaction to each other, and they argue that neither the baby nor the mother is a passive recipient of the other's emotions. Both are active participants in forming the attachment.

Temperament

During the earliest months of life, some infants smile or reach out to a new face and readily accept being held or cuddled. Others are more inhibited. Still others exhibit extreme reticence, even distress, in the presence of strangers. As adults, the xenophobic infants (those who fear strangers) are likely to be inhibited, meek, and wavering (Caspi, Elder, & Bem, 1988). Researchers know, however, that for most people there is relatively modest stability of such infant behaviors as evidenced by later behavioral styles (except for very extreme cases—intense shyness or diffidence, for example). This does not deny a genetic component to temperament but rather suggests that what is observed in infancy is not necessarily what is seen later on.

Temperament refers to long-lasting individual differences in the intensity and especially in the quality of a person's emotional reactions. Some psychologists believe that each person is born with a specific temperament: easygoing, willful, outgoing, or shy, to name a few. Newborns, infants, and children, like the adults they will eventually grow to be, are all different from one another. Generalizations from one child to all children are impossible, and even generalizations from a sample of children must be made with caution. So many variables can affect a child's growth and development that researchers painstakingly try to separate all the important ones. Thomas and Chess (1977), in their pioneering work in the New York Longitudinal Study, point out that temperament is not fixed and unchangeable. With these cautions in mind, let us look at studies of temperament.

Data from the New York Longitudinal Study show that children tend to fall into four broad categories: easy (40 percent of children), difficult (10 percent), slow-to-warm-up (15 percent), and unique (35 percent). *Easy* children are happy-go-lucky and adapt easily to new situations; *difficult* children are resistant to environmental change and often react poorly; *slow-to-warm-up* children respond slowly, have low-intensity responses, and are often negative. Many children are *unique* and show a varied blend of emotional reactions.

Temperament: Long-lasting individual differences in the intensity and especially in the quality of a person's emotional reactions.

Many researchers contend that some specific initial temperamental characteristics may be long-lasting and biologically based. For example, Jerome Kagan and his colleagues found that 2- and 3-year-olds who were *extremely* cautious and shy tended to remain that way for 4 more years. They also found physiological evidence (an increase in autonomic nervous system activity, for example) that these children may be more responsive to change and unfamiliarity (Kagan & Snidman, 1991a). Daniels and Plomin (1985) found an important relationship between the shyness of 2-year-old adopted infants and the shyness of their biological mothers. These findings suggest that genetic factors also play a role in shyness. Studies of identical twins on a range of emotional dimensions, especially temperament, also show support for a strong genetic component (Emde et al., 1992).

However, shyness and other aspects of temperament can be changed; human behavior is the product of deliberative thought processes as well as biological forces. A child's temperament affects his or her interaction with parents in important ways and may determine in part how the parents treat the child—there is a reciprocal and mutually reinforcing situation. Parents recognize that they affect their child's temperament and personality; they assume that their child-rearing practices will have important influences on development and that a child who may have been categorized as *difficult* by Thomas and Chess (1977) may as an adolescent be seen as *easy*. Moreover, shyness is somewhat culturally determined; in one cross-cultural study, researchers found that shyness among native Chinese students helps them gain acceptance from teachers; the opposite tends to be true for students in Western countries (Chen, Rubin, & Li, 1995). Finally, attachment theory has been criticized for being largely based on behaviors observed during momentary stressful situations, which are somewhat artificial (Field, 1996).

FOCUS

Review

- What evidence is there that attachment exists? pp. 364–365
- Cite evidence to suggest that some traits, such as shyness, are inborn. p. 367

Think Critically

- In what ways do you think that physical and emotional development might interact?
- What are the implications of cross-cultural differences in responsiveness toward infants for their later emotional development?

Social Development

In any bookstore, you'll find shelves lined with how-to books on child rearing written by physicians, parents, psychologists, and others. The variety of approaches and experts shows that ideas about child rearing are complicated and constantly changing. As society changes, so do beliefs and practices related to children's social development and ideas about how children form a sense of identity and self. As children move cognitively from egocentrism to a point where they can perceive themselves as different from the rest of the world, they also develop the ability to think about social relationships. As we will see, children have not one but many environments in which they develop socially. Parents exert a powerful influence on children, but not the sole influence. Thus, despite vast differences in the way parents treat children, most children turn out all right. Researchers such as Judith Rich Harris (1995) assert that this is because a child's many environments, especially his or her play groups, exert profound effects on social development, more than was ever thought possible.

Early Social Development

Social development begins soon after birth, with the development of an attachment between parents and their newborn. The nature of a child's early interactions with parents is a crucial part of personality development. Infants have a great need to be hugged and cuddled, nurtured, and made to feel good. However, as psychoanalyst Bruno Bettelheim (1987) said, "Love is not enough." Eventually, the most important job for parents is teaching their children both how to become independent and how to interact with others.

The First Months. In the 1st year of life, social interactions among children are limited; infants need constant attention and are largely egocentric. They are basically unable to recognize any needs other than their own. In about the second half of the 1st year, children exhibit strong attachments to parents and other caregivers, along with fear of strangers.

As early as 9 months, infants show they like to play games by indicating their unhappiness when an adult stops playing with them (Ross & Lollis, 1987). They play by themselves; but as they grow older, especially beyond 2 years of age, they engage in more social play with other children (Howes, Unger, & Seidner, 1989).

By the end of their 2nd year, children have begun to understand that they are separate from their parents—they are developing a sense of self. They learn to differentiate themselves from others, to manipulate the world, and to interact with other people. As they enter the preoperational stage, egocentrism gives way gradually to increased social interaction. At age 2, children are better at controlling their emotional responses than they were at 18 months. They generally play alone or alongside other children, but they prefer to play with an adult rather than with another 2-year-old (Jennings, Curry, & Connors, 1986). Gradually, however, they begin to socialize with their peers.

Sharing. The noted pediatrician Benjamin Spock once said that the only two things children will share willingly are communicable diseases and their mother's age. Actually, from age 2 until they begin school, children vacillate between quiet conformity and happy sharing, on the one hand, and making stubborn negative demands and exhibiting egocentric behavior, on the other. Because sharing is a socially desirable behavior, children's learning to share becomes a top priority when they enter a child-care center, nursery school, or kindergarten.

Very young children do not understand the concept of sharing—particularly the idea that if you share with another child, the other child is more likely to share with you. In a laboratory study of sharing, researchers observed groups of two children separated by a gate. Initially one child was given toys and the other wasn't; then the situation was reversed. The researchers found that none of the children shared spontaneously; however, 65 percent shared a toy when asked to do so by their mother. Moreover, a child who was deprived of a toy after having shared one often approached the child who now had the toy. One child even said, "I gave you a toy. Why don't you give me one?" Children do not initiate sharing at a young age; but once they share, they seem to exhibit knowledge about reciprocal arrangements (Levitt et al., 1985). Of course, sharing is more likely among children who are friends because they have more intense social activity and make more frequent attempts at conflict resolution (Newcomb & Bagwell, 1995).

Entry into kindergarten helps lead to a breakdown of egocentrism; however, many factors can either promote or retard this aspect of development. One variable is the type of toys children play with. Quilitch and Risley (1973) provided young children with two kinds of toys—those generally played with by one child at a time (isolate toys) and those designed for use by two or more children at the same time (social toys). All the children played with both kinds of toys, but some were first given social toys and others were first given isolate toys. After the initial play period, more of the children who had been given social toys first chose to play with other children. The researchers concluded that the kinds of toys given to children altered the degree of egocentrism exhibited in their play.

Gender Issues

In a 1959 study of masculinity and father–son relationships, Paul Mussen and Luther Distler concluded that a father's importance and involvement in his son's life are crucial in determining the child's gender-based interests. *The Research Process* on pages 370 and 371 explores the changing relationships of fathers and their children. A generation ago, when Mussen and Distler conducted their research, many parents tended to encourage "masculine" traits such as athletic prowess in their sons and "feminine" traits such as popularity in their daughters. Parents often accepted and promoted a gender-based social environment. Today, many parents de-emphasize gender-based interests in their children, seeking to reduce or eliminate society's tendency to stereotype people, their interests, and their occupations on the basis of gender. This trend is also reflected in children's literature through photographs and storylines (Kortenhaus & Demarest, 1993). Such de-emphasis on gender stereotyping has led to a more even distribution of scores on various measures of cognitive ability (Feingold, 1993).

There are gender similarities and gender differences. When young people are given equal schooling, measures of academic performance for boys and girls tend to be equal. Socially, both men and women value intelligence and a sense of humor in the opposite sex. But men and women differ in their biological makeup, and their experiences, biologically and environmentally, are not the same; for example, small but fairly consistent gender differences exist in domains closely related to sex and mating (Buss, 1995). Researchers are aware that their preexisting ideas and sometimes their politically correct desires to minimize differences may contaminate or obfuscate the truth. Thus, Alice Eagly (1995) argues that researchers must deal responsibly with issues of gender differences.

Gender Stereotyping. Socialization starts at the moment of birth, when parents may begin treating their children differently on the basis of gender. Psychologists are especially aware of *gender stereotyping*—patterns of behavior expected of people according to their gender. Young boys are given footballs; young girls are given Barbie dolls. Boys wear blue; girls wear pink. Is this a problem?

You may believe that most gender-stereotyped behavior comes from parents—that boys and girls are treated differently in their formative years and for this reason develop differently. The reality is that most of the differences in the way boys and girls are raised are small (Lytton & Romney, 1991). In Western cultures, some of the differences are the following: (1) Boys receive physical punishment more often than girls. (2) Fathers tend to differentiate between sons and daughters more than mothers do. (3) The extent to which parents treat boys and girls differently tends to decrease as the children grow older.

The gender differences that do exist in how parents raise their children tend to result from many factors, however. For example, boys tend to be assigned chores that take them away from people (such as yard work and walking the dog), whereas girls tend to be assigned in-house activities. As a consequence, some researchers assert, girls interact more with people and may therefore become more nurturing. In the same manner, boys may excel at manipulating objects and tools, while girls have fewer opportunities for inventive play. And both girls and boys may receive approval and praise for their "gender-appropriate" behaviors. Not only are reinforced behaviors important, but (as social learning theory shows) children learn gender-based ideas merely by watching the behavior of adults of their own gender (Luecke-Aleska et al., 1995).

Moreover, there exists evidence that there may be biological, especially hormonal, influences; that is, children may have preexisting preferences for gender-based behaviors (Berenbaum & Snyder, 1995). Researchers know that 18-month-old boys and girls show greater involvement with toys conventionally associated with

THE RESEARCH PROCESS

Is Dad's Time Quality Time?

The American family is undergoing dramatic changes. During the past two decades, women have entered the work force in unprecedented numbers and, in so doing, have changed the shape, structure, and fabric of family life. In some homes, men are staying home while their wives are working (Grbich, 1994). Regardless of who is the principal breadwinner, women are spending less time with their young children. Are fathers taking up the slack? Do fathers spend enough time with their children? Do fathers engage in basic caregiving, play, or both? Is Dad's time "quality" time? And down the road, how much do fathers contribute to adolescent maladjustment when compared to mothers?

The Quality of Time Concept. Today's fathers are more interested in their newborns and may be involved in their upbringing from the first moments of life, as evidenced by the fact that many more fathers are now present in the delivery room during their children's birth than was formerly true. Fathers are affectionate and responsive caregivers. Two words often used in describing fathers' interactions with children are *quality* and *quantity*. Fathers sometimes assert that they spend limited time with their children but that this time is "quality" time. Two Syracuse University researchers, Hoosain and Roopnarine (1994), looked at the quality and quantity of interactions between fathers and their children to determine whether this is true.

Methods. Among other groups, the researchers studied 23 two-parent African American families in which the father worked full-time and the mother worked part-time. Each family was middle-income and had a child younger than 2; all the families lived in Syracuse, New York. Both mothers and fathers were professionals, such as nurses, doctors, teachers, and social workers. Both parents were asked to fill out a parental involvement questionnaire to assess their involvement in child-care activities. Mothers and fathers rated their degree of involvement with their children in six areas: bedtime routines, physical care (such as diaper changing and bathing), feeding, singing, playing, and soothing the child.

Results. Some fathers spent large amounts of time with their children, others very little. Some spent quality time (time devoted to active involvement with a child, as opposed to mere presence); others did not. For example, compared with the mothers, the fathers rated themselves as being less involved in singing to infants, in bedtime routines, in the physical care of infants, in offering comfort when infants cried, in feeding and playing with the infants. In fact, the fathers spent about 42 percent as much time as the mothers in caregiving activities. The estimates for these African American fathers and children are quite similar to those of white Euro-American fathers and their children, as we will see.

Play turned out to be a prominent feature of the time men spent with their infants; in fact, the men were twice as likely to be involved in play as in basic caregiving activities. The gender of the infant seemed not to be important in determining the extent of play or basic caregiving for either mothers or fathers.

Conclusions. This study suggests that child care is a priority among middle-class African American fathers, but that the fathers play with their infants more than they do basic caregiving. It also suggests that they play with their sons and daughters equally. These data are consistent with other research. For example, Grossman, Pollack, and Golding (1988) looked at the quality and quantity of interactions between fathers and their first-born 5-year-old children. To measure quantity, the researchers had the fa-

their own gender—even if parents have not promoted play with gender-stereotyped toys (Caldera, Huston, & O'Brien, 1989). This suggests a biological influence (Berenbaum & Snyder, 1995). Further, starting at age 3 and continuing for several years, children prefer same-gender playmates. According to Eleanor Maccoby and Carol Jacklin (1987), this characteristic is reliable, cuts across a variety of situations, and is difficult to change. Gender segregation does not happen solely because children have been given "boy" toys or "girl" toys; nor does it result solely from inborn temperamental differences that lead to rough-and-tumble play for boys and more sedate play for girls (Berenbaum & Snyder, 1995). Children know they are members of one gender or the other. This knowledge binds members of each gender together and differentiates them from members of the other one. Children with widely different personalities are drawn together solely on the basis of their shared gender. Maccoby (1990) asserts that gender differences are minimal when children are observed individually but become more evident in social situations.

It is apparent that nurturing and biological influences on children are both important factors in determining gender differences. However, gender differences in behavior are small and are obvious only in certain situations, such as on the play-

thers estimate the average amount of time they spent with their children on weekdays and weekends, with respect to both playtime and caretaking. To measure quality, the researchers had the subjects perform a task that involved both parents and the child in their home. The researchers recorded the quality of the interactions during play in terms of warmth (was the parent critical or reinforcing?), attention, and responsiveness.

Grossman, Pollack, and Golding (1988) found that, as in the Hoosain and Roopnarine study, the men were good and attentive fathers; but they also found that the amount of time men spend with their children is directly affected by their wives. In general, men married to autonomous, self-sufficient, competent women spend less time with their children. The quality of the time a father spends with his children seems to be enhanced a great deal if the father is high in feelings of self-worth.

It is important to note that research on fathers and their children is limited; in a review of the impact of fathers on later adolescent maladjustment, only 1 percent of studies focused solely on fathers, while 48 percent focused exclusively on mothers (Phares & Compas, 1993). Further, the quality and quantity of time men spend with their children cannot be analyzed in isolation, because both aspects are affected by personal psychological variables as well as by marital factors and even the gender of the child (Ross & Taylor, 1989). For example, when a marriage is satisfying, fathers spend more time with their children (Willoughby & Glidden, 1995). Moreover, men are more likely to engage in affectionate touch with younger sons than older ones, and some studies find that daughters receive less attention from fathers than do sons (Harris & Morgan, 1991; Salt, 1991).

In general, fathers are seen as less affectionate than mothers and more likely to engage in play than in caregiving (Berndt et al., 1993; Hoosain & Roopnarine, 1994). But there are still many unanswered questions. Do some types of men marry autonomous women because they want little to do with their children? Do children seek out the more playful parent? Do children seek out the more autonomous parent? In what kinds of play do fathers engage? The research continues.

ground (Oliver & Hyde, 1993). As parents consider the implications of research on gender differences, they must use critical thinking skills. They should foster, among other things, children's achievement, moral values, and self-esteem. None of these values is gender-based; both boys and girls can and should be taught to play, learn, reason, and solve problems. All children should be taught basic human values, and these too are not gender-specific.

Self-Perception: Erik Erikson and the Search for Self

Developing an awareness of the self as different from others is a key to early childhood social development. Self-perception begins when the child recognizes that he or she is a separate person, different from other people; the self becomes more differentiated as a child develops an appreciation of his or her own inner mental world. As children develop a concept of themselves, they develop self-esteem and significant attachments to others. Such cognitive, and then social, changes do not

APPLICATIONS

Child Care

According to the Bureau of the Census (1995b), 60 percent of mothers with children under the age of 6 are working or looking for work outside the home; the figure increases to 75 percent for women whose children are between 6 and 17. For families in which both parents have jobs, as well as for single-parent families, child care can be a necessity. Child-care situations are becoming increasingly diverse as parents seek alternative arrangements for their children. While their mothers work, most preschool children are cared for in their own or other people's homes, often by babysitters, relatives, friends, fathers, or grandparents. Child-care centers provide care for about 23 percent of preschool children who have working mothers. Many Americans believe that when children are reared by people other than their parents, their development is less than optimal (Kagan, Kearsley, & Zelazo, 1980). In the past decade, this issue has been the subject of intensive research.

Because of numerous variables, it isn't easy to determine the effects of child care. The variables include, among other things, the child's age at entry into a child-care program, the child's family background, the security of the child's attachment to parents, and the stability of the child-care arrangement (Belsky, 1990). Infant care is stressful for parents; it is thus very important that such child-care environments be supportive not only for the infants but for their parents as well. If parents are overly anxious about child-care arrangements, this stress will affect their children (Harms, 1994). A child's home environment and socialization can, of course, moderate potential negative consequences of child care. For example, when there is parental harmony, parent–child relationships are enhanced, independent of child-care arrangements (Erel & Burman, 1995; Willoughby & Glidden, 1995).

Psychologists are especially interested in the relationship between child care and attachment, because they believe that a child's emotional security depends on a strong, loving bond with a mother or primary caretaker (Kagan, Kearsley, & Zelazo, 1980). Contrary to popular belief, studies of attachment behaviors find that nonparental care does not reduce a child's emotional attachment to the mother (Etaugh, 1980). Moreover, there is no firm evidence that temporary separations, such as those caused by child care for preschool children, create later psychological trauma (Bates et al., 1994).

Considerable evidence suggests that a stimulating, varied environment is necessary for optimal cognitive development and that high-quality child-care centers do provide a sufficiently stimulating environment. High-quality child care means an experienced, qualified, and well-paid staff, a low staff-to-child ratio, and a low staff turnover (Scarr, Eisenberg, & Deater-Deckard, 1994). In a study of middle-class children; Bates and his colleagues (1994) found no differences in intellectual functioning between children enrolled in high-quality child-care centers and children reared at home. In fact, high-quality child-care centers may increase children's positive social interactions with peers (Egeland & Hiester, 1995), may make children appear happier (Vandell, Henderson, & Wilson, 1988), and may help prevent the declines in cognitive functioning that sometimes occur in children from low-income families who are not exposed to varied environments (e.g., Burchinal, Lee, & Ramey, 1989). Further, in child-care centers there is often considerable sharing among children; this is an activity not normally done at home, and it can produce positive effects (Davis & Thornburg, 1994; Moorehouse, 1991). So first-class child-care centers can yield positive effects (Davis & Thornburg, 1994). When parents are involved, even a little, in the day-care situation, parental satisfaction and the child's behavior are even better (Cronan, Walen, & Cruz, 1994; Fagan, 1994a, 1994b).

However, some research has questioned the conventional wisdom on child care and asserts that there is a

take place in isolation. They are influenced by the nature of a child's early attachments, by the cultural world in which the child grows, by child-rearing practices, and by how children are taught and learn to think about the causes of events in the world. The construction of an identity—a self—occurs slowly and gradually and is affected by myriad variables. (As *Applications* discusses, child care arrangements may be one of those factors.)

Perhaps no one is more closely associated with the challenges of social development and self-understanding than the German-born psychoanalyst Erik H. Erikson (1902–1994), who studied with Freud in Austria. With sharp insight, a linguistic flair, and a logical, coherent approach to studying human behavior, Erikson developed a theory of *psychosocial* stages of development; each of his stages leads to the development of a unique self, and the stages help define how a person develops a role as a member of society. According to Erikson, a series of basic psychological conflicts determines the course of development. His theory is noted for its integration of a person's disposition and environment with historical forces in the shaping

basis for concern about the impact of child care on development (Bates et al., 1994). Some research suggests that infants who receive more than 20 hours of child care per week display more avoidance of their mothers when they are reunited than do infants who spend only a couple of hours in child care (Belsky & Rovine, 1988). Clarke-Stewart (1989) argues that studies indicate that children who spend extensive periods of time in child-care settings show increased disobedience, aggressiveness, bossiness, and brattiness. She suggests that this problem may be considered the "dark side" of children's social training: "In good or poor day-care programs, it seems children do not follow social rules or resolve social conflicts without resorting to aggression unless special efforts are made by their caregivers" (p. 271). There is no doubt that an understaffed center, lengthy periods spent in child care, peers who are difficult temperamentally, and parents who are not especially attentive to their child's needs may have deleterious effects. But more recent research (Caruso & Corsini, 1994) suggests that even when children enter day care at a young age, the impact of as much as 33 hours of child care a week is minimal.

Today, researchers generally assert that good quality child care "is neither a benefit nor a detriment to the development of children from stable low-risk families" (Scarr & Eisenberg, 1993, p. 638). The impact of child care on children grown to adulthood so far seems negligible (Morrison, Ispa, & Thornburg, 1994). Most psychologists are therefore maintaining an open mind regarding child care and its potential long-term effects. As Scarr, Phillips, and McCartney (1990) assert, it is necessary to consider the facts about child care—the evidence—not just the hopes and fears of parents and psychologists. This means looking at studies that show "no difference" as well as those that show better or worse performance or attachment later in life (Roggman et al., 1994). Further, and perhaps most important, young children's development must be studied within a context of multiple factors—home, parent harmony, school, playground relationships and activities, grandparents, nutrition. A child's development is usually not going to be determined by a single factor such as nonparental care (Bronfenbrenner, 1979). The research is far from complete and, to many, is still controversial and inconclusive (Roggman et al., 1994).

▲ *High-quality child-care centers provide young children with opportunities for positive growth by offering a stimulating environment, special group activities, and chances to share with others.*

of the self. Erikson's theory describes a continuum of stages (including dilemmas and crises) through which all individuals must pass. Each stage can have either a positive or a negative outcome. New dilemmas emerge as a person grows older and faces new responsibilities, tasks, and social relationships. A person may experience a dilemma as an opportunity and face it positively or may view the dilemma as a catastrophe and fail to cope with it effectively.

Table 10.5, on page 374, lists the first four psychosocial stages in Erikson's theory, with their age ranges and the important events associated with them. (We will look at Erikson's later stages, covering adolescence and adulthood, in Chapter 11.) Stages 1 through 4 of Erikson's theory cover birth through age 12. We now take a closer look at each of these stages.

Stage 1 (birth to 12–18 months) involves the development of *basic trust versus basic mistrust*. During their first months, according to Erikson, infants make distinctions about the world and decide whether it is a comfortable, loving place in which they can feel basic trust. At this stage, they develop beliefs about the essential truth-

TABLE 10.5 *Erikson's First Four Stages of Psychosocial Development*

Stage	Approximate Age	Important Event	Description
1. Basic trust versus basic mistrust	Birth to 12–18 months	Feeding	The infant must form a first loving, trusting relationship with the caregiver or develop a sense of mistrust.
2. Autonomy versus shame/doubt	18 months to 3 years	Toilet training	The child's energies are directed toward the development of physical skills, including walking and controlling the sphincter. The child learns control but may develop shame and doubt if not handled well.
3. Initiative versus guilt	3 to 6 years	Independence	The child continues to become more assertive and to take more initiative but may be too forceful, which can lead to guilt feelings.
4. Industry versus inferiority	6 to 12 years	School	The child must deal with demands to learn new skills or risk a sense of inferiority, failure, and incompetence.

fulness of people. If their needs are adequately met, they learn that the world is a predictable and safe place. Infants whose needs are not met learn to distrust the world.

During stage 2 (18 months to 3 years), the toddler must resolve the crisis of *autonomy versus shame and doubt*. Success in toilet training and other tasks involving control leads to a sense of autonomy and more mature behavior. Difficulties dealing with control during this stage result in fears and a sense of shame and doubt.

In Erikson's theory, stage 3 (3 to 6 years) is that of *initiative versus guilt*, when children develop the ability to use their own inventiveness, drive, and enthusiasm. During this stage they either gain a sense of independence and good feelings about themselves or develop a sense of guilt, lack of acceptance, and negative feelings about themselves. If children learn to dress themselves, clean their rooms, and develop friendships with other children, they can feel a sense of mastery; alternatively, they can be dependent or regretful.

During stage 4 (6 to 12 years), children must resolve the issue of *industry versus inferiority*. Children either develop feelings of competence and confidence in their abilities or experience inferiority, failure, and feelings of incompetence.

A key point of Erikson's theory is that children must go through each stage, resolving its crises as best they can. Many factors have a bearing on the successful navigation of these stages. Of course, children grow older whether or not they are ready for the next stage. A person may still have unresolved conflicts, opportunities, and dilemmas from previous stages. This can cause anxiety and discomfort and make resolution of advanced stages more difficult. Because adolescence is such a crucial stage for the formation of a firm identity, the environment surrounding an adolescent becomes especially important. We will turn to this topic in the context of the next chapter.

FOCUS

Review

- What is the research evidence as to why gender segregation occurs among boys and girls? p. 370
- Identify two key variables that affect the quality of child care. pp. 372–373

Think Critically

- What do you think happens in a modern American family when a child does not successfully master a stage of Erikson's development such as autonomy versus shame and doubt? How might the response be different in a Japanese family?
- Day care is becoming a reality for American households. What are the implications for workers and employers in terms of productivity? Should employers provide day care for their employees' children?

Summary and Review

Approaches to Child Development

What are the different views on and methods of studying development?

- The reductionistic view states that if psychologists can reduce an organism's behavior to its essential elements, they can explain the behavior; the organismic view asserts that people go through qualitatively different developmental stages that cannot be reduced to simple elements. In the contextual view, the social and cultural context and the events in an organism's life are seen as interrelated. p. 341
- In the cross-sectional method, researchers compare people of different ages to determine if they differ on some important dimension. In the longitudinal method, researchers study a group of people at different ages, usually over a long period of time, to determine whether changes have occurred. pp. 341–342

The First Ten Months

Describe the period from conception through birth.

- From about the 5th through the 49th day after conception, an unborn human being is called an *embryo*; from that point until birth, it is called a *fetus*. During the 1st month, the embryo begins to take shape. During the 2nd month, the embryo begins to resemble a human being. In the 3rd month, growth continues, features become more defined, and sex characteristics begin to appear. p. 343
- A *teratogen* is a substance that can produce developmental malformations in a fetus; common teratogens include alcohol and cocaine. In the first months of life, an embryo is especially sensitive to teratogens. p. 345
- *Labor* is the process in which the uterus contracts and the cervix opens so that the fetus can descend through the birth canal to the outside world. p. 345

How is a newborn equipped to deal with the world?

- When a child is born, it comes prepared with a set of primary reflexes; among them are the *Babinski reflex*, the *Moro reflex*, the *rooting reflex*, the *sucking reflex*, and the *grasping reflex*. Newborns also have surprisingly well-developed perceptual systems. pp. 347–350

KEY TERMS

Zygote, p. 342
Embryo, p. 342
Fetus, p. 343
Placenta, p. 343
Teratogen, p. 345
Labor, p. 345
Babinski reflex, p. 347
Moro reflex, p. 347
Rooting reflex, p. 347
Sucking reflex, p. 347
Grasping reflex, p. 347

Cognitive Development

What is the difference between assimilation and accommodation?

- Piaget's theory focuses on how people think, instead of on what they think. Piaget identified two processes that enable the individual to gain new knowledge: assimilation and accommodation. *Assimilation* is the process of absorbing, incorporating, and utilizing new information in a meaningful way. *Accommodation* is the process of modifying one's existing thought processes and framework of knowledge. p. 351

Describe Piaget's stages of cognitive development.

- Piaget believed that cognitive development occurs in four stages, each of which must be completed before the next stage begins. In the *sensorimotor stage*, covering roughly the first 2 years of life, the child begins to interact with the environment, and the rudiments of intelligence are established. pp. 353–354
- The *preoperational stage* lasts from about age 2 to age 7, when initial symbolic thought is developed. *Egocentrism,* the inability to perceive a situation or event except in relation to oneself, flourishes in this stage. At the end of the preoperational stage, children begin the process of *decentration*, gradually moving away from self-centeredness. p. 354
- The *concrete operational stage* lasts from approximately age 7 to age 12; the child develops the ability to understand constant factors in the environment, rules, and higher-order symbolism. pp. 354–355
- The *formal operational stage* begins at about age 12, when the individual can think hypothetically, consider all future possibilities, and use deductive logic. p. 355–356

How is Vygotsky's approach different from Piaget's?

- For Vygotsky, a child is part of an active social world in which communication with others and self-speech (private speech) help the child understand his or her world and that of other people. Vygotsky held that when children are presented tasks that are outside of their current abilities, they need the help of society to accomplish them. p. 358

KEY TERMS

Assimilation, p. 351
Accommodation, p. 351
Sensorimotor stage, p. 353
Preoperational stage, p. 354
Egocentrism, p. 354
Decentration, p. 354
Concrete operational stage, p. 354
Conservation, p. 354
Formal operational stage, p. 355

Moral Reasoning

How has morality been studied?

- *Morality* is a system of learned attitudes about social practices, institutions, and individual behavior that people use to evaluate situations and behavior as being right or wrong, good or bad. Piaget and Kohlberg studied moral reasoning, focusing on how people make moral judgments about hypothetical situations. Their theories differ in that Piaget thought of the stages of moral development as discrete, whereas Kohlberg viewed them as overlapping. Kohlberg proposed that children's interactions with parents and friends may influence their conceptions of morality. pp. 359–361

What was Gilligan's main criticism of Kohlberg's work?

- Whereas Kohlberg showed that young children base their decisions about right and wrong on the likelihood of avoiding punishment and obtaining rewards, Gilligan found that children were also concerned with caring, relationships, and connections with other people. Most important, Gilligan found important differences between boys and girls. As younger children, girls gravitate toward a morality of caring, while boys gravitate to a morality of justice. p. 362

KEY TERM

Morality, p. 359

Emotional Development

What evidence is there that attachment exists?

- *Attachment* is the strong emotional tie that a person feels toward a special other person in his or her life. Harlow found that infant monkeys clung to terry-cloth mother surrogates whether or not they provided milk. He concluded that a wire mother surrogate could not provide the comfort that a terry-cloth one could provide. p. 363
- *Bonding* is a special process of emotional attachment theorized to occur between parent and child in the minutes and hours immediately after birth; bonding is a controversial idea that is widely accepted but has little research support. p. 364
- Bowlby was one of the first to study the close attachment between mothers and their babies and to show that when removed from the mother, a baby develops characteristic responses of being secure, avoidant, resistant, or disoriented. Once established, early attachment is fairly permanent. Verbal exchanges between child and caregiver help establish ties, teach language, inform infants about the world, and socialize them. pp. 364–365

How permanent is temperament?

- *Temperament* refers to long-lasting individual differences in the intensity and especially in the quality of emotional reactions. Temperament is not fixed and unchangeable; still, many researchers contend that some specific initial temperamental characteristics may be long-lasting and may be biologically based. pp. 366–367

KEY TERMS

Attachment, p. 363
Bonding, p. 364
Temperament, p. 366

Social Development

How do children begin to develop a sense of self?

- By the end of their 2nd year, children have begun to understand that they are separate from their parents—they are developing a sense of self. Very young children do not understand the concept of sharing—particularly the idea that sharing with another child makes the other child more likely to share, too. p. 368

How do children learn gender roles?

- Gender stereotyping means having expectations for specific behavior patterns according to a person's gender. While parents do reinforce children selectively based on their gender, especially at young ages, gender differences in behavior are small and are apparent only in certain situations, such as on the playground and in groups. pp. 369–371

Describe Erikson's stage theory of psychosocial development.

- Erikson describes psychosocial development throughout life as a continuum of stages during which people resolve various psychosocial issues. His theory suggests that at each stage a successful or unsuccessful resolution of a dilemma determines personality and social interactions. pp. 372–374

Learning CONNECTIONS

Some students benefit from extra help with the concept of cognitive development. You can learn more about it in:

- The CD-ROM accompanying this book, Topic 8

- This book's study guide, *Keeping Pace Plus*, or the computerized study guide, Chapter 10
- The audiotape accompanying this book, *SoundGuide for Psychology*, Learning Unit 8
- The study aids found on the World Wide Web site for this book, at http://www.abacon.com/psych/lefton

Critical Thinking CONNECTIONS

Take a moment to think critically about how this chapter's topics are connected with the rest of psychology . . .

If you are interested in . . .	Ask yourself . . .	Then turn to . . .
The role of early childhood experiences in development 	In what ways do the brain structures of a newborn contribute to cognitive development through childhood?	Chapter 2, pp. 52–55
	Is it true that language development proceeds rapidly after it begins at about 18 months of age?	Chapter 7, pp. 256–258
Gender differences in development 	Are there in fact gender differences in cognitive development?	Chapter 7, pp. 234–235
	Do males and females exhibit aggressive behaviors differently?	Chapter 16, pp. 579–583
Social development in childhood 	How do children develop specific motives—for example, the desire to achieve or be successful?	Chapter 9, pp. 322–323
	What are the implications of Freud's view that the first 6 years of a child's life are crucial for later personality development?	Chapter 12, pp. 413–416
	Do a child's early interactions with parents, peers, religious institutions, and school shape his or her attitudes?	Chapter 16, pp. 557–558

11

Adolescence and Adulthood

During the past year, my daughter Jesse has matured physically into a woman, though I have to admit I sometimes still think of her as a child. She is eager to finish her high school years, but she occasionally worries about leaving friends and family to start college. She constantly asks herself what sort of career she should have. Although I know she finds her life exciting, she is looking forward to becoming an adult and leaving behind the uncertainty of adolescence.

At 75, Jesse's grandmother finds her life more rewarding now than it ever was before. Her youngest child left home to start his own family years ago, and since then she has devoted most of her spare time to painting. She and her husband have opened a gallery in which they sell her artwork. But she is struggling with the physical challenges of old age, including arthritis, which threatens to end her painting career.

Jesse and her grandmother are both facing new challenges. Every age—infancy, childhood, adolescence, adulthood, and late adulthood—brings its own joys and difficulties. Psychologists see human development as a process of natural, continuous growth that is influenced by a person's biological inheritance, life experiences, and frame of mind—and a certain amount of chance. For example, moving from one state to another changes people's lives; a divorce is unsettling; a death in the family can be devastating; winning the lottery can jolt a person from poverty to luxury and from anonymity to fame. So, in addition to normal, predictable maturational and developmental changes, a once-in-a-lifetime happening can permanently alter physical, social, and personality development.

This chapter discusses some of the developmental changes that occur during adolescence and adulthood and traces the psychological processes underlying these stages of development. You will see that a person's *chronological age* (actual age in years) is sometimes different from his or her *functional age* (the way the person actually performs in life). For example, some adolescents act "beyond their years," older and wiser than is expected of their age-matched peers. Among older adults—especially those over 65—some act in ways that seem more like expectations for people in their 40s and 50s (Neugarten, 1968).

Adolescence

Adulthood is the period in a person's life when the individual is relatively free of parental influence, especially financially, and accepts responsibility for himself or herself. In Western culture, the transition from childhood to adulthood brings dramatic physical, cognitive, social, and emotional changes. Generally, this transition occurs between the ages of 12 and 20, a period known as *adolescence*, which bridges childhood and adulthood but is like neither of those states. **Adolescence** is the period extending from the onset of puberty to early adulthood. **Puberty** is the period during which the reproductive system matures; it begins with an increase in production of sex hormones, occurring at and signaling the end of the childhood period. Although adolescents are in many ways like adults—they are nearly mature physically and mentally, and their moral development is fairly advanced—their emotional development may be far from complete.

Adolescence in Context

Adolescence is often referred to as a time of storm and stress—of raging hormones—and for some adolescents this is indeed the case. It is a popular stereotype that adolescents are in a state of conflict resulting in part from the lack of congruity in their physical, cognitive, social, and emotional development. And there is some truth to this image. Consider alcohol abuse. Most adolescents know that drinking is illegal, harmful, and potentially deadly when combined with driving. Yet most are not mature enough to stand up to peer pressure by making a conscious decision not to drink.

Storm and stress is not the whole of adolescence, though. Many adolescents go through this period of multiple changes without significant psychological difficulty. Although spurts of hormones are changing adolescents' reactions, nonbiological factors seem to be especially important in moderating the role of hormones in adolescents' moods (Buchanan, Eccles, & Becker, 1992; Eccles et al., 1993). Adolescence may be a challenging life period, just as adulthood is, but fewer than 30 percent of adolescents have serious difficulties (Eccles et al., 1993). Also, 57 percent of adolescents have basically positive, healthy emotional and social development during these years.

The current consensus among psychologists is that adolescence is not ordinarily a time of great psychological turmoil (Powers, Hauser, & Kilner, 1989) and that

Adolescence [add-oh-LESS-sense]: The period extending from the onset of puberty to early adulthood.

Puberty [PEW-burr-tee]: The period during which the reproductive system matures; it begins with an increase in sex hormone production and occurs at (and signals) the end of the childhood period.

adolescents have no more psychological disturbances than the rest of the population (Hauser & Bowlds, 1990). This does not mean that adolescence is conflict-free or that parent–child relationships do not change during this period (Larson & Ham, 1993); what it does mean is that adolescence does not *have* to be a stressful time (Galambos, 1992; Paikoff & Brooks-Gunn, 1991).

Although the physical changes experienced by adolescents may be universal, adolescence has not always been seen as a problem period in most societies. Some experts link the "invention" of the adolescent life stage with certain social and historical events. In the middle of the 19th century, waifs in large cities roamed the streets as pickpockets, prostitutes, and purse snatchers; and many used drugs, including opium. By 1860, the number of young people living by their wits on the streets of New York City had reached 30,000. The plight of these youths led to a reform movement that put many of them in school and helped stretch the age of dependence from 14 to 18.

▲ *The experiences of adolescents, like these South African boys, are not all alike, but many adolescents do experience common rituals of passage into adulthood.*

Nor are the feelings expressed by American adolescents universal. It may be common for a teenager in the United States to feel that "no one understands me," but it is difficult to imagine a teenage tribeswoman growing up in the jungles of New Guinea expressing the same sentiment; her focus during the teen years is not on self-expression but on learning specific skills. Thus, the problems of adolescence must be considered in a cultural context. Even when adolescents grow up in the same country, they experience life's joys and disappointments in different ways. Some teenagers come from disadvantaged economic groups, perhaps from a Chicago ghetto or a Native American reservation. Some grow up in luxury, perhaps in a wealthy suburb of Los Angeles. Others are exposed to racial prejudice, alcohol and other drug abuse, nonsupportive families, or other stressful situations that lead them to feel a lack of control over their own lives.

Unfortunately, most of the research on adolescence has been conducted on white, middle-class American teenagers. But researchers now understand that the life experiences of whites, Navajos, Hispanic Americans, African Americans, Asian Americans, and other groups are not all alike. Each year, more studies compare the experiences of different groups and sensitize both professionals and the public to cultural differences among groups as well as to the diversity that exists within cultural groups. The reality is that there is often more diversity within a given group than between groups. Researchers are recognizing the similarities between groups as well as the differences.

Physical Development in Adolescence

The words *adolescence* and *puberty* are often used interchangeably, but in fact they mean different things. As noted earlier, puberty is the period during which the reproductive system matures. The age when puberty begins varies widely; some girls begin to mature physically as early as age 8, some boys at 9 or 10 (Marshall & Tanner, 1969). The average age of puberty is 13, plus or minus a year or two (on average, girls enter puberty a year or two before boys). Just before the onset of puberty, boys and girls experience significant growth spurts, gaining as much as 5 inches in a single year.

By the end of the first or second year of the growth spurt, changes have occurred in body proportions, fat distribution, bones and muscles, and physical strength and agility. In addition, the hormonal system has begun to trigger the development of secondary sex characteristics. **Secondary sex characteristics** are the physical features of a person's gender identity that are not directly involved with reproduction but that help distinguish men from women. (Primary sex characteristics are those associated principally with the genitalia and gonads and are present at birth.) Boys experience an increase in body mass and a deepening of the voice, as well as the growth of pubic, underarm, and facial hair. Girls experience an increase in the size of the breasts, a widening of the hips, and the growth of underarm and pubic hair. Puberty ends with the maturation of the reproductive organs, at which time boys produce sperm and girls produce ova and begin to menstruate. These physical changes generally take several years to complete.

Puberty has received a good deal of research attention. For example, researchers have found that as boys pass through puberty, they feel more positive about their bodies, whereas girls are more likely to have negative feelings. Puberty itself does not create psychological maladjustment; but becoming an adolescent means emerging as an adult, socially and sexually, and this takes some significant adjustment. New forces affect the self-image of adolescents; and although these forces create new stresses, most adolescents perceive their new status as desirable. Maturation has implications for social development, because young people often gravitate to and choose environments and activities that complement their genetic tendencies. Researchers often find that in junior high school, early-maturing boys enjoy several advantages, including increased confidence, superior athletic prowess, greater sexual appeal, and higher expectations from teachers and parents (Apter et al., 1981). Early-maturing girls, on the other hand, seem to be at a disadvantage, because their female peers often treat them as outsiders.

Cognitive Development in Adolescence

As children mature physically, they also develop cognitively, in rather complex ways. Piaget and Vygotsky showed (see Chapter 10) that children's cognitive development has both biological and social components and proceeds chronologically, in stages. But cognitive development does not stop in adolescence. Because adolescents are now in the formal operational stage, can think about the world abstractly, and can develop hypotheses, they learn new cognitive strategies. Teenagers gain an expanding vocabulary, seek out creative solutions, and can now fully utilize higher mental functions. Problem solving often becomes a focus for adolescent thought. For a brief time, many adolescents become egocentric, idealistic, and critical of others—which may make decisions about everyday issues difficult for them. And, as is considered in *Diversity,* adolescents' cultural background may add another dimension.

Cognitive differences between boys and girls and between male and female adolescents are minimal. As we saw in Chapter 8, gender differences in verbal and mathematical abilities are exceedingly small (Hyde, Fennema, & Lamon, 1990). The cognitive differences found by recent research studies exist only in certain special populations—for example, among the very brightest mathematics students, where boys continue to outscore girls. However, boys' scores are especially variable (Hedges & Nowell, 1995). This does not mean that no differences are apparent; on certain tests (such as the SAT) males as a group outperform females in mathematics (Gustin & Corazza, 1994; Wainer & Steinberg, 1992). What it does mean is that when certain socioeconomic and cultural variables are discounted, differences are small and unimportant and refer only to overall group differences, not individual accomplishments.

Researchers are still trying to determine whether basic differences in intelligence exist between males and females and, if so, under what conditions. Biologically based mechanisms may account for some gender-based cognitive differences, but learning is far more potent in establishing and maintaining gender role stereotypes and gender-specific attitudes (see Chapter 5, p. 181).

Secondary sex characteristics: The physical features of a person's gender identity that are not directly involved with reproduction but that help distinguish men from women.

Diversity

Ethnic Differences in Achievement

Which group does best in school: Hispanic Americans, Asian Americans, or African Americans? There is a widely held belief that students of Asian American descent do better, thanks to inherited differences and to cultural values that stress achievement. Researchers have found that culture affects achievement in direct and indirect ways. Students in Asian nations spend more time in the classroom on academic subjects than do students in the United States; it is not surprising that their math scores are higher (Stigler & Baranes, 1988). Further, in Asian societies, families and teachers tend to treat all students as equal, emphasizing effort more than innate abilities—whereas in many Western cultures more attention is given to innate cognitive strengths.

One research team set out to determine how a person's ethnic background and worldview might affect academic achievement. Steinberg, Dornbusch, and Brown (1992) administered a 30-page questionnaire to more than 15,000 students at nine American high schools that varied geographically, ethnically, and socioeconomically. The questionnaire gathered information about the students' relationships, schooling, behavior problems, and potential maladjustment. The researchers focused on peer relationships, family relationships, and such family variables as ethnicity, socioeconomic status, immigration history, and patterns of language use.

Parental behavior was important. In the original study and in a follow-up study, the researchers found that adolescents having parents who are *authoritative*—not rigidly authoritarian but accepting, warm, democratic and firm—achieve more in school than do their peers (Steinberg et al., 1992). In addition, peer interactions also turn out to be important; strong peer support for academics can make up for a lack of positive parenting. Conversely, peer disdain of academics weakens a strong parental voice.

What about ethnic differences? Regardless of ethnic group, youngsters from authoritative homes fared better in social functioning than did their counterparts from permissive or neglectful homes. In school performance, there was a slight difference among ethnic groups: Authoritative parenting seemed to make more of a difference to white teenagers than to African American or Asian Americans teens. Why would authoritativeness benefit African Americans and Asian Americans less in academic performance than in social development? The difference in academic versus social development may have to do with worldviews (basic attitudes toward life) that are sharply different. The researchers found that whereas all of the students believed a good education would pay off, Asian Americans in particular had been taught to fear the consequences of a poor education. In contrast, African American students were more likely to be optimistic and believe that a positive life could still follow, even after a poor education. Not surprisingly, youngsters who are taught and believe that they can succeed without doing well in school will devote far less energy to academic pursuits than will students who are more fearful of negative consequences.

In a follow-up to their original study, Steinberg and his colleagues had students complete a battery of standardized tests to see if differences in achievement and adjustment were maintained over time. Results showed that the benefits of authoritative parenting were maintained and that "the deleterious effects of neglectful parenting continue to accumulate" (Steinberg et al., 1994, p. 754).

A child's worldview, taught by his or her parents and reinforced by peers, shapes future success. For example, when there is an absence of peer support for achievement, the positive influence of authoritative parenting is often undermined (Steinberg et al., 1993). Ethnic minorities may vary little in many ways; but when it comes to school, some distinctly different cultural views may alter motivation, performance, and later success in life and work. Steinberg, Dornbusch, and Brown (1992) have been careful in their conclusions; they realize that their study is of a small sample and that many different factors interact to affect performance. Still, they assert that their research provides a foundation for future research—an agenda for further questions.

Social Development in Adolescence

Adolescent social adjustment is profoundly affected by early childhood interactions. When children make poor adjustments early on, the likelihood of making good adolescent adjustments, social and otherwise, decreases. When Cairns and Cairns (1994) tracked 695 young people growing up over a 14-year period, they saw the youngsters' early patterns revealed forcefully as the years went by. These researchers argue that the trajectories of social development do not change much; troubled boys and girls stay troubled, and happy and well-adjusted children are more likely to stay well-adjusted.

Adolescents develop a self-image based on a set of beliefs about themselves; but other people also generate expectations and beliefs about adolescents, and these beliefs also have an impact (Cairns & Cairns, 1994). So an adolescent's personality and sense of self-esteem is affected by his or her childhood experiences, and by events such as the timing of puberty and how peers and parents react to that timing. Parents and teachers can help troubled children and both early- and late-maturing adolescents with feelings about body image. For example, research shows that involvement with athletics can be a buffer against the initial negative feelings that can sometimes arise during this period. For both girls and boys, increased time spent in sports is associated with increased satisfaction and higher self-ratings of strength and attractiveness. Physical activity is associated with higher levels of achievement, weight reduction, improved muscle tone, and stress reduction, all of which foster a positive self-image (Kirshnit, Richards, & Ham, 1988).

There are sharp individual differences in the development of adolescent self-esteem. One of the sources of these differences is gender. In spite of the rapidly changing role of women in American culture, American girls often develop low self-esteem by the time they reach high school, despite the fact that their early childhood ambitions and dreams may have been similar to those of boys. Television and the print media as well as school systems that still favor boys in many domains contribute to the disparity (Orenstein, 1994). Despite enormous gains, there are still many attitudes to change.

Two important sources of influence on self-esteem and personality are parents and peers. There is no question that adolescents are responsive to parental influence (Brown et al., 1993). Studies disagree about the relative influence of peers versus parents, but most indicate that adolescents' attitudes fall somewhere between those of their parents and those of their peers (Paikoff & Brooks-Gunn, 1991). The influence of peer groups is formidable. *Peer groups* are people who identify with and compare themselves to one another. They often consist of people of the same age, gender, and race, although adolescents may change their peer group memberships and may belong to more than one group. As adolescents spend more time away from parents and home, they experience increasing pressure to conform to their peer groups' values in relation to society, government, religion, music, and even fast-food restaurants; the desire for conformity is especially prevalent among same-sex peers (Bukowski et al., 1993). Peers sometimes praise, sometimes cajole, and constantly pressure one another to conform to behavioral standards, including standards for dress, social interaction—and forms of rebellion, such as shoplifting or drug taking (Farrell & Danish, 1993). Most important, peers influence the adolescent's developing self-concept.

Gender Development and Gender Differences

We saw in Chapter 10 that gender differences are differences between males and females in behavior or mental processes. Extensive research has revealed few important biologically determined behavioral differences between the genders. Although girls often reach developmental milestones earlier than boys, this difference between the genders usually disappears by late adolescence (L. Cohn, 1991). Experience and learning—the way a person is raised and taught—have a far more profound impact on behaviors than does biology.

Gender identity: A person's sense of being male or female.

Gender Identity. As noted earlier, a key feature of adolescence is that it is a period of transition and change. Adolescents must develop their own identity, a sense of themselves as independent, mature individuals. One important aspect of identity is **gender identity**—a person's sense of being male or female. Children develop gender identity by age 3. By age 4 or 5, children realize their gender identity is permanent; that is, they know that changing their hair, clothing, or behavior does not alter their gender.

Consider the experience that adolescents have when their bodies change in appearance very rapidly, sometimes in unpredictable ways. During the transition to adulthood, adolescents often try out various types of behaviors, including those relating to male–female relationships and dating. Some adolescents become extreme in their orientation toward maleness or femaleness. Boys, especially in groups, may become aggressive; girls may act submissively, be especially concerned with their looks, and focus on bonding with other girls. This exaggeration of traditional male or female behaviors is often short-lived but may be related to the increased feelings of self-esteem that boys feel during adolescence and the decreased self-esteem that girls experience (Block & Robins, 1993).

Many psychologists believe that once gender identity is firmly established, children and adolescents attempt to bring their behavior and thoughts within generally accepted gender-specific roles. **Gender schema theory** asserts that children and adolescents use gender as an organizing theme to classify and understand their perceptions about the world (S. L. Bem, 1985; Maccoby, 1988). (Recall from Chapter 6 that a schema is a conceptual framework that organizes information and makes sense of the world. See Figure 11.1 for a description of gender schema theory.) Young children decide on appropriate and inappropriate gender behaviors by processing a wide array of social information. They develop quick shorthand concepts of what boys and girls are like; then they try to behave consistently with those concepts. Thus, they show preferences for gender-related toys, activities, and vocations. In fact, children's and, later, adolescents' self-esteem and feelings of worth are often tied to their gender-based perceptions about themselves, many of which are determined by identification with the same-gender parent (Heilbrun, Wydra, & Friedberg, 1989). For example, young people may relate their self-worth to how much their behavior matches that of

FIGURE 11.1

Gender Schema Theory

According to gender schema theory, children and adolescents use gender as an organizing theme for classifying and understanding their perceptions about the world.

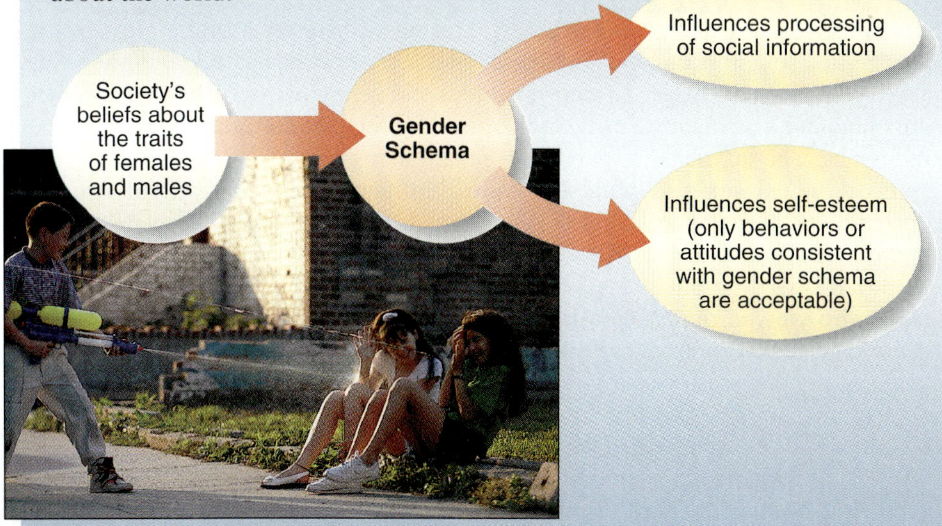

Gender schema theory: The theory that children and adolescents use gender as an organizing theme to classify and understand their perceptions about the world.

adult males or females or to how well they fulfill society's view of gender roles (see Hudak, 1993). There are some sharp differences between teenage boys and girls in self-esteem (Block & Robins, 1993) and in rates of depression, with girls being twice as likely to be depressed as boys (Nolen-Hoeksema & Girgus, 1994).

Gender Roles. **Gender roles** are the full range of behaviors generally associated with one's gender; these roles help people establish who they are. However, in the course of establishing a gender identity, people sometimes adopt a **gender role stereotype**—typical beliefs about gender-based behaviors that are strongly expected, regulated, and reinforced by society. Men, for example, may learn to hide their emotions; American society frowns on men who cry in public and reinforces men who appear strong and stoic when faced with sorrow or stress. In the workplace, gender role stereotypes still exist and heavily influence wages and promotions (Hoffman & Hurst, 1990; Pomerleau et al., 1990). According to the U.S. Bureau of the Census (1995b), on average, women in the United States earn about 72 cents for each dollar that a man earns—this discrepancy is referred to as the *wage gap*. The wage gap exists largely because women still predominate in many lower-paid jobs.

Androgyny. Developing a gender identity in adolescence has always been part of the transition to adulthood. Today, this task is more complicated, especially for women. In earlier decades of this century, most educated American women were expected to pursue marriage and homemaking, which were considered full-time careers. Today, women's plans often include a career outside the home, which may be interrupted for child rearing. In recent years, many women and men have developed new attitudes about gender roles—attitudes that encourage both traditionally masculine and traditionally feminine traits. They have adopted behaviors that are **androgynous**—shared by both genders. Thus, both men and women may fix cars, have careers, do housework, and help care for children. Several studies have found that people who rate high in androgynous characteristics tend to feel more fulfilled and more competent when dealing with social and personal issues (S. L. Bem, 1993). Gender-based characteristics have come under special scrutiny since so many children are reared in one-parent households; mothers and fathers try to ensure that their children have role models from whom to learn positive gender-related behaviors. This issue is discussed in *Applications*.

Sexual Behavior during Adolescence

In human beings, learned attitudes have a greater influence than biological factors in determining sexual behavior; and people first learn about such behavior at home. Children are affected by their parents' attitudes and behavior—whether, for instance, parents hug and kiss openly, seem embarrassed by their bodies, or talk freely about sexual issues. The influence of parents in sexual matters was shown in a study that examined how parents' discipline and control influence teenagers' sexual attitudes and behavior. Miller and colleagues (1986) surveyed more than 2,000 teenagers and their parents about parental discipline and teenage sexual behavior. The results showed that sexual permissiveness and intercourse were more frequent among adolescents who viewed their parents as not having rules or not being strict. Sexual behaviors, especially intercourse, were less frequent among teenagers who reported that their parents were strict. In addition, close relationships with parents and feelings of family support have been associated with later age at first intercourse (Brooks-Gunn & Furstenberg, 1989).

American adolescents view sexual intimacy as an important and normal part of growing up; premarital heterosexual activity has become increasingly common among adolescents, especially 13- to 17-year-olds. Three-fifths (60 percent) of white male teenagers have intercourse by age 18, and the same percentage of white female

Gender role: The full range of behaviors generally associated with one's gender, which help one establish who one is. Also known as *sex role*.

Gender role stereotype: Typical beliefs about gender-based behaviors that are expected, regulated, and reinforced by society.

Androgynous: Having both typically male and typically female characteristics.

APPLICATIONS

Life in One-Parent Families

Of the approximately 62 million family households in the United States, about 1 out of every 4 is a single-parent household; and most (85 percent) of these single parents are women. This family situation can be particularly problematic for some adolescents, although as the number of one-parent families has increased, some of the problems seem to have lessened.

A father's absence may be due to death, desertion, separation, or divorce. Well-known researcher Mavis Hetherington points out that almost half the children born since 1985 will experience the divorce of their parents (Hetherington, Stanley-Hagan, & Anderson, 1989). Most of these children will also experience the remarriage of one or both parents. The responses of children to these rapidly changing situations are diverse. Some children of divorced parents seem less able to cope than those who have lost a parent through death. They often have to deal with parental conflict, the divorce process itself, and continuing poor adjustment of parents (Forehand et al., 1990). The children may blame themselves; and as a result, their self-esteem, which is just beginning to strengthen, suffers. Children of divorce often refuse to accept its permanency (Wallerstein & Blakeslee, 1989). This is especially true of emerging adolescents, who tend to be more affected by divorce than are very young children or older adolescents (Amato, 1993; Amato & Keith, 1991).

The negative effects of an absent father are sometimes different for boys and girls. Boys seem to have a harder time, perhaps because they do not have as many opportunities to interact with adult men; they may end up learning from peers masculine behaviors, often highly stereotyped ones, such as that men do windows not dishes, carpentry not diapers, cookouts not soufflés (Wallerstein & Blakeslee, 1989). Girls can also have a hard time when their father is absent. They see boys having more freedom and status, while they must struggle for independence. Also, girls from one-parent homes report less positive attitudes toward the father and more sexual experimentation than do girls from two-parent homes. These gender differences are not always apparent, and sometimes they disappear by late adolescence. But Wallerstein and Blakeslee argue that although girls may not appear to be affected as much as boys, in later adolescence they show the negative effects.

One of the problems in researching children and divorce is that large representative samples are seldom used, so the negative outcomes of divorce may tend to be overemphasized (Barber & Eccles, 1992). Another problem is that preexisting behavior problems are rarely considered when the effects of divorce are evaluated (Cherlin et al., 1991). Some children and adolescents exhibit remarkable resiliency when faced with a divorce. In fact, Hetherington asserts that in the long run, some may actually be strengthened by having to cope with family transitions (Hetherington, Stanley-Hagan, & Anderson, 1989).

adolescents do so by just a year later, age 19. For African Americans, 60 percent of males have intercourse by age 16, and 60 percent of females do so by age 18. There are great individual differences in age at first intercourse and in the subsequent frequency of intercourse. It is not uncommon for first intercourse to occur at age 14 or 15 and then for the teenager not to have relations again for a year or two (Furstenberg, Brooks-Gunn, & Chase-Lansdale, 1989). Dreyer (1982) suggests four reasons for the early expression of sexual behavior. First, adolescents are reaching sexual maturity at younger ages than in previous decades. Second, knowledge and use of contraception are becoming more widespread, thus eliminating the fear of pregnancy. Third, adults' sexual attitudes and behaviors are changing. And finally, adolescents consider sexual behavior normal in an intimate relationship.

More relaxed attitudes about adolescent sexual behavior have brought about increased awareness of contraception and of the problems of teenage pregnancy. Nevertheless, each year in the United States, 1 in 10 teenage girls—more than 1 million girls—become pregnant. The consequences of childbearing for teenage mothers

FOCUS

Review

- What evidence exists to show that gender-based behaviors are strongly expected, regulated, and reinforced by society? pp. 385–386
- Identify several androgynous behaviors. p. 386

Think Critically

- What impact can a father's absence have on adolescents? How might things differ if the absent parent were the mother?

are great. A young woman's chances for education and employment become more limited, and many young women are forced to rely on public assistance. Most studies indicate that women who bear children early in their lives will not achieve economic equality with women who postpone parenthood until they are adults (Furstenberg, Brooks-Gunn, & Chase-Lansdale, 1989).

A variety of trends are affecting adolescents' sexual behavior. Today, almost 40 percent of 20-year-old women have had at least one pregnancy as a teenager, and 15 percent have had an abortion. In fact, current studies show that, despite the threat of AIDS, teenagers and college students still engage in regular sexual activity. Comprehensive school-based health-care programs that emphasize the complete picture of sexuality (attitudes, contraception, motivation, and behavior) reduce the risks of pregnancy in teenagers (Ford Foundation, 1989).

Adulthood

American adults in the 1990s often have vastly different life experiences than did adults of the 1950s, whose lives tended to follow more predictable and prescribed timetables. In the 1950s many people married when they were in their late teens or early 20s and had children soon after. Wives frequently stayed at home to raise the children, while husbands went to work to support the family. Today's adults are tending to marry later, and some not at all. Many people are postponing or rejecting parenting—for example, of the 60 million American women aged 15 to 44 in 1995, 25 million were childless. While some women choose to stay at home to raise children, many are concentrating on careers; some of these women's husbands raise the children. Many grown children are returning home after college, and divorce has broken up numerous families. The 1950s stereotype of a well-ordered, simple family structure has changed sharply, in a relatively short period of time.

The American adult life experience of the 1990s is also different from that of other cultures. Americans share some commonalities with people from other Western cultures, but very few with people in Third World countries. These ethnic differences have been studied little. In addition, until the 1970s, developmental psychologists in the United States concentrated largely on white middle-class children, especially those in infancy and early childhood.

Psychologists are now focusing on development across cultures and throughout the life span. They are recognizing that a person encounters new challenges in every stage of life. Researchers study adult development by looking at the factors that contribute to stability or change, to a sense of accomplishment or feelings of despair, and to physical well-being or diminished functioning. Researchers today are also examining the differences between men and women, with emphasis on the unique experiences of women in American culture. Minorities are being studied, and theories are recognizing and focusing on cultural diversity. Psychologists are also recognizing that a person's career, not just the person's family or life stage, is a defining characteristic of adulthood. Adults spend an enormous amount of time and energy on their careers, which have been examined relatively little by psychologists. Building Table 11.1 summarizes the major changes in functioning in young, early, and middle adulthood.

BUILDING TABLE 11.1

Major Changes in Important Domains of Adult Functioning

AGE	PHYSICAL CHANGE	COGNITIVE CHANGE	WORK ROLES	PERSONAL DEVELOPMENT	MAJOR TASKS
Young Adulthood, 18–25	Peak functioning in most physical skills; optimal time for childbearing	Cognitive skills high on most measures 	Choice of career, which may involve several job changes; low work satisfaction is common	Conformity; task of establishing intimacy	Separate from family; form partnership; begin family; find job; create individual life pattern
Early Adulthood, 25–40	Still good physical functioning in most areas; health habits during this time establish later risks	Peak period of cognitive skill on most measures	Rising work satisfaction; major emphasis on career or work success; most career progress steps made	Task of passing on skills, knowledge, love—generativity 	Rear family; establish personal work pattern and strive for success
Middle Adulthood, 40–65	Beginning signs of physical decline in some areas—strength, elasticity of tissues, height, cardiovascular function	Some signs of loss of cognitive skill on timed, unexercised skills	Plateau on career steps, but higher work satisfaction	Increase in self-confidence, openness; less use of immature defenses	Launch family; redefine life goals; redefine self outside of family and work roles; care for aging parents

Adult Stage Theories

Some people—perhaps the more poetic—think of life as a journey along a road from birth to death. The concept of a journey recalls Erik Erikson's stage theory, in which people move through a series of stages, resolving a different dilemma in each stage.

Erik Erikson—Revisited. An important aspect of Erikson's stage theory is that people progress in a specific direction from the beginning of life to the end—at each stage attempting to solve dilemmas. Stages 1–4 focused on childhood. Let's now consider those stages that begin with adolescence.

Erikson's stage 5, *identity versus role confusion*, marks the end of childhood and the beginning of adolescence. According to Erikson, the growth and turmoil of adolescence creates an "identity crisis." The major task for adolescents is to resolve that crisis successfully by forming an *identity*: a sense of who they are, where they perceive themselves to be going, and what their place is in the world. The failure to form an identity leaves the adolescent confused about adult roles and unable to cope with the demands of adulthood, including the development of mature relationships with members of the opposite sex (Erikson, 1963, 1968). The special prob-

TABLE 11.1 *Eriksons's Last Four Stages of Psychosocial Development*

Stage	Approximate Age	Important Event	Description
5. Identity versus role confusion	Adolescence	Peer relationships	The teenager must achieve a sense of identity in occupation, gender roles, politics, and religion.
6. Intimacy versus isolation	Young adulthood	Love relationships	The young adult must develop intimate relationships or suffer feelings of isolation.
7. Generativity versus stagnation	Middle adulthood	Parenting and work	Each adult must find some way to satisfy and support the next generation.
8. Ego integrity versus despair	Late adulthood	Reflection on and acceptance of one's life	The culmination is a sense of acceptance of oneself as one is and a sense of fulfillment.

lems of adolescence—which sometimes include rebellion, suicidal feelings, and drug problems—must also be dealt with at this stage.

Stage 6 (young adulthood) involves *intimacy versus isolation*. Young adults begin to select other people with whom they can form intimate, caring relationships. They learn to relate on a warm, social basis with members of the opposite sex. The alternative is to become isolated.

In stage 7 (middle adulthood), *generativity versus stagnation*, people become more aware of their mortality and develop a particular concern for future generations. They now hope to convey to the next generation, particularly their children, information, love, and warmth. As adults, they hope to influence their family and the world; otherwise they will stagnate, feeling that life is unexciting.

In stage 8 (late adulthood), *ego integrity versus despair*, people decide whether their existence is meaningful, happy, and cohesive or wasteful and unproductive. Many individuals never fully complete stage 8, and some do so with regrets and a feeling that time is too short. Those who do master and complete this stage feel fulfilled, with a sense that they understand, at least partly, what life is about.

Table 11.1 summarizes the last four stages of Erikson's theory.

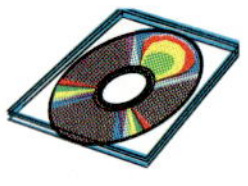

Fig. 8.13

Levinson's Life Structures. Another noted theorist, Daniel Levinson, has devised a different stage theory of adult development. He agrees that people go through stages and that they have similar experiences at certain points in their lives. He also agrees that studying those shared experiences allows psychologists to help people manage their lives. Unlike Erikson, however, Levinson does not see life as a journey toward some specific goal or objective, or as a blueprint that everyone must follow. Rather, he believes that a theory of development should lay out the stages (or eras) during which individuals work out various developmental tasks. In his words (Levinson, 1980, p. 289): "We change in different ways, according to different timetables. Yet, I believe that everyone lives through the same developmental periods in adulthood . . . though people go through them in their own ways."

Levinson (1978) suggests that, as people grow older, they adapt to the demands and tasks of life. He describes four basic eras in the adult life cycle, each with distinctive qualities and different life problems, tasks, and situations. Each era also brings with it different *life structures*—unique patterns of behavior and ways of interacting with the world, the "themes" of one's life at a given time, as reflected in two or three major areas of chosen commitment. However, because no two people have the same life situation, no two people adapt in exactly the same way. Each person develops a life structure to deal with each era. A young man in his early 30s, for example, may become involved in religious work and learn how groups function to achieve common goals; those skills may be less necessary during his 40s when he concentrates more on his sales career, or during his 60s when he focuses on retirement.

In each era, people develop stable life structures that get them through the era successfully. They then enter a new era, in which they encounter new life conditions, challenges, and dilemmas. Because the old life structures no longer work, the person must go through a period of transition, during which he or she adjusts to the new situation. Sometimes, the transition is difficult, characterized by anxiety and even depression. Thus, according to this theory, a person's life can be thought of as alternating between stable periods and transitional periods. The four eras outlined by Levinson are adolescence, early adulthood, middle adulthood, and late adulthood.

During *adolescence* (ages 11–17), young people enter the adult world but are still immature and vulnerable. During *early adulthood* (18–45), they make their first major life choices regarding family, occupation, and style of living. Throughout this period, adults move toward greater independence and senior positions in the community. They raise their children, strive to advance their careers, and launch their offspring into the adult world. Early adulthood is an era of striving for, gaining, and accepting responsibility. By the end of this era, at about age 45, most people are no longer caring for young children but may increasingly be involved in assisting aging parents.

The much discussed midlife crisis occurs at the end of early adulthood. During this era, people often realize that their lives are half over—that if they are to change their lives, they must do so now. Of those who are dissatisfied with the life they have made, some resign themselves to their original course; others decide to change, grow, and strive to achieve new goals. (This era is equivalent to Erikson's stage of generativity versus stagnation.)

Middle adulthood spans the years from 46 to 65. Adults who have gone through a midlife crisis now live with the decisions they made during early adulthood. Career and family are usually well established. People experience either a sense of satisfaction, self-worth, and accomplishment or a sense that much of their life has been wasted. It is often during this period that people reach their peak in creativity and achievement (Simonton, 1988). In the middle of this era, some people go through a crisis similar to that of early adulthood. Sometimes it is a continuation of the earlier crisis; at other times it is a new one.

The years after age 50 are ones of mellowing. People approaching their 60s begin to prepare for late adulthood, making whatever major career and family decisions are necessary before retirement. People in their early 60s generally learn to assess their lives not in terms of money or of day-to-day successes but according to whether life has been meaningful, happy, and cohesive. At this time, people stop blaming others for their problems. They are less concerned about disputes with other people. They try to optimize their life, because they know that at least two-thirds of it has passed and they wish to make the most of their remaining years. Depending on how well people come to accept themselves at this stage, the next decade may be one of great fulfillment or great despair.

Levinson's fourth and final era, *late adulthood*, covers the years from age 65 on. During retirement, many people relax and enjoy the fruits of their labors. Children, grandchildren, and even great-grandchildren can become the focus of an older person's life.

▲ *A midlife transition need not necessarily mean "midlife crisis." In fact, those who take up a new activity or interest in midlife may transform their lives for the better.*

Are Crises Unavoidable? Clearly, people go through transitions. At certain junctures, new decisions must be made and people must reassess who they are, where they are going, and how they want to get there. But does everyone go through a midlife crisis? A distinction should be drawn between a transition and a crisis. A *transition* suggests that a person has reached a time in life when old ways of coping are giving way to new ones, old tasks have been accomplished, and new methods of living are forthcoming. A person in transition must face new dilemmas, challenges, and responsibilities, which often require reassessment, reappraisal, and the development of new skills. A *crisis*, in contrast, occurs when old ways of coping become ineffective and a person is helpless—not knowing what to do and needing new, radically different coping strategies. Crises are often perceived as painful turning points and catastrophes in people's lives.

Not everyone experiences the infamous midlife crisis, but most people pass through a midlife transition; and some pass through two, three, or even more transitions. At around age 30, a transition may occur; during this transition, careers and relationships begun in a person's 20s are reevaluated and sometimes rejected. In the transitions of early and middle adulthood—including the midlife "crisis" at about age 40—people reorient their career and family choices. Sometimes parents experience another transition, called the *empty nest syndrome*, when their children leave home—although the empty nest is less likely to be a problem for people who are engaged in paid employment outside the home (Adelmann et al., 1989). Transitions also occur at retirement, not only for the retiree but for the spouse.

People who experience midlife transitions normally show no evidence of increased maladjustment or increased rates of suicide or alcoholism. In fact, suicide rates are at their lowest during midlife transitions. For some people, however, midlife changes can be difficult. These midlife changes must be examined for each individual, rather than across all individuals. Like adolescents, some adults grapple with the transitions in their lives, while others sail through them, not perceiving them as difficult or painful. Their attitudes depend on their unique personalities and ways of coping with the world. The term *midlife crisis* may be a misnomer. As Levinson (1980) suggests, it should more properly be called a midlife transition—a transition that may be more difficult for some individuals than others.

Gender Differences in Adult Stages. Levinson developed his theory by studying 40 men in detail over several years. His subjects were interviewed weekly for several months and again after 2 years. Spouses were interviewed, and extensive biographical data were collected. Levinson's theory has achieved wide acclaim, but it has also been challenged. A major shortcoming is that the theory was based on information gathered from a small sample of middle-class men. It did not consider gender differences, although researchers are working on a study of women based on data Levinson collected.

Women follow life stages similar to those for men—but they do it differently. As children, women are taught different values, goals, and approaches toward life, which are often reflected later in their choice of vocations, hobbies, and intellectual pursuits. Women have traditionally sought different career opportunities, although this is changing. In the field of law, for example, women now comprise nearly half of all law school students. However, female attorneys often choose careers that do not follow the traditional associate–partnership ladder chosen by males. In a follow-up book, *The Seasons of a Woman's Life* (1996), Levinson points out the complexities of women's lives. According to Levinson, women must deal with contradictory roles and responsibilities, which make their lives more complex and difficult to understand than men's. Career women and homemakers go through the same sequence of stages, but these scenarios differ in their details.

The developmental course of women, and especially of women's transitions, is similar to that of men; but some women tend to experience transitions and life events at later ages and in more irregular sequences (Smart & Peterson, 1994). In addition, women experience events such as midlife transitions differently than men; whereas some men approach a midlife crisis at age 40 as a last chance to hold on to their youth, many women see it as a time to reassess, refocus, and revitalize their creative energies (Apter, 1995; Levinson, 1996). At 50, many women become suddenly aware of their aging due to physical changes in their body—especially declining fertility—and this creates still a different type of "crisis" (Jarrett & Lethbridge, 1994; Pearlmann, 1993).

In a major study of women's transitions, Mercer, Nichols, and Doyle (1989) identified a developmental progression for women. They considered especially the role of motherhood and how it influences the life courses of women. In the *launch into adulthood era* (age 16 through 25), women break away from families to go to school, marry, and work. In the *leveling era* (age 26 through 30), many women readjust their life course; this is often a time for marriage, separation, or divorce. In the *liberation era* (age 36 through 40), women focus their aspirations, grow personally, and may initiate or change careers. The years from 40 through 60 were not ones in which Mercer and colleagues found major transitions; they found greater flux and crises in earlier and later years. In the *regeneration/redirection era* (age 61 through 65), women, like men, adjust to their lifetime choices and prepare for retirement and a more leisurely lifestyle. These two latter stages (liberation and regeneration) are times of great empowerment for women, when growth, regrowth, and purpose are often redefined and reinforced, resulting in a sense of true contentment. In the last stage of life, the *creativity/destructiveness era* (age 65 on), women are challenged to adapt to health changes and the loss of spouses and friends; this time may also be characterized by a surge of creativity or, sometimes, depression.

Today, many universities, recognizing that there are special issues relating to women, have departments of women's studies. Women still face discrimination in the workplace, and society continues to be ambivalent in its expectations for women. Women still have the primary burden of family responsibilities, especially child care; in the aftermath of a divorce, the woman usually gets physical custody of the children. Women often must juggle multiple roles, which place enormous burdens on them (K. J. Williams et al., 1991). The assumption of solo child-care responsibility after divorce has sharp economic consequences that alter the lifestyle, mental health, and course of life stages for women (McBride, 1990). Further, the issues in women's transitions are often different from those in men's; women tend to focus more on intimacy and relationships than do men (Caffarella & Olson, 1993). These are obvious differences in the life stages of men and women, whether upper-, middle-, or lower-class. Such differences are more dramatic in light of the fact that even greater differences exist *within* groups of demographically similar men or women. Even popular accounts of lifespan development such as Gail Sheehy's *New Passages* (1995) recognize the enormous individual differences that exist in people's ability to alter, customize, and create their life courses.

▲ *The Mercer study found that women between the ages of 36 and 65 often experience great empowerment in their careers, through reinforcement of growth, regrowth, and a sense of purpose. This has certainly proved true for Dr. Barbara Sanford, Director of the Jackson Lab, shown here consulting with a senior scientist.*

Physical Development in Adulthood

Although physical development in adulthood is slower, less dramatic, and sometimes less visible than in childhood and adolescence, it does occur.

Fitness Changes. Fitness involves both a psychological and a physical sense of well-being. Physically, human beings are at their peak of agility, speed, and strength between ages 18 and 30. From 30 to 40, there is some loss of agility and speed. And between 40 and 60, much greater losses occur. In general, strength, muscle tone, and overall fitness deteriorate from age 30 on. People become more susceptible to disease. Respiratory, circulatory, and blood pressure problems are more apparent; lung capacity and physical strength are significantly reduced. Decrease in bone mass and strength occur, especially in women; the resulting condition is called osteoporosis. Immune system responsitivity and the ability to fight disease diminish significantly among older adults.

Sensory Changes. In early adulthood, most sensory abilities remain fairly stable. As the years pass, however, adults must contend with inevitable sensory losses. Vision, hearing, taste, and smell require a higher level of stimulation to respond the way younger people's senses do. Older people, for example, usually are unable to make fine visual discriminations without the aid of glasses, have limited capacity for dark adaptation, and often have some degree of hearing loss, especially in the high-frequency ranges. Reaction time slows; visual acuity decreases; the risks of glaucoma, cataracts, and retinal detachment increase. By age 65, many people can no longer hear very high-frequency sounds, and some are unable to hear ordinary speech—the hearing loss is greater for men than for women.

Sexual Changes. In adults of both sexes, advancing years bring changes in sexual behavior and desire as well as physical changes related to sexuality. For example, in the child-rearing years, women's and men's sexual desires are sometimes moderated by the stresses of raising a family and juggling a work schedule. Women often experience an increase in sexual desire in their 30s and 40s, but at that age men achieve erections less rapidly. For women, midlife changes in hormones lead to the cessation of ovulation and menstruation at about 50 years, a process known as *menopause*. Menopause is not generally seen as a crisis but as a transition point at which women no longer have to deal with pregnancy issues; for some, however, it is perceived as the beginning of old age and a lack of youthful femininity. At about the same age, men's testosterone levels decrease, their ejaculations are weaker and briefer, and their desire for sexual intercourse decreases from adolescent levels (Rowland et al., 1993).

Theories of Aging. The quest for eternal youth has inspired extravagant attempts to slow, stop, or reverse the physical process of aging. Alchemists in the Middle Ages tried in vain to concoct an elixir of life. Ponce de Leon organized an expedition to the New World in 1512 to find the fabled fountain of youth. And in the past century, quacks have attempted to revive youthful vigor with everything from strong laxative therapy (to clean the colon) to injections of cells from lamb fetuses. In recent years, scientists seem to have dramatically increased the life span of some laboratory animals by feeding them calorie-restricted diets. So far, however, the maximum life span attained by a human being is about 120 years.

Despite the centuries-long search for the secret of eternal youth, psychologists and physicians have been examining the behavioral and physiological changes that accompany aging only since the early 1970s. Three basic types of theories have been developed to explain aging. Although each emphasizes a different cause for aging, it is most likely that aging results from a combination of all three. These theories are based on heredity, external factors, and physiology.

Genes determine much of a person's physical makeup; thus, it is probable that *heredity*, to some extent, determines how long a person will live. Much supporting evidence exists for this component. For example, long-lived parents tend to have long-lived offspring. However, researchers still do not know *how* heredity exerts its influence over the aging process.

Kimmel (1980) suggests that *external, or lifestyle, factors* affect how long a person will live. For example, people who live on farms live longer than those in cities; normal-weight people live longer than overweight people; and people who do not smoke cigarettes, who are not constantly tense, who wear seatbelts, and who are not exposed to disease or radiation live longer than others. Because these data on external factors are often obtained from correlational studies, cause-and-effect statements cannot be based on them; it is reasonable to assume, however, that external factors such as disease, smoking, and obesity affect a person's life span.

Several theories use *physiological explanations* to account for aging. Because a person's physiological processes depend on both hereditary and environmental factors, these theories rely on both concepts. The *wear-and-tear theory* of aging claims that the human organism simply wears out from overuse, like a machine (Hayflick, 1994). Research into how the body uses its energy stores suggests that in a way human beings are victims of the very act of living—the more we live, the quicker we age (Levine & Stadtman, 1992). A related theory, the *homeostatic theory*, suggests that the body's ability to adjust to varying situations decreases with age. For example, as the ability to maintain a constant body temperature decreases, cellular and tissue damage occur and aging results. Similarly, when the body can no longer control the use of sugar through the output of insulin, signs of aging appear. On the other hand, aging may be the *cause* of deviations from homeostasis, rather than the result.

It is also important to distinguish between primary and secondary aging. *Primary aging* is the normal, inevitable change that occurs among human beings and is irreversible, progressive, and universal. Such aging happens despite good health; a consequence of such aging is that a person is more vulnerable to American society's fast-paced and sometimes stressful life. *Secondary aging* is aging that is due to extrinsic factors such as disease, environmental pollution, or smoking. Lack of good nutrition is a secondary aging factor that is a principal cause of poor health and aging among the lower-income elderly of the U.S. population.

▲ *Positive changes in lifestyle—using seatbelts, quitting smoking, or learning to relax by practicing tai chi—affect how long a person will live.*

Cognitive Changes in Adulthood

Perhaps the most distressing change that may occur with aging is a decline in cognitive ability. Many researchers who once believed that general intellectual functioning remains stable throughout life now acknowledge that certain cognitive abilities deteriorate with age, especially in mathematics and memory functions.

However, it is difficult to know exactly what and how much change occurs in intellectual functioning. A major problem is defining intellectual functioning itself. Older people are likely to do poorly on standardized intelligence tests, not because their intelligence is low but because the tests require the manipulation of objects during a timed interval—and older people have a slower reaction time or decreased manual dexterity (often because of arthritis). To overcome these disadvantages, researchers have devised new methodologies for studying intelligence in older people.

Although most research indicates that cognitive and intellectual abilities decrease with advancing age, many of the changes are of little importance for day-to-day functioning (Schaie, 1994). For example, overall vocabulary decreases only slightly. Moreover, some of the changes observed in laboratory tasks (for example, reaction-time tasks) are either small and reversible or can be forestalled through cognitive interventions. In addition, many older persons do not do well on intelligence tests because they are not as motivated as younger persons to do well. Yet there is no doubt that the brain encodes information differently in the young than in the old. Memory changes, for example, probably result from changes in cortical activation during encoding (Grady et al., 1995).

For more than 35 years, K. Warner Schaie has been following thousands of men and women and testing them at regular intervals in various cognitive tasks. He argues that there is extreme variability in both the types and causes of cognitive deficits. He suggests that changes in health and family situation may produce severe biological and psychological consequences that in turn affect intellectual function-

TABLE 11.2 *Summary of Age-Related Changes in Intellectual Skills*

Ages 20–40	Ages 40–65	Age 65 and older
Peak intellectual ability between about 20 and 35	Maintenance of skill on measures of verbal intelligence; some decline of skill on measures of performance intelligence; decline usually not functionally significant till age 60 or older	Some loss of verbal intelligence; most noticeable in adults with poorer health, lower levels of activity, and less education
Optimal performance on memory tasks	Little change in performance on memory tasks, except perhaps some slowing later in this period	Slowing of retrieval processes and other memory processes; less-skillful use of coding strategies for new memories
Peak performance on laboratory tests of problem solving	Peak performance on real-life problem-solving tasks and many verbal abilities	Decline in problem-solving performance on both laboratory and real-life tests

Source: Adapted from Bee (1987).

ing (Schaie, 1994). See Table 11.2 for a summary of age-related changes in intellectual skills through adulthood.

Whatever the causes, changes in intellectual functioning that occur with age and that influence behavior are seldom devastating. Many researchers suggest a "use it and you are less likely to lose it" approach. Up to the ages of 60 through 65, there is little decline in learning or memory; motivation, interest, and recent educational experience (or lack of it) are probably more important in a person's ability to master complex knowledge than is age. At later ages, evidence exists for some modest decreases in abilities, particularly in such functions as short-term (working) memory (Craik, 1994; Craik, Morris, & Gick, 1990). Researchers generally concede that some age-related decrements do occur (e.g., Salthouse, 1995); however, such effects are often less apparent in cognitively active individuals (Simamura et al., 1995). For example, despite evidence that old age takes a toll, there exist many remarkable examples of intellectual achievement by people 70 years old or older. Golda Meir, for example, became prime minister of Israel at age 70. Benjamin Franklin invented bifocal eyeglasses at 74 and helped to frame the Constitution of the United States at 81. Arthur Rubinstein, the Polish-born American concert pianist, gave one of his greatest recitals (at New York's Carnegie Hall) at age 81.

Personality Development in Adulthood

A basic tenet of most personality theories is that, regardless of day-to-day variations, an individual's personality remains stable over time. That is, despite the frequently observed deviations from people's normal patterns or stages of development, the way a person copes with life tends to remain fairly consistent throughout that individual's lifetime. But research shows that personality may be sensitive to the unique experiences of the individual, especially during the adult years. According to Haan, Millsap, and Hartka (1986), children's and adolescents' personalities tend to remain stable, while those of adults change over time. The researchers collected data from a longitudinal sample of participants, who were asked to describe themselves on variables such as self-confidence, assertiveness, dependability, and warmth. Important shifts occurred in many variables once the participants reached adulthood. Adults are likely to be more assertive and self-confident than when they were younger, for example. Further, major life events—for example, a child's tragic death, a highly stressful job situation, or a divorce—can alter a person's overall outlook on life.

The data from this study are not easy to generalize from, because the researchers did not take into account changing societal values and expectations. Nevertheless, the data suggest that the adult years are filled with great personal challenges and opportunities and therefore are years in which people need to be innovative, flexible, and adaptive. Positive changes during adulthood—the development of a sense of generativity, the fulfillment of yearnings for love and respect—usually depend on some degree of success at earlier life stages. Adults who continue to have an especially narrow outlook are less likely to experience personality growth in later life.

Women have undergone special scrutiny since the early 1970s. As we have seen, researchers now recognize that the male-dominated psychology profession of the 1950s generated a host of personality theories based on studies of men that failed to highlight women's unique personality and development issues adequately. Personality researchers now acknowledge that contemporary women face challenges in the work force and the home that were not conceived of three decades ago. These challenges have given rise to the "supermom" phenomenon of women trying to have it all—home, family, career, personal satisfaction—within the same span of years. Serious research into the psychological life of women is just beginning to emerge.

Aspects of personality development are discussed in further detail in Chapter 12.

FOCUS

Review

- In each of Erikson's eight stages, people face dilemmas. What are the overall consequences of a poor outcome at any one stage? pp. 389–390
- What evidence suggests that there is a distinction between a transition and a crisis in an adult's life? p. 392
- What is the evidence that intelligence test scores decrease among aging people because of noncognitive factors? p. 395

Think Critically

- What do you think are the implications of the finding that women follow a different developmental progression than do men?

Late Adulthood

As people grow older, they age experientially as well as physically; that is, they gather experiences and expand their worlds. Nevertheless, in Western society, growing older is not always easy, especially because of the negative stereotypes associated with the aging process. Today, however, people are healthier than ever before, are approaching later years with vigor, and look forward to second and sometimes third careers. In general, being over age 65 brings with it new developmental tasks—retirement, health issues, and maintenance of a long-term standard of living.

How older people view themselves depends in part on how society treats them. Many Asian and African cultures greatly respect the elderly for their wisdom and maturity; in such societies, gray hair is a mark of distinction, not an embarrassment. In contrast, the United States is a youth-oriented society in which people spend a fortune on everything from hair dyes to facelifts to make themselves look younger. However, because the average age of Americans is climbing, how the elderly are perceived by their fellow Americans and how they perceive themselves may be changing.

Approximately 12 percent of the U.S. population—or more than 33 million Americans—are 65 years of age or older. According to the U.S. Bureau of the Census (1995a), the proportion of elderly people is expected to increase to between 20 and 25 percent of the total population by the year 2030, and the number of Americans past 65 will exceed 60 million (see Figure 11.2 on page 398). At present, the average life expectancy at birth in the United States is about 75 years, and the oldest of

FIGURE 11.2

A Nation Growing Older

In the year 2030, the U.S. population will be distributed fairly evenly among 10-year age groups ranging from birth through age 69. However, the number of elderly people in the United States will have increased sharply with the aging of the baby boomers.

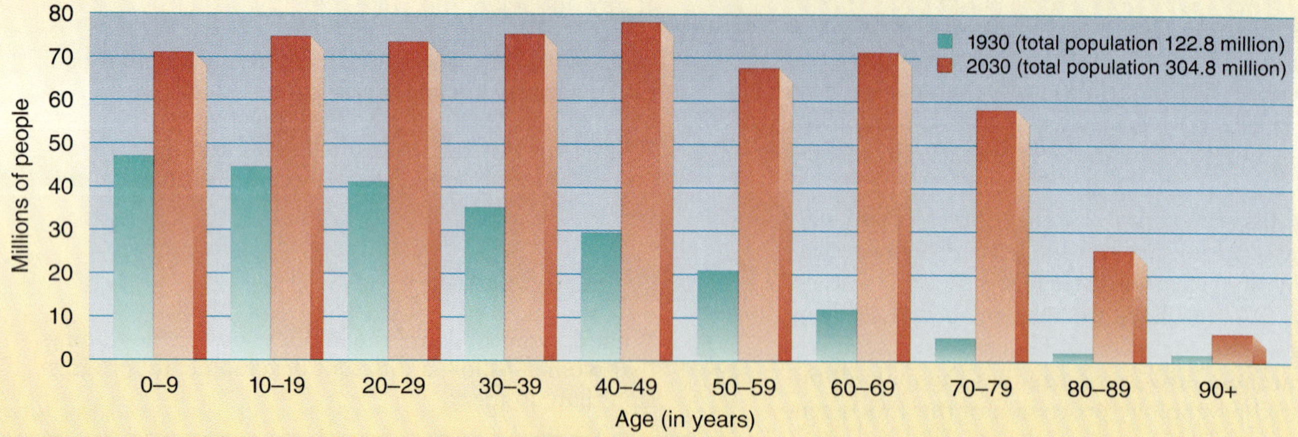

the old—those over 85—are the most rapidly growing elderly age group. Life expectancy is different for men and women, however. Women live about 4 years longer than men, on average.

For many people, the years after age 60 are filled with new activities and excitement. Both men and women enjoy doing things that they may not have been able to do before because of family commitments. Financially, two-thirds of American workers are covered by pension plans provided by their employers. Socially, most maintain close friendships and stay in touch with family members. Some, however, experience financial problems, and others experience loneliness and isolation because many of their friends and relatives have died or they have lost touch with their families. In the United States, there are now as many people over the age of 60 as there are under the age of 7; yet funding for programs to support the health and psychological well-being of older people is relatively limited.

Myths, Realities, and Stereotypes

There is a widely held myth that older people are less intelligent than younger people, less able to care for themselves, inflexible, and sickly. The reality is that many elderly people are as competent and capable as they were in their earlier adulthood. They work, play golf, run marathons, socialize, and stay politically aware and active. Older adults maintain a good sex life (Bretschneider & McCoy, 1988) and positive mental health. Of course, as was pointed out at the beginning of this chapter, some people will conduct life's activities in a frail, disorganized manner, even when young; others, who are in fact chronologically old, act youthful and vigorous. Building Table 11.2 summarizes important changes in adult functioning through late adulthood.

Ageism: Prejudice against the elderly and the discrimination that follows from it.

Ageism. Stereotypes about the elderly have given rise to **ageism**—prejudice against the elderly and the discrimination that follows from it. Ageism is prevalent in the job market, in which older people are not given the same opportunities as their younger coworkers, and in housing and health care. It is exceptionally preva-

BUILDING TABLE 11.2

Major Changes in Important Domains of Adult Functioning

AGE	PHYSICAL CHANGE	COGNITIVE CHANGE	WORK ROLES	PERSONAL DEVELOPMENT	MAJOR TASKS
Young Adulthood, 18–25	Peak functioning in most physical skills; optimum time for childbearing	Cognitive skills high on most measures	Choice of career, which may involve several job changes; low work satisfaction is common	Conformity; task of establishing intimacy	Separate from family; form partnership; begin family; find job; create individual life pattern
Early Adulthood, 25–40	Still good physical functioning in most areas; health habits during this time establish later risks	Peak period of cognitive skill on most measures	Rising work satisfaction; major emphasis on career or work success; most career progress steps made	Task of passing on skills, knowledge, love—generativity	Rear family; establish personal work pattern and strive for success
Middle Adulthood, 40–65	Beginning signs of physical decline in some areas—strength, elasticity of tissues, height, cardiovascular function	Some signs of loss of cognitive skill on timed, unexercised skills	Plateau on career steps, but higher work satisfaction	Increase in self-confidence, openness; less use of immature defenses	Launch family; redefine life goals; redefine self outside of family and work roles; care for aging parents
Late Adulthood, 65–75	Significant physical decline on most measures	Small declines for virtually all adults on some skills	Retirement 	Perhaps integrated level; perhaps more inferiority; or perhaps self-actualized; task of ego integrity	Cope with retirement; cope with declining health; redefine life goals and sense of self

lent in the media—on television and in newspapers, cartoons, and magazines—and in everyday language (Schaie, 1993). Schmidt and Boland (1986) examined everyday language to learn how people perceive older adults. They found interesting differences. For example, *elder statesman* implies that a person is experienced, wise, or perhaps conservative. However, *old statesman* might suggest that a person is past his prime, tired, or useless. The term *old people* may allude to positive elements in older adults—for example, being the perfect grandparent—or to negative qualities such as grouchiness or mental deficiencies. What does *old* mean?

Older people who are perceived to represent negative stereotypes are more likely to suffer discrimination than those who appear to represent more positive stereotypes. This means that an older person who appears healthy, bright, and alert is more likely to be treated with the same respect shown to younger people. By contrast, an older adult who appears less capable may not be given the same respect or treatment. In Chapter 16, we'll see that first impressions have a potent effect on people's behavior. This seems to be particularly true for older people: An older person's physical appearance may evoke ageism, whereas a younger person's appearance seems less likely to have such an immediate effect. In any case, ageism can be reduced if people recognize the diversity that exists among aging populations.

▲ *As the aging population of the United States continues to grow, many of the myths about aging are being dispelled. As this woman proves, growing old does not automatically relegate people to rocking chairs.*

Brain Disorders. You might assume that aging is inevitably accompanied by *senility*, a term once used to describe cognitive changes that occur in older people. Today, these cognitive deficits are known to be caused by brain disorders, sometimes termed *dementias,* that occur only in *some* older people. **Dementias** are long-standing impairments of mental functioning and global cognitive abilities in otherwise alert individuals, causing a loss of memory and related symptoms. The leading cause of degenerative dementia in the United States is Alzheimer's disease (see *The Research Process*). Only 0.4 percent of people aged 60 to 65 suffer from dementias. The percentage increases to 3.6 percent for people aged 75 to 79 and to 23.8 percent for those aged 85 to 93 (Selkoe, 1992).

More than 70 conditions cause dementias. Among them is AIDS; patients have a failing immune system, which can cause brain infections, which in turn can lead to dementia. Some conditions that cause dementia can be treated, and that treatment often halts (but does not reverse) the dementia. Memory loss can occur for recent events as well as for past events. Additional symptoms of dementias include loss of language skills, reduced capacity for abstract thinking, personality changes, and loss of a sense of time and place. Severe and disabling dementias affect about 1.5 million Americans. With the increasing number of elderly citizens, these statistics are on the rise.

Reversible dementias, which can be caused by malnutrition, alcoholism, or toxins (poisons), usually affect younger people. *Irreversible dementias* are of two types: multiple infarct dementia and Alzheimer's disease. *Multiple infarct dementia* is usually caused by two or more small strokes (ruptures of small blood vessels in the brain); it results in a slow degeneration of the brain.

Death: The End of the Life Span

Dementia: Long-standing impairment of mental functioning and global cognitive abilities in otherwise alert individuals, causing memory loss and related symptoms.

Alzheimer's disease [ALTZ-hy-merz]: A chronic and progressive disorder of the brain that is a major cause of degenerative dementia and may actually be a group of related disorders tied together loosely under one name.

People's overall health deteriorates as they age. For men, the probability of dying doubles in each decade after midlife. Blood pressure rises, cardiac output decreases, and the likelihood of stroke increases. One impact of this deterioration is that cardiovascular disease affects intellectual functioning by decreasing blood flow to the brain. Some individuals experience *terminal drop*—a rapid decline in intellectual functioning in the year before death. Some researchers attribute this change to cardiovascular disease, claiming that the decreased blood flow (and resulting decrease in oxygen) to the brain causes declining mental ability and, ultimately, failing health. However, although there is evidence for the terminal drop, no satisfactory method exists for predicting death on the basis of poor performance on intelligence or neuropsychological tests (Botwinick, 1984).

The leading causes of death in the United States are heart disease, cancer, strokes, and accidents; 7 out of 10 older Americans die from one of the first three—heart disease, cancer, or stroke. The number of Americans who succumb to heart

THE RESEARCH PROCESS

Alzheimer's Disease

The most common cause of degenerative dementia is **Alzheimer's disease,** a chronic and progressive disorder of the brain. It could well be the most widespread neurological disorder of all time. As the population grows older, the number of cases of Alzheimer's disease increases. Currently, there are about 1.5 to 2 million diagnosed Alzheimer's patients in the United States and nearly 20 million worldwide; in addition, there are a large number of undiagnosed cases. One recent estimate suggests that the numbers may be even greater than once thought: 1 in 10 people over 65 may have the disease, and almost half of those over 85 may have it (Evans et al., 1989). Because Alzheimer's is a degenerative disease, its progression cannot be stopped; it is irreversible and ultimately ends in death. To date, there is no fully effective method of prevention, treatment, or cure. What causes this disease? What is its psychological impact on the U.S. population? How does it affect families?

What Causes Alzheimer's Disease? A definitive diagnosis of Alzheimer's disease can be made only by an examination of brain tissue after death; tangled neurons is the typical finding. Brain scans usually confirm that the patient's neurons seem to be twisted, gnarled, and coated with *plaque* (fibrous tissue that impedes neural transmission). Levels of neurotransmitter substances—specifically actetycholine—are usually low.

Correlational research shows that Alzheimer's disease tends to run in families, which suggests a genetic basis or at least a predisposition to the disorder. Some researchers posit a depletion of enzymes; others suggest an accumulation of toxins; still others focus on neurotransmitters and metabolic patterns. Blood supply problems, immune system factors, head injuries, and viruses have also been proposed as contributors to the disease. Proteins that accumulate in the brain of Alzheimer's patients have been found elsewhere in the body, which makes the proteins easier to extract and study. Rabizadeh and others (1993) found a protein that seems to kill cells involved in memory unless another specific protein (called a *nerve growth factor,* or NGF) is bound to that protein. It is speculated that memory loss might be averted or stopped by treating cells with NGF or other drugs that mimic the action of NGF.

No one yet knows the causes of Alzheimer's disease or has developed an effective treatment. Researchers are beginning to think that there are many types of Alzheimer's disease, some of which may be hereditary (Bondareff et al., 1993) and some of which may have been generated by early life events, such as head injuries (Roberts, 1988). Research is showing that there may be a gene on chromosomes 1 and 14 that causes nearly all of the cases of early-onset familial Alzheimer's; such research may lead to an understanding of the biochemical causes of the disease (Levy-Lahad et al., 1995a, 1995b; Sherrington et al., 1995). The discovery of these genes may lead to diagnostic tests that can be offered to at-risk members of a family that harbors the genes.

Psychological Effects. The impact of Alzheimer's disease on the patient is enormous; the disease severely damages the quality of life. At the beginning patients are not necessarily stripped of their vigor or strength, but they slowly become confused and helpless. Initially, they may forget to do small things. Later, they may forget appointments, anniversaries, and the like. The forgetfulness is often overlooked at first. Jokes and other coping strategies cover up for memory losses and lapses. The memory losses are not always apparent; some days are better than others. Ultimately, however, the disorder grows worse. Alzheimer's patients start to have trouble finding their way home and remembering their own name and the names of their spouses and children. Sometimes fast retrieval is impaired more than general accumulated knowledge (Bäckman & Lipinska, 1993). Patients' personality also changes. They may become abrupt, abusive, and hostile to family members. Within months, or sometimes years, they lose their speech and language functions. Eventually, they lose all control of memory and even of basic bodily functions.

Implications for Families. In addition to studying the effects of Alzheimer's disease on patients, researchers are also studying the impact on patients' families. Caring for the patient imposes great physical, emotional, and financial hardships. The patient's loved ones "walk a tightrope between meeting the patient's needs and preserving their own well-being" (Heckler, 1985, p. 1241). Alzheimer's disease changes family life in irreversible ways; most patients are placed in nursing homes or hospitals after extensive and exhausting care at home. Brody, Lawton, and Liebowitz (1984, p. 1331) assert: "In the overwhelming majority of cases, nursing home placement occurs only after responsible family caregivers have endured prolonged, unrelenting caring (often for years) and no longer have the capacity to continue their caregiving efforts." The cost of nursing home care for Alzheimer's patients in the United States is currently more than $40 billion per year.

disease has decreased because of improved health, reduced smoking, and positive lifestyle changes among Americans. Strokes take their toll every year by cutting off the blood supply to the brain; rates of strokes are significantly lower among men and women who do not smoke, who manage their high blood pressure, and who regularly exercise. But cancer continues to increase; despite good cure rates, half of all cancers are found in men and women over the age of 65. A healthy lifestyle decreases the likelihood of disease (Hayflick, 1994), and research shows that older adults can achieve the fitness levels of younger adults (Danner & Edwards, 1992). Reducing risk factors can reduce needless early deaths, and this is best accomplished through health promotion and education (Hawranik, 1991; Becker, 1993).

Everyone recognizes that death is inevitable; but in the 20th century, few people actually witness death (Aiken, 1985). Before this century, most people died in bed at home, where other people were likely to be with them. Today, nearly 80 percent of Americans die in hospitals and nursing homes. About 8 million Americans experience the death of an immediate family member each year. **Thanatology,** the study of the psychological and medical aspects of death and dying, has become an interdisciplinary specialty. Researchers and theorists in several areas—including theology, law, history, psychology, sociology, and medicine—have come together to better understand death and dying. For psychologists, dealing with the process of dying is especially complicated because people do not like to talk or think about death. Nevertheless, considerable progress has been made toward understanding the psychology of dying.

Kübler-Ross's Stage Theory. Elisabeth Kübler-Ross has become famous for her studies of the way people respond psychologically to their impending death (see, e.g., Kübler-Ross, 1969, 1975). She believes that people in Western society fear death because it is unfamiliar, often hidden away in hospitals. She suggests that a way to reduce this fear is to involve members of a dying person's family more closely in what is, in fact, a very natural process. She contends that it is better for people to die at home than in an unfamiliar hospital room. In addition to imposing emotional stress on the terminally ill patient, impending death also causes stress for the patient's family. Kübler-Ross has drawn attention to the additional stress on family members created by interactions with doctors, especially in traditional impersonal hospital settings. Like many other physicians and psychologists, she believes that a more homelike setting can help patients and their families deal better with death. One answer to the problem of death in institutional settings is the hospice, discussed in *Applications*.

Kübler-Ross was one of the first researchers to use a stage theory to discuss people's fear of their own death and that of loved ones. People who learn they are terminally ill, in Kübler-Ross's view, typically go through five stages: *denial*, which serves as a buffer against the shocking news; *anger* directed against family, friends, or medical staff; *bargaining*, in which people try to gain more time by "making a deal" with God, themselves, or their doctors; *depression*, often caused by the pain of their illness and guilt over inconveniencing their family; and finally, *acceptance*, in which people stop fighting and accept death.

Criticisms of Kübler-Ross's Theory. Kübler-Ross's theory has been subject to considerable criticism. Not all researchers find the same sequence of events in the dying process (Stephenson, 1985). They argue that the sequence outlined by Kübler-Ross does not apply to all people and that the stages are not necessarily experienced in the order she suggests. However, Kübler-Ross contends that her theory was influenced to be an overall outline, not a strict set of stages or steps.

Kübler-Ross has also been criticized for her research techniques. Her interviews have not been very systematic; she offers few statistics, and some of her ideas rely more on intuition than on facts established through scientific methods. Specifically, her data-gathering techniques have been highly subjective. Schaie and Willis (1986)

Thanatology: The study of the psychological and medical aspects of death and dying.

APPLICATIONS

Hospice Care

Hospices were initially conceived of as special facilities established to provide efficient and humane care to terminally ill patients and their families. They were to address emotional, social, and spiritual needs in addition to physical ones, and to combine humane treatment with sensitivity to the financial costs of patient care (Butterfield-Picard & Magno, 1982; Smyser, 1982). Today, in the United States, hospices are not merely places—they are agencies. A hospice is thus an alternative source of care that helps provide a variety of resources to terminally ill patients and their families. Hospice care takes psychological principles used in therapy and puts them to work in the day-to-day care of the terminally ill. Hospice care focuses on the psychological needs of the patient, while acknowledging that death is inevitable and imminent.

The hospice approach is not appropriate for every dying person. It requires specific kinds of commitment from the patient and family members. Therefore, before providing care, hospices evaluate both the patient and the family. Hospices and their staff operate under a different set of guidelines from those used by hospitals and nursing homes that care for the terminally ill (Butterfield-Picard & Magno, 1982):

- Control of decisions concerning the patient's care rests with the patient and the family.
- Many aspects of traditional care, such as life-support procedures, are discontinued when the patient desires.
- Pain is kept to a minimum so that the patient can experience life as fully as possible until death.
- A team of professionals is available around the clock.
- Surroundings are homelike (often actually at home) rather than clinical.
- When possible, family members and the hospice team are the caregivers.
- Family members receive counseling before and after the patient dies.

There are currently hundreds of hospice care agencies in the United States. Yet relatively few terminally ill patients receive hospice care. For those who do, family members, friends, and practitioners have to deal with ethical and practical questions about care and costs, life-support systems, and medications. To help these concerned individuals, researchers and applied psychologists are exploring such issues as how to determine exactly when death occurs, how the dying should be treated, and how families and friends can cope better with the dying process. These researchers are examining questions such as how to help the families cope with grief over their loss and guilt about their feelings of relief.

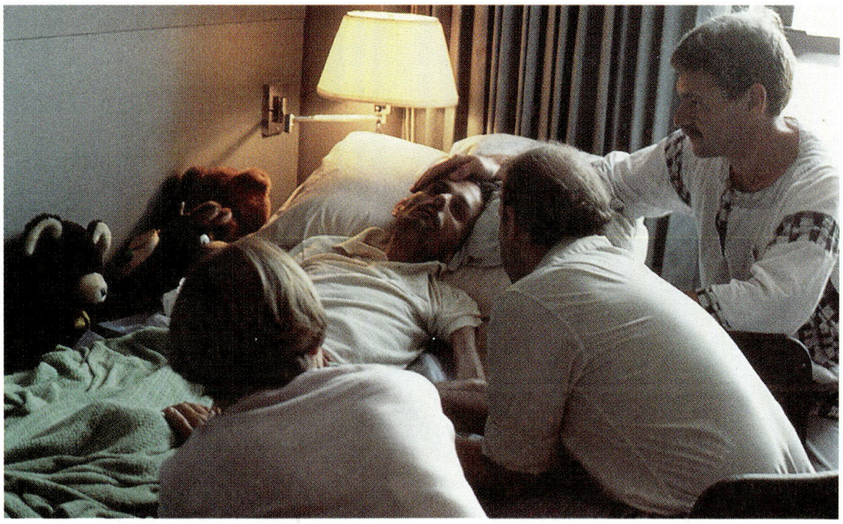

have suggested that the ideas put forth by Kübler-Ross should not be considered a theory but "an insightful discussion of some of the attitudes that are often displayed by people who are dying" (p. 483). Although Kübler-Ross's ideas about death and dying may not be valid in every case, many practitioners find them useful in guiding new medical staff through the difficult task of helping the dying, especially those who are facing premature death because of illnesses such as cancer.

Whether or not one accepts Kübler-Ross's stages as typical, it is clear that, as in all areas of life, different people approach death with

FOCUS

Think Critically

- How do you think that cognition might influence the health and well-being of older adults?
- What special emotional problems might need to be addressed when a terminally ill person enters a hospice program?

different attitudes and behaviors. In general, people fear the process of dying and the accompanying pain, disability, and dependency that often precedes death—although they are more fearful of death in middle age than at any other time in the life cycle. Religious people fear death less than others, older women fear it less than older men, and financially stable people have less negative attitudes toward death than do poor people. Moreover, most psychologists believe that the ways in which people have dealt with previous times of stress in their lives largely predict how they will deal with death.

Summary and Review

Adolescence

Distinguish between puberty and adolescence.

- *Puberty* is the period during which the reproductive system matures; it occurs at, and signals, the end of the childhood period. There is considerable variation among individuals as to its times of onset. *Adolescence* is the period extending from the onset of puberty to early adulthood. p. 380

What is the origin of the adolescent identity crisis?

- Changes in intellectual abilities, body proportions, and sexual urges (together with changing relationships with parents and peers) create the classic adolescent identity crisis of Western culture. However, the problems of adolescence must be considered in a cultural context, because most of the research on adolescence has been conducted with white, middle-class American teenagers—who are clearly not representative of all adolescents. pp. 380–381

- *Secondary sex characteristics* are the physical features of a person's gender identity that are not directly involved with reproduction but that help distinguish men from women. p. 382

Characterize cognitive and social development in adolescence, especially with respect to gender similarities and differences.

- Cognitive differences between male and female adolescents are minimal, but social differences are important and real. Adolescents develop a self-image based on a set of beliefs about themselves; but other people also generate expectations and beliefs about adolescents, and these beliefs affect them. The influence of peer groups, people who identify with and compare themselves to one another, is formidable. pp. 382–384

- *Gender identity* is a person's sense of being male or female. Parents are the first and most important forces shaping gender identity; they influence a child from birth. Peers and schools are important sources of information as well. *Gender schema theory* asserts that children and adolescents use gender as an organizing theme to classify and understand their perceptions about the world. pp. 384–385

- People sometimes adopt a *gender role stereotype*—a typical belief about gender-based behaviors that are strongly expected, regulated, and reinforced by society. But today, *androgyny*, the condition in which some typically male and some typically female characteristics are apparent in one individual, is more common than in the past. p. 386

How have adolescent sexual behavior and attitudes changed in recent years?

- Adolescents view sexual intimacy as a normal part of growing up, and premarital heterosexual activity has become more common among adolescents, especially 13- to 17-year-olds. More relaxed attitudes concerning adolescent sexual behavior have brought about increased awareness among adolescents about contraception and pregnancy. Yet teen pregnancy is on the rise; thus, increased awareness does not imply that the problem is being solved. pp. 386–388

KEY TERMS

Adolescence, p. 380
Puberty, p. 380
Secondary sex characteristics, p. 382
Gender identity, p. 384
Gender schema theory, p. 385
Gender role, p. 386
Gender role stereotype, p. 386
Androgynous, p. 386

Adulthood

Describe Erikson's last four stages of psychosocial development.

- Erikson's stage 5, identity versus role confusion, marks the end of childhood and the beginning of adolescence; adolescents must decide who they are and what they want to do in life. Stage 6 (young adulthood) involves intimacy versus isolation; young adults begin to select other people with whom they can form intimate, caring relationships. In stage 7 (middle adulthood), generativity versus stagnation, people become more aware of their mortality and develop a particular concern for future generations. Finally, in stage 8 (late adulthood), ego integrity versus despair, Erikson asserts that people decide whether their existence is meaningful, happy, and cohesive or wasteful and unproductive. pp. 389–390

Describe Levinson's theory of adult development.

- According to Levinson's stage theory of adulthood, all adults live through the same developmental periods, though people go through them in their own ways. His theory of adult development (which was generated from data on males) describes four basic eras, each with distinctive qualities and different life problems, tasks, and situations: adolescence, early adulthood, middle adulthood, and late adulthood. pp. 390–391

Differentiate life transitions and crises.

- Nearly everyone has transitions in life, but not everyone experiences them as crises. A transition suggests that a person has reached a time in life when old ways of coping are giving way to new ones. A crisis occurs when old ways of coping become ineffective and a person feels helpless, not knowing what to do. pp. 391–392

Do women's life stages parallel men's?

- Women do not necessarily follow the same life stages as men. Women tend to experience transitions and life events at later ages and in more irregular sequences than those reported by Levinson; consequently, Mercer, Nichols, and Doyle suggested a developmental progression for women that features five transitional eras: launch into adulthood, leveling, liberation, regeneration/redirection, and creativity/destructiveness. pp. 392–393

Describe the effects of aging.

- Physical development and aging continue throughout adulthood. In general, strength, muscle tone, and overall fitness deteriorate from age 30 on. There are also sensory changes, including increased reaction time after age 65. Sexual behavior, desire, and physical changes related to sexuality occur in adults of both sexes. pp. 393–394
- Primary aging is the normal, inevitable change that occurs in human beings and is irreversible, progressive, and universal. Secondary aging is aging that is due to extrinsic factors such as disease, environmental pollution, and smoking. p. 395
- Most research indicates that cognitive abilities decrease with advancing age, but many of the changes are of little importance for day-to-day functioning. p. 395
- Personality development is sensitive to the unique experiences of the individual, especially during the adult years. Major life events (deaths, divorce, etc.) can alter a person's overall outlook on life. pp. 396–397

Late Adulthood

Who are the aged, and how is life different in late adulthood?

- In general, being over age 65 classifies a person as being aged. Approximately 12 percent of the U.S. population—more than 33 million Americans—are 65 or older. p. 397
- *Ageism* is discrimination on the basis of age, often resulting in the denial of rights and services to the elderly. p. 399
- Brain disorders, sometimes called *dementias,* involve losses of cognitive or mental functioning. Reversible dementias, which may be caused by malnutrition, alcoholism, or toxins (poisons), usually affect younger people. Irreversible dementias are of two types, multiple infarct dementia and Alzheimer's disease. p. 400
- Currently, there are about 1.5 to 2 million diagnosed Alzheimer's patients in the United States. *Alzheimer's disease* is a degenerative disorder whose progression cannot be stopped; it is irreversible and ultimately ends in death. Individuals who suffer from Alzheimer's disease slowly lose their memory. Within months, or sometimes years, they lose their speech and language functions. Eventually, they lose all bodily and mental control. p. 401

What are the essential elements of Kübler-Ross's theory of dying?

- Kübler-Ross has described dying as a process involving five stages: denial, anger, bargaining, depression, and, finally, acceptance. Although controversial and not widely accepted by the scientific community, Kübler-Ross's ideas have generated much interest. p. 402

How can hospices aid the dying and their families?

- Hospice care is a special approach that helps provide efficient and humane care to terminally ill patients and their families. Hospice care is not appropriate for every dying person. It requires specific kinds of commitment from the patient and family members. p. 403

KEY TERMS

Ageism, p. 398
Dementia, p. 400
Alzheimer's disease, p. 401
Thanatology, p. 402

Learning CONNECTIONS

Some students benefit from extra help with stage theories of adult development. You can learn more about them in:

- The CD-ROM accompanying this book, Topic 8
- This book's study guide, *Keeping Pace Plus*, or the computerized study guide, Chapter 11
- The audiotape accompanying this book, *SoundGuide for Psychology*, Learning Unit 9
- The study aids found on the World Wide Web site for this book, at http://www.abacon.com/psych/lefton

Critical Thinking CONNECTIONS

Take a moment to think critically about how this chapter's topics are connected with the rest of psychology . . .

If you are interested in . . .	Ask yourself . . .	Then turn to . . .
Sexual behavior and the process of development 	What were the implications for personality theory when Freud assumed that a person's life energy is sexual in nature?	Chapter 12, pp. 411–412
	How do many psychological disorders exhibit themselves in the sexual domain of a person's life?	Chapter 14, pp. 491–492
	How are people attracted to those who share their attitudes and who like them?	Chapter 16, pp. 586–590
Midlife transitions and how people respond to stressful situations 	In what ways is a person's emotional life determined by how he or she appraises a situation?	Chapter 9, pp. 329–331
	How may people's health be affected by their reactions to life events, as well as to stressors in the environment?	Chapter 13, pp. 457–458
Stereotypes about certain types of people, including adolescents and the elderly 	In what ways does operant conditioning, used by parents to reinforce certain ideas in their children, lead to long-lasting ideas and evaluations?	Chapter 5, pp. 165–168
	How do stereotypes, which are usually based on wrong information from a limited or nonexistent sample of behavior, lead to prejudice?	Chapter 16, pp. 570–571

12

Personality and Its Assessment

From time to time, I ask my students to do some in-class writing. Often this is an exercise in which they must use critical thinking skills to evaluate a piece of research. But occasionally I ask them to speculate on other topics—for example, to describe their personality. Interestingly, most of my students write less than a paragraph about themselves. They tell me that they are outgoing and friendly, or perhaps that they are shy and quiet. Occasionally an eloquent student will compare herself or himself to an object like a car (sleek and fast), a plant (delicate and beautiful), or a computer (intelligent and logical). My students speak only infrequently of their emotional history or their aspirations for the future. Of course, this is just an in-class exercise. Perhaps they fear embarrassment. Certainly, they are not committed to telling me their deepest feelings about their past or their future.

Then there's usually someone who asks me to describe my own personality. I usually shrug off the question and tell them to do it for me. Even though we have spent more than 30 hours together in class, do my students have an accurate perception of what I am like at home, with my children, with my friends, at a party? My students will tell me about my sense of humor and my relationships with my wife and daughters—people whom I often use as examples. Yet they quickly realize that they have seen me in only limited circumstances, always doing much the same thing. Although we have spent many hours together—far more time than one spends on, say, a first or second date—it is hard to judge how I would act with my mother or how I felt about the Vietnam War. At this juncture, I usually point out the complexity of personality, of making judgments about what people are like, of the cultural vantage points everyone brings to assessments of personality. It is difficult to characterize people from a very small sample of the range of behaviors in which they engage. The reality is that no other phenomenon is as resistant to easy definition and assessment as the human character.

As my students do when speaking of themselves, most people describe the way they respond to the world by using catchwords. They say they are shy, sensitive, outgoing, concerned, or aggressive with other people or in certain situations. Psychologists, on the other hand, describe personality in a systematic and scientific way. For psychologists, **personality** is a set of relatively enduring behavioral characteristics (including thoughts) and internal predispositions that describe how a person reacts to the environment. Psychologists recognize that an individual's behavior is not consistent all the time or in every situation.

What gives people consistency in their behavioral characteristics? To answer this question, some personality theorists focus on day-to-day behaviors that characterize people; others focus on the inner conflicts that shape personality. Some see a human being as an individual who reacts to the environment. Others emphasize the internal, even genetic, influences that impel a person to action. Personality theorists must consider social psychological concepts such as attitudes, motivational concepts such as expectancies, and even biological theories such as those suggesting inherited predispositions toward such personality characteristics as shyness. The earliest personality theorists (for example, Freud) tended to think of personality as something stable within the individual. Later theorists began to recognize that personality depends on a host of environmental situations. Contemporary theorists, especially the behavioral and cognitive ones, often focus more on environmental determinants of personality than on internal predispositions.

Personality theories are a set of interrelated ideas and facts put forward to coherently explain and predict behavior and mental processes. Being able to predict and explain behavior enables psychologists to help people anticipate situations and express their feelings in manageable and reasonable ways. Personality theories focus on a few key questions:

- Does nature or nurture play a greater role in day-to-day behavior?
- Do unconscious processes direct behavior?
- Are human behavior patterns fixed?
- Does a person's behavior depend on the situation?
- What makes people consistent in their behavior?

No personality theory considers all these issues; nor does every theory explain all of personality. Thus, each theory we will consider is incomplete, but each is important because it addresses some key element. We will begin by examining psychoanalytic theory—an approach to personality that focuses on the unconscious and how thoughts and ideas contained therein direct day-to-day behavior. This approach is the well-known and widely disputed theory of Sigmund Freud.

Personality: A set of relatively enduring behavioral characteristics and internal predispositions that describe how a person reacts to the environment.

Psychoanalytic Theory

Sigmund Freud (1856–1939) was an Austrian physician whose influence on psychology became so great that some of his basic ideas and concepts are taken for granted. Such Freudian terms as *ego, oral fixation, death wish,* and *Freudian slip* and such Freudian concepts as *unconscious motivation* and *Oedipus complex* are part of everyday language. However, when Freud introduced his ideas, he was seen as strange, heretical, and simply off-base. Psychologists of the time thought that the proper subject matter of psychology was the study of the mind and how it works. Studying the unconscious and suggesting that children have sexual experiences were, to say the least, out of the mainstream.

▲ *Sigmund Freud*

Freud used hypnosis to treat people with physical and emotional problems. Most of his patients were from the middle and upper classes of Austrian society. Many were society matrons who, because they lived in a repressive society, had limited opportunities for the release of anxiety and tension. Freud noticed that many of them needed to discuss their problems and often felt better after having done so. From his studies of hypnosis and his work with these patients, he began to conceptualize a theory of behavior; many of his early conclusions focused on the role of sexual frustrations in producing physical symptoms. Over time, Freud developed an elaborate theory of personality and an accompanying approach to therapy. His approach to personality came to be called *psychoanalytic theory*, his method of therapy *psychoanalysis*.

Three Key Concepts

Many psychological theories have a key concept around which they grow. Freud's theory has three such concepts: psychic determinism, unconscious motivation, and conflict. **Psychic determinism** is a psychoanalytic assumption that all feelings, thoughts, actions, gestures, and speech have a purpose and are determined by some action or event that happened to an individual in the past. Adults, for example, do not have accidental slips of the tongue; nor do they frown or change mood by accident. Instead, past events affect all of today's actions. Moreover, most of a person's thoughts and behavior are determined by unconscious motivation. **Unconscious motivation** is a psychoanalytic assumption that behavior is determined by desires, goals, and internal states of which an individual is unaware, which are buried deep within the unconscious. By definition, people are unaware of the contents of the unconscious and even of its very existence.

Freud also theorized that people are constantly in *conflict.* They are energized and act the way they do because of two basic instinctual drives—*life*, which prominently features sex and sexual energy, and *death*, which features aggression. These instincts are buried deep within the unconscious and are not always socially acceptable. Freud wrote little about aggression until late in his life; he focused mainly on sexual instincts, which he termed the **libido**—the instinctual (and usually sexual) life force that, working on the pleasure principle and seeking immediate gratification, energizes the id. (The id will be discussed further in the next subsection.) In his later writings, Freud referred to the libido as "life energy." His critics assert that he was inordinately preoccupied with sexual matters.

When people exhibit socially unacceptable behaviors or have feelings they consider socially unacceptable, especially sexual feelings, they often experience self-punishment, guilt, and anxiety—conflict. Freud's theory thus describes a conflict between a person's instinctual (often unconscious) need for gratification and the demands of society for socialization. In other words, it paints a picture of human beings caught in a conflict between basic sexual and aggressive desires and society's demands. A Viennese gentleman of the Victorian era might have wished to strike an

Psychic determinism [SYE-kick]: Psychoanalytic assumption that everything a person feels, thinks, and does has a purpose and that all behaviors are caused by past events.

Unconscious motivation: Psychoanalytic assumption that behavior is determined by desires, goals, and internal states, buried deep within the unconscious, of which an individual is unaware.

Libido [lih-BEE-doe]: In Freud's theory, the instinctual (and usually sexual) life force that, working on the pleasure principle and seeking immediate gratification, energizes the id.

Conscious: Freud's first level of awareness, consisting of the thoughts, feelings, and actions of which people are aware.

Preconscious: Freud's second level of awareness, consisting of mental activities of which people can gain awareness by attending to them.

Unconscious: Freud's third level of awareness, consisting of mental activities beyond people's normal awareness.

Id: In Freud's theory, the source of instinctual energy, which works mainly on the pleasure principle.

Ego: In Freud's theory, the part of personality that seeks to satisfy the id and superego in accordance with reality.

offensive drunk, but social rules of that time did not allow such behavior. For Freud, a person's basic desire is to maximize instinctual gratification while minimizing punishment and guilt.

Structure of Consciousness and the Mind

In his theory, Freud considered the sources and consequences of conflict and how people deal with it. For Freud, a person's source of energy to deal with conflict is biologically determined and lies in the structure of consciousness.

Structure of Consciousness. According to Freud, consciousness consists of three levels of awareness. The first level, the **conscious**, consists of the thoughts, feelings, and actions of which people are aware. The second level, the **preconscious**, consists of mental activities of which people can become aware if they closely attend to them. The third level, the **unconscious**, consists of the mental activities beyond people's normal awareness. They become aware of these activities only through specific therapeutic techniques, such as dream analysis. Suppose a woman decides to become a psychotherapist for a *conscious* reason. She tells her family and friends that she wants to help people. Later, during an introspective moment, she realizes that her *preconscious* motivation for becoming a psychotherapist stems from a desire to resolve her own unhappiness. Finally, through psychoanalysis, she discovers that she hungers for love and intimacy, which her parents denied her. *Unconsciously*, she has been hoping that her future patients will satisfy that hunger by making her feel needed.

Id, Ego, and Superego. According to Freud's theory, the primary structural elements of the mind and personality are three mental forces (not physical structures of the brain) that reside, fully or partially, in the unconscious—the id, the ego, and the superego. Each force accounts for a different aspect of functioning (see Table 12.1).

The **id** is the source of a person's instinctual energy, which, according to Freud, is either sexual or aggressive. The id works through the *pleasure principle*; that is, it tries to maximize immediate gratification through the satisfaction of raw impulses. Deep within the unconscious, the demanding, irrational, and selfish id seeks pleasure. It does not care about morals, society, or other people.

While the id seeks to maximize pleasure and obtain immediate gratification, the **ego** (which grows out of the id) is the part of the personality that seeks to satisfy the individual's instinctual needs in accordance with reality; that is, it works by the *reality principle*. The ego acts as a manager, adjusting cognitive and perceptual processes to balance the person's functioning, to control the id, and to keep the person in touch with reality. For example, the id of a boy who wakes up shivering de-

TABLE 12.1 ***Comparison of Freud's Three Systems of Personality***

	Id	Ego	Superego
Nature	Represents biological aspect	Represents psychological aspect	Represents societal aspect
Level	Unconscious	Conscious and unconscious	Conscious and unconscious
Principle	Pleasure	Reality	Morality
Purpose	Seek pleasure and avoid pain	Adapt to reality; know true and false	Represent right and wrong
Aim	Immediate gratification	Safety and compromise	Perfection

FIGURE 12.1

Freud's View of Mental Forces

Freud viewed consciousness as having three levels: the conscious, the preconscious, and the unconscious. The *id* operates solely at an unconscious level. The *ego* is mainly a conscious and preconscious mental force. The *superego* operates mostly as a preconscious mental force.

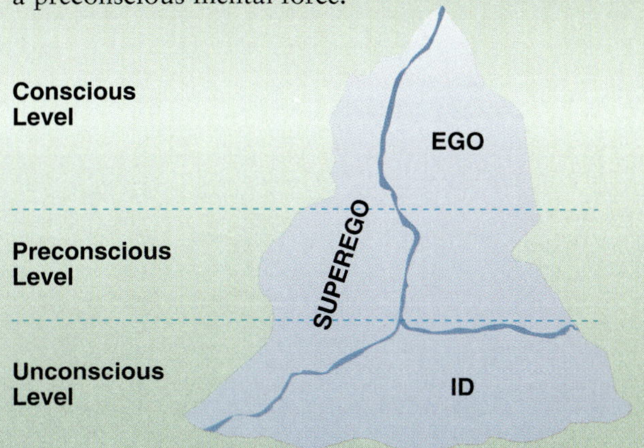

Mental Force	Level of Consciousness	Contents and Function
Ego	Mostly conscious	Executive mediating between id impulses and superego inhibitions; testing reality; rational
Superego	All levels, but mostly preconscious	Ideals and morals; striving for perfection; incorporated from parents; becoming a person's conscience
Id	Unconscious	Basic impulses (sex and aggression); seeking immediate gratification; irrational and impulsive

mands to be warmed. The ego may recognize that the boy could steal a blanket from his older brother, who is sleeping in the next bed. Working on the reality principle, the boy realizes that he can gratify his id by stealing the blanket.

The **superego** in Freud's theory is the moral aspect of mental functioning, comprising the ego ideal and the conscience and taught by parents and society. The superego tells the id and the ego whether gratification in a particular instance is ethical. It attempts to control the id by internalizing parental authority (whether rational or irrational) through the process of socialization and by punishing transgressions with feelings of guilt and anxiety. The superego may tell the boy just mentioned that stealing a blanket from his older brother, who may then become cold, is immoral and that his brother may punish him for stealing the blanket. By asking his parents for another blanket, the boy can satisfy his id without feeling guilty, fearful, or anxious. The ego and superego attempt to modulate the id and direct it toward appropriate ways of behaving. (See Figure 12.1 for a description of Freud's levels of consciousness and mental forces.)

Development of Personality

Freud strongly believed that if people looked at their past they could gain insight into their current behavior. This belief led him to create an elaborate psychosexual stage theory of personality development. Freud believed that the core aspects of personality are established early, remain stable throughout life, and are changed only with great difficulty. He argued that all people pass through five critical stages of personality development: oral, anal, phallic, latency, and genital (see Table 12.2 on page 414). At each of the key stages, Freud asserted, people experience conflicts and issues associated with *erogenous zones*—areas of the body that when stimulated give rise to erotic or sexual sensations.

Oral Stage. The concept of the **oral stage** is based on the fact that the instincts of infants (from birth to about age 2) are focused on the mouth as the primary pleasure-seeking center. Infants receive oral gratification through feeding, thumb sucking,

Superego [super-EE-go]: In Freud's theory, the moral aspect of mental functioning, comprising the ego ideal (what a person would ideally like to be) and the conscience, and taught by parents and society.

Oral stage: Freud's first stage of personality development, from birth to about age 2, during which infants obtain gratification primarily through the mouth.

TABLE 12.2 ***Freud's Five Psychosexual Stages of Personality Development***

Stage	Erogenous Zone	Conflicts/Experiences	Adult Traits (Especially Fixations) Associated with Problems at a Stage
Oral (birth to 2 years) 	Mouth	Infant achieves gratification through oral activities such as feeding, thumb sucking, and cooing.	Optimism, gullibility, passivity, hostility, substance abuse
Anal (2 to 3 years) 	Anus	The child learns to respond to some parental demands (such as for bladder and bowel control).	Excessive cleanliness, orderliness, messiness, rebelliousness
Phallic (3 to 7 years) 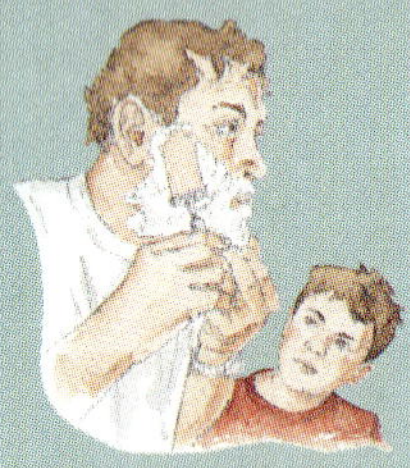	Genitals	The child learns to realize the differences between males and females and becomes aware of sexuality.	Flirtatiousness, vanity, promiscuity, chastity, disorder in gender identity
Latency (7 to puberty) 	None	The child continues developing but sexual urges are relatively quiet.	Not specified
Genital (puberty on) 	Genitals	The growing adolescent shakes off old dependencies and learns to deal maturely with the opposite sex.	Not specified

and cooing during the early months of life, when their basic feelings about the world are being established. Relying heavily on symbolism, Freud contended that adults who consider the world a bitter place (referring to the mouth and taste senses) probably had difficulty during the oral stage of development and may have traits associated with passivity and hostility. Their problems would tend to focus on nurturing, warmth, and love.

Anal Stage. The **anal stage** is Freud's second stage of personality development, from age 2 to about 3, during which children learn to control the immediate gratification they obtain through defecation and to become responsive to the demands of society. At about age 2 or 3, children learn to respond to some of parents' and society's demands. One parental demand is that children control their bodily functions of urination and defecation. Most 2- and 3-year-olds experience pleasure in moving their bowels, and the anal area is the focus of their pleasurable feelings. This stage therefore establishes the basis for conflict between the id and the ego—between the desire for infantile pleasure and the demand for adult, controlled behavior. Freud claimed that during the anal stage, children develop certain lasting personality characteristics related to control, such as neatness and orderliness, that reflect their toilet training. Thus, adults who had difficulty in the anal stage would tend to have problems that focus on orderliness (or lack of it) and also might be compulsive in many behaviors.

Phallic Stage. The **phallic stage** is Freud's third stage of personality development, from about age 4 to 7, during which children obtain gratification primarily from the genitals. At about age 4 or 5, children become aware of their sexuality. Freud claimed that numerous feelings are repressed so deeply during this stage that children (and later adults) are unaware of many of their sexual urges. Nonetheless, gender role development begins during this period.

During the phallic stage, children pass through the Oedipus (or Electra) complex. The **Oedipus complex** includes feelings of rivalry with the parent of the same sex and love of the parent of the opposite sex, ultimately resolved through identification with the parent of the same sex. The Oedipus complex for males thus refers to a boy's love for his mother, hostility toward his father, and consequent fear of castration and punishment by the father. In resolving the Oedipus complex, the boy eventually accepts his father's close relationship with his mother. Rather than feel excluded by it, he chooses to gratify his need for his mother's attention by identifying with his father. In this way, a young boy begins to model his behavior after that of his father. For females, Freud argued that the Oedipus complex, sometimes termed the *Electra complex*, follows a slightly different course. Freud held that when a young girl realizes that she has no penis, she develops what Freud called *penis envy*. He suggested that she can symbolically acquire a penis by attaching her love to her father. A young girl may then ask her father to marry her so they can raise a family together. When she realizes that this is unlikely, she may identify with her mother and copy her mother's behavior as a means of obtaining (or sharing in) her father's affection. Like the young boy, the young girl identifies with the parent of the same sex in the hope of obtaining affection from the parent of the opposite sex. For both boys and girls, the critical component in resolving the Oedipus complex is the development of identification with the parent of the same sex. Adult traits associated with problems at this stage usually involve sexuality and may be seen in vanity, promiscuity, or excessive worry about chastity.

The existence of an Oedipus complex is controversial and widely debated, especially because many people find the theory sexist and degrading to women. There is no doubt about Freud's views of women; he saw them as weaker and less rational than men and believed they should be subservient to men. Today, most researchers believe that Freud's notion of penis envy was imaginative but unconvincing, overdrawn, and lacking credibility (Stagner, 1988).

Latency Stage. Freud's fourth stage of development, the **latency stage**, lasts from about age 7 until puberty. During this period, children develop physically, but sexual urges are inactive (latent). Sexual urges, fears, and frustrations are repressed; much of children's energy is channeled into social or achievement-related activities. Some psychoanalysts (considered in the next section) believe that this stage has disappeared from American society because of rapid maturation into adolescence.

Anal stage: Freud's second stage of personality development, about age 2 to age 3, during which children learn to control the immediate gratification they obtain through defecation and to become responsive to the demands of society

Phallic stage [FAL-ick]: Freud's third stage of personality development, about age 4 to age 7, during which children obtain gratification primarily from the genitals.

Oedipus complex [ED-i-pus]: Occurring during the phallic stage, feelings of rivalry with the parent of the same sex and love of the parent of the opposite sex, ultimately resolved through identification with the parent of the same sex; in girls this process is called the *Electra complex*.

Latency stage [LAY-ten-see]: Freud's fourth stage of personality development, from about age 7 until puberty, during which sexual urges are inactive.

Genital Stage. When people reach the last stage of development, the **genital stage**, the sexuality, fears, and repressed feelings of earlier stages are once again exhibited. Many repressed sexual feelings toward the parents resurface at puberty. Over the course of the genital stage, the adolescent shakes off dependence on parents and learns to deal with members of the opposite sex in socially and sexually mature ways. Members of the opposite sex, who may have been ignored during the latency stage, are now seen as attractive and desirable. Many unresolved conflicts and repressed urges affect behavior during this stage. Ideally, if people have passed through previous stages of development without major incident, they will develop conventional relations with members of the opposite sex. If not, they may continue to have unresolved conflicts within their unconscious.

Unresolved Conflicts

As children proceed from one developmental stage to the next, they adjust their views of the world. However, according to Freud, if children do not successfully pass through a stage, they acquire a fixation and an unrelenting use of defense mechanisms.

Fixations. A **fixation** is an excessive attachment to some person or object that was appropriate only at an earlier stage of development. A person who becomes fixated is said to be arrested at a particular stage of development. Fixation at one developmental stage does not prevent all further development; but unless people master each stage successfully, they cannot fully master the later stages. For example, a child who does not successfully pass through the phallic stage probably has not resolved the Oedipus complex and may feel hostility toward the parent of the same sex. The child may suffer the consequences of this unresolved conflict throughout life.

Fixations or partial fixations usually occur because of frustration or overindulgence that hinders the expression of sexual or aggressive energy at a particular psychological stage. According to Freud, good personality adjustment generally involves a balance among competing forces. The child, and later the adult, should be neither too self-centered nor too moralistic. Parents who are restrictive, punitive, and overbearing or those who are indifferent, smothering, or overindulgent produce emotionally disturbed children who have a difficult time coping with life because of the resulting fixations. What happens when a person becomes fixated? According to Freud, the person develops defense mechanisms and sometimes maladjustment.

Defense Mechanisms. A **defense mechanism** is a largely unconscious way of reducing anxiety by distorting perceptions of reality. Everyone defends against anxiety from time to time. Defense mechanisms allow the ego to deal with the uncomfortable feelings that anxiety produces. In fact, people are typically unaware that they are using defense mechanisms. Nonetheless, people who use them to such an extent that reality is sharply distorted can become maladjusted.

Freud described many kinds of defense mechanisms but identified repression as the most important. In **repression**, anxiety-provoking thoughts and feelings are totally relegated to the unconscious. When people repress a feeling or desire, they become unaware of it. Thus, a young girl who has been taught that anger is inappropriate in women may repress her angry feelings.

In addition to repression, Freud observed five other key defense mechanisms:

- **Projection**—the mechanism by which people attribute their own undesirable traits to others. A woman with deep aggressive tendencies may see other people as acting in an excessively aggressive way. A man who is anxious about his own anger may see others as being overly hostile.
- **Denial**—the mechanism by which people refuse to accept reality or recognize the true source of their anxiety. Someone with strong sexual urges may deny interest in sex rather than deal with those urges.

Genital stage [JEN-it-ul]: Freud's last stage of personality development, from the onset of puberty through adulthood, during which the sexual conflicts of childhood resurface (at puberty) and are often resolved (during adolescence).

Fixation: An excessive attachment to some person or object that was appropriate only at an earlier stage of development.

Defense mechanism: A largely unconscious way of reducing anxiety by distorting perceptions of reality.

Repression: Defense mechanism by which people block anxiety-provoking feelings from conscious awareness and push them into the unconscious.

Projection: Defense mechanism by which people attribute their own undesirable traits to other people or objects.

Denial: Defense mechanism by which people refuse to recognize the true source of their anxiety.

- **Reaction formation**—the mechanism by which people defend against anxiety by adopting behaviors opposite to their true feelings. A classic example of the use of reaction formation as a defense mechanism is the behavior of a person who has strong sexual urges but becomes extremely chaste.
- **Sublimation**—the mechanism by which socially unacceptable impulses are redirected into acceptable ones. Thus, a man who has sexual desire for someone he knows is off limits (perhaps a cousin) may channel that desire into working 14-hour days at his office.
- **Rationalization**—the mechanism by which people reinterpret undesirable feelings or behavior to make them appear acceptable. For example, a shoplifter may rationalize that no one will miss the things she steals or that she needs the things more than other people do.

▲ *The work of a prison artist may represent sublimation, in which unacceptable impulses are rechanneled into socially acceptable behaviors.*

When a person's defense mechanisms cause reality to become distorted and maladaptive, that person must be concerned about using them. Overreliance on defense mechanisms leads to maladjustment.

Freud Today

When Freud's psychosexual theory of development was first proposed around 1900, it received considerable unfavorable attention. It was considered absurd to suggest that young children had sexual feelings toward their parents. Yet, if you watch young children and the ways in which they respond to and identify with their parents, you will see that there are elements of truth to Freud's conception of how personality development proceeds. Little girls do tend to idolize their fathers, and little boys often become strongly attached to their mothers.

Despite these observations, Freud's theories have been sharply criticized for numerous reasons. Some psychologists object to Freud's basic conception of human nature, his emphasis on sexual urges, and his idea that human behavior is biologically determined. Others reject his predictions about psychosexual stages and fixations. Still others assert that his theory does not account for changing situations and the differing cultures in which people live. Many people find Freud's ideas about women offensive. At a minimum, his ideas are controversial; many psychologists do not regard them as valid; some assert that Freud did not even remember his own work correctly (Schatzman, 1992). Almost all agree that his theory makes specific predictions about an individual's behavior almost impossible. Freud's theory also has to be considered in a cultural context. Austrian society, with its rigid standards of behavior, and Freud's wealthy patients biased him in directions that few theorists would adopt today.

Regardless of whether Freud was right or wrong, his influence on psychology and on Western culture exceeds that of any other personality theorist, present or past. His theory weaves together his clinical experiences with patients, his speculations about human nature, and his own extraordinary personality. In many ways, Freud's theory paved the way for other developmental stage theories, such as those of Piaget, Erikson, and Levinson, who made more specific predictions about specific behaviors.

Figure 12.2, on page 418, summarizes all four of these prominent stage theories of development, presenting a cross-comparison of the chronological order of their stages.

Reaction formation: Defense mechanism by which people behave in a manner opposite to their true but anxiety-provoking feelings.

Sublimation [sub-li-MAY-shun]: Defense mechanism by which people redirect socially unacceptable impulses into acceptable ones.

Rationalization: Defense mechanism by which people reinterpret undesirable feelings or behaviors in terms that make them appear acceptable.

FIGURE 12.2

A Comparison of Four Prominent Stage Theories

The stage theories of Freud, Piaget, Erikson, and Levinson all suggest that individuals must master each stage before they can pass successfully through the next.

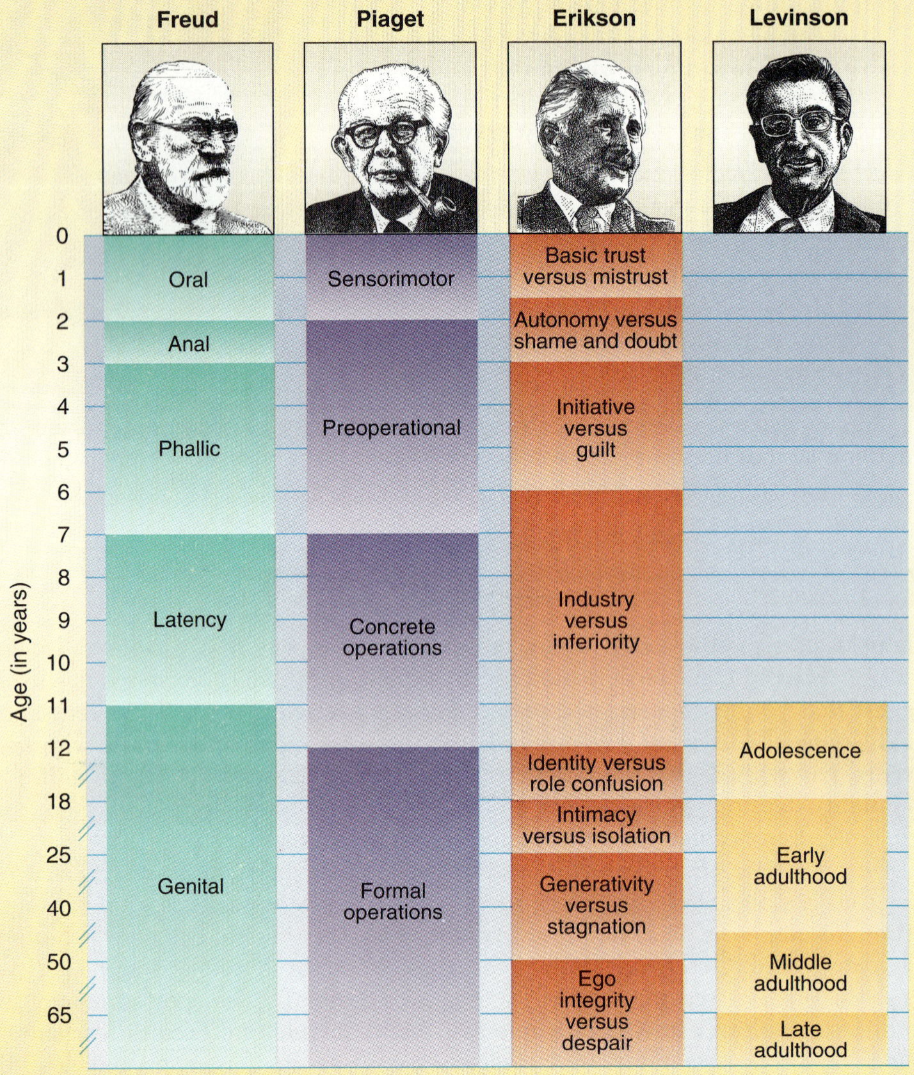

Cultural Determinants of Personality

When I first mentioned Freud, I noted that his practice was with Austrian society matrons. This seems simple enough, but consider the implications. Freud developed a theory from dealing with a particular group of patients whose day-to-day behavior, personalities, and problems were shaped by the culture in which they lived. *Culture*, as we have seen, refers to the norms, ideals, values, rules, patterns of communication, and beliefs adopted by a group of people. Within a culture, there may be different social classes, but all of the people have the same basic set of norms.

Cultural diversity is apparent as one travels from one country to another. For example, traveling from England, to Spain, through France, and then to Germany and onward to Turkey, one sees distinctly different value systems, lifestyles, and personalities. Modes of dress and attitudes about work, family, and religion all differ. Culture is significant, because the culture shapes how people raise their children, what values they teach, and what family life is like.

Cultural values shape personality. Therefore, personality theories must be considered in a cultural context. Western society values competitiveness, autonomy, and self-reliance; in addition, Western conceptions of personality focus on the individual. By contrast, non-Western cultures value interdependence and cooperation; they also focus more on groups in constructing conceptions of personality. For developing adolescents, one culture may stress conformity to rules, strict adherence to religious values, and obedience to parental authority. In contrast, another culture may stress independence, free thought, experimentation, and resistance to parental authority. Within American culture, there are significant variations based on heritage. People from a white Anglo-Saxon Protestant background bring to the culture a sharply different heritage than do people of African American descent.

The many variables make the study of culture and personality a complicated task. Adjustments and refinements must be made in order to take account of ethnicity, gender, age, and class, as well as culture. Accordingly, every personality theory, concept, and approach must be considered and evaluated from a multicultural perspective. For example, a person from Japan is likely to view embarrassment and saving face differently than does a person from the United States. We will come back to this multicultural theme later in this chapter, when we examine the theory of Walter Mischel. He argues that the context in which behavior occurs must be a focus of personality psychologists.

Neo-Freudians: Personality theorists who have proposed variations on the basic ideas of Freud, usually attributing a greater influence to cultural and interpersonal factors than Freud did.

Neo-Freudians—Dissent and Revision

There is no question that Freud has had an enormous impact on psychological thought. But modern theorists, including some of Freud's students, have found what they consider serious omissions, errors, and biases in Freudian theory. Many of these theorists have developed new ideas loosely based on Freud's original conception, but usually attributing greater influence to cultural and interpersonal factors; they have become known as **neo-Freudians**.

Some neo-Freudians (Alfred Adler, for instance) have argued that people are not driven solely by sexual instincts. Others (Erich Fromm, for example) have argued that the ego has more of a role than Freud thought in controlling behavior. Still others (Karen Horney, for instance) have focused on the central role of anxiety in shaping personality and maladjustment. Many theorists (Harry Stack Sullivan, for example) have attributed a greater influence to cultural and interpersonal factors. A number of the neo-Freudian theories (Carl Jung's, for instance) have been more optimistic and future-oriented. While traditional psychoanalysts begin by focusing on unconscious material in the id and only later try to increase the patient's ego control, many practicing neo-Freudians focus on helping people to develop stronger control of their ego and to feel better about their "selves." Carl Jung is one of the best known of the neo-Freudians; we'll explore his influential theory next.

Carl Gustav Jung ▼

Jung's Analytical Psychology

Carl Gustav Jung (1875–1961) was a psychiatrist who became a close friend and follower of Freud. However, Jung, a brilliant thinker, ultimately broke with Freud over several key issues. Compared to Freud, Jung placed relatively little emphasis on sex. He focused instead on people's desire to blend their basic drives (including sex) with real-world demands. Thus, Jung saw people's behavior as less rigidly fixed and determined. He also emphasized the search for meaning in life. In 1917, when Jung declared

Collective unconscious: In Jung's theory, a storehouse of primitive ideas and images in the shared unconscious that are inherited from one's ancestors.

Archetypes [AR-ki-types]: In Jung's theory, emotionally charged ideas and images that have rich meaning and symbolism and are contained within the collective unconscious.

his disagreements with Freud, he and Freud severed their relationship; Freud was intolerant of followers who deviated too much from his positions.

Jung chose to differentiate his approach from Freud's by terming it an *analytic approach* rather than a *psychoanalytic approach*. Like Freud, Jung emphasized unconscious processes as determinants of behavior, and he believed that each person houses past events in the unconscious. Jung's version of the unconscious was slightly different. Unlike Freud, Jung held that the unconscious anticipates the future and redirects a person's behavior when the person is leaning too much in one psychological direction. Thus, for example, if a person is using too many defense mechanisms, the unconscious can anticipate problems and help the person deal with anxiety rather than distort it.

In addition, Jung developed a new concept central to his ideas—that of the collective unconscious. The **collective unconscious** is a shared storehouse of primitive ideas and images in the unconscious that are inherited from one's ancestors. These inherited ideas and images are emotionally charged and rich in meaning and symbolism and are contained in the form of **archetypes** within a person's unconscious. The archetypes of the collective unconscious emerge in art, in religion, and especially in dreams. One especially important archetype is the *mandala*, a mystical symbol, generally circular in form, that in Jung's view represents the striving for unity within a person's self. Jung pointed out that many religions have mandalalike symbols; indeed, Hinduism and Buddhism use such symbols as aids to meditation. Another archetype is the concept of mother; each person is born with a predisposition to react to certain types of people or institutions as mother figures. Such figures are considered warm, accepting, and nurturing; some examples are the Virgin Mary, one's alma mater, and the Earth. There are archetypes for wise older men and wizards. Jung found rich symbolism in dreams and used archetypes such as the mandala and the mother to help people understand themselves.

Jung's ideas are widely read but not widely accepted by mainstream psychologists. Although his impact on psychoanalytic theory is important, Jung himself never achieved prominence in leading psychological thought because his ideas cannot be verified. Some theorists even view them as mere poetic speculation.

Another psychologist who broke with Freud—but who made a more lasting impact on psychological thought—was Alfred Adler, whom we consider next.

Adler believed that people are driven by the desire to overcome obstacles in their lives. Nearly every year Dick Hoyt and his son, Rick, who is confined to a wheelchair, run the Boston Marathon, a distance of 26 miles and 385 yards. ▼

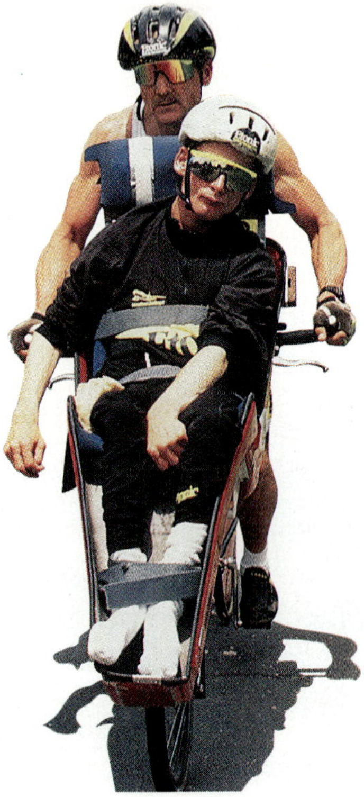

Adler's Fulfillment Approach

Alfred Adler (1870–1937) was heavily influenced by Freud, and some psychologists consider his theory simply an extension of Freud's. Adler was a Viennese physician who had an unhappy childhood. He recalled being compared to his older brother, who seemed to be better liked because of his physical prowess and attractiveness. Perhaps his unhappy childhood and feelings of inferiority led Adler to believe that people strive to become the best they can be. When Adler broke with Freudian traditions, he focused much more on human values and social interactions.

Adler differed with Freud concerning two key points: First, Adler viewed human beings as striving to overcome obstacles in order to fulfill themselves, rather than for pleasure. Second, Adler viewed the social nature of human beings as much more important than did Freud. Adler met with Freud weekly; in 1911, however, Freud denounced him because of sharp, irreconcilable differences in their views of personality.

Structure of Personality. According to Adler, people are motivated, or energized, by natural feelings of inferiority, which lead them to strive for completion, superiority, and ultimately perfection. Thus, feelings of inferiority are not always detrimental. A sense of inferiority can compel people to strive for superiority and thereby express their core tendencies, both as individuals and as members of society.

Adler recognized that people seek to express their need for superiority in different areas of life. Some seek to be superior artists; others seek to be superior social advocates, parents, or corporate executives. Thus, each person develops a unique lifestyle, in which attitudes and behaviors express a specific life goal or an ideal approach to achieving superiority. Adler eventually sought to develop an "individual" psychology, arguing that people have to be analyzed as unique human beings.

Adler stressed fulfillment through individual striving toward specific goals. Some life goals, which Adler called *fictional finalism,* are unrealistic and unlikely to be achieved by most people. Examples are winning the Pulitzer prize for literature, becoming a millionaire, or becoming a U.S. Senator (Adler, 1969). However, it is these fictional goals, which are often unconscious, that motivate people and set up unique patterns of striving.

FOCUS

Review

- What are the fundamental assumptions about human behavior on which Freud's theory is based? p. 411
- Why did Freud believe the unconscious to be so important in personality? pp. 411–412
- What is the fundamental function of all of Freud's defense mechanisms? p. 416
- To what fundamental assumptions of Freud did the neo-Freudians react? p. 419

Think Critically

- What was it about Austrian society that so shaped Freud's various points of view?
- Adler's view of personality development was radically different from Freud's. What implications did this difference have for Adler's theory of personality development?

Development of Personality. Adler believed that children's social interactions are particularly important in determining eventual personality characteristics. Adler and his followers relied heavily on the idea that early relationships with siblings, parents, and other family members determine the lifestyle an individual eventually chooses. It therefore follows, Adler asserted, that birth order is important. A first-born child, for example, is likely to have a different relationship with people and is thus likely to develop a lifestyle different from that of a third-born child. First-borns are pushed by parents toward success, leadership, and independence and so tend to have a high need for achievement. Their early experiences make it likely that they will choose careers reflecting that need for achievement, such as corporate executive or politician. Third-born children, on the other hand, are usually more relaxed about achievement. A young child who feels competitive with an older sibling, however, may develop a strong need for achievement that will drive the child toward public success. (See Table 12.3.)

Alfred Adler ▼

TABLE 12.3 ***Some of Adler's Hypotheses about Birth Order***

Birth Order	Hypothesis
Only child	The center of attention, dominant, often spoiled because of parental timidity and anxiety
First-born	Dethroned from a central position, has negative attitudes and feelings toward the second child and a passion for domination, protective and helpful toward others
Second-born	Actively struggling to surpass others
Last-born	The most pampered (the smallest and weakest), not unhappy, able to excel over others by being different
Only girl or boy	Extremely feminine or masculine in orientation

Humanistic Approaches

Unlike Freudians and neo-Freudians, who want to understand relationships between children and parents, humanistic theorists are more interested in people's conceptions of themselves and what they would like to become. In general, *humanistic theories* assume that people are motivated by internal forces to achieve personal goals. Humanistic psychology focuses not on disturbed individuals but on healthy people.

Humanistic theories, which emphasize fulfillment, were developed partly in response to Freud's theory, which stresses the conflict of inner forces. Whereas Freud saw people in conflict warding off evil thoughts and desires with defenses, humanists see people as basically decent (although some of their specific behaviors may not be). Moreover, humanistic fulfillment theories enable theoreticians and practitioners to make predictions about specific behaviors.

Sometimes humanistic theories are also called *phenomenological approaches,* because they focus on the individual's unique experiences with and ways of interpreting the things and people in the world (phenomena). These approaches are more likely to examine immediate experiences than past ones and are more likely to deal with an individual's perception of the world than with a therapist's perception of the individual. Finally, they focus on self-determination; people carve their own destinies, from their own vantage points, and in their own ways. The humanistic approaches are represented by two well-known psychologists, Abraham Maslow and Carl Rogers, whose theories are examined next.

Abraham Maslow

▲ *Abraham Maslow*

No single individual is more closely associated with humanistic phenomenological psychology than Abraham Maslow (1908–1970). In Chapter 9 we examined Maslow's theory of motivation, which states that human needs are arranged in a pyramidal hierarchy in terms of importance and potency. Lower needs—food and water, for example—are powerful and drive people toward fulfilling them. In the middle of the pyramid of needs are safety, then belongingness, then self-esteem. At the top of the pyramid is self-actualization. The higher a need is on the hierarchy, the more distinctly human the need.

As a humanist, Maslow believed human beings are born healthy and undamaged, and he had a strong bias toward studying well-adjusted people. Maslow spoke about personality in terms of human uniqueness and the human need for self-actualization—the process of growth and the realization of individual potential. He focused not on what was missing from personality or life but on what one might achieve in realizing one's full potential. The process of realizing potential and of growing is the process of becoming self-actualized. Critics of Maslow find his notions too fuzzy (as they do Freud's) and view his approach to psychology as romantic and never fully developed. Also, his theory is virtually untestable. A more complete and scientific humanistic approach was presented by Carl Rogers.

Rogers and Self Theory

Carl Rogers (1902–1987) began to formulate his personality theory during the first years of his practice as a clinician in Rochester, New York. He listened to thousands of patients and was among the first psychologists to record and transcribe his interactions with patients. What Rogers's patients said about their experiences, their thoughts, and themselves led him to make three basic assumptions about behavior: (1) Behavior is goal-directed and worthwhile. (2) People are innately good, so they will almost always choose adaptive, enhancing, and self-actualizing behaviors. (3) How people see their world determines how they will behave.

Key Concepts. Rogers believed that personal experiences provide an individual with a unique and subjective internal frame of reference and worldview. He believed that **fulfillment**—an inborn tendency directing people toward actualizing their essential nature and thus attaining their potential—is the motivating force of personality development. Thus, people strive naturally to express their capabilities, potential, and talents. Rogers's personality approach is *unidirectional,* because it always moves in the direction of fulfillment. This does not mean that an individual's personality undergoes uninterrupted growth. During some periods, no growth is evident. However, for Rogers, a person's core tendency is to actualize, maintain, and enhance life. Rogers liked the analogy of a seed, which if watered grows into a strong, healthy plant—a representative member of its species.

▲ *Carl Rogers*

Structure of Personality. Rogers's theory of personality is structured around the concept of self. By **self** he means the perceptions individuals have of themselves and of their relationships to other people and to various aspects of life. The self-concept is how people see their own behavior and internal characteristics. As mentioned before, Rogers's theory assumes that individuals are constantly engaged in the process of fulfilling their potential—of actualizing their true self.

Rogers suggested that each person has a concept not only of self but also of an ideal self. The **ideal self** is the self a person would ideally like to be (such as a competent professional, a devoted mate, or a loving parent). According to Rogerian theory, each person's happiness lies within that person's conception of self. A person is generally happy when agreement exists between the real (Rogers used the term *phenomenal*) self and the ideal self. Great discrepancies between the real and the ideal selves create unhappiness, dissatisfaction, and, in extreme cases, maladjustment.

Rogers's focus on the self led him to his basic principle—that people tend to maximize their self-concept through **self-actualization.** In the self-actualization process, the self grows, expands, and becomes social. People are self-actualized when they have expanded their self-concept and developed their potential to approximate their ideal selves by attempting to minimize ill health, be fully functioning, have a superior perception of reality, and feel a strong sense of self-acceptance. When people's self-concepts are not what they would like them to be, anxiety develops. Like Freud, Rogers saw anxiety as useful because it motivates people to try to actualize their best selves, to become all they are capable of being.

Development of Personality. Unlike Freud, Rogers suggested that personality development occurs continuously, not in stages. He contended that development involves learning self-assessment techniques in order to master the process of self-actualization—which takes a lifetime.

Rogers was particularly aware that children develop basic feelings about themselves early in life. This awareness led him to understand the role of social influences in the development of self-concepts. The self-assessments of children who are told that they are beautiful, intelligent, and good are radically different from those of children who are told that they are bad, dirty, stupid, and a general nuisance. Rogers did not claim that negative feelings toward children's behavior should not be expressed; rather, children should have a sense that they themselves are worthwhile and good, although a specific behavior that they exhibit might be unacceptable. Rogers suggested that children must grow up in an atmosphere in which they can experience life fully. This involves their recognizing both the good and the bad sides of their behavior.

The Importance of Self-Concepts. People with rigid self-concepts guard themselves against potentially threatening feelings and experiences. Rogers suggested that these people become unhappy when they are unable to fit new types of behavior into their existing self-concepts. They then distort their perceptions of their behavior in order to make the perceptions compatible with the self-concepts. A

Fulfillment: In Rogers's personality theory, an inborn tendency directing people toward actualizing their essential nature and thus attaining their potential.

Self: In Rogers's theory of personality, the perceptions individuals have of themselves and of their relationships to other people and to various aspects of life.

Ideal self: The self that a person would ideally like to be.

Self-actualization: The fundamental human need to strive to fulfill one's potential; from a humanistic view, a final level of psychological development in which a person attempts to minimize ill health, be fully functioning, have a superior perception of reality, and feel a strong sense of self-acceptance.

Fig. 10.7

man whose self-concept includes high moral principles, rigid religious observance, and strict self-control, for example, probably becomes anxious when he feels envy. Such a feeling is inconsistent with his self-concept. To avoid anxiety, he denies or distorts what he is truly experiencing. He may deny that he feels envy, or he may insist that he is entitled to the object he covets.

A changing world may threaten a person's self-concept. The person may then screen out difficult ideas or thoughts; this tends to create a narrow outlook, a limited conception of the world, and a restriction on personal growth. But individuals can reduce or eliminate their fear by broadening their frame of reference and by considering alternative behaviors. People with healthy self-concepts can allow new experiences into their lives and can accept or reject them. Such people move in a positive direction. With each new experience, their self-concepts become stronger and more defined, and the goal of self-actualization is brought closer.

Individual Development. Rogers's concept of personality shows an abiding concern for individual development. Rogers stressed that each person must evaluate her or his own situation from a personal (internal) frame of reference, not from the external framework of others.

Freud's and Rogers's theories of personality make fundamentally different assumptions about human nature and about how personality is expressed. Freud saw biologically driven human beings in conflict; Rogers saw human beings as inherently good and trying to be everything they could be. Freud was strongly deterministic, but humanists are strongly oriented toward free will. Humanists believe people can rise above biologically inherited traits and can use decision-making processes to guide behavior. The treatment procedures that developed out of the theories of Freud and Rogers—psychoanalysis and client-centered therapy (the latter will be discussed in Chapter 15)—are fundamentally different. (See Building Table 12.1 for a summary of the psychoanalytic and humanistic approaches.)

Next, we examine an approach to personality that focuses on traits and on the specific behavioral responses that individuals make throughout their lives.

BUILDING TABLE 12.1

Psychoanalytic and Humanistic Approaches to Personality

APPROACH	MAJOR PROPONENT	CORE OF PERSONALITY	STRUCTURE OF PERSONALITY	DEVELOPMENT	CAUSE OF PROBLEMS
Psychoanalytic	Sigmund Freud	Maximizes gratification while minimizing punishment or guilt; instinctual unconscious urges direct behavior	Id, ego, superego 	Five stages: oral, anal, phallic, latency, genital	Imbalances between the id, ego, and superego resulting in fixations
Humanistic	Carl Rogers	Actualizes, maintains, and enhances the experiences of life through the process of self-actualization	Self	Process of cumulative self-actualization and development of sense of self-worth	Wide incongruence between self and concept of ideal self

Trait and Type Theories

Both ancient philosophers and medieval physicians believed that the proportions of body fluids (called humors) determined a person's temperament and personality. Cheerful, healthy people, for example, were said to have a *sanguine* (cheerful, hopeful, and self-confident) personality because blood was their primary humor; those who had a preponderance of yellow bile were considered hot-tempered. Like their medieval counterparts, some early psychologists based their personality theories on the behaviors people openly exhibit, such as shyness, impulsiveness, and aggressiveness. And research shows that many of these easily observed characteristics do predict other behaviors. For example, extremely shy people are more likely than others to be anxious and lonely and to have low self-esteem (DePaulo et al., 1989), and adolescents with behavior problems often have low self-esteem (Harper & Marshall, 1991). Theories based on these observations—trait and type theories of personality—make intuitive sense and thus have been very popular.

Trait theorists study specific traits. A **trait** is any readily identifiable stable quality or behavior that characterizes the way in which an individual differs from other individuals. Someone might characterize Bill Clinton as being energetic and forward-looking and Bob Dole as tough and patriotic. Such characterizations present specific ideas about these people's traits. Traits can be evaluated on a continuum, so a person can be extremely shy, very shy, shy, or mildly shy. For some personality theorists, traits are the elements that personality is made of.

Type theorists group together traits common to specific personalities. **Types**, therefore, are categories in which broad collections of traits are loosely tied together and interrelated. Although the distinction between traits and types sometimes blurs, as Gordon Allport (1937, p. 295) explained, "A man can be said to *have* a trait; but he cannot be said to *have* a type. Rather he fits a type."

We now examine the trait and type theories of Gordon Allport, Raymond Cattell, and Hans Eysenck. Then we will examine a newer model of traits: the Big Five.

Allport's Trait Theory and Cattell's Factor Theory

Gordon Allport

The distinguished psychologist Gordon Allport (1897–1967) was a leading trait theorist who suggested that each individual has a unique set of personality traits. According to Allport (1937), if a person's traits are known, it is possible to predict how the person will respond to various events in the environment. Allport quickly discovered that while thousands of traits characterize people's behavior, some are more dominant than others. Indeed, psychologists have devised tests to measure many personality traits. *Applications,* on pages 426 and 427, looks at one such test.

Allport decided that traits could be grouped into three kinds: cardinal, central, and secondary. *Cardinal traits* are ideas and behaviors that determine the direction of a person's life. A clergyman's cardinal trait may be devotion to God; a civil rights leader's, the desire to rectify social and political injustices. Allport noted that many people have no cardinal traits. The more common *central traits* are reasonably easy to identify; they are the qualities and behaviors that characterize a person's daily interactions (the basic units of personality). Allport believed that central traits—including self-control, apprehension, tension, self-assuredness, forthrightness, and practicality—adequately describe many personalities. For example, tennis legend John McEnroe could be characterized as self-assured and hot-tempered, lacking emotional control; Woody Allen's typical film persona could be described as tense and apprehensive. *Secondary traits* are specific behaviors that occur in response to specific situations. For example, a person may have a secondary trait of a prejudice toward minorities or a love of spectator sports. Secondary traits are more easily modified than central traits and are not necessarily shown on a daily basis.

Trait: Any readily identifiable stable quality or behavior that characterizes the way in which an individual differs from other individuals.

Types: Categories of personality in which broad collections of traits are loosely tied together and interrelated.

APPLICATIONS

Can Psychologists Assess Personality Quickly?

The summer before my first year in college, I took a course called "How to Study." The instructor told us that if we had a better idea of our own personality style we would be better test takers. He argued that personality tests, along with interest and ability tests, were also useful in predicting vocational preferences. He then gave us a number of different personality tests. One of the key tests that he used was one developed in the 1960s by Peter Myers and Isabel Briggs.

The Myers–Briggs Type Indicator, often called the MBTI, is a test based on Jung's theory of personality. Jung proposed that each individual favors specific modalities, or ways of dealing with and learning about the world; the modalities that you prefer define a personality type that characterizes you. The MBTI asks you to choose between pairs of statements that deal with your preferences or inclinations. For instance,

> Do you think that having a daily routine is
> (a) an easy way to get things done,
> or
> (b) difficult even when necessary?

The MBTI is scored so that an individual is characterized as predominantly at one pole or another on four distinct dimensions: Extroversion–Introversion (E or I), Sensing–Intuition (S or N), Thinking–Feeling (T or F), and Judging–Perceptive (J or P). An individual can score high in each one of these bipolar dimensions. The various possible combinations thus yield 16 personality types. For example, an ENFP type is an individual whose principal modes are extroversion, intuition, feeling, and perception. A person who is summarized as an ENFP feels a greater relatedness to the outer world of people than to the inner world of ideas (E), tends to look for possibilities rather than to work with what is known (N), makes decisions based on personal values rather than logic (F), and shows a preference for a spontaneous way of life rather than an orderly existence (P).

Unfortunately, the MBTI has many problems. It can be scored in sophisticated ways, but often it is simply interpreted by unskilled examiners—much like my precollege study skills instructor—for purposes of vocational counseling. The MBTI was normed for students in grades 4 through 12, so it is best used for individuals of those ages. Cultural vantage points are not considered. Individual differences are not taken into account. Further, the likelihood of maladjustment is not considered, nor is the development of personality.

Everyone has different combinations of traits, which is why Allport claimed that each person is unique. To identify a person's traits, Allport recommended an in-depth study of that individual. If Allport's theory were followed to its logical conclusion, knowing a person's traits would allow a psychologist to predict how that person would respond to the environment—that is, what the person's behavior would be. This has not yet come about. Psychologists such as Allport and Raymond B. Cattell have argued, however, that it is possible to tell a great deal about a person just by knowing a few of the person's traits. Cattell (1965) used the technique of *factor analysis*—a statistical procedure in which psychologists analyze groups of variables (factors) to detect which are related—to show that groups of traits tend to cluster together. Thus, researchers find that people who describe themselves as warm and accepting also tend to rate themselves as high on nurturance and tenderness and low on aggression, suspiciousness, and apprehensiveness. Researchers also see patterns within professions; for example, artists may see themselves as creative, sensitive, and open, while accountants may describe themselves as careful, serious, conservative, and thorough-minded. Cattell termed obvious, day-to-day traits *surface traits* and higher-order traits *source traits*.

Hans Eysenck ▼

Eysenck's Type Theory

Whereas Allport and Cattell focused on traits, Hans Eysenck focused on higher levels of trait organization, or what he called *types*. Each type incorporates elements at a lower level (traits), and each trait incorporates lower-order qualities (habits). Eysenck (1970) argued that all personality traits can be grouped along three basic dimensions: emotional stability, introversion or extroversion, and psychoticism.

Emotional stability is the extent to which people control their feelings. At one extreme of this dimension, people can be spontaneous, genuine, and warm; at the other, they can be controlled, calm, flat, unresponsive, and stilted. The dimension of

In fairness, the MBTI is a quick and easy way to gather basic data about personality; when combined with other personality instruments such as the MMPI–2, the California Psychological Inventory, and the 16PF questionnaire (all of which will be discussed later), it can be useful in helping a skilled clinician judge important elements about an individual—for example, stress level (Ware, Rytting, & Jenkins, 1994). Research also shows that the MBTI can be used to assess the quality of therapeutic relationships and the extent to which people are able to perceive consumer messages, and that it can be helpful in designing techniques for classroom management (Carland et al., 1994; Claxton & McIntyre, 1994; Nelson & Stake, 1994). But, as we saw in Chapter 8, no single test score can reveal everything about an individual, as some might claim it can.

▲ *How do you think this teacher would score on the Extroversion–Introversion dimension of the MBTI? How about the boy in front of her?*

introversion or extroversion has to do with the extent to which people are withdrawn or open. Introverts are socially withdrawn and shy; extroverts are socially outgoing and open and like to meet new people. Eysenck's third dimension, *psychoticism*, is sometimes called tough- or tender-mindedness. At one extreme, people are troublesome, opposed to authority, sensation-seeking, insensitive, and risk-taking; at the other, they are warm, gregarious, and tender.

Eysenck argued that personality has a biological basis but emphasized that learning and experience also shape an individual's behavior. For example, he said that introverts and extroverts possess different levels of arousal in the cortex of the brain. Accordingly, persons of each type seek the amount of stimulation necessary to achieve their preferred level of arousal. For example, a person who prefers a low level of arousal, in which stimulation is less intense, may become a security guard or a librarian; a person who prefers a high level of arousal, which is reflected in outward behavior, may become a race-car driver or a politician. There are many people who may be characterized as sensation seekers; they climb mountains, ride dirt-bikes, gamble at the track, take drugs. The idea of a biological component to traits is hotly debated (Bullock & Gilliland, 1993; Heath & Martin, 1990). Most psychologists assert that some traits may be genetically passed on—at least to some extent (e.g., Plomin, 1994a)—but that environmental influences are so strong that most of a person's personality is shaped by day-to-day interactions.

The Big Five

Because of trait theory's popular appeal and commonsense approach, researchers today still find it attractive. However, rather than speaking of hundreds of traits or of a few types, many theorists now agree that there are five broad trait categories. These categories have become known as the *Big Five* (McCrae & Costa, 1987):

- *Extroversion–introversion,* or the extent to which people are social or unsocial, talkative or quiet, affectionate or reserved.
- *Agreeableness–antagonism,* or the extent to which people are good-natured or irritable, courteous or rude, flexible or stubborn, lenient or critical.
- *Conscientiousness–undirectedness,* or the extent to which people are reliable or undependable, careful or careless, punctual or late, well organized or disorganized.
- *Neuroticism–stability,* or the extent to which people are worriers or calm, nervous or at ease, insecure or secure.
- *Openness to experience,* or the extent to which people are open to experience or closed, independent or conforming, creative or uncreative, daring or timid.

Although dozens of traits can describe people, researchers think of the Big Five categories as "supertraits," the important dimensions that characterize personality (McCrea & Costa, 1990, 1994). Research has been supportive (Goldberg, 1990, 1993). However, you must remember this is only a model psychologists use to help them understand personality; it is not necessarily a final or complete description of personality. And not all researchers agree with the categories (Deniston & Ramanaiah, 1993; Wiggins & Trapnell, 1992). For example, recently researchers found evidence for two additional dimensions (excellent–ordinary, and evil–decent); the Big Five may soon be considered the Big Seven (Almagor, Tellegen, & Waller, 1995; Benet & Waller, 1995). Moreover, there are elements of personality that are not typed well by the Big Five, especially in the area of health-related concerns (Marshall et al., 1994); more research is needed into the meaning of the factors (Block, 1995).

Criticisms of Trait and Type Theories

Trait and type theories are appealing because they characterize people along important dimensions, providing simple explanations for how individuals behave. The idea of traits as accurate predictors of behavior has been supported by some research (Funder, 1995), but more often psychologists have criticized these theories on six basic fronts: First, they say trait theories are not actually personality theories. That is, they do not make good predictions about behaviors or explain why the behaviors occur. Some psychologists claim that trait theories are merely lists of behaviors arranged into a hierarchy. Second, most trait theories do not tell which personality characteristics last a lifetime and which are transient. Events that do not happen every day can alter traits and types. Third, since an individual's behavior depends on the situation or context, traits cannot predict behavior (Schmit & Ryan, 1993). Some researchers contend that the failure of trait theories to account for situational differences is a crucial weakness. Fourth, trait theories do not account for changing cultural elements. If you test the same person at 10-year intervals, the person's traits are likely to be different. But society will also be different, as will people's values and ideas. Trait and type theories do not account for these changing cultural norms. Fifth, not only does each culture change, but the differences between cultures (for example,

FOCUS

Review

- What does self-actualization mean in the context of Maslow's and Rogers's personality theories? pp. 422– 423
- Distinguish between a *trait* and a *type*. p. 425
- What is a fundamental criticism of trait and type theories? pp. 428–429

Think Critically

- Why would humanistic theory be seen as a reaction to Freudian theory?
- Many psychologists accept the Big Five, but perhaps they should think of a Big Six or Seven, or a Big Four. What do you think of the inclusiveness of the Big Five? Are five dimensions too many or not enough to characterize individual differences in personality?

between Western and Eastern cultures) are great, and trait theories do not account for them (Matsumoto, 1996). Finally, trait and type theories do not explain why people develop traits. Nor do they explain why traits change.

Trait and type theories continue to evolve, and debate continues as to the number of stable traits (Zuckerman, et al., 1993). However, psychologists want personality theories that (1) explain the development of personality, (2) predict maladjustment, and especially (3) explain why a person's behavior can be dramatically different in different situations. Theories that attempt to describe, explain, and predict behavior with more precision tend to be behavioral ones, the next major group of theories that we will examine.

Behavioral Approaches

Inner drives, psychic urges, and the need for self-actualization are hard-to-define concepts. Behaviorists assert that these concepts are not the proper subject matter of personality study. Behavioral theorists are practical. They believe that people often need to change aspects of their lives quickly and efficiently and that many people do not have the time, money, or energy for lengthy therapy or personality analysis. Consider the behavioral self-treatment Redford Williams proposes for Type A people—those hard-driving, ambitious, highly competitive people who, according to cardiologists, are at high risk of heart attacks (R. L. Williams, 1989). Williams says that in fact the lethal elements in Type A individuals are hostility and cynical mistrust, and he outlines steps such individuals can take to reduce hostility and develop a more trusting attitude and a healthier heart. One step is hostility monitoring—recording angry feelings in a "hostility" journal. Another is thought stopping—mentally yelling "Stop!" whenever hostile thoughts start forming. If behaviorists are correct in saying that personality is equivalent to the sum of a series of responses, then Williams's self-treatment program should help Type A individuals change their health-endangering personalities.

Key Behavioral Concepts

Behaviorists look at personality very differently than do any of the theorists described so far. They generally do not look inward; they look only at overt behavior. Behavioral approaches are often viewed as a reaction to the conceptual vagueness of traditional personality theories. Behavioral personality theorists assert that personality develops as people learn from their environments. The key word is *learn*. According to behaviorists, personality characteristics are not long-lasting and fixed; instead, they are subject to change. Thus, for behaviorists such as Skinner, personality is the sum of a person's learned tendencies.

Precisely Defined Elements. Behavioral theories tend to center on precisely defined elements, such as the relationship between stimuli and responses, the strength of stimuli, and the strength, duration, and timing of reinforcers. All of these can be tested in a laboratory or clinical setting. By focusing on stimuli and responses, behaviorists avoid conceptualizing human nature and concentrate instead on predicting behavior in specific circumstances. As a result, their assertions are more easily tested than are those of other theorists. Behaviorists see the development of personality simply as a change in response characteristics—a person learns new behaviors in response to new environments and stimuli.

Responses to Stimuli. For most behaviorists, the structural unit of personality is the response to stimuli. Any behavior, regardless of the situation, is seen as a response to a stimulus or a response in anticipation of reinforcement (or punishment). When an identifiable stimulus leads to an identifiable response, researchers predict that every time that stimulus occurs, so will the response. This stimulus–response relationship helps explain the constancy of personality. For example, whenever my wife has something unpleasant to discuss with me, she starts off the conversation in a really quiet voice, saying, "We need to talk about something." My response is often to tense up and become defensive. We have learned through repetition over the years that my initial response is predictable: The stimulus of a quiet voice announcing that we have to talk leads to my initial response of defensiveness.

Behavior Patterns. Using behavioral analysis, psychologists can discover how people develop behavior patterns (such as eating their vegetables or being hostile) and why behavior is in constant flux. The behavioral approach suggests that learning is the process that shapes personality and that learning takes place through experience. Because new experiences happen all the time, a person is constantly learning about the world and changing response patterns accordingly. Just as there are several learning principles involving the use of stimuli, responses, and reinforcement (for a review, see Chapter 5), there are several behavioral personality theories. These theories are based on classical conditioning, operant conditioning, and observational learning.

Classical Conditioning

Most people are fearful or anxious at some time. Some are fearful more often than not. How do people become fearful? What causes constant anxiety?

Many behavioral psychologists maintain that people develop fearfulness, anxiety, and a timid personality through classical conditioning, in which a neutral stimulus is paired with another stimulus that elicits some response. Eventually, the neutral stimulus can elicit the response on its own. For example, many people fear rats. Because rats are often encountered in dark cellars, a person may learn to fear dark cellars; that is, dark cellars become a feared stimulus. Later, the person may develop a generalized fear of dark places. If the first time the person sees a train, it's in a darkened station that looks like a cellar, the person may learn to fear trains. Classical conditioning thus allows researchers to explain the predictability of a person's day-to-day responses to specific stimuli. It describes the relationship between one stimulus and a person's expectation of another, as well as the predictable response the person makes (Rescorla, 1988).

Operant Conditioning

In operant conditioning, behavior is followed with a consequence, such as reinforcement or punishment. According to behaviorists, personality can be explained as spontaneous behavior that is reinforced. For example, when a person is affectionate and that behavior is reinforced with smiles and hugs, the person is likely to continue to be affectionate.

Behavioral psychologists often use the operant learning principles of reward and punishment to help children control themselves and shape their own personalities. Consider a problem of school discipline. A 10-year-old boy in a Florida public school frequently used obscenities (Lahey, McNees, & McNees, 1973). In an hour's time, the child would utter as many as 150 obscene words and phrases. To deal with the problem, whenever the child uttered an obscene word, the psychologists would take him out of the classroom for a minimum of 5 minutes and place him in a well-lit, empty room. They told him he would be placed in the time-out room every time he made an obscene utterance. In a few days, the average number of obscenities decreased dramatically, from more than 2 a minute to fewer than 5 an hour. Using operant conditioning, the researchers were able to modify an element of personality.

The time-out procedure is often used in learning situations in both classrooms and laboratories. As with any reinforcement or punishment procedure, the subject learns that the procedure is contingent on behavior. In the example, the time-out was punishment. The child found it rewarding to be in the classroom and punishing to be in the time-out room. Thus, to remain in the classroom and avoid being put in the time-out room, he learned not to utter obscenities.

Observational Learning

Observational learning theories assume that people learn new behaviors by watching the behaviors of others. The theory contends that an observer will imitate the behaviors of a model and thus develop a set of personality characteristics. Personality is thus seen as developing through the process of observation and imitation.

Observational learning theories stress the importance of the relationship between the observer and the model in eliciting imitative behavior. When children view the behavior of a parent or other important figure, their imitative behavior is significantly more extensive than when they observe the actions of someone less important to them. A son is more likely to adopt his father's hurried behavior than his neighbor's relaxed attitude, even if the boy spends roughly equal amounts of time in the presence of each.

People can learn abnormal, as well as acceptable, behavior and personality characteristics through imitation. In fact, the most notable behavior that people observe and then imitate may be violence on television. As we will see in Chapter 16, children who observe a violent TV program are more willing to hurt others after watching the program. If children observe people who are reinforced for violent, aggressive behavior, they are more likely to imitate that behavior than more socially desirable behaviors.

Observational learning theories assume that learning a new response through imitation can occur without reinforcement, but that later reinforcement acts to maintain such learned behavior and thus to maintain personality characteristics. Most people, for example, have observed aggressive, hostile behavior in others but still choose different ways to express emotions. Together, the imitative aspects of observational learning theories and the reinforcement properties of conditioned learning can account for most behaviors. For example, a daughter may become logical and forthright by watching her lawyer mother prepare arguments for court cases and seeing her win.

Researchers who focus on observational learning recognize that people choose to show some behaviors and to omit others. Accordingly, some researchers focus on observational learning in combination with another element—thought (cognition). The cognitive approaches to personality, which we will examine next, focus on the interaction of thoughts and behavior.

Cognitive Approaches

In some important ways, cognitive approaches to personality appeared as a reaction to strict behavioral models, adding a new dimension. The cognitive emphasis is on the interaction of thoughts and behavior. Cognitive approaches consider the uniqueness of human beings, especially of their thought processes, and assume that human beings are decision makers, planners, and evaluators of behavior.

Cognitive views have been influenced by the humanistic idea that people are essentially good and strive to be better. George Kelly (1955) was one of the first psychologists to assert that people make rational choices in trying to predict and manage events in the world. Many contemporary researchers claim that people can change their behavior, their conceptions of themselves, and their personalities in a short time if they are willing to change their thoughts.

Key Cognitive Concepts

From a cognitive point of view, the mere association of stimuli and responses is not enough for conditioning and learning to occur in human beings; thought processes also have to be involved. According to cognitive theory, a person exhibits learned behavior that is based on the situation and personal needs at a particular time. If thought and behavior are closely intertwined, then when something affects the person's thoughts, it should also affect his or her behavior. The man who mentally yells "Stop!" whenever his thoughts become hostile should be successful in quelling his disagreeable language.

One of the key concepts of the cognitive approach to personality is the idea that people develop self-schemata. As we saw in Chapters 6 and 11, a *schema* is a conceptual framework by which people make sense of the world. Self-schemata (*schemata* is the plural of *schema*) are series of ideas and self-knowledge that organize how people think about themselves. They are often global themes that help individuals define themselves. A man's self-schemata may comprise a self-schema that involves exercise, another that concerns his wife, and still others that are about schoolwork, family, and religious feelings. Cognitive researchers assert that people's self-schemata help shape their day-to-day behavior. They may affect people's adjustment, maladjustment, and ability to regulate their own behavior. Thus, someone who holds a self-schema for being in control of her emotions may find the death of a loved one a unique challenge to normal day-to-day coping mechanisms.

Over the years, a number of smaller cognitive theories (*microtheories*) have developed, dealing with how people perceive themselves and their relationship with the world. Many classic theories that attempt to explain all aspects of personality and behavior have been criticized because they are difficult to study scientifically. The ego in Freud's theory, for example, is not a physiological structure or state that can be manipulated or studied. Similarly, the concepts of self and of maximizing potential in Rogers's theory are difficult to measure and assess. As a reaction to imprecise grand theories, psychologists have developed smaller, better-researched theories. These microtheories, some of which follow a cognitive approach, account for specific behaviors in specific situations. Because of their smaller scope, they are easier to test.

We will consider three microtheories next: locus of control (developed by Julian Rotter), self-efficacy (Albert Bandura), and cognitive social learning (Albert Mischel). Each takes a different view and helps clarify different aspects of personality.

Locus of Control

One widely studied cognitive–behavioral theory is locus of control, introduced in the 1950s and 1960s and systematically developed by Julian Rotter and Herbert Lefcourt. *Locus of control* involves the extent to which individuals believe that a reinforcement or an outcome is contingent on their own behavior or personal characteristics versus the extent to which they believe that a reinforcement or outcome is a function of luck, chance, or fate or is simply unpredictable (Lefcourt, 1992; Rotter, 1990). Rotter focused on whether people place their locus of control inside themselves (internal) or in their environments (external). Locus of control influences how people view the world and how they identify the causes of success or failure in their lives. In an important way, it reflects people's personalities—their views of the world and their reactions to it.

To examine locus of control, Rotter developed a test consisting of a series of statements about oneself and other people. To determine whether your locus of control is internal or external, ask yourself to what extent you agree with the statements in Table 12.4. People with an internal locus of control (shown by their choice of statements) feel a need to control their environment. They are more likely to engage in preventive health measures and dieting than are external people. College

TABLE 12.4 *Statements Reflecting Internal versus External Locus of Control*

Internal Locus of Control		External Locus of Control
People's misfortunes result from the mistakes they make.	*versus*	Many of the unhappy things in people's lives are partly due to bad luck.
With enough effort, we can wipe out political corruption.	*versus*	It is difficult to have much control over the things politicians do in office.
There is a direct connection between how hard I study and the grade I get.	*versus*	Sometimes I can't understand how teachers arrive at the grades they give.
What happens to me is my own doing.	*versus*	Sometimes I feel that I don't have enough control over the direction my life is taking.

students characterized as internal are more likely than others to profit from psychotherapy and to show high academic achievement (Lefcourt & Davidson-Katz, 1991). Similarly, hospital nurses characterized as having a strong internal locus of control are more likely to want and attempt to reform unjust situations (Parker, 1993). In contrast, people with an external locus of control believe they have little control over their lives. A college student characterized as external may attribute a poor grade to a lousy teacher, feeling there was nothing he or she could have done to get a good grade. Individuals who develop an internal locus of control, on the other hand, feel they can master any course they take because they believe that through hard work they can do well in any subject.

People develop expectations based on their beliefs about the sources of reinforcement in their environments. These expectations lead to the specific behaviors psychologists call personality. Reinforcement of these behaviors in turn strengthens expectancy and leads to increased belief in internal or external control (see Figure 12.3).

Locus of control integrates personality theory, expectancy theories, and reinforcement theory. It describes several specific behaviors but is not comprehensive enough to explain all, or even most, of an individual's behavior. For example, people often develop disproportionately negative thoughts about themselves and acquire a poor sense of self-esteem. Sometimes this is shown in the behavior pattern known as

FIGURE 12.3

Locus of Control

A person's general expectations about life are determined in a three-part process: Specific expectancies result in specific behaviors, which are reinforced. This cycle eventually leads to a general expectancy about life, which underlies either an internal or external locus of control.

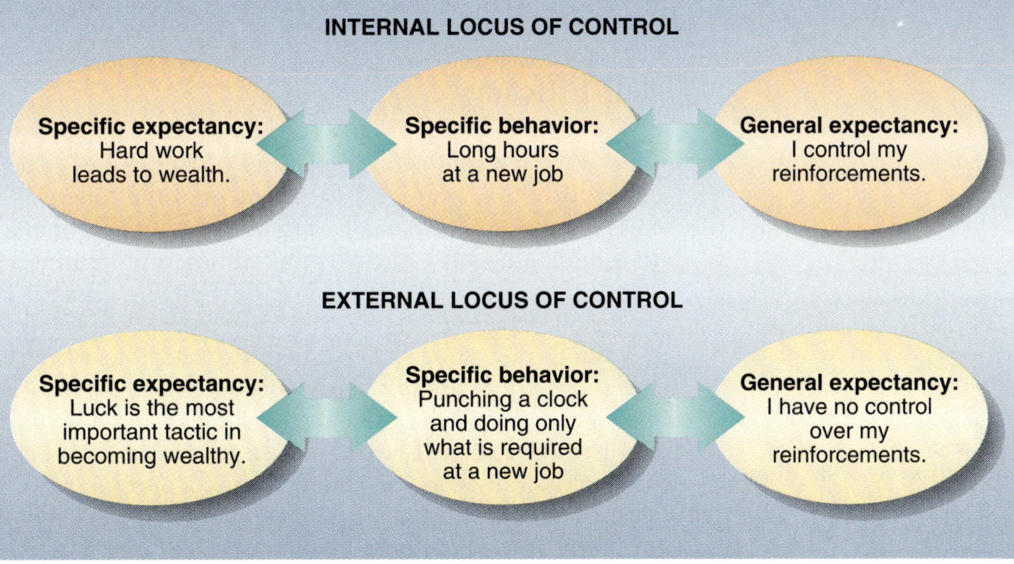

APPLICATIONS

Overcoming Shyness

About 40 percent of adults report being shy, and for at least 2 million adults, **shyness** is a serious behavior problem that inhibits personal, social, and professional growth. Shy people show extreme anxiety in social situations; they are extremely reticent and often overly concerned with how others view them. They fear acting foolishly; as a consequence, they may develop clammy hands, dry mouth, excessive perspiration, trembling, nausea, blushing, and a need to go to the bathroom frequently. Shyness makes people avoid social situations and makes them speak softly, when they speak at all. Shy people also avoid approaching other people (Asendorpf, 1989). Most shy people report that they have always been shy, and half of all shy people feel they are shyer than other people in similar situations (Carducci & Stein, 1988).

Personality researchers contend that certain personality traits, including shyness, are long-lasting. Jerome Kagan found that 2- and 3-year-olds who were extremely cautious and shy tended to remain that way for years (Kagan, 1989). Daniels and Plomin (1985) also found an important relationship between adopted infants' shyness at 2 years of age and the shyness of their biological mothers. This finding suggests that genetic factors play an important role in shyness (Lykken et al., 1992).

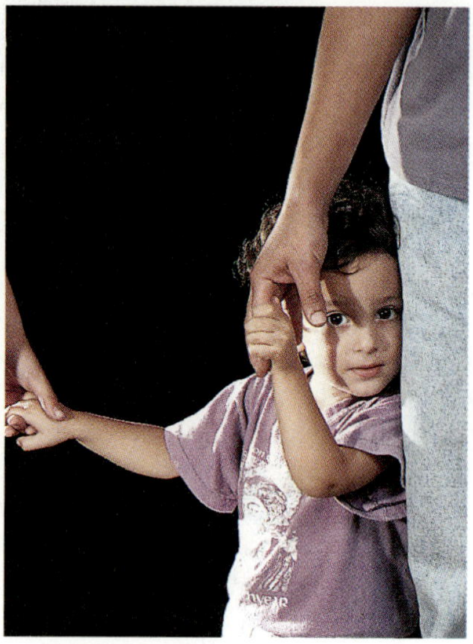

Although Kagan also suggests that extreme shyness may have a biological basis, he believes that shyness emerges because people develop distorted self-concepts—negative views about their competencies and a lack of self-esteem. Such individuals view themselves in a poor light, as having few social graces. These thoughts, combined with such actions as withdrawal and nervousness, set a person up for social failure. When negative events occur, the person then says, "See, I was right." A person's thoughts about her or his shyness, bodily reactions, and social behaviors thus perpetuate the shyness.

Treatment programs exist to help people overcome extreme shyness (Carducci & Stein, 1988). If you are shy, here are some things you can do:

- Rehearse what you want to say before speaking.
- Build your self-esteem by focusing on your good points.
- Accept who you are.
- Practice smiling and making eye contact.
- Observe the behavior of others whom you admire, and copy it.
- Think about how others feel; remember that about 40 percent of all people feel the way you do.
- Begin some relaxation training, perhaps involving self-hypnosis, yoga, or even biofeedback.
- Think positively; having a positive attitude about yourself and other people can go a long way toward helping to overcome shyness.

shyness, which is discussed in *Applications*. Bandura's theory, which we examine next, specifically addresses people's thoughts about their own effectiveness.

Self-Efficacy

One of the most influential cognitive microtheories of personality was developed by Albert Bandura, who is a past president of the American Psychological Association. His conception of personality began with observational learning theory and the idea that human beings observe, think about, and imitate behavior (Bandura, 1977a). Bandura played a major role in reintroducing thought processes into learning and personality theory.

Bandura argued that people's expectations of mastery and achievement and their convictions about their own effectiveness determine the types of behavior they will engage in and the amount of risk they will undertake (Bandura, 1977a, 1977b). He used the term **self-efficacy** to describe a person's belief about whether he or she can successfully engage in and execute a specific behavior. Judgments about self-efficacy determine how much effort people will expend and how long they will persist in the face of obstacles (Bandura, 1986).

Shyness: Extreme anxiety in individuals who are socially reticent and often overly concerned with how they appear to others, often leading to avoidance of social situations.

Self-efficacy: A person's belief about whether he or she can successfully engage in and execute a specific behavior.

A strong sense of self-efficacy allows people to feel free to select, influence, and even construct the circumstances of their own lives. Also, people's perceived self-efficacy in managing a situation heightens their sense that they can control it (Bandura & Wood, 1989). Thus, people who have a high level of self-efficacy are more likely than others to attribute success to variables within themselves rather than to chance factors and are more likely to pursue their own goals (Bandura, 1988; McAuley, Duncan, & McElroy, 1989). Because people can think about their motivation, and even their own thoughts, they can effect changes in themselves and persevere during tough times (Bandura, 1989; Haaga & Stewart, 1992).

Bad luck or nonreinforcing experiences can damage a developing sense of self-efficacy. Observation of positive, prosocial models during the formative years, on the other hand, can help people to develop a strong sense of self-efficacy that will encourage and reinforce them in directing their own lives. Bandura's theory allows individual flexibility in behavior. People are not locked into specific responses to specific stimuli, as some strict behaviorists might assert. According to Bandura, people choose the behaviors they will imitate, and they are free to adapt their behavior to any situation. Self-efficacy both determines and flows from feelings of self-worth. Accordingly, people's sense of self-efficacy determines how they may present themselves to other people. For example, a man whom others view as successful may not share that view, and a man who has achieved little of note to society may consider himself a capable and worthy person; each of these men will present himself as he sees himself (as a failure or a worthy person), not as others see him.

Bandura's theory is optimistic. It is a long way from Freud's view, which argues that conflicting biologically based forces determine human behavior. It is also a long way from a strict behavioral theory, which suggests that environmental contingencies shape behavior. Bandura believes that human beings have choices, that they direct the course of their lives. He also believes that society, parents, experiences, and even luck help shape those lives.

Gender and Self-Efficacy. Men and women develop differently, both physiologically and socially, and this difference affects their self-efficacy. As children, boys are more likely than girls to play in large groups where opportunities for discussion are minimized; girls, in contrast, more frequently play in small groups in which interpersonal awareness is more likely to be heightened. In addition, boys may be encouraged more than girls to become involved in competitive, achievement-related activities (L. D. Cohn, 1991). In general, adult males have higher self-esteem than females, and this gender difference stays fairly constant across ages, educational levels, and cultures (Feingold, 1994).

Self-efficacy is affected by the cultural variables that define men's and women's roles. Research that has manipulated participants' view of performance on various tasks shows that a person's sense of self-efficacy is related to the person's fulfillment of culturally mandated, gender-appropriate norms (Josephs, Markus, & Tafarodi, 1992). Men more than women focus on independence and distinctiveness; women more than men focus on interdependence and good relations. From these different focuses, both men and women derive a sense of self-efficacy.

Mischel's Cognitive Social Learning

Like Bandura, Walter Mischel claims that thought is crucial in determining human behavior; but Mischel also believes that both past experiences and current reinforcement are important. What's more, Mischel is an *interactionist*—he focuses on the interaction of people and their environment (Mischel, 1983). Mischel and other cognitive theorists (e.g., Cantor & Kihlstrom, 1982) argue that people respond flexibly to various situations. They change their responses on the basis of their past experiences and their current assessment of the present situation. This process of adjustment is called *self-regulation*. People make subtle adjustments in their tone of

THE RESEARCH PROCESS

Women's Personality Changes from College to Midlife

Does personality change over time, or does it stay the same from adolescence through old age? Are personality changes the same for men and women? Trait theorists assume that personality remains much the same over the life span. Shy people stay shy; high school pranksters become retirement home pranksters. Stage theorists such as Erik Erikson and Daniel Levinson (Chapter 11), on the other hand, contend that people change during their life span. These psychologists believe in an adult life cycle. But are there gender differences in the course of personality development? Many researchers think there are, particularly before and during adolescence (L. D. Cohn, 1991).

Hypotheses. Unfortunately, most personality and adult life cycle studies have been conducted with men—who represent less than half of the population. Do women's personalities change in a similar way? Or do the personalities of career-oriented women change and those of family-oriented women stay the same? Helson and Moane (1987), of the University of California at Berkeley, studied the personalities of a group of women, starting when the women were of college age and continuing to when they were at midlife. In a second study, husbands and wives were studied (Wink & Helson, 1993). A third study compared three samples of women who were adults in the 1950s, early 1960s, and late 1960s (Helson, Stewart, & Ostrove, 1995). The primary objective was to discover whether personality changes are obvious across different life paths and whether those changes support theories of adult development and personality. A second objective was to compare the life cycles of men and women, since previous long-term studies had failed to address that vital issue. The researchers asked whether life cycles for adulthood need to be rethought. Do women have midlife transitions, as men do?

Method. Helson and Moane began their work in 1958 at Mills College, a private women's college located in Oakland, California. They gathered information from the same 81 women at ages 21, 27, and 43. In using this longitudinal method, they studied a single group of people at different times to determine whether changes had occurred over time. (For a review of this method, see Chapter 10, page 341.) The researchers used several measures of personality, including the California Psychological Inventory (CPI). The CPI, which is commonly used to study people from midadolescence to old age, is a test of normal personality. Designed to assess effectiveness in interpersonal functioning, it examines confidence, independence, responsibility, socialization, self-control, tolerance, and flexibility, among other dimensions.

Correlational Results. The results, reported as correlations among the different measures of personality, showed interesting stabilities and changes. For example, when the women were between the ages of 21 and 27, they took control of their lives, acknowledged differences between the way the world ought to be and the way it was, and scored higher on tolerance, social maturity, and femininity than they did later in life. At ages 27 to 43, they scored higher in the areas of dominance, independence, and confidence, but lower in flexibility and femininity. The changes from 27 to 43 were greater than the changes from 21 to 27. As the women grew older, they became more organized, committed, and work-oriented, but less open to change.

The results of this study are consistent with adult life cycle theories of development that have focused on men. From ages 21 to 43, there were increases in self-discipline and commitment to duties; this typically occurs with men, too. The women became more confident, independent, and work-oriented. Until age 27, the

voice and overt behavior (their personality), depending on the context in which they find themselves. Those who tend to be warm, caring, and attentive, for example, can in certain situations become hostile and aggressive.

People's personalities, and particularly their responses to any given stimulus, are determined by the following (Mischel, 1979): *competencies* (what people know and can do), *encoding strategies* (the way they process, attend to, and select information), *expectancies* (their anticipation of outcomes), *personal values* (the importance they attach to various aspects of life), and *self-regulatory systems* (the systems of rules people have established for themselves to guide their behavior).

Mischel has had a great impact on psychological thought, because he has challenged researchers to consider the idea that traits alone cannot predict behavior, that the context of the situation must be considered. The context means not only the immediate situation but also the culture in which a person lives and was raised, as well as other variables such as the gender and age of the person whose behavior is being predicted.

changes were small; but after age 27, the women focused less on gender-specific tasks such as child care and more on gaining independence and confidence and on developing a career. Later in life, women became happier than their husbands were, but both men and women were happier in late adulthood than in their child-rearing years (Wink & Helson, 1993).

Conclusions. Like Daniel Levinson (1996), both Helson and Moane (1987) and Wink and Helson (1993) maintain that women's and men's personalities change in consistent and predictable ways between the ages of 21 (young adulthood) and 43 (middle age). They believe, for example, that a career requires a person to develop skills, confidence, and insight into others—things that were not necessary at earlier life stages for some women. From the researchers' view, personality is not static; rather, personality is a constantly evolving set of skills and abilities acquired to cope with the demands and dilemmas that face maturing individuals. This view is consistent with that of stage theorists like Levinson, but it presents problems for trait theorists, who assert that personality is stable during the life span (e.g., McCrae & Costa, 1994).

Implications. The researchers conducted their studies during a time of rapid change in women's roles in society, from 1960 through 1985. Were the changes that occurred then similar to the changes that are taking place now or to the changes that will occur in the next 20 years? Is the United States likely to experience a decade similar to the one that saw the Vietnam War, the women's liberation movement, and Watergate? Women aged 21 to 27 today may not show the same patterns. Research is addressing various possibilities. For example, Helson and Picano (1990) have shown that women who filled more traditional roles early in life but later joined the labor force are able to adapt their personalities to new sets of demands; this is especially true if they are well educated and seek independence—traits more typically found in women of the most recent generations than in older, more traditionally raised participants (Helson, Stewart, & Ostrove, 1995).

The 1960–1985 research did not specifically address the implications for personality of certain lifestyle variations; many women, for example, opt for a career first and children later. Socioeconomic status and societal changes determine so many lifestyle, educational, and work issues that they need to be examined, too. Further, new research must consider results in a historical context, taking into account changing political, social, and moral values. Last, it will take a longitudinal study of college women of the 1990s traced over 20 years to determine whether Helson and Moane's findings are still valid for today's generation.

The Research Process discusses how two researchers studied the constancy of personality by examining the behavioral characteristics of a group of women over a period of 20 years.

Cognitive Theories Evolve

From the view of cognitive personality theorists, human uniqueness can best be explained by the idea that reinforcement, past experiences, current feelings, future expectations, and subjective values all influence people's responses to their environments. Human beings have characteristic ways of responding, but those ways—their personalities—change, depending on specific circumstances.

Cognitive theories of personality are well researched but not yet complete; they do not, for example, clearly explain the development of personality from childhood to adulthood. They are also not well integrated. Bandura, for example, has shifted

BUILDING TABLE 12.2

Psychoanalytic, Humanistic, Trait and Type, Behavioral, and Cognitive Approaches to Personality

APPROACH	MAJOR PROPONENT	CORE OF PERSONALITY	STRUCTURE OF PERSONALITY	DEVELOPMENT	CAUSE OF PROBLEMS
Psychoanalytic	Sigmund Freud	Maximizes gratification while minimizing punishment or guilt; instinctual unconscious urges direct behavior	Id, ego, superego	Five stages: oral, anal, phallic, latency, genital	Imbalances between the id, ego, and superego resulting in fixations
Humanistic	Carl Rogers	Actualizes, maintains, and enhances the experiences of life through the process of self-actualization	Self	Process of cumulative self-actualization and development of sense of self-worth	Wide incongruence between self and concept of ideal self
Trait and Type	Gordon Allport	Organizes responses in characteristic modes	Traits	Process of learning new traits	Having learned faulty or inappropriate traits
Behavioral	B. F. Skinner	Reduction of social and biological needs that energize behavior through the emission of learned responses	Responses	Process of learning new responses	Having learned faulty or inappropriate behaviors
Cognitive	Several, including Rotter, Bandura, and Mischel	Responses depend on a changing environment, and the person responds after thinking about the context of the environment	Responses determined by thoughts	Process of thinking about new responses	Inappropriate thoughts or faulty reasoning

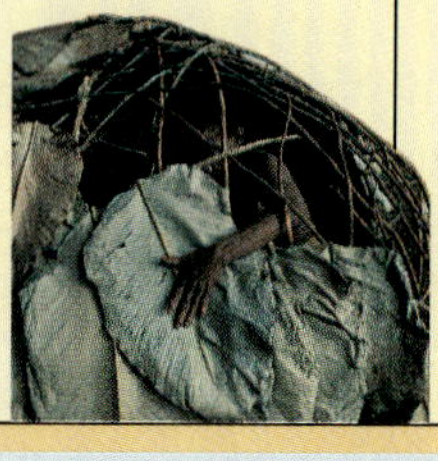

his focus from observational learning to self-regulation to self-efficacy without tying the threads of those research areas together. What this incompleteness and lack of coherence signify is that personality research and theory are still in their infancy, with further research and new ideas needed to tie up loose ends and generate more complete, sophisticated theories.

Personality theories are diverse, and their explanations and accounts of specific behaviors vary sharply; each one views the development of personality and maladjustment from a different vantage point. See Building Table 12.2 for an overall summary of the theories presented in this chapter.

When a practitioner, regardless of orientation, meets a client, there are several ways the client can be evaluated. These techniques are the focus of psychological assessment, the topic we will consider next.

FOCUS

Review

- Identify three key behavioral concepts used to explain personality development. p. 432
- What is locus of control? p. 432
- Why is Mischel called an interactionist? p. 435

Think Critically

- For a cognitive psychologist, what are some possible explanations of the constancy of personality?
- If a person has an internal locus of control, under what conditions is he or she more likely to have a strong sense of self-efficacy?

Personality Assessment

Assessment is the process of evaluating individual differences among human beings by means of techniques such as tests, interviews, observations, and recordings of physiological processes. Psychologists who conduct assessments are constantly seeking ways to evaluate personality in order to explain behavior, to diagnose and classify maladjusted people, and to develop treatment plans when necessary. Many individuals and organizations give tests—school systems often give IQ tests, for example—but these are not assessments. An assessment is done by a psychologist who has a relationship with a client, and the type of examination used is determined by the client's needs (Matarazzo, 1990). Often, more than one assessment procedure is needed to provide all the necessary information, and many psychologists administer a group, or *battery*, of tests. The goal of the examiner is to use a variety of available tests so that when the information taken together is added up, an intelligent, informed conclusion can be drawn. As Kaufman (1990, p. 29) asserts, "Psychologists need to be shrewd detectives to uncover test interpretations that are truly 'individual' . . . and will ultimately help the person referred for evaluation."

A psychologist may assess personality with the Minnesota Multiphasic Personality Inventory–2nd Edition (MMPI–2) (discussed later in this section), intelligence with the WAIS–R (described in Chapter 8), and a specific skill (such as coordination) with some other specific test. More confidence can be placed in the data from several tests than in the data from a single test; furthermore, with several measures, current levels of functioning are better characterized. Hundreds of psychological tests exist; there are more than 100 tests just for measuring the various elements of anxiety. The purpose of the testing determines the type of tests administered.

Objective Personality Tests

Next to intelligence tests, the most widely given tests are *objective personality tests*. These tests, sometimes termed *personality inventories*, generally consist of true/false or check-the-best-answer questions. The aims of objective personality tests vary. Raymond Cattell developed a test called the 16PF (16PF refers to 16 personality

Assessment: The process of evaluating individual differences among human beings by means of tests and direct observation of behavior.

TABLE 12.5 *The Clinical and Validity Scales of the MMPI–2*

Scale Name	Interpretation
Clinical Scales	
1. Hypochondriasis (Hs)	High scorers reflect an exaggerated concern about their physical health.
2. Depression (D)	High scorers are usually depressed, despondent, and distressed.
3. Hysteria (Hy)	High scorers complain often about physical symptoms, with no apparent organic cause.
4. Psychopathic deviate (Pd)	High scorers show a disregard for social and moral standards.
5. Masculinity/femininity (Mf)	Extreme scorers show "traditional" masculine or feminine attitudes and values.
6. Paranoia (Pa)	High scorers demonstrate extreme suspiciousness and feelings of persecution.
7. Psychasthenia (Pt)	High scorers tend to be highly anxious, rigid, tense, and worrying.
8. Schizophrenia (Sc)	High scorers tend to be socially withdrawn and to engage in bizarre and unusual thinking.
9. Hypomania (Ma)	High scorers are highly emotionally excitable, energetic, and impulsive.
10. Social introversion (S)	High scorers tend to be modest, self-effacing, and shy.
Validity Scales	
1. Cannot say (?)	High scorers may be evasive in filling out the questionnaire.
2. Lie (L)	High scorers attempt to present themselves in a very favorable light and possibly tell lies to do so.
3. Infrequency (F)	High scorers are presenting themselves in a particularly bad way and may well be "faking bad."
4. Defensiveness (K)	High scorers may be very defensive in filling out the questionnaire.

factors) to screen job applicants and to examine individuals who fall within a normal range of personality functioning. The California Psychological Inventory (CPI) is used primarily to identify and assess normal aspects of personality. Using a large sample of normal subjects as a reference group, it examines personality traits such as sociability, self-control, and responsibility.

One of the most widely used and best-researched personality tests is the Minnesota Multiphasic Personality Inventory–2nd Edition (the MMPI–2). The original MMPI was widely used, and the second edition, published in 1989, is considered a major revision. The MMPI–2 consists of 567 true/false statements that focus on attitudes, feelings, motor disturbances, and bodily complaints. A series of subscales examine different aspects of functioning and measure the truthfulness of the examinee's responses; these subscales, called the clinical and validity scales, are shown in Table 12.5. In 1992 a special version of the MMPI was developed for adolescents, called the MMPI–A. Items on this test cover adolescent issues such as eating disorders, substance abuse, and family and school problems. Typical statements on the MMPI–2 are as follows:

> I tire easily.
>
> I become very anxious before examinations.

I worry about sex matters.

I become bored easily.

The MMPI–2 can be administered individually or to a group. The test takes 90 minutes to complete and can be scored in less than a half-hour. It provides a profile that lets psychologists assess an individual's current level of functioning and characteristic way of dealing with the world, and it provides a description of some specific personality characteristics. The MMPI–2 also enables psychologists to make reasonable predictions about a person's ability to function in specific situations, such as working in a mental hospital or as a security guard. Generally, the MMPI–2 is used as a screening device for maladjustment. Its norms are based on the profiles of thousands of normal people and a smaller group of psychiatric patients. Each scale tells how most normal individuals score. In general, a score significantly above normal may be considered evidence of maladjustment.

Nearly 5,000 published studies have examined the validity and reliability of the original MMPI. For the most part, these studies have supported the MMPI as a valid and useful predictive tool. The MMPI–2 has a much larger sample (2,600 people) of subjects for standardization, and these subjects are also more representative of the overall population than were the initial group of subjects. The MMPI–2 includes questions that focus on eating disorders and drug abuse. Older questions that had a gender bias have been revised. Because many of the test's traditional features remain unchanged, the refinements and modifications should only improve its predictive validity (Butcher et al., 1990). Yet the MMPI–2 is by no means a perfect instrument for valid predictions about future behavior; it should be considered as only one in a battery of tests (Helmes & Reddon, 1993).

Projective Tests

The fundamental idea underlying the use of projective tests is that a person's unconscious motives direct daily thoughts and behavior. **Projective tests** are devices or instruments used to assess personality in which an examinee is shown a standard set of ambiguous stimuli and asked to respond in an unrestricted manner. The examinees are assumed to project their unconscious feelings, drives, and motives onto the ambiguous stimuli. Clinicians assess the deeper levels of an examinee's personality structure and uncover motives of which the individual may not be aware. Projective tests are used when it is important to determine whether the examinee is trying to hide something from the psychologist. They tend to be less reliable than objective personality tests, but they help complete a picture of psychological functioning.

FIGURE 12.4

The Rorschach Inkblot Test

In a Rorschach Inkblot Test, the psychologist asks a person to describe what he or she sees in an inkblot such as this one. From the person's descriptions, the psychologist makes inferences about his or her drives, motivations, and unconscious conflicts.

Rorschach Inkblot Test. One widely used projective test is the *Rorschach Inkblot Test* (see Figure 12.4). Ten inkblots are shown to the person, one at a time. Five are black and white, two have some red ink, and three have various pastel colors. The blots are symmetrical, with a specific shape or form. Examinees tell the clinician what they see in the design, and a detailed report of the response is made for later interpretation. Aiken (1988, p. 390) reports a typical response:

> My first impression was a big bug, a fly maybe. I see in the background two facelike figures pointing toward each other as if they're talking. It also has a resemblance to a skeleton—the pelvis area. I see a cute little bat right in the middle. The upper half looks like a mouse.

After the inkblots have been shown, the examiner asks specific questions, such as these: "Describe the facelike figures." "What were the figures talking about?"

Projective tests: Personality-assessing devices or instruments in which examinees are shown a standard set of ambiguous stimuli and asked to respond in an unrestricted manner.

Although norms are available for responses, skilled interpretation and good clinical judgment are necessary for placing an individual's responses in a meaningful context. Long-term predictions can be formulated only with great caution (Exner, Thomas, & Mason, 1985) because of a lack of substantive supporting research (Wood, Nezworski, & Stejskal, 1996).

Thematic Apperception Test. The *Thematic Apperception Test* (TAT) is much more structured than the Rorschach. (The TAT was discussed in Chapter 9 as one way to assess a person's need for achievement.) It consists of black-and-white pictures, each depicting one or more people in an ambiguous situation; examinees are asked to tell a story describing the situation. Specifically, they are asked what led up to the situation, what will happen in the future, and what the people are thinking and feeling. The TAT is particularly useful as part of a battery of tests to assess a person's characteristic way of dealing with others and of interacting with the world.

To some extent, projective tests have a bad reputation among nonpsychologists. Most argue that the interpretation of pictures is too subjective and prone to error. Practicing clinicians, even when they use projective tests, are likely to rely heavily on behavioral assessment approaches, discussed next.

Behavioral Assessment

Traditionally, *behavioral assessment* focused on overt behaviors that could be examined directly. Today, practitioners and researchers examine cognitive activity as well. Their aim is to gather information in order to both diagnose maladjustment and to prescribe treatment. Four popular and widely used behavioral assessment techniques are behavioral assessment interviews, naturalistic observation, self-monitoring, and neuropsychological assessment.

Behavioral Assessment Interviews. Any psychological assessment is likely to begin with an interview. Interviews are personal, giving the client (and the client's family) an opportunity to express feelings, facts, and experiences that might not be expressed through other assessment procedures. Interviews yield important information about the client's family situation, occupational stresses, and other events that affect the behavior being examined. They also allow psychologists to evaluate the client's motivations as well as to inform the client about the assessment process.

Behavioral assessment interviews tend to be systematic and structured, focusing on overt and current behaviors and paying attention to the situations in which these behaviors occur. The interviewer will ask the examinee about the events that led up to a specific response, how the examinee felt while making the response, and whether the same response might occur in other situations. Through this type of interview, the clinician has the opportunity to select the problems to be dealt with in therapy and to set treatment goals. Many clinicians consider their first interview with a client a key component in the assessment process. Interviews reveal only what the interviewee wishes to disclose, however, and are subject to bias on the part of the interviewer. Nonetheless, when followed up with other behavioral measures, interviews are a good starting point.

Naturalistic Observation. In behavioral assessment, naturalistic observation involves two or more observers entering a client's natural environment and recording the occurrence of specified behaviors at predetermined intervals. In a personality assessment, for example, psychologists might observe how often a child in a classroom uses obscene words or how often a hospitalized patient refers to her depressed state. The purpose of naturalistic observation as a behavioral assessment technique is to observe people without interfering with their behavior. The strength of the approach is in providing information that might otherwise be unavailable or difficult to piece together. For example, observation can help psychologists learn what sequences of events can lead up to an outburst of antisocial behaviors.

Naturalistic observation is not without its problems, however. How does a researcher record behavior in a home setting without being observed? Do naturalistic samples of behavior in one setting represent interactions in other settings? Does the observer have any biases, make inaccurate judgments, or collect inadequate data? Although naturalistic observation is not perfect, it is a powerful technique.

Self-Monitoring. **Self-monitoring** is an assessment procedure in which a person systematically counts and records the frequency and duration of specific behaviors in himself or herself. One person might record the number and duration of evidences of specific personality traits—or of such symptoms as migraine headaches, backaches, or feelings of panic. Another person might self-monitor his or her eating or sleeping patterns, sexual behavior, or smoking. Self-monitoring is inexpensive, easy to do, and applicable to a variety of problems. It reveals information that might otherwise be inaccessible, and it enables practitioners to probe the events that preceded the monitored activity to see if some readily identifiable pattern exists. In addition, self-monitoring helps clients become more aware of their own behaviors and the situations in which they occur.

FOCUS

Review

- What evidence is there that the MMPI–2 is a good test of potential maladjustment? p. 441
- What is the goal of a projective test? p. 441
- Identify the techniques of behavioral assessment. pp. 442–443

Think Critically

- What do the TAT and the Rorschach Inkblot Test aim to do, and do you think they achieve that goal?
- In what ways do you think a personality test cannot accurately characterize your personality?

Self-monitoring: An assessment procedure in which a person systematically counts and records the frequency and duration of specific behaviors in himself or herself.

Neuropsychological Assessment. Personality changes and some forms of maladjustment often result from a brain disorder or a malfunction in the nervous system (see Figure 12.5 for examples). The newest way to detect such disorders is

FIGURE 12.5

Some Brain–Behavior Characteristics for Selected Sites in the Brain

(Adapted from Cohen et al., 1988.)

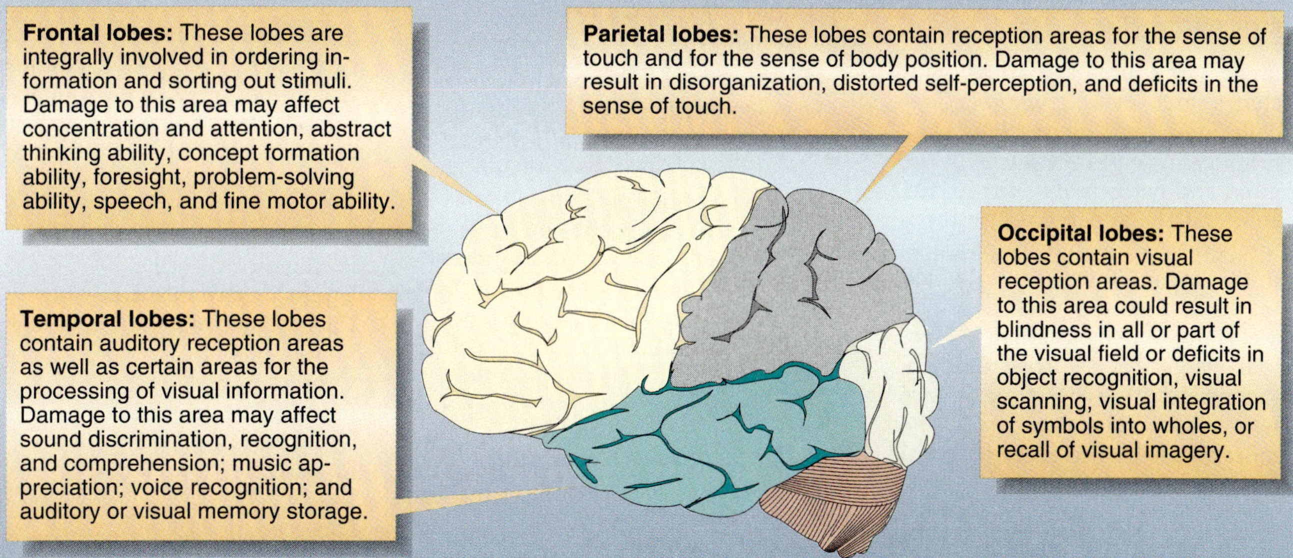

neuropsychological assessment. (Neurologists are physicians who study the physiology of the brain and its disorders; neuropsychologists are psychologists who study the brain and its disorders as they relate to behavior.) Though neuropsychology is a traditional area in experimental psychology, employment of its techniques by practitioners is a new development. Practitioners now routinely watch for signs of neuropsychological disorders. The signs may become evident through the use of traditional assessment devices such as histories (a history of headaches, for example), intelligence tests (showing slow reaction times), or observation of the client during a session (the occurrence of head motions or muscle spasms). Thus, if a child who makes obscene gestures or remarks frequently and inappropriately accompanies them with facial tics, the practitioner may suspect the existence of the neurological disorder known as Tourette's disorder, in which such behaviors are often evident. Psychologists who see evidence of neuropsychological deficits often refer the client with the problem to a neuropsychologist or neurologist for further evaluation.

Summary and Review

Psychoanalytic Theory

What are the fundamental assumptions about human behavior and the mind on which Freud's theory is based?

- *Psychic determinism* suggests that all thoughts, feelings, actions, gestures, and speech are determined by some action or event that happened to an individual in the past. *Unconscious motivation* suggests that behavior is determined by desires, goals, and internal states of which an individual is unaware. Freud also theorized that people are constantly in conflict because of two basic instinctual drives buried deep within the unconscious—life, which prominently features sex and sexual energy, and death, which features aggression. p. 411

- Freud's structure of *personality* includes three levels: *conscious, preconscious*, and *unconscious*. The primary structural elements of the mind and personality—the id, the ego, and the superego—are three forces that reside, fully or partially, in the unconscious. The *id*, which works through the pleasure principle, is the source of human instinctual energy. The *ego* tries to satisfy the instinctual needs in accordance with reality. The *superego* is the moral branch or aspect of mental functioning. pp. 412–413

- Freud described the development of personality in terms of five consecutive stages: oral, anal, phallic, latency, and genital. In the *oral stage* newborns' instincts are focused on the mouth—their primary pleasure-seeking center. In the *anal stage* children learn to control the immediate gratification obtained through defecation and become responsive to the demands of society. In the *phallic stage* children obtain gratification primarily from the genitals. During this stage, children pass through the *Oedipus complex* (or Electra complex). In the *latency stage*, sexual urges are inactive. The *genital stage* is Freud's last stage of personality development, during which the sexual conflicts of childhood resurface at puberty and are resolved in adolescence. pp. 413–416

What is the fundamental function of all of Freud's defense mechanisms?

- *Defense mechanisms* such as *projection, denial*, *reaction formation*, *sublimation*, and *rationalization* are ways to reduce anxiety by distorting one's perceptions of reality. Defense mechanisms allow the ego to deal with anxiety. For Freud, the most important defense mechanism is *repression*—in which people block anxiety-provoking feelings from conscious awareness and push them into the unconscious. pp. 416–417

To what fundamental assumptions of Freud did the neo-Freudians react?

- A *neo-Freudian* (such as Jung or Adler) is a psychologist who modified or varied some of the basic ideas of Freud; these theorists usually attributed a greater influence to cultural and interpersonal factors than did Freud. Some neo-Freudians argued that Freud overemphasized sex and left out many key issues. Other neo-Freudians asserted that the ego has more of a role than Freud thought in controlling behavior and shaping personality. p. 419

- Jung emphasized unconscious processes as determinants of behavior and believed that each person houses past events in the unconscious. The *collective unconscious* is a collection of emotionally charged ideas and images that have rich meaning and symbolism. In Adler's theory, people strive for superiority or perfection. This tendency is often prompted by feelings of inferiority. According to Adler, individuals develop a lifestyle that allows them to express their goals in the context of human society. pp. 419–420

KEY TERMS

Personality, p. 410
Psychic determinism, p. 411
Unconscious motivation, p. 411
Libido, p. 411
Conscious, p. 412
Preconscious, p. 412
Unconscious, p. 412
Id, p. 412
Ego, p. 412
Superego, p. 413
Oral stage, p. 413
Anal stage, p. 415

Phallic stage, p. 415
Oedipus complex, p. 415
Latency stage, p. 415
Genital stage, p. 416
Fixation, p. 416
Defense mechanism, p. 416
Repression, p. 416
Projection, p. 416
Denial, p. 416
Reaction formation, p. 416
Sublimation, p. 417
Rationalization, p. 417
Neo-Freudians, p. 419
Collective unconscious, p. 420
Archetypes, p. 420

Humanistic Approaches

What does self-actualization mean in the context of Maslow's and Rogers's personality theories?

- In Maslow's theory, *self-actualization* is the process of realizing one's innate human potential to become the best one can be. The process of realizing potential, and of growing, is the process of becoming self-actualized. p. 422
- The humanistic approach of Rogers states that *fulfillment* is the motivating force of personality development. Rogers focuses on the concept of *self;* the *ideal self* is the self a person would ideally like to be. Persons with rigid self-concepts guard themselves against threatening feelings; they become unhappy when they are unable to fit new types of behavior into their current self-concepts. pp. 423–424

KEY TERMS
Fulfillment, p. 423
Self, p. 423
Ideal self, p. 423
Self-actualization, p. 423

Trait and Type Theories

Distinguish between a trait and a type.

- A *trait* is any readily identifiable stable quality or behavior that characterizes the way in which an individual differs from other people; a *type* is a category in which broad collections of traits are loosely tied together and interrelated. A person can be said to have a trait; a person fits a type. p. 425

Describe the ideas of Allport, Cattell, and Eysenck regarding traits.

- Allport argued that if you know a person's traits, it is possible to predict how he or she will respond to stimuli. Cardinal traits are ideas and behaviors that determine the direction of a person's life. Central traits are the qualities and behaviors that characterize a person's daily interactions. Secondary traits are specific behaviors that occur in response to specific situations. Cattell used the technique of factor analysis to show that groups of traits tend to cluster together. Cattell termed obvious, day-to-day traits surface traits and called higher-order traits source traits. Eysenck focused on types, which are higher levels of trait organization. Eysenck argued that all personality traits can be grouped along three basic dimensions: emotional stability, introversion–extroversion, and psychoticism. pp. 425–427

What are the Big Five?

- Although dozens of traits exist, researchers think of the Big Five as "supertraits," the important dimensions that characterize personality. These are extroversion–introversion, or the extent to which people are social or calm; agreeableness–antagonism, or the extent to which people are good-natured or irritable; conscientiousness–undirectedness, or the extent to which people are reliable or undependable; neuroticism–stability, or the extent to which people are nervous or at ease; and openness to experience, or the extent to which people are independent or conforming. pp. 427–428

KEY TERMS
Trait, p. 425
Types, p. 425

Behavioral Approaches

What are the key aspects of behavioral approaches to personality?

- Behavioral theories of personality center on precisely defined elements, such as the relationship between stimuli and responses, the strength of stimuli, and the strength, duration, and timing of reinforcers. For behaviorists, the structural unit of personality is the response. All behaviors are seen as responses to stimuli or as responses waiting for reinforcement. Behavioral psychologists try to discover behavior patterns and to use learning principles to help clients control their behavior and shape their personalities. pp. 429–430

Identify three key behavioral concepts used to explain personality development.

- Behavioral psychologists who focus on classical conditioning maintain that people develop fearfulness and anxiety through the process in which a neutral stimulus is paired with another stimulus that elicits some response. According to behaviorists who focus on operant conditioning, personality can be explained as spontaneous behavior that is reinforced. Observational learning theorists see personality as developing through the process of observation and imitation and points out that learning can occur independent of reinforcement. pp. 430–431

Cognitive Approaches

What are the key ideas of the cognitive approach to personality?

- The cognitive approach emphasizes the interaction of a person's thoughts and behavior. It considers the uniqueness of human beings and assumes that human beings are decision makers, planners, and evaluators of behavior. Cognitive views assert that people make rational choices in trying to predict and manage events in the world. One of the key concepts of the cognitive approach is the idea that people develop self-schemata—series of ideas and self-knowledge that organize how a person thinks about himself or herself. p. 432
- Locus of control, according to Rotter, is the extent to which individuals believe that a reinforcement or an outcome is contingent on their own behavior or personal characteristics as opposed to luck, chance, fate, or external forces. People clas-

sified as having an internal locus of control feel in control of their environment and future; people with an external locus of control believe that they have little control over their lives. pp. 432–433

- *Self-efficacy,* in Bandura's theory, is a person's belief about whether he or she can successfully engage in and execute a specific behavior. Judgments about self-efficacy determine how much effort people will expend and how long they will persist in the face of obstacles. A strong sense of self-efficacy allows people to feel free to select, influence, and even construct the circumstances of their lives. pp. 434–435

- Cognitive theories of personality have reintroduced thought into the equation of personality and situational variables. They have focused on how people interpret the situations in which they find themselves and then alter their behavior. Mischel argues that people change their responses based on their past experiences and their current assessment of the situation to suit the present situation. This process of adjustment is called *self-regulation.* p. 435

KEY TERMS
Shyness, p. 434
Self-efficacy, p. 434

Personality Assessment

Describe assessment.

- *Assessment* is the process of evaluating individual differences among human beings by means of techniques such as tests, interviews, observations, and recordings of physiological processes. Many psychologists administer a group, or battery, of tests. The goal is to use the variety of tests available so that when the information taken together is added up, intelligent, informed conclusions can be drawn. p. 439

What is the MMPI–2?

- The MMPI–2 consists of over 500 true/false statements that focus on attitudes, feelings, motor disturbances, and bodily complaints. Clinical and validity subscales examine different aspects of functioning and measure the truthfulness of the examinee's responses. The MMPI–2 is used as a screening device for maladjustment. pp. 440– 441

What is the goal of a projective test?

- *Projective tests* such as the Rorschach Inkblot Test and the TAT use ambiguous stimuli and ask examinees to respond in an unrestricted manner. Examinees are thought to project unconscious feelings, drives, and motives onto the ambiguous stimuli. p. 441

Identify the techniques of behavioral assessment.

- Four popular and widely used behavioral assessment techniques are behavioral assessment interviews, naturalistic observation, self-monitoring, and neuropsychological assessment. Behavioral assessment interviews tend to be systematic and structured, focusing on overt and current behaviors and paying attention to the situations in which these behaviors occur. Naturalistic observation involves observing a client in the natural environment and recording the occurrence of specified behaviors at predetermined intervals. In *self-monitoring,* a person systematically records the frequency and duration of specific behaviors in himself or herself. Neuropsychological assessment is the study of the brain and its disorders as they relate to behavior. pp. 442–443

KEY TERMS
Assessment, p. 439
Projective tests, p. 441
Self-monitoring, p. 443

Learning CONNECTIONS

Some students benefit from extra help with personality theories. You can learn more about them in:

- The CD-ROM accompanying this book, Topic 10

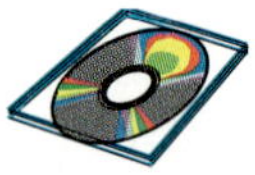

- This book's study guide, *Keeping Pace Plus*, or the computerized study guide, Chapter 12
- The audiotape accompanying this book, *SoundGuide for Psychology*, Learning Unit 12
- The study aids found on the World Wide Web site for this book, at http://www.abacon.com/psych/lefton

Critical Thinking CONNECTIONS

Take a moment to think critically about how this chapter's topics are connected with the rest of psychology . . .

If you are interested in . . .	Ask yourself . . .	Then turn to . . .
Freud's psychoanalytic approach and the broad array of theories that developed from it 	How does Erikson's stage theory of adult development relate to Freud's?	Chapter 11, pp. 389–390
	How do people use defense-oriented coping skills, some of which are Freudian in nature, to deal with stress?	Chapter 13, pp. 463–465
	How do Freudian approaches to the treatment of abnormal behavior help people uncover hidden motivations and biological urges?	Chapter 15, pp. 524–526
The relationship between personality and stress 	What traits motivate people to compete against others?	Chapter 9, pp. 322–323
	What are some of the symptoms of anxiety disorders?	Chapter 14, pp. 484–485
How personality and intelligence are assessed by psychologists 	How are tests of intelligence and their various subscales constructed?	Chapter 8, pp. 273–275
	How do psychologists use testing in the business environment?	Chapter 17, pp. 604–606

13

Stress and Health Psychology

Every year hundreds of students move into the dorms on my school's campus. Anxious families unload carloads of stereos, bedding, and computer equipment. Books, clothing, portable shelves are trundled up flights of concrete stairs to cramped dorm rooms. The weather is invariably hot. The orientation schedule is frantic and confusing. The roommate's family is tense and unfriendly. An overtired younger sibling has a tantrum about being dragged from one end of the campus to the other. Family patience is worn paper thin.

The move-in weekend and freshman orientation are exciting. There are new roommates, new courses, and new freedom—from handling money to doing one's own laundry. Excitement, change, and freedom can be stressful for everyone involved. Eventually parents go back home, peers and counselors take over, stress levels go down a bit, and students become acclimated to campus life. But some stress remains. As a student, you face a variety of stressors: studying for several exams in the same week, juggling studies with a part-time job, getting along with a difficult roommate in cramped quarters. Stressors, from the hassles of freshman orientation to the traumas of war, are a reality for everyone. People can deal with stress in either positive or negative ways; unfortunately, many don't cope effectively with stress. Some suffer from stress-related health problems, such as high blood pressure and insomnia. Others try to escape from stress by turning to alcohol and other drugs.

In this chapter, we will examine the nature of stress, learn how to cope with it, and look at the interrelationship of health and stress. We will also look into how motivation, learning, and personality work together to influence the ability to cope with stress in day-to-day life.

Stress

Popping antacid tablets like candy, launching into tirades at coworkers or friends, pounding their fists on a table, and downing cocktails each night are a way of life for many people who succumb to stress caused by their jobs, families, and financial burdens. One person may have a high-pressure job that affects her social life and causes daily migraines. A coworker may manage the same amount of stress in more positive ways, without suffering negative health consequences. Herein lies an important point: Different people evaluate and handle stress different ways.

What Is Stress?

A **stressor** is an environmental stimulus that affects an organism in physically or psychologically injurious ways, usually producing anxiety, tension, and physiological arousal. **Anxiety** is a generalized feeling of fear and apprehension that may be related to a particular event or object and is often accompanied by increased physiological arousal. Physiological arousal, often the first change that appears when a person responds to a stressor, includes changes in the autonomic nervous system that bring about increased heart rate, faster breathing, higher blood pressure, sweating palms, and dilation of the pupils.

Whenever something negatively affects someone, physically or psychologically, the person may experience the effect as stress. **Stress** is a nonspecific, often global, response by an organism to real or imagined demands made on it; it is an emotional response. The key is that not all people view a stimulus or a situation in the same way; *a person must appraise a situation as stressful for it to be stressful*. This broad definition recognizes that everyone experiences stress at some time, but that stress is also an interpreted state; stress is a response on the part of an individual. Richard Lazarus (1993), a leader in the study of emotion and stress, asserts that people *actively negotiate* between the demands of the environment (stressors) and personal beliefs and behaviors. This active negotiation is what cognitive researchers refer to as *cognitive appraisal*. Sometimes the arousal that stressors bring about initiates positive actions; sometimes the arousal's effects are detrimental. Thinking "I can't possibly handle this!" is likely to lead to a less positive response than is thinking "This is my chance to really show my stuff!" See Figure 13.1 for an overview of the responses to stressors that occur after a cognitive appraisal.

What determines whether a particular event will be stressful? Beyond cognitive appraisal, the answer lies in the extent to which people are familiar with the event, how much they have anticipated the event, and how much control they have over the event and their response to it. The first day of a new course brings excitement and some apprehension about an instructor's expectations and whether the time commitments for the course will be burdensome; the second or third time a class meets is usually much less worrisome. When people can predict events and are familiar with them, they feel that they are more in control and can have some impact on the future.

Stressor: An environmental stimulus that affects an organism in physically or psychologically injurious ways, usually producing anxiety, tension, and physiological arousal.

Anxiety: A generalized feeling of fear and apprehension that may be related to a particular event or object and is often accompanied by increased physiological arousal.

Stress: A nonspecific, often global, response by an organism to real or imagined demands made on it (a person must appraise a situation as stressful for it to be stressful).

FIGURE 13.1

The Effect of Cognitive Appraisal on Responses to Stressors

Depending on how a potential stressor (for example, entering a tied game in overtime) is evaluated, its impact can vary emotionally, physiologically, and behaviorally.

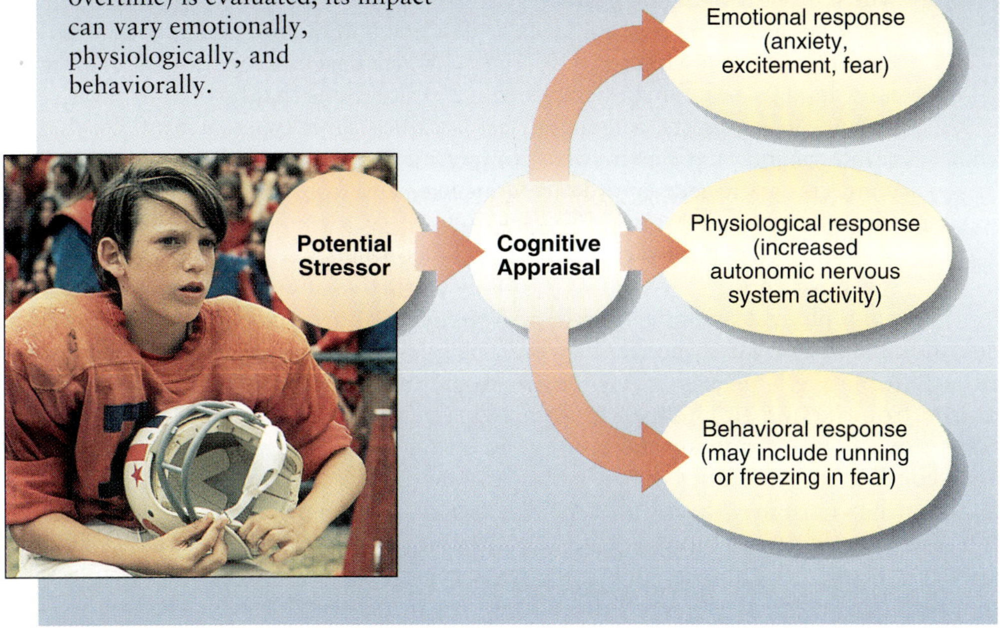

Sources of Stress

During rehearsal for a choral concert, a number of elementary school children developed nausea, shortness of breath, and abdominal pains. At the choir performance that evening, several of the children collapsed on stage. At another school, sixth-graders became dizzy and fainted during their graduation program. In both cases, the children were diagnosed as suffering from stress-related disorders. Feeling stress and trapped in situations that didn't allow them to escape from it, the children responded with symptoms of physical illness. There are three broad types of situations that cause stress: frustration, conflict, and pressure.

Frustration. When people are hindered from meeting their goals, they often feel frustrated. **Frustration** is the emotional state or condition that results when a goal—work, family, or personal—is thwarted or blocked. When people believe they cannot achieve a goal (often because of situations beyond their control), they may experience frustration. When you are unable to obtain a summer job because of a lack of experience, it can cause feelings of frustration. When a grandparent becomes ill, you may feel helpless; this can cause frustration. When there is an environmental threat over which people have no control, frustration is often the result (Hallman & Wandersman, 1992).

Some frustrations are externally caused. Examples are your lack of experience for a specific job or your grandparent's illness. Other frustrations are caused by specific people; your boss may be unfair in his appraisal of you, or your roommate may watch television too late at night. You can sometimes alleviate the frustration of dealing with other people by taking some action; this action, however, may place you in conflict, another type of stress.

Conflict. When people must make difficult decisions, they may be in a state of conflict. **Conflict** is the emotional state or condition in which people have to make

Frustration: The emotional state or condition that results when a goal—work, family, or personal—is thwarted or blocked.

Conflict: The emotional state or condition in which a person has to make difficult decisions about two or more competing motives, behaviors, or impulses.

▲ *Stress-related disorders are by no means unique to U.S. students. Failing to pass grade-level examinations in Japanese schools is tantamount, in the eyes of many, to future career failure. Thus, the stress experienced by Japanese schoolchildren is severe enough to cause many to become ill and some even to attempt suicide.*

difficult decisions about two or more competing motives, behaviors, or impulses. Consider the difficult decisions of American draftees who did not want to fight in the Vietnam War but also did not want to flee to Canada or face imprisonment. Or what happens if a person's goals and needs conflict—if a student must choose between two equally desirable academic courses, which will both advance the student's career plans but which meet at the same hour?

One of the first psychologists to describe and quantify such conflict situations was Neal Miller (1944, 1959). Miller developed hypotheses about how animals and human beings behave in situations that have both positive and negative aspects. In general, he described three types of conflicts that result when situations involve competing demands: approach–approach conflicts, avoidance–avoidance conflicts, and approach–avoidance conflicts.

Approach–approach conflict is the conflict that results when a person must choose between two equally attractive alternatives or goals (for example, two wonderful jobs). Approach–approach conflict generates discomfort and a stress response; however, people can usually tolerate it because either alternative is pleasant. **Avoidance–avoidance conflict** is the conflict that results from having to choose between two equally distasteful alternatives or goals (for example, mowing the lawn or painting the garage). **Approach–avoidance conflict** is the conflict that results from having to choose an alternative or goal that has both attractive and repellent aspects. Studying for an exam, which can lead to good grades but is boring and difficult, is an approach–avoidance situation. As Figure 13.2 shows, any of the three types of conflict situations will lead to a different degree of stress. Miller developed principles to predict behavior in conflict situations, particularly in approach–avoidance situations: (1) The closer a person is to a goal, the stronger the tendency is to approach the goal. (2) When two incompatible responses are available, the stronger one will be expressed. (3) The strength of the tendency to approach or avoid is correlated with the strength of the motivating drive. (Thus, someone on a diet who is considering a hot fudge sundae may yield to temptation if desire for the sundae is stronger than the desire to lose weight.) People regularly face conflict situations that may cause them to become anxious. Moreover, if conflicts affect day-to-day behavior, people may exhibit symptoms of maladjustment.

Pressure from Work, Time, and Life Events. Arousal and stress may occur when people feel **pressure**—the emotional state or condition resulting from the real or imagined expectations of others for certain behaviors or results. Although individual situations differ, pressure is common to almost everyone. Most of the time, it is associated with work, a lack of time, and life events.

Work that is either too overstimulating or understimulating can cause stress. Work-related stress also can come from fear of retirement, of being passed over for promotion, or of organizational changes. In addition, the physical work setting may be too noisy or crowded or isolated. Work-related pressure from deadlines, competition, and professional relationships (to name just a few possibilities) can cause a variety of physical problems. People suffering from work stress may experience migraines, sleeplessness, hunger for sweets, overeating, and intestinal distress. Stress at work often leads to an impaired immune system, which in turn leads to illness, resulting in lost efficiency and absenteeism (Levi, 1990).

Individuals with high-stress jobs, particularly where the stress is constant and the stressors are beyond the individual's control, show the effects most dramatically. Air traffic controllers and surgeons, for example, are responsible for the lives of other people every day and must be alert and organized at all times. If they work too many hours without relief, they may even make a fatal mistake. Others with high-stress jobs include inner-city high school teachers, customer service agents, waiters and waitresses, and emergency workers.

Approach–approach conflict: Conflict that results from having to choose between two equally attractive alternatives or goals.

Avoidance–avoidance conflict: Conflict that results from having to choose between two equally distasteful alternatives or goals.

Approach–avoidance conflict: Conflict that results from having to choose an alternative or goal that has both attractive and repellent aspects.

Pressure: Emotional state or condition resulting from others' expectations of specific behaviors or results.

FIGURE 13.2

Three Types of Conflict

In approach–approach conflict, people have to choose between equally appealing situations. In avoidance–avoidance conflict, people have to choose between equally distasteful situations. In approach–avoidance conflict, people are faced with a single alternative that is both appealing and distasteful.

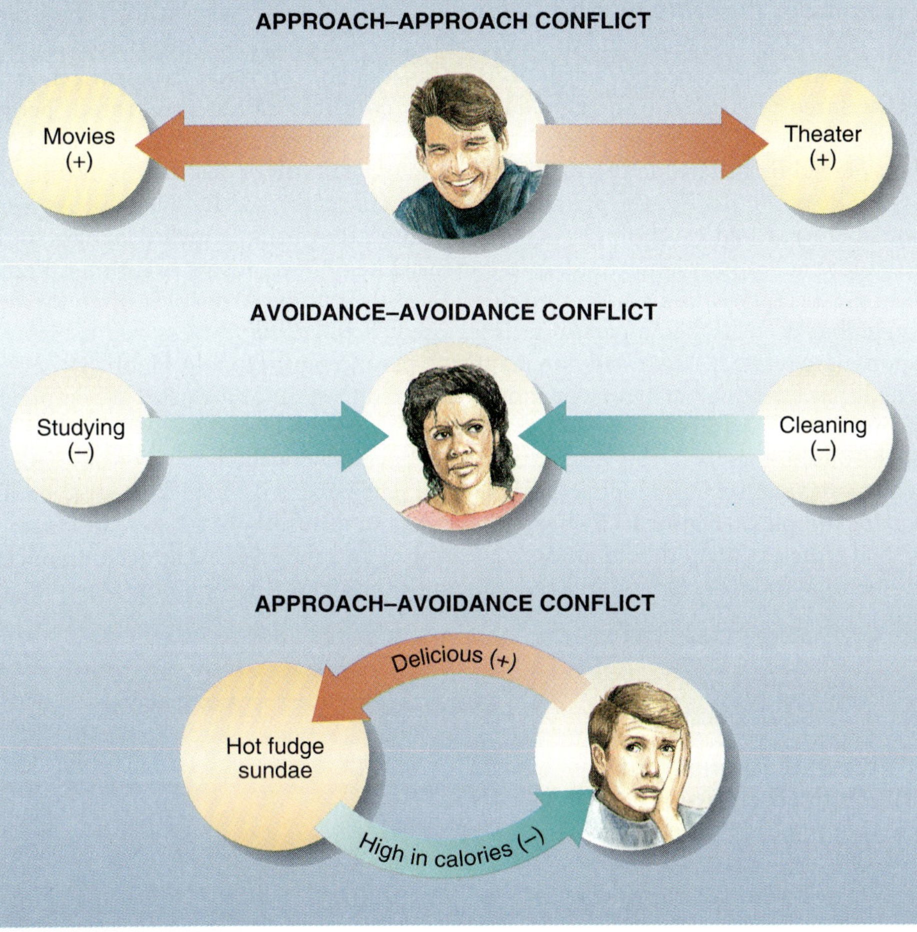

Lack of time is another common source of stress. Everyone faces deadlines: Students must complete tests before class ends, auto workers must keep pace with the assembly line, and taxpayers must file their returns by April 15. People have only a limited number of hours each day in which to accomplish tasks; therefore, many people carefully allocate their time to reduce time pressure. They may establish routines, make lists, set schedules, leave optional meetings early, and set aside leisure time in which to rid themselves of stressful feelings. If they do not handle time pressures successfully, they may begin to feel overloaded and stressed.

A third common source of stress is life events, which may be both positive and stressful at the same time. Consider marriage. Marriage unites people as partners, companions, lovers, and friends. Nonetheless, adjusting to married life means becoming familiar with new experiences, responding to unanticipated events, and having less control over many aspects of day-to-day experiences—all of which can be stressful. Also, at times, interpersonal discord arises. One partner may not be fulfilling marital or role obligations or may be causing the spouse to feel left out; both possibilities may bring about stress and even health problems (Burman & Margolin, 1992). We will examine stressful life events in more detail on pages 457–458.

Responses to Stress

People experience stress in a wide variety of ways. Some individuals experience modest increases in physiological arousal, while others may exhibit significant physical symptoms. In extreme cases, people become so aroused, anxious, and disorganized that their behavior becomes maladaptive or maladjusted. The basic idea underlying the work of many researchers is that stress activates a biological predisposition toward maladjustment (Monroe & Simons, 1991).

Emotion, Physiology, and Behavior. Psychologists who study stress typically divide the stress reaction into emotional, physiological, and behavioral components. *Emotionally*, people's reactions often depend on their frustration, their work-related pressures, and their day-to-day conflicts. When frustrated, people become angry or annoyed; when pressured, they become aroused and anxious; when placed in situations of conflict, they may vacillate or become irritable and hostile. *Physiologically*, the stress response is characterized by arousal. As mentioned before, when psychologists refer to arousal, they usually mean changes in the autonomic nervous system that cause increased heart rate, faster breathing, higher blood pressure, sweating palms, and dilation of the pupils. Arousal is often the first change that occurs when a person feels stressed. *Behaviorally*, stress and its arousal response are related. As we saw in Chapter 9, psychologist Donald Hebb (1972) has argued that effective behavior depends on a person's state of arousal. When people are moderately aroused, they behave with optimal effectiveness. When they are underaroused, they lack the stimulation to behave effectively. Overarousal tends to produce disorganized and ineffective behavior, particularly if the tasks people undertake are complex. (Figure 13.3 shows the effects of arousal on task performance.)

Nevertheless, a moderate amount of arousal and the stress that accompanies it may be unavoidable. Stress and the concomitant arousal keep people active and

FIGURE 13.3

Effects of Arousal on Task Performance

When arousal is low, task performance is poor or nonexistent. Performance is usually best at moderate levels of arousal. High levels of arousal usually impair performance on complex tasks such as surgery.

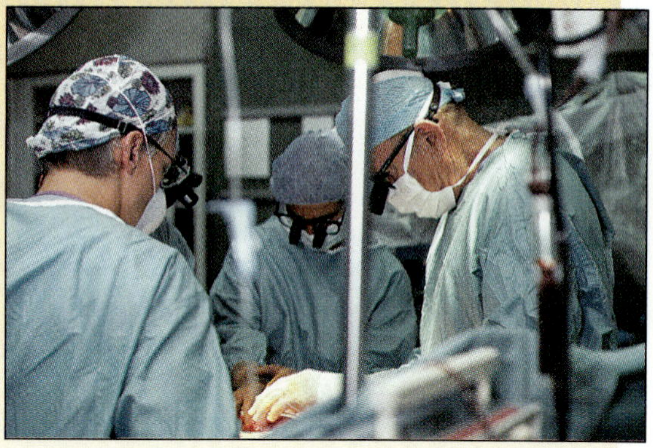

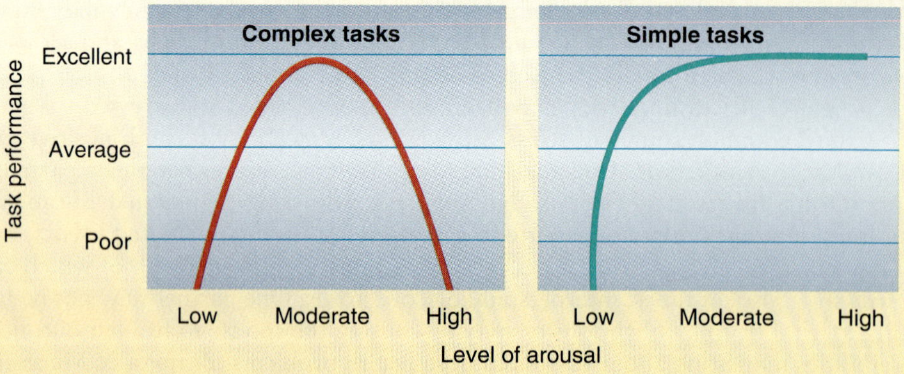

involved. They impel students to study, drive athletes to excel during competition, and help businesspeople to strive for further success. In short, stress and arousal can help people achieve their potential.

Burnout. A stress reaction especially common in people with high standards is burnout. **Burnout** is a state of emotional and physical exhaustion, lowered productivity, and feelings of isolation, often caused by work-related pressures (Kalimo & Mejman, 1987). People who face high-pressure conditions on a daily basis often feel debilitated, hopeless, and emotionally drained and may eventually stop trying. Although burnout is most often work-related, pressures caused by family, financial, or social situations can create the same feelings. Burnout victims develop negative self-concepts because they are unable to maintain the high standards they have set for themselves. They often cease to be concerned about others and have physical as well as social problems.

Health Consequences. A recent research study found that stress contributes to a person's susceptibility to the common cold (Cohen, Tyrrell, & Smith, 1993). Mothers and self-help books have long told people to reduce their levels of stress to keep from getting sick, and research now supports their advice. Stress does not directly cause disease. However, it contributes to many diseases, including the six major causes of death in the United States: heart disease, cancer, lung ailments, accidental injuries, cirrhosis of the liver, and suicide. In general, stress affects the immune system, making people more vulnerable to disease (Cohen, Tyrrell, & Smith, 1991; Cohen & Williamson, 1991; Herbert et al., 1994). More specifically, when stress responses go unexpressed, people show increased levels of autonomic nervous system activity (Hughes, Uhlmann, & Pennebaker, 1994). This, in turn, can lead to higher blood pressure which has been linked to heart disease and other ailments. Stress may also lead to headaches, backaches, decreased productivity, and family arguments. At a minimum, stress-related illnesses are causing an increase in medical costs for both individuals and employers. Extreme stress has been implicated in sudden heart attacks (Kamarck & Jennings, 1991).

Stress afflicts children as well as adults. Children are particularly unable to change or control the circumstances in which they find themselves (Band & Weisz, 1988). They may experience stress in school, stress caused by an abusive parent, stress from their parents' divorce, or stress from peer pressure. Like adults, they often show their stress response in physical symptoms. Also like adults, children have to appraise a situation as stressful for it to be stressful; and some children are more vulnerable than others.

Ethnic Differences in Responses to Stressors. In March 1989, the oil tanker *Exxon Valdez* ran aground on the rocks of Prince William Sound in Alaska and created an ecologically disastrous oil spill. It also had profound effects on the people living in the region, who experienced a marked increase in physical and psychological disorders. A research team sought to explore whether perceptions of the event and subsequent stress reactions to the disaster varied with the ethnicity of the residents (Palinkas et al., 1992). The team examined Native Alaskans and white Euro-Americans in 13 communities in Alaska that were affected by the oil spill. The Native Alaskans have a distinctly different lifestyle and work in different types of jobs compared to the Euro-Americans. The Euro-Americans are more likely to resemble the population of the rest of the United States.

Although both groups reported more psychological problems than usual, the Native Alaskans reported more participation in clean-up activities than did the Euro-Americans. The Native Alaskans were also more affected in their business dealings (fishing, for example), and the clean-up activities dominated their work, social, and cultural lives. Consequently, they saw the *Exxon Valdez* accident as having a far greater social and psychological impact, and they experienced far more stress than did the Euro-Americans. As we have seen before, people have a cultural

Burnout: State of emotional and physical exhaustion, lowered productivity, and feelings of isolation, often caused by work-related pressures.

framework that shapes their point of view; that framework also determines which events they will see as stressful.

Studying Stress: Focus on Physiology

Psychologists want to know how today's increasingly complex lifestyles affect the physical and psychological well-being of individuals. For example, does intense competition make businesspeople more susceptible to heart attacks? How can psychologists help people cope with life stressors, such as having a baby? How can therapists help veterans who are traumatized by war? These questions have helped researchers develop theories of stressors. One of the best-known theories is Hans Selye's general adaptation syndrome, which we will look at next.

Selye's General Adaptation Syndrome. In the 1930s, Hans Selye (1907–1982) began a systematic study of stressors and stress. He investigated the physiological changes in people who were experiencing various amounts of stress. Selye conceptualized people's responses to stress in terms of a *general adaptation syndrome* (1956, 1976). (A *syndrome* is a set of responses; in the case of stress, it is a set of behaviorally defined physical symptoms.) Selye's work initiated thousands of studies on stress and stress reactions, and Selye himself published more than 1,600 articles on the topic.

According to Selye, people's response to a stressor occurs in three stages: (1) an initial short-term stage of alarm, (2) a longer period of resistance, and (3) a final stage of exhaustion (see Figure 13.4). During the *alarm stage*, people experience increased physiological arousal. They become excited, anxious, or frightened. Bodily resources are mobilized. Metabolism speeds up dramatically, and blood is diverted from the skin to the brain, resulting in a pale appearance. (The response is much like the fight-or-flight syndrome, in which the sympathetic nervous system is activated; see Chapter 2.) Later on in the stress response, people also may experi-

FIGURE 13.4

Selye's General Adaptation Syndrome
According to Hans Selye, a person's response to a stressor can be divided into three stages: alarm, resistance, and exhaustion.

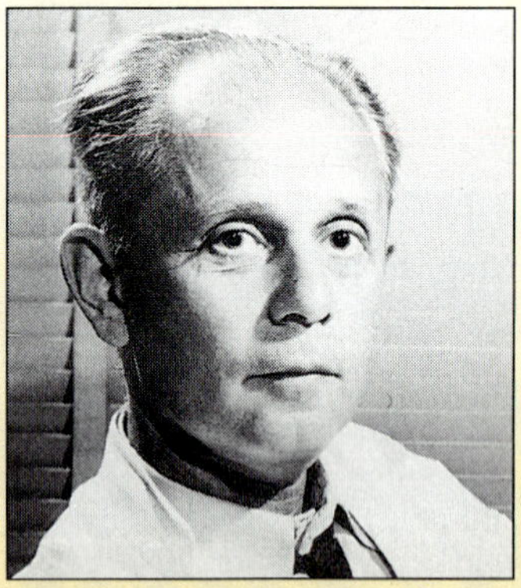

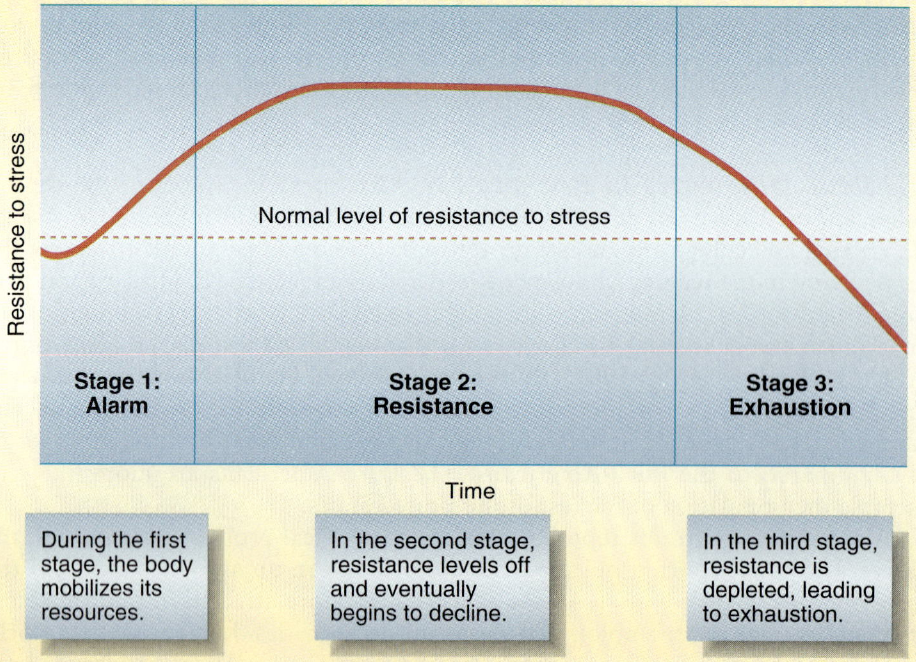

ence loss of appetite, sleeplessness, headaches, ulcers, or hormone imbalances; their normal level of ability to cope with stressors decreases.

Because people cannot stay highly aroused for very long, the initial alarm response usually leads to *resistance*. During this stage, physiological and behavioral responses become more moderate and sustained. People in the resistance stage often are irritable, impatient, and angry; and they may be constantly tired. This stage can persist for a few hours, several days, or even years, although eventually resistance begins to decline. Couples who suffer traumatic divorces sometimes exhibit anger and emotional fatigue years after the conflict has been resolved in court.

The final stage is *exhaustion*. Stress saps psychological energy; adaptability is depleted. If people don't reduce their level of stress, they can become too exhausted to adapt. At that point, they again become extremely alarmed, and they finally give up. The air traffic controller who takes no vacations, works long shifts, and is being expected to do more with less help may show the symptoms of maladjustment or withdrawal. In extreme cases of constant stress, as in war, serious illness and death may occur. Of course, not everyone shows the same behaviors.

Holmes–Rahe Scale. Among the many researchers Selye inspired to study stressors and refine his theory are Holmes and Rahe. Their basic assumption is that stressful life events, especially occurring in combination, will damage health (Holmes & Rahe, 1967; Rahe, 1989). *Stressful life events* are prominent events in a person's day-to-day circumstances that necessitate change.

To test their assumption, the researchers devised the Social Readjustment Rating Scale—a scale on which individuals circle significant life events (changes) that they've recently experienced (Table 13.1 shows part of this scale). Each event is

TABLE 13.1 ***A Portion of the Holmes–Rahe Social Readjustment Rating Scale***

Rank	Life Event	Value	Rank	Life Event	Value
1	Death of spouse	100	22	Change in responsibilities at work	29
2	Divorce	73	23	Son or daughter leaving home	29
3	Marital separation	65	24	Trouble with in-laws	29
4	Jail term	63	25	Outstanding personal achievement	28
5	Death of close family member	63	26	Wife begins or stops work	26
6	Personal injury or illness	53	27	Begin or end school	26
7	Marriage	50	28	Change in living conditions	20
8	Fired at work	47	29	Revision of personal habits	24
9	Marital reconciliation	45	30	Trouble with boss	23
10	Retirement	45	31	Change in work hours or conditions	20
11	Change in health of family member	44	32	Change in residence	20
12	Pregnancy	40	33	Change in schools	20
13	Sex difficulties	39	34	Change in recreation	19
14	Gain of new family member	39	35	Change in church activities	19
15	Business readjustment	39	36	Change in social activities	18
16	Change in financial state	38	37	Loan for lesser purchase (under $10,000)	17
17	Death of close friend	37	38	Change in sleeping habits	16
18	Change to different line of work	36	39	Change in number of family get-togethers	15
19	Change in number of arguments with spouse	35	40	Change in eating habits	15
			41	Vacation	13
20	Mortgage or loan for major purchase	31	42	Christmas	12
21	Foreclosure of mortgage or loan	30	43	Minor violations of the law	11

TABLE 13.2 *Life's Little Hassles—The Top Ten*

1.	Concerns about weight
2.	Health of a family member
3.	Rising prices of common goods
4.	Home maintenance
5.	Too many things to do
6.	Misplacing or losing things
7.	Yard work or outside home maintenance
8.	Property, investment, or taxes
9.	Crime
10.	Physical appearance

Source: Kanner et al., 1981.

rated for its influence on a person. The death of a spouse, divorce, and illness are rated as high stressors; changes in eating habits, vacations, and holidays are rated lower. A person's total score is an index of stress and the likelihood of illness in the next 2 years. According to Holmes and Rahe, a person who scores above 300 points will be likely to suffer a stress-induced physical illness.

Although widely used, the Holmes–Rahe scale has been sharply criticized on a number of dimensions. First, for many people who score high on the scale, a direct relationship between health and life events has not been found (Krantz, Grunberg, & Baum, 1985). People have support systems, friends, and activities that influence how, when, and under what conditions stressors will affect them. Some psychologists therefore question the validity of the scale in predicting illness (Theorell et al., 1986). Another criticism stems from the fact that the scale was based on a study of young male Navy personnel, whose characteristics do not necessarily match those of the general U.S. population, especially older people and women (Dohrenwend & Shrout, 1985). In addition, the scale includes only major life events. The stressors faced by most people are seldom crises; they are day-to-day irritations, but they do cause stress over the years (Kanner et al., 1981; Whisman & Kwon, 1993). Table 13.2 presents the 10 most frequently cited daily hassles.

The results of a study of the effect of both major life events and daily hassles on the reported health of elderly subjects showed that hassles are more closely related to psychological and physical ill health than are major life events (Chamberlain & Zika, 1990). Other studies found that flu, headaches, sore throats, and backaches also were related to daily hassles and stressors (DeLongis, Folkman, & Lazarus, 1988) and that there may be a genetic predisposition to high levels of autonomic system activity in response to stressful life events (Kendler et al., 1993). It is not surprising that people with an external locus of control (see Chapter 12, pages 432–433), little social support (to be discussed in a later section), and high levels of stress see life as much more difficult than others do (Jorgensen & Johnson, 1990). *Diversity* examines the influence of culture on the ways people perceive and handle stressors.

Heart Disease and Stress

Heart disease and high blood pressure account for more than half the deaths each year in the United States. Physicians and psychologists view this silent killer as a disorder of lifestyle (R. M. Kaplan, 1988). Three components of day-to-day life that

Stress and Hispanic Americans

Researchers have long known that stress depletes people's psychological resources. They also recognize that stress is often a result of daily hassles, certain life events such as loss of a job, and long-term strains such as poor economic conditions. A relatively unexplored research area has been differences in ways of experiencing and coping with such stressors among different cultural groups in the U.S. population. For example, are Hispanic Americans more vulnerable than non-Hispanic whites? This question was investigated by three California researchers, Jacqueline Golding, Marilyn Potts, and Carol Aneshensel.

Question and Method. Golding, Potts, and Aneshensel (1991) questioned whether Hispanic Americans are more at risk for stress and strain than are non-Hispanic whites. They examined the data from a large epidemiological study by the National Institute of Mental Health, which estimated the prevalence of mental disorders in the general population.

More than 2,300 individuals responded to interviews that asked a set of questions about psychiatric disorders, use of health services, and demographic characteristics. The study was conducted in Los Angeles County, California, and it included 1,244 respondents who were Hispanic (538 of whom were born in the United States and 706 of whom were born in Mexico and immigrated to the United States). In addition, there were 1,149 non-Hispanic white respondents.

Measures. Respondents indicated whether they had experienced stress from life events in the past 6 months. These events included such items as undesirable family or relationship events, such as divorce; undesirable work- or money-related events, such as being fired or getting into financial trouble; legal events, such as arrests; crime victimization, such as being burglarized; housing changes, such as moving; medical or psychological problems, such as a physical illness or drug problems; and deaths in the family. In addition to questions about psychological stress, the researchers investigated whether persistent economic strain was evident among respondents, by asking about any difficulty affording clothes, food, and medical care or paying bills.

To make appropriate comparisons, the researchers had to ensure that equivalent subjects were studied. They did not want to compare more wealthy Hispanic American participants with poor ones, for example; thus, they used a variety of statistical and sampling techniques to ensure comparable groups of subjects—this is a strength of the research study.

Results. Golding, Potts, and Aneshensel (1991) found that rates of life events were fairly similar among Hispanic and non-Hispanic white participants. Among both Hispanic Americans and non-Hispanic whites, the uneducated were more likely to be burglarized, to suffer from unemployment, and to have marital problems. The only important differences were related to economic strain. Hispanic participants, especially those who were immigrants, reported more economic strain than did whites. Being poor, female, and coming from a large household was also associated with greater strains.

Conclusions. There are few differences between Hispanic Americans and non-Hispanic whites in terms of stressful life events (Golding, Potts, and Aneshensel 1991). The stressors of divorce, unemployment, and moving occurred equally frequently when comparable groups were analyzed. But the economic strains and the day-to-day hassles of being economically disadvantaged and unable to afford life's necessities seemed to affect the Hispanic participants especially the immigrants, more than the non-Hispanic whites. The researchers point out that stresses resulting from adverse life events and economic strains are difficult to separate because these stressors invariably occur together.

Research into ethnicity and behavior often shows striking differences because the worldview and life experiences of different groups are unique. Everyone, regardless of ethnicity, is similarly and adversely affected by the difficult times in life. Nevertheless, how individuals respond is in part dependent on their culture and the values that it espouses, reinforces, and expects (Crystal et al., 1994).

are being studied in conncection with high blood pressure and heart disease are work-site stress, Type A behavior, and physiological reactivity. Intense research into each of these biobehavioral factors has altered heart patient treatment.

Work-Site Stress. Work-site stress increases the prevalence of heart attacks (Levi, 1990). Researchers theorize that this may happen because physiological components of the stress response place extra burdens on the heart over many years. The likelihood that you will have a heart attack increases significantly if you are an air traffic controller or a surgeon, because these kinds of work are loaded with potential stressors. Other jobs may cause stress by demanding too little or too much of a worker. Stress is also affected by a person's degree of *autonomy*—the extent to which the person controls the speed, flow, and level of work. A position with high demands and low control increases stress. A factory worker, for example, usually has little control over the work and may therefore experience stress.

Men are more likely than women to develop heart disease related to work-site stress. However, in recent years, the work and home situations of men and women have become much more parallel. When their situations are similar, men and women seem to have similar rates of heart disease (Hamilton & Fagot, 1988).

Type A Behavior. In the late 1950s, physicians Friedman and Rosenman identified a pattern of behavior that they believe contributes to heart disease: Type A behavior (Friedman & Rosenman, 1974). **Type A behavior** occurs in individuals who are competitive, impatient, hostile, and always striving to do more in less time. (**Type B behavior** occurs in people who are calmer, more patient, and less hurried.)

Early studies of Type A behavior showed a positive association with heart disease; that is, Type A individuals were more likely than Type B individuals to have heart attacks. More recent research, however, suggests that no such relationship exists (Matthews, 1988). Some elements of Type A behavior do seem to be related to heart disease (Byrne & Reinhart, 1989), but the overall Type A behavior pattern is not. For example, hostility and anger have been related to heart disease (Miller et al., 1996), as have suspiciousness and mistrust (Weidner et al., 1989). One important research finding is that expressing the emotions associated with stress verbally or in writing decreases the risk of health problems (Berry & Pennebaker, 1993). People who are extremely anxious, depressed, angry, and unhappy have a higher rate of heart disease than do normally adjusted people (T. Q. Miller et al., 1991), although the physiological mechanism underlying this is unclear (Suls & Wan, 1993). In sum, Type A behavior patterns exist; however, a direct relationship to heart disease is minimal or nonexistent (Friedman & Booth-Kewley, 1988; Matthews, 1988).

Physiological Reactivity. A possible third factor relating stress to heart disease is how the body reacts to stressors. This is called *reactivity*, or *physiological reactivity*. A situation interpreted as stressful may cause the body to react physiologically, triggering processes that lead to heart disease. Research shows that Type A behavior patterns are associated with increased physiological reactivity (Contrada, 1989), long-lasting emotional distress (Suls & Wan, 1989a, 1989b), and feelings of anger and hostility (Suarez & Williams, 1989). But it is still not clear whether the reactivity predisposes people to high blood pressure and heart disease or whether those predisposed to those problems show reactivity. People who are physically fit react better physiologically to stressful situations than those who are not fit.

Although work-site stress, aspects of Type A behavior, and physiological reactivity may be individually linked to heart disease, research suggests that these factors are interactive; that is, they affect one another (Krantz et al., 1988). From a psychologist's viewpoint, this is an important finding requiring further investigation. First, much more research is needed to sort out the factors. Laboratory studies of stress are not the same as real-world situations (Lassner, Matthews, & Stoney, 1994). Second, although behavioral factors contribute to heart disease, researchers

Type A behavior: Behavior characterized by competitiveness, impatience, hostility, and constant efforts to do more in less time.

Type B behavior: Behavior characterized by more calmness, more patience, and less hurrying than that of Type A individuals.

need to learn how important they are. Third, psychologists need to find interventions that will lessen the feelings arising from excessive stress and so decrease the likelihood of heart disease (Frasure-Smith, Lespérance, & Talajic, 1993). Fourth, and most important, an individual's culture and worldview affect work-site stress, Type A behavior, and physiological reactivity. Research shows that Japanese Americans who were the most traditional in Japanese cultural views (collectivistic, for example) had the lowest incidence of heart disease when compared with Japanese Americans who were the least traditional in terms of Japanese values (Matsumoto, 1996). Thus, culture does, in part, shape people's health.

Posttraumatic Stress Disorder

In 1989, a group of U.S. Army veterans returned with several therapists to Vietnam, where they had waged war more than two decades earlier. This time, however, their mission was not to fight an enemy but to heal their own psychological wounds. One veteran reported that he had been haunted for years by nightmares of his combat experiences. This severe stress-related disorder is termed **posttraumatic stress disorder (PTSD)**—a mental disorder that may become evident after a person has undergone severe stress caused by some type of disaster.

▲ *The floods that swept the Midwest in the spring of 1993 left in their wake not only devastation of physical property, but numerous victims of posttraumatic stress disorder.*

Origins and Symptoms. Victims of rape, natural disasters (tornados, earthquakes, hurricanes, floods), and disasters caused by human beings (wars, train wrecks, toxic chemical spills) often suffer from PTSD. Many survivors of the 1989 San Francisco earthquake still fear the double-decker freeways of California, which took several lives when they collapsed in the quake. Posttraumatic stress disorder is also still evident long after the 1980 volcanic eruption of Mount St. Helens (Shore, Vollmer, & Tatum, 1989). The bombings at New York City's World Trade Center in 1993 and Oklahoma City's federal building in 1995 still affect hundreds of people who were trapped and many others who witnessed the event. The 1993 floods along the Missouri and Mississippi rivers left in their wake many people suffering from PTSD. The likelilhood that a person will experience PTSD at some time during his or her life is about 8 percent (Kessler et al., 1995).

Common symptoms of posttraumatic stress disorder are vivid, intrusive recollections or reexperiences of the traumatic event and occasional lapses of normal consciousness (Wood et al., 1992). People may develop anxiety, depression, or exceptionally aggressive behavior; they may avoid situations that resemble the traumatizing events. Such behaviors may eventually interfere with daily functioning, family interactions, and health. Research on PTSD is attempting to identify a possible genetic predisposition (True et al., 1993) and to examine psychological causes such as motivated forgetting of difficult circumstances (Foa & Riggs, 1995). An increasing number of studies are focusing on the psychological aftermath of natural disasters such as earthquakes, tornados, and floods (Wood et al., 1992). Many more studies have focused on Vietnam veterans and those exposed to sudden death (e.g., Pitman et al., 1990; Ursano et al., 1995).

Posttraumatic stress disorder (PTSD): Mental disorder that may become evident after a person has undergone extreme stress caused by some type of disaster; common symptoms include vivid, intrusive recollections or reexperiences of the traumatic event and occasional lapses of normal consciousness.

The Vietnam Veteran. Vietnam veterans are particularly vulnerable to posttraumatic stress disorder. Although most veterans of the Vietnam War do not suffer from the disorder, thousands of them do. Decades later, these people still endure sleeping problems, the reliving of painful experiences, difficulty in concentrating, and feelings of alienation.

Many Vietnam veterans did not experience symptoms until months or even years after their return home. Those who suffer from the disorder seem more likely than others to have other stressful events in their lives and other adjustment problems, which in turn make the disorder worse—a vicious circle (McFall, Mackay, & Donovan, 1991).

The Vietnam War created unique psychological problems. Survival—not heroism—was the primary concern of many military personnel. Some turned to drugs or alcohol to alleviate fear. Moreover, the combatants, most of whom were drafted, knew that many people in the United States vehemently opposed the conflict. Finally, many of the soldiers were whisked home without ceremony or a chance to reacclimate gradually (Hobfoll et al., 1991).

For many complicated psychological, political, and social reasons, mental health practitioners have not always been as responsive as they might have been to veterans suffering from posttraumatic stress disorder. This has occured in part because, as we will see in the next section, other variables (such as a high degree of resilience) can lessen the impact of the trauma of war on many individuals (Sutker et al., 1995). Still, too often, clients have been held responsible for how they experience traumatic stress. Now that psychologists recognize the disorder, special help in the form of workshops and therapy is becoming available, and drug therapies are being assessed (Lerer et al., 1987).

FOCUS

Review

- Why is appraisal such a key component of stress? p. 450
- What is the link between stress and ill health? p. 455

Think Critically

- Do you see yourself as a Type A person or a Type B person? Do you know any Type A people, and does their health seem to be affected?

Coping

Most people need a way to cope with anxiety and with the physical ailments produced by stress. Some people seek medical and psychological help; others turn to alcohol and other drugs.

What Is Coping?

In general, *coping* means dealing with a situation. However, for a psychologist, **coping** is the process by which a person takes some action to manage environmental and internal demands that cause or might cause stress and that will tax the individual's inner resources. This definition of coping involves five important components. First, the coping is constantly changing and being evaluated and is therefore a process or a strategy. Second, coping involves managing situations, not necessarily bringing them under complete control. Third, coping is effortful; it does not happen automatically. Fourth, coping aims to manage cognitive as well as behavioral events. Finally, coping is a learned process.

Coping: Process by which a person takes some action to manage environmental or internal demands that cause or might cause stress and that will tax the individual's inner resources.

Many types of coping strategies exist; a person may use a few or many of them. Coping begins at the biological level. People's bodies respond to stress with specific reactions, including changes in hormone levels, in autonomic nervous system activity, and in the amount of neurotransmitters in the brain. Effective coping strategies occur at the psychological level when people learn new ways of dealing with their vulnerabilities.

Resilience, Coping Skills, and Social Support

A crucial factor that determines how well people cope with their problems is resilience. **Resilience** is the extent to which people are flexible, are less easily impaired by events, and respond adaptively to external or internal demands. A person who is resilient is said to be less vulnerable to stressors. Resilience depends on **coping skills**—the techniques people use to deal with changing situations and stress. People who have effective coping skills to guide them are prepared to deal with stress-related situations and are thus less vulnerable (Wiebe, 1991). People with poor or less well-developed coping skills may be extremely vulnerable and incapable of dealing with stress. Hilsman & Garber (1995) showed that this was especially true in children, who, because they are young, are less likely to have well-developed coping skills. In some cases, children may even develop a sense of *learned helplessness*; they may have found that rewards and punishments are not contingent on their behavior, so they learn not to try to cope, thereby remaining helpless (Job & Barnes, 1995). Faced with poor coping skills and a loss of control, some adults, too, stop responding. (We examined learned helplessness in Chapter 9.)

People's resilience and vulnerability are also affected by the level of social support available to them. **Social support** consists of the comfort, recognition, approval, and encouragement from available other people, including friends, family, members of organizations, and coworkers. When people feel supported by others' emotional concern and displays of caring, such as phone calls or notes, they can cope better with extraordinary pressure. The support is especially valuable when it is offered by someone who is important to the vulnerable person (Dakof & Taylor, 1990; Kessler et al., 1992). In addition to (and sometimes in place of) friends and family, group therapy (examined in Chapter 15) can be especially effective in alleviating anxiety. In group therapy, other people in similar situations can offer concern and emotional support. Even animals can provide social support (J. M. Siegel, 1990).

Defense-Oriented and Task-Oriented Coping Strategies

According to psychologist Richard S. Lazarus (1982), people faced with constant stress use either defense- or task-oriented coping strategies. *Defense-oriented coping strategies* do not reduce stressors; however, they help people protect themselves from their effects. These strategies ease stress, thereby enabling people to tolerate and deal with disturbances. As we saw in Chapter 12, people may use defense mechanisms to distort reality in order to defend themselves against life's difficulties. One such mechanism is *rationalization*, in which people reinterpret reality to make it more palatable. If your boyfriend or girlfriend dumps you, you may cope by telling your friends that you "never really liked him/her that much anyway." Similarly, a person who is turned down for a job may rationalize that he didn't want to work for the company after all. Another defense mechanism is *reaction formation*. A woman who is feeling a lot of stress and fear at work but who raves about her job has developed a reaction formation. She is expressing a feeling that is the opposite of her true one.

Stress management is becoming increasingly important to highly stressed individuals. Counselors commonly treat stress by first identifying the stressor and then helping the client modify behavior to cope with it. Through therapy, a person troubled by stressful situations can learn to cope by untangling personal feelings, understanding the sources of the stress, and then modifying behavior to alleviate it. Students about to enter college, for example, often show signs of stress. They're worried about academic pressures, social life, and overall adjustment. At some schools, incoming college students can receive counseling to learn how to deal with

Resilience: The extent to which people are flexible, are less easily impaired by events, and respond adaptively to external or internal demands.

Coping skills: Techniques people use to deal with stress and changing situations.

Social support: The comfort, recognition, approval, and encouragement available from other people, including friends, family, members of organizations, and coworkers.

FIGURE 13.5

Developing a Stress Reduction Program

The first step in developing a stress reduction program is identifying the stressor.

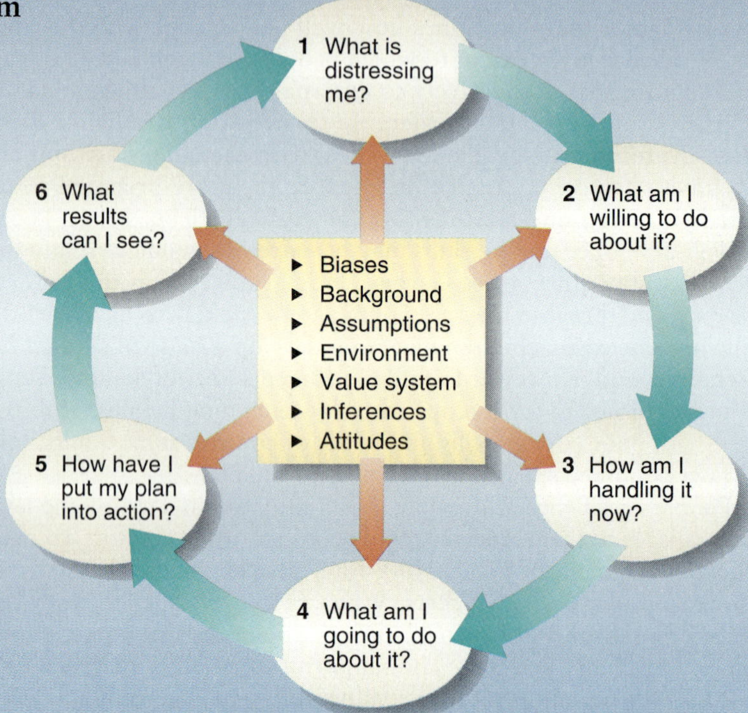

their stress. Similarly, stress management seminars, in which psychologists help business executives deal with stress in the corporate world, are becoming popular. The aim of both the counseling and the seminars is the same: to modify people's responses to stressors by replacing maladaptive responses with more useful ones.

Most psychologists, and especially behavioral psychologists, recommend *task-oriented coping strategies* for managing stress. The strategies usually involve several tasks, or steps (see Figure 13.5). Essentially, these steps are (1) identifying the stressor, (2) choosing an appropriate course of action for stress reduction, (3) implementing the plan, and (4) evaluating its success. Each of these steps (which are not always undertaken in order) is affected by a person's biases, attitudes, value systems, and previous environmental stressors.

Identifying the Stressor. Since stress-producing situations exist in many areas, identifying the stressor is often difficult. A woman may be experiencing problems with her workload, her finances, her social life, and her roommate. She must decide what is causing her the most stress and whether her problems with her social life, for example, are in some way tied to her work situation. Older people seem to have as much difficulty as younger people in identifying and controlling the sources of stress (Lazarus & DeLongis, 1983).

Choosing the Action. Once the stressor is found, people need to choose among several coping strategies. For example, they can withdraw from a stress-inducing situation by quitting work, leaving a spouse, or declaring bankruptcy. More often, they turn to other people or other methods of coping.

Because stress is usually accompanied by arousal and excitement, people may cope by using *relaxation techniques*. These techniques include biofeedback, hypnosis, and meditation, all of which help people to refocus their energies. Exercise such as aerobics, jogging, or racquetball is another effective way for a person to relax, relieve stress, and improve mood states (Aganoff & Boyle, 1994; Thayer, Newman, & McClain, 1994).

Many people manage stress and anxiety with *cognitive coping strategies*; that is, they prepare themselves to handle pressure through gradual exposure to increasingly intense stressors (Janis, 1985). Chapter 9 discussed a study in which subjects viewing a film with painful scenes were able to control their emotional responses (Lazarus & Alfert, 1964). This study suggests that people can learn to manage their stress by using their thought processes. A major goal of current research on stress is to prepare people to react in constructive ways to early warning signs of stress.

Research shows that people can help with stress by talking to themselves and using imagery (Ilacqua, 1994). The self-talk procedure, which is used widely, is effective in helping people confront stressors and cope with pain and the feeling of being overwhelmed (Turk, Meichenbaum, & Genest, 1983). By talking to themselves, people gain control over their emotions, arousal, and stress reactions; this technique is especially useful before noxious or painful medical procedures such as chemotherapy (Ludwick-Rosenthal & Neufeld, 1988).

Stress inoculation [in-OK-you-LAY-shun]: Procedure of giving people realistic warnings, recommendations, and reassurances to help them prepare for and cope with impending dangers or losses.

Implementing the Plan. Stress management counselors help people prepare for stressful situations by providing them with new ideas—a process called stress inoculation. **Stress inoculation** is the procedure of giving people realistic warnings, recommendations, and reassurances to help them prepare for and cope with impending dangers or losses. Sometimes stress inoculation involves a single technique, such as breathing deeply and regularly. At other times it is more elaborate, involving graded exposure to various levels of threats or detailed information about a forthcoming procedure (Janis, 1985). Janis likens stress inoculation to an antibiotic given to ward off disease. It helps people to defend themselves and to cope with stressors when they occur. Essentially, stress inoculation does the following:

- Increases the predictability of stressful events.
- Fosters coping skills.
- Generates self-talking.
- Encourages confidence about successful outcomes.
- Builds a commitment to personal action and responsibility for an adaptive course of action.
- Gives people realistic warnings, recommendations, and reassurances to help them prepare for and cope with impending dangers or losses.

To cope well both at home and at work, people should be task-oriented, self-monitoring, realistic, open to supportive relationships, and patient (Sarason & Sarason, 1987). They also need to eat sensibly, get enough sleep, stand up to the boss from time to time, find a hobby, take refuge in family—and sometimes, when things get too extreme, quit. Most important, people have to believe in themselves and in their ability to cope well with stress (Bandura et al., 1988). *Applications,* on pages 466 and 467, examines the importance of a positive attitude in coping with stress.

Evaluating the Success of the Plan. A well-designed coping plan includes evaluation of the plan's success. Have the techniques been effective? Is there still more to do? Are new or further actions needed? All of these questions need to be answered as part of the task-oriented coping strategy.

FOCUS

Review

- What is the evidence that the immune system is implicated in the relationship of attitudes and health? p. 466

Think Critically

- From your own experience, what coping techniques are more effective than others?

APPLICATIONS

Coping, Health, and a Positive Attitude

Applied psychologists claim that simply maintaining a positive attitude can help a person cope with stress and can even reduce its physical symptoms. People who believe they have control over their lives, health, and well-being are more relaxed and happier than those who do not (Rodin, 1986; Thompson et al., 1993). An upbeat mood, a positive sense of personal control, and even a self-serving bias can facilitate such worthwhile behaviors as helping others and evaluating people favorably (Meyers & Diener, 1995). Applied psychologists suggest that people who have positive attitudes may even live longer.

Sometimes, reframing or rethinking a situation serves as a rationalization to make it less anxiety-producing, as we saw in Chapter 12. One study, however, showed that people who engage in such small self-deceptions may be healthier than people who focus on their anxiety. In an unpublished study of people from 1946 through 1988, Peterson, Seligman, and Vaillant (reported in DeAngelis, 1988) found that those who made excuses for negative events in 1946 had better health in 1988. Such results indicate that people who emphasize the downside of life's events may develop learned helplessness. They may then choose inaction because they believe themselves to be powerless in controlling events. Taking a positive approach and believing in your own abilities will help you ward off stress and avoid the fear and arousal that come from feelings of despair and low self-esteem (Bandura et al., 1988). Seligman (1988) argues that optimism helps people achieve goals and cope more effectively; for example, optimistic salespeople substantially outsell their pessimistic colleagues. Maintaining an optimistic attitude is likely to help people engage in self-protective behaviors that will foster change for the better (Ewart, 1991; Scheier & Carver, 1993).

The Conservation of Resources. People can develop a positive attitude by conserving resources. A person's home, marriage, and status as a valued worker, good student, or community leader are all resources. Hobfoll (1989) suggests that people strive to retain, protect, and build their resources; the potential or actual loss of these valued resources is threatening. In Hobfoll's view, when these resources are under attack, people try to defend themselves. They attempt to ward off the attack or replace the lost resources by, say, seeking a new marriage or leadership position or by gaining some new competence or financial strength. When someone is experiencing stress because of a threat to his or her personal resources, treatment might mean shifting the person's focus of attention, reinterpreting the threat, helping the person see how he or she might replace the lost resource (for example, by finding a new job), and reevaluating the threat.

Positive Attitudes and Psychoneuroimmunology. One effect of a positive approach is that it may harness the body's own defense mechanisms. **Psychoneuroimmunology (PNI)** is the study of how psychological processes and the nervous system affect, and in turn are affected by, the body's natural defense system—the immune system. Research in PNI shows that the immune system (which fights disease) responds to a person's moods, stress level, and basic attitudes about life (Herbert et al., 1994; Stanford & Salmon, 1993). According to PNI researchers, the brain provides information to the immune system about how and when to respond. The nervous and immune systems seem to be linked, each producing substances that alter the functions of the other. The brain—especially after activation of the sympathetic nervous system—sends to the immune system signals that trigger its disease-fighting ability, including the production of white blood cells and other types of disease-fighting cells (Herbert et al., 1994; Shurin et al., 1994). The immune system sends signals to the brain that alter its functioning (Maier, Watkins, & Fleshner, 1994). Thus, the immune system of a person with a positive, upbeat attitude responds better and faster than does that of a person who is depressed and lethargic (Ader & Cohen, 1993; O'Leary, 1990). Consider people who have recently lost loved ones to death: They consistently show higher rates of illness. Today, many AIDS patients are provided with counseling designed to

Health Psychology

At least half of all the premature deaths in the United States are the result of unhealthy lifestyles. In the past, most people died from causes beyond their control—influenza, tuberculosis, and pneumonia, for example. Today, the leading causes of death in the United States—heart disease, cancer, stroke, and accidents—can be controlled to some extent by environmental and behavioral variables. Psychologists believe there is a direct relationship between people's health and their behavior. **Health psychology** is the psychological subfield concerned with the use of psychological ideas and principles in health enhancement, illness prevention, diagnosis and treatment of disease, and rehabilitation processes. It is an action-oriented

Psychoneuroimmunology (PNI) [SYE-ko-NEW-ro-IM-you-NOLL-oh-gee]: The study of how psychological processes and the nervous system affect and in turn are affected by the body's natural defense system—the immune system.

bolster their immune systems by improving their attitudes; this may help them live longer.

Not all researchers agree about the role of positive illusions and thoughts (e.g., Colvin & Block, 1994), but most psychologists agree that thoughts and ideas play an important role both in preventing illness and in determining people respond to becoming sick. Some psychologists still find it difficult to accept the idea that the immune system responds to mental attitudes. Researchers, however, are beginning to realize the power that positive thinking may have on certain bodily processes (Herbert & Cohen, 1993; O'Leary, 1990). Of course, even though positive attitudes and thoughts can be beneficial, they can go only so far in helping to alleviate illness, and only with some people (Manuck et al., 1991). Sometimes having a positive attitude and practicing meditation, exercise, and other traditional coping techniques fail to reduce stress. This failure sometimes occurs because attempts have been half-hearted; at other times, the problem is a lack of expertise. More often, though, people just lack coping skills or even the knowledge that such skills exist. Wearing rose-colored glasses from time to time can be beneficial; however, continuous self-deception can lead to maladjustment, lies, and a badly distorted view of reality.

Effective Coping Strategies. Taking responsibility for preventive behaviors can be an important step toward better physical and mental health (Ewart, 1991). There are a number of steps you can take to cope, manage stress, and stay healthy:

- *Increase exercise.* People are able to cope better when they improve their physical fitness, usually by exercising. In addition, increased exercise will lower blood pressure and reduce the risk of heart disease.
- *Eat well.* People feel better and cope better when they eat well and have a balanced diet. This also means not being overweight.
- *Sleep well.* People react better to life when they have had a good night's sleep; reaction time improves, as does judgment.
- *Be flexible.* Life is unpredictable; accept that fact, and day-to-day changes and surprises will be easier to handle.
- *Keep stress at school or the office.* Work-related stressors should be kept in the work environment. Bringing stressors home will only make stress worse. People are more likely to be involved in substance abuse and domestic violence when they bring stressors home with them.
- *Communicate.* Share your ideas, feelings, and thoughts with the significant people in your life. This will decrease misunderstanding, mistrust, and stress.
- *Learn to relax.* In this fast-paced society, seldom people take the time to relax and let uncomfortable ideas and feelings leave them. Learn meditation, yoga, or deep breathing. Schedule some time each day for yourself.
- *Seek support.* Social support from family, friends, and self-help groups helps you appraise situations differently. Remember, you have to appraise a situation as stressful for it to be stressful. Social support helps you keep stressful situations in perspective.

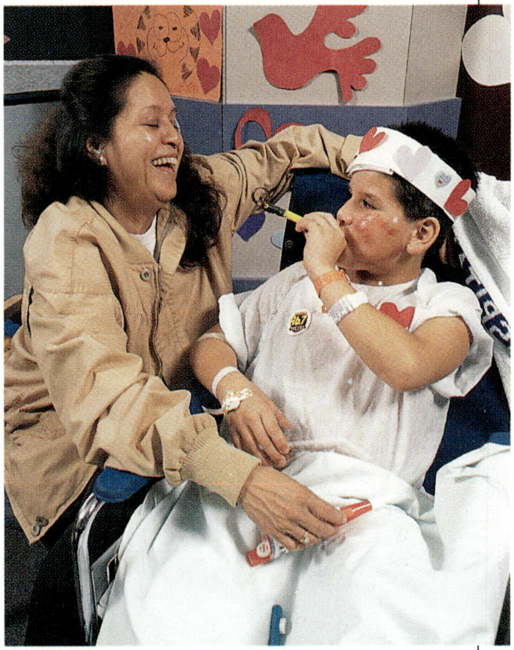

▲ *Laughter really can be the best medicine.*

discipline that assumes that people's ideas and behaviors contribute to the onset and prevention of illness. A closely related field, *behavioral medicine*, integrates behavioral science with biomedical knowledge and techniques; it is narrower in focus than health psychology (Agras, 1992).

Traditionally, physicians have looked at health as the absence of disease. A person who was not experiencing adverse effects from infection, an injury, or an abnormal condition of some kind was considered healthy. Now, however, physicians and psychologists acknowledge that health refers not just to the absence of disease but to the total welfare of a person in terms of social, physical, and mental well-being. This concentration on social, physical, and mental well-being places health and psychology in the same corner, with a focus on the positive side—health promotion. Health and wellness are now seen as conditions people can actively pursue by eating well, exercis-

Health psychology: Subfield concerned with the use of psychological ideas and principles in health enhancement, illness prevention, diagnosis and treatment of disease, and rehabilitation processes.

ing regularly, and managing stress effectively (Cowen, 1991). Unlike medicine, which focuses on specific diseases, health psychology looks at the broad principles of thought and behavior that clarify fundamental psychosocial mechanisms and affect all areas of a person's life. Today, researchers are focusing on the positive effects of health-promoting behaviors (Millar & Millar, 1995).

Variables That Affect Health and Illness

Health and illness are affected by complex interrelationships among many events. Accordingly, health researchers have explored five variables that correlate strongly with health and illness: personality, cognitions, social environment, gender, and sociocultural variables (Rodin & Salovey, 1989).

Personality. Do certain personality variables predispose people to illness? Or does illness predispose a person to a specific personality? Some evidence suggests that angry, hostile people are more prone to illness than are optimists. But which comes first? Perhaps the lack of illness causes optimism, or at least a positive lifestyle. The role of personality variables in illness and health is still unclear, and much more research is needed (as we saw when we examined the role of Type A behavior in heart disease, page 460).

Cognitions. People's thoughts and beliefs about themselves, other people, and situations affect health-related behaviors. For example, one important variable is the extent to which people believe they control their lives, including health and illness. People with an internal locus of control (examined in Chapter 12) are more likely to take charge of their illnesses and attempt to get better than are people with an external locus of control. When people sense that they can control their own health, they are more likely to engage in health-conscious behaviors, such as eating complex carbohydrates, decreasing their consumption of saturated fat, and exercising more (Taylor, 1990).

Social Environment. Family, close friends, and work can be sources of social support—a key element in helping a person maintain health and recover from illness. Greater self-esteem, positive feelings about the future, and a sense of control are characteristic of people with strong social support. Adults in stable long-term relationships such as marriage are less likely to be ill than are people devoid of strong social support networks; in addition, the children of stable marriages are likely to be healthier (Gottman & Katz, 1989). Support from coworkers and supervisors in the work environment may also facilitate health (Repetti, Matthews, & Waldron, 1989). Individuals with social support are more likely to engage in preventive dental health, proper eating habits, and the use of safety practices that extend life, such as wearing seat belts.

Gender. Some health concerns apply only to women (menopause, for example), and others affect women disproportionately (for example, eating disorders). Therefore, the health concerns of women differ from those of men. Seventy percent of all psychoactive medications prescribed are for women, and two-thirds of all surgical procedures are performed on women (Ogur, 1986; Travis, 1988). While women have generally enjoyed an advantage in longevity, the gap in average life span between men and women has been decreasing. Women's changing lifestyles and work patterns are highly correlated with increased medical problems and decreased average life span. Further, as Rodin and Ickovics (1990) assert, the redefinition of gender roles and the changing social support structure for women affect health, medical treatment, and psychological functioning.

Sociocultural Variables. Not only gender but cultural background, age, ethnic group, and socioeconomic class are all important variables that affect health.

Although women tend to visit physicians more often than men, in some cultures the quality of their treatment is not equal to that given men. With advancing age, people are more likely to become ill or depressed (although there is much individual variation) (Dura, Stukenberg, & Kiecolt-Glaser, 1990). Often, illness among the elderly is affected by other variables, such as loneliness and isolation from family. Ethnicity is also an important variable. Some ethnic minorities and people from lower socioeconomic groups may lack knowledge, funds, or access to preventive care. In addition, older, less educated, and less affluent individuals are far less likely to engage in exercise, which helps to prevent illness. In the end, researchers know that socioeconomic status, with the many variables that make it hard to define, is positively correlated with health (Adler et al., 1994).

Disease prevention is the focus of many health psychologists. For example, preventing the spread of AIDS, considered in *Applications* (on pages 470 and 471), is of great concern.

The Psychology of Being Sick

When a person is sick with an illness that impairs day-to-day functioning, the effects can be devastating. The impact on the individual can be profound, both psychologically and economically. Illness seriously affects both the sick person and family members. Health psychologists are concerned not only with the links between stress and illness but with how people cope with illness when it occurs.

Seeking Medical Care. When do people seek medical care? What are the variables that prompt a person to try to get help to become well and healthy? Most people avoid medical care and advice except when it becomes absolutely necessary. Usually, when people have a visible symptom (rashes, cuts, swellings, fever) and the symptom appears threatening, painful, and persistent, they seek professional help. They are more likely to seek such help when they are sure the problem is physical rather than psychological and when they think medical attention will provide a cure. If they think medical attention will be a waste of time, or if they dread a diagnosis, they often delay seeking help.

There are gender differences in people's willingness to seek medical attention. Women seek medical help more than men do, have more medical visits, and take more prescription medication (Rosenstock & Kirscht, 1979). However, men have a shorter life span than do women and have higher rates of ulcers, heart disease, and stroke. Men may be less willing to seek medical attention because they perceive it as a weakness in character. Because some women are not in the work force, they may have more time to think about their symptoms or to pay a medical visit. In addition, women often seek a doctor's care for normal, nonpathological conditions (situations not caused by disease) such as pregnancy, childbirth, and menopause.

Major cultural differences also exist in health-care seeking; a country's technological, economic, and political system shape health-care delivery, as does its level of economic development. These factors, in turn, affect individuals' willingness to seek health care and to trust health-care providers. Matsumoto (1996) describes research showing that Japanese women trust their physicians less than American women do, yet are more likely to comply with a physician's advice for an invasive medical procedure. Power relationships and trust, two culturally determined variables, affect greatly health-care seeking.

The Sick Role. When people do what they think will help them get well, they are adopting a *sick role*. For most people, this means taking specific steps to get well, relieving themselves of normal responsibilities, and realizing that they are not at fault for their illness. Of course, a person can also adopt behaviors associated with illness when in fact there is no illness or pathology.

APPLICATIONS

AIDS (Acquired Immune Deficiency Syndrome)

A major concern of health psychologists is AIDS (acquired immune deficiency syndrome). People who are infected with the human immunodeficiency virus (HIV—the virus that causes AIDS) can harbor it for many years without developing AIDS. However, once people develop this deadly infectious disease, they generally die within 2 years of diagnosis, because their immune systems can no longer fight off diseases and infections. A great deal is known about AIDS, but at present there are no preventative vaccines or cures and few treatments to slow the virus's destructive course. Moreover, some people, fearing contamination, shun AIDS patients. Because most people with AIDS are infected through sexual contact or intravenous drug use, some attach a moral stigma to the disease. For all these reasons, AIDS is accompanied by devastating psychological consequences.

One in 250 persons in the United States is infected with HIV. Most people who have AIDS are between 20 and 49 years of age. HIV infection/AIDS is the leading cause of death among adults aged 25 to 40. Reports from the Centers for Disease Control show that more than 230,000 deaths from AIDS have occurred so far in the United States, and an estimated 1.1 million U.S. inhabitants are infected with HIV. Worldwide, 13 to 14 million persons are infected. Although at present some states have a greater percentage of cases than others (especially New York and California), most experts believe that this unevenness will disappear in time (Rosenberg, 1995).

Few other diseases are accompanied by so many losses. AIDS patients face the loss of physical strength, mental acuity, ability to work and care for their families, self-sufficiency, social roles, income and savings, housing, the emotional support of friends and loved ones, and ultimately life itself. Some schools have prohibited any children who have AIDS, or even those who have family members with AIDS, from attending classes. People with AIDS have been fired, and coworkers have quit their jobs to avoid them; judges have held legal hearings on closed-circuit television to avoid contact with people who have AIDS. For many people with AIDS, self-esteem fades rapidly as they blame themselves for having contracted the disease. This self-blame leads to depression, anxiety, self-anger, and a negative outlook on life. Families and friends become similarly affected as they cope with a dying loved one and face their own inability to understand the disease.

In AIDS prevention efforts, psychologists pay particular attention to high-risk behaviors so as to help individuals avoid risky situations. High-risk behaviors are those that directly

Unfortunately, many people blame the ailing person for being sick, even though the illness may be unrelated to any preventive measures a person might have taken. Sick people usually are relieved of normal responsibilities, such as working or taking care of the family. When they are in the hospital, they give over to physicians and nurses the responsibility for their care. Although American culture fosters an attitude that says people should be cheerful when sick, it is normal for sick people to be slightly depressed or even angry, especially when hospitalized (R. S. Lazarus, 1984). Because sickness is generally seen as a temporary state, we expect people to get well and to work toward that end—taking medication, sleeping, and, especially, complying with medical advice.

Compliance with Medical Advice. Getting people to adhere to health regimens or to follow their physicians' advice has long been a focus of health psychologists. People will comply with specific recommendations for a particular health problem, such as "Take three tablets a day for 10 days." However, they are less likely to adhere to general recommendations for diet, exercise, and overall health conditions, such as quitting smoking or relaxing more. For example, cigarette smoking is one of the largest health concerns today, causing about a half million deaths annually in the United States alone. Yet many people continue to smoke.

Compliance with medical advice depends on the severity of the problem. If an illness causes pain or discomfort, people are more likely to comply with a regimen of treatment to alleviate the discomfort. And people are more receptive to medical treatment when it is specific, simple, and easy to do, has minimal side effects, and brings about immediate relief (Klonoff, Annechild, & Landrine, 1994). Also, people

expose people to the blood or semen of others who are likely to have been exposed to the virus—in other words, to others who are likely to have engaged in high-risk behaviors. Often, individuals who have engaged in high-risk behaviors are sexually promiscuous men and women, homosexual or bisexual men, or present or past intravenous drug abusers. Heterosexuals who have had sexual contact with carriers of AIDS are at significant risk. In the United States, about 9 percent of known cases of AIDS occur from heterosexual sex. But, according to the Centers for Disease Control, heterosexual sex accounts for 71 percent of reported AIDS cases in other parts of the world. (See Figure 13.6.) Everywhere, adolescents are at especially high risk because they, more than adults, are likely to engage in unprotected sexual activity (St. Lawrence, 1993).

AIDS education aimed at young people is critically important, because education has proved to be effective in changing behavior (Fisher & Fisher, 1992). AIDS education, and research in general, has ignored gender as a crucial variable; but recent analyses show that women often respond better than men do to education about high-risk behaviors (Amaro, 1995). Further, when men and women communicate better, they are more likely to minimize the risks of transmission (Dolcini et al., 1995).

FIGURE 13.6

Sources of HIV Infection in Adults

Worldwide estimates are for adults infected with HIV; U.S. figures are for reported AIDS cases.

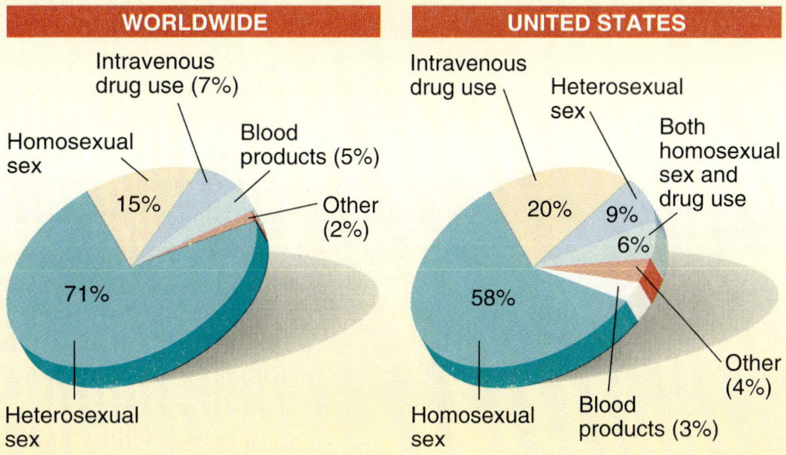

seeking a cure or relief of specific symptoms are more likely to be cooperative than are people merely seeking wellness or prevention. When long-term exercise is the prescribed treatment, most people drop out of a program within 6 months. Even when the impact of not taking a preventive medication is serious, people are not especially compliant; this is especially true for lengthy or difficult treatments, such as four-times-daily insulin injections (Hanson et al., 1989).

Compliance with a health-care regimen is increased when the regimen is tailored to the person's lifestyle and habits. Even written agreements between practitioners and clients can be helpful. Health psychologists have found clients more likely to adhere to treatments when a physician's influence and the family support systems are substantial. Social support from family and friends turns out to be especially valuable in getting even very sick people to comply with guidelines for treatment (DiMatteo & DiNicola, 1982). Helping people to build resourcefulness, manage stress, and understand the implications of their medical regimen is key to improved compliance (Aikens et al., 1992).

Health Psychology and Adaptive Behavior

Health psychologists focus on adaptive behaviors that will improve people's day-to-day lives. They encourage preventive programs at work and educate people about ways to manage stress and about other positive approaches toward health that will enhance and prolong life. They frequently conduct stress management workshops to help managers and workers cope with increasing pressures and workloads; they are also involved in helping people quit smoking, control their alcohol intake, follow exercise programs, and practice good nutrition.

Today, health psychologists attempt to change people's behavior before it gets out of hand. Health psychology is an action-oriented discipline, and as men and women seek more healthful lifestyles in the 1990s, psychologists are playing an instrumental role in their quest. Sometimes, health psychologists focus on preventive behaviors—use of condoms to prevent the spread of AIDS, regular exercise, and so on. At other times, they help people deal with existing problems such as obesity, diabetes, and high stress levels. Let's examine three ways of dealing with health problems: behavioral interventions, pain management, and stress management.

Behavioral Interventions. To manage existing health disorders and help prevent disease, behavioral interventions are necessary and important. Health psychologists know that many lifestyle behavior problems can be modified; these include smoking, excessive drinking, drug abuse, and overeating (relative to exercise). Excess caloric intake leads to obesity—and obesity in turn often leads to hypertension (high blood pressure), which causes heart disease.

Some interventions are community-based. Consider drug abuse. The principal places where people are introduced to drugs are schools, in both city and suburban settings. As a result, in the mid-1980s, under the direction of the Secretary of Education, a national plan was laid out for achieving drug-free schools. To a great extent, the moderately successful plan was an effort to help students cope without drugs; it was an action-oriented and incorporated effort to educate students and involve the community in dealing with drug use and abuse and especially prevention. Other interventions are on an individual level. For example, the likelihood that a person will stick to an exercise regime is increased when prompts and phone calls are made by friends, relatives, and coaches (Lombard, Lombard, & Winett, 1995).

Pain Management. Severe and disabling pain is symptomatic of some illnesses. Such pain can take three forms: (1) *chronic pain*, which is long-lasting and ever-present; (2) *periodic pain*, which comes and goes; (3) and *progressive pain*, which is ever-present and increases in severity as the illness progresses. Many people suffer from chronic pain, such as headache pain, lower back pain, and arthritis pain. Some types of chronic pain can be treated with drugs, surgery, or other medical interventions; but other types may call for nontraditional psychological techniques.

Two nontraditional techniques for pain management are hypnosis and biofeedback (examined in Chapter 4). Other techniques include behavior modification and cognitive therapy. Behavior modification uses learning principles (see Chapter 5) to teach people new effective behaviors and to help them unlearn old maladaptive behaviors. People undergoing this type of therapy learn to relax after a twinge of pain rather than focusing on the pain and thus making it worse. Chapter 15 looks into how cognitive therapy uses behavior modification techniques to help people acquire new thoughts, beliefs, and values that can help in pain management.

Stress Management. Because stressors exist in everyone's life—whether school exams, parent or peer demands, natural disasters, illness, death, divorce, inflation, or financial difficulties—many health psychologists focus on stress and its management. With the help of health psychologists, employers are sponsoring programs for managing stress in the workplace (Glasgow & Terborg, 1988). The pro-

FOCUS

Review

- Under what conditions do people comply with medical advice? pp. 470–471

Think Critically

- What are the implications of the finding that women seem to respond better than men to education about high-risk behaviors that transmit AIDS?

grams usually involve education, exercise, nutrition, and counseling. The results are fewer workdays lost to illness and lower health-care costs.

Stress management also results in fewer lost lives (Gebhardt & Crump, 1990). When patients who were hospitalized for heart attacks were treated for stress symptoms after their release from the hospital, they had fewer subsequent heart attacks than did a control group who did not receive specific stress treatments (Frasure-Smith & Prince, 1989).

The task of managing stress in people's daily lives is becoming greater each day, as new and potent forces impinge on people's health (Ilgen, 1990). In the 1990s, people are concerned about managing not only day-to-day illness and stress but also turmoil in the health-care professions that threatens them and their families.

Summary and Review

Stress

Why is appraisal such a key component of stress?

- *Stress* is a nonspecific, often global, response by an organism to real or imagined environmental demands. It is a normal part of living and depends on a person's appraisal of a situation. Stress is caused by *stressors*—environmental stimuli that affect an organism in either physically or psychologically injurious ways. p. 450

What kinds of conflicts result in stress?

- *Approach–approach conflicts* arise when a person must choose between two equally pleasant alternatives, such as two wonderful jobs. *Avoidance–avoidance conflicts* occur when a choice involves two equally distasteful alternatives, such as mowing the lawn or painting the garage. *Approach–avoidance conflicts* result when a choice or goal has both attractive and repellent aspects, such as eating a delicious but fattening dessert. p. 452
- Emotionally, people's reactions often depend on their *frustration*, their work-related *pressures*, and their day-to-day *conflicts*. Physiologically, the stress response is characterized by arousal. Behaviorally, stress and its arousal response are related. When people are moderately aroused, they behave with optimal effectiveness; when they are underaroused, they lack the stimulation to behave effectively. pp. 451–454

Describe three stages of Selye's general adaptation syndrome.

- Selye characterized stress responses as a general adaptation syndrome with three stages: alarm, resistance, and exhaustion. During the alarm stage, people experience increased physiological arousal and mobilize bodily resources. During resistance, physiological and behavioral responses become more moderate and sustained. During exhaustion, if people don't relieve their stress, they can become too exhausted to adapt; at that point, they again become extremely alarmed, and they finally give up. pp. 456–457

Characterize Type A behavior.

- *Type A behavior* occurs in individuals who are competitive, impatient, hostile, and always striving to do more in less time. Some elements of Type A behavior seem related to heart disease, but not the overall Type A behavior pattern. p. 460

What is the link between stress and ill health?

- People exposed to high levels of stress for long periods of time may develop stress-related disorders, including physical illness. *Posttraumatic stress disorder (PTSD)* is a disorder that may become evident after a person has undergone extreme stress caused by some type of disaster. pp. 458, 460–461

KEY TERMS

Stressor, p. 450
Anxiety, p. 450
Stress, p. 450
Frustration, p. 451
Conflict, p. 451
Approach–approach conflict, p. 452
Avoidance–avoidance conflict, p. 452
Approach–avoidance conflict, p. 452
Pressure, p. 452
Burnout, p. 455
Type A behavior, p. 460
Type B behavior, p. 460
Posttraumatic stress disorder (PTSD), p. 461

Coping

Distinguish various forms of coping.

- *Coping* is the process by which a person takes some action to manage environmental and internal demands that cause or might cause stress and that will tax the individual's inner resources. *Coping skills* are the techniques people use to deal with changing situations and stress. pp. 462–463
- Defense-oriented coping strategies do not reduce stressors but instead help people protect themselves from their effects. Most psychologists recommend task-oriented coping strategies. These strategies usually involve several tasks, or steps: (1) identifying the stressor, (2) choosing an appropriate course of action for stress reduction, (3) implementing the plan, and (4) evaluating its success. pp. 463–465
- *Stress inoculation* increases the predictability of stressful events, fosters coping skills, generates self-talking,

encourages confidence about successful outcomes, builds a commitment to personal action and responsibility for an adaptive course of action, and gives people realistic warnings, recommendations, and reassurances to help them prepare for and cope with impending dangers or losses. p. 465

- *Psychoneuroimmunology (PNI)* is the study of how psychological processes and the nervous system affect the body's immune system and how, in turn, the immune system influences psychological processes. pp. 466–467

KEY TERMS

Coping, p. 462
Resilience, p. 463
Coping skills, p. 463
Social support, p. 463
Stress inoculation, p. 465
Psychoneuroimmunology (PNI), p. 466

Health Psychology

What is the role of health psychology?

- *Health psychology* is the use of psychological ideas and principles to help enhance health, prevent illness, diagnose and treat disease, and rehabilitate people. Health psychology is an action-oriented discipline that focuses on preventive health measures as well as intervention in existing conditions. pp. 466–467
- Health psychologists can highlight the distinction between high-risk and low-risk behavior in AIDS prevention. They can be involved in educating youth, the uneducated, and other high-risk populations; they can also counsel AIDS patients and their families. pp. 470–471

Under what conditions do people comply with medical advice?

- When people do what they think will help them get well, they are adopting a sick role. Research shows that people are more receptive to medical treatments when the treatments are specific, simple, and easy to do and have minimal side effects. p. 469–471

KEY TERM

Health psychology, p. 467

Learning CONNECTIONS

Some students benefit from extra help with the concept of conflict. You can learn more about it in:

- The CD-ROM accompanying this book, Topic 11

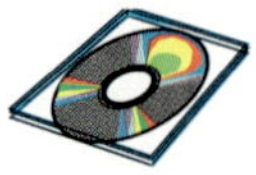

- This book's study guide, *Keeping Pace Plus*, or the computerized study guide, Chapter 13
- The audiotape accompanying this book, *SoundGuide for Psychology*, Learning Unit 13
- The study aids found on the World Wide Web site for this book, at http:/ /www.abacon.com/psych/lefton

Critical Thinking CONNECTIONS

Take a moment to think critically about how this chapter's topics are connected with the rest of psychology . . .

If you are interested in . . .	Ask yourself . . .	Then turn to . . .
How people cope with everyday problems 	What are some coping techniques you can practice at home to effectively manage stressors?	Chapter 4, pp. 130–133
	How can you learn to control your emotional responses to situations through self-instruction?	Chapter 9, p. 333
	How do you think seriously depressed people come to feel that they cannot cope any longer?	Chapter 14, pp. 500–501
	Is there a form of therapy that focuses on changing people's distorted ideas of reality?	Chapter 15, pp. 539–540
The role of stress in everyday life 	What relationship exists between arousal and stress?	Chapter 9, pp. 302–303
	Which psychological disorders have a strong component of anxiety?	Chapter 14, pp. 484–487
	What are the social implications of the fact that frustration leads to stress and, ultimately, to aggression?	Chapter 16, pp. 579–583
Psychology's role in health and well-being 	What is the best evidence that the immune system can be conditioned to respond to environmental stimulation?	Chapter 5, pp. 160–161

14

Psychological Disorders

Under a 1987 directive issued by Mayor Edward Koch to help New York City's mentally ill homeless, Joyce Brown was forcibly committed to Bellevue Hospital. The 40-year-old former secretary had lived on a Manhattan sidewalk for a year, feeding herself on $7 a day and huddling over a hot-air vent in winter to stay warm. She was dirty and incoherent, cursed at passersby, defecated in her clothes, and tore up and burned dollar bills given to her. Brown, however, didn't want to be "helped." She said, "Some people are street people; that's the life they choose to lead."

Brown took her battle to court, and the judge found her to be educated, intelligent, and fiercely independent. In explaining her odd behavior, Brown said that after she had eaten enough for the day, she burned any excess money because carrying cash at night was dangerous. She attributed her filthy condition to the inaccessibility of public toilets. Neither suicidal nor malnourished, Brown seemingly posed little threat to herself or others.

Three psychiatrists hired by Brown's attorneys testified that the woman was odd but not crazy. Four psychiatrists for the city said she was maladjusted. The judge ruled in Brown's favor, noting that street life may be aesthetically offensive but that the mentally ill are as entitled as everyone else to freedom.

Joyce Brown's case raises important questions about mental illness: How different must a person's behavior be to qualify as abnormal? Is Brown's behavior any stranger than that of an old man who leaves a multimillion-dollar fortune to his cats? Is it any more eccentric than taking a midwinter bath in an ice-covered lake, as members of the Polar Bear Club do, or undergoing extensive cosmetic surgery to obtain a "perfect" face and body? What should public policy be regarding mental illness? When a man rapes and murders a little girl, should he be judged criminally insane? In this chapter we will consider these and related questions.

What Is Abnormal Behavior?

Is Joyce Brown merely odd, or is her behavior abnormal? To some extent, it depends on where you live, because every society has its own definition of abnormal behavior. In Russia, for example, people were once regularly placed in mental institutions for political dissent. Generally, however, behavior classified as abnormal is more than odd. In any single month, about 15 percent of adults in the U.S. population meet the criteria for having a mental disorder; that is, they exhibit symptoms of abnormality (Reiger et al., 1988).

A Definition

Abnormal behavior is behavior characterized as (1) atypical, (2) socially unacceptable, (3) distressing, (4) maladaptive, and/or (5) the result of distorted cognitions. Let's consider these five distinguishing characteristics in turn.

First, abnormal behavior is *atypical*. Many behaviors are unusual; however, abnormal behaviors tend to be so unusual as to be statistically rare. For example, you would not consider ear piercing among teenage boys to be abnormal, because the practice is fairly common in the United States today. However, washing one's hands every few minutes during the day until they are raw is abnormal. Of course, not all atypical behavior is necessarily abnormal. The Olympic feats of runner Carl Lewis are statistically uncommon but not abnormal.

Second, in addition to being atypical, abnormal behavior is also often *socially unacceptable*. To some degree, ideas about what is normal and abnormal vary according to cultural values, which are in a constant state of flux. What is acceptable in one culture may be labeled unacceptable in another. Similarly, behavior that was considered unacceptable 20 years ago, such as a woman calling a man for a date, may be considered acceptable today. A behavior that is judged abnormal, however, is one that is unacceptable to society in general.

Third, a person's abnormal behavior often causes *distress* to the person or to those around the person. While feelings of anxiety or distress are normal in many situations, prolonged anxiety (distress) may result from abnormal behavior. You may feel anxious while you are preparing to speak in front of a group; but constant, unrelenting anxiety, the avoidance of any situation that might require public speaking, and fear of people in general suggest a problem.

Fourth, abnormal behavior is usually *maladaptive*, or self-defeating to the person exhibiting it. Maladaptive behavior, such as drug abuse, is harmful and nonproductive. It often leads to more misery and prevents people from making positive changes in their lives.

Last, abnormal behavior is often the result of *distorted cognitions* (thoughts). For example, a young man with distorted cognitions may falsely believe that people

Abnormal behavior: Behavior characterized as atypical, socially unacceptable, distressing, maladaptive, and/or the result of distorted cognitions.

are out to get him. A woman suffering from major depression may believe that she is worthless, stupid, and unlovable.

In recent years, psychologists have begun to describe behavior in terms of *maladjustment* rather than *abnormality*. The distinction is important because it implies that maladaptive behavior can, with treatment, be adjusted—and become adaptive and productive. The term *maladjustment* also emphasizes specific behaviors rather than labeling the entire person.

Using the sociocultural approach (described on page 481), researchers such as Thomas Szasz go so far as to assert that maladjustment and mental illness are socially constructed and defined. Szasz argues that there is, in fact, a myth of mental illness; for Szasz, once a practitioner labels a person as "abnormal," the person starts to act that way (Szasz, 1984, 1987). The patient confirms the therapist's expectations about his or her abnormality, even when the expectations may not reflect the patient's real condition. From Szasz's view, a patient in therapy unwittingly creates situations that lead to results that the therapist has predicted—I referred to this phenomenon in Chapter 1 as a *self-fulfilling prophecy* (page 17). Because of the phenomenon of the self-fulfilling prophecy, it is important for a therapist to label people as little as possible. Giving a person or the person's behavior a label or tag rarely helps; so, in Szasz's view, *mental illness* is a label that serves no good purpose.

To summarize, abnormal behavior is characterized as atypical, socially unacceptable, distressing, maladaptive, and/or the result of distorted cognitions. There are, of course, exceptions to this definition. For example, most people would not hesitate to label drug abuse as abnormal behavior, but it is not as atypical as it once was. Nevertheless, this definition provides psychologists with a solid framework from which to explore abnormal behavior and its treatment.

▲ *Certain behaviors may be atypical, yet not meet the descriptive criteria for abnormality.*

Perspectives on Abnormality

Before prescribing treatment, mental health practitioners want to know why a person is maladjusted, because establishing the cause of a disorder can sometimes help mental health professionals define a treatment plan. Therefore, practioners often turn to theories and models that attempt to explain the causes of abnormality. A **model** is an analogy, a perspective, or an approach that helps scientists discover relationships among data; it uses a structure from one field to help describe data in another. Psychologists use models to make predictions about behavior. These models form the basis of **abnormal psychology**, the field of psychology concerned with the assessment, treatment, and prevention of maladaptive behavior. Several models help explain abnormal behavior: medical–biological, psychodynamic, humanistic, behavioral, cognitive, sociocultural, legal, and interactionist.

Medical–Biological Model. Thousands of years ago, people believed that abnormal behavior was caused by demons that invaded an individual's body. The "cure" often involved a surgeon performing *trephination*—drilling a hole into the skull to allow the evil force to escape. Even as recently as a few hundred years ago, people with psychological disorders were caged and treated like animals. Early reformists, such as Philippe Pinel, advocated the medical model and proposed that abnormal behavior could be treated and cured, like an illness. When scientists showed that syphilis could cause mental disorders, the medical model gained even greater acceptance and led to more humane treatment and better conditions for those with psychological disorders.

Model: A perspective or approach derived from data in one field, used to help describe data in another field.

Abnormal psychology: The field of psychology concerned with the assessment, treatment, and prevention of maladaptive behavior.

The *medical–biological model* of abnormal behavior focuses on the biological and physiological conditions that initiate abnormal behaviors. This model adequately deals with a range of mental ailments, such as those caused by mercury poisoning or viral attacks on brain cells. It focuses on genetic abnormalities, problems in the central nervous system, and hormonal changes. It also helps explain and treat substance abuse problems and schizophrenia, two disorders that may have a strong biological component. Proponents of the medical–biological model might explain Joyce Brown's behavior (described at the beginning of this chapter) as resulting from a chemical or hormonal imbalance that altered her judgment.

Many of the terms and concepts used in psychology and psychiatry are borrowed from medicine; they include *treatment*, *case*, *symptom*, *syndrome*, and also the term *mental illness*. The medical model assumes that abnormal behavior, like other illnesses, can be diagnosed, treated, and often cured. This approach has not gone unchallenged, however. Its critics say that it does not take advantage of modern psychological insights, such as those of learning theory. A major—but not surprising—disadvantage of the medical model is that it emphasizes hospitalization and drug treatment rather than solving psychological problems by psychological means. Use of the medical model also has fostered the notion that abnormal behavior can be infectious, much like a disease.

Psychodynamic Model. The *psychodynamic model* of abnormal behavior is loosely rooted in Freud's theory of personality (discussed in Chapter 12). This model assumes that psychological disorders result from anxiety produced by unresolved conflicts and forces of which a person may be unaware. It asserts that maladjustment occurs when a person relies on too many defense mechanisms or when defense mechanisms fail. Joyce Brown's behavior might be explained as anger turned inward. Although Brown is bright and capable, her behavior might be seen as a reaction to her fear of competing caused by low self-esteem that was initiated in childhood. Treatment usually involves helping a patient become aware of motivations and conflicts so that the person can have a healthier lifestyle. We will explore psychodynamic approaches to treatment in more detail in Chapter 15.

Humanistic Model. Like the psychodynamic model, the *humanistic model* of abnormal behavior assumes that inner psychic forces are important in establishing and maintaining a normal lifestyle. Unlike psychodynamic theorists, however, humanists believe that people have a good deal of cognitive control over their lives. The humanistic model focuses on individual uniqueness and decision making. It contends that people become maladjusted when their expectations far exceed their achievements. In Joyce Brown's case, a humanist might focus on her dignity, self-respect, and quest for independence. Humanistic treatment usually involves helping maladjusted people to discover and accept their true selves, formulate more realistic self-concepts and expectations, and become more like their ideal selves.

Behavioral Model. The *behavioral model* of abnormal behavior states that such behavior is caused by faulty or ineffective learning and conditioning patterns. Two fundamental assumptions of behavioral (learning) theorists are that disordered behavior can be reshaped and that more appropriate, worthwhile behaviors can be substituted through traditional learning techniques (see Chapter 5). Behavioral theorists assume that events in a person's environment reinforce or punish various behaviors selectively and, in doing so, shape personality and may create maladjustment. They thus contend that an abusive husband may have learned to assert dominance over women through physical abuse because as a child he was rewarded for typically "masculine" behaviors (such as fighting) and punished for typically "feminine" behaviors (such as nurturance). Proponents of the behavioral model might explain Joyce Brown's behavior by noting that she did not find significant reinforcers in the work world and she felt she could take care of herself and manage better on a day-to-day basis on the streets.

Cognitive Model. The *cognitive model* of abnormal behavior asserts that human beings engage in both prosocial and maladjusted behaviors because of their thoughts. As thinking organisms, individuals decide how to behave; abnormal behavior is based on false assumptions or unrealistic coping strategies. Practitioners of the cognitive perspective treat people with psychological disorders by helping them develop new thought processes that instill new values. Joyce Brown might be assumed to have developed wrong ideas about the world; these ideas might be irrational and might have led her to maladaptive behaviors. Using the cognitive model, a practitioner might assert that a client such as Brown could replace maladjusted behaviors with worthwhile ones. The practitioner might treat Brown by helping her to formulate more rational self-concepts and to adopt more effective coping strategies.

Sociocultural Model. According to the *sociocultural model* of abnormal behavior, people develop abnormalities within and because of a context—the context of the family, the community, and the society. Researchers, especially cross-cultural researchers, have shown that people's personality development and their disorders reflect their culture, the stressors in their society, and the types of disorders prevalent in their society. Relying heavily on the learning and cognitive frameworks, the sociocultural model focuses on cultural variables as key determinants of maladjustment.

As researchers examine the frequency and types of disorders that occur in different societies, they also note some sharp differences within each society. Within a specific society, disorders vary as a function of the decade in which they occur and the age and gender of the clients. In China, for example, depression is relatively uncommon, but stress reactions in the form of physical ailments are frequent. Americans and Europeans report guilt and shame when they are depressed; depressed individuals in Africa, on the other hand, are less likely to report these symptoms but more likely to report somatic (physical) complaints. Specific disorders seem highly culture-specific; for example, a*mok* (as in "running amok") is a disorder that is characterized by sudden rage and homicidal aggression and is seen in some Asian countries, such as Malaysia and Thailand. Brought on by stress, sleep deprivation, and alcohol consumption, the behavior can be broken down into a series of stages. Similarly, *anorexia nervosa,* discussed in Chapter 9, is a disorder primarily confined to the West. Researchers now recognize, therefore, that some disorders are *culturally indigenous;* that is, specific to a culture (Simons & Hughes, 1993).

Legal Model. The *legal model* of abnormal behavior defines such behavior strictly in terms of guilt, innocence, and sanity. Think about John W. Hinckley Jr., the man who attempted to assassinate President Ronald Reagan. A jury declared him "not guilty by reason of insanity," and he was acquitted of attempted murder charges. During the public outcry that followed, states sought to prohibit the insanity plea. At least half the states changed their insanity plea, 12 adopted the new plea "guilty but mentally ill," and 3 chose to eliminate the insanity plea altogether.

The term *insane* is a legal term, not a psychological one. Insanity refers to a condition that excuses people from responsibility and protects them from punishment. From the legal point of view, a person cannot be held responsible for a crime if, at the time of the crime, the person lacked the capacity to recognize right from wrong or to obey the law.

Think again about Joyce Brown. Do legal criteria for guilt or innocence by reason of insanity describe her situation? The answer is no. Although useful for judicial purposes, the legal definition of abnormal behavior is too focused to be useful in treating clients; it is also a misconception that it is widely used as a defense.

In one of the rare instances of successful use of insanity as a legal defense, John W. Hinckley, Jr., was acquitted of attempted murder charges in connection with his assassination attempt against former President Ronald Reagan. ▼

Interactionist Model. Each of the models we've examined—medical–biological, psychodynamic, humanistic, behavioral, cognitive, sociocultural, and legal—looks at maladjustment from a different perspective. No single model can explain every kind of abnormal behavior; however, each has value. For some disorders (such as phobias), learning theory explains the cause and prescribes an effective course of treatment. For other disorders (such as schizophrenia), medical–biological theory explains a significant part of the problem. Consequently, many psychologists use an *interactionist model* (sometimes termed an *eclectic model*) of abnormal behavior, one drawing on all these perspectives. For example, a therapist could treat a depressed patient by arranging for antidepressant drugs (medical–biological approach), helping the patient develop new, optimistic thought processes (cognitive approach), and teaching the patient adaptive behaviors to eliminate depression-inducing stress (behavioral approach).

As you examine each of the psychological disorders presented in this chapter, think about why you favor one model of maladjustment over another. Do you have a cognitive bent, or do you favor a more psychodynamic approach? Perhaps you are more behavioral in your beliefs. Regardless of a practitioner's predispositions, it is important that symptoms be carefully evaluated so proper diagnoses can be made. People who are suffering need to be helped, not ignored, especially since a wide variety of treatments are available (Isaac & Armat, 1990).

Next, we will consider a system that has been developed to help practitioners make diagnoses. The system is presented in the work known as the *Diagnostic and Statistical Manual of Mental Disorders*.

Diagnosing Maladjustment: The *DSM–IV*

Three psychiatrists hired by Joyce Brown's attorneys testified that she was odd but not crazy. Four psychiatrists hired by the city of New York said she was insane. This controversy underscores the fact that diagnosing maladjusted behavior is a complicated process.

Diagnostic and Statistical Manual of Mental Disorders. The American Psychiatric Association has devised a system for diagnosing maladjusted behavior—the *Diagnostic and Statistical Manual of Mental Disorders*. Its goals are (1) to improve the reliability of diagnoses by categorizing disorders according to observable behaviors, and (2) to make sure that the diagnoses are consistent with research evidence and practical experience (Widiger et al., 1991). The system designates 16 major categories of maladjustment and more than 200 subcategories. (Table 14.1 lists some of the major classifications.) The *DSM* also cites the **prevalence** of each disorder—the percentage of the population displaying the disorder during any specified period. For most psychological disorders, researchers also know the lifetime prevalence—the statistical likelihood that a person will develop the disorder during his or her lifetime.

An important feature of the *DSM* is that diagnostic information for any individual is laid out on five different dimensions. The *DSM* refers to these dimensions as axes; the manual thus uses what is called a *multiaxial* system, in order to be as informative, precise, reliable, and valid as possible about an individual's condition. Axis I describes the *major disorders* themselves, many of which yielded this chapter's main headings. Axis II describes *personality disorders and prominent maladaptive personality features*, as well as defense mechanisms—an example might be inflexible thinking strategies. Axis III describes *current medical conditions* that might be pertinent to understanding or managing the individual's mental disorder—diabetes may interact with eating behavior, for instance, which is a relevant factor in anorexia nervosa. Axis IV, *psychosocial or environmental problems*, refers to life stresses or familial support systems that may or may not facilitate a person's treatment or recovery. Finally, Axis V comprises a *global assessment of functioning*, which reports the clinician's overall assessment of functioning in the psychological, social, and occupational domains of the person's life. These five axes, when viewed

Prevalence: The percentage of a population displaying a disorder during any specified period.

TABLE 14.1 ***Major Classifications of the* Diagnostic and Statistical Manual of Mental Disorders, *Fourth Edition***

Disorders First Diagnosed in Infancy, Childhood, and Adolescence
Delirium, Dementia, and Other Cognitive Disorders
Substance-Related Disorders
Schizophrenia and Other Psychotic Disorders
Mood Disorders
Anxiety Disorders
Somatoform Disorders
Factitious Disorders
Dissociative Disorders
Sexual and Gender Identity Disorders
Eating Disorders
Sleep Disorders
Impulse Control Disorders

Note: Each classification is further broken down into subtypes (with some minor modifications).

together, help a clinician fully describe the nature of a person's maladjustment. It is important to note that there may not be an assessment on a particular axis. So, for example, there may be no medical condition to report on Axis III.

You might think that such a diagnostic manual would be straightforward, like an encyclopedia of mental disorders. However, the *DSM* has met with some resistance and controversy; because it was written by committees, it represents various compromises. Some psychologists applaud its recognition of social and environmental influences on behavior. Others take issue with the way it places disorders together based on symptoms rather than causes. Still others argue that the *DSM* is too precise and complicated. Some assert that, despite its rigor, it is still not precise enough. Others worry about a bias against women. Still others believe the *DSM* should go beyond its descriptive approach with diagnosis and include problem-oriented and problem-solving information rather than just symptoms. Many psychologists are unhappy with the use of psychiatric terms that perpetuate a medical rather than a behavioral model. The manual is continually being revised to reflect the latest scientific knowledge and thus is an evolving system of classification (Clark, Watson, & Reynolds, 1995). The current edition is the fourth, the *DSM–IV,* published in 1994.

Diversity and Diagnoses. The *DSM* is by no means the final word in diagnosing maladjustment, and its reliability is not completely known; it is a developing system of classification. In addition, it needs to become more sensitive to issues of diversity. Not all ethnic groups exhibit symptoms of every disorder; nor do all members of one ethnic group have an equal likelihood of exhibiting specific symptoms.

Research shows that the likelihood of a specific diagnosis is indeed related to ethnicity. For example, Asian Americans and African Americans receive more diagnoses of schizophrenia than do whites (Paradis, Hatch, & Friedman, 1994), despite the fact that Asians in general do not seek mental health services as often as whites do (Uba, 1994). Hispanic Americans receive fewer diagnoses of schizophrenia than do whites (Flaskerud & Hu, 1992). Similarly, Koreans are more likely to be diagnosed as depressed than are people in Taiwan, the Philippines, or the United States (Crittenden et al., 1992). The rates of a specific disorder in a particular country

FOCUS

Review

- What are the advantages and disadvantages of the medical–biological model of abnormal behavior? pp. 479–480
- Identify the distinguishing characteristics of the psychodynamic, humanistic, and cognitive models of abnormal behavior. pp. 480–481
- What are the goals of the *DSM*, and what are its potential advantages and disadvantages? pp. 482–483

Think Critically

- Do you think there are some behaviors that are perceived as abnormal in all cultures? Explain.
- If you had a say in what the next edition of the *DSM* would look like, what would you add to make it more useful?

probably reflect racial, religious, and cultural biases; they especially reflect the specific culture-bound symptomatology that a society considers normal. As suggested earlier, various cultures allow for, and perhaps encourage, specific symptomatology. Culture and its effects on clinical diagnosis and treatment plans are under-researched and constitute an important area of concern for practicing psychologists. The American Psychological Association (1993) suggests that practitioners must:

- Recognize cultural diversity.
- Understand the role of culture and ethnicity in development.
- Help clients understand their own sociological identification.
- Understand how culture, race, gender, and sexual orientation interact to affect behavior.

In the remainder of this chapter, we will explore some of the most important disorders described in *DSM–IV* and their consequences. We begin with anxiety disorders.

Anxiety, Somatoform, and Dissociative Disorders

Everyone experiences anxiety. Most people feel anxious in specific situations, such as before taking an examination, competing in a swim meet, or delivering a speech. Although anxiety can be a positive, motivating force, its effects can also be debilitating; left untreated, chronic anxiety may eventually impair a person's health. Those who have had serious enough anxiety problems to have been hospitalized are at increased risk for suicide (Allgulander, 1994). Anxiety disorders are so common in the general population that they warrant special consideration. Research into them, however, is not extensive; and there is a real paucity of research on special populations—for example, African Americans (Last & Perrin, 1993).

Karen Horney

Anxiety: A generalized feeling of fear and apprehension that may be related to a particular event or object and is often accompanied by increased physiological arousal.

Defining Anxiety

Karen Horney (pronounced HORN-eye), a neo-Freudian renowned for her work on anxiety, described anxiety as the central factor in both normal and abnormal behavior (Horney, 1937). **Anxiety** is customarily considered a generalized feeling of fear and apprehension that may be related to a particular event or object and is often accompanied by increased physiological arousal. Horney considered it a motivating force, an intrapsychic urge, and a signal of distress. She also argued that it is anxiety that underlies many forms of maladjustment. She believed that maladjustment occurs when too many defenses against anxiety pervade the personality.

Freud, in contrast, saw anxiety as the result of constant conflict among the id, ego, and superego; he called nearly all forms of behavior associated with anxiety *neurotic*. Freud's term *neurosis* has made its way into everyday language, to the point where nonpsychologists tend to describe any behavioral quirk as neurotic.

Today psychologists believe that, as a general catchall term, *neurosis* is neither appropriate nor efficient. Precise and consistent diagnosis of maladjustment is essential to appropriate treatment; however, anxiety (and what Freud called neurotic behavior) refers to a wide range of symptoms, including fear, apprehension, inattention, palpitations, respiratory distress, and dizziness.

Psychologists recognize that anxiety is a key symptom of maladjustment—not necessarily the cause of maladjustment. Apprehension, fear, and its accompanying autonomic nervous system arousal are caused by thoughts, environmental stimuli, or perhaps some long-standing and as yet unresolved conflict. This is clearly the case with generalized anxiety disorders, considered next.

Generalized Anxiety Disorders

Every disorder represents a different pattern of behavior and maladjustment, and *DSM–IV* classifies disorders under a variety of diagnostic categories. Those in which anxiety is the prominent feature are designated generalized anxiety disorders. **Generalized anxiety disorders** are anxiety disorders characterized by persistent anxiety occurring more days than not for at least 6 months, sometimes with autonomic hyperactivity, apprehension, problems with motor tension, and difficulty in concentrating. People with a generalized anxiety disorder feel anxious almost constantly. They often report sleep disturbances, excessive sweating, muscle tension, headaches, and insomnia. They are tense and irritable, are unable to concentrate, have difficulty making decisions, and may hyperventilate (Rapee, 1986).

DSM–IV states that a person must show persistent anxiety to receive this diagnosis. When such chronic anxiety has no obvious source, it is called free-floating anxiety. **Free-floating anxiety** is persistent anxiety not clearly related to any specific object or situation, accompanied by a sense of impending doom. Of course, the source of such extreme anxiety may be, and often is, a specific stressor in the environment, such as having been in a prisoner-of-war camp.

People with a generalized anxiety disorder show impairment in three areas of functioning. One area is *motor tension*—the person is unable to relax and exhibits jumpiness, restlessness, and tension. The second area is *autonomic hyperactivity*—the person sweats, has a dry mouth, has a high resting pulse rate, urinates frequently, and may complain of a lump in the throat. The third area is *vigilance*—the person has difficulty concentrating and is irritable and impatient. Unlike people who feel anxious almost constantly, those who suffer from phobic disorders, considered next, have far more focused anxiety and fear.

Phobic Disorders

Do you know someone who is petrified at the thought of an airplane ride, who avoids crowds at all cost, or who shudders at the sight of a harmless garden snake? That person may suffer from a **phobic disorder**—an anxiety disorder involving an excessive, unreasonable, and irrational fear of, and consequent attempt to avoid, specific objects or situations. People with phobic disorders exhibit avoidance and escape behaviors, show increased heart rate and irregular breathing patterns, and report thoughts of disaster and severe embarrassment. Many psychologists agree that, once established, phobias are maintained by the relief a person derives from escaping or avoiding the feared situation.

One key to diagnosing a phobic disorder is that the fear must be excessive and disproportionate to the situation. Most people who fear heights would not avoid visiting a friend who lived on the top floor of a tall building; a person with a phobia of heights would, however. Fear alone does not distinguish a phobia; both fear and avoidance must be evident.

Generalized anxiety disorders: Anxiety disorders characterized by persistent anxiety for at least a month, sometimes with problems in motor tension, autonomic hyperactivity, apprehension, and concentration.

Free-floating anxiety: Persistent anxiety not clearly related to any specific object or situation and accompanied by a sense of impending doom.

Phobic disorder: Anxiety disorder characterized by unreasonable fear of, and consequent attempted avoidance of, specific objects or situations.

People suffering from extreme cases of agoraphobia are afraid to leave their homes. ▶

Mild phobic disorders occur in about 7.5 percent of the U.S. population. They are, in fact, relatively common in well-adjusted people. Severe, disabling phobias occur in less than 0.05 percent of the population and typically appear in patients with other disorders (Seif & Atkins, 1979). Phobias occur most frequently between the ages of 30 and 60 and about equally in men and women (Marks, 1977). There are an infinite number of objects and situations toward which people become fearful. Because of the diversity and number of phobias, *DSM* classifies three basic kinds: agoraphobia, social phobia, and specific phobia. We consider these next.

Agoraphobia. **Agoraphobia** is a marked fear and avoidance of being alone or isolated in open and public places from which escape might be difficult or embarrassing. This phobia is accompanied by avoidance behaviors that may eventually interfere with normal activities. It can become so debilitating that it prevents the individual from going into any open space, traveling in airplanes or through tunnels, or being in crowds. People with a severe case may decide never to leave their home, fearing that they will lose control, panic, or cause a scene in a public place. Agoraphobia is often brought on by stress, particularly interpersonal stress. It is far more common in women than in men, and it is often accompanied by other disorders.

The disorder brings about hyperventilation, extreme tension, and even cognitive disorganization (Zitrin, 1981). Agoraphobics feel weak and dizzy when they have an attack and often suffer from severe panic attacks. *Panic attacks* are characterized as acute anxiety, accompanied by sharp increases in autonomic nervous system arousal, that is not triggered by a specific event; persons who experience such attacks often avoid the situations that are associated with them, thus perpetuating the agoraphobia (McNally, 1990, 1994). Agoraphobics often are seriously depressed (Breier, Charney, & Heninger, 1984).

Agoraphobia is complicated, incapacitating, and extraordinarily difficult to treat. According to Freud and other psychoanalysts, traumatic childhood experiences may cause people to avoid particular objects, events, and situations that produce anxiety. Freudians speculate that as young children, agoraphobics may have feared abandonment by a cold or nonnurturing mother and the fear has generalized to a fear of abandonment or helplessness. Most researchers today find Freudian explanations of phobic behavior unconvincing. As an alternative, modern learning theory suggests that agoraphobia may develop because people avoid situations they have found painful or embarrassing. Failed coping strategies and low self-esteem have been implicated (Williams, Kinney, & Falbo, 1989). Despite much research, no simple cause for the disorder has been found.

Agoraphobia [AG-or-uh-FOE-bee-uh]: Anxiety disorder characterized by fear and avoidance of being alone or in public places from which escape might be difficult.

Social phobia [FOE-bee-uh]: Anxiety disorder characterized by fear of, and desire to avoid, situations in which the person might be exposed to scrutiny by others and might behave in an embarrassing or humiliating way.

Social Phobia. Whereas a person with agoraphobia may avoid all situations involving other people, a person with a social phobia tends to avoid situations involving possible exposure to the scrutiny of other people. A **social phobia** is an anxiety disorder characterized by fear of, and desire to avoid, situations in which

TABLE 14.2 *Some Common Specific Phobias*

Acrophobia (fear of high places)	Hematophobia (fear of blood)
Ailurophobia (fear of cats)	Mysophobia (fear of contamination)
Algophobia (fear of pain)	Nyctophobia (fear of darkness)
Anthropophobia (fear of men)	Pathophobia (fear of disease)
Aquaphobia (fear of water)	Pyrophobia (fear of fire)
Astraphobia (fear of storms, thunder, and lightning)	Thanatophobia (fear of death)
Claustrophobia (fear of closed places)	Xenophobia (fear of strangers)
Cynophobia (fear of dogs)	Zoophobia (fear of animals)

one might be exposed to scrutiny by others and might behave in an embarrassing or humiliating way. A person with a social phobia avoids eating in public or speaking before other people. Such a person also avoids evaluation by refusing to deal with people or situations in which evaluation and a lowering of self-esteem might occur (Williams, Kinney, & Falbo, 1995).

Specific Phobia. A **specific phobia** is an anxiety disorder characterized by irrational and persistent fear of a specific object or situation, along with a compelling desire to avoid it. Most people are familiar with specific phobias; see Table 14.2 for some examples. Among specific phobias are *claustrophobia* (fear of closed spaces), *hematophobia* (fear of the sight of blood), and *acrophobia* (fear of heights). Many specific phobias develop in childhood, adolescence, or early adulthood. Most people who have fears of heights, small spaces, water, doctors, or flying can calm themselves and deal with their fears; but those who cannot (true phobics) often seek the help of a psychotherapist when the phobia interferes with their health or with day-to-day functioning. Treatment using behavior therapy is typically effective.

Diversity, on page 488, examines the prevalence of specific phobias and other anxiety disorders among African Americans.

Obsessive–Compulsive Disorders

Being orderly and organized is an asset for most people in today's fast-paced, complex society. However, when orderliness becomes a driving concern, a person may be suffering from an obsessive–compulsive disorder. An **obsessive–compulsive disorder** is an anxiety disorder characterized by persistent and uncontrollable thoughts and irrational beliefs that cause performance of intrusive and inappropriate compulsive rituals that interfere with daily life. The unwanted thoughts, urges, and actions of people with obsessive–compulsive disorders focus on maintaining order and control. About 2 to 4 percent of the U.S. population suffers from obsessive–compulsive disorders. Males are far more likely than females to be diagnosed as having this disorder (Douglas et al., 1995). Of the people with the disorder, about 20 percent have only obsessions or compulsions; about 80 percent have both.

People with obsessive–compulsive disorders combat anxiety by carrying out ritual behaviors that reduce tension; they feel that they have to *do* something. Their thoughts have extraordinary power to control actions (Meares, 1994). For example, a man obsessed with avoiding germs may wash his hands a hundred times a day and may wear white gloves to avoid touching contaminated objects. If he does not perform these compulsive acts, he may develop severe anxiety. A woman obsessed with punctuality may become extremely anxious if dinner guests arrive 5 minutes late. Adolescents with obsessive–compulsive disorders tend to wash and rewash, check, count, repeat, touch, and straighten their environment (March, Leonard, & Swedo,

People with obsessive–compulsive disorders carry out ritual behaviors that interfere with the tasks of daily life, such as repeatedly sharpening pencils and precisely lining them up. ▼

Specific phobia: Anxiety disorder characterized by irrational and persistent fear of a particular object or situation, along with a compelling desire to avoid it.

Obsessive–compulsive disorder: Anxiety disorder characterized by persistent and uncontrollable thoughts and irrational beliefs that cause the performance of compulsive rituals that interfere with daily life.

DIVERSITY

The Dilemma of Anxiety Disorders among Ethnic Minorities

Here are three important facts: (1) Anxiety disorders, as a group, are one of the most common problems presented to clinical psychologists. (2) By the year 2000, one-third of the U.S. population will be composed of ethnic minorities. (3) There are higher rates of mental disturbances among some ethnic minorities than among others. For example, Asian Americans have a higher rate of mental disturbances than any other ethnic minority. In addition, African American clients have many more unnecessary psychiatric hospitalizations than do white clients (Friedman, Paradis, & Hatch, 1994).

Though relatively little attention has been given to anxiety disorders among ethnic minorities, there has been some research. Two researchers from the University of Pittsburgh, Neal and Turner (1991), found that African Americans had a higher prevalence of specific phobias and agoraphobia than any other ethnic group. African Americans are nearly twice as likely as whites to report recent specific and social phobias (Brown, Eaton, & Sussman, 1990). The percentage of African Americans who are diagnosed as agoraphobic is 1.5 times that of whites. Further, the percentage of African American Vietnam veterans who suffer from posttraumatic stress disorder is also higher than the percentage of white veterans. Like the other disorders, childhood anxiety disorders are less likely among white adolescents than among African American adolescents (Beidel, Turner, & Trager, 1994; Kashani & Orvaschel, 1988); the same pattern emerges with posttraumatic stress disorder (Last & Perrin, 1993).

Researchers such as Neal and Turner (1991) and Last and Perrin (1993) are not sure why these differences exist. They see these patterns of disorders among African Americans as a dilemma. And research on the situation is made especially difficult by certain problems. Among these problems are the following five: (1) Within the African American community, research does not have an honorable reputation, because of abuses that occurred in the past. As a consequence, few individuals wish to participate in research studies. (2) At times of emotional distress, African Americans are more likely to seek help from an emergency room physician or a minister than from a mental health professional. Again, lack of treatment yields few participants for research (Paradis, Hatch, & Friedman, 1994). (3) Researchers have unwittingly neglected anxiety disorders in African Americans. (4) The number of African Americans who are themselves engaged in clinical research is exceptionally small. (5) It is not clear how African Americans view anxiety, anxiety disorders, and coping with anxiety.

Today, the researchers who are asking the questions are often community psychologists. They know the appropriate questions to ask. However, they often lack the personnel and the resources to fully implement their ideas. There is a high frequency of disorders among ethnic minorities in general, and of anxiety disorders among African Americans in particular; there are complicated social and cultural factors that may underlie these disorders. These factors are part of the multicultural research problems that psychologists are only now beginning to recognize.

▲ *Complicating research efforts on African Americans is the fact that they are more likely to seek help from a doctor or minister than a mental health professional.*

1995). A person may compulsively write notes about every detail of every task before permitting herself or himself to take any action. Here is an account of fairly severe obsessive–compulsive behavior:

> I used to write notes to remind myself to do a particular job, so in my mind there was a real risk that one of these notes might go out of the window or door. . . . My fear was that if one of these papers blew away, this would cause a fatality to

the person carrying out my design project. . . . I found it difficult to walk along the street, as every time I saw paper I wondered if it was some of mine. I had to pick it all up, unless it was brown chocolate paper, or lined paper, which I didn't use. And before I got on my bike, I checked that nothing was sticking out of my pockets and got my wife to recheck. . . . I couldn't smoke a cigarette without taking it to bits and checking there was no document between the paper and tobacco. I couldn't even have sex because I thought a piece of paper might get intertwined into the mattress. (Melville, 1977, pp. 66–67)

Freud and other psychodynamic theorists believed that obsessive–compulsive disorders come largely from difficulties during the anal stage of development, when orderliness and cleanliness are often stressed. Learning theorists argue that bringing order to a person's environment reduces uncertainty and risk and thus is reinforcing. Because reinforced behaviors tend to recur, these behaviors become exaggerated during times of stress. Neuroscience-oriented theorists now believe strongly that such factors as dysfunction in the basal ganglia, chronic levels of elevated arousal, a genetic link, and brain trauma explain obsessive–compulsive disorders (Last et al., 1991; Turner, Beidel, & Nathan, 1985).

Practitioners report that full-blown and dramatic cases of obsessive–compulsive disorders are relatively rare. Treatment often includes drugs (such as Anafrinil, Prozac, or Zoloft; see Chapter 15) combined with relaxation exercises (March, Leonard, & Swedo, 1995). Such treatment helps change ideas about stress and the consequences of anxiety. Family support and family psychotherapy are also helpful; families are taught that they should neither encourage the behaviors nor participate in the person's rituals. In fact, research shows that when clients are given specific instructions to refrain from compulsive behaviors after exposure to anxiety-producing ideas, people, or events, the training decreases compulsive acts and associated anxiety (Marks et al., 1986). Today, self-help groups, greater awareness of the disorders, and drug therapies are leading to successful treatment. Somatoform and dissociative disorders, discussed next, are harder to understand and treat.

Somatoform Disorders

If you were a writer for a TV soap opera, you might have on your desk a copy of *DSM–IV,* with the page turned down at somatoform and dissociative disorders. These disorders are relatively rare and are studied less than other disorders; however, they make for fascinating reading and study.

Somatoform disorders are disorders that involve real physical symptoms that are not under voluntary control and for which no apparent physical cause exists. Evidence suggests that the causes are psychological. Three types of somatoform disorders are somatization disorders, conversion disorders, and hypochondriasis. People suffering from these disorders often are also diagnosed as having personality disorders, which we will discuss later (Bass & Murphy, 1995).

Somatization Disorders. **Somatization disorders** are somatoform disorders characterized by recurrent and multiple physical complaints of several years' duration for which medical attention has been ineffective. Despite physicians' inability to help, those with the disorder tend to seek medical attention at least once a year. The disorder typically begins before age 30. It is diagnosed in only about 1 percent of females and is even rarer in males.

Patients with such disorders feel sickly for much of their lives and may report muscle weakness, double vision, memory loss, and hallucinations. Other commonly reported symptoms include gastrointestinal problems; painful menstrual periods with excessive bleeding; sexual indifference; and pains in the back, chest, and genitals. Patients are often beset by anxiety and depression.

Individuals with somatization disorders often have a host of emotional problems that cause their physical complaints. However, some of the physical conditions

Somatoform disorders [so-MAT-oh-form]: Disorders characterized by real physical symptoms not under voluntary control and for which no evident physical cause exists.

Somatization disorders: Somatoform disorders characterized by recurrent and multiple physical complaints of several years' duration for which medical attention has been ineffective.

are not psychologically caused, and physicians must be especially careful to treat medically those conditions that need treatment and not to dismiss all the patient's problems as psychological.

Conversion Disorders. **Conversion disorders** are somatoform disorders characterized by the loss or alteration of physical functioning for no apparent physiological reason. People suffering from conversion disorders often lose the use of their arms, hands, or legs or their vision or other sensory modality. They may develop a combination of ailments. For example, a patient may become not only blind but also deaf, mute, or totally paralyzed. Although patients may be unaware of the relationship, conversion disorders are generally considered a way to escape from or avoid upsetting situations. Also, the attention and support patients sometimes receive because of the symptoms may cause them to maintain the disorder. Conversion disorders are often associated with a history of psychosomatic illness. Men and women are equally likely to develop conversion disorders, which, like somatization disorders, are rare.

Hypochondriasis. When a person spends a lot of time going to physicians with all types of bodily complaints for which the physicians can find no cause, psychologists suspect hypochondriasis. **Hypochondriasis** is a somatoform disorder characterized by an inordinate preoccupation with health and illness, coupled with excessive anxiety about disease. Hypochondriacs believe, erroneously, that they have grave afflictions. They become preoccupied with minor aches and pains and often miss work and create alarm among family members. Every ache, every minor symptom is examined, interpreted, and feared.

Psychodynamic views of hypochondriasis focus on how the symptoms of the illness keep the person from dealing with some other painful source of stress. Behavioral psychologists focus on how the illness can be reinforcing: People are given extra attention and care, and the illness diverts attention from tasks at which the individual may not be succeeding. By focusing on illness, a person may avoid dealing with marital problems, financial affairs, and educational goals. Of course, to the hypochondriac, the fears and anxiety are real. Only through psychotherapy can the true causes of the overattention to symptoms be addressed.

Dissociative Disorders

Dissociative disorders are disorders characterized by a sudden but temporary alteration in consciousness, identity, sensory/motor behavior, or memory. Although relatively rare, these disorders are quite noticeable and sharply delineated. They include dissociative amnesia and dissociative identity disorder.

Dissociative Amnesia. Dissociative amnesia (formerly called *psychogenic amnesia*), one of several dissociative disorders, used to be grouped with other disorders. Today, however, psychologists recognize it as a separate disorder. **Dissociative amnesia** is a dissociative disorder characterized by the sudden and extensive inability to recall important personal information, usually information of a traumatic or stressful nature. The memory loss is too extensive to be explained by ordinary forgetfulness. Often the amnesia is brought on by a traumatic incident involving the threat of physical injury or death. The condition, which is relatively rare, occurs most often during wars or natural disasters.

Dissociative Identity Disorder: Multiple Personality. Another form of dissociative disorder, often associated with dissociative amnesia but presenting a dramatically different kind of behavior, is **dissociative identity disorder**, more commonly known as *multiple personality.* Dissociative identity disorder is characterized by the existence within an individual of two or more distinct personalities, each of which is dominant at particular times and directs the individual's behavior at those

Conversion disorders: Somatoform disorders characterized by the loss or alteration of physical functioning for no apparent physiological reason.

Hypochondriasis [hy-po-kon-DRY-a-sis]: Somatoform disorder characterized by an inordinate preoccupation with health and illness, coupled with excessive anxiety about disease.

Dissociative disorders: Disorders characterized by a sudden but temporary alteration in consciousness, identity, sensory/motor behavior, or memory.

Dissociative amnesia: Dissociative disorder characterized by the sudden and extensive inability to recall important personal information, too extensive to be explained by ordinary forgetfulness.

Dissociative identity disorder: Dissociative disorder characterized by the existence within an individual of two or more distinct personalities, each of which is dominant at particular times and directs the individual's behavior at those times.

times. Each personality has unique traits and different memories and behavioral patterns. For example, one personality may be adaptive and efficient at coping with life, while another may exhibit maladaptive behavior. Some people's alternate personalities are of the opposite sex. Each personality is usually unaware of any other one, although in some cases they eavesdrop on each other (Schacter et al., 1989). Each personality, when active, acknowledges that time has passed but cannot account for it. The switch from one personality to another is usually brought on by stress.

Despite the impression given by popular movies and books such as *The Three Faces of Eve* and *Sybil*, multiple personality is an extremely rare diagnosed disorder, with only a few hundred actual well-documented cases in history. Many people confuse multiple personality with schizophrenia, a much more common disorder that we'll examine later in this chapter (Steinberg et al., 1994).

Psychologists have little data on the causes of dissociative identity disorder and debate about how best to classify it. For some, there is doubt as to whether multiple personality actually exists; some assert that it is unrecognized by practitioners (Huapaya, 1994). Other psychologists assert that it can nearly always be traced back to severe, prolonged child abuse. Some psychologists think people invent multiple personalities to avoid taking responsibility for their own behavior, especially when they have committed criminal acts. Others think some therapists subtly encourage patients to show symptoms of this disorder so that the therapists can achieve recognition. In any case dissociative identity disorder is well-known; it is vivid and interesting, and much more research is needed before comprehensive theories and effective treatments will become available.

> **FOCUS**
>
> ***Review***
>
> - When is anxiety called free-floating? p. 485
> - Identify the central elements of an obsessive–compulsive disorder. p. 487
> - What evidence might suggest that a person is displaying the symptoms of dissociative identity disorder (multiple personality)? pp. 490–491
>
> ***Think Critically***
>
> - What are the implications of dissociative identity disorder for traditional theories of personality?

Sexual Disorders

Few behaviors arouse more anxiety, fear, and superstition than those involving human sexuality. Many sexual problems (for example, orgasmic dysfunction) are often temporary symptoms of some other type of problem that is not really sexual in nature (for example, anxiety or poor communication between partners). True *sexual disorders*, however, range from disorders of desire, arousal, and orgasm to disorders that focus on pain to disorders induced by substance abuse. In the next few paragraphs, we will focus on the subcategory of sexual disorders consisting of sexual deviations, which are also known as paraphilias.

Sexual deviations, or *paraphilias*, are sexual practices directed toward objects rather than people, sexual encounters involving real or simulated suffering or humiliation, or sexual activities with nonconsenting partners. The *DSM* classifies only a few true sexual deviations; some researchers, however, maintain that there are many more (Money, 1984). A diagnosis of sexual deviation is made when the causes are psychological rather than physical and when these behaviors are the primary source of sexual stimulation or gratification for the individual. Following are some of the urges and behaviors that characterize sexual deviations. A person can be characterized as having such a disorder if he or she has the urges and acts on them, allows them to be his or her primary source of sexual gratification, or is markedly distressed by them.

Fetishism, which is more common in men than in women, involves sexual arousal and gratification brought about by nonliving objects rather than by people.

Sexual deviations: Sexual practices directed toward objects rather than people, sexual encounters involving real or simulated suffering or humiliation, or sexual activities with a nonconsenting partner. Also known as *paraphilias*.

For example, a man may have a fetish about a woman's shoes and may receive sexual gratification from them instead of from her.

In *transvestic fetishism*, also known as transvestitism or *cross-dressing*, a man receives gratification (often, but not always, sexual) by dressing in the clothing of a woman. (The number of women diagnosed with this disorder is very small.) Interference with cross-dressing produces frustration. Transvestites consider themselves members of their own sex, and most are heterosexual.

A person who achieves sexual satisfaction by watching other people in different states of undress or sexual activity is practicing *voyeurism*. Most voyeurs, or "peeping Toms," are men. Some researchers suggest that because voyeurs generally do not want to be seen, they are excited by the risk of discovery involved in watching other people. Another unconventional sexual activity is *exhibitionism*, in which adult men expose their genitals to unsuspecting observers, who are almost always female. Exhibitionists find the startled reactions of their victims sexually arousing.

Some people derive sexual satisfaction through sexual contact with children, a disorder known as *pedophilia*. Most pedophiles are well acquainted with the child; sometimes they are even close relatives. Many are married and appear to neighbors and friends to be well adjusted, both sexually and socially. Pedophiles may suffer from loneliness or schizophrenia, however. Fifty percent were themselves sexually abused as children (Ames & Houston, 1990).

Two other types of deviations are *sexual sadism* and *sexual masochism*. A sadist achieves sexual gratification by inflicting pain on a sexual partner. A masochist achieves sexual gratification from experiencing pain inflicted by someone else. Sadists and masochists are often sexual partners; the sadist provides the pain for the masochist, and both achieve sexual satisfaction. The pain involved can be physical or emotional.

Most psychologists agree that sexual disorders are learned behaviors. According to Freudians, problems during the Oedipal period create sexual problems later in life. Most behavioral practitioners agree in part with Freud, saying that sexual deviants are people whose normal gender identification went haywire early in their lives. They also argue that a difficult adolescence and a poor emerging self-concept are learning factors that may predispose someone to sexual disorders. Individuals who had a difficult time with their parents and peers, for example, may display some of those problems through sexual disorders when they are adults. Often, anger, hostility, shame, and doubt are present in people who suffer from sexual disorders.

Unfortunately, the causes and treatment of sexual disorders have not been studied much. Thus, psychologists know less than they would like to know about biological and environmental contributions. Most practitioners focus on behavioral treatments and on teaching people new, more adaptive ways of expressing feelings, fears, and sexual urges. These techniques can be effective and do not require hospitalization or drug therapy, unlike treatment for some of the more debilitating disorders considered in the remainder of this chapter.

Personality Disorders

People who exhibit inflexible and longstanding maladaptive ways of dealing with the environment that typically cause stress and/or social or occupational difficulties may have one of the **personality disorders**. Often, these disorders begin in childhood or adolescence and persist throughout adulthood. People with personality disorders are easy to spot but difficult to treat.

Personality disorders: Disorders characterized by inflexible and long-standing maladaptive ways of dealing with the environment, which typically cause stress and/or social or occupational problems.

Types of Personality Disorders

People with personality disorders are divided into three broad clusters: those whose behavior appears (1) odd or eccentric, (2) fearful or anxious, or (3) dramatic, emotional, and erratic. We will now consider five specific personality disorders: paranoid, dependent, histrionic, narcissistic, and antisocial.

Paranoid Personality Disorder. Fitting into the first cluster, by showing odd or eccentric behavior, are people suffering from *paranoid personality disorder,* who have unwarranted feelings of persecution and who mistrust almost everyone. They are hypersensitive to criticism and have a restricted range of emotional responses. They have strong fears of being exploited, and of losing control and independence. Sometimes they appear cold, humorless, even scheming. As you might expect, people with paranoid personality disorder are suspicious and seldom able to form close, intimate relationships with others.

Dependent Personality Disorder. Fitting into the second behavior cluster, by acting fearful or anxious, are individuals whose behavior is characteristic of *dependent personality disorder*. Such people are submissive and clinging; they let others make all the important decisions in their lives. They try to appear pleasant and agreeable at all times. They act meek, humble, and affectionate in order to keep their protectors. Battered wives often suffer from the dependent personality disorder. Overprotective, authoritarian parenting seems to be a major initiating cause of dependency (R. F. Bornstein, 1992).

Histrionic Personality Disorder. Fitting into the third cluster, because of dramatic, emotional, and erratic behaviors, are those people with the disorder called *histrionic personality disorder*. Individuals with this disorder seek attention by exaggerating situations in their lives. They have stormy personal relationships, are excessively emotional, and demand constant reassurance and praise.

Narcissistic Personality Disorder. Closely related to histrionic personality disorder, and also classified in the third cluster, is *narcissistic personality disorder*. People with this disorder have an extremely exaggerated sense of self-importance, expect favors, and need constant admiration and attention. They show a lack of caring for others, and they react to criticism with rage, shame, or humiliation.

Antisocial Personality Disorder. Still another disorder of the third cluster, and perhaps the most widely recognized personality disorder, is the antisocial personality disorder. An **antisocial personality disorder** is characterized by egocentricity, behavior that is irresponsible and that violates the rights of other people (lying, theft, delinquency, and other violations of social rules), a lack of guilt feelings, an inability to understand other people, and a lack of fear of punishment. Individuals with this disorder may be superficially charming, but their behavior is destructive and often reckless. A person so diagnosed must be at least 18 years old and usually displays a blatant disregard for others.

A person who frequently changes jobs, does not take proper care of his or her children, is arrested often, fails to pay bills, and lies constantly displays behaviors typical of antisocial personality disorder. Such people are relatively unsocialized adults: They are unwilling to conform to and live by society's rules, and their behavior often brings them into conflict with society. Antisocial people consistently blame others for their behavior. They seldom feel guilt or learn from experience or punishment. The disorder occurs six times more often in men than in women. Extreme forms of this disorder are displayed by cold-blooded killers, such as Charles Manson and Ted Bundy, although most people with the disorder exhibit it through less deadly and sensational behaviors. As many as 3 percent of all individuals may be diagnosed with antisocial personality disorder.

Adopted children separated at birth from antisocial biological parents are likely to show antisocial behavior later in life; this and other evidence suggests a genetic (nature) contribution to the disorder (Lyons et al., 1995; Nigg & Goldsmith, 1994).

Antisocial personality disorder: Personality disorder characterized by egocentricity, behavior that is irresponsible and that violates the rights of other people (lying, theft, delinquency, and other violations of societal rules), a lack of guilt feelings, an inability to understand other people, and a lack of fear of punishment.

▲ *Serial killer Theodore Robert Bundy, who assaulted and murdered as many as 36 victims between 1974 and 1978, is an extreme example of a person with antisocial personality disorder. Bundy proclaimed that he felt no guilt for his actions and "felt sorry" for those who did.*

Another fact that suggests a genetic factor is that the nervous systems of people diagnosed as having antisocial personality disorder may be different from those of normal people. When normal people do something wrong, their autonomic nervous system reacts with symptoms of anxiety, such as fear, heart palpitations, and sweating. Evidence suggests that *decreased* autonomic arousal is characteristic in people with antisocial personality disorders (Patrick, 1994). These people do not function at sufficiently high levels of autonomic nervous system arousal, do not experience the physiological symptoms of anxiety, and thus do not learn to associate those symptoms with antisocial behavior.

On the environmental (nurture) side, some psychologists believe that poor child-rearing practices and unstable family situations render individuals with antisocial personality disorder unable to learn fear, guilt, and punishment avoidance. Such people seem to have learned maladaptive functioning from their family situations and consequently to have developed inappropriate behaviors. Also, the symptoms of antisocial personality disorder are often seen first in a person's interactions with family members. Family relationships become strained, and some people suffering with the disorder may become involved in domestic violence—including child abuse, which we examine next. If the environmental viewpoint is correct, antisocial personality disorder may be a learned behavior. (*Applications* examines another behavior that, while it is not a *DSM–IV* classification, is an urgent problem for individuals and society—rape.)

Psychological Maltreatment of Children

The psychological maltreatment of children often takes the form of child abuse. Child abuse is not classified as a personality disorder, but many child abusers suffer from personality and other disorders. Many practitioners see child abuse as an outcome of previous psychological maltreatment of the abuser. **Child abuse** is the physical, emotional, or sexual mistreatment of children and is implicated in children's development of antisocial personality disorder. The impact on an abused child's self-esteem is profound (Romans et al., 1995; Trickett & Putnam, 1993), although victimized children can recover well with treatment (Kendall-Tackett, Williams, & Finkelhor, 1993).

Over 1 million children in the United States are the victims of maltreatment each year (National Research Council Panel on Child Abuse & Neglect, 1993). Females are victimized more than males (Knutson, 1995). Victimization is easier to detect through overt behaviors in young children than it is in school-age children (Campis, Hebden-Curtis, & DeMaso, 1993). Research shows that not all cases are reported and that even some treated cases go unreported by therapists, though the therapists are bound by law to report them; further, the rate of child abuse has not decreased in recent years (Kalichman & Craig, 1991; Knutson & Selner, 1994).

The Child Abuser. Who are the child abusers? Only about 5 percent of child abusers exhibit symptoms of very disturbed behavior. Most abusive parents seem quite normal by traditional social standards and sometimes have a prominent place in the community.

A distinction must be made between those who physically abuse children and those who sexually abuse them. Physically abusive parents often have unusually high expectations for their children and distorted perceptions of the children's behavior. They are generally less satisfied with their children than are nonabusive parents, and they perceive child rearing as more difficult than do nonabusive parents (Trickett & Susman, 1988). Abusive parents are not necessarily more discipline-oriented, power-oriented, or authoritarian with their children, but they tend to rely on ineffective child management techniques, including aversive control, blaming, scapegoating, threats, verbal degradations, and physical punishment (Emery, 1989a, 1989b; Milner & Chilamkurti, 1991). Parents who were abused as children are far more likely

Child abuse: Physical, emotional, or sexual mistreatment of children.

APPLICATIONS

Rape

Rape is not a classification in the *DSM,* but it is a crime that often is committed by an individual with an antisocial personality disorder. **Rape** is forcible sexual assault on an unwilling partner, usually a woman. The legal definition of *rape* varies from state to state, but it is generally being broadened to include any sexual assault (usually intercourse) that occurs without freely given consent.

Most rapes are planned, often in a meticulous manner; relatively seldom is rape an impulsive act that is prompted by a spur-of-the-moment sexual or aggressive feeling. Rape should be considered a violent crime rather than a sexual crime. Labeling rape a sexual assault obscures the violent, brutal nature of the crime and often places the woman on the defensive in the courtroom, even though she was the victim. Research shows that people often blame the victim, particularly if she knew the rapist (Kanekar et al., 1991).

More than 100,000 rapes are reported each year, according to the FBI; many experts assert, however, that this is only one-fourth of the actual number. Rape is in fact underreported to the criminal justice system (Koss, 1993). For example, one research study found that 27 percent of college women had experienced situations in which rape was attempted, and 7.5 percent of college men reported initiating acts that meet the definition of rape (Koss, Gidycz, & Wisniewski, 1987). Although these results are not necessarily generalizable to the entire population, rape and attempted rape seem to be far more common than was previously believed. Many rape victims know their assailants. On college campuses today, rape or attempted rape by an acquaintance—sometimes known as *date rape*—is receiving increased attention from law enforcement officials, who acknowledge its high prevalence (Ellis, 1994).

The Rapist. Because rape is a violent crime, it has come under the critical eye of researchers seeking to understand the characteristics and motivations of the rapist. Several facts about rapists are coming into focus. They tend to be young, often between 15 and 25. Many are poor and uneducated. Many have willing sexual partners other than their rape victims; half of all convicted rapists are married, although their high level of aggressiveness probably precludes happy and stable marriages or other satisfactory relationships.

Rapists may have some history of sexual dysfunctions; however, this finding is not consistent across all studies. They often have committed another sex-related offense, although this finding also is not consistent across all studies (Furby, Weinrott, & Blackshaw, 1989). Rapists tend to be more responsive to violence than are other men and less able to understand cues and messages from women who say no. Rapists' levels of maladjustment vary from slight to extreme when measured on psychological tests (Kalichman et al., 1989). Men who assault and rape women often view their attacks not as rape but as "mere" assault (Bourque, 1989). Various classifications of rapists have emerged—from rapists who rape on a whim, to angry rapists, to violent, sadistic rapists. No firm classification system is yet in place.

Most research shows that between 15 and 25 percent of male college students engage in some level of sexual aggression, usually toward women (Malamuth & Sockloskie, 1991). Most rapists think the likelihood of being punished is small, and this is considered one of the contributory factors in rape (L. Ellis, 1991). A comprehensive theory of rape is going to have to account for both its aggressive and its sexual nature (Barbaree & Marshall, 1991).

than others to be abusers themselves, especially if they do not have a stable, emotionally satisfying, supportive relationship with a mate (Egeland, Jacobvitz, & Sroufe, 1988; Worling, 1995). Societal attitudes toward family privacy, poverty, and difficult children all act together with the other factors to play a role. Belsky summarizes it well (1993, p. 427): "There is no one pathway to these disturbances in parenting; rather maltreatment seems to arise when stressors outweigh supports and risks are greater than protective factors."

Rape: Forcible sexual assault on an unwilling partner, usually a woman.

Prevention. Most psychologists and social workers consider child abuse an interactive process involving parental incompetence, environmental stress, and poor

FOCUS

Review

- Identify the distinguishing characteristics of a person diagnosed as having an antisocial personality disorder. p. 493

Think Critically

- Describe a preventive program that could be instituted to help decrease child abuse.
- How do you think colleges can help prevent date rape?

child management techniques. Therefore, both psychologists and social workers attempt to change family systems and patterns of interaction. Parents can be taught different coping skills, impulse control, effective child management techniques, and constructive ways to interact with their children. When these techniques are applied in an early intervention program for parents at risk of child abuse, they produce encouraging results. Children of potentially abusive parents who have undergone such therapy seem to have fewer and less intense behavior problems. Yet evaluations of such programs are equivocal. Reppucci and Haugaard (1989), for example, conclude: "We cannot be sure whether prevention programs are working, nor can we be sure that they are doing more good than harm" (p. 1274). These researchers argue that extensive investigation of the full range of preventive efforts is urgent. It is impossible not to concur.

Mood Disorders

Everyone experiences depression at one time or another. Ending a long-term intimate relationship, feeling overwhelmed during final exams, mourning the death of a close friend, and experiencing serious financial problems can all be sources of depression. But when people become so depressed or sad that a change occurs in their outlook and overt behavior, they may be suffering from clinical depression. Depression is considered to be a type of mood disorder. Mood disorders, which include *bipolar disorders* and *depressive disorders*, may sometimes be precipitated by a specific event, although for many individuals the symptoms develop gradually.

Bipolar Disorders

Gustav Mahler, a 19th-century Austrian composer and conductor, apparently suffered from a bipolar disorder. At age 19, he wrote to a friend:

> Much has happened within me since my last letter; I cannot describe it. Only this: I have become a different person. I don't know whether this new person is better; he certainly is not happier. The fires of a supreme zest for living and the most gnawing desire for death alternate in my heart, sometimes in the course of a single hour.

Bipolar disorders, which originally were known as *manic–depressive disorders*, get their name from the fact that patients' behavior vacillates between two extremes: mania and depression. The *manic phase* is characterized by rapid speech, inflated self-esteem, impulsiveness, euphoria, and decreased need for sleep. Patients in the manic phase are easily distracted, get angry when things do not go their way, and seem to have boundless energy. A person in the *depressed phase*, which often follows the manic phase, is moody and sad, with feelings of hopelessness.

Almost 2 million Americans suffer from bipolar disorders; men and women are equally likely to be affected. Although Mahler's bipolar disorder started when he was still in his teens, people who suffer from bipolar disorders are often in their late 20s before they begin to manifest the symptoms overtly, and these disorders often continue throughout life. Patients can be relatively normal for a few days, weeks, or months between episodes of excitement and depression, or they can rapidly vacil-

Bipolar disorders: Mood disorders characterized by vacillation between two extremes, mania and depression; originally known as manic–depressive disorders.

TABLE 14.3 *Bipolar Disorder Involves Cycles of Mania and Depression*

	Manic Behavior	Depressive Behavior
Emotional characteristics	Elation, euphoria Extreme sociability, expansiveness Impatience Distractibility Inflated self-esteem	Gloominess, hopelessness Social withdrawal Irritability Cognitive indecisiveness
Cognitive characteristics	Desire for action Impulsiveness Talkativeness Grandiosity	Slowness of thought Obsessive worrying about death Negative self-image Delusions of guilt Difficulty in concentrating Decreased motor activity
Motor characteristics	Hyperactivity Decreased need for sleep Sexual indiscretion Increased appetite	Fatigue Difficulty in sleeping Decreased sex drive Decreased appetite

late between excitement and depression. The key component of bipolar disorders is the shift from excited states to depressive states of sadness and hopelessness. The disorder seems to have a biological basis (Leber, Beckham, & Danker-Brown, 1985), and patients often respond fairly well to drug treatment, especially to lithium (which will be discussed in the next chapter) (Gitlin et al., 1995). As many as 50 percent of individuals who suffer from bipolar disorder also exhibit maladaptive personality traits, such as experiencing obsessions and compulsions or being overly dependent or narcissistic (Peselow, Sanfilipo, & Fieve, 1995). Table 14.3 lists the signs and symptoms of mania and depression in bipolar disorders.

Depressive Disorders

Bonnie Strickland, former president of the American Psychological Association, said during the 1988 APA meetings, "Depression has been called the common cold of psychological disturbances . . . which underscores its prevalence, but trivializes its impact." Strickland noted that at any time, about 14 million people are suffering from this disabling disorder.

Depressive disorders are a general category of mood disorders in which people on a day-to-day basis show extreme and persistent sadness, despair, and loss of interest in life's usual activities. The main difference between depressive disorders and bipolar disorders is that people with depressive disorders show no vacillation between excitement and depression; they tend to be depressed constantly. One type of depressive disorder is major depressive disorder; it is eight times more common than bipolar disorders.

Major depressive disorder, one of several depressive disorders, is characterized by loss of interest in almost all of life's usual activities; a sad, hopeless, or discouraged mood; sleep disturbance; loss of appetite; loss of energy; and feelings of unworthiness and guilt. Someone experiencing it is not merely experiencing fleeting anxiety or sadness, although this disorder may be triggered by to a specific event, such as the loss of a loved one, a job, or a home or some failure in life. Sufferers show at least some impairment of social and occupational functioning, although their behavior is not necessarily bizarre.

Depressive disorders: General category of mood disorders in which people show extreme and persistent sadness, despair, and loss of interest in life's usual activities.

Major depressive disorder: Depressive disorder characterized by loss of interest in almost all of life's usual activities, as evidenced by a sad, hopeless, or discouraged mood, sleep disturbance, loss of appetite, loss of energy, and feelings of unworthiness and guilt.

Symptoms. The symptoms of major depressive disorder include poor appetite, insomnia, weight loss, loss of energy, feelings of worthlessness and intense guilt, inability to concentrate, and sometimes thoughts of death and suicide (Benca et al., 1992; Buchwald & Rudick-Davis, 1993; Irwin, Smith, & Gillin, 1992). Depressed patients have a gloomy outlook on life, an extremely distorted view of current problems, a tendency to blame themselves, and low self-esteem (Maddux & Meier, 1995). They often withdraw from social and physical contact with others. Every task seems to require a great effort, thought is slow and unfocused, and problem-solving abilities are impaired (Danion et al., 1991; Hartlage et al., 1993; Marx, Williams, & Claridge, 1992). Individuals who display symptoms have other problems as well; for example, decrease in bone density and heightened risk of osteoporosis occur in those who suffer from depression, and depression is associated with abnormal brain activity in the frontal lobes and with immune system problems (George, Ketter, & Post, 1993; Herbert & Cohen, 1993; Schweiger et al., 1994).

Depressed people may also have **delusions**—false beliefs that are inconsistent with reality, held in spite of evidence that negates them, and often induce feelings of guilt, shame, and persecution. Seriously disturbed patients show even greater disruptions in thought and motor processes and a total lack of spontaneity and motivation. Such patients typically report that they have no hope for themselves or the world; nothing seems to interest them. They are often extremely self-critical (Blatt, 1995). Some feel responsible for serious world problems such as economic depression, disease, or hunger. They report strange diseases and may insist that their body is disintegrating or that their brain is being eaten from the inside out. Most people who exhibit symptoms of major depressive disorder can describe their reasons for feeling sad and dejected; however, they may be unable to explain why their response is so deep and so prolonged.

Psychologists say that many people suffering from major depressive disorder are poor at reality testing. *Reality testing* is a person's ability to judge the demands of the environment accurately and to deal with those demands. People with poor reality testing are unable to cope with the demands of life in rational ways because their reasoning ability is grossly impaired.

Onset and Duration. A major depressive episode can occur at any age, although people who experience these episodes usually undergo the first one before age 40. Symptoms are rapidly apparent and last for a few days, weeks, or months. Because so many different circumstances can be involved in depressive reaction, the extent of depression varies dramatically from individual to individual. Episodes may occur once or many times. Sometimes a depressive episode may be followed by years of normal functioning—followed by two or three brief incidents of depression a few weeks apart. Stressful life events are sometimes predictors of depression (Monroe, Simons, & Thase, 1991). Major depressive disorder is not exclusively an adult disorder; researchers find evidence of it in children and adolescents (Larson et al., 1990). When children show depression, they often have other symptoms, especially anxiety and loneliness. Treatment plans must be flexible and must take into account the wide array of family situations in which children find themselves—divorce or foster care or an environment of alcoholism or child abuse, for example.

Prevalence. According to the National Institutes of Mental Health, major depressive disorders strike about 14 to 15 million Americans each year. Women are twice as likely as men to be diagnosed as depressed and are more likely to express feelings of depression openly (Allgood-Merten, Lewinsohn, & Hops, 1990). In the United States, about 19 to 23 percent of women and 8 to 11 percent of men have experienced a major depressive episode at some time. About 6 percent of women and 3 percent of men have experienced episodes sufficiently severe to require hospitalization. It is unclear why women experience more depression than men; research on gender differences in both causes and treatment is limited (Strickland, 1992).

Delusions: False beliefs, which are inconsistent with reality and held in spite of evidence that negates them.

According to several studies, Americans born around 1960 suffer up to 10 times as many episodes of major depressive disorder as did their grandparents or great-grandparents (Lewinsohn et al., 1993). This may be due to changes in diagnosis, in reporting frequency, or perhaps in the stressors in society; the answer is not yet clear. In addition, people in developing cultures are far less likely to develop the passivity, feelings of hopelessness, diminished self-esteem, and suicidal tendencies that typify Westerners afflicted by major depressive disorder. Martin Seligman (1988) suggests that the increased incidence of depression in the United States stems from too much emphasis on the individual, coupled with a loss of faith in such supportive institutions as family, country, and religion.

Clinical Evaluation. How does a practitioner know if a person is suffering from major depressive disorder? A complete clinical evaluation comprises three parts: a physical examination, a psychiatric history, and a mental status examination. The *physical examination* is given to rule out thyroid disorders, viral infection, and anemia—all of which cause a slowing down of behavior. A neurological check of coordination, reflexes, and balance is part of this exam, to rule out brain disorders. The *psychiatric history* attempts to trace the course of the apparent disorder, genetic or family factors, and past treatments. Finally, the *mental status examination* scrutinizes thought, speaking processes, and memory; it may include interviews, tests for psychiatric symptoms (among them the MMPI–2), and projective tests such as the TAT (see Chapter 12 for details). All of this is done because, among other things, it is important to distinguish between major depressive disorder and dysthymic disorder. In *dysthymic disorder* people experience a mild but chronic depressed mood for more days than not, for at least 2 years, along with poor appetite, insomnia, low self-esteem, and feelings of hopelessness. This disorder often goes undiagnosed and untreated; people begin to act, and to be treated, as if this "sad" personality is normal. Yet dysthymic disorder spreads a thin veil of sadness over a person's life; individuals with the disorder are less likely to marry and more likely to divorce and are often underemployed or unemployed. They report being self-critical, have low interest in life's activities, and show occupational and social impairment. Dysthymic disorder is not as severe as major depressive disorder but lasts longer and often occurs alongside it; clinicians often diagnose dysthymic disorder in persons who were initially seeking help for a major depressive episode.

Causes of Major Depressive Disorder

Most psychologists believe major depressive disorder is caused by a combination of biological, learning, and cognitive factors. Biological theories suggest that chemical and genetic processes can account for depression. Learning theories suggest that people develop faulty behaviors. Cognitive theories suggest that irrational ideas guide behavior. Learned helplessness theories suggest that people may choose not to respond and give up. Let's look at each theory in more detail.

Biological Theories. Are people born with a predisposition to depression? Depression may be genetically based, according to Tsuang and Faraone (1990). Children of depressed patients are more likely than other children to be depressed; further, twin studies also indicate that genetic factors play a substantial role in depression (Kendler et al., 1992, 1993).

A different approach is the *norepinephrine hypothesis*, which states that an insufficient amount of norepinephrine (a neurotransmitter in the brain, discussed in Chapter 2) may cause depression. Research has shown that if the level of norepinephrine at receptor sites in the brain is increased, depression is alleviated. Because aversive stimuli decrease norepinephrine levels, however, being in a stressful situation could bring about depression. Research suggests that, although the norepinephrine hypothesis is not false, the biological underpinnings of depression are more complex. That is, depression may be caused by many substances in the brain (norepinephrine and others) that are not functioning properly or by genetic factors, or both (Faraone, Kremen, & Tsuang, 1990). Evidence even suggests a relationship between allergies and depression; this research suggests that in a small group of depressed patients, allergic reactions may accentuate brain chemical imbalances and abnormal brain activity (George, Ketter, & Post, 1993; P. S. Marshall, 1993).

Other evidence for a biological explanation of depression is that antidepressant drugs (tricyclics) seem to help certain types of depressed patients. In one study, every depressed patient was given one of three treatments: psychotherapy alone, an antidepressant drug alone, or a combination of psychotherapy and drug therapy. In this study, psychotherapy and drug therapy proved equally effective in reducing depressive symptoms. However, the combination of psychotherapy and drug therapy helped the most (DiMascio et al., 1979). In Chapter 16 we will see that this finding is hotly debated; some researchers assert that a talking therapy is as or more effective than drug therapy (Antonuccio, Danton, & DeNelsky, 1995).

Learning and Cognitive Theories. Learning and cognitive theorists argue that people learn depressive behaviors and thoughts. People with poor social skills who never learn to express prosocial behaviors and who are punished for the behaviors they do exhibit experience the world as aversive and depressing. In support of this idea is the finding that children of depressed patients, having been exposed to depressive behaviors so much, are more likely than other children to be depressed (Downey & Coyne, 1990). In addition, Peter Lewinsohn (1974) believes that people who have few positive reinforcements in their lives (often the old, the sickly, and the poor) become depressed. Other people find them unpleasant and avoid them, thus creating a nonreinforcing environment (Lewinsohn & Talkington, 1979). Lewinsohn stresses that depressed people often lack the social skills needed to obtain reinforcement, such as asking a neighbor or friend for help with a problem. See Figure 14.1 for details of Lewinsohn's view.

Psychiatrist Aaron Beck proposed another influential learning theory. Beck (1967) suggested that depressed people already have negative views of themselves, the environment, and the future; and these views cause them to magnify their errors. They compare themselves to other people, usually unfairly; and when they come up short, they see the difference as disastrous. They see the human condition as universally wretched, become angry, and view the world as a place that defeats positive behavior. Their poor self-concept and negative expectations about the world produce negative future expectations that lead to depression. All of this is magnified in adolescents, who are going through many bodily changes that may heighten their risk of depression (Allgood-Merton, Lewinsohn, & Hops, 1990).

Beck (1967, 1972, 1976) theorized that depression does not cause negative feelings but that negative feelings and expectations cause depression. Research supports Beck's theory. Depressed people are harsher on themselves than nondepressed people are, and they have particularly low levels of self-expectations and self-esteem (Maddux, 1995). They make judgments based on insufficient data, they overgeneralize, and they exaggerate the negative outcomes in their lives. According to Beck, being depressed causes poor judgments and thus affects people's cognitions. Beck's theory is influential among psychologists for two reasons. First, it is consistent with the notion that depression stems from a lack of appropriate positive reinforcements in people's environments. Second, it acknowledges both cognitive and environmental variables such as family interactions.

Learned helplessness: The behavior of giving up or not responding, exhibited by people or animals exposed to negative consequences or punishment over which they have no control.

Learned Helplessness. What would you do if you failed every exam you took, regardless of your efforts? What happens when a person's hopes and dreams are constantly thwarted, regardless of the person's behavior? The result may be **learned helplessness** (which we considered in more detail in Chapter 9)—the behav-

FIGURE 14.1

Lewinsohn's View of Depression

According to Lewinsohn, few reinforcers are available in the environment for some people. This lack of reinforcers causes depression, which then leads to even fewer reinforcers.

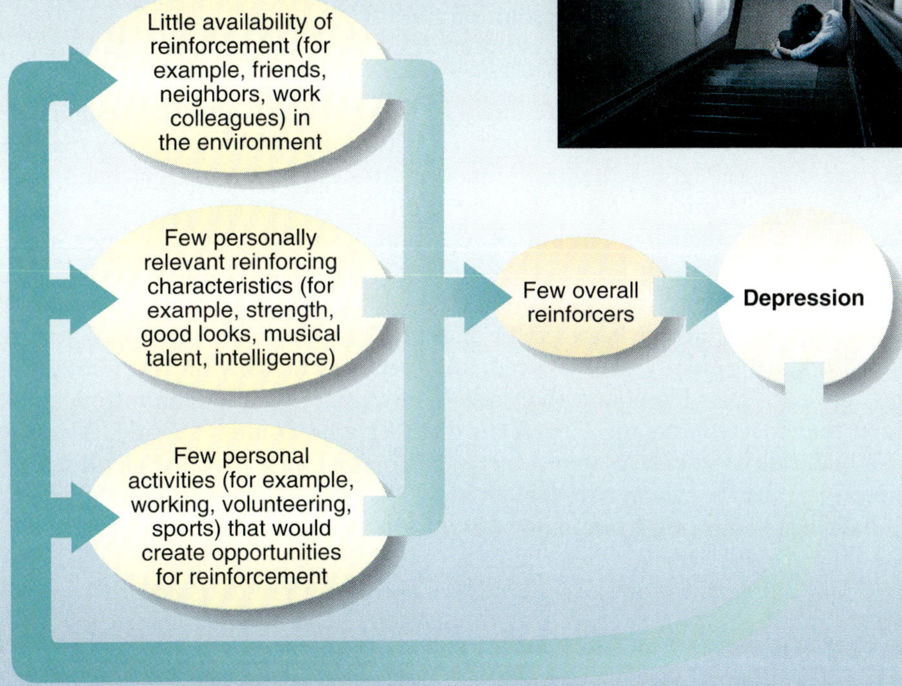

ior of giving up or not responding, exhibited by people or animals who have learned that rewards and punishments are not contingent on behavior.

Seligman (1976) has suggested that people's beliefs about the causes of their failures determine whether they will become depressed. When they attribute their failures to unalterable conditions within themselves ("my own weakness, which is unlikely to change"), they acquire low self-esteem (Maddux & Meier, 1995). That is, when people come to believe that eventual outcomes are unrelated to anything under their control, they develop learned helplessness and become pessimistic rather than optimistic. For example, a man who comes to believe that his effort to meet new people by being outgoing and friendly never works may stop trying. Eventually, he will choose not to respond to the environment, because he has learned that his behavior makes no difference (Peterson & Seligman, 1984). Seligman (1988) argues that the environment, not genetics, is the cause of pessimism, depression, and helplessness, especially when people believe that they are responsible for long-standing failures in many areas of their lives. When learned helplessness is operative, people adopt the view that they cannot change highly aversive life events (Abramson, Metalsky, and Alloy, 1989).

The idea that learned helplessness is a key factor in depression has received research support, although the way this factor operates is not yet fully understood (DeVellis & Blalock, 1992; Metalsky & Joiner, 1992). The effects of helplessness and depression are poignant and painful. They influence a person's day-to-day life, work environment, and family roles—especially parenting (Downey & Coyne, 1990).

Suicide

As suggested earlier, depressed individuals are at greater risk for suicide than are nondepressed individuals. Fortunately, most people who think about suicide do not actually commit the act; but when people become depressed and feel hopeless, the likelihood that they will commit suicide increases sharply, especially among older white males (Rifai et al., 1994). Each day, about 80 people in the United States commit suicide; that's almost 30,000 people each year. These individuals are often lonely, guilt-ridden, and depressed. They believe things cannot and will not get better, and that suicide is their best resolution.

A distinction must be drawn between attempters and completers. *Attempters* try to commit suicide but are unsuccessful. They tend to be young, impulsive, more often women than men, and more likely to make nonfatal attempts such as wrist slashing. *Completers* succeed in taking their lives. They tend to be white, male, and older, and they use highly lethal techniques of self-destruction, such as handguns.

Who commits suicide? More than three times as many men as women actually succeed in ending their lives, although four times as many women as men attempt (but fail) to do so. Among adolescents, suicide is the second leading cause of death (after accidents); 1 out of every 1,000 adolescents attempts suicide each year, and nearly 5,000 young people between the ages of 15 and 24 are successful (Garland & Zigler, 1993). The elderly, the divorced, and former patients with psychological disorders have a higher likelihood than others of attempting and committing suicide. In fact, the elderly make up 23 percent of those who commit suicide. Alcoholics have a high rate of suicide; Native Americans do, too, partly because alcoholism is a common problem for them (Murphy et al., 1992; Young & French, 1993). People who have been suffering from major depression are more likely to attempt suicide while they are recovering, when their energy level is higher, than at the depths of depression; during the worst of a depressive episode, a person is usually too weak, divided, and lacking in energy to commit suicide. Although only 15 percent of depressed people are suicidal, most suicide-prone individuals are depressed.

Are there warning signs of suicide? Research shows that predicting suicide is difficult, but not impossible (Shneidman, 1994). There are several indicators: changes in personal appearance, a dramatic drop in quality of schoolwork, changes in drug abuse patterns, decreased appetite, the giving away of prized possessions, and, most important, a depressed attitude. Nearly everyone who is suicidal exhibits depression, shown by changes in sleeping patterns (especially insomnia), a diminished ability to concentrate, fatigue, feelings of worthlessness, and decreased problem-solving abilities (Hughes & Neimeyer, 1993). In addition, 86 percent of those who are successful have attempted suicide before. Clearly, suicide attempters may become suicide completers if no one intervenes.

Heavily publicized suicides of pop culture idols such as Kurt Cobain, lead singer of the rock group Nirvana, glamorize this self-destructive act, adding to the pressures on adolescents at risk for attempting suicide. ▼

Causes. The causes of suicide are as complex as the people who commit suicide. For some individuals who take their own lives, societal pressures serve as a catalyst. For others, the catalysts may be the responsibility of aging parents, substance abuse that impairs judgment, or traumatic events. For still other people, a long-standing series of psychological disorders may predispose them to suicide. The psychological antecedents for suicide are about the same in non-Western as in Western cultures (Cheng, 1995). Table 14.4 presents some of the many myths about suicide and counters them with facts.

Psychologists cite a broad array of factors that may influence a suicide attempt. *Biological psychologists* assert that certain neurotransmitters, especially serotonin, have been linked to disorders that predispose individuals to suicide; for example, research shows that there are alterations in the serotonin system of those who attempt and complete suicide (Arango, Underwood, & Mann, 1992; Rifai,

TABLE 14.4 *Myths and Facts about Suicide*

Myth	Fact
1. Suicide happens without warning.	1. Suicidal individuals give many clues; 80 percent have to some degree discussed with others their intent to commit suicide.
2. Once people become suicidal, they remain so.	2. Suicidal persons remain so for limited periods—thus the value of restraint.
3. Suicide occurs almost exclusively among affluent or very poor individuals.	3. Suicide tends to occur proportionately in all economic levels of society.
4. Virtually all suicidal individuals are mentally ill.	4. This is not so, although most are depressed to some degree.
5. Suicidal tendencies are inherited or run in families.	5. There is no evidence for a direct genetic factor.
6. Suicide does not occur in primitive cultures.	6. Suicide occurs in almost all societies and cultures.
7. In Japan ritual suicide is common.	7. In modern Japan ritual suicide is rare; the most common method is barbiturate overdose.
8. Writers and artists have the highest suicide rates because they are "a bit crazy to begin with."	8. Physicians and police officers have the highest suicide rates; they have access to the most lethal means, and their work involves a high level of frustration.
9. Once a person starts to come out of a depression, the risk of suicide dissipates.	9. The risk of suicide is highest in the initial phase of an upswing from the depth of depression.
10. People who attempt suicide fully intend to die.	10. People who attempt suicide have diverse motives.

Source: Meyer & Salmon, 1988.

Reynolds, & Mann, 1992; Roy et al., 1991). *Behavioral psychologists* suggest that past experiences with suicide (such as seeing the effects of suicides on friends and relatives of a person who committed suicide) reinforce people's attempts to commit suicide. Other people who have taken their lives may also serve as models for suicidal behavior, but this is not always the case (Gibson & Range, 1991). *Psychodynamically oriented psychologists* suggest that the suicidal person is turning hostility and anger inward. Freud might argue that the act of suicide is the ultimate release of the aggressive instinct. *Cognitive psychologists* assert that suicide is the failure of a person's problem-solving abilities in response to stress or, alternatively, that the person's cognitive assessment is that the future is hopeless. *Humanistic psychologists* see suicide as a waste of a human being's potential, and they attempt to help suicidal and depressed patients focus on the meaning in their lives so that they can fulfill rather than destroy themselves. Many theorists, regardless of orientation, focus on a person's attempt to avoid self-awareness (Baumeister, 1990).

Adolescent suicide has received a great deal of attention because it is uncommonly prevalent. Also, 60 percent of all youths aged 15 to 19 who commit suicide use a gun. The suicide rate among teenage males is six times higher than that among teenage females (O'Donnell, 1995). Adolescents who attempt suicide often see a wide discrepancy between their high personal ambitions and seemingly meager results. The causes of adolescent suicide are complex and still not fully understood, but the increasing pressures and stress encountered by adolescents in the United States today certainly contribute to the rising number of suicides. Adolescents face an extremely competitive work force, alternating pressures to conform and to be an individual, and a social situation teeming with violence, crime, and drugs. Often, angry and frustrated adolescents exhibit other self-destructive behaviors, such as drug use, in addition to feeling hopelessness and low self-esteem (Kashani, Reid, & Rosenberg, 1989). Prevention efforts must focus on counseling, education, and reduction of the risk factors that lead to suicide.

Prevention. Most individuals who attempt suicide really want to live. However, their stress and their sense of helplessness about the future tell them that death is the only way out. This is even more true of adults than of adolescents (Cole, 1989). Some people are helped by crisis intervention and by counselors they can talk to on suicide hotlines. But a primary goal should be to help eliminate conditions that lead to and foster suicide, including availability of guns, alcoholism, drug abuse, and emotional isolation (Maris & Silverman, 1995).

When a person makes a suicide threat, take it seriously. Most people who commit suicide leave clues to their intentions ahead of time. Statements such as "I don't want to go on" or "I'm a burden to everyone, so maybe I should end it all" should be taken as warning signs. When people begin to give things away or to write letters with ominous overtones to relatives and friends, these are signs, too. If you know someone you think may be contemplating suicide, here are some steps you can take (Curran, 1987):

- Talk about stressors with the person who is at risk. The more the suicidal individual talks, the better. Don't be afraid to talk about suicide; it will not influence your friend or relative to commit suicide.
- Help the person who is contemplating suicide to seek out a psychologist, psychiatrist, counselor, or parent. A person thinking of suicide needs counseling.
- Do not keep a contemplated suicide a secret. Resist the person's attempt to keep you quiet about such confidences.
- Tell the person's spouse, parent, guardian, or counselor. Unless you are certain that these people already know, you should tell someone responsible for your friend's or relative's welfare.

The inability to function on a day-to-day basis becomes especially apparent in the study of an even more disabling disorder, schizophrenia, which we examine next.

FOCUS

Review

- Identify the key characteristics of a bipolar disorder. p. 496
- What are the essential characteristics of major depression? p. 487
- Describe how learned helplessness can lead to depression. p. 501

Think Critically

- What are the implications of the finding that many people who experience manic episodes also suffer from personality disorders?
- How might Szasz (who claimed mental illness is just a label) explain the behavior of a person showing depressive symptoms?
- If you have known someone who has committed suicide, do the psychological theories discussed in this section make sense with respect to that person? Why or why not?

Schizophrenia

Schizophrenia is considered the most devastating, complex, and frustrating of all mental disorders; people with this disorder lose touch with reality and are often unable to function in a world that makes no sense to them. A person with schizophrenia is said to have a schizophrenic disorder; this is because schizophrenia really represents a range of disorders. **Schizophrenic disorders** are a group of disorders characterized by a lack of reality testing and by deterioration of social and intellectual functioning, beginning before age 45 and lasting at least 6 months. People diagnosed as having a schizophrenic disorder often show serious personality disintegration. They may be considered **psychotic**—suffering from a gross impairment in reality testing that is wide-ranging and interferes with their ability to meet the ordinary demands of life.

FIGURE 14.2

Cultural Factors in the Diagnosis of Schizophrenia and Mood Disorders

African Americans are more likely than whites to be diagnosed as suffering from schizophrenia. In contrast, whites and Hispanic Americans are more likely than African Americans to be diagnosed as having some kind of mood disorder.
(Based on data from Snowden & Cheung, 1990.)

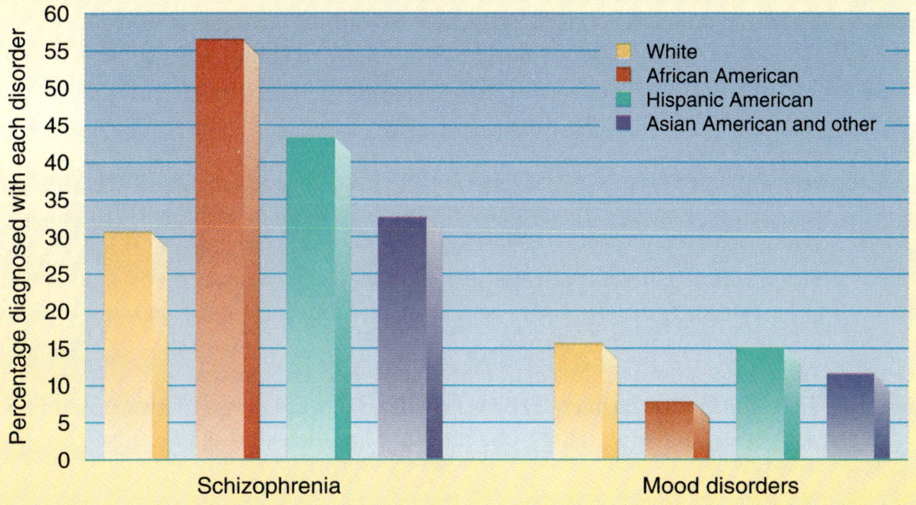

Schizophrenia begins slowly, with more symptoms developing as time passes. It affects 1 of every 100 people in the United States and accounts for almost 25 percent of all mental hospital admissions each year. The diagnosis occurs more frequently among lower socioeconomic groups and nonwhites and more frequently among younger people (Lindsey & Paul, 1989). As Figure 14.2 shows, African Americans are more likely than whites to be diagnosed as schizophrenic. Cultural biases against poor people and nonwhites, as well as these groups' higher stress levels, may account for this higher incidence of diagnosis.

Essential Characteristics of Schizophrenic Disorders

People with schizophrenic disorders display sudden significant changes in thought, perception, mood, and overall behavior. Those changes are often accompanied by distortions of reality and an inability to respond appropriately in thought, perception, or emotion.

Thought Disorders. One of the first signs of schizophrenia is difficulty maintaining logical thought and coherent conversation. People with schizophrenia disorders show disordered thinking and impaired memory (Sengel & Lovallo, 1983). They may also suffer from *delusions*. Many have delusions of persecution and believe that the world is a hostile place. These delusions are often accompanied by delusions of grandeur, in which the patient erroneously believes that he or she is a particularly important person. This importance becomes the reason for the persecution. Sometimes patients take on the role of an important character in history—for example, Jesus Christ or the Queen of England—and imagine that people are con-

Schizophrenic disorders [SKIT-soh-FREN-ick]: A group of disorders characterized by a lack of reality testing and by deterioration of social and intellectual functioning, beginning before age 45 and lasting at least 6 months; persons with these disorders often show serious personality disintegration with significant changes in thought, mood, perception, and behavior.

Psychotic [sye-KOT-ick]: Suffering from a gross impairment in reality testing that interferes with the ability to meet the ordinary demands of life.

spiring to harm them. Delusional thought is often apparent in schizophrenics' speech, in which sentence structure, words, and ideas become jumbled and disordered, creating a "word salad" of thoughts. Thus, a patient might be heard to say, "Your highness, may I more of some engine to my future food, for his lowness." Both thought and speech patterns become disorganized and often incoherent.

Perceptual Disorders. Another sign of schizophrenic disorders is the presence of **hallucinations**—compelling perceptual (visual, tactile, olfactory, or auditory) experiences without a real physical stimulus. Auditory hallucinations are the most common. The patient reports hearing voices originating outside his or her head. The voices may comment on the patient's behavior or direct the patient to behave in certain ways (Bentall, 1990). For example, convicted murderer David Berkowitz (known to the media as Son of Sam) claimed that his neighbor's dog told him to kill. Hallucinations have a biological basis and are caused by abnormal brain responses (Asaad & Shapiro, 1986).

Emotional Disorders. One of the most striking characteristics of schizophrenia is the display of inappropriate **affect**—emotional responses. A patient with schizophrenia may become depressed and cry when her favorite food falls on the floor, yet laugh hysterically at the death of a close friend or relative. Some patients display no emotion (either appropriate or inappropriate) and seem incapable of experiencing a normal range of feeling. Their affect is constricted, or *flat*. They show blank, expressionless faces, even when presented with a deliberately provocative remark or situation. Other patients exhibit *ambivalent* affect. They go through a wide range of emotional behaviors in a brief period, seeming happy one moment and dejected the next.

Types of Schizophrenia

The term *schizophrenia* is a catchall for patients displaying many symptoms; however, there are actually five types of schizophrenia—disorganized, paranoid, catatonic, residual, and undifferentiated—each with different symptoms, diagnostic criteria, and causes (see Table 14.5). Regardless of the type, a diagnosis of schizophrenia requires the presence of the following features:

- Lack of reality testing
- Involvement of more than one area of psychological functioning
- Deterioration in social and intellectual functioning
- Onset of illness generally before age 45
- Duration of illness of at least 6 months

Disorganized Type. The **disorganized type of schizophrenia** is characterized by severely disturbed thought processes, frequent incoherence, delusions, and inappropriate affect. Patients may exhibit bizarre emotions, with periods of giggling, crying, or irritability for no apparent reason. Their behavior can be silly, inappropriate, or even obscene. They show a severe disintegration of normal personality, a loss of reality testing, and often poor personal hygiene. Their chances for recovery are poor.

Paranoid Type. The paranoid type of schizophrenia is one of the most difficult to identify and study, because outward behavior often seems appropriate to the situation. **The paranoid type of schizophrenia** is characterized by hallucinations and delusions of persecution or grandeur (or both), and sometimes irrational jealousy. Paranoid schizophrenics may actively seek out other people and not show extreme withdrawal from social interaction. Their degree of disturbance varies over time. (The paranoid type of schizophrenia is different from the paranoid personality disorder, which is discussed on page 493 and which has less likelihood of being biologically caused.)

Hallucinations [ha-LOOSE-in-AY-shuns]: Compelling perceptual (visual, tactile, olfactory, or auditory) experiences without a real physical stimulus.

Affect: A person's emotional responses.

Disorganized type of schizophrenia: A major type of schizophrenia, characterized by frequent incoherence; absence of systematized delusions; and blunted, inappropriate, or silly affect.

Paranoid type of schizophrenia [PAIR-uh-noid]: A major type of schizophrenia, characterized by delusions and hallucinations of persecution or grandeur (or both), and sometimes irrational jealousy.

TABLE 14.5 *Types and Symptoms of Schizophrenia*

Type	Symptoms
Disorganized	Frequent incoherence, absence of systematized delusions, and blunted, inappropriate, or silly affect
Paranoid	Delusions and hallucinations of persecution or grandeur (or both) and sometimes irrational jealousy
Catatonic	Stupor in which there is a negative attitude and marked decrease in reactivity to the environment, or an excited phase in which there is agitated motor activity not influenced by external stimuli and which may appear or disappear suddenly ▶
Residual	History of at least one previous episode of schizophrenia with prominent psychotic symptoms but at present a clinical picture without any prominent psychotic symptoms; continuing evidence of the illness, such as inappropriate affect, illogical thinking, social withdrawal, or eccentric behavior
Undifferentiated	Prominent delusions, hallucinations, incoherence, or grossly disorganized behavior, without meeting the criteria for any of the other types or meeting the criteria for more than one type

Paranoid schizophrenics may be alert, intelligent, and responsive. However, their delusions and hallucinations impair their ability to deal with reality, and their behavior is often unpredictable and sometimes hostile. They may see bizarre images and are likely to have auditory hallucinations. They may think they are being chased by ghosts or by intruders from another planet. They may believe certain events in the world have a particular significance to them. If, for example, the President of the United States makes a speech deploring crime, a paranoid schizophrenic patient may believe that the President is referring specifically to the patient's crimes. Patients with the paranoid type of schizophrenia have a better chance of recovery than do patients with other types of schizophrenia.

Catatonic Type. **The catatonic type of schizophrenia** is characterized by displays of excited or violent motor activity or by stupor. That is, there are actually two subtypes of the catatonic type of schizophrenia—excited and withdrawn—both of which involve extreme overt behavior. *Excited* catatonic patients show excessive activity. They may talk and shout continuously and engage in seemingly uninhibited, agitated, and aggressive motor activity. These episodes usually appear and disappear suddenly. *Withdrawn* catatonic patients tend to appear stuporous—mute, negative, and basically unresponsive. Although they occasionally exhibit some signs of the excited type, they usually show a high degree of muscular rigidity. They are not immobile but have a decreased level of speaking, moving, and responding, although they are usually aware of events around them. Withdrawn catatonic patients may use immobility and unresponsiveness to maintain control over their environment; their behavior relieves them of the responsibility of responding to external stimuli.

Residual and Undifferentiated Type. People who show symptoms attributable to schizophrenia but who remain in touch with reality are said to have the **residual type of schizophrenia.** Such patients show inappropriate affect, illogical thinking, or eccentric behavior. They have a history of at least one previous schizophrenic episode.

Sometimes it is difficult to determine which category a patient most appropriately fits into (Gift et al., 1980). Some patients exhibit all the essential features of

Catatonic type of schizophrenia [CAT-uh-TONN-ick]: A major type of schizophrenia, characterized by displays of excited or violent motor activity or by stupor (in which the individual is mute, negative, and basically unresponsive).

Residual type of schizophrenia: A schizophrenic disorder in which the patient exhibits inappropriate affect, illogical thinking, and/or eccentric behavior but seems generally in touch with reality.

schizophrenia—prominent delusions, hallucinations, incoherence, and grossly disorganized behavior—but do not fit neatly into the categories of disorganized, catatonic, paranoid, or residual. Individuals with these characteristics are said to have the **undifferentiated type of schizophrenia.**

Causes of Schizophrenia

What causes people to lose their grasp on reality with such devastating results? Are people born with schizophrenia, or do they develop it as a result of painful childhood experiences? Researchers of schizophrenia take markedly different positions about its origins. Biologically oriented psychologists focus on chemicals in the brain and a person's genetic heritage; their basic argument is that schizophrenia is a brain disease. Learning theorists argue that a person's environment and early experiences cause schizophrenia. The arguments for each approach are compelling.

Biological Causes. Evidence exists to suggest the presence of some kind of biological determinant of, or predisposition to, schizophrenia. People born with that predisposition have a greater probability of developing schizophrenia than do other people. In early or middle fetal development, brain connections may go awry and result in later cerebral malfunctioning (Waddington, 1993). This may be because key RNA molecules may be missing when the major neurotransmitters, such as GABA (discussed in Chapter 2), are forming (Akbarian et al., 1995). Using this evidence, researchers assert that schizophrenia is caused by brain chemistry and perhaps an impaired autonomic nervous system response (Hollister et al., 1994).

About 1 percent of the U.S. population is schizophrenic; when one parent has schizophrenia, however, the probability that an offspring also will develop the disorder increases to between 3 and 14 percent. If both parents have schizophrenia, their children have about a 35 percent probability of developing it. (Figure 14.3 shows the likelihood of the relatives of schizophrenics developing the disorder.) It is now generally accepted that schizophrenia runs in families; the children and siblings of schizophrenic patients are more likely to exhibit maladjustment and schizophrenic symptoms than are other people (Kety et al., 1994). Researchers have been looking for a gene that might carry specific traits associated with schizophrenia, although such efforts have had only limited success (Markow, 1992).

Researchers are aware that the family environment of children of schizophrenics is typically unusual, and they acknowledge that the genetic evidence is only suggestive and that environment is also likely to play a role in the development of the disorder. If schizophrenia were totally genetic, then the likelihood that identical (monozygotic) twins, who have identical genes, would show the disorder would be 100 percent. (This likelihood of shared traits is referred to as the **concordance rate.**) But studies of schizophrenia in identical twins show concordance rates that range from 15 to 86 percent (DiLalla & Gottesman, 1995; Torrey et al., 1994), suggesting that other factors are involved. In one important study, analysis of brain structures showed subtle but important brain abnormalities in a schizophrenic individual whose identical twin did not show the abnormality. Such studies assert that nongenetic factors must exert an important influence on schizophrenia and be critical in its development (DiLalla & Gottesman, 1995; Gottesman, 1991; Suddath et al., 1990).

Nevertheless, most researchers agree that genetics is a fundamental factor in the disorder. The concordance rate for schizophrenia in identical twins is almost five times that in fraternal twins. Moreover, identical twins reared apart from their natural parents and from each other show a higher concordance rate than do fraternal twins or controls (Stone, 1980). Other support for a biological basis for schizophrenia comes from researchers who discovered that chemicals in the bloodstream may contribute to the development of schizophrenia. Several studies note the importance of the neurotransmitter *dopamine* in schizophrenia. Dopamine pathways are consid-

Undifferentiated type of schizophrenia: A schizophrenic disorder characterized by a mixture of symptoms and which does not meet diagnostic criteria of other categories, or may meet criteria of more than one category.

Concordance rate: The percentage of occasions when two groups or individuals show the same trait.

FIGURE 14.3

The Risk That Various Relatives of a Schizophrenic Person Will Develop Schizophrenia

The more closely two individuals are related, the greater the likelihood that if one develops schizophrenia, the other will, too. The Genain quadruplets—three of whom were diagnosed as schizophrenic—provide a classic example of genetic influence.

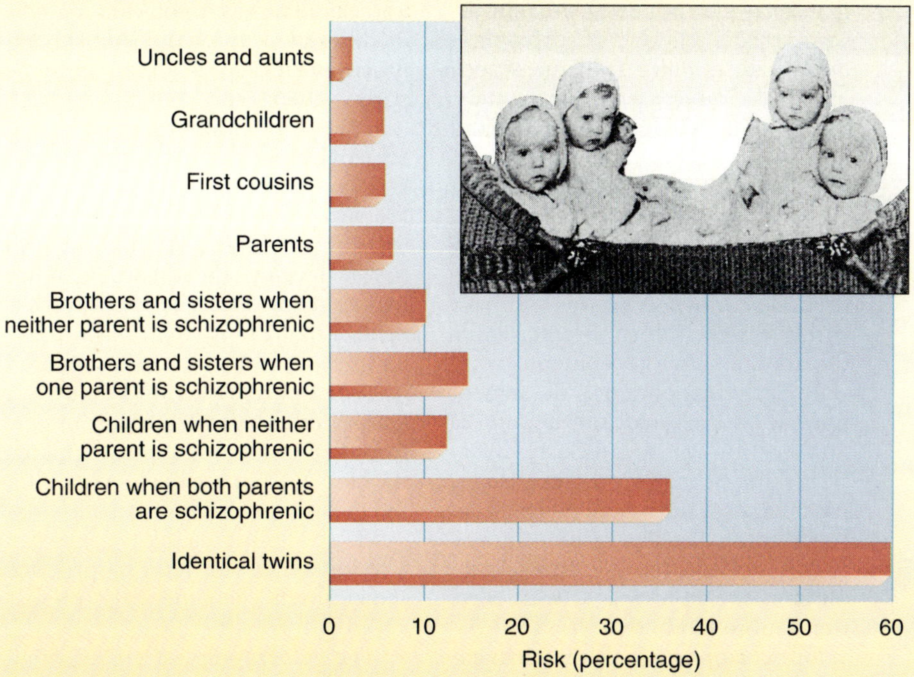

ered one of the main sites of biochemical disturbance in the brain (M. B. Bowers, Jr., 1982). A class of drugs, the *phenothiazines*, appears to block receptor sites in the dopamine pathways. When patients with schizophrenia are given phenothiazines, many of their disturbed thought processes and hallucinations disappear. Conversely, drugs that stimulate the dopamine system and increase brain dopamine levels (such as amphetamines) aggravate existing schizophrenic disorders.

Certain portions of the brains of schizophrenic patients and their relatives exhibit abnormalities, although it is not yet clear whether schizophrenia causes the abnormalities or the abnormalities cause schizophrenia (Cannon & Marco, 1994). For example, the *brain ventricles* (hollow areas normally filled with fluid) are enlarged in some schizophrenic patients (Raz & Raz, 1990; Suddath et al., 1990). Furthermore, some structures, notably the frontal lobes, show reduced blood flow and functioning in schizophrenics (Buchsbaum, 1990; Resnick, 1992).

In sum, researchers now assert that biological and genetic factors predict a specific risk for schizophrenia. While many stress factors (which are the focus of environmental researchers) may contribute to schizophrenia, a genetic component seems to be essential. *The Research Process,* on page 510, looks more closely at this question.

These PET scans show decreased neural activity in the brain of a person diagnosed with schizophrenia compared with that in a normal brain. ▼

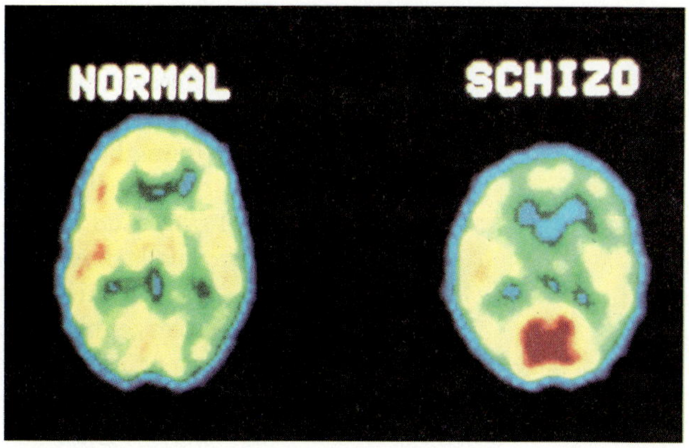

THE RESEARCH PROCESS

High-Risk Children and Schizophrenia

Can schizophrenia be prevented? Do some people have a vulnerability to schizophrenia that is triggered by stressful situations? According to the vulnerability–stress hypothesis, a person's susceptibility to schizophrenia depends on genetic factors, birth factors, and stress during infancy, childhood, and adolescence. This approach assumes that when stressors appear, schizophrenia and its symptoms may appear; the more stressors, the more likely that schizophrenia will surface. Some people can tolerate a great deal of stress; others can tolerate very little before schizophrenia materializes.

Psychologists have conducted longitudinal studies of schizophrenia, following children of schizophrenic mothers and fathers from birth to adulthood. These studies, known as *high-risk studies* because the participants are assumed to be at higher risk than the general population, have produced landmark results. The high-risk approach is effective because:

- Participants can be studied before the disorder develops.
- The data are relatively unbiased, because it is not known whether the child will become schizophrenic.
- Data can be gathered from the individuals and their families (not from doctors or hospital records) and are therefore not influenced by patients' likelihood of seeking particular medical assistance.

Many high-risk studies under way throughout the world, including some that started in the 1960s, are now assessing the likelihood of schizophrenia in mature adults. The Copenhagen High-Risk Project is one such study. Since 1962, Mednick, Parnas, and Schulsinger (1987) have followed a sample of 207 people who were at high risk for schizophrenia, as well as 104 control individuals. This study focused on mothers and their children. The mothers of the high-risk children were schizophrenic, while the mothers in the control group were not schizophrenic. The schizophrenic and control mothers were matched for age, social class, education, and urban–rural differences. Psychological tests were given at periodic intervals. The results showed that if a child's mother was schizophrenic, the child was at least eight times more likely than usual to develop schizophrenia. If the birth experience was traumatic, there was increased likelihood of schizophrenia. The results also showed that poor maternal supervision was related to the development of schizophrenia.

Other high-risk projects offer similar results. The University of Rochester Child and Family Study, which began in 1972, shows that when parents are maladjusted, their children often need psychological care (Wynne, Cole, & Perkins, 1987). The Stony Brook High-Risk Project has reported that considerable family discord, poor parenting skills, and marital conflict are related to psychological problems in children. The relationship is magnified when there is a schizophrenic parent (Weintraub, 1987).

There is no doubt that children of schizophrenic parents are at greater risk for developing schizophrenia. However, researchers are most interested in the high-risk children who never develop the disorder. What makes them different? Researchers believe that family relationships are an important dimension. If children of schizophrenic parents live in a household filled with discord, fighting, alcoholism, and poor discipline, they are much more likely to develop the disorder. Burman and colleagues (1987, p. 364) conclude: "Stressful environments will tend to produce schizophrenia in genetically predisposed individuals."

The vulnerability–stress hypothesis may prove to be the most accurate predictor of schizophrenia. It appears that in some people who are more vulnerable than others, stressors may spark the psychiatric disorder (or relapse). The longitudinal research continues.

Environmental Factors. Some psychologists believe that in addition to genetic factors, environmental interactions determine the development of schizophrenia (see Figure 14.4). Freudian psychologists, for example, suggest that early childhood relationships determine whether a person will become fixated at the oral stage and develop a disorder such as schizophrenia. Such a person has not developed an ego and will make judgments based on the id's pleasure principle. Lacking the ego, which uses the reality principle in making judgments, the individual will seek immediate gratification and thus be unable to deal effectively with reality. Freudian psychologists assert that a person who has successfully passed through the oral stage and has developed a strong ego is unlikely to suffer from schizophrenia; there is a lack of rigorous scientific evidence to support this assertion, however.

Behavioral explanations of schizophrenia are based on traditional learning principles (explored in Chapter 5). The behavioral approach argues that faulty reinforcement and extinction procedures, as well as social learning processes, can account for schizophrenia. Imagine a child brought up in a family where the parents constantly argue, where the father is an alcoholic, and where neither parent shows much affection for the other or for anyone else. Such a child, receiving no reinforce-

FIGURE 14.4

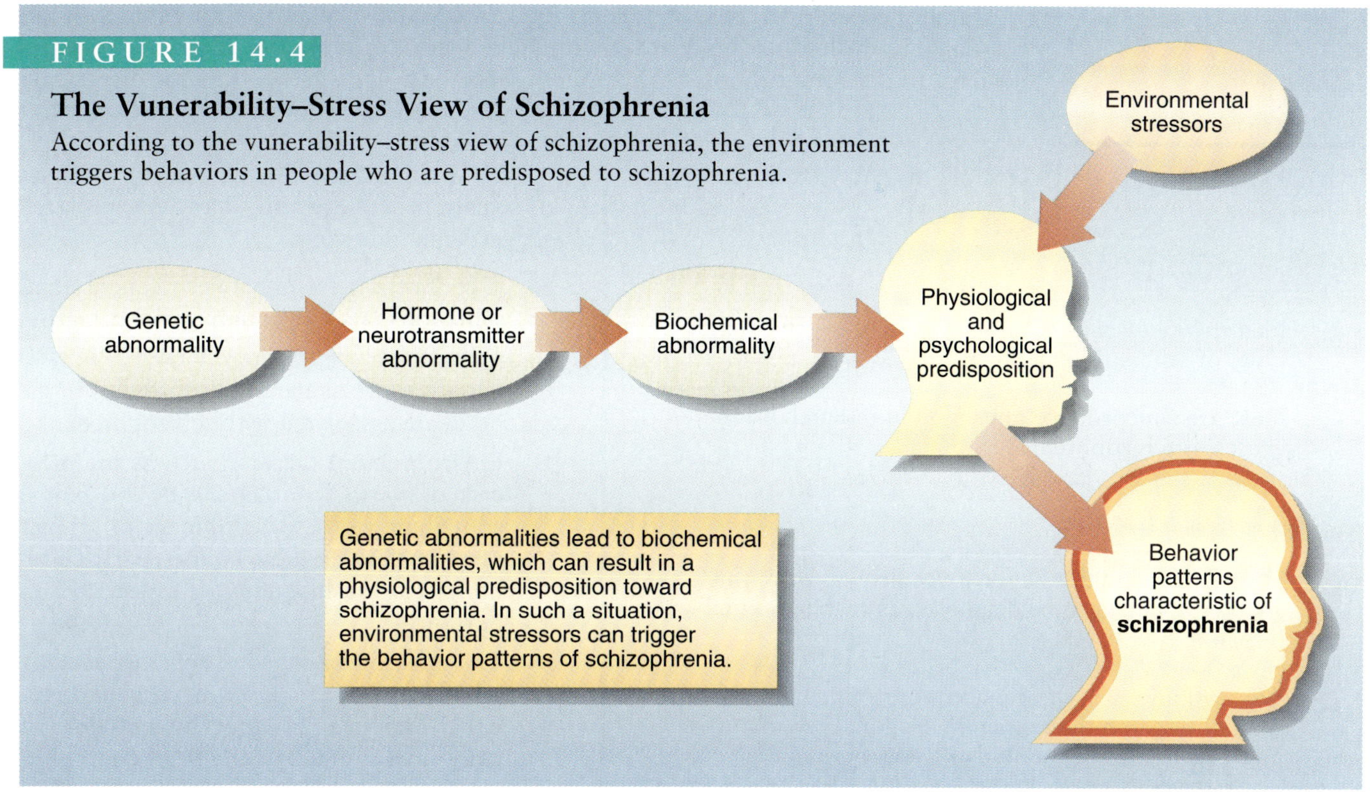

The Vunerability–Stress View of Schizophrenia
According to the vunerability–stress view of schizophrenia, the environment triggers behaviors in people who are predisposed to schizophrenia.

ment for interest in events, people, and objects in the outside world, may become withdrawn and begin to exhibit schizophrenic behavior. Lidz (1973) argues that children who grow up in such homes adopt the family's faulty view of the world and of relationships and thus are likely to expect reinforcement for abnormal behaviors. Growing up in such an emotionally fragmented environment may predispose individuals to emotional disorder and eventual schizophrenia (Miklowitz, 1994; Walker et al., 1983). In addition, if the parents themselves are schizophrenic and they mistreat the child, this increases the likelihood of problems such as schizophrenia in the child's future.

Even in families in which marital conflict is absent, parents sometimes confuse their children. Some parents, for example, frequently place their children in a situation that offers two different and inconsistent messages, a **double bind**. Initially described by Bateson (Bateson et al., 1956), double bind situations usually occur between individuals with a strong emotional attachment, such as a child and a parent (Mishler & Waxler, 1968). In play, a parent may hold up a toy and say, "No, you may not have this," while smiling and giving other nonverbal assurances that the child may have the toy. Generally, the child understands that the parent is teasing. However, not all children understand this and not all situations are so clearly cued. Games of this kind, if played consistently, may shape an environment of confusion conducive to the development of schizophrenia.

According to learning theory, a person who receives a great deal of attention for behaviors that other people see as bizarre is likely to continue those behaviors. People who fail to develop effective social skills are more at risk for bizarre behaviors (Mueser et al., 1990). Other reinforcement theories suggest that bizarre behavior and thoughts are themselves reinforcing, because they allow the person to escape from both acute anxiety and an overactive autonomic nervous system.

Nature or Nurture? Many variables determine whether an individual will develop schizophrenia. Some people, because of family environment, genetic history, or brain chemistry, are more vulnerable than others. **Vulnerability** is a person's

Double bind: A situation in which an individual is given two different and inconsistent messages.

Vulnerability: A person's diminished ability to deal with demanding life events.

diminished ability to deal with demanding life events. The more vulnerable the individual is, the less necessary are environmental stress or other disorders (such as anxiety) to the initiation of a schizophrenic episode. This is the vulnerability–stress hypothesis, sometimes termed the *diathesis–stress model.*

To summarize, although the exact causes of schizophrenia are still unknown, research suggests the following:

- A connection exists between genetics and schizophrenia, although genetic factors alone cannot account for its development.
- Specific types of chemical substances in the brain are associated with schizophrenia.
- Environmental factors (such as the presence of marital conflict and double binds) contribute to the development of schizophrenia. Among these factors, early childhood relationships may be especially important.
- The most likely cause of schizophrenia is a biological predisposition in the individual, which is aggravated by a climate of emotional immaturity, lack of communication, and emotional instability.

FOCUS

Review

- Identify the essential characteristics of the five major types of schizophrenia. p. 506
- How are concordance rates used in research on the causes of schizophrenia? p. 508

Think Critically

- How likely would it be for Joyce Brown, from the chapter opening, to be diagnosed as schizophrenic? Explain.
- Why would researchers place more emphasis on longitudinal research than on cross-sectional research (see pages 341–342) in the study of schizophrenia?

Summary and Review

What Is Abnormal Behavior?

Provide a definition of abnormal behavior and explain the major perspectives on abnormality.

- *Abnormal behavior* is atypical, socially unacceptable, distressing, maladaptive, and/or the result of distorted cognitions. p. 478
- The medical–biological model focuses on the biological and physiological conditions that initiate abnormal behaviors. The psychodynamic model focuses on unresolved conflicts and forces of which a person may be unaware. The humanistic model assumes that people can control their own lives; it focuses on individual uniqueness and decision making. The behavioral model states that abnormal behavior is caused by faulty or ineffective learning and conditioning patterns. The cognitive model looks at people's ideas and thoughts. The sociocultural model examines abnormalities within the context of culture, the family, the community, and society. The legal model defines abnormal behavior strictly in terms of guilt, innocence, and sanity. The interactionist model draws on all of these perspectives. pp. 479–482

What are the goals of the DSM, *and what are its potential advantages and disadvantages?*

- The *DSM–IV* is the latest edition of the diagnostic manual that mental health practitioners use to diagnose and classify mental disorders. It describes behavior in terms of its characteristics and its *prevalence.* The manual uses what is called a multiaxial system in order to be as informative, precise, reliable, and valid as possible about an individual's condition. Its goals are to improve the reliability of diagnoses and to make sure that diagnoses are consistent with research evidence and practical experience. Some psychologists applaud the *DSM* for its recognition of social and environmental influences on behavior; others take issue with the way it places disorders together based on symptoms rather than causes. Still others argue that it is too precise and complicated, and that it has a bias against women. pp. 482–483

KEY TERMS

Abnormal behavior, p. 478
Model, p. 479
Abnormal psychology, p. 479
Prevalence, p. 482

Anxiety, Somatoform, and Dissociative Disorders

What are the chief characteristics of anxiety, somatoform, and dissociative disorders?

- *Anxiety* is a generalized feeling of fear and apprehension, which is often accompanied by increased physiological arousal and may or may not be related to a specific event or object. p. 484

- A *generalized anxiety disorder* is characterized by persistent anxiety of at least a month's duration. It can include autonomic hyperactivity, impairments in motor tension, and vigilance. A *phobic disorder* is characterized by irrational fear and avoidance of certain objects or situations; people are not truly phobic unless they avoid situations that make them fearful. p. 485

- Individuals with *obsessive–compulsive disorders* have persistent and uncontrollable thoughts and irrational beliefs, which cause them to perform compulsive rituals that interfere with normal daily functioning. The focus of these behaviors is often on maintaining order and control. p. 487

- People with *somatoform disorders* have real physical symptoms with no apparent physical cause. *Somatization disorders* are somatoform disorders characterized by recurrent and multiple complaints of several years' duration for which medical attention has not been effective. *Conversion disorders* are somatoform disorders characterized by the loss or alteration of physical functioning for no apparent physiological reason. *Hypochondriasis* is a somatoform disorder characterized by an extreme preoccupation with health and illness, anxiety about disease, and imagined afflictions. pp. 489–490

- *Dissociative disorders* are disorders characterized by a sudden but temporary alteration in consciousness, identity, sensory/motor behavior, or memory. These disorders, though quite noticeable, are relatively rare. p. 490

KEY TERMS

Anxiety, p. 484
Generalized anxiety disorders, p. 485
Free-floating anxiety, p. 485
Phobic disorder, p. 485
Agoraphobia, p. 486
Social phobia, p. 486
Specific phobia, p. 487
Obsessive–compulsive disorder, p. 487
Somatoform disorders, p. 489
Somatization disorders, p. 489
Conversion disorders, p. 490
Hypochondriasis, p. 490
Dissociative disorders, p. 490
Dissociative amnesia, p. 490
Dissociative identity disorder, p. 490

Sexual Disorders

What are the essential components of sexual deviations?

- *Sexual deviations* are sexual practices directed toward objects rather than people or involving real or simulated suffering, humiliation, or nonconsenting partners. p. 491

KEY TERM

Sexual deviations, p. 491

Personality Disorders

What are the chief characteristics of five key personality disorders?

- People who have unwarranted feelings of persecution and who mistrust almost everyone are said to be suffering from the type of *personality disorder* called paranoid personality disorder. Submissive and clinging behaviors are characteristic of people with a dependent personality disorder. Dramatic, emotional, and erratic behaviors are characteristic of the histrionic personality disorder. The narcissistic personality disorder is characterized by an extremely exaggerated sense of self-importance, an expectation of special favors, and a constant need for attention; people with the disorder show a lack of caring for others and react to criticism with rage, shame, or humiliation. The *antisocial personality disorder* is characterized by behavior that is irresponsible and destructive and violates the rights of others; persons with antisocial personality disorder have no fear of punishment and are egocentric. pp. 492–493

KEY TERMS

Personality disorders, p. 492
Antisocial personality disorder, p. 493
Child abuse, p. 494
Rape, p. 495

Mood Disorders

What are the major mood disorders and their essential characteristics?

- *Bipolar disorders* get their name from the fact that patients' behavior vacillates between two extremes: mania and depression. p. 496

- Patients diagnosed with *major depressive disorder* have a gloomy outlook on life, especially slow thought processes, loss of appetite, an exaggerated view of current problems, loss of energy, and a tendency to blame themselves. p. 497

- The norepinephrine hypothesis suggests that an insufficient amount of norepinephrine in the brain causes depression. Learning theories argue that reinforcement patterns and social interactions determine the course and nature of depression. pp. 499–500

Who attempts suicide?

- Most people who think about suicide do not actually commit the act. Attempters try to commit suicide but are unsuccessful; completers succeed in taking their lives. More than three times as many men as women actually succeed in ending their lives, although four times as many women as men attempt to do so; each year 1 out of every 1,000 adolescents attempts suicide. p. 502

KEY TERMS

Bipolar disorders, p. 496
Depressive disorders, p. 497
Major depressive disorder, p. 497
Delusions, p. 498
Learned helplessness, p. 500

Schizophrenia

Identify the essential characteristics of the five major types of schizophrenia.

- Schizophrenia is a group of disorders characterized by a lack of reality testing and by deterioration of social and intellectual functioning. Individuals with *schizophrenic disorders* often show serious personality disintegration, with significant changes in thought, mood, perception, and behavior. p. 505

- The *disorganized type of schizophrenia* is characterized by severely disturbed thought processes. Patients have *hallucinations* and delusions and are frequently incoherent. The *paranoid type of schizophrenia* is among the most difficult to identify and study, because outward behavior often seems appropriate to the situation. Patients may actively seek out other people and may not show extreme withdrawal from social interaction. There are actually two subtypes of the *catatonic type of schizophrenia*—excited and withdrawn. People who show symptoms attributable to schizophrenia but who remain in touch with reality are diagnosed as having the *residual type of schizophrenia*. Some patients exhibit all the essential features of schizophrenia but do not fall clearly into any one of the other categories—these individuals are classified as suffering from the *undifferentiated type of schizophrenia*. pp. 506–508

How are concordance rates used in research on the causes of schizophrenia?

- The *concordance rate* is the percentage of occasions when two groups or individuals show the same trait. Concordance rates between siblings are often examined, especially those for twins, who share a genetic heritage. Biological studies suggest that the cause of schizophrenia must be to some extent genetic, as is shown by higher concordance rates for identical twins than for fraternal twins. p. 508

KEY TERMS

Schizophrenic disorders, p. 505
Psychotic, p. 505
Hallucinations, p. 506
Affect, p. 506
Disorganized type of schizophrenia, p. 506
Paranoid type of schizophrenia, p. 506
Catatonic type of schizophrenia, p. 507
Residual type of schizophrenia, p. 507
Undifferentiated type of schizophrenia, p. 508
Concordance rate, p. 508
Double bind, p. 511
Vulnerability, p. 511

Learning CONNECTIONS

Some students benefit from extra help with the different types of psychological disorders. You can learn more about them in:

- The CD-ROM accompanying this book, Topic 12

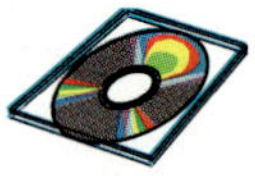

- This book's study guide, *Keeping Pace Plus*, or the computerized study guide, Chapter 14
- The audiotape accompanying this book, *SoundGuide for Psychology*, Learning Unit 14
- The study aids found on the World Wide Web site for this book, at http://www.abacon.com/psych/lefton

Critical Thinking CONNECTIONS

Take a moment to think critically about how this chapter's topics are connected with the rest of psychology . . .

If you are interested in . . .	Ask yourself . . .	Then turn to . . .
The role of anxiety in normal behavior and in maladjustment 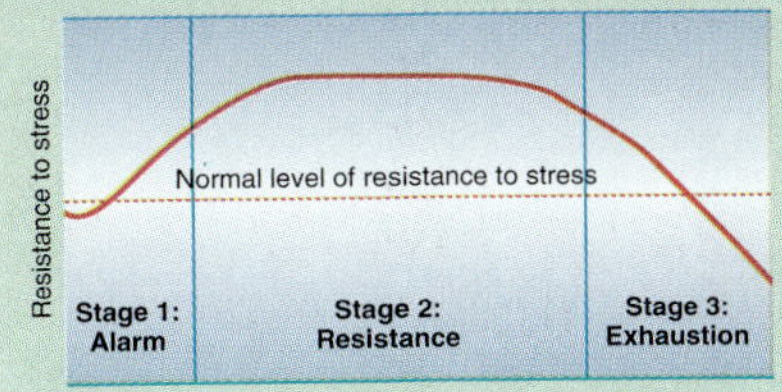	How is behavior affected when a person is feeling anxious and aroused?	Chapter 9, pp. 302–303
	How might continually high levels of anxiety, stress, and autonomic nervous system arousal induce disorders?	Chapter 13, pp. 454–455
The biological bases of psychological disorders 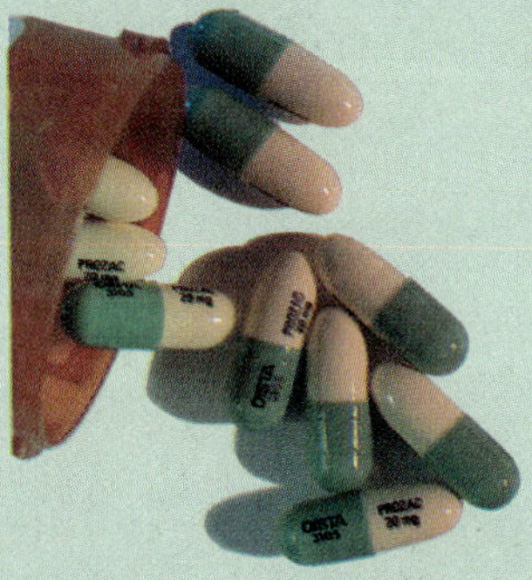	What hormonal and genetic influences produce disorders?	Chapter 2, pp. 41–42, 62–63
	How do drugs produce effects similar to those of disorders?	Chapter 4, pp. 134, 136–143
	What are the implications of the finding that certain disorders are specific to Western culture?	Chapter 9, p. 327
	How do you think drugs should be used to treat various forms of maladjustment?	Chapter 15, pp. 547–549
The role of learning in the development of various forms of maladjustment 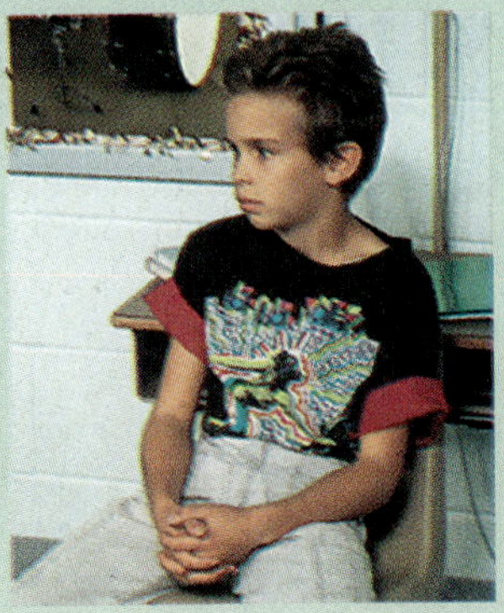	In what ways might children's maladjusted behavior be learned through conditioning?	Chapter 5, pp. 185–188
	How have different theories evolved regarding the origins and treatments of various disorders?	Chapter 1, pp. 25–30 and Chapter 15, pp. 531–537

15

Approaches to Treatment

A good friend's life changed drastically 2 years ago. Tricia was working with a therapist in an effort to sort out some career and marital problems when one day she started to remember some awful events that had taken place many years before. As a young adolescent, Tricia had been sexually abused by her father. Over a period of several months in therapy, she slowly and painfully began to recall the details of her ordeal. After her memories surfaced, she began waking up in the middle of the night, drenched in a cold sweat. Her dreams were terrifying re-creations of the horrors she had experienced. She became depressed, unable to concentrate at work, and increasingly withdrawn from her family. As a consequence of her depression, she lost weight, had great difficulty sleeping, developed an array of physical complaints, and lost interest in her usual activities. This once vibrant, active woman was taken over by her memories. Her stress level became unbearable. She was angry and despondent, and her mood affected all areas of her life.

A software consultant and sales manager, Tricia became distraught about her declining monthly sales totals and began trying to relieve her tension by joining coworkers at a local bar after work. Often she telephoned her husband to say she was going to be home late. Over time, there were many harsh words between them. Tricia soon began to come in to work late and sometimes skipped work altogether. Her work performance was clearly slipping. Angry and anxious, losing sleep, losing weight, and abusing alcohol, Tricia ultimately was involved in months of therapy dealing with numerous issues, including her self-esteem, her distorted ideas about work demands, and her marital relationship; and for a short time, she also received medication to combat anxiety.

People often find it difficult to cope with problems such as worksite stress or peer pressure or enduring abuse at home. When problems become overwhelming, people need help.

Therapy Comes in Many Forms

Many types of treatment are available for people who are having difficulty coping with their problems (see Figure 15.1). When a person seeks help from a physician, mental health counseling center, or drug treatment center, an initial working diagnosis is necessary. Does the person have medical problems? Should the person be hospitalized? Is the person dangerous? If talking therapy is in order, what type of practitioner is best suited for the person? There are two broad types of therapy: biologically based therapy and psychotherapy.

FIGURE 15.1

Types of Treatment

A 1993 study of nearly 23 million people with mental health or substance abuse problems showed that such people seek help from a variety of sources.
(Adapted from Narrow et al., 1993.)

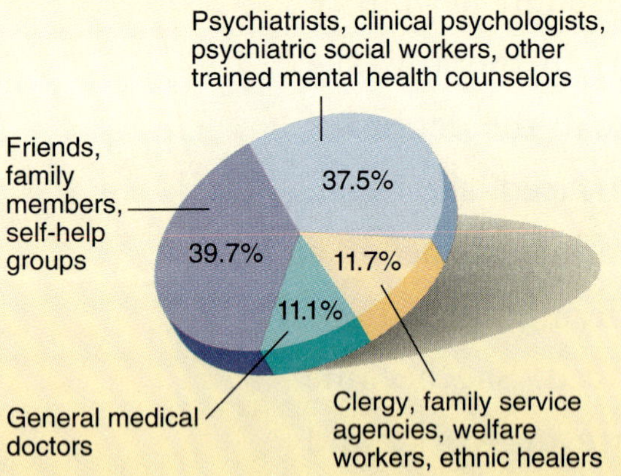

Biologically Based Therapy and Psychotherapy

Biologically based therapy has traditionally been called *somatic therapy*; this term refers to treatment of psychological disorders by means of treatments for the body, including therapy that affects hormone levels and the brain. For example, severely depressed individuals may need antidepressants; those diagnosed as having schizophrenia may need antipsychotic drugs; those with less severe disorders may be advised to change their diet and exercise more, because exercise has mood-enhancing effects with many disorders (Byrne & Byrne, 1993). We will examine some of these biological therapies later in this chapter. But first, we will explore the broad array of psychological therapies that are available for people suffering from life problems or maladjustment.

Psychotherapy is the treatment of emotional or behavioral problems through psychological techniques. It is a change-oriented process whose goal is to help individuals cope better with their problems and achieve more emotionally satisfying lifestyles. Psychotherapy accomplishes its goal by teaching people how to relieve stress, improve interpersonal communication, understand previous events in their lives, and modify their faulty ideas about the world. Psychotherapy helps people improve their self-image and adapt to new and challenging situations.

Of course, different cultures perceive different outcomes as optimal. Thus, in the United States, enhancing self-esteem through accomplishment may be seen as an

DIVERSITY

Asian Americans and Mental Health

Asian Americans are as difficult as African Americans or Protestants to characterize as a group. That is, there are considerable differences within each group, including diversity in language, education, traditions, and socioeconomic levels. However, like any other ethnic experience, the Asian American experience requires a unique perspective in the study of psychology. This perspective raises psychologists' sensitivity and understanding of the rich Asian American cultural heritage. This is important because Asian Americans comprise a rapidly increasing percentage of the U.S. population. To understand the mental health of Asian Americans, psychologists must understand what healing means, what family means, and the role of spirituality in Asian cultural traditions—and the relationship of these variables to therapy (Gerber, 1994). As Tsai and Uemura (1988) assert, one must understand at least three core cultural values that shape the responses of Asian Americans to stress and to the world: family, harmony, and stoicism.

In traditional Asian cultures, the *family* is the primary source of emotional support. The most important family relationship is not the global husband–wife–children relationship but rather the parent–child relationship. A person is defined by roles in the family, which include parent roles, grandparent roles, and child roles. A deferential and respectful relationship to elders is maintained, with an emphasis on prescribed roles; these family roles and responsibilities provide support.

Harmony results from minimizing shame and keeping dignity intact. This is a key goal if an Asian American is to have a good relationship with family and self. Preserving dignity, or "face," maintains a person and the person's family and community. If everyone preserves such dignity, interpersonal harmony is optimized.

Asian Americans also rely on personal strength and a sense of *stoicism*; that is, restraint is valued, and emotional maturity means suffering silently and suppressing emotions. The open expression of emotion is discouraged.

These three values—family, harmony, and stoicism—tend to keep Asian Americans from utilizing mental health services provided in the community (Tsai & Uemura, 1988). Asian Americans may subject themselves to enormous levels of stress before seeking outside help; they tend, as a group, to seek such help only in extreme crises. They are far more likely to ask for help from family, thus maintaining harmony and saving face by being stoic. For example, Japanese Americans suffered many emotional problems during World War II, when they were incarcerated at the Manzanar relocation center in California. (Asian Americans were ordered by the U.S. government to be held in camps isolated from the rest of the population during that war.) Those who were confined at the Manzanar camp and at other, similar camps suffered with great dignity and stoicism; to this day, however, survivors of the camps still bear emotional burdens.

A challenge for psychologists is to reach out to the Asian American community by making psychological services available in a way that minimizes shame, improves family unity, and respects cultural differences. The therapeutic alliance must respect the Asian family, its life cycle, its traditions, and the types of problems presented to practitioners (McGoldrick et al., 1991). This often means that utilizing family bonds—perhaps through family therapy—is an effective technique, as is relying on traditional and familiar Asian American philosophical traditions. Not all Americans have exactly the same needs.

optimal goal of psychotherapy. In Asia, an outcome that improves family harmony may enhance self-esteem, even though achieving that goal means working for collective rather than personal good. This difference in goals is highlighted in *Diversity;* it is also recognized by professional organizations such as the American Psychological Association (1993) and the American Psychiatric Association (1995).

Psychotherapy [SYE-ko-THER-uh-pee]: The treatment of emotional or behavioral problems through psychological techniques.

Is Psychotherapy Necessary and Effective?

The reputation of psychotherapy is often shaped by the mass media and the images it presents to the public. Talk-show psychologist Frasier Crane on *Frasier* bumbles through his own life; Barbara Streisand, in her role as psychiatrist in the film *Prince of Tides,* stretched the ethical boundaries by sleeping with her client's brother. These images, as well as talk-show pop psychology, make many ask, "Is psychotherapy really necessary or effective?" Some researchers note that many clients could outgrow or otherwise find relief from their symptoms without psychotherapy. Others assert that psychotherapy is more art than science. Still others believe psychotherapy provides only temporary relief. Let's consider some of the arguments.

Placebo Effects. A **placebo effect** is a nonspecific therapeutic change that occurs as a result of a person's expectations of change rather than as a result of any specific treatment. Is the benefit of psychotherapy largely a placebo effect? Physicians report that sometimes people experience relief from their symptoms when they are given sugar pills and are told that the pills are medicine. In much the same way, some patients in psychotherapy may show relief from their symptoms simply because they have entered therapy and now expect change. For some people, just the attention of a therapist and the chance to express their feelings can be therapeutic. One research study even showed that clients who paid for therapy had a better therapeutic outcome than clients who did not pay; researchers recognize and pay particular attention to such nonspecific effects (Roberts et al., 1993; Yoken & Berman, 1984).

But any placebo effect in psychotherapy is likely to be temporary. Any long-lasting therapeutic benefits will generally come about from the client's and therapist's efforts. Research studies that compare traditional psychotherapies with placebo treatments show that the traditional therapies are consistently more effective (Lipsey & Wilson, 1993).

Psychotherapy Research. In 1952, an important paper by Hans Eysenck challenged the effectiveness of psychotherapy, claiming that it produces no greater change in maladjusted individuals than do naturally occurring life experiences. Thousands of studies attempting to investigate the effectiveness of therapy followed. These studies showed what clients and therapists have known for decades: that Eysenck was wrong. Analyses of large amounts of data using sophisticated statistical techniques found psychotherapy effective (Lipsey & Wilson, 1993; Smith, Glass, & Miller, 1980). Although many psychologists challenge the data, techniques, and conclusions of these analyses, most are still convinced that psychotherapy is effective with a wide array of clients (e.g., Kazdin, 1991b; Matt, 1989; Seligman, 1995). The effectiveness of therapy and people's speed of response do vary with the type of problem—anxiety and depression respond more rapidly than do personality disorders, for example (Kopta et al., 1994).

Is one type of therapy more effective than another? Many researchers contend that most psychotherapies are equally effective; that is, regardless of the approach a therapist uses, the results are often the same. Some newer and trendier approaches—ones that often appear in popular magazines—tend to be less reliable and reflect a culture eager to try the new, unproved, and fascinating. Critics such as Robyn Dawes (1994) assert that many therapists do not pay attention to known data and that some therapists—often those with little training—don't do the right thing for their clients by ignoring the facts and looking for the exotic or easy way out. But if most of the legitimate therapies are effective, there must be some common underlying component that makes them successful. Both the American Psychological Association and many individual researchers are seeking to systematize research strategies to investigate

Placebo effect [pluh-SEE-bo]: A nonspecific therapeutic change that occurs as a result of a person's expectations of change rather than as a direct result of any specific treatment.

TABLE 15.1 *Signs of Good Progress in Therapy*

The client is providing personally revealing and significant material.
The client is exploring the meanings of feelings and occurrences.
The client is exploring material avoided earlier in therapy.
The client is expressing significant insight into personal behavior.
The client's method of communicating is active, alive, and energetic.
There is a valued client–therapist working relationship.
The client feels free to express strong feelings toward the therapist—either positive or negative.
The client is expressing strong feelings outside of therapy.
The client moves toward a different set of personality characteristics.
The client is showing improved functioning outside of therapy.
The client indicates a general state of well-being, good feelings, and positive attitudes.

Source: Mahrer & Nadler, 1986.

effectiveness; this research will lead to a clearer picture of which approaches are best for certain disorders and for particular types of clients (Beutler, 1991). Table 15.1 presents some generally recognized signs of good progress in therapy.

Which Therapy, Which Therapist?

Before 1950, there were about 15 types of psychotherapy; today, there are about 200 different approaches. Some focus on individuals, some on groups of individuals (group therapy), and others on families (family therapy). Some psychologists even deal with whole communities; these *community psychologists* focus on helping individuals, groups, and communities develop a more action-oriented approach to individual and social adjustment. A therapist's training will usually determine the type of treatment approach he or she takes. Rather than using just one type of psychotherapy, many therapists take an *eclectic approach*—that is, they combine several different techniques in their treatment.

A number of systematic psychotherapeutic approaches are in use today. Each can be applied in several formats—with individuals, couples, or groups—and each will be defined and examined in greater detail in later sections of this chapter. Some practitioners use *psychodynamically based approaches*, which loosely or closely follow Freud's basic ideas. These therapists' aim is to help patients understand the motivations underlying their behavior. They assume that maladjustment and abnormal behavior occur when people do not understand themselves adequately. Practitioners of *humanistic therapy* assume that people are essentially good—that they have an innate disposition to develop their potential and to seek beauty, truth, and goodness. This type of therapy tries to help people realize their full potential and find meaning in life. In contrast, *behavior therapy* is based on the assumption that most behaviors, whether normal or abnormal, are learned. Behavior therapists encourage their clients to learn new adaptive behaviors. Growing out of behavior therapy and cognitive psychology (see Chapters 1 and 7) is *cognitive therapy*, which focuses on changing a client's behavior by changing his or her thoughts and perceptions.

Let's return for a moment to my friend Tricia. What type of therapy would best suit her situation? As mentioned before, the appropriateness and effectiveness of the different kinds of therapy vary with the type of disorder being treated and the goal of the client. Research to discover the best treatment method is often conducted for specific disorders, such as depression (Robinson, Berman, & Neimeyer, 1990). Results from such studies usually limit their conclusions to a specific method for a specific problem. For example, individual psychodynamic therapy has a good success rate for people with anxiety and maladjustment disorders, but it is less successful for those with schizophrenia. Long-term group therapy is more effective than short-term individual therapy for people with personality disorders. Behavior therapy is usually the most effective approach with children, regardless of the disorder.

Tricia could therefore receive effective treatment from a variety of therapists. One therapist might focus on the root causes of her maladjustment. Another might concentrate on eliminating her symptoms: anxiety, drinking, and declining work performance. Besides the therapeutic approaches, some characteristics of the therapists themselves affect the treatment; among these characteristics are gender, ethnicity, personality, level of experience, and degree of empathy.

Although there are differences among the various psychotherapies and therapists, there are also some commonalities. In all the therapies, clients usually expect a positive outcome, which helps them strive for change. Figure 15.2 presents an overview of outcomes when psychotherapy is combined with efforts to change. In addition, clients receive attention, which helps them maintain a positive attitude. Moreover, no matter what type of therapy is involved, certain characteristics must be present in both therapist and client for therapeutic changes to occur. For example, good therapists communicate interest, understanding, respect, tact, maturity, and ability to help. They respect clients' ability to cope with their troubles (C.T. Fischer, 1991). They use suggestion, encouragement, interpretation, examples, and

FIGURE 15.2

Goals of Psychotherapy

An important goal of psychotherapy is engaging people in the process of change. Once initiated, psychotherapy, along with efforts to change, can affect a host of problems, including specific maladaptive behaviors, distorted thoughts, inner conflicts, and interpersonal relationships.

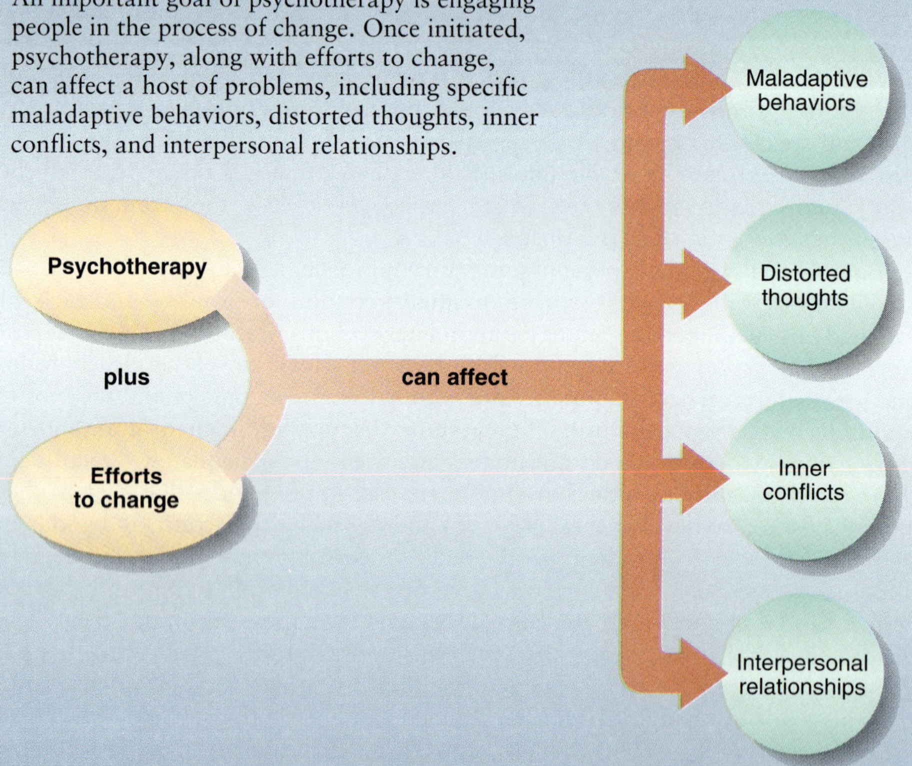

TABLE 15.2 *Psychotherapy Practitioners and Their Activities*

Type of Practitioner	Degree	Years beyond Undergraduate Degree	Activities
Clinical or counseling psychologist	PhD (Doctor of Philosophy) or PsyD (Doctor of Psychology)	5–8	Diagnosis, testing, and treatment using a wide array of techniques, including insight and behavior therapy
Psychiatrist	MD (Doctor of Medicine)	8	Biomedical therapy, diagnosis, and treatment, often of a psychoanalytic nature
Social worker	MSW (Master of Social Work)	2	Family therapy or behavior therapy, often in community-based settings such as hospitals
Psychiatric nurse	BSN or MA (Bachelor of Science in Nursing or Master of Arts)	0–2	Inpatient psychiatric care, supportive therapy of various types
Counselor	MA (Master of Arts, often in counseling)	2	Supportive therapy, family therapy, vocational readjustment, alcoholism and drug abuse counseling

perhaps rewards to help clients change or rethink their situations. But clients must be willing to make some changes in their lifestyles and ideas. A knowledgeable, accepting, and objective therapist can facilitate behavior changes, but the client is the one who makes the changes (Lafferty, Beutler, & Crago, 1989).

Variables such as the client's social class, gender, age, education, therapeutic expectations, and level of anxiety are also important. For example, therapists need to understand the unique life stresses experienced by women. Similarly, they must address the special obstacles facing clients of various ethnic and other minority groups (Sue, 1988). In general, the therapist and client must form an alliance to work together purposefully (Luborsky, Barber, & Crits-Cristoph, 1990); such alliances are helped if the therapist and client share some values (Kelly & Strupp, 1992). Because psychoanalysis is based on the development of a unique relationship between the therapist and the patient, compatibility is especially critical. The patient and the therapist usually decide within the first few sessions whether they feel comfortable working with each other.

Table 15.2 presents an overview of the major practitioners of psychotherapy, including their earned degrees and their activities. The table includes some practitioners who do not have as much training in psychotherapy as do psychologists—for example, nurses and social workers. These types of practitioners often work as part of a team, along with a clinical psychologist or psychiatrist, in delivering mental health services to clients.

In the next sections, we will look more closely at the four major psychotherapeutic approaches: psychodynamic, humanistic, behavior, and cognitive therapies.

FOCUS

Review

- What is the essential difference between biologically based therapy and psychotherapy? p. 518

Think Critically

- Identify some things you think might happen as a result of treatment for anxiety or depression. What would you expect to gain, lose, or change during therapy?
- Why do you think some disorders respond more quickly to therapy than others do?
- What are the implications of the fact that in Central and South America there are dramatically different mental health services available for the rich and the poor?

Psychoanalysis and Psychodynamic Therapies

▲ *Anna O. was typical of the Viennese matrons treated in the early days of psychotherapy. She had developed a number of peculiar symptoms, including partial paralysis, which Freud attributed to unresolved and suppressed events in her past.*

Psychoanalysis is a lengthy insight therapy developed by Freud that aims at uncovering conflicts and unconscious impulses through special techniques, including free association, dream analysis, and transference. It is used by therapists who are specifically trained in its theory and practice. There are about 3,000 practicing psychoanalysts in the United States. Many other psychologists use a therapy loosely connected to or rooted in Freudian theory. These psychologists refer to their therapies as **psychodynamically based therapies**—therapies that use theory, approach, or techniques derived from Freud, but that sometimes reject some of the elements of Freud's theory.

Sigmund Freud believed that the exchange of words in psychoanalysis causes therapeutic change. According to Freud (1920/1966, p. 21):

> The patient talks, tells of his past experiences and present impressions, complains, and expresses his wishes and his emotions. The physician listens, attempts to direct the patient's thought-processes, reminds him, forces his attention in certain directions, gives him explanations and observes the reactions of understanding or denial thus evoked.

Freud's therapy is an **insight therapy**—a therapy that attempts to discover relationships between unconscious motivations and current abnormal behavior. Insight therapy has two basic assumptions: (1) that becoming aware of one's motivations helps one change and become more adaptable, and (2) that the causes of maladjustment are unresolved conflicts that the person was unaware of and therefore unable to deal with. The goal of insight therapy is to treat the causes of abnormal behaviors rather than the behaviors themselves. In general, insight therapists try to help people see life from a different perspective so they can choose more adaptive lifestyles.

Goals of Psychoanalysis

Many individuals who seek psychotherapy are unhappy with their behavior but are unable to change it. As we saw in the discussion of Freud's theory of personality (Chapter 12), Freud believed that conflicts among a person's unconscious thoughts and processes produce maladjusted behavior. The general goal of psychoanalysis is to help patients understand the unconscious motivations that direct their behavior. Only when they become aware of those motivations can they begin to choose behaviors that lead to more fulfilling lives. In psychoanalysis, patients are encouraged to express healthy impulses, strengthen day-to-day functioning based on reality, and perceive the world as a positive rather than a punishing place.

To illustrate the psychoanalytic approach, suppose that Tricia seeks the help of a psychologist who uses a psychodynamically based therapy. The psychologist might attempt to discover the source of Tricia's problems by asking her to describe how she relates to her parents—especially to her father. Tricia realizes that she has sought her father's love all her life. Through therapy, she realizes she is torn between her love for her father and her rage toward him. She discovers that she has been incapable of expressing anger appropriately toward him. In addition, she confronts the fact that she hates being in sales—in fact, she thinks she might prefer being a photographer. Frustrated and hostile, she has lost interest in work and begun using alcohol to numb the pain of her past memories and her diminishing self-esteem.

Psychoanalysis [SYE-ko-uh-NAL-uh-sis]: A lengthy therapy developed by Freud that aims at uncovering conflicts and unconscious impulses through special techniques, including free association, dream analysis, and transference.

Psychodynamically based therapies [SYE-ko-dye-NAM-ick-lee]: Therapies based loosely on Freud's psychoanalytic theory, using a part of that approach but rejecting some elements.

Insight therapy: Therapy that attempts to discover relationships between unconscious motivations and current abnormal behavior in order to change that behavior.

Techniques of Psychoanalysis

In general, psychoanalytic techniques are geared toward the exploration of early experiences. In traditional psychoanalysis, the patient lies on a couch and the therapist sits in a chair out of the patient's view. Freud believed this arrangement would allow the patient to be more relaxed and feel less threatened than if the therapist were in view. Today, however, many followers of Freud prefer face-to-face interactions with patients.

Two major techniques used in psychoanalysis are free association and dream analysis. In **free association**, the patient is asked to report whatever comes to mind, regardless of how disorganized it might be, how trivial it might seem, or how disagreeable it might feel. A therapist might say, "I can help you best if you say whatever thoughts and feelings come to your mind, even if they seem irrelevant, immaterial, foolish, embarrassing, upsetting, or even if they're about me, even very personally, just as they come, without censoring or editing" (Lewin, 1970, p. 67). The purpose of free association is to help patients learn to recognize connections and patterns among their thoughts and to allow the unconscious to express itself freely.

In **dream analysis**, patients are asked to describe their dreams in detail; the dreams are interpreted and used to provide insight into unconscious motivations. Sometimes lifelike, sometimes chaotic, sometimes incoherent, dreams may at times replay a person's life history and at other times venture into the person's current problems. Freud believed dreams represent some element of the unconscious seeking expression. Psychodynamically oriented therapists see much symbolism in dreams; they assert that the content of a dream hides its true meaning. Many therapists use patients' dreams to gain insight into patients' current problems. The goal of dream analysis is to help therapists reveal patients' unconscious desires and motivations by discovering the meaning of their dreams.

Both free association and dream analysis involve the therapist's interpretation. **Interpretation,** in Freud's theory, is the technique of providing a context, meaning, or cause of a specific idea, feeling, or set of behaviors; it is the process of tying a set of behaviors to its unconscious determinant. With this technique, the therapist tries to find common threads in a patient's behavior and thoughts. Patients' use of *defense mechanisms* (ways of reducing anxiety by distorting reality, examined in Chapter 12) is often a sign of an area that may need to be explored. For example, if a male patient avoids the subject of women, invariably deflecting the topic with an offhand remark or a joke, the therapist may wonder if some kind of denial is going on. The therapist may then encourage the patient to explore his attitudes and feelings about women in general and about his mother in particular.

Two processes are central to psychoanalysis: resistance and transference. **Resistance** is an unwillingness to cooperate by which a patient signals a reluctance to provide the therapist with information or to help the therapist understand or interpret a situation, sometimes to the point of belligerence. For example, a patient disturbed by her analyst's unsettling interpretations might become angry and start resisting treatment by missing appointments or failing to pay for therapy. Analysts usually interpret resistance as meaning either that the patient wishes to avoid discussing a particular subject or that an especially difficult stage in psychotherapy has been reached. To minimize resistance, analysts try to accept patients' behavior. When a therapist does not judge but merely listens, a patient is more likely to describe feelings thoroughly.

In transference, patients transfer feelings from earlier relationships to the therapist. **Transference** is a psychoanalytic phenomenon in which a therapist becomes the object of a patient's emotional attitudes about an important person in the patient's life, such as a parent. For example, if Tricia's therapist is a man and she becomes hostile toward him, a psychoanalyst would say that she is acting as though the therapist were her father; that is, she is acting out toward the therapist attitudes and emotional reactions from an earlier relationship (Butler & Strupp, 1991). Most importantly, because the psychotherapist will respond differently than Tricia's father might have, Tricia can experience the conflict differently, which will lead her to a better understanding of the issue. By permitting transference, the therapist gives patients a new opportunity to understand their feelings and can guide them in the

Free association: Psychoanalytic technique in which a person reports to the therapist his or her thoughts and feelings as they occur, regardless of how trivial, illogical, or objectionable their content may appear.

Dream analysis: Psychoanalytic technique in which a patient's dreams are interpreted and used to provide insight into the individual's unconscious motivations.

Interpretation: In Freud's theory, the technique of providing a context, meaning, or cause of a specific idea, feeling, or set of behaviors; the process of tying a set of behaviors to its unconscious determinant.

Resistance: In psychoanalysis, an unwillingness to cooperate by which a patient signals a reluctance to provide the therapist with information or to help the therapist understand or interpret a situation.

Transference: Psychoanalytic phenomenon in which a therapist becomes the object of a patient's emotional attitudes about an important person in the patient's life, such as a parent.

exploration of repressed or difficult material. The examination of thoughts or feelings that were previously considered unacceptable (and therefore were often repressed) helps patients understand and identify the underlying conflicts that direct their behavior.

Psychoanalysis, with its slowly gained insights into the unconscious, is a gradual and continual process. Through their insights, patients learn new ways of coping with instinctual urges and develop more mature means of dealing with anxiety and guilt. The cycle of interpretation, resistance to interpretation, and transference occurs repeatedly in the process of psychoanalysis and is sometimes referred to as **working through**.

Ego Analysts

Freud's theory has not been universally accepted; even his followers have disagreed with him. One group of psychoanalysts, referred to as *ego analysts,* or *ego psychologists,* have modified some of Freud's basic ideas. **Ego analysts** are psychoanalytic practitioners who assume that the ego has greater control over behavior than Freud suggested and who are more concerned with reality testing and control over the environment than with unconscious motivations and processes. Like Freud, ego analysts believe that psychoanalysis is the appropriate method for treating patients with emotional problems. Unlike Freud, however, they assume that people have voluntary control over whether, when, and in what ways their biological urges will be expressed.

A major disagreement between ego analysts and traditional psychoanalysts has to do with the role of the id and the ego. (Recall from Chapter 12 that the id operates on the pleasure principle, while the ego operates on the reality principle and tries to control the id's impulsive behavior.) A traditional Freudian asserts that the ego grows out of the id and controls it—but an ego analyst asserts that the ego is independent of the id, controls memory and perception, and is conflict-free. Whereas traditional psychoanalysts begin by focusing on unconscious material in the id and only later try to increase the patient's ego control, ego analysts aim at helping clients develop stronger egos. They may ask a client to assertively take control of a situation—to let reason, rather than feeling, guide a specific behavior pattern. From an ego analyst's point of view, a weak ego may cause maladjustment by its failure to perceive, understand, and control the id. Thus, by learning to master and develop their egos—including moral reasoning and judgment—people gain greater control over their lives.

Criticisms of Psychoanalysis

Critics of psychoanalysis contend that the approach is unscientific, imprecise, and subjective; they assert that psychoanalytic concepts such as id, ego, and superego are not linked to real things or to day-to-day behavior. Other critics object to Freud's biologically oriented approach, which suggests that a human being is a mere bundle of energy caught in conflict and driven toward some hedonistic goal. These critics ask: Where in this approach does human free will come in? Also, elements of Freud's theory are untestable, and some are sexist. Freud conceived of men and women in prescribed roles; most practitioners today find this idea objectionable.

Quite aside from these criticisms, the effectiveness of psychoanalysis is open to question. Research shows that psychoanalysis is more effective for some people than for others. It is more effective, for example, for people with anxiety disorders than for those diagnosed as schizophrenic. In addition, younger patients improve more than older ones. In general, studies show that psychoanalysis can be as effective as other therapies, but it is no more so (Garfield & Bergin, 1986).

Working through: In psychoanalysis, the repetitive cycle of interpretation, resistance to interpretation, and transference.

Ego analyst: Psychoanalytic practitioner who assumes that the ego has greater control over behavior than Freud suggested and who is more concerned with reality testing and control over the environment than with unconscious motivations and processes. Also known as an *ego psychologist*.

BUILDING TABLE 15.1

Key Issues in Psychoanalytic Therapy

THERAPY	NATURE OF PSYCHO-PATHOLOGY	GOAL OF THERAPY	ROLE OF THERAPIST	ROLE OF UNCONSCIOUS MATERIAL	ROLE OF INSIGHT	TECHNIQUES
Psychoanalytic	Maladjustment reflects inadequate conflict resolution and fixation in early development.	Attainment of maturity, strengthened ego functions, reduced control by unconscious or repressed impulses	An *investigator,* uncovering conflicts and resistances 	Primary in classical psychoanalysis, less emphasis in ego analysis	Includes not solely intellectual understanding but also emotional experiences	Analyst takes an active role in interpreting the dreams and free associations of patients.

Psychoanalysis also has certain disadvantages. The problems addressed in psychoanalysis are difficult, and a patient must be highly motivated and articulate to grasp the complicated and subtle relationships being explored. Further, because traditional psychoanalysis involves meeting with the analyst for an hour at a time, 5 days a week, for approximately 5 years, psychoanalysis is typically extremely costly. Many people who seek therapy cannot afford the money or the time for this type of treatment, nor will most insurance companies foot the bill.

Building Table 15.1 presents a summary of the key components of the psychoanalytic view of therapy. Humanistic therapies, which we will examine next, are neither as time-consuming nor as comprehensive in their goals as is psychoanalysis.

FOCUS

Review

- Explain what is meant by resistance and transference. p. 525
- What basic criticism of psychoanalysis do ego analysts offer? p. 526
- Identify the disadvantages of psychoanalysis. p. 526

Think Critically

- Why do you think most practitioners feel that psychoanalysis is not the most appropriate treatment for marital discord?

Humanistic Therapies

Humanistic therapies, unlike psychoanalytic therapies, emphasize the uniqueness of the human experience and the idea that human beings have free will to determine their destinies. Humanistic psychologists assert that human beings are conscious, creative, and born with an innate desire to fulfill themselves. To some extent, humanistic approaches are an outgrowth of psychodynamically based insight therapies: They help basically healthy people understand the causes of their behavior, both normal and maladjusted. Client-centered therapy and Gestalt therapy are two types of humanistic therapies.

Client-Centered Therapy

Client-centered therapy is an insight therapy that seeks to help people evaluate the world and themselves from their own perspective by providing them with a nondirective environment and unconditional positive regard (which we will soon look at in more detail). Client-centered therapy, or *person-centered therapy,* was developed by Carl Rogers (1902–1987). Rogers was a quiet, caring man who turned the psychoanalytic world upside-down when he introduced his approach. He focused on the person, listening intently to his clients and encouraging them to define their own "cures." Rogers saw people as basically good, competent, social beings who move forward and grow. He believed that people move toward their ideal selves throughout life, maturing into fulfilled individuals through the process of self-actualization.

▲ *Carl Rogers (upper right) held that the therapist in client-centered therapy must be a warm, accepting person who projects positive feelings toward a client.*

Rogerian therapists hold that problem behaviors occur when the environment prevents a person from developing his or her own innate potential. If children are given love and reinforcement only for their achievements, for example, as adults they may see themselves and others almost solely in terms of achievement. Rogerian treatment involves helping people evaluate the world from their own perspective and improve their self-regard. A Rogerian therapist might treat my friend Tricia by encouraging her to explore her past goals, current desires, and expectations for the future, and then asking whether she can achieve what she wants through sales, photography, or some other option. Table 15.3 presents the basic assumptions underlying Rogers's approach to treatment.

Techniques of Client-Centered Therapy. Because its goal is to help clients discover and actualize their as-yet-undiscovered selves, client-centered therapy is nondirective. **Nondirective therapy** is a form of therapy in which the client determines the direction of therapy while the therapist remains permissive, almost passive, and accepts totally the client's feelings and behavior. In nondirective therapy the therapist does not dominate the client, but instead encourages the client's search for growth.

The use of the word *client* rather than *patient* is a key aspect of Rogers's approach to therapy (*patient* connotes a medical model). In psychoanalysis, the therapist *directs* patients' "cure" and helps patients understand their behavior; in client-centered therapy, the therapist *guides* clients and helps them realize what they feel is right for themselves. The clients direct the conversation, and the therapist helps them organize their thoughts and ideas simply by asking the right questions, by

Client-centered therapy: An insight therapy, developed by Carl Rogers, that seeks to help people evaluate the world and themselves from their own perspective by providing them with a nondirective environment and unconditional positive regard. Also known as *person-centered therapy*.

Nondirective therapy: A form of therapy in which the client determines the direction of therapy while the therapist remains permissive, almost passive, and accepts totally the client's feelings and behavior.

TABLE 15.3 ***Rogers's Assumptions about Human Beings***

1. People are innately good and are effective in dealing with their environments.
2. Behavior is purposeful and goal-directed.
3. Healthy people are aware of all their behavior; they choose their behavior patterns.
4. A client's behavior can be understood only from the client's point of view. Even if a client has misconstrued events in the world, the therapist must understand how the client sees those events.
5. Effective therapy occurs only when a client modifies his or her behavior, not when the therapist manipulates it.

responding with words such as "oh," and by reflecting back the clients' feelings. Even a small movement, such as a nod or gesture, can help clients stay on the right track. Clients learn to evaluate the world from their own vantage point, with little interpretation by the therapist.

A basic tenet of client-centered therapy is that the therapist must be a warm, accepting person who projects positive feelings toward clients. To counteract clients' negative experiences with people who were unaccepting, and who thus have taught them that they are bad or unlikable, client-centered therapists accept clients as they are, with good and bad points; they respect them for their worth as individuals, showing them *unconditional positive regard* and respect. *Empathic understanding*, whereby therapists communicate acceptance and recognition of clients' emotions and encourage clients to discuss whatever feelings they have, is an important part of the therapeutic relationship.

Client-centered therapy can be viewed as a consciousness-raising process that helps people expand their awareness. Initially, clients tend to express the attitudes and ideas they have adopted from other people. Thus, Tricia might say, "I should make top sales figures," implying "because my father counts on my success." As therapy progresses and she experiences the empathic understanding of the therapist, she will begin to use her own ideas and standards when evaluating herself (Rogers, 1951). As a result, she may begin to talk about herself in more positive ways and try to please herself rather than others. She may say, "I should make top sales figures only if they mean something to me," reflecting a more positive, more accepting attitude about herself. As she begins to feel better about herself, she will eventually suggest to the therapist that she knows how to deal with the world and may be ready to leave therapy.

Criticisms of Client-Centered Therapy. Client-centered therapy is acclaimed for its focus on the therapeutic relationship. No other therapy makes clients feel so warm, accepted, and safe. These are important characteristics of any therapy, but critics argue that they may not be enough to bring about long-lasting change.

Critics of client-centered therapy assert that lengthy discussions about past problems do not necessarily help people with their present difficulties and that an environment of unconditional positive regard may not be enough to bring about desired behavior changes. They believe that this therapy may be making therapeutic promises that cannot be fulfilled and that it focuses on concepts that are hard to define, such as self-actualization.

A therapy session with Fritz Perls might find clients role-playing the objects or characters in their dreams in order to become free of unfinished business or unresolved conflicts. ▼

Gestalt Therapy

With the aim of creating an awareness of a person's whole self, Gestalt therapy differs significantly from psychoanalysis. **Gestalt therapy** is an insight therapy that emphasizes the importance of a person's being aware of current feelings and situations. It assumes that human beings are responsible for themselves and their lives and that they need to focus not on the past but on the present, the "here and now." As such, Gestalt therapy is concerned with current feelings and behaviors and their representation in a meaningful, coherent whole.

Frederick S. ("Fritz") Perls (1893–1970), a physician and psychoanalyst trained in Europe, was the founder and principal proponent of Gestalt therapy. He was a dynamic, charismatic therapist, and many psychologists followed him and his ideas closely. Perls assumed that the best way to help clients come to terms with anxiety and other unpleasant feelings was to focus on their current understanding and awareness of the world, not on past situations and experiences.

Gestalt therapy [Gesh-TALT]: An insight therapy that emphasizes the importance of a person's being aware of current feelings and situations.

Goals of Gestalt Therapy. The goals of Gestalt therapy are to help clients be in touch with current feelings and old conflicts and to enable them to resolve future conflicts. The therapy aims at expanding clients' awareness of their current attitudes and feelings so they can respond more fully and appropriately to current situations. Gestalt therapy does not attempt to "cure" people; rather, it helps them become complete and enables them to continue to adapt in the future. Gestalt psychologists help people deal with feelings of what Perls termed *incomplete Gestalts*—that is, unfinished business or unresolved conflicts, such as previously unrecognized feelings of anger toward a spouse or envy of a brother or sister.

From Perls's point of view, the client needs to expand conscious awareness by reconnecting fragments of past and current experience. Perls argued that people develop false lives and are not in touch with their real selves. Only when they become aware of the here and now can they become sensitive to the tension and repression that made their previous behavior maladaptive. Also, once they become aware of their current feelings and accept themselves, clients can understand earlier behaviors and plan appropriate future behaviors. From a Gestalt viewpoint, healthy people are in touch with their feelings and with reality. Thus, a major goal of therapy is to get people in touch with their feelings so they can construct an accurate picture of their psychological world.

Guided by a Gestalt-oriented therapist, Tricia might explore her past and current relationship with her parents. She might realize that her anger and her poor work performance reflect low self-esteem and hostile feelings toward her father. After constructing an accurate picture of her psychological world, she could adopt new behaviors that would help her explore other careers while she continued her sales work.

Techniques of Gestalt Therapy. Gestalt therapy examines current feelings and behaviors of which a client may be unaware. Usually, the therapist asks the client to concentrate on current feelings about a difficult past experience. For example, a Gestalt therapist may ask a client to relive a situation and discuss it as if it were happening in the present. The underlying assumption is that feelings expressed in the present can be understood and dealt with more easily than can feelings remembered from the past.

Many Gestalt techniques are designed to help clients become more alert to significant sensations in themselves and to their surroundings. One such technique is to have clients change the way they talk; a client who thinks she has trouble being assertive might be asked to speak assertively to each member of a group. Another technique is to ask clients to behave in a manner opposite to the way they feel; a man who feels hostile or aggressive toward his boss, for example, might be asked to behave as though their relationship were warm and affectionate. For these reasons, Gestalt therapy is considered an experiential therapy.

Hypnosis (described in Chapter 4), while not exactly a psychodynamic or humanistic technique, is used by many practitioners as an adjunct to their therapies. Gestalt therapists use it from time to time to help bring clients to a more complete awareness of their surroundings. Evidence suggests that a client's susceptibility to hypnosis can affect the outcome of some therapeutic interventions, although Spanos, Lush, and Gwynn (1989) assert that other techniques work just as well. Therapists may use hypnosis to help clients relax, remember past events, reduce their anxiety, quit smoking, raise their consciousness, or even lose weight.

FOCUS

Review

- Why is Rogers's therapy termed *client-centered*? p. 528
- What is the fundamental aim of Gestalt therapy? p. 529
- Briefly describe the major differences between client-centered therapy and Gestalt therapy. pp. 528–531

Think Critically

- What are the implications for a theory about therapy of assuming that people are inherently good, as Rogers did?
- How might psychodynamic and humanistic therapists use hypnosis differently?

BUILDING TABLE 15.2

Key Issues in Psychoanalytic and Humanistic Therapy

THERAPY	NATURE OF PSYCHO-PATHOLOGY	GOAL OF THERAPY	ROLE OF THERAPIST	ROLE OF UNCONSCIOUS MATERIAL	ROLE OF INSIGHT	TECHNIQUES
Psychoanalytic	Maladjustment reflects inadequate conflict resolution and fixation in early development.	Attainment of maturity, strengthened ego functions, reduced control by unconscious or repressed impulses	An *investigator,* uncovering conflicts and resistances	Primary in classical psychoanalysis, less emphasis in ego analysis	Includes not solely intellectual understanding but also emotional experiences	Analyst takes an active role in interpreting the dreams and free associations of patients.
Humanistic	Pathology reflects an incongruity between the real self and the potential, desired self. Overdependence on others for gratification and self-esteem.	To foster self-determination, release human potential, expand awareness	An *empathic person* in true encounter with client, sharing experience	Emphasis is primarily on conscious experience 	Used by many, but there is more emphasis on *how* and *what* questions than on *why* questions	Client is asked to see the world from a different perspective and is encouraged to focus on current situations rather than past ones.

Criticisms of Gestalt Therapy. Gestalt therapy encourages clients to get in touch with their feelings. This approach is seen as both a strength and a weakness. Some critics believe Perls was too focused on individuals' happiness and growth, that he encouraged the attainment of these goals at the expense of other goals. Gestalt therapy is also criticized for focusing too much on feelings and not enough on thought and decision making. Some psychologists think Gestalt therapy may work well for healthy people who want to grow but that it may not be as successful for severely maladjusted people who cannot make it through the day.

Building Table 15.2 presents a summary of the key components of the psychoanalytic and humanistic views of therapy.

Behavior Therapy

Sometimes people have problems that may not warrant an in-depth discussion of early childhood experiences, an exploration of unconscious motivations, a lengthy discussion about current feelings, or a resolution of inner conflicts. Examples of such problems are fear of heights, anxiety about public speaking, marital conflicts, and sexual dysfunction. In these cases, behavior therapy may be more appropriate than psychodynamically based or humanistic therapies.

Goals of Behavior Therapy

Behavior therapy is a therapy based on the application of learning principles to human behavior. Also called *behavior modification*, it focuses on changing overt behaviors rather than on understanding subjective feelings, unconscious processes, or motivations. It uses learning principles to help people replace maladaptive behaviors with new, better ones. Behavior therapists assume that people's behavior is influenced by changes in their environment, in the way they respond to that environment, and in the way they interact with other people. Unlike psychodynamically based therapies, behavior therapy does not aim to discover the origins of a behavior; it works only to alter it. For a person with a nervous twitch, for example, the goal would be to eliminate the twitch. Thus, behavior therapists treat people by having them first unlearn old, faulty behaviors and then learn new, more acceptable or effective ones.

Behavior therapists do not always focus on the problems that caused the client to seek therapy. If they see that the client's problem is caused by some other situation, they may focus on changing that situation. For example, a man may seek therapy because of a faltering marriage. However, the therapist may discover that the marriage is suffering because of the client's excessive arguments with his wife, each of which is followed by a period of heavy drinking. The therapist may then discover that both the arguments and the drinking are brought on by stress at work, aggravated by the client's unrealistic expectations regarding his performance (Goldfried & Davison, 1976). In this situation, the therapist may focus on helping the client develop standards that will ease the original cause of the problem—the tension felt at work—and that will be consistent with the client's capabilities, past performance, and realistic likelihood of future performance.

Unlike psychodynamic and humanistic therapies, behavior therapy does not encourage clients to interpret past events to find their meaning. Although a behavior therapist may uncover a chain of events leading to a specific behavior, that discovery will not generally prompt a close examination of the client's early experiences.

When people enter behavior therapy, many aspects of their behavior may change, not just those specifically being treated. Thus, a woman being treated for extreme shyness may find not only that the shyness decreases but also that she can engage more easily in discussions about emotional topics and can perform better on the job. Behaviorists argue that once a person's behavior has changed, it may be easier for the person to manage attitudes, fears, and conflicts.

Behavior Therapy versus Psychodynamic and Humanistic Therapies

Behaviorists are dissatisfied with psychodynamic and humanistic therapies for three basic reasons: (1) psychodynamic and humanistic therapies use concepts that are almost impossible to define and measure (such as the id and self-actualization); (2) some studies show that patients who do not receive psychodynamic and humanistic therapies improve anyway; and (3) once a therapist has labeled a person as abnormal, the label itself may lead to maladaptive behavior. (Although this is true of any type of therapy, psychodynamic therapy tends to use labels more than behavior therapy does.) Behavior therapists assume that people display maladaptive behavior not because they are abnormal but because they are having trouble adjusting to their life situations; if they are taught new ways of coping, the maladjustment will disappear. A great strength of behavior therapy is that it provides a coherent conceptual framework.

However, behavior therapy is not without its critics. Most insight therapists, especially those who are psychodynamically based, believe that if only *overt* behavior is treated, as is often done in behavior therapy, symptom substitution may occur.

Behavior therapy: A therapy that is based on the application of learning principles to human behavior and focuses on changing overt behaviors rather than on understanding subjective feelings, unconscious processes, or motivations. Also known as *behavior modification*.

Symptom substitution is the appearance of one overt symptom to replace another that has been eliminated by treatment. Thus, insight therapists argue that if a therapist eliminates a nervous twitch without examining its underlying causes, the client will express the underlying disorder by developing some other symptom, such as a speech impediment. Behavior therapists, on the other hand, contend that symptom substitution does not occur if the treatment makes proper use of behavioral principles. Research shows that behavior therapy is at least as effective as insight therapy and is more effective in some cases (Jacobson, 1991; McGlynn, 1990; Snyder, Wills, & Grady-Fletcher, 1991).

Techniques of Behavior Therapy

Behavior therapists use an array of techniques often in combination, to help people change their behavior; chief among these techniques are operant conditioning, counterconditioning, and modeling. In addition to using several behavioral techniques, the therapist may use some insight techniques. A good therapist will use whatever combination of techniques will help a client most efficiently and effectively. The more complicated the disorder being treated, the more likely it is that a practitioner will use a mix of therapeutic approaches—a *multimodal approach* (e.g., Blanchard et al., 1990).

Behavior therapy usually involves three general procedures: (1) identifying the problem behavior and its frequency; (2) treating the client, perhaps by reeducation, communication training, or some type of counterconditioning; and (3) assessing whether there is a lasting behavior change. If the client exhibits the new behavior for several weeks or months, the therapist concludes that treatment was effective. Let's now explore the three major behavior therapy techniques: operant conditioning, counterconditioning, and modeling.

Operant Conditioning

Operant conditioning procedures are used with different people in different settings to achieve a wide range of desirable behaviors, including increased reading speed, improved classroom behavior, and the maintenance of personal hygiene. As we saw in Chapter 5, operant conditioning to establish new behaviors often depends on a *reinforcer*—any event or circumstance that increases the probability that a particular response will recur. Tricia could employ operant conditioning to help herself adopt more positive responses toward herself. For example, she could ask her husband to praise her every time she honors her own best instincts, uses her own good judgment, or is honest about her feelings.

One of the most effective uses of operant conditioning is with children who are antisocial, slow to learn, or in some way maladjusted. Operant conditioning is also effective with patients in mental hospitals. Ayllon and Haughton (1964), for example, instructed hospital staff members to reinforce patients for psychotic, bizarre, or meaningless verbalizations during one period and for neutral verbalizations (such as comments about the weather) during another. As expected, the relative frequency of each type of verbalizations increased when it was reinforced and decreased when it was not reinforced (see Figure 15.3 on page 534).

Token Economies. One way of rewarding adaptive behavior is with a **token economy**—an operant conditioning environment in which individuals who engage in appropriate behavior receive tokens that they can exchange for desirable items or activities. In a hospital setting, for example, some rewards might be candy, new clothes, games, or time with important people in the patients' lives. The more tokens people earn, the more items or activities they can obtain.

Symptom substitution: The appearance of one overt symptom to replace another that has been eliminated by treatment.

Token economy: An operant conditioning procedure in which individuals who engage in appropriate behavior receive tokens that they can exchange for desirable items or activities.

FIGURE 15.3

Reinforcement Increases Desired Behaviors

A study by Ayllon and Haughton (1964) found that reinforcement affected the frequency of psychotic and neutral verbal behavior in hospitalized patients.

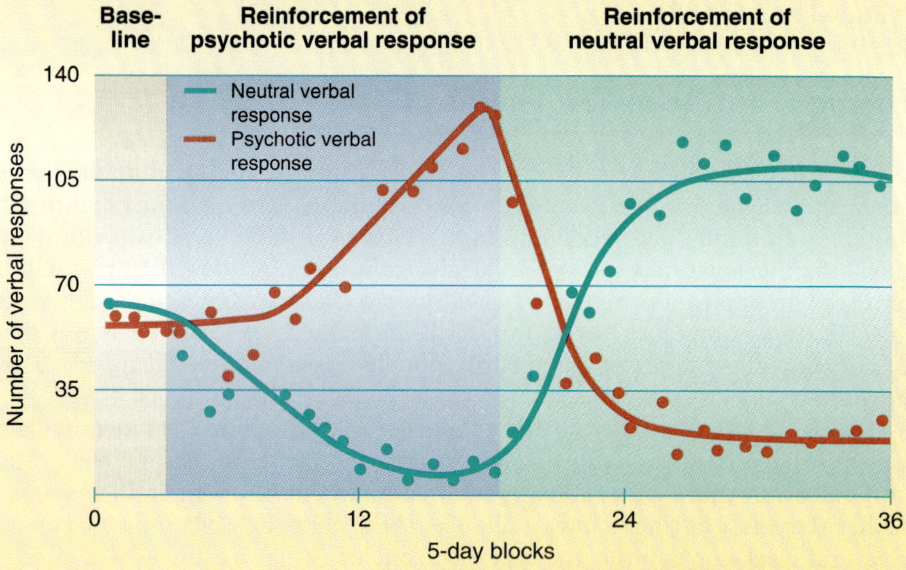

Token economies are used to modify behavior in social settings, usually with groups of people. They aim to strengthen behaviors that are compatible with social norms. For example, a patient in a mental hospital might receive tokens for cleaning tables, helping in the hospital laundry, and maintaining certain standards of personal hygiene and appearance. The number of tokens earned is determined by the level of difficulty of the behavior or task and how long the person performs it. Thus, patients might receive 3 tokens for brushing their teeth but 40 tokens for engaging in helping behaviors.

Ayllon and Azrin (1965) monitored the performance of a group of hospitalized patients who were involved in doing simple work tasks for 45 days. They found that when tokens (reinforcement) were contingent on performance, the patients produced about four times as much work per day as when tokens were not delivered. (See Figure 15.4, in which some of the researchers' results are presented.) Token economies become especially effective when combined with other behavioral techniques (Miller, Cosgrove, & Doke, 1990). We will examine two of these techniques next—extinction and punishment first, followed by time-out.

Time-out: A punishment procedure in which a person is physically removed from a desired or reinforcing situation to decrease the likelihood that an undesired behavior will recur.

Counterconditioning: A process of reconditioning in which a person is taught a new, more adaptive response to a familiar stimulus.

Extinction and Punishment. As we saw in Chapter 5, extinction and punishment can decrease the frequency of a behavior. For example, if reinforcers are withheld, extinction of an undesired behavior will occur. Suppose a 6-year-old girl refuses to go to bed at the designated time. When she is taken to her bedroom, she cries and screams violently. If the parents give in and allow her to stay up, they are reinforcing the crying behavior: The child cries; the parents give in. A therapist might suggest that the parents stop reinforcing the crying behavior by insisting that their daughter go to bed and stay there. Chances are that the child will cry loudly and violently for two or three nights, but the behavior will eventually be extinguished (C. D. Williams, 1959).

FIGURE 15.4

Token Economies Change Performance Effectively

Aylon and Azrin (1965) found that tokens increased the number of hours worked by patients. Token economies have also proved effective in some school settings.

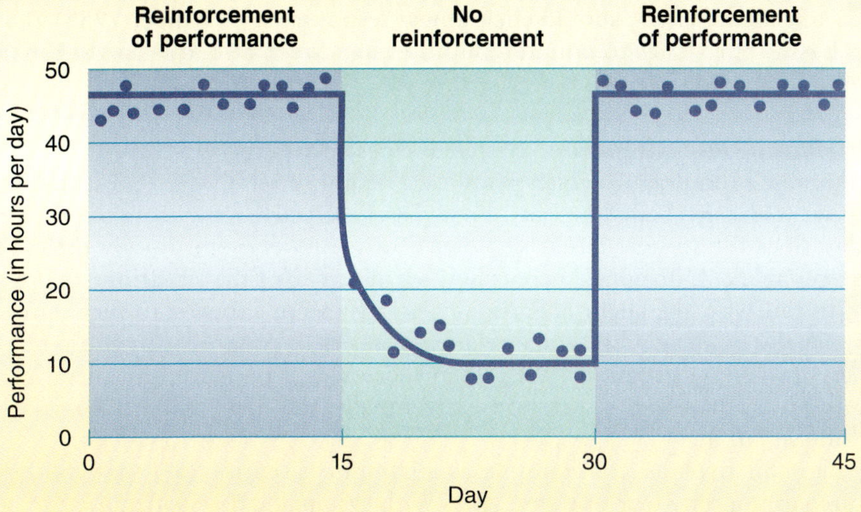

Another way to decrease the frequency of an undesired behavior is to punish it. Punishment often involves the presentation of an aversive stimulus. In the laboratory, researchers might provide slight electric shocks to get adult participants to stop performing a specific behavior. Usually, punishment for undesired behaviors is combined with positive reinforcement for desired behaviors.

Time-Out. As we saw in Chapter 5, **time-out**—the physical removal of a person from sources of reinforcement in order to decrease the occurrence of undesired behaviors—is an effective operant conditioning procedure. Suppose a boy regularly throws a temper tantrum each time he wants a piece of candy, an ice-cream cone, or his little brother's toys. With the time-out procedure, whenever the child misbehaved, he would be placed in a restricted area away from the rest of the family, without sweets, toys, television, or other people. He would be required to stay in the restricted area (such as a chair or a time-out room) for a short period, such as 5 or 10 minutes; if he left, more time would be added. Not only would the child not be getting what he wanted, he would also be removed from any potential source of reinforcement. Time-out is principally used with children; it is especially effective when it is combined with positive reinforcers for appropriate behavior and is administered by a knowledgeable parent or child-care specialist (Crespi, 1988).

Although the use of time-out has been questioned by some researchers, this technique can be effective if combined with positive reinforcement of appropriate behaviors. ▼

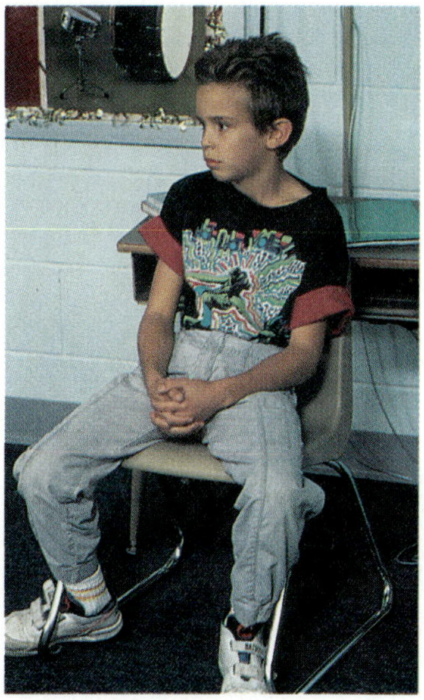

Counterconditioning

A second major technique of behavior therapy is **counterconditioning**—a process of reconditioning in which a person is taught a new, more adaptive response to a familiar stimulus. For example, anxiety is one of the first responses people show when they are maladjusted, fearful, or lacking in self-esteem. If a therapist can condition a person to respond with something other than anxiety—that is, *countercondition* the person—a real breakthrough will be achieved, and the person's anxiety will be reduced.

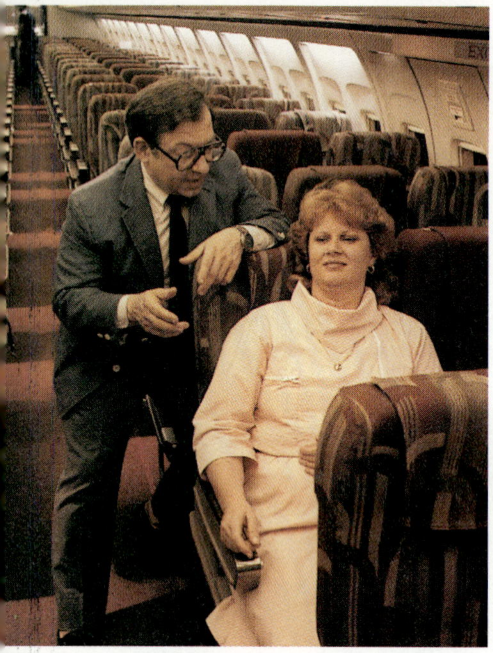

▲ *Using systematic desensitization, this therapist is gradually acclimating his client to a previously terrifying situation—flying.*

Joseph Wolpe was one of the initial proponents of counterconditioning. His work in classical conditioning, especially in situations in which animals show conditioned anxiety responses, led him to attempt to inhibit or decrease anxiety as a response in human beings. His therapeutic goal was to replace anxiety with some other response, such as relaxation, amusement, or pleasure.

Behavior therapy using counterconditioning begins with a specific stimulus (S^1) which elicits a specific response (R^1). After the person undergoes counterconditioning, the same stimulus (S^1) should elicit a new response (R^2) (Wolpe, 1958). There are two basic approaches to counterconditioning: systematic desensitization and aversive counterconditioning.

Systematic Desensitization. **Systematic desensitization** is a three-stage counterconditioning procedure in which people are taught to relax when presented with stimuli that formerly elicited anxiety. First the client learns how to relax; then the client describes the specific situations that arouse anxiety; and finally the client, while deeply relaxed, imagines increasingly vivid scenes of the situations that elicit anxiety. In this way, the client is gradually, step by step, exposed to the source of anxiety, usually by imagining (while relaxed) a series of progressively more fearful or anxiety-provoking situations. With each successive experience, the client learns relaxation rather than fear as a response. Eventually, the client actually approaches the real-life situation.

Flying in an airplane, for example, is a stimulus situation (S^1) that can bring about an inappropriate fear response (R^1). With systematic desensitization therapy, the idea of flying (S^1) can eventually elicit a response of curiosity or even relaxation (R^2). The therapist might first ask the relaxed client to imagine sitting in an airplane on the ground, then to imagine the airplane taxiing, and eventually to imagine flying though the billowing clouds. As the client practices relaxation while imagining the scene, he or she becomes able to tolerate more stressful imagery and may eventually perform the imagined behavior—in this case, flying in an airplane.

Systematic desensitization is most successful for people who have problems such as impulse control or who exhibit forms of anxiety, such as phobias. It is not especially effective for people who exhibit serious psychotic symptoms; nor is it the best treatment for situations involving interpersonal conflict.

Systematic desensitization: A counterconditioning procedure in which a person first learns deep relaxation and then imagines a series of progressively fearful situations; with each successive experience, the person learns relaxation rather than fear as a new response to a formerly fearful stimulus.

Aversive counterconditioning: A counterconditioning technique that seeks to teach a new response by pairing an aversive or noxious stimulus with the stimulus that elicits an undesirable response so that the subject will learn to adopt a new, more worthwhile behavior in response to the familiar stimulus and cease the undesired behavior.

Aversive Counterconditioning. Before therapy, clients often do not avoid a stimulus that prompts inappropriate behavior. This is where aversive counterconditioning, another form of counterconditioning, can be used. **Aversive counterconditioning** is a counterconditioning technique in which an aversive or noxious stimulus is paired with a stimulus that elicits an undesired behavior so that the client will adopt a new, more worthwhile behavior in response to the familiar stimulus and thus cease the undesired behavior. As with systematic desensitization, the objective is to teach a new response to the original stimulus. A behavior therapist might use aversive counterconditioning to teach an alcoholic client to avoid alcohol. The first step might be to teach the person to associate alcohol (the original stimulus) with the sensation of nausea (a noxious stimulus). If verbal instruction is not enough, the therapist might administer a drug that causes nausea whenever alcohol is consumed. The goal is to make the drinking of alcohol unpleasant. Eventually, the treatment will make the client experience nausea just at the thought of consuming alcohol, thus causing the client to avoid alcohol.

Modeling

Both children and adults learn behaviors by watching and imitating other people—in other words, by observing models. Children learn table manners, toilet behavior, and appropriate responses to animals by observing and imitating their parents and other models. Similarly, the music you listen to, the clothing styles you wear, and the social or political causes you support are determined, in part, by the people around you.

According to Albert Bandura (1977a), as part of behavior therapy, modeling is most effective in three areas: (1) teaching new behavior, (2) helping to eliminate fears, especially phobias, and (3) enhancing already existing behavior. By watching the behavior of others, people learn to exhibit more adaptive and appropriate behavior. Bandura, Blanchard, and Ritter (1969), for example, asked people with snake phobia to watch other people handling snakes. Afterward, the watchers' fear of snakes was reduced.

One problem with modeling is that people may observe and imitate the behavior of inappropriate models. We will see in Chapter 16 that people imitate violent behaviors that they have observed on television and in movies. Further, many adolescents become involved in abuse of alcohol and other drugs because they imitate their peers. Such imitation often occurs because of faulty thinking about situations, people, or lifelong goals. When people have developed a faulty set of expectations that guide their behavior, cognitive therapy may be in order.

Building Table 15.3, on page 538, presents a summary of the key components of the psychoanalytic, humanistic, and behavioral views of therapy.

FOCUS

Review

- Identify the fundamental reasons why behaviorists are dissatisfied with psychodynamic and humanistic therapies. p. 532
- For what disorders is the behavior therapy technique of operant conditioning especially effective? p. 533

Think Critically

- How would the therapy process differ if a practitioner used behavior therapy or Gestalt therapy with a person who was suffering from low self-esteem?
- Why do you think modeling is especially effective in the treatment of phobias?

Cognitive Therapy

Cognitive psychologists have had a profound impact in many areas of psychology, especially in therapy. In the past, most behavior therapists were concerned only with overt behavior; today, many incorporate thought processes into their treatments. Researchers now suggest that thought processes may hold the key to managing many forms of maladjustment.

Therapists who use *cognitive restructuring* (cognitive therapy) are interested in modifying the faulty thought patterns of disturbed people (Mahoney, 1977). This type of therapy is effective for people who have attached overly narrow or otherwise inappropriate labels to certain situations; for example, such a person may believe that sex is dirty or that assertiveness is unwomanly. Whenever presented with a situation that involves sex or assertiveness, the person will respond in a way that is determined by his or her thoughts about the situation rather than by the facts of the situation.

Cognitive therapy is derived from three basic propositions:

- Cognitive activity affects behavior.
- Cognitive activity can be monitored.
- Behavior changes can be effected through cognitive changes.

Like other forms of behavior therapy, cognitive therapy focuses on current behavior and current thoughts. It is not especially concerned with uncovering forgotten childhood experiences, although it can be used to alter thoughts about those experiences. It has been used effectively to treat depression, bulimia, weight loss,

BUILDING TABLE 15.3

Key Issues in Psychoanalytic, Humanistic, and Behavior Therapy

THERAPY	NATURE OF PSYCHO-PATHOLOGY	GOAL OF THERAPY	ROLE OF THERAPIST	ROLE OF UNCONSCIOUS MATERIAL	ROLE OF INSIGHT	TECHNIQUES
Psychoanalytic	Maladjustment reflects inadequate conflict resolution and fixation in early development.	Attainment of maturity, strengthened ego functions, reduced control by unconscious or repressed impulses	An *investigator,* uncovering conflicts and resistances	Primary in classical psychoanalysis, less emphasis in ego analysis	Includes not solely intellectual understanding but also emotional experiences	Analyst takes an active role in interpreting the dreams and free associations of patients.
Humanistic	Pathology reflects an incongruity between the real self and the potential, desired self. Overdependence on others for gratification and self-esteem.	To foster self-determination, release human potential, expand awareness	An *empathic person* in true encounter with client, sharing experience	Emphasis is primarily on conscious experience	Used by many, but there is more emphasis on *how* and *what* questions than on *why* questions	Client is asked to see the world from a different perspective and is encouraged to focus on current situations rather than past ones.
Behavior	Symptomatic behavior stems from faulty learning or learning of maladaptive behaviors. The symp tom is the problem; there is no "underlying disease."	To relieve symptomatic behavior by suppressing or replacing maladaptive behaviors	A *helper* helping client unlearn old behaviors and learn new ones	No concern with unconscious processes	Irrelevant and unnecessary	Clients learn new responses; purpose is to establish new behaviors and eliminate faulty or undesirable ones.

anger, and adolescent behavior problems (e.g., Kendall, 1993; Shapiro et al., 1994; Whisman, 1993). When cognitive restructuring is combined with other psychological techniques, such as reinforcement, which help the person make behavioral changes, findings are even more supportive (Kirsch, Montgomery, & Sapirstein, 1995). Cognitive therapy has gone through three decades of development, and its effectiveness and future look promising (Beck et al., 1994; Brown & Barlow, 1995; Gaffer, Tsaousis, & Kemp-Wheeler, 1995; Mahoney, 1993).

Rational–Emotive Therapy

The best-known cognitive therapy is **rational–emotive therapy**—a cognitive behavior therapy that emphasizes the importance of logical, rational thought processes. This therapy was developed by researcher Albert Ellis more than 30 years ago. Most behavior therapists assume that abnormal behavior is caused by faulty and irrational *behavior* patterns. Ellis and his colleagues, however, assume that it is caused by faulty and irrational *thinking* patterns (Ellis, 1970; Ellis & Harper, 1961). They believe that if faulty thought processes can be replaced with rational ones, maladjustment and abnormal behavior will disappear.

According to Ellis, psychological disturbance is a result of events in a person's life that give rise to irrational beliefs leading to negative emotions and behaviors. Moreover, these beliefs are a breeding ground for further irrational ideas (Dryden & Ellis, 1988). Ellis (1988) argues that people make formal demands on themselves and on other people, and they rigidly hold onto them no matter how unrealistic and illogical they are.

Thus, a major goal of rational–emotive therapy is to help people examine the past events that produced the irrational beliefs. Ellis, for example, tries to focus on a client's basic philosophy of life and how it is self-defeating. He thus tries to uncover the client's thought patterns and help the client recognize that the underlying beliefs are faulty. Table 15.4 lists 10 irrational assumptions that, according to Ellis, cause emotional problems and maladaptive behaviors. They are based on people's needs to be liked, to be competent, to be loved, and to feel secure. When people place irrational or exaggerated value on these needs, the needs become maladaptive and lead to emotional disturbance, anxiety, and abnormal behavior. If rational–emotive therapy is successful, the client adopts different behaviors based on new, more rational thought processes. Research supports the effectiveness of the approach (Abrams & Ellis, 1994; Haaga & Davison, 1993), and Ellis (1993) asserts that rational–emotive therapy has broad applications in both therapy and classroom settings.

TABLE 15.4 *Ellis's Outline of Ten Irrational Assumptions*

1. It is a necessity for an adult to be loved and approved of by almost everyone for virtually everything.
2. A person must be thoroughly competent, adequate, and successful in all respects.
3. Certain people are bad, wicked, or villainous and should be punished for their sins.
4. It is catastrophic when things are not going the way one would like.
5. Human unhappiness is externally caused. People have little or no ability to control their sorrows or to rid themselves of negative feelings.
6. It is right to be terribly preoccupied with and upset about something that may be dangerous or fearsome.
7. It is easier to avoid facing many of life's difficulties and responsibilities than it is to undertake more rewarding forms of self-discipline.
8. The past is all-important. Because something once strongly affected someone's life, it should continue to do so indefinitely.
9. People and things should be different from the way they are. It is catastrophic if perfect solutions to the grim realities of life are not immediately found.
10. Maximal human happiness can be achieved by inertia and inaction or by passively and without commitment "enjoying oneself."

Source: Ellis & Harper, 1961.

Rational–emotive therapy: A cognitive behavior therapy that emphasizes the importance of logical, rational thought processes.

Beck's Approach

Another cognitive therapy that focuses on irrational ideas is that of Aaron Beck (1963). As we saw in Chapter 14, Beck's theory assumes that depression is caused by people's distorted cognitive views of reality, which lead to negative views about the world, themselves, and the future, and often to gross overgeneralizations. For example, people who think they have no future—that all of their options are blocked—and who undervalue their intelligence are likely to be depressed. Such individuals form appraisals of situations that are distorted and based on insufficient (and sometimes wrong) data. The goal of therapy, therefore, is to help them to develop realistic appraisals of the situations they encounter and to solve problems (Beck, 1991). The therapist acts as a trainer and coinvestigator, providing data to be examined and guidance in understanding how cognitions influence behavior (Beck & Weishaar, 1989).

According to Beck (1976), a successful client passes through four stages in the course of correcting faulty views and moving toward improved mental health: "First, he has to become aware of what he is thinking. Second, he needs to recognize what thoughts are awry. Then he has to substitute accurate for inaccurate judgments. Finally, he needs feedback to inform him whether his changes are correct" (p. 217).

Meichenbaum's Approach

Some researchers, among them Donald Meichenbaum, believe that what people *say* to themselves determines what they will do. Therefore, a key goal of therapy is to change the things people say to themselves. According to Meichenbaum, the therapist has to change the client's appraisal of stressful events and the client's use of self-instructions, thus normalizing his or her reactions (Meichenbaum, 1993).

A strength of Meichenbaum's theory is that self-instruction can be used in many settings for many different problems (Dobson & Block, 1988). It can help people who are shy or impulsive, people with speech impediments, and even those who are schizophrenic (Meichenbaum, 1974; Meichenbaum & Cameron, 1973). Rather than attempting to change their irrational beliefs, clients learn a repertoire of activities they can use to make their behavior more adaptive. For example, they may learn to conduct a private monologue in which they work out adaptive ways of thinking and coping with situations. They can then discuss with a therapist the quality and usefulness of these self-instructional statements. They may learn to organize their responses to specific situations in an orderly, more easily exercised set of steps.

Building Table 15.4 provides an overall summary of the psychoanalytic, humanistic, behavioral, and cognitive approaches to individual therapy.

Cognitive therapy in its many forms has been used with adults and children, and with specialized groups such as women and the elderly (Davis & Padesky, 1989; DiGiuseppe, 1989; Glantz, 1989). It can be applied to such problems as anxiety disorders, marital difficulties, chronic pain, and (as is evident from Beck's work) depression. Cognitive therapy continues to make enormous strides. It is influencing an increasing number of theorists and practitioners who conduct both long-term therapy and brief therapy (the latter type of therapy is considered in *Applications* on page 542).

Group Therapy

Group therapy: Psychotherapeutic process in which several people meet as a group with a therapist.

When several people meet as a group to receive psychological help, the treatment is referred to as **group therapy**. This technique was introduced in the early 1900s and

BUILDING TABLE 15.4

Key Issues in Psychoanalytic, Humanistic, Behavior, and Cognitive Therapy

THERAPY	NATURE OF PSYCHO-PATHOLOGY	GOAL OF THERAPY	ROLE OR THERAPIST	ROLE OF UNCONSCIOUS MATERIAL	ROLE OF INSIGHT	TECHNIQUES
Psychoanalytic	Maladjustment reflects inadequate conflict resolution and fixation in early development.	Attainment of maturity, strengthened ego functions, reduced control by unconscious or repressed impulses	An *investigator,* uncovering conflicts and resistances	Primary in classical psychoanalysis, less emphasis in ego analysis	Includes not solely intellectual understanding but also emotional experiences	Analyst takes an active role in interpreting the dreams and free associations of patients.
Humanistic	Pathology reflects an incongruity between the real self and the potential, desired self. Overdependence on others for gratification and self-esteem.	To foster self-determination, release human potential, expand awareness	An *empathic person* in true encounter with client, sharing experience	Emphasis is primarily on conscious experience	Used by many, but there is more emphasis on *how* and *what* questions than on *why* questions	Client is asked to see the world from a different perspective and is encouraged to focus on current situations rather than past ones.
Behavior	Symptomatic behavior stems from faulty learning or learning of maladaptive behaviors. The symptom is the problem; there is no "underlying disease."	To relieve symptomatic behavior by suppressing or replacing maladaptive behaviors	A *helper* helping client unlearn old behaviors and learn new ones	No concern with unconscious processes	Irrelevant and unnecessary	Clients learn new responses; purpose is to establish new behaviors and eliminate faulty or undesirable ones.
Cognitive	Maladjustment occurs because of faulty, irrational thought patterns.	To change the way clients think about themselves and the world	A *trainer* and *coinvestigator* helping the client learn new, rational ways to think about the world	Little or no concern with unconscious processes	Irrelevant, but may be used if it does occur	Clients learn to think situations through logically and to reconsider many of their irrational assumptions.

APPLICATIONS

Brief Therapy

There is a new model for psychotherapy in town—and it is often a cognitive one. The new model rejects many of the traditional ideas of the various therapies discussed so far in this chapter. Its proponents reject the idea that any one therapeutic approach can help all people with any behavioral or emotional problem. They also reject the belief that a person's unconscious or life history must be understood fully before the client can end therapy. They disavow the idea that the therapist and the client have to resolve past or future psychological problems during one series of psychotherapy sessions. Finally, therapists using the new model assert that it works with a wide array of clients, including adolescents and families (Swift, 1993) in a short period of time (Huber, 1994).

Sometimes termed **brief therapy,** or *brief intermittent therapy,* this new therapeutic approach is based on a blend of psychotherapeutic orientations and skills (Cummings, 1986). A basic goal of brief therapy is to give clients what they need; the therapy therefore focuses on treating clients' problems efficiently and getting clients back on their own as quickly as possible. One of its objectives is to save clients time and money. There are no limits on the number of sessions, however, and clients remain in therapy as long as they find it necessary. They can also return if they need help in the future. The key distinction of this changing approach to therapy is that more and more therapists are thinking in terms of *planned* short-term treatments (Huber, 1994; Wells & Phelps, 1990).

The therapist makes sure that treatment begins in the first session of brief therapy. He or she strives to perform an *operational diagnosis* that answers this question: Why is the client here today instead of last week, last month, last year, or next year? The answer indicates to the therapist the specific problem for which the client is seeking help. Also in the first session, "every client makes a therapeutic contract with every therapist" (N. A. Cummings, 1986, p. 430; Goulding, 1990). The goals of therapy are established and agreed on by the client and the therapist; and the therapy is precise, active, and directive, with no unnecessary steps (Clarkin & Hull, 1991; Lazarus & Fay, 1990).

Published research on brief therapy is encouraging, suggesting that the therapy is effective and that the effects are long-lasting (e.g., Huber, 1994; Shefler, Dasberg, & Ben-Shakhar, 1995). Research has been limited to relatively few clients with a narrow range of problems. Nonetheless, researchers have found brief therapy to be effective when treatment goals and procedures are tailored to the client's needs and the time available (Brom, Kleber, & Defares, 1989). It can be especially effective when combined with cognitive restructuring (Ellis, 1990) and is effective for relapse prevention for alcoholics (Sandahl & Ronnberg, 1990).

Brief therapy is not a cure-all. As with all therapies, its aim is to help relieve clients' suffering (L. Segal, 1991), and it will be effective with some clients and with some problems some of the time (Clarkin & Hull, 1991). Further research on brief therapy is being conducted now, and its future will depend on the results of that research.

has become increasingly popular since World War II. One reason for its popularity is that in the United States the demand for therapists exceeds the number available. Individually, a therapist can generally see up to 40 clients a week for 1 hour each. But in a group, the same therapist might see 8 to 10 clients in just 1 hour. Another reason for the popularity is that the therapist's fee is shared among the members of the group, making group therapy less expensive than individual therapy.

Brief therapy: A therapeutic approach that focuses on identifying the client's current problem and solving it with the most effective treatment as quickly as possible. Also known as *brief intermittent therapy.*

Group therapy can also be more effective than individual therapy in the treatment of interpersonal conflicts (Rose, 1991), since the social pressures that operate in a group can help shape the members' behavior. In addition, group members can be useful models of behavior for one another, and groups provide frequent and varied opportunity for mutual reinforcement and support. Successful self-help organizations such as Weight Watchers, Gamblers Anonymous, and Alcoholics Anonymous practice a form of group therapy. Such self-help groups grow in popularity each year; currently, about 6 million American adults are members of such groups.

Technique and Formats

The techniques used in group therapy are determined largely by the nature of the group and the orientation of its therapist. The group may follow a psychoanalytic, client-centered, Gestalt, behavioral, or other approach. No two groups are alike, and no two groups deal with individual members in the same way.

In traditional group therapy, 6 to 12 clients meet on a regular basis (usually once a week) with a therapist in a clinic or hospital or in the therapist's office. Generally, the therapist selects members on the basis of what they can gain from and offer to the group. The goal is to construct a group whose members are compatible (though not necessarily the same) in terms of age, needs, and problems. The duration of group therapy varies; it usually takes longer than 6 months, but there are a growing number of short-term groups (under 12 weeks) (Rose, 1991). The format of traditional group therapy varies, but generally each member describes her or his problems to the other members, who in turn relate their experiences with similar problems and how they coped with them. This gives individuals a chance to express their fears and anxieties to people who are warm and accepting; each member eventually realizes that everyone has emotional problems. Group members also have opportunities to role play (try out) new behaviors in a safe but evaluative environment. In a mental health center, for example, a therapist might help members relive past traumas and cope with their continuing fears. Finally, in group therapy, members can exert pressure on an individual to behave in more appropriate ways. Sometimes the therapist is directive in helping the group cope with a problem. At other times the therapist allows the group to resolve a problem independently.

▲ *Group therapy can be an effective alternative to individual psychotherapy for people having problems with interpersonal relationships. In traditional group therapy, the group meets weekly with the therapist to talk about members' current issues in a warm and accepting environment.*

Nontraditional Group Therapy

Two nontraditional techniques sometimes used in group therapy are psychodrama and encounter groups. **Psychodrama** is a group therapy procedure in which members act out their situations, feelings, and roles. It stems from the work of J. L. Moreno, a Viennese psychiatrist who used this technique in the 1920s and 1930s. Those who participate can practice expressing their feelings and responding to the feelings of others. Even those who do not participate can see how others respond to different emotions and situations. Psychodrama can help open the floodgates of emotion and can be used to refine social skills and define problem areas that need to be worked on further (Naar, 1990).

All kinds of other groups come together to learn more about their feelings, behavior, and interactions. In the 1960s and 1970s such groups were termed **encounter groups**; today they often taken on specialized names such as "The 1990s Special Awareness Group" or the "Mediation as a Way of Life Group." These groups are designed to offer people experiences that will help them self-actualize and develop better interpersonal relationships and a sense of authenticity or gen-

Psychodrama [SYE-ko-drama]: A group therapy procedure in which members act out their situations, feelings, and roles.

Encounter group: Group of people who meet to learn more about their feelings, behavior, and interactions.

Family therapy: Therapy in which two or more people who are committed to one another's well-being are treated at once, in an effort to change the ways in which they interact.

uineness. (Self-actualization, which we examined in Chapters 9 and 12, is the process by which people move toward fulfilling their potential.) These special encounter groups also enable their members to work on resolving their own problems and perceiving—and ultimately minimizing—the effects of their problems on others. Each encounter group is unique. Some are like regular therapy groups. In others, the therapist participates minimally, if at all. Some researchers believe that encounter groups made up of specific types of people—such as female athletes, drug addicts, alcoholics, homosexuals, or singles—have an advantage in therapy.

Family Therapy

A special form of group therapy is family therapy. **Family therapy** is therapy in which two or more people who are committed to each other's well-being are treated at once in an effort to change the ways in which they interact. (Marital, or couple, therapy is thus a subcategory of family therapy.) A *family* is defined as any group of people who are committed to one another's well-being, preferably for life (Bronfenbrenner, 1989). Today it is widely recognized that families are often nontraditional; there are blended families and single-parent families, among others. Different kinds of families are shaping the way people respond to the world and must be considered as part of the cultural context in which psychologists view behavior. Families are now more complicated; few consist simply of Ward, June, Wally, and the Beaver. And even for traditional families, life has grown more complicated by the increasing need to juggle work and family responsibilities and cope with crime and health problems such as AIDS.

With families facing new kinds of problems, family therapy is now widely used by a large number of practitioners, especially social workers. Family therapy aims to change the ways in which family members interact. From a family therapist's point of view, the real patient in family therapy is the family's structure and organization. While parents may identify one member of their family—perhaps a delinquent child—as the problem, family therapists believe that that person, in many cases, may simply be a scapegoat. The so-called problem member diverts the family's attention from structural problems that are difficult to confront. Any clinician who works with a person who has some type of adjustment problem must also consider the impact of this problem on other people. This is one of the main focuses of the study of codependence, which is considered in *Applications*.

Sometimes family therapy is termed *relationship therapy*, because relationships are often the focus of the intervention, especially with couples (Becvar & Becvar, 1988; Jacobson & Addis, 1993). Research on effectiveness indicates that, like other forms of therapy, family therapy and marital (couple) therapy are effective (Shadish et al., 1993). However, because of the myriad of variables found within families, doing such research is complicated to say the least (Lebow & Gurman, 1995).

Family therapists attempt to change *family systems*. This means that treatment takes place within the ongoing, active social system that is a marriage or a family (Fruzzetti & Jacobson, 1991). Therapists assume that there are multiple sources of psychological influence: Individuals within a family affect family

FOCUS

Review

- According to Ellis, what are the consequences of developing irrational beliefs? p. 539
- Identify the advantages of various forms of group therapy over individual therapy. pp. 542–543

Think Critically

- Compare and contrast rational–emotive therapy and Beck's approach to cognitive therapy.
- Why do you think that having several people in treatment together makes such a difference in group therapy? Isn't getting a great deal of one-on-one attention—individual therapy—likely to produce superior results?

APPLICATIONS

Codependence

Recently, practitioners have focused on how families often become enmeshed in one member's problems—for example, depression, alcoholism, drug abuse, child abuse, or anxiety disorders. Such involvement often becomes devastating for the whole family. This problem is termed *codependence*. Codependence is not a disorder in the *DSM–IV*. In fact, the families of people with disorders such as substance abuse have often gone relatively unnoticed. But practitioners who treat whole families, not just the person suffering from maladjustment, view codependence as an additional type of adjustment problem—not for the patient but for the patient's family and friends.

Families often become enmeshed in supporting and protecting one member who has serious problems. The codependents—the family members or friends—are often plagued by intense feelings of shame, fear, anger, or pain; they cannot express those feelings, however, because of an intense desire to please and care for the person suffering from the disorder or addiction. Codependent children may believe their job is to take care of their maladjusted parents. Codependent adults may strive to help their maladjusted spouses, relatives, or friends with the problems. They often think that if they were perfect, they could help the maladjusted individual. In some cases, people actually *need* the person to stay disordered; for example, families sometimes unwittingly want a member with a problem to remain dependent on them so they can stay in a controlling position. Practitioners often see patients with alcoholism or cocaine addiction whose friends or family members are codependent.

Here are some warning signs that people may be codependent:

- They always choose to be with the wrong people—alcoholics or verbally or physically abusive people, for example.
- They assume responsibility for others with whom they have relationships.
- They avoid confronting their feelings about their current relationships.
- They are anxious a great deal of the time, especially about their friend, spouse, or relative with problems.
- They close out all of their own feelings because they are focused on other people's feelings.

Pia Mellody and colleagues (Mellody, Miller, & Miller, 1989) assert that people who suffer from codependence lack the necessary skills to lead mature, satisfying, adult lives. Codependents have difficulty experiencing positive self-esteem, setting psychological boundaries between themselves and others, and defining and meeting their own day-to-day needs. They become wrapped up in another person; in doing so, they not only suffer themselves but retard the growth of the other person. The problem of codependence has only recently been recognized and is still being evaluated. Mellody suggests a family-oriented therapeutic approach for treating codependence, and future research will evaluate this idea.

Groups such as Alanon and Alateen help family members acknowledge and deal with codependence.

interactions, and family interactions affect individuals; the family is thus an interactive system (Sturges, 1994). For example, when a mother labels a son "lazy" because he is not working, the son may feel shame but may act out his feeling as anger. He may lash out at his father's poor work habits and lack of success. This may be followed by a squabble over who "brings home the bacon," and so forth. The mother's attitude may lead to a clash among all the individuals within the closed system, the family. The family systems approach has become especially popular in colleges of social work, in departments of psychology, and even in colleges of medicine, where patients are often seen in a family setting. A useful technique in family therapy is to *restructure* the family's interactions. If a son is responding too submissively to his domineering mother, for example, the therapist may suggest that the son be assigned chores only by his father.

Many psychologists, social workers, and psychiatrists use family therapy to help individuals and families change. Some researchers believe the family systems approach is as effective as individual therapy—and more effective in some situations (Bednar, Burlingame, & Masters, 1988). Not all families profit equally from such interventions, however. Family therapy is difficult with families that are disorganized or in which not all members participate. Younger couples and families seem to have better outcomes; when depression is evident, outcomes are not as good (Lebow & Gurman, 1995). In addition, some family members may drop out of therapy; this almost always has negative consequences (Prinz & Miller, 1994).

Biologically Based Therapies

When an individual is referred to a practitioner for help, the usual approach involves some form of psychological treatment. This generally means a talking therapy that may be based on psychodynamic, humanistic, behavioral, or cognitive theories. For some patients, however, talking therapy is not enough. Some may be too profoundly depressed; others may be exhibiting symptoms of bipolar disorders (manic depression) or schizophrenia; still others may need hospitalization because they are suicidal. This is where biologically based therapies enter the picture. These therapies may include medication, hospitalization, and the involvement of physicians. They are generally used in combination with traditional forms of psychotherapy, in a multimodal approach. Biologically based therapies fall into three broad classes: psychosurgery (rarely used), electroconvulsive shock therapy (occasionally used), and drug therapy (often used).

Psychosurgery and Electroconvulsive Shock Therapy

Psychosurgery is brain surgery; it was used in the past to alleviate symptoms of serious mental disorders. A particular type of psychosurgery commonly performed in the 1940s and 1950s was *prefrontal lobotomies,* in which the surgeon would sever parts of the brain's frontal lobes from the rest of the brain. The frontal lobes were thought to control emotions; their removal destroyed connections within the brain, making patients docile. Patients lost the symptoms of their mental disorders, but they also became overly calm and completely unemotional. Some became unable to control their impulses, and an estimated 1 to 4 percent died from the operation. President John F. Kennedy's younger sister, Rosemary, underwent this surgery in 1941 after a series of outbursts of violent behavior and after being diagnosed with mild retardation.

Today, despite advances in technology and in the precision of the operation, psychosurgery is rarely used, for three basic reasons. First, drug therapy has proved more effective than surgical procedures. Second, the long-term effects of psychosurgery are questionable. Third, and most important, the procedure is irreversible and therefore morally objectionable to most practitioners and to patients and their families. Its widespread use during the 1940s and 1950s is considered by many to have been a serious mistake.

Electroconvulsive shock therapy (ECT) [eel-ECK-tro-con-VUL-siv]: A treatment for severe mental illness in which a brief application of electricity to the head is used to produce a generalized seizure. Also known as *shock treatment.*

Electroconvulsive shock therapy (**ECT**), or *shock treatment*, once widely employed with depressed individuals, is a treatment for severe mental illness in which a brief application of electricity to the head is used to produce a generalized seizure (convulsion). The duration of the shock is less than a second, and patients are treated in 3 to 12 sessions over several weeks. In the 1940s and 1950s, ECT was routinely given to severely disturbed patients in mental hospitals. Unfortunately, it was often used on patients who did not need it (mostly women) and by overzealous physicians who wished to control unruly patients. Today, ECT is not a common treatment. According to the National Institutes of Health, fewer than 2.5 percent of all psychiatric hospital patients are treated with ECT.

Is ECT at all effective? Could drug therapy or traditional psychotherapy be used in its place? ECT is effective in the short-term management of severely depressed individuals and those suffering from extreme episodes of mania; it is sometimes used when a particular patient is at risk of suicide (Abrams, Swartz, & Vedak, 1991; Mukherjee, Sackeim, & Schnurr, 1994). However, its effects are only temporary if it is not followed by drug therapy and psychotherapy (Parker et al., 1992). Generally speaking, ECT should be used as a last resort, when other forms of treatment have been ineffective and when a patient is not responsive to medications. ECT is not appropriate for treating schizophrenia or for managing unruly behaviors associated with other disorders.

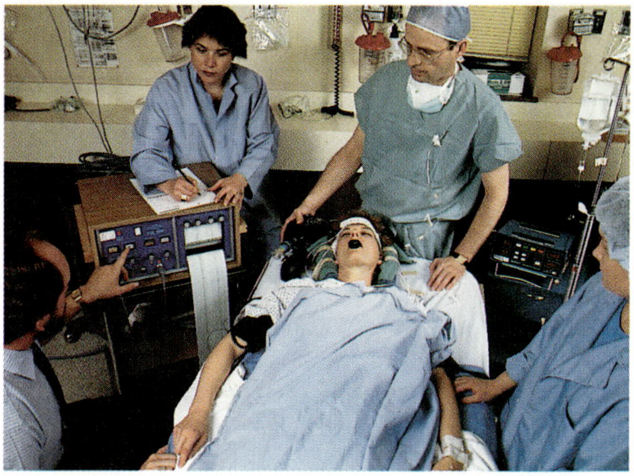

▲ *In electroconvulsive shock therapy, an electric current passes through the brain for less than a second, causing a brief seizure.*

The medical risk of death during the administration of ECT is low (Coffey et al., 1991). However, there is a potential for memory loss and for a decreased ability to learn and retain new information that may endure for several weeks. In addition, ECT may frighten patients and can leave them with feelings of shame and of being stigmatized. If practitioners determine that ECT is warranted, the law requires (and medical ethics demand) that the patient has the right to accept or reject the treatment. Much more research is needed to determine the full effects of ECT and the groups for whom the treatment may be beneficial.

Drug Therapy

In this fast-paced society, people seem to want quick fixes. Every 4 years, politicians promise a quick fix for the economy, a new plan to eliminate poverty, or a simple solution to racial tension. In the same manner, people often want to take drugs to alleviate emotional problems. Drug therapy is an important form of treatment, especially for anxiety, depression, and schizophrenia. It is the most widely used biologically based therapy, and it is effective when used correctly and carefully. But several key issues must be stressed. Dosages are especially important and must be monitored; too much or too little of certain drugs is dangerous. Long-term usage of many drugs is ill-advised. Further, no drug will permanently cure the maladjustments of people who are not coping well. Last, physicians and psychiatrists must be sensitive to the issues of overmedication and long-term dependence on drugs.

Drug therapy can be an effective method for treating a variety of disorders. But often clinicians are reluctant to turn to drug therapy until after traditional forms of psychotherapy have failed—which may cause a delay in the patient's healing. Drug therapy is sometimes used in combination with traditional talking therapy, (as is shown in *Applications* on page 548).

When physicians (often psychiatrists) do administer drugs, people may experience relief from symptoms of anxiety, mania, depression, and schizophrenia. Drugs for the relief of mental problems are sometimes termed *psychotropic drugs*; they are usually grouped into four classes: antianxiety drugs, antidepressant drugs, antimania drugs, and antipsychotic drugs.

Antianxiety Drugs. Antianxiety drugs, or tranquilizers, (technically *anxiolytics*) are mood-altering substances. Widely used in the United States (and probably overprescribed), these drugs reduce stressful feelings, calm patients, and lower excitability. Librium, Xanax, and Valium are trade names of the most widely prescribed antianxiety drugs. When taken occasionally to help a person through a

APPLICATIONS

Talking Therapy, Drug Therapy, and Depression

Depression is the most common disorder seen by the medical, psychiatric, and psychological communities. Nearly 20 percent of the population will experience a depressive episode at one time or another. Women are twice as likely as men to be diagnosed as depressed; the aged are more likely than others to be depressed, as are widows and people with lower incomes (Coryell, Endicott, & Keller, 1992; Umberson, Wortman, & Kessler, 1992).

Treatment for depression has traditionally involved insight-oriented therapy, drug therapy, or a combination of the two. Insight therapy has been used to help patients gain an understanding of the causes of their feelings of sadness. Drug therapy has proved especially effective in altering brain activity in ways that alleviate depressive symptoms. Prozac and Zoloft are two popular and effective drugs.

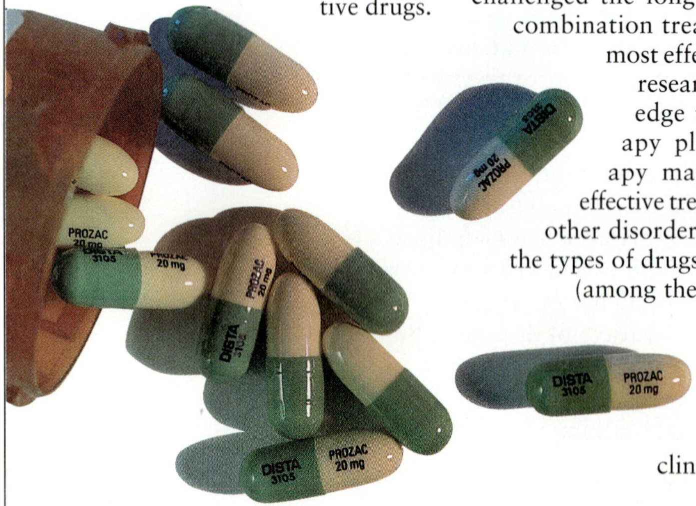

A commonly held belief of practitioners and theoreticians is that the most effective treatment is drugs in combination with psychotherapy.

New research is challenging this idea, however. In the last decade, psychologists have found that (1) psychotherapy is especially effective for depression; (2) the benefits of psychotherapy for depression are long-lasting; and (3) most important, combinations of psychotherapy and drug therapy are *not* necessarily more effective than either of the treatments alone. In important reviews of the research literature on the treatment of depression, Muñoz and colleagues (1994) argued that psychotherapy is more effective than medicine in depression; Antonuccio, Danton, and DeNelsky (1995) came to the same conclusion. Robinson, Berman, and Neimeyer earlier argued (1990) that drug therapy alone or traditional psychotherapy alone is equally effective for patients suffering from depression. These researchers' findings startled some members of the psychological community, because they challenged the long-held idea that combination treatments are the most effective. The three researchers acknowledge that drug therapy plus psychotherapy may be the most effective treatment for some other disorders. However, for the types of drugs they examined (among the many different types available) and with patients suffering from clinical depression, the result was clear: The combination treatment provided no additional benefit over drug therapy alone or psychotherapy alone.

The work of these researchers raises a question: How many widows, other women, and people from lower socioeconomic levels are being given drugs when they don't need them? The answer is unclear; but with each passing month, new research on various disorders and on the role of psychotherapy and drug therapy continues to emerge (Southwick & Yehuda, 1993). For example, Wexler and Cicchetti (1992), like Muñoz and colleagues (1994), argue that psychotherapy alone has the advantage. These studies led Antonuccio to assert that "when treating depression, there is no stronger medicine than psychotherapy" (1995, p. 451). In a review of studies on psychotherapy and depression, Antonuccio, Danton, and DeNelsky (1995, p. 582) wrote: "there is a tendency to underestimate the power and cost-effectiveness of a caring, confidential psychotherapeutic relationship in the treatment of depression . . . for those who do not respond to psychotherapy, the costs and benefits of drug treatments or combined treatments can then be carefully weighed." Today, most therapists are practical and say that an initial treatment with psychotherapy alone might perhaps be followed by combination treatment. There are likely to be further studies showing which types of depressive disorders can best benefit from drug therapy, which from traditional insight therapy, which from cognitive therapy, and which from combinations of drug therapy and traditional talking therapies.

stressful situation, such drugs are useful. They also help manage anxiety in a person who is extremely anxious, particularly when the person is also receiving some form of psychotherapy. However, long-term use of antianxiety drugs without some adjunct therapy is usually ill-advised. Today, physicians are wary of patients seeking antianxiety drugs for management of daily stress; they worry about substance abuse and an overreliance on drugs to get through the day.

Antidepressant Drugs. As their name suggests, antidepressants (technically *thymoleptics*) are sometimes considered mood elevators. They work by altering the level of neurotransmitters in the brain. When a neuron sends a key neurotransmitter (usually serotonin or norepinepherine) across a synapse, there is often an excess of the neurotransmitter; this excess is then reabsorbed into the transmitting neuron (a process called *reuptake*). In depressed individuals, there is often too little of the neurotransmitter absorbed into the next cell because of the reuptake—but antidepressants block such reuptake.

One major category of antidepressants includes drugs such as Prozac, Zoloft, and Paxil. These drugs block the reuptake of serotonin—they are thus often referred to as serotonin reuptake inhibitors—and account for 60 percent of antidrepessant sales in the United States. Extremely depressed people who take such antidepressants often become more optimistic and less sad and redevelop a sense of purpose in their lives. These medications allow many people to function outside a hospital setting. The drugs can take as long as 4 weeks to reach their full effectiveness, and daily use is necessary.

Antidepressants also include two other major categories of drugs: tricylics and monoamine oxidase (MAO) inhibitors. Both types of drugs are potent. The tricylics are prescribed much more often than the MAO inhibitors because they pose less danger of medical complications. (Patients on MAO inhibitors have to adhere to special diets and some other restrictions to prevent adverse physical reactions to the drugs.) To help a patient suffering from a severe bout of depression, a physician might prescribe a commonly used tricyclic such as imipramine (Tofranil) or amitriptyline (Elavil), which will have fewer serious side effects and alleviate symptoms in the majority of people with depressive problems.

Research on the effectiveness of antidepressant drugs is controversial. Some researchers assert that these drugs have major effects, and others report only modest help from the drugs (Greenberg et al., 1992; Schulberg & Rush, 1994.) Research using double-blind procedures and carefully controlled conditions continues, especially with drugs that have specific actions on depressive behaviors (Dubovsky & Thomas, 1995; Roose et al., 1994). The impact of new research findings will be profound, because the number of people with depressive disorders is substantial.

Antimania Drugs. Lithium carbonate, the only effective antimania drug (also technically a *thymoleptic*), has come into wide use for patients with bipolar (manic–depressive) disorders because it relieves the manic elements. Psychiatrists find that when a daily maintenance dose is taken, lithium is especially helpful in warding off future episodes of mania. The dosage of any drug is important, but in the case of lithium it is especially important. Too much produces noxious side effects; too little has no effect. No drug will cure individuals with bipolar disorder of all their symptoms and solve all their problems (for example, lithium is less effective with young patients); in general, however, lithium allows most patients to cope better, to control their symptoms, and to seek other therapies that allow them to manage their lives in the most productive way possible. The same is true of other drugs in this class, including valproic acid, or valproate.

FOCUS

Review

- What are the ethical implications of psychosurgery and of electroconvulsive shock therapy (ECT)? pp. 546–547
- What are the major classes of psychotropic drugs, and what evidence exists to show their effectiveness in which situations? pp. 547–550

Think Critically

- The use of ECT has increased in the 1990s because of improved techniques and medical monitoring. Do you think that ECT is ever useful?
- What is the solution to the problem of the overprescription of medications, especially antidepressants?

TABLE 15.5 ***Common Drugs Used to Treat Psychiatric Disorders***

Effect Group	Chemical Group	Generic Name	Trade Name
Antianxiety (anxiolytic)	Benzodiazepines	Diazepam Chlordiazepoxide Alprazolam Clonazepam	Valium Librium Xanax Klonapin
	Nonbenzodiazepine	Buspirone	Buspar
Antidepressant (thymoleptic)	Tricylics	Amitriptyline Imipramine Nortriptyline Desipramine Doxepin Clomipramine	Elavil Tofranil Pamelor Norpramin Sinequan Anafranil
	Monoamine oxidase inhibitors	Phenelzine Tranylcypromine	Nardil Parnate
	Serotonin reuptake inhibitors	Fluoxetine Sertraline Paroxetine Fluvoxamine	Prozac Zoloft Paxil Luvox
Antimanic (thymoleptic)	Lithium carbonate	Lithium	Eskalith, Lithonate, Lithobid
	GABA agonist Unknown (antiepileptic)	Valproic acid Carbamazepine	Depakene Tegretol
Antipsychotic (neuroleptic)	Phenothiazines	Chlorpromazine Trifluoperazine Fluphenazine Thioridazine	Thorazine Stelazine Prolixin Mellaril
	Butyrophenones Atypicals	Haloperidol Clozapine Risperidone	Haldol Clozaril Risperdal

Antipsychotic Drugs. Antipsychotic drugs (technically *neuroleptics*) are used mainly for people who suffer from the disabling disorder of schizophrenia. These drugs reduce hostility and aggression in violent patients and make their disorders more manageable. They also reduce delusions and allow some patients to manage life outside a hospital setting.

Most of the antipsychotic drugs prescribed are phenothiazines, the most common of which is chlorpromazine (Thorazine). They seem to work by altering the level and uptake of brain neurotransmitters—but this is uncertain (Goldenberg, 1990). As with antidepressants, dosages of antipsychotic drugs are crucial. Further, if patients are maintained on antipsychotic drugs for too long, other problems can emerge. One such problem is *tardive dyskinesia*—a central nervous system disorder characterized by involuntary, spasmodic movements of the upper body, especially the face and fingers, and including leg jiggling and tongue protrusions, facial tics, and involuntary movements of the mouth and shoulders. See Table 15.5 for a detailed listing of some common drugs used to treat psychiatric disorders.

Summary and Review

Therapy Comes in Many Forms

What is the essential difference between biologically based therapy and psychotherapy?

- Two broad types of therapy are biologically based therapy and psychotherapy. *Biologically based therapy* refers to treatment of emotional or behavioral problems by means of treating the body. *Psychotherapy* is treatment through psychological techniques. p. 518

Is therapy necessary and effective in the long run?

- A *placebo effect* is a nonspecific therapeutic change that occurs as a result of a person's expectations of change rather than as a direct result of a certain treatment. However, any long-term therapeutic effects come from the client's and therapist's efforts. p. 520

KEY TERMS
Psychotherapy, p. 519
Placebo effect, p. 520

Psychoanalysis and Psychodynamic Therapies

According to psychoanalytic theory, what causes maladjustment and what processes are involved in treatment?

- *Insight therapies*, which include *psychodynamically based therapies*, assume that maladjustment and abnormal behavior are caused by people's failure to understand their own motivations and needs. Insight therapists believe that once patients understand the motivations that produce maladjusted behavior, the behavior can be changed. p. 524
- According to Freud, conflicts among a person's unconscious thoughts and processes produce maladjusted behavior. Classical Freudian *psychoanalysis* often involves a process of *free association, dream analysis, interpretation, resistance*, and *transference*; collectively, this repetitive cycle is referred to as *working through*. pp. 524–526

What are the basic criticisms of psychoanalysis?

- *Ego analysts* are psychoanalytic practitioners who are often critical of classical Freudian analysis and believe that the ego has greater control over behavior than Freud suggested. They are more concerned with reality testing and control over the environment than with unconscious motivations and processes. p. 526
- Critics of psychoanalysis contend that the approach is unscientific, imprecise, and subjective. Other critics object to Freud's biologically oriented approach, which suggests that a human being is a mere bundle of energy caught in conflict and driven toward some hedonistic goal. Further, many elements of Freud's theory are sexist or untestable. p. 526

KEY TERMS
Psychoanalysis, p. 524
Psychodynamically based therapies, p. 524
Insight therapy, p. 524
Free association, p. 525
Dream analysis, p. 525
Interpretation, p. 525
Resistance, p. 525
Transference, p. 525
Working through, p. 526
Ego analyst, p. 526

Humanistic Therapies

Briefly describe the major differences between client-centered therapy and Gestalt therapy.

- *Client-centered therapy* aims to help clients realize their potential by learning to evaluate the world and themselves from their own point of view. This approach is a *nondirective therapy*, and the therapist conveys unconditional positive regard while letting the client set the agenda for therapy. p. 528
- *Gestalt therapy* encourages individuals to get in touch with their current feelings and become aware of their current situations. Gestalt techniques are designed to help clients become more alert to their significant feelings and to their surroundings in the "here and now." p. 529

KEY TERMS
Client-centered therapy, p. 528
Nondirective therapy, p. 528
Gestalt therapy, p. 529

Behavior Therapy

Identify the basic assumptions and techniques of behavior therapy.

- *Behavior therapy*, or behavior modification, is a therapy based on the application of learning principles to human behavior. It focuses on changing overt behaviors rather than on understanding subjective feelings, unconscious processes, or motivations. It attempts to replace old behaviors with new, more adaptive ones. p. 532
- Techniques of behavior therapy include *token economies, time-out*, and *counterconditioning*. *Systematic desensitization* is a three-stage counterconditioning procedure in which a person is taught to relax while imagining increasingly fearful situations. pp. 533–536
- As part of behavior therapy, modeling is especially effective in three areas: (1) teaching new behavior, (2) helping to eliminate fears, especially phobias, and (3) enhancing already existing behavior. p. 537

KEY TERMS
Behavior therapy, p. 532
Symptom substitution, p. 533
Token economy, p. 533
Time-out, p. 534
Counterconditioning, p. 534
Systematic desensitization, p. 536
Aversive counterconditioning, p. 536

Cognitive Therapy

What are the basic propositions of cognitive therapy?

- The three basic propositions of cognitive therapy are: (1) Cognitive activity affects behavior; (2) cognitive activity can be monitored; (3) behavior changes can be effected through cognitive changes. p. 537

- *Rational–emotive therapy* emphasizes the role of logical, rational thought processes in behavior. It assumes that faulty, irrational thinking patterns are the cause of abnormal behavior. p. 539

KEY TERMS
Rational–emotive therapy, p. 539
Brief therapy, p. 542

Group Therapy

What is group therapy, and what is the function of family therapy?

- *Group therapy* is therapy used to treat several people simultaneously for emotional and behavioral problems. The techniques used by a therapy group are determined by the nature of the group and the orientation of its therapist. pp. 540–543
- *Family therapy* attempts to change family systems, because individuals affect family processes and family processes affect individuals. Treatment takes place within an ongoing, active social system such as a marriage or family. p. 544

KEY TERMS
Group therapy, p. 540
Psychodrama, p. 543
Encounter group, p. 543
Family therapy, p. 544

Biologically Based Therapies

What are the major types of biologically based therapies and the major classes of psychotropic drugs?

- The major biologically based therapies are psychosurgery, electroconvulsive shock therapy, and drug therapy. Psychosurgery (brain surgery) is a generally outmoded method of treatment used to alleviate symptoms of serious mental disorders. *Electroconvulsive shock therapy* (ECT) is a treatment for severe mental illness in which a brief application of electricity to the head is used to produce a generalized seizure. pp. 546–547
- Drugs for the relief of mental problems are usually grouped into four classes: antianxiety drugs, antidepressant drugs, antimania drugs, and antipsychotic drugs. Such drugs often work by altering the level of neurotransmitters in the brain. For example, when a neuron sends a key neurotransmitter across a synapse, there is often an excess of the neurotransmitter; this excess is then reabsorbed into the transmitting neuron—reuptake. In depressed individuals, too little of the neurotransmitter is often absorbed into the next cell because of the reuptake—but antidepressants block such reuptake. pp. 547–549

KEY TERM
Electroconvulsive shock therapy (ECT), p. 546

Learning CONNECTIONS

Some students benefit from extra help with the many different forms of therapy. You can learn more about them in:

- The CD-ROM accompanying this book, Topic 13

- This book's study guide, *Keeping Pace Plus,* or the computerized study guide, Chapter 15
- The audiotape accompanying this book, *SoundGuide for Psychology,* Learning Unit 15
- The study aids found on the World Wide Web site for this book, at http://www.abacon.com/psych/lefton

Critical Thinking CONNECTIONS

Take a moment to think critically about how this chapter's topics are connected with the rest of psychology . . .

If you are interested in . . .	Ask yourself . . .	Then turn to . . .
Freud's theory of psychoanalysis as a therapeutic approach 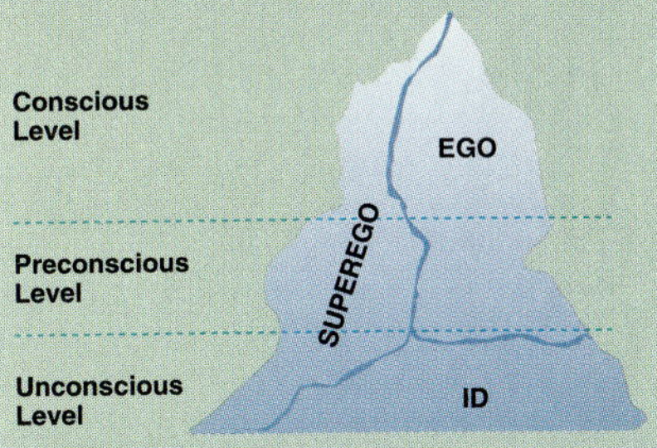	How did Freud develop his theory of personality into a full-blown treatment approach?	Chapter 12, pp. 411–416
	How could defense mechanisms be overused by individuals in need of therapy?	Chapter 12, pp. 416–417
The behavioral approach to therapy 	Why do you think the earliest behaviorists focused on overt, observable behavior?	Chapter 1, pp. 28–29
	How might classical conditioning, operant conditioning, and modeling explain long-standing behaviors—some of which may become maladaptive?	Chapter 5, pp. 153–155, 165, 185–188
	Why might disorders such as depression have a cognitive basis, requiring a change in thought processes and overt behavior?	Chapter 14, p. 500
Biological approaches to therapy 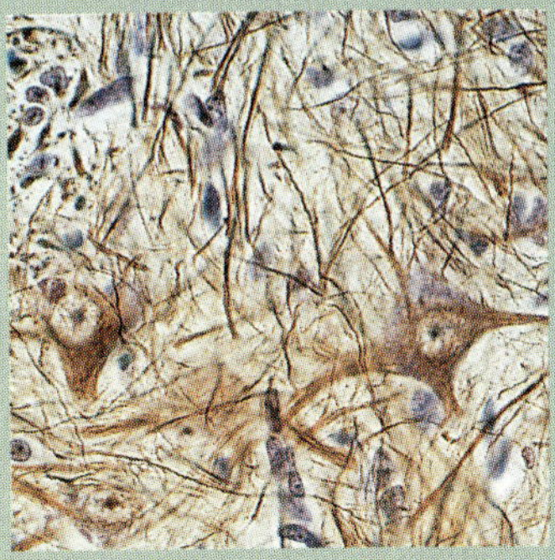	How could certain chemicals in the blood and brain that affect behavior be exploited as part of a multimodal treatment approach?	Chapter 2, pp. 47–48, 62–63
	How might stress lead to health problems that can be alleviated in part through psychotherapy and in part through drug treatments?	Chapter 13, pp. 456–462
	What does the fact that depression is sometimes alleviated by drug therapy indicate about its causes?	Chapter 14, pp. 499–500

16

Social Psychology

How much my friends had changed! I had vowed to stay friends forever with my high school buddies. We had known each other for years and had gone through a lot together. We had gone fishing, attended our first dances, and with a great flurry of excitement double-dated for the first time. But now, after I'd been away a year, my high school friends had changed. The instant bond, the easy understanding, the shared agreements now seemed neither instant nor easy. Our political views were different. Even our tastes in music had changed.

My high school buddies were still my friends, but our year away from one another had created distance. Life had influenced them, and none of them was the same. My best friend had started playing harmonica and thought that he was going to be a blues musician in New Orleans. Another friend had started questioning his sexuality and declared himself homosexual. And I had changed, too. I had started to listen to cool jazz, and I had taken up a new interest—psychology. I no longer wanted to cruise the neighborhoods of former girlfriends; there was now a girl at school who totally mesmerized me. We had all indeed changed a great deal.

Psychologists recognize that people's behavior is shaped by early experiences, by others in their lives, and by such daily influences as advertising, new friends, and school experiences. People are not programmed machines that stay the same forever; they examine other people's nonverbal messages, looking beyond their smiles, and they resist (or give in to) attempts to change their attitudes or to gain their compliance. No person is an island, unaffected by other people's attitudes and behavior. This became apparent to me when I left for college. My high school friends and I were influenced greatly by others. We changed how we dressed, how we voted, who we paid attention to. I realized then, and I know now, that what people wear, whom they vote for, and what they value are affected by an array of social variables.

In this chapter, we examine the social world of interactions among individuals and within groups We will see that other people affect each individual's attitudes and self-perceptions and exert powerful influences on individual behavior. **Social psychology** is this study of how individuals influence and are influenced by the thoughts, feelings, and behaviors of others.

This chapter looks at some of the traditional concepts in social psychology: attitudes, social cognition, and social interactions. These concepts help psychologists form an understanding of behavior when more than one person is involved—that is, of social behavior. Our focus at first will be on how individual attitudes are affected by other people.

Attitudes

Attitudes are long-lasting patterns of feelings and beliefs about other people, ideas, or objects that are based in a person's past experiences and shape his or her future behavior. They are usually evaluative and serve certain functions, such as guiding new behaviors and helping the individual interpret the world efficiently (Eagly & Chaiken, 1993). Attitudes are shaped by how a person perceives other people, how others perceive him or her, and how the person *thinks* others see him or her. For example, my new interest in cool jazz was initiated by my roommate, who, I had decided, was "with it." It also was influenced by listening to this music at a club where I met my new girlfriend, who had been a devoted listener for 2 years. It was further shaped by the reinforcement I received when I announced my new interest to my dad and by praise from an uncle who loved jazz. Roommates, situations, relatives, and praise were changing me.

Dimensions and Functions of Attitudes

Football fans are often fanatical in their attitudes; their enthusiasm is earnest, and they often back up their feelings with visible support for the team. Yet not everybody appreciates football, and even people who like it may find the hoopla that surrounds a game to be a bit much. People's feelings and beliefs about football, or any other subject, are a crucial part of their attitudes. Attitudes have three dimensions—cognitive, emotional, and behavioral—each of which serves a specific function. The *cognitive dimension* of an attitude consists of thoughts and beliefs. When someone forms attitudes about a group of people, a series of events, or a political philosophy, the cognitive dimension of those attitudes serves a function by helping the person categorize, process, and remember the people, events, and philosophy (Hymes, 1986).

The *emotional dimension* of an attitude involves evaluative feelings, such as like or dislike. For example, some people like the abstract mood of cool jazz; others prefer the down-to-earth sound of country and western. When people have strongly held attitudes about a specific topic, they are said to have a *conviction*. Once people

Social psychology: The study of how individuals influence and are influenced by the thoughts, feelings, and behaviors of other people.

Attitudes: Long-lasting patterns of feelings and beliefs about other people, ideas, or objects that are based in a person's past experiences, shape his or her future behavior, are evaluative in nature, and serve certain functions.

form a conviction, they think about it and become involved with it (which makes convictions long-lasting and resistant to change). This is especially true of religious and political convictions (Abelson, 1988). For example, despite strong scientific evidence to the contrary, many people still believe that the Shroud of Turin, a piece of cloth that bears an image resembling Jesus Christ's face, was actually used as Christ's burial cloth. Once people have adopted a conviction, it functions to justify a wide range of behaviors and to interpret new information about events in the world.

The *behavioral dimension* of an attitude determines how people actually show their beliefs and evaluative feelings (Eagly, 1992), such as by voting in accordance with their political beliefs. Behaviorally, attitudes function to shape specific actions. Individuals do not always publicly display their attitudes, of course, especially when their attitudes are not yet firmly established or when their attitudes and behaviors are inconsistent. For example, many more people cognitively and emotionally support a nuclear arms freeze than give their time, energy, or money to organizations supporting this cause (Gilbert, 1988).

What variables determine how attitudes are formed, displayed, or changed? Why are some attitudes hard to modify and others relatively easy? We will take up each of these questions in the following sections, beginning at the beginning—with attitude formation.

Forming Attitudes

Attitudes are formed through learning that begins early in life. Thus, psychologists rely on learning theories to explain how children form attitudes. Three learning theory concepts that help explain attitude formation are classical conditioning, operant conditioning, and observational learning (see Chapter 5 for a review and detailed explanation of these concepts).

The association of people, events, and ideologies with certain attitudes often goes unnoticed because it happens so effortlessly. However, such associations can shape children's views of and emotional responses to the world, thereby forming the basis of their future attitudes as adults. (See Figure 16.1 for an application of this

FIGURE 16.1

Classical Conditioning in Attitude Formation

In attempting to form positive attitudes toward a product or idea, advertisers use classical conditioning techniques. They pair the product or idea with an attractive, desirable individual or situation to evoke a positive response.

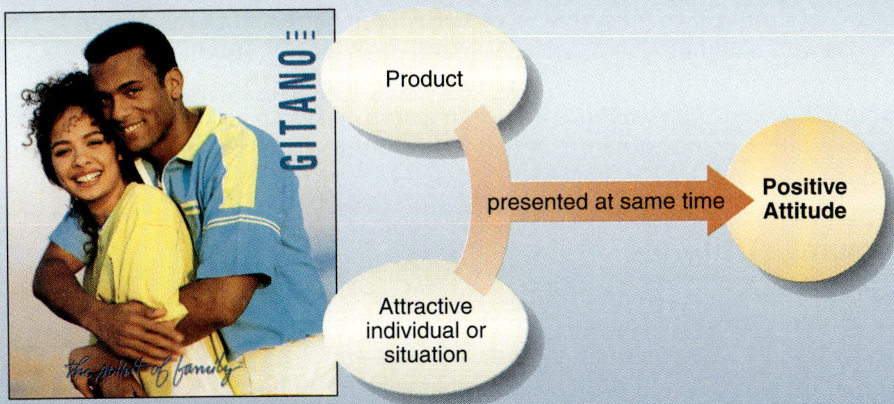

process to attitude formation in adults.) For example, suppose a parent never has a good word to say about Democrats ("bleeding-heart liberals" and so on). *Classical conditioning* pairs the formerly neutral stimulus (a person, the "Democrat") with an unconditioned stimulus (derogatory comments). Because derogatory comments naturally elicit negative feelings as a response, the resulting negative feelings can be considered an unconditioned response. If a child overhears such remarks repeatedly, the Democratic party will eventually evoke a response of negative feelings (now a conditioned response) in the child.

A key principle of *operant conditioning* is that reinforced behaviors are likely to recur; this principle helps explain how attitudes are maintained over time. In socializing their children, parents express approval for and reinforce ideas and behaviors consistent with their own "correct" view of the world. Such approval and reinforcement help children adopt their parents' "correct" attitudes.

According to the concept of *observational learning*, people establish attitudes by watching the behavior of those they consider significant and then imitating that behavior. The new attitudes people learn eventually become their own. Suppose that a young girl sees her father react angrily to a TV news story that contradicts a tenet of the family's religious faith. The next time the child hears a similar argument, she will be likely to mimic her father's attitude, which will partially affect her own attitude.

Predicting Behavior from Attitudes

Social psychologists can assess people's attitudes, but whether those attitudes predict behavior depends on numerous variables. Among these, four key variables are attitude strength, vested interest, specificity of attitudes, and accessibility of attitudes.

Attitudes are better predictors of behavior when the attitude strength is strong and there are few competing outside influences, such as conflicting advertising appeals or advice from friends. A person who believes strongly in the health hazards of cigarette smoke, even after bombardment by Camel advertisements, may work actively for a nonsmoking environment. Furthermore, attitudes people consider personally important (in which they have a vested interest) are more likely to be shown in behavior and to stay intact, regardless of how situations change over time (Krosnick, 1988). If a parent believes strongly in improving her child's educational opportunities, she will be far more likely to attend PTA meetings. The extent to which a belief is tied up with a person's self-concept is also a good predictor of both the strength of the belief and the likelihood that the person will act on it (Pomerantz, Chaiken, & Tordesillas, 1995).

Attitudes are also more likely to foretell behavior when they are specific and the situation requiring a decision closely matches the situation to which the attitude applies. Global attitudes, and even stereotypes about people, do not predict specific behaviors very well (Haddock, Zanna, & Esses, 1994). For example, a person may have a broadly liberal political attitude, but only a specific attitude about health care, welfare reform, or government waste will predict whether the person will vote for a specific candidate. Last, attitudes predict behavior best when they are accessible, that is, well formed and easily remembered (Fazio, 1990). When people have sharply delineated ideas about a political position, they can easily decide how favorably they rate a new candidate. When they cannot easily remember or articulate their views, making such judgments is more time-consuming and less predictable.

Changing Attitudes

Since people learn attitudes, they can change them or learn new ones. Changed attitudes may impel a person to do almost anything—from trying a new brand of soap, to voting Democratic, to undergoing a religious conversion, to becoming a lover of jazz. Social psychologists have identified four key components of attitude change: the communicator, the communication, the medium, and the audience.

The Communicator. To be persuasive, a communicator—the person trying to effect attitude change—must project integrity, credibility, and trustworthiness. If people don't respect, believe, or trust the communicator, they are unlikely to change their attitudes. Researchers have also found that the perceived power, prestige, celebrity, prominence, and attractiveness of the communicator are extremely important (Chaiken & Eagly, 1993; Cialdini, 1994). For example, the Surgeon General has a greater ability to change your views about cigarette smoking in the workplace than does a local school board member.

Information received from friends is considered more influential than information from the communications media. For example, Costanzo and colleagues (1986, p. 528) suggest: "Media sources are effective in creating awareness of a new technology, but interpersonal sources exert a far greater influence on the decision to adopt a new technology." Leonard-Barton (1981) showed that the best predictor of whether a customer will purchase solar energy equipment is the number of the person's acquaintances who currently own such devices. Similarly, a teenager is more likely to follow a close friend's advice on the use of condoms than that of an unknown public health official (Jaccard et al., 1990).

The Communication. A clear, convincing, and logical argument is the most effective tool for changing attitudes—especially attitudes with emotional content, such as those concerning capital punishment or school desegregation (Millar & Millar, 1990). This is especially true in Western culture, where appeals to logic and reason, rather than to authority and tradition, are more prevalent than in Japan, for example.

Communications that arouse fear are effective in motivating attitude change, especially when health issues are concerned and the communicator does not overdo the fear appeal (Robberson & Rogers, 1988). For example, think of some of the antismoking messages you've seen on television. What techniques do they use to induce fear? Fear works; college students who come to fear AIDS are more likely to use condoms (Boyd & Wandersman, 1991), and fear of cancer can be motivating in some situations (Wandersman & Hallman, 1993).

Researchers have also found that if people hear a persuasive message often enough, they begin to believe it, regardless of its validity. Repeated exposure to certain situations can also change attitudes (R. F. Bornstein, 1989). For example, after seeing numerous TV commercials that show the Energizer battery outperforming the competition, a viewer may change his or her attitude toward the product from neutral to positive. Similarly, a name that is heard often is more likely to be viewed positively than is one heard infrequently; this is called the *mere exposure effect* (Jacoby et al., 1989).

The Medium. The way in which communication is presented—its medium—influences people's receptiveness to attitude change. Today, one of the most common avenues for attempts at attitude change is the mass media, particularly television. After all, the goal of TV commercials is either to change or to strengthen people's behavior. Commercials exhort viewers to drink Pepsi instead of Coke, to say no to drugs, or to vote for a Democrat instead of a Republican. Research shows that TV advertising is one of the most influential media of attitude change in the Western world; this is no surprise, given the fact that in the average American household, the television is on for more than 4 hours every day.

Nevertheless, face-to-face communication often has more impact than communication through television or in writing. Thus, even though candidates for public office rely heavily on TV, radio, and printed ads, they also try to meet people face-to-face, sometimes taking to the road by bus to give their message directly to the people. This is important because research shows that in politics the impact of the mass media through bursts of advertising is often overrated; television may serve only to strengthen preexisting ideas, except when there are massive (and expensive) advertising campaigns and preexisting ideas are weak (Sears & Kosterman, 1994).

The Audience. From time to time, people actually want to have their attitudes changed and seek out alternative views. At other times, they fold their arms firmly and announce, "It's going to take an act of Congress to change my mind" (Johnson & Eagly, 1989). Openness to attitude change is in part age- and education-related. People are most susceptible to attitude change in their early adult years; susceptibility to change drops off in later years (Krosnick & Alwin, 1989). People of high intelligence are less likely to have their opinions changed, and those of high self-esteem tend to be similarly unyielding (Rhodes & Wood, 1992). Furthermore, if you are a friend of the person trying to change your attitudes, attitude change is far more likely (Cialdini, 1994).

Attitude change is complicated, and researchers have shown that a wide array of other variables are important as well. For example, attitude change is more likely when the targeted attitude is not too different from an existing one; it is also more likely when the audience is not highly involved with a particular point of view (Johnson & Eagly, 1989). Changing the attitudes of politically involved citizens, for instance, is more difficult than altering those of noninvolved citizens (Johnson & Eagly, 1989; Ottati, Fishbein, & Middlestadt, 1988). Research also shows that people who positively anticipate a new idea, or who feel that others around them are inclined to change their views, are likely to exhibit attitude change (Boninger et al., 1990; Cialdini, 1994). The extent of attitude change is even affected by prevalent attitudes in the particular region of the country; this was seen in the case of Anita Hill, where regional variations predicted students' attitudes—Southern students, being more conservative, tended to believe Judge Thomas rather than Professor Hill (Eisenman, 1993).

Changing attitudes, and ultimately behavior, can be difficult if people have well-established habits (which often come with advancing age) or are highly motivated in the opposite direction. Consider attitudes toward seatbelts. Although people generally believe in the effectiveness of seatbelts and hold positive attitudes about using them, few people use them all the time. Mittal (1988) showed that getting people to use seatbelts takes more than fostering positive attitudes; it also requires instilling a new habit in people. Mittal found that the more often people use seatbelts, the more likely they will be to use them in the future. Thus, education and devices to promote remembering (such as warning buzzers) can be helpful (Geller, Patterson, & Talbot, 1982).

Cognitive Approaches: The Elaboration Likelihood Model. Decades of research have identified the components of attitude change. But for all their knowledge about to whom and how persuasion takes place, only recently have researchers begun to focus on what happens cognitively to individuals whose attitudes are being changed. Various theories attempt to understand such individuals' thought processes so as to be able to predict actual attitude change. One such theory, proposed by Richard Petty and John Cacioppo (1981, 1985), suggests that people generally want to have valid attitudes and beliefs that will prove helpful in the face of day-to-day challenges and problems (Petty et al., 1994). These researchers' model is called the **elaboration likelihood model**—a view of attitude change suggesting that there are two routes to attitude change: central and peripheral. (See Figure 16.2 for an overview of this model.)

The *central route* emphasizes conscious, thoughtful consideration and elaboration of arguments concerning a given issue. Attitude change via this route depends on how effective, authoritative, and logical a communication is. Confronted with scientific evidence on the effects of secondhand smoke on people's health and especially on the prevalence of respiratory diseases, most people conclude through the central route that such smoke is in fact detrimental to health. That is, unless they are highly motivated to believe otherwise, they conclude that the scientific arguments against smoking are too strong to refute.

Elaboration likelihood model: A theory suggesting that there are two routes to attitude change: central, which focuses on thoughtful, elaborative considerations; and peripheral, which focuses on less careful, more emotional, and even superficial considerations.

The *peripheral route* emphasizes less careful, more emotional, and even superficial evaluation of the message. This route has an indirect but nevertheless powerful

FIGURE 16.2

Elaboration Likelihood Model

According to the elaboration likelihood model, attitude change can occur through the central route or the peripheral route.

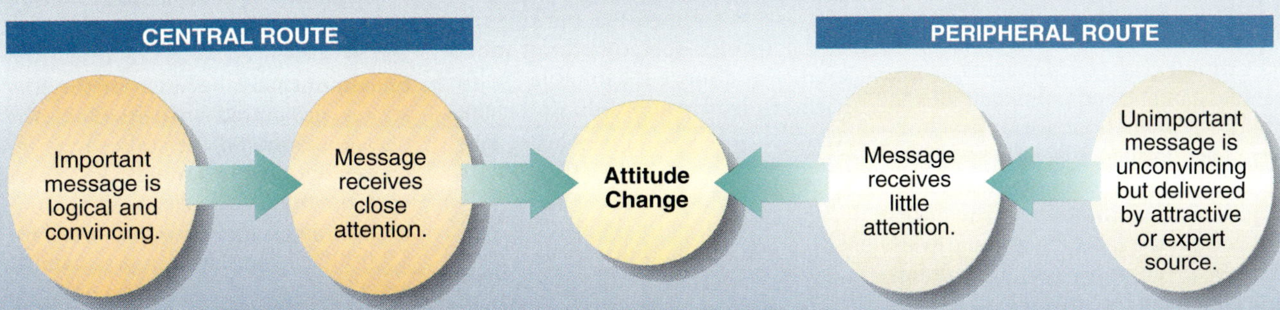

effect, especially when there are no convincing or powerful arguments that can force the use of the central route. This is what happens frequently in political messages (DeBono, 1992; Petty et al., 1993). Whether a person accepts a message through this route depends on how the person perceives its pleasantness, its delivery, its similarity to well-established personal attitudes, and the communicator. Think of an infomercial you may have seen on television that attempts to sell exercise equipment, such as the one done by Jane Fonda. Such commercials often make their pitch while featuring attractive models and an upbeat, eager (and trim) audience. You may believe the evidence presented only because a respected, convincing, and seemingly honest person has expressed the ideas. The attitude change that you may show—desire to buy the product—often stems largely from emotional or personal rather than logical arguments and therefore may not be long-lasting (Petty et al., 1993).

The key idea of the elaboration likelihood model is that sometimes people form or change attitudes because of thoughtful conscious decisions (central route) or because of emotional, quick, simple ideas or feelings (peripheral route). The central route is used when people have the ability, time, and energy to think through arguments carefully; the peripheral route is more likely to be used when motivation is low, time is short, or ability to think through arguments is impaired (Petty et al., 1994).

Applications, on page 562, shows some tried-and-true techniques that have been used for decades to influence attitudes, change behaviors, and obtain favors.

▲ *The scientific evidence linking secondhand smoke with an increased incidence of respiratory disease can change people's attitudes via the central route.*

Searching for Cognitive Consistency

Although basic ideas about life and morals are established early, attitudes continually develop and change. Some people seek change, trying to keep pace with friends or relatives; others resist change. Most people, however, try to maintain consistency among their various attitudes and between their attitudes and their behavior. *Consistency* refers to a high degree of coherence among elements of behavior and mental processes; such coherence leads to orderly living and enables people to make decisions about their future behavior without having to filter out numerous alternatives.

APPLICATIONS

Techniques to Induce Attitude Change

How do people influence one another? What techniques promote attitude change? Managers, salespeople, parents, and politicians all apply the principles of social psychology. They influence people regularly by using social psychological techniques such as the foot in the door, the door in the face, the ask-and-you-shall-be-given approach, lowballing, modeling, and incentives.

Foot-in-the-Door Technique. To get someone to change an attitude or grant a favor, begin by asking for a small attitude change or a small favor. In other words, get your foot in the door. Ask to borrow a quarter today, a dollar next week, and money for your tuition within a month.

The essence of the *foot-in-the-door technique* is that a person who grants a small request is likely to comply with a larger request later. It works, however, only if the person first grants the small favor, and it works best if there is some time between the first, small request and the later, large one. A person who says no to the first favor may find it even easier to say no to subsequent ones. Although the foot-in-the-door technique is relatively common in American society, cross-cultural studies show that it is not as easily found in all countries (Kilbourne, 1989).

Door-in-the-Face Technique. To use the *door-in-the-face technique*, first ask for something outrageous; then later ask for something much smaller and more reasonable. Ask a friend to lend you $100; after being turned down, ask to borrow $5. Your friend may be relieved to grant the smaller favor.

The principle of the door-in-the-face technique is that a person may be more likely to grant a small request after turning down a larger one. It appears to work because people do not want to be seen as turning someone down twice, and it works best if there is little time between requests. To look good and maintain a positive self-image, people agree to the lesser of two requests.

Ask-and-You-Shall-Be-Given Technique. When people ask for money for a good cause, whether the request is large or small, they usually will get a positive response. Ask someone who has given before, and the request is even more likely to be granted (Doob & McLaughlin, 1989). Fundraisers for universities, churches, and museums know that asking usually will get a positive response. Research indicates that asking in an unusual way can pique a person's interest, turn the donor aside from his or her well-rehearsed script of saying no, and increase the likelihood of giving (Santos, Leve, & Pratkinis, 1994).

Lowballing Technique. *Lowballing* is a technique by which a person is influenced to make a decision or commitment because of the low stakes associated with it. Once the decision is made, the stakes may increase; but the person will likely stick with the original decision. For example, if a man agrees to buy a car for $9,000, he may still buy it even if several options are added on, increasing the price to $10,000. Lowballing works because people tend to stick to their commitments, even if the stakes are raised. Changing one's mind may suggest a lack of good judgment, may cause stress, and may make the person feel as if she or he were violating an (often imaginary) obligation.

Modeling. Showing good behavior, such as conserving energy or saying no to drugs, to someone increases the likelihood that the person will behave similarly. The person being observed is a model for the desired behavior. *Modeling*, which we examined in Chapters 5 and 15, is a powerful technique for influencing behaviors and attitudes by demonstrating those behaviors and expressing those attitudes. When well-known athletes exhibit generosity of spirit and act like good sports, they serve as models for youngsters who aspire to careers such as theirs.

Incentives Technique. Nothing succeeds better in eliciting a particular behavior than a desired incentive. Offering a 16-year-old unlimited use of the family car for setting the dinner table every day usually results in a neatly set dinner table. Offering a large monetary bonus to a sales agent for achieving higher than usual year-end sales performance usually boosts sales efforts.

Cognitive Dissonance. Imagine the dilemma faced by a scientist who smokes cigarettes and who finds through her research that cigarettes do indeed cause cancer. As a scientist, she must find the physical evidence compelling; as a smoker, she recognizes that she has smoked for years, feels fine, and has a 92-year-old grand-

FIGURE 16.3

Cognitive Dissonance

A person often holds inconsistent attitudes or behaves in ways that are inconsistent with his or her attitude. When an event challenges one of those attitudes or the behavior, the person is motivated to change the attitude or behavior because of cognitive dissonance.

mother who still smokes. How does she reconcile these opposite facts? Moreover, what further confusion would she suffer if she learned that a chest X ray found her grandmother's lungs totally clear?

Whenever people's attitudes conflict with one another or with their behavior, they feel uncomfortable. Leon Festinger (1919–1989) termed this feeling **cognitive dissonance**—the state of discomfort that results when a discrepancy exists between two or more of a person's beliefs or between a person's beliefs and overt behavior. Based on the premise that people seek to reduce such dissonance, Festinger (1957) proposed a *cognitive dissonance theory*. According to the theory, when people experience conflict among their attitudes (see Figure 16.3) or between their attitudes and their behavior, they are motivated to change either their attitudes or their behavior. Most psychologists consider cognitive dissonance theory to be a type of motivation theory, because it suggests that people become energized to do something. Consider an example of behavior–attitude conflict. Suppose you are a strong proponent of animal rights. You support the American Society for the Prevention of Cruelty to Animals (ASPCA) and Greenpeace, refrain from eating meat, and are repulsed by fur coats. Then you win a raffle and are awarded a stylish black leather coat. Wearing the coat goes against your beliefs; but it feels good, you know it looks great on you, and all your friends admire it. According to cognitive dissonance theory, you are experiencing conflict between your attitudes (animal rights) and your behavior (wearing the coat). To relieve the conflict, you either stop wearing the coat or modify your beliefs (leather becomes an acceptable choice). Psychologists have devised measures for a person's preference for consistency (Cialdini, Trost, & Newsom, 1995); but

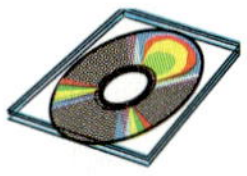

Fig. 14.5A

Cognitive dissonance [COG-nuh-tiv DIS-uh-nins]: A state in which individuals feel uncomfortable because they hold two or more thoughts, attitudes, or behaviors that are inconsistent with one another.

FIGURE 16.4

Two Views of Attitudes

Does behavior follow from attitudes (the traditional view), or do attitudes follow from behavior (Bem's view)?

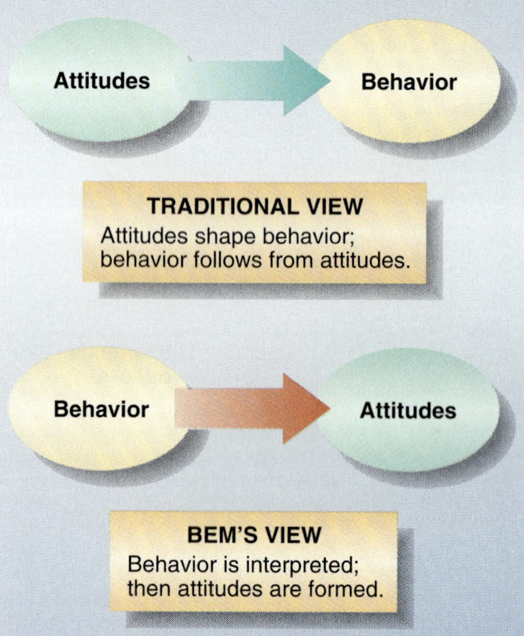

not all people are consistent, nor do all psychologists suggest that consistency is important.

An Alternative to Cognitive Dissonance Theory. Social psychologist Daryl Bem (1972) claims that people do not change their attitudes because of internal states such as dissonance. He has proposed **self-perception theory**—an approach to attitude formation in which people are assumed not to know what their attitudes are until they stop and examine their behavior. Bem holds that people infer their attitudes and emotional states from their behavior. That is, people simply look at their behavior and say, "If I behaved in this way, I must have had this (consistent) attitude." See Figure 16.4 for a comparison of the traditional view of attitude formation with Bem's view.

Bem's research is supported to some extent by the cognitive work of Stanley Schachter (which we reviewed in Chapter 9). Schachter showed that research participants inferred aspects of their emotional states from both their physical states and the situations in which they found themselves. Thus, a person who is physically aroused and surrounded by happy people reports feeling happy. A person who is physically aroused and in a tense situation reports feeling angry.

Reactance Theory. Leading a consistent and coherent life with a clear set of attitudes may feel good, but attitudes are often challenged. Have you ever been ordered (perhaps by a parent) to do something and found that you wanted to do the exact opposite? According to social psychologist Jack Brehm (1966), whenever people feel their freedom of choice is being unjustly restricted, they are motivated to reestablish that freedom. Brehm terms this form of negative influence *reactance*. In **reactance**, the inconsistency lies between a person's self-image as being free to choose and the person's realization that someone else is trying to force him or her to choose a particular alternative.

Reactance theory is consonant with the notion of forbidden fruit. Forbidden activities often become more attractive. Choosing the forbidden fruit may provide an individual with a sense of autonomy. An adolescent who is told he cannot be friends with members of a minority group may seek out members of that group more often. When coercion is used, resistance follows. According to reactance theory, the extent of reactance is directly related to the extent of the restriction on freedom of choice. If a person does not consider the choice very important and if the restriction is slight, little reactance develops. The wording or delivery of the restriction also affects the extent of reactance. People who are told they *must* respond in a certain way are more likely to react negatively than if they merely receive a suggestion or are given a relatively free choice.

FOCUS

Review

- What is the relationship between attitudes and behavior? pp. 556, 558
- What is the evidence that a good communicator can effectively change attitudes? p. 559
- What evidence exists to show that modeling is a way of inducing attitude change? p. 562

Think Critically

- Under what conditions are attitudes most likely to predict behaviors? Can you think of situations where existing attitudes will not predict future behaviors?
- Why do some researchers consider cognitive dissonance theory a motivational theory?

Social Cognition

On meeting someone for the first time, you might say, "I really like him!" or "I can't put my finger on why, but she irritates me." Often, first impressions are based on nothing more than the other person's appearance, body language, and speech patterns. Yet these impressions can have lasting effects. How do people form such attitudes about others? In this section, we will move outward from individual attitudes to the broader world of social cognition—one's view of the entire social milieu.

Social cognition is the thought process involved in making sense of events, other people, oneself, and the world in general through analyzing and interpreting them. It focuses on social information in memory, which affects judgments, choices, evaluations, and, ultimately, behavior (Fiske, 1992). Social cognition is a useful and pragmatic process in which people often use mental shortcuts to help them organize the world. The process often begins with attempts to understand other people's communications, which can be verbal (words) or nonverbal (looks, gestures, body movements, and other means of expression), and to form impressions of the people. The process by which people use the behavior and appearance of others to infer their internal states and intentions is known as **impression formation;** sometimes the impressions are accurate, but certainly not always. We will look at impression formation in more depth later in this section, when we study attribution.

Organizing the World Using Mental Shortcuts

We saw earlier that people use their attitudes to help them make decisions and organize their lives. In a related way, using mental shortcuts helps people process information and decreases the information overload that they might otherwise experience in their complex lives. People seek to be "cognitive misers," processing information superficially unless they are motivated to do otherwise. As Susan Fiske (1992, p. 879) asserts, "Social cognition operates in the service of practical consequences." To help themselves make decisions, people develop pragmatic (result-oriented) rules of thumb.

One rule of thumb is *representativeness*; individuals or events that appear to be representative of other members of a group are quickly classified as such, often despite a complete lack of evidence. Another rule of thumb is *availability*; the easier it is to bring to mind instances of one category, type, or idea, the more likely it is that the category, type, or idea will be used to describe an event. Still another rule of thumb is the *false consensus effect*; people tend to believe that others believe the way they do. The last rule of thumb is *framing*; the way in which information is presented to people helps determine whether they are likely to accept it easily.

When other people's behavior fits neatly into a person's conceptions of the world, the individual can use little effort to make judgments about it. One of the most powerful ways of sending easily interpreted signals is nonverbal communication.

Assessing the World Using Nonverbal Communication

Impression formation often begins with nonverbal communication. **Nonverbal communication** is provided by cues or actions that involve movements of the body, especially the face. When a person irritates you, it may be a gesture, a grimace, or an averting of the eyes that generates your bad feelings—not the words that are spoken (Ambady & Rosenthal, 1993). Nonverbal communication is difficult to suppress and is easily accessible to observers (DePaulo, 1992). Three major sources of nonverbal communication are facial expressions, body language, and eye contact.

Self-perception theory: Approach to attitude formation in which people are assumed to infer their attitudes on the basis of observations of their own behavior.

Reactance: Pattern of feelings and subsequent behaviors aimed at reestablishing a sense of freedom when there is an inconsistency between a person's self-image as being free to choose and the person's realization that someone is trying to force him or her to choose a particular alternative.

Social cognition: The thought process involved in making sense of events, people, oneself, and the world in general through analyzing and interpreting them.

Impression formation: The process by which a person uses the behavior and appearance of others to infer their internal states and intentions.

Nonverbal communication: Information provided by cues or actions that involve movements of the body, especially the face.

▲ *Facial expressions like that of a delighted Thai woman (left) and body language such as that exhibited in a makeshift Iraqi courtroom (right) are universal means of nonverbal communication.*

Facial Expressions and Body Language. Many of the conclusions you draw about other people are based on their facial expressions. Most people, across cultures, can distinguish six basic emotions in the facial expressions of other people: love, joy, anger, sadness, fear, and surprise (Shaver et al., 1987). A simple expression such as a smile, for example, gives others a powerful cue about a person's truthfulness. Research shows that when a person smiles, both the smile and the muscular activity around the eyes help determine if the truth is being told or if the person is smiling to mask another emotion (Ekman, Friesen, & O'Sullivan, 1988). *The Research Process* examines this research in more detail.

People also convey information about their moods and attitudes through body positions and gestures—**body language.** Such movements as crossing the arms, lowering the head, and standing rigidly can all communicate negative attitudes. On the other hand, when a server in a restaurant squats down next to a table and comes closer to making direct eye contact, tips increase (Lynn & Mynier, 1993). Body language may differ according to culture and gender. In the United States, the energetic and forceful way younger people walk makes them appear sexier, more carefree, and happier than older people (Montepare & Zebrowitz-McArthur, 1988); yet this is culture-bound—body language is not viewed in the same way in non-Western cultures. A pensive, reflective posture or a deferential movement or head position might signal composure, confidence, and status in Japan, for example (Matsumoto & Kudoh, 1993). In addition, gestures have different meanings in different societies. For example, the American A-OK sign is a rude gesture referring to sexual acts in many cultures. Research also shows that in Western cultures women are often better than men at communicating and interpreting nonverbal messages, especially facial expressions (Sogon & Izard, 1987). Women are more likely to send nonverbal facial messages but are also more cautious in interpreting nonverbal messages sent to them by men.

Eye Contact. Researchers are well aware of another source of nonverbal communication: *eye contact.* The eyes convey a surprising amount of information about feelings. A person who is looking at you may glance briefly or may stare. You may glance or stare back. You would probably gaze tenderly at someone you were fond of but avoid eye contact with someone you did not trust or like or did not know well (Teske, 1988). Frequent eye contact between two people may indicate that they are sexually attracted to each other.

People tend to judge others based on the eye contact they engage in, making inferences (attributions) about others' internal dispositions from the degree of eye contact. Americans generally prefer modest amounts of eye contact rather than constant or no eye contact. Job applicants, for example, are rated more favorably when they make moderate amounts of eye contact; speakers who make more rather than

Body language: Communication of information through body positions and gestures.

THE RESEARCH PROCESS

Hiding the Truth

Can you deceive others by smiling when you're telling a lie? Not very well, according to Ekman, Friesen, and O'Sullivan (1988). Back in the early 1970s, two of these researchers noted that facial features and gestures provide complex information to an observer, especially when a person tries to be deceitful. They observed that subtle facial cues accompany various types of smiling and that people cannot mask true emotions with a grin. They tested their idea experimentally by having participants view people telling about pleasant experiences and then view people lying about experiences, trying to make unpleasant ones seem pleasant.

Method. Ekman and his colleagues identified several types of smiles: happy smiles, false smiles, listening smiles, and masking smiles (smiles meant to deceive or hide a real emotion). They hypothesized that facial muscles around the eyes and nose signal the real meaning of a smile. The research team videotaped (using a concealed camera) participants who first truthfully described a film that was mildly enjoyable. Then the participants watched an unpleasant film about skin burns and amputations and were asked to conceal negative feelings when describing the film. Could the participants convince another person that they had watched a pleasant film?

Results. The researchers scored close-ups of the participants' faces with respect to which facial muscles moved. Facial muscle movements such as pulling the brows together, wrinkling the nose, and raising the brows were categorized; the results showed that smiles of true enjoyment involved eye muscle activity more often than did feigned smiles of enjoyment. When a participant tried to conceal negative emotions with a happy but false smile, specific changes occurred in the muscles. The results support the researchers' contention that genuinely happy smiles differ from other smiles in that they appear more quickly and take longer before fading.

▲ *School picture day has a way of eliciting a particular kind of smile.*

Conclusions. This study shows that smiles are not a single category of behavior but are multifaceted. A person can convey different social signals through a smile. From a social psychologist's view, this is important because it confirms that people are tuned in to fine elements of behavior; a person can discriminate between types of smiles and can assign different meanings to them. Thus, for example, research shows that deceptive salespersons reveal their falseness through nonverbal cues (DePaulo & DePaulo, 1989). Similarly, your boss may be smiling, but a mere lift of an eyebrow or a couple of millimeters' change in the distance between the eyebrows can have a dramatic impact on your thoughts or overt behavior.

less eye contact are preferred; and witnesses testifying in a court trial are perceived as more credible when they make eye contact with the attorney (DePaulo, 1992). However, all this is true only in Western cultures, which foster an individualistic stance; in some non-Western cultures—for example, Japan—making direct eye contact may be a sign of disrespect, arrogance, and even a challenge.

Inferring the Causes of Behavior: Attribution

If you see people standing in line at a bus stop, you can be fairly certain that they are queued up because they wish to take a bus. Similarly, if you saw a man at the bus stop reading the Muslim holy book, the Koran, you might infer that he is a devout Muslim. In getting to know others, people often infer the causes of their behavior. When they do, they are making attributions. **Attribution** is the process by which a person infers other people's motives and intentions through observing their behavior and deciding whether the causes of the behavior are *dispositional* (internal) or *situational* (external). Through attribution, people decide how they will react toward others, in an attempt to evaluate and to make sense of their social world. Attribution may seem like a fairly straightforward process based on common sense. However, it must

Attribution: The process by which a person infers other people's motives and intentions through observing their behavior and deciding whether the causes of the behavior are dispositional (internal) or situational (external).

take into account internal as well as external causes of behavior. Someone making an *internal attribution* thinks the behavior comes from within the person, from the individual's personality or abilities. Someone making an *external attribution* believes that person's behavior is caused by outside events, such as the weather or luck.

People can be mistaken when they infer the causes of another person's behavior. Suppose that the man you saw reading the Koran is actually a Catholic taking a world religion class that uses the book as a text. In that case, your original attribution (that he is a Muslim) was wrong. It is also easy to see that culture shapes attributions; Morris and Peng (1994) found that accounts of certain crimes in English-language newspapers were dispositional in tone, but that Chinese newspapers were more situational in their explanations of the same crimes.

To learn about attribution and how it can be more precise, researchers have conceptualized its processes. Harold Kelley's (1972, 1973) theory of attribution suggests that people use three criteria to decide whether the causes of a behavior are internal or external: *consensus*, *consistency*, and *distinctiveness* (see Figure 16.5). According to Kelley, to infer that someone's behavior is caused by internal characteristics, you must believe: (1) that few other people in the same situation would act in the same way (low consensus), (2) that the person has acted in the same way in similar situations in the past (high consistency), and (3) that the person acts in the same way in different situations (low distinctiveness). To infer that a person's behavior is caused by external factors, you must believe: (1) that most people would act that way in that sort of situation (high consensus), (2) that the person has acted that way in similar situations in the past (high consistency), and (3) that the person acts differently in other situations (high distinctiveness).

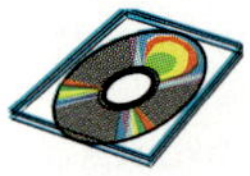

Fig. 14.1

FIGURE 16.5

Attributional Thinking

Assigning an internal attribution to a person's behavior is usually the result of low consensus, high consistency, and low distinctiveness. When a person's behavior shows high consensus, consistency, and distinctiveness, others tend to attribute the causes of the behavior to external reasons. These are the fundamental guidelines of Kelley's attributional model.

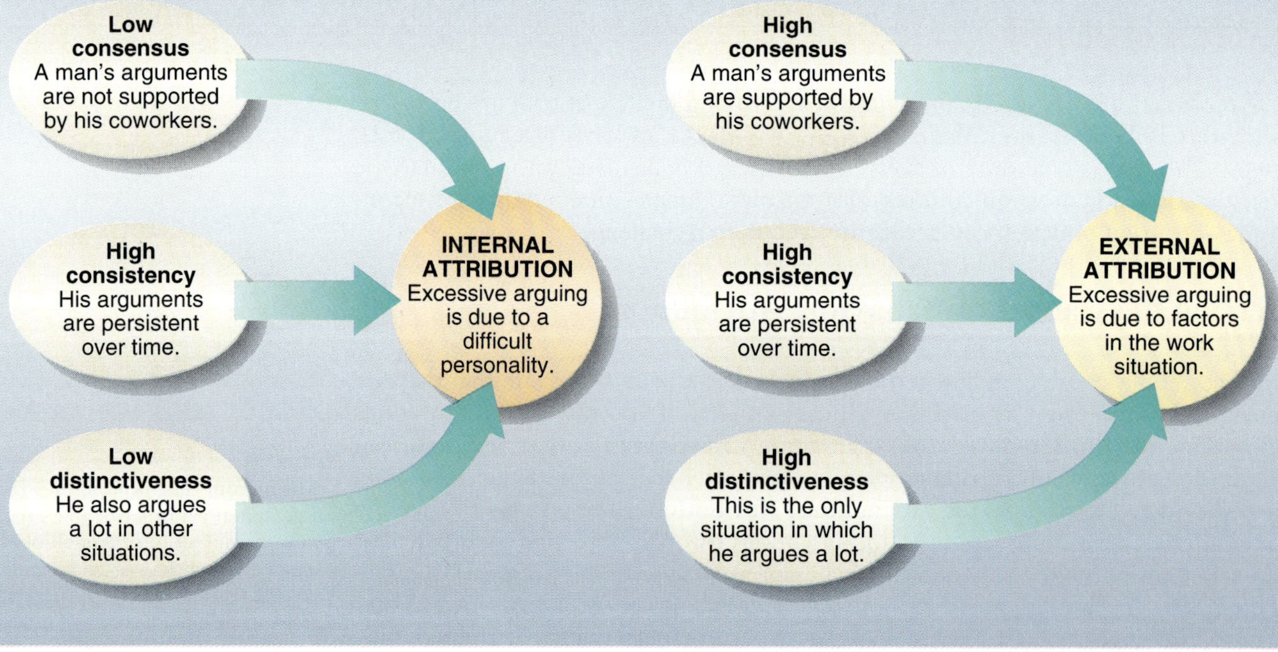

To see how Kelley's theory works, suppose that a man in an office gets into an argument with his supervisor, but other people in the same office do not enter into the discussion (low consensus). Also suppose that the man has argued about the same issue on other occasions (high consistency). Finally, assume that he argues with everybody (low distinctiveness). In such a case, people would no doubt attribute the argument to the individual's personality; the man is simply argumentative. Now suppose (1) that many of the man's coworkers join in and support him in the debate (high consensus), (2) that the man has argued about the same issue in the past (high consistency), but (3) that he does not argue in other situations (high distinctiveness). People would then be more likely to attribute the argument to situational factors, such as the supervisor's incompetence.

It's difficult to avoid making attributions about other people. Would your first impression of these boys have been different if they were not making peace signs and were not members of the Gang Peace group? ▼

Why People Make Attributions. Why do people make attributions? What motivates a person to want to know the causes of other people's behavior? The accepted explanation is that individuals engage in the process of attribution to maintain a sense of control over their environment. It helps people feel competent and masterful, because they think that knowledge about the causes of behavior will help them control and predict similar events in the future (Burger & Hemans, 1988). People also make attributions in order to quickly make sense of their world. If a person's behavior fits in with a pattern you have seen before, why analyze it in depth? People are quick to make causal attributions if the behavior being observed is not unusual.

Errors in Attribution. Social psychologists have found, however, that people are often mistaken or biased in their attributions concerning the behaviors of others. Sometimes they make errors because they use mental shortcuts that are not accurate. Two of the common types of errors that have been identified are the fundamental attribution error and the actor–observer effect.

When people commit the **fundamental attribution error**, they assume that other people's behavior is caused by internal dispositions and underestimate situational influences: A man may have lost his temper, but only *because* he was overcharged for an item; a woman may have become hostile *because* a waiter spilled soup on her and did not apologize.

The **actor–observer effect** is the tendency to attribute the behavior (especially failings) of others to dispositional causes but to attribute one's own behavior to situational causes. A young child who gets hurt may say, "You made me hurt myself." When a friend gets hurt, however, the same child may say, "You're clumsy." If you fail an exam, you may blame it on your roommate, whose radio kept you from concentrating on your studies. But when someone else fails an exam, you may wonder about the person's intelligence.

Errors in attribution are often judgments made in a limited context, with limited knowledge. Often they do not help people cope any better—they simply assign blame (Funder, 1987; Tennen & Affleck, 1990). Some errors in attribution come from the fact that people generally perceive themselves as having more positive traits than others do and as being more flexible in their ability to adapt (Sande, Goethals, & Radloff, 1988). This tendency has been seen cross-culturally (Liebrand, Messick, & Wolters, 1986) but often does not exist to the same extent or have the same meaning in other cultures (Matsumoto, 1994). This has important implications in business relationships, where good will and trust are important; if a businessperson tends to see others as less (or more) flexible than the people in his or her company, this may alter a negotiation in a fundamental way.

Fundamental attribution error: The tendency to attribute other people's behavior to dispositional (internal) causes rather than situational (external) causes.

Actor–observer effect: The tendency to attribute the behavior of others to dispositional causes but to attribute one's own behavior to situational causes.

Self-Serving Bias. The **self-serving bias** is people's tendency to evaluate their own positive behaviors as due to their own internal traits and characteristics but to blame their failures and shortcomings on external, situational factors. People may develop a self-serving bias because it helps meet their *need for self-esteem*. This bias can be seen as an adaptive response that helps people deal with their limitations and gives them the courage to venture into areas they normally might not explore. People also make such attributions about themselves to help maintain a sense of balance by resolving inconsistencies between old and new information about themselves (Snyder & Higgins, 1988). Often, a person who makes an excuse about some negative personal behavior has shifted the cause of the behavior to a less central element of personality or to situational factors. This behavior results in enhanced image building and a sense of control. Furthermore, a self-serving bias allows people to present themselves to others in a positive light (Celuch & Slama, 1995; Weary et al., 1982).

Errors in attribution contribute to the self-serving bias. People tend to take credit for their successes but to blame others for their failures; that is, people assume that good things happen to them because they deserve it and that bad things happen to other people because those individuals deserve that. When something bad happens to you, you may blame it on bad luck or circumstances; when something bad happens to others, you may blame it on their careless or reckless behavior. This combination of attribution errors and self-serving bias helps some people maintain self-esteem and appear competent. Such an attitude, however, may inhibit people from having realistic goals, thus setting them up for disappointment.

People constantly seek the reasons for other people's behavior in order to make judgments about them. Most people also regularly reflect on their own behavior and in doing so form self-perceptions. *Diversity* further examines the influence of ethnicity on self-perception.

Prejudice

People's ideas, about themselves and others, help define who they are, how they view the world, and ultimately how they behave. But what happens when the ideas, values, or activities of another person or another group of people are different from yours? What happens when you do not know the other group of people well, or at all? Why do some people form negative evaluations of certain groups, such as African Americans, Asians, Jews, or homosexuals? In the pages that follow, we will explore the darker side of attitudes and attributions about others—prejudice—and how it can be prevented.

Prejudice is a negative evaluation of an entire group of people that is typically based on unfavorable (and often wrong) ideas or stereotypes about the group. It is usually based on a small sample of experience with an individual from the group being evaluated, or even on no experience. **Stereotypes** are fixed, overly simple, often wrong, and often negative ideas about traits, attitudes, and behaviors attributed to groups of people. People hold stereotyped ideas about Native Americans, Catholics, women, and mountain folk; the stereotypes can lead to prejudice.

Prejudice, as an attitude, is composed of a cognitive belief (all Xs are stupid), an emotional element (I hate those Xs), and often a behavior (I am doing everything I can to keep those Xs out of my neighborhood). When prejudice is translated into behavior, it is called **discrimination**—behavior targeted at individuals or groups, with the aim of holding them apart and treating them differently. One widely held type of discrimination is *sexism* (prejudice based on gender), which involves accepting the strong and widely held beliefs of rigid gender role stereotyping. We examined gender role stereotyping in Chapter 11. Overt discrimination based on gender is illegal, but it still exists, and many women's expectations for themselves are still based on old stereotypes about their gender (Swim et al., 1995).

Sometimes people are prejudiced but do not show that attitude in their behavior; that is, they do not discriminate. Merton (1949) referred to such individuals as

Self-serving bias: People's tendency to evaluate their own positive behaviors as due to their own internal traits and characteristics, but their failures and shortcomings to external, situational factors.

Prejudice: Negative evaluation of an entire group of people, typically based on unfavorable (often wrong) ideas about the group.

Stereotypes: Fixed, overly simple, often wrong, and often negative ideas about traits, attitudes, and behaviors attributed to groups of people.

Discrimination: Behavior targeted at individuals or groups, with the aim of holding them apart and treating them differently.

Diversity

Self-Perceptions of African American Women

Psychologists know that men and women perceive themselves differently. So do teenagers and people over age 65, people from the North and those from the South, and African Americans and white Americans.

Victoria Binion (1990) undertook a study of self-perception in a sample of African American and white women. Among other things, she was interested in the relationship between culture and gender role attitudes and perceptions. Binion interviewed more than 175 women in a low-income community close to downtown Detroit. In her questionnaire, she asked the participants about their gender identity, gender role attitudes, and self-perceptions. The participants either agreed or disagreed (on a scale of 1 to 5) with statements such as "The only way for women to survive is to have men protect them" and "Women can handle a lot more hurt than men can." The women were young (about 26 years of age) and were all high school graduates.

The results of the study showed that African American women characterized themselves as either androgynous (37 percent), masculine (24 percent), feminine (18 percent), or undifferentiated (none of the above) (22 percent). Women who saw themselves as masculine showed traits such as independence and courage. Women who saw themselves as feminine tended to view themselves as weak and needing help. Women self-described as androgynous showed traits and agreed with statements that were both masculine and feminine.

There is a strong cultural component in self-perception and gender identity. The African American women in Binion's study were more than twice as likely as the white women (37 percent compared to 16 percent) to characterize themselves as androgynous (having many characteristics of both genders), and they were less likely (16 percent) than the white women were (22 percent) to characterize themselves as feminine. Further, the responses of the African American women indicated that they were less liberal than the white women about the female role in the family: They expressed less cultural freedom and less liberal gender role attitudes than did the white women. Paradoxically, although the African American women tended to report more traditional gender role attitudes (women as weaker and dependent), many identified themselves as being androgynous.

The relationships among culture, gender identity, and self-perceptions are complex. For example, women who are college graduates have more liberal views about the female role regardless of their culture. A woman's relationship with her parents is linked to her self-report of masculinity or femininity; for example, women who were brought up with a father in the home tended to have more liberal views about the woman's role in the family.

There exists enormous diversity among individual women, individual families, and cultural values within any community. Each person's self-perception is affected by parenting, education, and ethnicity. When social psychologists develop theories of self-perception, ethnicity is one variable they are going to have to take into account. People are diverse, and the data show that culture affects how they perceive themselves.

cautious bigots (unlike true bigots, who are prejudiced and do discriminate). Also, people sometimes show *reverse discrimination*, bending over backward to treat an individual more positively than they should, solely to counter their own preexisting biases or stereotypes (Chidester, 1986). That is, someone prejudiced toward African Americans may treat an African American person oversolicitously and may evaluate

▲ *Children learn prejudice, in part, from the attitudes and actions of their parents and other adults.*

the person favorably on the basis of standards different from those used for others. This, too, is discrimination. (Table 16.1 illustrates the interaction between prejudice and discrimination.)

A related concept is *tokenism*, in which prejudiced people engage in positive but trivial actions toward members of a group they dislike. A male executive may make a token gesture toward the women on his staff, or a manager may hire a token Hispanic American. By engaging in tokenism, a person often attempts to put off more important actions, such as changing overall personnel or hiring practices. The trivial behavior justifies, in this person's mind, the idea that he or she has done something for the disliked group. Tokenism has negative consequences for the self-esteem of the person it is applied to, and it perpetuates discrimination.

What Causes Prejudice? The causes of prejudice cannot be tied to a single theory or explanation. Like so many other psychological phenomena, prejudice has multiple causes and can be examined within an individual, between individuals, within a group, or within society (Duckitt, 1992). We will consider four theories to explain prejudice: social learning theory, motivational theory, cognitive theory, and personality theory.

According to *social learning theory*, children learn to be prejudiced; they watch parents, other relatives, and neighbors engaged in acts of discrimination, which often include stereotyped judgments and racial slurs; they then incorporate those ideas into their own behavioral repertoire. After children have observed such behaviors, they are then reinforced (operant conditioning) for exhibiting similar behaviors. Thus, through imitation and reinforcement, a prejudiced view is transmitted from parents to children, from one generation to the next.

We saw in Chapter 9 that people are motivated to succeed, to get ahead, and to provide for basic as well as high-level emotional needs. If people are raised to compete against others for scarce resources, the competition can foster negative views against competitors. *Motivational theory* thus asserts that individuals learn to dislike specific individuals (competitors) and then generalize that dislike to whole

TABLE 16.1 ***Prejudice and Discrimination***

Prejudice and discrimination interact in such a way that one can be evident without the other.

	Presence of Prejudice	Absence of Prejudice
Presence of Discrimination	An employer believes that nonwhites cannot do quality work and does not promote them, regardless of their performance.	An employer believes that all people can do quality work but does not promote minorities because of long-held company policies.
Absence of Discrimination	An employer believes that nonwhites cannot do quality work, but promotes them on the basis of their performance rather than following preconceived ideas.	An employer believes that all people can do quality work and promotes people on the basis of their performance on the job.

classes of similar individuals (races, religions, or cultures). Gordon Allport asserted that the arousal of competition followed by erroneous generalizations creates specific prejudice toward minority groups (Allport, 1954/1979; Gaines & Reed, 1995). This helps make minorities that are seen as economic competitors into scapegoats—for example, Jews in Nazi Germany and Japanese Americans during World War II. Research with children, adolescents, and adults shows that people who are initially seen as friends or as neutral others are sometimes treated badly when turned into competitors. Competition for jobs among immigrants can also create prejudice, particularly in times of economic hardship.

Cognitive theorists assert that people think about individuals and their groups of origin as a way of organizing the world. Cialdini (1993) argues that there are so many events, circumstances, and changing variables in their lives that people cannot easily analyze all the relevant data about any one thing. People thus devise mental shortcuts to help them make decisions. One of those shortcuts is to stereotype individuals and the groups they belong to—for example, all Hispanics, all homeless people, all men, all lawyers. By devising such shortcuts in thinking, people develop ideas about who is in an *in-group*—that is, who is a member of a group to which they belong or want to belong. People tend to see themselves and other members of an in-group in a favorable light.

As we saw earlier in this chapter, when judging other people, individuals make fundamental attribution errors. They assume that other people's behavior is caused by "internal dispositions"—which may not be true—and that other people are all alike, at least most of the time (Lambert, 1995). They underestimate situational influences and overestimate dispositional influences on other people's behavior, and then they use those behaviors as evidence for their attitudes (prejudices). Thus, hostilities between Arabs and Israelis in the Middle East, Catholics and Protestants in Ireland, and blacks and whites in South Africa are perpetuated.

Personality psychologists assert that a person who develops prejudices has a "prejudice-prone personality." In fact, some personality tests examine the extent to which people are likely to be prejudiced. For example, one common personality type is the *authoritarian personality*. Authoritarian people may have been fearful and anxious as children and may have been raised by cold, love-withholding parents who regularly used physical punishment. To gain control and mastery as adults, such individuals become aggressive and controlling over others. They see the world in absolutes—good versus bad, black versus white. They also tend to blame others for their problems and to become prejudiced toward those people (Adorno et al., 1950). The relationship between personality and prejudice has its roots in psychoanalytic theory and is hotly debated.

How to Reduce and Eliminate Prejudice. To reduce and eliminate prejudice, people as individuals can teach rational thinking, try to judge others based on their behavior, promote equality, and avoid labels that perpetuate stereotypes (Jussim et al., 1995). For example, once people have worked on a community project with a member of a different culture, lived with a person of another race, or prayed

FOCUS

Review

- Identify key characteristics of nonverbal communication. p. 565
- Describe the fundamental difference between dispositional and situational interpretations of the causes of behavior. pp. 567–568
- How do psychological theories explain the development of prejudice? pp. 572–573

Think Critically

- Can you describe any useful functions that errors in attribution have served for you or a friend in the last few months? Have such errors helped someone feel more intelligent, more worthwhile, or less at fault?
- In the United States prejudice has been instrumental in poor treatment of African Americans, women, the aged, homosexuals, and many minority groups. What do you think are some effective techniques (not necessarily governmental policies) that can be used to help eliminate prejudice, right previous injustices, and make for a better, more tolerant society?

with members of a different church, their views of them as individuals change (Wilder & Thompson, 1980).

A society can pass laws that mandate equal treatment for all people—for example, those that forbid discrimination in the workplace or in the housing market. Voters can elect officials on the basis of their competence, throw them out on the basis of their incompetence, and make gender-neutral judgments of performance. Margaret Thatcher, former prime minister of Great Britain, was widely judged by her performance, not by her gender.

Psychologists (and you, as a student of psychology) must be especially sensitive to the need to think about *individuals* rather than about groups. Through examination of individuals, psychologists become sensitive to the wide diversity of human behavior. Although it is tempting to derive broad generalizations about behavior when making attributions about the causes of behavior, researchers must focus on individuals. When they focus on individuals, they see that human beings are engaged in and are affected by a whole array of behaviors.

Social Interactions

It is one thing to think about oneself and others in a variety of ways, both positive and negative. It is quite another to "reach out and touch someone." When people interact with one another, complex new realms of possibility open up. For this reason, social psychologists pay close attention to the interactions among individuals. From obeying authority to watching television to helping a person in distress, day-to-day social interactions can be exceedingly complex, with intricate variables. This is what makes the study of social behaviors so exciting.

Social Influence

Parents try to instill specific values in their children. An adolescent may admire the hairstyle or mannerisms of an attractive peer and decide to adopt them. Professors urge students to shed preconceived ideas. The behavior or appearance of a celebrity may be emulated by adoring fans. Religious leaders exhort their followers to live in certain ways. Social interactions affect individual behavior in profound ways; when people are members of a group, their social interactions are often even more striking than their individual behavior.

One kind of social interaction is **social influence,** or the way in which one or more people alter the attitudes or behavior of others, either directly or indirectly. People exert powerful influences on others, and psychologists have attempted to understand how this influence operates. Studies of social influence have focused on two topics: conformity and obedience.

Conformity. When someone changes attitudes or behaviors to be consistent with other people or with social norms, the person is exhibiting **conformity**; he or she is trying to fit in. The behaviors the person may adopt include positive, prosocial behaviors such as wearing seatbelts, volunteering time and money for a charity, or buying only products that are safe for the environment. Sometimes, however, people conform to counterproductive, antisocial behaviors, such as drug abuse, fraternity hazing, or mob action.

People conform to the behaviors and attitudes of their peer or family groups. A successful young executive may wear conservative dark suits and drive a BMW in order to fit in with office colleagues. Similarly, the desire to conform can induce people to do things they might not do otherwise. An infamous example is the My Lai massacre, in which American soldiers slaughtered Vietnamese civilians during the

Social influence: The way in which one or more people alter the attitudes or behavior of others.

Conformity: People's tendency to change attitudes or behaviors to be consistent with other people or with social norms.

Vietnam War. While several factors account for the soldiers' behavior (including combat stress, hostility toward the Vietnamese, and obedience to authority), the soldiers also yielded to extreme group pressure. The few soldiers who refused to kill the civilians hid that fact from their comrades. One soldier even shot himself in the foot to avoid becoming part of the slaughter.

Groups strongly influence conformity. Solomon Asch (1908–1996) found that people in a group adopt its standard. Examples of conformity to group standards range from an individual refraining from speaking during a public address to a whole nation discriminating against a particular ethnic group. Studies also show that individuals conform to group norms even when they are not pressured to do so. Consider what happens when an instructor asks a class of 250 students to answer a relatively simple question, but no one volunteers. When asked, most students will report that they did not raise their hand because no one else did. Asch (1955, p. 6) stated:

> The tendency to conformity in our society [is] so strong that reasonably intelligent and well-meaning young people [being] willing to call white black is a matter of concern. It raises questions about our ways of education and about the values that guide our conduct.

Suppose you have agreed to participate in an experiment. You are seated at the end of a table next to four other students. The experimenter holds up a card and asks each of you to pick which of two lines is longer, A or B. You quickly discover that the task is simple. The experimenter proceeds to hold up successive pairs of lines, with each participant correctly identifying the longest. Suddenly, after several rounds, you notice that the first person has chosen line A instead of line B, though B is obviously longer. You are surprised when the second person also chooses line A, then the third, then the fourth. Your turn is next. You are sure that line B is longer. What do you do?

In 1951, Asch performed a similar experiment to explore conformity. Seven to nine individuals were brought into a room and asked to judge which of three lines matched a standard (see Figure 16.6). However, only one group member—the naive participant—was unaware of the purpose of the study. The others were collaborators of the researcher, and they deliberately gave false answers to try to influence the naive participant. Asch found that the naive participant would generally go along with the group, even though the majority answer was obviously wrong and even though the group exerted no explicit or directly observable pressure on that person.

Although only some of the naive participants conformed in Asch's experiments, enough did so that psychologists researched the phenomenon further. They found that the relative number of individuals collaborating with the researcher is a critical

FIGURE 16.6

Asch's Classic Study of Conformity

Participants were shown cards like those above the photo and asked to choose the line on the card at the right that was the same length as the line on the card at the left. The confederates deliberately chose incorrect answers to see if the unsuspecting participant (fifth from the left in the photo) would go along with the majority.

variable. When 1 or 2 individuals collaborate with the researcher, the tendency to conform is considerably less than when 10 do. Another important variable is the number of dissenting votes. If even 1 of 15 people disagrees with the other collaborating participants, the naive participant is more likely to choose the correct line.

How do groups influence individual behavior? One conformity variable is the *amount of information* provided when a decision is to be made. When people are uncertain of how to behave in ambiguous situations, they seek the opinions of others. For example, people who are unsure of how they should vote in an election will often ask trusted friends for advice. People tend to accept the advice of those whom they like and who are like them.

Another important variable that affects the degree of conformity is the *relative competence* of the group. People are more likely to conform to the decision of a group if they perceive its members as being more competent than they themselves are. This pressure becomes stronger as group size increases. A first-year student in a large class, for example, may not answer even a simple question if no one else speaks up, because he assumes that his classmates are more competent than he is.

Position within a group also affects individual behavior. A person who confidently believes that a group holds her in high esteem will respond independently. If she feels insecure about her status, even though it may be high, she may respond as the group does because she fears losing status.

The *public nature of behavior* also determines people's responses. Individuals are more willing to make decisions that are inconsistent with those of their group when the behavior is private. In a democracy, for example, voting is done privately so as to minimize group pressure on how individuals vote.

Why do people tend to conform? Several theories have attempted to explain this phenomenon. The *social conformity approach* states that people conform to avoid the stigma of being wrong, deviant, out of line, or different from others. According to this view, people want to do the right thing, and people define as right whatever is generally accepted (Festinger, 1954). For example, in high school, a boy may be considered socially correct if he joins the football team but not if he enrolls in a modern dance class. The boy doesn't want to rock the boat or be thought of as different or odd; he conforms in order to reap the benefits of group membership.

Another explanation for why individuals in a group conform—or don't conform—lies in *attribution*. When a person can identify causes for other people's behavior in a group, and strongly disagrees with those causes, conformity disappears (Ross, Bierbrauer, & Hoffman, 1976). Suppose you hear many people arguing vehemently in favor of the construction of a toxic waste incinerator near your town because it will boost the local economy. At first you agree, but later you discover that all the leading incinerator proponents own land at the proposed building site and stand to make money by selling the land to the incinerator company. After attributing the incinerator proponents' attitude to a desire for personal profit, you may no longer agree with their arguments.

The issue of *independence* also helps explain conformity (or the lack of it). Although most people would like to be independent, independence is risky. People in a group may have to face the consequences of their independence, such as serious disapproval, peer pressure to conform, being seen as deviant, becoming less powerful, or simply being left out.

Last, conformity is partly a matter of *expediency;* conforming conserves mental energy. Recall Cialdini's (1993) argument that too many events, circumstances, and changing variables exist for people to be able to analyze all the relevant data. People therefore need shortcuts to help them make decisions. It is efficient and easy for people to go along with others whom they trust and respect, especially if key elements of a situation fit in with their views.

All four variables—social conformity, attribution, the risks of independence, and expediency—interact to produce individual conformity. As psychologists try to sort out the variables and examine different theories, they approach an understanding of how groups manipulate and influence the behavior of individuals. But not everyone conforms to group pressures all the time—especially when other people disagree with the group. Both everyday experience and research show that *dissenting opinions* help counteract group influence and conformity. Even one or two people in a large group can seriously influence decision making. Moreover, when group decision making occurs, a consistent opposing voice (think of South African leader Nelson Mandela) can exert substantial influence and foster a sense of liberation, even when the opposition is devoid of power or status (Kitayama & Burnstein, 1994). Not surprisingly, analysis of cross-cultural studies shows that countries with collectivistic cultures exhibit more conformity than do countries with individualistic cultures (Bond & Smith, 1996).

▲ *Conformity is the course chosen by most people, but some want a greater degree of independence and are willing to risk a certain degree of social disapproval to gain it.*

Obedience and Milgram's Study. **Obedience** is compliance with the orders of another person or group of people. The studies on obedience by Stanley Milgram (1933–1984) are classic. Milgram's results and interpretations still generate debate today. Milgram's work focused on the extent to which an individual will obey a significant person. His studies showed that ordinary people were remarkably willing to comply with the wishes of others, especially if they saw the others as legitimate authority figures.

Imagine that you are one of the participants in Milgram's 1963 study at Yale University. You and a man you do not know are brought into a laboratory and are told that you will be participating in an experiment on paired-associate learning. You draw lots to determine who will be the teacher and who will be the learner. The drawing is actually rigged so that you will be the teacher and the man, who is collaborating with the experimenter, will be the learner.

The learner/collaborator is taken to an adjoining room, where you cannot see him. You are shown a shock-generating box containing 30 switches, with labels that range from "Slight Shock" to "Danger: Severe Shock." You are told to shock the learner by hitting one of the switches every time he makes an error on a test he will be given.

As the test continues, the experimenter and an assistant, both wearing white lab coats, encourage you to increase the shock voltage one level each time the learner makes a mistake. As the shock level rises, the learner/collaborator screams as if he is suffering increasing pain. When the intensity reaches the point of intense shock, the learner stops responding vocally to the test stimulus and pounds on the walls of the booth. The experimenter tells you to treat the learner's lack of vocal response as an error and to continue increasing the levels of shock. What would you do?

This was the basic scenario of the Milgram study. As Figure 16.7 on page 578 shows, 65 percent of the participants in the study continued to shock the learner until shocks at all levels were delivered. (As you may have guessed by now, the learner/collaborators were not actually receiving shocks; they were only pretending to be in pain.) However, not all of Milgram's participants were obedient. Moreover, the presence of others who refused to participate reduced the probability of obedience to as little as 10 percent (Milgram, 1965; Powers & Geen, 1972). These data suggest that obedience is sensitive to both authority and peer behavior. The fact that an individual's ability to resist coercion improves in the presence of an ally who also resists indicates the importance of other social influences on behavior.

Did conducting the study at the prestigious Yale University influence the participants? Milgram (1965) suggested that his experiment might have involved a particular type of experimental bias—*background authority*. To investigate the issue,

Obedience: Compliance with the orders of another person or group of people.

FIGURE 16.7

Milgram's Obedience Study

(Based on data from Milgram, 1963.)

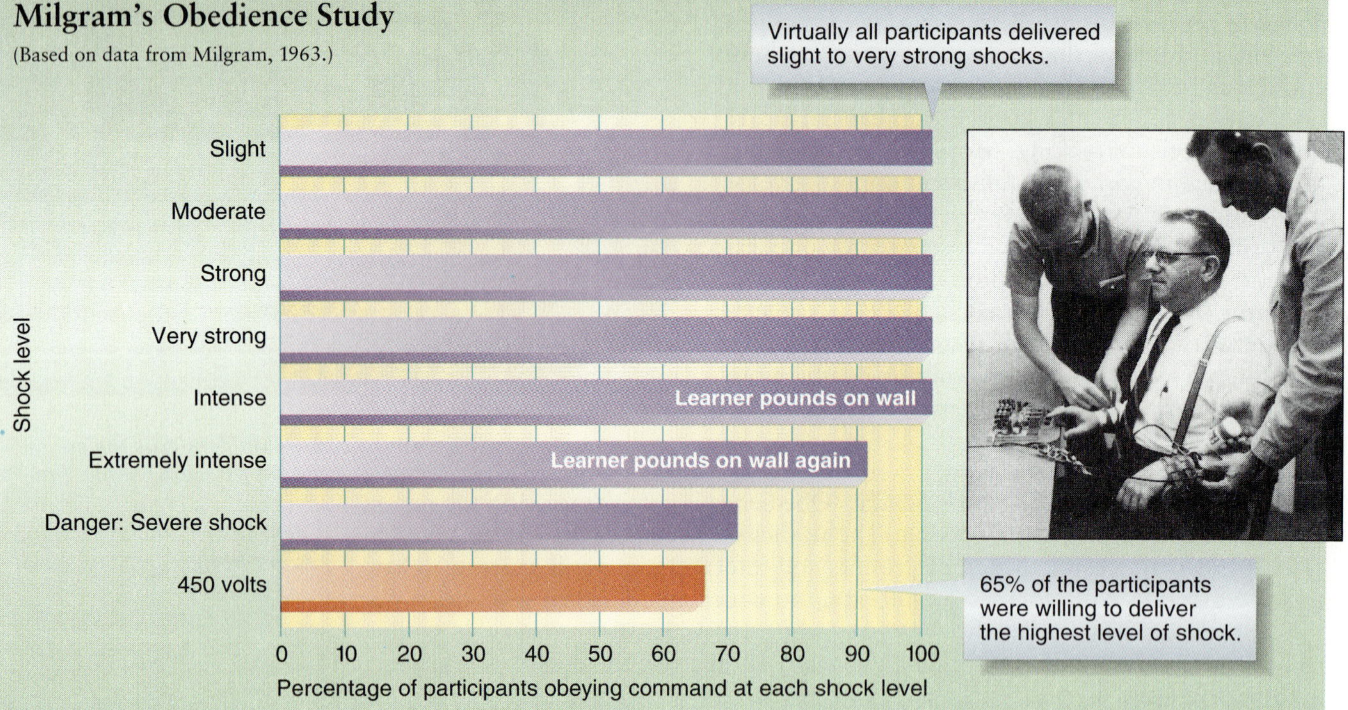

Milgram conducted a second study in an office building in Bridgeport, Connecticut. Participants were contacted by mail and had no knowledge that Milgram or his associates were from Yale. In this second study, 48 percent of the participants, as compared with the 65 percent at Yale, delivered the maximum level of shock. Milgram therefore concluded that the perceived function of an institution can induce obedience in participants. Moreover, an institution's qualitative position within a category (for example, a prestigious versus a little-known university) may be less important than the type of institution it is (for example, a university rather than an office building).

Explaining Milgram's Results. Why did so many participants in Milgram's experiments obey the wishes of the authority figure? One reason is that they were volunteers. Volunteers often bring undetected biases to an experimental situation, and one such bias is a willingness to go along with authority. When instructed to shock, Milgram's participants did what they were told. Another explanation derives from learning theories. Children learn that authority figures, such as teachers and parents, know more than they do and that taking their advice generally proves beneficial. As adults, they maintain those beliefs, with the authority figures being employers, judges, government leaders, and so on. Cialdini (1993) also notes that obedience has practical advantages, such as helping people make decisions quickly: "It is easy to allow ourselves the convenience of automatic obedience. . . . We don't have to think, therefore we don't" (p. 178).

Researchers repeated Milgram's methods, and the results of one study suggest that obedience to authority is not specific to Western cultures (Shanab & Yahya, 1978). People tend to obey those in authority, and such obedience is even more highly valued in many non-Western cultures. Students at the University of Jordan participated in a similar study; as in the original Milgram study, about 65 percent were willing to give high levels of shock to other students. Milgram's findings apply to men and women, old and young; they show that the social world and people's interactions within it are strongly affected by others.

In any study of social influence, researchers worry about ethical issues, and Milgram's experimental methods certainly raised ethical issues. The primary issue was one of deception and potential harm to those who participated. Obtaining unbiased responses in psychological research often requires deceiving naive participants. To ensure that participants do not have any lasting ill effects, researchers debrief them after the experiment. **Debriefing** is a procedure to inform participants about the true nature of the experiment after its completion, including an explanation of hypotheses, methods, and expected or potential results. Researchers do debriefing *after* the experiment, to preserve the validity of the responses while taking ethical considerations into account. Of course, debriefing must be done clearly and with sensitivity, especially in studies like Milgram's, which could affect a participant's self-esteem.

Milgram's participants were fully debriefed and shown that they had not actually harmed the other person. Nevertheless, critics argued, the participants came to realize that they were capable of inflicting severe pain on other people. Milgram therefore had a psychiatrist interview a sample of his obedient participants a year after the study. No evidence of psychological trauma or injury was found. Moreover, one study reported that participants viewed participation in the obedience experiment as a positive experience. They did not regret having participated; nor did they report any short-term negative psychological effects (Ring, Wallston, & Corey, 1970).

Aggression

Social interactions are shaped by a wide array of events in people's lives. Whether someone succumbs to pressure, develops prejudices, or acts submissively is shaped by that person's day-to-day experiences. We have seen, through the study of social influence, that people can act to *sway* others. Social influence can even go to the extreme at which people are swayed to *harm* others.

> We killed, killed, killed. The Malays would stop and go through people's pockets and take their watches and money. We did not think of watches or money. We thought only of killing. . . . [W]e were drunk with blood.

A Semai soldier told that tale to American anthropologist Robert K. Dentan (1968), who lived with the man's tribe for more than a year. What is most remarkable about the story is that the Semais are among the most gentle people on earth. Not a single murder has been recorded among this central Malayan tribe, adults never physically attack one another, children are taught to be nonviolent, and the tribe has no police force. The Semai regret even having to kill their chickens for food. Yet, despite their pacifist heritage, Semai tribesmen were recruited and trained by the British to fight Communist guerrillas in the early 1950s. When their comrades fell in battle, the Semai avenged themselves on the enemy with terrible ferocity. One veteran reported drinking the blood of a man he killed. Upon their return home, however, the Semai soldiers returned to their pacifist ways.

In contrast to the Semai, the Yanomamo of Brazil and Venezuela are among the most violent people on earth. Their murder rate is three times that of the city of Detroit, and an estimated 44 percent of the men aged 25 or older have participated in at least one killing. Yet other South American tribes are as peaceful as the Yanomamo are violent. If people can be either loving or violent, what compels them to act one way or the other?

When people feel unable to control situations that affect their lives, they may become frustrated, angry, and aggressive. Social psychologists define **aggression** as any behavior designed to harm another person or thing. An aggressive person may attempt to harm others physically through force, to harm them verbally through gossip, rumors, or irritating comments, or to harm them emotionally by withholding love. On a larger scale, whole countries attempt to harm others by acts of war. Three major theoretical explanations for aggressive behavior are instincts, acquired drives, and cognitive psychology.

Debriefing: A procedure to inform participants about the true nature of an experiment after its completion.

Aggression: Any behavior designed to harm another person or thing.

Instincts. Some psychologists believe that many aspects of behavior, including aggression, are inborn (see DiLalla & Gottesman, 1991); but most psychologists and the American Psychological Association (1990) do not agree. Those who believe that people are genetically predisposed toward aggression are termed *nativists.* An early nativist was Freud, who suggested that people have a destructive desire to release aggression against themselves, a death instinct he called *thanatos.* However, Freud never fully developed this concept, and today his death instinct is not widely accepted.

Another nativist was the ethologist and Nobel laureate Konrad Lorenz (1903–1989), who investigated aggressive behavior through naturalistic observation. He noted that although animals of the same species fight with one another, they often use signals that tell them to avoid fighting or to stop fighting well before serious injury or death occur. According to Lorenz (1964), aggression is instinctive and spontaneous; the aggressive instinct serves to maximize the use of food, space, and resources. Lorenz stressed the social implications of people's aggressive instincts, focusing on their adaptive values.

Both animals and human beings can be aggressive; whether that aggression is inhibited or expressed depends on the organism's previous experiences and current social context, such as whether the organism is being provoked or whether it has been raised in a hostile environment (Lore & Schultz, 1993).

Acquired Drives. Another explanation for aggressive behavior is that the frustration of goal-directed behavior leads to aggression—this is the *frustration–aggression hypothesis,* initially proposed by Dollard and colleagues (1939). This theory relies on observations demonstrating that people involved in everyday goal-oriented tasks often become aggressive or angry when frustrated. For example, ordinarily, you may be unlikely to become upset if another car pulls out into traffic in front of you. However, if you are in a hurry to get to work, you might honk or mutter angrily at the other driver. On a larger scale, the violence between Catholics and Protestants in Northern Ireland is fueled in part by intense competition for decent jobs in a depressed economy.

Berkowitz (1964) examined the evidence for the frustration–aggression hypothesis and proposed a modified version of it. He suggested that frustration creates a *readiness* for aggressive acts rather than producing actual aggression. He showed that, even when frustration is present, certain events or situations must exist before aggression occurs—for example, a weapon lying on a table. In a later reformulation, Berkowitz (1989) suggested that frustrations generate aggressive inclinations to the extent that they arouse negative feelings in the frustrated individual (Berkowitz, 1990). Berkowitz's conception accounts for the instances when people don't become aggressive when frustrated. Although many psychologists find the frustration–aggression hypothesis too simplistic, it is beneficial—in part because it has led to other research that helps describe behavior, for example, cognitive theory.

Cognitive Psychology. Theories are perishable; they eventually become outdated and are replaced. This has been especially true in the study of aggression. Old ideas about aggression being inborn and people having inherited tendencies to violence have come to be considered wrong; see Table 16.2. Early research (described in Chapter 5) was based on learning theory explanations of how children learn aggressive behavior, which were popular in the 1950s and 1960s. Later, with the increasing influence of Skinner's behaviorism, researchers focused on more refined, operant interpretations of aggression. They studied the effects of punishing children for aggressive behavior and rewarding them for nonaggressive behavior. A shift toward observational (social) learning theory occurred in the 1970s, and the effects of television viewing were a prime focus (see *Applications* on page 582). In the 1980s, cognitive explanations of aggression became prevalent, and researchers began to speak in terms of thought, interpretations, and expectations

Leonard Eron's work is typical of much contemporary social psychological research. He shifted his explanations of aggression from simple motivational drive

TABLE 16.2 *A Tendency to Violence Is Not Inherited*

Scientific groups, including the American Psychological Association, have adopted a statement called the "Seville Statement on Violence," which asserts that the misuse of scientific data to support war is wrong and is based on erroneous assumptions.

It is scientifically incorrect to say:

We have inherited a tendency to make war from our animal ancestors.

War on any other violent behavior is programmed into our human nature.

Through the course of human evolution, aggression more than any other characteristic has been programmed into human behavior.

Humans have a violent brain.

War is caused by instinct or any other specific inborn motivation.

Source: Adapted from the Seville Statement on Violence, 1994.

reduction ideas (described in Chapter 9) to social learning ideas, and finally to a cognitive–behavioral analysis. Eron (1987) conducted a longitudinal study of aggression over 22 years. He examined and tracked the entire third-grade population (870 students) of Columbia County, a semirural area in New York State. Eron's early work, in the 1960s, examined external psychological conditions that might cause aggression, especially parental attitudes toward children (Lefkowitz et al., 1977). In the late 1970s, Eron and other aggression researchers began to probe the influences in children's lives that cause them to *interpret* the world in a way that makes them aggressive. These researchers started looking at the data within a cognitive frame of reference: An aggressive child responds to the world with combativeness because the child has internalized aggressive ideas. Eron (1987, p. 441) argued: "It was what the subjects were saying to themselves about what they wanted . . . what might be an effective or appropriate response . . . that helped determine how aggressive they are today." So, like Eron, researchers today are examining how stimuli in an individual's environment may elicit thoughts and emotional responses that give way to aggressive behavior (Bushman & Geen, 1990.) These stimuli include a difficult personal situation and frustrating social conditions (Staub, 1996). They are also considering the possibility of some genetic link or defect that may predispose individuals toward aggression (Brunner et al., 1993; Cadoret et al., 1995).

Gender Differences in Aggression. Many people believe that men are naturally more aggressive than women. They refer to aggressive contact sports such as football and boxing, the aggressive role of men in business, the overwhelming number of violent crimes committed by men, and the traditional view that men are more likely than women to be ruthless and unsympathetic. It is also generally accepted that more masculine people are more aggressive (Kogut, Langley, & O'Neal, 1992). But are men really more aggressive than women?

To learn more about gender differences in aggression, two psychologists at Purdue University, Alice Eagly and Valerie Steffen (1986), searched the psychological literature from a 15-year period for studies of adults exposed to standardized situations designed to induce aggressive behavior. They found 63 experiments that compared gender differences in aggressive behaviors. Most of the studies were conducted in laboratories, although some were conducted in field settings. The laboratory experiments were often teacher–learner situations, where a teacher had to deliver shocks to a learner (similar to the Milgram studies). The field experiments typically involved the experimenter cutting in line in front of an unsuspecting person, causing mild frustration that could turn into anger and aggression.

APPLICATIONS

Exposure to Violence

Exposure to violence in its many forms has been likened to a public health epidemic; violence is seen on city streets, in rural communities, and on the worldwide stage. Violence is almost commonplace, and its impact on childhood development grows daily (Osofsky, 1995). Nowhere is violence more prevalent

than on television. And most children aged 2–11 spend more hours watching television (an average of almost 22 hours a week) than they spend in any other activity except sleep; they are also often indiscriminate viewers (Huston et al., 1992; Kubey & Csikszentmihalyi, 1990). Television thus serves as a major source of children's imitative behavior. For example, watching television has been shown to affect children's career aspirations. Furthermore, it may alter their overall aggressive thoughts and their views of life and may decrease their creativity (Bushman & Geen, 1990; Valkenberg & van der Voort, 1994). The fact that television portrays so much aggressive behavior concerns parents and educators, as well as social psychologists: Half of all prime-time TV characters are involved in violent activity of some kind; about one-tenth kill or are killed; the perpetrators of these crimes go unpunished in nearly three-quarters of violent scenes. Moreover, about 20 percent of males appearing on TV shows are engaged in law enforcement, whereas fewer than 1 percent are in law enforcement in the real world.

Research generally supports the contention that viewers who frequently watch violent programs on television are more likely to be aggressive than are viewers who see less TV violence (Wood, Wong, & Chachere, 1991). Further, one study found that children exposed to large doses of TV violence are less likely to help a real-life victim of violence; and another found that viewers of violence were less sympathetic to victims than were nonviewers (Huston et al., 1992). Viewers of violence also are more fearful of becoming victims of violent acts. One study found that the viewing of violence at age 8 predicted aggressive behavior at age 19 (Eron & Huesmann, 1980). Children who play violent video games also seem to act more aggressively at later ages (Schutte et al., 1988), and even infants can become fearful by watching television (Meltzoff, 1988). How does watching violence on television affect viewers? Baron and Byrne (1991) describe four primary effects of viewing violence on television:

- It weakens the inhibitions of viewers.
- It may suggest new ideas and techniques to the uninitiated.
- It may activate or stimulate existing aggressive ideas.
- It may reduce a person's overall emotional sensitivity to violence.

Television can also have positive effects on children. In one study, children exposed to shows such as *Sesame Street* and *Mister Rogers' Neighborhood*, which focus on topics such as sharing and caring, were more likely to engage in prosocial behavior with other children than were children in a control group who did not watch those shows (Coates, Pusser, & Goodman, 1976).

Research on the effects of television has important social implications. Social psychologists interested in public policy are suggesting requirements for at least a certain amount of educational programming for children on every station and for controls to protect children from advertising that exploits their special vulnerability (Huston et al., 1992; Huston, Watkins, & Kunkel, 1989).

Eagly and Steffen confirmed what people had already observed—men are more *physically* aggressive than women. But they also found that both men and women use *psychological* aggression such as verbal abuse and angry gestures. They offer an interesting interpretation of the findings. They suggest that the differences in aggression that appear between men and women are directly related to the perceived consequences of the aggression. Women in many cultures have been raised with values that make them feel especially guilty if they cause physical pain; men have not been raised with those values, at least not to the same extent. However, gender roles in American society are changing, so it may be that gender differences in willingness to cause pain—and act aggressively—will diminish in the future. Research supports

TABLE 16.3 *Myths about Physical Abuse in Close Relationships*

Violence in close relationships never happens to people like me.
People never tell anyone about violence in their relationships.
Only males inflict violence on their partners.
Women stay in abusive relationships only because they are passive.
In couples, there is a cycle of violence.
Battered women are masochistic; their batterers are mentally ill.
Violence nearly always involves the use of alcohol.

Source: Adapted from Marshall & Vitanza, 1994, p. 263.

the idea that the context and situation in which people find themselves alters the nature and extent of aggression in men and women toward individuals of their own and the opposite gender (Harris, 1994; Olson, 1994).

Domestic Assault. Will today's children create a gentler society? Will they deal with marital conflict through reason and caring? Or will the couples of tomorrow be even more violent than today's adults? As many as 2 million women a year may be beaten by their husbands, and nearly 30 percent of all married couples report at least one violent episode. Sexual abuse and assault have been experienced by 38 to 67 percent of adult women before age 18 (Koss, 1990). Many women have thus experienced assault in various forms long before marriage. High levels of conflict, low socioeconomic status, alcohol abuse, and exposure to violence as a child are correlated with domestic violence (Pan, Neidig, & O'Leary, 1995; Sugarman & Hotaling, 1989). Further, younger adults (under age 30) are more likely to engage in domestic violence than are older adults (O'Leary et al., 1989); and such behaviors (pushing, shoving, slapping) are fairly stable—a person who is aggressive early in a relationship stays that way. While domestic violence against men exists, the vast majority of cases involve men abusing women. There continue to be many myths about physical abuse in close relationships; Table 16.3 describes some of them.

Is there some event, action, or predisposition that makes a man abuse his partner? Early explanations of domestic violence focused on mental disorders, and many research studies show that men who assault women suffer from personality disorders such as those we examined in Chapter 14. Other explanations of domestic violence focus on biological predispositions (e.g., Cadoret et al., 1995). Sociobiological theory, for example, explains aggressive behaviors as attempts to maximize the likelihood that the aggressors and their offspring will survive.

Differing from these psychiatric and biological theorists, many sociologists and psychologists believe that assaults on women by their partners are generated by social rules supporting male dominance. Although society is changing, there is a traditional image of couples that places the male in the dominant role (e.g., Stets & Pirog-Good, 1989). According to this view, men are merely living up to cultural expectations (Sommers-Flanagan, Sommers-Flanagan, & Davis, 1993).

But none of these explanations is substantiated by all the data. Dutton (1988) proposes a *nested ecological approach*. This approach views people as growing and developing within a social context and suggests that a valid explanation of domestic violence must examine at least four factors:

- The cultural values of the individuals (Do they see men and women as equal?)
- Their social situation (Are they employed?)
- The cohesiveness of the family unit (Do they communicate?)
- Their level of individual development (Do they express feelings well? Do they excuse violence? Have they witnessed family violence?)

FOCUS

Review

- Identify the key findings and the ethical issues for Milgram's study. pp. 577–578
- What is the evidence that allows psychologists to assert that the key factor in aggressive behavior is thought? pp. 580–581

Think Critically

- Do you think that some societies may be less aggressive overall than other societies? What evidence could you cite that suggests that it might be possible to shape a society's aggressiveness?

In a comprehensive theory of domestic violence, a potentially assaultive male must be evaluated in each of the four areas suggested. Although some interpretations see violence against women as the misuse of power by men (L. Walker, 1989), the nested ecological approach considers a complex mix of variables as the determinants of assaultive behavior. Unlike most domestic assault models, which focus on one level of analysis (communication, personal values, or, perhaps, job stress), the nested ecological approach suggests multiple levels, with the importance of each level differing for each assault case. Although it is often tempting to rely on simple models of domestic assault, the reality is that human beings are complex, and the causes of assault must be understood in a broader context.

Prosocial Behavior

Are small-town people more helpful than city people? It turns out that they are, and that this is true all over the world (Yousif & Korte, 1995); but what factors are at work, and under what conditions are people helpful? For example, if you are walking down the street with a bag of groceries and you drop them, what is the likelihood that someone will help you pick them up? Will a bystander who observes a serious accident or a crime help the victim? What attributions will the bystander make about the causes of an incident? What attitudes about helping behavior or about people being victims will the bystander bring to the incident? Psychologists want to find out when, and under what conditions, someone will help a stranger. They are examining the likelihood of **prosocial behavior**—behavior that benefits someone else or society but that generally offers no obvious benefit to the person performing it and that may even involve some personal risk or sacrifice.

Altruism: Helping without Rewards. Why does Peter Beneson, the founder of Amnesty International, devote so much time and effort to helping "prisoners of conscience" around the world? What compels Mother Teresa to wander Calcutta's streets and attend to the wounds and diseases of people no one else will touch? Why did Oskar Schindler risk his life to save 1,100 Jews from the Nazi death camps during World War II?

Altruism consists of behaviors that benefit other people and for which there is no discernible extrinsic reward, recognition, or appreciation (Quigley, Gaes, & Tedeschi, 1989). However, does an altruistic person truly expect no reward for good acts? Isn't the feeling of well-being after performing an altruistic act a type of reward? Does the altruist expect a reward in an afterlife?

Many behaviorists contend that it is an element of personality that directs people to seek social approval by helping. From this view, people with a high need for achievement are more likely than others to be helpful, and people may continue to be helpful because the positive consequences of their actions are self-reinforcing (Batson et al., 1991; Puffer, 1987). From a behavioral view, intrinsically rewarding activities become powerful behavior initiators; thus, when you have a relationship with a person, the person's affection and approval make you more likely to be caring and helpful (Batson, 1990). Further, once kindness and helpfulness become well established and even routine, individuals are more likely to help others, such as the homeless, disadvantaged senior citizens, and orphans.

Prosocial behavior: Behavior that benefits someone else or society but that generally offers no obvious benefit to the person performing it and that may even involve some personal risk or sacrifice.

Altruism [AL-true-ism]: Behaviors that benefit other people and for which there is no discernible extrinsic reward, recognition, or appreciation.

Other theorists would argue that biological drives underlie altruistic behavior. Consider the following scenario. An infant crawls into a busy street. A truck is approaching. The mother darts in front of the oncoming vehicle and carries her child to safety. Most people would say that love impelled the mother to risk her life to save the child. Sociobiologists would argue that the mother committed her brave deed so her genes would be passed on to another generation.

The idea that people are genetically predisposed toward certain behaviors was described by Edward Wilson, a Harvard University zoologist, in his 1975 book *Sociobiology: A New Synthesis*. Wilson argued that biological, genetic factors underlie all behavior. But he went one step further. He asserted, in his theory of **sociobiology**, that even day-to-day behaviors are determined by the process of natural selection—that social behaviors that contribute to the survival of a species are passed on through the genes from one generation to the next and account for the mechanisms that have evolved to produce behaviors like altruism (Crawford & Anderson, 1989). For the sociobiologist, genetics is the key to daily behavior.

Sociobiological theory is hotly debated by psychologists, because it places genetics in a position of primary importance and minimizes the role of learning. Most psychologists feel strongly that learning plays a key role in the day-to-day activities of human beings. People *learn* to love, to become angry, to help or hurt others, and to develop relationships with those around us. But although sociobiology is too fixed and rigid for most psychologists, it does raise interesting questions about the role of biology and genetics in social behavior.

Behavioral theories and sociobiology are two ways of explaining why people help others. People don't always help, however. One important area of research seeks to explain why.

Bystander Apathy: Failing to Help. The study of helping behavior has taken some interesting twists and turns. For example, psychologists have found that in large cities, where potentially lethal emergencies (accidents, thefts, stabbings, rapes, and murders) occur frequently, people often exhibit bystander apathy—they watch, but seldom help. **Bystander apathy** is the unwillingness of witnesses to an event to help; this unwillingness increases with the number of observers, a fact that has been termed the *bystander effect*. In a well-known incident in New York City in 1964, Kitty Genovese was walking home when a man approached her with a knife. A chase ensued, during which she screamed for help. He stabbed her, and she continued screaming. When lights came on in nearby buildings, the attacker fled. But when he saw that no one was coming to his victim's aid, he returned and stabbed her again. The assault lasted more than 30 minutes and was heard by dozens of neighbors; yet no one came to the victim's aid. This is a classic case of bystander apathy.

Bibb Latané and John Darley (1970) investigated bystander apathy in a long series of studies. They found that in situations requiring uncomfortable responses, people must choose between helping and standing by apathetically. They must decide whether to introduce themselves into a situation, especially when there are other bystanders. But they first have to decide what is going on (is this an emergency or not?) and often are misled by the *apparent* lack of concern among other bystanders to conclude that nothing really bad is going on after all—so they don't help. Latané and Darley reasoned that when people are aware of other bystanders in an emergency situation, they may also be less likely to help because they experience *diffusion of responsibility* (the feeling that they cannot be held responsible). To test their hypothesis, the researchers brought college students to a laboratory and told them they were going to be involved in a study of people who were interested in discussing college life in New York City. They explained that, in the interest of preserving people's anonymity, a group discussion would be held over an intercom system rather than face-to-face, and that each person in the group would talk in turn. In fact, in each experimental session there was only one true participant. All the other conversations were prerecorded by assistants who worked for the researchers.

Sociobiology: Theory based on the premise that even day-to-day behaviors are determined by the process of natural selection—that social behaviors that contribute to the survival of a species are passed on genetically from one generation to the next and account for the mechanisms producing behaviors such as altruism.

Bystander apathy: The unwillingness of witnesses to an event to help, an effect that increases when there are more observers.

FIGURE 16.8

The Bystander Effect

In a classic bystander apathy study, as the number of people in the group increased, the willingness of the naive participant to inform the experimenter that the victim had suffered a seizure decreased.
(From Latané & Darley, 1970.)

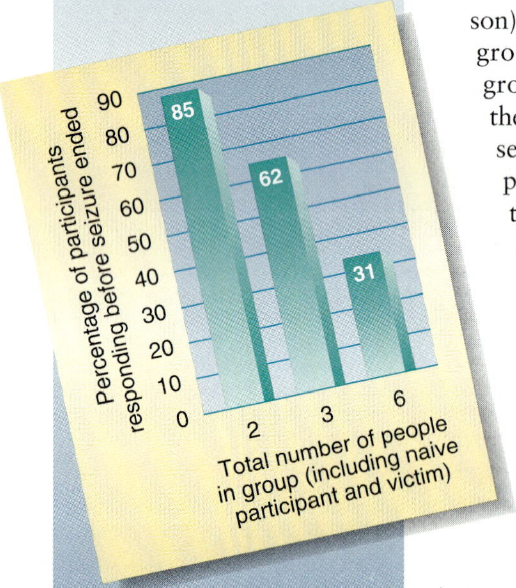

The independent variable was the number of people the naive participant thought were in the discussion group. The dependent variable was whether and how fast the naive participant reported as an emergency an apparently serious seizure affecting one of the "other participants." The future "seizure victim" spoke first; he talked about his difficulties getting adjusted to New York and mentioned that he was prone to seizures, particularly when studying hard. Next, the naive participant spoke. Then came the prerecorded discussions by assistants. Then the "seizure victim" talked again. After a few relatively calm remarks, his speech became increasingly loud and incoherent; he stuttered and indicated that he needed help because he was having "a-a-a real problem—er—right now and I—er—if somebody could help me out it would—it would—er—er sh-sure be good." At this point, the experimenters began timing the speed of the naive participant's response.

Each naive participant was led to believe that his or her discussion group contained two (participant and victim), three (participant, victim, and one other person), or six (participant, victim, and four other people). That is, in the two-person group, participants believed they were the only bystander; in the three-person group, they thought there was one other bystander. When participants thought they were the only bystander, 85 percent of them responded before the end of the seizure. If they thought there was only one other bystander, 62 percent of the participants responded by the end of the seizure. When participants thought there were four additional bystanders, only 31 percent responded by the end of the seizure (see Figure 16.8).

In general, research has shown that bystanders will help under some conditions. For one thing, people's self-concepts and previous experiences affect their willingness to intercede. Bystanders who see themselves as being especially competent in emergencies (such as doctors and nurses) are likely to help a victim regardless of the number of people present (Pantin & Carver, 1982). If the person who needs help has a relationship with the person who can offer help, help is more likely to be given (Batson, 1990). Research in cities of various sizes shows that people who live in small communities are more likely to help (Levine et al., 1994). Also, personality characteristics of the individual involved in a bystander situation are important. Men respond more often than women (Salminen & Glad, 1992). Tice and Baumeister (1985) found, however, that participants with a high degree of masculinity were less likely to respond. They contended that highly masculine subjects might be especially fearful of embarrassment. In American society, the personality characteristics of men, in general, emphasize strength and aggression rather than sensitivity and nurturing. This finding is supported by work showing that women are more likely than men to help friends, and that when women do so, they do it in a nurturing rather than a problem-solving way (Belansky & Boggiano, 1994).

Relationships and Attraction

If people are inclined to engage in prosocial behavior toward those with whom they have a relationship, what is it about your friends that attracts you and makes you want to maintain a relationship with them in the first place? We saw in Chapter 9 that people develop relationships to fulfill their needs for warmth, understanding, and emotional security. Psychologists also know that people are attracted to those who live or work near them, whom they consider good-looking, who share their attitudes, and with whom they spend time. Social psychologists in particular study **interpersonal attraction,** the tendency of one person to evaluate another person (or a symbol or image of another person) in a positive way.

Interpersonal attraction: The tendency of one person to evaluate another person (or a symbol or image of another person) in a positive way.

Proximity. People are more likely to develop a relationship with a neighbor than with someone who lives several blocks or miles away. Three decades of re-

◀ *Culture helps define people's standards or ideals for physical attractiveness.*

search show that the closer people are geographically—whether where they work or where they live—the more attracted they will be. A simple explanation is that they are likely to see each other more often, and repeated exposure leads to familiarity, which leads to attraction. Another reason is that attraction is facilitated by the anticipation of a relationship with someone one encounters frequently. In addition, if people are members of a group, such as a computer club, a volunteer organization, or an aerobics class, they perceive themselves as sharing the same feelings, attitudes, and values as others in the group. That perception leads to attraction.

Physical Attractiveness. Within seconds of seeing a person, you are able to decide if they are attractive to you (Locher et al., 1993). Research shows that people feel more personal regard and ascribe more power, status, and competence to individuals they find physically attractive than to those they don't; we saw this earlier when we looked into who could best change people's attitudes (Dion, Pak, & Dion, 1990; Feingold, 1992a, 1992b). Volumes of research show that people are attracted romantically, at least at first, to those whom they find attractive (Cunningham, Barbee, & Pike, 1990). In general, people will judge an attractive individual to have more positive traits and characteristics than an unattractive one, especially when appearance is the first information provided (Benassi, 1982). Attractive people are granted more freedom and are perceived as being more fair and competent than unattractive people (Cherulnik, Turns, & Wilderman, 1990). For example, attractive college professors are seen as better teachers and are less likely to be blamed if a student receives a failing grade in a course (Romano & Bordieri, 1989). But such findings about attractiveness are a distinctly Western phenomenon; values about attractiveness differ cross-culturally, and different cultures appraise various elements of life in a different way (Matsumoto & Kudoh, 1993).

How important is attractiveness when it comes to dating? Do people always select the most attractive person for a date? Research shows that people prefer attractive dates, and some studies show that people seek out those of their own level of attractiveness. But other variables also seem to play an important role; educational level, intelligence, socioeconomic status, and similarity of previous experiences all weigh heavily in the choice of whom to date and eventually marry (Feingold, 1988a). Although physical attractiveness and youthfulness are initially important in the selection of dates and mates (especially among men), appearance is just one variable among many (Sprecher, Sullivan, & Hatfield, 1994).

In a typical physical attractiveness experiment, participants are given two identical job résumés, each with a different picture attached to it. Results show that people will evaluate the résumé of the person they find physically attractive more positively than that of the other person, even though the qualifications of the "applicants" are the same (e.g., Frieze, Olson, & Russell, 1991). Attractive people are preferred in the workplace, as dates, and as friends; they are also thought to be less menacing (Eagly et al., 1991). In one research study, for example, participants were given information about a hypothetical sex offender, including a facial photograph and a conviction record (Esses & Webster, 1988). The subjects judged physically unattractive sex offenders as less likely to restrain their behavior in the future than better-looking but equally dangerous sex offenders.

Liking Those Who Share the Feeling and Who Hold Similar Attitudes. Learning theorists contend that people are attracted to and form relationships with those who give them positive reinforcement and that they dislike those who punish them. The basic idea is simple: You like the people who like you. Moreover, if you like someone, you tend to assume (sometimes incorrectly) that the other person likes you in return and that the two of you share similar qualities. This tendency is especially prevalent in people who need social approval—for example, people with low self-esteem (Jacobs, Berscheid, & Walster, 1971).

Another attribute that affects the development of relationships is real or perceived similarity in attitudes and opinions. If you perceive someone's attitudes as similar to your own, there is an increased probability that you will like that person. Having similar values, interests, and background is a good predictor of a friendship (e.g., L. Miller, 1990). Similarly, voters who agree with the views of a particular candidate tend to rate that person as more honest, friendly, and persuasive than the politicians with whom they disagree.

Researchers have also found that, conversely, if you already like someone, you will perceive that person's attitudes as being similar to your own. For example, voters who like a particular candidate, perhaps because the candidate is warm-hearted or physically attractive, will tend to minimize their attitudinal differences. The slogan "I Like Ike" helped elect Eisenhower, and some political analysts have suggested that Bill Clinton defeated George Bush in the 1992 presidential election because voters perceived him as being a more caring person.

That you like those who like you is explained by cognitive consistency theory, which suggests that sharing similar attitudes reduces cognitive dissonance (the phenomenon we examined earlier). In your natural inclination to avoid dissonance, you feel attracted to those you believe share similar attitudes; shared attitudes in turn lead to attraction and liking. Learning theories also suggest that you like people with similar attitudes because similar attitudes are reinforcing to you. As long as you think the other person's attitudes are genuine, such liking will continue.

Friendships and the Role of Equity. Laverne and Shirley, Tom Sawyer and Huck Finn, Lucy and Ethel—liking each other and sharing ideas and values has been the basis of many friendships. *Friendship* is a special two-way relationship between people. According to one influential group of researchers, if two people's behaviors, emotions, and thoughts are related, and the people are dependent on one another, a close relationship exists (Kelley et al., 1983). Closeness is reported by many researchers as the key variable that defines a friendship, although *close* must be defined so that all researchers mean the same thing when they use the word (Berscheid, Snyder, & Omoto, 1989).

Ideally, friends participate as equals, enjoy each other's company, have mutual trust, provide mutual assistance, accept each other as they are, respect each other's judgment, feel free to be themselves with each other, understand each other in fundamental ways, and are intimate and share confidences (Davis & Todd, 1984). Reciprocity and commitment between people who see themselves as equals are essentials of friendship (Hartup, 1989). Compared with casual friends, close friends interact more frequently across a wider range of settings, are more exclusive, and offer each other more benefits (Hays, 1989).

As we saw in Chapter 10, elementary school children tend to form same-gender friendships; cross-gender friendships are rare. With youngsters, friendships lead to cooperation rather than competition, at least more than with nonfriends (Hartup, 1989). Furthermore, when children have friends in the classroom, they do better in school (Ladd, 1990). Adolescent friendships sometimes provide a place for sharing and intimacy, although they can also be filled with conflict over social or political issues, drugs, gangs, and sexual behavior (Berndt, 1992). Among adults, friendships between two women differ from those between two men; and both differ from friendships between a man and a woman. Western cultural expectations for specific gender-based behaviors, such as who helps with child care or who initiates sexual activity, often control male-female interactions in friendship. Women talk more about family, personal matters, and doubts and fears than men do; men talk more about sports and work than do women. Women in general find friendships more satisfying than men do (Elkins & Peterson, 1993).

Equity plays an important role in close relationships. **Equity theory** states that people attempt to maintain stable, consistent interpersonal relationships in which the ratio of members' contributions is balanced. This ensures that all members are treated fairly. People in close relationships usually have a sense of balance in the relationships and believe they will stay together for a long time (Clark & Reis, 1988).

According to equity theory, one way in which people maintain a balanced relationship is to make restitution when it is demanded. Apologies help restore a sense of autonomy and fairness to an injured individual. Similarly, people who do favors expect favors in return, often using the principle of equity unconsciously in day-to-day life. If a friend helps you move into your new apartment, you may be expected to lend her a hand when she has to take an old refrigerator to the dump. Research shows that when a person senses inequity in a situation, this affects her or his feeling about the other person—especially when the other person is being treated better (Griffeth, Vecchio, & Logan, 1989).

Intimate Relationships and Love. People involved in a close relationship may also be intimate with one another. In **intimacy** each person is willing to self-disclose and to express important feelings and information to the other person; in response, the other person usually acknowledges the first person's feelings, making each person feel valued and cared for (Reis & Shaver, 1988). Research shows that self-disclosure tends to be reciprocal; people who disclose themselves to others are usually recipients of intimate information (Collins & Miller, 1994).

Unfortunately, there is little research on intimate relationships outside of marriage. Communication, affection, consideration, and self-disclosure between friends have been studied relatively little. However, important individual and gender differences do exist in friendships. For example, men are more self-disclosing with a woman than they are with another man; in general, men are less likely to be self-disclosing and intimate than are women (Dindia & Allen, 1992). Psychologists know much more about intimate relationships between pairs of people, especially men and women, when sex, love, and marriage become involved (Miller, 1990).

Love, emotional commitment, and sex are the parts of intimate relationships that most people think of when they hear the word *intimacy*. People in love relationships often express feelings in unique ways—they give flowers, take moonlit walks, write lengthy letters, and have romantic dinners. According to psychologists, love has psychological, emotional, biochemical, and social factors. Consider this array of definitions of *love*:

- Fromm (1956) focused on the idea that mature love is possible only if a person achieves a secure sense of self-identity. He said that when people are in love, they become one and yet remain two individuals.
- Heinlein (1961) wrote that love "is a condition in which the happiness of the other person is essential to your own."

Equity theory: In social psychology, the theory that people attempt to maintain stable, consistent interpersonal relationships in which the ratio of members' contributions is balanced.

Intimacy: A state of being or feeling in which each person is willing to self-disclose and to express important feelings and information to the other person; such behaviors are usually reciprocated.

- Branden (1980) suggested that love is "a passionate spiritual, emotional, sexual attachment between a man and a woman that reflects a high regard for the value of each other's person."
- Tennov (1981) believed that the ultimate state of romantic love is one called "limerance": a head-over-heels involvement and preoccupation with thoughts of the loved one.

All are right, and none are. Many classifications of love have been suggested, and all have some overlapping components. One influential classification is Sternberg's (1986b) view, which sees love as having three components: intimacy, commitment, and passion. *Intimacy* is a sense of emotional closeness. *Commitment* is the extent to which a relationship is permanent and long-lasting. *Passion* is arousal, some of it sexual, some intellectual, and some inspirational. When all three components are present, the highest type of love—*consummate love*—results. Another view of love (Hendrick & Hendrick, 1986) includes six distinct varieties: passionate, game-playing, friendship, logical, possessive, and selfless (see Table 16.4).

Different as these classifications may be, researchers have nonetheless identified some common elements in love relationships. Love usually involves the idealization of another person; people see their loved ones in a positive light. It also involves caring for another person and being fascinated with that person. Love includes trust, respect, liking, honesty, companionship, and sexual attraction. A central element is commitment; however, researchers disagree as to whether love and commitment can be separated, because one usually follows from, or is part of, the other (Fehr, 1988; Fehr & Russell, 1991).

What happens when love disappears? People in a close emotional relationship who break up, whether married or not, experience emotional distress. Sadness, anger, loss, and despair are among the emotions experienced by people at the end of a close relationship. However, research shows that the extent of those feelings is determined by an individual's level of security. If you lose a lover or spouse, your

TABLE 16.4 *Varieties of Love*

Hendrick and Hendrick's (1986) description of love includes six distinct varieties.

Varieties of Love	Sample Items Measuring Each Variety
Passionate love	My lover and I were attracted to each other immediately after we first met. My lover and I became emotionally involved rather quickly.
Game-playing love	I have sometimes had to keep two of my lovers from finding out about each other. I can get over love affairs pretty easily and quickly.
Friendship love	The best kind of love grows out of a long friendship. Love is really a deep friendship, not a mysterious, mystical emotion.
Logical love	It is best to love someone with a similar background. An important factor in choosing a partner is whether or not he (she) will be a good parent.
Possessive love	When my lover doesn't pay attention to me, I feel sick all over. I cannot relax if I suspect that my lover is with someone else.
Selfless love	I would rather suffer myself than let my lover suffer. Whatever I own is my lover's to use as he (she) chooses.

reaction will be determined not only by the loss of your relationship but also by your own basic feelings of security, attachment, and anxiety (Simpson, 1990).

Love is a state, but it is also an act and a series of behaviors. Thus, although a person may be in love, most psychologists think of love in terms of the behaviors that demonstrate it, including remaining faithful sexually and showing caring behaviors (D. Buss, 1988). Yet researchers also wish to know whether love has a biological basis.

According to David McClelland (1986), two sources exist for understanding love: analytical self-reports ("I think I have fallen in love") governed by the left side of the brain, and emotional reports governed by the right side of the brain (an idea we examined in Chapters 2 and 4). In McClelland's view, the right brain can tell the individual about emotional experiences that are not consciously processed. McClelland argues that these emotional processes influence physiological processes and behaviors (the sweaty palms, the racing heart) that are not directly under our conscious control. In some ways, McClelland writes, there are two psychologies of love: an analytic left-brain understanding and an emotional right-brain understanding. McClelland's view, particularly his physiologically based explanation of love, has yet to achieve wide acceptance, because most researchers assert that love derives from environmental rather than biological variables (Waller & Shaver, 1994).

Love is expressed differently in every culture, and even within a culture there are enormous variations in the expression of love. Two researchers from the University of Keele in England, Robin Goodwin and Daniel Tang (1991), used questionnaires to examine whether British and Chinese university students in Hong Kong valued the same traits in friends and romantic partners. Results showed that, overall, romantic partners were expected to be more honest and caring than friends were expected to be. In addition, the British students stressed sensitivity and humor in both romantic partners and friends, but the Chinese students stressed creativity and astuteness about money. Other results support these conclusions. When Susan Sprecher and her colleagues (1992) compared love attitudes and experiences among Japanese, Americans, and Russians, they found distinct cultural differences. For example, the Japanese were less romantic than the other groups; the Americans were more likely to associate love with marriage than were the other groups; and the Russians were the most excitable and had the most trouble staying calm when in love.

Cultural differences in love relationships vary in part because of the nature of marriages themselves. In cultures where marriages are arranged by parents, love comes about slowly over time. In cultures where passionate love is equated with happiness, such as the United States, love is often seen to wane over time; but in cultures where romantic, passionate love is valued less, the depth of relationships and the waning of passion are viewed differently and have a different time course. Even within American culture, there are differences in decisions to marry among ethnic groups; for example, African American women are more likely than white women to insist on having economic supports, such as a steady job or family help, in place before marriage (Bulcroft & Bulcroft, 1993). Psychologists know far too little about love relationships in this and other cultures; yet love is a basic human emotion that is nurtured from birth to death and is easily seen in every culture. As psychologists discern the key elements of friendships, they will be more likely to tackle the even more complicated topic of love and how it should be nurtured.

Behavior in Groups

"Membership has its privileges," according to American Express. In appealing to people's desire to be part of a group, the charge card company is employing psychological principles to sell its product and engender loyalty. To make the American Express group as attractive as possible, the company has run magazine ads featuring famous athletes, actors, politicians, and businesspeople who are cardholders. Who wouldn't want to identify with such an elite group?

FIGURE 16.9

Social Facilitation

The presence of others may have opposite effects, either helping or hindering a person's performance. The presence of others heightens arousal, and heightened arousal leads to better performance on tasks a person is good at and worse performance on difficult tasks.

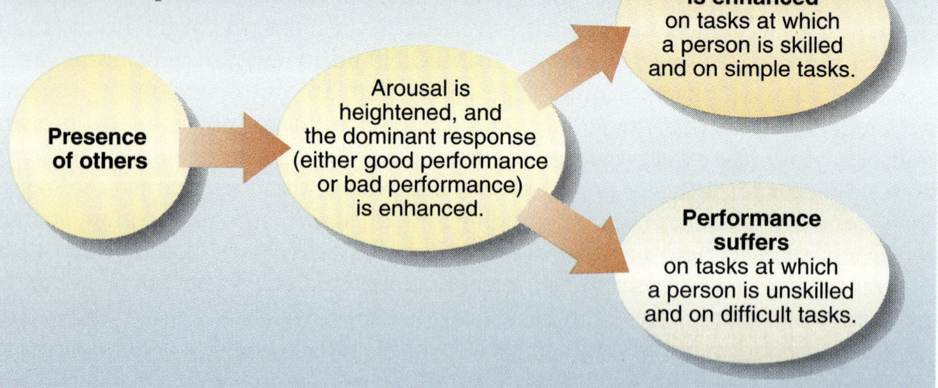

Membership does confer certain advantages, which is why people belong to all kinds of groups. There are formal groups, such as the American Association of University Students, and informal ones, such as a lunch group of coworkers. A **group** can be either a large number of people working toward a common purpose or a small number of people (even two) who are loosely related and have some common goals or interests. By joining a group, people indicate that they agree with or have a serious interest in its purpose. If a major function of the American Cancer Society is to raise money for cancer research, a person's membership indicates an interest in finding a cure for cancer. It has generally been thought that groups function well and enhance performance; research shows, however, that such effects of groups are modest and that the larger effect that emanates from a group is a sense of cohesion, solidarity, and commitment to a task (Mullen & Copper, 1994).

Social Facilitation. Individual behavior is affected not only by membership in a group but also by the mere presence of a group. **Social facilitation** is a change in performance that occurs when people believe they are in the presence of other people. For example, there is anecdotal evidence that a person practicing a sport at which he or she is accomplished may do even better when other people are watching. A person who is less accomplished, however, may do worse when other people are around. Research studies that examine people's performance at various tasks—for example, keyboard data entry—show this effect (Aiello & Kolb, 1995).

How the presence of others changes a person's behavior, and whether it changes the behavior for better or worse, is illustrated in Figure 16.9. This figure is based on Robert Zajonc's (1965) drive theory of social facilitation. According to Zajonc, the presence of others produces heightened arousal, which leads to a greater likelihood that an individual will exhibit a particular response (Jackson & Latané, 1981; Zajonc, 1965).

But just what is the nature of the heightened arousal? This is a source of some debate. One theory of social facilitation suggests that fear of evaluation—not the mere presence of people—brings about changes in performance (see Innes & Young, 1975). If an auto mechanic knows that a customer is watching him repair an engine, he is likely to increase his work speed to convince the observer of his efficiency and

Group: Two or more individuals who are loosely or cohesively related and who share some common characteristics and goals.

Social facilitation: Change in performance that occurs when people believe they are in the presence of other people.

professionalism. Bond and Titus (1983) suggest that the effects of social facilitation are often overestimated and the effects of believing oneself to be observed are often underestimated. They caution that a model of social facilitation must take into account the actual and believed presence of observers, as well as the perceived importance of the evaluation by the perceived observers. Thus, being evaluated by a friend has a different effect than being evaluated by a stranger (Buck et al., 1992).

A decrease in an individual's effort and productivity as a result of working in a group is known as **social loafing**. Suppose you and your friends are asked to help someone move a grand piano; in order to move the piano, you join forces with your friends and accomplish the task. Did you expend as much effort as a member of the group as you would have expended if you had had to move the piano by yourself? Research confirms the social loafing effect. In an experiment in which individuals were instructed to clap their hands and cheer, they clapped and cheered less loudly when they were part of a group (Latané, Williams, & Harkins, 1979).

Most psychologists claim that social loafing occurs when individual performance within a group cannot be evaluated; that is, poor performance may go undetected, and exceptional performance may go unrecognized. Consequently, people feel less pressure to work hard or efficiently. One study showed that as group size increased, individual members believed their own efforts were more dispensable—the group could function without their help. "Let George do it" became the prevailing attitude (Kerr & Bruun, 1983). Such findings are evident cross-culturally; even Jordanian students, who come from a society that stresses cohesion and group cooperation, worked less hard when they were working together than when working alone (Atoum & Farah, 1993).

Social loafing is minimized when the task is attractive and rewarding and the group is committed to high task performance (Zaccaro, 1984). It is also less apparent when a group is small, when the members know one another well, and when a group leader calls on individuals by name or lets it be known that individual performance may be evaluated (Williams, Harkins, & Latané, 1981). Some researchers have noted decreased social loafing when individuals have the opportunity to assess their own performance relative to an objective standard or relative to other people's performance, even though no one else is evaluating them (Harkins & Szymanski, 1988; Szymanski & Harkins, 1993). As with so many other social phenomena, a wide array of variables can alter the extent of social loafing; yet researchers conclude that social loafing is a robust phenomenon that occurs across a wide variety of tasks and situations (Karau & Williams, 1993, 1995; Prattarelli & McIntyre, 1994).

Group Polarization. In groups, people may be willing to adopt behaviors slightly more extreme than their individual behavior tendencies. They may be willing to make decisions that are risky or even daring. A woman who by herself is unwilling to invest money in a venture may change her mind on hearing that other members of her group are investing. Some early research on group decision making focused on the willingness of individuals to accept more risky alternatives when other members of the group did so; this research described such individuals as making a *risky shift* in their decisions.

In a group, individuals initially perceive themselves as being more extreme than the other members of the group. They also believe they are more fair, more right-minded, more liberal, and so on. When they discover that their positions are not very different from those of others in the group, they shift, or become *polarized*, to show that they are even more right-minded, more fair, or more liberal. They also may become more assertive in expressing their views. Shifts or exaggerations that take place among group members after group discussions are referred to as **group polarization**; in individuals, such a shift is known as a *choice shift* (Zuber, Crott, & Werner, 1992).

A *persuasive arguments* explanation of the polarization phenomenon asserts that people tend to become more extreme after hearing views similar to their own. A

Social loafing: Decrease in productivity that occurs when an individual works in a group instead of alone.

Group polarization: Exaggeration of individuals' preexisting attitudes as a result of group discussion.

person who is mildly liberal on an issue becomes even more liberal, more polarized. The explanation therefore suggests that people in a group often become more wedded to their initial views instead of becoming more moderate. If other people in the group hold similar views, that may polarize them even more. The effects of group polarization are particularly evident among juries. After group discussion, jury members are likely to decide on their initial views and argue for them more strongly. Thus, individual jury members with an initially doubting view toward a witness will have even deeper doubts after group discussions; their initial view becomes a verdict.

Another explanation for group polarization is *diffusion of responsibility*—the feeling of individual members of a group that they cannot be held responsible for the group's actions. If a church youth group makes a decision to invest money, for example, no single individual is responsible. Diffusion of responsibility may allow the teenagers to make far more extreme investment decisions as a group than they would individually.

Social comparison may also play a role in group polarization. People compare their view with the ideas of others whom they respect and who may hold more extreme attitudes than theirs. Feeling as right-minded as their colleagues, they become at least as liberal or as conservative as their peer group—they polarize their views.

After a group becomes polarized, many people in the group may share the same opinion. When such an event occurs (as it often does with government officials), people sometimes fall into a trap called *groupthink*.

Groupthink. Studies of decision making in government have often focused on the concept of **groupthink**—the tendency of people in a group to seek concurrence with one another when reaching a decision, usually prematurely. Groupthink occurs when group members reinforce shared beliefs in the interest of getting along, rather than effectively evaluating alternative solutions to the problem. The group does not allow its members to disagree, to accept dissenting opinions, or to evaluate options realistically (Janis, 1983). Groupthink discredits or ignores information not held in common, and thus cohesive groups are more likely to exhibit it (Mullen et al., 1994). See Figure 16.10 for a summary of the factors leading to groupthink.

Studies of history and government offer several examples of groupthink resulting in defective decision making. Consider the Bay of Pigs invasion, cited by Janis (1982) and McCauley (1989) as an example of groupthink. In the Bay of Pigs incident, President John F. Kennedy decided to go ahead with a CIA plan, devised by anti-Castro exiles, to invade Cuba. When the President asked for counsel from his

FIGURE 16.10

Groupthink: Development and Results

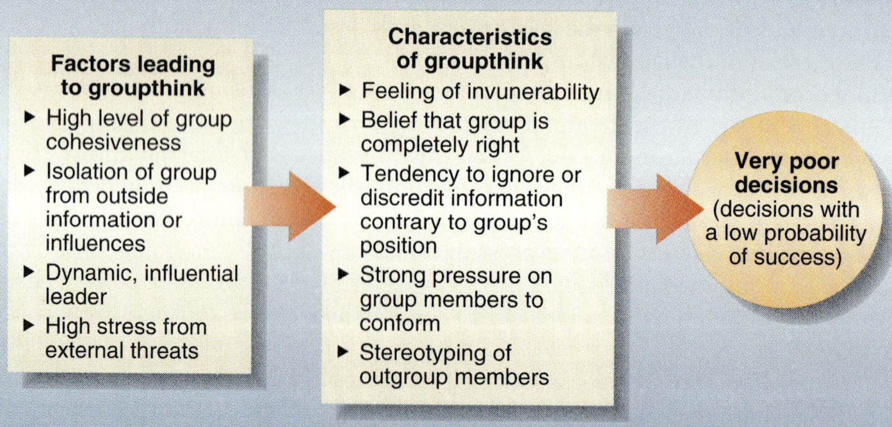

Groupthink: The phenomenon of people in a group reinforcing one another and seeking concurrence and group cohesiveness, rather than effectively evaluating choices and reasoning.

advisers—an impressive group with wide political experience—no one voted against the plan, and the mission was carried out. The Bay of Pigs invasion was a result of groupthink and the unwillingness of group members to upset each other (or the boss), and it turned out to be a major political fiasco that nearly resulted in war between the United States and the Soviet Union.

Social psychologist Ivan Steiner (1982) suggests that groupthink occurs when members' overriding concern is to maintain group cohesiveness and harmony. Maintaining cohesiveness helps individuals believe that the group cannot make mistakes. In addition, strong leaders often insulate a group from information or from other people to keep the group thinking in one direction (McCauley, 1989).

Despite the intuitive appeal of the groupthink concept, however, research support for it is minimal. Nevertheless, Aldag and Fuller (1993) assert that despite its lack of empirical support, groupthink is a defective process that people should guard against. They argue that groupthink can happen and that research into leaders, committees, and technology needs to focus on the variables that may create it or help defend against it (Miranda, 1994).

Unrestrained Group Behavior. The presence of other people can arouse people (social facilitation), can make them less active (social loafing), can cause them to make extreme decisions (group polarization), or can lead to consensus-making poor decisions (groupthink). So, when placed in a group, normally thoughtful people have been known to take part in bad decision making and even very irrational behaviors. Consider mob violence. When people engage in a riot, looting, or a beating, individuals explain their behavior not in terms of individual responsibility but as a group decision.

A key component of unrestrained behavior such as mob violence is *anonymity*. Anonymity produces a lack of self-awareness and self-perception that leads to decreased concern with social evaluation. When people have fewer concerns about being evaluated, they are more willing to engage in inappropriate or irrational behaviors. When there is violence or illegal drug use among the crowd at a rock concert, people feel less responsible. The view that no single individual can be held responsible for the behavior of a group arises out of **deindividuation**—the process by which individuals lose their self-awareness and distinctive personalities in the context of a group (Diener et al., 1980). Deindividuation (and its accompanying arousal) can lead to shifts in people's perceptions of how their behavior will be viewed—and thus to less controlled, less self-conscious, or less careful decisions about behavior (see Prentice-Dunn & Rogers, 1984). With deindividuation, people alter their thoughts about decisions. Groups such as the military, prisons, and cults use deindividuation to encourage their members to conform. In boot camp, military recruits are made to feel that they are there to serve the group, not their conscience. In prisons, inmates are made to wear uniforms and cut their hair short and are assigned numbers. With

FOCUS

Review

- What is the key psychological explanation for bystander apathy? p. 585
- Identify the fundamental characteristics of a close relationship. p. 588
- Distinguish between social facilitation and social loafing. pp. 592–593
- Identify the social variables that are important in explaining unrestrained group behavior. p. 595

Think Critically

- Provide a psychological explanation of why, if you perceive someone's attitudes as similar to your own, you will probably like that person. Why might you be able to influence that person to do things that he or she might otherwise not do?
- Psychologists know that people like (and love) those who are like themselves. What are some things that you can do (based on psychological principles) that will increase the likelihood that you will get a job or be promoted in the job you are in?
- Can you think of any famous dissenters in history? How did their refusal to conform to group pressure affect their lives? How did their dissent influence society?

Deindividuation: The process by which individuals in a group lose their self-awareness and concern with evaluation.

their unique personality stripped away, they are no longer treated as individuals and are made to behave as members of one large prison group. A cult persuades members to go along with group beliefs and acquire a sense of obligation to the group by asking individual members to perform increasingly taxing services on the group's behalf. In the end, an individual's behavior in a group often becomes distorted, more extreme, and less rational; the group makes members feel less accountable for their own actions.

Summary and Review

Attitudes

What is social psychology?

- *Social psychology* is the study of how individuals influence and are influenced by the thoughts, feelings, and behaviors of others. p. 556

What is the relationship between attitudes and behavior?

- *Attitudes* are long-lasting patterns of feelings and beliefs about other people, ideas, or objects, which are based in people's experiences and shape their future behavior. Attitudes are usually evaluative and have cognitive, emotional, and behavioral dimensions, each of which serves a function. Attitudes are formed early in life, through learning processes. Social psychologists can assess people's attitudes, but whether those attitudes predict behavior depends on a number of variables including attitude strength, vested interest, specificity of attitudes, and accessibility of attitudes. pp. 556–558

What are the key components of attitude change?

- There are four key components of attitude change, each of which affects the extent of change that may take place: the communicator, the communication, the medium, and the audience. The *elaboration likelihood model,* proposed by Petty and Cacioppo, asserts that there are two routes to attitude change: central and peripheral. The central route emphasizes rational decision making; the peripheral route, which is more indirect and superficial, emphasizes emotional and motivational influences. pp. 559–560
- Cognitive explanations of attitudes and attitude change include cognitive dissonance and reactance theory. *Cognitive dissonance* is the discomfort that results when an individual maintains two or more beliefs, attitudes, or behaviors that are inconsistent with one another. *Reactance* is the pattern of feelings and subsequent behaviors aimed at reestablishing a person's sense of freedom when there is an inconsistency between the person's self-image as being free to choose and the person's realization that someone is trying to force him or her to choose a particular alternative. pp. 560–561

KEY TERMS

Social psychology, p. 556
Attitudes, p. 556
Elaboration likelihood model, p. 560
Cognitive dissonance, p. 563
Self-perception theory, p. 565
Reactance, p. 565

Social Cognition

What is social cognition?

- *Social cognition* is the thought process of making sense of events, people, oneself, and the world in general through analyzing and interpreting them. Often, to save time, people use mental shortcuts to make sense of the world, developing rules of thumb. p. 565

How are nonverbal communication and attribution theory used in the study of social cognition?

- *Nonverbal communication* is information provided by cues or actions that involve movements of the body, especially the face. These sources of information help people make judgments about other people and about events in the world. pp. 565–568
- *Attribution* is the process by which someone infers other people's motives and intentions from observing their behavior and deciding whether the causes of the behavior are dispositional (internal) or situational (external). Attribution helps people make sense of the world, organize their thoughts quickly, and maintain a sense of control over the environment. It helps people feel competent and masterful and maintain a sense of balance, because it helps them predict similar events in the future. pp. 567–569

Describe the most common attribution errors.

- Two of the most common errors in attribution are the fundamental attribution error and the actor–observer effect. The *fundamental attribution error* is the tendency to attribute other people's behavior to dispositional rather than situational causes. The *actor–observer effect* is the tendency for people to attribute the failings of others to dispositional causes but to attribute their own failings to situational causes. Sometimes these errors occur because of a *self-serving bias;* that is, people's tendency to evaluate their own behavior as worthwhile, regardless of the situation. pp. 569–570

Define prejudice and identify the theories that explain it.

- *Prejudice* is a negative evaluation of an entire group of people. Prejudice is typically based on *stereotypes*—fixed, overly simple, often wrong, and often negative ideas, usually about traits, attitudes, and behaviors attributed to groups of people. Prejudice often leads to *discrimination*, behaviors targeted at individuals or groups with the aim of holding them apart and treating them differently. Prejudice has multiple causes and can be accounted for, at least to some extent, by social learning theory, motivational theory, cognitive theory, and personality theory. pp. 570–573

KEY TERMS

Social cognition, p. 565
Impression formation, p. 565
Nonverbal communication, p. 565
Body language, p. 566
Attribution, p. 567
Fundamental attribution error, p. 569
Actor–observer effect, p. 569
Self-serving bias, p. 570
Prejudice, p. 570
Stereotypes, p. 570
Discrimination, p. 570

Social Interactions

Explain social influence and conformity.

- *Social influence* is the way in which one or more people alter the attitudes or behavior of others, either directly or indirectly. Social influence is easily seen in studies of conformity. *Conformity* occurs when a person changes attitudes or behaviors to be consistent with other people or with social norms. pp. 574–575

What is obedience, and what did Milgram's studies of obedience demonstrate?

- *Obedience* is the process by which a person complies with the orders of another person or group of people. Milgram's studies demonstrated that an individual's ability to resist coercion is limited (65 percent of participants in one study delivered what they thought were the highest possible levels of shock to another person), although the presence of an ally who refuses to participate reduces obedience and underscores the importance of social influences on behavior. p. 577

Describe aggression, prosocial behavior, and bystander apathy.

- *Aggression* is viewed by social psychologists as any behavior designed to harm another person or thing. *Prosocial behavior* exhibits itself in *altruism*, behaviors that benefit someone else or society but that generally offer no obvious benefit to the person performing them. In contrast, *bystander apathy* is the unwillingness of witnesses to an event to help, especially when they are among numerous observers. pp. 579, 584–585

Define interpersonal attraction and indicate some key findings in studies of it.

- *Interpersonal attraction* is the tendency of one person to evaluate another person (or a symbol or image of another person) in a positive way. The process of attraction involves the characteristics of both the people involved and the situation. People give more personal regard and ascribe more power, status, and competence to people they find attractive than to those they don't. p. 586

Define friendship and love and distinguish between them.

- Reciprocity, closeness, and commitment between people who see themselves as equals are essentials of friendship. *Equity theory* holds that people attempt to maintain stable, consistent relationships in which the ratio of members' contributions is balanced. Love usually involves the idealization of another person. People see their loved ones in a positive light, care for them, and are fascinated with them; love also involves trust and commitment. According to Sternberg, love has three components: *intimacy* (a sense of emotional closeness), commitment (the extent to which a relationship is permanent), and passion (arousal, some of it sexual, some intellectual, and some inspirational). pp. 588–589

What are social facilitation and social loafing?

- *Social facilitation* in groups is a change in performance that occurs when people believe they are in the presence of other people. The change can be either positive or negative. *Social loafing* is a decrease in an individual's effort and productivity as a result of working in a group. pp. 592–593

Identify three processes that may occur in group decision making that may or may not be helpful.

- Extremes of group behavior include *group polarization*, the exaggeration of preexisting attitudes as a result of group discussion; *groupthink*, the tendency of people in a group to seek concurrence with one another; and *deindividuation*, the process by which the individuals in a group lose their self-awareness, self-perception, and concern with evaluation. pp. 593–595

KEY TERMS

Social influence, p. 574
Conformity, p. 574
Obedience, p. 577
Debriefing, p. 579
Aggression, p. 579
Prosocial behavior, p. 584
Altruism, p. 584
Sociobiology, p. 585
Bystander apathy, p. 585
Interpersonal attraction, p. 586
Equity theory, p. 589
Intimacy, p. 589
Group, p. 592
Social facilitation, p. 592
Social loafing, p. 593
Group polarization, p. 593
Groupthink, p. 594
Deindividuation, p. 595

Learning CONNECTIONS

Some students benefit from extra help with the various social psychological phenomena. You can learn more about them in:

- The CD-ROM accompanying this book, Topic 14 
- This book's study guide, *Keeping Pace Plus,* or the computerized study guide, Chapter 16
- The audiotape accompanying this book, *SoundGuide for Psychology,* Learning Unit 16
- The study aids found on the World Wide Web site for this book, at http://www.abacon.com/psych/lefton

Critical Thinking CONNECTIONS

Take a moment to think critically about how this chapter's topics are connected with the rest of psychology . . .

If you are interested in . . .	Ask yourself . . .	Then turn to . . .
How people form ideas about themselves and their behavior 	How do early interactions with parents, friends, and relatives help shape a child's developing self-concept?	Chapter 10, pp. 371–373
	How do humanists such as Carl Rogers focus their theories around the idea of an emerging and satisfying self-concept?	Chapter 12, pp. 422–424
	How do cognitive psychologists claim that a person's self-concept can be bolstered through cognitive (thought) reshaping?	Chapter 15, pp. 539–540
Gender and social behavior 	What are the implications of gender segregation beginning in childhood?	Chapter 10, pp. 369–371
	Why is it that men and women follow different life courses, especially when it comes to midlife transitions?	Chapter 11, pp. 392–393
	What are the implications of the fact that some psychological disorders are more prevalent in women than in men?	Chapter 14, pp. 486, 487, 489, 491, 498
The formation of attitudes 	According to social (observational) learning theory, how do people learn attitudes by observing the behavior and attitudes of others?	Chapter 5, pp. 185–188
	In what ways do children's and adolescents' developing attitudes, which are often based on gender role stereotypes, have their roots in childhood learning?	Chapter 10, pp. 363–365, 367–374

17

Applied Psychology

Ted, a fellow mountain biking enthusiast, had worked for the same textile manufacturing company for 20 years. He was a loyal, hard-working, company-oriented sales representative. With two decades of experience and a traditional all-American work ethic, he earned a fine living. He was convinced that he had not only a good job, but job security to boot.

Was he wrong! About two years ago, Ted was summoned—that's the way he described it—to a managing partner's office and handed a pink slip. He was given 3 weeks' pay, 2 weeks' vacation pay owed to him, his employer's best wishes, and some optional counseling. Ted's economic life came crashing down around him—mortgages, car payments, tuition for a child in college, a younger son who also hoped to go to a private college.

For 16 months Ted insisted on staying with what he knew best—textiles. This was his mistake; textiles is a dwindling industry in the United States. It took a full 16 months before Ted was so desolate that he sought the help of the counseling service that was a benefit of his dismissal. The firm employed traditional clinical psychologists as well as industrial/organizational psychologists; both types helped Ted enormously. A clinician worked with Ted to restore his self-esteem; an industrial/organizational psychologist—his job counselor—worked with him to develop a new résumé and better job goals, and helped him into a series of retraining courses that eased the transition to a new industry. The same industrial/organizational psychologist was also working with several other textile companies in the Southeast that were helping their employees make transitions into new technologies, new careers, and new lives.

My fellow cyclist Ted is one of thousands of workers who have borne the brunt of corporate downsizing. But the plight of companies in their struggles to stay competitive is quite real. Stockholders are demanding more; the global economy is extraordinarily competitive; to stay in business, companies have to be nimble. In an effort to help employees stay on the cutting edge, to improve productivity, and to help both managers and workers solve problems, companies are turning to applied psychologists.

Applied psychology is the branch of psychology that uses psychological principles to help solve practical problems of everyday living—whether those problems come up on the job, at school, or even on the playing field. Consider sport psychology, for example. Applied psychologists examine how the basics of behavior, such as learning and memory, affect day-to-day athletic activities—even a pickup basketball game. They also consider how coaches can motivate athletes to demonstrate peak performance by using common psychological mechanisms to help them visualize possibilities, overcome obstacles, and achieve fulfillment. To a great extent, applied psychologists help people better manage their own behavior.

In this chapter we consider an array of fields in which psychology is indeed applied to modern life. We begin with the workplace, because this is the place where psychological principles have for so long been systematically studied and applied—even as far back as John B. Watson, who applied psychology to a Maxwell House coffee advertising campaign in 1915.

Industrial/Organizational Psychology

Increased global competition, changes in information technology, and industrial reengineering are fast changing the world of work. As productivity has become increasingly important to business, industrial/organizational psychology has grown in importance. **Industrial/organizational (I/O) psychology** is the study of how individual behavior is affected by the work environment, by coworkers, and by organizational practices. It is the study of people not only in industry but in government, in hospitals, universities, and other nonprofit organizations. I/O psychologists study behavior in large and small businesses—from small biotech start-ups to large multinational corporations. In all of these environments, key concerns are how well individuals perform their duties and relate to one another; I/O psychology is increasingly being applied to address those concerns through provision of research-based answers to pressing organizational problems (Cascio, 1995). Large companies have I/O psychologists on site, working in their human resources departments, and small ones hire them as consultants.

I/O psychologists pay close attention to the type of company in which they work, because companies vary in their organizational structures, and worldwide companies vary even more. Given today's increasingly global economy, I/O psychologists must take into account global multicultural differences among organizations. Many companies reflect an organizational structure that in turn reflects their society. Asian companies—in Korea, for example—often reflect a family orientation, where people work hard for the good of the entire family. This affects hiring decisions, firing, promotions, hierarchies, and the general work ethic. Culture especially

Applied psychology: The branch of psychology that uses psychological principles to help solve practical problems of everyday living.

Industrial/organizational (I/O) psychology: The study of how individual behavior is affected by the work environment, by coworkers, and by organizational practices.

affects how decisions are made; in Japan, for example, plans for new ideas are often drafted from the bottom up, rather than emanating from higher levels of an organization as they often do in the United States. The entire corporate mind-set may vary from culture to culture, and from company to company within each culture. Some companies, especially those in Latin American countries, are extremely hierarchical in nature, according high respect to authority figures; some companies in Third World countries are more loosely organized in terms of who does what; in the United States, there is often some flexibility as to who is allowed to assume various roles.

In general, I/O psychology can be divided into four broad areas: human resources psychology, motivation of job performance, job satisfaction, and leadership. *Human resources psychology* focuses on the personnel functions of placing people in their jobs, training them, promoting, determining benefits, and evaluating performance. Such functions take place both before people begin to work for an organization and as an ongoing process within the organization. *Motivation of job performance* is a key area for I/O psychologists; they study not only rewards and success at work but also workers' influence on management and management's concerns about itself. *Job satisfaction* and other aspects of happiness at work are concerns of workers and employers alike. Last, the study of *leadership* focuses on the key attributes of leaders—people who influence other people's behavior toward the attainment of agreed-upon goals.

Human Resources Psychology

Human resources, or personnel psychologists are involved in a broad array of activities related to employment—from helping employers choose among prospective job candidates, to determining compensation packages, to facilitating on-the-job training, to arranging termination programs when businesses must downsize. To help organizations succeed, human resources psychologists must consider the internal conditions of an organization (its size, structure, and business strategies) as well as external conditions (legal, social, political, cultural) (Jackson & Schuler, 1995). Among the most important tasks is helping organizations select among well-trained, qualified candidates for specific positions. Today, finding the right people for jobs occurs within the overall context of an organization's *strategic planning*. This high-level planning, which is finalized at the top levels of the organization, includes forecasting the organization's future needs, establishing specific objectives, and implementing programs to ensure that appropriate people will be available when needed (Jackson & Schuler, 1990).

Job Analyses. An important step in the strategic planning process is ensuring that there are well-qualified personnel to fill all of the company's needs. Companies often prepare **job analyses**—careful descriptions of the various tasks and activities that are required for employees to do their jobs, along with the necessary knowledge, skills, and abilities. Thus, there is an analysis of *what* gets done and *how* it gets done. This means specifying performance criteria—behaviors—that are required of employees. For example, a computer programmer might be expected to write code, debug the code of other programmers, and evaluate the efficiency of the code. Job analysis also means enumerating the qualifications for employment. For example, a computer programmer might need a college degree in computer science, 2 or 3 years of experience, and top-notch hands-on computing skills.

The federal government has taken a leading role in preparing what it terms a *functional job analysis*, sometimes called an FJA, to describe each type of work and the level of complexity of each job. An FJA is appealing to I/O psychologists because—like operationally defined behavior in a research study—it is concrete, observable, and measurable. In an FJA there are three hierarchies of worker functions, and in each hierarchy there is an analysis of what gets done and how. In most jobs, workers have to deal with data (information), people (coworkers, subordinates,

Job analyses: Careful descriptions of the various tasks and activities that will be required for employees to do their jobs, along with the necessary knowledge, skills, and abilities; such analyses describe what gets done and how it gets done.

or customers), and things (objects). Within each of these types of work there are various levels of complexity. With data, individuals may have to compare, contrast, or copy data; on a more complex level, they may also have to analyze or synthesize data from different sources. With people, individuals may have to take instructions, help others, or serve others; on a more complex level, they may have to supervise, instruct, negotiate with, or mentor other people. With things, individuals may handle, carry, sort, or tend; on a more complex level, they may be altering, preparing, or fixing equipment.

There are other ways to measure what a job is, what gets done on a job, and who is best suited to specific work. For example, the *position analysis questionnaire* is widely used to ask those who know the job best to analyze their own jobs. On this questionnaire, workers fill out up to 194 statements describing a given job (McCormick, Jeanneret, & Mecham, 1972). The position analysis questionnaire has questions in six major areas: information sources (where the worker gets data from), mental processes (what decision making is required), work output (what physical work is required), relationships with others (communication skills), job context (physical working conditions), and other (licensing, criticality of position, special clothes, etc.).

The FJA and the position analysis questionnaire are widely used instruments, but there are many other such tests and analysis instruments, and most of them work equally well (Levine et al., 1983). All have a similar goal: Employers need to ensure that jobs are appropriate and have the correct scope. A job should not be too big or encompass too many tasks; nor should it be too limiting and so focused that it becomes boring and repetitive. Ideally, jobs should allow employees some level of responsibility for and control over how they do their work. Two of the key tasks of an I/O psychologist are balancing the scope and complexity of jobs and helping employers create jobs that will be motivating.

Selection Procedures. Employers want to hire individuals who will enjoy their work, suit the company's needs, and be productive. I/O psychologists develop specific selection procedures, including tests, to produce the best match between employers and employees. The selection procedures for jobs with large firms are often complicated and time-consuming.

Selection procedures have one basic goal—predicting the success of job candidates in order to help an employer determine which candidates to hire and which to reject. Employers and researchers use application forms, interviews, work samples, and tests to make comparisons between people looking for a job. Subtle factors can be at work in selection procedures, and evaluators have to pay particular attention to these factors—for example, to guard against the influence of their own moods (Baron, 1993), an applicant's expensive clothes or unattractive looks, and other non–job-related characteristics that have nothing to do with an applicant's true capabilities (Forsythe, 1990).

Paper-and-pencil tests can be administered in groups or individually. They can focus on measures of general or specific abilities, on motivation, or on personality variables. Intelligence tests are widely used measures of general ability in jobs that require high-level cognitive skills. Other standardized cognitive tests, such as those for general ability and specific verbal or mathematical knowledge, are good predictors of both academic success and certain types of job performance (Ree, Earles, & Teachout, 1994; Schmidt, Onex, & Hunter, 1992). However, an important question for I/O psychologists is whether such tests (or any tests for that matter) are the *best* predictors of job performance. This question has become especially important because of a large number of lawsuits filed by those who think the tests discriminate against them. *Applications* addresses this issue of equal employment opportunity further.

Standardized tests are not limited to intellectual abilities. Depending on the job, there may be tests of spatial abilities (for air traffic controllers), perceptual accuracy (stenographers, proofreaders), or motor abilities (firefighters). Each test is used to

APPLICATIONS

The Law and I/O Psychology—A Dynamic Tension

Since 1964, the federal government has enacted a series of laws to ensure that discrimination does not take place in the workplace. For example, the Civil Rights Act of 1964 made it illegal to discriminate against certain "protected" groups (Native Americans, Hispanic Americans, women, and blacks, among others) in housing, education, and employment. To enforce that legislation, the Equal Employment Opportunity Commission (EEOC) was established to investigate, eliminate, and prevent such discrimination. A key provision of the act was to ensure that no unlawful employment practices based on discrimination because of race, color, religion, sex, or national origin were used in hiring, firing, pay, or other terms or conditions of employment. It should come as no surprise that I/O psychologists are often called in to ensure that the guidelines used to select and promote employees are based on truly job-related knowledge and skills.

I/O psychologists may be hired as expert witnesses by individuals who file suit against employers; in this capacity, they help the aggrieved individuals establish that employers engaged in bias, discrimination, and/or unfair practices. They sometimes assert that the validity of a particular employment criterion (such as attractiveness and youthfulness for flight attendants) is questionable. Of course, employers hire their own expert witnesses. In court, these I/O psychologists testify to the validity, reliability, and predictability of various tests and selection procedures.

The challenge for I/O psychologists grew even more complex in 1992, when the Americans with Disabilities Act (ADA) went into effect. This law requires that employers make reasonable accommodations for employees who have disabilities but are otherwise qualified to perform various jobs. As expert witnesses in cases arising from this act, I/O psychologists help the courts answer questions like these: What exactly is a disability? (Is an employee with attention deficit disorder "disabled"?) What exactly is a reasonable accommodation? (Should such an employee be given extended deadlines?) What tests shall be used to decide if an employee is disabled? (Who says the employee has ADD? Is he or she "self-diagnosed"?) What if psychologists and medical doctors disagree?

Because of the lack of definitive answers to some of these questions, the courts have become clogged with lawsuits. Psychologists who are willing and qualified to act as expert witnesses are in high demand. And there is a dynamic and healthy tension between the law and psychology—something like the relationship between art and science. Psychological science has much to offer individuals, employers, and the courts. Like medical diagnoses, legal judgments are sometimes less precise than either employers or employees would like. With each passing year, however, psychological research is helping to sharpen the decision-making rules and to bring legal criteria into focus.

help the employer determine if a job candidate's abilities match the job's requirements. Tests of managerial ability, which sometimes present the applicant with a simulated in-box to sort through, have also been devised and have proved successful at indicating who will be a good manager (Berman & Miner, 1985).

The United States has become a service-based economy, with jobs in the service sector accounting for about 79 percent of all employment. Thus, many employers want their employees to be able to provide high-quality customer service and to be creative, adaptable, resilient, empathic, and understanding with customers. Since these abilities are now being considered important as job qualifications (Cascio, 1995), it is not surprising that the use of tests to measure elements of personality in the workplace has increased markedly in the last decade. Several million such tests are administered yearly. Personality tests are used more to find specific behavior patterns that are well suited to a type of job than to screen out people who may be abnormal. For example, some people who exhibit Type A behavior patterns (discussed in Chapter 13) do better at some types of high-pressure work, such as being a commodities trader, than at others, such as meticulously checking a manuscript for typographical errors (Lee, Ashford, & Bobko, 1990). Tests of personality and interests, however, are difficult to correlate with job performance; for example, outgoing individuals may be good salespeople, but quiet, introspective individuals can often be just as persuasive.

One type of test that has seen significantly increased use across different kinds of jobs is the test of integrity. Some such tests focus on attitudes about theft, including rationalizations about "acceptably" small amounts of on-the-job theft. Other tests examine integrity more indirectly, by looking at such characteristics as dependability, conscientiousness, and thrill seeking. Finally, tests such as the MMPI–2, which screens for maladjustment, are also used to reveal people of low integrity. Although such tests are controversial—many feel that individuals may be misdiagnosed or wrongly classified as lacking in integrity—their usage is on the increase, and they are seen as an alternative that is better than not testing at all (Camara & Schneider, 1994; Sackett, 1994).

Tests are just one way to gather information about applicants. Biographical data can help paint an accurate picture of an individual, as can work samples, letters of recommendation, and exercises in which job candidates take part in general discussions about work. Interviews can be important in determining the fit of an applicant with a position—but research shows that interviewers often make final decisions about applicants within the first minutes of an interview! Also, sometimes interviewers' judgments are based more on negative information provided than on positive information. Structured interviews—in which each applicant is asked the same questions in a certain way, in a certain order, and in the same manner—work better than do unstructured interviews (Arvey & Campion, 1982).

Training. Once a company has made a hiring decision about a new employee, a period of training nearly always follows. *Training* is the process by which organizations systematically teach employees skills to improve their job performance. Most corporations offer systematic training, which typically begins by teaching employees about the organization and its goals. A new employee may need to learn specific skills, such as how to use a computer program or how to sell in a new industry. Training individuals about specific tasks can be simple or complex. For example, a new sales manager must learn not only about the products she will sell but also about the territory she will manage, the employees she will supervise, and the specific needs of her customers.

A variety of methods are available for training. At the simplest levels are lectures, films, and videotapes. Self-paced instruction, whereby a person works with materials at his or her own pace, is often used. Training programs often also use discussion groups, simulations, and on-the-job procedures; a training program may involve an apprenticeship or a mentoring relationship, with regular performance appraisals by a more senior person on the job. Letting employees watch others so that they can observe and imitate is particularly effective. There are problems; for example, some people react better to certain training methods than do others, and finding appropriate mentors for women has often been difficult because of smaller numbers of senior women in the work force.

In today's fast-paced, highly technological workplace, even seasoned employees need training and retraining. In large organizations, training is an ongoing process, as new products and technologies are introduced. I/O psychologists typically break training into a multistep set of learning objectives. Because it provides very specific goals for knowledge and skill acquisition, this method of training is often particularly effective at helping employees identify their strengths and weaknesses. It also helps employees pinpoint specific obstacles to overcome and opportunities for improvement.

In order to keep pace with today's rapidly changing workplace, even seasoned employees and managers require specialized training sessions, such as this seminar on a new software application. ▼

Training may be the simple process of reviewing a new tool or procedure, such as introducing an executive to the information superhighway, teaching a secretary a new word-processing program, or working with custodians to promote recycling efforts. It may also be an elaborate process that involves the employee in active on-the-job participation—perhaps programming a robot or pitching a product to clients. Training may include repetitive practice, particularly with highly technical equipment. It often involves moving from a teaching classroom or sales meeting to the field, store, or actual workplace. Last, training usually involves feedback, so employees can learn whether the new skill or knowledge has been successfully acquired.

I/O psychologists take training especially seriously, because business or organizational success requires well-trained employees. Accordingly, to ensure good training, researchers seek to know what successful outcomes of training are—that is, what constitutes good work performance. In a way, researchers look at the desired outcome and work backward to determine how employees should be trained. I/O psychologists look at how employees have reacted to recent training by examining work products, final exams, or results immediately after a training procedure. Results are, after all, what employers want. Effective training produces changes in employees' ability to deliver results, whether in the form of better-quality products, clearer communications, or more effective supervision.

Performance Appraisal. Have you ever been evaluated by an employer? Bosses are sometimes good at appraising work, but they may overlook your best efforts and remember your mistakes, or they may not accurately convey how they feel about your performance. What makes a boss good at evaluating employees?

The process by which a supervisor periodically evaluates job-relevant strengths and weaknesses of a subordinate is called **performance appraisal**. Performance appraisals are especially important because they are often used to determine salaries, layoffs, firings, transfers, and promotions (Cleveland, Murphy, & Williams, 1989). Supervisors have always made such appraisals, and researchers have tried in the past 70 years to find ways for them to do it more systematically. Ways to improve the appraisal process typically involve more active thinking on the part of supervisors, as *The Research Process* on page 608 points out.

The problem with performance appraisals is that they are often done inaccurately by people with few skills in evaluation and with few diagnostic aids. Supervisors generally report that they dislike conducting appraisals. They don't like to review their subordinates, and many acknowledge that they do not have strong evaluative skills. Further, managers have just as many inappropriate biases as anyone else (Swim et al., 1989), as Chapter 16's discussion of attribution errors pointed out.

What are the criteria, or standards, on which a worker is judged? There is usually no ultimate criterion, no comprehensive yardstick of performance, by which to judge a worker, because multiple performance criteria enter into evaluation. A worker's quantity of work is often important, but so is the quality. Relationships with other workers enter into an appraisal of performance. Researchers have devised scales of performance in areas such as sales volume, relationship with customers, and quality of interworker communication; these can be helpful diagnostic tools. But because these skills often overlap, multiple or composite scales have been devised. None has proved totally satisfactory.

Because of the "soft" nature of some criteria, such as how well people "get along," most psychologists today recommend a focus on the best available criteria. This means focusing on those elements of performance that *best* describe satisfactory performance, recognizing that many criteria can be used. A sales manager will look first at a salesperson's "measurables," such as sales volume, gross sales, or net profits; then the manager will assess other variables that may be important, such as customer relations or coworker communication. Other measurable criteria might include a keyboarder's number of words or characters typed, a bank teller's number of shortages, or a nursery worker's number of saplings planted.

The task of doing performance appraisal requires objective measures whenever possible. But managers often compare individuals with one another, rank employees from best to worst, or rate employees in groups such as the top 10 percent, the next 20 percent, and so on. Such ratings may help differentiate among employees, but they fall short of fairness in a variety of areas. What about workers evaluated by different supervisors, one of them "easy" and the other demanding? What if subjective, "soft" criteria such as camaraderie and friendliness with management are

Performance appraisal: The process by which a supervisor periodically evaluates the job-relevant strengths and weaknesses of subordinates.

THE RESEARCH PROCESS

Performance Appraisal and Cognition

"I distinctly remember you goofing off last Thursday. On Friday, I saw you behaving rudely to a customer. Don't do it again!" the boss shouted at an intimidated clerk. The frightened clerk shook his head and walked away muttering. He had been out sick on Thursday; furthermore, his boss didn't know the nature of his interaction with the customer, who had yelled at him and insulted him and done everything but slap him. He felt that his performance appraisal was inaccurate, to say the least.

Managers have to observe employees, evaluate their performance, remember it after intervening activities have taken place, and then recall specific behaviors accurately. Cognitive processes are crucial in performance appraisals, because the evaluators often focus on the negative (Ganzach, 1995). One important cognitive process in appraisals is memory. Do supervisors remember their appraisals of workers? Does a worker's most recent work bias a performance appraisal?

Hypotheses and Questions. Although an employee's work may be consistently good, a bad period of performance just before an appraisal can bias an observer toward a poor decision. Steiner and Rain (1989) argue that there are recency effects in performance appraisals, just as there are in memory in general (as we saw in Chapter 6). Do other memory effects also affect performance appraisals? Are there techniques managers can use to ensure more accurate appraisals, such as taking notes?

Method. DeNisi, Robbins, and Cafferty (1989) asked the participants in a study to watch videotapes of carpenters who were sawing, sanding, and staining wood and then to evaluate the worker's performance. The participants were provided with a guide to good performance, and some received a set of diary cards with tabs on them. The tabbed cards either included the names of the carpenters or the task names, or were blank. The participants who were not given cards were asked to remember the workers' performance without help. The researchers wanted to know if using diaries would help people make better performance evaluations.

Results and Conclusion. The results showed that the diaries produced better recall and more accurate ratings. Keeping a diary provided participants with a structure for organizing information and made them less dependent on memory, which would help to eliminate the recency effects found by Steiner and Rain. Performance appraisals are a cognitive task affected by traditional cognitive variables, such as intervening activity, memory loss, and recency effects. The research shows that keeping a diary can minimize the negative effects and improve appraisals. Diary recording is not a complete solution to improving performance evaluations. A wide range of factors influence the evaluations, including who was evaluated just before the employee and how the employee was rated last time, among other things (Maurer, Palmer, & Ashe, 1993). Still, the use of diaries has a generally positive impact on the process of performance evaluations.

Implications. Employers need to be sensitive to how and when they do performance appraisals (Kluger & DeNisi, 1996). I/O psychologists help employers to be fair, professional, and accurate. In addition, because laws have been passed to protect employees from discrimination, employers have been forced to be more responsive to employees by doing regular appraisals. In the process, larger companies with better-trained staffs are helping workers by specifying tasks to be mastered during the next appraisal period. I/O psychologists have also worked to develop better rating forms, to train managers to evaluate performance more effectively, and especially to help managers conduct unbiased appraisals.

used? Might that discriminate against ethnic minorities and women, who don't necessarily have easy access to or common personal interests with management?

You can see that even when objective measures are used, certain problems can be associated with them; these include leniency, central tendency, halo effects, and reliability. Some raters always judge people with *leniency*, giving them higher evaluations than they may deserve. The rater may simply want to be liked, or he or she may want to avoid confrontation or even to have the employee's positive evaluation reflect well on himself or herself. In addition, some raters always judge people "about average," giving them a *central* rating. These raters are unwilling to rank people very high or very low but give "safe" judgments that are unlikely to raise eyebrows. *Halo effects* in job performance evaluations occur when a rater is unable to discriminate among the many conceptually discrete parts of a job. Thus, a strong first impression or strong work on one part of a job may lead to a good rating on later work or on other parts of a job—regardless of the quality or quantity of later or different work. *Reliability* refers to the consistency of observations. Good raters consistently rate similar work in similar ways; many others, however, deviate in rating from one occasion to the next and from one employee to the next based on events that are hard to quantify, such as a worker's unique ability to work well in a team.

Many companies require periodic evaluations, but reluctant managers do them as infrequently as possible, and sometimes in a cursory manner. They often evaluate everybody about the same—average, or perhaps very good, which may leave employees feeling unappreciated.

Motivation of Job Performance

I/O psychologists help people work together in organizations; they work at satisfying the emotional and social needs of employees, and they help organizations motivate management and workers. One obvious motivator is the fact that people need money to live. But both employers and psychologists know that different people are motivated by different things. Monetary rewards are important, of course—but so is the likelihood of praise for success. Such values are very much culturally determined; the value placed on hard work varies from culture to culture. Some cultures stress a person's duties to contribute to society; others stress a person's right to meaningful work; and still others stress a person's need for happiness at work. I/O psychologists study especially carefully the impact of rewards and success within the context of culture.

When Hofstede (1983) examined attitudes in more than 50 countries, he found that organizations and culture varied on four main dimensions. *Power distance* is the extent to which there is a rigid hierarchy, or pecking order, in a company, limiting employees' independence of action. *Uncertainty avoidance* is a lack of tolerance for ambiguity or uncertainty in the workplace, which may be found in risk-averse countries such as Japan. Cultures varied in the extent to which they valued *individualism* as opposed to the collective good of the organization. Finally, Hofstede found that emphasis on work goals as opposed to interpersonal goals, a trait that he labeled *masculinity*, also varied from culture to culture. Not surprisingly, Hofstede found that most Western companies fostered a combination he called independent individualism; Asian companies fostered collectivism; and some other societies fostered unique combinations. Israel, for instance, fosters dependent collectivism (high power distance, low individualism). Such cultural values will affect what people's needs and goals are, what they value, what they consider equitable, and how they can most effectively be managed.

▲ *The high degree of collectivism in Asian cultures is reflected in the attire and togetherness of this group of Japanese coworkers having lunch under the cherry blossoms at the Shinjuku National Garden.*

In American culture at least, job performance is affected by *intrinsically motivated behavior*—behavior engaged in strictly because it brings pleasure. (We examined intrinsic and extrinsic motivation in Chapters 5 and 9.) Recall that when intrinsically motivated behaviors are constantly reinforced with direct external rewards (such as money), productivity often drops. Money often is not that important to job performance. A well-paid plumber may find plumbing work tedious and unfulfilling, whereas a lower-paid clerical worker who finds the job important and challenging will perform well and be given increased responsibilities. With the help of I/O psychologists' theoretical work, employers can find ways to motivate employees to be more productive (and thus to provide companies with more profits).

Need and Goal-Setting Theory. As we saw in Chapter 9, need theory suggests that people are motivated to work toward a goal because of primary drives—often physiological, such as needs for food or shelter. But human beings also have desires and needs that are much more complex than the basic ones addressed by need theory. Workers will often perform difficult tasks for long hours, not for pay or for food or for praise, but merely to reach a goal or to compare their present performance with new performance. Mountain climbers tackle a new peak "because it's there." **Goal-setting theory** asserts that setting specific, clear, attainable goals for a given task will lead to better performance. In mountain biking, I challenge myself to ride harder and longer, not to break records for middle-aged men, but to meet artificial goals that I have set for myself.

Goal-setting theory states that goals work best when they are somewhat challenging but attainable and personally agreed to by a worker. Goals work especially well when they enhance a worker's sense of self-esteem or self-efficacy. For example, if a sales manager and her staff agree to a 50 percent increase in annual sales, rather than an unrealistic 200 percent increase, chances are that they will perform well (see Figure 17.1).

Goal-setting theory can account for some work behaviors, but it will not explain why people will work on projects for years, at low pay, or under difficult conditions. More fully developed expectancy theories take the next step forward—explaining the motivation for this type of performance.

Expectancy Theories. A successful employer–employee relationship relies on many factors beyond economic motivation. **Expectancy theories**, which we discussed in Chapter 9, suggest that a worker's effort and desire to maintain goal-

FIGURE 17.1

Need Theory versus Goal-Setting Theory

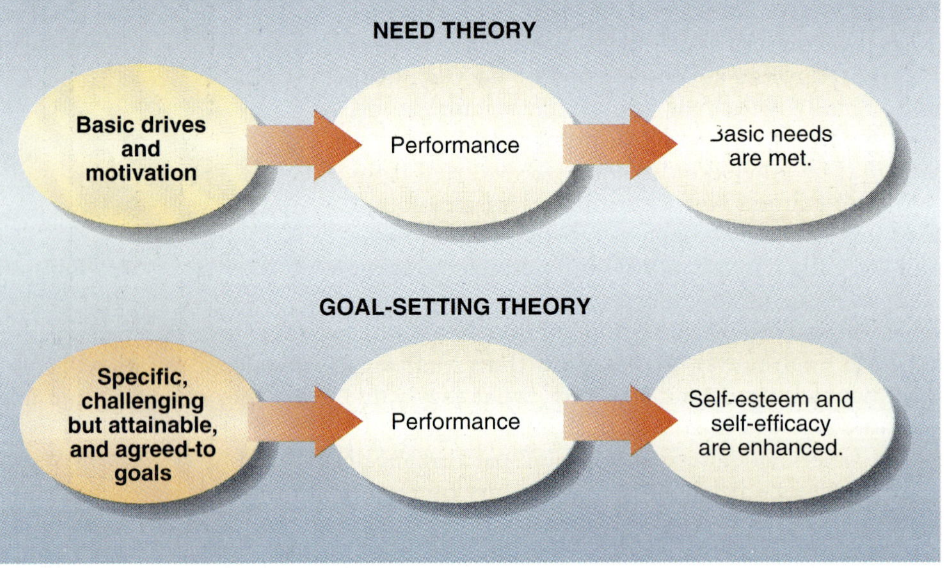

Goal-setting theory: Theory that asserts that setting specific, clear, attainable goals for a given task will lead to better performance.

Expectancy theories: Theories that suggest that a worker's effort and desire to maintain goal-directed behavior (to work) is determined by expectancies regarding the outcomes of that work.

directed behavior (in other words, to work) is determined by expectations regarding the outcomes of that work.

One expectancy theory, proposed by Victor Vroom (1964), suggests that job performance is determined by both motivation and ability. Vroom's proposal is considered an expectancy theory because it states that motivation is determined by what people expect to experience in performing a task—a rewarding outcome or a frustrating one. According to Vroom, a person must first have the willingness and the ability to perform the task; without that, the experience will be frustrating and thus nonmotivating. Given willingness and ability, Vroom's theory holds that motivation results from a three-part equation made up of expectancy, instrumentality, and valence. *Expectancy* is the belief that hard or extra work will lead to good or improved performance; *instrumentality* refers to a worker's belief that good performance will be rewarded; and *valence* refers to the value placed on the rewards that are offered. A person who gets a big raise but later gets the cold shoulder from coworkers because of it may then give the raise lower valence.

Edward Lawler and Lyman Porter (1967) modified and expanded on Vroom's theory. They contended that performance is determined by ability, effort, and *role perceptions*—the ways people believe they should be doing their jobs (see Figure 17.2). These researchers believed that workers must fully understand the nature of their positions and all that is required of them. Too often, people fail not because of lack of effort or ability, but because they do not know what is expected of them or how to achieve a sense of control or power in the organization (Ragins & Sundstrom, 1989). For example, an employee may burn a great deal of midnight

FIGURE 17.2

Expectancy Theories

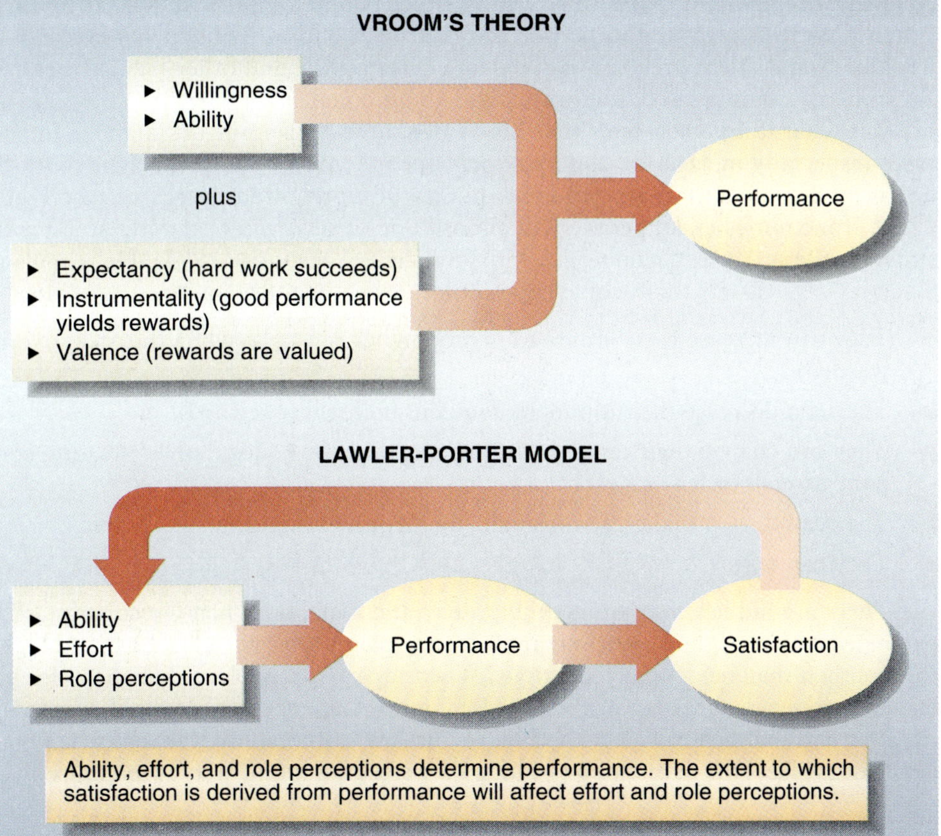

Ability, effort, and role perceptions determine performance. The extent to which satisfaction is derived from performance will affect effort and role perceptions.

oil, but if he or she has misread what it really takes to succeed in the organization, actual performance may be low.

Today, researchers claim that the motivation to work can be explained more by integrative theories that focus on goals, experiences, and thoughts (Locke & Latham, 1990a). Locke and Latham (1990b) assert that, if a high challenge is accompanied by high expectations for success, then high performance is likely; however, employees must also be committed to the goals of the company and be open to feedback. Success is also based on effort, persistence, and specific task strategies. When people are given incentives, when they think their contributions are important, and when the effort required of them is not excessive, productivity will be high (Shepperd, 1993). When performance is high, job satisfaction is likely; this in turn facilitates commitment to the organization and its goals.

Equity Theory. Being treated fairly is a prime concern for almost everyone. People want to be compensated for their work, to earn as much as they can, and most feel that they are worth more than they are paid. As radio personality Garrison Keillor implied when he described the inhabitants of Lake Wobegon, most people feel that they are "above average." But what happens when people feel that they are being unfairly treated? My psychology faculty colleagues all feel that they are underpaid, and I agree—there is not a single faculty member of my psychology department who earns what he or she should. Yet we are all treated fairly compared to one another, and our salaries are not too far out of line with those in the rest of the psychology departments in the United States.

In I/O psychology, **equity theory** asserts that what people bring to a work situation should be balanced by what they receive compared with other workers; thus, workers' input (what they bring or do) should be balanced by their compensation (what they receive). If input and compensation are not balanced, people will adjust their work level and potentially their job satisfaction accordingly. According to equity theories, each individual privately weighs the balance between input and compensation and compares this ratio to other people's input/compensation ratio. When the ratios are similar, people are relatively happy. Thus, if my colleagues' workloads and talent are compensated at a certain level and other faculty members are similarly compensated, their ratios are about equal.

But what if a person feels that his or her ratio is way out of balance? In such cases (especially in cases of underpayment) people may slow down their work behavior and gripe and groan, and the quality of work often decreases (see Figure 17.3). If inequities exist, people will choose one of several alternatives to alter the situation (Berg, 1991; Greenberg, 1990; Summers & Hendrix, 1991). Hellriegel and Slocum (1992) assert that people have choices when they feel an inequity exists:

- They can increase their inputs to justify higher rewards (when they feel overrewarded).
- They can decrease their inputs to compensate for low rewards.
- They can change their rewards through legal actions, illegal ones (stealing company assets), or leaving early.
- They can distort reality by rationalizing inequities, and thus feel better.
- They can quit.

There are hidden costs of inequity in pay and benefits. When Greenberg (1990) examined employee theft rates in manufacturing plants after pay cuts, he found higher rates of theft than before pay reductions. When supervisors explained the basis for pay cuts to workers, feelings became less bruised, ratios were not perceived as being so out of kilter, and the theft rate decreased. A key finding of this study was that when management explains the nature of pay shifts, the perception of inequity is minimized.

Equity theory: In I/O psychology, the theory that suggests that what people bring to a work situation should be balanced by what they receive compared with other workers; thus, input should be balanced by compensation, or rewards, or workers will adjust their work level and potentially their job satisfaction.

Motivation Management: Three Approaches. Recognizing the complexity of motivation management, I/O psychologists have developed three basic approaches

FIGURE 17.3

Equity Theory

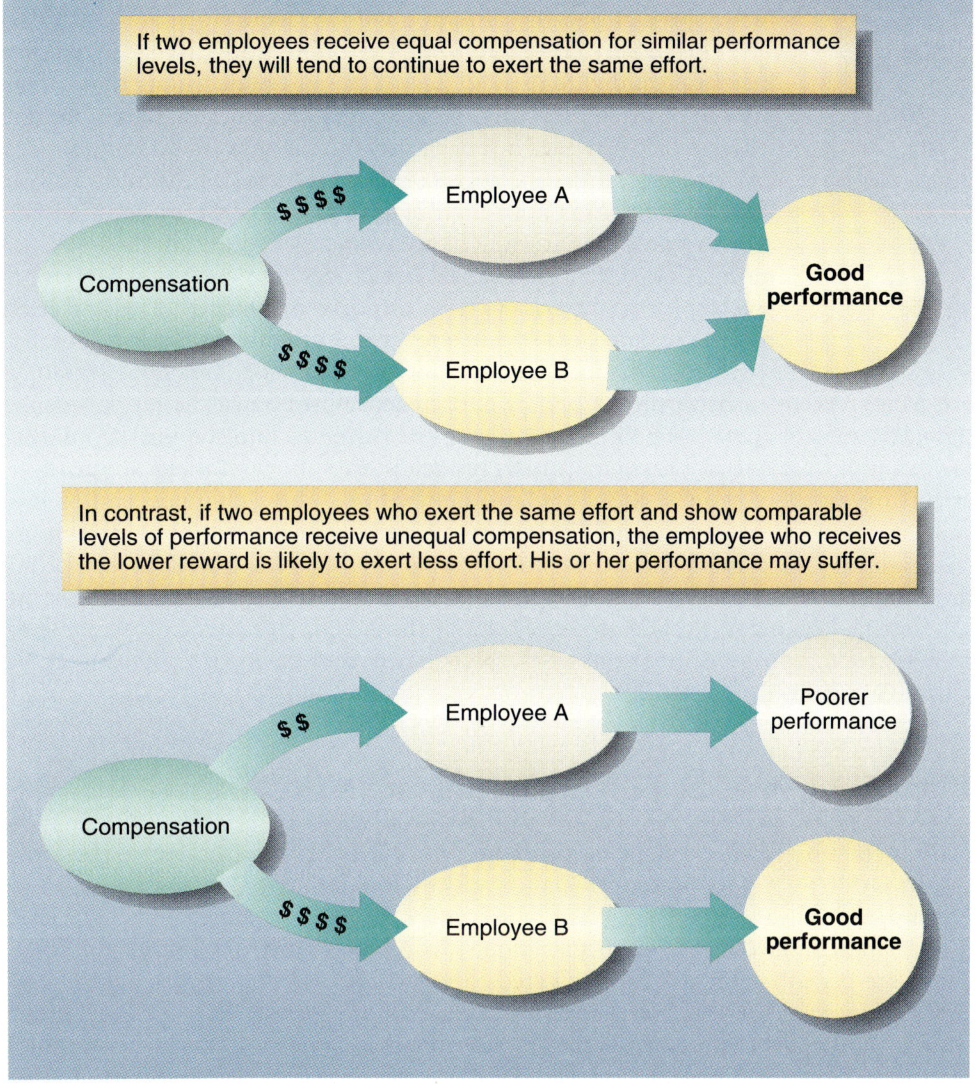

to motivation in the workplace: paternalistic, behavioral, and participatory. The fundamental idea of the *paternalistic approach* to motivation is that a company takes care of its employees' needs and desires in a fatherly manner. Early in this century, this approach was common in the mining companies of Appalachia and in the mills of Massachusetts, which provided housing, schools, recreation, and churches for employees. This approach is common today in some Japanese companies, which promote lifelong employment and support employees' needs, from recreation to drug rehabilitation. Nevertheless, such approaches are contrary to many American psychologists' views on behavior. Instrumental (operant) conditioning studies show that for a behavior (such as work) to be established and maintained—at least in Western cultures—reinforcement must be contingent on performance. In a paternalistic system all employees, productive as well as nonproductive, are given reinforcement if they fulfill their role as workers. Reinforcement without the need for performance does not encourage people to work hard, as equity theory predicts.

Behavioral approaches to motivation assume that people will work only if they receive tangible rewards for specific task performance. Examples include paying a

▲ *Quality circles, like this one at a plant in Tokyo, originated in Japan as a means of involving both workers and supervisors in improving the quality of production processes from the bottom up. These groups usually meet after working hours to identify, analyze, and solve quality issues.*

factory worker by the piece and a typist by the page. In such a system, hardworking employees obtain more rewards—commissions, salary increases, bonuses, and so on—because they produce more; but little attention is paid to the emotional needs of workers. In the long run, goal-setting theory and, to some extent, expectancy theory predict that this situation will not work.

The *participatory approach* to motivation is based on the belief that individuals who have a say in the decisions that affect their lives are motivated to work harder and smarter. Participation, it is argued, provides a setting in which managers and employees can exchange information to solve problems (Tjosvold, 1987). Supporters of this approach believe that a sense of competence and self-determination is likely to increase individuals' levels of motivation (Deci, 1975). *Quality circles*, in which workers at all levels meet to discuss ways to improve product quality and promote excellence, constitute one technique employers use to involve workers in the management process (Matsui & Onglatco, 1990).

Many variables affect the success of participatory programs: the work setting, the individuals involved, the kinds of decisions to be made, and the hiring policies, for example. When truly participatory approaches are followed, there are positive effects on workers' values, thoughts, and motivation. These changes lead to less conflict among workers, increased productivity, and better overall job performance (see Figure 17.4). When workers feel comfortable and involved with their work and their organization, they are more likely to be spontaneous, to help coworkers, to protect the organization, and so on. Many of these behaviors depend on the employee's feeling positive about the work environment and having a good attitude at work (George & Brief, 1992).

Job Satisfaction

Job satisfaction is different from job motivation. Motivation (the internal conditions that direct a person to act) is always shown in behavior; job satisfaction (a person's attitude about the work and workplace) may not be shown in behavior. A tired, bored, and overworked electrician may feel discouraged and angry—and may even hate her job—but still be motivated to work. Her motivation may stem from the high pay she receives, from her obligation to complete a job, or from some other source. Thus, although her job satisfaction is low, it does not affect her performance. In general, however, a satisfied worker is a high-performing worker who will remain in the organization. This is why I/O psychologists seek to identify the sources of job satisfaction.

There are probably more sources of job satisfaction than I can list here, but they tend to cluster in five basic categories. These categories, as well as examples of each, are summarized in Table 17.1 on page 616. They are the work itself, the perceived rewards of the work (which we just discussed), the quality of supervision, the support of coworkers, and the work setting. The overall level of satisfaction depends on the extent to which people feel their expectations for satisfaction are matched by their actual satisfaction. The closeness of that match, in turn, depends on various aspects of a job. People can be pleased or dissatisfied about hours, pay, client contact, and promotion opportunities, among other things (Algera, 1990). People have standards for comparison that determine the extent to which they feel they are doing well or poorly. As we saw earlier, in the discussion of equity theory, one of those standards is fairness; when people believe decisions, evaluations, and resource allocations are made fairly, their job satisfaction tends to be high. This finding is true for both men and women in many different settings (Witt & Nye, 1992).

FIGURE 17.4

The Participatory Approach to Motivation Leads to Increased Work Effectiveness

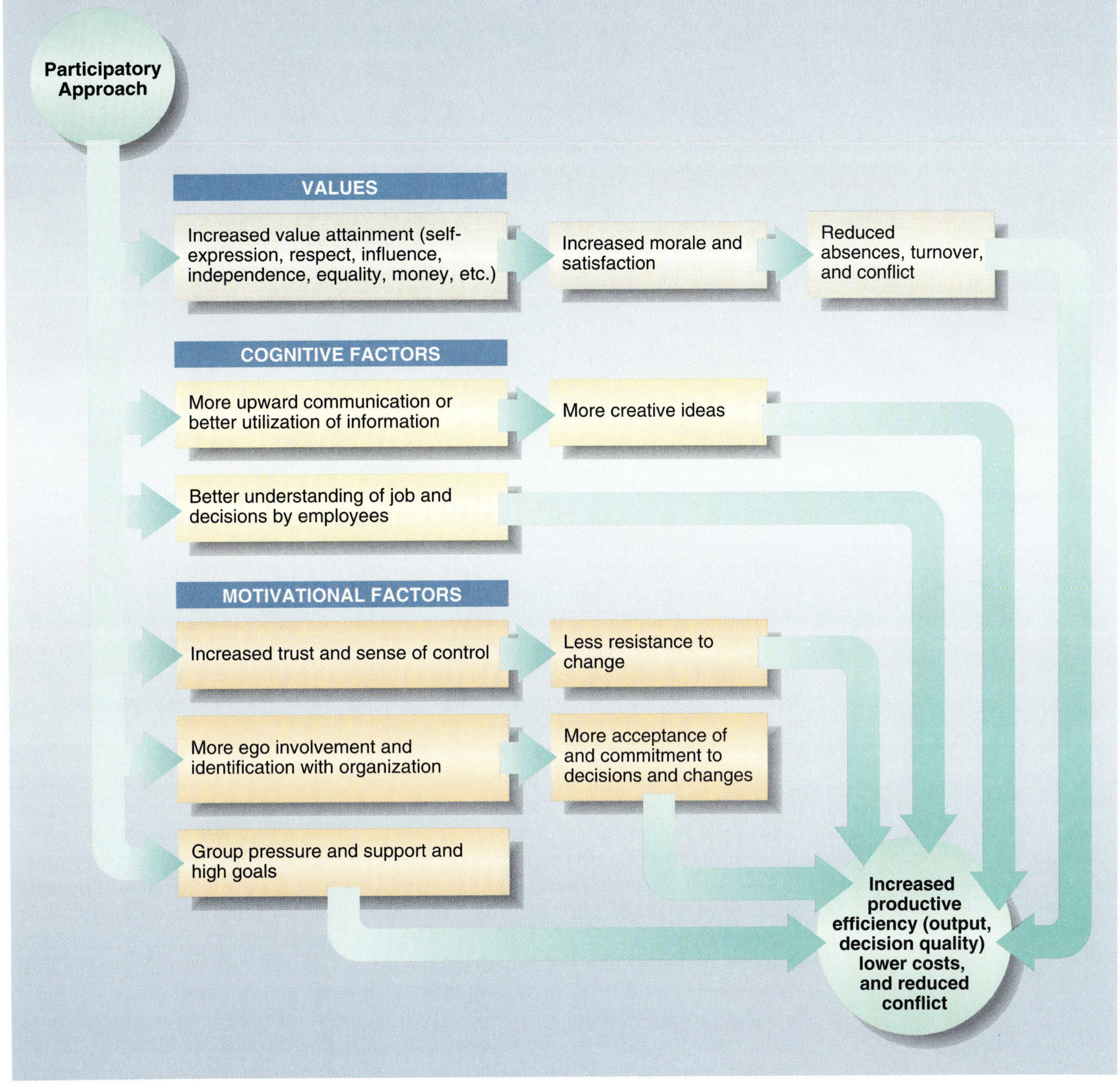

Leadership

In every organization, some individuals emerge as *leaders*—people who influence other people's behavior toward the attainment of agreed-upon goals. Informal leaders may emerge spontaneously in any group, or they may be formally chosen by higher management. Leaders are expected to help further the purposes of their organization. Thus, one of their primary roles is to persuade and motivate employees to

TABLE 17.1 *Key Factors Related to Job Satisfaction*

Area	Factors
The work itself	The work is interesting. The work is perceived to be challenging. There are opportunities to apply one's own judgment. There is some degree of autonomy.
Perceived rewards	There is adequate recognition. The pay is adequate and equitable. The work contributes to self-esteem and self efficacy. There are opportunities for advancement.
Quality of supervision	Supervisors offer encouragement, support, and help (Huebner, 1994).
Support from coworkers	There are opportunities to interact socially. Coworkers are supportive and compatible.
The work setting	There is job security. There are positive attitudes toward the work environment (it is seen as pleasant, attractive, and comfortable). There are opportunities to influence company policy and procedures. Adequate information and equipment is available.

perform at a high level. It is important to note, however, that not all managers are leaders; nor are all leaders managers. Truly effective leadership is so close to being an art that it should come as no surprise that I/O psychologists have studied it intensively in an effort to understand it. The study of leadership has gone through three major phases, each with a characteristic focus: traits, behaviors, or situations. The right combination of these elements ultimately describes an effective leader.

Trait Theories of Leadership. The specific personality traits of individual organizational leaders were studied intensively in the early 1950s and are receiving increased attention again. This research tries to isolate the characteristics that make individuals good or poor leaders; for example, are good leaders assertive, directive, or authoritarian? But the trait approach troubles some researchers. Leaders cannot be universally characterized by traits such as assertiveness, self-confidence, or drive. Many business leaders are assertive, but many others are not. In fact, individual differences among leaders are extreme. Although an individual leader's personality traits will tell psychologists something about leadership, the differences among leaders tend to be greater than the similarities. One reason that studies are unable to find a common denominator is that each leader and each organization has different goals. Today, researchers also recognize that a key, and sometimes defining, trait of effective business leaders is *flexibility*—the ability to adapt to a rapidly changing workplace, organization, and global economy.

Leadership Behaviors. Another focus of research in leadership is specific leadership behaviors. Many research studies try to find characteristic ways in which leaders interact with other members of their organizations. Some of the pioneering work on leadership was done at the University of Michigan's Institute for Social Research. The Michigan studies (as they are often called) found that business leaders tend to be either employee- or task-oriented. Whether a leader is employee- or task-oriented has to do with how the leader chooses to influence behavior. An employee-oriented leader acts so as to maintain and enhance individual employees' feelings of self-worth or self-esteem. Such leaders try to empower employees and coworkers and make them feel valued and important. A task-oriented leader focuses on getting the job done efficiently and quickly, with as little effort as possible.

Leadership styles are sometimes related to gender, with women being more employee-oriented and men more task-oriented (Eagly & Johnson, 1990). Recent studies show that the gender of the leader and of the followers has other important effects. For example, female leaders or managers tend to be evaluated as positively as their male counterparts. However, when they behave in stereotypically male ways, they are devalued—especially if the evaluators are men (Eagly, Makhijani, & Klonsky, 1992).

Further research has confirmed that behavioral differences among leaders are great and that a leader's behavior is determined by personal traits, by overall orientation (employee or task), and sometimes by the group of people being led. Some groups of individuals have characteristics that demand an employee orientation on the leader's part. For example, an underpaid, overworked, but dedicated social worker may have a great need for self-esteem, feel that his work is worthwhile, but also know that he is underpaid. A supervisor must motivate this person not with authoritarian task-oriented directions but with concern for his need for self-worth. Highly paid executives, however, may be more easily motivated by a task-oriented approach, because they recognize that their salaries reflect their higher levels of creativity and productivity. Job performance, job satisfaction, and the way a worker is treated are closely related. In motivating workers, leaders must consider their own personal traits, the various possible behaviors they might use to influence others, and the conditions in which they and their coworkers work.

Situational Leadership Theory. Many researchers have shifted from investigating leader behavior to investigating the *situations* in which these behaviors are performed. Some situations lend themselves to leadership, and even to specific forms of leadership; others call for little leadership. Thus, a warm, friendly, employee-oriented leader (or supervisor) is generally very useful for a group of service workers. But if the organization encounters financial trouble and its workers must be laid off, with the supervisor having no control over who is let go, the climate of uncertainty may undermine the usefulness of the warm and friendly approach. To continue functioning, the organization may then have to find a task-oriented leader who is trusted for his or her integrity and fairness.

Theories of Leadership Effectiveness. A complex interplay of factors determines the most effective style of leadership for different situations, even within one organization. Effective leaders may simply be those who are best at perceiving the goals and needs of their organization and fitting their style to those needs. Two major theories that try to account for leadership effectiveness are the *Fiedler contingency model* and *Vroom's leadership model.*

Fred Fiedler (1964, 1974) developed a contingency model of leadership that acknowledges that traits, behaviors, and situations can vary among individuals and over time and that effective leadership is contingent on all these factors. Fiedler's model assumes that there are numerous possible situations in which leaders may find themselves. Relationships between leaders and followers can be good or bad; tasks for the organization can be structured (or routine) or unstructured (or complex); and the leader's power can be weak or strong. A leader is obviously in a favorable position if he or she has good relations with employees, has a task that is structured, and is in a position of power. Fiedler developed scales for rating leadership ability and effectiveness and correlated them with the various possible situations. His results show that employee-oriented leaders have the best overall functioning, and that leaders who are task-oriented can have very effective organizations, but only in extremely favorable circumstances.

The key element of Fiedler's theory is that leaders can change their behavior according to the situation in which they find themselves and adopt the most effective leadership approach possible for that situation. Fiedler made a great inferential leap in assuming that a combination of factors affects leaders' behavior. Ultimately, his approach may not explain leadership, but it provides a solid theory with practical implications.

Unlike Fiedler, Vroom and Yetton focused on the various ways in which leaders may make decisions in organizations. In this leader-participation model, Vroom and Yetton laid out a flowchart for determining the amount of advice a leader should seek out, depending on the task to be accomplished. A leader can make an authoritarian decision and simply announce it; a leader can present a problem, solicit advice, and then make the final decision; or a leader can allow other people to make the decision. As a leader's use of authority increases, the freedom of others in the group decreases. That is, when a manager makes a decision and announces it, subordinates and coworkers have little freedom of choice; this style of leadership is called *boss-centered* (Vroom, 1974; Vroom & Yetton, 1973). According to Vroom's view, each time a decision is to be made, managers or leaders can ask themselves a series of questions to arrive the best possible leadership approach for the situation.

The strength of Vroom's model is that it recognizes that leaders have options—that they can choose how to behave in light of their own previous experiences and knowledge and on the basis of situations or conditions. Vroom's model has received some research support, but its practical implications in the workplace have not been evaluated systematically. Like Fiedler's model, it emphasizes the important role of situational variables in determining which leadership approach is most appropriate to a situation.

Bill Gates, the founder of Microsoft, may be an example of a transformational leader, since his influence can be felt at every level of that organization. Many younger managers at the company carry their Gates impressions almost to the point of caricature, using his slang and intonations in their own conversations. ▼

Transformational Leadership. If one person took an organization or company and provided it with direction, a new vision, and a sense of purpose, that person would be considered a first-rate leader. Such leaders are hard to find, but occasionally someone emerges who is considered charismatic, having extraordinary effects on followers. These leaders are often called **transformational leaders**; they provide inspiration, intellectual stimulation, and individual care to followers and are able to draw extra creativity and effort out of organization members (Bass, 1985, 1990). Often such individuals do not have formal authority based on their position; because of their personality, style, and interpersonal skills, however, they seem to be able to influence and empower others. Transformational leaders have a strong sense of moral purpose, have an aura of authority and dignity, and define people's roles in terms of their own ideological values. Such leaders often have a strong vision, use unconventional techniques or ideas, and communicate extreme confidence in their own abilities to lead and solve problems.

Transformational leaders often take advantage of organizational weaknesses, and create opportunities to re-create, or transform, an organization and its employees or constituents. This occurs when the charismatic leader can distinguish the forest from the trees well enough to give individuals help and courage to reach and achieve heretofore unthought-of goals. Such leaders are often able to create a willingness on the part of employees to go along with their ideas and a reluctance to criticize their ideas or them (Deluga, 1990). When such an individual operates within the context of an organization, the organization often becomes something new. New values, ideas, and ways of operating are adopted by the members of the organization (Howell & Avolio, 1993). When new values are adopted, new levels of performance are often expected.

Transformational leader: Charismatic leader who inspires and provides intellectual stimulation to re-create an organization.

Transformational leadership is hard to create and generally is seen as competing with traditional values in organizations that focus on profits, personnel, productivity, and cost-efficiency. Transformational leaders, many feel, are born, not made, and are individually unique. But contrary arguments are made by some researchers, who assert that transformational skills can be learned (Hackman & Johnson, 1991) and that men and women are both quite capable of being effective transformational leaders (Hackman et al., 1992).

Psychologists' knowledge of how people influence and manage others has grown dramatically. Researchers now know that effective leadership depends not only on personal traits and on specific techniques or behaviors, but also on the situation. Workers may exaggerate the leadership effectiveness of a boss if their environment is productive and they are happy (Shamir, 1992). Thus, leadership, workers' perceptions of leadership, and motivation are interrelated.

So what goes into effective leadership? Sensitivity to worker motivation, satisfaction, and performance can help a leader set solid personnel selection policies. Good selection procedures help establish a favorable working situation, and a favorable situation makes for better leadership possibilities. Better leadership, in turn, may make workers more productive and more satisfied. Through carefully conducted I/O research, psychologists can help organizations more effectively meet their own goals by seeking out effective leaders who can persuade, motivate, build confidence, and create a better workplace with more satisfied workers and stockholders (Hogan, Curphy, & Hogan, 1994).

FOCUS

Review

- What are the goals of selection procedures and training efforts in today's workplace? pp. 604–606
- Identify and differentiate three theories of motivation management. pp. 613–614
- Describe key elements of transformational leadership. p. 618

Think Critically

- What are the motivational implications of the fact that jobs increasingly require more cognitive than physical skills?
- Many companies have relaxed their dress codes to allow more casual modes of dress. If you were running a large multinational corporation, what would your stance on workplace dress codes be? Why?
- If you were setting up your own company, what approach would you use to motivate your workers? Would you be the paternalistic boss, would you set objectives to be met, or would you let workers participate in decision making?
- How can leaders meet the goals of their organizations and at the same time attempt to be transformational leaders creating new and different organizations? Are these goals mutually contradictory?

Human Factors and Ergonomics

When I stand at an ATM, I often recall how frustrating it used to be to see a teller in a bank and wait in line for 10 minutes. At first, banks designed more efficient, roped-off waiting lines. Now, I can bank at my convenience with a machine. In addition, from my phone at home I can check my balance, move money between accounts, and pay bills—all rather easily. Applied psychologists who study human factors have played an important role in streamlining banking experiences as well as many other day-to day routines. Donald Norman, a psychologist who has studied applied issues, wrote a best-selling book that I regularly recommend to my students: *Design of Everyday Things* (1990). Entertaining and enlightening reading, it focuses on how clever machines are making life easier.

Human factors is the study of the relationship of human beings to machines and to workplaces and other environments. A human factors psychologist might focus on the creation of health-care products for use by the handicapped, on the design of cooking utensils or educational products, or on the interaction of robots and people. Most human factors research focuses on the work environment, especially in the areas of efficiency and safety.

Human factors: The study of the relationship of human beings to machines and to workplaces and other environments.

Efficiency

In the work environment, researchers have examined workers' ability to operate machines effectively. Much of this research centers on **ergonomics**—the study of the fit between human anatomy or physiology, the demands of a particular task or piece of equipment, and the environment in which the task occurs. Human factors researchers seek to develop person–machine interfaces that minimize frustration and errors, maximize output, and are reliable. Such researchers have focused on studying machines and interfaces to ensure that speed and accuracy of work are optimized and that workplaces minimize fatigue and stress (Sanders & McCormick, 1993).

A key difference between a human factors researcher and an I/O psychologist is that the I/O researcher might examine what can be done to the human being to change his or her behavior to improve efficiency. A human factors researcher, on the other hand, will look at what can be changed about the machine, computer, or interface. It is often easier to change a machine than to change a human being!

In the early part of this century, working with machinery meant reading dials, turning wheels, and lifting equipment. Human factors researchers then focused on creating machine–human interfaces that required as little energy as possible and resulted in as few errors as possible on the part of the machine operator. Today, working with machinery often means operating a computer, monitoring computer-controlled devices, programming equipment, and working in teams with other highly skilled employees. To a great extent, *controlling* equipment, rather than operating it, has become a focus of human factors research. If equipment is to be properly controlled, dials, computer screens, and display devices have to be designed to minimize errors. For example, a pilot must be able to read a computer screen accurately, under all possible conditions, in order to land a plane safely; a nuclear power plant operator must be able to read the temperature of nuclear devices. The design of computer display screens has thus dominated recent research in human factors (Howell, 1993).

Computer displays are everywhere. You often type at a computer, pay a restaurant check at a computer-controlled cash register, and bank at automated teller machines, ATMs. Well-designed machines and computer interfaces minimize errors; but the ability to create good interfaces depends on knowledge of how human beings see, manipulate, and interact with the machine. This means studying perception, human information processing, and complex decision making. The ATM is an example of an interface that has been studied well by human factors researchers. My local bank has an ATM that is easy to operate—I have never made a mistake there. But the ATM at a bank next door to mine has a confusing, gaudy interface, and I have seen many users kick, curse, and lose their cards. It is usually the human factors psychologist who can take the credit for a well-designed interface that minimizes errors, confusion, and angry customers.

Computer screens are important, but displays are only one part of the study of human factors. Workers are also increasingly dependent on one another to get a task done in today's workplace, so there has been increased emphasis on social factors in the workplace. For example, researchers are studying interactions of pilots and navigators in the cockpit, in addition to the instrumentation displays they use.

Many jobs are complex and require advanced technology. In industries such as auto manufacturing, for instance, robotic equipment has been programmed to do many tasks that human beings once did. These devices must be designed effectively to duplicate the abilities of human beings. Much of the work of robotics engineers is dedicated to making sure that robots are both effective and safe.

Even the tools of carpenters, tailors, and technicians can be designed using the principles of human factors. For example, what is the best weight for a hammer? How tall should a drill press be? Can the design of sewing machines, computers, and robotic controls take into account the size of an operator's hand? Today, Apple

Ergonomics: The study of the fit between human anatomy or physiology, the demands of a particular task or piece of equipment, and the environment in which the task occurs.

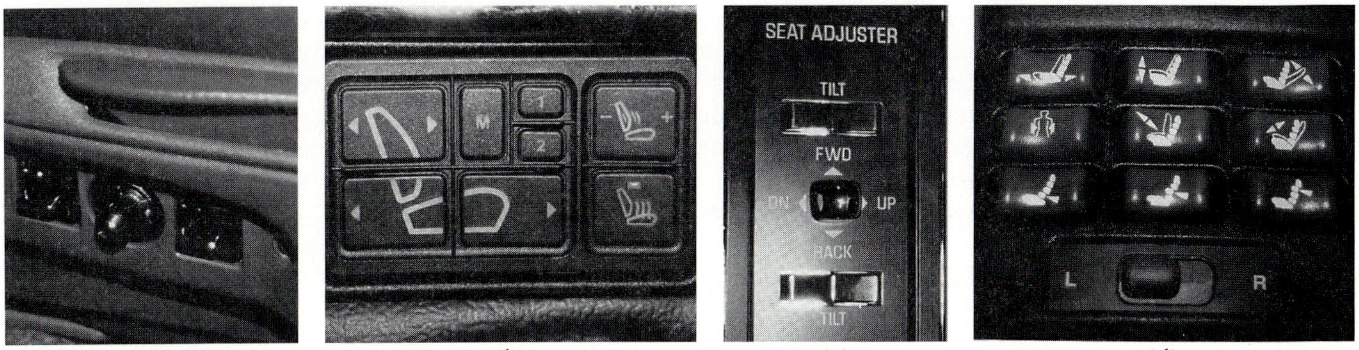

(a) (b) (c) (d)

▲ *If equipment is to be operated properly, control devices must be designed to be clear and easy to use. All of these controls operate automobile seats, but not all are equally well designed. From a human factors point of view, the controls in photo (b) are the most effective; those in photo (d), the least effective.*

Computer ships keyboards that have been designed to be easy to type on, to minimize typing errors, and to reduce carpal tunnel syndrome. These keyboards are split in the center, with the two parts angled in different directions. The human factors psychologists at Apple are convinced that they have designed a keyboard that meets the important human factors considerations of accuracy, productivity, and safety.

Safety

Human factors research can provide a work environment that is not only efficient but also safe. Many industrial accidents occur despite attempts to protect workers' safety; human factors research can help reduce accidents through design improvements. Human factors psychologists can also help estimate how quickly people become fatigued and lose accuracy and then can design work schedules that optimize the safe use of equipment—especially of potentially dangerous equipment. Such psychologists can help promote safety through programs that improve people's attitudes about safety and therefore promote safer work behavior. Only when workers believe that safety is valued and personally desirable are they likely to make safety-promoting changes

It is often easier to design a safe, or nearly safe, work environment than to influence workers to work safely. Researchers classify efforts to design safe work environments in three categories (Sanders & McCormick, 1993). *Exclusion designs* make it impossible for a specific error to occur; *prevention designs* make it difficult though not impossible for an error to happen; and *fail-safe designs* do not reduce the likelihood of an accident, but lessen its consequences should it occur. For a nuclear power plant, human factors psychologists might develop prevention designs that greatly decrease the likelihood of a nuclear accident (or so they hope). In efforts to ensure safe work environments, the federal government has invoked legislation; the Occupational Safety and Health Act (OSHA) has established standards for health and safety in the workplace that act as prevention designs. These fall short of exclusion designs, of course, because establishing standards is easier than enforcing them. Workers must accept safety standards before they can be effective, and the government really does not have an adequate staff to regulate, enforce, or inspect all places of business. Since OSHA was enacted, however, the death rate from workplace accidents has been cut in half.

Research in an array of other subdisciplines in psychology helps to establish and maintain workplace safety. *Perceptual research* investigates light levels that are appropriate for reading computer screens. Which color is most easily seen in the dark? (Yellow.) Is it easier to see white letters on a dark background, or the reverse? (White letters on dark backgrounds are easier.) *Environmental research* (which we will examine in more detail later) has focused on efficiency and safety when looking at variables such as temperature and noise. When temperature or noise is too high, performance decreases. Moderate, comfortable temperatures, and machine-related noise levels that are not too distracting, improve not only efficiency but also safety. Environmental research also reveals that signs and warnings help motivate people to follow regulations. Specific instructions that are personalized for a user—for example, using that person's name as part of the instructions—work better still. If the user has to do something before using a machine, such as remove a warning label first, labels are especially effective (Duffy, Kalsher, & Wogalter, 1993). Even if people can attend to specific warnings about equipment safety and even if they are given clear directions, incentives and proper reinforcements must be put into play to ensure compliance; this is the domain of learning and social psychologists, who study how reinforcements and social influence can be used to induce worthwhile and helpful behaviors.

Warnings, labels, and compliance techniques are all helpful in establishing safety. These efforts constitute a form of outreach that has been successful in improving the efficiency and safety of the workplace.

FOCUS

Review

- What is an effective technique to ensure that people will take safety measures when using equipment? p. 622

Think Critically

- Why do you think some businesses have been slow to adopt safety measures? What can psychologists do to help convince business leaders that it is in their best interest to improve safety?

Psychology and the Law

In the workplace, as elsewhere, the laws that govern society help regulate both public and private behavior. Laws determine, among other things, how people make fair hiring or firing decisions and how old individuals have to be to work in the first place. To some extent, laws determine whom people can marry and when. People's thoughts and behaviors shape laws, and laws in turn shape people's behaviors; there is a reciprocal relationship in which each affects the other. The interface between the law and psychology is thus as complex as are people and the legal system.

Psychologists play several roles in the legal system: researchers, policy or program evaluators, advocates, and expert witnesses. As *researchers*, they help determine why individuals behave in ways that are unacceptable to society. For instance, psychologists do basic research in intelligence, personality, mathematical ability, and the role of genetics in determining aggressiveness, to name just a few areas. This basic research often helps solve some very practical problems. For example, some psychologists develop tests to determine who is mentally ill and who is capable of standing trial, as well as tests to evaluate truthfulness and integrity among defendants and witnesses. Other psychologists look for the causes of aggressiveness in order to develop programs to avert it among accused criminals and to help convicted criminals channel their aggressive energy productively.

Psychologists often serve as *policy or program evaluators,* who help governments and other institutions determine whether various policies, agencies, or programs actually work. For example, psychologists interpret what remedial education has accomplished and whether IQ testing has been valid. When legislators wondered whether Head Start programs were making a difference, they turned to psychologists. When new laws calling for equal educational opportunities for the handicapped were being considered, lawyers and judges turned to psychologists for insight into how well various programs might work.

Psychologists are also often asked to be *advocates* for individuals and society, helping to shape social policy in such areas as minority, remedial, and gifted education. When state and federal governments seek to trim budgets of social programs affecting children, they turn to psychologists to ascertain what the impact for the future might be. Boards of education consult psychologists to determine how best to mainstream exceptional students. Psychologists advise government agencies at all levels on how to help those who suffer posttraumatic stress after a flood, earthquake, or other disaster and on how to respond more effectively to such disasters in the future.

Finally, psychologists often serve as *expert witnesses*, bringing their knowledge to the courts as consultants. They do not try to address legal issues directly or to make the ultimate decisions for the courts. Psychologists help the courts in their area of competence—psychology. Psychologists have often been asked to determine who is a good eyewitness (we examined such studies in Chapter 6). They also address specific questions like these: "Is this person insane?" "What are the implications of a divorce on this child?" "Is this woman competent to stand trial?"

Psychologists can help determine whether there was any link between a person's mental state or problem and a crime that occurred. From a legal standpoint, a person who deliberately plans a crime is more accountable than one who accidentally commits one. In many states, when an accused person is convicted of a serious crime, a jury can judge the person "guilty, but mentally ill." This verdict is seen by many as a reasonable alternative because it reduces the number of outcomes of "not guilty by reason of insanity" (a finding that many find unsatisfying), encourages treatment for the seriously mentally ill, and takes a potentially dangerous offender off the street.

There is, of course, an uneasy alliance between the legal and the psychological professions (Melton et al., 1987). Lawyers assert that psychology is an inexact, or "fuzzy," science and that psychologists should not be allowed to testify as expert witnesses. Psychologists argue that lawyers always want simple answers to complicated human questions and insist on seeking facts even when theories may best describe the truth. In the area of child custody, for example, psychologists are asked to testify in a divorce settlement as to who would be the best custodian of the children and what the psychological consequences of living with one parent or the other will be for a child. Yet, because the legal system is adversarial, each side is likely to have a psychologist testifying that the children will do best with the parent who hired him or her. In fact, there may be no right or wrong answer in some cases. Further research into the relationship between the law and psychology will help. However, the fact is that answers to various legal questions are not always clear and definitive—this is especially true when psychologists look at environmental issues.

Environmental Psychology

Two years ago, a toxic waste spill contaminated a stream that flowed into a small lake in my neighborhood. Children occasionally swim in this lake, and people regularly catch fish there. The reaction of the neighborhood was swift; people became alarmed about their health and welfare. Signs went up warning people to stay away from the lake, and property owners began to worry about the value of their homes.

My neighbors feared cancer and worried about monetary losses from the disintegration of their community. The phone lines hummed, the press was brought in, and the local environmental control agency sprang into action. In the end, the spill turned out to be very localized, the levels of toxins were low, and no one was hurt. There were some small legal claims against the chemical company that had spilled the waste. From an applied psychologist's point of view, however, the mobilization of the residents in my neighborhood was classic. In a neighborhood group, people became empowered; discussions ensued, and people were energized. Individuals who had never met one another started sharing ideas, and people who had never given much thought to hazardous waste became knowledgeable and outspoken on the subject.

A particular group of applied psychologists, known as environmental psychologists, study how physical settings such as people's homes and neighborhoods affect behavior. They are interested in such issues as the effects of crowding, how personal space can be changed to meet changing needs, and group reactions to environmental threats. These psychologists examine not only whole neighborhoods but also smaller groups. **Environmental psychology** is the study of how physical settings affect human behavior and how people change their environment, often to make it more comfortable and acceptable. Environmental psychologists focus on the human interactions with the environment; they recognize that people are affected by the environment in which they live, work, and play and that the environment is affected by human behavior. Today, the field of environmental psychology has expanded to embrace the idea that human beings affect and to a great extent can control environmental quality for future generations. Behavioral interventions are now being designed to preserve and protect the environment (e.g., Dwyer et al., 1993; Porter, Leeming, & Dwyer, 1995). Because of the large number of variables that enter into studies in environmental psychology, the field has become a multidisciplinary one, encompassing research from many other fields, such as architecture, geography, and sociology (Stokols, 1995).

Environmental psychologists often conduct studies and consult for institutions, such as governments, schools, hospitals, and churches. For example, consider the design of a nursing station in a hospital. The station is the center of activity on each floor, and in traditional hospital floor plans it is usually placed at the junction of two long corridors. An alternative is to place it at the hub of a wheellike arrangement of rooms (a radial design). Most of the patient rooms will then be closer to the nursing station, and nurses can reach them faster and more efficiently. When Trites and his coworkers (1970) investigated worker satisfaction with different hospital designs, they found a distinct preference for the radial design. That result led to the redesigning of many hospital floors (Proshansky & O'Hanlon, 1977).

Environmental Variables

The environment includes not only the shape of a building, the layout of a hospital floor or a dormitory, or the arrangement of buildings in a housing development or shopping mall. It also includes such variables as furniture and fixtures, climate, noise level, and the number of people per square foot. Environmental psychologists study the relationships among the many variables. Whether a room is perceived as crowded, for example, depends not only on the number of people in it but also on the room's size and shape, furniture layout, ceiling height, number of windows, wall colors, and lighting—as well as on the time of day. Researchers who look at global environmental systems such as cities, communities, and neighborhoods must consider all these variables and more. Three of the environmental variables that are easiest to control in order to promote people's well-being are temperature, noise, and environmental toxins.

Temperature. Very hot or very cold climates can cause behavioral effects that range from annoyance to inability to function. New England industrial workers, for example, would never survive the winter without proper shelter, heating, and warm clothes; and Southern workers would be far less productive without air conditioning during the summer.

Environmental variables that impair work performance are considered stressors. As we saw in Chapter 13, a **stressor** is a stimulus that affects an organism in physically or psychologically injurious ways and usually elicits feelings such as anxiety, tension, and physiological arousal. Temperature can be a stressor that affects many behaviors, including academic performance, driving an automobile, and being attracted toward others. In general, performance is optimal at moderate temperatures and becomes progressively worse at high or low temperatures.

Environmental psychology: The study of how physical settings affect human behavior and how people change their environment.

Stressor: A stimulus that affects an organism in physically or psychologically injurious ways and usually elicits feelings such as anxiety, tension, and physiological arousal.

When the temperature rises and people become uncomfortable, they are more likely to make risky decisions and to behave erratically and less likely to be accurate (Kudoh et al., 1991). Research shows that as temperature rises, aggression increases. In hotter regions of the world, people show more aggression; hotter years, months, and days have all been associated with more aggressive behaviors, such as murders, riots, and wife beatings (C. A. Anderson, 1989). Laboratory research on temperature can never be identical to situations in a real-life setting; therefore, ongoing field-based work is likely to provide better evidence about the exact nature of a relationship between heat and aggression (Anderson & DeNeve, 1992; Bell, 1992).

Noise. Another environmental variable that often affects human behavior is *noise*—unwanted sound. Noise is a stressor that can overstimulate people—they become uncommonly aroused—and often leads to poor work performance and social functioning.

Some noises are almost always present: the buzzing of fluorescent lights, the humming of refrigerators, the banging of doors as they open or close, the chirping of birds, the engine sounds of moving cars, and the murmur of people talking. Although some of these sounds may be unwanted, they are usually not too disruptive; nor are they stressors. They rarely raise levels of arousal or interfere with daily activities.

However, an unpredictable and intermittent noise of moderate intensity, such as a train whistle, can impair performance on tasks that involve sustained attention or memory. And if noise raises physiological arousal to very high levels, it may impair performance in general and even cause hearing damage (see Chapter 3). Thus, noise acts as a stressor when it interferes with communication, raises physiological arousal, or is so loud that it causes pain. More commonly, noise simply interferes with the ability to concentrate, learn, and remember—thus, it induces stress (Evans, Hygge, & Bullinger, 1995).

Environmental Toxins (Pollutants). As you drive into a congested city such as Los Angeles, Detroit, or New York, it is distressing to see how the skyline is at once beautiful and polluted with airborne toxins. Cities continue to become more congested; crowding continues to be a problem; people continue to drive big gas-guzzling cars; industry continues to develop new products made from new chemicals. Adding to all of this is the array of chemicals and substances such as carbon monoxide and sulfur that fill the air from automobiles and from the burning of high-sulfur coal and oil in industrial cities. Nearly any airborne substance, whether an industry-based chemical or a naturally occurring substance such as pollen, can trigger respiratory problems and result in deleterious work performance and health consequences. Airborne toxins, which are often deeply breathed and absorbed by the lungs, can impair motor tasks that involve reaction time, as well as affect long-term health; for example, even in cities that meet federal standards for clean air, the risk of premature death is 3 to 8 percent higher than in the cleanest areas.

While smokestacks have been made taller and in some communities have even been banned, the automobile is not becoming any less common. Thus waste and pollution continue to be major urban problems. One pollutant that has received enormous attention in the last few years has been cigarette smoke. This pollutant of restaurants, bars, and the urban workplace has come under great criticism because of the damaging effects of secondhand smoke; increasingly, local governments are making buildings smoke-free.

Crowding

Another environmental variable is simply the number of people. In some situations that involve many people, you may feel closed in and crowded. In other situations, the excitement of a crowd may be exhilarating. It is generally not the size of a space or the number of people that causes you to feel crowded; rather, **crowding** is the

Crowding: The perception that one's space is too restricted.

perception that your space is too limited. Thus, crowding is a psychological state. One person may feel crowded and uncomfortable in a mall filled with Christmas shoppers; someone else may feel that the throngs create a happy holiday ambiance.

Personal Space. Crowding is affected by both social density and spatial density. *Social density* is the number of people in a given space; *spatial density* is the amount of space allocated to a fixed number of people. For example, in an empty theater, a person might feel lonely; but in a full, or even half-full, theater, the person might feel crowded (social density). In contrast, eight people may feel comfortable in a large modern elevator, but the same eight people might feel intolerably cramped in a small old-fashioned elevator (spatial density). Researchers must be careful to separate the variables of social and spatial density (Baum, 1987).

A study on the effects of architectural design in dormitories was done in 1973 by Valins and Baum. The dormitories were of two designs: (1) corridors with long hallways, 2 people per room, 34 people per floor, and a shared bathroom and lounge; or (2) suites, with 4 or 6 students sharing a bathroom and lounge, and several suites per floor (see Figure 17.5). The actual square footage per student was about the same in both types of dormitories; but 67 percent of corridor residents found their living space crowded, compared with only 25 percent of suite residents. Corridor residents reported too many people on their floor and too many unwanted interactions. Valins and Baum (1973) concluded that corridor designs promoted "excessive social interaction and that such interaction is associated with the experience of crowding" (p. 249).

If some dormitories produce feelings of crowding, as Valins and Baum have suggested, these feelings should be evident in people's behavior. In a classic study, Bickman and colleagues (1973) compared the helping behavior shown by students living in housing of different densities. They used a measure called the *lost-letter technique*, in which unmailed letters were purposely dropped in dormitory corridors. They reasoned that someone finding the letter would assume that a person in the dormitory had dropped it by mistake on the way to the mailbox.

The dependent variable was the number of "lost" letters that were subsequently mailed. The independent variable was the density of housing. The experiment involved

FIGURE 17.5

The Psychological Effects of Architectural Design

A corridor dorm and a suite have different psychological effects on students, even when actual space per student is about the same. Valins and Baum reported that students living in corridor dorms complained about being crowded more than students living in suites did. (Based on Valins & Baum, 1973.)

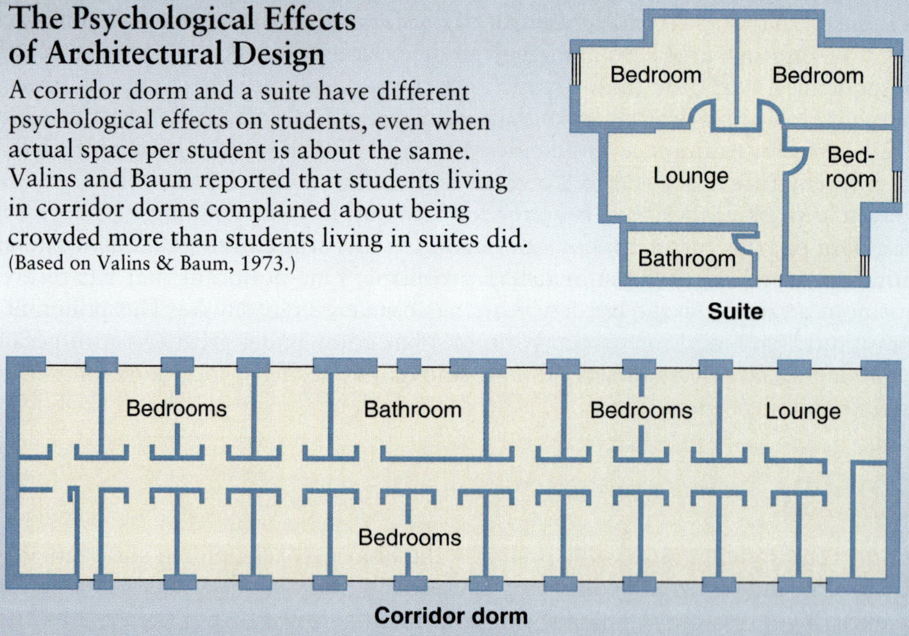

high-density dormitories (high-rise, 22-story towers, each housing more than 500 students), medium-density dorms (4- to 7-story buildings, each housing about 165 students), and low-density dorms (2- to 4-story buildings, with about 58 students each). Letters were left unobtrusively in areas near stairwells and elevators, with no more than one letter per corridor. The letters were addressed, sealed, and stamped but had no return address.

The results showed that helping behavior was 63 percent in high-density dorms, 87 percent in medium-density dorms, and 100 percent in low-density dorms. And when questionnaires were distributed to the students in the various dorms, the answers generally reflected attitudes related to the kind of housing in which the students lived. For example, students in high-density dorms reported feeling less trust, cooperativeness, and responsibility than did students in the lower-density dorms. The researchers concluded that students living in the higher-density dormitories behaved in a less socially responsible manner toward other dormitory residents. Baum believes that in situations of high density, people feel stressed, out of control, and crowded. All of this contributes to potential problems in situations of high density—for example, in prisons (Fleming, Baum, & Weiss, 1987).

Although many of the effects of crowding are not consistent across all situations or populations, certain effects seem to be universal. In high-density situations, people feel stressed and sometimes overaroused. They may feel alone or anonymous, and they may withdraw from the situation. They may become apathetic, may exhibit impaired task performance, and may even become hostile. Maintaining a sense of control and of personal space seems to be a crucial variable (Evans, Lepore, & Shroeder, 1996; Ruback & Pandey, 1991).

Personal Space and Culture. To help assert their individuality and maintain a sense of personal control, human beings generally try to establish appropriate degrees of personal space. **Personal space** is the area or invisible boundary around an individual that the person considers private. Encroachment on that space causes displeasure and often withdrawal.

The size of your personal space can change, depending on the situation and the people near you. For example, you may walk arm in arm with a family member, but you will avoid physical contact with a stranger. You may stand close to a friend and whisper in his ear, but you will keep a certain distance from an elevator operator or a store clerk.

Anthropologist Edward Hall (1966) suggested that personal space is a mechanism by which people communicate with others. He proposed that people adhere to established norms of personal space that are learned in childhood. Hall also observed that the use of personal space varies from culture to culture. In the United States, especially in suburban and rural areas, people are used to large homes and generous personal space. In Japan, on the other hand, where there is little space available per person, people are used to small homes that provide little personal space. In general, Western cultures insist on a fair amount of space for people, reserving proximity for intimacy and close friends, while Arab cultures allow much smaller distances between strangers (Rustemli, 1991).

To explain the concept of personal space in the United States, Hall classified four *spatial zones*, or distances, used in social interactions with other people. The distances are intimate, personal, social, and public. An *intimate distance* (from 0 to 18 inches) is reserved for people who have great familiarity with one another. It is acceptable for comforting someone who is hurt, for lovers, for physicians, and for athletes. The closeness enables a person to hold another person, examine the other's hair and eyes, and hear the other's breath. An acceptable distance for close friends and everyday interactions is *personal distance* (1.5 to 4 feet). It is the distance used for most social interactions. At 1.5 to 2 feet, someone might tell a secret to a close friend. At 2 feet, people can walk and talk together. At 2 to 4 feet, a person can maintain good contact with a coworker without seeming too personal or too impersonal. *Social distance* (4 to 12 feet) is used for business and for interactions with

Personal space: The area around an individual that is considered private and around which the person feels an invisible boundary.

FIGURE 17.6

People's Use of Personal Space When Seated and Standing

(Based on Altman & Vinsel, 1977.)

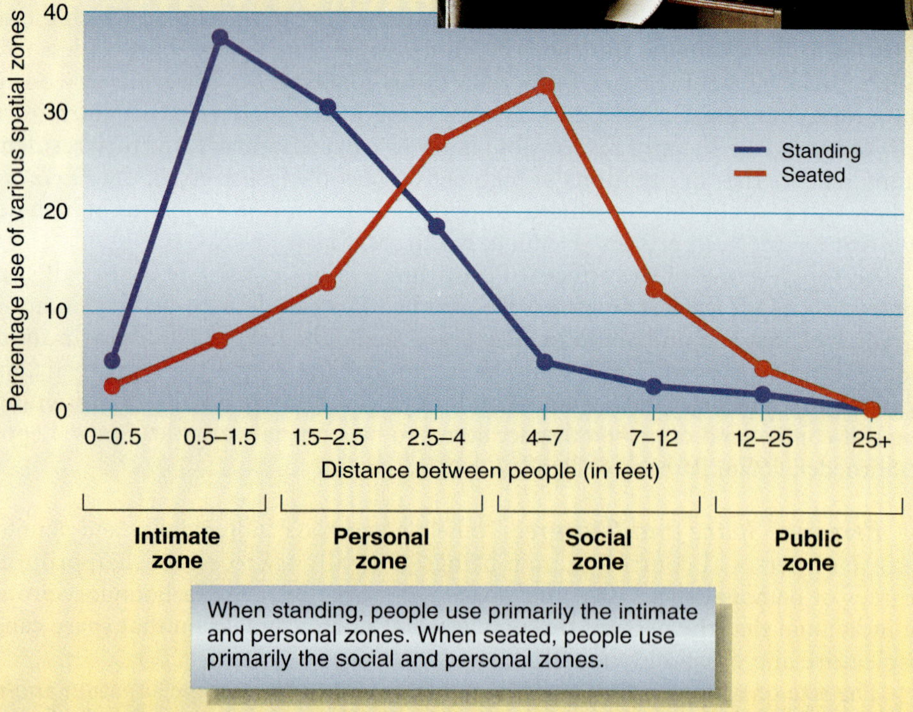

strangers. At 4 to 6 feet, people are close enough to communicate their ideas effectively but far enough away to remain separated. Personal space in the social zone may be controlled by physical barriers, such as a desk to separate a clerk, receptionist, or boss from the people with whom the person interacts. *Public distance* (12 to 25 feet or more) minimizes personal contact. It is the distance at which politicians speak at lunch clubs, teachers instruct classes of students, and actors and musicians perform. Public distance is sufficiently great to eliminate personal interaction between individuals and their audiences.

Of course, determining personal space is a tricky endeavor, and researchers are trying to sort out distance estimations (Zakay, Hayduk, & Tsal, 1992). Figure 17.6 presents generally accepted estimates of the spaces people use when seated and when standing.

Territoriality. Irwin Altman (1975) has suggested that the key to understanding why people feel crowded and need personal space is privacy. **Privacy** is the result of the process of controlling boundaries between people so that access is limited. Everyone needs privacy. According to Altman, privacy allows people to develop and nurture a sense of self. Without it, people feel they have no control over who and what can intrude on them. This sense of helplessness can lead to low self-esteem and poor social adaptations. Understanding people's need for privacy is central to understanding the behavior of human beings in their environment.

Privacy: The result of the process of controlling the boundaries between people so that access is limited.

One way in which people maintain a sense of privacy is to change their immediate environment. When a teenage girl goes into a room and closes the door, she closes herself off from other people; she limits their access to her. The teenager has set up a boundary—a closed door—behind which she can do what she wants when she wants to. Similarly, two people may enter a room and close the door, thereby controlling other people's access to them.

Maintaining a sense of privacy is closely related to territoriality, another important aspect of many people's lives. **Territorial behavior** is behavior involved in establishing, maintaining, personalizing, and defending a delineated space. It helps regulate the exclusive use of a specific area by a person or a group of people by marking a space as a private area where intruders are not welcome. Homeowners put up fences and signs reading "No Trespassing," teenagers lock their bedroom doors, street gangs defend their turf, and nations wage war in defense of their national boundaries. Like personal space behaviors, territorial behaviors are privacy-regulating mechanisms.

Preserving the Environment

Elementary school children often come home from special school programs reminding parents of the need to recycle, reuse, and cut back on waste. Starting with the youngest, people are being encouraged to do their part to preserve this fragile planet. An emerging area of environmental research focuses on doing something to actually control people's behavior in the environment. For example, research studies by Scott Geller at Virginia Polytechnic Institute found that littering can be significantly reduced if instructions for proper disposal of objects are provided; the more specific the instructions, the less littering occurs (Geller, 1975; Geller, Witmer, & Tuso, 1977).

Another area of research seeks the variables that make people want to preserve the environment. Aside from their children's reminders, what makes people want to conserve energy and reduce pollution by driving smaller, more fuel-efficient cars and investing in solar panels for their homes? Research on these issues has shown that tax laws that reward energy savings, signs about energy conservation, and new energy-saving equipment help people adopt more energy-saving behaviors. As with littering, when people are given specific energy-saving instructions and prompts, they are more likely to comply (Geller, Winett, & Evertt, 1982).

Some tremendous worldwide environmental problems must be solved. Geller (1989) suggests that marketing principles be combined with behavioral analysis to solve such problems as preserving the earth's rain forests and managing waste. First, environmentally beneficial ideas and behaviors must be advanced; this helps move people to at least intend to engage in such behaviors (Stasson & Fishbein, 1990). Products or ideas can be promoted as being affordable, accessible, easy to use, and desirable (Burn, 1991). Keeping in mind all the means of attitude change that we discussed in Chapter 16, psychologists must then analyze the wants, needs, and perceptions of the people being targeted. After these steps have been taken, researchers should evaluate the results of efforts to change attitudes and behavior to see whether the strategy has been effective. Geller claims that behavioral interventions combined with social marketing and policy strategies can provide an integrative program for

FOCUS

Review

- How does each type of environmental stressor affect behavior? pp. 624–625
- Describe the hypothesis and results of the lost-letter experiment. pp. 626–627
- What is the purpose of each of the four spatial zones that define personal space? pp. 627–628

Think Critically

- What are the implications of the study of environmental variables such as noise, temperature, and pollutants for architectural firms, heating and cooling companies, and window designers?
- How can people seek intimacy in their lives and still maintain personal space and a sense of territory and privacy?

Territorial behavior: Behavior involved in establishing, maintaining, personalizing, and defending a delineated space.

environmental preservation (e.g., Geller, 1992). He also calls for a collaboration of social action research and scholarship to preserve the quality of the environment. Many cost-effective traditional interventions are still not as effective as they might be (Needleman & Geller, 1992). Once people stop being reinforced for recycling or other pro-environment behaviors, they often discontinue the behavior; psychologists have to work at fostering long-term changes in behavior. As William Dwyer and his colleagues assert (1993, p. 317): "Even the most effective techniques for the initiation of behavior change is of minimal importance unless that behavior can be maintained or if the intervention can remain in place for a long-period of time . . . behavioral scientists need to give much greater consideration to the development of lifelong behaviors that will help maintain environmental quality. Only then can behavior science meaningfully contribute to saving planet Earth."

Social change begins with individual change, and community psychologists, considered next, attempt to foster such change.

Community Psychology

In the 1960s, many psychologists recognized that individual therapy was at best imprecise and at worst inefficient for treating large numbers of people. Researchers and practitioners, as well as politicians, sought a more efficient and effective approach. President John F. Kennedy's 1963 message to Congress called for "a bold new approach" to the treatment of mental illness and was followed by legislation and funding for community mental health centers. Community psychology has emerged in response to a widespread desire for a more action-oriented approach to individual and social adjustment. **Community psychology** is a branch of psychology that seeks to reach out to society to provide services, such as community mental health centers, and especially to effect social change.

The general aims of community psychology are to strengthen existing social support networks and to stimulate the formation of new networks to meet new challenges (Gonzales et al., 1983). A key element is community involvement leading to social change. A church or synagogue group, for example, could mobilize its senior citizens for a foster grandparent program. A community psychologist might help a group develop better fire safety procedures in public housing—the focus of community psychology is often on solving applied behavior problems. A key element of community psychology is **empowerment**—helping people in the community to enhance their existing skills and develop new skills, knowledge, and motivation so that they can gain control over their own lives (Rappaport, 1987). Community psychologists work in schools, churches, planning commissions, and prisons. They plan and set up programs for bringing psychological skills and knowledge into the community. Community psychologists work especially hard at prevention of psychological problems. Prevention operates at three levels: primary, secondary, and tertiary.

One focus of community psychology is *primary prevention*—reducing the risk of *new* cases of a disorder or counteracting harmful circumstances before they lead to maladjustment. Primary prevention usually targets groups rather than individuals. It may focus on an entire community, on mild-risk groups (such as children from families of low socioeconomic status), or on high-risk groups (such as children of schizophrenic parents). Community psychologists may establish drug prevention centers, safe houses for battered women, and suicide hotlines.

In response to growing public awareness of mental health problems, a special kind of primary prevention service agency—the *neighborhood clinic*—came into being. Such clinics help communities cope with problems that may be created by mental illness, unemployment, and lack of education. Some clinics provide free, confidential treatment for such problems as drug addiction, alcoholism, and emotional and psychological disorders. They offer a variety of services, including partial hospitalization programs for people who require hospitalization during the day and

Community psychology: The branch of psychology that seeks to reach out to society to provide services such as community mental health centers and especially to effect social change—through empowerment of individuals, planning, prevention, early intervention, research, and evaluation.

Empowerment: Facilitating the development of skills, knowledge, and motivation in individuals so that they can act for themselves and gain control over their own lives.

outpatient care for people who live at home while receiving therapy. They also offer consultation, education programs, and lectures and literature on such topics as therapy, family planning, and drug rehabilitation.

Secondary prevention involves catching problems and identifying new cases in the early stages. Community psychologists offer secondary prevention services in *crisis intervention centers,* which help people deal with short-term stressful situations requiring immediate therapeutic attention. Often the crisis is a specific event; for example, a person may be contemplating suicide, or a woman may have been raped. The focus of crisis intervention is on the immediate circumstances, not on past experiences. Studies show that crisis intervention therapy can be especially effective (Sawicki, 1988), but one problem in evaluating such therapy is that a variety of techniques are used, making controlled comparisons difficult (Slaikeu, 1990).

Tertiary prevention focuses on the treatment of full-blown psychological problems. There is considerable overlap between secondary and tertiary prevention, as sometimes issues and problems that are presented as short-term or in their early stages may have a long-standing basis. Community psychologists offer help to eliminate or reduce a problem as well as to strengthen existing family or community resources. Sometimes this help is an intervention to protect family members; other times, it consists of counseling, consulting with schools, or calling in other social service agencies. Again, the emphasis is on utilizing existing community resources and empowering individuals to manage their own lives more effectively.

An important aim of community psychology is to serve all members of the community, including people who might not otherwise be able to afford the services of a psychotherapist or counselor. Community psychologists are change-oriented. Because they believe that some social conditions and organizational procedures result in maladjusted individuals, they often advocate changes in community institutions and organizations. For example, they seek to improve the court system, develop programs to prevent drug use in schools, help energy conservation groups educate the public, consult with industry about reducing stress on the job, help religious organizations develop volunteer programs to aid the homeless, help hospitals set up preventive-medicine programs, and foster community involvement in educational issues.

Educational Psychology

When I was in elementary school, the teachers were often old and strict; they usually believed that children should be seen and not heard. Students were grouped according to ability, but that ability was inferred only from the teacher's observations of classroom behavior. If we acted out in any way (as I unfortunately did far too often), we were assigned seats in the seventh row. Little attention was paid to those of us relegated to the seventh row.

Things have changed. Today all teachers have undergraduate college degrees; most have advanced degrees. Teachers are now required to be trained not only in their content areas but also in sophisticated educational techniques. History teachers need to know history and how to teach it, as well as how to manage classrooms and help individual students meet their special challenges. And this is where educational psychology comes in.

Educational psychology is the systematic application of psychological principles to learning and teaching. Psychology has had a long tradition of studying learning principles; psychological researchers have thoroughly explored how people study, learn, and forget. Educators have long focused on instructional techniques and principles of classroom management. *Educational psychologists* bring these two disciplines together. They show how psychological ideas, methods, and theories can be applied to improve learning in individual students and in whole classrooms and to improve the process of teaching itself. In short, they help create better classroom managers (Fox, 1993). A distinction exists between educational psychologists and

Educational psychology: The systematic application of psychological principles to learning and teaching.

school psychologists. Although both share many similar concerns, educational psychologists are likely to focus on strategies to improve overall learning and classroom techniques. School psychologists are more likely to focus on interventions to affect individuals, on diagnoses of psychological and learning problems, and on consultations with parents and educators about an individual child's progress or plans.

Problems Studied by Educational Psychologists

Educational psychologists need to know a great deal about students to help promote effective teaching. For example, they seek to discover information about students' backgrounds, interests, abilities, and past learning and to understand how they interact with other students and other teachers and how they go about solving problems. Psychologists usually study these issues in the context of five areas of inquiry in order to put theory into practice. You will recognize these areas from earlier chapters, because educational psychologists apply the lessons of many psychological subdisciplines—from learning, to developmental, to social psychology.

A key focus for educational psychologists is *developmental change*—how and when individuals develop physically, socially, and intellectually. In children these processes are rapid, change each year, and dramatically alter the ways a child or adolescent learns and interacts with teachers and other students.

Educational psychologists also study students' backgrounds to learn how *environmental conditions* can affect the learning process. Socioeconomic status is but one of those conditions; parental marital status, use of drugs in the home, and how learning is talked about at home are other important environmental factors.

Classroom learning styles are important to educational psychologists. These psychologists study *behavioral principles of learning* to ensure that the classroom has appropriate order; they study *cognitive processes* to learn how students learn and process new information; and they examine *social interactions* to find out how students are influenced by others and how they can be influenced in positive ways.

FOCUS

Review

- Why did community psychology emerge, and what do community psychologists mean by *empowerment*? p. 630
- What are the goals of and the problems studied by educational psychologists? pp. 631–632

Think Critically

- Many community psychologists focus on helping groups of people, such as churches, neighborhoods, schools, and even whole communities, to change. What is the role of community psychology for individuals?
- If you wanted to be a teacher, what do you think would be the most challenging part of ensuring effective instruction? How do you think that aspect of teaching would vary with the grade or the subject matter that you might teach?
- Many schools are moving toward the concept of block scheduling, in which two periods are joined to provide one long class. What are the advantages and/or disadvantages for effective instruction of block scheduling, compared with traditional classes of shorter duration?

Putting Theory into Practice

Studying the principles of psychology is obviously a key prerequisite of effective classroom technique. But what are effective classroom techniques? Educational psychologists try to bridge the gap between theory and practice by developing approaches to learning and instruction that optimize student outcomes. For example, educational psychologists have focused on developing individualized educational plans to personalize instruction; they work to develop mastery learning—breaking learning down into a series of discrete steps in which all students can gain competence. They also foster immediate feedback and seek to establish clearly defined

APPLICATIONS

Classroom Management

There is a difference between the amount of time that is allocated to a class and the amount of time students are actually engaged in learning. Both time allocation and management of engaged time are key issues for teachers (Slavin, 1991). Establishing clear classroom rules and pacing a class effectively are important.

Time Allocation. Because teachers have such small amounts of time with students, they must manage allocated time effectively. How much time is actually spent on learning? In many elementary schools only about 60 percent of classroom time is actually spent on the task at hand (Karweit & Slavin, 1981). Researchers have found that carefully dividing up the allocated class time is key. Other recommendations are to avoid late starts and early finishes to class periods. Late starts signal to students that the lesson is not of importance. This leads to further late starts by students and a general lackadaisical attitude. A teacher should avoid interruptions at all costs; interruptions break a lesson's momentum and steal substantial time from engaged learning. When students are actively engaged with learning, they are said to be *on task*. To encourage on-task behaviors, effective teachers minimize time spent on recurring activities by ensuring smooth and efficient handling of routine procedures. Finally, efficient teachers minimize time spent on discipline by quickly and efficiently imposing penalties in private, and then seeking to reestablish a positive relationship with the offender (Weinstein & Mignano, 1993).

Engaged Time. If time is well allocated, then students' on-task time is more likely to be well spent. Effective teachers try to maintain momentum and smoothness of instruction by setting up a meaningful sequence of instructional ideas. Managing transitions from one topic to the next helps keep students engaged and focused.

Maintaining an entire class's focus is also an important task. Letting students know that the teacher is aware of the activities of the class keeps students on task (Brooks, 1985). Instructors who can juggle many tasks at one time and can work well with both individuals and small groups help ensure effective on-task instruction (Charles, 1985). Teachers who make the basics clear, monitor work in progress, and give frequent feedback are more effective in engaging students.

Classroom Rules. When instructors start the year with a clear set of guidelines for students, in which students are systematically introduced to the procedures and teachers' expectations, on-task and engaged student behaviors are more likely to occur. When rules are limited in number and clear, they are far more likely to be easily enforced. In addition, when students are asked to help establish ground rules, such as not talking without raising one's hand, offenders know that they are breaking their own rules, not arbitrary regulations. Educational psychologists assert that it is necessary to "let the punishment fit the crime" (Notterman & Drewry, 1993), and that students themselves may be the best judges of appropriate punishments.

Pacing. The tempo of a class is like the tempo of a symphony. A conductor does not want the musicians to play too quickly or with too much enthusiasm; engaging concerts, like good classes, use silences effectively. Phrases and ideas are not repeated too often, and the voice of the band, or the teacher, needs to change often to keep attention. The pace needs to be varied—short segments are more likely to hold attention than long ones.

Pacing is determined by the nature of the students, the material to be covered, and the instructor's own personal style. But combined with classroom rules and effective allocation of time to ensure on-task behavior, pacing is an important element of effective instruction.

Each of these four elements—time allocation, engaged time, classroom rules, and pacing—helps establish effective instruction. There are other important tactics, too, of course: summarizing, using feedback, encouraging student interaction, and even planning seating arrangements. All of these topics are part of the discipline of educational psychology. Each has been explored in depth by learning researchers, classroom teachers, and educational psychologists.

objectives and to develop effective classroom management techniques (as described in *Applications*).

Educational psychologists are both theoreticians and practitioners. They try to implement instructional techniques in innovative ways that have measurable outcomes. What if a student acts out in class by verbally abusing another child? There are dozens of things an instructor can do—and such situations happen throughout the day. Should a teacher *scold* the child, *ignore* the child, *banish* the child to the school office, *punish* the child for classroom misbehavior, or *instruct* the child on respect for peers? The answers lie in psychological principles: Scolding is punishment; ignoring is another form of punishment; banishment is a form of time-out—but instruction tries to focus on positive future behaviors. It is research in each of these areas, plus a little common sense and knowledge of children, that makes for effective teaching.

Sport Psychology

Imagine lining up a shot—any kind of shot will do. You picture the ball, you think about its final destination, you visualize its trajectory. You shoot. When golfers such as Jack Nicklaus, basketball players such as Michael Jordan, or quarterbacks such as Joe Montana prepare to take their shots, they usually imagine them first. In using mental imagery, they are using principles of sport psychology.

Sport psychology is the systematic application of psychological principles in sports. Sport psychologists, like any psychologists, recognize that behavior (in this case, athletic performance) is affected by the individual athlete, the athlete's team, the team leader or coach, and the environment in which these individuals interact. The characteristics of athlete, coach, and environment are each multidimensional; people, their own personal characteristics, how they interact with others, and how the environment affects them are all influenced by years of past events, relationships, and successes or failures. Nevertheless, sport psychologists have tried to bring some order to the study of athletic performance. Sport psychologists study the behaviors associated with sports in the traditional ways that psychologists go about things: Some do basic research in sports; others take an educational role, teaching about sport psychology; still others are applied practitioners who help athletes overcome obstacles to achieve their highest potential. There exist a whole range of sports behaviors that researchers consider appropriate for study, education, and intervention. Among the most important are the topics we will consider here: motivation, activation and arousal, anxiety and performance, and intervention strategies (Cox, Qiu, & Liu, 1993).

Motivation

If there were simple answers to explain what motivates an athlete—what factors energize, direct, and sustain athletic performance—then the task for sport psychologists, and especially for an athlete's coach, would be dramatically different. But athletic performance is exceedingly complicated. According to one researcher, it takes at least four levels of analysis to understand what motivates a person to perform a sport well (Roberts, 1992):

- *What is the goal*? Is the person seeking competitive abilities or merely mastery of a sport? Is the goal learning to play squash at a national level of competition, or is the goal to have a friendly game in which the athlete knows the rules, feels competent, and has fun playing? Based on such a recognition of personal goals, the athlete must then accept goals set up by a coach.
- *Is the motivational climate set by friends, parents, and coaches geared toward competition or mastery*? When the climate is geared toward mastery, the athlete's energy level is usually much lower, and so is anxiety.
- *How does the athlete perceive his or her abilities—as high, low, or not relevant?* When people have a strong self-concept of their abilities, they do better in sports. As we saw in Chapter 12, when people have a positive sense of self-efficacy, they do much better at a task.

Sport psychology: The systematic application of psychological principles in sports.

- *Is the athlete's achievement behavior adaptive or maladaptive?* Does the athlete set up realistic goals, practice schedules, and follow training routines, or does the athlete engage in self-defeating behaviors?

To a great extent, this four-step analysis of motivation looks at what energizes and sustains an athlete in sports. But a person who seeks to understand sport psychology must recognize that human beings are not always rational or goal-directed and do not always behave consistently. People's behavior is affected by their health, love life, family situation, and financial status, to name just a few variables. The complexity of these situations makes the study of sport psychology harder but also more exciting. Researchers have so much to learn, especially about the energizing of behavior in activation and arousal, our next topic.

Activation and Arousal

In our study of motivation in Chapter 9, we saw that, given moderate levels of arousal and moderately difficult tasks, as arousal increased, performance also increased. Arousal is generally viewed as stimulation and excitement—a performance enhancer. But excessive levels of arousal are associated with poor performance. Yerkes and Dodson characterized such a learning curve as an inverted U (see page 302 for a review of the Yerkes–Dodson law). One need not be a psychologist to recognize that when people are extremely frightened, aroused, or activated, performance suffers. This is certainly true in athletics; dozens of research studies have shown that being activated and aroused increases athletic performance—but only up to a point.

The inverted U–shape relationship for arousal and performance is not always orderly, however, especially in sports situations that involve a heavy level of cognitive activity, such as quarterbacking in football or catching in baseball. Researchers know that for every increase in a person's arousal, a corresponding increase (or decrease) in performance is not necessarily evident. Sometimes a small increase in arousal can push some people "over the top" to acute anxiety and poor performance. Young children are less affected by pressure; older children, in contrast, think about options ("The player at second base doesn't catch very well, so it makes more sense to throw to first") and are more affected by pressure (French, Spurgeon, & Nevett, 1995). How then is arousal distinct from anxiety?

Anxiety and Performance

When an athlete is fearful, tense, and apprehensive and such feelings are associated with arousal, the athlete is suffering from anxiety. Some people, including athletes, feel this way most of the time—trait personality theorists would say that such people have a strong or dominant anxiety trait. A whole range of tests has been developed to measure anxiety in athletes and to discern whether anxiety is related to specific events or is a general trait in a given athlete.

Unlike weekend or casual sports enthusiasts, competitive athletes often reach their peak of anxiety significantly before an athletic event begins, and their highest levels of anxiety may disappear immediately before the event. As they step up to the plate, hoop, skating arena, or scrimmage line, professional athletes often become cool, collected, and in control. Three hours earlier they may have felt overwhelmed by their arousal and fear, but when they have to perform, their anxiety is gone.

If this relationship between anxiety and performance were tidy, psychologists wouldn't fret about precompetitive anxiety. But, like so many other psychological phenomena, anxiety is related to other aspects of an athlete's performance and life. If an athlete's arousal exceeds the level needed for effective performance, anxiety can take over. Similarly, an underaroused athlete may also become anxious and stay anxious through an event. So arousal and anxiety are closely related and hard to separate. But separation can be achieved through good intervention strategies.

In a key game near the end of the college baseball season, a second baseman's anxiety level could be high enough to interfere with his skill at making a double play.

Intervention Strategies

When a person's level of anxiety is sufficiently high that arousal leads to lower performance, interventions can be put in place to help relieve anxiety and arousal. Stress management approaches described in Chapter 13 have proved to be effective. There exist a broad array of such anxiety-reducing techniques.

One widely used technique is *progressive relaxation,* in which athletes are taught to relax slowly and progressively as time passes. Individual muscle relaxation, with progressively deeper muscle-group relaxation, is the goal. Typical steps are suggestions to relax the limbs, to feel heaviness or warmth in the arms and legs, to feel a reduced heart rate, and to sense coolness on the forehead.

Hypnosis, the state encouraging uncritical acceptance of suggestions, has been widely used to help athletes achieve deep relaxation, as well as to help them focus their energy and attention. Closely associated with hypnosis is instruction in *meditation* to help an athlete relax and gain control of his or her focus. The technique of meditation is to focus energy and attention on a single thought, idea, sound, or object. (Hypnosis and meditation can help athletes relax and focus, of course, but they will never make a bad athlete into a good one.)

Using *mental imagery* to promote relaxation has been shown to be worthwhile in many sports activities (Overby, 1990), and when mental imagery is combined with other relaxation strategies, the results have proved especially effective (Murphy & Jowdy, 1992). As described earlier, athletes also use mental imagery to "psych up," or practice for a sports activity in their thoughts (Murphy, 1990).

Cognitive interventions that focus on changing thought patterns about a sport, an event, abilities, or strategies have been especially helpful (Boutcher, 1992). Cognitive strategies often focus on educational issues in the sport in combination with training in relaxation, such as thinking calm thoughts just before a pole vault. Cognitive interventions may teach athletes to think positively, to block out distractions, and to focus on the one part of their body that is crucial in their sport.

Sport Psychology: The Future

As sport psychologists gain a stronger sense of the variables that underlie sports, there is likely to be a more comprehensive growth of theory to help explain performance in various sports, as well as increased specialization focusing on areas such as motivation, personality variables, coaches, specific behavioral training, relaxation, imagery, and aggression. And since sport is a worldwide activity, there will be significant growth in cross-cultural research in sport psychology. Sport behavior cannot be examined in isolation—different countries have coaches, environments, and cultural expectations that shape athletic performance differently. For example, Chinese athletes see the causes of their failures as more internal and controllable than do German athletes (Si, Rethorst, & Willimczik, 1995). Researchers need to understand how variables such as locus of control (see Chapter 12 for a review of this concept) operate in sports, how the family affects an athlete's development, and how such factors vary cross-culturally (Hellstedt, 1995). Such research may begin to reveal why Russian athletes are such wonderful ice dancers, why Canadians play hockey so well, and why rugby and soccer are not the national sports of the United States. Stay tuned.

FOCUS

Review

- Identify four levels of analysis needed for an understanding of motivation in sports. pp. 634–635

Think Critically

- Sport psychologists seek to enhance athletes' performance on physical, emotional, and motivational fronts. Is there an ethical problem for sport psychologists with such behavior management?

Summary and Review

Industrial/Organizational Psychology

What is I/O psychology?

- *Industrial/organizational (I/O) psychology* is the study of how individual behavior is affected by the work environment, by coworkers, and by organizational practices. It can be divided into four broad areas: human resources psychology, motivation of job performance, job satisfaction, and leadership. pp. 602–603

What are the goals of job analyses, selection procedures, and training efforts in today's workplace?

- The functional job analysis and the position analysis questionnaire are instruments that have been developed by I/O psychologists for *job analyses*. All such analyses have a similar goal: Employers need to ensure that jobs are appropriate and have the correct scope. Two of the key tasks of an I/O psychologist are to balance the scope and complexity of jobs and to help employers create jobs that will be motivating. pp. 603–604

- Selection procedures have the basic goal of predicting the success of job candidates in order to help an employer determine which candidates to hire and which to reject. Application forms, interviews, samples of work, and tests are some of the instruments used in selection. Training is the process by which organizations systematically teach employees skills to improve their job performance. pp. 604–607

What is a performance appraisal?

- *Performance appraisal* is the process whereby a supervisor periodically evaluates the job-relevant strengths and weaknesses, of subordinates. The problem with performance appraisals is that they are often done inaccurately by people with few skills in evaluation and with few diagnostic aids. Multiple performance criteria must enter into an appraisal. pp. 607–609

How have psychologists tried to help managers motivate workers?

- I/O psychologists help employers find ways to motivate employees to be more productive. *Goal-setting theory* asserts that setting specific, clear, attainable goals for a given task will lead to better performance. p. 610

- *Expectancy theories* assert that performance is determined by both motivation and ability. Vroom suggests further that work motivation is determined by expectancy (the belief that hard or extra work will lead to good or improved performance); instrumentality (the belief that good performance will be rewarded); and valence (the value put on rewards that are offered). Lawler and Porter contended that performance is determined by motivation, ability, and role perceptions—the ways people believe they should be doing their jobs. pp. 610–611

How have psychologists analyzed worker performance and job satisfaction?

- The view that what people bring to a work situation should be balanced by what they receive there compared with others is captured in *equity theory*. Thus, workers' input (what they bring or do) should be balanced by the rewards they receive. If input is not balanced with compensation, people will adjust their work input accordingly. p. 612

- I/O psychologists have developed three basic approaches to motivation management: paternalistic, behavioral, and participatory. pp. 613–615

- There are many sources of job satisfaction, including the work itself, the perceived rewards of the work, the quality of supervision, the support of coworkers, and the work setting. In the end, the overall level of satisfaction depends on the extent to which people feel their expectations for satisfaction are matched by their actual satisfaction. p. 614

What makes a good leader?

- A leader is a person who influences other people's behavior toward the attainment of agreed-upon goals. Business leaders can be employee-oriented or task-oriented; the context of the situation or the organization is a key determinant of which type of leader will be more effective. *Transformational leaders*—charismatic leaders who inspire and provide intellectual stimulation— create opportunities to transform an organization, often by empowering employees. pp. 615–619

KEY TERMS

Applied psychology, p. 602
Industrial/organizational (I/O) psychology, p. 602
Job analyses, p. 603
Performance appraisal, p. 607
Goal-setting theory, p. 610
Expectancy theories, p. 610
Equity theory, p. 612
Transformational leader, p. 618

Human Factors and Ergonomics

Describe the field of human factors and ergonomics.

- *Human factors* is the study of the relationship of human beings to machines and to workplaces and other environments. *Ergonomics* is the study of the fit between human anatomy or physiology, the demands of a particular task or piece of equipment, and the environment in which the task occurs. Human factors research can provide a work environment that is not only efficient but also safe. Warnings, labels, and compliance techniques are all helpful in improving safety. pp. 619–621

KEY TERMS

Human factors, p. 619
Ergonomics, p. 620

Psychology and the Law

What key roles do psychologists play in the legal system?

- As researchers, psychologists help determine why individuals behave in ways that are unacceptable to society. Psychologists also act as policy or program evaluators, helping governments and other institutions determine whether various policies, agencies, or programs actually work. Psychologists work as advocates for individuals and society, helping shape social policy in such areas as minority, remedial, and gifted education. Finally, psychologists often serve as expert witnesses, bringing their knowledge to the courts as consultants. pp. 622–623

Environmental Psychology

What do environmental psychologists study?

- *Environmental psychology* is the study of how physical settings and aspects of the environment affect human behavior, as well as how people can change their environment to meet their psychological needs. *Crowding* is the perception that one's space is too limited. Social density is the number of people in a given space, while spatial density is the amount of space allocated to a fixed number of people. *Personal space*, as defined by Hall, is the immediate area around an individual that the person considers private. Four spatial zones, or distances, in social interactions in the United States are intimate, personal, social, and public. pp. 623–628

KEY TERMS

Environmental psychology, p. 624
Stressor, p. 624
Crowding, p. 625
Personal space, p. 627
Privacy, p. 628
Territorial behavior, p. 629

Community Psychology

Why did community psychology emerge, and what do community psychologists mean by empowerment*?*

- *Community psychology* seeks to reach out to society to provide psychological services to people who might not otherwise receive them. The general aims of community psychologists are to empower people and to use three levels of prevention strategies to help ward off, treat, or stop psychological problems in the community. *Empowerment* refers to helping people to enhance existing skills and develop new skills, knowledge, and motivation so that they can gain control over their own lives. p. 630

KEY TERMS

Community psychology, p. 630
Empowerment, p. 630

Educational Psychology

What are the goals of and problems studied by an educational psychologist?

- *Educational psychology* is the systematic application of psychological principles to learning and teaching. To help create effective teaching, educational psychologists seek to discover information about students' backgrounds, interests, abilities, and past learning; about how they interact with other students and other teachers; and about how they go about solving problems. Key areas for educational psychologists are developmental changes—how and when individuals grow physically, socially, and intellectually. Educational psychologists study students' backgrounds to learn how environmental conditions affect the learning process. Classroom learning styles are also important to educational psychologists. Both time allocation and management of engaged time are key issues for effective teachers. pp. 631–633

KEY TERM

Educational psychology, p. 631

Sport Psychology

What is sport psychology?

- *Sport psychology* is the systematic application of psychological principles in sports. Sport psychologists recognize that athletic performance is affected by the athlete, the team leader or coach, and the environment. Sport psychologists study issues such as arousal and performance and have found an inverted U–shape relationship between arousal and performance; but researchers know that as arousal increases, performance may or may not increase or decrease smoothly. pp. 634–635

What occurs when an athlete is anxious?

- When an athlete is fearful, tense, and apprehensive and such feelings are associated with arousal, the athlete is suffering from anxiety. When anxiety is too high and arousal lowers performance, interventions can help lower arousal and relieve anxiety. pp. 635–636

KEY TERM

Sport psychology, p. 634

Learning CONNECTIONS

Some students benefit from extra help with expectancy theories. You can learn more about them in:

- The CD-ROM accompanying this book, Topic 4
- This book's study guide, *Keeping Pace Plus*, or the computerized study guide, Chapter 17
- The study aids found on the World Wide Web site for this book, at http:/ /www.abacon.com/psych/lefton

Critical Thinking CONNECTIONS

Take a moment to think critically about how this chapter's topics are connected with the rest of psychology . . .

If you are interested in . . .	Ask yourself . . .	Then turn to . . .
The influence of the environment on people's perceptions of the world 	How do people's perceptions of the world depend on past experiences as well as on current stimuli in the environment?	Chapter 3, pp. 87–88, 93–96
	In what ways can stressors in the environment such as work-site pressure eventually lead to health problems?	Chapter 13, pp. 452–453
	How do people make decisions about the causes of other people's behavior, especially if the causes are due to environmental situations?	Chapter 16, pp. 567–569
Community psychology 	What are the implications of practitioners' moving toward group therapy, which is less expensive for clients?	Chapter 15, pp. 542–543
	How do people sometimes make worse decisions in groups than individually?	Chapter 16, pp. 593–595
Sport psychology 	How can people use conditioned responses to improve sports performance?	Chapter 5, pp. 178, 185–188
	Can achievement-oriented theories be applied to motivate people to achieve more than they do?	Chapter 9, pp. 303–304, 322–323
	How do adolescents conform, and how might this affect their attitudes about sports?	Chapter 11, pp. 383–384

Appendix

Statistical Methods

Scientific progress is in many ways directly linked to researchers' ability to measure and quantify data. **Statistics** is the branch of mathematics that deals with collecting, classifying, and analyzing data. To rule out coincidence and discover the true causes of behavior, psychologists control the variables in experiments (topics discussed in detail in Chapter 1), then use statistics to describe, summarize, and present results. These methods and procedures for analyzing data are the topics of this appendix.

Descriptive Statistics

Researchers use statistics to evaluate and organize data. Specifically, they use **descriptive statistics**—procedures used to summarize, condense, and describe sets of data. Descriptive statistics make it possible for researchers to interpret the results of their experiments. For example, your professors use descriptive statistics to interpret exam results. A statistical description of a 100-point midterm exam may show that 10 percent of a class scored more than 60 points, 70 percent scored between 40 and 60 points, and 20 percent scored fewer than 40 points. On the basis of this statistical description, the professor might conclude that the test was exceptionally difficult and might arrange the grades so that anyone who earned 61 points or more received an A. But before inferences can be drawn or grades can be arranged, the data from a research study must be organized in a meaningful way.

Statistics: The branch of mathematics that deals with collecting, classifying, and analyzing data.

Descriptive statistics: A general set of procedures used to summarize, condense, and describe sets of data.

Frequency distribution: A chart or array of scores, usually arranged from the highest to the lowest, showing the number of instances for each score.

Organizing Data: Frequency Distributions

When psychologists do research, they often produce large amounts of data that must be assessed. Suppose a social psychologist asked parents to monitor the number of hours their children watch television. The parents might report between 0 and 20 hours of television watching a week. Here is a list of the actual number of hours of television watched by 100 children in a particular week:

11	18	5	9	6	20
9	7	15	3	6	11
6	1	10	3	4	4
8	8	9	10	13	12
16	1	15	9	4	3
10	5	6	12	8	2
14	12	6	9	8	12
10	7	3	14	13	7
10	17	11	13	16	7
15	11	9	11	16	8
14	7	10	10	12	8
11	1	12	7	6	0
19	18	9	8	2	5
9	14	7	10	9	2
10	4	13	8	5	4
9	8	5	17	15	17
5	13	10	11		

The first step in making these numbers meaningful is to arrange them in a chart or array, organized from the highest to the lowest, showing the number of times each number occurs; this type of organization is known as a **frequency distribution**. As the frequency distribution in Table A.1 shows, 10 children were reported to have watched 9 hours of television in a week—a greater number of children than watched any other number of hours.

TABLE A.1 ***A Frequency Distribution of the Number of Hours of Television Watched in a Week by 100 Children***

Note that few individuals score very high or very low—most score in the middle range.

Number of Hours of Television Watched	Individuals Watching Each Number of Hours	Total Number of Individuals Watching
0	I	1
1	III	3
2	III	3
3	IIII	4
4	IIIII	5
5	IIIIII	6
6	IIIIIII	7
7	IIIIIII	7
8	IIIIIIIII	9
9	IIIIIIIIII	10
10	IIIIIIIII	9
11	IIIIIII	7
12	IIIIII	6
13	IIIII	5
14	IIII	4
15	IIII	4
16	III	3
17	III	3
18	II	2
19	I	1
20	I	1
		100

FIGURE A.1

A Frequency Polygon Showing Hours of Television Watched Weekly by 100 Children

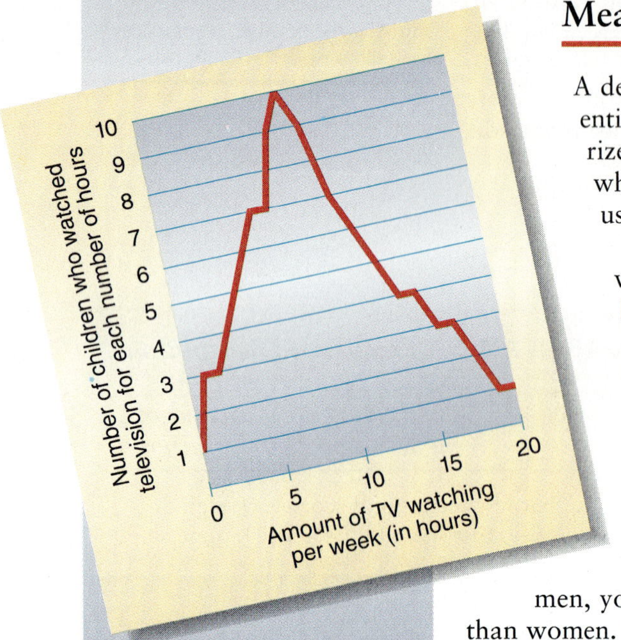

Researchers often construct graphs from the data in frequency distributions. Such graphs, called **frequency polygons,** show the range of possible results or scores (for example, numbers of hours of TV watching) on the horizontal axis, or *abscissa,* and the frequency of each score (for example, the number of children who watched television for each number of hours) on the vertical axis, or *ordinate.* Figure A.1 is a frequency polygon of the data from the frequency distribution in Table A.1. Straight lines connect the data points.

Measures of Central Tendency

A descriptive statistic that tells which result or score best represents an entire set of scores is a **measure of central tendency.** It is used to summarize and condense data. Also, because almost every group has members who score higher or lower than the rest of the group, researchers often use a measure of central tendency to describe the group *as a whole.*

People often use the word *average* in a casual way to describe a variety of commonalities or tendencies. A woman asks a clerk to help her find a sweater for her "average-sized" husband. The owner of a new sedan boasts that his car "averages" 40 miles to a gallon of gasoline. A doctor tells her patient that his serum cholesterol level is "average" because it falls halfway between low and high measurements. In each of these cases, the person is using *average* to depict a type of norm, and others understand what the person means, even though not all of these examples are technically "averages." As another example, consider this statement: Men are taller than women. Because you know that some women are taller than some men, you assume that the statement means: *On the average,* men are taller than women. In other words, comparing the heights of all the men and all the women in the world would show that, *on the average,* men are taller.

Let's look more closely at three measures of central tendency: mean (arithmetic average), mode, and median.

Mean. How could a researcher investigate the truth of the statement that men are taller than women? One way would be to measure the heights of thousands of men and women, taking a careful sample from each country, race, and age group. The researcher could then calculate the average heights of the men and the women in the sample and plot the results on a graph. Table A.2 lists height data from a small sample of men and women. For each group, the heights of the men or women were measured, added together, and divided by the number of people in the group. The resulting number is the **mean,** or *arithmetic average* (in this case, of the heights of men or women in the group). The mean is the most frequently used measure of central tendency.

Mode. Another statistic used to describe the central tendency of a set of data is the mode. The **mode** is the most frequently observed data point. Table A.3 plots the frequencies of different heights for all the heights in Table A.2. It shows, for example, that only one person is 58 inches tall, three people are 79 inches, and more people are 70 inches tall than any other single height. The mode of the heights of this group is therefore 70 inches.

Median. The **median** is the 50-percent point: Half the observations (or scores) fall above it and the other half fall below it. Table A.4 on page 644 arranges all the heights for men and women given in Table A.2 from lowest to highest. It shows that half the heights fall above 68 and half fall below 68. The median of the data set,

Frequency polygon: Graph of a frequency distribution that shows the number of instances of obtained scores, usually with the data points connected by straight lines.

Measure of central tendency: A descriptive statistic that tells which result or score best represents an entire set of scores.

Mean: The measure of central tendency that is calculated by dividing the sum of the scores by the total number of scores. Also known as the *arithmetic average.*

Mode: The measure of central tendency that is the most frequently observed data point.

Median: The measure of central tendency that is the data point having 50 percent of all the observations (scores) above it and 50 percent below it.

TABLE A.2 *Calculation of Mean Height for 20 Men and 20 Women*

Men	Height (in inches)	Women	Height (in inches)
Davis	62	Leona	58
Baird	62	Golde	59
Jason	64	Marcy	61
Ross	67	Mickey	64
David	68	Sharon	64
Cary	68	Rozzy	66
Mark	69	Bonnie	66
Evan	70	Dianne	66
Michael	70	Cheryl	66
Davey	70	Carol	67
Steven	70	Iris	67
Morry	70	Nancy	67
Alan	70	Theresa	67
Bernie	70	Sylvia	67
Lester	70	Jay	68
Al	70	Linda	68
Arnold	73	Elizabeth	71
Andrew	79	Jesse	75
Corey	79	Gabrielle	76
Stephen	79	Sarah	77
Total height	**1400**	***Total height***	**1340**

Mean: $\frac{\Sigma S}{N} = \frac{1400}{20} = 70$ inches   Mean: $\frac{\Sigma S}{N} = \frac{1340}{20} = 67$ inches

Note: ΣS means add up the scores; N means number of scores.

TABLE A.3 *The Mode for Men's and Women's Heights*

The mode is 70 inches, the most frequently observed height.

Height (in inches)	Number of Individuals of Each Height	
58	I	
59	I	
60		
61	I	
62	II	
63		
64	II	
65		
66	IIIII	
67	IIIIII	
68	IIII	
69		
70	IIIIIIII	**Mode**
71	I	
72		
73	I	
74	I	
75	I	
76	I	
77	I	
78		
79	III	

therefore, is 68. You have probably read news reports that refer to medians, for example: "According to the U.S. Census Bureau, the median family income in United States rose to $36,000 this year." What this means is that half of U.S. families earned more than this amount and half earned less.

Table A.5 on page 644 presents a set of data from an experiment on memory. The scores are the numbers of correctly recalled items. There are three groups of participants: a control group, which received no special treatment; one experimental group, which received task-motivating instructions (such as think hard, focus your attention); and a second experimental group, which was hypnotized and told under hypnosis that its members would have better recall. The results of the study show that the task-motivated group did slightly worse than the control groups: its mean was 10.3 words recalled, compared with the control group's mean of 10.6. But the hypnosis group did better, recalling 15.4 words on average, compared with the control group's average recall of 10.6 words—a difference of 4.8 words. Hypnosis therefore *seemed* to have a positive effect on memory. But let's look at it another way before coming to that conclusion.

The medians for the control group and the task-motivated group were equal: 10.5 words. The difference between the medians of the control group and the hypnosis group was 4 words. Hypnosis still seems to have a positive effect, but the

TABLE A.4
The Median of Men's and Women's Heights

The median is the height in the middle of the range of heights measured—half the heights are above the median and half are below.

Height (in inches)	
58	
59	
61	
62	
62	
64	
64	
66	
66	
66	
66	
66	
67	
67	
67	
67	
67	
67	
68	
68	— **Median**
68	
68	
70	
70	
70	
70	
70	
70	
70	
70	
70	
71	
73	
74	
75	
76	
77	
79	
79	

TABLE A.5 ***Calculations of Mean and Median Memory Scores for Three Groups (with 10 People in Each Group)***

Person	Scores of Control Group	Scores of Task-Motivated Group	Scores of Hypnosis Group
1	10	11	16
2	12	13	14
3	14	14	16
4	10	12	12
5	11	12	10
6	9	8	9
7	5	10	15
8	12	5	12
9	16	10	18
10	7	8	32
Total	106	103	154
Mean	10.6	10.3	15.4
Median	10.5	10.5	14.5

Control Group (scores are reordered lowest to highest)

$$\text{Mean} = \frac{5 + 7 + 9 + 10 + 10 + 11 + 12 + 12 + 14 + 16}{10} = \frac{106}{10} = 10.6$$

Median = 5 7 9 10 [10 11] 12 12 14 16
↓
10.5

The point at which half the scores fall above and half the scores fall below is 10.5; that is, 10.5 is the median.

Task-Motivated Group (scores are reordered lowest to highest)

$$\text{Mean} = \frac{5 + 8 + 8 + 10 + 10 + 11 + 12 + 12 + 13 + 14}{10} = \frac{103}{10} = 10.3$$

Median = 5 8 8 10 [10 11] 12 12 13 14
↓
10.5

The point at which half the scores fall above and half the scores fall below is 10.5; that is, 10.5 is the median.

Hypnosis (scores are reordered lowest to highest)

$$\text{Mean} = \frac{9 + 10 + 12 + 12 + 14 + 15 + 16 + 16 + 18 + 32}{10} = \frac{154}{10} = 15.4$$

Median = 9 10 12 12 [14 15] 16 16 18 32
↓
14.5

The point at which half the scores fall above and half the scores fall below is 14.5; that is, 14.5 is the median.

median difference (4 words) is smaller than the mean difference (4.8 words) because the median discounts very high and very low scores. For example, if you get a test score of 0 after obtaining five other scores whose average is about 70, the sixth score will drop that *average* substantially; averaging in a sixth score of 60 would not have as large an impact. But with a median, a single extreme score (such as 0 or 120) would count the same. With a sample as small as this one, where a single score can have a big impact, the median is often a better measure of central tendency.

The mean, mode, and median are descriptive statistics that measure central tendency. Each tells researchers something about the average (or typical) person or item being scored. Sometimes the mean, the mode, and the median are the same number; but more often, enough variability exists (one very tall or very short person in a group of height measurements, for example) for each central tendency measure to yield a slightly different result and to be used for different purposes. If you had to guess the height of a woman you had never met, a good guess would be the mean, or average, height for women. If you were a buyer for a clothing store and had to pick one dress size or one shoe size to order, you might be more likely to pick the modal size—the size that will occur more often than any other.

Measures of Variability

A measure of central tendency is a single number that describes a hypothetical "average." In real life, however, people do not always reflect the central tendency. Consequently, knowing how an average person or item scores is more useful when accompanied by knowledge of how the scores in the group are distributed relative to one another. If you know that the mean of a group of numbers is 150, you still do not know how widely dispersed are the scores that are averaged to calculate that mean. In other words, in your psychology class the mean on your final examination may be 150, and though you may have scored 170 (above the mean), you still do not know how much you can celebrate. Are there few others above your score? If there are many others, how much better than you did they do?

A statistic that describes the extent to which scores in a distribution differ from one another is called a *measure of variability*. **Variability** is the extent to which scores differ from one another, especially the extent to which they differ from the mean. If all scores obtained are the same, no variability exists; this, however, is unlikely to occur. It is more usual that, in any group of people being tested or measured in some way, personal and situational characteristics will cause some to score high and some to score low. If researchers know the extent of the variability, they can estimate the extent to which subjects differ from the mean, or "average," subject. Two important and useful measures of variability are range and standard deviation.

Range. The **range** shows the spread of scores in a distribution; it is calculated by subtracting the lowest score from the highest score. If the lowest score on a test is 20 points and the highest is 85, the range is 65 points. In this example, whether the mean is 45, 65, or 74 points, the range remains 65; that is, there is a 65-point spread from the lowest score to the highest.

The range is a relatively crude measure of the extent to which subjects vary within a group. In a group of 100 students, for example, the mean score might be 80, and nearly all the students might have scored within 10 points of that mean. But if the lowest score is 20 and the highest is 85, the range will be 65. More precise measures of the spread of scores within a group are available, however. They indicate how scores are distributed as well as the extent of their spread.

Standard Deviation. Consider a reaction-time study that measures how fast people press a button when a light flashes. The following list gives the number of milliseconds it took each of 30 randomly chosen 10th graders to press the button when the light flashed; clearly, the reaction times vary.

450	490	500	610	520	470
480	492	585	462	600	490
740	700	595	500	493	495
498	455	510	470	480	540
710	722	575	490	495	570

Variability: The extent to which scores differ from one another, especially the extent to which they differ from the mean.

Range: A measure of variability that describes the spread between the highest and the lowest scores in a distribution.

TABLE A.6 *Computation of the Standard Deviation for a Small Distribution of Scores*

Score	Score − Mean	(Score − Mean)^2
10	10 − 6 = 4	16
10	10 − 6 = 4	16
10	10 − 6 = 4	16
5	5 − 6 = −1	1
4	4 − 6 = −2	4
4	4 − 6 = −2	4
4	4 − 6 = −2	4
1	1 − 6 = −5	25
48		86

Standard deviation = $\sqrt{\frac{\Sigma(X-\overline{X})^2}{N-1}}$, where Σ means "sum up," X is a score, $\overline{X}$ is the mean of the scores, and N is the number of scores.

Sum of scores = 48.

$\overline{X}$ = sum of scores ÷ 8 = 6.

Sum of squared differences from mean = 86.

Average of squared differences from mean (dividing by the number of scores − 1) = 86 ÷ 7 = 12.3.

Square root of average squared difference from the mean = 3.5.

Standard deviation = 3.5.

TABLE A.7 *Reaction Times, Mean Reaction Times, and Standard Deviations for Responses to a Light*

Group 1 shows a wider range of scores and thus great variability. Group 2, in contrast, shows a narrow range of scores and little variability.

Times for Group 1 (in milliseconds)	Times for Group 2 (in milliseconds)
380	530
400	535
410	540
420	545
470	550
480	560
500	565
720	570
840	575
935	580
Mean = 555	Mean = 555
Standard deviation = 197	Standard deviation = 17

If you were told only that the mean reaction time was 540 milliseconds, you might assume that 540 was the best estimate of how long it takes a 10th grader to respond to the light. But of course not everyone took 540 milliseconds; some took more time and some took less. Psychologists say that the data were variable, or that variability existed.

To find out how much variability exists among data, and to quantify it in a meaningful manner, researchers need to know the standard deviation. A **standard deviation** is a descriptive statistic that measures the variability of data from the mean of the sample—that is, the extent to which each score differs from the mean. The calculations for a standard deviation are shown in Table A.6. Here is the general procedure: First, subtract the mean from each score and then square that difference. Next, add up the squared differences and divide by the number of scores minus 1. (For a small sample, to get a better estimate of the sample's standard deviation, researchers typically divide by 1 less than the number of scores.) Last, take the square root of the answer. You have now calculated a standard deviation.

A standard deviation gives information about all the members of a group, not just an average member. Knowing the standard deviation—that is, the variability associated with a mean—enables a researcher to make more accurate predictions. Table A.7 shows the reaction times for two groups of participants responding to a light. The mean is the same for both groups; but group 1 shows a large degree of variability, while group 2 shows little variability. The standard deviation (the estimate of variability) for group 1 participants will be substantially higher than that for group 2 participants because the scores differ from the mean much more in the first group than in the second. Since the standard deviation for subjects in group 2 is small, a researcher can more confidently predict that any one individual in that group will respond to the light in about 555 milliseconds (the mean response time). However, the researcher cannot confidently make the same prediction for individuals in group 1, since that group's standard deviation is high.

Standard deviation: A descriptive statistic that measures the variability of data from the mean of the sample.

Normal distribution: The approximately expected distribution of scores when a sample is drawn from a large population, drawn as a frequency polygon that often takes the form of a bell-shaped curve. Also known as a *normal curve.*

The Normal Distribution

When a large number of scores are involved, a frequency polygon often takes the form of a bell-shaped curve; this curve depicts the **normal distribution**, or *normal curve*. Normal distributions usually have a few scores at each extreme and progressively more scores toward the middle. Height, for example, is approximately normally distributed: More people are of average height than are very tall or very short (see Figure A.2). Weights, shoe sizes, IQs, and scores on psychology exams also tend to be normally distributed.

FIGURE A.2

A Normal Curve for Height

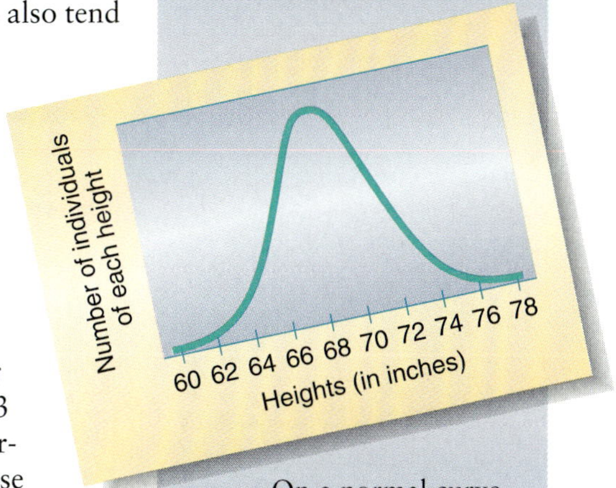

On a normal curve for height, many more people are of average height than are at the extremes.

Characteristics of a Normal Curve. A normal curve has certain characteristics. The mean, mode, and median are assumed to be the same; the distribution of scores around that central point is symmetrical; also, most individuals have a score that occurs within 6 standard deviations—3 above the mean and 3 below it (see Figure A.3).

To explain this phenomenon, Figure A.4 shows a normal curve for test scores. The mean is 50, and the standard deviation is 10 points. Note how each increment of 10 points above or below the mean accounts for fewer and fewer individuals. Scores between 50 and 60 account for 34.13 percent of those tested; scores between 60 and 70 account for 13.59 percent; and scores above 70 account for under 2.5 percent. The sum of these percentages (34.13 + 13.59 + 2.14 + 0.13) represents 50 percent of the scores.

When you know the mean and standard deviation of a set of data, you can estimate where an individual in the sample population stands relative to others. In Figure A.5 on page 648, for example, Dennis is 74 inches tall. His height is 1 standard deviation above the mean, which means that he is taller than 84 percent of the population (0.13 + 2.14 + 13.59 + 34.13 + 34.13 = 84.12 percent). Rob, who is 66 inches tall, is taller than only 16 percent of the population. His height is 1 standard deviation below the mean.

FIGURE A.3

Percentages of Population for a Normal Curve

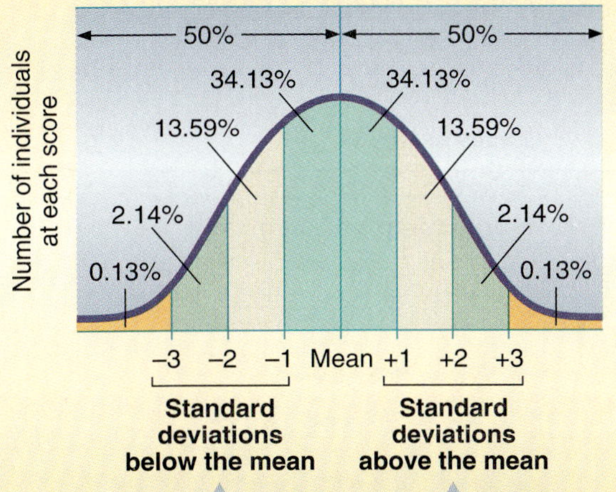

On a normal curve, most individuals score within 6 standard deviations, 3 on either side of the mean.

FIGURE A.4

A Normal Curve with a Standard Deviation of 10 Points

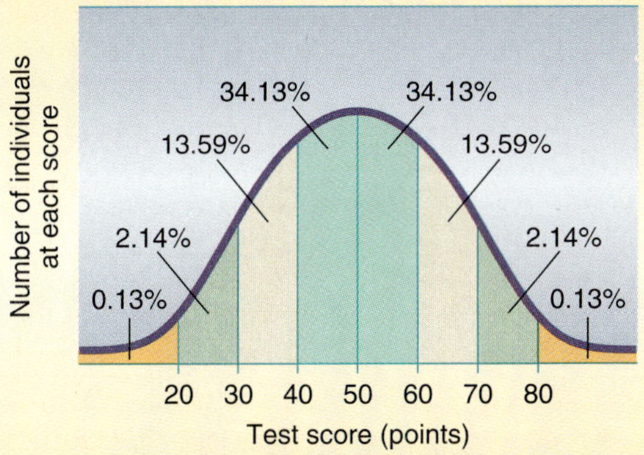

The mean of 50 is at the midpoint of the distribution of test scores: 50% of the scores fall below the mean, and 50% of the scores fall above the mean.

FIGURE A.5

A Normal Curve with a Mean of 70 and a Standard Deviation of 4 Inches

On this normal curve, Dennis's height of 74 inches is 1 standard deviation above the mean height of 70 inches. Rob's height is 66 inches, which is 1 standard deviation below the mean.

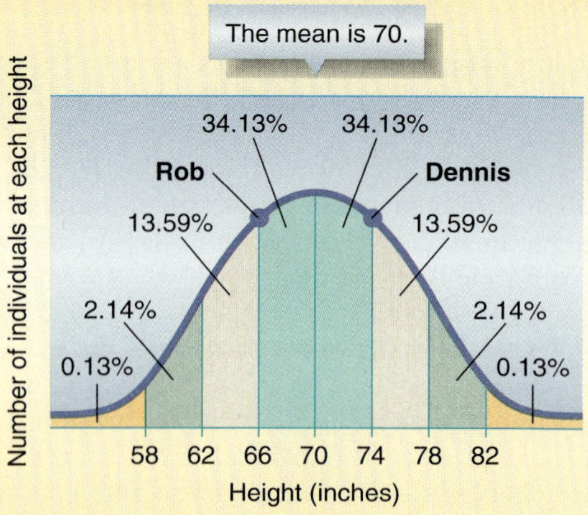

Normal Curves: A Practical Example. Your grade on an examination is often determined by how other members of your class do on the exam. This is what instructors mean when they say that a grade is on a "sliding scale" or a "curve." If the average student in a class answers only 50 percent of the questions correctly, a student who answers 70 percent correctly has done a good job. But if the average student scores 85 percent, then someone who scores only 70 percent has not done so well.

Before they assign grades on a sliding scale, testing services and instructors generally plot the test results on a graph in order to calculate a mean. They then inspect the scores and "slide the scale" to an appropriate level. Figure A.6 shows scores achieved and grades assigned on a calculus test. The average score is 65 percent; the instructor decides to give students who score 65 percent a C, those who do better an A or a B, and those who do worse a D or an F.

FIGURE A.6

Grading on a Sliding Scale

To calculate grades on a sliding scale, instructors often draw a graph like this one, showing the number of individuals at each score. They then figure out the cutoff points for assigning letter grades (A, B, C, D, and F).

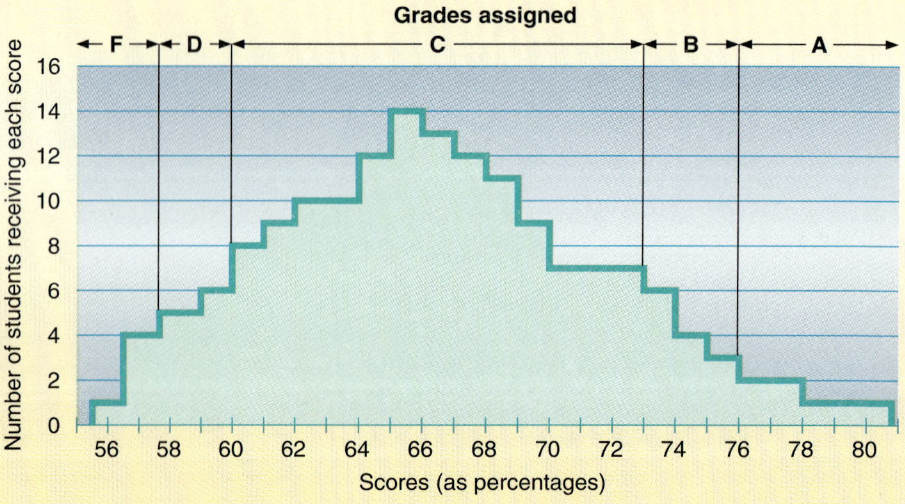

Inferential Statistics and Correlation

Confidence in predictions turns out to be a key issue for statisticians; they want to be as sure as possible that the mean of a group (sample) actually represents the mean of the larger population that the group represents. This concern is important because researchers want to be able to tell whether a difference between a control group and an experimental group is due to statistical manipulations, to extraneous variables, or to one or two deviant scores. It turns out that many of the manipulations and controls that researchers devise are necessary if they wish to make sound inferences, the topic we will consider next.

Researchers use inferential statistics in making decisions about data. **Inferential statistics** are procedures used to reach reasonable conclusions (generalizations) about larger populations from small samples of data. There are usually two issues to be explored: First, does the mean of a sample (a small group of people) actually reflect the mean of the larger population? Second, is a difference found between two means (for example, between the mean for a control group and the mean for an experimental group) a real and important difference, or is it a result of chance?

Significant Differences

Psychologists hope to find a **significant difference**—a difference that is statistically unlikely to have occurred because of chance alone and thus is more likely to be due to the experimental conditions. To find a significant difference, a researcher shows that a performance difference between two or more groups is not a result of chance variations and can be repeated experimentally. Generally, psychologists assume that a difference is statistically significant if the likelihood of its occurring by chance is less than 5 percent—that is, it would occur by chance less than 5 out of 100 times. But many researchers assume a difference is significant only if the likelihood of its occurring by chance is less than 1 percent.

It is sometimes difficult to decide whether a difference is significant. Let's go back to Table A.5, where calculations were performed for a set of memory scores. The results showed that the task-motivated group recalled no more words, on average, than the control group did (in fact, 0.3 fewer words). The hypnosis group recalled 4.8 more words, on average, than the control group. Since the hypnosis group did better than the control group, can the researcher conclude that hypnosis is a beneficial memory aid? Did the hypnosis group do *significantly* better than the control group? Was a 4.8-word difference significant? It is easy to see that if the recall difference between the two groups had been 10 words, and if the variability within each group had been very small, the difference would be considered significant. Similarly, a 1- or 2-word difference would not be considered significant if the variability within each group was large. In the present case, a 4.8-word difference was not significant; the scores were highly variable, and only a small sample of people was used. When scores are variable (widely dispersed), both statistical analysts and researchers are unlikely to view a small difference between two groups as significant or important. (See Figure A.7 on page 650 for an illustration of this point.)

Even if statistically significant differences are obtained, most researchers require that an experiment be repeated and that the results be the same. Repeating an experiment to verify a result is called *replicating* the experiment. If the results of a replicated experiment remain the same, a researcher will generally say that the observed difference between the two groups is important.

Inferential statistics: Procedures used to reach reasonable conclusions (generalizations) about larger populations from small samples of data.

Significant difference: An experimentally obtained statistical difference that is unlikely to have occurred because of chance alone.

Correlation

For many reasons, it is sometimes impractical or impossible to collect experimental data for control groups or experimental groups or to do research that involves

FIGURE A.7

The Possible Outcomes of Experiments Whose Means Are Identical

In the first graph, the observed scores all cluster around the means—there is little variability. The difference between the means in the first graph is therefore likely to be significant. The means in the second graph (although identical to the ones in the first graph) are unlikely to be deemed significantly different—the scores are too widely distributed. Here, there is too much variability; the means may be affected by extreme scores. Thus, a scientist is less likely to accept these means as different from one another.

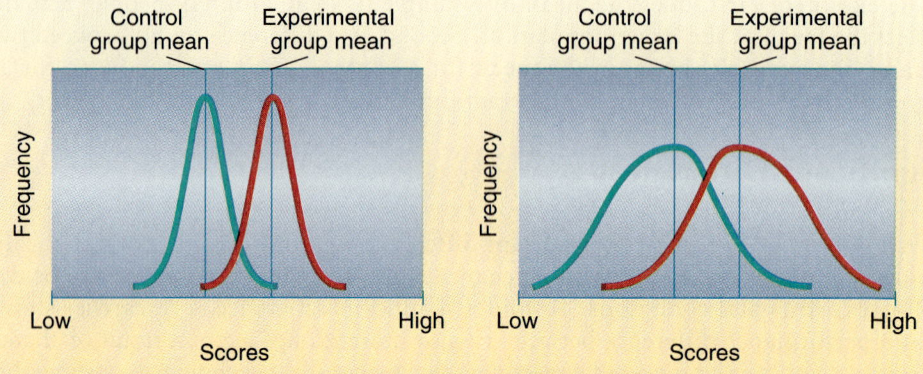

manipulations of an experimental variable. Sometimes a researcher wants to compare data that were gathered by others in different kinds of surveys and questionnaires, for instance. In such cases, the researcher may calculate correlations.

A correlation exists when an increase in the value of one variable is regularly accompanied by an increase or a decrease in the value of a second variable. The degree and direction of relationship between two variables is expressed by a numerical value called the **correlation coefficient**. Correlation coefficients range from –1, through 0, to +1. Any correlation coefficient greater or less than 0, regardless of its sign, indicates that the variables *are* somehow related. When two variables are perfectly correlated, they are said to have a correlation coefficient of 1. A perfect correlation occurs when knowing the value of one variable allows a researcher to predict *precisely* the value of the second; this is, of course, a rare occurrence in psychological research.

Most variables are not perfectly correlated. One example of imperfectly correlated variables is the incidence of schizophrenia in children of schizophrenic parents. Research shows that if a parent is schizophrenic, the likelihood that his or her child will be schizophrenic increases sharply. Thus, there is a correlation between parents' and children's rates of schizophrenia. But this correlation is not perfect; that is, not every child born to a schizophrenic parent will develop the disorder. Because of this imperfect correlation, psychologists conclude that genetics is only one of several contributing factors in the development of the disorder.

Correlation coefficient: A number that expresses the degree and direction of a relationship between two variables, ranging from –1 (a perfect negative correlation) to +1 (a perfect positive correlation).

Before calculating a correlation coefficient, researchers often plot, or graph, the data that they obtain in a scatter plot. A *scatter plot* is a diagram of data points that shows the relationship between two variables. An individual's score on one variable is measured on the horizontal axis, or x axis; the score on the second variable is measured on the vertical axis or y axis. Thus, a scatter plot might show 10 individuals' heights and weights; for each person, there is a height and weight pair. For example,

FIGURE A.8

Three Types of Correlation: A Summary

(a) In a positive correlation, an increase in one variable is associated with an increase in the other variable. (b) In a negative correlation, an increase in one variable is associated with a decrease in the other variable. (c) No correlation exists when changes in one variable are not associated in any systematic way with changes in the other variable.

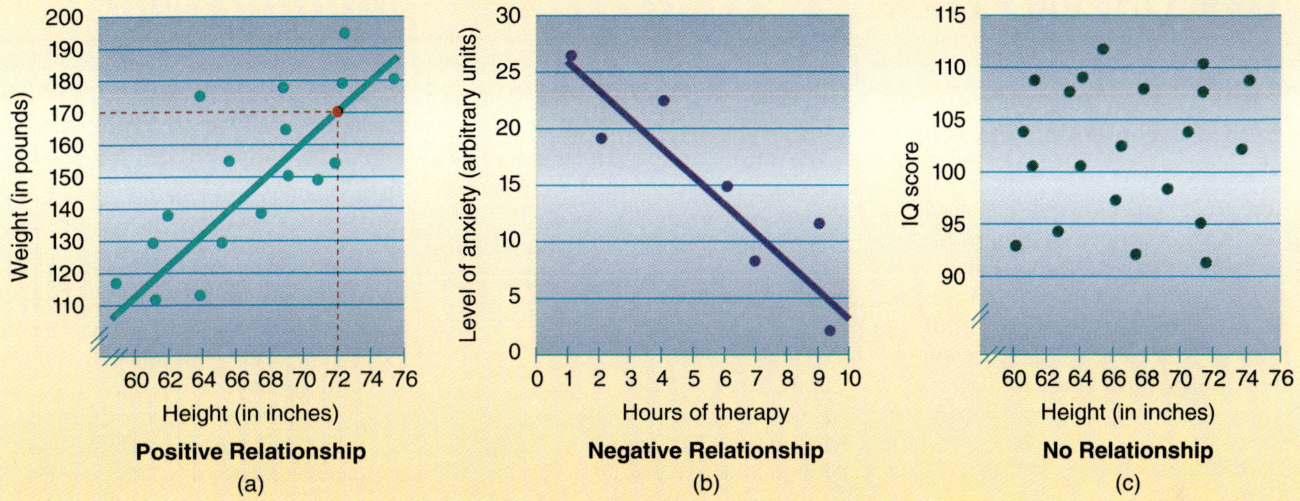

in Figure A.8(a) the first person's height may be 6 feet and weight, 170 pounds; a dot is made on the graph at the point where 6 feet on the x axis and 170 pounds on the y axis intersect. Plotting all 10 points in this way gives a graphic sense of the extent to which these two variables are related. Tall people do tend to weigh more than short people in general, and when height/weight data are plotted, the graph usually shows that as height increases, so does weight (at least most of the time).

When one variable shows an increase in value and a second also shows an increase, the two variables are said to be positively related, and the relationship is known as a *positive correlation*. Height and weight show a positive correlation: Generally, as height increases, so does weight. Although knowing a person's height does not allow one to predict his or her weight precisely, the scatter plot in Figure A.8(a) shows a positive direction overall—upward and to the right. These two variables have a correlation coefficient of about 0.65.

On the other hand, if one variable decreases as the other increases, the variables are said to be negatively correlated, and the relationship is known as a *negative correlation*. For example, the relationship between the number of hours of therapy and the extent of anxiety shows a negative correlation; see Figure A.8(b). As the number of hours of therapy increases, anxiety decreases. The scatter plot shows a corresponding movement downward and to the right. These two variables have a negative correlation of about –0.6 or –0.7.

A correlation coefficient of +0.7 is no stronger than one of –0.7. That is, the plus or minus sign changes the *direction*, not the strength, of a relationship. The strength is shown by the number: The larger the number, the greater the strength of the correlation. A correlation coefficient of –0.8 is stronger than one of +0.7; a correlation coefficient of +0.6 is stronger than one of –0.5.

Some variables show absolutely no correlation; absence of correlation is expressed by a correlation coefficient of 0. Figure A.8(c) plots data for IQ and height. The figure shows no pattern in the scatter plot and no correlation between IQ and height; the two variables are said to have a correlation coefficient of 0.

As we saw in Chapter 1, a correlation in no way implies a cause-and-effect relationship. A correlation between two variables simply indicates that if there is an increase in one variable, there will probably be an increase or decrease in the other variable. It is only through experimental studies that researchers can make cause-and-effect statements. Many of the studies reported in this text are correlational, but far more are experimental. Whenever possible, researchers wish to draw causal inferences.

Summary and Review

Descriptive Statistics

How do descriptive statistics help researchers organize data?

- *Researchers use descriptive statistics* to summarize, condense, and describe sets of data. A *frequency distribution* is a way of organizing data to show the number of times each item occurs; the graphic version of a frequency distribution is a *frequency polygon.* pp. 641–642

How are measures of central tendency used?

- *Measures of central tendency* are descriptive statistics that indicate which single score best represents an entire set of scores. The most frequently used measure of central tendency is the *mean*, or arithmetic average. Also used are the *mode*, or most frequently observed data point, and the *median*, the 50-percent point. p. 642

What is a measure of variability?

- A measure of *variability* is any statistic that describes the extent to which scores in a distribution differ from one another. One such measure, the *range*, shows the spread of scores in a distribution. Another measure of variability, the *standard deviation*, shows the extent to which individual scores in a distribution vary from the mean. pp. 645–646

What are the key characteristics of a normal distribution?

- The mean, mode, and median of a *normal distribution,* or normal curve, are generally assumed to be the same, and the distribution of scores around that central point is symmetrical. p. 647

KEY TERMS

Statistics, p. 641
Descriptive statistics, p. 641
Frequency distribution, p. 641
Frequency polygon, p. 642
Measure of central tendency, p. 642
Mean, p. 642
Mode, p. 642
Median, p. 642
Variability, p. 645
Range, p. 645
Standard deviation, p. 646
Normal distribution, p. 647

Inferential Statistics and Correlation

What is the role of inferential statistics?

- *Researchers use inferential statistics* to determine whether two or more groups differ from one another and whether the difference is a result of chance. A *significant difference* is one that most likely did not occur by chance and that can be repeated experimentally with similar groups of people. Repeating an experiment to verify a result is called replicating the experiment. p. 649

What are the essential characteristics of a correlation coefficient?

- The *correlation coefficient* expresses the degree of relationship between two variables. When two variables are perfectly correlated, they are said to have a correlation coefficient of 1. A plus or minus sign in front of the correlation coefficient indicates the direction, not the strength, of a correlation relationship. The strength is shown by the number: The larger the number, the greater the strength of the correlation. pp. 650–651

Compare correlational and experimental studies with regard to cause and effect.

- Correlational studies make no statements about cause and effect. They simply show that if there is an increase in one variable, there will probably be an increase or decrease in another variable. Only through experimental studies can researchers make cause-and-effect statements. p. 652

KEY TERMS

Inferential statistics, p. 649
Significant difference, p. 649
Correlation coefficient, p. 650

References

Abed, F. (1991). Cultural influences on visual scanning patterns. *Journal of Cross-Cultural Psychology, 22,* 525–534.

Abelson, R. P. (1988). Conviction. *American Psychologist, 43,* 267–276.

Abrams, M., & Ellis, A. (1994). Stress management and counselling: Rational emotive behaviour therapy in the treatment of stress. *British Journal of Guidance and Counselling, 22,* 39–50.

Abrams, R., Swartz, C. M., & Vedak, C. (1991). Antidepressant effects of high-dose right unilateral electroconvulsive therapy. *Archives of General Psychiatry, 48,* 746–748.

Abramson, L. Y., Metalsky, G. I., & Alloy, L. B. (1989). Hopelessness depression: A theory-based subtype of depression. *Psychological Review, 96,* 358–372.

Adelmann, P. K., Antonucci, T. C., Crohan, S. E., & Coleman, L. M. (1989). Empty nest, cohort, and employment in the well-being of midlife women. *Sex Roles, 20,* 173–180.

Ader, R., & Cohen, N. (1993). Psychoneuroimmunology: Conditioning and stress. *Annual Review of Psychology, 44,* 53–85.

Ader, R., Cohen, N., & Bovbjerg, D. (1982). Conditioned suppression of humoral immunity in the rat. *Journal of Comparative and Physiological Psychology, 96,* 517–521.

Adler, A. (1969). *The science of living.* Garden City, NY: Anchor Books. (Original work published 1929.)

Adler, N. E., Boyce, T., Chesney, M. A., Cohen, S., Folkman, S., Kahn, R. L., & Syme, S. L. (1994). Socioeconomic status and health: The challenge of the gradient. *American Psychologist, 49,* 15–24.

Adorno, T., Frenkel-Brunswick, E., Levinson, D., & Sanford, R. (1950). *The authoritarian personality.* New York: Harper & Row.

Aganoff, J. A., & Boyle, G. J. (1994). Aerobic exercise, mood states and menstrual cycle symptoms. *Journal of Psychosomatic Research, 38,* 183–192.

Agnew, H. W., Jr., & Webb, W. B. (1973). The influence of time course variable on REM sleep. *Bulletin of the Psychonomic Society, 2,* 131–133.

Agras, W. S. (1992). Some structural changes that might facilitate the development of behavioral medicine. *Journal of Consulting and Clinical Psychology, 4,* 499–509.

Aiken, L. R. (1985). *Dying, death, and bereavement.* Boston: Allyn & Bacon.

Aiken, L. R. (1988). *Psychological testing and assessment* (6th ed). Boston: Allyn & Bacon.

Aikens, J. E., Wallander, J. L., Bell, D. S. H., & Cole, J. A. (1992). Daily stress variability, learned resourcefulness, regimen adherence, and metabolic control in type I diabetes mellitus: Evaluation of a path model. *Journal of Consulting and Clinical Psychology, 60,* 113–118.

Aiello, J. R., & Kolb, K. J. (1995). Electronic performance monitoring and social context: Impact on productivity and stress. *Journal of Applied Psychology, 80,* 339–353.

Ainsworth, M. D. S. (1979). Infant–mother attachment. *American Psychologist, 34,* 932–937.

Akbarian, S., Kim, J. J., Potkin, S. G., Hagman, J. O., Tafazzoli, A., Bunney, W. E., Jr., & Jones, E. G. (1995). Gene expression for glutamic acid decarboxylase is reduced without loss of neurons in prefrontal cortex of schizophrenics. *Archives of General Psychiatry, 52,* 258–266.

Alan Guttmacher Institute (1991). *Facts in brief.* New York: Author.

Aldag, R. J., & Fuller, S. R. (1993). Beyond Fiasco: A reappraisal of the groupthink phenomenon and a new model of group decision processes. *Psychological Bulletin, 113,* 533–552.

Algera, J. A. (1990). The job characteristics model of work motivation revisited. In U. Kleinbeck, H. Quast, H. Thierry, & H. Hacker (Eds.), *Work motivation.* Hillsdale, NJ: Erlbaum.

Alkon, D. L. (1989, July). Memory storage and neural systems. *Scientific American,* 42–50.

Allen, B. P. (1987). Youth suicide. *Adolescence, 22,* 271–290.

Allen, G. L. (1981). A developmental perspective on the effects of "subdividing" macrospatial experience. *Journal of Experimental Psychology: Human Learning and Memory, 7,* 120–132.

Allen, G. L. (1987). Cognitive influences on the acquisition of route knowledge in children and adults. In P. Ellen & C. Thinus-Blanc (Eds.), *Cognitive processes and spatial orientation in animal and man: Vol. 2. Neurophysiology and developmental aspects,* Boston: Martinus Nijhoff.

Allen, K. E., Turner, K. D., & Everett, P. M. (1970). A behavior modification classroom for Head Start children with problem behaviors. *Exceptional Children, 37,* 119–127.

Allgood-Merten, B., Lewinsohn, P. M., & Hops, H. (1990). Sex differences and adolescent depression. *Journal of Abnormal Psychology, 99,* 55–63.

Allgulander, C. (1994). Suicide and mortality patterns in anxiety neurosis and depressive neurosis. *Archives of General Psychiatry, 51,* 708–712.

Allington, R. L. (1981). Sensitivity to orthographic structure in educable mentally retarded children. *Contemporary Educational Psychology, 6,* 135–139.

Allison, T., Ginter, H., McCarthy, G., Nobre, A. C., Puce, A., Luby, M., & Spencer, D. D. (1994). Face recognition in human extrastriate cortex. *Journal of Neurophysiology, 71,* 821–825.

Allport, G. W. (1937). *Personality: A psychological interpretation.* New York: Holt.

Allport, G. W. (1979). *The nature of prejudice.* Cambridge, MA: Addison-Wesley. (Original work published in 1954.)

Almagor, M., Tellegen, A., & Waller, N. G. (1995). The big seven model: A cross-cultural replication and further exploration of the basic dimensions of natural language trait descriptors. *Journal of Personality and Social Psychology, 69,* 300–307.

Altman, I. (1975). *The environment and social behavior.* Monterey, CA: Brooks/Cole.

Altman, I., & Vinsel, A. M. (1977). Personal space: An analysis of E. T. Hall's proxemics framework. In I. Altman, A. Rapoport, & J. F. Wohlwill (Eds.), *Human behavior and environment: Vol. 2. Advances in theory and research.* New York: Plenum.

Amaro, H. (1995). Love, sex, and power: Considering women's realities in HIV prevention. *American Psychologist, 50,* 437–447.

Amato, P. R. (1993). Children's adjustment to divorce: Theories, hypotheses, and empirical support. *Journal of Marriage and the Family, 55,* 23–38.

Amato, P. R., & Keith, B. (1991). Parental divorce and the well-being of children: A meta-analysis. *Psychological Bulletin, 110,* 26–46.

Ambady, N., & Rosenthal, R. (1993). Half a minute: Predicting teacher evaluations from thin slices of nonverbal behavior and physical attractiveness. *Journal of Personality and Social Psychology, 64,* 431–441.

American Association on Mental Retardation (1992). *Mental retardation.* Washington, DC: Author.

American Psychiatric Association (1994). *Diagnostic and statistical manual of mental disorders* (4th ed.) *(DSM–IV).* Washington, DC: Author.

American Psychiatric Association (1995). Practice guideline for psychiatric evaluation of adults. *American Journal of Psychiatry, 152,* 67–80.

American Psychological Association (1992). Ethical principles of psychologists and code of conduct. *American Psychologist, 47,* 1597–1611.

American Psychological Association (1993). Guidelines for providers of psychological services to ethnic, linguistic, and culturally diverse populations. *American Psychologist, 48,* 45– 48.
American Psychological Association (1994). The Seville statement on violence. *American Psychologist, 49,* 845–846.
American Psychological Association (1995). *Demographic characteristics of APA members by membership status, 1993.* Washington, DC: Office of Demographic, Employment, and Educational Research, APA Education Directorate.
Ames, M. A., & Houston, D. A. (1990). Legal, social, and biological definitions of pedophilia. *Archives of Sexual Behavior, 19,* 333–342.
Amir, S., & Stewart, J. (1996). Resetting of the circadian clock by a conditioned stimulus. *Nature, 379,* 542–544.
Anderson, C. A. (1989). Temperature and aggression: Ubiquitous effects of heat on occurrence of human violence. *Psychological Bulletin, 106,* 74–96.
Anderson, C. A., & DeNeve, K. M. (1992). Temperature, aggression, and the negative affect escape model. *Psychological Bulletin, 111,* 347–351.
Anderson, K. J. (1990). Arousal and the inverted-U hypothesis: A critique of Neiss's "reconceptualizing arousal." *Psychological Bulletin, 107,* 96–100.
Anderson, N. B. (1989). Racial differences in stress-induced cardiovascular reactivity and hypertension: Current status and substantive issues. *Psychological Bulletin, 105,* 89–105.
Anderson, R., Manoogian, S., & Reznick, J. (1976). Undermining and enhancing of intrinsic motivation in pre-school children. *Journal of Personality and Social Psychology, 34,* 915–922.
Andrews, J. D. W. (1989). Integrating visions of reality: Interpersonal diagnosis and the existential vision. *American Psychologist, 44,* 803–817.
Angoff, W. H. (1988). The nature–nuture debate, aptitudes, and group differences. *American Psychologist, 43,* 713–720.
Antonovsky, A. (1987). Health promoting factors at work: The sense of coherence. In R. Kalimo, M. A. El-Batawi, & C. L. Cooper (Eds), *Psychological factors at work and their relation to health.* Geneva: World Health Organization.
Antonuccio, D. (1995). Psychotherapy for depression: No stronger medicine. *American Psychologist, 50,* 450–451.
Antonuccio, D. O., Danton, W. G. (1995). Psychotherapy versus medication for depression: Challenging the conventional wisdom with data. *Professional Psychology: Research and Practice, 26,* 574–585.
Antonuccio, D. O., Danton, W. G., & DeNelsky, G. Y. (1995). Psychotherapy vesus medication for depression: Challenging the conventional wisdom with data. *Professional Psychology: Research and Practice, 26,* 574–585.
Aoki, C., & Siekevitz, P. (1988, December). Plasticity in brain development. *Scientific American,* pp. 56–64.
Appel, J. B., & Peterson, N. J. (1965). What's wrong with punishment? *Journal of Criminal Law, Criminology, and Police Science, 156,* 450–453.
Apter, A., Galatzer, A., Beth-Halachmi, N., & Laron, Z. (1981). Self-image in adolescents with delayed puberty and growth retardation. *Journal of Youth and Adolescence, 10,* 501–505.
Apter, T. (1995). *Secret paths: Women in the new midlife.* New York: Norton.
Arango, V., Underwood, M. D., & Mann, J. J. (1992). Alterations in monoamine receptors in the brain of suicide victims. *Journal of Clinical Psychopharmacology, 12,* 8S–12S.
Argyle, M. (1991). *Cooperation.* New York: Routledge.
Arvey, R. D., & Campion, J. E. (1982). The employment interview: A summary and review of recent research. *Personnel Psychology, 35,* 281–322.
Asaad, G., & Shapiro, B. (1986). Hallucinations: Theoretical and clinical overview. *American Journal of Psychiatry, 143,* 1088– 1097.
Asch, S. E. (1955, November). Opinions and social pressure. *Scientific American,* pp. 31–35.
Asendorpf, J. B. (1989). Shyness as a final common pathway for two different kinds of inhibition. *Journal of Personality and Social Psychology, 57,* 481–492.
Ashcraft, M. H. (1989). *Human memory and cognition,* Glenview, IL: Scott, Foresman.
Atoum, A. O., & Farah, A. M. (1993). Social loafing and personal involvement among Jordanian college students. *The Journal of Social Psychology, 133,* 785–789.
Attie, I., & Brooks-Gunn, J. (1989). Development of eating problems in adolescent girls: A longitudinal study. *Developmental Psychology, 25,* 70–79.
Ayllon, T., & Azrin, N. H. (1965). The measurement and reinforcement behavior of psychotics. *Journal of the Experimental Analysis of Behavior, 8,* 357–383.
Ayllon, T., & Haughton, E. (1964). Modification of symptomatic verbal behavior of mental patients. *Behavior Research and Therapy, 2,* 87–97.
Azrin, N. H., & Holtz, W. C. (1966). Punishment. In W. K. Honig (Ed.), *Operant behavior: Areas of research and application.* New York: Appleton-Century-Crofts.
Bäckman, L., & Lipinska, B. (1993). Monitoring of general knowledge: Evidence for preservation in early Alzheimer's disease. *Neuropsychologia, 31,* 335–345.
Baddeley, A. (1994). The magical number seven: Still magic after all these years? *Psychological Review, 101,* 353–356.
Baddeley, A. D., & Hitch, G. (1974). Working memory. In G. Bower (Ed.), *Recent advances in learning and motivating* (Vol. 8). New York: Academic.
Baddeley, A. D., & Hitch, G. J. (1994). Developments in the concept of working memory. *Neuropsychology, 6,* 485–493.
Baillargeon, R. (1991). Reasoning about the height and location of a hidden object in 4.5- and 6.5-month-old infants. *Cognition, 38,* 2–17.
Baillargeon, R. (1994). How do infants learn about the physical world? *Current Directions in Psychological Science, 3,* 133–140.
Baird, J. C., Wagner, M., & Fuld, K. (1990). A simple but powerful theory of the moon illusion. *Journal of Experimental Psychology: Human Perception and Performance, 16,* 675–677.
Bak, M., Girvin, J. P., Hambrecht, F. T., Kufta, C. V., Loeb, G. E., & Schmidt, E. M. (1990). Visual sensations produced by intracortical microstimulation of the human occipital cortex. *Medical and Biological Engineering and Computing, 28,* 257–259.
Balay, J., & Shevrin, H. (1988). The subliminal psychodynamic activation method. *American Psychologist, 3,* 161–174.
Baldwin, E. (1993). The case for animal research in psychology. *Journal of Social Issues, 49,* 121–131.
Band, E. B., & Weisz, J. R. (1988). How to feel better when it feels bad: Children's perspectives on coping with everyday stress. *Developmental Psychology, 24,* 247–253.
Bandura, A. (1969). *Principles of behavior modification.* New York: Holt, Rinehart & Winston.
Bandura, A. (1977a). Self-efficacy: Toward a unifying theory of behavioral change. *Psychological Review, 84,* 191–215.
Bandura, A. (1977b). *Social learning theory.* Englewood Cliffs, NJ: Prentice-Hall.
Bandura, A. (1986) *Social foundations of thought and action: A social cognitive theory.* Englewood Cliffs, NJ: Prentice Hall.
Bandura, A. (1988). Self-regulation of motivation and action through goal systems. In V. Hamilton, G. H. Bower, & N. H. Frijda (Eds.), *Cognitive perspectives on emotion and motivation* (pp. 37–61). Dordrecht, Netherlands: Kluwer Academic.
Bandura, A. (1989). Human agency in social cognitive theory. *American Psychologist, 44,* 1175–1184.
Bandura, A., Blanchard, E. B., & Ritter, B. (1969). Relative efficacy of desensitization and modeling approaches for inducing behavioral, affective, and attitudinal changes. *Journal of Personality and Social Psychology, 13,* 173–199.
Bandura, A., Cioffi, D., Taylor, B., & Brouillard, M. E. (1988). Perceived self-efficacy in coping with cognitive stressors and opioid activation. *Journal of Personality and Social Psychology, 55,* 479–488.
Bandura, A., & Menlove, F. L. (1968). Factors determining vicarious extinction of avoidance through symbolic modeling. *Journal of Personality and Social Psychology, 8,* 99–108.
Bandura, A., Ross, D., & Ross, S. A. (1963). A comparative test of the status envy, social power, and secondary reinforcement theories of identificatory learning. *Journal of Abnormal and Social Psychology, 67,* 527–534.
Bandura, A., Ross, D., & Ross, S. A. (1963). Imitation of film-mediated aggressive models. *Journal of Abnormal and Social Psychology, 66,* 3–11.
Bandura, A., & Walters, R. (1963). *Social learning and personality development.* New York: Holt, Rinehart & Winston.
Bandura, A., & Wood, R. (1989). Effect of perceived controllability and performance standards on self-regulation of complex decision

making. *Journal of Personality and Social Psychology, 56,* 805–814.
Banich, M. T. (1995). Interhemispheric interaction: Mechanisms of unified processing. In F. L. Kitterle (Ed.), *Hemispheric communication: Mechanisms and models* (pp. 271–300). Hillsdale, NJ: Erlbaum.
Barbaree, H. E., & Marshall, W. L. (1991). The role of male sexual arousal in rape: Six models. *Journal of Consulting and Clinical Psychology, 59,* 621–630.
Barbato, G., Barker, C., Bender, C., Giesen, H. A., & Wehr, T. A. (1994). Extended sleep in humans in 14 hour nights (LD 10:14): Relationship between REM density and spontaneous awakening. *Electroencephalography and Clinical Neurophysiology, 90,* 291–297.
Barber, B. L., & Eccles, J. S. (1992). Long-term influence of divorce and single parenting on adolescent family and work-related values, behaviors, and aspirations. *Psychological Bulletin, 111,* 108–126.
Barber, T. X., Spanos, N. P., & Chaves, J. F. (1974). *Hypnosis, imagination, and human potentialities.* New York: Pergamon.
Bard, P. (1934). Emotion: The neuro-humoral basis of emotional reactions. In C. Murchison (Ed.), *Handbook of General Experimental Psychology.* Worcester, MA: Clark University Press.
Bardon, J. I. (1983). Psychology applied to education: A specialty in search of an identity. *American Psychologist, 38,* 185–196.
Baron, R. A. (1993). Interviewers' moods and evaluations of job applicants: The role of applicant qualifications. *Journal of Applied Social Psychology, 23,* 253–271.
Baron, R. A., & Byrne, D. (1991). *Social psychology* (6th ed.). Boston: Allyn & Bacon.
Barrett, G. V., & Depinet, R. L. (1991). A reconsideration of testing for competence rather than for intelligence. *American Psychologist, 46,* 1012–1024.
Bashore, T. R., & Rapp, R. E. (1993). Are there alternatives to traditional polygraph procedures? *Psychological Bulletin, 113,* 3–22.
Bass, B. M. (1985). *Leadership and performance beyond expectations.* New York: Free Press.
Bass, B. M. (1990). From transactional to transformational leadership: Learning to share the vision. *Organizational Dynamics, 18,* 19–31.
Bass, C., & Murphy, M. (1995). Somatoform and personality disorders: Syndromal comorbidity and overlapping developmental pathways. *Journal of Psychosomatic Research, 39,* 403–427.
Bates, J. E., Marvinney, D., Kelly, T., Dodge, K. A., Bennett, D. S., & Pettit, G. S. (1994). Child-care history and kindergarten adjustment. *Developmental Psychology, 30,* 690–700.
Bateson, G., Jackson, D. D., Haley, J., & Weakland, J. (1956). Toward a theory of schizophrenia. *Behavioral Science, 1,* 251–264.
Batson, C. D. (1990). How social an animal? *American Psychologist, 45,* 336–346.
Batson, C. D., Batson, J. G., Slingsby, J. K., Harrell, K. L., Peekna, H. M., & Todd, R. M. (1991). Empathic joy and the empathy–altruism hypothesis. *Journal of Personality and Social Psychology, 61,* 413–426.
Baum, A. (1987). Crowding. In D. Stokols & I. Altman (Eds.), *Handbook of environmental psychology.* New York: Wiley.
Baum, A., Grunberg, N. E., & Singer, J. E. (1992). Biochemical measurements in the study of emotion. *Psychological Science, 3,* 56–62.
Baumeister, R. F. (1990). Suicide as escape from self. *Psychological Review, 97,* 90–113.
Baumeister, R. F., & Tice, D. M. (1985). Self-esteem and responses to success and failure: Subsequent performance and intrinsic motivation. *Journal of Personality, 53,* 450–467.
Bayley, N. (1969). *Bayley scales of infant development.* New York: Psychological Corporation.
Bayley, N. (1969). Consistency and variability in the growth of intelligence from birth to eighteen years. *Journal of Genetic Psychology, 25,* 165–196.
Bechara, A., Tranel, D., Damasio, H., Adolphs, R., Rockland, C., & Damasio, A. R. (1995). Double dissociation of conditioning and declarative knowledge relative to the amygdala and hippocampus in humans. *Science, 269,* 1115–1118.
Beck, A. T. (1963). Thinking and depression: 1. Idiosyncratic content in cognitive distortions. *Archives of General Psychiatry, 9,* 324– 333.
Beck, A. T. (1967). *Depression: Clinical, experimental, and theoretical aspects.* New York: Hober.
Beck, A. T. (1972). *Depression: Causes and treatment.* Philadelphia: University of Pennsylvania Press.
Beck, A. T. (1976). *Cognitive therapy and emotional disorders.* New York: International Universities Press.
Beck, A. T. (1991). Cognitive therapy. *American Psychologist, 46,* 368–375.
Beck, A. T., & Weishaar, M. (1989). Cognitive therapy. In A. Freeman, K. M. Simon, L. E. Beutler, & H. Arkowitz (Eds.), *Comprehensive handbook of cognitive therapy.* New York: Plenum.
Beck, J. (1966). Effects of orientation and of shape similarity on perceptual grouping. *Perception and Psychophysics, 1,* 311–312.
Beck, J. G., Stanley, M. A., Baldwin, L. E., Deagle, E. A., III, & Averill, P. M. (1994). Comparison of cognitive therapy and relaxation training for panic disorder. *Journal of Consulting and Clinical Psychology, 62,* 818–826.
Becker, M. H. (1993). A medical sociologist looks at health promotion. *Journal of Health and Social Behavior, 34,* 1–6.
Becvar, D. S., & Becvar, R. J. (1988). *Family therapy: A systemic integration.* Boston: Allyn & Bacon.
Bednar, R. L., Burlingame, G. M., & Masters, K. S. (1988). Systems of family treatment: Substance or semantics? *Annual Review of Psychology, 39,* 401–434.
Beech, H. R. (1987). The use of behavioural therapy in somatic stress reactions. In R. Kalimo, M. A. El-Batawi, & C. L. Cooper (Eds.), *Psychological factors at work and their relation to health.* Geneva: World Health Organization.
Begg, I. M., Needham, D. R., & Bookbinder, M. (1993). Do backward messages unconsciously affect listeners? No. *Canadian Journal of Experimental Psychology, 47,* 1–14.
Beidel, D. C., Turner, M. W., & Trager, K. N. (1994). Test anxiety and childhood anxiety disorders in African-American and white school children. *Journal of Anxiety Disorders, 8,* 169–179.
Bekerian, D. A., & Bowers, J. M. (1983). Eyewitness testimony: Were we misled? *Journal of Experimental Psychology: Learning, Memory, and Cognition, 9,* 139–145.
Belansky, E. S., & Boggiano, A. K. (1994). Predicting helping behaviors: The role of gender and instrumental/ expressive self-schemata. *Sex Roles, 30,* 647–662.
Belenky, M. F., Clinchy, B. M., Goldberger, N. R., & Tarule, J. M. (1986). *Women's ways of knowing.* New York: Basic Books.
Bell, B. E., & Loftus, E. F. (1989). Trivial persuasion in the courtroom: The power of (a few) minor details. *Journal of Personality and Social Psychology, 56,* 669–679.
Bell, P. A. (1992). In defense of the negative affect escape model of heat and aggression. *Psychological Bulletin, 111,* 342–346.
Belmont, L., & Marolla, F. A. (1973). Birth order, family size, and intelligence. *Science, 182,* 1096–1101.
Belsky, J. (1990). Parental and nonparental child care and children's socioemotional development: A decade in review. *Journal of Marriage and the Family, 52,* 885–903.
Belsky, J. (1993). Etiology of child maltreatment: A developmental–ecological analysis. *Psychological Bulletin, 114,* 413– 434.
Belsky, J., & Rovine, M. J. (1988). Nonmaternal care in the first year of life and the security of infant–parent attachment. *Child Development, 59,* 157–167.
Bem, D. J. (1972). Self-perception theory. In L. Berkowitz (Ed.), *Advances in experimental social psychology.* New York: Academic.
Bem, S. L. (1985). Androgyny and gender schema theory: A conceptual and empirical integration. In T. B. Sonderegger (Ed.), *Nebraska symposium on motivation.* Lincoln: University of Nebraska Press.
Bem, S. L. (1993). *The lenses of gender.* New Haven: Yale University Press.
Benassi, M. A. (1982). Effects of order of presentation, primacy, and attractiveness on attributions of ability. *Journal of Personality and Social Psychology, 43,* 48–58.
Benca, R. M., Obermeyer, W. H., Thisted, R. A., & Gillin, C. (1992). Sleep and psychiatric disorders. *Archives in General Psychiatry, 49,* 651–655.
Benet, V., & Waller, N. G. (1995). The big seven factor model of personality description: Evidence for its cross-cultural generality in a Spanish sample. *Journal of Personality and Social Psychology, 69,* 701– 718.
Benjamin, L. T., Jr., Durkin, M., Link, M., Vestal, M., & Acord, J. (1992). Wundt's American doctoral students. *American Psychologist, 47,* 123–131.
Bentall, R. P. (1990). The illusion of reality: A review and integration of psychological research on hallucinations. *Psychological Bulletin, 107,* 82–95.
Berenbaum, S. A., & Snyder, E. (1995). Early hormonal influences on childhood sex-typed activity and playmate preferences: Implications

for the development of sexual orientation. *Developmental Psychology, 3,* 31–42.
Berg, T. R. (1991). The importance of equity perception and job satisfaction in predicting employee intent to stay at television stations. *Group and Organizational Studies, 16,* 268–284.
Berk, L. E. (1994). *Child development* (3rd. ed.). Boston: Allyn & Bacon.
Berkowitz, L. (1964). *The effects of observing violence.* San Francisco: Freeman.
Berkowitz, L. (1989). Frustration-aggression hypothesis: Examination and reformulation. *Psychological Bulletin, 106, 59–73.*
Berkowitz, L. (1990). On the formation and regulation of anger and aggression. *American Psychologist, 45,* 494–503.
Berkowitz, L. (1993). Pain and aggression: Some findings and implications. *Motivation and Emotion, 17,* 277–294.
Berlin, B., & Kay, P. (1969). *Basic color terms: Their universality and evolution.* Berkeley: University of California Press.
Berman, F. E., & Miner, J. B. (1985). Motivation to manage at the top executive level: A test of the hierarchic role-motivation theory. *Personnel Psychology, 38,* 377–391.
Bernal, G., & Berger, S. M. (1976). Vicarious eyelid conditioning. *Journal of Personality and Social Psychology, 34,* 62–68.
Berndt, T. J. (1992). Friendship and friends' influence in adolescence. *Psychological Science, 1,* 156–159.
Berndt, T. J., Cheung, P. C., Lau, S., Hau, K. T., & Lew, W. J. F. (1993). Perceptions of parenting in mainland China, Taiwan, and Hong Kong: Sex differences and societal differences. *Developmental Psychology, 29,* 156–164.
Bernstein, D. & Ebbesen, E. (1978). Reinforcement and substitution in humans: A multiple-response analysis. *Journal of the Experimental Analysis of Behavior, 30,* 243–253.
Bernstein, I. L. (1988, September). *What does learning have to do with weight loss and cancer?* Paper presented at a science and public policy seminar sponsored by the Federation of Behavioral, Psychological, and Cognitive Sciences, Washington, DC.
Beroldi, G. (1994). Critique of the Seville statement on violence. *American Psychologist, 49,* 847–848.
Berridge, K. C., & Robinson, T. E. (1995). The mind of an addicted brain: Neural sensitization of wanting versus liking. *Current Directions in Psychological Science. 4,* 71–76.
Berry, D. S., & Pennebaker, J. W. (1993). Nonverbal and verbal emotional expression and health. *Psychotherapy and Psychosomatics, 59,* 11–19.
Berry, D. S., & Wero, J. L. F. (1993). Accuracy in face perception: A view from ecological psychology. *Journal of Personality, 61,* 497–520.
Berscheid, E., Snyder, M., & Omoto, A. M. (1989). The relationship closeness inventory: Assessing the closeness of interpersonal relationships. *Journal of Personality and Social Psychology, 57,* 792–807.
Bertenthal, B. I., Campos, J. J., & Kermoian, R. (1994). An epigenetic perspective on the development of self-produced locomotion and its consequences. *Current Directions in Psychological Science, 3,* 140–145.
Best, C. T., & Queen, H. F. (1989). Baby, it's in your smile: Right hemiface bias in infant emotional expressions. *Developmental Psychology, 25,* 264–276.
Betancourt, H., & Lopez, S. R. (1993). The study of culture, ethnicity, and race in American psychology. *American Psychologist, 48,* 629–637.
Bettelheim, B. (1987). *A good enough parent: A book on child-rearing.* New York: Knopf.
Beutler, L. E. (1991). Have all won and must all have prizes? Revisiting Luborsky et al.'s verdict. *Journal of Consulting and Clinical Psychology, 59,* 226–232.
Beutler, L. E., Williams, R. E., Wakefield, P. J., & Entwistle, S. R. (1995). Bridging scientist and practitioner perspectives in clinical psychology. *American Psychologist, 50,* 984–994.
Bexton, W. H., Heron, W., & Scott, T. H. (1954). Effects of decreased variation in the sensory environment. *Canadian Journal of Psychology, 8,* 70–76.
Bickman, L., Teger, A., Gabriele, T., McLaughlin, C., Berger, M., & Sunaday, E. (1973). Dormitory density and helping behavior. *Environment and Behavior, 5,* 465–466.
Binion, V. J. (1990). Psychological androgyny: A black female perspective. *Sex Roles, 22,* 487–507.
Bishop, J. E. (1986, February 14). Technology. Researchers track pain's path, develop new kind of reliever. *Wall Street Journal,* p. 23.
Bivens, J. A., & Berk, L. E. (1990). A longitudinal study of the development of elementary school children's private speech. *Merrill-Palmer Quarterly, 36,* 443–463.
Blakemore, C., & Cooper, G. F. (1970). Development of the brain depends on the visual environment. *Nature, 228,* 477–478.
Blanc-Garin, J., Fauré, S., & Sabio, P. (1993). Right hemisphere performance and competence in processing mental images in a case of partial interhemispheric disconnection. *Brain and Cognition, 22,* 118–133.
Blanchard, E. B., Appelbaum, K. A., Radnitz, C. L., Michultka, D., Morrill, B., Kirsch, C., Hillhouse, J., Evans, D. D., Guarnieri, P., Attanasio, V., Andrasik, F., Jaccard, J., & Dentinger, M. P. (1990). Placebo-controlled evaluation of abbreviated progressive muscle relaxation and of relaxation combined with cognitive therapy in the treatment of tension headache. *Journal of Consulting and Clinical Psychology, 58,* 210–215.
Blasi, A. (1980). Bridging moral cognition and moral action: A critical review of the literature. *Psychological Bulletin, 88,* 1–45.
Blass, T. (1991). Understanding behavior in the Milgram obedience experiment: The role of personality, situations, and their interactions. *Journal of Personality and Social Psychology, 60,* 398–413.
Blatt, S. J. (1995). The destructiveness of perfectionism. *American Psychologist, 50,* 1003–1020.
Block, J. (1995). A contrarian view of the five-factor approach to personality description. *Psychological Bulletin, 117,* 187–215.
Block, J., & Robins, R. W. (1993). A longitudinal study of consistency and change in self-esteem from early adolescence to early adulthood. *Child Development, 64,* 909–923.
Bloom, F. E. (1981, October). Neuropeptides. *Scientific American,* pp. 148–168.
Blum, K., Cull, J. G., Braverman, E. R., & Comings, D. E. (1996). Reward deficiency syndrome. *American Scientist, 84,* 132–145.
Blum, K., Noble, E. P., Sheridan, P. J., Montgomery, A., Ritchie, T., Ozkaragoz, T., Fitch, R. J., Wood, R., Finley, O., & Sadlack, F. (1993). Genetic predisposition in alcoholism: Association of the D^2 dopamine receptor TaqI B1 RFLP with severe alcoholics. *Alcohol, 10, 59–67.*
Bohannon, J. N., III (1988). Flashbulb memories for the space shuttle disaster: A tale of two theories. *Cognition, 29,* 179–196.
Bohmer, P., & Sitton, S. (1993). The influence of birth order and family size on notable American women's selection of careers. *Psychological Record, 43,* 375–380.
Boivin, D. B., Duffy, J. F., Kronauer, R. E., & Czeisler, C. A. (1996). Dose-response relationships for resetting of human circadian clock by light. *Nature, 379,* 540–542.
Bond, C. F., Jr., & Titus, L. J. (1983). Social facilitation: A meta-analysis of 241 studies. *Psychological Bulletin, 94,* 265–292.
Bond, R., & Smith, P. B. (1996). Culture and conformity: A meta-analysis of studies using Asch's (1952b, 1956) line judgement task. *Psychological Bulletin, 119,* 111–137.
Bondareff, W., Mountjoy, C. Q., Wischik, C. M., Hauser, D. L., LaBree, L. D., & Roth, M. (1993). Evidence of subtypes of Alzheimer's disease and implications for etiology. *Archives in General Psychiatry, 50,* 350–354.
Boninger, D. S., Brock, T. C., Cook, T. D., Gruder, C. L., & Romer, D. (1990). Discovery of reliable attitude change persistence resulting from a transmitter tuning set. *Psychological Science, 1,* 268–271.
Bonnet, M. H. (1980). Sleep, performance, and mood after the energy-expenditure equivalent of 40 hours of sleep deprivation. *Psychophysiology, 17,* 56–63.
Borg, E., & Counter, S. A. (1989, August). The middle-ear muscles. *Scientific American,* pp. 74–80.
Bornstein, M. H. (1989). Sensitive periods in development: Structural characteristics and causal interpretations. *Psychological Bulletin, 105,* 179–197.
Bornstein, M. H., Tal, J., Rahn, C., Galperin, C. Z., Pecheux, M. G., Lamour, M., Toda, S., Azuma, H., Ogino, M., & Tamis-Lemonda, C. S. (1992). Functional analysis of the contents of maternal speech to infants of 5 and 13 months in four cultures: Argentina, France, Japan, and the United States. *Developmental Psychology, 28,* 593–603.
Bornstein, R. F. (1989). Exposure and affect: Overview and meta-analysis of research, 1968–1987. *Psychological Bulletin, 106,* 265–289.

Bornstein, R. F. (1992). The dependent personality: Developmental, social, and clinical perspectives. *Psychological Bulletin, 112,* 3–23.

Bornstein, R. F. (1992). Subliminal mere exposure effects. In R. F. Bornstein & T. S. Pittman (Eds.), *Perception without awareness: Cognitive, clinical and social perspectives* (pp. 191–210). New York: Guilford.

Borrie, R. A. (1991). The use of restricted environmental stimulation therapy in treating addictive behaviors. *International Journal of the Addictions, 25,* 995–1015.

Bors, D. A., & Forrin, B. (1995). Age, speed of information processing, recall, and fluid intelligence. *Intelligence, 20,* 229–248.

Botwinick, J. (1984). *Aging and behavior: A comprehensive integration of research findings* (3rd ed.). New York: Springer-Verlag.

Bouchard, T. J., Jr., Lykken, D. T., McGue, M., Segal, N. L., & Tellegen, A. (1990). Sources of human psychological differences: The Minnesota study of twins reared apart. *Science, 250,* 223–228.

Bouchard, T. J., Jr., & McGue, M. (1981). Familial studies of intelligence: A review. *Science, 212,* 1055–1058.

Bourque, L. B. (1989). *Defining rape.* Durham, NC: Duke University Press.

Bourtchuladze, R., Frenguelli, B., Blendy, J., Cioffi, D., Schutz,G., & Silva, A. J. (1994). Deficient long-term memory in mice with a targeted mutation of the camp-responsive element-binding protein. *Cell, 79,* 59–68.

Boutcher, S. H. (1992). Attention and athletic performance: An integrated approach. In Thelma S. Horn (Ed.), *Advances in sport psychology* (pp. 251–265), Champaign, IL: Human Kinetics.

Bouton, M. E. (1994). Conditioning, remembering, and forgetting. *Journal of Experimental Psychology: Animal Behavior Processes, 20,* 219–231.

Bovbjerg, D. H., Redd, W. H., Jacobsen, P. B., Manne, S. L., Taylor, K. L., Surbone, A., Crown, J. P., Norton, L., Gilewski, T. A., Hudis, C. F., Reichman, B. S., Kaufman, R. J., Currie, V. E., & Hakes, T. B. (1992). An experimental analysis of classically conditioned nausea during cancer chemotherapy. *Psychosomatic Medicine, 54,* 623–637.

Bower, G. H. (1981). Mood and memory. *American Psychologist, 36,* 126–148.

Bower, T. G. R. (1966, December). The visual world of infants. *Scientific American,* pp. 80–92.

Bowers, K. S. (1979). Time distortion and hypnotic ability: Underestimating the duration of hypnosis. *Journal of Abnormal Psychology, 88,* 435–439.

Bowers, K. S., Regehr, G., Balthazard, C., & Parker, K. (1990). Intuition in the context of discovery. *Cognitive Psychology, 22,* 72– 110.

Bowers, M. B., Jr. (1982). Biochemical processes in schizophrenia: An update. *Schizophrenia Bulletin, 6,* 393–403.

Bowlby, J. (1977). The making and breaking of affectional bonds: Etiology and psychopathology in the light of attachment theory. *British Journal of Psychiatry, 130,* 201–210.

Bowlby, J. (1988). *A secure base.* New York: Basic Books.

Boyd, B., & Wandersman, A. (1991). Predicting undergraduate condom use with the Fishbein and Ajzen and the Triandis attitude–behavior models: Implications for public health interventions. *Journal of Applied Social Psychology, 21,* 1810–1830.

Boynton, R. M. (1988). Color vision. *Annual Review of Psychology, 39,* 69–101.

Boysen, S. T., & Berntson, G. G. (1989). Numerical competence in a chimpanzee (Pan troglodytes). *Journal of Comparative Psychology, 103,* 23–31.

Bradley, B. P. (1990). Behavioural addictions: Common features and treatment implications. *British Journal of Addiction, 85,* 1417–1419.

Brainerd, C. J., Reyna, V. F., & Brandse, E. (1995). Are children's false memories more persistent than their true memories? *Psychological Science, 6,* 359–364.

Branden, N. (1980). *The psychology of romantic love.* Los Angeles: Tarcher.

Brehm, J. W. (1966). *A theory of psychological reactance.* New York: Academic.

Brehm, J. W., & Self, E. A. (1989). The intensity of motivation. *Annual Review of Psychology, 40,* 109–131.

Breier, A., Charney, D., & Heninger, G. R. (1984). Major depression in patients with agoraphobia and panic disorder. *Archives of General Psychiatry, 41,* 1129–1135.

Bretschneider, J. G., & McCoy, N. L. (1988). Sexual interest and behavior in healthy 80- to 102-year-olds. *Archives of Sexual Behavior, 17,* 109–129.

Bridges, K. M. B. (1932). Emotional development in early infancy. *Child Development, 3,* 324–341.

Broadbent, D. E. (1958). *Perception and communication.* London: Pergamon.

Brody, E. M., Lawton, M. P., and Liebowitz, B. (1984). Senile dementia: Public policy and adequate institutional care. *American Journal of Public Health, 74,* 1381–1383.

Brom, D., Kleber, R. J., & Defares, P. B. (1989). Brief psychotherapy for posttraumatic stress disorders. *Journal of Consulting and Clinical Psychology, 57,* 607–612.

Bronfenbrenner, U. (1979). *The ecology of human development.* Cambridge, MA: Harvard University Press.

Bronfenbrenner, U. (1989, September). *Who cares for children?* Invited address, UNESCO, Paris.

Brooks, D. (1985). Beginning the year in junior high: The first day of school. *Educational Leadership, 42,* 76–78.

Brooks-Gunn, J., & Furstenberg, F. F., Jr. (1989). Adolescent sexual behavior. *American Psychologist, 44,* 249–257.

Broughton, R. J. (1991). Field studies of sleep/wake patterns and performance: A laboratory experience. *Canadian Journal of Psychology, 45,* 240–253.

Brown, A. S. (1989). *How to increase your memory power.* Glenview, IL: Scott, Foresman.

Brown, B. B., Mounts, N., Lamborn, S. D., & Steinberg, L. (1993). Parenting practices and peer group affiliation in adolescence. *Child Development, 64,* 467–482.

Brown, D. R., Eaton, W. W., & Sussman, L. (1990). Race differences in prevalence of phobic disorders. *Journal of Nervous and Mental Disease, 178,* 434–441.

Brown, G. M. (1994). Light, melatonin and the sleep–wake cycle. *Journal of Psychiatry & Neuroscience, 19,* 345–353.

Brown, L. M., & Gilligan, C. (1992). *Meeting at the crossroads.* Cambridge, MA: Harvard University Press.

Brown, R. (1970). The first sentences of child and chimpanzee. In R. Brown (Ed.), *Psycholinguistics: Selected Papers.* New York: Free Press.

Brown, R., & Kulik, J. (1977). Flashbulb memories. *Cognition, 5,* 73–99.

Brown, T. A., & Barlow, D. H. (1995). Long-term outcome in cognitive-behavioral treatment of panic disorder: Clinical predictors and alternative strategies for assessment. *Journal of Consulting and Clinical Psychology, 63,* 754–765.

Brownell, K. D., & Rodin, J. (1994). The dieting maelstrom: Is it possible and advisable to lose weight? *American Psychologist, 49,* 781–791.

Brownell, K. D., & Wadden, T. A. (1992). Etiology and treatment of obesity: Understanding a serious, prevalent, and refractory disorder. *Journal of Consulting and Clinical Psychology, 60,* 505–517.

Bruner, J. (1990). *Acts of meaning.* Cambridge, MA: Harvard University Press.

Brunner, H. G., Nelen, M., Breakefield, X. O., Ropers, H. H., & van Oost, B. A. (1993). Abnormal behavior associated with a point mutation in the structural gene for monoamine oxidase A. *Science, 262,* 578–580.

Bryant, R. A., & McConkey, K. M. (1989). Hypnotic blindness: A behavioral and experiential analysis. *Journal of Abnormal Psychology, 98,* 71–77.

Buchanan, C. M., Eccles, J. S., & Becker, J. B. (1992). Are adolescents the victims of raging hormones: Evidence for activational effects of hormones on moods and behavior at adolescence. *Psychological Bulletin, 111,* 62–107.

Buchsbaum, M. S. (1990). The frontal lobes, basal ganglia, and temporal lobes as sites for schizophrenia. *Schizophrenia Bulletin, 16,* 379–382.

Buchsbaum, M. S. (1995). Charting the circuits. *Nature, 378,* 128–130.

Buchwald, A. M., & Rudick-Davis, D. (1993). The symptoms of major depression. *Journal of Abnormal Psychology, 102,* 197–205.

Buck, R., Losow, J. I., Murphy, M. M., & Costanzo, P. (1992). Social facilitation and inhibition of emotional expression and communication. *Journal of Personality and Social Psychology, 6,* 962–968.

Bukowski, W. M., Gauze, C., Hoza, B., & Newcomb, A. F. (1993). Differences and consistency between same-sex and other-sex peer relationships during early adolescence. *Developmental Psychology, 29,* 255–263.

Bulcroft, R. A., & Bulcroft, K. A. (1993). Race differences in attitudinal and motivational factors in the decision to marry. *Journal of Marriage and the Family, 55,* 338–355.

Bullock, W. A., & Gilliland, K. (1993). Eysenck's arousal theory of introversion–extraversion: A converging measures investigation. *Journal of Personality and Social Psychology, 64,* 113–123.

Burchinal, M., Lee, M., & Ramey, C. (1989). Type of day-care and preschool intellectual development in disadvantaged children. *Child Development, 60,* 128–137.

Burg, B., & Belmont, I. (1990). Mental abilities of children from different cultural backgrounds in Israel. *Journal of Cross-Cultural Psychology, 21,* 90–108.

Burger, J. M., & Hemans, L. T. (1988). Desire for control and the use of attribution processes. *Journal of Personality, 56,* 531–546.

Burman, B., & Margolin, G. (1992). Analysis of the association between marital relationships and health problems: An interactional perspective. *Psychological Bulletin, 112,* 39–63.

Burman, B., Mednick, S. A., Machon, R. A., Parnas, J., & Schulsinger, F. (1987). Children at high risk for schizophrenia: Parent and offspring perceptions of family relationships. *Journal of Abnormal Psychology, 96,* 364–366.

Burn, S. M. (1991). Social psychology and the stimulation of recycling behaviors: The block leader approach. *Journal of Applied Social Psychology, 21,* 611–629.

Bushman, B. J., & Geen, R. G. (1990). Role of cognitive–emotional mediators and individual differences in the effects of media violence on aggression. *Journal of Personality and Social Psychology, 58,* 156–163.

Buss, D. M. (1988). Love acts: The evolutionary biology of love. In R. J. Sternberg & M. L. Barnes (Eds.), *The psychology of love.* New Haven: Yale University Press.

Buss, D. M. (1995). Psychological sex differences: Origins through sexual selection. *American Psychologist, 50,* 164–168.

Butcher, J. N., Graham, J. R., Dahlstrom, W. G., & Bowman, E. (1990). The MMPI-2 with college students. *Journal of Personality Assessment, 54,* 1–15.

Butler, R., & Nisan, M. (1986). Effects of no feedback, task-related comments, and grades on intrinsic motivation and performance. *Journal of Educational Psychology, 78,* 210–216.

Butler, S. F., & Strupp, H. H. (1991). Psychodynamic psychotherapy. In M. Hersen, A. E. Kazdin, & A. S. Bellack (Eds.), *The clinical psychology handbook* (2nd Ed.). New York; Pergamon.

Butterfield-Picard, H., & Magno, J. B. (1982). Hospice the adjective, not the noun: The future of a national priority. *American Psychologist, 37,* 1254–1259.

Byne, W. (1994, May). The biological evidence challenged. *Scientific American,* pp. 50–55.

Byrne, A., & Byrne, D. G. (1993). The effect of exercise on depression, anxiety, and other mood states. *Journal of Psychosomatic Research, 37,* 565–574.

Byrne, D. G., & Reinhart, M. I. (1989). Occupation, type A behavior and self-reported angina pectoris. *Journal of Psychosomatic Research, 33,* 609–619.

Cacioppo, J. T., Petty, R. E., Feinstein, J. A., & Jarvis, W. B. G. (1996). Dispositional differences in cognitive motivation: The life and times of individuals varying in need for cognition. *Psychological Bulletin, 119,* 197–253.

Cadoret, R. J., Yates, W. R., Troughton, E., Woodworth, G., & Stewart, M. A. (1995). Genetic-environmental interaction in the genesis of aggressivity and conduct disorders. *Archives of General Psychiatry, 52,* 916–924.

Caffarella, R. S., & Olson, S. K. (1993). Psychosocial development of women: A critical review of the literature. *Adult Education Quarterly, 43,* 125–151.

Cairns, R. B., & Cairns, B. D. (1994). *Lifelines and risks: Pathways of youth in our time.* Cambridge, England: Cambridge University Press.

Caldera, Y. M., Huston, A. C., & O'Brien, M. (1989). Social interactions and play patterns of parents and toddlers with feminine, masculine, and neutral toys. *Child Development, 109,* 70–76.

Camara, W. J., & Schneider, D. L. (1994). Integrity tests: Facts and unresolved issues. *American Psychologist, 49,* 112–119.

Campis, L. B., Hebden-Curtis, C. J., & DeMaso, D. R. (1993). Developmental differences in detection and disclosure of sexual abuse. *Journal of the American Academy of Child and Adolescent Psychiatry, 32,* 920–924.

Camras, L. A., Oster, H., Campos, J. J., Miyake, K., & Bradshaw, D. (1992). Japanese and American infants' responses to arm restraint. *Developmental Psychology, 28,* 578–583.

Canavan-Gumpert, D. (1977). Generating reward and cost orientations through praise and criticism. *Journal of Personality and Social Psychology, 35,* 501–513.

Cannon, T. D., & Marco, E. (1994). Structural brain abnormalities as indicators of vulnerability to schizophrenia. *Schizophrenia Bulletin, 20,* 89–102.

Cannon, W. B. (1927). The James–Lange theory of emotion: A critical examination and an alternative theory. *American Journal of Psychology, 39,* 106–124.

Cantor, N., & Kihlstrom, J. F. (1982). Cognitive and social processes in personality. In G. T. Wilson & C. M. Franks (Eds.), *Contemporary behavior therapy.* New York: Guilford.

Carducci, B. J., & Stein, N. D. (1988, April). *The personal and situational pervasiveness of shyness in college students: A nine-year comparison.* Paper presented at the meeting of the Southeastern Psychological Association, New Orleans.

Carland, J. C., Carland, J. W., Ensley, M. D., & Stewart, H. W. (1994). The implications of cognition and learning styles for management education. *Management Learning, 25,* 413–431.

Carlson, C. R., Gantz, F. P., & Masters, J. C. (1983). Adults' emotional states and recognition of emotion in young children. *Motivation and Emotion, 7,* 81–102.

Carr, M., Borkowski, J. G., & Maxwell, S. E. (1991). Motivational components of underachievement. *Developmental Psychology, 27,* 108–118.

Caruso, G. A. L., & Corsini, D. A. (1994). The prevalence of behavior problems among toddlers in child care. *Early Education and Development, 5,* 27–40.

Carver, C. S., & Scheier, M. F. (1990). Origins and functions of positive and negative affect: A control-process view. *Psychological Review, 97,* 19–35.

Cascio, W. F. (1995). Whither industrial and organizational psychology in a changing world of work? *American Psychologist, 50,* 928–939.

Casey, R. J., & Berman, J. S. (1985). The outcome of psychotherapy with children. *Psychological Bulletin, 98,* 388–400.

Caspi, A., Elder, G. H., & Bem, D. J. (1988). Moving away from the world: Life-course patterns of shy children. *Developmental Psychology, 24,* 824–831.

Cassidy, J., & Berlin, L. J. (1994). The insecure/ambivalent pattern of attachment: Theory and research. *Child Development, 65,* 971–991.

Cattell, R. B. (1965). *The scientific analysis of personality.* Baltimore: Penguin.

Cavanagh, P., & Leclerc, Y. G. (1989). Shape from shadows. *Journal of Experimental Psychology: Human Perception and Performance, 15,* 3–27.

Ceci, S. J. (1991). How much does schooling influence general intelligence and its cognitive components? A reassessment of the evidence. *Developmental Psychology, 27,* 703–722.

Ceci, S. J., & Bronfenbrenner, U. (1991). On the demise of everyday memory. *American Psychologist, 46,* 27–31.

Ceci, S. J., & Bruck, M. (1993). Suggestibility of the child witness: A historical review and synthesis. *Psychological Bulletin, 113,* 403–439.

Celuch, K., & Slama, M. (1995). Getting along and getting ahead as motives for self-presentation: Their impact on advertising effectiveness. *Journal of Applied Social Psychology, 25,* 1700–1713.

Cermak, L. S. (1975). *Improving your memory.* New York: Norton.

Chaiken, S., & Eagly, A. H. (1983). Communication modality as a determinant of persuasion: The role of communicator salience. *Journal of Personality and Social Psychology, 45,* 241–256.

Chamberlain, K., & Zika, S. (1990). The minor events approach to stress: Support for the use of daily hassles. *British Journal of Psychology, 81,* 469–481.

Chamizo, V. D., & Mackintosh, N. J. (1989). Latent learning and latent inhibition in maze discriminations. *Quarterly Journal of Experimental Psychology, 41B,* 21–31.

Chang, F. I. F., Isaacs, K. R., & Greenough, W. T. (1991). Synapse formation occurs in association with the induction of long-term potentiation in two-year-old rat hippocampus in vitro. *Neurobiology of Aging, 12,* 517–522.

Charles, C. M. (1985). *Building classroom discipline: From models to practice* (2nd ed.). New York: Longman.
Chassin, L., Pillow, D. R., Curran, P. J., Molina, B. S. G., & Barrera, M., Jr. (1993). Relation of parental alcoholism to early adolescent substance use: A test of three mediating mechanisms. *Journal of Abnormal Psychology, 102,* 3–19.
Chen, X., Li, Z., & Rubin, K. H. (1995). Social functioning and adjustment in Chinese children: A longitudinal study. *Developmental Psychology, 31,* 531–539.
Cheng, A. T. A. (1995). Mental illness and suicide: A case-control study in East Taiwan. *Archives of General Psychiatry, 52,* 594–603.
Cherlin, A. J., Furstenberg, F. F., Jr., Chase-Lansdale, L., Kiernan, K. E., Robins, P. K., Morrison, D. R., & Teitler, J. O. (1991). Longitudinal studies of effects of divorce on children in Great Britain and the United States. *Science, 252,* 1386–1389.
Cherulnik, P. D., Turns, L. C., & Wilderman, S. K. (1990). Physical appearance and leadership: Exploring the role of appearance-based attribution in leader emergence. *Journal of Applied Social Psychology, 20,* 1530–1539.
Chidester, T. R. (1986). Problems in the study of interracial interaction: Pseudo-interracial dyad paradigm. *Journal of Personality and Social Psychology, 50,* 74–79.
Chomsky, N. (1957). *Syntactic structures.* The Hague, Netherlands: Mouton.
Chomsky, N. (1986). *Knowledge of language: Its nature, origin, and use.* New York: Praeger.
Chomsky, N. (1990). On the nature, use and acquisition of language. In W. G. Lycan (Ed.), *Mind and cognition* (pp. 627–646). Oxford, England: Blackwell.
Cialdini, R. B. (1993). *Influence* (3rd ed.). New York: HarperCollins.
Cialdini, R. B. (1994). Interpersonal influence. In S. Shavitt & T. C. Brock (Eds.), *Persuasion: Psychological insights and perspectives* (pp. 195–218). Boston: Allyn & Bacon.
Cialdini, R. B., Trost, M. R., & Newsom, J. T. (1995). Preference for consistency: The development of a valid measure and the discovery of surprising behavioral implications. *Journal of Personality and Social Psychology, 69,* 318–328.
Cicero, T. J. (1994). Effects of paternal exposure to alcohol on offspring development. *Alcohol Health and Research World, 18,* 37–41.
Cioffi, F. (1974). Was Freud a liar? *The Listener,* 172–174.
Clarizio, H., & Veres, V. (1984). A short-form version of the WISC–R for the learning disabled. *Psychology in the Schools, 21,* 154–157.
Clark, L. A., Watson, D., & Reynolds, S. (1995). Diagnosis and classification of psychopathology: Challenges to the current system and future directions. *Annual Review of Psychology, 46,* 121–153.
Clark, M. S., & Reis, H. T. (1988). Interpersonal processes in close relationships. *Annual Review of Psychology, 39,* 609–672.
Clarke-Stewart, A. (1973). Interactions between mothers and their young children: Characteristics and consequences. *Monographs of the Society of Research in Child Development, 38.*
Clarke-Stewart, A. (1989). Infant day care: Maligned or malignant? *American Psychologist, 44,* 266–273.
Clarke-Stewart, A., Friedman, S., & Koch, J. B. (1985). *Child development: A topical approach.* New York: Wiley.
Clarkin, J. F., & Hull, J. W. (1991). The brief psychotherapies. In M. Hersen, A. E. Kazdin, & A. S. Bellack (Eds.), *The clinical psychology handbook* (2nd ed.). New York: Pergamon.
Claxton, R. P., & McIntyre, R. P. (1994). Empirical relationships between need for cognition and cognitive style: Implications for consumer psychology. *Psychological Reports, 74,* 723–732.
Cleveland, J. N., Murphy, K. R., & Williams, R. E. (1989). Multiple uses of performance appraisal: Prevalence and correlates. *Journal of Applied Psychology, 74,* 130–135.
Clifton, R. K., Muir, D. W., Ashmead, D. H., & Clarkson, M. G. (1993). Is visually guided reaching in early infancy a myth? *Child Development, 64,* 1099–1110.
Coates, B., Pusser, H. E., & Goodman, I. (1976). The influence of "Sesame Street" and "Mister Rogers' Neighborhood" on children's social behavior in the preschool. *Child Development, 47,* 138–144.
Cochrane, G. J. (1987). Hypnotherapy in weight-loss treatment: Case illustrations. *American Journal of Clinical Hypnosis, 30,* 20–27.
Coffey, C. W., Weiner, R. D., Djang, W. T., Figiel, G. S., Soady, S. A. R., Patterson, L. J., Holt, P. D., Spritzer, C. E., & Wilinson, W. E. (1991). Brain anatomic effects of electroconvulsive therapy. *Archives of General Psychiatry, 48,* 1013–1021.
Cohen, R. J., Montague, P., Nathanson, L. S., & Swerdlik, M. E. (1988). *Psychological testing.* Mountain View, CA: Mayfield.
Cohen, S., Tyrrell, D. A. J., & Smith, A. P. (1991). Psychological stress and susceptibility to the common cold. *New England Journal of Medicine, 325,* 606–612.
Cohen, S., Tyrrell, D. A. J., & Smith, A. P. (1993). Negative life events, perceived stress, negative affect, and susceptibility to the common cold. *Journal of Personality and Social Psychology, 64,* 131–140.
Cohen, S., & Williamson, G. M. (1991). Stress and infectious disease in humans. *Psychological Bulletin, 109,* 5–24.
Cohn, D. A. (1990). Child–mother attachment of six-year-olds and social competence at school. *Child Development, 61,* 152–162.
Cohn, J. F., & Tronick, E. Z. (1983). Three-month-old infants' reaction to simulated maternal depression. *Child Development, 54,* 185–193.
Cohn, L. (1991). Sex differences in the course of personality development: A meta-analysis. *Psychological Bulletin, 109,* 252–266.
Cole, D. A. (1989). Psychopathology of adolescent suicide: Hopelessness, coping beliefs, and depression. *Journal of Abnormal Psychology, 98,* 248–255.
Collins, N. L., & Miller, L. C. (1994). Self-disclosure and liking: A meta-analytic review. *Psychological Bulletin, 116,* 457–475.
Colvin, C. R., & Block, J. (1994). Do positive illusions foster mental health? An examination of the Taylor and Brown formulation. *Psychological Bulletin, 116,* 3–20.
Comer, J. P. (1988, November). Educating poor minority children. *Scientific American,* pp. 42–51.
Contrada, R. J. (1989). Type A behavior, personality hardiness, and cardiovascular responses to stress. *Journal of Personality and Social Psychology, 57,* 895–903.
Conway, M. A. (1991). In defense of everyday memory. *American Psychologist, 46,* 19–26.
Conway, M. A., Anderson, S. J., Larsen, S. F., Donnelly, C. M., McDaniel, M. A., McClelland, A. G. R., Rawles, R. E., & Logie, R. H. (1994). The formation of flashbulb memories. *Memory & Cognition, 22,* 326–343.
Coppola, D. M., & O'Connell, R. J. (1988). Behavioral responses of peripubertal female mice towards puberty-accelerating and puberty-delaying chemical signals. *Chemical Senses, 13,* 407–424.
Corbetta, M., Shulman, G. L., Miezin, F. M., & Petersen, S. E. (1995). Superior parietal cortex activation during spatial attention shifts and visual feature conjunction. *Science, 270,* 802–805.
Coren, S., & Aks, D. J. (1990). Moon illusion in pictures: A multimechanism approach. *Journal of Experimental Psychology: Human Perception and Performance, 16,* 365–380.
Coren, S., & Halpern, D. F. (1991). Left-handedness: A marker for decreased survival fitness. *Psychological Bulletin, 109,* 90–106.
Corina, D. P., Vaid, J., & Bellugi, U. (1992). The linguistic basis of left hemisphere specialization. *Science, 255,* 1258–1260.
Coryell, W., Endicott, J., Keller, M. (1992). Major depression in a nonclinical sample. *Archives of General Psychiatry, 49,* 117–125.
Costanzo, M., Archer, D., Aronson, E., & Pettigrew, T. (1986). Energy conservation behavior: The difficult path from information to action. *American Psychologist, 41,* 521–528.
Covin, T. M., & Sattler, J. M. (1985). A longitudinal study of the Stanford–Binet and WISC–R with special education students. *Psychology in the Schools, 22,* 274–276.
Cowen, E. L. (1991). In pursuit of wellness. *American Psychologist, 46,* 404–408.
Cox, R. H., Qiu, Y., & Liu, Z. (1993). Overview of sport psychology. In R. N. Singer, M. Murphey, & L. K. Tennant (Eds.), *Handbook of research on sport psychology* (pp. 3–31). New York: Macmillan.
Craik, F. I. (1994). Memory changes in normal aging. *Current Directions in Psychological Science, 3,* 155–158.
Craik, F. I. M., & Lockhart, R. S. (1972). Levels of processing: A framework for memory research. *Journal of Verbal Learning and Verbal Behavior, 11,* 671–784.
Craik, F. I. M., Morris, R. G., & Gick, M. L. (1990). Adult age differences in working memory. In G. Vallar and T. Shallice (Eds.), *Neuropsychological impairments of short-term memory* (pp. 247–267). New York: Cambridge University Press.
Crandall, C. S. (1994). Prejudice against fat people: Ideology and self-interest. *Journal of Personality and Social Psychology, 66,* 882–894.

Crane, J. (1994). Exploding the myth of scientific support for the theory of black intellectual inferiority. *Journal of Black Psychology, 20,* 189–209.

Crawford, C. B., & Anderson, J. L. (1989). Sociobiology. *American Psychologist, 44,* 1449–1459.

Crawford, H. J. (1994). Brain dynamics and hypnosis: Attentional and disattentional processes, *The International Journal of Clinical and Experimental Hypnosis, 42,* 204–232.

Crawford, M., & MacLeod, M. (1990). Gender in the college classroom: An assessment of the "chilly climate" for women. *Sex Roles, 23,* 101–122.

Crespi, T. D. (1988). Effectiveness of time-out: A comparison of psychiatric, correctional and day-treatment programs. *Adolescence, 23,* 805–811.

Crick, F., & Koch, C. (1992, September). The problem of consciousness. *Scientific American,* pp. 153–159.

Crittenden, K. S., Fugita, S. S., Bae, H., Lamug, C. B., & Lin, C. (1992). A cross-cultural study of self-report depressive symptoms among college students. *Journal of Cross-Cultural Psychology, 23,* 163–178.

Cronan, T. A., Walen, H. R., Cruz, S. G. (1994). The effects of community-based literacy training on Head Start parents. *Journal of Community Psychology, 22,* 248–258.

Crowder, R. G. (1993). Short-term memory: Where do we stand? *Memory and Cognition, 21,* 142–145.

Crowl, R. K., & MacGinitie, W. H. (1974). The influence of students' speech characteristics on teachers' evaluations of oral answers. *Journal of Educational Psychology, 66,* 304–308.

Crystal, D. S., Chen, C., Fuligni, A. J., Stevenson, H. W., Hsu, C., Ko, H., Kitamura, S., & Kimura, S. (1994). Psychological maladjustment and academic achievement: A cross-cultural study of Japanese, Chinese, and American high school students. *Child Development, 65,* 738–753.

Cummings, N. A. (1986). The dismantling of our health system: Strategies for the survival of psychological practice. *American Psychologist, 41,* 426–431.

Cunningham, M. R., Barbee, A. P., & Pike, C. L. (1990). What do women want? Facialmetric assessment of multiple motives in the perception of male facial physical attractiveness. *Journal of Personality and Social Psychology, 59,* 61–72.

Curran, D. K. (1987). *Adolescent suicidal behavior.* Washington, DC: Hemisphere.

Cutler, W. B., Preti, G., Krieger, A., Huggins, G. R., Garcia, C. R., & Lawley, H. J. (1986). Human axillary secretions influence women's menstrual cycles: The role of donor extract from men. *Hormones and Behavior, 20,* 463–473.

Czeisler, C. A., Johnson, M. P., Duffy, J. F., Brown, E. N., Ronda, J. M., & Kronauer, R. E. (1990). Exposure to bright light and darkness to treat physiologic maladaptation to night work. *New England Journal of Medicine, 322,* 1253–1259.

Dakof, G. A., & Taylor, S. E. (1990). Victims' perceptions of social support: What is helpful from whom? *Journal of Personality and Social Psychology, 58,* 80–89.

Damasio, A. R. (1994). *Descartes' error: Emotion, reason, and the human brain.* New York: Putnam.

Damasio, A. R., & Damasio, H. (1992, September). Brain and language. *Scientific American,* pp. 89–95.

Damasio, A. R., Tranel, D., & Damasio, H. (1990). Face agnosia and the neural substrates of memory. *Annual Review of Neuroscience, 13,* 89–109.

Daniels, D., & Plomin, R. (1985). Origins of individual differences in infant shyness. *Developmental Psychology, 21,* 118–121.

Danion, J. M., Willard-Schroeder, D., Zimmermann, M. A., Grange, D., Schlienger, J. L., & Singer, L. (1991). Explicit memory and repetition priming in depression. *Archives of General Psychiatry, 48,* 707–711.

Danner, R., & Edwards, D. (1992). Life is movement: Exercise for the older adult. *Activities, Adaptation & Aging, 17,* 15–26.

Daum, I., Ackermann, H., Schugens, M. M., Reimold, C., Dichgans, J., & Birbaumer, N. (1993). The cerebellum and cognitive functions in humans. *Behavioral Neuroscience, 107,* 411–419.

Davidson, R. J. (1992). Emotion and affective style: Hemispheric substrates. *Psychological Science, 3,* 39–43.

Davis, D., & Padesky, C. (1989). Enhancing cognitive therapy with women. In A. Freeman, K. M. Simon, L. E. Beutler, & H. Arkowitz (Eds.), *Comprehensive handbook of cognitive therapy.* New York: Plenum.

Davis, K. E., & Todd, M. J. (1982). Friendship and love relationships. In K. E. Davis & M. J. Todd (Eds.), *Advances in descriptive psychology* (Vol. 2). Greenwich, CT: JAI.

Davis, N. S., & Thornburg, K. R. (1994). Child care: A synthesis of research. *Early Child Development and Care, 98,* 39–45.

Dawes, R. M. (1994). *House of cards: Psychology and psychotherapy built on myth.* New York: Free Press.

Dawson, G., Grofer, L., Panagiotides, H., Hill, D., & Spieker, S. (1992). Frontal lobe activity and affective behavior of infants of mothers with depressive symptoms. *Child Development, 63,* 725–737.

Dawson, G., Klinger, L. G., Panagiotides, H., Spieker, S., & Frey, K. (1992). Infants of mothers with depressive symptoms: Electroencephalographic and behavioral findings related to attachment status. *Development and Psychopathology, 4,* 67–80.

DeAngelis, T. (1988). In praise of rose-colored specs. *APA Monitor, 19,* 11.

DeBono, K. G. (1992). Pleasant scents and persuasion: An information processing approach. *Journal of Applied Social Psychology, 22,* 910–919.

Deci, E. L. (1972). Effects of contingent and non-contingent rewards and controls on intrinsic motivation. *Organizational Behavior and Human Performance, 8,* 217–229.

Deci, E. L. (1975). *Intrinsic motivation.* New York: Plenum.

Deci, E. L., Driver, R. E., Hotchkiss, L., Robbins, R. J., & Wilson, I. M. (1993). The relation of mothers' controlling vocalizations to children's intrinsic motivation. *Journal of Experimental Child Psychology, 55,* 151–162.

Deffenbacher, K. A. (1994). Effects of arousal on everyday memory. *Human Performance, 7,* 141–161.

DeLongis, A., Folkman, S., & Lazarus, R. S. (1988). The impact of daily stress on health and mood: Psychological and social resources as mediators. *Journal of Personality and Social Psychology, 54,* 486–495.

Deluga, R. J. (1990). The effects of transformational, transactional, and laissez faire leadership characteristics on subordinate influencing behavior. *Basic and Applied Social Psychology, 11,* 191–203.

Dement, W. C., Greenberg, S., & Klein, R. (1966). The effect of partial REM sleep deprivation and delayed recovery. *Journal of Psychiatric Research, 4,* 141–152.

Dement, W. C., & Kleitman, N. (1957). The relation of eye movements during sleep to dream activity: An objective method for the study of dreaming. *Journal of Experimental Psychology, 53,* 339–346.

Dement, W. C., & Wolpert, E. A. (1958). The relation of eye movements, body motility, and external stimuli to dream content. *Journal of Experimental Psychology, 55,* 543–553.

DeNisi, A. S., Robbins, T., & Cafferty, T. P. (1989). Organization of information used for performance appraisals: Role of diary-keeping. *Journal of Applied Psychology, 74,* 124–129.

Deniston, W. M., & Ramanaiah, N. V. (1993). California psychological inventory and the five-factor model of personality. *Psychological Reports, 73,* 491–496.

Denmark, F. I. (1994). Engendering psychology. *American Psychologist, 49,* 329–334.

Dennett, D. C. (1991). *Consciousness explained.* Boston: Little, Brown.

Dentan, R. K. (1968). *The Semai: A nonviolent people of Malaya.* New York: Holt, Rinehart & Winston.

DePaulo, B. M. (1992). Nonverbal behavior and self-presentation. *Psychological Bulletin, 111,* 230–243.

DePaulo, B. M., Dull, W. R., Greenberg, J. M., & Swaim, G. W. (1989). Are shy people reluctant to ask for help? *Journal of Personality and Social Psychology, 56,* 834–844.

DePaulo, P. J., & DePaulo, B. M. (1989). Can deception by salespersons and customers be detected through nonverbal behavioral cues? *Journal of Applied Social Psychology, 19,* 1552–1577.

Deregowski, J. B. (1980). Perception. In H. C. Triandis & J. W. Berry (Eds.), *Handbook of cross-cultural psychology: Vol. 3. Basic processes.* Boston: Allyn & Bacon.

Dershowitz, A. M. (1986). *Reversal of fortune inside the Von Bulow case.* New York: Random House.

D'Esposito, M., Detre, J. A., Alsop, D. C., Shin, R. K., Atlas, S., & Grossman, M. (1995). The neural basis of the central executive system of working memory. *Nature, 378,* 279–281.

DeValois, R. L., & Jacobs, G. H. (1968). Primate color vision, *Science, 162,* 533–540.

DeValois, R. L., Thorell, L. G., & Albrecht, D. G. (1985). Periodicity of striate-cortex-cell receptive fields. *Journal of the Optical Society of America (A), 2,* 1115–1123.

DeVellis, B. M., & Blalock, S. J. (1992). Illness attributions and hopelessness depression: The role of hopelessness expectancy. *Journal of Abnormal Psychology, 101,* 257–264.

DeVries, B., & Walker, L. J. (1986). Moral reasoning and attitudes toward capital punishment. *Developmental Psychology, 22,* 509–513.

Deyo, R. A., Straube, K. T., & Disterhoft, J. F. (1989). Nimodipine facilitates associative learning in aging rabbits. *Science, 243,* 809–811.

Diener, E., Lusk, R., DeFour, D., & Flax, R. (1980). Deindividuation: Effects of group size, density, number of observers, and group member similarity on self-consciousness and disinhibited behavior. *Journal of Personality and Social Psychology, 39,* 449–459.

Dietvorst, T. F. (1978). Biofeedback assisted relaxation training with patients recovering from myocardial infarction. *Dissertation Abstracts International, 38,* 3389.

DiGiuseppe, R. (1989). Cognitive therapy with children. In A. Freeman, K. M. Simon, L. E. Beutler, & H. Arkowitz (Eds.), *Comprehensive handbook of cognitive therapy.* New York: Plenum Press.

DiLalla, D. L., & Gottesman, I. I. (1995). Normal personality characteristics in identical twins discordant for schizophrenia. *Journal of Abnormal Psychology, 104,* 490–499.

DiLalla, L. F., Thompson, L. A., Plomin, R., Phillips, K., Fagan, J. F., III, Haith, M. M., Cyphers, L. H., & Fulker, D. W. (1990). Infant predictors of preschool and adult IQ: A study of infant twins and their parents. *Development Psychology, 26,* 759–769.

DiMascio, A., Weissman, M. M., Prusoff, B. A., Neu, C., Zwilling, M., & Klerman, G. L. (1979). Differential symptom reduction by drugs and psychotherapy in acute depression. *Archives of General Psychiatry, 36,* 1450–1456.

DiMatteo, M. R., & DiNicola, D. D. (1982). *Achieving patient compliance: The psychology of the medical practitioner's role.* New York: Pergamon.

Dindia, K., & Allen, M. (1992). Sex differences in self-disclosure: A meta-analysis. *Psychological Bulletin, 112,* 106–124.

Dinges, N. G., & Hull, P. V. (1993). Personality, culture, and international studies. In D. Lieberman (Ed.), *Revealing the world: An interdisciplinary reader for international studies.* Dubuque, IA: Kendall-Hunt.

Dion, K. K., Pak, A. W., & Dion, K. L. (1990). Stereotyping physical attractiveness. *Journal of Cross-Cultural Psychology, 21,* 158–179.

Dobson, K. S., & Block L. (1988). Historical and philosophical bases of the cognitive–behavioral therapies. In K. S. Dobson (Ed.), *Handbook of cognitive–behavioral therapies.* New York: Guilford.

Dohrenwend, B. P., & Shrout, P. E. (1985). "Hassles" in the conceptualization and measurement of life stress variables. *American Psychologist, 40,* 780–785.

Dolcini, M. M., Coates, T. J., Catania, J. A., Kegeles, S. M., & Hauck, W. W. (1995). Multiple sexual partners and their psychosocial correlates: The population-based AIDS in multiethnic neighborhoods (AMEN) study. *Health Psychology, 14,* 22–31.

Dollard, J., Doob, L. W., Miller, N. E., Mowrer, O. H., & Sears, R. R. (1939). *Frustration and agrression.* New Haven, CT: Yale University Press.

Dollins, A. B., Lynch, H. J., Wurtman, R. J., Deng, M. H., Kischka, K. U., Gleason, R. E., & Lieberman, H. R. (1993). Effect of pharmacological daytime doses of melatonin on human mood and performance. *Psychopharmacology, 112,* 490–496.

Dollins, A. B., Lynch, H. J., Wurtman, R. J., Deng, M. H., et al. (1993). Effects of illumination on human nocturnal serum melatonin levels and performance. *Physiology and Behavior, 53,* 153–160.

Domino, G. (1986). Sleep habits in the elderly: A study of three Hispanic cultures. *Journal of Cross-Cultural Psychology, 17,* 109– 120.

Domino, G. (1992). Cooperation and competition in Chinese and American children. *Journal of Cross-Cultural Psychology, 23,* 456–467.

Donnelly, C. M., & McDaniel, M. A. (1993). Use of analogy in learning scientific concepts. *Journal of Experimental Psychology: Learning, memory, and cognition, 19,* 975–987.

Doob, A. N., & McLaughlin, D. S. (1989). Ask and you shall be given: Request size and donations to a good cause. *Journal of Applied Social Psychology, 19,* 1049–1056.

Douglass, H. M., Moffitt, T. E., Dar, R., McGee, R., & Silva, P. (1995). Obssessive–compulsive disorder in a birth cohort of 18-year-olds: Prevalence and predictors. *Journal of the American Academy of Child and Adolescent Psychiatry, 34,* 1424–1429.

Dowling, J. E., & Boycott, B. B. (1996). *Proceedings of the Royal Society* (London) (series), *166,* 80–111.

Downey, G., & Coyne, J. C. (1990). Children of depressed parents: An integrative review. *Psychological Bulletin, 108,* 50–76.

Drennen, W. T., & Holden, E. W. (1984). Trait/set interactions in EMG biofeedback. *Psychological Reports, 54,* 843–849.

Dreyer, P. H. (1982). Sexuality during adolescence. In B. B. Wolman (Ed.), *Handbook of developmental psychology.* Englewood Cliffs, NJ: Prentice-Hall.

Dryden, W., & Ellis A. (1988). Rational–emotive therapy. In K. S. Dobson (Ed.), *Handbook of cognitive–behavioral therapies.* New York: Guilford.

Dubovsky, S. L., & Thomas, M. (1995). Beyond specificity: Effects of serotonin and serotonergic treatments on psychobiological dysfunction. *Journal of Psychosomatic Research, 39,* 429–444.

Duckitt, J. (1992). Psychology and prejudice. *American Psychologist, 47,* 1182–1193.

Duffy, R. D., Kalsher, M. J., & Wogalter, M. S. (1993). The effectiveness of an interactive warning in a realistic product-use situation. *Proceedings of the Human Factors and Ergonomics Society, 37th Annual Meeting,* 935–939.

Dunant, Y., & Israel, M. (1985, April). The release of acetylcholine. *Scientific American,* pp. 58–83.

Duncan, J. (1980). The locus of interference in the perception of simultaneous stimuli. *Psychological Review, 87,* 272–300.

Dunn, J. (1992). Siblings and development. *Current Directions in Psychological Science, 1,* 6–9.

Dunn, J., & Plomin, R. (1990). *Separate lives.* New York: Basic.

Dura, J. R., Stukenberg, K. W., & Kiecolt-Glaser, J. K. (1990). Chronic stress and depressive disorders in older adults. *Journal of Abnormal Psychology, 99,* 284–290.

Dutton, D. G. (1988). *The domestic assault of women.* Boston: Allyn & Bacon.

Dweck, C. S. (1986). Motivational processes affecting learning: Special issue. Psychological science and education. *American Psychologist, 41,* 1040–1048.

Dweck, C. S., & Leggett, E. L. (1988). A socio-cognitive approach to motivation and personality. *Psychological Review, 95,* 256–273.

Dwyer, W. O., Leeming, F. C., Cobern, M. K., Porter, B. E., & Jackson, J. M. (1993). Critical review of behavioral interventions to preserve the environment research since 1980. *Environment and Behavior, 25,* 275–321.

Eagly, A. H. (1992). Uneven progress: Social psychology and the study of attitudes. *Journal of Personality and Social Psychology, 63,* 693–710.

Eagly, A. H. (1995). The science and politics of comparing women and men. *American Psychologist, 50,* 145–158.

Eagly, A. H., Ashmore, R. D., Makhijani, M. G., & Longo, L. C. (1991). What is beautiful is good, but . . . : A meta-analytic review of research on the physical attractiveness stereotype. *Psychological Bulletin, 110,* 109–128.

Eagly, A. H., & Chaiken, S. (1993). *The psychology of attitudes.* Fort Worth, TX: Harcourt Brace Jovanovich.

Eagly, A. H., & Johnson, B. T. (1990). Gender and leadership style: A meta-analysis. *Psychological Bulletin, 108,* 233–256.

Eagly, A. H., Makhijani, M. G., & Klonsky, B. G. (1992). Gender and the evaluation of leaders: A meta-analysis. *Psychological Bulletin, 111,* 1, 3–22.

Eagly, A. H., & Steffen, V. J. (1986). Gender and aggressive behavior: A meta-analytic review of the social psychological literature. *Psychological Bulletin, 100,* 309–330.

Eccles, J. S., Wigfield, A., Midgley, C., Reuman, D., Buchanan, C. M., Flanagan, C., & MacIver, D. (1993). Development during adolescence: The impact of stage–environment fit on young adolescents' experiences in schools and families. *American Psychologist, 48,* 90–101.

Egeland, B., & Hiester, M. (1995). The long-term consequences of infant day-care and mother–infant attachment. *Child Development, 66,* 474–485.

Egeland, B., Jacobvitz, D., & Sroufe, L. A. (1988). Breaking the cycle of abuse. *Child Development, 59,* 1080–1088.

Egeth, H. E. (1993). What do we not know about eyewitness identification? *American Psychologist, 48,* 577–580.

Eich, E. (1995). Searching for mood dependent memory. *Psychological Science, 6,* 67–75.

Eisenberger, R., & Selbst, M. (1994). Does reward increase or decrease creativity? *Journal of Personality and Social Psychology, 66,* 1116–1127.
Eisenman, R. (1993). Professor Anita Hill versus Judge Clarence Thomas: The view of students at a Southern university. *Bulletin of the Psychonomic Society, 31,* 179–180.
Ekman, P. (1992). Facial expressions of emotion: New findings, new questions. *Psychological Science, 3,* 34–38.
Ekman, P. (1993). Facial expression and emotion. *American Psychologist, 48,* 384–392.
Ekman, P. (1994). Strong evidence for universals in facial expressions: A reply to Russell's mistaken critique. *Psychological Bulletin, 115,* 268–287.
Ekman, P., Friesen, W. V., & O'Sullivan, M. (1988). Smiles when lying. *Journal of Personality and Social Psychology, 54,* 414–420.
Elbert, T., Pantev, C., Wienbruch, C., Rockstroh, B., & Taub, E. (1995). Increased cortical representation of the fingers of the left hand in string players. *Science, 270,* 305–307.
Elkind, D. (1981a). Giant in the nursery—Jean Piaget. In E. M. Hetherington & R. D. Parke (Eds.), *Contemporary readings in child psychology* (2nd ed.). New York: McGraw-Hill.
Elkind, D. (1981b). *The hurried child.* Reading, MA: Addison-Wesley.
Elkind, D. (1987). *Miseducation.* New York: Knopf.
Elkins, L. E., & Peterson, C. (1993). Gender differences in best friendships. *Sex Roles, 29,* 497–508.
Elliott, E. S., & Dweck, C. S. (1988). Goals: An approach to motivation and achievement. *Journal of Personality and Social Psychology, 54,* 5–12.
Elliott, R. (1987). *Litigating intelligence: IQ tests, special education, and social science in the courtroom.* Dover, MS: Auburn House.
Ellis, A. (1970). *The essence of rational psychotherapy: A comprehensive approach to treatment.* New York: Institute for Rational Living.
Ellis, A. (1988, August). *The philosophical basis of rational–emotive therapy (RET).* Paper presented at the 96th Annual Convention of the American Psychological Association, Atlanta.
Ellis, A. (1990). How can psychological treatment aim to be briefer and better? The rational–emotive approach to brief therapy. In J. K. Zeig & S. G. Gilligan (Eds.), *Brief therapy myths, methods, and metaphors,* New York: Brunner/Mazel.
Ellis, A. (1993). Reflections on rational–emotive therapy. *Journal of Consulting and Clinical Psychology, 61,* 199–201.
Ellis, A., & Harper, R. A. (1961). *A guide to rational living.* North Hollywood, CA: Wilshire.
Ellis, G. M. (1994). Acquaintance rape. *Perspectives in Psychiatric Care, 30,* 11–16.
Ellis, L. (1991). A synthesized (biosocial) theory of rape. *Journal of Consulting and Clinical Psychology, 59,* 631–642.
Ellis, R. J., & Oscar-Berman, M. (1989). Alcoholism, aging, and functional cerebral asymmetries. *Psychological Bulletin, 106,* 128–147.
Ellsworth, P. C. (1994). William James and emotion: Is a century of fame worth a century of misunderstanding? *Psychological Review, 101,* 222–229.
Embretson, S. E. (1995). The role of working memory capacity and general control processes in intelligence. *Intelligence, 20,* 169–189.
Emde, R. N., Plomin, R., Robinson, J., Corley, R., DeFries, J., Fulker, D. W., Reznick, J. S., Campos, J., Kagan, J., & Zahn-Waxler, C. (1992). Temperament, emotion, and cognition at fourteen months: The MacArthur longitudinal twin study. *Child Development, 63,* 1437–1455.
Emery, R. E. (1989a). Family violence. *American Psychologist, 44,* 321–328.
Emery, R. E. (1989b, September 15). *Family violence: Has science met its match?* Edited transcript of a science and public policy seminar presented by the Federation of Behavioral, Psychological, and Cognitive Sciences in the Rayburn House Office Building, Washington, DC.
Eppinger, M. G., Craig, P. L., Adams, R. L., & Parsons, O. A. (1987). The WAIS–R index for estimating premorbid intelligence: Cross-validation and clinical utility. *Journal of Consulting and Clinical Psychology, 55,* 86–90.
Epstein, R. (1991). Skinner, creativity, and the problem of spontaneous behavior. *Psychological Science, 2,* 362–370.
Erel, O., & Burman, B. (1995). Interrelatedness of marital relations and parent–child relations: A meta-analytic review. *Psychological Bulletin, 118,* 108–132.
Ericsson, K. A., & Charness, N. (1994). Expert performance: Its structure and acquisition. *American Psychologist, 49,* 725–747.
Ericsson, K. A., Chase, W. G., & Faloon, S. (1980). Acquisition of a memory skill. *Science, 208,* 1181–1182.
Ericsson, K. A., & Kintsch, W. (1995). Long-term working memory. *Psychological Review, 102,* 211–245.
Ericsson, K. A., Krampe, R. T., & Tesch-Römer, C. (1993). The role of deliberate practice in the acquisition of expert performance. *Psychological Review, 100,* 363–406.
Erikson, E. H. (1963). *Childhood and society* (2nd ed.). New York: Norton.
Erikson, E. H. (1968). *Identity: Youth and crisis.* New York: Norton.
Erlenmeyer-Kimling, L., & Jarvik, L. F. (1963). Genetics and intelligence: A review. *Science, 142,* 1477–1479.
Eron, L. D. (1987). The development of aggressive behavior from the perspective of a developing behaviorism. *American Psychologist, 42,* 435–442.
Eron, L. D., & Huesmann, L. R. (1980). Adolescent aggression and television. *Annals of the New York Academy of Sciences, 347,* 319–331.
Eslinger, P. J., Grattan, L. M., Damasio, H., & Damasio, A. R. (1992). Developmental consequences of childhood frontal lobe damage. *Archives of Neurology, 49,* 764–769.
Esses, V. M., & Webster, C. D. (1988). Physical attractiveness, dangerousness, and the Canadian criminal code. *Journal of Applied Social Psychology, 18,* 1017–1031.
Etaugh, C. (1980). Effects of nonmaternal care on children. *American Psychologist, 35,* 309–319.
Evans, D. A., Funkenstein, H. H., Albert, M. S., Scherr, P. A., Cook, N. R., Chown, M. J., Hebert, L. E., Hennekens, C. H., & Taylor, J. O. (1989). Prevalence of Alzheimer's disease in a community population of older persons. *Journal of the American Medical Association, 262,* 2551–2556.
Evans, G. W., Hygge, S., & Bullinger, M. (1995). Chronic noise and psychological stress. *Psychological Science, 6,* 333–338.
Evans, G. W., Schroeder, A., & Lepore, S. J. (1996). The role of interior design elements in human responses to crowding. *Journal of Personality and Social Psychology, 70,* 41–46.
Ewart, C. K. (1991). Social action theory for a public health psychology. *American Psychologist, 46,* 931–946.
Exner, J. E., Jr., Thomas, E. A., & Mason, B. (1985). Children's Rorschachs: Description and prediction. *Journal of Personality Assessment, 49,* 13–14.
Eyer, D. E. (1992). *Mother–infant bonding: A scientific fiction.* New Haven, CT: Yale University Press.
Eysenck, H. J. (1970). *The structure of human personality* (3rd ed.). London: Methuen.
Eysenck, H. J. (1995). *Genius: The natural history of creativity.* Cambridge, England: Cambridge University Press.
Fagan, J. (1994). Correlates of maternal involvement in on-site and off-site day care centers. *Child and Youth Care Forum, 23,* 275– 290.
Fagan, J. F., III (1992). Intelligence: A theoretical viewpoint. *Current Directions in Psychological Science, 1,* 82–86.
Fagan, T. K. (1992). Compulsory schooling, child study, clinical psychology, and special education. *American Psychologist, 47,* 236–243.
Fairburn, C. G., Jones, R., Peveler, R. C., Carr, S. J., Solomon, R. A., O'Connor, M. E., Burton, J., & Hope, R. A. (1991). Three psychological treatments of bulimia nervosa. *Archives of General Psychiatry, 48,* 463–469.
Fantz, R. L. (1961, May). The origin of form perception. *Scientific American,* pp. 66–72.
Faraone, S. V., Kremen, W. S., & Tsuang, M. T. (1990). Genetic transmission of major affective disorders: Quantitative models and linkage analyses. *Psychological Bulletin, 108,* 109–127.
Farrell, A. D., & Danish, S. J. (1993). Peer drug associations and emotional restraint: Causes or consequences of adolescents' drug use? *Journal of Consulting and Clinical Psychology, 61,* 327–334.
Fazio, R. H. (1990). Multiple processes by which attitudes guide behavior: The MODE model as an integrative framework. In M. P. Zanna (Ed.), *Advances in experimental social psychology* (Vol. 23, pp. 75–109). San Diego: Academic.
Feeney, D. M. (1987). Human rights and animal welfare. *American Psychologist, 42,* 593–599.

Fehr, B. (1988). Prototype analysis of the concepts of love and commitment. *Journal of Personality and Social Psychology, 55,* 557–579.
Fehr, B., & Russell, J. A. (1991). The concept of love viewed from a prototype perspective. *Journal of Personality and Social Psychology, 60,* 425–438.
Feingold, A. (1988a). Cognitive gender differences are disappearing. *American Psychologist, 43,* 95–103.
Feingold, A. (1988b). Matching for attractiveness in romantic partners and same-sex friends: A meta-analysis and theoretical critique. *Psychological Bulletin, 104,* 226–235.
Feingold, A. (1992a). Gender differences in mate selection preferences: A test of the parental investment model. *Psychological Bulletin, 112,* 125–139.
Feingold, A. (1992b). Good-looking people are not what we think. *Psychological Bulletin, 111,* 304–341.
Feingold, A. (1993). Cognitive gender differences: A developmental perspective. *Sex Roles, 29,* 91–111.
Feingold, A. (1994). Gender differences in personality: A meta-analysis. *Psychological Bulletin, 116,* 429–456.
Fenwick, P., Donaldson, S., Gillies, L., Bushman, J., Fenton, G., Perry, I., Tilsley, C., & Serafinowicz, H. (1977). Metabolic and EEG changes during transcendental meditation. *Biological Psychology, 5,* 101–118.
Fernandez, E., & Turk, D. C. (1992). Sensory and affective components of pain: Separation and synthesis. *Psychological Bulletin, 112,* 205–217.
Festinger, L. (1954). A theory of social comparison processes. *Human Relations, 7,* 117–140.
Festinger, L. (1957). *A theory of cognitive dissonance.* Evanston, IL: Row, Petersen.
Fiedler, F. E. (1964). A contingency model of leadership effectiveness. In L. Berkowitz (Ed.), *Advances in experimental social psychology* (Vol. 1). New York: Academic.
Fiedler, F. E. (1974). Personality, motivational systems, and behavior of high and low LPC persons. *Human Relations, 25,* 391–412.
Field, T. (1996). Attachment and separation in young children. *Annual Review of Psychology, 47,* 541–561.
Fine, A. (1986, August). Transplantation in the central nervous system. *Scientific American,* pp. 52–67.
Finn, P. R., Kessler, D. N., & Hussong, A. M. (1994). Risk for alcoholism and classical conditioning to signals for punishment: Evidence for a weak behavioral inhibition system? *Journal of Abnormal Psychology, 103,* 293–301.
Finn, P. R., & Pihl, R. O. (1987). Men at high risk for alcoholism: The effect of alcohol on cardiovascular response to unavoidable shock. *Journal of Abnormal Psychology, 96,* 230–236.
Fischer, C. T. (1991). Phenomenological–existential psychotherapy. In M. Hersen, A. E. Kazdin, & A. S. Bellack (Eds.), *The clinical psychology handbook* (2nd ed.). New York: Pergamon.
Fischer, J., & Gochros, H. L. (1975). *Planned behavior change: Behavior modification in social work.* New York: Free Press.
Fischer, K. W., & Silvern, L. (1985). Stages and individual differences in cognitive development. *Annual Review of Psychology, 36,* 613–648.
Fisher, C. B., & Fyrberg, D. (1994). Participant partners: College students weigh the costs and benefits of deceptive research. *American Psychologist, 49,* 417–427.
Fisher, J. D., & Fisher, W. A. (1992). Changing AIDS-risk behavior. *Psychological Bulletin, 111,* 455–474.
Fiske, S. T. (1992). Thinking is for doing: Portraits of social cognition from daguerreotype to laserphoto. *Journal of Personality and Social Psychology, 63,* 877–889.
Fitzgerald, L. F., & Osipow, S. H. (1986). An occupational analysis of counseling psychology. *American Psychologist, 41,* 535–544.
Flaskerud, J. H., & Hu, L. T. (1992). Relationship of ethnicity to psychiatric diagnosis. *Journal of Nervous and Mental Disease, 180,* 296–303.
Flavell, J. H. (1986). The development of children's knowledge about the appearance-reality distinction. *American Psychologist, 41,* 418– 425.
Flavell, J. H., Green, F. L., & Flavell, E. R. (1989). Young children's ability to differentiate appearance–reality and level 2 perspectives in the tactile modality. *Child Development, 60,* 201–213.
Flavell, J. H., Green, F. L., & Flavell, E. R. (1993). Children's understanding of the stream of consciousness. *Child Development, 64,* 387–398.
Fleming, I., Baum, A., & Weiss, L. (1987). Social density and perceived control as mediators of crowding stress in high-density residential neighborhoods. *Journal of Personality and Social Psychology, 52,* 899–906.
Fleming, J. D. (1974, July). Field report: The state of the apes. *Psychology Today,* pp. 31–46.
Flor, H., & Turk, D. C. (1989). Psychophysiology of chronic pain: Do chronic pain patients exhibit symptom-specific psychophysiological responses? *Psychological Bulletin, 105,* 215–259.
Flynn, J. R. (1987). Massive gains in 14 nations: What IQ tests really measure. *Psychological Bulletin, 101,* 171–191.
Flynn, J. R. (1988). The decline and rise of scholastic aptitude scores. *American Psychologist, 43,* 479–480.
Foa, E. B., & Riggs, D. S. (1995). Posttraumatic stress disorder following assault: Theoretical considerations and empirical findings. *Current Directions in Psychological Science, 4,* 61–65.
Ford Foundation (1989). *The common good, social welfare, and the American future.* New York: Author.
Forehand, R., Thomas, A. M., Wierson, M., Brody, G., & Fauber, R. (1990). Role of maternal functioning and parenting skills in adolescent functioning following parental divorce. *Journal of Abnormal Psychology, 99,* 278–283.
Forsythe, S. M. (1990). Effect of applicant's clothing on interviewer's decision to hire. *Journal of Applied Social Psychology, 20,* 1579–1595.
Foster, R. G. (1993). Photoreceptors and circadian systems. *Current Directions in Psychological Science, 2,* 34–39.
Fox, M. (1993). *Psychological perspectives in education.* New York: Cassell Educational.
Fox, N. A. (1991). If it's not left, it's right. *American Psychologist, 46,* 863–872.
Frable, D. E. (1989). Sex typing and gender ideology: Two facets of the individual's gender psychology that go together. *Journal of Personality and Social Psychology, 56,* 95–108.
Frasure-Smith, N., Lespérance, F., & Talajic, M. (1993). Depression following myocardial infarction: Impact on 6-month survival. *Journal of the American Medical Association, 270,* 1819–1825.
Frasure-Smith, N., & Prince, R. (1989). Long-term follow-up of the ischemic heart disease life stress monitoring program. *Psychosomatic Medicine, 51,* 485–513.
Frederiksen, N. (1986). Toward a broader conception of human intelligence. *American Psychologist, 41,* 445–452.
French, K. E., Spurgeon, J. H., & Nevett, M. E. (1995). Expert–novice differences in cognitive and skill execution components of youth baseball performance. *Research Quarterly for Exercise and Sport, 66,* 194–201.
Freud, S. (1933). *New introductory lectures on psycho-analysis.* New York: Norton.
Freud, S. (1966). *A general introduction to psychoanalysis* (J. Riviere, Trans.) New York: Washington Square. (Original work published 1920.)
Frezza, M., di Padova, C., Pozzato, G., Terpin, M., Baraona, E., & Lieber, C. S. (1990). High blood alcohol levels in women. *New England Journal of Medicine, 322,* 95–99.
Friedman, H. S., & Booth-Kewley, S. (1988). Validity of the Type A construct: A reprise. *Psychological Bulletin, 104,* 381–384.
Friedman, M., & Rosenman, R. H. (1974). *Type A behavior and your heart.* Greenwich, CT: Fawcett.
Friedman, S., Paradis, C. M., & Hatch, M. (1994). Characteristics of African-American and white patients with panic disorder and agoraphobia. *Hospital and Community Psychiatry, 45,* 798–803.
Friedman, W. J. (1993). Memory for the time of past events. *Psychological Bulletin, 113,* 44–66.
Frieze, I. H., Olson, J. E., & Russell, J. (1991). Attractiveness and income for men and women in management. *Journal of Applied Social Psychology, 21,* 1039–1057.
Frijda, N. H., Kuipers, P., & ter Schure, E. (1989). Relations among emotion, appraisal, and emotional action readiness. *Journal of Personality and Social Psychology, 57,* 212–228.
Fromm, E. (1956). *The art of loving.* New York: Harper & Row.
Fromme, K., Marlatt, G. A., Baer, J. S., & Kivlahan, D. R. (1994). The alcohol skills training program: A group intervention for young adult drinkers. *Journal of Substance Abuse Treatment, 11,* 143–154.
Fruzzetti, A. E., & Jacobson, N. S. (1991). Marital and family therapy. In M. Hersen, A. E. Kazdin, & A. S. Bellack (Eds.), *The clinical psychology handbook* (2nd ed.). New York: Pergamon.

Funder, D. C. (1995). On the accuracy of personality judgment: A realistic approach. *Psychological Review, 102,* 652–670.

Furby, L., Weinrott, M. R., & Blackshaw, L. (1989). Sex offender recidivism: A review. *Psychological Bulletin, 105,* 3–30.

Furstenberg, F. F., Jr., Brooks-Gunn, J., & Chase-Lansdale, L. (1989). Teenaged pregnancy and childbearing. *American Psychologist, 44,* 313–320.

Furumoto, L., & Scarborough, E. (1986). Placing women in the history of psychology: The first American women psychologists. *American Psychologist, 41,* 35–42.

Gaffan, E. A., Tsaousis, J., & Kemp-Wheeler, S. M. (1995). Researcher allegiance and meta-analysis: The case of cognitive therapy for depression. *Journal of Consulting and Clinical Psychology, 63,* 960–980.

Gaines, S. O., Jr., & Reed, E. S. (1995). Prejudice: From Allport to DuBois. *American Psychologist, 50,* 96–103.

Galambos, N. L. (1992). Parent–adolescent relations. *Current Directions, 1,* 146–149.

Galin, D. (1974). Implications for psychiatry of left and right cerebral specialization: A neurophysiological context for unconscious processes. *Archives of General Psychiatry, 31,* 572–583.

Gallup, G. G., Jr., & Suarez, S. D. (1985). Alternatives to the use of animals in psychological research. *American Psychologist, 40,* 1104–1111.

Galotti, K. M. (1989). Approaches to studying formal and everyday reasoning. *Psychological Bulletin, 105,* 331–351.

Ganzach, Y. (1995). Negativity (and positivity) in performance evaluation: Three field studies. *Journal of Applied Psychology, 80,* 491–499.

Garcia, J., & Koelling, R. A., (1971). The use of ionizing rays as a mammalian olfactory stimulus. In H. Autrum, R. Jung, W. R. Loewenstein, D. M. MacKay, & H. L. Teuber (Eds.), *Handbook of sensory physiology: Vol. 4. Chemical senses,* (Pt. 1). New York: Springer-Verlag.

Garcia, J., Gustavson, C. R., Kelly, D. J., & Sweeney, M. (1976). Preynlithium aversions: I. Coyotes and wolves. *Behavioral Biology, 16,* 61–72.

Gardner, H., & Hatch, T. (1989). Multiple intelligences go to school: Educational implications of the theory of multiple intelligences. *Educational Research, 18,* 6.

Gardner, R. A., & Gardner, B. T. (1969). Teaching sign language to a chimp. *Science, 165,* 664–672.

Gardner, W., Scherer, D., & Tester, M. (1989). Asserting scientific authority: Cognitive development and adolescent legal rights. *American Psychologist, 6,* 895–902.

Garfield, S. L., & Bergin, A. E. (1986). *Handbook of psychotherapy and behavior change* (3rd ed.). New York: Wiley.

Garfinkel, P. E., Moldofsy, H., & Garner, D. M. (1980). The heterogeneity of anorexia nervosa. Bulimia as a distinct subgroup. *Archives of General Psychiatry, 37,* 1036–1040.

Garland, A. F., & Zigler, E. (1993). Adolescent suicide prevention. *American Psychologist, 48,* 169–182.

Garry, M. & Loftus, E. F. (1994). Pseudomemories without hypnosis. *The International Journal of Clinical and Experimental Hypnosis, 42,* 363–378.

Garza, R. T., & Borchert, J. E. (1990). Maintaining social identity in a mixed-gender setting: Minority/majority status and cooperative/competitive feedback. *Sex Roles, 22,* 679–691.

Gazzaniga, M. S. (1983). Right hemisphere language following brain bisection: A 20-year perspective. *American Psychologist, 38,* 525–537.

Gazzaniga, M. S. (1989). Organization of the human brain. *Science, 245,* 947–952.

Gebhardt, D. L., & Crump, C. E. (1990). Employee fitness and wellness programs in the workplace. *American Psychologist, 45,* 262–272.

Geen, R. G. (1991). Social motivation. *Annual Review of Psychology, 42,* 377–399.

Geller, E. S. (1975). Increasing desired waste disposals with instructions. *Man–Environment Systems, 5,* 125–128.

Geller, E. S. (1989). Applied behavior analysis and social marketing: An integration for environmental preservation. *Journal of Social Issues, 45,* 17–36.

Geller, E. S. (1992). It takes more than information to save energy. *American Psychologist, 47,* 814–815.

Geller, E. S., Patterson, L., & Talbot, E. (1982). A behavioral analysis of incentive prompts for motivating safety belt use. *Journal of Applied Behavior Analysis, 15,* 403–415.

Geller, E. S., Winett, R. A., & Evertt, P. B. (1982). *Preserving the environment: New strategies for behavior change.* New York: Pergamon.

Geller, E. S., Witmer, J. F., & Tuso, M. E. (1977). Environmental intervention for litter control. *Journal of Applied Psychology, 62,* 344–351.

George, J. M., & Brief, A. P. (1992). Feeling good—doing good: A conceptual analysis of the mood at work–organizational spontaneity relationship. *Psychological Bulletin, 112,* 310–329.

George, M. S., Ketter, T. A., Parekh, P. I., Horwitz, B., Herscovitch, P., & Post, R. M. (1995). Brain activity during transient sadness and happiness in healthy women. *American Journal of Psychiatry, 152,* 341–351.

George, M. S., Ketter, T. A., & Post, R. M. (1993). SPECT and PET imaging in mood disorders. *Journal of Clinical Psychiatry, 54,* 6–13.

Gerber, L. (1994). Psychotherapy with southeast Asian refugees: Implications for treatment of Western patients. *American Journal of Psychotherapy, 48,* 280–293.

German, D. (1983). Analysis of word-finding disorders on the Kaufman Assessment Battery for Children (K-ABC). *Journal of Psychoeducational Assessment, 1,* 121–134.

Geschwind, N. (1972, April). Language and the brain. *Scientific American,* pp. 76–83.

Gibson, E. J. (1988). Exploratory behavior in the development of perceiving, acting, and the acquiring of knowledge. *Annual Review of Psychology, 39,* 1–41.

Gibson, E. J. (1992). How to think about perceptual learning: Twenty-five years later. In H. L. Pick, Jr., P. van den Broek, & D. C. Knill (Eds.), *Cognition: Conceptual and methodological issues* (pp. 215–238). Washington, DC: American Psychological Association.

Gibson, J. A. P., & Range, L. M. (1991). Are written reports of suicide and seeking help contagious? High schoolers' perceptions. *Journal of Applied Social Psychology, 21,* 1517–1523.

Gift, T. E., Strauss, J. S., Ritzler, B. A., Kokes, R. F., & Harder, D. W. (1980). How diagnostic concepts of schizophrenia differ. *Journal of Nervous and Mental Disease, 168,* 3–8.

Gilbert, R. K. (1988). The dynamics of inaction. *American Psychologist, 43,* 755–764.

Gilligan, C. (1982). *In a different voice: Psychological theory and women's development.* Cambridge, MA: Harvard University Press.

Gitlin, M. J., Swendsen, J., Heller, T. L., & Hammen, C. (1995). Relapse and impairment in bipolar disorder. *American Journal of Psychiatry, 152,* 1635–1640.

Glantz, M. D. (1989). Cognitive therapy with the elderly. In A. Freeman, K. M. Simon, L. E. Beutler, & H. Arkowitz (Eds.), *Comprehensive handbook of cognitive therapy.* New York: Plenum.

Glasgow, R. E., & Terborg, J. R. (1988). Occupational health promotion programs to reduce cardiovascular risk. *Journal of Consulting and Clinical Psychology, 56,* 365–373.

Goff, K. (1992). Enhancing creativity in older adults. *Journal of Creative Behavior, 26,* 40–49.

Goldberg, L. R. (1990). An alternative "description of personality": The Big Five factor structure. *Journal of Personality and Social Psychology, 59,* 1216–1229.

Goldenberg, M. M. (1990). *Pharmacology for the psychotherapist.* Muncie, IN: Accelerated Development.

Goldfried, M. R., & Davison, G. C. (1976). *Clinical behavior therapy.* New York: Holt, Rinehart & Winston.

Golding, J. M., Potts, M. K., & Aneshensel, C. S. (1991). Stress exposure among Mexican Americans and non-Hispanic whites. *Journal of Community Psychology, 19,* 37–59.

Goldman, M. S., Brown, S. A., Christiansen, B. A., & Smith, G. T. (1991). Alcoholism and memory: Broadening the scope of alcohol-expectancy research. *Psychological Bulletin, 110,* 137–146.

Goleman, D. (1995). *Emotional intelligence.* New York: Bantam.

Gonzales, L. R., Hays, R. B., Bond, M. A., & Kelly, J. G. (1983). Community mental health. In M. Hersen, A. E. Kazdin, & A. S. Bellack (Eds.), *The clinical psychology handbook.* New York: Pergamon.

Gonzales, R. R., & Roll, S. (1985). Relationship between acculturation, cognitive style, and intelligence. *Journal of Cross-Cultural Psychology, 16,* 190–205.

Goodwin, R., & Tang, D. (1991). Preferences for friends and close relationship partners: A cross-cultural comparison. *Journal of Social Psychology, 131,* 579–581.

Gopnik, A. (1993). How we know our minds: The illusion of first-person knowledge of intentionality. *Behavioral and Brain Sciences, 16,* 1–14.

Gottesman, I. I. (1991). *Schizophrenia genesis.* New York: Freeman.

Gottman, J. M., & Katz, L. F. (1989). Effects of marital discord on young children's peer interaction and health. *Developmental Psychology, 25,* 373–381.

Goulding, M. M. (1990). Getting the important work done fast: Contract plus redecision. In J. K. Zeig & S. G. Gilligan (Eds.), *Brief therapy myths, methods, and metaphors.* New York: Brunner/Mazel.

Grady, C. L., McIntosh, A. R., Horwitz, B., Maisog, J. M., Ungerleider, L. G., Mentis, M. J., Pietrini, P., Schapiro, M. B., & Haxby, J. V. (1995). Age-related reductions in human recognition memory due to impaired encoding. *Science, 269,* 218–220.

Gray, C. M., König, P., Engel, A. K., & Singer, W. (1989). Oscillatory responses in cat visual cortex exhibit inter-columnar synchronization which reflects global stimulus properties. *Nature, 338,* 334–337.

Graziano, M. S. A., & Gross, C. G. (1994). Mapping space with neurons. *Current Directions in Psychological Science, 3,* 164–167.

Grbich, C. (1994). Women as primary breadwinners in families where men are primary caregivers. *Australian New Zealand Journal of Sociology, 30,* 105–118.

Green, R. J., & Stanton, M. E. (1989). Differential ontogeny of working memory and reference memory in the rat. *Behavioral Neuroscience, 103,* 98–105.

Greenberg, J. (1990). Employee theft as a reaction to underpayment inequity: The hidden cost of pay cuts. *Journal of Applied Psychology, 75,* 561–568.

Greenberg, R. P., Bornstein, R. F., Greenberg, M. D., Fisher, S., & Seymour, F. (1992). A meta-analysis of antidepressant outcome under "blinder" conditions. *Journal of Consulting and Clinical Psychology, 60,* 664–669.

Greenfield, P. M., & Savage-Rumbaugh, E. S. (1990). Grammatical combination in Pan paniscus: Processes of learning and invention in the evolution and development of language. In S. T. Parker and K. R. Gibson (Eds.), *"Language" and intelligence in monkeys and apes.* New York: Cambridge University Press.

Greeno, C. G., & Wing, R. R. (1994). Stress-induced eating. *Psychological Bulletin, 115,* 444–464.

Greeno, J. G. (1989). A perspective on thinking. *American Psychologist, 44,* 134–141.

Griffeth, R. W., Vecchio, R. P., & Logan, J. W., Jr. (1989). Equity theory and interpersonal attraction. *Journal of Applied Psychology, 74,* 394–401.

Grilo, C. M., & Pogue-Geile, M. F. (1991). The nature of environmental influences on weight and obesity: A behavior genetic analysis. *Psychological Bulletin, 110,* 520–537.

Grilo, C. M., & Shiffman, S. (1994). Longitudinal investigation of the abstinence violation effect in binge eaters. *Journal of Consulting and Clinical Psychology, 62,* 611–619.

Gross, J. J., Fredrickson, B. L., & Levenson, R. W. (1994). The psychophysiology of crying. *Psychophysiology, 31,* 460–463.

Grossberg, S. (1995). The attentive brain. *American Scientist, 83,* 438–449.

Grossman, F. K., Pollack, W. S., & Golding, E. (1988). Fathers and children: Predicting the quality and quantity of fathering. *Developmental Psychology, 1,* 91–92.

Guilford, J. P. (1967). *The nature of human intelligence.* New York: McGraw-Hill.

Guilford, J. P. (1985). The structure of intellect model. In B. B. Wolman (Ed.), *Handbook of intelligence: Theories, measurements, and applications.* New York: Wiley.

Gulevich, G., Dement, W., & Johnson, L. (1966). Psychiatric and EEG observations on a case of prolonged (264 hours) wakefulness. *Archives of General Psychiatry, 15,* 29–35.

Gur, R. C., Mozley, L. H., Mozley, P. D., Resnick, S. M., Karp, J. S., Alavi, A., Arnold, S. E., & Gur, R. E. (1995). Sex differences in regional cerebral glucose metabolism during a resting state. *Science, 267,* 528–531.

Gustin, W. C., & Corazza, L. (1994). Mathematical and verbal reasoning as predictors of science achievement. *Roeper Review, 16,* 160–162.

Haaga, D. A. F., & Davison, G. C. (1993). An appraisal of rational–emotive therapy. *Journal of Consulting and Clinical Psychology, 61,* 215–220.

Haaga, D. A. F., & Stewart, B. L. (1992). Self-efficacy for recovery from a lapse after smoking cessation. *Journal of Consulting and Clinical Psychology, 60,* 24–28.

Haan, N., Millsap, R., & Hartka, E. (1986). As time goes by: Change and stability in personality over fifty years. *Psychology and Aging, 1,* 220–232.

Haber, R. N. (1979). Twenty years of haunting eidetic imagery: Where's the ghost? *Behavioral and Brain Sciences, 2,* 583–629.

Hackman, M. Z., Furniss, A. H., Hills, M. J., & Paterson, T. J. (1992). Perceptions of gender-role characteristics and transformational and transactional leadership behaviors. *Perceptual and Motor Skills, 75,* 311–319.

Hackman, M. Z., & Johnson, C. E. (1991). *Leadership: A communication perspective.* Prospect Heights, IL: Waveland.

Haddock, G., Zanna, M. P., & Esses, V. M. (1994). The (limited) role of trait-laden stereotypes in predicting attitudes toward native peoples. *British Journal of Social Psychology, 33,* 83–106.

Haith, M. M., & McCarty, M. E. (1990). Stability of visual expectations at 3.0 months of age. *Developmental Psychology, 26,* 68–74.

Halaas, J. L., Gajiwala, K. S., Maffei, M., Cohen, S. L., Chait, B. T., Rabinowitz, D., Lallone, R. L., Burley, S. K., & Friedman, J. M. (1995). Weight-reducing effects of the plasma protein encoded by the obese gene. *Science, 269,* 543–546.

Hale, R., Nevels, R. M., Lott, C., & Titus, T. (1990). Cultural insensitivity to sexist language toward men. *Journal of Social Psychology, 130,* 697–698.

Halgren, E., Walter, R. D., Cherlow, A. G., & Crandall, P. H. (1978). Mental phenomena evoked by electrical stimulation of the human hippocampal formation and amygdala. *Brain, 101,* 83–117.

Hall, E. T. (1966). *The hidden dimension.* Garden City, NY: Doubleday.

Hall, S. M., Havassy, B. E., & Wasserman, D. A. (1991). Effects of commitment to abstinence, positive moods, stress, and coping on relapse to cocaine use. *Journal of Consulting and Clinical Psychology, 59,* 526–532.

Hallman, W. K., & Wandersman, A. H. (1992). Attribution of responsibility and individual and collective coping with environmental threats. *Journal of Social Issues, 48,* 101–118.

Halpern, D. F. (1986). *Sex differences in cognitive abilities.* Hillsdale, NJ: Erlbaum.

Hamann, S. B., & Squire, L. R. (1995). On the acquisition of new declarative knowledge in amnesia. *Behavioral Neuroscience, 109,* 1027–1044.

Hamer, D. H., Hu, S., Magnuson, V. L., Hu, N., & Pattatucci, A. M. L. (1993). A linkage between DNA markers on the X chromosome and male sexual orientation. *Science, 261,* 321–327.

Hamilton, S., & Fagot, B. I. (1988). Chronic stress and coping styles: A comparison of male and female undergraduates. *Journal of Personality and Social Psychology, 5,* 819–823.

Hanson, C. L., Cigrang, J. A., Harris, M. A., Carle, D. L., Relyea, G., & Burghen, G. A. (1989). Coping styles in youths with insulin-dependent diabetes mellitus. *Journal of Consulting and Clinical Psychology, 57,* 644–651.

Harkins, S. G., & Szymanski, K. (1988). Social loafing and self-evaluation with an objective standard. *Journal of Experimental Social Psychology, 24,* 354–365.

Harlow, H. F. (1962). The heterosexual affectional system in monkeys. *American Psychologist, 17,* 1–9.

Harlow, H. F., & Zimmerman, R. R. (1958). The development of affectional responses in infant monkeys. *Proceedings of the American Philosophic Society, 102,* 501–509.

Härmä, M., Laitinen, J., Partinen, M., & Suvanto, S. (1994). The effect of four-day round trip flights over 10 time zones on the circadian variation of salivary melatonin and cortisol in airline flight attendants. *Ergononics, 37,* 1479–1489.

Harmon, T. M., Hynan, M. T., & Tyre, T. E. (1990). Improved obstetric outcomes using hypnotic analgesia and skill mastery combined with childbirth education. *Journal of Consulting and Clinical Psychology, 58,* 525–530.

Harms, T. (1994). Humanizing infant environments for group care. *Children's Environments, 11,* 155–167.

Harper, J. F., & Marshall, E. (1991). Adolescents' problems and their relationship to self-esteem. *Adolescence, 26,* 799–803.

Harris, C. M., Hainline, L., Abramov, I., Lemerise, E., & Camenzuli, C. (1988). The distribution of fixation durations in infants and naive adults. *Vision Research, 28,* 419–432.

Harris, J. R. (1995). Where is the child's environment? A group socialization theory of development. *Psychological Review, 102,* 458–489.

Harris, K. M., & Morgan, S. P. (1991). Fathers, sons, and daughters: Differential paternal involvement in parenting. *Journal of Marriage and the Family, 53,* 531–544.
Harris, M. B. (1994). Gender of subject and target as mediators of aggression. *Journal of Applied Social Psychology, 24,* 453–471.
Harris, V. A., & Katkin, E. S. (1975). Primary and secondary emotional behaviour: An analysis of the role of autonomic feedback on affect, arousal, and attribution. *Psychological Bulletin, 82,* 904–916.
Harrison, J. R., & Barabasz, A. F. (1991). Effects of restricted environmental stimulation therapy on the behavior of children with autism. *Child Study Journal, 21,* 153–166.
Harrison, Y., & Horne, J. A. (1996). Long-term extension to sleep—are we really chronically sleep deprived? *Psychophysiology, 33,* 22–30.
Hartlage, S., Alloy, L. B., Vazquez, C., & Dykman, B. (1993). Automatic and effortful processing in depression. *Psychological Bulletin, 113,* 247–278.
Hartup, W. W. (1989). Social relationships and their developmental significance. *American Psychologist, 44,* 120–126.
Hauser, S. T., & Bowlds, M. K. (1990). Stress, coping, and adaptation. In S. S. Feldman & G. R. Elliott (Eds.), *At the threshold.* Cambridge, MA: Harvard University Press.
Hawkins, J. D., Catalano, R. F., & Miller, J. Y. (1992). Risk and protective factors for alcohol and other drug problems in adolescence and early adulthood: Implications for substance abuse prevention. *Psychological Bulletin, 112,* 64–105.
Hawranik, P. (1991). A clinical possibility: Preventing health problems after the age of 65. *Journal of Gerontological Nursing, 17,* 20–25.
Hayflick, L. (1994). *How and why we age.* New York: Ballantine.
Hays, R. B. (1989). The day-to-day functioning of close versus casual friendships. *Journal of Social and Personal Relationships, 6,* 21–37.
Heath, A. C., & Martin, N. G. (1990). Psychoticism as a dimension of personality: A multivariate genetic test of Eysenck and Eysenck's psychoticism construct. *Journal of Personality and Social Psychology, 58,* 111–121.
Heatherton, T. F., & Baumeister, R. F. (1991). Binge eating as escape from self-awareness. *Psychological Bulletin, 100,* 86–108.
Heatherton, T. F., Polivy, J., & Herman, C. P. (1991). Restraint, weight loss, and variability of body weight. *Journal of Abnormal Psychology, 100,* 78–83.
Hebb, D. O. (1949). *Organization of behavior.* New York: Wiley.
Hebb, D. O. (1955). Drives and the C. N. S. (conceptual nervous system). *Psychological Review, 62,* 243–254.
Hebb, D. O. (1972). *Textbook of psychology* (3rd ed.). Philadelphia: Saunders.
Heckler, M. M. (1985). Psychology in the public forum: The fight against Alzheimer's disease. *American Psychologist, 40,* 1240– 1244.
Hedges, L. V., & Nowell, A. (1995). Sex differences in mental test scores, variability, and numbers of high-scoring individuals. *Science, 269,* 41–45.
Heeger, D. J. (1994). The representation of visual stimuli in primary visual cortex. *Current Directions in Psychological Science, 3,* 159–163.
Heider, E. R. (1971). "Focal" color areas and the development of color names. *Developmental Psychology, 4,* 447–455.
Heider, E. R. (1972). Universals in color naming and memory. *Journal of Experimental Psychology, 93,* 10–21.
Heider, E. R., & Olivier, D. C. (1972). The structure of the color space in naming and memory for two languages, *Cognitive Psychology, 3,* 337–354.
Heider, K. G. (1991). *Landscapes of emotion: Lexical maps and scenarios of emotion terms in Indonesia.* Cambridge, England: Cambridge University Press.
Heider, K. G. (1994, March). *An anthropologist discovers emotion in the New Guinea Highlands.* Paper presented at the University of South Carolina Educational Foundation Research Award in Humanities and Social Sciences Lecture, Columbia, South Carolina.
Heilbrun, A. B., Jr., Wydra, D., & Friedberg, L. (1989). Parent identification and gender schema development. *Journal of Genetic Psychology, 150,* 293–299.
Heinlein, R. (1961). *Stranger in a strange land.* New York: Putnam.
Hellriegel, D., & Slocum, J. (1992). *Management* (6th ed). Reading, MA: Addison-Wesley.
Hellstedt, J. C. (1995). Invisible players: A family systems model. In S. M. Murphy (Ed.), *Sport psychology interventions* (pp. 117–146). Champaign, IL: Human Kinetics.
Helmes, E., & Reddon, J. R. (1993). A perspective on developments in assessing psychopathology: A critical review of the MMPI and MMPI–2. *Psychological Bulletin, 113,* 453–471.
Helms, J. E. (1992). Why is there no study of cultural equivalence in standardized cognitive ability testing? *American Psychologist, 47,* 1083–1101.
Helson, R., & Moane, G. (1987). Personality change in women from college to midlife. *Journal of Personality and Social Psychology, 53,* 176–186.
Helson, R., & Picano, J. (1990). Is the traditional role bad for women? *Journal of Personality and Social Psychology, 59,* 311– 320.
Helson, R., Stewart, A. J., & Ostrove, J. (1995). Identity in three cohorts of midlife women. *Journal of Personality and Social Psychology, 69,* 544–557.
Hendrick, C., & Hendrick, S. S. (1986). A theory and method of love. *Journal of Personality and Social Psychology, 50,* 392–402.
Herbert, T. B., & Cohen, S. (1993). Depression and immunity: A meta-analytic review. *Psychological Bulletin, 113,* 472–486.
Herbert, T. B., Cohen, S., Marsland, A. L., Bachen, E. A., et al. (1994). Cardiovascular reactivity and the course of immune response to an acute psychological stressor. *Psychosomatic Medicine, 56,* 337–344.
Herrnstein, R. J., & Murray, C. (1994). *The bell curve: Intelligence and class structure in American life.* New York: Free Press.
Hetherington, E. M., Stanley-Hagan, M., & Anderson, E. R. (1989). Marital transitions: A child's perspective. *American Psychologist, 44,* 303–312.
Hildebrandt, K. A. (1983). Effect of facial expression variations on ratings of infant's physical attractiveness. *Developmental Psychology, 29,* 414–417.
Hilgard, E. R. (1965). *Hypnotic susceptibility.* New York: Harcourt, Brace & World.
Hilgard, E. R., & Morgan, A. H. (1975). Heart rate and blood pressure in the study of laboratory pain in man under normal conditions and as influenced by hypnosis. *Acta Neurobiologiae Experimentalis, 35,* 501–513.
Hilsman, R., & Garber, J. (1995). A test of the cognitive diathesis–stress model of depression in children: Academic stressors, attributional style, perceived competence, and control. *Journal of Personality and Social Psychology, 69,* 370–380.
Hinton, G. (1992, September). How neural networks learn from experience. *Scientific American,* pp. 145–151.
Hinton, G., Plaut, D. C., & Shallice, T. (1993, April). Simulating brain damage. *Scientific American,* pp. 76–83.
Hirsch, H. V. B., & Spinelli, D. N. (1971). Modification of the distribution of receptive field orientation in cats by selective exposure during development. *Experimental Brain Research, 13,* 509–527.
Hirsch, J., & Leibel, R. L. (1988). New light on obesity. *The New England Journal of Medicine, 318,* 509–510.
Hobfoll, S. E. (1989). Conservation of resources: A new attempt at conceptualizing stress. *American Psychologist, 44,* 513–524.
Hobfoll, S. E., Spielberg, C. D., Breznitz, S., Figley, C., Folkman, S., Lepper-Green, B., Meichenbaum, D., Milgram, N. A., Sandler, I., Sarason, I., & Van der Kolk, B. (1991). War-related stress. *American Psychologist, 46,* 848–855.
Hobson, J. A. (1989). *Sleep.* New York: Freeman.
Hobson, J. A. (1994). *The chemistry of conscious states: How the brain changes its mind.* Boston: Little, Brown.
Hobson, J. A., & McCarley, R. W. (1977). The brain as a dream state generator: An activation-synthesis of the dream process. *American Journal of Psychiatry, 134,* 1335–1348.
Hoffman, C., & Hurst, N. (1990). Gender stereotypes: Perception or rationalization? *Journal of Personality and Social Psychology, 58,* 197–208.
Hofstede, G. (1983). National cultures revisited. *Behavior Science Research, 18,* 285–305.
Hogan, R., Curphy, G. J., & Hogan, J. (1994). What we know about leadership: Effectiveness and Personality. *American Psychologist, 49,* 493–504.
Holder, M. D., Yirmiya, R., Garcia, J., & Raizer, J. (1989). Conditioned taste aversions are not readily disrupted by external excitation. *Behavioral Neuroscience, 103,* 605–611.
Holland, M. K. (1975). *Using psychology: Principles of behavior and your life.* Boston: Little, Brown.
Hollister, J. M., Mednick, S. A., Brennan, P. A., & Cannon, T. D. (1994). Impaired autonomic nervous system habituation in those at genetic risk for schizophrenia. *Archives of General Psychiatry, 51,* 552–558.

Holloway, F. A. (1977). State-dependent retrieval based on time of day. In B. Ho, D. Chute, & D. Richards (Eds.), *Drug discrimination and state-dependent learning*. New York: Academic.
Holmes, D. S. (1984). Mediation and somatic arousal reduction. *American Psychologist, 39,* 1–10.
Holmes, T. H., & Rahe, R. H. (1967). The social readjustment rating scale. *Journal of Psychosomatic Research, 11,* 213–218.
Hom, H. L., Jr., & Arbuckle, B. (1988). Mood induction effects upon goal setting and performance in young children. *Motivation and Emotion, 12,* 113–122.
Honts, C. R. (1994). Psychophysiological detection of deception. *Current Directions in Psychological Science, 3,* 77–82.
Hoosain, Z., & Roopnarine, J. L. (1994). African-American fathers' involvement with infants: Relationship to their functioning style, support, education, and income. *Infant Behavior and Development, 17,* 175–184.
Hoptman, M. J., & Davidson, R. J. (1994). How and why do the two cerebral hemispheres interact? *Psychological Bulletin, 116,* 195–219.
Horne, J. (1988). *Why we sleep*. New York: Oxford University Press.
Horney, K. (1937). *The neurotic personality of our time.* New York: Norton.
Hornstein, G. A. (1992). The return of the repressed. *American Psychologist, 47,* 254–263.
Howard, K. I., Kopta, S. M., Krause, M. S., & Orlinsky, D. E. (1986). The dose–effect relationships in psychotherapy. *American Psychologist, 41,* 159–164.
Howard, R. W. (1993). On what intelligence is. *British Journal of Psychology, 84,* 27–37.
Howe, M. J. A., & Smith, J. (1988). Calendar calculating in "idiots savants": How do they do it? *British Journal of Psychology, 79,* 371–386.
Howell, J. M., & Avolio, B. J. (1993). Transformational leadership, transactional leadership, locus of control, and support for innovation: Key predictors of consolidated-business-unit performance. *Journal of Applied Psychology, 78,* 891–902.
Howell, W. C. (1993). Engineering psychology in a changing world. *Annual Review of Psychology, 44,* 231–263.
Howes, C., Unger, O., & Seidner, L. B. (1989). Social pretend play in toddlers: Parallels with social play and with solitary pretend. *Child Development, 60,* 77–84.
Hoyt, I. P., Nadon, R., Register, P. A., Chorny, J., Fleeson, W., Grigorian, E. M., & Otto, L. (1989). Daydreaming, absorption, and hypnotizability. *The International Journal of Clinical and Experimental Hypnosis, 37,* 332–342.
Huapaya, L. V. M. (1994). Four cases of supposed multiple personality disorder: Evidence of unjustified diagnoses. *Canadian Journal of Psychiatry, 39,* 247.
Hubel, D. H., & Wiesel, T. N. (1962). Receptive fields, binocular interaction, and functional architecture in the cat's visual cortex. *Journal of Physiology, 160,* 106–164.
Huber, C. H. (1994). Brief therapy: The 20-minute hour. In J. L. Ronch, W. V. Ornum, & N. C. Stilwell (Eds.), *The couseling sourcebook: A practical reference on contemporary issues* (pp. 72–85). New York: Crossroad Publishing.
Hudak, M. A. (1993). Gender schema theory revisited: Men's stereotypes of American women. *Sex Roles, 28,* 279–293.
Hudspeth, A. J. (1983, January). The hair cells of the inner ear. *Scientific American,* pp. 54–73.
Huebner, E. S. (1994). Relationships among demographics, social support, job satisfaction and burnout among school psychologists. *School Psychology International Thousand Oaks, 15,* 181–186.
Hughes, S. L., & Neimeyer, R. A. (1993). Cognitive predictors of suicide risk among hospitalized psychiatric patients: A prospective study. *Death Studies, 17,* 103–124.
Hughes, C. F., Uhlmann, C., & Pennebaker, J. W. (1994). The body's response to processing emotional trauma: Linking verbal text with autonomic activity. *Journal of Personality, 62,* 564–585.
Humphreys, K. (1996). Clinical psychologists as psychotherapists: History, future, and alternatives. *American Psychologist, 51,* 190–197.
Hunt, E. (1995). The role of intelligence in modern society. *American Scientist, 83,* 356–368.
Hunt, E. B., & Agnoli, F. (1991). The Whorfian hypothesis: A cognitive psychology perspective. *Psychological Review, 98,* 377–389.
Hunt, M. (1974). *Sexual behavior in the 1970s*. New York: Dell.
Hurvich, L., & Jameson, D. (1974). Opponent processes as a model of neural organization. *American Psychologist, 30,* 88–102.
Huston, A. C., Donnerstein, E., Fairchild, H., Feshback, N. D., Katz, P. A., Murray, J. P., Rubinstein, E. A., Wilcox, B. L., & Zuckerman, D. (1992). *Big world, small screen.* Lincoln: University of Nebraska Press.
Huston, A. C., Watkins, B. A., & Kunkel, D. (1989). Public policy and children's television. *American Psychologist, 44,* 424–433.
Hwong, N. C., Caswell, A., Johnson, D. W., & Johnson, R. T. (1993). Effects of cooperative and individualistic learning on prospective elementary teachers' music achievement and attitudes. *The Journal of Social Psychology, 133,* 53–64.
Hyde, J. S., Fennema, E., & Lamon, S. J. (1990). Gender differences in mathematics performance: A meta-analysis. *Psychological Bulletin, 107,* 139–155.
Hyde, J. S., & Linn, M. C. (1988). Gender differences in verbal ability: A meta-analysis. *Psychological Bulletin, 104,* 53–69.
Hymes, R. W. (1986). Political attitudes as social categories: A new look at selective memory. *Journal of Personality and Social Psychology, 51,* 233–241.
Ilacqua, G. E. (1994). Migraine headaches: Coping efficacy of guided imagery training. *Headache, 34,* 99–102.
Ilgen, D. R. (1990). Health issues at work: Opportunities for industrial/organizational psychology. *American Psychologist, 45,* 273–283.
Ingbar, D. H., & Gee, J. B. L. (1985). Pathophysiology and treatment of sleep apnea. *Annual Review of Medicine, 36,* 369–395.
Inhelder, B., & Piaget, J. (1958). *The growth of logical thinking from childhood to adolescence.* New York: Basic Books.
Inhoff, A. W., Morris, R., & Calabrese, J. (1986). Eye movements in skilled transcription typing. *Bulletin of the Psychonomic Society, 2,* 113–114.
Innes, J. M., & Young, R. F. (1975). The effect of presence of an audience, evaluation apprehension, and objective self-awareness on learning. *Journal of Experimental Social Psychology, 11,* 35–42.
Insua, A. M. (1983). WAIS–R factor structures in two cultures. *Journal of Cross-Cultural Psychology, 14,* 427–438.
Intraub, H. (1980). Presentation rate and the representation of briefly glimpsed pictures in memory. *Journal of Experimental Psychology: Human Learning and Memory, 6,* 1–12.
Intraub, H., & Nicklos, S. (1985). Levels of processing and picture memory: The physical superiority effect. *Journal of Experimental Psychology: Learning, Memory, and Cognition, 11,* 284–298.
Irwin, M., Smith, T. L., & Gillin, J. C. (1992). Electroencephalographic sleep and natural killer activity in depressed patients and control subjects. *Psychosomatic Medicine, 54,* 10–21.
Isaac, R. J., & Armat, V. C. (1990). *Madness in the streets: How psychiatry and the law abandoned the mentally ill.* New York: Free Press.
Isabella, R. A., Belsky, J., & von Eye, A. (1989). Origins of infant–mother attachment: An examination of interactional synchrony during the infant's first year. *Developmental Psychology, 25,* 12–21.
Itzkoff, S. W. (1994). *The decline of intelligence in America: A strategy for national renewal.* Westport, CT: Praeger.
Iwata, B. A., Pace, G. M., Cowdery, G. E., & Miltenberger, R. G. (1994). What makes extinction work: An analysis of procedural form and function. *Journal of Applied Behavior Analysis, 27,* 131–144.
Izard, C. E. (1993). Four systems for emotion activation: Cognitive and noncognitive processes. *Psychological Review, 100,* 68–90.
Izard, C. E. (1994). Innate and universal facial expressions: Evidence from developmental and cross-cultural research. *Psychological Bulletin, 115,* 288–299.
Izard, C. E., & Saxton, P. M. (1988). Emotions. In R. C. Atkinson, R. J. Herrnstein, G. Lindzey, & R. D. Luce (Eds.), *Stevens handbook of experimental psychology: Vol. 1. Perception and motivation.* New York: Wiley.
Jaccard, J., Helbig, D. W., Wan, C. K., Gutman, M. A., & Kritz-Silverstein, D. C. (1990). Individual differences in attitude–behavior consistency: The prediction of contraceptive behavior. *Journal of Applied Social Psychology, 20,* 575–617.
Jacklin, C. N. (1989). Female and male: Issues of gender. *American Psychologist, 44,* 127–133.
Jackson, J. M., & Latané, B. (1981). All alone in front of all those people: Stage fright as a function of number and type of co-performers and audience. *Journal of Personality and Social Psychology, 40,* 73–85.
Jackson, S. E., & Schuler, R. S. (1990). Human resource planning: Challenges for industrial/organizational psychologists. *American Psychologist, 45,* 223–239.

Jackson, S. E., & Schuler, R. S. (1995). Understanding human resource management in the context of organizations and their environments. *Annual Review of Psychology, 46,* 237–264.
Jacobs, L., Berscheid, E., & Walster, E. (1971). Self-esteem and attraction. *Journal of Personality and Social Psychology, 17,* 84–91.
Jacobs, R. A., & Kosslyn, S. M. (1994). Encoding shape and spatial relations: The role of receptive field size in coordinating complementary representations. *Cognitive Science, 18,* 361–386.
Jacobson, N. S. (1991). Behavioral versus insight-oriented marital therapy: Labels can be misleading. *Journal of Consulting and Clinical Psychology, 59,* 142–145.
Jacobson, N. S., & Addis, M. E. (1993). Research on couples and couple therapy: What do we know? Where are we going? *Journal of Consulting and Clinical Psychology, 61,* 85–93.
Jacobson, N. S., & Bussob, N. (1983). Marital and family therapy. In M. Herson, A. E. Kazdin, & A. S. Bellack (Eds.), *The clinical psychology handbook.* New York: Pergamon.
Jacoby, L. L., Kelley, C., Brown, J., & Jasechko, J. (1989). Becoming famous overnight: Limits on the ability to avoid unconscious influences of the past. *Journal of Personality and Social Psychology, 56,* 326–338.
James, W. (1884). What is an emotion? *Mind, 9,* 188–205.
James, W. (1890). *Principles of psychology.* New York: Dover.
Jan, J. E., Espezel, H., & Appleton, R. E. (1994). The treatment of sleep disorders with melatonin. *Developmental Medicine and Child Neurology, 36,* 97–107.
Janis, I. L. (1982). *Groupthink* (2nd ed.). Boston: Houghton Mifflin.
Janis, I. L. (1983). The role of social support in adherence to stressful decisions. *American Psychologist, 38,* 142–160.
Janis, I. L. (1985). Stress inoculation in health care: Theory and research. In A. Monat & Richard S. Lazarus (Eds.), *Stress and Coping* (2nd ed.). New York: Columbia University Press.
Jansen, A. S. P., Nguyen, X. V., Karpitskiy, V., Mettenleiter, T. C., & Loewy, A. D. (1995). Central command neurons of the sympathetic nervous system: Basis of the fight-or-flight response. *Science, 270,* 644–646.
Jarrett, M. E., & Lethbridge, D. J. (1994). Looking forward, looking back: Women's experience with waning fertility during midlife. *Qualitative Health Research, 4,* 370–384.
Jaynes, J. (1976). *The origin of consciousness in the breakdown of the bicameral mind.* Boston: Houghton Mifflin.
Jenkins, H. M., & Harrison, R. H. (1960). Effect of discrimination training on auditory generalization. *Journal of Experimental Psychology, 59,* 244–253.
Jennings, K. D., Curry, N. E., & Connors, R. (1986). Toddlers' social behaviors in dyads and groups. *Journal of Genetic Psychology, 147,* 515–528.
Jensen, A. R. (1969). How much can we boost IQ and scholastic achievement? *Harvard Educational Review, 39,* 1–123.
Jensen, A. R. (1970). Can we and should we study race differences? In J. Hellmuth (Ed.), *Disadvantaged child* (Vol. 3). New York: Brunner/Mazel.
Jensen, A. R. (1984). The black–white difference on the K–ABC: Implications for future tests. *Journal of Special Education, 18,* 377–408.
Jensen, A. R. (1987). Psychometric g as a focus on concerted research effort. *Intelligence, 11,* 193–198.
Jensen, A. R., & Weng, L. J. (1994). What is a good g? *Intelligence, 18,* 231–258.
Job, R. F. S., & Barnes, B. W. (1995). Stress and consumption: Inescapable shock, neophobia, and quinine finickiness in rats. *Behavioral Neuroscience, 109,* 106–116.
John, E. R., Chesler, P., Bartlett, F., & Victor, I. (1968). Observational learning in cats. *Science, 159,* 1489–1491.
Johnson, B. T., & Eagly, A. H. (1989). Effects of involvement on persuasion: A meta-analysis. *Psychological Bulletin, 106,* 290–314.
Johnson, C., & Larson, R. (1982). Bulimia: An analysis of moods and behavior. *Psychosomatic Medicine, 44,* 341–351.
Johnson, F. W. (1991). Biological factors and psychometric intelligence: A review. *Genetic, Social, and General Psychology Monographs, 117,* 315–357.
Johnson, L. C., Slye, E. S., & Dement, W. (1965). Electroencephalographic and autonomic activity during and after prolonged sleep deprivation. *Psychosomatic Medicine, 27,* 415–423.
Jones, F. D., & Koshes, R. J. (1995). Homosexuality and the military. *American Journal of Psychiatry, 152,* 16–21.
Jones, L. V. (1984). White-black achievement differences: The narrowing gap. *American Psychologist, 39,* 1207–1213.
Jones, S. S., & Raag, T. (1989). Smile production in older infants: The importance of a social recipient for the facial signal. *Child Development, 60,* 811–818.
Jorgensen, R. S., & Johnson, J. H. (1990). Contributors to the appraisal of major life changes: Gender, perceived controllability, sensation seeking, strain, and social support. *Journal of Applied Social Psychology, 20,* 1123–1138.
Josephs, R. A., Markus, H. R., & Tafarodi, R. W. (1992). Gender and self-esteem. *Journal of Personality and Social Psychology, 63,* 391–402.
Jussim, L., Nelson, T. E., Manis, M., & Soffin, S. (1995). Prejudice, stereotypes, and labeling effects: Sources of bias in person perception. *Journal of Personality and Social Psychology, 68,* 228–246.
Kagan, J. (1989). Temperamental contributions to social behavior. *American Psychologist, 44,* 668–674.
Kagan, J., & Snidman, N. (1991). Infant predictors of inhibited and uninhibited profiles. *Psychological Science, 2,* 40–44.
Kagan, J., Kearsley, R. B., & Zelazo, P. R. (1980). *Infancy: Its place in human development.* Cambridge, MA: Harvard University Press.
Kaitz, M., Lapidot, P., Bronner, R., & Eidelman, A. I. (1992). Parturient women can recognize their infants by touch. *Developmental Psychology, 28,* 35–39.
Kaitz, M., Meschulach-Sarfaty, O., & Auerbach, J. (1988). A reexamination of newborns' ability to imitate facial expressions. *Developmental Psychology, 1,* 3–7.
Kales, A., Tan, T. L., Kollar, E. J., Naithoh, P., Preson, T. A., & Malmstrom, E. J. (1970). Sleep patterns following 205 hours of sleep deprivation. *Psychosomatic Medicine, 32,* 189–200.
Kalichman, S. C., & Craig, M. E. (1991). Professional psychologists' decisions to report suspected child abuse: Clinician and situation influences. *Professional Psychology: Research and Practice, 22,* 84–89.
Kalichman, S. C., Szymanowski, D., McKee, G., Taylor, J., & Craig, M. E. (1989). Cluster analytically derived MMPI profile subgroups of incarcerated adult rapists. *Journal of Clinical Psychology, 45,* 149–155.
Kalil, R. E. (1989, December). Synapse formation in the developing brain. *Scientific American,* 76–85.
Kalimo, R., & Mejman, T. (1987). Psychological and behavioural responses to stress at work. In R. Kalimo, M. A. El-Batawi, & C. L. Cooper (Eds), *Psychosocial factors at work and their relation to health.* Geneva: World Health Organization.
Kamarck, T., & Jennings, J. R. (1991). Biobehavioral factors in sudden cardiac death. *Psychological Bulletin, 109,* 42–75.
Kandel, E., & Abel, T. (1995). Neuropeptides, adenylyl cyclase, and memory storage. *Science, 268,* 825–826.
Kanekar, S., Shaherwalla, A., Franco, B., Kunju, T., & Pinto, A. J. (1991). The acquaintance predicament of a rape victim. *Journal of Applied Social Psychology, 21,* 1524–1544.
Kanner, A. D., Coyne, J. C., Schaefer, C., & Lazarus, R. S. (1981). Comparison of two modes of stress measurement: Daily hassles and uplifts versus major life events. *Journal of Behavioral Medicine, 4,* 1–39.
Kaplan, A. S., & Woodside, D. B. (1987). Biological aspects of anorexia nervosa and bulimia nervosa. *Journal of Consulting and Clinical Psychology, 55,* 645–653.
Kaplan, C. A., & Simon, H. A. (1990). In search of insight. *Cognitive Psychology, 22,* 374–419.
Kaplan, R. M. (1988). Health-related quality of life in cardiovascular disease. *Journal of Consulting and Clinical Psychology, 56,* 382–392.
Karau, S. J., & Williams, K. D. (1993). Social loafing: A meta-analytic review and theoretical integration. *Journal of Personality and Social Psychology, 65,* 681–706.
Karau, S. J., & Williams, K. D. (1995). Social loafing: Research findings, implications, and future directions. *Current Directions in Psychological Science, 4,* 134–140.
Karweit, N., & Slavin, R. E. (1981). Measurement and modeling choices in studies of time and learning. *American Educational Research Journal, 18,* 157–171.
Kashani, J. H., & Orvaschel, H. (1988). Anxiety disorders in mid-adolescence: A community sample. *American Journal of Psychiatry, 145,* 960–964.
Kashani, J. H., Reid, J. C., & Rosenberg, T. K. (1989). Levels of hopelessness in children and adolescents: A developmental perspective. *Journal of Consulting and Clinical Psychology, 57,* 496–499.

Katsuki, Y. (1961). Neutral mechanisms of auditory sensation in cats. In W. A. Rosenblith (Ed.), *Sensory communication.* Cambridge, MA: MIT Press.

Katz, S., Lautenschlager, G. J., Blackburn, A. B., & Harris, F. H. (1990). Answering reading comprehension items without passages on the SAT. *Psychological Science, 1,* 122–127.

Kaufman, A. S. (1983). Some questions and answers about the Kaufman Assessment Battery for Children (K–ABC). *Journal of Psychoeducational Assessment, 1,* 205–218.

Kaufman, A. S. (1984). K–ABC and controversy. *Journal of Special Education, 18,* 409–444.

Kaufman, A. S. (1990). *Assessing adolescent and adult intelligence.* Boston: Allyn & Bacon.

Kazdin, A. E. (1991a). Treatment research: The investigation and evaluation of psychotherapy. In M. Hersen, A. E. Kazdin, & A. S. Bellack (Eds.), *The clinical psychology handbook* (2nd ed.). New York: Pergamon.

Kazdin, A. E. (1991b). Effectiveness of psychotherapy with children and adolescents. *Journal of Consulting and Clinical Psychology, 59,* 785–798.

Keesey, R. E., & Powley, T. L. (1986). The regulation of body weight. *Annual Review of Psychology, 37,* 109–135.

Kelley, H. H. (1972). Attribution in social interaction. In E. E. Jones et al. (Eds.), *Attribution: Perceiving the causes of behavior.* Morristown, NJ: General Learning Press.

Kelley, H. H. (1973). Process of causal attribution. *American Psychologist, 28,* 107–128.

Kelley, H. H., Berscheid, E., Christensen, A., Harvey, J. H., Huston, T. L., et al. (1983). *Close relationships.* New York: Freeman.

Kelly, G. (1955). *The psychology of personal constructs.* New York: W. W. Norton.

Kelly, T. A., & Strupp, H. H. (1992). Patient and therapist values in psychotherapy: Perceived changes, assimilation, similarity, and outcome. *Journal of Consulting and Clinical Psychology, 60,* 34–40.

Kendall, P. C. (1993). Cognitive–behavioral therapies with youth: Guiding theory, current status, and emerging developments. *Journal of Consulting and Clinical Psychology, 61,* 235–247.

Kendall-Tackett, K. A., Williams, L. M., & Finkelhor, D. (1993). Impact of sexual abuse on children: A review and synthesis of recent empirical studies. *Psychological Bulletin, 113,* 164–180.

Kendler, K. S., Neale, M., Kessler, R., Heath, A., & Eaves, L. (1992). A population-based twin study of major depression in women. *Archives of General Psychiatry, 49,* 257–266.

Kendler, K. S., Neale, M., Kessler, R., Heath, A., & Eaves, L. (1993). A twin study of recent life events and difficulties. *Archives of General Psychiatry, 50,* 789–796.

Kendler, K. S., Neale, M. C., Heath, A. C., Phil, D., et al. (1994). A twin-family study of alcoholism in women. *American Journal of Psychiatry, 151,* 707–715.

Kendler, K. S., Neale, M., MacLean, C. J., Heath, A., Eaves, L., & Kessler, R. (1993). Smoking and major depression. *Archives of General Psychiatry, 50,* 36–43.

Kennell, J. H., Voos, D. K., & Klaus, M. H. (1979). Parent–infant bonding. In J. D. Osofsky (Ed.), *Handbook of infant development.* New York: Wiley.

Kerr, N., & Bruun, S. E. (1983). Dispensability of member effort and group motivation losses: Free-rider effects. *Journal of Personality and Social Psychology, 44,* 78–94.

Kessler, R. C., Kendler, K. S., Heath, A. C., Neale, M. C., & Eaves, L. J. (1992). Social support, depressed mood, and adjustment to stress: A genetic epidemiologic investigation. *Journal of Personality and Social Psychology, 62,* 257–272.

Kessler, R. C., Sonnega, A., Bromet, E., Hughes, M., & Nelson, C. B. (1995). Posttraumatic stress disorder in the National Comorbidity Survey. *Archives of General Psychiatry, 52,* 1048–1060.

Kety, S. S., Wender, P. H., Jacobsen, B., Ingraham, L. J., Jansson, L., Faber, B., & Kinney, D. K. (1994). Mental illness in the biological and adoptive relatives of schizophrenic adoptees: Replication of the Copenhagen study in the rest of Denmark. *Archives of General Psychiatry, 51,* 442–455.

Kihlstrom, J. F., Barnhardt, T. M., & Tataryn, D. J. (1992). The psychological unconscious. *American Psychologist, 47,* 788–791.

Kilbourne, B. K. (1989). A cross-cultural investigation of the foot-in-the-door compliance induction procedure. *Journal of Cross-Cultural Psychology, 20,* 3–38.

Kim, J. J., & Fanselow, M. S. (1992). Modality-specific retrograde amnesia of fear. *Science, 256,* 675–677.

Kimball, M. M. (1989). A new perspective on women's math achievement. *Psychological Bulletin, 105,* 198–214.

Kimmel, D. C. (1980). *Adulthood and aging: An interdisciplinary view* (2nd ed.). New York: Wiley.

Kimura, D. (1992, September). Sex difference in the brain. *Scientific American,* pp. 119–125.

Kingstone, A., Enns, J. T., Mangun, G. R., & Gazzaniga, M. S. (1995). Guided visual search is a left-hemisphere process in split-brain patients. *American Psychological Society, 6,* 118–121.

Kinsbourne, M. (1975). The ontogeny of cerebral dominance. In D. Aaronson & R. W. Rieber (Eds.), *Developmental Psycholinguistics and Communication Disorders. Annals of the New York Academy of Science, 263,* 244–250.

Kinsey, A. C., Pomeroy, W. B., & Martin, C. E. (1948). *Sexual behavior in the human male.* Philadelphia: W. B. Saunders.

Kinsey, A. C., Pomeroy, W. B., Martin, C. E., & Gebhard, P. H. (1953). *Sexual behavior in the human female.* Philadelphia: W. B. Saunders.

Kirsch, I., & Lynn, S.J. (1995). The altered state of hypnosis. *American Psychologist, 50,* 846–858.

Kirsch, I., Montgomery, G., & Sapirstein, G. (1995). Hypnosis as an adjunct to cognitive–behavioral psychotherapy: A meta-analysis. *Journal of Consulting and Clinical Psychology, 63,* 214–220.

Kirshnit, C. E., Richards, M. H., & Ham, M. (1988, August). *Athletic participation and body-image during early adolescence.* Paper presented at the 96th Annual Convention of the American Psychological Association, Atlanta.

Kitayama, S., & Burnstein, E. (1994). Social influence, persuasion, and group decision making. In S. Shavitt & T. C. Brock (Eds.), *Persuasion: Psychological insights and perspectives* (pp. 175–194). Boston: Allyn & Bacon.

Kitwood, T. (1990). *Concern for others.* New York: Routledge.

Klaus, M. H., & Kennell, J. H. (1983). *Bonding: The beginnings of parent–infant attachment* (Rev. ed.). New York: New American Library.

Kleinginna, P. R., Jr., & Kleinginna, A. M. (1981). A categorized list of definitions with suggestions for a consensual definition. *Motivation and Emotion, 5,* 345–380.

Kleinmuntz, B., & Szucko, J. J. (1984). Lie detection in ancient and modern times: A call for contemporary scientific study. *American Psychologist, 39,* 766–776.

Klesges, R. C., Isbell, T. R., & Klesges, L. M. (1992). Relationship between dietary restraint, energy intake, physical activity, and body weight: A prospective analysis. *Journal of Abnormal Psychology, 101,* 668–674.

Klingenspor, B. (1994). Gender identity and bulimic eating behavior. *Sex Roles, 31,* 407–432.

Klonoff, E. A., Annechild, A., & Landrine, H. (1994). Predicting exercise adherence in women: The role of psychological and physiological factors. *Preventive Medicine, 23,* 257–262.

Kluger, A. N., & DeNisi, A. (1996). The effects of feedback interventions on performance: A historical review, a meta-analysis, and preliminary feedback intervention theory. *Psychological Bulletin, 119,* 254–284.

Knutson, J. F. (1995). Psychological characteristics of maltreated children: Putative risk factors and consequences. *Annual Review of Psychology, 46,* 401–431.

Knutson, J. F., & Selner, M. B. (1994). Punitive childhood experiences reported by young adults over a 10-year period. *Child Abuse and Neglect, 18,* 155–166.

Kogut, D., Langley, T., & O'Neal, E. C. (1992). Gender role masculinity and angry aggression in women. *Sex Roles, 26,* 355–365.

Kohlberg, L. (1969). The cognitive-developmental approach to socialization. In D. A. Goslin (Ed.), *Handbook of socialization theory and research.* Chicago: Rand McNally.

Köhler, W. (1973). *The mentality of apes* (2nd ed.). New York: Liveright. (Original work published 1927.)

Kohn, A. (1986). *No contest: The case against competition.* Boston: Houghton Mifflin.

Kohn, A. (1992). *No contest.* Boston: Houghton Mifflin.

Kohout, J., & Pion, G. (1990). Participation of ethnic minoirities in psychology: Where do we stand? In G. Stricker, E. Davis-Russell, E. Bourg, E. Duran, W. R. Hammond, J. McHolland, K. Polite, & B. E. Vaughn (Eds.), *Toward ethnic diversification in psychology education and training.* Hyattsville, MD: American Psychological Association.

Kohout, J., Wicherski, M., & Cooney, B. (1992). *Characteristics of graduate departments of psychology: 1989–1990.* Washington, DC: Office of Demographic, Employment, and Educational Research, American Psychological Association.

Kolb, B. (1989). Brain development, plasticity, and behavior. *American Psychologist, 44,* 1203–1212.

Koocher, G. P. (1991). Questionable methods in alcoholism research. *Journal of Consulting and Clinical Psychology, 59,* 246–248.

Kopp, C. B. (1989). Regulation of distress and negative emotions: A developmental view. *Developmental Psychology, 25,* 343–354.

Kopp, C. B., & Kaler, S. R. (1989). Risk in infancy: Origins and implications. *American Psychologist, 44,* 224–230.

Kopta, S. M., Howard, K. I., Lowry, J. L., & Beutler,L. E. (1994). Patterns of symptomatic recovery in psychotherapy. *Journal of Consulting and Clinical Psychology, 62,* 1009–1016.

Kortenhaus, C. M., & Demarest, J. (1993). Gender role stereotyping in children's literature: An update. *Sex Roles, 28,* 219–232.

Koss, M. P. (1990). The women's mental health research agenda. *American Psychologist, 45,* 374–380.

Koss, M. P. (1993). Rape: Scope, impact, interventions, and public policy responses. *American Psychologist, 48,* 1062–1069.

Koss, M. P., Gidycz, C. A., & Wisniewski, N. (1987). The scope of rape: Incidence and prevalence of sexual aggression and victimization in a national sample of higher education students. *Journal of Consulting and Clinical Psychology, 55,* 162–170.

Kosslyn, S. M. (1975). Information representation in visual images. *Cognitive Psychology, 7,* 341–370.

Kosslyn, S. M. (1987). Seeing and imagining in the cerebral hemispheres: A computational approach. *Psychological Review, 94,* 148–175.

Kosslyn, S. M., LeSueur, L. L., Dror, I. E., & Gazzaniga, M. S. (1993). The role of the corpus callosum in the representation of lateral orientation. *Neuropsychologia, 31,* 675–686.

Koulack, D. (1991). *To catch a dream.* Albany: State University of New York Press.

Krantz, D. S., Contrada, R. J., Hill, D. R., & Friedler, E. (1988). Environmental stress and biobehavioral antecedents of coronary heart disease. *Journal of Consulting and Clinical Psychology, 56,* 333–341.

Krantz, D. S., Grunberg, N. E., & Baum, A. (1985). Health psychology. *Annual Review of Psychology, 36,* 349–383.

Kranzler, H. R., & Anton, R. F. (1994). Implications of recent neuropsychopharmacologic research for understanding the etiology and development of alcoholism. *Journal of Consulting and Clinical Psychology, 62,* 1116–1126.

Kranzler, J. H., & Jensen, A. R. (1991). The nature of psychometric g: Unitary process or a number of independent processes? *Intelligence, 15,* 397–422.

Krosnick, J. A. (1988). Attitude importance and attitude change. *Journal of Experimental Social Psychology, 24,* 240–255.

Krosnick, J. A., & Alwin, D. F. (1989). Aging and susceptibility to attitude change. *Journal of Personality and Social Psychology, 57,* 416–425.

Kruley, P., Sciama, S. C., & Glenberg, A. M. (1994). On-line processing of textual illustrations in the visuospatial sketchpad: Evidence from dual-task studies. *Memory and Cognition, 22,* 261–272.

Krupa, D. J., Thompson, J. K., & Thompson, R. F. (1993). Localization of a memory trace in the mammalian brain. *Science, 260,* 989–991.

Kubey, R., & Csikszentmihalyi, M. (1990). *Television and the quality of life.* Hillsdale, NJ: Erlbaum.

Kübler-Ross, E. (1969). *On death and dying.* New York: Macmillan.

Kübler-Ross, E. (1975). *Death: The final stage of growth.* Englewood Cliffs, NJ: Prentice-Hall.

Kudoh, N., Tajima, H., Hatayama, T., Maruyama, K., Shoji, Y., Hayashi, T., & Nakanishi, M. (1991). Effects of room environment on human cognitive activities. *Tohoku Psychologica Folia, 50,* 45–54.

Kuhl, P. K., Williams, K. A., Lacerda, F., Stevens, K. N., & Lindblom, B. (1992). Linguistic experience alters phonetic perception in infants by 6 months of age. *Science, 255,* 606–655.

Ladd, G. W. (1990). Having friends, keeping friends, making friends, and being liked by peers in the classroom: Predictors of children's early school adjustment? *Child Development, 61,* 1081–1100.

LaFerla, J. J., Anderson, D. L., & Schalch, D. S. (1978). Psychoendocrine response to sexual arousal in human males. *Psychosomatic Medicine, 40,* 166–172.

Lafferty, P., Beutler, L. E., & Crago, M. (1989). Differences between more and less effective psychotherapists: A study of select therapist variables. *Journal of Consulting and Clinical Psychology, 57,* 76–80.

Lahey, B. B., McNees, M. P., & McNees, M. C. (1973). Control of an obscene "verbal tic" through timeout in an elementary school classroom. *Journal of Applied Behavior Analysis, 6,* 101–104.

Lambert, A. J. (1995). Stereotypes and social judgment: The consequences of group variability. *Journal of Personality and Social Psychology, 68,* 388–403.

Landrine, H., Klonoff, E. A., & Brown-Collins, A. (1992). Cultural diversity and methodology in feminist psychology. *Psychology of Women Quarterly, 16,* 145–163.

Lang, P. J. (1994). The varieties of emotional experience: A meditation on James–Lange theory. *Psychological Review, 101,* 211–221.

Lange, C. G. (1922). *The emotions* (English translation). Baltimore: Williams & Wilkins. (Original work published 1885.)

Langlois, J. H., Ritter, J. M., Casey, R. J., & Sawin, D. B. (1995). Infant attractiveness predicts maternal behaviors and attitudes. *Developmental Psychology, 31,* 464–472.

Langlois, J. H., Ritter, J. M., Roggman, L. A., & Vaughn, L. S. (1991). Facial diversity and infant preferences for attractive faces. *Developmental Psychology, 27,* 79–84.

Langlois, J. H., Roggman, L. A., & Rieser-Danner, L. A. (1990). Infants' differential social responses to attractive and unattractive faces. *Developmental Psychology, 26,* 153–159.

Langman, B., & Cockburn, A. (1975). Sirhan's gun. *Harper's, 250,* 16–27.

Larrick, R. P., Morgan, J. N., & Nisbett, R. E. (1990). Teaching the use of cost–benefit reasoning in everyday life. *Psychological Science, 1,* 362–370.

Larson, R., & Ham, M. (1993). Stress and "storm and stress" in early adolescence: The relationship of negative events with dysphoric affect. *Developmental Psychology, 29,* 130–140.

Larson, R. W., Raffaelli, M., Richards, M. H., Ham, M., & Jewell, L. (1990). Ecology of depression in late childhood and early adolescence: A profile of daily states and activities. *Journal of Abnormal Psychology, 99,* 92–102.

Lassner, J. B., Matthews, K. A., & Stoney, C. M. (1994). Are cardiovascular reactors to asocial stress also reactors to social stress? *Journal of Personality and Social Psychology, 66,* 69–77.

Last, C. G., Hersen, M., Kazdin, A., Orvaschel, H., & Perrin, S. (1991). Anxiety disorders in children and their families. *Archives of General Psychiatry, 48,* 928–931.

Last, C. G., & Perrin, S. (1993). Anxiety disorders in African-American and white children. *Journal of Abnormal Child Psychology, 21,* 153–164.

Latané, B., & Darley, J. M. (1970). *The unresponsive bystander: Why doesn't he help?* New York: Meredith.

Latané, B., Williams, K., & Harkins, S. (1979). Many hands make light work: The causes and consequences of social loafing. *Journal of Personality and Social Psychology, 37,* 822–832.

Laumann, E. O., Gagnon, J. H., Michael, R. T. & Michaels, S. (1994). *The social organization of sexuality: Sexual practices in the United States.* Chicago, IL: The University of Chicago Press.

Lavach, J. R. (1991). Cerebral hemisphericity, college major and occupational choices. *Journal of Creative Behavior, 25,* 218–222.

Lawler, E. E., & Porter, L. W. (1967). Antecedent attitudes of effective managerial performance. *Organizational Behavior and Human Performance, 2,* 122–142.

Lazarus, A. A., & Fay, A. (1990). Brief psychotherapy: Tautology or oxymoron? In J. K. Zeig & S. G. Gilligan (Eds.), *Brief therapy myths, methods, and metaphors.* New York: Brunner/Mazel.

Lazarus, R. S. (1982). The psychology of stress and coping, with particular reference to Israel. In C. D. Spielberger, I. G. Sarason, & N. A. Milgram (Eds.), *Stress and anxiety* (Vol. 8). Washington, DC: Hemisphere.

Lazarus, R. S. (1984). The trivialization of distress. In B. L. Hammonds & C. J. Scheirer (Eds.), *Psychology and health: The master lecture series.* Washington, DC: American Psychological Association.

Lazarus, R. S. (1991a). Cognition and motivation in emotion. *American Psychologist, 46,* 352–367.

Lazarus, R. S. (1991b). The cognitive–motivational–relational theory. In R. S. Lazarus (Ed.), *Emotion and adaptation.* New York: Oxford University Press.

Lazarus, R. S. (1991c). *Emotion and adaptation.* New York: Oxford University Press.

Lazarus, R. S. (1991d). Progress on a cognitive–motivational–relational theory of emotion. *American Psychologist, 46,* 819–834.

Lazarus, R. S. (1993). From psychological stress to the emotions: A history of changing outlooks. *Annual Review of Psychology, 44,* 1–21.

Lazarus, R. S., & Alfert, E. (1964). Short-circuiting of threat by experimentally altering cognitive appraisal. *Journal of Abnormal and Social Psychology, 69,* 195–205.

Lazarus, R. S., & DeLongis, A. (1983). Psychological stress and coping in aging. *American Psychologist, 38,* 245–254.

Leahey, T. H. (1992). The mythical revolutions of American psychology. *American Psychologist, 47,* 308–318.

Leber, W. R., Beckham, E. E., & Danker-Brown, P. (1985). Diagnostic criteria for depression. In E. E. Beckham & W. R. Leber (Eds.), *Handbook of depression: Treatment, assessment, and research.* Homewood, IL: Dorsey Press.

Lebow, J. L., & Gurman, A. S. (1995). Research assessing couple and family therapy. *Annual Review of Psychology, 46,* 27–57.

LeDoux, J. E. (1992). Emotion and the amygdala. In J. P. Aggleton (Ed.), *The amygdala: Neurobiological aspects of emotion, memory, and mental dysfunction,* (pp. 339–351). New York: Wiley-Liss.

LeDoux, J. E. (1993). Emotional memory systems in the brain. *Behavioural Brain Research, 58,* 69–79.

LeDoux, J. E. (1994, June). Emotion, memory and the brain. *Scientific American,* pp. 50–57.

LeDoux, J. E. (1995). Emotion: Clues from the brain. *Annual Review of Psychology, 46,* 209–235.

LeDoux, J. E., Romanski, L., & Xagoraris, A. (1989). Indelibility of subcortical emotional memories. *Journal of Cognitive Neuroscience, 1,* 238–243.

Lee, C., Ashford, S. J., & Bobko, P. (1990). Interactive effects of "Type A" behavior and perceived control on worker performance, job satisfaction, and somatic complaints. *Academy of Management Journal, 33,* 870–881.

Lefcourt, H. M. (1992). Durability and impact of the locus of control construct. *Psychological Bulletin, 112,* 411–414.

Lefcourt, H. M., & Davidson-Katz, K. (1991). Locus of control and health. In C. R. Snyder & D. R. Forsyth (Eds.), *Handbook of social and clinical psychology* (pp. 246–266). New York: Pergamon.

Lefkowitz, M. M., Eron, L. D., Walder, L. O., & Huesmann, L. R. (1977). *Growing up to be violent.* New York: Pergamon.

Leibowitz, H. W. (1971). Sensory, learned, and cognitive mechanisms of size perception. *Annals of the New York Academy of Sciences, 1988,* 47–62.

Leiner, H. C., Leiner, A. L., & Dow, R. S. (1986). Does the cerebellum contribute to mental skills? *Behavioral Neuroscience, 100,* 443–454.

Lenneberg, E. H. (1967). *Biological foundations of language.* New York: Wiley.

Leon, M. (1992). The neurobiology of filial learning. *Annual Review of Psychology, 43,* 377–399.

Leonard-Barton, D. (1981). The diffusion of active residential solar energy equipment in California. In A. Shama (Ed.), *Marketing solar energy innovations* (pp. 243–257). New York: Praeger.

Lepper, M. R., & Greene, D. (1978). Overjustification research and beyond: Toward a means–end analysis of intrinsic motivation. In M. R. Lepper & D. Greene (Eds.), *The hidden cost of reward.* Hillsdale, NJ: Erlbaum.

Lepper, M. R., Greene, D., & Nisbett, R. E. (1973). Undermining children's intrinsic interest with extrinsic reward: A test of the overjustification hypothesis. *Journal of Personality and Social Psychology, 28,* 129–137.

Lerer, B., Bleich, A., Kotler, M., Garb, R., Hertzberg, M., & Levin. B. (1987). Posttraumatic stress disorder in Israeli combat veterans. *Archives of General Psychiatry, 44,* 976–977.

Lester, B. M., & Dreher, M. (1989). Effects of marijuana use during pregnancy on newborn cry. *Child Development, 60,* 765–771.

LeVay, S. (1991). A difference in hypothalamic structure between heterosexual and homosexual men. *Science, 253,* 1034–1037.

LeVay, S., & Hamer, D. H. (1994, May). Evidence for a biological influence in male homosexuality. *Scientific American,* pp. 44–49.

Levenson, R. W. (1992). Autonomic nervous system differences among emotions. *Psychological Science, 3,* 23–27.

Levenson, R. W., Ekman, P., Heider, K., & Firesen, W. V. (1992). Emotion and autonomic nervous system activity in the Minangkabau of West Sumatra. *Journal of Personality and Social Psychology, 62,* 972–988.

LeVere, T. E., Brugler, T., Sandin, M., & Gray-Silva, S. (1989). Recovery of function after brain damage: Facilitation by the calcium entry blocker nimodipine. *Behavioral Neuroscience, 103,* 561– 565.

Levi, L. (1990). Occupational stress. *American Psychologist, 46,* 1142–1145.

Levin, D. J. (1990). *Alcoholism.* New York: Hemisphere.

Levine, E. L., Ash, R. A., Hall, H., & Sistrunk, F. (1983). Evaluation of job analysis methods by experienced job analysts. *Academy of Management Journal, 26,* 339–348.

Levine, M. (1975). *Hypothesis testing: A cognitive theory of learning.* Hillsdale, NJ: Erlbaum.

Levine, R. L., & Stadtman, E. R. (1992). Oxidation of proteins during aging. *Generations, 16,* 39–42.

Levine, R. V., Martinez, T. S., Brase, G., & Sorenson, K. (1994). Helping in 36 U.S. cities. *Journal of Personality and Social Psychology, 67,* 69–82.

Levinson, D. J. (1978). *The seasons of a man's life.* New York: Knopf.

Levinson, D. J. (1980). Toward a conception of the adult life course. In N. J. Smelser & E. H. Erikson (Eds.), *Themes of work and love in adulthood.* Cambridge, MA: Harvard University Press.

Levinson, D. J. (1996). *The seasons of a woman's life.* New York: Alfred A. Knopf.

Levitt, M. J., Weber, R. A., Clark, M. C., & McDonnell, P. (1985). Reciprocity of exchange in toddler sharing behavior. *Developmental Psychology, 21,* 122–123.

Levy-Lahad, E., Wasco, W., Poorkaj, P., Romano, D. M., Oshima, J., Pettingell, W. H., Yu, C., Jondro, P. D., Schmidt, S. D., Wang, K., Crowley, A. C., Fu, Y. H., Guenette, S. Y., Galas, D., Nemens, E., Wijsman, E. M., Bird,T. D., Schellenberg, G. D., & Tanzi, R. E. (1995a). Candidate gene for the chromosome 1 familial Alzheimer's disease locus. *Science, 269,* 973–977.

Levy-Lahad, E., Wijsman, E. M., Nemens, E., Anderson, L., Goddard, K. A. B., Weber, J. L., Bird, T. D., & Schellenberg, G. D. (1995b). A familial Alzheimer's disease locus on chromosome I. *Science, 269,* 970–973.

Lewin, K. K. (1970). *Brief psychotherapy.* St. Louis: Warren H. Green.

Lewinsohn, P. M. (1974). Classical and theoretical aspects of depression. In I. S. Calhoun, H. E. Adams, & K. M. Mitchell (Eds.), *Innovative treatment methods in psychopathology.* New York: Wiley Interscience.

Lewinsohn, P. M., & Talkington, J. (1979). Studies on the measurement of unpleasant events and relations with depression. *Applied Psychological Measurement, 3,* 83–101.

Lewis, M. (1995). Self-conscious emotions. *American Scientist, 83,* 68–78.

Lewis, M., & Feiring, C. (1989). Infant, mother, and mother–infant interaction behavior and subsequent attachment. *Child Development, 60,* 831–837.

Lewis, M., & Saarni, C. (1985). Culture and emotions. In M. Lewis & C. Saarni (Eds.), *The socialization of emotions.* New York: Plenum.

Lidz, T. (1973). *The origin and treatment of schizophrenic disorders.* New York: Basic Books.

Liebrand, W. B. G., Messick, D. M., & Wolters, F. J. M. (1986). Why we are fairer than others: A cross-cultural replication and extension. *Journal of Experimental Social Psychology, 22,* 590–604.

Lilly, J. C. (1956). Mental effects of reduction of ordinary levels of physical stimuli in intact, healthy persons. *Psychiatric Research Reports, 5,* 1–28.

Linberg, M. A., Beggs, A. L., Chezik, D. D., & Ray, D. (1982). Flavor–toxicosis associations: Tests of three hypotheses of long delay learning. *Physiology and Behavior, 29,* 439–442.

Lindsay, D. S. (1993). Eyewitness suggestibility. *Current Directions in Psychological Science, 2,* 86–89.

Lindsey, K. P., & Paul, G. L. (1989). Involuntary commitments to public mental institutions: Issues involving the overrepresentation of blacks and assessment of relevant functioning. *Psychological Bulletin, 106,* 171–183.

Lindvall, O. (1991). Prospects of transplantation in human neurodegenerative diseases. *Trends in Neurosciences, 14,* 376–384.

Lindvall, O., Brundin, P., Widner, H., Rehncrona, S., Gustavi, B., Frackowiak, R., Leenders, K. L., Sawle, G., Rothwell, J. C., Marsden, C. D., & Bjorklund, A. (1990). Grafts of fetal dopamine neurons survive and improve motor function in Parkinson's disease. *Science, 247,* 374–577.

Linn, M. C., & Petersen, A. C. (1985). Emergence and characterization of sex differences in spatial ability: A meta-analysis. *Child Development, 56,* 1479–1498.

Linney, J. A., & Seidman, E. (1989). The future of schooling. *American Psychologist, 44,* 336–340.

Lipsey, M. W., & Wilson, D. B. (1993). The efficacy of psychological, educational, and behavioral treatment: Confirmation from meta-analysis. *American Psychologist, 48,* 1181–1209.

Locher, P., Unger, R., Sociedade, P., & Wahl, J. (1993). At first glance: Accessibility of the physical attractiveness stereotype. *Sex Roles, 28,* 729–743.

Locke, E. A., & Latham, G. P. (1990a). Work motivation: The high performance cycle. In U. Kleinbeck, H. Quast, H. Thierry, & H. Hacker (Eds.), *Work Motivation.* Hillsdale, NJ: Erlbaum.

Locke, E. A., & Latham, G. P. (1990b). Work motivation and satisfaction: Light at the end of the tunnel. *Psychological Science, 1,* 240–246.

Loehlin, J. C., Horn, J. M., & Willerman, L. (1994). Differential inheritance of mental abilities in the Texas adoption project. *Intelligence, 19,* 325–336.

Loftus, E. F. (1979). The malleability of human memory. *American Scientist, 67,* 310–320.

Loftus, E. F. (1991). *Witness for the defense.* New York: St. Martin's.

Loftus, E. F. (1993). The reality of repressed memories. *American Psychologist, 48,* 518–537.

Loftus, E. F., Garry, M., & Feldman, J. (1994). Forgetting sexual trauma: What does it mean when 38% forget? *Journal of Consulting and Clinical Psychology, 62,* 1177–1181.

Loftus, E. F., & Hoffman, H. G. (1989). Misinformation and memory: The creation of new memories. *Journal of Experimental Psychology: General, 118,* 100–104.

Lombard, D. N., Lombard, T. N., & Winett, R. A. (1995). Walking to meet health guidelines: The effect of prompting frequency and prompt structure. *Health Psychology, 14,* 164–170.

Lore, R. K., & Schultz, L. A. (1993). Control of human aggression. *American Psychologist, 48,* 16–25.

Lorenz, K. (1964). Ritualized fighting. In J. D. Carthy & F. J. Ebling (Eds.), *The natural history of agrression.* New York: Academic Press.

Lowe, M. R. (1993). The effects of dieting on eating behavior: A three-factor model. *Psychological Bulletin, 114,* 100–121.

Lowell, E. L. (1952). The effect of need for achievement on learning and speed of performance. *Journal of Psychology, 33,* 31–40.

Luborsky, L., Barber, J. P., & Crits-Christoph, P. (1990). Theory-based research for understanding the process of dynamic psychotherapy. *Journal of Consulting and Clinical Psychology, 58,* 281–287.

Luck, S. J., Hillyard, S. A., Mangun, G. R., & Gazzaniga, M. S. (1994). Independent attentional scanning in the separated hemispheres of split-brain patients. *Journal of Cognitive Neuroscience, 6,* 84–91.

Ludwick-Rosenthal, R., & Neufeld, W. J. (1988). Stress management during noxious medical procedures: An evaluative review of outcome studies. *Psychological Bulletin, 3,* 326–342.

Luecke-Aleksa, D., Anderson, D. R., Collins, P. A., & Schmitt, K. L. (1995). Gender constancy and television viewing. *Developmental Psychology, 31,* 773–780.

Luger, G. F., Bower, T. G. R., & Wishart, J. G. (1983). A model of the development of the early infant object concept. *Perception, 12,* 21–34.

Lummis, M., & Stevenson, H. W. (1990). Gender differences in beliefs and achievement: A cross-cultural study. *Developmental Psychology, 26,* 252–263.

Lundin, R. W. (1961). *Personality: An experimental approach.* New York: Macmillan.

Luus, C. A. E., & Wells, G. L. (1994). The malleability of eyewitness confidence: Co-witness and perseverance effects. *Journal of Applied Psychology, 79,* 714–723.

Lykken, D. T., McGue, M., Tellegen, A., & Bouchard, T. J., Jr. (1992). Emergenesis. *American Psychologist, 47,* 1565–1577.

Lynch, G., & Baudry, M. (1984). The biochemistry of memory: A new and specific hypothesis. *Science, 224,* 1057–1063.

Lynn, M., & Mynier, K. (1993). Effect of server posture on restaurant tipping. *Journal of Applied Social Psychology, 23,* 678–685.

Lyons, M. J., True, W. R., Eisen, S. A., Goldberg, J., Meyer, J. M., Faraone, S. V., Eaves, L. J., & Tsuang, M. T. (1995). Differential heritability of adult and juvenile antisocial traits. *Archives of General Psychiatry, 52,* 906–915.

Lytton, H., & Romney, D. M. (1991). Parents' differential socialization of boys and girls: A meta-analysis. *Psychological Bulletin, 109,* 267–296.

Maccoby, E. E. (1988). Gender as a social category. *Developmental Psychology, 24,* 755–765.

Maccoby, E. E. (1990). Gender and relationships. *American Psychologist, 45,* 513–520.

Maccoby, E. E., & Jacklin, C. N. (1987). Gender segregation in childhood. *Advances in Child Development and Behavior, 20,* 239–287.

MacLeod, C. M. (1991). Half a century of research on the stroop effect: An integrative review. *Psychological Bulletin, 109,* 163–203.

MacNichol, E. F. (1964, December). Three-pigment color vision. *Scientific American,* pp. 48–56.

Maddux, J. E. (1995). Self-efficacy theory: An introduction. In J. E. Maddux (Ed.), *Self-efficacy, adaptation, and adjustment: Theory, research, and application* (pp. 3–33). New York: Plenum.

Maddux, J. E., & Meier, L. J. (1995). Self-efficacy and depression. In J. E. Maddux (Ed.), *Self-efficacy, adaptation, and adjustment: Theory, research, and application* (pp. 143–169). New York: Plenum.

Madrazo, I., Drucken-Colin, R., Diaz, V., Martinez-Mata, J., Toress, C., & Becerril, J. J. (1987). Open microsurgical autograft of adrenal medulla to the right caudate nucleus in two patients with intractable Parkinson's disease. *New England Journal of Medicine, 316,* 831–834.

Magolda, M. B. (1990). Gender differences in epistemological development. *Journal of College Student Development, 31,* 555–561.

Mahoney, M. J. (1977). Reflections on the cognitive–learning trend in psychotherapy. *American Psychologist, 32,* 5–13.

Mahoney, M. J. (1993). Introduction to special section: Theoretical developments in the cognitive psychotherapies. *Journal of Consulting and Clinical Psychology, 61,* 187–193.

Mahrer, A. R., & Nadler, W. P. (1986). Good moments in psychotherapy: A preliminary review, a list, and some promising research avenues. *Journal of Consulting and Clinical Psychology, 54,* 10–15.

Maier, N. R. F., & Klee, J. B. (1941). Studies of abnormal behavior in the rat: 17. Guidance versus trial and error and their relation to convulsive tendencies. *Journal of Experimental Psychology, 29,* 380–389.

Maier, S. F., Watkins, L. R., & Fleshner, M. (1994). Psychoneuroimmunology: The interface between behavior, brain, and immunity. *American Psychologist, 49,* 1004–1017.

Malamuth, N. M., & Sockloskie, R. J. (1991). Characteristics of aggressors against women: Testing a model using a national sample of college students. *Journal of Consulting and Clinical Psychology, 59,* 670–681.

Mamelak, M. (1991). A model for narcolepsy. *Canadian Journal of Psychology, 45,* 194–220.

Mangan, B. (1993). Dennett, consciousness, and the sorrows of functionalism. *Consciousness and Cognition, 2,* 1–17.

Mann, L., Mitsui, H., Beswick, G., & Harmoni, R. V. (1994). A study of Japanese and Australian children's respect for others. *Journal of Cross-Cultural Psychology, 25,* 133–145.

Manuck, S. B., Cohen, S., Rabin, B. S., Muldoon, M. F., & Bachen, E. A. (1991). Individual differences in cellular immune response to stress. *Psychological Science, 2,* 111–115.

March, J. S., Leonard, H. L., & Swedo, S. E. (1995). Obsessive–compulsive disorder. In J. S. March (Ed.), *Anxiety disorders in children and adolescents* (pp. 251–275). New York: Guilford.

Maris, R., & Silverman, M. M. (1995). *Suicide prevention: Toward the year 2000.* New York: Guilford.

Markow, T. M. (1992). Genetics and developmental stability: An integrative conjecture on aetiology and neurobiology of schizophrenia. *Psychological Medicine, 22,* 295–305.

Markowitsch, H. J., & Tulving, E. (1994). Cognitive processes and cerebral cortical fundi: Findings from positron emission tomography studies. *Proceedings of the National Academy of Sciences of the United States of America, 91,* 10507–10511.

Marks, I. M. (1977). Clinical phenomena in search of laboratory models. In J. D. Maser & M. E. P. Seligman (Eds.), *Psychopathology experimental models.* San Francisco: Freeman.

Marks, I. M., et al. (1986). *Behavioral psychotherapy: Pocketbook of clinical management.* Bristol, England: John Wright.

Marks, W. B., Dobell, W. H., & MacNichol, J. R. (1964). The visual pigments of single primate cones. *Science, 142,* 1181–1183.

Marlatt, G. A., Baer, J. S., Donovan, D. M., & Kivlahan, D. R. (1988). Addictive behaviors: Etiology and treatment. *Annual Review of Psychology, 39,* 223–252.

Marlatt, G. A., Larimer, M. E., Baer, J. S., & Quigley, L. A. (1993). Harm reduction for alcohol problems: Moving beyond the controlled drinking. *Behavior Therapy, 24,* 461–504.

Marschark, M., Yuille, J. C., Richman, C. L., & Hunt, R. R. (1987). The role of imagery in memory: On shared and distinctive information. *Psychological Bulletin, 102,* 28–41.

Marshall, G. N., Wortman, C. B., Vickers, R. R., Jr., Kusulas, J. W., & Hervig, L. K. (1994). The five-factor model of personality as a framework for personality–health research. *Journal of Personality and Social Psychology, 67,* 278–286.

Marshall, L. L., & Vitanza, S. A. (1994). Physical abuse in close relationships: Myths and realities. In A. L. Weber & J. H. Harvey (Eds.), *Perspectives on close relationships* (pp. 263–284). Boston: Allyn & Bacon.

Marshall, P. S. (1993). Allergy and depression: A neurochemical threshold model of the relation between the illnesses. *Psychological Bulletin, 113,* 23–43.

Marshall, W. A., & Tanner, J. M. (1969). Variations in the pattern of pubertal changes in girls. *Archives of Disease in Childhood, 44,* 291–303.

Martin, A., Haxby, J. V., Lalonde, F. M., Wiggs, C. L., & Ungerleider, L. G. (1995). Discrete cortical regions associated with knowledge of color and knowledge of action. *Science, 270,* 102–105.

Martin, R., & Haroldson, S. (1977). Effect of vicarious punishment on stuttering frequency. *Journal of Speech and Hearing Research, 20,* 21–26.

Marx, E. M., Williams, J. M. G., & Claridge, G. C. (1992). Depression and social problem solving. *Journal of Abnormal Psychology, 101,* 78–86.

Maslow, A. H. (1962). *Toward a psychology of being.* New York: Van Nostrand.

Maslow, A. H. (1969). Toward a humanistic biology. *American Psychologist, 24,* 734–735.

Massaro, D. W., & Cowan, N. (1993). Information processing models: Microscopes of the mind. *Annual Review of Psychology, 44,* 383–425.

Masters, W. H., Johnson, V. E., & Kolodny, R. C. (1994). *Heterosexuality.* New York: HarperCollins.

Matarazzo, J. D. (1990). Psychological assessment versus psychological testing. *American Psychologist, 45,* 999–1017.

Matsui, T., & Onglatco, M. L. U. (1990). Relationships between employee quality circle involvement and need fulfillment in work as moderated by work type: A compensatory or a spillover model? In U. Kleinbeck, H. Quast, H. Thierry, & H. Hacker (Eds.), *Work motivation.* Hillsdale, NJ: Erlbaum.

Matsumoto, D. (1994). *People: Psychology from a cultural perspective.* Pacific Grove, CA: Brooks/Cole.

Matsumoto, D. (1996). *Culture and psychology,* Pacific Grove, CA: Brooks/Cole.

Matsumoto, D., & Kudoh, T. (1993). American–Japanese cultural differences in attributions of personality based on smiles. *Journal of Nonverbal Behavior, 17,* 231–243.

Matt, G. E. (1989). Decision rules for selecting effect sizes in meta-analysis: A review and reanalysis of psychotherapy outcome studies. *Psychological Bulletin, 105,* 106–115.

Matthews, K. A. (1988). Coronary heart disease and Type A behaviors: Update on and alternative to the Booth-Kewley and Friedman (1987) quantitative review. *Psychological Bulletin, 104,* 373–380.

Matthies, H. (1989). Neurobiological aspects of learning and memory. *Annual Review of Psychology, 40,* 381–404.

Mauer, D., & Salapatek, P. (1976). Development changes in the scanning of faces by young infants. *Child Development, 47,* 523–527.

Maunsell, J. H. R. (1995). The brain's visual world: Representation of visual targets in the cerebral cortex. *Science, 270,* 764–769.

Maurer, T. J., Palmer, J. K., & Ashe, D. K. (1993). Diaries, checklists, evaluations, and contrast effects in measurement of behavior. *Journal of Applied Psychology, 78,* 226–231.

Mauro, R., Sato, K., & Tucker, J. (1992). The role of appraisal in human emotions: A cross-cultural study. *Journal of Personality and Social Psychology, 62,* 301–317.

May, J., & Kline, P. (1987). Measuring the effects upon cognitive abilities of sleep loss during continuous operations. *The British Psychological Society, 78,* 443–455.

McAuley, E., Duncan, T. E., & McElroy, M. (1989). Self-efficacy cognitions and causal attributions for children's motor performance: An exploratory investigation. *Journal of Genetic Psychology, 150,* 65–73.

McBride, A. B. (1990). Mental health effects of women's multiple roles. *American Psychologist, 45,* 381–384.

McCall, R. B. (1983). Environmental effects on intelligence: The forgotten realm of discontinuous nonshared within-family factors. *Child Development, 54,* 408–415.

McCarty, D., Argeriou, M., Huebner, R. B., & Lubran, B. (1991). Alcoholism, drug abuse, and the homeless. *American Psychologist, 46,* 1139–1148.

McCaslin, M., Tuck, D., Wiard, A., Brown, B., LaPage, J., & Pyle, J. (1994). Gender composition and small-group learning in fourth-grade mathematics. *The Elementary School Journal, 94,* 467–482.

McCauley, C. (1989). The nature of social influence in groupthink: Compliance and internalization. *Journal of Personality and Social Psychology, 57,* 250–260.

McClearn, G. E., Plomin, R., Gora-Maslak, G., & Crabbe, J. C. (1991). The gene chase in behavioral science. *Psychological Science, 2,* 222–229.

McClelland, D. C. (1958). Methods of measuring human motivation. In J. W. Atkinson (Ed.), *Motives in fantasy, action, and society.* Princeton, NJ: Van Nostrand.

McClelland, D. C. (1961). *The achieving society.* Princeton, NJ: Van Nostrand.

McClelland, D. C. (1986). Some reflections on the two psychologies of love. *Journal of Personality, 54,* 334–353.

McClelland, D. C. (1987). Characteristics of successful entrepreneurs. *The Journal of Creative Behavior, 21,* 219–233.

McClintock, M. K. (1971). Menstrual synchrony and suppression. *Nature, 229,* 244–245.

McCloskey, M., Wible, C. G., & Cohen, N. J. (1988). Is there a special flashbulb-memory mechanism? *Journal of Experimental Psychology: General, 117,* 171–181.

McConkey, K. M., & Kinoshita, S. (1988). The influence of hypnosis on memory after one day and one week. *Journal of Abnormal Psychology, 97,* 48–53.

McConkie, G. W., Kerr, P. W., Reddix, M. D., & Zola, D. (1988). Eye movement control during reading: 1. The location of initial eye fixations on words. *Vision Research, 28,* 1107–1118.

McCormick, E. J., Jeanneret, P. R., & Mecham, R. C. (1972). A study of job characteristics and job dimensions as based on the Position Analysis Questionnaire (PAQ) [Monograph]. *Journal of Applied Psychology, 56,* 347–368.

McCrady, B. S. (1994). Alcoholics anonymous and behavior therapy: Can habits be treated as diseases? Can diseases be treated as habits? *Journal of Consulting and Clinical Psychology, 62,* 1159– 1166.

McCrae, R. R., & Costa, P. T., Jr. (1987). Validation of the five-factor model of personality across instruments and observers. *Journal of Personality and Social Psychology, 52,* 81–90.

McCrae, R. R., & Costa, P. T., Jr. (1990). *Personality in adulthood.* New York: Guilford.

McCrae, R. R., & Costa, P. T., Jr. (1994). The stability of personality: Observations and evaluations. *Current Directions in Psychological Science, 3,* 173–175.

McDonaugh, G. R. (1992). *An examination of racial stereotypes: The differential effects of gender and social class on their content.* Dissertation research, Purdue University, West Lafayette, Indiana.

McFall, M. E., Mackay, P. W., & Donovan, D. M. (1991). Combat-related PTSD and psychosocial adjustment problems among substance abusing veterans. *Journal of Nervous and Mental Disease, 179,* 33–38.

McGaugh, J. L. (1990). Significance and remembrance: The role of neuromodulatory systems. *Psychological Science, 1,* 15–25.

McGinty, D., & Szymusiak, R. (1988). Neuronal unit activity patterns in behaving animals: Brainstem and limbic system. *Annual Review of Psychology, 39,* 135–168.

McGlynn, S. M. (1990). Behavioral approaches to neuropsychological rehabilitation. *Psychological Bulletin, 108,* 420–441.

McGoldrick, M., Preto, N. G., Hines, P. M., & Lee, E. (1991). Ethnicity and family therapy. In A. S. Gurman & D. P. Kniskern (Eds.), *Handbook of family therapy* (Vol. 2). New York: Brunner/Mazel.

McGraw, K. O., & Fiala, J. (1982). Undermining the Zeigarnik effect: Another hidden cost of reward. *Journal of Personality, 50,* 58–66.

McGue, M., Pickens, R. W., & Svikis, D. S. (1992). Sex and age effects on the inheritance of alcohol problems: A twin study. *Journal of Abnormal Psychology, 101,* 3–17.

McKeachie, W. J. (1988). Teaching thinking. *Update: National Center for Research to Improve Postsecondary Teaching and Learning, 2,* 1.

McKeachie, W. J., Pintrich, P. R., & Lin, Y. (1985). Learning to learn. In G. d'Ydewalle (Ed.), *Cognition, information processing, and motivation.* New York: Elsevier– North Holland.

McKenzie, B. E., Tootell, H. E., & Day, R. H. (1980). Development of visual size constancy during the 1st year of human infancy. *Developmental Psychology, 16,* 163–174.

McManus, I. C., & Bryden, M. P. (1991). Geschwind's theory of cerebral lateralization: Developing a formal, causal model. *Psychological Bulletin, 110,* 235–237.

McMinn, M. R., Lindsay, S. F., Hannum, L. E., & Troyer, P. K. (1990). Does sexist language reflect personal characteristics? *Sex-Roles, 23,* 389–396.

McMinn, M. R., Troyer, P. K., Hannum, L. E., & Foster, J. D. (1991). Teaching nonsexist language to college students. *Journal of Experimental Education, 59,* 153–161.

McNally, R. J. (1990). Psychological approaches to panic disorder: A review. *Psychological Bulletin, 108,* 403–419.

McNally, R. J. (1994). Cognitive bias in panic disorder. *Current Directions in Psychological Science, 3,* 129–132.

McNeill, D. (1970). Explaining linguistic universals. In J. Morton (Ed.), *Biological and social factors in psycholinguistics.* London: Logos.

McNemar, Q. (1964). Lost: Our intelligence. Why? *American Psychologist, 19,* 871–882.

McReynolds, P. (1996). Lightner Witmer: A centennial tribute. *American Psychologist, 51,* 237–240.

Meares, R. (1994). A pathology of privacy: Towards a new theoretical approach to obsessive–compulsive disorder. *Contemporary Psychoanalysis, 30,* 83–100.

Medin, D. L. (1989). Concepts and conceptual structure. *American Psychologist, 44,* 1469–1481.

Mednick, S. A., Parnas, J., & Schulsinger, F. (1987). The Copenhagen high-risk project, 1962–1986. *Schizophrenia Bulletin, 13,* 485–495.

Meichenbaum, D. (1974). *Cognitive behavior modification.* Morristown, NJ: General Learning.

Meichenbaum, D. (1977). *Cognitive behavior modification.* New York: Plenum.

Meichenbaum, D. (1993). Changing conceptions of cognitive behavior modification: Retrospect and prospect. *Journal of Consulting and Clinical Psychology, 61,* 202–204.

Meichenbaum, D., & Cameron, R. (1973). Training schizophrenics to talk to themselves: A means of developing attentional controls. *Behavior Therapy, 4,* 515–534.

Mellody, P., Miller, A. W., & Miller, J. K. (1989). *Facing codependence.* New York: Harper & Row.

Melton, G. B., Petrila, J., Poythress, N. G., & Slobogin, C. (1987). *Psychological evaluations for the courts.* New York: Guilford.

Meltzoff, A. N. (1988). Imitation of televised models by infants. *Child Development, 59,* 1221–1229.

Melville, J. (1977). *Phobias and compulsions.* New York: Penguin.

Melzack, R. (1990, February). The tragedy of needless pain. *Scientific American,* 27–33.

Melzack, R., & Wall, P. D. (1970). Psychophysiology of pain. *International Anesthesiology Clinics, 8,* 3–34.

Mercer, R. T., Nichols, E. G., & Doyle, G. C. (1989). *Transitions in a woman's life* (Vol. 12). New York: Springer.

Merton, R. K. (1949). Merton's typology of prejudice and discrimination. In R. M. MacIver (Ed.), *Discrimination and national welfare.* New York: Harper & Row.

Merzenich, M. M., Jenkins, W. M., Johnston, P., Schreiner, C., Miller, S. L., & Tallal, P. (1996). Temporal processing deficits of language-learning impaired children ameliorated by training. *Science, 271,* 77–81.

Mesquita, B., & Frijda, N. H. (1992). Cultural variations in emotions: A review. *Psychological Bulletin, 112,* 179–204.

Metalsky, G. I., & Joiner, T. E., Jr. (1992). Vulnerability to depressive symptomatology: A prospective test of the diathesis–stress and causal mediation components of the hopelessness theory of depression. *Journal of Personality and Social Psychology, 63,* 667–675.

Metcalfe, J., Funnell, M., & Gazzaniga, M. S. (1995). Right-hemisphere memory superiority: Studies of a split-brain patient. *Psychological Science, 6,* 157–164.

Meyer, R. G., & Salmon, P. (1988). *Abnormal psychology* (2nd ed.). Boston: Allyn & Bacon.

Meyers-Levy, J., & Maheswaran, D. (1991). Exploring differences in males' and females' processing strategies. *Journal of Consumer Research, 18,* 63–70.

Middaugh, S. J. (1990). On clinical efficacy: Why biofeedback does—and does not—work. *Biofeedback and Self-Regulation, 15,* 191–208.

Mikhailova, N. G., Zukhar, A. V., Loseva, E. V., & Ermakova, I. V. (1991). Influence of transplantation of embryonal brain tissue (early periods) on reactions of avoidance of artificial and zoosocial stimuli in rats. *Neuroscience and Behavioral Physiology, 21,* 34–37.

Miklowitz, D. J. (1994). Family risk indicators in schizophrenia. *Schizophrenia Bulletin, 20,* 137–150.

Milgram, S. (1963). Behavioral study of obedience. *Journal of Abnormal and Social Psychology, 67,* 371–378.

Milgram, S. (1965). Liberating effects of group pressure. *Journal of Personality and Social Psychology, 1,* 127–134.

Millar, M. G., & Millar, K. (1990). Attitude change as a function of attitude type and argument type. *Journal of Personality and Social Psychology, 39,* 217–228.

Millar, M. G., & Millar, K. (1995). Negative affective consequences of thinking about disease detection behaviors. *Health Psychology, 14,* 141–146.

Miller, B. C., McCoy, J. K., Olson, T. D., & Wallace, C. M. (1986). Parental discipline and control attempts in relation to adolescent sexual attitudes and behavior. *Journal of Marriage and the Family, 48,* 503–512.

Miller, G. A. (1956). The magical number seven plus or minus two: Some limits on our capacity for processing information. *Psychological Review, 63,* 81–97.

Miller, G. A. (1965). Some preliminaries to psycholinguistics. *American Psychologist, 20,* 15–20.

Miller, K. F., & Baillargeon, R. (1990). Length and distance: Do preschoolers think that occlusion brings things together? *Developmental Psychology, 26,* 103–114.

Miller, L. C. (1990). Intimacy and liking: Mutual influence and the role of unique relationships. *Journal of Personality and Social Psychology, 59,* 50–60.

Miller, M. E., & Bowers, K. S. (1993). Hypnotic analgesia: Dissociated experience or dissociated control? *Journal of Abnormal Psychology, 102,* 29–38.

Miller, N. E. (1944). Experimental studies of conflict. In J. M. Hunt (Ed.), *Personality and behavioral disorders* (Vol. 1). New York: Ronald Press.

Miller, N. E. (1959). Liberalization of basic S–R concepts: Extensions to conflict behavior, motivation, and social learning. In S. Koch (Ed.), *Psychology: A study of a science* (Vol. 2). New York: McGraw-Hill.

Miller, N. E. (1969). Learning of visceral and glandular responses. *Science, 163,* 434–445.

Miller, P. F., Light, K. C., Bragdon, E. E., Ballenger, M. N., Herbst, M. C., Maixner, W., Hinderliter, A. L., Atkinson, S. S., Koch, G. G., & Sheps, D. S. (1993). Beta-endorphin response to exercise and mental stress in patients with ischemic heart disease. *Journal of Psychosomatic Research, 37,* 455–465.

Miller, P. H., & Aloise, P. A. (1989). Young children's understanding of the psychological causes of behavior: A review. *Child Development, 60,* 257–285.

Miller, R. P., Cosgrove, J. M., & Doke, L. (1990). Motivating adolescents to reduce their fines in a token economy. *Adolescence, 25,* 97–104.

Miller, T. Q., Smith, T. W., Turner, C. W., Guijarro, M. L., & Hallet, A. J. (1996). A meta-analytic review of research on hostility and physical health. *Psychological Bulletin, 119,* 322–348.

Miller, T. Q., Turner, C. W., Tindale, R. S., Posavac, E. J., & Dugoni, B. L. (1991). Reasons for the trend toward null findings in research on Type A behavior. *Psychological Bulletin, 110,* 469–485.

Milner, B. (1966). Amnesia following operation on the temporal lobes. In C. W. M. Whitty & O. L. Zangwill (Eds.), *Amnesia.* London: Butterworth.

Milner, B., Corkin, S., & Teuber, H. L. (1968). Further analysis of hippocampal amnesic syndrome: 14-year follow-up study of H. M. *Neuropsychologia, 6,* 215–234.

Milner, J. S., & Chilamkurti, C. (1991). Physical child abuse perpetrator characteristics: A review of the literature. *Journal of Interpersonal Violence, 6,* 345–366.

Milner, P. M. (1989). A cell assembly theory of hippocampal amnesia. *Neuropsychologia, 27,* 23–30.

Milner, P. M. (1991). Brain stimulation reward: A review. *Canadian Journal of Psychology, 45,* 1–36.

Miranda, S. M. (1994). Avoidance of groupthink meeting management using group support systems. *Small Group Research, 25,* 105–136.
Mischel, W. (1979). On the interface of cognition and personality: Beyond the person–situation debate. *American Psychologist, 34,* 740–754.
Mischel, W. (1983). Alternatives in the pursuit of the predictability and consistency of persons: Stable data that yield unstable interpretations. *Journal of Personality, 51,* 578–604.
Mischel, W., & Grusec, J. E. (1966). Determinants of the rehearsal and transmission of neutral and averse behaviors. *Journal of Personality and Social Psychology, 3,* 197–205.
Mishima, K., Okawa, M., Hishikawa, Y., Hozumi, S., Hori, H., & Takahashi, K. (1994). Morning bright light therapy for sleep and behavior disorders in elderly patients with dementia. *Acta Psychiatrica Scandinavica, 89,* 1–7.
Mishler, E. G., & Waxler, N. E. (1968). Family interaction processes and schizophrenia: A review of current theories. In E. G. Mishler & N. E. Waxler (Eds.), *Family processes and schizophrenia.* New York: Science House.
Mittal, B. (1988). Achieving higher seat belt usage: The role of habit in bridging the attitude–behavior gap. *Journal of Applied Social Psychology, 18,* 993–1016.
Money, J. (1984). Paraphilias: Phenomenology and classification. *American Journal of Psychotherapy, 38,* 164–168.
Monroe, S. M., & Simons, A. D. (1991). Diathesis-stress theories in the context of life stress research: Implications for the depressive disorders. *Psychological Bulletin, 110,* 406–425.
Monroe, S. M., Simons, A. D., Thase, M. E. (1991). Onset of depression and time to treatment entry: Roles of life stress. *Journal of Consulting and Clinical Psychology, 59,* 566–573.
Montepare, J. M., & Zebrowitz-McArthur, L. (1988). Impressions of people created by age-related qualities of their gaits. *Journal of Personality and Social Psychology, 55,* 547–556.
Montgomery-St. Laurent, T., Fullenkamp, A. M., & Fischer, R. B. (1988). A role for the hamster's flank gland in heterosexual communication. *Physiology and Behavior, 44,* 759–762.
Moorehouse, M. J. (1991). Linking maternal employment patterns to mother–child activities and children's school competence. *Developmental Psychology, 27,* 295–303.
Morgan, W. P. (1992). Hypnosis and sport psychology. In J. Rhue, S. J. Lynn & I. Kirsch (Eds.), *Handbook of clinical hypnosis.* Washington, DC: American Psychological Association.
Morin, C. M., Stone, J., McDonald, K., & Jones, S. (1994). Psychological management of insomnia: A clinical replication series with 100 patients. *Behavior Therapy, 25,* 291–309.
Morris, M. W., & Peng, K. (1994). Culture and cause: American and Chinese attributions for social and physical events. *Journal of Personality and Social Psychology, 67,* 949–971.
Morris, R. G. M. (1989). *Parallel distributed processing: Implications for psychology and neurobiology.* Oxford, England: Clarendon.
Morrison, J. W., Ispa, J. M., & Thornburg, K. R. (1994). African American college students' psychosocial development as related to care arrangements during infancy. *Journal of Black Psychology, 20,* 418–429.
Moskowitz, B. A. (1978, November). The acquisition of language. *Scientific American,* pp. 92–108.
Mueser, K. T., Bellack, A. S., Morrison, R. L., & Wade, J. H. (1990). Gender, social competence, and symptomatology in schizophrenia: A longitudinal analysis. *Journal of Abnormal Psychology, 99,* 138–147.
Mukherjee, S., Sackeim, H. A., & Schnurr, D. B. (1994). Electroconvulsive therapy of acute manic episodes: A review. *American Journal of Psychiatry, 151,* 169–176.
Mullen, B., Anthony, T., Salas, E., & Driskell, J. E. (1994). Group cohesiveness and quality of decision making: An integration of tests of the groupthink hypothesis. *Small Group Research, 25,* 189–204.
Mullen, B. & Copper, C. (1994). The relation between group cohesiveness and performance: An integration. *Psychological Bulletin, 115,* 210–227.
Muñoz, R. F., Hollon, S. D., McGrath, E., Rehm, L. P., & VandenBos, G. R. (1994). On the AHCPR *Depression in primary care* guidelines: Further considerations for practitioners. *American Psychologist, 49,* 42–61.
Murphy, G. E., Wetzel, R. D., Robins, E., & McEvoy, L. (1992). Multiple risk factors predict suicide in alcoholism. *Archives of General Psychiatry, 49,* 459–463.
Murphy, S. M. (1990). Models of imagery in sport psychology: A review. *Journal of Mental Imagery, 14,* 153–172.
Murphy, S. M., & Jowdy, D. P. (1992). Imagery and mental practice. In Thelma S. Horn (Ed.), *Advances in sport psychology* (pp. 221–250). Champaign, IL: Human Kinetics.
Muray, H. A. (1983). *Explorations in personality.* New York: Oxford University Press.
Mussen, P. H., & Distler, L. (1959). Masculinity, identification, and father–son relationships. *Journal of Abnormal and Social Psychology, 59,* 350–356.
Myers, D. G., & Diener, E. (1995). Who is happy? *Psychological Science, 6,* 10–19.
Naar, R. (1990). Psychodrama in short-term psychotherapy. In R. A. Wells & V. J. Giannetti (Eds.), *Handbook of the brief psychotherapies.* New York: Plenum.
Nace, E. P. (1987). *The treatment of alcoholism.* New York: Brunner/Mazel.
Nahm, F. K. D., Tranel, D., Damasio, H., & Damasio, A. R. (1993). Cross-modal associations and the human amygdala. *Neuropsychologia, 31,* 727–744.
Narrow, W. E., Regier, D. A., & Rae, D. S. (1993). Use of services by persons with mental and addictive disorders: Findings from the National Institute of Mental Health Epidemiologic Catchment Area Program. *Archives of General Psychiatry, 50,* 95–107.
Nash, M. (1987). What, if anything, is regressed about hypnotic age regression? A review of the empirical literature. *Psychological Bulletin, 102,* 42–52.
Nathan, B. R., & Tippins, N. (1990). The consequences of halo "error" in performance ratings: A field study of the moderating effect of halo on test validation results. *Journal of Applied Psychology, 75,* 290–296.
Nathan, P. E. (1988). The addictive personality is the behavior of the addict. *Journal of Consulting and Clinical Psychology, 56,* 183–188.
Nathan, P. E., & Skinstad, A. H. (1987). Outcomes of treatment for alcohol problems: Current methods, problems, and results. *Journal of Consulting and Clinical Psychology, 55,* 332–340.
Nathans, J. (1989, February). The genes for color vision. *Scientific American,* pp., 42–49.
National Research Council Panel on Research on Child Abuse and Neglect, Commission on Behavioral and Social Sciences and Education. (1993). *Understanding child abuse and neglect.* Washington, DC: National Academic Press.
Navon, D. (1990). How critical is the accuracy of an eyewitness's memory? Another look at the issue of lineup diagnosticity. *Journal of Applied Psychology, 75,* 506–510.
Neal, A. M., & Turner, S. M. (1991). Anxiety disorders research with African Americans: Current status. *Psychological Bulletin, 109,* 400–410.
Needleman, L. D., & Geller, E. S. (1992). Comparing interventions to motivate work-site collection of home-generated recyclables. *American Journal of Community Psychology, 20,* 775–785.
Neisser, U. (1967). *Cognitive Psychology.* Englewood Cliffs, NJ: Prentice-Hall.
Neisser, U. (1992). Two themes in the study of cognition. In H. L Pick, Jr., P. van den Broek, & D. C. Knill (Eds.), *Cognition: Conceptual and methodological issues* (pp. 333–340). Washington, DC: American Psychological Association.
Neisser, U., Boodoo, G., Bouchard, T. J., Jr., Boykin, A. W., Brody, N., Ceci, S. J., Halpern, D. F., Loehlin, J. C., Perloff, R., Sternberg, R. J., & Urbina, S. (1996). Intelligence: Knowns and unknowns. *American Psychologist, 51,* 77–101.
Nelson, B. A., & Stake, J. E. (1994). The Myers–Briggs type indicator personality dimensions and perceptions of quality of therapy relationships. *Psychotherapy, 31,* 449–455.
Nelson, C. A., & Ludemann, P. M. (1989). Past, current, and future trends in infant face perception research. *Canadian Journal of Psychology, 43,* 183–198.
Nelson, K. (1993). The psychological and social origins of autobiographical memory. *Psychological Science, 4,* 7–14.
Nemeroff, C. B., Knight, D. L., Kirshnan, R. R., Slotkin, T. A., Bissette, G., Melville, M. L., Blazer, D. G. (1988). Marked reduction in the number of platelet-tritiated imipramine binding sites in geriatric depression. *Archives of General Psychiatry, 45,* 919–923.

Neugarten, B. (1968). Adult personality: Toward a psychology of the life cycle. In B. Neugarten (Ed.), *Middle age and aging* (pp. 137–147). Chicago: University of Chicago Press.

Newcomb, A. F., & Bagwell, C. L. (1995). Children's friendship relations: A meta-analytic review. *Psychological Bulletin, 117,* 306–347.

Newcomb, M. D., & Bentler, P. M. (1989). Substance use and abuse among children and teenagers. *American Psychologist, 44,* 242–248.

Newcombe, N., & Huttenlocher, J. (1992). Children's early ability to solve perspective-taking problems. *Developmental Psychology, 28,* 635–643.

Newell, A., & Simon, H. A. (1972). *Human problem solving.* Englewood Cliffs, NJ: Prentice-Hall.

Nigg, J. T., & Goldsmith, H. H. (1994). Genetics of personality disorders: Perspectives from personality and psychopathology research. *Psychological Bulletin, 115,* 346–380.

Nilsson, K. M. (1990). The effect of subject expectations of "hypnosis" upon vividness of visual imagery. *The International Journal of Clinical and Experimental Hypnosis, 38,* 17–24.

Nisbett, R. E. (1972). Hunger, obesity, and the ventromedial hypothalamus. *Psychological Review, 79,* 433–453.

Nolen-Hoeksema, S., & Girgus, J. S. (1994). The emergence of gender differences in depression during adolescence. *Psychological Bulletin, 115,* 424–443.

Norman, D. A. (1990). *Design of everyday things.* New York: Doubleday.

Norris, J. (1989). Normative influence effects on sexual arousal to nonviolent sexually explicit material. *Journal of Applied Social Psychology, 19,* 341–352.

Noton, D., & Stark, L. (1971, June). Eye movements and visual perception, *Scientific American,* pp. 35–44.

Notterman, J. M., & Drewry, H. N. (1993). *Psychology and education: Parallel and interactive approaches.* New York: Plenum.

Novak, M. A., & Suomi, S. J. (1988). Psychological well-being of primates in captivity. *American Psychologist, 43,* 765–773.

Nucci, L., & Turiel, E. (1993). God's word, religious rules, and their relation to Christian and Jewish children's concepts of morality. *Child Development, 64,* 1475–1491.

Nuechterlein, K. H., & Holroyd, J. C. (1980). Biofeedback in the treatment of tension headache: Current status. *Archives of General Psychiatry, 37,* 866–873.

O'Donnell, C. R. (1995). Firearm deaths among children and youth. *American Psychologist, 50,* 771–776.

Ofshe, R. J., & Singer, M. T. (1994). Recovered-memory therapy and robust repression: Influence and pseudomemories. *The International Journal of Clinical and Experimental Hypnosis, 42,* 391–410.

Ogur, B. (1986). Long day's journey into night: Women and prescription drug abuse. *Women and Health, 11,* 99–115.

Olds, J. (1955). Physiological mechanisms of reward. *Nebraska Symposium on Motivation, 3,* 73–139.

Olds, J. (1969). The central nervous system and the reinforcement of behavior. *American Psychologist, 24,* 114–132.

Olds, J., & Milner, P. (1954). Positive reinforcement produced by electrical stimulation of septal area and other regions of rat brain. *Journal of Comparative and Physiological Psychology, 47,* 419–427.

O'Leary, A. (1990). Stress, emotion, and human immune function. *Psychological Bulletin, 108,* 363–382.

O'Leary, K. D., Barling, J., Arias, I., Rosenbaum, A., Malone, J., & Tyree, A. (1989). Prevalence and stability of physical aggression between spouses: A longitudinal analysis. *Journal of Consulting and Clinical Psychology, 57,* 263–268.

Olio, K. A. (1994). Truth in memory. *American Psychologist, 49,* 442–443.

Olivardia, R., Pope, H. G., Jr., Mangweth, B., & Hudson, J. L. (1995). Eating disorders in college men. *American Journal of Psychiatry, 152,* 1279–1283.

Oliver, M. B., & Hyde, J. S. (1993). Gender differences in sexuality: A meta-analysis. *Psychological Bulletin, 114,* 29–51.

Olson, E. (1994). Female voices of aggression in Tonga. *Sex Roles, 30,* 237–248.

Orenstein, P. (1994). *School girls: Young women, self-esteem, and the confidence gap.* New York: Doubleday.

Ornstein, R. E. (1976). A science of consciousness. In P. R. Lee, R. E. Ornstein, D. Galin, A. Deikman, & C. T. Tart (Eds.), *Symposium on consciousness* (San Francisco, 1974). New York: Viking.

Ornstein, R. E. (1977). *The psychology of consciousness* (2nd ed.). New York: Harcourt Brace Jovanovich.

Osofsky, J. D. (1995). The effects of exposure to violence on young children. *American Psychologist, 50,* 782–788.

Ottati, V., Fishbein, M., & Middlestadt, S. E. (1988). Determinants of voters' beliefs about the candidates' stands on the issues: The role of evaluative bias heuristics and the candidates' expressed message. *Journal of Personality and Social Psychology, 55,* 517–529.

Overby, L. Y. (1990). A comparison of novice and experienced dancers' imagery ability. *Journal of Mental Imagery, 14,* 173–184.

Owens, M. E., Bliss, E. L., Koester, P., & Jeppsen, E. A. (1989). Phobias and hypnotizability: A reexamination. *The International Journal of Clinical and Experimental Hypnosis, 37,* 207–216.

Pagano, R. W., Rose, R. M., Stivers, R. M., & Warrenburg, S. (1976). Sleep during transcendental meditation. *Science, 191,* 308–310.

Paikoff, R. L., & Brooks-Gunn, J. (1991). Do parent–child relationships change during puberty? *Psychological Bulletin, 110,* 47–66.

Paivio, A. (1971). *Imagery and verbal processes.* New York: Holt, Rinehart & Winston.

Palinkas, L. A., Russell, J., Downs, M. A., & Petterson, J. S. (1992). Ethnic differences in stress, coping, and depressive symptoms after the Exxon *Valdez* oil spill. *Journal of Nervous and Mental Disease, 180,* 287–295.

Pan, H. S., Neidig, P. H., & O'Leary, K. D. (1994). Predicting mild and severe husband-to-wife physical aggression. *Journal of Consulting and Clinical Psychology, 62,* 975–981.

Pantin, H. M., & Carver, C. S. (1982). Induced competence and the bystander effect. *Journal of Applied Social Psychology, 12,* 100–111.

Papini, M. R., & Bitterman, M. E. (1990). The role of contingency in classical conditioning. *Psychological Review, 97,* 396–403.

Paradis, C. M., Hatch, M., & Friedman, S. (1994). Anxiety disorders in African Americans: An update. *Journal of the National Medical Association, 86,* 609–612.

Parker, D. E. (1980, November). The vestibular apparatus. *Scientific American,* pp. 118–135.

Parker, G., Roy, K., Hadzi-Pavlovic, D., & Pedic, F. (1992). Psychotic (delusional) depression: A meta-analysis of physical treatments. *Journal of Affective Disorders, 24,* 17–24.

Parker, L. E. (1993). When to fix it and when to leave: Relationships among perceived control, self-efficacy, dissent, and exit. *Journal of Applied Psychology, 78,* 949–959.

Parkin, A. J., Reid, T., & Russo, R. (1990). On the differential nature of implicit and explicit memory. *Memory and Cognition, 18,* 507–514.

Parrott, W. G., & Schulkin, J. (1993). Neuropsychology and the cognitive nature of the emotions. *Cognition and Emotion, 7,* 43–59.

Patrick, C. J. (1994). Emotion and psychopathy: Startling new insights. *Psychophysiology, 31,* 319–330.

Patrick, C. J., & Iacono, W. G. (1989). Psychopathy, threat, and polygraph test accuracy. *Journal of Applied Psychology, 74,* 347–355.

Pavlov, I. P. (1927). *Conditioned reflexes.* London: Oxford University Press.

Payne, J. W., Bettman, J. R., & Johnson, E. J. (1992). Behavioral decision research: A constructive processing perspective. *Annual Review of Psychology, 43,* 87–132.

Pearlman, C. (1991). Electroconvulsive therapy. *General Hospital Psychiatry, 13,* 128–137.

Pearlmann, S. F. (1993). Late mid-life astonishment: Disruptions to identity and self-esteem. *Women and Therapy, 14,* 1–12.

Pedersen, D. M., & Wheeler, J. (1983). The Müller-Lyer illusion among Navajos. *Journal of Social Psychology, 121,* 3–6.

Pedersen, N. L., Plomin, R., & McClearn, G. E. (1994). Is there g beyond g? (Is there genetic influence on specific cognitive abilities independent of genetic influence on general cognitive ability?) *Intelligence, 18,* 133–143.

Pedersen, N. L., Plomin, R., Nesselroade, J. R., & McClearn, G. E. (1992). A quantitative genetic analysis of cognitive abilities during the second half of the life span. *Psychological Science, 3,* 346–353.

Pelleymounter, M. A., Cullen, M. J., Baker, M. B., Hecht, R., Winters, D., Boone, T., & Collins, F. (1995). Effects of the obese gene product on body weight regulation in ob/ob mice. *Science, 269,* 540–543.

Penfield, W. W. (1958). *The excitable cortex in conscious man.* Springfield, IL: Charles Thomas.

Penfield, W. W., & Jasper, H. (1954). *Epilepsy and the functional anatomy of the human brain.* Boston: Little, Brown.

Penfield, W. W., & Mathieson, G. (1974). Memory: Autopsy findings and comments on the role of hippocampus in experiential recall. *Archives of Neurology, 31,* 145–154.

Penfield, W. W., & Milner, B. (1958). Memory deficit produced by bilateral lesions in the hippocampal zone. *Archives of Neurological Psychiatry, 79,* 475–497.
Penfield, W. W., & Perot, P. (1963). The brain's record of auditory and visual experience. *Brain, 86,* 595–696.
Persky, H. (1978). Plasma testosterone level and sexual behavior of couples. *Archives of Sexual Behavior, 7,* 157–173.
Peselow, E. D., Sanfilipo, M. P., & Fieve, R. R. (1995). Relationship between hypomania and personality disorders before and after successful treatment. *American Journal of Psychiatry, 152,* 232– 238.
Pesut, D. J. (1990). Creative thinking as a self-regulatory metacognitive process: A model for education, training and further research. *Journal of Creative Behavior, 24,* 105–110.
Peterson, C., & Seligman, M. E. P. (1984). Causal explanations as a risk factor for depression: Theory and evidence. *Psychological Review, 91,* 347–374.
Peterson, L. R., & Peterson, M. J. (1959). Short-term retention of individual verbal items. *Journal of Experimental Psychology, 58,* 193–198.
Petty, R. E., & Cacioppo, J. T. (1981). *Attitudes and persuasion: Classic and contemporary approaches.* Dubuque, IA: Wm. C. Brown.
Petty, R. E., and Cacioppo, J. T. (1985). The elaboration likelihood model of persuasion. In L. Berkowitz (Ed.), *Advances in experimental social psychology* (Vol. 19). New York: Academic.
Petty, R. E., Cacioppo, J. T., Strathman, A. J., & Priester, J. R. (1994). To think or not to think: Exploring two routes to persuasion. In S. Shavitt & T. C. Brock (Eds.), *Persuasion: Psychological insights and perspectives* (pp. 113–148). Boston: Allyn & Bacon.
Petty, R. E., Schumann, D. W., Richman, S. A., & Strathman, A. J. (1993). Positive mood and persuasion: Different roles for affect under high- and low-elaboration conditions. *Journal of Personality and Social Psychology, 64,* 5–20.
Pfister, H. P., & Muir, J. L. (1992). Prenatal exposure to predictable and unpredictable novelty stress and oxytocin treatment affects offspring development and behavior in rats. *International Journal of Neuroscience, 62,* 227–241.
Phares, V., & Compas, B. E. (1993). Fathers and developmental psychopathology. *Current Directions in Psychological Science, 2,* 162–165.
Piaget, J. (1932). *The moral judgment of the child.* London: Routledge & Kegan Paul.
Piaget, J. (1963). The attainment of invariants and reversible operations in the development of thinking. *Social Research, 30,* 283–299.
Pickens, R. W., Svikis, D. S., McGue, M., Lykken, D. T., Heston, L. L., & Clayton, P. J. (1991). Heterogeneity in the inheritance of alcoholism. *Archives of General Psychiatry, 48,* 19–28.
Pine, J. M. (1995). Variation in vocabulary development as a function of birth order. *Child Development, 66,* 272–281.
Pitman, R. K., Orr, S. P., Forgue, D. F., Altman, B., de Jong, J. B., & Herz, L. R. (1990). Psychophysiologic responses to combat imagery of Vietnam veterans with posttraumatic stress disorder versus other anxiety disorders. *Journal of Abnormal Psychology, 99,* 49–54.
Pittam, J., Gallois,C., Iwawaki, S., Kroonenberg, P. (1995). Australian and Japanese concepts of expressive behavior. *Journal of Cross-Cultural Psychology, 26,* 451–473.
Pittman, T. S., & Heller, J. F. (1987). Social motivation. *Annual Review of Psychology, 38,* 461–490.
Plomin, R. (1989). Environment and genes: Determinants of behavior. *American Psychologist, 44,* 105–111.
Plomin, R. (1994a). *Genetics and experience: The interplay between nature and nuture.* Thousand Oaks, CA: Sage.
Plomin, R. (1994b). Nature, nurture, and social development. *Social Development, 3,* 37–53.
Plomin, R., & Neiderhiser, J. (1991). Quantitative genetics, molecular genetics, and intelligence. *Intelligence, 15,* 369–387.
Plomin, R., Reiss, D., Hetherington, E. M., & Howe, G. W. (1994). Nature and nurture: Genetic contributions to measures of the family environment. *Developmental Psychology, 30,* 32–43.
Plotkin, W. B. (1980). The role of attributions of responsibility in the facilitation of unusual experiential states during alpha training: An analysis of the biofeedback placebo effect. *Journal of Abnormal Psychology, 89,* 67–78.
Plutchik, R. (1980). *Emotion: A psychoevolutionary synthesis.* New York: Harper & Row.
Pollatsek, A., Raney, G. E., Lagasse, L., & Rayner, K. (1993). The use of information below fixation in reading and in visual search. *Canadian Journal of Experimental Psychology, 47,* 179–200.
Pomerantz, E. M., Chaiken, S., & Tordesillas, R. S. (1995). Attitude strength and resistance processes. *Journal of Personality and Social Psychology, 69,* 408–419.
Pomerleau, A., Bolduc, D., Malcuit, G., & Cossette, L. (1990). Pink or blue: Environmental gender stereotypes in the first two years of life. *Sex Roles, 22,* 359–367.
Porter, B. E., Leeming, F. C., & Dwyer, W. O. (1995). Solid waste recovery: A review of behavioral programs to increase recycling. *Environment and Behavior, 27,* 122–152.
Posner, M. I., & Mitchell, R. F. (1967). Chronometric analysis of classification. *Psychological Review, 74,* 392–409.
Powell, B., & Steelman, L. C. (1990). Beyond sibship size: Sibling density, sex composition, and educational outcomes. *Social Forces, 69,* 181–206.
Powers, P. C., & Geen, R. G. (1972). Effects of the behavior and the perceived arousal of a model on instrumental aggression. *Journal of Personality and Social Psychology, 23,* 175–184.
Powers, S. I., Hauser, S. T., Kilner, L. A. (1989). Adolescent mental health. *American Psychologist, 44,* 200–208.
Powley, T. L. (1977). The ventromedial hypothalamic syndrome, satiety, and a cephalic phase hypothesis. *Psychological Review, 84,* 89–126.
Pratarelli, M. E., & McIntyre, J. A. (1994). Effects of social loafing on word recognition. *Perceptual and Motor Skills, 78,* 455–464.
Pratkanis, A. R., Eskenazi, J., & Greenwald, A. G. (1994). What you expect is what you believe (but not necessarily what you get): A test of the effectiveness of subliminal self-help audiotapes. *Basic and Applied Social Psychology, 15,* 251–276.
Premack, D. (1962). Reversibility of the reinforcement relation. *Science, 136,* 255–257.
Premack, D. (1965). Reinforcement theory. In D. Levine (Ed.), *Nebraska Symposium on Motivation* (Vol. 13, pp. 123–180). Lincoln: University of Nebraska Press.
Premack, D. (1971). Language in chimpanzees? *Science, 172,* 808– 822.
Prentice-Dunn, S., & Rogers, R. W. (1984). Effects of deindividuating situational cues and aggressive models on subjective deindividuation and aggression. *Journal of Personality and Social Psychology, 39,* 104–113.
Preti, G., Cutler, W. B., Garcia, C. R., Huggins, G. R., & Lawley, H. J. (1986). Human axillary secretions influence women's menstrual cycles: The role of donor extract of females. *Hormones and Behavior, 20,* 474–482.
Price, D. D., et al. (1984). A psychophysical analysis of acupuncture analgesia. *Pain, 19,* 27–42.
Prinz, R. J., & Miller, G. E. (1994). Family-based treatment for childhood antisocial behavior: Experimental influences on dropout and engagement. *Journal of Consulting and Clinical Psychology, 62,* 654–660.
Prinz, R. N., Vitiello, M. V., Raskind, M. A., & Thorphy, M. J. (1990). Geriatrics: Sleep disorders and aging. *New England Journal of Medicine, 323,* 520–526.
Proshansky, H. M., & O'Hanlon, T. (1977). Environmental psychology: Origins and development. In D. Stokols (Ed.), *Perspectives on environment and behavior: Theory, research, and application.* New York: Plenum.
Puffer, S. M. (1987). Prosocial behavior, noncompliant behavior, and work performance among commission salespeople. *Journal of Applied Psychology, 72,* 615–621.
Putnam, W. H. (1979). Hypnosis and distortions in eyewitness memory. *International Journal of Clinical and Experimental Hypnosis, 27,* 437–448.
Quigley, B., Gaes, G. G., & Tedeschi, J. T. (1989). Does asking make a difference? Effects of initiator, possible gain, and risk on attributed altruism. *Journal of Social Psychology, 129,* 259–267.
Quilitch, H. R., & Risley, T. R. (1973). The effects of play materials on social play. *Journal of Applied Behavior Analysis, 6,* 573–578.
Rabizadeh, S., et al. (1993). Induction of apoptosis by the low affinity NGF receptor. *Science, 261,* 345–348.
Rachlin, H. (1995). Things that are private and things that are mental. In J. T. Todd & E. K. Morris (Eds.), *Modern perspectives on B. F. Skinner and contemporary behaviorism* (pp. 179–183). Westport, CT: Greenwood.
Rafaeli, A. (1989). When clerks meet customers: A test of variables related to emotional expressions on the job. *Journal of Applied Psychology, 74,* 385–393.

Ragins, B. R., & Sundstrom, E. (1989). Gender and power in organizations: A longitudinal perspective. *Psychological Bulletin, 105,* 51–88.

Rahe, R. H. (1989). Recent life change stress and psychological depression. In T. W. Miller (Ed.), *Stressful life events.* Madison, WI: International Universities Press.

Raichle, M. E. (1994, April). Visualizing the mind: Strategies of cognitive science and techniques of modern brain imaging open a window to the neural systems responsible for thought. *Scientific American,* pp. 58–64.

Raisman, G., Morris, R. J., & Zhou, C. F. (1987). Specificity in the reinnervation of adult hippocampus by embryonic hippocampal transplants. In F. J. Seil, E. Herbert, & B. M. Carlson (Eds.), *Progress in brain research* (Vol. 71, pp. 325–333). New York: Elsevier.

Rapee, R. (1986). Differential response to hyperventilation in panic disorder and generalized anxiety disorder. *Journal of Abnormal Psychology, 95,* 24–28.

Rappaport, J., (1987). Terms of empowerment/exemplars of prevention: Toward a theory for community psychology. *American Journal of Community Psychology, 2,* 121–148.

Ravussin, E., Lillioja, S., Knowler, W. C., Christin, L., Freymond, D., Abbott, W. G. H., Boyce, V., Howard, B. V., & Bogardus, C. (1988). Reduced rate of energy expenditure as a risk factor for body-weight gain. *New England Journal of Medicine, 318,* 467– 472.

Rayner, K., & Pollatsek, A. (1992). Eye movements and scene perception. *Canadian Journal of Psychology, 46,* 342–376.

Raz, S., & Raz, N. (1990). Structural brain abnormalities in the major psychoses: A quantitative review of the evidence from computerized imaging. *Psychological Bulletin, 208,* 93–108.

Ree, M. J., & Earles, J. A. (1992). Intelligence is the best predictor of job performance. *Current Directions in Psychological Science, 1,* 86–89.

Ree, M. J., & Earles, J. A. (1993). G is to psychology what carbon is to chemistry: A reply to Sternberg and Wagner, McClelland, and Calfee. *Current Directions in Psychological Science, 2,* 11–12.

Ree, M. J., Earles, J. A., & Teachout, M. S. (1994). Predicting job performance: Not much more than g. *Journal of Applied Psychology, 79,* 518–524.

Reed, C. F. (1984). Terrestrial passage theory of the moon illusion. *Journal of Experimental Psychology: General, 113,* 489–516.

Reiger, D. A., Boyd, J. H., Burke, J. D., Rae, D. S., Myers, J. K., Kramer, M., Robins, L. N., George, L. K., Karno, M., & Locke, B. Z. (1988). One-month prevalence of mental disorders in the United States. *Archives of General Psychiatry, 45,* 977–986.

Reis, H. T., Shaver, P. (1988). Intimacy as an interpersonal process. In S. Duck (Ed.), *Handbook of personal relationships: Theory, relationships and interventions.* Chichester, England: Wiley.

Reis, S. M. (1989). Reflections on policy affecting the education of gifted and talented students. *American Psychologist, 44,* 399–408.

Reisenzein, R. (1983). The Schachter theory of emotion: Two decades later. *Psychological Bulletin, 94,* 239–264.

Reiss, D. (1995). Genetic influence on family systems: Implications for development. *Journal of Marriage and the Family, 57,* 543–560.

Repa, B. K. (1988). Is there life after partnership? *American Bar Association Journal, 74,* 70–75.

Repetti, R. L., Matthews, K. A., & Waldron, I. (1989). Employment and women's health. *American Psychologist, 44,* 1394–1401.

Reppucci, N. D., & Haugaard, J. J. (1989). Prevention of child sexual abuse. *American Psychologist, 44,* 1266–1275.

Rescorla, R. A. (1977). Pavlovian 2nd-order conditioning: Some implications for instrumental behavior. In H. Davis & H. Herwit (Eds.), *Pavlovian–operant interactions.* Hillsdale, NJ: Erlbaum.

Rescorla, R. A. (1978). Some implications of a cognitive perspective on Pavlovian conditioning. In S. H. Hulse, H. Fowler, & W. Honig (Eds.), *Cognitive process in animal behavior.* Hillsdale, NJ: Erlbaum.

Rescorla, R. A. (1988). Pavlovian conditioning: It's not what you think it is. *American Psychologist, 43,* 151–160.

Resnick, S. M. (1992). Positron emission tomography in psychiatric illness. *Psychological Science, 1,* 92–98.

Restak, R. M. (1994). *The modular brain: How new discoveries in neuroscience are answering age-old questions about memory, free will, consciousness, and personal identity.* New York: Macmillan.

Restle, F. (1970). Moon illusion explained on the basis of relative size. *Science, 167,* 1092–1096.

Rhodes, N., & Wood, W. (1992). Self-esteem and intelligence affect influenceability: The mediating role of message reception. *Psychological Bulletin, 111,* 156–171.

Richardson, J. T. E., & Zucco, G. M. (1989). Cognition and olfaction: A review. *Psychological Bulletin, 105,* 352–360.

Richman, A. L., Miller, P. M., & LeVine, R. A. (1992). Cultural and educational variations in maternal responsiveness. *Developmental Psychology, 28,* 614–621.

Rifai, A. H., George, C. J., Stack, J. A., Mann, J. J., & Reynolds, C. F. (1994). Hopelessness in suicide attempters after acute treatment of major depression in late life. *American Journal of Psychiatry, 151,* 1687–1690.

Rifai, A. H., Reynolds, C. F., & Mann, J. J. (1922). Biology of elderly suicide. *Suicide and Life Threatening Behavior, 22,* 48–61.

Riger, S. (1992). Epistemological debates, feminist voices. *American Psychologist, 47,* 730–740.

Riley, W. T., Treiber, F. A., & Woods, M. G. (1989). Anger and hostility in depression. *Journal of Nervous and Mental Disease, 177,* 668–669

Ring, K., Wallston, K., & Corey, M. (1970). Mode of debriefing as a factor affecting subjective reaction to a Milgram-type obedience experiment: An ethical inquiry. *Representative Research in Social Psychology, 1,* 67–88.

Rips, L. J. (1990). Reasoning. *Annual Review of Psychology, 41,* 321–353.

Ritter, J. M., & Langlois, J. H. (1988). The role of physical attractiveness in the observation of adult–child interactions: Eye of the beholder or behavioral reality? *Developmental Psychology, 24,* 254–263.

Robberson, M. R., & Rogers, R. W. (1988). Beyond fear appeals: Negative and positive persuasive appeals to health and self-esteem. *Journal of Applied Social Psychology, 18,* 277–287.

Robbins, M., & Meyer, D. (1970). Motivational control of retrograde amnesia. *Journal of Experimental Psychology, 84,* 220–225.

Roberts, A. H., Kewman, D. G., Mercier, L., & Hovell, M. (1993). The power of nonspecific effects in healing: Implications for psychosocial and biological treatments. *Clinical Psychology Review, 13,* 375–391.

Roberts, G. W. (1988). Immunocytochemistry of neurofibrillary tangles in dementia pugilistica and Alzheimer's disease: Evidence for common genesis. *Lancet, II,* 1456–1457.

Roberts, G. C. (1992). *Motivation in sport and exercise: Conceptual constraints and convergence.* (pp. 3–29). Champaign, IL: Human Kinetics.

Robinson, L. A., Berman, J. S., & Neimeyer, R. A. (1990). Psychotherapy for the treatment of depression: A comprehensive review of controlled outcome research. *Psychological Bulletin, 108,* 30–49.

Rodin, J. (1981). Current status of the internal–external hypothesis for obesity: What went wrong? *American Psychologist, 36,* 361– 372.

Rodin, J. (1986). Aging and health: Effects of the sense of control. *Science, 233,* 1271–1276.

Rodin, J., & Ickovics, J. R. (1990). Women's health. *American Psychologist, 45,* 1018–1034.

Rodin, J., & Salovey, P. (1989). Health psychology. *Annual Review of Psychology, 40,* 533–581.

Roehrs, T., Timms, V., Zwyghuizen-Doorenbos, A., & Roth, T. (1989). Sleep extension in sleepy and alert normals. *Sleep, 12,* 449–457.

Rogers, C. R. (1951). *Client-centered therapy.* Boston: Houghton Mifflin.

Roggman, L. A., Langlois, J. H., Hubbs-Tait, L., & Rieser-Danner, L. A. (1994). Infant day-care, attachment, and the file drawer problem. *Child Development, 65,* 1429–1443.

Rogoff, B. & Morelli, G. (1989). Perspectives on children's development from cultural psychology. *American Psychologist, 44,* 343–348.

Romano, S. T., & Bordieri, J. E. (1989). Physical attractiveness stereotypes and students' perceptions of college professors. *Psychological Reports, 64,* 1099–1102.

Romans, S. E., Martin, J. L., Anderson, J. C., Herbison, G. P., & Mullen, P. E. (1995). Sexual abuse in childhood and deliberate selfharm. *American Journal of Psychiatry, 152,* 1336–1342.

Roose, S. P., Glassman, A. H., Attia, E., & Woodring, S. (1994). Comparative efficacy of selective serotonin reuptake inhibitors and tricyclics in the treatment of melancholia. *American Journal of Psychiatry, 151,* 1735–1739.

Rorty, M., Yager, J., & Rossotto, E. (1994). Childhood sexual, physical, and psychological abuse in bulimia nervosa. *American Journal of Psychiatry, 151,* 1122–1126.

Rosch, E. (1973). Natural categories. *Cognitive Psychology, 4,* 328–350.

Rosch, E. (1978). Principles of categorization. In E. Rosch & B. B. Lloyd (Eds.), *Cognition and categorization* (pp. 27–48). Hillsdale, NJ: Erlbaum.

Rose, S. A., & Feldman, J. F. (1995). Prediction of IQ and specific cognitive abilities at 11 years from infancy measures. *Developmental Psychology, 31,* 685–696.

Rose, S. D. (1991). The development and practice of group treatment. In M. Hersen, A. E. Kazdin, & A. S. Bellack (Eds.), *The clinical psychology handbook* (2nd ed.). New York: Pergamon.

Rosenberg, H. (1993). Prediction of controlled drinking by alcoholics and problem drinkers. *Psychological Bulletin, 113,* 129– 139.

Rosenberg, P. S. (1995). Scope of the AIDS epidemic in the United States. *Science, 270,* 1372–1375.

Rosenstock, I. M., & Kirscht, J. P. (1979). Why people seek health care. In G. C. Stone, F. Cohen, & N. E. Adler (Eds.), *Health psychology—A handbook.* San Francisco: Jossey-Bass.

Rosenthal, R., & Rubin, D. (1982). Further meta-analytic procedures for assessing cognitive gender differences. *Journal of Educational Psychology, 74,* 708–712.

Ross, H. S., & Lollis, S. P. (1987). Communication within infant social games. *Developmental Psychology, 2,* 241–248.

Ross, H. S., & Taylor, H. (1989). Do boys prefer daddy or his physical style of play? *Sex Roles, 20,* 23–26.

Ross, L., Bierbrauer, G., & Hoffman, S. (1976). The role of attribution processes in conformity and dissent. *American Psychologist, 31,* 148–157.

Rothbart, M. K., Taylor, S. B., & Tucker, D. M. (1989). Right-sided facial asymmetry in infant emotional expression. *Neuropsychologia, 27,* 675–687.

Rotter, J. B. (1990). Internal versus external control of reinforcement. *American Psychologist, 45,* 489–493.

Rowland, D. L., Greenleaf, W. J., Dorfman, L. J., & Davidson, J. M. (1993). Aging and sexual function in men. *Archives of Sexual Behavior, 22,* 545–558.

Roy, A., Segal, N. L., Ceterwall, B. S., & Robinette, C. D. (1991). Suicide in twins. *Archives of General Psychiatry, 48,* 29–32.

Ruback, R. B., & Pandey, J. (1991). Crowding, perceived control, and relative power: An analysis of households in India. *Journal of Applied Social Psychology, 21,* 315–344.

Rubin, R. T., Villanueva-Meyer, J., Ananth, J., Trajmar, P. G., & Mena, I. (1992). Regional xenon 133 cerebral blood flow and cerebral technetium 99m HMPAO uptake in unmedicated patients with obsessive–compulsive disorder and matched normal control subjects. *Archives of General Psychiatry, 49,* 695–702.

Rumbaugh, D. M., Gill, T. V., & Von Glaserfeld, E. D. (1973). Reading and sentence completion by a chimpanzee (Pan). *Science, 182,* 731–733.

Rumbaugh, D. M., & Savage-Rumbaugh, S. (1978). Chimpanzee language research: Status and potential. *Behavior Research Methods and Instrumentation, 10,* 119–131.

Rumbaugh, D. M., Savage-Rumbaugh, S., & Hegel, M. T. (1987). Summation in the chimpanzee (Pan troglodytes). *Journal of Experimental Psychology: Animal Behavior Processes, 13,* 107–115.

Rushton, J. P. (1995). *Race, evolution, and behavior: A life history perspective.* New Brunswick, NJ: Transaction.

Russell, J. A. (1991). Culture and the categorization of emotions. *Psychological Bulletin, 110,* 426–450.

Russell, J. A. (1994). Is there universal recognition of emotion from facial expression? A review of the cross-cultural studies. *Psychological Bulletin, 115,* 102–141.

Russell, J. A. (1995). Facial expressions of emotion: What lies beyond minimal universality? *Psychological Bulletin, 118,* 379–391.

Russo, N. F., & Denmark, F. L. (1987). Contributions of women to psychology. *Annual Review of Psychology, 38,* 279–297.

Rustemli, A. (1991). Crowding effects of density and interpersonal distance. *The Journal of Social Psychology, 132,* 51—58.

Ryan, R. M., Mims, V., & Koestner, R. (1983). Relation of reward contingency and interpersonal context to intrinsic motivation: A review and test using cognitive evaluation theory. *Journal of Personality and Social Psychology, 45,* 736–750.

Sackett, P. R. (1994). Integrity testing for personnel selection. *Current Directions in Psychological Science, 3,* 73–76.

Sadock, V. (1980). Special areas of interest. In H. Kaplan, A. Freeman, & B. Sadock (Eds.), *Comprehensive Textbook of Psychiatry* (Vol. 3). Baltimore: Williams & Wilkins.

St. Lawrence, J. S. (1993). African-American adolescents' knowledge, health-related attitudes, sexual behavior, and contraceptive decisions: Implications for the prevention of adolescent HIV infection. *Journal of Consulting and Clinical Psychology, 61,* 104–112.

Sakitt, B., & Long, G. M. (1979). Cones determine subjective offset of a stimulus but rods determine total persistence. *Vision Research, 19,* 1439–1443.

Salminen, S., & Glad, T. (1992). The role of gender in helping behavior. *The Journal of Social Psychology, 132,* 131–133.

Salt, R. E. (1991). Affectionate touch between fathers and preadolescent sons. *Journal of Marriage and the Family, 53,* 545–554.

Salthouse, T. A. (1995). Selective influences of age and speed on associative memory. *American Journal of Psychology, 108,* 381–396.

Salzberg, H. C., & DePiano, F. A. (1980). Hypnotizability and task motivating suggestions: A further look at how they affect performance. *International Journal of Clinical and Experimental Hypnosis, 28,* 261–271.

Sandahl, C., & Ronnberg, S. (1990). Brief group psychotherapy in relapse prevention for alcohol dependent patients. *International Journal of Group Psychotherapy, 40,* 453–476.

Sande, G. N., Goethals, G. R., & Radloff, C. E. (1988). Perceiving one's own traits and others: The multifaceted self. *Journal of Personality and Social Psychology, 54,* 13–20.

Sanders, G. S., & Simmons, W. L. (1983). Use of hypnosis to enhance eyewitness accuracy: Does it work? *Journal of Applied Psychology, 68,* 70–77.

Sanders, M. S., & McCormick, E. J. (1993). *Human factors in engineering and design* (7th ed.). New York: McGraw-Hill.

Sanders, R. J. (1985). Teaching apes to ape language: Explaining the imitative and nonimitative signing of a chimpanzee *(Pan troglodytes). Journal of Comparative Psychology, 99,* 197–210.

Santos, M. D., Leve, C., & Pratkanis, A. R. (1994). Hey buddy, can you spare seventeen cents? Mindful persuasion and the pique technique. *Journal of Applied Social Psychology, 224,* 755–764.

Sarason, I. G., & Sarason, B. R. (1987). *Abnormal psychology: The problem of maladaptive behavior* (5th ed.). Englewood Cliffs, NJ: Prentice-Hall.

Sattler, J. M. (1992). *Assessment of children: Revised and updated* (3rd ed.). San Diego: Jerome M. Sattler.

Savage-Rumbaugh, S. (1987). A new look at ape language: Comprehension of vocal speech and syntax. In R. A. Dienstbier & D. W. Leger (Eds.), *Comparative perspectives in modern psychology.* Lincoln: University of Nebraska Press.

Savage-Rumbaugh, S., Pate, J. L., Lawson, J., Smith, S. T., & Rosenbaum, S. (1983). Can a chimpanzee make a statement? *Journal of Experimental Psychology: General, 112,* 457–492.

Sawicki, S. (1988). Effective crisis intervention. *Adolescence, 23,* 83–88.

Saxe, L. (1994). Detection of deception: Polygraph and integrity tests. *Current Directions in Psychological Science, 3,* 69–73.

Scarr, S. & Eisenberg, M. (1993). Child care research: Issues, perspectives, and results. *Annual Review of Psychology, 44,* 613–644.

Scarr, S., Eisenberg, M., Deater-Deckard, K. (1994). Measurement of quality in child care centers. *Early Childhood Research Quarterly, 9,* 131–151.

Scarr, S., Phillips, D., & McCartney, K. (1990). Facts, fantasies, and the future of child care in the United States. *Psychological Science, 1,* 26–35.

Scarr, S., & Weinberg, R. A. (1983). The Minnesota adoption studies: Genetic differences and malleability. *Child Development, 54,* 260–267.

Schachter, S. (1971). Some extraordinary facts about obese humans and rats. *American Psychologist, 26,* 129–144.

Schachter, S., Goldman, R., & Gordon, A. (1968). Effects of fear, food deprivation, and obesity on eating. *Journal of Personality and Social Psychology, 10,* 91–97.

Schachter, S., & Singer, J. E. (1962). Cognitive, social, and physiological determinants of emotional state. *Psychological Review, 69,* 379–399.

Schacter, D. L. (1992). Understanding implicit memory. *American Psychologist, 47,* 559–569.

Schacter, D. L., Alpert, N. M., Savage, C. R., Rauch, S. L., & Albert, M. S. (1996). Conscious recollection and the human hippocampal formation: Evidence from positron emission tomography. *Proceedings of the National Academy of Sciences of the USA, 93,* 321– 325.

Schachter, D. L., Kihlstrom, J. F., Kihlstrom, L. C., & Berren, M. B. (1989). Autobiographical memory in a case of multiple personality disorder. *Journal of Abnormal Psychology, 98,* 508–514.

Schaie, K. W. (1993). The Seattle longitudinal studies of adult intelligence. *Current Directions in Psychological Science, 2,* 171–175.

Schaie, K. W. (1994). The course of adult intellectual development. *American Psychologist, 49,* 304–313.

Schaie, K. W., & Willis, S. L. (1986). *Adult development and aging* (2nd ed.). Boston: Little, Brown.

Schatzman, M. (1992). Freud: Who seduced whom? *New Scientist,* pp. 34–37.

Scheier, M. F., & Carver, C. S. (1993). On the power of positive thinking: The benefits of being optimistic. *Current Directions in Psychological Science, 2,* 26–30.

Schiff, M., Duyme, M., Dumaret, A., & Tomkiewicz, S. (1982). How much could we boost scholastic achievement and IQ scores? A direct answer from a French adoption study. *Cognition, 12,* 165– 196.

Schiller, P. H. (1994). Area V4 of the primate visual cortex. *Current Directions in Psychological Science, 3,* 89–92.

Schlaug, G., Jäncke, L., Huang, Y., & Steinmetz, H. (1995). In vivo evidence of structural brain asymmetry in musicians. *Science, 267,* 699–701.

Schmidt, D. F., & Boland, S. M. (1986). Structure of perceptions of older adults: Evidence for multiple stereotypes. *Psychology and Aging, 1,* 255–260.

Schmidt, F. L., Onex, D. S., & Hunter, J. E. (1992). Personnel selection. *Annual Review of Psychology, 43,* 627–670.

Schmidt, S. R. (1991). Can we have a distinctive theory of memory? *Memory and Cognition, 19,* 523–542.

Schmit, M. J., & Ryan, A. M. (1993). The big five in personnel selection: Factor structure in applicant and nonapplicant populations. *Journal of Applied Psychology, 78,* 966–974.

Schneider, W., & Detweiler, M. (1987). A connectionist/control, architecture, and working memory. In G. H. Bower (Ed.). *The psychology of learning and motivation.* San Diego: Academic.

Schnur, E., Brooks-Gunn, J., & Shipman, V. C. (1992). Who attends programs serving poor children? The case of Head Start attendees and nonattendees. *Journal of Applied Developmental Psychology, 13,* 405–421.

Schuckit, M. A. (1994). Low level of response to alcohol as a predictor of future alcoholism. *American Journal of Psychiatry, 151,* 184–189.

Schulberg, H. C., & Rush, A. J. (1994). Clinical practice guidelines for managing major depression in primary care practice: Implications for psychologists. *American Psychologist, 49,* 34–41.

Schutte, N. S., Malouff, J. M., Post-Gorden, J. C., & Rodasta, A. L. (1988). Effects of playing video games on children's aggressive and other behaviors. *Journal of Applied Social Psychology, 18,* 454–460.

Schwartz, J. C., & Shaver, P. (1987). Emotions and emotion knowledge in interpersonal relations. *Advances in Personal Relationships, 1,* 197–241.

Schwartzman, A. E., Gold, D., Andres, D., Arbuckle, T. Y., & Chaikelson, J. (1987). Stability of intelligence: A 40-year follow-up. *Canadian Journal of Psychology, 41,* 244–256.

Schwarz-Stevens, K. S., & Cunningham, C. L. (1993). Pavlovian conditioning of heart rate and body temperature with morphine: Effects of CS duration. *Behavioral Neuroscience, 107,* 1039–1048.

Schweickert, R., & Boruff, B. (1986). Short-term memory capacity: Magic number or magic spell? *Journal of Experimental Psychology: Learning, Memory, and Cognition, 12,* 419–425.

Schweiger, U., Deuschle, M., Körner, A., Lammers, C. H., Schmider, J., Gotthardt, U., Holsboer, F., & Heuser, I. (1994). Low lumbar bone mineral density in patients with major depression. *American Journal of Psychiatry, 151,* 1691–1693.

Sears, D. O., & Kosterman, R. (1994). Mass media and political persuasion. In S. Shavitt & T. C. Brock (Eds.), *Persuasion: Psychological insights and perspectives* (pp. 251–278). Boston: Allyn & Bacon.

Segal, L. (1991). Brief therapy: The MRI approach. In A. S. Gurman & D. P. Kniskern (Eds.), *Handbook of family therapy* (Vol. 2). New York: Brunner/Mazel.

Seif, M. N., & Atkins, A. L. (1979). Some defensive and cognitive aspects of phobias. *Journal of Abnormal Psychology, 88,* 42–51.

Sejnowski, T. J., Koch, C., & Churchland, P. S. (1988). Computational neuroscience. *Science, 24,* 1299–1306.

Seligman, M. E. P. (1975). *Helplessness.* San Francisco: Freeman.

Seligman, M. E. P. (1976). *Learned helplessness and depression in animals and humans.* Morristown, NJ: General Learning.

Seligman, M. E. P. (1988, August). *Learned Helplessness.* G. Stanley Hall lecture at the American Psychological Association Convention, Atlanta.

Seligman, M. E. P. (1991). *Learned optimism.* New York: Knopf.

Seligman, M. E. P. (1995). The effectiveness of psychotherapy. *American Psychologist, 50,* 965–974.

Selkoe, D. J. (1992, September). Aging brain, aging mind. *Scientific American,* pp. 135–142.

Sell, R. L., Wells, J. A., & Wypij, D. (1995). The prevalence of homosexual behavior and attraction in the United States, the United Kingdom and France: Results of national population-based samples. *Archives of Sexual Behavior, 24,* 235–248.

Selye, H. (1956). *The stress of life.* New York: McGraw-Hill.

Selye, H. (1976). *Stress in health and disease.* London: Butterworth.

Sengel, R. A., & Lovallo, W. R. (1983). Effects of cueing on immediate and recent memory in schizophrenics. *Journal of Nervous and Mental Disease, 171,* 426–430.

Sevcik, R. A., & Savage-Rumbaugh, E. S. (1994). Language comprehension and use by great apes. *Language and Communication, 14,* 37–58.

Shadish, W. R., Montgomery, L. M., Wilson, P., Wilson, M. R., Bright, I., & Okwumabua, T. (1993). Effects of family and marital psychotherapies: A meta-analysis. *Journal of Consulting and Clinical Psychology, 61,* 992–1002.

Shallice, T., Fletcher, P., Frith, C. D., Grasby, P., Frackowiak, R. S. J., & Dolan, R. J. (1994). Brain regions associated with acquisition and retrieval of verbal episodic memory. *Nature, 368,* 633–635.

Shamir, B. (1992). Attribution of influence and charisma to the leader: The romance of leadership revisited. *Journal of Applied Social Psychology, 22,* 386–407.

Shanab, M. E., & Yahya, K. A. (1978). A cross-cultural study of obedience. *Bulletin of the Psychonomic Society, 11,* 267–269.

Shapiro, D. A., Barkham, M., Rees, A., Hardy, G. E., Reynolds, S., & Startup, M. (1994). Effects of treatment duration and severity of depression on the effectiveness of cognitive–behavioral and psychodynamic–interpersonal psychotherapy. *Journal of Consulting and Clinical Psychology, 62,* 522–534.

Shatz, C. J. (1992, September). The developing brain. *Scientific American,* pp. 61–67.

Shatz, M., & Gelman, R. (1973). The development of communication skills: Modifications in the speech of young children as a function of listener. *Monographs of the Society for Research in Child Development, 38* (2, Serial No. 152).

Shaver, P. R., Schwartz, J., Kirson, D., & O'Connor, C. (1987). Emotion knowledge: Further exploration of a prototype approach. *Journal of Personality and Social Psychology, 52,* 1061–1086.

Shaw, J. S., III, Bjork, R. A., & Handal, A. (1995). Retrieval-induced forgetting in an eyewitness-memory paradigm. *Psychonomic Bulletin and Review, 2,* 249–253.

Shaywitz, B. A., Shaywitz, S. E., Pugh, K. R., Constable, R. T., Skudlarski, P., Fulbright, R. K., Bronen, R. A., Fletcher, J. M., Shankweiler, D. P., Katz, L., & Gore, J. C. (1995). Sex differences in the functional organization of the brain for language. *Nature, 373,* 607–609.

Shedler, J., & Block, J. (1990). Adolescent drug use and psychological health. *American Psychologist, 45,* 612–630.

Sheehy, G. (1995). *New passages: Mapping your life across time.* New York: Random House.

Shefler, G., Dasberg, H., & Ben-Shakhar, G. (1995). A randomized controlled outcome and follow-up study of Mann's time-limited psychotherapy. *Journal of Consulting and Clinical Psychology, 63,* 585–593.

Shepard, S., & Metzler, D. (1988). Mental rotation: Effects of dimensionality of objects and type of task. *Journal of Experimental Psychology: Human Perception and Performance, 14,* 3–11.

Shepperd, J. A. (1993). Productivity loss in performance groups: A motivation analysis. *Psychological Bulletin, 113,* 67–81.

Sheridan, M. S. (1985). Things that go beep in the night: Home monitoring for apnea. *Health and Social Work, 10,* 63–70.

Sherin, J. E., Shiromani, P. J., McCarley, R. W., & Saper, C. B. (1996). Activation of ventrolateral preoptic neurons during sleep. *Science, 271,* 216–219.

Sherman, M., & Key, C. B. (1932). The intelligence of isolated mountain children. *Child Development, 3,* 279–290.

Sherrington, R., Rogaev, E. I., Liang, Y., Rogaeva, E. A., Levesque, G., Ikeda, M., Chi, H., Lin, C., Li, G., Holman, K., Tsuda, T., Mar, L., Foncin, J. F., Bruni, A. C., Montesi, M. P., Sorbi, S., Rainero, I., Pinessi, L., Nee, L., Chumakov, I., Pollen, D., Brookes, A., Sanseau, P., Polinsky, R. J., Wasco, W., Da Silva, H. A. R., Haines, J. L., Pericak-Vance, M. A., Tanzi, R. E., Roses, A. D., Fraser, P. E., Rommens, J. M., & St. George-Hyslop, P. H. (1995). Cloning of a gene bearing missense mutations in early-onset familial Alzheimer's disease. *Nature, 375,* 754–760.

Shiffrin, R. M. (1993). Short-term memory: A brief commentary. *Memory and Cognition, 21,* 193–197.

Shimamura, A. P., Berry, J. M., Mangels, J. A., Rusting, C. L., & Jurica, P. J. (1995). Memory and cognitive abilities in university professors: Evidence for successful aging. *Psychological Article, 6,* 271–277.

Shimamura, A. P., & Squire, L. R. (1986). Memory and metamemory: A study of the feeling-of-knowing phenomenon in amnesic patients. *Journal of Experimental Psychology: Learning, Memory, and Cognition, 12,* 452–460.

Shimberg, M. E. (1929). An investigation into the validity of norms with special reference to urban and rural groups. *Archives of Psychology, 104,* 1–62.

Shneidman, E. S. (1994). Clues to suicide, reconsidered. *Suicide and Life-Threatening Behavior, 24,* 395–397.

Shore, J. H., Vollmer, W. M., & Tatum, E. L. (1989). Community patterns of posttraumatic stress disorders. *Journal of Nervous and Mental Disease, 177,* 681–685.

Shurin, M. R., Shou, D., Kusnecov, A., Rassnick, S., et al. (1994). Effect of one or more footshocks on spleen and blood lymphocyte proliferation in rats. *Brain, Behavior and Immunity, 8,* 57–65.

Shute, V. J., Pellegrino, J. W., Hubert, L., & Reynolds. R. W. (1983). The relationship between androgen levels and human spatial abilities. *Bulletin of the Psychonomic Society, 21,* 465–468.

Si, G., Rethorst, S., & Willimczik, K. (1995). Causal attribution perception in sports achievement: A cross-cultural study on attributional concepts in Germany and China. *Journal of Cross-Cultural Psychology, 26,* 537–553.

Siegel, E. F. (1979). Control of phantom limb pain by hypnosis. *American Journal of Clinical Hypnosis, 21,* 285–286.

Siegel, J. M. (1990). Stressful life events and use of physician services among the elderly: The moderating role of pet ownership. *Journal of Personality and Social Psychology, 58,* 1081–1086.

Siegel, S. (1988). State dependent learning and morphine tolerance. *Behavioral Neuroscience, 102,* 228–232.

Sigman, M. (1995). Nutrition and child development: More food for thought. *Current Directions in Psychological Science, 4,* 52–55.

Silverman, L. H. (1983). The subliminal psychodynamic activation method: Overview and comprehensive listing of studies. In J. Masling (Ed.), *Empirical studies of psychoanalytic theories* (Vol. 1, pp. 69–100). Hillsdale, NJ: Erlbaum.

Simons, R. C., & Hughes, C. C. (1993). Culture-bound syndromes. In A. C. Gaw (Ed.), *Culture, ethnicity and mental illness* (pp. 75–99). Washington, DC: American Psychiatric Press.

Simonton, D. K. (1988). Age and outstanding achievement: What do we know after a century of research? *Psychological Bulletin, 104,* 251–267.

Simpson, J. A. (1990). Influence of attachment styles on romantic relationships. *Journal of Personality and Social Psychology, 59,* 971–980.

Singer, D. G., & Singer, J. L. (1990). *The house of make-believe.* Cambridge, MA: Harvard University Press.

Singer, L. M., Brodzinsky, D. M., Ramsay, D., Steir, M., & Waters, E. (1985). Mother–infant attachment in adoptive families. *Child Development, 56,* 1543–1551.

Skaalvik, E. M., & Rankin, R. J. (1994). Gender differences in mathematics and verbal achievement, self-perception and motivation. *British Journal of Educational Psychology, 64,* 419–428.

Skinner, B. F. (1948). Superstition in the pigeon. *Journal of Experimental Psychology, 38,* 168–172.

Skinner, B. F. (1988, June). Skinner joins aversives debate. *American Psychological Association APA Monitor,* 22.

Skinner, B. F. (1989). The origins of cognitive thought. *American Psychologist, 44,* 13–18.

Slaikeu, K. A. (1990). *Crisis intervention* (2nd ed.). Boston: Allyn & Bacon.

Slavin, R. E. (1991). *Educational psychology: Theory into practice* (3rd ed). Englewood Cliffs, NJ: Prentice Hall.

Smart, R., & Peterson, C. (1994). Stability versus transition in women's career development: A test of Levinson's theory. *Journal of Vocational Behavior, 45,* 241–260.

Smith, C. A. (1989). Dimensions of appraisal and physiological response in emotion. *Journal of Personality and Social Psychology, 56,* 339–353.

Smith, E. P., & Davidson, W. S., II. (1992). Mentoring and the development of African-American graduate students. *Journal of College Student Development, 33,* 531–539.

Smith, K. H., & Rogers, M. (1994). Effectiveness of subliminal messages in television commercials: Two experiments. *Journal of Applied Psychology, 79,* 866–874.

Smith, M. C. (1983). Hypnotic memory enhancement of witnesses: Does it work? *Psychological Bulletin, 94,* 387–407.

Smith, M. L., Glass, G. V., & Miller, T. I. (1980). *The benefits of psychotherapy.* Baltimore: Johns Hopkins University Press.

Smyser, A. A. (1982). Hospices: Their humanistic and economic value. *American Psychologist, 37,* 1260–1262.

Snowden, L. R., & Cheung, F. K. (1990). Use of inpatient mental health services by members of ethnic minority groups. *American Psychologist, 45,* 347–355.

Snyder, C. R., & Higgins, R. L. (1988). Excuses: Their effective role in the negotiation of reality. *Psychological Bulletin, 104,* 23–35.

Snyder, D. K., Wills, R. M., & Grady-Fletcher, A. (1991). Long-term effectiveness of behavioral versus insight-oriented marital therapy: A 4-year follow-up study. *Journal of Consulting and Clinical Psychology, 59,* 138–141.

Snyder, S. H. (1980). Brain peptides as neurotransmitters. *Science, 209,* 976–983.

Snyderman, M., & Rothman, S. (1987). Survey of expert opinion on intelligence and aptitude testing. *American Psychologist, 42,* 137– 144.

Sobal, J., & Stunkard, A. J. (1989). Socioeconomic status and obesity: A review of the literature. *Psychological Bulletin, 105,* 260–275.

Sobell, M. B., & Sobell, L. C. (1982). Controlled drinking: A concept coming of age. In K. R. Blanstein & J. Polivy (Eds.), *Self-control and self-modification of emotional behavior.* New York: Plenum.

Sogon, S., & Izard, C. (1987). Sex differences in emotion recognition by observing body movements: A case of American students. *Japanese Psychological Research, 29,* 89–93.

Sogon, S., & Masutani, M. (1989). Identification of emotion from body movements: A cross-cultural study of Americans and Japanese. *Psychological Reports, 65,* 35–46.

Solso, R. L. (1979). *Cognitive psychology.* New York: Harcourt, Brace & Jovanovich.

Somer, E. (1990). Brief simultaneous couple hypnotherapy with a rape victim and her spouse: A brief communication. *International Journal of Clinical and Experimental Hypnosis, 38,* 1–5.

Sommers-Flanagan, R., Sommers-Flanagan, J., & Davis, B. (1993). What's happening on music television? A gender role content analysis. *Sex Roles, 28,* 745–754.

Sorce, J. F., & Emde, R. N. (1981). Mother's presence is not enough: Effect of emotional availability on infant exploration. *Developmental Psychology, 17,* 737–745.

Southwick, S. M., & Yehuda, R. (1993). The interaction between pharmacotherapy and psychotherapy in the treatment of posttraumatic stress disorder. *American Journal of Psychotherapy, 47,* 404–410.

Spangler, W. D. (1992). Validity of questionnaire and TAT measures of need for achievement: Two meta-analyses. *Psychological Bulletin, 112,* 140–154.

Spanos, N. P., Lush, N. I., & Gwynn, M. I. (1989). Cognitive skill-training enhancement of hypnotizability: Generalization effects and trance logic responding. *Journal of Personality and Social Psychology, 56,* 795–804.

Specker, S., de Zwaan, M., Raymond, N., & Mitchell, J. (1994). Psychopathology in subgroups of obese women with and without binge eating disorder. *Comprehensive Psychiatry, 35,* 185–190.

Sperling, G. (1960). The information available in brief visual presentations. *Psychological Monographs, 15,* 201–293.

Sperry, R. W. (1985). Consciousness, personal identity, and the divided brain. In D. F. Benson & E. Zaidel (Eds.), *The dual brain: Hemispheric specialization in humans* (pp. 11–26). New York: Guilford.

Speth, C., & Brown, R. (1990). Effects of college students' learning styles and gender on their test preparation strategies. *Applied Cognitive Psychology, 4,* 189–202.

Sporer, S. L. (1993). Eyewitness identification accuracy, confidence, and decision times in simultaneous and sequential lineups. *Journal of Applied Psychology, 78,* 22–33.

Sporer, S. L., Penrod, S., Read, D., & Cutler, B. (1995). Choosing, confidence, and accuracy: A meta-analysis of the confidence-accuracy relation in eyewitness identification studies. *Psychological Bulletin, 118,* 315–327.

Sprecher, S., Aron, A., Hatfield, E., Cortese, A., Potapova, E., & Levitskaya, A. (1992, July). *Love: American style, Russian style, and Japanese style.* Paper presented at the Sixth International Conference on Personal Relationships, Orono, Maine.

Sprecher, S., Sullivan, Q., & Hatfield, E. (1994). Mate selection preferences: Gender differences examined in a national sample. *Journal of Personality and Social Psychology, 66,* 1074–1080.

Squire, L. R. (1987). *Memory and brain.* New York: Oxford University Press.

Stagner, R. (1988). *A history of psychological theories.* New York: Macmillan.

Standing, L. (1973). Learning 10,000 pictures. *Quarterly Journal of Experimental Psychology, 25,* 207–222.

Stanford, S. C., & Salmon, P. (1993). *Stress: From synapse to syndrome.* London: Academic.

Stanley, B. G., & Gillard, E. R. (1994). Hypothalamic neuropeptide Y and the regulation of eating behavior and body weight. *Current Directions in Psychological Science, 3,* 9–15.

Stasson, M., & Fishbein, M. (1990). The relation between perceived risk and preventive action: A within-subject analysis of perceived driving risk and intentions to wear seatbelts. *Journal of Applied Social Psychology, 20,* 1541–1557.

Staszewski, J. J. (1987). The psychological reality of retrieval structures: An investigation of expert knowledge (doctoral dissertation, Cornell University, 1987). *Dissertation Abstracts International, 48,* 2168B.

Staszewski, J. J. (1988). Skilled memory and expert mental calculation. In M. T. H. Chi, R. Glaser, & M. J. Farr (Eds.), *The nature of expertise.* Hillsdale, NJ: Erlbaum.

Staub, E. (1996). Cultural-societal roots of violence. *American Psychologist, 51,* 117–132.

Steele, C. M., & Aronson, J. (1995). Stereotype threat and the intellectual test performance of African Americans. *Journal of Personality and Social Psychology, 69,* 797–811.

Steele, C. M., & Josephs, R. A. (1990). Alcohol myopia. *American Psychologist, 45,* 921–933.

Steele, C. M., Spencer, S. J., & Lynch, M. (1993). Self-image, resilience, and dissonance: The role of affirmational resources. *Journal of Personality and Social Psychology, 64,* 885–896.

Stein, M. I. (1974). *Stimulating creativity.* New York: Academic.

Steinberg, L., Dornbusch, S. M., & Brown, B. B. (1992). Ethnic difference in adolescent achievement. *American Psychologist, 47,* 723–729.

Steinberg, L., Dornbusch, S. M., & Brown, B. B. (1993). Ethnic differences in adolescent achievement: An ecological perspective. *Annual Progress in Child Psychiatry and Child Development,* 528–543.

Steinberg, L., Lamborn, S. D., Darling, N., Mounts, N. S., & Dornbusch, S. M. (1994). Over-time changes in adjustment and competence among adolescents from authoritative, authoritarian, indulgent, and neglectful families. *Child Development, 65,* 754–770.

Steinberg, L., Lamborn, S. D., Dornbusch, S. M., & Darling, N. (1992). Impact of parenting practices on adolescent achievement: Authoritative parenting, school involvement, and encouragement to succeed. *Child Development, 63,* 1266–1281.

Steinberg, M., Cicchetti, D., Buchanan, J., Rakfeldt, J., & Rounsaville, B. (1994). Distinguishing between multiple personality disorder (dissociative identity disorder) and schizophrenia using the structured clinical interview for DSM–IV dissociative disorders. *Journal of Nervous and Mental Disease, 182,* 495–502.

Steiner, D. D., & Rain, J. S. (1989). Immediate and delayed primacy and recency effects in performance evaluation. *Journal of Applied Psychology, 74,* 136–142.

Steiner, I. D. (1982). Heuristic models of groupthink. In M. Brandstatter, J. H. Davis, & G. Stocker-Kreichgauer (Eds.), *Group decision making.* New York: Academic.

Stephan, C. W., & Langlois, J. H. (1984). Baby beautiful: Adult attributions of infant competence as a function of infant attractiveness. *Child Development, 55,* 576–585.

Stephenson, J. S. (1985). *Death, grief, and mourning: Individual and social realities.* New York: Macmillan.

Sternberg, R. J. (1984). The Kaufman Assessment Battery for Children: An information-processing analysis and critique. *Journal of Special Education, 18,* 269–279.

Sternberg, R. J. (1985). *Beyond IQ.* Cambridge, England: Cambridge University Press.

Sternberg, R. J. (1986a). *Intelligence applied: Understanding and increasing your intellectual skills.* New York: Harcourt Brace Jovanovich.

Sternberg, R. J. (1986b). A triangular theory of love. *Psychological Review, 93,* 119–135.

Sternberg, R. J. (1995). For whom the bell curve tolls: A review of *The Bell Curve. Psychological Science, 6,* 257–261.

Sternberg, R. J., & Detterman, D. L. (Eds.). (1986). *What is intelligence? Contemporary viewpoints on its nature and definition.* Norword, NJ: Ablex Publishing.

Sternberg, R. J., & Wagner, R. K. (1993). The g-ocentric view of intelligence and job performance is wrong. *Current Directions in Psychological Science, 2,* 1–4.

Sternberg, R. J., Wagner, R. K., Williams, W. M., & Horvath, J. A. (1995). Testing common sense. *American Psychologist, 50,* 912– 927.

Stets, J. E., & Pirog-Good, M. A. (1989). Sexual aggression and control in dating relationships. *Journal of Applied Social Psychology, 19,* 1392–1412.

Stigler, J. W., & Baranes, R. (1988). Culture and mathematics learning. In E. Rothkpof (Ed.), *Review of Research in Education, 15* (pp. 253–306). Washington, DC: American Educational Research Association.

Stimpson, D., Jensen, L., & Neff, W. (1992). Cross-cultural gender differences in preference for a caring morality. *Journal of Social Psychology, 132,* 317–322.

Stitzer, M. L. (1988). Drug abuse in methadone patients reduced when rewards/punishments clear. *Alcohol, Drug Abuse, and Mental Health, 14,* 1.

Stokols, D. (1995). The paradox of environmental psychology. *American Psychologist, 50,* 821–837.

Stone, M. H. (1980). *The borderline syndromes.* New York: McGraw-Hill.

Strayer, D. L, & Kramer, A. R. (1990). Attentional requirements of automatic and controlled processing. *Journal of Experimental Psychology: Learning, Memory, and Cognition, 16,* 67–82.

Streissguth, A. P., Barr, H. M., & Martin, D. C. (1983). Maternal alcohol use and neonatal habituation assessed with the Brazelton Scale. *Child Development, 54,* 1109–1118.

Streissguth, A. P., Barr, H. M., Sampson, P. D., Darby, B. L., & Martin, D. C. (1989). IQ at age 4 in relation to maternal alcohol use and smoking during pregnancy. *Developmental Psychology, 25,* 3–11.

Stricker, G. (1992). The relationship of research to clinical practice. *American Psychologist, 47,* 543–549.

Strickland, B. R. (1988). Clinical psychology comes of age. *American Psychologist, 43,* 104–107.

Strickland, B. R. (1992). Women and depression. *Psychological Science, 1,* 132–135.

Striegel-Moore, R. H., Silberstein, L. R., & Rodin, J. (1986). Toward an understanding of risk factors for bulimia. *American Psychologist, 41,* 246–263.

Stroop, J. R. (1935). Studies of interference in serial verbal reactions. *Journal of Experimental Psychology, 18,* 643–662.

Strughold, H. (1924). Ueber die Dichte und Schwellen der Smerzpunkete der Epidermis in der verschiedenen Korperregionen. *Z. Biol., 80,* 367–380.

Stuart, E. W., Shimp, T. A., & Engle, R. W. (1987). Classical conditioning of consumer attitudes: Four experiments in an advertising context. *Journal of Consumer Research, 14,* 334–349.

Stunkard, A., Coll, M., Lundquist, S., & Meyers, A. (1980). Obesity and eating style. *Archives of General Psychiatry, 37,* 1127– 1129.

Stunkard, A. J., & Sørensen, T. I. A. (1993). Obesity and socioeconomic status—a complex relation. *The New England Journal of Medicine, 329,* 1036–1037.

Sturges, J. S. (1994). Family dynamics. In J. L. Ronch, W. V. Ornum & N. C. Stilwell (Eds.), *The counseling sourcebook: A practical reference on contemporary issues* (pp. 358–372). New York: Crossroad.

Suarez, E. C., & Williams, R. B. (1989). Situational determinants of cardiovascular and emotional reactivity in high and low hostile men. *Psychosomatic Medicine, 51,* 404–418.

Suddath, R. L, Christinson, G. W., Torrey, E. F., Casanova, M. F., & Weinberger, D. R. (1990). Anatomical abnormalities in the brains of monozygotic twins discordant for schizophrenia. *New England Journal of Medicine, 322,* 789–794.

Sue, S. (1988). Psychotherapeutic services for ethnic minorities. *American Psychologist, 43,* 301–308.

Suedfeld, P. (1990). Restricted environmental stimulation and smoking cessation: A 15-year progress report. *International Journal of the Addictions, 25,* 861–888.

Sugarman, D. B., & Hotaling, G. T. (1989). Violent men in intimate relationships: An analysis of risk markers. *Journal of Applied Social Psychology, 19,* 1034–1048.

Suls, J., & Wan, C. K. (1989a). Effects of sensory and procedural information on coping with stressful medical procedures and pain: A meta-analysis. *Journal of Consulting and Clinical Psychology, 57,* 372–379.

Suls, J., & Wan, C. K. (1989b). The relation between Type A behavior and chronic emotional distress: A meta-analysis. *Journal of Personality and Social Psychology, 57,* 503–512.

Suls, J., & Wan, C. K. (1993). The relationship between trait hostility and cardiovascular reactivity: A quantitative review and analysis. *Psychophysiology, 30,* 615–626.

Summers, T. P., & Hendrix, W. H. (1991). Modeling the role of pay equity perceptions: A field study. *Journal of Occupational Psychology, 64,* 145–157.

Sutker, P. B. & Allain, A. N. (1988). Issues in personality conceptualizations of addictive behaviors. *Journal of Consulting and Clinical Psychology, 56,* 172–182.

Sutker, P. B., Davis, J. M., Uddo, M., & Ditta, S. R. (1995). War zone stress, personal resources, and PTSD in Persian Gulf War returnees. *Journal of Abnormal Psychology, 104,* 444–452.

Swaab, D. F., & Hofman, M. A. (1995). Sexual differentiation of the human hypothalamus in relation to gender and sexual orientation. *Trends in Neuroscience, 18,* 264–270.

Swets, J. A. (1992). The science of choosing the right decision threshold in high-stakes diagnostics. *American Psychologist, 47,* 522– 532.

Swift, W. J. (1993). Brief psychotherapy with adolescents: Individual and family approaches. *American Journal of Psychotherapy, 47,* 373–386.

Swim, J., Borgida, E., Maruyama, G., & Myers, D. G. (1989). Joan McKay versus John McKay: Do gender stereotypes bias evaluations? *Psychological Bulletin, 105,* 409–429.

Swim, J. K., Aikin, K. J., Hall, W. S., & Hunter, B. A. (1995). Sexism and racism: Old-fashioned and modern prejudices. *Journal of Personality and Social Psychology, 68,* 199–214.

Szasz, T. (1984). *The therapeutic state: Psychiatry in the mirror of current events* (p. 502). Buffalo, NY: Prometheus.

Szasz, T. (1987). *Insanity:* The idea and its consequences New York: Wiley.

Szymanski, K., & Harkins, S. G. (1993). The effect of experimenter evaluation on self-evaluation within the social loafing paradigm. *Journal of Experimental Social Psychology, 29,* 268–286.

Tanenhaus, M. K., Spivey-Knowlton, M. J., Eberhard, K. M., & Sedivy, J. C. (1995). Integration of visual and linguistic information in spoken language comprehension. *Science, 268,* 1632–1634.

Tarter, R. E., & Vanyukov, M. (1994). Alcoholism: A developmental disorder. *Journal of Consulting and Clinical Psychology, 62,* 1096–1107.

Taylor, S. H. (1990). Health psychology. *American Psychologist, 45,* 40–50.

Teevan, R. C., & McGhee, P. E. (1972). Childhood development of fear of failure motivation. *Journal of Personality and Social Psychology, 21,* 345–348.

Tennen, H., & Affleck, G. (1990). Blaming others for threatening events. *Psychological Bulletin, 108,* 209–232.

Tennov, D. (1981). *Love and limerance.* Briarcliffe Manor, NY: Stein & Day.

Terrace, H. S. (1979, November). How Nim Chimpski changed my mind. *Psychology Today,* pp. 65–76.

Terrace, H. S. (1980). *Nim.* New York: Knopf.

Terrace, H. S. (1985). In the beginning was the "name." *American Psychologist, 40,* 1011–1028.

Teske, J. A. (1988). Seeing her looking at you: Acquaintance and variation in the judgment of gaze depth. *American Journal of Psychology, 101,* 239–257.

Thayer, R. E., Newman, J. R., & McClain, T. M. (1994). Self-regulation of mood: Strategies for changing a bad mood, raising energy, and reducing tension. *Journal of Personality and Social Psychology, 67,* 910–925.

Thelen, E. (1994). Three-month-old infants can learn task-specific patterns of interlimb coordination. *Psychological Science, 5,* 280–285.

Theorell, T., Svensson, J., Knox, S., Waller, D., & Alvarez, M. (1986). Young men with high blood pressure report few recent life events. *Journal of Psychosomatic Research, 30,* 243–249.

Thomas, A., & Chess, S. (1977). *Temperament and development.* New York: Brunner/Mazel.

Thompson, R. F. (1991). Are memory traces localized or distributed? *Neuropsychologia, 29,* 571–582.

Thompson, R. F., & Krupa, D. J. (1994). Organization of memory traces in the mammalian brain. *Annual Review of Neuroscience, 17,* 519–549.

Thompson, S. C., Sobolew-Shubin, A., Galbraith, M. E., Schwankovsky, L., & Cruzen, D. (1993). Maintaining perceptions of control: Finding perceived control in low-control circumstances. *Journal of Personality and Social Psychology, 64,* 293–304.

Thorkildsen, T. A. (1989). Justice in the classroom: The student's view. *Child Development, 60,* 323–334.

Tice, D. M., & Baumeister, R. F. (1985). Masculinity inhibits helping in emergencies: Personality does predict the bystander effect. *Journal of Personality and Social Psychology, 49,* 420–428.

Tilley, A., & Warren, P. (1983). Retrieval from semantic memory at different times of day. *Journal of Experimental Psychology: Learning, Memory, and Cognition, 9,* 718–724.

Timberlake, W., & Farmer-Dougan, V. A. (1991). Reinforcement in applied settings: Figuring out ahead of time what will work. *Psychological Bulletin, 110,* 379–391.

Tjosvold, D. (1987). Participation: A close look at its dynamics. *Journal of Management, 13,* 739–750.

Tjosvold, D., & Chia, L. C. (1989). Conflict between managers and workers: The role of cooperation and competition. *Journal of Social Psychology, 129,* 235–247.

Torrey, E. F., Bowler, A. E., Taylor, E. H., & Gottesman, I. I. (1994). *Schizophrenia and manic–depressive disorder: The biological roots of mental illness as revealed by the Landmark study of identical twins.* New York: Basic Books.

Tracy, R. J., & Barker, C. H. (1994). A comparison of visual versus auditory imagery in predicting word recall. *Imagination, Cognition and Personality, 13,* 147–161.

Travis, C. B. (1988). *Women and health psychology: Biomedical issues.* Hillsdale, NJ: Erlbaum.

Travis, R., & Kohli, V. (1995). The birth order factor: Ordinal position, social strata, and educational achievement. *Journal of Social Psychology, 135,* 499–507.

Trickett, P. K., & Putnam, F. W. (1993). Impact of child sexual abuse on females: Toward a developmental, psychobiological integration. *Psychological Science, 4,* 81–87.

Trickett, P. K., & Susman, E. J. (1988). Parental perceptions of childrearing practices in physically abusive and nonabusive families. *Developmental Psychology, 24,* 270–276.

Trites, D., Galbraith, F. D., Sturdavent, M., & Leckwart, J. F. (1970). Influence of nursing-unit design on the activities and subjective feelings of nursing personnel. *Environment and Behavior, 2,* 203–234.

Tronick, E. Z. & Cohn, J. F. (1989). Infant–mother face-to-face interaction: Age and gender differences in coordination and the occurrence of miscoordination. *Child Development, 60,* 85–92.

Tronick, E. Z., Morelli, G. A., & Ivey, P. K. (1992). The Efe forager infant and toddler's pattern of social relationships: Multiple and simultaneous. *Developmental Psychology, 28,* 568–577.

True, W. R., Rice, J., Eisen, S. A., Heath, A. C., Goldberg, J., Lyons, M. J., & Nowak, J. (1993). A twin study of genetic and environmental contributions to liability for posttraumatic stress symptoms. *Archives of General Psychiatry, 50,* 257–264.

Tsai, M., & Uemura, A. (1988). Asian Americans: The struggles, the conflicts, and the successes. In P. Bronstein & K. Quina (Eds.), *Teaching a psychology of people.* Washington, DC: American Psychological Association.

Tsuang, M. T., & Faraone, S. V. (1990). *The genetics of mood disorders.* Baltimore: Johns Hopkins University Press.

Tulving, E. (1991). Memory research is not a zero-sum game. *American Psychologist, 46,* 41–42.

Tulving, E. (1993). What is episodic memory? *Current Directions in Psychological Science, 2,* 67–70.

Tulving, E., Schacter, D. L., & Stark, H. A. (1982). Priming effects in word fragment completion are independent of recognition memory. *Journal of Experimental Psychology: Learning, Memory, and Cognition, 8,* 336–342.
Turk, D. C. (1978). Cognitive behavioral techniques on the management of pain. In J. P. Foreyt & D. J. Rathgen (Eds.), *Cognitive behavior therapy: Research and application.* New York: Plenum.
Turk, D. C., Meichenbaum, D., & Genest, M. (1983). *Pain and behavioral medicine: A cognitive–behavioral perspective.* New York: Guilford.
Turkheimer, E. (1991). Individual and group differences in adoption studies of IQ. *Psychological Bulletin, 110,* 392–405.
Turner, S. M., Beidel, D. C., & Nathan, R. S. (1985). Biological factors in obsessive–compulsive disorders. *Psychological Bulletin, 97,* 430–450.
Turner, T. J., & Ortony, A. (1992). Basic emotions: Can conflicting criteria converge? *Psychological Review, 99,* 566–571.
Tversky, A., & Kahneman, D. (1973). Availability: A heuristic for judging frequency and probability. *Cognitive Psychology, 4,* 207–232.
Uba, L. (1994). *Asian Americans: Personality patterns, identity, and mental health.* New York: Guilford.
Umberson, D., Wortman, C. B., & Kessler, R. C. (1992). Widowhood and depression: Explaining long-term gender differences in vulnerability. *Journal of Health and Social Behavior, 33,* 10–24.
Underwood, G. (1994). Subliminal perception on TV. *Nature, 370,* 103.
Ursano, R. J., Fullerton, C. S., Kao, T., & Bhartiya, V.R. (1995). Longitudinal assessment of posttraumatic stress disorder and depression after exposure to traumatic death. *Journal of Nervous and Mental Disease, 183,* 36–42.
U.S. Bureau of the Census (1995a). *Statistical Brief* (Sixty-five plus in the United States, SB/95-8). Washington, DC: U.S. Government Printing Office.
U.S. Bureau of the Census (1995b). *Statistical Brief* (American women: A profile, SB/95-19). Washington, DC: U.S. Government Printing Office.
Vaillant, G. E., & Milofsky, E. S. (1982). The etiology of alcoholism: A prospective view. *American Psychologist, 37,* 494– 503.
Valins, S. (1966). Cognitive effects of false heart-rate feedback. *Journal of Personality and Social Psychology, 4,* 400–408.
Valins, S., & Baum, A. (1973). Residential group size, social interaction, and crowding. *Environment and Behavior, 5,* 421–435.
Valkenburg, P. M., & van der Voort, T. H. A. (1994). Influence of TV on daydreaming and creative imagination: A review of research. *Psychological Bulletin, 116,* 316–339.
Vandell, D. L., Henderson, V. K., & Wilson, K. S. (1988). A longitudinal study of children with day-care experiences of varying quality. *Child Development, 59,* 1286–1292.
Vasquez, B., Johnson, D. W., & Johnson, R. T. (1994). The impact of cooperative learning on the performance and retention of U.S. Navy air traffic controller trainees. *The Journal of Social Psychology, 133,* 769–783.
Vernon, P. (1979). *Intelligence: Heredity and environment.* San Francisco: W. H. Freeman.
Vitiello, M. V. (1989). *Unraveling sleep disorders of the aged.* Paper presented at the annual meeting of the Association of Professional Sleep Societies, Washington, DC.
Von Senden, M. (1932). *Raum- und Gaestaltauffassung bei operierten: Blindgeborernin vor und nach der Operation.* Leipzig, Germany: Barth.
Vroom, V. H. (1964). *Work and motivation.* New York: Wiley.
Vroom, V. H. (1974). A new look at managerial decision making. *Organizational Dynamics, 5,* 66–80.
Vroom, V. H., & Yetton, P. W. (1973). *Leadership and decision-making.* Pittsburgh: University of Pittsburgh Press.
Vygotsky, L. S. (1962). *Thought and language* (E. Hanfmann & G. Vakar, Eds. and Trans.). Cambridge, MA: MIT Press. (Original work published in 1934.)
Vygotsky, L. S. (1978). *Mind in society: The development of higher mental processes.* Cambridge, MA: Harvard University Press. (Original works published 1930, 1933, and 1935).
Waddington, J. L. (1993). Neurodynamics of abnormalities in cerebral metabolism and structure in schizophrenia. *Schizophrenia Bulletin, 19,* 55–69.
Wainer, H., & Steinberg, L. S. (1992). Sex differences in performance on the mathematics section of the scholastic aptitude test: A bidirectional validity study. *Harvard Educational Review, 62,* 323–336.
Walk, R. D., & Gibson, E. J. (1961). A comparative and analytical study of visual depth perception. *Psychological Monographs, 75* (15).
Walker, E., Hoppes, E., Mednick, S., Emory, E., & Schulsinger, F. (1983). Environmental factors related to schizophrenia in psychophysiologically labile high-risk males. *Journal of Abnormal Psychology, 90,* 313–320.
Walker, E. A. (1989). Psychology and violence against women. *American Psychologist, 44,* 695–702.
Walker-Andrews, A. S. (1986). Intermodal perception of expressive behaviors: Relation of eye and voice? *Developmental Psychology, 22,* 373–377.
Waller, N. G., & Shaver, P. R. (1994). The importance of nongenetic influences on romantic love styles: A twin-family study. *Psychological Science, 5,* 268–274.
Wallerstein, J. S., & Blakeslee, J. (1989). *Second chances.* New York: Ticknor & Fields.
Walters, E. E., & Kendler, K. S. (1995). Anorexia nervosa and anorexic-like syndromes in a population-based female twin sample. *American Journal of Psychiatry, 152,* 64–67.
Walton, G. E., & Bower, T. G. R. (1993). Newborns form "prototypes" in less than 1 minute. *Psychological Science, 4,* 203–205.
Wandersman, A. H., & Hallman, W. K. (1993). Are people acting irrationally? *American Psychologist, 48,* 681–686.
Ware, R., Rytting, M., & Jenkins, D. (1994). The effect of stress on MBTI scores. *Journal of Psychological Type, 30,* 39–44.
Washton, A. M. (1989). *Cocaine addiction.* New York: Norton.
Watkins, M. J. (1990). Mediationism and the obfuscation of memory. *American Psychologist, 45,* 328–335.
Watson, J. B. (1924). *Behaviorism.* Chicago: University of Chicago Press.
Weary, G., Harvey, J. H., Schwieger, P., Olson, C. T., Perloff, E., & Pritchard, S. (1982). Self-presentation and the moderation of self-serving biases. *Social Cognition, 1,* 140–159.
Weaver, C. A., III (1993). Do you need a "flash" to form a flashbulb memory? *Journal of Experimental Psychology: General, 122,* 39–46.
Webb, W. B., & Agnew, H. W., Jr. (1975). The effects on subsequent sleep of an acute restriction of sleep length. *Psychophysiology, 12,* 367–370.
Wechsler, D. (1958). *The measurement and appraisal of adult intelligence* (4th ed.). Baltimore: Williams & Wilkins.
Weidner, G., Friend, R., Ficarrotto, T. J., & Mendell, N. R. (1989). Hostility and cardiovascular reactivity to stress in women and men. *Psychosomatic Medicine, 51,* 36–45.
Weingartner, H. (1977). Human state-dependent learning. In B. T. Ho, D. Richards, & D. L. Chute (Eds.), *Drug discrimination and state-dependent learning.* New York: Academic.
Weingartner, H., Adefris,W., Eich, J. E., & Murphy, D. L. (1976). Encoding-imagery specificity in alcohol state-dependent learning. *Journal of Experimental Psychology, 2,* 83–87.
Weinstein, C. S., & Mignano, A. (1993). *Organizing the elementary school classroom: Lessons from research and practice.* New York: McGraw-Hill.
Weintraub, S. (1987). Risk factors in schizophrenia: The stony brook high-risk project. *Schizophrenia Bulletin, 13,* 439–443.
Wells, G. L. (1993). What do we know about eyewitness identification? *American Psychologist, 48,* 553–571.
Wells, G. L., Luus, C. A. E., & Windschitl, P. D. (1994). Maximizing the utility of eyewitness identification evidence. *Current Directions in Psychological Science, 3,* 194–197.
Wells, R. A., & Phelps, P. A. (1990). The brief psychotherapies: A selective overview. In R. A. Wells & V. J. Giannetti (Eds.), *Handbook of the brief psychotherapies.* New York: Plenum.
Werler, M. M., Mitchell, A. A., & Shapiro, M. B. (1989). The relation of aspirin use during the first trimester of pregnancy to congenital cardiac defects. *New England Journal of Medicine, 321,* 1639– 1642.
West, M. A. (1980). Meditation and the EEG. *Psychological Medicine, 10,* 369–375.
West, M. A. (1982). Meditation and self-awareness: Physiological and phenomenological approaches. In G. Underwood (Ed.), *Aspects of consciousness: Vol. 3. Awareness and self-awareness.* London: Academic.
Wexler, B. E., & Cicchetti, D. V. (1992). The outpatient treatment of depression. *Journal of Nervous and Mental Disease, 180,* 277– 286.

Whisman, M. A. (1993). Mediators and moderators of change in cognitive therapy of depression. *Psychological Bulletin, 114,* 248–265.
Whisman, M. A., & Kwon, P. (1993). Life stress and dysphoria: The role of self-esteem and hopelessness. *Journal of Personality and Social Psychology, 65,* 1054–1060.
White, N. M., & Milner, P. M. (1992). The psychobiology of reinforcers. *Annual Review of Psychology, 43,* 443–471.
Whorf, B. L. (1956). *Language, thought, and reality: Selected writings of Benjamin Lee Whorf* (J. B. Carroll, Ed.). New York: Wiley.
Widiger, T. A., Frances, A. J., Pincus, H. A., Davis, W. W., & First, M. B. (1991). Toward an empirical classification for the *DSM–IV. Journal of Abnormal Psychology, 100,* 280–288.
Wiebe, D. J. (1991). Hardiness and stress moderation: A test of proposed mechanisms. *Journal of Personality and Social Psychology, 60,* 89–99.
Wiggins, J. G. (1994). Would you want your child to be a psychologist? *American Psychologist, 49,* 485–492.
Wiggins, J. S., & Trapnell, P. D. (1992). Personality structure: The return of the Big Five. In S. R. Briggs, R. Hogan, & W. H. Jones (Eds.), *Handbook of personality psychology.* Orlando, FL: Academic.
Wilder, D. A., & Thompson, J. E. (1980). Intergroup contact with independent manipulations of in-group and out-group interaction. *Journal of Personality and Social Psychology, 38,* 589–603.
Williams, C. D. (1959). Case report: The elimination of tantrum behavior by extinction procedures. *Journal of Abnormal and Social Psychology, 59,* 269.
Williams, K., Harkins, S., & Latané, B. (1981). Identifiability as a deterrent to social loafing: Two cheering experiments. *Journal of Personality and Social Psychology, 40,* 303–311.
Williams, K. J., Suls, J., Alliger, G. M., Learner, S. M., & Wan, C. K. (1991). Multiple role juggling and daily mood states in working mothers: An experience sampling study. *Journal of Applied Psychology, 76,* 664–674.
Williams, L. M. (1994). Recall of childhood trauma: A prospective study of women's memories of child sexual abuse. *Journal of Consulting and Clinical Psychology, 62,* 1167–1176.
Williams, R. L. (1989). *The trusting heart: Great news about Type A behavior.* New York: Random House.
Williams, S. L., Kinney, P. J., & Falbo, J. (1989). Generalization of therapeutic changes in agoraphobia: The role of perceived self-efficacy. *Journal of Consulting and Clinical Psychology, 57,* 436–442.
Williamson, R. C. (1991). *Minority languages and bilingualism: Case studies in maintenance and shift.* Norwood, NJ: Ablex.
Willoughby, J. C., & Glidden, L. M. (1995). Fathers helping out: Shared child care and marital satisfaction of parents of children with disabilities. *American Journal on Mental Retardation, 99,* 399–406.
Wilson, D., Mundy-Castle, A., & Panditji, L. (1990). Birth order and intellectual development among Zimbabwean children. *Journal of Social Psychology, 130,* 409–411.
Wilson, D. A., & Sullivan, R. M. (1994). Neurobiology of associative learning in the neonate: Early olfactory learning. *Behavioral and Neural Biology, 61,* 1–18.
Wilson, E. O. (1975). *Sociobiology: A new synthesis.* Cambridge, MA: Harvard University Press.
Wilson, F. A. W., & Goldman-Rakie, P. S. (1994). Viewing preferences of rhesus monkeys related to memory for complex pictures, colours and faces. *Behavioral Brain Research, 60,* 79–89.
Wilson, R. S. (1983). The Louisville twin study: Developmental synchronies in behavior. *Child Development, 54,* 298–315.
Wing, R. R., Epstein, L. H., Nowalk, M. P., & Lamparski, D. M. (1986). Behavioral self-regulation in the treatment of patients with diabetes mellitus. *Psychological Bulletin, 99,* 78–89.
Wink, P., & Helson, R. (1993). Personality change in women and their partners. *Journal of Personality and Social Psychology, 65,* 597–605.
Wirth, S., & Wolf, B. (1994). Zur brauchbarkeit des konfluenzmodells—erklären familienstrukturvariablen kognitive leistungen? *Psychologie in Erziehung und Unterricht, 41,* 31–48.
Wise, R. A., & Bozarth, M. A. (1987). A psychomotor stimulant theory of addiction. *Psychological Review, 94,* 469–492.
Witt, L. A., & Nye, L. G. (1992). Gender and the relationship between perceived fairness of pay or promotion and job satisfaction. *Journal of Applied Psychology, 77,* 910–917.
Wittrock, M. C. (1987, August 29). *The teaching of comprehension.* Thorndike Award Address, 1987 American Psychological Association annual meeting, New York.
Wolpe, J. (1958). *Psychotherapy by reciprocal inhibition.* Stanford, CA: Stanford University Press.
Wong, R. O. L., Chernjavsky, A., Smith, S. J., & Shatz, C. J. (1995). Early functional neural networks in the developing retina. *Nature, 374,* 716–718.
Wood, J. M., Bootzin, R. R., Rosenhan, D., Nolen-Hoeksema, S., & Jourden, F. (1992). Effects of the 1989 San Francisco earthquake on frequency and content of nightmares. *Journal of Abnormal Psychology, 101,* 219–224.
Wood, J. M., Nezworski, M. T., & Stejskal, W. J. (1996). The comprehensive system for the Rorschach: A critical examination. *American Psychological Society, 7,* 3–10.
Wood, N. L., & Cowan, N. (1995). The cocktail party phenomenon revisited: Attention and memory in the classic selective listening procedure of Cherry (1953). *Journal of Experimental Psychology: General, 124,* 243–262.
Wood, W., Wong, F. Y., & Chachere, J. G. (1991). Effects of media violence on viewers' aggression in unconstrained social interaction. *Psychological Bulletin, 109,* 371–383.
Woodward, W. R. (1982). The "discovery" of social behaviorism and social learning theory, 1870–1980. *American Psychologist, 37,* 396–410.
Worling, J. R. (1995). Sexual abuse histories of adolescent male sex offenders: Differences on the basis of the age and the gender of their victims. *Journal of Abnormal Psychology, 104,* 610–613.
Wright, J. C., Huston, A. C., Truglio, R., Fitch, M., Smith, E., & Piemyat, S. (1995). Occupational portrayals on television: Children's role schemata, career aspirations, and perceptions of reality. *Child Development, 66,* 1706–1718.
Wright, R. (1994). *The moral animal: The new science of evolutionary psychology.* New York: Pantheon.
Wundt, W. (1896). *Grundress er psychologie.* Leipzig, Germany: Engleman.
Wyatt, G. E. (1994). The sociocultural relevance of sex research: Challenges for the 1990s and beyond. *American Psychologist, 49,* 748–754.
Wynn, K. (1992). Addition and subtraction by human infants. *Letters to Nature, 358,* 749–750.
Wynne, L. C., Cole, R. E., & Perkins, P. (1987). University of Rochester child and family study: Risk research in progress. *Schizophrenia Bulletin, 13,* 463–467.
Wyszecki, G., & Stiles, W. S. (1967). *Color science: Concepts and methods, quantitative data, and formulas.* New York: Wiley.
Yoken, C., & Berman, J. S. (1984). Does paying a fee for psychotherapy alter the effectiveness of treatment? *Journal of Consulting and Clinical Psychology, 52,* 254–260.
York, J. L., & Welte, J. W. (1994). Gender comparisons of alcohol consumption in alcoholic and nonalcoholic populations. *Journal of Studies on Alcohol, 55,* 743–750.
Young, A. W., & Ellis, A. W. (1981). Asymmetry of cerebral hemispheric function in normal and poor readers. *Psychological Bulletin, 89,* 183–190.
Young, S. N., Smith, S., Pihl, R. O., & Ervin, F. R. (1985). Tryptophan depletion causes a rapid lowering of mood in normal males. *Psychopharmacology, 87,* 173–177.
Young, T. J., & French, L. A. (1993). Suicide and social status among Native Americans. *Psychological Reports, 73,* 461–462.
Yousif, Y., & Korte, C. (1995). Urbanization, culture, and helpfulness: Cross-cultural studies in England and the Sudan. *Journal of Cross-Cultural Psychology, 26,* 474–489.
Yuille, J. C. (1993). We must study forensic eyewitnesses to know about them. *American Psychologist, 48,* 572–573.
Yuille, J. C., & Cutshall, J. L. (1986). A case study of eyewitness memory of a crime. *Journal of Applied Psychology, 71,* 291–301.
Yuille, J. C., Davies, G., Gibling, F., Marxsen, D., & Porter, S. (1994). Eyewitness memory of police trainees for realistic role plays. *Journal of Applied Psychology, 79,* 931–936.
Zaccaro, S. J. (1984). Social loafing: The role of task attractiveness. *Personality and Social Psychology Bulletin, 10,* 99–106.
Zaidel, E. (1983). A response to Gazzaniga: Language in the right hemisphere, convergent perspectives. *American Psychologist, 38,* 542–546.
Zaidel, E., Aboitiz, F., Clarke, J., Kaiser, D., & Matteson, R. (1995). Sex differences in interhemispheric relations for language. In F. L. Kitterle (Ed.), *Hemispheric communication: Mechanisms and models* (pp. 85–175). Hillsdale, NJ: Erlbaum.

Zajonc, R. B. (1965). Social facilitation. *Science, 149,* 269–274.
Zajonc, R. B. (1993). The confluence model: Differential or difference equation. *European Journal of Social Psychology, 23,* 211–215.
Zajonc, R. B., Berbaum, M. L., Markus, G. B., Bargh, J. A., & Moreland, R. L. (1991). One justified criticism plus three flawed analyses equals two unwarranted conclusions: A reply to Retherford and Sewell. *American Sociological Review, 56,* 159–165.
Zajonc, R. B., & Markus, G. B. (1975). Birth order and intellectual development. *Psychological Review, 82,* 74–88.
Zajonc, R. B., Murphy, S. T., & Inglehart, M. (1989). Feeling and facial efference: Implications of the vascular theory of emotion. *Psychological Review, 96,* 395–416.
Zakay, D., Hayduk, L. A., & Tsal, Y. (1992). Personal space and distance misperception: Implications of a novel observation. *Bulletin of the Psychonomic Society, 30,* 33–35.
Zangwill, O. L., & Blakemore, C. (1972). Dyslexia: Reversal of eye movements during reading. *Neuropsychologia, 10,* 371–373.
Zhang, Y., Proenca, R., Maffei, M., Barone, M., Leopold, L., & Friedman, J. M. (1994). Positional cloning of the mouse obese gene and its human homologue. *Nature, 372,* 425–432.
Zigler, E. F. (1987). Formal schooling for four-year-olds? No. *American Psychologist, 42,* 254–260.
Zigler, E. F. (1994). Reshaping early childhood intervention to be a more effective weapon against poverty. *American Journal of Community Psychology, 22,* 37–47.
Zigler, E. F., & Hodapp, R. M. (1991). Behavioral functioning in individuals with mental retardation. *Annual Review of Psychology, 42,* 29–50.
Zins, J. E., & Barnett, D. W. (1983). The Kaufman Assessment Battery for Children and school achievement: A validity study. *Journal of Psychoeducational Assessment, 1,* 235–241.
Zitrin, C. M. (1981). Combined pharmacological and psychological treatment of phobias. In M. Navissakalian & D. H. Barlow (Eds.), *Phobias: Psychological and pharmacological treatments.* New York: Guilford.
Zola-Morgan, S., Squire, L. R., & Mishkin, M. (1982). The neuroanatomy of amnesia: Amygdala–hippocampus versus temporal stem. *Science, 218,* 1337–1339.
Zuber, J. A., Crott, H. W., & Werner, J. (1992). Choice shift and group polarization: An analysis of the status of arguments and social decision schemes. *Journal of Personality and Social Psychology, 62,* 50–61.
Zuckerman, M. (1969). Variables affecting deprivation results and hallucinations, reported sensations, and images. In J. P. Zubek (Ed.), *Sensory deprivation.* New York: Appleton-Century-Crofts.
Zuckerman, M. (1990). Some dubious premises in research and theory on racial differences. *American Psychologist, 45,* 1297–1303.
Zuckerman, M., Kuhlman, D. M., Joireman, J., Teta, P., & Kraft, M. (1993). A comparison of three structural models for personality: The big three, the big five, and the alternative five. *Journal of Personality and Social Psychology, 65,* 757–768.

Glossary

Abnormal behavior: Behavior characterized as atypical, socially unacceptable, distressing, maladaptive, and/or the result of distorted cognitions.
Abnormal psychology: The field of psychology concerned with the assessment, treatment, and prevention of maladaptive behavior.
Absolute threshold: The statistically determined minimum level of stimulation necessary to excite a perceptual system.
Accommodation: (1) In perception, the change in the shape of the lens of the eye to keep an object in focus on the retina when the object is moved closer to or farther away from the observer. (2) In developmental theory, according to Piaget, the process by which new concepts and experiences modify existing cognitive structures and behaviors.
Action potential: An electrical current sent down the axon of a neuron, initiated in an all-or-none fashion by a rapid reversal of the electrical balance of the cell membrane. Also known as a *spike discharge.*
Actor-observer effect: The tendency to attribute the behavior of others to dispositional causes but to attribute one's own behavior to situational causes.
Addictive drug: A drug that causes a compulsive physiological need and that, when withheld, produces withdrawal symptoms.
Adolescence [add-oh-LESS-sense]: The period extending from the onset of puberty to early adulthood.
Affect: A person's emotional responses.
Afferent neuron: Neurons that send messages to the spinal cord and brain.
Ageism: Prejudice against the elderly and the discrimination that follows from it.
Aggression: Any behavior designed to harm another person or thing.
Agonist [AG-oh-nist]: Chemical that mimics the actions of a neurotransmitter, usually by occupying receptor sites and facilitating neurochemical transfers.
Agoraphobia [AG-or-uh-FOE-bee-uh]: Anxiety disorder characterized by fear and avoidance of being alone or in public places from which escape might be difficult.
Alcoholic: A problem drinker who also has both a physiological and a psychological need to consume alcohol and to experience its effects.
Algorithm [AL-go-rith-um]: Simple, specific, exhaustive problem-solving procedure that follows a set of rules to implement a step-by-step analysis, as in working out a math problem.
All-or-none: Either at full strength or not at all; a principle by which neurons fire.
Allele [A-leel]: Each member of a pair of genes, which occupies a particular place on a paired chromosome.
Altered state of consciousness: A state of consciousness that is dramatically different from that of ordinary awareness and responsiveness.
Altruism [AL-true-ism]: Behaviors that benefit other people and for which there is no discernible extrinsic reward, recognition, or appreciation.
Alzheimer's disease [ALTZ-hy-merz]: A chronic and progressive disorder of the brain that is a major cause of degenerative dementia and may actually be a group of related disorders tied together loosely under one name.
Amnesia [am-NEE-zhuh]: Inability to remember information (typically all events within a specific period) usually due to physiological trauma.
Amplitude: The total energy of a sound wave, which determines the loudness of a sound. Also known as *intensity.*
Amygdala [a-MIG-duh-luh]: A set of cells that is part of the limbic system; involved in the control of many emotional behaviors and considered especially important in the recognition of fear.
Anal stage: Freud's second stage of personality development, about age 2 to age 3, during which children learn to control the immediate gratification they obtain through defecation and to become responsive to the demands of society.
Androgynous: Having both typically male and typically female characteristics.
Anorexia nervosa [an-uh-REX-see-uh ner-VOH-suh]: An eating disorder characterized by an intense fear of becoming obese, dramatic weight loss, concern about weight, disturbances in body image, and an obstinate and willful refusal to eat.
Antagonist: Chemical that opposes the actions of a neurotransmitter, usually by preventing the neurotransmitter from occupying a receptor site.
Anterograde amnesia: Loss of memory for events and experiences occurring after the amnesia-causing event.
Antisocial personality disorder: Personality disorder characterized by egocentricity, behavior that is irresponsible and that violates the rights of other people (lying, theft, delinquency, and other violations of societal rules), a lack of guilt feelings, an inability to understand other people, and a lack of fear of punishment.
Anxiety: A generalized feeling of fear and apprehension that may be related to a particular event or object and is often accompanied by increased physiological arousal.
Applied psychology: The branch of psychology that uses psychological principles to help solve practical problems of everyday living.
Approach–approach conflict: Conflict that results from having to choose between two equally attractive alternatives or goals.

Approach–avoidance conflict: Conflict that results from having to choose an alternative or goal that has both attractive and repellent aspects.
Archetypes [AR-ki-types]: In Jung's theory, emotionally charged ideas and images that have rich meaning and symbolism and are contained within the collective unconscious.
Arousal: Activation of the central nervous system, the autonomic nervous system, and the muscles and glands; according to some motivational theorists, organisms may seek to maintain optimal levels of arousal by actively varying their exposure to arousing stimuli.
Assessment: The process of evaluating individual differences among human beings by means of tests and direct observation of behavior.
Assimilation: According to Piaget, the process by which new concepts and experiences are incorporated into existing mental frameworks so as to be used in a meaningful way.
Attachment: The strong emotional tie that a person feels toward a special other person in his or her life.
Attitudes: Long-lasting patterns of feelings and beliefs about other people, ideas, or objects that are based in a persons's past experiences, shape his or her future behavior, are evaluative in nature, and serve certain functions.
Attribution: The process by which a person infers other people's motives and intentions through observing their behavior and deciding whether the causes of the behavior are dispositional (internal) or situational (external).
Autonomic nervous system [au-toe-NOM-ick]: The part of the peripheral nervous system that controls the vital and automatic processes of the body, such as the heart rate, digestive processes, blood pressure, and functioning of internal organs.
Aversive counterconditioning: A counterconditioning technique that seeks to teach a new response by pairing an aversive or noxious stimulus with the stimulus that elicits an undesirable response so that the subject will learn to adopt a new, more worthwhile behavior in response to the familiar stimulus and cease the undesired behavior.
Avoidance–avoidance conflict: Conflict that results from having to choose between two equally distasteful alternatives or goals.
Axon: A thin, elongated process that leads from the neuron cell body and serves to transmit signals from the cell body and through the axon terminal to adjacent neurons, muscles, or glands.
Babinski reflex: A reflex in which a newborn projects its toes outward and up when the soles of its feet are touched.
Backward search: Heuristic procedure in which a problem solver starts at the end of a problem and systematically works in reverse steps to discover the subparts necessary to achieve a solution.
Behavior therapy: A therapy that is based on the application of learning principles to human behavior and focuses on changing overt behaviors rather than on understanding subjective feelings, unconscious processes, or motivations. Also known as *behavior modification.*
Behaviorism: The school of psychological thought that rejects the study of the contents of consciousness and focuses on describing and measuring only that which is observable directly or through assessment instruments.
Binocular depth cues: Any visual cues for depth perception that require the use of both eyes.
Biofeedback: Technique by which individuals can monitor and learn to control the involuntary activity of some of the body's organs and functions.
Biological perspective: The school of psychological thought that examines psychological issues based on how heredity and biological structures affect mental processes and behavior and focuses on how physical mechanisms affect emotions, feelings, thoughts, desires, and sensory experiences. Also known as the *neuroscience perspective.*
Bipolar disorders: Mood disorders characterized by vacillation between two extremes, mania and depression; originally known as *manic-depressive disorders.*
Body language: Communication of information through body positions and gestures.
Bonding: A special process of emotional attachment that may occur between parents and babies in the minutes and hours immediately after birth.
Brain: The part of the central nervous system that is located in the skull and that regulates, monitors, processes, and guides other nervous system activity.
Brainstorming: A problem-solving technique that involves considering all possible solutions without making prior evaluative judgments.
Brief therapy: A therapeutic approach that focuses on identifying the client's current problem and solving it with the most effective treatment as quickly as possible. Also known as *brief intermittent therapy.*
Brightness: The lightness or darkness of reflected light, determined in large part by the light's intensity.
Bulimia nervosa [boo-LEE-me-uh ner-VOH-suh]: An eating disorder characterized by repeated episodes of binge eating (and a fear of not being able to stop eating) followed by purging.
Burnout: State of emotional and physical exhaustion, lowered productivity, and feelings of isolation, often caused by work-related pressures.
Bystander apathy: The unwillingness of witnesses to an event to help, an effect that increases when there are more observers.
Case study: Method of interviewing participants to gain information about their background, including data on such factors as childhood, family, education, and social and sexual interactions.
Catatonic type of schizophrenia [CAT-uh-TONN-ick]: A major type of schizophrenia, characterized by displays of excited or violent motor activity or by stupor (in which the individual is mute, negative, and basically unresponsive).
Central nervous system: One of the two major parts of the nervous system, consisting of the brain and the spinal cord.
Cerebellum [seh-rah-BELL-um]: A large structure that is attached to the back surface of the brain stem and that influences balance, coordination, and movement.
Child abuse: Physical, emotional, or sexual mistreatment of children.
Chromosome: Strand of DNA in the nuclei of all cells, which carries genetic information.
Chunks: Manageable and meaningful units of information that can be easily encoded, stored, and retrieved.

Circadian rhythms [sir-KAY-dee-an]: Internally generated patterns of body functions, including hormonal signals, sleep, blood pressure, and temperature regulation, which have an approximate 24-hour cycle and occur even when normal day and night cues are removed.

Classical conditioning: Conditioning process in which an originally neutral stimulus, by repeated pairing with a stimulus that normally elicits a response, comes to elicit a similar or even identical response. Also known as *Pavlovian conditioning*.

Client-centered therapy: An insight therapy, developed by Carl Rogers, that seeks to help people evaluate the world and themselves from their own perspective by providing them with a nondirective environment and unconditional positive regard. Also known as *person-centered therapy*.

Clinical psychologist: Mental health practitioner who views behavior and mental processes from a psychological perspective and who uses knowledge to treat persons with serious emotional or behavioral problems or to do research into the causes of behavior.

Cognitive dissonance [COG-nuh-tiv DIS-uh-nins]: A state in which individuals feel uncomfortable because they hold two or more thoughts, attitudes, or behaviors that are inconsistent with one another.

Cognitive psychology: The study of the overlapping fields of learning, perception, memory, and thought with a special emphasis on how people attend to, acquire, transform, store, and retrieve knowledge.

Cognitive theory: In motivation, an explanation of behavior that emphasizes the role of thought and individual choices regarding life goals and the means of achieving them.

Collective unconscious: In Jung's dream theory, a storehouse of primitive ideas and images in the unconscious that are inherited from one's ancestors; these inherited ideas and images, called *archetypes*, are emotionally charged and rich in meaning and symbolism.

Color blindness: The inability to perceive different hues.

Community psychology: The branch of psychology that seeks to reach out to society to provide services such as community mental health centers and especially to effect social change—through empowerment of individuals, planning, prevention, early intervention, research, and evaluation.

Concept: Mental category used to classify an event or object according to some distinguishing property or feature.

Concordance rate: The percentage of occasions when two groups or individuals show the same trait.

Concrete operational stage: Piaget's third stage of cognitive development (lasting from approximately age 6 or 7 to age 11 or 12), during which the child develops the ability to understand constant factors in the environment, rules, and higher-order symbolism.

Conditioned response: Response elicited by a conditioned stimulus.

Conditioned stimulus: A neutral stimulus that, through repeated association with an unconditioned stimulus, begins to elicit a conditioned response.

Conditioning: Systematic procedure through which associations and responses to specific stimuli are learned.

Conduction deafness: Deafness resulting from interference with the transmission of sound to the neural mechanism of the inner ear.

Conflict: The emotional state or condition in which a person has to make difficult decisions about two or more competing motives, behaviors, or impulses.

Conformity: People's tendency to change attitudes or behaviors to be consistent with other people or with social norms.

Conscious: Freud's first level of awareness, consisting of the thoughts, feelings, and actions of which people are aware.

Consciousness: The general state of being aware of and responsive to events in the environment, including one's own mental processes.

Conservation: The ability to recognize that something that has changed in some way (such as the "shape" of a liquid put in a different container) still has the same weight, substance, or volume.

Conservative focusing: A hypothesis-testing strategy that involves the successive elimination of alternative possibilities from a narrow range of options.

Consolidation [kon-SOL-ih-DAY-shun]: The evolution of a temporary neural circuit into a more permanent circuit.

Control group: In an experiment, the comparison group—the group of participants who are tested on the dependent variable in the same way as the experimental group but for whom the independent variable is not manipulated.

Convergence: The movement of the eyes toward each other to keep information at corresponding points on the retinas as an object moves closer to the observer.

Convergent thinking: In problem solving, the process of narrowing down choices and alternatives to arrive at a suitable answer.

Conversion disorders: Somatoform disorders characterized by the loss or alteration of physical functioning for no apparent physiological reason.

Convolution: Characteristic fold in the tissues of the cerebral hemispheres and the overlying cortex.

Coping: Process by which a person takes some action to manage environmental or internal demands that cause or might cause stress and that will tax the individual's inner resources.

Coping skills: Techniques people use to deal with stress and changing situations.

Cortex: The convoluted, or furrowed, exterior covering of the brain's hemispheres, which is about 2 millimeters thick, consists of six thin layers of cells, and is traditionally divided into a series of lobes, or areas, each with characteristic structures; thought to be involved in both sensory interpretation and complex thought processes. Also known as the *neocortex*.

Counterconditioning: A process of reconditioning in which a person is taught a new, more adaptive response to a familiar stimulus.

Creativity: A quality of thought and problem solving, generally considered to include originality, novelty, and appropriateness.

Crowding: The perception that one's space is too restricted.

Dark adaptation: Increased sensitivity to light in a dark environment; when a person moves from a light environment to a dark one, chemicals in the rods and cones regenerate and return to their inactive state, and light sensitivity increases.

Debriefing: A procedure to inform participants about the true nature of an experiment after its completion.
Decay: Loss of information from memory as a result of disuse and the passage of time.
Decentration: The process of changing from a totally self-oriented point of view to one that recognizes other people's feelings, ideas, and viewpoints.
Decision making: Assessing and choosing among alternatives.
Declarative memory: Memory for specific facts.
Deep structure: The organization of a sentence that is closest to its underlying meaning.
Defense mechanism: A largely unconscious way of reducing anxiety by distorting perceptions of reality.
Deindividuation: The process by which individuals in a group lose their self-awareness and concern with evaluation.
Delusions: False beliefs, which are inconsistent with reality and held in spite of evidence that negates them.
Demand characteristics: Elements of a study situation that might set things up in a specific way or tip off a participant as to the purpose of the study and perhaps thereby elicit specific behavior from the participant.
Dementia: Long-standing impairment of mental functioning and global cognitive abilities in otherwise alert individuals, causing memory loss and related symptoms.
Dendrites: Thin, widely branching fibers extending from the neuron cell body, which receive signals from neighboring neurons and carry them back to the cell body.
Denial: Defense mechanism by which people refuse to recognize the true source of their anxiety.
Dependent variable: The variable in a controlled experiment that is expected to change because of the manipulation of the independent variable.
Depressive disorders: General category of mood disorders in which people show extreme and persistent sadness, despair, and loss of interest in life's usual activities.
Deviation IQ: A standard IQ test score for which the mean and standard deviation remain constant at all ages.
Diabetes mellitus [mel-LIGHT-us]: A condition in which too little insulin is produced, causing sugar to be insufficiently transported out of the blood and into body cells.
Dichromats [DIE-kroe-MATZ]: People who can distinguish only two of the three basic hues.
Discrimination: Behavior targeted at individuals or groups, with the aim of holding them apart and treating them differently.
Disorganized type of schizophrenia: A major type of schizophrenia, characterized by frequent incoherence; absence of systematized delusions; and blunted, inappropriate, or silly affect.
Dissociative amnesia: Dissociative disorder characterized by the sudden and extensive inability to recall important personal information, too extensive to be explained by ordinary forgetfulness.
Dissociative disorders: Disorders characterized by a sudden but temporary alteration in consciousness, identity, sensory/motor behavior, or memory.
Dissociative identity disorder: Dissociative disorder characterized by the existence within an individual of two or more distinct personalities, each of which is dominant at particular times and directs the individual's behavior at those times.
Divergent thinking: In problem solving, widening the range of possibilities and expanding the options for solutions.
Double bind: A situation in which an individual is given two different and inconsistent messages.
Double-blind technique: Research technique in which neither the experimenter nor the participants know who is in the control or the experimental group.
Down syndrome: A human genetic defect in which more than two whole chromosomes are present for the 21st pair; usually accompanied by characteristic physical abnormalities and mental retardation.
Dream: A state of consciousness that occurs largely during REM sleep and is usually accompanied by vivid visual, tactile, or auditory imagery.
Dream analysis: Psychoanalytic technique in which a patient's dreams are interpreted and used to provide insight into the individual's unconscious motivations.
Drive: An internal aroused condition that directs an organism to satisfy physiological needs.
Drive theory: An explanation of behavior emphasizing internal factors that energize organisms to attain, reestablish, balance, or maintain some goal that helps with survival.
Drug: Any chemical substance that alters normal biological processes.
Eating disorders: Psychological disorders characterized by gross disturbances in eating behavior and in the way individuals respond to food.
Eclecticism [ek-LECK-ti-sizm]: In psychology, a combination of theories, facts, or techniques; the practice of using whatever clinical and counseling techniques are appropriate for an individual client rather than relying exclusively on the techniques of one school of psychology.
Educational psychology: The systematic application of psychological principles to learning and teaching.
Efferent neuron: Neurons that send messages from the brain and spinal cord to other structures in the body.
Ego: In Freud's theory, the part of personality that seeks to satisfy the id and superego in accordance with reality.
Ego analyst: Psychoanalytic practitioner who assumes that the ego has greater control over behavior than Freud suggested and who is more concerned with reality testing and control over the environment than with unconscious motivations and processes. Also known as an *ego psychologist.*
Egocentrism [ee-go-SENT-rism]: The inability to perceive a situation or event except in relation to oneself. Also known as *self-centeredness.*
Elaboration likelihood model: A theory suggesting that there are two routes to attitude change: central, which focuses on thoughtful, elaborative considerations; and peripheral, which focuses on less careful, more emotional, and even superficial considerations.
Elaborative rehearsal: Rehearsal involving repetition (often in short-term memory) in which the stimulus may be associated with other events and be further processed (transferred to long-term memory).
Electroconvulsive shock therapy (ECT) [eel-ECK-tro-con-VUL-siv]: A treatment for severe mental illness in which a brief application of electricity to the head is used to produce a generalized seizure. Also known as *shock treatment.*

Electroencephalogram (EEG) [eel-ECK-tro-en-SEFF-uh-low-gram]: Record of an organism's electrical brain-wave patterns, obtained through electrodes placed on the scalp.
Electromagnetic radiation [ee-LEK-tro-mag-NET-ick]: The entire spectrum of waves initiated by the movement of charged particles.
Embryo [EM-bree-o]: The human organism from the 5th through the 49th day after conception.
Emotion: A subjective response, usually accompanied by a physiological change, which is interpreted by an individual and then readies the individual for some action that is associated with a change in behavior.
Empowerment: Facilitating the development of skills, knowledge, and motivation in individuals so that they can act for themselves and gain control over their own lives.
Encoding: The process by which information is put into memory, through conversion of an experience into electrochemical energy.
Encoding specificity principle: The finding that the value or effectiveness of a specific retrieval cue depends on how well it compares with and contains information from when the original memory was encoded.
Encounter group: Group of people who meet to learn more about their feelings, behavior, and interactions.
Endocrine glands [END-oh-krin]: Ductless glands that secrete hormones directly into the bloodstream, rather than through a specific duct, or opening, into a target organ.
Endorphins [en-DOR-finz]: Painkillers produced naturally in the brain and pituitary gland.
Environmental psychology: The study of how physical settings affect human behavior and how people change their environment.
Episodic memory [ep-ih-SAH-dick]: Memory for specific events, objects, and situations.
Equity theory: (1) In social psychology, the theory that people attempt to maintain stable, consistent interpersonal relationships in which the ratio of members' contributions is balanced. (2) In I/O psychology, the theory that suggests that what people bring to a work situation should be balanced by what they receive compared with other workers; thus, input should be balanced by compensation, or rewards, or workers will adjust their work level and potentially their job satisfaction.
Ergonomics: The study of the fit between human anatomy or physiology, the demands of a particular task or piece of equipment, and the environment in which the task occurs.
Ethics: Rules of proper and acceptable conduct that investigators use to guide psychological research; these rules concern the treatment of animals, the rights of human beings, and the responsibilities of investigators.
Excitement phase: The first phase of the sexual response cycle, during which there are initial increases in heart rate, blood pressure, and respiration.
Expectancy theories: (1) Explanations of behavior that focus on people's expectations of success in reaching a goal and the need for achievement as energizing factors. (2) In I/O psychology, theories that suggest that a worker's effort and desire to maintain goal-directed behavior (to work) is determined by expectancies regarding the outcomes of that work.
Experiment: Procedure in which a researcher systematically manipulates and observes elements of a situation in order to answer a question and, usually to test hypotheses and make inferences about cause and effect.
Experimental group: In an experiment, the group of participants for whom the independent variable is manipulated.
Explicit memory: Memory for specific events; a conscious, voluntary, active memory store that is relatively easily accessed.
Extinction [egg-STINK-shun]: (1) In classical conditioning, the process through which withholding of the unconditioned stimulus gradually reduces the probability of a conditioned response. (2) In operant conditioning, the process by which the probability of an organism's emitting a conditioned response is reduced when reinforcement no longer follows the response.
Extrinsic rewards [ecks-TRINZ-ick]: Rewards that come from the external environment.
Factor analysis: A statistical procedure designed to discover the mutually independent elements (factors) in any set of data.
Family therapy: Therapy in which two or more people who are committed to one another's well-being are treated at once, in an effort to change the ways in which they interact.
Fetus [FEET-us]: The human organism from the 49th day after conception until birth.
Fixation: An excessive attachment to some person or object that was appropriate only at an earlier stage of development.
Fixed-interval schedule: A reinforcement schedule in which a reinforcer (reward) is delivered after a specified interval of time, provided that the required response occurs at least once after the interval.
Fixed-ratio schedule: A reinforcement schedule in which a reinforcer (reward) is delivered after a specified number of responses has occurred.
Forebrain: The largest, most complicated, and most advanced organizationally and functionally of the three divisions of the brain, with many interrelated parts: the thalamus and hypothalamus, the limbic system, the basal ganglia and corpus callosum, and the cortex.
Formal operational stage: Piaget's fourth and final stage of cognitive development (beginning at about age 12), during which the individual can think hypothetically, can consider all future possibilities, and is capable of deductive logic.
Fraternal twins: Double births resulting from the release of two ova that are fertilized by two sperm; fraternal twins are no more or less genetically similar than non-twin siblings.
Free association: Psychoanalytic technique in which a person reports to the therapist his or her thoughts and feelings as they occur, regardless of how trivial, illogical, or objectionable their content may appear.
Free-floating anxiety: Persistent anxiety not clearly related to any specific object or situation and accompanied by a sense of impending doom.
Frequency: In sound waves, a measure of the number of times a complete change in air pressure occurs per unit of time; expressed in hertz (Hz), or cycles per second.
Frustration: The emotional state or condition that results when a goal—work, family, or personal—is thwarted or blocked.

Fulfillment: In Rogers's personality theory, an inborn tendency directing people toward actualizing their essential nature and thus attaining their potential.
Functional fixedness: The inability to see that an object can have a function other than its stated or usual one.
Functionalism: The school of psychological thought (an outgrowth of structuralism) that was concerned with how and why the conscious mind works; its main aim was to know how the contents of consciousness functioned and worked together.
Fundamental attribution error: The tendency to attribute other people's behavior to dispositional (internal) causes rather than situational (external) causes.
Gender identity: A person's sense of being male or female.
Gender role: The full range of behaviors generally associated with one's gender, which help one establish who one is. Also known as *sex role.*
Gender role stereotype: Typical beliefs about gender-based behaviors that are expected, regulated, and reinforced by society.
Gender schema theory: The theory that children and adolescents use gender as an organizing theme to classify and understand their perceptions about the world.
Gene: The unit of hereditary transmission carried in chromosomes and consisting of DNA and protein.
Generalized anxiety disorders: Anxiety disorders characterized by persistent anxiety for at least a month, sometimes with problems in motor tension, autonomic hyperactivity, apprehension, and concentration.
Genetics: The study of heredity, the biological transmission of traits and characteristics from parents to offspring.
Genital stage [JEN-it-ul]: Freud's last stage of personality development, from the onset of puberty through adulthood, during which the sexual conflicts of childhood resurface (at puberty) and are often resolved (during adolescence).
Gestalt psychology [gesh-TALT]: The school of psychological thought that argued that behavior cannot be studied in parts but must be viewed as a whole; the focus was on the unity of perception and thinking.
Gestalt therapy [gesh-TALT]: An insight therapy that emphasizes the importance of a person's being aware of current feelings and situations.
Goal-setting theory: Theory that asserts that setting specific, clear, attainable goals for a given task will lead to better performance.
Grammar: The linguistic description of how a language functions, especially the rules and patterns used for generating appropriate and comprehensible sentences.
Grasping reflex: A reflex in which a newborn grasps vigorously any object touching its palm or fingers or placed in its hand.
Group: Two or more individuals who are loosely or cohesively related and who share some common characteristics and goals.
Groupthink: The phenomenon of people in a group reinforcing one another and seeking concurrence and group cohesiveness, rather than effectively evaluating choices and reasoning.
Group polarization: Exaggeration of individuals' preexisting attitudes as a result of group discussion.
Group therapy: Psychotherapeutic process in which several people meet as a group with a therapist.
Hallucinations [ha-LOOSE-in-AY-shuns]: Compelling perceptual (visual, tactile, olfactory, or auditory) experiences without a real physical stimulus.
Halo effect: The tendency for one of an individual's characteristics to influence the evaluation of other characteristics.
Hawthorne effect: The finding, based on early research studies at the Hawthorne industrial plant, that people behave differently (usually better) when they know they are being observed.
Health psychology: Subfield concerned with the use of psychological ideas and principles in health enhancement, illness prevention, diagnosis and treatment of disease, and rehabilitation processes.
Heuristics [hyoo-RISS-ticks]: Sets of strategies, not strict rules, that act as guidelines for discovery-oriented problem solving.
Higher-order conditioning: Process by which a neutral stimulus takes on conditioned properties through pairing with a conditioned stimulus.
Hindbrain: The most primitive organizationally of the three functional divisions of the brain, consisting of the medulla, reticular formation, pons, and cerebellum.
Hippocampus: Part of the limbic system, a large structure lying just next to the corpus callosum; involved in memory, learning, and emotional functions.
Hormones: Endocrine gland chemicals that regulate the activities of specific organs or cells.
Hue: The psychological property of light referred to as color and determined by the wavelength reflected from an object.
Human factors: The study of the relationship of human beings to machines and to workplaces and other environments.
Humanistic psychology: The school of psychological thought that emphasizes the uniqueness of each human being and the idea that human beings have free will to determine their destiny.
Humanistic theory: An explanation of behavior that emphasizes the entirety of life rather than individual components of behavior; focuses on human dignity, individual choice, and self-worth.
Hyperopic [HY-per-OP-ick]: Having trouble seeing things that are nearby but able to see objects at a distance. Also known as *farsighted.*
Hypnosis: Altered state of consciousness brought about by procedures that may induce a trance.
Hypochondriasis [hy-po-kon-DRY-a-sis]: Somatoform disorder characterized by an inordinate preoccupation with health and illness, coupled with excessive anxiety about disease.
Hypoglycemia [hi-po-gly-SEE-me-uh]: A condition in which overproduction of insulin results in very low blood sugar levels.
Hypothalamus: A relatively small structure of the forebrain, lying just below the thalamus, which acts through its connections with the rest of the forebrain and the midbrain and affects many complex behaviors, such as eating, drinking, and sexual activity.

Hypothesis: Tentative statement or idea expressing a causal relationship between two events or variables that are to be evaluated in a research study.
Hypothesis-testing theory: A view of concept formation as an active process in which people acquire new information by generating hypotheses about stimuli, testing those hypotheses, discarding old hypotheses if necessary, and making inferences about the stimuli.
Id: In Freud's theory, the source of instinctual energy, which works mainly on the pleasure principle.
Ideal self: The self that a person would ideally like to be.
Identical twins: Double births resulting from the splitting of a zygote into two identical cells, which then separate and develop independently; identical twins have exactly the same genetic makeup.
Illusion: A perception of a physical stimulus that differs from measurable reality and normal expectations about its appearance.
Imagery: Cognitive process in which a mental picture of a sensory or perceptual experience is created.
Implicit memory: Memory for previously experienced events that occurs passively, almost unconsciously, without a person deliberately attempting to learn or remember the event.
Impression formation: The process by which a person uses the behavior and appearance of others to infer their internal states and intentions.
Independent variable: The variable in a controlled experiment that the experimenter directly and purposely manipulates to see how the variables under study will be affected.
Industrial/organizational (I/O) psychology: The study of how individual behavior is affected by the work environment, by coworkers, and by organizational practices.
Informed consent: The agreement of participants expressed through a signed document that indicates that they understand the nature of their participation in upcoming research and have been fully informed about the general nature of the research, its goals, and its methods.
Insight therapy: Therapy that attempts to discover relationships between unconscious motivations and current abnormal behavior in order to change that behavior.
Insomnia: Prolonged inability to sleep.
Insulin: Hormone produced by the pancreas; facilitates the transport of sugar from the blood into body cells, where it is metabolized.
Intelligence: According to Wechsler, "the aggregate or global capacity of the individual to act purposefully, to think rationally, and to deal effectively with the environment."
Interference: Suppression or confusion of one bit of information with another that was received either earlier or later.
Interpersonal attraction: The tendency of one person to evaluate another person (or a symbol or image of another person) in a positive way.
Interpretation: In Freud's theory, the technique of providing a context, meaning, or cause of a specific idea, feeling, or set of behaviors; the process of tying a set of behaviors to its unconscious determinant.
Interview: Face-to-face meeting in which a series of standardized questions are used to gather detailed information.
Intimacy: A state of being or feeling in which each person is willing to self-disclose and to express important feelings and information to the other person; such behaviors are usually reciprocated.
Intrinsically motivated behaviors [in-TRINZ-ick-lee]: Behaviors engaged in for no apparent reward except the pleasure and satisfaction of the activity itself.
Introspection: Description and analysis by a person of what he or she is thinking and feeling. Also known as *self-examination.*
Job analyses: Careful descriptions of the various tasks and activities that will be required for employees to do their jobs, along with the necessary knowledge, skills, and abilities; such analyses describe what gets done and how it gets done.
Kinesthesis [kin-iss-THEE-sis]: The awareness aroused by movements of the muscles, tendons, and joints.
Labor: The process in which the uterus contracts and the cervix opens so that the fetus can descend through the birth canal to the outside world.
Latency stage [LAY-ten-see]: Freud's fourth stage of personality development, from about age 7 until puberty, during which sexual urges are inactive.
Latent content: The deeper meaning of a dream, usually involving symbolism, hidden content, and repressed or obscured ideas and wishes.
Latent learning: Learning that occurs in the absence of any direct reinforcement and that is not necessarily demonstrated in any observable behavior, though it has the potential to be exhibited.
Law of Prägnanz [PREG-nants]: The Gestalt principle that when items or stimuli can be grouped together and seen as a whole, they will be.
Learned helplessness: Behavior of giving up or not responding, exhibited by organisms exposed to negative consequences or punishment over which they have no control; the major cause is an organism's belief that its response will not affect what happens to it in the future.
Learning: A relatively permanent change in an organism that occurs as a result of experiences in the environment.
Levels-of-processing approach: A memory theory that is considered a distinct alternative to the information-processing approach and that suggests that information does not move from one stage of memory to another in a linear way but is processed in different ways, to different extents, and at different levels, depending on the degree of analysis.
Libido [lih-BEE-doe]: In Freud's theory, the instinctual (and usually sexual) life force that, working on the pleasure principle and seeking immediate gratification, energizes the id.
Light: The portion of the electromagnetic spectrum visible to the eye.
Limbic system: An interconnected group of structures (including parts of the cortex, thalamus, and hypothalamus) located deep within the temporal lobe and involved in emotions, memory, social behavior, and brain disorders such as epilepsy; within the limbic system are the hippocampus and the amygdala.
Linguistics [ling-GWIS-ticks]: The study of language, including speech sounds, meaning, and grammar.
Logic: The procedure used to reach a valid conclusion.
Long-term memory: The memory storage system that keeps a relatively permanent record of information.

Lucid dream [LOO-sid]: Dream in which the person is aware of dreaming while it is happening.
Mainstreaming: The administrative practice of placing children with special needs in regular classroom settings with the support of special education services.
Maintenance rehearsal: The repetitive review of information (usually in short-term memory) with little or no interpretation.
Major depressive disorder: Depressive disorder characterized by loss of interest in almost all of life's usual activities, as evidenced by a sad, hopeless, or discouraged mood, sleep disturbance, loss of appetite, loss of energy, and feelings of unworthiness and guilt.
Manifest content: The overt story line, characters, and setting of a dream—the obvious, clearly discernible events of the dream.
Means–ends analysis: Heuristic procedure in which the problem solver tries to move closer to a solution by comparing the current situation with the desired goal and determining the most efficient way to get from one to the other.
Meditation: State of consciousness induced by a variety of techniques and characterized by concentration, restriction of incoming stimuli, and deep relaxation to produce a sense of detachment.
Medulla [meh-DUH-lah]: The most primitive and lowest portion of the hindbrain; controls basic bodily functions such as breathing.
Memory: The ability to remember past events, images, ideas, or previously learned information or skills; the storage system that allows for retention and retrieval of previously learned information.
Memory span: The limited number of items that can be easily reproduced after presentation to short-term memory, usually confined to one or two chunks of information.
Mental retardation: Below-average intellectual functioning, as measured on an IQ test, accompanied by substantial limitations in functioning that originate before age 18.
Midbrain: The second level of the three organizational structures of the brain, which receives afferent signals from other parts of the brain and from the spinal cord, interprets the signals, and either relays the information to a more complex part of the brain or causes the body to act at once; considered important in the regulation of movement.
Model: A perspective or approach derived from data in one field, used to help describe data in another field.
Monochromats [MON-o-kroe-MATZ]: People who cannot perceive any color, usually because their retinas contain only rods.
Monocular depth cues [mah-NAHK-you-ler]: Depth cues that do not depend on the use of both eyes.
Morality: A system of learned attitudes about social practices, institutions, and individual behavior used to evaluate situations and behavior as being right or wrong, good or bad.
Moro reflex: A reflex in which a newborn stretches out its arms and legs and cries when there is a loud noise or abrupt change in the environment.
Morpheme [MORE-feem]: A basic unit of meaning in a language.
Motivation: Any internal condition that appears by inference to initiate, activate, or maintain an organism's goal-directed behavior.
Motive: A specific (usually internal) condition, usually involving some sort of arousal, that directs an organism's behavior toward a goal.
Myopic [my-OP-ick]: Able to see things that are close but having trouble seeing objects at a distance. Also known as *nearsighted.*
Naturalistic observation: Careful and objective observation of events from a distance, without observer intervention.
Nature: An individual's genetically inherited characteristics.
Need: A state of physiological imbalance usually accompanied by arousal.
Need for achievement: A social need that directs people to strive constantly for excellence and success.
Negative reinforcement: Removal of an aversive stimulus after a particular response to increase the likelihood that the response will recur.
Neo-Freudians: Personality theorists who have proposed variations on the basic ideas of Freud, usually attributing a greater influence to cultural and interpersonal factors than Freud did.
Nervous system: The structures and organs that act as the communication system for the body, allowing all behavior and mental processes to take place.
Neuromodulator: Chemical substance that functions to increase or decrease the sensitivity of widely distributed neurons to the specific effects of neurotransmitters.
Neuron [NEW-ron]: The basic unit (a single cell) of the nervous system, comprising dendrites, which receive neural signals; a cell body, which generates electrical signals; and an axon, which transmits neural signals. Also known as a *nerve cell.*
Neurotransmitter [NEW-roh-TRANS-mitt-er]: Chemical substance that resides in the axon terminals and within synaptic vesicles and that, when released, moves across the synaptic space and binds to a receptor site on adjacent neurons.
No rapid eye movement (NREM) sleep: Four distinct stages of sleep during which no rapid eye movements occur.
Nondirective therapy: A form of therapy in which the client determines the direction of therapy while the therapist remains permissive, almost passive, and accepts totally the client's feelings and behavior.
Nonverbal communication: Information provided by cues or actions that involve movements of the body, especially the face.
Normal curve: A bell-shaped graphic representation of data arranged to show what percentage of the population falls under each part of the curve.
Norms: The scores and corresponding percentile ranks of a large and representative sample of individuals from the population for which a test was designed.
Nurture: An individual's experiences in the environment.
Obedience: Compliance with the orders of another person or group of people.
Observational learning theory: Theory that suggests that organisms learn new responses by observing the behavior of a model and then imitating it. Also known as *social learning theory.*
Obsessive–compulsive disorder: Anxiety disorder characterized by persistent and uncontrollable thoughts and irrational beliefs that cause the performance of compulsive rituals that interfere with daily life.

Oedipus complex [ED-i-pus]: Occurring during the phallic stage, feelings of rivalry with the parent of the same sex and love of the parent of the opposite sex, ultimately resolved through identification with the parent of the same sex; in girls this process is called the *Electra complex*.
Olfaction [ole-FAK-shun]: The sense of smell.
Operant conditioning [OP-er-ant]: Conditioning in which the probability that an organism will emit a response is increased or decreased by the subsequent delivery of a reinforcer or punisher. Also known as *instrumental conditioning*.
Operational definition: Definition of a variable in terms of the set of methods or procedures used to measure or study that variable.
Opiate: Drugs with pain-relieving and sedative properties that are addictive and produce tolerance.
Opponent–process theory: The theory, proposed by Herring, that color is coded by stimulation of three types of paired receptors; each pair of receptors is assumed to operate in an antagonistic way so that stimulation by a given wavelength produces excitation in one receptor of the pair and inhibition of the other receptor.
Optic chiasm [KI-azm]: The point at which half of the optic nerve fibers from each eye cross over and project to the other side of the brain.
Oral stage: Freud's first stage of personality development, from birth to about age 2, during which infants obtain gratification primarily through the mouth.
Orgasm phase: The third phase of the sexual response cycle, during which autonomic nervous system activity reaches its peak and muscle contractions occur throughout the body, but especially in the genital area, in spasms.
Parallel distributed processing (PDP): Organization of the brain in neural networks with many operations taking place simultaneously and at many locations within the brain.
Paranoid type of schizophrenia [PAIR-uh-noid]: A major type of schizophrenia, characterized by delusions and hallucinations of persecution or grandeur (or both), and sometimes irrational jealousy.
Parasympathetic nervous system [PAIR-uh-sim-puh-THET-ick]: The part of the autonomic nervous system that controls the ongoing maintenance processes of the body, such as the heart rate, digestive processes, and blood pressure.
Participant: Individual who takes part in an experiment and whose behavior is observed for research data collection. Also known as a *subject*.
Percentile score: A score indicating what percentage of the test population would obtain a lower score.
Perception: Process by which an organism selects and interprets sensory input so that it acquires meaning.
Performance appraisal: The process by which a supervisor periodically evaluates the job-relevant strengths and weaknesses of subordinates.
Peripheral nervous system [puh-RIF-er-al]: The part of the nervous system that carries information to and from the central nervous system through a network of spinal and cranial nerves.
Personal space: The area around an individual that is considered private and around which the person feels an invisible boundary.
Personality: A set of relatively enduring behavioral characteristics and internal predispositions that describe how a person reacts to the environment.
Personality disorders: Disorders characterized by inflexible and long-standing maladaptive ways of dealing with the environment, which typically cause stress and/or social or occupational problems.
Phallic stage [FAL-ick]: Freud's third stage of personality development, about age 4 to age 7, during which children obtain gratification primarily from the genitals.
Phenylketonuria (PKU) [fee-nil-key-ton-NYEW-ree-uh]: A human genetic disorder that prevents an individual from processing the amino acid phenylalanine.
Phobic disorder: Anxiety disorder characterized by unreasonable fear of, and consequent attempted avoidance of, specific objects or situations.
Phoneme [FOE-neem]: A basic unit of sound in a language.
Photoreceptors: The light-sensitive cells in the retina: rods and cones.
Pitch: The psychological experience that corresponds with the frequency of an auditory stimulus. Also known as *tone*.
Pituitary gland [pit-YOU-ih-tare-ee]: The body's master gland, located at the base of the brain and closely linked to the hypothalamus; regulates the actions of other endocrine glands; major function is the control of growth hormones.
Placebo effect [pluh-SEE-bo]: A nonspecific therapeutic change that occurs as a result of a person's expectations of change rather than as a direct result of any specific treatment.
Placenta [pluh-SENT-uh]: A mass of tissue in the uterus connected to the fetus by the umbilical cord and serving as the mechanism for the exchange of nutrients and waste products.
Plateau phase: The second phase of the sexual response cycle, during which the sexual partners are preparing for orgasm, autonomic nervous system activity increases, and there is further vasoconstriction.
Pons: A structure of the hindbrain that connects with the medulla and the cerebellum, provides a link with the rest of the brain, and is involved in sleep.
Positive reinforcement: Presentation of a rewarding or pleasant stimulus after a particular response, to increase the likelihood that the response will recur.
Posttraumatic stress disorder (PTSD): Mental disorder that may become evident after a person has undergone extreme stress caused by some type of disaster; common symptoms include vivid, intrusive recollections or reexperiences of the traumatic event and occasional lapses of normal consciousness.
Preconscious: Freud's second level of awareness, consisting of mental activities of which people can gain awareness by attending to them.
Prejudice: Negative evaluation of an entire group of people, typically based on unfavorable (often wrong) ideas about the group.
Preoperational stage: Piaget's second stage of cognitive development (lasting from about age 2 to age 6 or 7), during which initial symbolic thought is developed.
Pressure: Emotional state or condition resulting from others' expectations of specific behaviors or results.
Prevalence: The percentage of a population displaying a disorder during any specified period.
Primacy effect: The more accurate recall of items that were presented first in a series.

Primary punisher: Any stimulus or event that is naturally painful or aversive to an organism.
Primary reinforcer: A reinforcer (such as food, water, or the termination of pain) that has survival value for an organism and thus its value does not have to be learned.
Privacy: The result of the process of controlling the boundaries between people so that access is limited.
Proactive interference [pro-AK-tiv]: Decrease in accurate recall of information as a result of the effects of previously learned or presented information. Also known as *proactive inhibition.*
Problem solving: The behavior of individuals when confronted with a situation or task that requires some insight or some unknown elements to be determined.
Procedural memory: Memory for the perceptual, motor, and cognitive skills required to complete a task.
Projection: Defense mechanism by which people attribute their own undesirable traits to other people or objects.
Projective tests: Personality-assessing devices or instruments in which examinees are shown a standard set of ambiguous stimuli and asked to respond in an unrestricted manner.
Prosocial behavior: Behavior that benefits someone else or society but that generally offers no obvious benefit to the person performing it and that may even involve some personal risk or sacrifice.
Psychedelics: Consciousness-altering drugs that affect moods, thoughts, memory, judgment, and perception and that are usually self-administered for the purpose of producing those results.
Psychiatrist: Physician (medical doctor) specializing in the treatment of patients with emotional disorders.
Psychic determinism [SYE-kick]: Psychoanalytic assumption that everything a person feels, thinks, and does has a purpose and that all behaviors are caused by past events.
Psychoactive drug [SYE-koh-AK-tiv]: A drug that alters behavior, thought, or emotions by altering biochemical reactions in the nervous system, thereby affecting consciousness.
Psychoanalysis [SYE-ko-uh-NAL-uh-sis]: A lengthy therapy developed by Freud that aims at uncovering conflicts and unconscious impulses through special techniques, including free association, dream analysis, and transference.
Psychoanalyst: Psychiatrist or, occasionally, nonmedical practitioner who has studied the technique of psychoanalysis and uses it in treating people with emotional problems.
Psychoanalytic approach [SYE-ko-an-uh-LIT-ick]: The school of psychological thought developed by Freud, which assumes that psychological maladjustment is a consequence of anxiety resulting from unresolved conflicts and forces of which a person may be unaware; includes therapeutic technique known as *psychoanalysis.*
Psychodrama [SYE-ko-drama]: A group therapy procedure in which members act out their situations, feelings, and roles.
Psychodynamically based therapies [SYE-ko-dye-NAM-ick-lee]: Therapies based loosely on Freud's psychoanalytic theory, using a part of that approach but rejecting some elements.
Psycholinguistics: The study of how language is acquired, perceived, understood, and produced.
Psychological dependence: A compelling desire to use a drug, along with an inability to inhibit that desire.
Psychologist: Professional who studies human behavior and uses behavioral principles in scientific research or in applied settings.
Psychology: The science of behavior and mental processes.
Psychoneuroimmunology (PNI) [SYE-ko-NEW-ro-IM-you-NOLL-oh-gee]: The study of how psychological processes and the nervous system affect and in turn are affected by the body's natural defense system—the immune system.
Psychophysics [SYE-co-FIZ-icks]: The subfield that focuses on the relationship between physical stimuli and people's conscious experience of them.
Psychostimulant: A drug that in low to moderate doses increases alertness, reduces fatigue, and elevates mood.
Psychotherapy [SYE-ko-THER-uh-pee]: The treatment of emotional or behavioral problems through psychological techniques.
Psychotic [sye-KOT-ick]: Suffering from a gross impairment in reality testing that interferes with the ability to meet the ordinary demands of life.
Puberty [PEW-burr-tee]: The period during which the reproductive system matures; it begins with an increase in sex hormone production and occurs at (and signals) the end of the childhood period.
Punishment: The process of presenting an undesirable or noxious stimulus, or removing a desirable stimulus, to decrease the probability that a particular preceding response will recur.
Questionnaire: Printed form with questions, usually given to a large group of people; used by researchers to gather a substantial amount of data in a short time. Also known as a *survey.*
Rape: Forcible sexual assault on an unwilling partner, usually a woman.
Rapid eye movement (REM) sleep: Stage of sleep characterized by high-frequency, low-voltage brain-wave activity, rapid and systematic eye movements, and dreams.
Rational–emotive therapy: A cognitive behavior therapy that emphasizes the importance of logical, rational thought processes.
Rationalization: Defense mechanism by which people reinterpret undesirable feelings or behaviors in terms that make them appear acceptable.
Raw score: An examinee's test score that has not been transformed or converted in any way.
Reactance: Pattern of feelings and subsequent behaviors aimed at reestablishing a sense of freedom when there is an inconsistency between a person's self-image as being free to choose and the person's realization that someone is trying to force him or her to choose a particular alternative.
Reaction formation: Defense mechanism by which people behave in a manner opposite to their true but anxiety-provoking feelings.
Reasoning: The process by which people generate logical and coherent ideas, evaluate situations, and reach conclusions.
Recency effect: The more accurate recall of items presented last in a series.
Receptive fields: The areas of the retina that, when stimulated, produce a change in the firing of cells in the visual system.
Reflex: Involuntary, automatic behavior that occurs in response to a stimulus without prior learning and usually shows little variability from instance to instance.

Refractory period: The recovery period of a neuron after it fires, during which it cannot fire again; this period allows the neuron to reestablish electrical balance with its surroundings.
Rehearsal: The process of repeatedly verbalizing, thinking about, or otherwise acting on information in order to keep that information in memory.
Reinforcer: Any event that increases the probability of a recurrence of the response that preceded it.
Reliability: A test's ability to yield the same score for the same individual through repeated testings.
Representative sample: A sample of individuals who match the population with whom they are to be compared with regard to key variables such as socioeconomic status and age.
Repression: Defense mechanism by which people block anxiety-provoking feelings from conscious awareness and push them into the unconscious.
Residual type of schizophrenia: A schizophrenic disorder in which the patient exhibits inappropriate affect, illogical thinking, and/or eccentric behavior but seems generally in touch with reality.
Resilience: The extent to which people are flexible, are less easily impaired by events, and respond adaptively to external or internal demands.
Resistance: In psychoanalysis, an unwillingness to cooperate by which a patient signals a reluctance to provide the therapist with information or to help the therapist understand or interpret a situation.
Resolution phase: The fourth phase of the sexual response cycle, during which the body naturally returns after orgasm to its resting, or normal, state.
Reticular formation [reh-TICK-you-lar]: Extending out from the medulla, a latticelike network of neurons that directly controls a person's state of arousal, waking, and sleeping, as well as other bodily functions.
Retinal disparity: The slight difference between the visual images projected on the two retinas.
Retrieval: The process by which stored information is recovered from memory.
Retroactive interference [RET-ro-AK-tiv]: Decrease in accurate recall of information as a result of the subsequent presentation of different information. Also known as *retroactive inhibition.*
Retrograde amnesia [RET-ro-grade]: Loss of memory for events and experiences occurring in a period preceding the amnesia-causing event.
Rooting reflex: A reflex in which a newborn turns its head toward a mild stimulus applied to its lips or cheek.
Saccades [sack-ADZ]: Rapid voluntary movements of the eyes, to focus on different points.
Sample: A group of participants who are assumed to be representative of the population about which an inference is being made.
Saturation: The depth of hue of reflected light, as determined by the homogeneity of the wavelengths contained in the light. Also known as *purity.*
Schema [SKEEM-uh]: A conceptual framework that organizes information and makes sense of the world by laying out a structure in which events can be encoded.
Schizophrenic disorders [SKIT-soh-FREN-ick]: A group of disorders characterized by a lack of reality testing and by deterioration of social and intellectual functioning, beginning before age 45 and lasting at least 6 months; persons with these disorders often show serious personality disintegration with significant changes in thought, mood, perception, and behavior.
Scientific method: In psychology, the techniques used to discover knowledge about human behavior and mental processes; in experimentation, the scientific method involves stating the problem, forming a theory, developing hypotheses, observation (which often includes manipulating some part of the environment to better understand previous conditions that led to a behavior or phenomenon), and replicating results.
Secondary punisher: A neutral stimulus with no intrinsic negative effect on an organism that acquires punishment value through repeated pairing with a punishing stimulus.
Secondary reinforcer: A neutral stimulus that has no intrinsic value for an organism initially but that can become rewarding when linked with a primary reinforcer.
Secondary sex characteristics: The physical features of a person's gender identity that are not directly involved with reproduction but that help distinguish men from women.
Sedative–hypnotic: Drug that relaxes and calms people and, in higher doses, induces sleep.
Self: In Rogers's theory of personality, the perceptions individuals have of themselves and of their relationships to other people and to various aspects of life.
Self-actualization: The fundamental human need to strive to fulfill one's potential, thus a state of motivation according to Maslow; from a humanist's view, a final level of psychological development in which a person attempts to minimize ill health, be fully functioning, have a superior perception of reality, and feel a strong sense of self-acceptance.
Self-efficacy: A person's belief about whether he or she can successfully engage in and execute a specific behavior.
Self-fulfilling prophecy: The unwitting creation by a researcher of a situation that leads to specific prophesied results.
Self-monitoring: An assessment procedure in which a person systematically counts and records the frequency and duration of specific behaviors in himself or herself.
Self-perception theory: Approach to attitude formation in which people are assumed to infer their attitudes on the basis of observations of their own behavior.
Self-serving bias: People's tendency to evaluate their own positive behaviors as due to their own internal traits and characteristics, but their failures and shortcomings to external, situational factors.
Semantic memory: Memory for ideas, rules, and general concepts about the world.
Semantics [se-MAN-ticks]: The analysis of the meaning of language components.
Sensation: Process by which the sense organ receptor cells are stimulated and relay their initial information to higher brain centers for further processing.
Sensorimotor stage: The first of Piaget's four stages of cognitive development (covering roughly the first 2 years of life), during which the child begins to interact with the environment and the rudiments of memory are established.
Sensorineural deafness [sen-so-ree-NEW-ruhl]: Deafness resulting from damage to the cochlea, the auditory nerve, or higher auditory processing centers.

Sensory memory: The mechanism that performs initial encoding and brief storage of stimuli. Also known as the *sensory register.*
Sexual deviations: Sexual practices directed toward objects rather than people, sexual encounters involving real or simulated suffering or humiliation, or sexual activities with a nonconsenting partner. Also known as *paraphilias.*
Shape constancy: The ability to recognize a shape despite changes in the orientation or angle from which it is viewed.
Shaping: Gradual training of an organism to give the proper responses through selective reinforcement of behaviors as they approach the desired response.
Short-term memory: The memory storage system that temporarily holds current or recently attended-to information for immediate or short-term use.
Shyness: Extreme anxiety in individuals who are socially reticent and often overly concerned with how they appear to others, often leading to avoidance of social situations.
Signal detection theory: Theory that holds that an observer's perception is dependent on the intensity of a stimulus, on the observer's motivation, on the criteria he or she sets up, and on the "noise" that is present.
Significant difference: In an experiment, a difference that is unlikely to have occurred because of chance alone and is most likely due to the systematic manipulations of the researcher.
Size constancy: The ability of the perceptual system to recognize that an object remains constant in size regardless of its distance from the observer or the size of its image on the retina.
Skinner box: Named (by others) for its developer, B. F. Skinner, a box that contains a responding mechanism (usually a lever) capable of delivering a consequence, often a reinforcer, to an organism.
Sleep: Nonwaking state of consciousness characterized by general unresponsiveness to the environment and general physical immobility.
Social cognition: The thought process involved in making sense of events, people, oneself, and the world in general through analyzing and interpreting them.
Social facilitation: Change in performance that occurs when people believe they are in the presence of other people.
Social influence: The way in which one or more people alter the attitudes or behavior of others.
Social loafing: Decrease in productivity that occurs when an individual works in a group instead of alone.
Social need: An aroused condition that directs people toward establishing feelings about themselves and others and toward establishing and maintaining relationships.
Social phobia [FOE-bee-uh]: Anxiety disorder characterized by fear of, and desire to avoid, situations in which the person might be exposed to scrutiny by others and might behave in an embarrassing or humiliating way.
Social psychology: The study of how individuals influence and are influenced by the thoughts, feelings, and behaviors of other people.
Social support: The comfort, recognition, approval, and encouragement available from other people, including friends, family, members of organizations, and coworkers.
Sociobiology: Theory based on the premise that even day-to-day behaviors are determined by the process of natural selection—that social behaviors that contribute to the survival of a species are passed on genetically from one generation to the next and account for the mechanisms producing behaviors such as altruism.
Somatic nervous system [so-MAT-ick]: The part of the peripheral nervous system that carries information to skeletal muscles and thereby affects bodily movement; it controls voluntary, conscious sensory and motor functions.
Somatization disorders: Somatoform disorders characterized by recurrent and multiple physical complaints of several years' duration for which medical attention has been ineffective.
Somatoform disorders [so-MAT-oh-form]: Disorders characterized by real physical symptoms not under voluntary control and for which no evident physical cause exists.
Sound: The psychological experience that occurs when changes in air pressure take place at the receptive organ for hearing; the resulting tone, or sounds, vary in frequency and amplitude.
Specific phobia: Anxiety disorder characterized by irrational and persistent fear of a particular object or situation, along with a compelling desire to avoid it.
Spinal cord: The portion of the central nervous system that is contained within the spinal column and transmits signals from the senses to the brain, controls reflexive responses, and conveys signals from the brain to the muscles and glands.
Split-brain patients: People whose corpus callosum, which normally connects the two cerebral hemispheres, has been surgically severed, usually because of uncontrollable epilepsy.
Spontaneous recovery: Recurrence of an extinguished conditioned response following a rest period.
Sport psychology: The systematic application of psychological principles in sports.
Standard score: A score that expresses an individual's position relative to the mean, based on the standard deviation.
Standardization: The process of developing uniform procedures for administering and scoring a test and for establishing norms.
State-dependent learning: The tendency to recall information learned in a particular physiological state most accurately when one is again in that physiological state.
Stereotypes: Fixed, overly simple, often wrong, and often negative ideas about traits, attitudes, and behaviors attributed to groups of people.
Stimulus discrimination: Process by which an organism learns to respond only to a specific reinforced stimulus.
Stimulus generalization: Occurrence of a conditioned response with a stimulus that is similar but not identical to the original conditioned stimulus.
Storage: The process of maintaining information in memory.
Stress: A nonspecific, often global, response by an organism to real or imagined demands made on it (a person must appraise a situation as stressful for it to be stressful).
Stress inoculation [in-OK-you-LAY-shun]: Procedure of giving people realistic warnings, recommendations, and reassurances to help them prepare for and cope with impending dangers or losses.
Stressor: A stimulus that affects an organism in physically or psychologically injurious ways and usually elicits feelings such as anxiety, tension, and physiological arousal.

Structuralism: The school of psychological thought that considered the organized structure of immediate, conscious experience to be the proper subject matter of psychology.
Subgoal analysis: Heuristic procedure in which a task is broken down into smaller, more manageable parts.
Sublimation [sub-li-MAY-shun]: Defense mechanism by which people redirect socially unacceptable impulses into acceptable ones.
Subliminal perception: Perception below the threshold of awareness.
Substance abusers: People who overuse and rely on drugs to deal with stress and anxiety.
Sucking reflex: A reflex in which a newborn makes sucking motions when presented with a stimulus to the lips, such as a nipple.
Superego [super-EE-go]: In Freud's theory, the moral aspect of mental functioning, comprising the ego ideal (what a person would ideally like to be) and the conscience, and taught by parents and society.
Superstitious behavior: Behavior learned through coincidental association with reinforcement.
Surface structure: The organization of a sentence that is closest to its written or spoken form.
Syllogism [SILL-oh-jiz-um]: A sequence of statements, or premises (usually two), followed by a conclusion; the task is to decide (deduce) whether the conclusion is warranted.
Sympathetic nervous system: The part of the autonomic nervous system that become most active in response to emergency situations; it calls up bodily resources as needed for major energy expenditures.
Symptom substitution: The appearance of one overt symptom to replace another that has been eliminated by treatment.
Synapse [SIN-apps]: The microscopically small space between the axon terminals of one neuron and the receptor sites of another neuron.
Syntax [SIN-tacks]: The way words and groups of words are related and combine to form phrases and sentences.
Systematic desensitization: A counterconditioning procedure in which a person first learns deep relaxation and then imagines a series of progressively fearful situations; with each successive experience, the person learns relaxation rather than fear as a new response to a formerly fearful stimulus.
Temperament: Long-lasting individual differences in the intensity and especially in the quality of a person's emotional reactions.
Teratogen [ter-AT-oh-jen]: Substance that can produce developmental malformations (birth defects) in a fetus.
Territorial behavior: Behavior involved in establishing, maintaining, personalizing, and defending a delineated space.
Thalamus: A large structure of the forebrain that acts primarily as a routing station to send information to other parts of the brain but probably also performs some interpretive functions; nearly all sensory information proceeds through the thalamus.
Thanatology: The study of the psychological and medical aspects of death and dying.
Theory: In psychology, a collection of interrelated ideas and facts put forward to explain and predict behavior and mental processes.
Time-out: A punishment procedure in which a person is physically removed from a desired or reinforcing situation to decrease the likelihood that an undesired behavior will recur.
Token economy: An operant conditioning procedure in which individuals who engage in appropriate behavior receive tokens that they can exchange for desirable items or activities.
Tolerance: Progressive insensitivity to repeated use of a specific drug in the same dosage and at the same frequency of use.
Trait: Any readily identifiable stable quality or behavior that characterizes the way in which an individual differs from other individuals.
Transduction: The process by which a perceptual system analyzes stimuli and converts them into electrical impulses. Also known as *coding*.
Transference: Psychoanalytic phenomenon in which a therapist becomes the object of a patient's emotional attitudes about an important person in the patient's life, such as a parent.
Transformational grammar: An approach to the study of language that assumes that each surface structure of a sentence has a deep structure associated with it.
Transformational leader: Charismatic leader who inspires and provides intellectual stimulation to re-create an organization.
Trichromatic theory [try-kroe-MAT-ick]: The visual theory, stated by Young and Helmholtz, that all colors can be made by mixing three basic colors: red, green, and blue. Also known as the *Young-Helmholtz theory*.
Trichromats [TRY-kroe-MATZ]: People who can perceive all three primary colors and thus can distinguish any color.
Type A behavior: Behavior characterized by competitiveness, impatience, hostility, and constant efforts to do more in less time.
Type B behavior: Behavior characterized by more calmness, more patience, and less hurrying than that of Type A individuals.
Types: Categories of personality in which broad collections of traits are loosely tied together and interrelated.
Unconditioned response: Unlearned or involuntary response to an unconditioned stimulus.
Unconditioned stimulus: A stimulus that normally produces a measurable involuntary response.
Unconscious: Freud's third level of awareness, consisting of mental activities beyond people's normal awareness.
Unconscious motivation: Psychoanalytic assumption that behavior is determined by desires, goals, and internal states, buried deep within the unconscious, of which an individual is unaware.
Undifferentiated type of schizophrenia: A schizophrenic disorder characterized by a mixture of symptoms and which does not meet diagnostic criteria of other categories, or may meet criteria of more than one category.
Validity: The ability of a test to measure what it is supposed to measure and to predict what it is supposed to predict.
Variable: Condition or characteristic of a situation or person that is subject to change (that varies) within or across situations or individuals.
Variable-interval schedule: A reinforcement schedule in which a reinforcer (reward) is delivered after predetermined but varying intervals of time, provided that the required response occurs at least once after each interval.

Variable-ratio schedule: A reinforcement schedule in which a reinforcer (reward) is delivered after a predetermined but variable number of responses has occurred.
Vasocongestion: In the sexual response cycle, engorgement of the blood vessels, particularly in the genital area, due to increased blood flow.
Vestibular sense [ves-TIB-you-ler]: The sense of bodily orientation and postural adjustment.
Visual cortex: The most important area of the brain's occipital lobe, which receives information from the lateral geniculate nucleus. Also known as the *striate cortex*.
Vulnerability: A person's diminished ability to deal with demanding life events.
Withdrawal symptoms: Physiological reactions that occur when an addictive drug is no longer administered to an addict.
Working memory: A conception of short-term memory that focuses on several subsystems: a component to encode and rehearse auditory information, a visual-spatial scratch pad, and a central processing mechanism, or executive, that balances and controls information flow.
Working through: In psychoanalysis, the repetitive cycle of interpretation, resistance to interpretation, and transference.
Zygote [ZEYE-goat]: A fertilized egg.

Name Index

Subject Index